RELIGION AND THE CONSTITUTION

Second Edition

Michael W. McConnell
Circuit Judge, U.S. Court of Appeals for the Tenth Circuit
Presidential Professor, University of Utah,
S.J. Quinney College of Law

John H. Garvey
Dean and Professor of Law
Boston College

Thomas C. Berg
Professor of Law
University of St. Thomas School of Law (Minnesota)

ΛSPEN

PUBLISHERS

76 Ninth Avenue, New York, NY 10011
http://lawschool.aspenpublishers.com

Aspen Publishers
Attn: Permissions Department
76 Ninth Avenue, 7th Floor
New York, NY 10011-5201

Printed in the United States of America.

1 2 3 4 5 6 7 8 9 0

ISBN 0-7355-6137-0

Library of Congress Cataloging-in-Publication Data

McConnell, Michael W.
  Religion and the constitution/Michael W. McConnell, John H. Garvey, Thomas C. Berg.—2nd ed.
    p. cm.
  ISBN 0-7355-6137-0
  1. Church and state—United States—Cases. 2. Freedom of religion—United States—Cases. I. Garvey, John H., 1948- II. Berg, Thomas C., 1960- III. Title.

KF4865.A7M235 2006
342.7308'52—dc22

2006018082

RELIGION
AND THE
CONSTITUTION

About Aspen Publishers

Aspen Publishers, headquartered in New York City, is a leading information provider for attorneys, business professionals, and law students. Written by preeminent authorities, our products consist of analytical and practical information covering both U.S. and international topics. We publish in the full range of formats, including updated manuals, books, periodicals, CDs, and online products.

Our proprietary content is complemented by 2,500 legal databases, containing over 11 million documents, available through our Loislaw division. Aspen Publishers also offers a wide range of topical legal and business databases linked to Loislaw's primary material. Our mission is to provide accurate, timely, and authoritative content in easily accessible formats, supported by unmatched customer care.

To order any Aspen Publishers title, go to *http://lawschool.aspenpublishers.com* or call 1-800-638-8437.

To reinstate your manual update service, call 1-800-638-8437.

For more information on Loislaw products, go to *www.loislaw.com* or call 1-800-364-2512.

For Customer Care issues, e-mail *CustomerCare@aspenpublishers.com*; call 1-800-234-1660; or fax 1-800-901-9075.

Aspen Publishers
a Wolters Kluwer business

SUMMARY OF CONTENTS

CONTENTS

ix

PREFACE

The subject of religion and the state has unquestionably come of age in recent years. There is now a large enough body of court decisions on the First Amendment's religion provisions to support a full-length casebook—indeed, more than one. And the relationship of religion to government and public life has doubtless provoked even greater interest since the September 2001 terrorist attacks, which were inspired by a religious view radically opposed to the modern Western arrangement of religious liberty.

This casebook on religion and the U.S. Constitution reflects the authors' thinking on the subject over the period of a number of years. It reflects several premises about how to teach and understand the relations between government and religion.

The heart of the book is organized according to three fundamental ways in which government interacts with religion:

- the regulation of religious activity (Part III),
- the funding of religious activity (Part IV), and
- the treatment of religion in government's culture-shaping activities such as public schools (Part V).

Each of these ties together a number of sections—a structure that is designed to help students see logical relationships between cases that may involve quite different sets of facts. In each of these three major areas, we examine doctrines under both components of the First Amendment's religion provision:

- free exercise of religion and
- nonestablishment of religion.

One of the chief reasons why the Supreme Court's case law on religion has been so inconsistent and shifting is that for years the Court treated these two First Amendment concepts in isolation from each other, labeling cases as "Free Exercise Clause cases" or "Establishment Clause cases." The structure of this casebook—with free exercise rulings immediately followed by nonestablishment rulings in the same area, and vice versa—is designed to help teachers and students think about the two clauses together, to consider the implications of nonestablishment in every free exercise dispute, and vice versa. The interaction of these two clauses is the key point of Part I; it continues to be emphasized throughout the text.

This casebook seeks throughout to integrate current issues concerning religion and the state with historical and theoretical perspectives on those issues. One of the great rewards of studying church-state relations is the rich history of reflection and debate on the subject that extends back for centuries. The questions that underlie today's debates—for example, how to maintain a moral framework for society and at the same time respect the rights of conscientious dissenters—are truly perennial questions, even though they may take different forms in different times and places. Accordingly, Part II of the book provides a concentrated historical background on the development of religious liberty in America from the established churches of the colonial era up through the enactment of the First Amendment. Subsequently, each of the three largest parts of the book (III through V listed above) begins with a historically oriented section, and the text returns to historical and theoretical materials throughout.

To make possible the integration of these rich historical and theoretical perspectives, the casebook relies on fairly significant notes following the leading cases. It is difficult to make sense of the Supreme Court's case law under the Religion Clauses, which is so shifting and inconsistent taken on its own terms, without understanding that there are various historical and theoretical tensions that pull the Justices in different directions. The notes following the cases aim to help students by summarizing the holding and rationale of the case before delving into its complications and variations.

The authors have worked hard to include questions on both sides of the issues. People who look through the book will find citations to a wide range of authors. For example, see the material on Charitable Choice (in Part IV, the very last section). It includes several quotes from Carl Esbeck, a proponent of charitable choice; but following it are two or three notes that raise constitutional objections, including quotes from Alan Brownstein, the leading academic critic of charitable choice.

The richness of the subject of religion and the state means that it is difficult to cover every page of these materials in one course. Different emphases are possible: basic Religion Clause doctrines, the historical background of current issues, the legal problems faced by religious organizations, and so forth. The Teacher's Manual accompanying the book provides instructors with suggested syllabi for these varying emphases.

New developments following the publication of this edition, such as Supreme Court decisions and significant lower court decisions and scholarly commentary, will be posted on the supplemental website at http://www.bc.edu/ReligionAndTheConstitution.

A word about editing style. Another advantage of a subject as focused as religion and the Constitution is that students can read opinions in something resembling their actual form, without the need for constant severe editing. Therefore, a number of the cases here are lightly edited. We have, however, tried to streamline the reading by eliminating reported citations within excerpts. (The case citation almost always appears somewhere else in the materials.) We have indicated the editing out of text within an excerpt by ellipses, but we have not indicated where citations or footnotes have been dropped.

Finally, as with the first edition, we welcome comments from teachers and readers on all aspects of the book.

Michael W. McConnell
John H. Garvey
Thomas C. Berg

July 2006

ACKNOWLEDGMENTS

Judge McConnell thanks the many colleagues and students who have helped him to grapple with these issues over the years, and the law schools of the University of Chicago and University of Utah, which have supported his research.

Dean Garvey thanks his students and colleagues at Boston College Law School for their thoughtful contributions, and Pat Parlon for logistical support.

Professor Berg thanks colleagues and students at the University of St. Thomas School of Law (Minnesota) and Cumberland Law School for their insights, and Mary Edel-Joyce for logistical support.

The authors together thank the many colleagues at law schools and elsewhere who have used the first edition and provided comments on it, and those who generously permitted the use of excerpts from their own publications. As with the first edition, we especially thank Douglas Laycock, who contributed not only a wealth of advice and encouragement on the book, but also years of intellectual inspiration and challenge on its subject matter.

RELIGION
AND THE
CONSTITUTION

I

INTRODUCTION

Congress shall make no law respecting an establishment of religion,
or prohibiting the free exercise thereof.

—U.S. Const., amend. I

The religion provision(s) of the first amendment to the U.S. Constitution—is it one clause or two?—is (or are) America's primary effort to answer a perennial question: How should civil government treat the religious beliefs and institutions of the society? History has presented an almost endless variety of answers to that question: from ancient empires where the rulers were seen as gods, to the medieval- and Reformation-era arrangements where the state was distinct from the Christian church but each state nevertheless established and promoted a particular Christian institutional body, to modern Western arrangements in which the state gives most or all religions a substantial and equal degree of freedom.

Religion, in all its many forms, has traditionally been one of the most potent influences on both individuals and groups—their understanding of right and wrong, the nature and origins of the universe, their conception of the human person, and much more. Some sociologists have maintained a so-called "secularization" thesis, which holds that with increasing scientific awareness and educational attainment, religious conviction will tend to wither away. But this shows no sign of taking place. In some cases the resurgence of religion has been very troubled and has contributed to horrible consequences—witness the role of a certain kind of radical Islam in the attacks of September 11, 2001. But in the United States itself, the very heart of modernity, religion is potent, too. Consider the role of religious groups and ideas on both sides of today's political debates—and the fact that the most prevalent song at patriotic services after the September 11 attacks was "God Bless America." Well over 90 percent of Americans claim to believe in God; and while that mere claim does not necessarily indicate a real commitment, there are many millions of Americans for whom religion truly is a source of worldview, identity, and community.

The last three or four centuries in the West have generally (with important exceptions) seen a gradual movement away from state-enforced unity on religious

1

matters, and toward greater freedom for a wide variety of religious positions. This has happened partly because efforts to coerce religious unity through the state failed, with horrific results, such as the "wars of religion" in the 1600s. The Thirty Years' War of 1618 to 1648, pitting Protestant nations and princes against the Catholic Holy Roman Empire and its allies, devastated large parts of Germany. Hundreds of cities were ruined and villages wiped out, and a quarter of the population died from the war "and its apocalyptic secondary manifestations—price increases, hunger, epidemics, diseases." Herbert Langer, Thirty Years War 8-9 (C.S.V. Salt trans. 1980). In England, the Catholic-Protestant conflict beginning with Henry VIII produced hundreds of martyrs on each side, and the civil war between the Puritan-oriented Parliament and the Anglican Royalists in the 1640s caused the death of nearly 4 percent of the English population (almost 200,000) through battle, disease, or other effects. See, e.g., Charles Carlton, Going to the Wars: The Experience of the British Civil Wars, 1638-1651, at 339 (1992).

These traumas were very much on the minds of early Americans as they ratified the first amendment. As James Madison put it in his Memorial and Remonstrance Against Religious Assessments (1785): "Torrents of blood have been spilt in the old world, by vain attempts of the secular arm to extinguish Religious discord, by proscribing all difference in Religious opinions." Increased toleration for religious differences has also been fueled by increased religious diversity, by religious theologies themselves (especially the belief that coerced faith is not valid), and finally by secularization, which has indeed occurred to some degree. There has been an increase in the number and prominence of citizens who claim no religious beliefs at all.

But this last factor raises another question. Some critics claim that increased religious freedom in modern America has been purchased at the price of "privatizing" religion, of cutting it off from public life—that a healthy "separation of church and state" has turned into an unhealthy separation of government from religious norms and values. A common example is the general absence of religious elements in public schools, which is perhaps necessary to protect children of varying faiths, but which gives many people the impression that the schools think religion is unimportant. In a society such as ours—where government is such an important force, but so is religion—to what extent can government be separate from religion? How can a complex society have religious freedom for all faiths without unduly privatizing religion, which itself can be seen as a restriction on religious freedom?

In addition to these complexities about the relation of government to religion, there is a complexity in the text of the First Amendment's religion provision itself. The religion provision is unique among the rights-protecting provisions of the Constitution in that it has a dual aspect: It forbids both laws "respecting an establishment of religion" and laws "prohibiting the free exercise thereof." What is the relationship between these clauses? Surprisingly, more than 200 years after these 16 words were added to the Constitution, that basic question remains contested. There are several possibilities (this is not a complete list):

- The two clauses are overlapping ways of expressing essentially the same idea.
- The two clauses are harmonious but apply to different types of government action. The Free Exercise Clause applies to government action hindering

religious practice, and the Establishment Clause applies to government action benefiting religion. The two clauses, working together, minimize governmental power or influence with respect to religion.

- The two clauses are in tension with each other. The Establishment Clause prohibits government action that benefits religion, and the Free Exercise Clause requires protection for religion, which is a benefit. The task is to determine when each principle applies, and to maintain the balance between them.
- The Free Exercise Clause protects individual or corporate religious conscience from governmental coercion. The Establishment Clause protects the processes of democratic government from religious control.

This book is organized to encourage you to think about both clauses in every case. In "free exercise cases" you should think about the implications for the Establishment Clause, and in "establishment" cases you should think about the implications for the Free Exercise Clause.

In addition, in many cases religious activity takes the form of speech or expression: for example, a student passing out evangelistic tracts at a public school, or a group of believers assembling for services in a municipal park. In such cases, you will need also to consider the First Amendment's rights of freedom of speech and assembly and even the freedom of the press.

Our major emphasis, however, will be on the Free Exercise and Establishment Clauses. In the next few pages, we introduce some key general principles that aid in the interpretation of these two provisions. We also reiterate the point mentioned above: The two clauses interact with each other, and in considering a particular case about religion and government you should consider the implications of both free exercise and nonestablishment.

A. THE RELIGION CLAUSES AND UNDERLYING VALUES: THE CASE OF SABBATH OBSERVANCES

We begin with a common situation where religious conviction can conflict with the practices of government or of society: observance of the Sabbath by religious believers. The first case, from Pennsylvania, is the very first reported case raising what appears to be a free exercise claim in the United States after adoption of the Constitution. The second case, arising in Connecticut, reflects the Supreme Court's current understanding of the Establishment Clause. Think about what underlying value(s) should guide the constitutional approach to the problem in both cases.

1. Testifying on the Sabbath.   In Stansbury v. Marks, 2 Dall. 213 (Pa. 1793), a Jewish citizen was subpoenaed to testify in a civil case on Saturday, which was treated at that time as an ordinary day for public business. The opinion for the Pennsylvania Supreme Court read in its entirety:

In this cause (which was tried on Saturday, the 5th of April) the defendant offered Jonas Phillips, a Jew, as a witness; but he refused to be sworn, because it was his Sabbath. The Court, therefore, fined him £10; but the defendant, afterwards, waiving the benefit of his testimony, he was discharged from the fine.

Phillips could not testify in court in *Stansbury* without violating the Jewish law. Five of the 613 *mitzvot*, or commandments, of the orthodox Jewish faith involve keeping the Sabbath day holy. As stated in the Code of Maimonides: "Scripture says . . . *And thou shalt honor* [*the Sabbath*], *not doing thy wonted ways, nor pursuing thy business, nor speaking thereof* (Is. 58:13). Accordingly, one is forbidden to go anywhere on the Sabbath in connection with his business, or even to talk about it." The Code of Maimonides, Book Three: The Book of Seasons, Ch. 24, at 157 (Solomon Gandz & Hyman Klein trans. 1961).

On the other hand, as a resident of Pennsylvania, Phillips was subject to legal process to compel testimony in court. In those days the Pennsylvania courts were in session for six days a week, including Saturday. He was faced with a clear conflict between the requirements of civil and religious law. One possible resolution of this conflict would be to obey God's law and suffer the civil consequences (in this case, a substantial fine). Another would be to obey the civil law and suffer the spiritual consequences. Phillips did neither. Instead, he contended that under the laws of Pennsylvania he was entitled to a special dispensation that would allow him to avoid testifying on Saturday, on account of his religious principles. What could be the legal basis for such a claim?

Consider the issue in *Stansbury* and what it tells us about the nature of the constitutional right of religious freedom and the values or principles underlying it.

2. Free Exercise Arguments: Liberty and Neutrality. Note that *Stansbury* involved the law of a state, not the federal government, in 1793. At that time the First Amendment did not apply to the actions of the states, and therefore the federal Free Exercise Clause was of no use to him. The Pennsylvania constitution of 1790, however—like the constitutions of all other states at the time but one—contained a provision analogous to the Free Exercise Clause. It read (Art. IX, § 3):

> That all men have a natural and indefeasible right to worship Almighty God according to the dictates of their own consciences; that no man can of right be compelled to attend, erect, or support any place of worship, or maintain any ministry, against his consent; that no human authority can, in any case whatever, control or interfere with their rights of conscience; and that no preference shall ever be given, by law, to any religious establishment or modes of worship.

Phillips might have made several arguments under this provision.

(a) The right to "worship Almighty God according to the dictates of [his] own conscience." If Phillips relied on this clause, his argument would raise several questions. Is refraining from work on the Sabbath an act of worship? Does it matter whether Phillips would attend worship services that day? Alternatively, would he base his claim on the clause prohibiting human authorities from "control[ing] or interfer[ing] with the[ ] rights of conscience?" What is the difference, if any, between these clauses? Is the phrase "rights of conscience" broader than "the right to worship"? How does either clause compare to the language of the First Amendment's "no law prohibiting the free exercise of religion"?

(b) The "no preference" clause: "no preference shall ever be given, by law, to any religious establishment or modes of worship." Could Phillips rely on this clause? The courts of the Commonwealth were closed on Sunday, the day recognized by most Christians as the day of rest. Is it persuasive to argue that operating courts on the Sabbath day of a minority religion and not on the Sabbath day of the predominant religion is giving a "preference" to one "establishment" or "mode of worship" over another? If so, what is the remedy? Is Pennsylvania required to open its courts on Sunday? Would this advance the purposes of the constitutional provision? How does accommodating Phillips solve the constitutional problem?

(c) **If testimony can be postponed for important secular reasons, similar consideration and respect should be given to his religious reason.** Suppose that the state allowed a witness to postpone his testimony for important secular reasons, such as health problems or work-scheduling conflicts. Phillips might argue that an exemption must likewise be given for his religiously based refusal to testify on Saturday.

To summarize: we have identified three different types of argument Phillips might make in support of his claim that he could not be compelled to testify in court on the Sabbath. First is a claim of a specific **substantive liberty** (whether denominated a "right to worship according to conscience," a "right of conscience," or the "free exercise of religion"). Such a liberty gives the person a presumptive right to exercise his religion, unless it falls within an explicit or implicit limitation (of which we will say more in a moment). In addition, Phillips might have two different claims based on **neutrality or equality**. He could raise a claim of *denominational neutrality*, a claim to be treated as favorably as the most favored religion. Thus, if citizens who observe a day of rest on Sunday are spared the possibility of inconsistent civil obligations, a comparable protection should be extended to those who observe a day of rest on Saturday. Or he could make a claim of *neutrality between religious and nonreligious reasons* for not appearing in court. This raises a serious difficulty: Which nonreligious reasons provide the baseline for his claim of equal treatment? Presumably, some secular reasons would be judged too insubstantial to justify a change of court schedule; some would be honored by most judges. Should religious reasons automatically be treated as comparable in importance to the most important secular reasons? Why?

3. Limits on the Free Exercise of Religion. Construct also the arguments against Phillips's position. (Remember, the trial court rejected his argument.) Was Pennsylvania's decision to conduct public business six days a week made for religious reasons? Was it made for the purpose of interfering with the Jewish Sabbath? Does that matter? Does the imposition of a general civic obligation to testify in court amount to an attempt to control or interfere with the rights of conscience? What negative consequences would you predict if Phillips's interpretation were accepted? Is the Pennsylvania Constitution's protection for the "rights of conscience" absolute? If not, what are its limitations?

Most comparable state constitutional provisions of the period explicitly answered this question. For example, the New York Constitution of 1777, Art. XXXVIII, provided:

> The free exercise and enjoyment of religious profession and worship, without discrimination or preference, shall forever hereafter be allowed, within this State, to all mankind: *Provided*, That the liberty of conscience, hereby granted, shall not be so construed as to excuse acts of licentiousness, or justify practices inconsistent with the peace or safety of this State.

How would Phillips's case come out under this provision? What legal issues are raised by the New York Constitution that were not relevant to the Pennsylvania Constitution? How should we interpret the *lack* of a "peace or safety" proviso in the Pennsylvania Constitution?

4. Differing Conceptions of "Free and Equal": Form or Impact? In 1793, the vast majority of citizens of the United States were Protestant Christians. There were Jewish communities of sufficient size to form houses of worship in only five American cities: Savannah, Charleston, Philadelphia, New York, and Newport. It was common at that time for Jews to suffer various civic disabilities. In 11 of the states, as of 1793, Jews were denied the right to vote or hold office. See Morton Borden, Jews, Turks, and Infidels 11-15 (1984). With independence and with the adoption of free exercise clauses both at the federal level and in all but one of the state constitutions, Jewish Americans had hopes of becoming free and equal citizens, virtually for the first time in Western history.

But what it means to be "free and equal" may be a contested question. We have described three different ways in which Jonas Phillips may have understood it. There is another possibility that he might have found less appealing. Under this view, all legal distinctions based on religion would be abolished. Disabilities would be lifted. Jewish Americans would become just Americans, with the same rights and obligations as every other citizen. Under this vision, the state itself is secular, and knows not the creed of its citizens; religious practice is purely private, and receives neither the encouragement nor even the acknowledgment of the state. This would leave Phillips without a remedy.

Such a vision was adopted in France at this time as a result of the French Revolution:

> Jews, according to the terms of emancipation, were expected to divest themselves entirely of their national character—they were to give up the civil aspects of Talmudic law; disavow the political implications of Jewish messianism; abandon the use of Yiddish; and, most importantly, relinquish their semi-autonomous communal institutions. They were to become like other Frenchmen in every respect, save religion.

Vicki Caron, French-Jewish Assimilation Reassessed: A Review of the Recent Literature, 42 Judaica 134, 138 (Spring 1993) (summarizing Simon Schwarzfuchs, Du Juif à l'Israélite: Histoire d'une Mutation, 1770-1879 (1989)). One prominent French legislator explained that no one could be his fellow citizen "who does not wish to drink or eat with me, who cannot give me his daughter in marriage, whose son cannot become my son-in-law, and who, by the religion he professes is separated from all other men. Only when Jews do what other men do," he said, "what the constitution and law requires of us all, will we welcome them as citizens." Frances Malino, A Jew in the French Revolution: The Life of Zalkind Hourwitz 145 (1996).

The problem, though, was that this vision of secular equality would force Jews to abandon aspects of their Jewishness. To be sure, it would protect them from laws that explicitly singled out Jews for disabilities, and it would maintain a secular public order in which all citizens could participate on the basis of their shared characteristics. But it would not protect the ability of religious minorities to maintain their *differences* from secular society. It would provide no protection for religious practices at odds with the secular interests of the majority. To put it another way, forcing Phillips to testify on Saturday would **formally** treat him equally with other citizens, but its **impact** on him and other Jews would be quite unequal compared with the Protestant majority. You might consider an analogy to the issue of disabilities: In order to ensure that individuals with disabilities have an equal opportunity to participate, it is sometimes necessary to make special accommodations (wheelchair ramps, sign language interpretation, and so forth). For discussion of the relation between equality and difference, see Martha Minow, Making All the Difference: Inclusion, Exclusion, and American Law (1990); Timothy L. Hall, Religion, Equality, and Difference, 65 Temple L. Rev. 1 (1992).

Differing visions of religious liberty and equality thus come in conflict with each other in many cases under the Religion Clauses. The choice between these visions was contested in 1793, and it remains contested today.

5. The Other Side of the Coin: The Interaction of Free Exercise and Nonestablishment. Now add in another complication to the analysis: the fact that in the case of religious issues, more than one constitutional provision is in play.

Can it be argued that excusing Phillips from appearing in court on account of his religious beliefs would actually *violate* the Pennsylvania Constitution? Consider the fact that an individual with a powerful *secular* reason for not appearing in court that day—perhaps the need to visit a sick relative or to attend an important activity with his or her children—might be required to appear. If that were the case, would excusing Phillips because of his Sabbath violate any provision of Art. IX, §3? Or consider the fact that other parties to the case might be inconvenienced if Phillips were excused on his Sabbath. Why should they be burdened on account of his religion? Suppose the state enacted a law providing that "no person may be compelled to testify in court on a day that that person observes as his Sabbath." Does such a law promote religious freedom? Is there a sense in which it violates religious freedom? Would it violate the Establishment Clause if enacted today?

ESTATE OF THORNTON v. CALDOR, INC.
472 U.S. 703 (1985)

Chief Justice BURGER delivered the opinion of the Court.

We granted certiorari to decide whether a state statute that provides employees with the absolute right not to work on their chosen Sabbath violates the Establishment Clause of the First Amendment.

I

In early 1975, petitioner's decedent Donald E. Thornton began working for respondent Caldor, Inc., a chain of New England retail stores; he managed the men's and boys' clothing department in respondent's Waterbury, Connecticut, store. At that time, respondent's Connecticut stores were closed on Sundays pursuant to state law.

In 1977, following the state legislature's revision of the Sunday-closing laws, respondent opened its Connecticut stores for Sunday business. In order to handle the expanded store hours, respondent required its managerial employees to work every third or fourth Sunday. Thornton, a Presbyterian who observed Sunday as his Sabbath, initially complied with respondent's demand and worked a total of 31 Sundays in 1977 and 1978. In October 1978, Thornton was transferred to a management position in respondent's Torrington store; he continued to work on Sundays during the first part of 1979. In November 1979, however, Thornton informed respondent that he would no longer work on Sundays because he observed that day as his Sabbath; he invoked the protection of Conn. Gen. Stat. §53-303e(b), which provides:

> No person who states that a particular day of the week is observed as his Sabbath may be required by his employer to work on such day. An employee's refusal to work on his Sabbath shall not constitute grounds for his dismissal.

Thornton rejected respondent's offer either to transfer him to a management job in a Massachusetts store that was closed on Sundays, or to transfer him to a nonsupervisory position in the Torrington store at a lower salary.[8] In March 1980, respondent transferred Thornton to a clerical position in the Torrington store; Thornton resigned two days later and filed a grievance with the State Board of Mediation and Arbitration alleging that he was discharged from his manager's position in violation of Conn. Gen. Stat. §53-303e(b). . . .

The [Board sustained his grievance; but the] Supreme Court of Connecticut reversed, holding the statute did not have a "clear secular purpose." By authorizing each employee to designate his own Sabbath as a day off, the statute evinced the "unmistakable purpose . . . [of] allow[ing] those persons who wish to worship on a particular day the freedom to do so." The court then held that the "primary effect" of the statute was to advance religion because the statute "confers its 'benefit' on an explicitly religious basis. Only those employees who designate a Sabbath are entitled not to work on that particular day, and may not be penalized for so doing." The court noted that the statute required the State Mediation Board to decide which religious activities may be characterized as an "observance of Sabbath" in order to assess employees' sincerity, and concluded that this type of inquiry is "exactly the type of 'comprehensive, discriminating and continuing state surveillance' . . . which creates excessive governmental entanglements between church and state."

We granted certiorari. We affirm.

II

Under the Religion Clauses, government must guard against activity that impinges on religious freedom, and must take pains not to compel people to act in the name of any religion. In setting the appropriate boundaries in Establishment Clause cases, the Court has frequently relied on our holding in Lemon v. Kurtzman (1971) for guidance, and we do so here. To pass constitutional muster under *Lemon* a statute must not only have a secular purpose and not foster excessive entanglement of government with religion, its primary effect must not advance or inhibit religion.

8. The collective-bargaining agreement in effect for nonsupervisory employees provided that they were not required to work on Sunday if it was "contrary [to their] personal religious convictions."

The Connecticut statute challenged here guarantees every employee, who "states that a particular day of the week is observed as his Sabbath," the right not to work on his chosen day. The State has thus decreed that those who observe a Sabbath any day of the week as a matter of religious conviction must be relieved of the duty to work on that day, no matter what burden or inconvenience this imposes on the employer or fellow workers. The statute arms Sabbath observers with an absolute and unqualified right not to work on whatever day they designate as their Sabbath.

In essence, the Connecticut statute imposes on employers and employees an absolute duty to conform their business practices to the particular religious practices of the employee by enforcing observance of the Sabbath the employee unilaterally designates. The State thus commands that Sabbath religious concerns automatically control over all secular interests at the workplace; the statute takes no account of the convenience or interests of the employer or those of other employees who do not observe a Sabbath. The employer and others must adjust their affairs to the command of the State whenever the statute is invoked by an employee.

There is no exception under the statute for special circumstances, such as the Friday Sabbath observer employed in an occupation with a Monday through Friday schedule—a school teacher, for example; the statute provides for no special consideration if a high percentage of an employer's work force asserts rights to the same Sabbath. Moreover, there is no exception when honoring the dictates of Sabbath observers would cause the employer substantial economic burdens or when the employer's compliance would require the imposition of significant burdens on other employees required to work in place of the Sabbath observers.[9] Finally, the statute allows for no consideration as to whether the employer has made reasonable accommodation proposals.

This unyielding weighting in favor of Sabbath observers over all other interests contravenes a fundamental principle of the Religion Clauses, so well articulated by Judge Learned Hand: "The First Amendment . . . gives no one the right to insist that in pursuit of their own interests others must conform their conduct to his own religious necessities." Otten v. Baltimore & Ohio R. Co. (2d Cir. 1953). As such, the statute goes beyond having an incidental or remote effect of advancing religion. The statute has a primary effect that impermissibly advances a particular religious practice.

III

We hold that the Connecticut statute, which provides Sabbath observers with an absolute and unqualified right not to work on their Sabbath, violates the Establishment Clause of the First Amendment.

---

9. Section 53-303e(b) gives Sabbath observers the valuable right to designate a particular weekly day off—typically a weekend day, widely prized as a day off. Other employees who have strong and legitimate, but non-religious, reasons for wanting a weekend day off have no rights under the statute. For example, those employees who have earned the privilege through seniority to have weekend days off may be forced to surrender this privilege to the Sabbath observer; years of service and payment of "dues" at the workplace simply cannot compete with the Sabbath observer's absolute right under the statute. Similarly, those employees who would like a weekend day off, because that is the only day their spouses are also not working, must take a back seat to the Sabbath observer.

Justice O'CONNOR, with whom Justice MARSHALL joins, concurring.

The Court applies the test enunciated in Lemon v. Kurtzman and concludes that Conn. Gen. Stat. §53-303e(b) has a primary effect that impermissibly advances religion. I agree, and I join the Court's opinion and judgment. In my view, the Connecticut Sabbath law has an impermissible effect because it conveys a message of endorsement of the Sabbath observance.

All employees, regardless of their religious orientation, would value the benefit which the statute bestows on Sabbath observers—the right to select the day of the week in which to refrain from labor. Yet Connecticut requires private employers to confer this valued and desirable benefit only on those employees who adhere to a particular religious belief. The statute singles out Sabbath observers for special and, as the Court concludes, absolute protection without according similar accommodation to ethical and religious beliefs and practices of other private employees. There can be little doubt that an objective observer or the public at large would perceive this statutory scheme precisely as the Court does today. The message conveyed is one of endorsement of a particular religious belief, to the detriment of those who do not share it. As such, the Connecticut statute has the effect of advancing religion, and cannot withstand Establishment Clause scrutiny.

I do not read the Court's opinion as suggesting that the religious accommodation provisions of Title VII of the Civil Rights Act of 1964 are similarly invalid. These provisions preclude employment discrimination based on a person's religion and require private employers to reasonably accommodate the religious practices of employees unless to do so would cause undue hardship to the employer's business. . . . In my view, a statute outlawing employment discrimination based on race, color, religion, sex, or national origin has the valid secular purpose of assuring employment opportunity to all groups in our pluralistic society. Since Title VII calls for reasonable rather than absolute accommodation and extends that requirement to all religious beliefs and practices rather than protecting only the Sabbath observance, I believe an objective observer would perceive it as an anti-discrimination law rather than an endorsement of religion or a particular religious practice.

NOTES AND QUESTIONS

1. Why Did the Statute in *Caldor* Violate the Establishment Clause? There are several possible answers, each with a different implication for the relationship between free exercise and nonestablishment. How would each of these rationales affect the analysis of Jonas Phillips's situation in *Stansbury*?

(a) Favoring one religious interest over others. Perhaps the problem in *Caldor* is that it is unconstitutional for the state to extend a benefit to "a particular religious practice," resting on the Sabbath, and not to all religious practices. As we will see, a prime purpose of the Establishment Clause was to prohibit the government from explicitly giving one particular church favored status (as, for example, England did with the Anglican church, or colonial Massachusetts with the Congregational church). Earlier we referred to this as "denominational neutrality." Does the Connecticut statute violate this principle? If so, is it unconstitutional for the legislature to make accommodations to specific laws—such as military draft exemptions for religious pacifists, exemptions for kosher butchers from meat preparation laws, or exemptions for peyote use by Native American religions?

   (b) Favoring religious over secular interests.   Perhaps *Caldor* means that it is unconstitutional for the state to extend a benefit to religious employees that it does not extend to other employees who have "strong and legitimate, but nonreligious reasons" for objecting to work on a particular day: for example, spending time with spouses or children. As we will see, the Establishment Clause has been interpreted to prevent official favoritism for religion in general, not just favoritism for one religion. Is an exemption such as this unconstitutional favoritism for religion? Suppose that the statute were one of many statutes allowing employees to take days off for various reasons, such as jury or military service, pregnancy, the need to care for sick dependents, voting or attendance at nominating conventions, and so forth?

   In thinking about "favoritism for religion," do not forget about the implications of the Free Exercise Clause. When the First Amendment protects the "free exercise of religion" but not the free exercise of other convictions or activities, does that constitute favoritism for religion? This again raises the question whether, taken as a whole, the First Amendment treats **religious liberty** and religious exercise as a matter worthy of distinctive protection, or whether it gives only **equality** of protection, that is, only as much protection as other convictions and activities receive.

   (c) Burdening others.   Perhaps, in the light of the Free Exercise Clause, it is not always unconstitutional to give unique protection to religious convictions, but it becomes unconstitutional if the state thereby forces some other citizens to bear costs on account of those religious convictions: for example, the employee who must work the Saturday shift to make up for the Sabbath observer, or the employer who must pay premium overtime wages to that replacement. Or perhaps the state may require some citizens to bear "reasonable" costs on account of the religious convictions of others, but that requirement must not be absolute or "unyielding" (as the Court found the Connecticut rule to be): Religious interests must be properly balanced against other interests. Would you decide the case differently if it could be shown that the employer could staff its stores on Saturday and Sunday at reasonable cost, by paying premium wages on those days?

   2. The *Lemon* Establishment Clause Test: Purpose, Effect, and Entanglement. As seen in Thornton v. Caldor, the Supreme Court's most prominent attempt to define a test for an establishment of religion is the three-part test of Lemon v. Kurtzman, 403 U.S. 602 (1971): A law must (1) have a secular purpose; (2) have a "primary effect" that "neither advances nor inhibits religion"; and (3) not foster an "excessive entanglement" between government and religion.

   Since its announcement in 1971, the *Lemon* test has been widely criticized both on and off the Court. Several former or current Justices have called for abandonment or substantial modification of the *Lemon* test, and the Court has often decided cases without reference to it. This has led one scholar to declare that "*Lemon* is dead." Michael S. Paulsen, *Lemon* Is Dead, 43 Case West. Res. L. Rev. 795 (1993) (criticizing the *Lemon* test and proposing a "noncoercion" alternative). Of course, the test has received equally strong support from other quarters. See, e.g., Daniel O. Conkle, Toward a General Theory of the Establishment Clause, 82 Nw. U. L. Rev. 1113 (1988).

The most common complaints about *Lemon* are (1) that it is ambiguous and indeterminate, producing inconsistent and unprincipled results; (2) that it often requires discrimination against religion; and (3) that it creates unnecessary conflicts with the Free Exercise Clause, the Free Speech Clause, and sometimes other portions of the First Amendment. Are any of these criticisms valid with respect to the decision in Thornton v. Caldor? As you read other Establishment Clause cases in this course, consider whether the criticisms have any validity in those situations. Consider also whether any other doctrinal "test" would be superior.

B. THE CASE OF PUBLIC SCHOOL PRAYERS

Now consider another recent case involving the Establishment Clause. In Lee v. Weisman, 505 U.S. 577 (1992), a middle-school principal planning the graduation ceremony invited a local rabbi to offer an invocation and benediction; the principal advised the rabbi that the prayer should be "nonsectarian" and gave him a copy of a pamphlet of guidelines for civic prayers, written by the National Conference of Christians and Jews, an ecumenical group. The rabbi's invocation went as follows:

> God of the Free, Hope of the Brave: For the legacy of America where diversity is celebrated and the rights of minorities are protected, we thank You. May these young men and women grow up to enrich it. For the liberty of America, we thank You. May these new graduates grow up to guard it. For the political process of America in which all its citizens may participate, for its court system where all may seek justice, we thank You. May those we honor this morning always turn to it in trust. For the destiny of America, we thank You. May the graduates of Nathan Bishop Middle School so live that they might help to share it. May our aspirations for our country and for these young people, who are our hope for the future, be richly fulfilled. Amen.

A graduating student, Deborah Weisman, and her family objected to the prayer. Put yourself in their shoes. Why did they object? As it happened, the Weismans were Jewish. Why would they object to having a rabbi offer a prayer? Compare the claims of the Weismans to that of Jonas Phillips. Both felt the effects of government policies that differed from their own religious views. In what way were the injuries different?

The Supreme Court agreed with the Weismans and held that the school had violated the Establishment Clause. The Court held that the graduation prayer unconstitutionally coerced participation in a religion, because "[s]tate officials direct the performance of a formal religious exercise at [the] graduation ceremonies," and students' "attendance and participation in the state-sponsored religious activity are in a fair and real sense obligatory, though the school district does not require attendance as a condition for receipt of the diploma." The Court explained that the ceremony "places public pressure, as well as peer pressure, on attending students to stand as a group or, at least, maintain respectful silence during the Invocation and Benediction. . . . [G]iven our social conventions, a reasonable dissenter in this milieu could believe that the group exercise signified her own participation or approval of it."

Justice Scalia dissented. He pointed out that "[f]rom our Nation's origin, prayer has been a prominent part of governmental ceremonies and proclamations." He added that "[t]he coercion that was a hallmark of historical establishments of religion was coercion of religious orthodoxy and of financial support by force of law and threat of penalty," not the subtler pressure involved in *Weisman*.

We will consider Lee v. Weisman in greater detail later (p. 498), in looking at the role of religion in public schools. For now, the decision helps raise further questions about the no-establishment principle and its relationship to religious freedom.

1. Establishment Clause Arguments: Liberty, Neutrality, and Separation. Is there any overlap between the types of argument the Weismans would make against the graduation prayer and the types of argument that might have been available to Jonas Phillips? In connection with *Stansbury*, we suggested two quite different bases for Jonas Phillips's claim: (1) a **substantive liberty** to exercise religion, in the absence of a sufficient governmental purpose to the contrary; and (2) a claim of **neutrality or equality**, either among religious denominations or between religious and nonreligious claims. Can you see how Deborah Weisman might make parallel claims? Her interest in not being coerced to participate in a public prayer is a claim of substantive liberty: the liberty not to exercise religion against one's will. And she might also argue that the practice of public prayer constitutes a preference for some religions over others (perhaps for the kind of ecumenical prayer encouraged by the National Conference of Christians and Jews pamphlet), or for religious speech over secular speech. Claims such as these would treat the Establishment Clause as symmetrical to the Free Exercise Clause: Both reflect principles of (1) substantive liberty and/or (2) neutrality or equal treatment.

But many would say that claims of this sort do not fully capture what is wrong with the practice of officially sponsored public prayer. The problem, they might say, is not just "coercion" and not just "favoritism," but a third principle—that it is deeply wrong for the government of a pluralistic republic to be engaged in the sponsorship of religious worship. For example, some statements in *Weisman* suggested other constitutional problems with the graduation prayer besides its coercive aspect. The Court noted that "the potential for divisiveness over the [school's] choice of a particular member to conduct the ceremony is apparent," and that by advising the rabbi ahead of time "the principal directed and controlled the content of the prayer." Perhaps the governmental touch degrades religion; perhaps the involvement of government with religion is insulting to nonbelievers, or creates social division; perhaps all of these. Religion is simply not the proper business of government. This type of concern often goes under the rubric of **church-state separation**.

Unfortunately, the intuition behind church-state separation, while widely held, is difficult to define or express in legally manageable terms. Aren't religion and government bound to have some contact in the real world? If total separation between the two is impossible, what kinds of contacts are forbidden? What would the principle of church-state separation call for in Jonas Phillips's case: exempting him from the civil duty of testifying, or applying that duty without regard to his religion?

Consider the following argument for a strict church-state separation, made by Justice Blackmun in a concurrence in *Weisman*:

> When the government arrogates to itself a role in religious affairs, it abandons its obligation as a guarantor of democracy. Democracy requires the nourishment of dialogue and dissent, while religious faith puts its trust in an ultimate divine authority above all human deliberation. When the government appropriates religious truth, it "transforms rational debate into theological decree." Those who disagree no longer are questioning the policy judgment of the elected but the rules of a higher authority who is beyond reproach. . . . Democratic government will not last long when proclamation replaces persuasion as the medium of political exchange.

Is this an accurate picture of religion? Of democracy? Of the reasons for church-state separation? If it is accurate, what should it mean for Deborah Weisman's problem? For Jonas Phillips's problem in *Stansbury*?

2. The Limits of the Establishment Clause: Public Religious Speech by Individuals. Just as we saw boundaries on the right of free exercise in *Stansbury*, are there limits on the principle that religion and government must never mix? Suppose that precisely the same prayers as those in *Weisman* were offered under precisely the same conditions—but instead of being offered at the instigation of the principal, they were offered by the class valedictorian, who was chosen to speak based on her grades and who included a prayer in her presentation without the advance knowledge of the principal. See Doe v. Madison Joint School Dist. No. 321, 147 F.3d 832, vacated as moot, 177 F.3d 789 (9th Cir. 1999) (en banc). Presumably, dissenting students would be under the same "psychological coercion" to "participate" in the prayer (or at least to stand in respectful silence), but the government would have no direct involvement with the prayer. Would the valedictorian's speech violate the Constitution as interpreted in *Weisman*? Is "coercion" enough to violate the Establishment Clause without any governmental involvement in the decision to have a prayer?

The question can be put another way: Is the school constitutionally obligated to screen the words of speakers at graduation ceremonies to ensure that they do not include prayers? Is this consistent with the freedom of speech of the valedictorian? With free exercise? Just as a very broad statute accommodating free exercise was held to be an establishment in Thornton v. Caldor, a broad application of the Establishment Clause—holding that religious expression even without government control is unconstitutional in a public setting—might conflict with rights of free exercise and free speech. Again, remember that the two religion clauses in the First Amendment must be considered together. Does a very broad rule of church-state separation promote religious freedom, or conflict with it?

II

HISTORY

A. THE THEORY AND PRACTICE OF RELIGIOUS ESTABLISHMENTS

The classic form of "establishment of religion" known to the framers of the First Amendment was the religion "by law established" in the British Empire: the Church of England (sometimes called the Anglican Church). Not only was this the official church in the mother country, but it was established by law in all the southern colonies (including Maryland after 1688), plus the four metropolitan counties of New York. The middle colonies of Pennsylvania, Delaware, and upstate New York, plus Rhode Island, had no formal religious establishment. The New England colonies outside of Rhode Island had a somewhat different kind of religious establishment, based upon the religious judgments of the people of each town.

Under the English system, the establishment of religion had these legal features (among others):

1. Governmental Control over Doctrine and Personnel. The Act of Supremacy, passed in 1534, made the King or Queen of England the official head of the Church, and gave the monarch power to correct "the ecclesiastical state and persons, and . . . all manner of errors, heresies, schisms, [etc.]." 1 Eliz., c.1, § 8. During the reign of Edward VI, Parliament enacted the Thirty-Nine Articles—the doctrinal tenets of the Church of England—as well as the Book of Common Prayer, which prescribes the liturgy for religious worship. The Uniformity Act required all ministers (with the exception of certain trinitarian Protestant ministers exempted under the Toleration Act of 1689) to conform to these requirements. The Archbishop of Canterbury and other high church officials were (and are) appointed by the government. See William Blackstone, Commentaries on the Laws of England Bk. I, ch. 11.

2. Suppression of Alternative Faiths. Not only did the government appoint church leaders, it forbade the public preaching of alternative doctrines. As noted above, only ministers from denominations that shared most of the Anglicans' theological doctrines were permitted to preach under the Act of Toleration. Particularly severe punishments were prescribed for Catholics, partly because the Roman Catholic Church recognized the Stuart Pretenders as the legitimate kings of England between 1688 and 1745. See Blackstone's Commentaries Bk. IV, ch. 4. The preaching of Unitarianism remained illegal (at least, formally) until well into the nineteenth century. Prior to the English Civil War, so-called "puritan" Protestants (who wished to "purify" Anglican worship of its "popish" elements) were also prohibited from engaging in public worship. These restrictions were the immediate reason why the Pilgrims fled their homes in England, first to Holland and then to Plymouth Bay.

In the Anglican colonies, colonial governors reserved to themselves the right to license preachers; in New England the colonial legislatures set qualifications for ministers. Many colonies prohibited itinerant preaching (can you speculate why?); this was the issue that occasioned Elisha Williams's sermon, reprinted later in this chapter. In Virginia, until the eve of the Revolution, Baptist preachers were imprisoned for preaching without a license. The sight of Baptist ministers jailed in Culpepper County inspired the young James Madison to write his first words on the subject of religious freedom, in a letter to his college friend, William Bradford, on January 24, 1774:

> That diabolical Hell conceived principle of persecution rages among some and to their eternal Infamy the Clergy can furnish their Quota of Imps for such business. This vexes me the most of any thing whatever. There are at this [time?] in the adjacent County not less than 5 or 6 well meaning men in close [jail] for publishing their religious Sentiments which in the main are very orthodox. I have neither patience to hear talk or think of any thing relative to this matter, for I have squabbled and scolded abused and ridiculed so long about it, [to so lit]tle purpose that I am without common patience. So I [leave you] to pity me and pray for Liberty of Conscience [to revive among us].

These requirements bear a close resemblance to the licensing of the press. Both maintained government control over the key means for the propagation of opinion.

3. Political Connections.   The Church of England had an official, and prominent, position in the governmental structure of the country. Bishops, by virtue of their office, sat in the House of Lords. Pursuant to the Test Act, 25 Car. II, c.2, and the Corporation Act, 13 Car. II, st. 2, c.1, only those who had received communion in the Church of England in the preceding year and who swore that they did not believe in the Catholic doctrine of transubstantiation—the idea that the bread and wine of communion turn into the body and blood of Christ—could hold offices in government, including public corporations, military positions, and academic positions. (Isaac Newton, a non-trinitarian, thus had to obtain special leave of Parliament to teach at Cambridge.) Even after Independence, almost all of the states retained religious tests for office, some excluding Catholics, some excluding Jews, and some excluding atheists. Article VI of the U.S. Constitution forbids such "religious tests for office" at the federal level. See Gerard V. Bradley, The No Religious Test Clause and the Constitution of Religious Liberty: A Machine That Has Gone of Itself, 37 Case W. Res. L. Rev. 674 (1987).

4. Compelled Attendance and Support.   In the days of Queen Elizabeth I, subjects were required to attend church, and were fined one shilling if they did not. 1 Eliz. 1, c.2 (1559). This law remained on the books until 1846, but by the time of American Independence it was essentially unenforced. Financial support for the established church principally came in the form of land grants (profit-making lands, called "glebe lands," were expected to defray the basic needs of the minister) and mandatory tithes. (There was little in the way of direct appropriations by Parliament.) In most of the colonies—as in many European countries today—individuals were taxed for the support of the church. In the Anglican colonies, these mandatory payments went to the established Church of England; in New England they went to the minister selected by the particular town, which in practice almost always meant a Congregationalist (Puritan) minister.

The Anglican establishments of the South and metropolitan New York did not survive the American Revolution, in part because Anglican ministers tended to support the Crown, thus discrediting the church in the eyes of newly Republican America. (Can you see why Anglican theology would tend to be associated with support for England in the War of Independence?) By contrast, the Congregationalist (or Puritan) ministers of New England were enthusiastic proponents of independence (also for theological reasons, which were more complicated). The New England establishments thus emerged from the American Revolution with renewed prestige. Speaking of the Massachusetts establishment, John Adams commented that "we might as well expect a change in the solar system as to expect they would give up their establishment." By this time, however, the Massachusetts establishment had lost its earlier rigor. Adams called it "the most mild and equitable establishment of religion that was known in the world." Here are the constitutional provisions regarding toleration and establishment in Massachusetts, adopted in 1780:

CONSTITUTION OF MASSACHUSETTS (1780)
Part the First.
A Declaration of the Rights of the Inhabitants
of the Commonwealth of Massachusetts. . . .

ART. II.

It is the right as well as the duty of all men in society, publicly and at stated seasons, to worship the Supreme Being, the great Creator and Preserver of the universe. And no subject shall be hurt, molested, or restrained, in his person, liberty, or estate, for worshiping God in the manner and season most agreeable to the dictates of his own conscience, or for his religious profession or sentiments, provided he doth not disturb the public peace or obstruct others in their religious worship.

ART. III.

As the happiness of a people and the good order and preservation of civil government essentially depend upon piety, religion, and morality, and as these cannot be generally diffused through a community but by the institution of the public worship of God and of public instructions in piety, religion, and morality: Therefore, To promote their happiness and to secure the good order and preservation of their government, the people of this commonwealth have a right to invest their legislature with power to authorize and require, and the legislature shall, from time to time, authorize and require, the several towns, parishes, precincts, and other bodies-politic or religious societies to make suitable provision, at their own expense, for the institution of the public worship of God and for the support and maintenance of public Protestant teachers of piety, religion, and morality in all cases where such provision shall not be made voluntarily.

And the people of this commonwealth have also a right to, and do, invest their legislature with authority to enjoin upon all the subjects an attendance upon the instructions of the public teachers aforesaid, at stated times and seasons, if there be any on whose instructions they can conscientiously and conveniently attend.

Provided, notwithstanding, That the several towns, parishes, precincts, and other bodies-politic, or religious societies, shall at all times have the exclusive right of electing their public teachers and of contracting with them for their support and maintenance.

And all moneys paid by the subject to the support of public worship and of the public teachers aforesaid shall, if he require it, be uniformly applied to the support of the public teacher or teachers of his own religious sect or denomination, provided there be any on whose instructions he attends; otherwise it may be paid toward the support of the teacher or teachers of the parish or precinct in which the said moneys are raised.

And every denomination of Christians, demeaning themselves peaceably and as good subjects of the commonwealth, shall be equally under the protection of the law; and no subordination of any one sect or denomination to another shall ever be established by law.

Note that Massachusetts combined compelled support for religion (and especially the majority religion of the town) with protection for the free exercise of other religions, and allowed those who were in regular attendance in another church to direct their financial support to that church. There was no coercion to participate in religious worship or punishment for participation in a dissenting denomination. This combination of a noncoercive establishment with protection for free exercise was a serious possibility for the new United States. It is a combination frequently found in liberal nations today, such as Great Britain and Germany, where public support for a range of churches is combined with principles of noncoercion. What was the rationale for this kind of establishment? Consider the following opinion, written by Chief Justice Theophilus Parsons, one of the framers of the Massachusetts provision:

BARNES v. FIRST PARISH IN FALMOUTH
6 Mass. 400 (1810)

PARSONS, C.J. The plaintiff claims to be a public teacher of piety, religion, and morality, within the third article of the declaration of rights prefixed to the constitution of this commonwealth, but of a sect of Christians different from the inhabitants of the first parish in Falmouth, and publicly instructing several of the said inhabitants, who are of the same sect with himself, who usually attend on his preaching, and who have directed their taxes, paid for supporting public worship in the parish, to be paid over for his support; and he has instituted this suit to recover those taxes of the parish.

Not pretending to be the public teacher of any incorporated religious society obliged by law to maintain a public teacher, to maintain the issue on his part, he offered evidence, that in fact he was the teacher of a voluntary society of Universalists, who usually attended on his instruction. This evidence was rejected by the judge, on the ground that no person could maintain this action but a Protestant teacher of piety, religion, and morality, of some incorporated religious society; and to this rejection the plaintiff excepts.

[We must] consider the motives which induced this people to introduce into the constitution a religious establishment, the nature of the establishment introduced, and the rights and privileges it secured to the people, and to their teachers. If these points shall be clearly and justly explained, it will be easy to infer the principles by which the present action must be decided.

The object of a free civil government is the promotion and security of the happiness of the citizens. These effects cannot be produced, but by the knowledge and practice of our moral duties, which comprehend all the social and civil obligations of man to man, and of the citizen to the state. If the civil magistrate in any state could procure by his regulations a uniform practice of these duties, the government of that state would be perfect.

To obtain that perfection, it is not enough for the magistrate to define the rights of the several citizens, as they are related to life, liberty, property, and reputation, and to punish those by whom they may be invaded. Wise laws, made to this end, and faithfully executed, may leave the people strangers to many of the enjoyments of civil and social life, without which their happiness will be extremely imperfect. Human laws cannot oblige to the performance of the duties of imperfect obligation; as the duties of charity and hospitality, benevolence and good neighborhood; as the duties resulting from the relation of husband and wife, parent and child; of man to man, as children of a common parent; and of real patriotism, by influencing every citizen to love his country, and to obey all its laws. These are moral duties, flowing from the disposition of the heart, and not subject to the control of human legislation.

Neither can the laws prevent, by temporal punishment, secret offences, committed without witness, to gratify malice, revenge, or any other passion, by assailing the most important and most estimable rights of others. For human tribunals cannot proceed against any crimes, unless ascertained by evidence; and they are destitute of all power to prevent the commission of offences, unless by the feeble examples exhibited in the punishment of those who may be detected. . . .

In selecting a religion, the people [of Massachusetts] were not exposed to the hazard of choosing a false and defective religious system. Christianity had long been promulgated, its pretensions and excellences well known, and its divine authority admitted. This religion was found to rest on the basis of immortal truth; to contain a system of morals adopted to man, in all possible ranks and conditions, situations and circumstances, by conforming to which he would be meliorated and improved in all the relations of human life; and to furnish the most efficacious sanctions, by bringing to light a future state of retribution. And this religion, as understood by Protestants, tending, by its effects, to make every man submitting to its influence, a better husband, parent, child, neighbor, citizen, and magistrate, was by the people established as a fundamental and essential part of their constitution.

The manner in which this establishment was made, is liberal, and consistent with the rights of conscience on religious subjects. As religious opinions, and the time and manner of expressing the homage due to the Governor of the universe, are points depending on the sincerity and belief of each individual, and do not concern the public interest, care is taken, in the second article of the declaration of rights, to guard these points from the interference of the civil magistrate; and no man can be hurt, molested, or restrained, in his person, liberty, or estate, for worshiping God in the manner and season most agreeable to the dictates of his own conscience, or for his religious profession or sentiment, provided he does not disturb the public peace, or obstruct others in their religious worship in which case he is punished, not for his religious opinions or worships, but because he interrupts others in the enjoyment of the rights he claims for himself, or because he has broken the public peace.

Having secured liberty of conscience, on the subject of religious opinion and worship, for every man, whether Protestant or Catholic, Jew, Mahometan, or Pagan, the constitution then provides for the public teaching of the precepts and maxims of the religion, of Protestant Christians to all the people. And for this purpose it is made the right and the duty of all corporate religious societies, to elect and support a public Protestant teacher of piety, religion, and morality; and the election and support of the teacher depend exclusively on the will of a majority of each society incorporated for those purposes. As public instruction requires persons who may be taught, every citizen may be enjoined to attend on some one of these teachers, at times and seasons to be stated by law, if there be any on whose instructions he can conscientiously attend.

In the election and support of a teacher, every member of the corporation is bound by the will of the majority; but as the great object of this provision was to secure the election and support of public Protestant teachers by corporate societies, and as some members of any corporation might be of a sect or denomination of Protestant Christians different from the majority of the members, and might choose to unite with other Protestant Christians of their own sect or denomination, in maintaining a public teacher, who by law was entitled to support, and on whose instructions they usually attended, indulgence was granted, that persons thus situated might have the money they contributed to the support of public worship, and of the public teachers aforesaid, appropriated to the support of the teacher on whose instructions they should attend.

Several objections have at times been made to this establishment, which may be reduced to three: that when a man disapproves of any religion, or of any supported doctrines of any religion, to compel him by law to contribute money for public instruction in such religion or doctrine, is an infraction of his liberty of conscience; that to compel a man to pay for public religious instructions, on which he does not attend, and from which he can therefore derive no benefit, is unreasonable and intolerant; and that it is anti-christian for any state to avail itself of the precepts and maxims of Christianity, to support civil government, because the Founder of it has declared that his kingdom is not of this world. . . .

When it is remembered that no man is compellable to attend on any religious instruction, which he conscientiously disapproves and that he is absolutely protected in the most perfect freedom of conscience in his religious opinions and worship, the first objection seems to mistake a man's conscience for his money and to deny the state a right of levying and of appropriating the money of the citizens, at the will of the legislature, in which they all are represented. But as every citizen derives the security of his property, and the fruits of his industry, from the power of the state, so, as the price of this protection, he is bound to contribute, in common with his fellow-citizen, for the public use, so much of his property, and for such public uses, as the state shall direct. . . . The great error lies in not distinguishing between liberty of conscience in religious opinions and worship, and the right of appropriating money by the state. The former is an unalienable right; the latter is surrendered to the state, as the price of protection.

The second objection is, that it is intolerant to compel a man to pay for religious instruction, from which, as he does not hear it, he can derive no benefit. This objection is founded wholly in mistake. The object of public religious instruction is to teach, and to enforce by suitable arguments, the practice of a system of correct morals among the people, and to form and cultivate reasonable and just habits and manners; by which every man's person and property are protected from outrage, and his personal and social enjoyments promoted and multiplied. From these effects every man derives the most important benefits; and whether he be, or be not, an auditor of any public teacher, he receives more solid and permanent advantages from this public instruction, than the administration of justice in courts of law can give him. The like objection may be made by any man to the support of public schools, if he have no family who attend; and any man, who has no lawsuit, may object to the support of judges and jurors on the same ground; when, if there were no courts of law, he would unfortunately find that causes for lawsuits would sufficiently abound.

The last objection is founded upon the supposed anti-christian conduct of the state, in availing itself of the precepts and maxims of Christianity, for the purposes of a more excellent civil government. It is admitted that the Founder of this religion did not intend to erect a temporal dominion, agreeable to the prejudices of his countrymen; but to reign in the hearts of men, by subduing their irregular appetites and propensities, and by moulding their passions to the noblest purposes. And it is one great excellence of his religion, that, not pretending to worldly pomp and power, it is calculated and accommodated to meliorate the conduct and condition of man, under any form of civil government.

The objection goes further, and complains that Christianity is not left, for its promulgation and support, to the means designed by its Author, who requires not the assistance of man to effect his purposes and intentions. Our constitution certainly provides for the punishment of many breaches of the laws of Christianity, not for the purpose of propping up the Christian religion, but because those breaches are offences against the laws of the state; and it is a civil as well as a religious duty of the magistrate, not to bear the sword in vain. But there are many precepts of Christianity, of which the violation cannot be punished by human laws; and as obedience to them is beneficial to civil society, the state has wisely taken care that they should be taught, and also enforced by explaining their moral and religious sanctions, as they cannot be enforced by temporal punishments. And from the genius and temper of this religion, and from the benevolent character of its Author, we must conclude that it is his intention that man should be benefited by it in his civil and political relations, as well as in his individual capacity. And it remains for the objector to prove, that the patronage of Christianity by the civil magistrate, induced by the tendency of its precepts to form good citizens, is not one of the means by which the knowledge of its doctrines was intended to be disseminated and preserved among the human race.

The last branch of the objection rests on the very correct position that the faith and precepts of the Christian religion are so interwoven, that they must be taught together; whence it is inferred that the state, by enjoining instruction in its precepts, interferes with its doctrines, and assumes a power not intrusted to any human authority.

If the state claimed the absurd power of directing or controlling the faith of its citizens, there might be some ground for the objection. But no such power is claimed. The authority derived from the constitution extends no further than to submit to the understanding of the people the evidence of truths deemed of public utility, leaving the weight of the evidence, and the tendency of those truths, to the conscience of every man. . . .

These objections to our constitution cannot be made by the plaintiff, who, having sought his remedy by an action at law, must support it as resting on our religious establishment, or his claim can have no legal foundation.

The last point for our consideration is, whether this establishment, according to the true intent and design of its provisions, will, or will not, enable the plaintiff to maintain his claim to the money he demands. [The court concluded that Art. III authorized payment only to ministers in legally incorporated churches. Since Barnes belonged to an unincorporated voluntary society, his claim failed.]

NOTES AND QUESTIONS

1. Theological and Political Establishments of Religion.   There are two distinct rationales for the establishment of religion, which we might call "theological" and "political." Theological justifications are based on the idea that the power of the state should be used for the support of the true religion—either for the glory of God or for the spiritual welfare of the people. Political justifications are based on idea that the inculcation of certain common ideas and values is useful for civil purposes (whether or not they are true). In most (all?) societies, there are efforts to unite the people around certain shared symbols, values, virtues, and ideas. Where such efforts carry the official weight of government, they may be called an "establishment." When those symbols, values, virtues, and ideas have a religious foundation, the system can be called an "establishment of religion." What are some examples of "establishment" of nonreligious ideas? Consider such things as "English only" laws, Flag Day, Martin Luther King Day, or public school inculcation of virtues such as honesty, hard work, or racial tolerance.

2. The Massachusetts Establishment.   The Massachusetts establishment was originally predominantly theological in nature. The Pilgrims and Puritans who traveled to the "wilderness" of New England did so in order to create a commonwealth governed on genuinely Christian principles (by their lights), a "City on a Hill" that would serve as an inspiration to the world. They believed that government had an obligation to God to uphold the truth. They thought that allowing the teaching of religious error was an affront to God and bad for the people. The leading Boston clergyman, John Cotton, commented: "It is no impeachment of church liberty, but an enlargement of its beauty and honor, to be bound by strict laws and holy commandments, to observe the pure worship of God[.]" Irwin H. Polishook, Roger Williams, John Cotton and Religious Freedom 76 (1967). He maintained that "[t]he word of God in such things [religious fundamentals] is so clear, that [a person] *cannot but be convinced* in conscience of the dangerous error of his way, after once or twice admonition wisely and faithfully dispenses. . . . If such a man, after such admonition, shall still persist in the error of his way and be punished, he is not persecuted for cause of conscience, but *for sinning against his own conscience.*" John Cotton, The Bloudy Tenet, Washed (1647).

To what extent did Chief Justice Parsons rely on theological justifications of this sort? Did he advocate the public teaching of religion because it would be pleasing to God, or an advancement of the truth? Or because it would induce people to behave as better citizens? Note the rationale offered by Article III of the Massachusetts Constitution:

> As the happiness of a people and the good order and preservation of civil govern-
> ment essentially depend upon piety, religion, and morality, and as these cannot
> be generally diffused through a community but by the institution of the public
> worship of God and of public instructions in piety, religion, and morality:
> Therefore . . .

Is this a "theological" or a "political" justification?

The idea that government should control religion for reasons of state has deep roots. Consider this passage from philosopher Thomas Hobbes:

LEVIATHAN
Thomas Hobbes, Ch. 42 (1651)

[T]he right of judging what doctrines are fit for peace, and to be taught the subjects, is in all commonwealths inseparably annexed . . . to the sovereign power civil, whether it be in one man, or in one assembly of men. For it is evident to the meanest capacity, that men's actions are derived from the opinions they have of the good or evil, which from those actions redound unto themselves; and consequently, men that are once possessed of an opinion, that their obedience to the sovereign power will be more hurtful to them than their disobedience, will disobey the laws, and thereby overthrow the commonwealth, and introduce confusion and civil war; for the avoiding whereof, all civil government was ordained. And therefore in all commonwealths of the heathen, the sovereigns have had the name of pastors of the people, because there was no subject that could lawfully teach the people, but by their permission and authority.

This right of the heathen kings cannot be thought taken from them by their conversion to the faith of Christ; who never ordained that kings, for believing in him, should be deposed, that is, subjected to any but himself, or, which is all one, be deprived of the power necessary for the conservation of peace amongst their subjects, and for their defense against foreign enemies. And therefore Christian kings are still the supreme pastors of their people, and have power to ordain what pastors they please, to teach the Church, that is, to teach the people committed to their charge. . . .

Seeing then in every Christian commonwealth, the civil sovereign is the supreme pastor, to whose charge the whole flock of his subjects is committed, and consequently that it is by his authority that all other pastors are made, and have power to teach, and perform all other pastoral offices; it followeth also, that it is from the civil sovereign that all other pastors derive their right of teaching, preaching, and other functions pertaining to that office, and that they are but his ministers; in the same manner as the magistrates of towns, judges in courts of justice, and commanders of armies, are all but ministers of him that is the magistrate of the whole commonwealth, judge of all causes, and commander of the whole militia, which is always the civil sovereign. And the reason hereof, is not because they that teach, but because they that are to learn, are his subjects. For let it be supposed, that a Christian king commit the authority of ordaining pastors in his dominions to another king, as divers Christian kings allow that power to the Pope; he doth not thereby constitute a pastor over himself, nor a sovereign pastor over his people; for that were to deprive himself of the civil power; which, depending on the opinion men have of their duty to him and the fear they have of punishment in another world, would depend also on the skill and loyalty of doctors, who are no less subject, not only to ambition, but also to ignorance, than any other sort of men. So that where a stranger hath authority to appoint teachers, it is given him by the sovereign in whose dominions he teacheth.

NOTES AND QUESTIONS

1. What Is Wrong with Establishment of Religion?   Hobbes, who wrote during a time of civil war among religious factions, thought it was too dangerous to allow the authority of the Church to be at odds with the civil power. The result could only be to encourage subjects to disobey the law, and to "introduce confusion and civil war." If civil and spiritual authorities were combined, however, the moral suasion of ministers and the promise and threat of eternal rewards and punishments could be harnessed to state purposes as an auxiliary form of social control over the population. What, if anything, is wrong with Hobbes's argument? Are there any ways in which our government attempts to shape behavior by inculcating certain values or attitudes?

Note that Hobbes's argument is not dependent on the particular values that a regime might wish to inculcate. Hobbes was particularly concerned about national unity and the prevention of civil war. Under other circumstances, regimes might emphasize other issues, and thus foster a different kind of religion. One regime might wish to foster an ideal of citizenship based on thoughtless obedience to authority, military valor, and honor. Another might wish to develop citizens who think for themselves, question authority, and dare to speak out. One might emphasize the virtues of tolerance, equality, or environmental awareness, another the virtues of hard work and personal responsibility. Whatever the content,

Hobbes would say that the government must be able to make use of the institutions for formation and inculcation of values, to serve its civic ends.

Thomas Jefferson wrote that "it is time enough for the rightful purposes of civil government for its officers to interfere when principles break out into overt acts against peace and good order." Hobbes, by contrast, claimed that "it is evident to the meanest capacity, that men's actions are derived from the opinions they have." In effect, Hobbes argued, it is too late to seek to control human behavior after bad acts have already taken place. A wise ruler will attempt to shape the character of the people. As the English statesman Edmund Burke argued: "[I]t is the right of government to attend much to opinions; because, as opinions soon combine with passions, even when they do not produce them, they have much influence on actions." Edmund Burke, Speech on the Petition of the Unitarians (1791). Chief Justice Parsons agreed, noting that many evil deeds are done in secret, and that much good conduct—what he called "imperfect obligations"—cannot be coerced by law. Which side in this conflict is correct?

Perhaps the answer to Hobbes is to say that governments have a right to be concerned about opinion and character, but that religion is not relevant to such things. Government could attempt to inculcate public virtue through secular means, but not by controlling or fostering religion. Jefferson wrote that "our civil rights have no dependence on our religious opinions, any more than our opinions in physicks or geometry." But is this a good analogy? Our opinions in physics and geometry have little bearing on how we behave as citizens and neighbors. Is the same thing true of religion?

The drafters of Article III of the Massachusetts Constitution of 1780 evidently disagreed with Jefferson. They presupposed that the "happiness of a people and the good order and preservation of civil government essentially depend upon piety, religion, and morality," and that "these cannot be generally diffused through a community but by the institution of the public worship of God and of public instructions in piety, religion, and morality." One does not have to agree with them that religion is *necessary* for these purposes; perhaps other means would be helpful as well. But can it be denied that religion is often one of the most powerful influences on human behavior? If so, what is wrong with Hobbes's position? Or Parsons's? Does Jefferson's argument depend on the proposition that religion is irrelevant to behavior?

Jefferson also argued that attempts to shape opinion by means of governmental power were doomed to failure. He wrote that "all attempts to influence [the mind] by temporal punishments or burdens, or by civil incapacitations, tend only to beget habits of hypocrisy and meanness." That might well be true of the overt coercion of adults. But is it true of what might be called a "soft" establishment: government control over education and use of public symbols, holidays, and other means for inculcation of values? When public schools engage in character education, or seek to encourage environmental responsibility or discourage smoking or drug use, does this merely "beget habits of hypocrisy and meanness"? Or does it sometimes work?

What was wrong with the Massachusetts establishment? Did it violate principles of liberty of conscience? Baptists complained that requiring them to contribute money even to their own church was an interference with their relationship with God, and hence a violation of conscience. Chief Justice

Parsons responded that this argument "seems to mistake a man's conscience for his money." Who is right? Do you think that a taxpayer's conscience is violated when tax money is spent for things he disapproves of? Does a taxpayer who conscientiously disapproves of abortion have a right to exemption from public payments for abortions? Is the conscience of a Quaker violated by forcing him to pay for the military? Is the conscience of a smoker violated when he pays for government antismoking campaigns?

Did the Massachusetts establishment violate principles of neutrality? Article III of the Declaration of Rights envisioned various "towns, parishes, precincts, and other bodies-politic" establishing separate churches. There were religious as well as political reasons for this arrangement. Unlike the Church of England, which was organized hierarchically (different parish priests reporting to the same bishop, ultimately accountable to the sovereign), the Massachusetts establishment was congregational. It consisted of autonomous local churches. This ecclesiastical form was one legacy of the Protestant Reformation, a conscious rejection of the hierarchy in the Roman Catholic Church. Because the Puritan (or Congregational, as they were called in Massachusetts) churches were organized in this way, the government could plausibly claim that there was no one established church. Anglicans, if they were a majority in the town of Holyoke, could make the Church of England the established church of that town; their neighbors in Chicopee might choose Presbyterianism.

This was truer in theory than in practice. First, most towns had a Congregational majority. Smaller sects were dispersed rather than clustered in one place where they might take control. Second, the system satisfied a majority of people in each town, but it did nothing for local dissenters. Article III tried to deal with this problem by allowing a citizen to direct that his taxes be "applied to the support of the public teacher or teachers of his own religious sect or denomination." But as the court held in *Barnes*, this was limited to "incorporated societies." That excluded a lot of churches. Was it neutral? This restriction was repealed in 1811. Did that solve the neutrality problem? Note that the default position, which applied to anyone who did not regularly attend a church, was to give the money to the town-established church. Note also that taxpayers could not direct their taxes to secular nonprofit organizations. If these provisions were amended, would the scheme be "neutral"?

The Massachusetts establishment was eventually repealed, in 1833, but only partly because of principled objections. In the years after *Barnes*, Unitarians grew significantly in numbers, and began to control more and more of the towns around Boston. The Supreme Judicial Court ruled that even when the majority of members of a parish church were trinitarian Congregationalists, the right to levy taxes rested with the majority of voters, who in that case were Unitarian. Baker v. Fales, 16 Mass. (5 Tyng) 488 (1820). With trinitarians now finding themselves in the unaccustomed position of having to provide certificates like other dissenting groups, "[t]he problem of religious taxes was now a matter of concern to the ruling elite as well as to the minorities." William G. McLoughlin, Soul Liberty: The Baptists' Struggle in New England, 1630-1833, at 299 (1991). Eventually the supporters of state assessments gave up, and in 1833 Massachusetts effectively ended the system by passing a constitutional amendment stating that "all religious sects and denominations, demeaning themselves peaceably and as good citizens of the commonwealth, shall be equally under the protection of the law and no subordination of any one sect or denomination to another shall ever be established by law."

2. Do Establishments Injure Religion? It may not be accurate to view religious establishment as a special "benefit" to religion. Many observers thought that establishment was injurious to religion—not only to dissenting religions, which suffered discrimination, but to the established church itself. Observe that the established churches of Europe today are plagued with low attendance and seemingly low levels of enthusiasm or belief. As early as the 1830s, Alexis de Tocqueville, a Frenchman who traveled extensively in the United States, found that Americans were far more religiously observant than most Europeans, and he attributed this difference to the separation of church and state. See Alexis de Tocqueville, 1 Democracy in America 292, 295-301 (J.P. Mayer ed., 1969) (1835).

How does government aid harm an established church? Government-enforced monopoly privileges tend to produce inefficiencies in commercial markets. Maybe this is true for churches, too. One of the earliest arguments against governmental support for religion was made by the economist Adam Smith in The Wealth of Nations, the first comprehensive argument for free market economics:

> The teachers of [religious] doctrine . . . may depend altogether for their subsistence upon the voluntary contributions of their hearers; or they may derive it from some other fund to which the law of their country may entitle them. . . . Their exertion, their zeal and industry, are likely to be much greater in the former situation than in the latter. In this respect the teachers of new religions have always had a considerable advantage in attacking those ancient and established systems of which the clergy, reposing themselves upon their benefices, had neglected to keep up the fervour of faith and devotion in the great body of the people; and having given themselves up to indolence, were become altogether incapable of making any vigorous exertion in defence even of their own establishments. . . . [Clergy who have been given state support] have many of them become very learned, ingenious, and respectable men; but they have in general ceased to be very popular preachers.

Adam Smith, An Inquiry into the Nature and Causes of the Wealth of Nations (1776).

The British philosopher David Hume, who believed that enthusiastic religion was dangerous to the public good, advised the civil magistrate for this very reason "to bribe their [the clergy's] indolence, by assigning stated salaries to their profession, and rendering it superfluous for them to be farther active, than merely to prevent their flock from straying in quest of new pastures." David Hume, 4 History of England 30-31 (1773). One of the first acts of the French revolutionaries was to make ministers, priests, and rabbis salaried employees of the Republic.

Moreover, with government support may come government control—hence, the subordination of religious to governmental or political objectives. An established church may be forced to "water down" its message in order to maintain consensus and avoid offending segments of the population. Is there a parallel to this in the instructions that the school principal gave to the rabbi about the content of his graduation prayer in Lee v. Weisman?

The Baptists of Virginia opposed a proposal to provide financial support to churches on the following ground:

> If, therefore, the State provide a Support for Preachers of the Gospel, and they receive it in Consideration of their Services, they must certainly when they Preach act as Officers of the State, and ought to be Accountable thereto for their Conduct, not only as Members of civil Society, but also *as Preachers*. The Consequence of this is, that those whom the State employs in its Service it has a Right to *regulate* and *dictate to*; it may judge and determine *who* shall preach; *when* and *where* they shall preach; and *what* they must preach.

Declaration of the Virginia Association of Baptists (Dec. 25, 1776), in 1 The Papers of Thomas Jefferson 660-661 (J. Boyd ed., 1950). This helps explain why, as we will see, the most "enthusiastic" and evangelical denominations were in the forefront of the struggle against established churches at the time of the founding.

3. Violations of Neutrality/Equality. Another feature of the classic establishment of religion is that it treated different faiths and beliefs unequally, according special privileges to the favored religion(s) and imposing penalties or disadvantages on others. By contrast, one of the most common claims about our disestablishmentarian constitutional system is that it is "neutral" toward and among religions. This proposition was affirmed repeatedly during the founding period. Every one of the 12 state constitutional free exercise provisions in 1789 contained language referring to denominational equality (though in two states this equality was extended only to Christian denominations). New York and South Carolina both specified that the right of free exercise was to be "without discrimination or preference," and Virginia provided that "all men are equally entitled to the free exercise of religion." Other states used words like "every," "all," "no," "equal," or "equally" to make the same point. Rhode Island's proposed amendment to the federal Constitution stated that "no particular sect or society ought to be favored or established by law." J. Elliot, ed., 1 The Debates in the Several States on the Adoption of the Federal Constitution 334 (1854). In a similar vein, Jonas Phillips, leader of the Jewish community in Philadelphia, whom we encountered in Stansbury v. Marks (p. 3), drafted a petition to the Convention asking that the Constitution be framed to ensure that "all Religious societies are on an Equal Footing." M. Schappes, ed., A Documentary History of the Jews in the United States, 1654-1875, at 69 (1950). Madison's initial draft of the Free Exercise Clause referred to "the full and equal rights of conscience." Clearly, equality is a major value underlying the Religion Clause.

But remember, from the free exercise materials above, that equality (or neutrality) can have different and even conflicting meanings. Does it merely require that the government treat all religions equally (what we have called "denominational equality")? Or does it mean that the government should be neutral as between religion and comparable secular ideas or commitments? Chief Justice Rehnquist has suggested that "[t]he evil to be aimed at . . . appears to have been the establishment of a national church, and perhaps the preference of one religious sect over another; but it was definitely not concerned about whether the Government might aid all religions evenhandedly." Wallace v. Jaffree, 472 U.S. 38, 99 (1985) (Rehnquist, J., dissenting). The majority on the Supreme

Court, however, has consistently held that the Establishment Clause requires neutrality not only among religions but between religion and "nonreligion" (whatever that might mean). For a historical defense of this position, see Douglas Laycock, "Nonpreferential" Aid to Religion: A False Claim About Original Intent, 27 Wm. & Mary L. Rev. 875 (1986).

A second question is whether the "neutrality" of a policy toward religion should be determined by its **form** or by its **impact**. A government policy is "formally neutral" if it makes no reference (explicit or through deliberate proxy) to religion. Such policies could be said to be "religion-blind"—like requiring Saturday testimony from a witness without considering his Jewish faith. A policy is neutral in its impact if it creates neither incentive nor disincentive to engage in a religious practice. This kind of neutrality is sometimes called "substantive neutrality." See Douglas Laycock, Formal, Substantive, and Disaggregated Neutrality Toward Religion, 39 DePaul L. Rev. 993 (1990). Formal and substantive neutrality are quite different, since the former disregards religion while the other seeks to minimize the impact on religion. Obviously, substantive neutrality can never be entirely achieved. Every government action has *some* impact on religious practice. Paving roads makes it easier to go to church, and military recruitment efforts tend to dampen enthusiasm for religious pacifism. So, theories of substantive neutrality are principally directed at government policies, like the Saturday court sessions in *Stansbury*, that have a disproportionate effect on religious minorities that could be avoided without injury to important governmental purposes.

B. MAJOR INFLUENCES ON THE IDEA OF RELIGIOUS LIBERTY

With the possible exception of the Netherlands, the United States was the first nation to adopt what Roger Williams, over a century before, had called the "livelie experiment" in religious liberty. It had always been thought necessary that nations be united by religion as well as allegiance, and that the government rest on religious as well as political authority. The founders were taking a risk. They were charting unknown territories. But the idea of religious liberty did not originate with the Congress that drafted the Bill of Rights. Some of the colonies had experienced religious liberty for more than 150 years before Independence. Let us examine the influences that combined to produce the American idea of religious liberty.

THE ESSENTIAL RIGHTS AND LIBERTIES OF RELIGION IN THE AMERICAN CONSTITUTIONAL EXPERIMENT

John Witte, Jr.
71 Notre Dame L. Rev. 371, 377-388 (1996)

Within the eighteenth century sources at hand, two theological perspectives on religious liberties and rights were critical to constitutional formation: those of congregational Puritans and of free church evangelicals. Two contemporaneous political perspectives were equally influential: those of enlightenment thinkers and civic republicans. Exponents of these four perspectives often found common cause and used common language, particularly during the Constitutional Convention and ratification debates. Yet each group cast its views in a distinctive ensemble, with its own emphases and its own applications. . . .

1. Puritan Views

The New England Puritans were the direct heirs of the theology of religious liberty taught by European Calvinists. They had revised and refined this European legacy through the efforts of John Winthrop, John Cotton, Cotton Mather, Jonathan Edwards, Charles Chauncy, Jonathan Mayhew, and a host of other eminent writers. Since the 1630s, the Puritans had dominated the New England colonies and thus had ample occasion to cast their theological and political principles into constitutional practice.

The Puritans who wrote on religious liberties and rights were concerned principally with the nature of the church, of the state, and of the relationship between them. They conceived of the church and the state as two separate covenantal associations, two seats of Godly authority in the community. Each institution, they believed, was vested with a distinct polity and calling. The church was to be governed by pastoral, pedagogical, and diaconal authorities who were called to preach the word, administer the sacraments, teach the young, [and] care for the poor and the needy. The state was to be governed by executive, legislative, and judicial authorities who were called to enforce law, punish crime, cultivate virtue, and protect peace and order.

In the New England communities where their views prevailed, the Puritans adopted a variety of safeguards to ensure the basic separation of the institutions of church and state. Church officials were prohibited from holding political office, serving on juries, interfering in governmental affairs, endorsing political candidates, or censuring the official conduct of a statesman. Political officials, in turn, were prohibited from holding ministerial office, interfering in internal ecclesiastical government, performing sacerdotal functions of clergy, or censuring the official conduct of a cleric. To permit any such officiousness on the part of church or state officials, Governor John Winthrop averred, "would confound [ ] those Jurisdictions, which Christ hath made distinct."

Although church and state were not to be confounded, however, they were still to be "close and compact." For, to the Puritans, these two institutions were inextricably linked in nature and in function. Each was an instrument of Godly authority. Each did its part to establish and maintain the community. As one mid-eighteenth century writer put it, "I look upon this as a little model of the Gloriou[s] Kingdome of Christ on earth. Christ Reigns among us in the Common wealth as well as in the Church, and hath his glorious Interest involved and wrapt up in the good of both Societies respectively." The Puritans, therefore, readily countenanced the coordination and cooperation of church and state.

State officials provided various forms of material aid to churches and their officials. Public properties were donated to church groups for meeting houses, parsonages, day schools, and orphanages. Tax collectors collected tithes and special assessments to support the ministers and ministry of the congregational church. Tax exemptions and immunities were accorded to some of the religious, educational, and charitable organizations that they operated. Special subsidies and military protections were provided for missionaries and religious outposts. Special criminal laws prohibited interference with religious properties and services. State officials also provided various forms of moral support to the church. Sabbath day laws prohibited all forms of unnecessary labor and uncouth leisure on Sundays and holy days, and required faithful attendance at worship services.

Church officials, in turn, provided various forms of material aid and accommodation to the state. Church meetinghouses and chapels were used not only to conduct religious services, but also to host town assemblies, political rallies, and public auctions, to hold educational and vocational classes, to house the community library, to maintain census rolls and birth, marriage, and death certificates. Parsonages were used not only to house the minister and his family, but also to harbor orphans and widows, the sick and the aged, victims of abuse and disaster. Church officials also afforded various forms of moral support to the state. They preached obedience to the authorities and imposed spiritual discipline on parishioners found guilty of crime. They encouraged their parishioners to be active in political affairs and each year offered "election day sermons" on Christian political principles. They offered learned expositions on the requirements of Godly law, and occasionally offered advice to legislatures and courts.

Puritan leaders of colonial New England left little room for individual religious experimentation. Despite their adherence to a basic separation of the institutions of church and state, the New England authorities insisted on general adherence to the creeds and canons of Puritan Calvinism. Already in the 1630s, dissidents from this faith, such as Anne Hutchinson and Roger Williams, were summarily dismissed from the colony. Immigration restrictions in Massachusetts Bay throughout the seventeenth century left little room to Quakers, Catholics, Jews, "Familists, Antinomians, and other Enthusiasts." Although in the eighteenth century, religious dissidents of many kinds came to be tolerated in the New England colonies, they enjoyed only limited political rights and social opportunities and were subject to a variety of special governmental restrictions, taxes, and other encumbrances.

2. Evangelical Views

Though the evangelical tradition of religious liberty is sometimes traced to the seventeenth century—particularly to Roger Williams, the founder of colonial Rhode Island and William Penn, the founder of Pennsylvania—it did not emerge as a strong political force until after the Great Awakening of circa 1720-1780. Numerous spokesmen for the evangelical cause rose up in the course of the later eighteenth century all along the Atlantic seaboard—Isaac Backus, John Leland, John Wesley, and a host of other pastors and pamphleteers. Though the evangelicals had enjoyed fewer opportunities than the Puritans to institutionalize their views, they nonetheless had a formidable influence on the early American constitutional experiment.

Like the Puritans, the evangelicals advanced a theological theory of religious rights and liberties. They likewise advocated the institutional separation of church and state—the construction of a "wall of Separation between the Garden of the Church and the Wilderness of the world," to quote Roger Williams. The evangelicals went beyond the Puritans, however, both in their definition of

individual and institutional religious rights and in their agitation for a fuller
separation of the institutions of church and state. The evangelicals sought to
protect the liberty of conscience of every individual and the freedom of association of every religious group. Their solution was thus to prohibit all legal
establishments of religion, and, indeed, all admixtures of religion and politics.
As John Leland, the fiery Baptist preacher, put it in a proposed amendment to
the Massachusetts Constitution:

> To prevent the evils that have heretofore been occasioned in the world by religious
> establishments, and to keep up the proper distinction between religion and pol-
> itics, no religious test shall ever be requested as a qualification of any officer, in any
> department of this government; neither shall the legislature, under this constitu-
> tion, ever establish any religion by law, give any one sect a preference to another, or
> force any man in the commonwealth to part with his property for the support of
> religious worship, or the maintenance of ministers of the gospel.

Later, Leland put the matter even more bluntly: "The notion of a Christian commonwealth should be exploded forever." Religious voluntarism lay at the heart of
the evangelical view. Every individual, they argued, must be given the liberty of
conscience to choose or to change his or her faith. "[N]othing can be true religion
but a voluntary obedience unto [God's] revealed will," declared the Baptist Isaac
Backus. State coercion or control of this choice—either directly through persecution and forced collection of tithes and services, or indirectly through withholding civil rights and benefits from religious minorities—was an offense both
to the individual and to God. A plurality of religions should coexist in the community, and it was for God, not the state, to decide which of these religions should
flourish and which should fade. "Religious liberty is a divine right," wrote the
evangelical preacher Israel Evans, "immediately derived from the Supreme Being,
without the intervention of any created authority. . . . [T]he all-wise Creator
invested [no] order of men with the right of judging for their fellow-creatures
in the great concerns of religion."

Every religious body was likewise to be free from state control of their assembly and worship, state regulations of their property and polity, state incorporation of their society and clergy, state interference in their discipline and
government. Every religious body was also to be free from state emoluments
like tax exemptions, civil immunities, property donations, and other forms of
state support for the church, that were readily countenanced by Puritan and
other leaders. The evangelicals feared state benevolence towards religion and
religious bodies almost as much as they feared state repression. For those religious bodies that received state benefits would invariably become beholden to
the state, and distracted from their divine mandates. "[I]f civil Rulers go so far
out of their Sphere as to take the Care and Management of religious affairs upon
them," reads a 1776 Baptist Declaration, " Yea . . . Farewel to 'the free exercise
of Religion.'"

The chief concern of the evangelicals was theological, not political. Having
suffered for more than a century as a religious minority in colonial America, and
even longer in Europe, they sought a constitutional means to free all religion
from the fetters of the law, to relieve the church from the restrictions of the state.
In so doing, they developed only the rudiments of a political theory. They were

content with a state that created a climate conducive to the cultivation of a plurality of religions and accommodated all religious believers and religious bodies without conditions or controls.

3. ENLIGHTENMENT VIEWS

Exponents of the enlightenment tradition in America provided a political theory that complemented the religious rights theology of the evangelicals. Though American exponents of the enlightenment claimed early European visionaries such as John Locke and David Hume, they did not emerge as a significant political voice until the mid-eighteenth century. The American Revolution served to transform the American enlightenment tradition from scattered groups of elite philosophers into a sizeable company of intellectual and political lights. Members of this company, though widely divergent in theological perspective and social position, were united in their efforts to convert enlightenment ideals into constitutional imperatives and in their adherence to the political views of such spokesmen as Thomas Jefferson, Benjamin Franklin, and others.

The primary purpose of enlightenment writers was political, not theological. They sought not only to free religion and the church from the interference of politics and the state, as did the evangelicals, but, more importantly, to free politics and the state from the intrusion of religion and the church. Exponents of the enlightenment movement taught that the state should give no special aid, support, privilege, or protection to organized religion in the form of tax exemptions, special criminal protections, administrative subsidies, or the incorporation of religious bodies. Nor should the state predicate its laws or policies on explicitly religious grounds or religious arguments, or draw on the services of religious officials or bodies to discharge state functions. As Madison put it in 1822: "[A] perfect separation between ecclesiastical and civil matters" is the best course, for "religion & Gov. will both exist in greater purity, the less they are mixed together." Madison, however, did not press this logic to absolutist conclusions—particularly when it came to the "adiaphora" or nonessentials of church-state relations. In an 1832 letter to Rev. Jasper Adams, he wrote:

> [I]t may not be easy, in every possible case, to trace the line of separation between the rights of religion and the Civil authority with such distinctness as to avoid collisions & doubts on unessential points. The tendency to a usurpation on one side or the other, or to a corrupting coalition or alliance between them, will be best guarded against by an entire abstinence of the Gov. from interference in any way whatever, beyond the necessity of preserving public order, & protecting each sect ag. trespasses on its legal rights by others.

Such views were based on a profound skepticism about organized religion and a profound fear of an autocratic state. To allow church and state to be unrestricted, it was thought, would be to invite arbitrariness and abuse. To allow them to combine would be to their mutual disadvantage—to produce, in Thomas Paine's words, "a sort of mule-animal, capable only of destroying, and not of breeding up." Such views were also based on the belief that a person is fundamentally an individual being and that religion is primarily a matter of private reason and conscience and only secondarily a matter of communal association and corporate confession. Every person, James Madison wrote, has the right to form a rational opinion about the duty he owes the Creator and the manner in which that duty is to be discharged. Whether that religious duty is to be discharged individually or corporately is of secondary importance. Such views were also based on a contractarian political philosophy that called for the state to ensure the maximum liberty of citizens and their associations and to intervene only where one party's exercise of liberty intruded on that of the other.

Post-revolutionary Virginia proved to be fertile ground for political exponents of the enlightenment tradition to cultivate these views. . . .

4. CIVIC REPUBLICAN VIEWS

The "civic republicans," as they have come to be called in recent histories, were an eclectic group of politicians, preachers, and pamphleteers who strove to cultivate a set of common values and beliefs for the new nation. Their principal spokesmen were John Adams, Samuel Adams, Oliver Ellsworth, George Washington, James Wilson, and other leaders—though the movement attracted considerable support among the spiritual and intellectual laity of the young republic as well. Just as the enlightenment leaders found their theological allies among the evangelicals, so the republican leaders found their theological allies among the Puritans.

To be sure, the civic republicans shared much common ground with evangelical and enlightenment exponents. They, too, advocated liberty of conscience for all and state support for a plurality of religions in the community. They, too, opposed religious intrusions on politics that rose to the level of political theocracy and political intrusions on religion that rose to the level of religious establishment. But, contrary to evangelical and enlightenment views and consistent with Puritan views, civic republicans sought to imbue the public square with a common religious ethic and ethos—albeit one less denominationally specific and rigorous than that countenanced by the Puritans.

"Religion and Morality are the essential pillars of Civil society," George Washington declared. "[W]e have no government," John Adams echoed, "armed with power capable of contending with human passions unbridled by morality and religion." "Religion and liberty are the meat and the drink of the body politic," wrote Yale President Timothy Dwight. According to the civic republicans, society needs a fund of religious values and beliefs, a body of civic ideas and ideals that are enforceable both through the common law and through communal suasion. This was what Benjamin Franklin had called the "Publick Religion" (and what is now called the "civil religion") of America, which undergirded the plurality of sectarian religions. This "Publick Religion" taught a creed of honesty, diligence, devotion, public spiritedness, patriotism, obedience, love of God, neighbor, and self, and other ethical commonplaces taught by various religious traditions at the time of the founding. Its icons were the Bible, the Declaration of Independence, the bells of liberty, and the Constitution. Its clergy were public-spirited Christian ministers and religiously devout politicians. Its liturgy was the proclamations of prayers, songs, sermons, and Thanksgiving Day offerings by statesmen and churchmen. Its policy was government appointment of legislative and military chaplains, government sponsorship of general religious education and organization, and government enforcement of a religiously based morality through positive law.

Civic republicans countenanced state support and accommodation for religious institutions, for they were regarded as allies and agents of good government. . . . Civic republicans, therefore, endorsed tax exemptions for church properties and tax support for religious schools, charities, and missionaries; donations of public lands to religious organizations; and criminal protections against blasphemy, sacrilege, and interruption of religious services. In theory, such state emoluments were to be given indiscriminately to all religious groups. In reality, certain Protestant groups received the preponderance of such support, while Quakers, Catholics, and the few Jewish groups about were routinely excluded.

Post-revolutionary Massachusetts proved to be fertile ground for the cultivation of these civic republican views. [They] also found favor in the Continental Congress, which authorized the appointment of tax-supported chaplains to the military, tax appropriations for religious schools and missionaries, diplomatic ties to the Vatican, and recitations of prayer at its opening sessions and during the day of Thanksgiving. The Continental Congress also passed the Northwest Ordinance in 1787, which provided, in part: "Religion, morality, and knowledge, being necessary to good government and the happiness of mankind, schools and the means of education shall forever be encouraged."

NOTES AND QUESTIONS

The theological and political thinkers whom Witte describes were concerned with religious rights and liberties in a world very different from ours. Still, it might be of some help in understanding their similarities and differences to think about how they might have dealt with some of the questions we debate today.

1. Exemptions from the Law. Consider the plight of religious minorities like Jonas Phillips in Stansbury v. Marks (p. 3). Would he have had to testify on a Saturday in Puritan Massachusetts? Who would have offered the strongest support to his argument for an exemption? Would any of the groups Witte considers have opposed exemptions in principle?

2. Government Sponsored Prayer. What about prayer at public gatherings like the commencement in Lee v. Weisman (p. 12)? Would it have been forbidden in the Massachusetts Bay Colony? Would eighteenth century evangelicals have frowned on it as an improper mixing of religion and politics? (Do evangelical Protestants support it today, and if so why? Do they agree among themselves?) Would enlightenment writers have allowed it? Civic republicans like George Washington?

3. Tax Support for Religious Institutions. Would their answers be the same if the issue were tax support for parochial schools? It is unlikely that the Massachusetts Bay Colony would have supported Catholic or Jewish schools, but what about Congregational schools? Would there have been any enthusiasm for such assistance among citizens who were not themselves seriously religious? Would evangelicals and enlightenment thinkers have opposed such aid?

Suppose the state were to offer vouchers that students could spend at any school they chose—including parochial schools?

Witte begins his review with the observation that there were two theological perspectives on religious liberty critical to the constitutional formation: Congregational Puritans and Free Church Evangelicals. Elisha Williams, rector of Yale University and later Justice of the Connecticut Supreme Court, was a Congregationalist minister inspired by the Great Awakening. He was therefore, in a sense, a combination of the two theological positions. The following sermon was delivered in opposition to a proposed bill that would have prohibited itinerant preaching.

THE ESSENTIAL RIGHTS AND LIBERTIES OF PROTESTANTS
Elisha Williams (1744)

Every man has an equal right to follow the dictates of his own conscience in the affairs of religion. Every one is under an indispensable obligation to search the scripture for himself (which contains the whole of it) and to make the best use of it he can for his own information in the will of GOD, the nature and duties of Christianity. And as every Christian is so bound; so he has an unalienable right to judge of the sense and meaning of it, and to follow his judgment wherever it leads him; even an equal right with any rulers be they civil or ecclesiastical. This I say, I take to be an original right of the humane nature, and so far from being given up by them if they should be so weak as to offer it. Man by his constitution as he is a reasonable being capable of the knowledge of his Maker; is a moral & accountable being; and therefore as every one is accountable for himself, he must reason, judge and determine for himself. That faith and practice which depends on the judgment and choice of any other person, and not on the person's own understanding judgment and choice, may pass for religion in the synagogue of Satan, whose tenet is that ignorance is the mother of devotion; but with no understanding Protestant will it pass for any religion at all. No action is a religious action without understanding and choice in the agent. Whence it follows, the rights of conscience are sacred and equal in all, and strictly speaking unalienable. This *right of judging every one for himself in matters of religion* results from the nature of man, and is so inseparable connected therewith, that a man can no more part with it than he can with his power of thinking: and it is equally reasonable for him to attempt to strip himself of the power of reasoning, as to attempt the vesting of another with this right. And whoever invades this right of another, be he pope or Caesar, may with equal reason assume the other's power of thinking, and so level him with the brutal creation. A man may alienate some branches of his property and give up his right in them to others; but he cannot transfer the right of conscience, unless he could destroy his rational and moral powers, or substitute some other to be judged for him at the tribunal of GOD . . .

Now inasmuch as the scriptures are the only rule of faith and practice to a Christian; hence every one has an unalienable right to read, enquire into, and impartially judge of the sense and meaning of it for himself. For if he is to be governed and determined therein by the opinions and determinations of any others, the scriptures cease to be a rule to him, and those opinions or determinations of others are substituted in the room thereof. . . .

This is a truth of too great importance for a Christian ever in any measure to give up; and is so clear and obvious a truth, as may well pass for a self-evident maxim, *That a Christian is to receive his Christianity from* CHRIST *alone.* For what is it which is necessarily implied and supposed in the very notion of a Christian but this, that he is a follower and disciple of CHRIST, one who receives and professes to believe his doctrines as true, and submits to his commands? And so far only as any does this, is he a Christian: and so far therefore as he receives or admits any other doctrines or laws, is he to be denominated from that person or sect, from whose authority or instruction he receives them. . . .

Again, if CHRIST be the Lord of the conscience, the sole King in his own kingdom; then it will follow, that all such as in any manner or degree assume the power of directing and governing the consciences of men, are justly chargeable with invading his rightful dominion; He alone having the right they claim. Should the king of France take it into his head to prescribe laws to the subjects of the king of Great Britain; who would not say, it was an invasion of and insult offer'd to the British legislature.

I might also add, that for any to assume the power of directing the consciences of men, not leaving them to the scriptures alone, is evidently declaring them to be defective and insufficient to that purpose, did not know what was necessary and sufficient for us, and has given us a law, the defects of which were to be supplied by the wisdom of some of his own wiser disciples. How high an impeachment this is of his infinite wisdom, such would do well to consider, who impose their own doctrines, interpretations or decisions upon any men by punishments, legal incapacities, or any other methods besides those used and directed to in the sacred scriptures.

And as all imposers on men's consciences are guilty of rebellion against GOD and CHRIST, of manifest disobedience to and contempt of their authority and commands; so all they who submit their consciences to any such unjust usurp'd authority, besides the share which such persons necessarily have in the guilt of the usurpers, as countenancing and giving in to their illegal claim and supporting their wicked pretensions, they do likewise renounce subjection to the authority and laws of CHRIST.

NOTES AND QUESTIONS

1. Theological Premises for Religious Freedom. What are Elisha Williams's premises and what is his argument for liberty of conscience? Note that his argument depends on the proposition that each believer must read and interpret the scriptures for himself or herself. This idea originated in Protestant opposition to the Roman Catholic claim that the scriptures could best be understood in light of the teaching authority of the Church. Note the anti-Catholic rhetoric of the sermon (such as the reference to the "synagogue of Satan," which is a reference to the Catholic Church). For an insightful discussion of the Protestant theological argument for religious freedom, see Nicholas Wolterstorff, A Religious

Argument for the Civil Right to Freedom of Religious Exercise, Drawn from American History, 36 Wake Forest L. Rev. 535 (2001).

Does it matter that the argument for liberty of conscience proceeds from Protestant sectarian premises? Is it possible to have a theory of freedom of religion that is wholly neutral on theological issues?

Note that Williams's argument for liberty of conscience is *not* based on any theory of individual autonomy, but rather on the theory that laws governing religious practice are an invasion of the proper authority of God. What is the significance of that?

Note also that Williams supplies a "theological" counter to Hobbes's (and Parsons's) "political" argument for establishment: essentially, that the freedom of each person to act upon his own understanding of the will of God is more important than anything that might be achieved by a political establishment. It seems quite different from Jefferson's answers, which were fundamentally based on the idea that religion could be irrelevant to the state. Williams does not argue for liberty of conscience on the ground that religion is irrelevant, but on the ground that it is supremely important, and that governmental involvement with religion is an invasion of the sovereignty of God.

2. Political Arguments for Religious Freedom: The Enlightenment.   Witte observes that alongside these two theological views were two political strands in our idea of religious liberty. One of these—the enlightenment tradition—complements the religious theory of the evangelicals. The most prominent figure in this tradition was the seventeenth century political philosopher John Locke. The following is his first Letter on Toleration, written in 1689. This letter had considerable currency in the United States during the founding period. It was quoted and paraphrased in many a sermon and political pamphlet. It had a major influence on the thinking of Thomas Jefferson. See Charles Kessler, Locke's Influence on Jefferson's Bill for Establishing Religious Freedom, 25 J. Church & State 231 (1983).

A LETTER CONCERNING TOLERATION
John Locke (1689)

I esteem it above all things necessary to distinguish exactly the business of civil government from that of religion and to settle the just bounds that lie between the one and the other. If this be not done, there can be no end put to the controversies that will be always arising between those that have, or at least pretend to have, on the one side a concernment for the interest of men's souls, and, on the other side, a care of the commonwealth.

The commonwealth seems to me to be a society of men constituted only for the procuring, preserving, and advancing their own civil interests.

Civil interests I call life, liberty, health, and indolency of body; and the possession of outward things, such as money, lands, houses, furniture, and the like. . . .

Now that the whole jurisdiction of the magistrate reaches only to these civil concernments, and that all civil power, right and dominion, is bounded and confined to the only care of promoting these things; and that it neither can nor ought in any manner to be extended to the salvation of souls, these following considerations seem unto me abundantly to demonstrate.

First, because the care of souls is not committed to the civil magistrate, any more than to other men. It is not committed unto him, I say, by God; because it appears not that God has ever given any such authority to one man over another as to compel anyone to his religion. Nor can any such power be vested in the magistrate by the consent of the people, because no man can so far abandon the care of his own salvation as blindly to leave to the choice of any other, whether prince or subject, to prescribe to him what faith or worship he shall embrace. For no man can, if he would, conform his faith to the dictates of another. All the life and power to true religion consist in the inward and full persuasion of the mind; and faith is not faith without believing. Whatever profession we make, to whatever outward worship we conform, if we are not fully satisfied in our own mind that the one is true and the other well pleasing unto God, such profession and such practice, far from being any furtherance, are indeed great obstacles to our salvation. For in this manner, instead of expiating other sins by the exercise of religion, I say, in offering thus unto God Almighty such a worship as we esteem to be displeasing unto Him, we add unto the number of our other sins those also of hypocrisy and contempt of His Divine Majesty.

In the second place, the care of souls cannot belong to the civil magistrate, because his power consists only in outward force; but true and saving religion consist in the inward persuasion of the mind, without which nothing can be acceptable to God. And such is the nature of the understanding, that it cannot be compelled to the belief of anything by outward force. Confiscation of estate, imprisonment, torments, nothing of this nature can have any such efficacy as to make men change the inward judgement that they have framed of things.

It may indeed be alleged that the magistrate may make use of arguments, and, thereby draw the heterodox into the way of truth, and procure their salvation. I grant it; but this is common to him with other men. In teaching, instructing, and redressing the erroneous by reason, he may certainly do what becomes any good man to do. Magistracy does not oblige him to put off either humanity or Christianity; but it is one thing to persuade, another to command; one thing to press with arguments, another with penalties. This civil power alone has a right to do; to the other, goodwill is authority enough. . . .

In the third place, the care of the salvation of men's souls cannot belong to the magistrate; because, though the rigour of laws and the force of penalties were capable to convince and change men's minds, yet would not that help at all to the salvation of their souls. For there being but one truth, one way to heaven, what hope is there that more men would be led into it if they had no rule but the religion of the court and were put under the necessity to quit the light of their own reason, and oppose the dictates of their own consciences, and blindly to resign themselves up to the will of their governors and to the religion which either ignorance, ambition, or superstition had chanced to establish in the countries where they were born? In the variety and contradiction of opinions in religion, wherein the princes of the world are as much divided as in their secular interests, the narrow way would be much straitened; one country alone would be in the right, and all the rest of the world put under an obligation of following their princes in the ways that lead to destruction; and that which heightens the absurdity, and very ill suits the notion of a Deity, men would owe their eternal happiness or misery to the places of their nativity.

These considerations, to omit many others that might have been urged to the same purpose, seem unto me sufficient to conclude that all the power of civil government relates only to men's civil interests, is confined to the care of the things of this world, and hath nothing to do with the world to come.

Let us now consider what a church is. A church, then, I take to be a voluntary society of men, joining themselves together of their own accord in order to the public worshiping of God in such manner as they judge acceptable to Him, and effectual to the salvation of their souls. . . .

But as in every Church there are two things especially to be considered—the outward form and rites of worship, and the doctrines and articles of faith—these things must be handled each distinctly that so the whole matter of toleration may the more clearly be understood.

Concerning outward worship, I say, in the first place, that the magistrate has no power to enforce by law, either in his own Church, or much less in another, the use of any rites or ceremonies whatsoever in the worship of God. And this, not only because these Churches are free societies, but because whatsoever is practised in the worship of God is only so far justifiable as it is believed by those that practise it to be acceptable unto Him. Whatsoever is not done with that assurance of faith is neither well in itself, nor can it be acceptable to God. . . .

But some may ask: "What if the magistrate should enjoin anything by his authority that appears unlawful to the conscience of a private person?" I answer that, if government be faithfully administered and the counsels of the magistrates be indeed directed to the public good, this will seldom happen. But if, perhaps, it do so fall out, I say, that such a private person is to abstain from the action that he judges unlawful, and he is to undergo the punishment which it is not unlawful for him to bear. For the private judgement of any person concerning a law enacted in political matters, for the public good, does not take away the obligation of that law, nor deserve a dispensation. But if the law, indeed, be concerning things that lie not within the verge of the magistrate's authority (as, for example, that the people, or any party amongst them, should be compelled to embrace a strange religion, and join in the worship and ceremonies of another Church), men are not in these cases obliged by that law, against their consciences. For the political society is instituted for no other end, but only to secure every man's possession of the things of this life. . . .

But what if the magistrate believe such a law as this to be for the public good? I answer: As the private judgement of any particular person, if erroneous, does not exempt him from the obligation of law, so the private judgement (as I may call it) of the magistrate does not give him any new right of imposing laws upon his subjects, which neither was in the constitution of the government granted him, nor ever was in the power of the people to grant, much less if he make it his business to enrich and advance his followers and fellow-sectaries with the spoils of others. But what if the magistrate believe that he has a right to make such laws and that they are for the public good, and his subjects believe the contrary? Who shall be judge between them? I answer: God alone. For there is no judge upon earth between the supreme magistrate and the people.

NOTES AND QUESTIONS

1. Locke's Theory of Separate Spheres: Civil and Religious.   Is it possible, as Locke says, to "distinguish exactly the business of civil government from that of religion?" Are there some areas of life in which both church and state are concerned? What about education of the young, care for the poor, marriage and family life, and so forth? Many of the activities of churches concern the government: their buildings must comply with health and fire codes, their employment is subject to labor law, their use of funds affects their tax status, and their pronouncements can help or hinder government action. By the same token, many of the activities of the government concern the churches. How can we draw the line? Who is to say which aspects of life are purely civil or which have a religious dimension? Isn't this one of the issues about which the various religions disagree? Note that Locke draws the line by assigning to the civil magistrate authority over everything that concerns the public good, excluding only the care of souls and the rites or ceremonies of worship. In the case of a conflict between an order of the magistrate and the dictates of divine law, the believer must obey the magistrate or suffer the civil penalty. Is there any room for accommodation in such a system? How would Locke have responded to Jonas Phillips in *Stansbury*?

2. The Effect of the Expanded State on the Two Spheres.   In Locke's time, the government largely confined its attentions to protecting the public peace from foreign invasion and domestic disturbance. Education, care of the poor and the sick, and many other areas of moral/cultural concern were largely left to the church. In such a world, Locke's separationism left a wide field of authority to religious institutions. In modern times, however, the welfare-regulatory state has vastly expanded its powers into areas formerly private and frequently religious. The scope of governmental interests now vastly exceeds that anticipated by Locke. Under Locke's conception of the division of "business" between church and state, what is the effect of this expansion of government? Is there any way for the government to expand its scope without shrinking the scope of religion?

3. Political Arguments for Religious Freedom: Civic Republicanism and the Enlightenment.   The other political ingredient in our idea of religious liberty is the civic republican tradition. It is instructive to see that influence at work in the thought of George Washington—and to compare it with the enlightenment ideals of our third president, Thomas Jefferson.

FAREWELL ADDRESS
George Washington (1796)

Of all the dispositions and habits which lead to political prosperity, religion and morality are indispensable supports. In vain would that man claim the tribute of patriotism who should labor to subvert these great pillars of human happiness— these firmest props of the duties of men and citizens. The mere politician, equally with the pious man, ought to respect and to cherish them. A colume could not trace all their connections with private and public felicity. . . . And let us with caution indulge the supposition that morality can be maintained without religion. Whatever may be conceded to the influence of refined education on minds of peculiar structure, reason and experience both forbid us to expect that national morality can prevail in exclusion of religious principle.

. . . It is substantially true that virtue or morality is a necessary spring of popular government. The rule indeed extends with more or less force to every species of free government. Who that is a sincere friend to it can look with indifference upon attempts to shake the foundation of the fabric? Promote, then, as an object of primary importance, institutions for the general diffusion of knowledge. In proportion as the structure of a government gives force to public opinion, it is essential that public opinion should be enlightened.

LETTER TO THE RELIGIOUS SOCIETY CALLED QUAKERS

George Washington (1789)

Your principles and conduct are well known to me; and it is doing the people called Quakers no more than justice to say, that (except their declining to share with others the burden of common defense) there is no denomination among us, who are more exemplary and useful citizens.

I assure you very explicitly, that in my opinion the conscientious scruples of all men should be treated with great delicacy and tenderness: and it is my wish and desire, that the laws may always be as extensively accommodated to them, as a due regard for the protection and essential interests of the nation may justify and permit.

LETTER TO A COMMITTEE OF THE DANBURY BAPTIST ASSOCIATION

Thomas Jefferson, Washington (January 1, 1802)

Gentlemen,—The affectionate sentiments of esteem and approbation which you are so good as to express towards me, on behalf of the Danbury Baptist Association, give me the highest satisfaction. My duties dictate a faithful and zealous pursuit of the interests of my constituents, and in proportion as they are persuaded of my fidelity to those duties, the discharge of them becomes more and more pleasing.

Believing with you that religion is a matter which lies solely between man and his God, that he owes account to none other for his faith or his worship, that the legislative powers of government reach actions only, and not opinions, I contemplate with sovereign reverence that act of the whole American people which declared that their legislature should "make no law respecting an establishment of religion, or prohibiting the free exercise thereof," thus building a wall of separation between Church and State. Adhering to this expression of the supreme will of the nation in behalf of the rights of conscience, I shall see with sincere satisfaction the progress of those sentiments which tend to restore to man all his natural rights, convinced he has no natural right in opposition to his social duties.

I reciprocate your kind prayers for the protection and blessing of the common Father and Creator of man, and tender you for yourselves and your religious association, assurances of my high respect and esteem.

NOTES ON THE STATE OF VIRGINIA

Thomas Jefferson, Query 17, 157-161 (1784)

The error seems not sufficiently eradicated, that the operations of the mind, as well as the acts of the body, are subject to the coercion of the laws. But our rulers can have authority over such natural rights only as we have submitted to them. The rights of conscience we never submitted, we could not submit. We are answerable for them to our God. The legitimate powers of government extend to such acts only as are injurious to others. But it does me no injury for my neighbour to say there are twenty gods, or no god. It neither picks my pocket nor breaks my leg.

NOTES AND QUESTIONS

1. Enlightenment Versus Civic Republican Views of Religion. Washington and Jefferson shared a commitment to the rights of conscience, but in what ways did their understandings of religious freedom differ? Jefferson advocated a "wall of separation" between church and state, while Washington maintained that "religion and morality" are "indispensable supports" to "political prosperity." What are the implications of these positions?

Perhaps more strikingly, Jefferson commented that "the legislative powers of government reach actions only, and not opinions," and that a person has "no natural right in opposition to his social duties." Does this mean that the First Amendment protects only opinions, but not actions based on those opinions? Is that consistent with the term "free *exercise* of religion"? How are a person's "social duties" to be defined? By the legislature? Does this mean that the "natural right" of free exercise of religion places no limit on "social duties" as defined by the legislature? Contrast these statements with Washington's "wish and desire" that the laws be "accommodated" to the religious "scruples" of the Quakers—which presumably included exemption from such "social duties" as service in the military and the taking of oaths.

Is there any connection between the two Presidents' respective positions on the connection between religion and government (totally separated, according to Jefferson; religion an "indispensable support" to Washington) and their positions on free exercise accommodations? Which position is most in the interest of religious minorities? Which position is most in the interest of atheists and unbelievers? Which position best reflects the meaning of the First Amendment?

2. Religious Teachings and Public Life. In his *Notes on the State of Virginia*, Jefferson advocated the rights of conscience on the ground that "The legitimate powers of government extend to such acts only as are injurious to others. But it does me no injury for my neighbor to say there are twenty gods, or no god. It neither picks my pocket nor breaks my leg." But what happens when religious teachings *do* have an effect on others, for good or ill? (When religions proclaim that a war in which the country is engaged is unjust, this can undermine the war effort; when religions teach the supremacy of one race or the hatefulness of another, it affects civil rights; when religions inspire people to overcome their dependency on alcohol or drugs, or to become productive citizens, this can benefit the entire community.) Does Jefferson's freedom of conscience apply only when religious teachings are irrelevant to life on earth? Did Washington think that the Quakers' refusal to serve in the military was a matter of indifference to the public? Should religion be protected because it is of no importance to the public, or because it is of such high importance that it outweighs other public purposes?

3. The "Wall of Separation."   Jefferson's Letter to the Danbury Baptists is famous for its metaphor of the "wall of separation between Church and State." This metaphor has proven very influential in the Supreme Court's thinking about the Establishment Clause. The Court first quoted it in Reynolds v. United States, 98 U.S. 145, 164 (1879), where the Court said that it was "an authoritative declaration of the scope and effect of the [First A]mendment." When the Establishment Clause was first applied against the states, the Court invoked Jefferson again. Everson v. Board of Education, 330 U.S. 1, 15 (1947). For many people his wall of separation is synonymous with nonestablishment. But what, exactly, did Jefferson mean by a "wall of separation"?

The metaphor of the "wall" was not new with Jefferson. It may have originated with Roger Williams, a devout and obstreperous religious malcontent who founded the colony of Rhode Island on principles of religious toleration. In 1644, in *The Bloudy Tenent of Persecution,* Williams had written that

> the church of the Jews under the old testament in the type, and the church of the Christians under the new testament in the antitype, were both separate from the world; and that when they have opened a gap in the hedge or wall of separation between the garden of the church and the wilderness of the world, God has ever broken down the wall itself, removed the candlestick, etc. and made his garden a wilderness, as at this day. And that therefore if he will ever please to restore his garden and paradise again, it must of necessity be walled in peculiarly unto himself from the world, and that all that shall be saved out of the world are to be transplanted out of the wilderness of the world, and added unto his church or garden.

Did Jefferson's use of the "wall" metaphor mean the same thing as Roger Williams's did? Probably not. To begin with, Jefferson was not greatly concerned about harm to religious institutions as such. Notice his observation that "religion is a matter which lies solely between man and his God." Jefferson was hostile to orthodox Christianity, as well as Judaism, and contemptuous of religious enthusiasm. His own religious faith is probably best described as "deist"—the view that there is a Creator God, but that He plays no active role in human affairs. Hence reference to "the common Father and Creator of man" in this letter, and to the "Creator" in the Declaration of Independence. Jefferson viewed Jesus as a good man and excellent moral teacher, but not as divine. Jefferson composed his own version of the gospels, *The Life and Morals of Jesus of Nazareth,* carefully excising all references to miracles from the New Testament account. He wrote in a letter late in his life:

> If, by *religion*, we are to understand *sectarian dogmas*, in which no two of them agree, then your exclamation is just, that this would be the best of all possible worlds, if there were no religion in it.

Letter to John Adams, May 5, 1817, in 2 The Adams-Jefferson Letters 512 (L. Cappon ed., 1959).

Unlike Washington, Jefferson thought that the effects of religion on the polity were largely deleterious. In particular, he was concerned that efforts to establish a religion led to persecution and civil war. He observed in his Notes on the State of Virginia that "Millions of innocent men, women, and children, since the introduction of Christianity, have been burnt, tortured, fined, imprisoned; yet we have not advanced one inch toward uniformity." But quite apart from that, Jefferson saw an inherent inconsistency between an established religion (like the Anglican Church in Virginia) and the natural right to equality that made democracy possible. The problem with orthodox forms of Christianity was that they depended on divine revelation to explain the truths of religion. And revelation is not a book that everyone can read. The faithful and their ministers have access to a special form of knowledge. This was not Jefferson's approach to religion. He preferred Nature's God (the term he used in the Declaration of Independence) to the Bible's. How does this compare to Washington's understanding of the civic function of religion?

C. THE VIRGINIA ASSESSMENT CONTROVERSY

In a colony named for Queen Elizabeth (the Virgin Queen), whose first town was named for King James (Jamestown), it is not surprising that settlers would transplant the established English church. King James required as much in the charters he granted in 1606 and 1609. The early laws of the colony directed new arrivals to repair to the minister for an examination of their faith. Those who settled were required to attend church and forbidden to blaspheme. The legislature created glebe lands for the support of the clergy and a system of mandatory tithes. Sanford H. Cobb, The Rise of Religious Liberty in America 74-82 (1902).

The provisions for clerical support were still in place on the eve of the Revolutionary War, but they had begun to fall apart. As in New England, there were various religious groups—Baptists and Presbyterians most prominent among them—who resented the obligation to support a church from which they dissented. Quite apart from that, the Anglican establishment's connections with the mother country caused disaffection even among people who were not religiously fervent. The state convention that formally severed relations with England in 1776 also adopted a Declaration of Rights guaranteeing the free exercise of religion. The Declaration was drafted by George Mason; Madison assisted him with the section on religious freedom.

VIRGINIA DECLARATION OF RIGHTS (1776)

A Declaration of Rights made by the Representatives of the good people of Virginia, assembled in full and free Convention; which rights do pertain to them and their posterity, as the basis and foundation of Government.

1. That all men are by nature equally free and independent, and have certain inherent rights, of which, when they enter into a state of society, they cannot, by

any compact, deprive or divest their posterity; namely, the enjoyment of life and liberty, with the means of acquiring and possessing property, and persuing and obtaining happiness and safety. . . .

16. That Religion, or the duty which we owe to our Creator, and the manner of discharging it, can be directed only by reason and conviction, not by force or violence: and, therefore, all men are equally entitled to the free exercise of religion, according to the dictates of conscience; and that it is the mutual duty of all to practise Christian forbearance, love, and charity, towards each other.

NOTES AND QUESTIONS

1. The Language of the Declaration of Rights. The Declaration of Rights was a product of legislative deliberation in which George Mason and James Madison were the principal participants. Mason produced the initial draft: "that all men should enjoy the fullest toleration in the exercise of religion, according to the dictates of conscience, unpunished and unrestrained by the magistrate, unless under color of religion any man disturb the peace, the happiness, or safety of society." Madison objected to the word "toleration" on the ground that it implied legislative grace. As George Washington was later to write to the Jewish Congregation of Newport, Rhode Island, "It is now no more that toleration is spoken of, as if it was by the indulgence of one class of people, that another enjoyed the exercise of their inherent natural rights." 31 The Writings of George Washington 93 n.65 (J. Fitzpatrick ed., 1939). In place of Mason's "toleration" language, Madison proposed that "all men are equally entitled to the full and free exercise of religion according to the dictates of conscience." Madison also argued that the "peace, happiness, and safety" language of the Mason draft was insufficiently protective. He proposed that free exercise of religion be protected "unless under color of religion the preservation of equal liberty and the existence of the State are manifestly endangered." The Mason proposal would have been less protective than most of the other states (because the "happiness" of society is such a generous standard for governmental justification), while the Madison proposal would have been far more protective than any other state. The Virginia legislature ultimately adopted language that did not spell out the nature of the state interest that could outweigh a free exercise claim. Most likely, this was a compromise through silence. See Michael W. McConnell, The Origins and Historical Understanding of Free Exercise of Religion, 103 Harv. L. Rev. 1409, 1443-1444, 1462-1463 (1990).

2. The New Religious Assessment Proposal. The Declaration of Rights did not address the issue of assessments, but it made it more difficult to uphold a system that required all citizens to contribute to the support of one Church. The legislature abolished the tax for nonmembers of the Anglican Church in 1776 and for members in 1779. Hening's Statutes 9:164, 10:197. Five years later the issue arose again, although in a different form. In the 1780s, after the excitement of the successful War of Independence had cooled, the nation (under the Articles of Confederation) entered a period of economic recession and cultural self-doubt. Many believed that the new nation was lacking in the "public virtue" needed to sustain republican government. Many attributed this to the decline in the public teaching and proclamation of religion. In 1784 the General Assembly considered Patrick Henry's Bill Establishing a Provision for Teachers of the Christian Religion, more popularly known as the Assessment Bill, reprinted below.

Supporters of the bill, as its preamble indicated, believed that the "diffusion of Christian knowledge" would promote civil tranquility by "correcting the morals of men, restraining their vices, and preserving the peace of society." Although the bill aided only Christian teachers, this limitation made little difference in the proposed law's effect: "[F]or all practical purposes Christianity and religion were synonymous in Virginia in 1784." There were no non-Christian teachers of religion. Leo Pfeffer, Church, State and Freedom 109-110 (1967).

A BILL ESTABLISHING A PROVISION FOR TEACHERS OF THE CHRISTIAN RELIGION (1784)

Whereas the general diffusion of Christian knowledge hath a natural tendency to correct the morals of men, restrain their vices, and preserve the peace of society; which cannot be effected without a competent provision for learned teachers, who may be thereby enabled to devote their time and attention to the duty of instructing such citizens, as from their circumstances and want of education, cannot otherwise attain such knowledge; and it is judged that such provision may be made by the Legislature, without counteracting the liberal principle heretofore adopted and intended to be preserved by abolishing all distinctions of pre-eminence amongst the different societies or communities of Christians;

Be it therefore enacted by the General Assembly, That for the support of Christian teachers, _____ per centum on the amount, or _____ in the pound on the sum payable for tax on the property within this Commonwealth, is hereby assessed, and shall be paid by every person chargeable with the said tax at the time the same shall become due; and the Sheriffs of the several Counties shall have power to levy and collect the same in the same manner and under the like restrictions and limitations, as are or may be prescribed by the laws for raising the Revenues of this State.

And be it enacted, That for every sum so paid, the Sheriff or Collector shall give a receipt, expressing therein to what society of Christians the person from whom he may receive the same shall direct the money to be paid, keeping a distinct account thereof in his books. The Sheriff of every County, shall, on or before the _____ day of _____ in every year, return to the Court, upon oath, two alphabetical lists of the payments to him made, distinguishing in columns opposite to the names of the persons who shall have paid the same, the society to which the money so paid was by them appropriated; and one column for the names where no appropriation shall be made. One of which lists, after being recorded in a book to be kept for that purpose, shall be filed by the Clerk in his office; the other shall by the Sheriff be fixed up in the Court-house, there to remain for the inspection of all concerned. . . .

And be it further enacted, That the money to be raised by virtue of this Act, shall be by the Vestries, Elders, or Directors of each religious society, appropriated to a provision for a Minister or Teacher of the Gospel of their denomination, or the providing places of divine worship, and to none other use whatsoever; except in the denominations of Quakers and Menonists, who may receive what is collected from their members, and place it in their general fund, to be disposed of in a manner which they shall think best calculated to promote their particular mode of worship.

And be it enacted, That all sums which at the time of payment to the Sheriff or Collector may not be appropriated by the person paying the same, shall be accounted for with the Court in manner as by this Act is directed; and after deducting for his collection, the Sheriff shall pay the amount thereof (upon account certified by the Court to the Auditors of Public Accounts, and by them to the Treasurer) into the public Treasury, to be disposed of under the direction of the General Assembly, for the encouragement of seminaries of learning within the Counties whence such sums shall arise, and to no other use or purpose whatsoever.

THIS Act shall commence, and be in force, from and after the ____ day of ____ in the year ____.

NOTES AND QUESTIONS

1. The "Nonpreferential" Assessment. Far more than Article III of the Massachusetts Declaration of Rights, the Assessment Bill embodies a theory of nonpreferentialism. The preamble expresses the intention of adhering to "the liberal principle . . . abolishing all distinctions of pre-eminence amongst the different societies or communities of Christians." In fact Henry's Bill is more neutral than that. The Bill allows each taxpayer to designate the church to which his payment would be sent. Moreover, unlike the 1780 Massachusetts arrangement (p. 17), there is no established church that gets people's taxes in default of other arrangements; if one fails to make a designation, his money goes "for the encouragement of seminaries of learning." What harm is there in this system to individual taxpayers? To religious societies?

2. Opposition to the Assessment. Opponents of the Assessment Bill, led by James Madison, believed that their primary task would be "to overcome the tremendous influence which Henry's oratory exerted in the Virginia Assembly." Indeed, passage of the bill seemed so imminent in 1784 that Jefferson, writing Madison from Paris, quipped: "What we have to do, I think, is devotedly to pray for his death." With the measure all but enacted, the opposition convinced the General Assembly, in Madison's words, "that the Bill should be postponed till the ensuing session; and in the meantime, be printed for public consideration."

Once printed, the bill drew a lot of opposition. A remonstrance from the Hanover Presbytery, submitted to the General Assembly in 1785, is representative:

> The end of Civil Government is security as to the temporal liberty and property of Mankind; and to protect them in the free Exercise of Religion—Legislators are invested with powers from their Constituents, for these purposes only; and their duty extends no further—Religion is altogether personal, and the right of exercising it unalienable; and it is not, cannot, and ought not be, resigned to the will of the society at large; and much less to the Legislature[.]

By far the most enduring contribution to this debate was Madison's own Memorial and Remonstrance Against Religious Assessments. Widely distributed by his friends before the General Assembly reconvened, the Memorial and Remonstrance generated such popular and political opposition to the Assessment Bill that the measure collapsed in committee shortly before Christmas, 1785.

Because it is probably the fullest and most thoughtful exposition of the disestablishmentarian thinking at the time of the founding, as well as the reasoning of the principal author of the Bill of Rights, we reproduce Madison's Memorial and Remonstrance in full. Read it carefully, and think about each of its arguments.

MEMORIAL AND REMONSTRANCE AGAINST RELIGIOUS ASSESSMENTS

James Madison (1785)

TO THE HONORABLE THE GENERAL ASSEMBLY OF THE COMMONWEALTH OF VIRGINIA. A MEMORIAL AND REMONSTRANCE

We, the subscribers, citizens of the said Commonwealth, having taken into serious consideration, a Bill printed by order of the last Session of General Assembly, entitled "A Bill establishing a provision for Teachers of the Christian Religion," and conceiving that the same, if finally armed with the sanctions of a law, will be a dangerous abuse of power, are bound as faithful members of a free State, to remonstrate against it, and to declare the reasons by which we are determined. We remonstrate against the said Bill,

1. Because we hold it for a fundamental and undeniable truth, "that Religion or the duty which we owe to our Creator and the Manner of discharging it, can be directed only by reason and conviction, not by force or violence."[1] The Religion then of every man must be left to the conviction and conscience of every man; and it is the right of every man to exercise it as these may dictate. This right is in its nature an unalienable right. It is unalienable; because the opinions of men, depending only on the evidence contemplated by their own minds, cannot follow the dictates of other men: It is unalienable also; because what is here a right towards men, is a duty towards the Creator. It is the duty of every man to render to the Creator such homage, and such only, as he believes to be acceptable to him. This duty is precedent both in order of time and degree of obligation, to the claims of Civil Society. Before any man can be considered as a member of Civil Society, he must be considered as a subject of the Governor of the Universe: And if a member of Civil Society, who enters into any subordinate Association, must always do it with a reservation of his duty to the general authority; much more must every man who becomes a member of any particular Civil Society, do it with a saving of his allegiance to the Universal Sovereign. We maintain therefore that in matters of Religion, no man's right is abridged by the institution of Civil Society, and that Religion is wholly exempt from its cognizance. True it is, that no other rule exists, by which any question which may

---

1. [1776 Virginia] Declaration of Rights, Art. 16. [EDITORS' NOTE: Footnote in original. The quotations in the Memorial and Remonstrance are generally from that Declaration.]

divide a Society, can be ultimately determined, but the will of the majority; but it is also true, that the majority may trespass on the rights of the minority.

2. Because if religion be exempt from the authority of the Society at large, still less can it be subject to that of the Legislative Body. The latter are but the creatures and vicegerents of the former. Their jurisdiction is both derivative and limited: it is limited with regard to the co-ordinate departments, more necessarily is it limited with regard to the constituents. The preservation of a free government requires not merely, that the metes and bounds which separate each department of power may be invariably maintained; but more especially, that neither of them be suffered to overleap the great Barrier which defends the rights of the people. The Rulers who are guilty of such an encroachment, exceed the commission from which they derive their authority, and are Tyrants. The People who submit to it are governed by laws made neither by themselves, nor by an authority derived from them, and are slaves.

3. Because, it is proper to take alarm at the first experiment on our liberties. We hold this prudent jealousy to be the first duty of citizens, and one of [the] noblest characteristics of the late Revolution. The freemen of America did not wait till usurped power had strengthened itself by exercise, and entangled the question in precedents. They saw all the consequences in the principle, and they avoided the consequences by denying the principle. We revere this lesson too much, soon to forget it. Who does not see that the same authority which can establish Christianity, in exclusion of all other Religions, may establish with the same ease any particular sect of Christians, in exclusion of all other Sects? That the same authority which can force a citizen to contribute three pence only of his property for the support of any one establishment, may force him to conform to any other establishment in all cases whatsoever?

4. Because, the Bill violates that equality which ought to be the basis of every law, and which is more indispensable, in proportion as the validity or expediency of any law is more liable to be impeached. If "all men are by nature equally free and independent," all men are to be considered as entering into Society on equal conditions; as relinquishing no more, and therefore retaining no less, one than another, of their natural rights. Above all are they to be considered as retaining an "*equal* title to the free exercise of Religion according to the dictates of conscience." Whilst we assert for ourselves a freedom to embrace, to profess and to observe the Religion which we believe to be of divine origin, we cannot deny an equal freedom to those whose minds have not yet yielded to the evidence which has convinced us. If this freedom be abused, it is an offence against God, not against man: To God, therefore, not to men, must an account of it be rendered. As the Bill violates equality by subjecting some to peculiar burdens; so it violates the same principle, by granting to others peculiar exemptions. Are the Quakers and Menonists the only sects who think a compulsive support of their religions unnecessary and unwarrantable? Can their piety alone be intrusted with the care of public worship? Ought their Religions to be endowed above all others, with extraordinary privileges, by which proselytes may be enticed from all others? We think too favorably of the justice and good sense of these denominations, to believe that they either covet preeminencies over their fellow citizens, or that they will be seduced by them, from the common opposition to the measure.

5. Because the bill implies either that the Civil Magistrate is a competent Judge of Religious truth; or that he may employ Religion as an engine of

Civil policy. The first is an arrogant pretension falsified by the contradictory opinions of Rulers in all ages, and throughout the world: The second an unhallowed perversion of the means of salvation.

6. Because the establishment proposed by the Bill is not requisite for the support of the Christian Religion. To say that it is, is a contradiction to the Christian Religion itself; for every page of it disavows a dependence on the powers of this world: it is a contradiction to fact; for it is known that this Religion both existed and flourished, not only without the support of human laws, but in spite of every opposition from them; and not only during the period of miraculous aid, but long after it had been left to its own evidence, and the ordinary care of Providence: Nay, it is a contradiction in terms; for a Religion not invented by human policy, must have preexisted and been supported, before it was established by human policy. It is moreover to weaken in those who profess this Religion a pious confidence in its innate excellence, and the patronage of its Author; and to foster in those who still reject it, a suspicion that its friends are too conscious of its fallacies, to trust it to its own merits.

7. Because experience witnesseth that ecclesiastical establishments, instead of maintaining the purity and efficacy of Religion, have had a contrary operation. During almost fifteen centuries, has the legal establishment of Christianity been on trial. What have been its fruits? More or less in all places, pride and indolence in the Clergy; ignorance and servility in the laity; in both, superstition, bigotry and persecution. Enquire of the Teachers of Christianity for the ages in which it appeared in its greatest lustre; those of every sect, point to the ages prior to its incorporation with Civil policy. Propose a restoration of this primitive state in which its Teachers depended on the voluntary rewards of their flocks; many of them predict its downfall. On which side ought their testimony to have greatest weight, when for or when against their interest?

8. Because the establishment in question is not necessary for the support of Civil Government. If it be urged as necessary for the support of Civil Government only as it is a means of supporting Religion, and it be not necessary for the latter purpose, it cannot be necessary for the former. If Religion be not within [the] cognizance of Civil Government, how can its legal establishment be said to be necessary to civil Government? What influence in fact have ecclesiastical establishments had on Civil Society? In some instances they have been seen to erect a spiritual tyranny on the ruins of Civil authority; in many instances they have been seen upholding the thrones of political tyranny; in no instance have they been seen the guardians of the liberties of the people. Rulers who wished to subvert the public liberty, may have found an established clergy convenient auxiliaries. A just government, instituted to secure & perpetuate it, needs them not. Such a government will be best supported by protecting every citizen in the enjoyment of his Religion with the same equal hand which protects his person and his property; by neither invading the equal rights of any Sect, nor suffering any Sect to invade those of another.

9. Because the proposed establishment is a departure from that generous policy, which, offering an asylum to the persecuted and oppressed of every Nation and Religion, promised a lustre to our country, and an accession to the number of its citizens. What a melancholy mark is the Bill of sudden degeneracy? Instead of holding forth an asylum to the persecuted, it is itself a signal of persecution. It degrades from the equal rank of Citizens all those whose

opinions in Religion do not bend to those of the Legislative authority. Distant as it may be, in its present form, from the Inquisition it differs from it only in degree. The one is the first step, the other the last in the career of intolerance. The magnanimous sufferer under this cruel scourge in foreign Regions, must view the Bill as a Beacon on our Coast, warning him to seek some other haven, where liberty and philanthropy in their due extent may offer a more certain repose from his troubles.

10. Because, it will have a like tendency to banish our Citizens. The allurements presented by other situations are every day thinning their number. To superadd a fresh motive to emigration, by revoking the liberty which they now enjoy, would be the same species of folly which has dishonoured and depopulated flourishing kingdoms.

11. Because, it will destroy that moderation and harmony which the forbearance of our laws to intermeddle with Religion, has produced amongst its several sects. Torrents of blood have been spilt in the old world, by vain attempts of the secular arm to extinguish Religious discord, by proscribing all difference in Religious opinions. Time has at length revealed the true remedy. Every relaxation of narrow and rigorous policy, wherever it has been tried, has been found to assuage the disease. The American Theatre has exhibited proofs, that equal and compleat liberty, if it does not wholly eradicate it, sufficiently destroys its malignant influence on the health and prosperity of the State. If with the salutary effects of this system under our own eyes, we begin to contract the bonds of Religious freedom, we know no name that will too severely reproach our folly. At least let warning be taken at the first fruits of the threatened innovation. The very appearance of the Bill has transformed that "Christian forbearance, love and charity," which of late mutually prevailed, into animosities and jealousies, which may not soon be appeased. What mischiefs may not be dreaded should this enemy to the public quiet be armed with the force of a law?

12. Because, the policy of the bill is adverse to the diffusion of the light of Christianity. The first wish of those who enjoy this precious gift, ought to be that it may be imparted to the whole race of mankind. Compare the number of those who have as yet received it with the number still remaining under the dominion of false Religions; and how small is the former! Does the policy of the Bill tend to lessen the disproportion? No; it at once discourages those who are strangers to the light of [revelation] from coming into the Region of it; and countenances, by example the nations who continue in darkness, in shutting out those who might convey it to them. Instead of levelling as far as possible, every obstacle to the victorious progress of truth, the Bill with an ignoble and unchristian timidity would circumscribe it, with a wall of defence, against the encroachments of error.

13. Because attempts to enforce by legal sanctions, acts obnoxious to so great a proportion of Citizens, tend to enervate the laws in general, and to slacken the bands of Society. If it be difficult to execute any law which is not generally deemed necessary or salutary, what must be the case where it is deemed invalid and dangerous? and what may be the effect of so striking an example of impotency in the Government, on its general authority.

14. Because a measure of such singular magnitude and delicacy ought not to be imposed, without the clearest evidence that it is called for by a majority of citizens: and no satisfactory method is yet proposed by which the voice of the majority in this case may be determined, or its influence secured. "The people of

the respective counties are indeed requested to signify their opinion respecting the adoption of the Bill to the next Session of Assembly." But the representation must be made equal, before the voice either of the Representatives or of the Counties, will be that of the people. Our hope is that neither of the former will, after due consideration, espouse the dangerous principle of the Bill. Should the event disappoint us, it will still leave us in full confidence, that a fair appeal to the latter will reverse the sentence against our liberties.

15. Because, finally, "the equal right of every citizen to the free exercise of his Religion according to the dictates of conscience" is held by the same tenure with all our other rights. If we recur to its origin, it is equally the gift of nature; if we weigh its importance, it cannot be less dear to us; if we consult the Declaration of those rights which pertain to the good people of Virginia, as the "basis and foundation of Government," it is enumerated with equal solemnity, or rather studied emphasis. Either then, we must say, that the will of the Legislature is the only measure of their authority; and that in the plentitude of this authority, they may sweep away all our fundamental rights; or, that they are bound to leave this particular right untouched and sacred: Either we must say, that they may control the freedom of the press, may abolish the trial by jury, may swallow up the Executive and Judiciary Powers of the State; nay that they may despoil us of our very right of suffrage, and erect themselves into an independent and hereditary assembly; or we must say, that they have no authority to enact into law the Bill under consideration. We the subscribers say, that the General Assembly of this Commonwealth have no such authority: And that no effort may be omitted on our part against so dangerous an usurpation, we oppose to it, this remonstrance; earnestly praying, as we are in duty bound, that the Supreme Lawgiver of the Universe, by illuminating those to whom it is addressed, may on the one hand, turn their councils from every act which would affront his holy prerogative, or violate the trust committed to them: and on the other, guide them into every measure which may be worthy of his [blessing, may re]dound to their own praise, and may establish more firmly the liberties, the prosperity, and the Happiness of the Commonwealth.

NOTES AND QUESTIONS

1. Madison's Variety of Arguments.   Madison and Jefferson were friends and fought together against the religious establishment in Virginia. But Madison makes arguments against the Assessment Bill that Jefferson would not have made. In fact, part of the enduring appeal of the Memorial and Remonstrance is that it draws on such a broad range of disestablishmentarian thought.

(a) Where have we seen arguments like those made in ¶¶5-7?   Would these claims appeal to atheists? Agnostics? Non-Christians? Which of the four groups discussed by Witte (p. 29) would support these arguments?

(b) What kinds of harm does Madison threaten in ¶¶9-11, 13-15?   Which of the groups discussed by Witte might oppose religious assessments for reasons like these?

(c) In ¶4 Madison invokes the Virginia Declaration of Rights, which says that "all men are equally entitled to the free exercise of religion."   How does the Assessment Bill deny this right? What kind of theory would see this as the principal argument against a religious establishment?

(d) **The first argument Madison makes (¶1) is a religious version of social contract theory.** He asserts that we have a duty to the Universal Sovereign which is "precedent both in order of time and degree of obligation, to the claims of Civil Society." We come into society "with a reservation of [this] duty." What theory of disestablishment would find this argument most congenial? What appeal would this claim have for nonbelievers? How does this argument compare to Elisha Williams's plea for "the essential rights and liberties of Protestants"?

2. Jefferson's Religious Freedom Statute. The last document that we include in this review of Virginia's history is Thomas Jefferson's Bill for Establishing Religious Freedom. Jefferson drafted the bill in 1777 and submitted it to the General Assembly in 1779. The bill declared religious observance and belief to be a natural right and prohibited discrimination along religious lines—"religious beliefs shall in no wise diminish, enlarge or affect one's civil capabilities." When Jefferson left in 1784 on a diplomatic mission to France his friends, Madison, Mason, and others, carried on the fight to make the bill law. Their efforts culminated in passage of the bill in 1786, less than one month after the defeat of the Assessment Bill. Particularly noteworthy was an attempt to amend the bill's preamble, which Jefferson described thus: "Where the preamble declares that coercion is a departure from the plan of the holy author of our religion, an amendment was proposed by inserting the words 'Jesus Christ,' so that it should read 'a departure from the plan of Jesus Christ, the holy author of our religion'; the insertion was rejected by a great majority, in proof that they meant to comprehend within the mantle of its protection, the Jew and the Gentile, the Christian and the Mahometan, the Hindoo, the infidel of every denomination." Although Jefferson's bill did not explicitly disestablish the Anglican (we should now say Episcopalian) Church, its passage sounded the death knell for its establishment and marked the beginning of separation of church and state in Virginia.

A BILL FOR ESTABLISHING RELIGIOUS FREEDOM (1786)

Well aware that Almighty God hath created the mind free; that all attempts to influence it by temporal punishments or burdens, or by civil incapacitations, tend only to beget habits of hypocrisy and meanness, and are a departure from the plan of the Holy Author of our religion, who being Lord both of body and mind, yet chose not to propagate it by coercions on either, as was in his Almighty power to do; that the impious presumption of legislators and rulers, civil as well as ecclesiastical, who, being themselves but fallible and uninspired men, have assumed dominion over the faith of others, setting up their own opinions and modes of thinking as the only true and infallible, and as such endeavoring to impose them on others, hath established and maintained false religions over the greatest part of the world, and through all time: that to compel a man to furnish contributions of money for the propagation of opinions which he disbelieves is sinful and tyrannical, that even forcing him to support this or that teacher of his own religious persuasion, is depriving him of the comfortable liberty of giving his contributions to the particular pastor whose morals he would make his pattern, and whose powers he feels most persuasive to righteousness, and is withdrawing from the ministry those temporal rewards, which proceeding from an approbation of their personal conduct, are an additional incitement to earnest and unremitting labors for the instruction of mankind; that our civil rights have no dependence on our religious opinions, any more than our opinions in physics or geometry; that, therefore, the proscribing [of] any citizen as unworthy [of] the public confidence by laying upon him an incapacity of being called to the offices of trust and emolument, unless he profess or renounce this or that religious opinion, is depriving him injuriously of those privileges and advantages to which, in common with his fellow-citizens, he has a natural right; that it tends also to corrupt the principles of that very religion it is meant to encourage, by bribing, with a monopoly of worldly honors and emoluments, those who will externally profess and conform to it; that though indeed these are criminal who do not withstand such temptation, yet neither are those innocent who lay the bait in their way; that to suffer the civil magistrate to intrude his powers into the field of opinion and to restrain the profession or propagation of principles, on the supposition of their ill tendency is a dangerous fallacy, which at once destroys all religious liberty, because he being of course judge of that tendency will make his opinions the rule of judgment, and approve or condemn the sentiments of others only as they shall square with or differ from his own; that it is time enough for the rightful purposes of civil government for its officers to interfere when principles break out into overt acts against peace and good order; and finally, that truth is great and will prevail if left to herself; that she is the proper and sufficient antagonist to error, and has nothing to fear from the conflict unless by human interposition disarmed of her natural weapons, free argument and debate; errors ceasing to be dangerous when it is permitted freely to contradict them.

Be it therefore enacted by the General Assembly, That no man shall be compelled to frequent or support any religious worship, place, or ministry whatsoever, nor shall be enforced, restrained, molested, or burthened in his body or goods, nor shall otherwise suffer, on account of his religious opinions or belief; but that all men shall be free to profess, and by argument to maintain, their opinions in matters of religion, and that the same shall in no wise diminish, enlarge, or affect their civil capacities.

And though we know well that this Assembly, elected by the people for the ordinary purposes of legislation only, have no power to restrain the acts of succeeding Assemblies, constituted with the power equal to our own, and that therefore to declare this act irrevocable would be of no effect in law; yet we are free to declare, and do declare, that the rights hereby asserted are of the natural rights of mankind, and that if any act shall be hereafter passed to repeal the present or to narrow its operation, such act will be an infringement of natural right.

NOTES AND QUESTIONS

1. Jefferson's Religious Freedom Bill. Compare the arguments Jefferson made in the preamble of this bill with the ones Madison made in his Memorial and Remonstrance. What good did he think would come from a regime of religious freedom? What harms would it avoid? Was Jefferson's position here consistent with the one he took 16 years later in his letter to the Danbury Baptists?

2. Are "Religious Opinions" Publicly Relevant?   What did Jefferson mean by saying that "our civil rights have no dependence on our religious opinions, any more than our opinions in physics or geometry"? Was he making a statement of fact? Why had the English Parliament a century earlier asked putative office-holders to make a declaration of their religious beliefs? Did Parliament ever have office-seekers take an oath affirming the principles of geometry?

D. THE CONSTITUTIONAL PROVISIONS

1. Framing the First Amendment

The original Constitution drafted by the Convention in 1787 and ratified by 11 states in 1788 contained no provision protecting the general freedom of religion. It did, however, prohibit religious tests for federal office and allow affirmations in lieu of oaths. Toward the end of the Convention, George Mason (the principal author of the Virginia Declaration of Rights) proposed addition of a Bill of Rights, but this proposal was rejected, probably because it came so late in the process and the delegates were anxious to bring the drafting to an end. During the ratification debates, the absence of a Bill of Rights became one of the major points of contention. The absence of protection for religious freedom was particularly noted. The Baptist General Committee, for example, announced opposition to the proposed Constitution solely because it had not "made sufficient provision for the secure enjoyment of religious liberty."

Federalists (the advocates of the Constitution) argued that a Bill of Rights was unnecessary because the powers of the new federal government were so limited. "There is not a shadow of right in the general government to intermeddle with religion," Madison told the Virginia ratifying convention. Critics were not satisfied, and insisted that a Bill of Rights be added. Seven states drafted proposals for amendments, and five of them (plus the minority report in Pennsylvania) proposed religious freedom guarantees. Virginia proposed an amendment modeled on its own Declaration of Rights:

> That religion, or the duty which we owe to our Creator, and the manner of discharging it, can be directed only by reason and conviction, not by force or violence; and therefor all men have an equal, natural, and unalienable right to the free exercise of religion, according to the dictates of conscience.

Two other states made proposals almost identical to Virginia's. Meanwhile, New Hampshire, a state with an established church and a strong states' rights orientation toward the church-state question, proposed that "Congress shall make no laws touching religion, or to infringe the rights of conscience."

In the First Congress, James Madison was the first draftsman, and principal exponent, of a Bill of Rights. The following excerpt from a speech he made introducing his proposal gives an indication of the tone of his advocacy:

> The first of these amendments relates to what may be called a bill of rights. I will own that I never considered this provision so essential to the Federal Constitution

as to make it improper to ratify it, until such an amendment was added; at the same time, I always conceived, that in a certain form, and to a certain extent, such a provision was neither improper nor altogether useless.

1 Annals of Congress 436 (June 8, 1789) (J. Gales ed., 1834). For a more complete account of this interesting episode in our history, see Paul Finkelman, James Madison and the Bill of Rights: A Reluctant Paternity, 1990 Sup. Ct. Rev. 301.

Madison's principal argument in favor of the Bill of Rights was frankly political: Many constituents wanted it; the proponents of the Constitution had promised it; a failure to carry through would give ammunition to opponents of the new government. See, for example, an earlier passage in the speech quoted above:

I do most sincerely believe, that if Congress will devote but one day to this subject, so far as to satisfy the public that we do not disregard their wishes, it will have a salutary influence on the public councils, and prepare the way for a favorable reception of our future measures. It appears to me that this House is bound by every motive of prudence, not to let the first session pass over without proposing [amendments to the Constitution].

Madison's own political fortunes were closely connected to the question. Denied a Senate seat by a Virginia legislature dominated by his political adversary, Patrick Henry, and thrown into a congressional district with an anti-federalist majority, Madison faced a tough election campaign for a seat in the House of Representatives. (Ironically, his opponent was James Monroe, who later became a close political friend and ally, his Secretary of State, and successor as President.) Madison's opponents spread the rumor that he was opposed to any amendments to the Constitution. This charge was particularly potent among Madison's Baptist constituents, who were a large and potentially decisive swing vote. On advice of his political advisor, Madison composed a letter to George Eve, a Baptist minister, proclaiming his support for "the most satisfactory provisions for all essential rights, particularly the rights of Conscience in the fullest latitude, the freedom of the press, trials by jury, security against general warrants & c." Letter to Rev. George Eve (Jan. 2, 1789), in 11 Papers of James Madison 404-405 (R. Rutland & C. Hobson eds., 1977). The Baptists shifted their support to Madison. At a political rally at the Blue Run Baptist Church, Reverend Eve "took a very Spirited and decided Part in [Madison's] favor" and "Spoke Long" on Madison's contributions to the cause of religious freedom. Madison won the election. (This incident provides historical perspective on the frequent claim that religious groups should not be involved in politics. It also dramatizes the tie between evangelical dissenting groups and the First Amendment.)

Having won his seat in the First Congress, Madison drafted a proposed Bill of Rights, differing substantially from the proposals that had emanated from the state ratifying conventions. Among his proposals were two amendments relevant to religious liberty. First, he proposed that Art. I, §9 (the section containing express limitations on the power of Congress) be amended by adding:

The civil rights of none shall be abridged on account of religious belief or worship, nor shall any national religion be established, nor shall the full and equal rights of conscience be in any manner, or on any pretext, infringed.

1 Annals of Congress at 434. Second, he proposed that Art. I, § 10 (the section containing express limitations on the powers of the States) be amended by adding:

> No State shall violate the equal rights of conscience, or the freedom of the press, or the trial by jury in criminal cases.

After discussion, Madison's proposals were referred to a select committee. On August 15, 1789, the House of Representatives met as a Committee of the Whole to consider the select committee's proposals. The following debate ensued on the committee's version of Madison's first proposal (i.e., the proposal applicable to the federal government):

1 ANNALS OF CONGRESS 757-759 (J. Gales ed., 1834)
Saturday, August 15, 1789

AMENDMENTS TO THE CONSTITUTION

The House again went into a Committee of the Whole on the proposed amendments to the Constitution. Mr. BOUDINOT in the Chair.

The fourth proposition being under consideration, as follows:

Article 1. Section 9. Between paragraphs two and three insert "no religion shall be established by law, nor shall the equal rights of conscience be infringed."

Mr. SYLVESTER had some doubts of the propriety of the mode of expression used in this paragraph. He apprehended that it was liable to a construction different from what had been made by the committee. He feared it might be thought to have a tendency to abolish religion altogether.

Mr. VINING suggested the propriety of transposing the two members of the sentence.

Mr. GERRY said it would read better if it was, that no religious doctrine shall be established by law.

Mr. SHERMAN thought the amendment altogether unnecessary, inasmuch as Congress had no authority whatever delegated to them by the Constitution to make religious establishments; he would, therefore, move to have it struck out.

Mr. CARROLL—As the rights of conscience are, in their nature, of peculiar delicacy, and will little bear the gentlest touch of governmental hand; and as many sects have concurred in opinion that they are not well secured under the present Constitution, he said he was much in favor of adopting the words. He thought it would tend more towards conciliating the minds of the people to the Government than almost any other amendment he had heard proposed. He would not contend with gentlemen about the phraseology, his object was to secure the substance in such a manner as to satisfy the wishes of the honest part of the community.

Mr. MADISON said, he apprehended the meaning of the words to be, that Congress should not establish a religion, and enforce the legal observation of it by law, nor compel men to worship God in any manner contrary to their conscience. Whether the words are necessary or not, he did not mean to say, but they had been required by some of the State Conventions, who seemed to entertain an opinion that under the clause of the Constitution, which gave power to Congress to make all laws necessary and proper to carry into execution the Constitution and the laws made under it, enabled them to make laws of such a nature as might infringe the rights of conscience, and establish a national religion; to prevent these effects he presumed the amendment was intended, and he thought it as well expressed as the nature of the language would admit.

Mr. HUNTINGTON said that he feared with the gentleman first up on this subject that the words might be taken in such latitude as to be extremely hurtful to the cause of religion. He understood the amendment to mean what had been expressed by the gentleman from Virginia; but others might find it convenient to put another construction upon it. The ministers of their congregations to the Eastward were maintained by the contributions of those who belonged to their society; the expense of building meeting houses was contributed in the same manner. These things were regulated by by-laws. If an action was brought before a Federal Court on any of these cases, the person who had neglected to perform his engagements could not be compelled to do it; for a support of ministers or building of places of worship might be construed into a religious establishment.

By the charter of Rhode Island, no religion could be established by law; he could give a history of the effects of such a regulation, indeed the people were now enjoying the blessed fruits of it. He hoped, therefore, the amendment would be made in such a way as to secure the rights of conscience, and a free-exercise of the rights of religion, but not to patronise those who professed no religion at all.

Mr. MADISON thought, if the word "national" was inserted before religion, it would satisfy the minds of honorable gentlemen. He believed that the people feared one sect might obtain a pre-eminence, or two combine together, and establish a religion to which they would compel others to conform. He thought if the word "national" was introduced, it would point the amendment directly to the object it was intended to prevent.

Mr. LIVERMORE was not satisfied with that amendment; but he did not wish them to dwell long on the subject. He thought it would be better if it were altered, and made to read in this manner, that Congress shall make no laws touching religion, or infringing the rights of conscience.

Mr. GERRY did not like the term national, proposed by the gentleman from Virginia, and he hoped it would not be adopted by the House. It brought to his mind some observations that had taken place in the conventions at the time they were considering the present Constitution. It had been insisted upon by those who were called anti-federalists, that his form of Government consolidated the Union; the honorable gentleman's motion shows that he considers it in the same light. Those who were called anti-federalists at that time, complained that they had injustice done them by the title, because they were in favor of a Federal Government, and the others were in favor of a national one; the federalists were for ratifying the Constitution as it stood, and the others not until amendments were made. Their names then ought not to have been distinguished by federalists and anti-federalists, but rats and anti-rats.

Mr. MADISON withdrew his motion, but observed that the words "no national religion shall be established by law," did not imply that the Government was a national one; the question was then taken on Mr. LIVERMORE's motion, and passed in the affirmative, thirty-one for, and twenty against it.

Five days later, without further recorded discussion, the House adopted a motion by Fisher Ames, of Massachusetts, to alter the wording as follows:

> Congress shall make no law establishing religion, or to prevent the free exercise thereof, or to infringe the rights of conscience.

1 Annals of Congress 796. Mysteriously, the House and Senate Journals record that the Senate received a proposed amendment slightly different from the Ames's version: "Congress shall make no law establishing Religion, or prohibiting the free exercise thereof, nor shall the rights of conscience be infringed." Unlike House debates, Senate debates were not recorded at that time. Nonetheless, the first Senate Journal records the following discussion on September 3, 1789:

JOURNAL OF THE FIRST SESSION OF THE SENATE OF THE UNITED STATES OF AMERICA 116
September 3, 1789

On motion to amend article third, and to strike out these words: "religion, or prohibiting the free exercise thereof," and insert "one religious sect or society in preference to others":
It passed in the negative.
On motion for reconsideration:
It passed in the affirmative.
On motion that article the third be striken out:
It passed in the negative.
On motion to adopt the following, in lieu of the third article: "Congress shall not make any law infringing the rights of conscience, or establishing any religious sect or society":
It passed in the negative.
On motion to amend the third article, to read thus:
"Congress shall make no law establishing any particular denomination of religion in preference to another, or prohibiting the free exercise thereof, nor shall the rights of conscience be infringed":
It passed in the negative.

Six days later, the Senate took up the issue again, as follows:

SENATE JOURNAL 129
September 9, 1789

On motion to amend article the third, to read as follows: "Congress shall make no law establishing articles of faith or a mode of worship, or prohibiting the free exercise of religion, or abridging the freedom of speech, or the press, or the right of the people peaceably to assemble, and petition to the government for the redress of grievances."

It was passed in the affirmative.

A conference committee was appointed to iron out the differences on this and other issues arising from proposed amendments to the Constitution. Madison headed the House delegation. The Senate Journal, at 141-142, reports that the House agreed to the Senate proposals, with the exception of the third article. The House proposed that the third article be amended to read:

> Congress shall make no law respecting an establishment of religion, or prohibiting the free exercise thereof; or abridging the freedom of speech, or of the press; or the right of the people peaceably to assemble, and petition the government for a redress of grievances.

On September 25, 1789 (Senate Journal at 150-151), the Senate concurred in the House proposal, and the amendment was approved for transmission to the states for ratification. It was numbered the third. (Many writers have found it significant that the First Amendment is the first, but this is only because the original First and Second Amendments were not ratified.*) The "First Amendment" was ratified on December 15, 1791.

Madison's second proposal, which would have prohibited the states from violating the "equal rights of conscience," was debated and approved by the House on August 17, 1789:

1 ANNALS OF CONGRESS 783-784 (J. Gales ed., 1834)
August 17, 1789

The committee then proceeded to the fifth proposition:

Article I, section 10, between the first and second paragraph, insert "no State shall infringe the equal rights of conscience, nor the freedom of speech, or of the press, nor the right of trial by jury in criminal cases."

Mr. TUCKER—This is offered, I presume, as an amendment to the Constitution of the United States, but it goes only to the alteration of the constitutions of particular States. It will be much better, I apprehend, to leave the State Governments to themselves, and not to interfere with them more than we already do; and that is thought by many to be rather too much. I therefore move, sir, to strike out these words.

Mr. MADISON conceived this to be the most valuable amendment in the whole list. If there were any reason to restrain the Government of the United States from infringing upon these essential rights, it was equally necessary that they should be secured against the State Governments. He thought that if they

---

*The original Second Amendment was finally ratified as the Twenty-Seventh Amendment in 1992, 203 years after it was proposed. It deals with the compensation of senators and representatives.

provided against the one, it was as necessary to provide against the other, and was satisfied that it would be equally grateful to the people.

Mr. LIVERMORE had no great objection to the sentiment, but he thought it not well expressed. He wished to make it an affirmative proposition; "the equal rights of conscience, the freedom of speech or of the press, and the right of trial by jury in criminal cases, shall not be infringed by any State."

This transposition being agreed to, and Mr. TUCKER's motion being rejected, the clause was adopted.

[This proposal was rejected by the Senate on September 21, 1789, and never revived. See Senate Journal at 142.]

What interpretive issues are raised by these debates and votes? Although the debates covered both the Establishment and Free Exercise Clauses together, different interpretive issues have emerged for each clause, and so here it is useful to separate them.

a. Issues Concerning Establishment

1. Concerns About Disestablishment.   In the House, the debates over establishment were dominated by concerns—expressed most forcefully by Sylvester and Huntington—that the Establishment Clause "might be taken in such latitude as to be extremely hurtful to the cause of religion." Why might this have been a worry? (The only example given was that federal courts would not be able to enforce Connecticut's requirement of paying for the support of ministers and houses of worship. It is difficult to see why such cases would be in federal court.)

Huntington's reference to the "blessed fruits" of Rhode Island's history of disestablishment should not be misunderstood: Huntington was being sarcastic. In this period, Rhode Island (sometimes called "Rogue's Island") was the butt of jokes and allegations of lawlessness and lack of civic virtue. Huntington, a representative of the Puritan tradition of Connecticut, was implying that if disestablishment were interpreted in a way that was hostile to religion, this would undermine civic virtue and civil order. He thought it important to "secure the rights of conscience, and a free exercise of the rights of religion, but not to patronise those who professed no religion at all."

Madison responded to these remarks by construing his proposal narrowly. He said that he "apprehended the meaning of the words to be, that Congress should not establish a religion, and enforce the legal observation of it by law, nor compel men to worship God in any manner contrary to their conscience," and that the impetus for the proposal was that "the people feared one sect might obtain a pre-eminence, or two combine together, and establish a religion to which they would compel others to conform." Does this mean that the Establishment Clause is directed solely at laws that would require everyone to conform to a single church or combination of churches? What else might it mean?

2. Federalism.   Madison also responded to the critics by proposing that the word "national" be inserted before "religion." This emphasizes the "federalism" aspect of the original Amendment—an aspect also emphasized by Livermore's proposal that "Congress shall make no laws touching religion."

As noted above, this had been the language proposed by Livermore's home state, New Hampshire, one of the states with an established Church. The "no laws touching religion" would have prevented the federal government not only from establishing its own church, but also from disturbing New Hampshire's establishment: It would have been a "state rights" barrier to federal action.

Madison's suggestion was rejected for semantic reasons: Arch antifederalists such as Elbridge Gerry objected to using the term "nation" to describe the United States. But does the ultimate text of the First Amendment still reflect a "federalism" element, affirmatively protecting state establishments of religion? If so, what part of the text? See, e.g., Elk Grove Unified School Dist. v. Newdow, 542 U.S. 1, 49-54 (2004) (Thomas, J., concurring in the judgment) (p. 74). If there is such a federalism element, does it extend only to protecting a state's power to establish an official church, or does it also protect a state's power to interfere with free exercise? See, e.g., Steven D. Smith, Foreordained Failure: The Quest for a Constitutional Principle of Religious Freedom ch. 2 (1995); Joseph Snee, Religious Disestablishment and the Fourteenth Amendment, 1954 Wash. U. L.Q. 371.

The federalism question also influenced Madison's second proposal: to prohibit the states from violating the "equal rights of conscience." Madison averred that this was "the most valuable amendment in the whole list." Why? Under Madison's theory of the dangers of factions in politics, set forth in his great essays in The Federalist Papers (especially No. 10), a more extensive republic is less prone to the oppression of factions (including religious factions) because there will be more numerous and divided factions. It follows that the danger of such oppression is greater at the state level. This might seem to be borne out by the religious circumstances of the day. While different religious denominations were dominant in various states, no one religion was dominant at the national level.

Madison's proposal met with the opposition of those who believed that a new, distant, powerful, and potentially unaccountable federal government posed a greater threat to liberty than did government closer to the people and more under their direct control. While the Senate debates were not recorded, it may be presumed that this was the reason for the defeat of Madison's second proposal in that chamber. This may be taken to suggest that the majority (in the Senate, at least) rejected Madison's theory about the relative dangers of oppression at the state and national level. Alternatively, the vote could be taken as confirmation of Madison's view: At the state level, where a single religion was often dominant, many states continued to maintain some form of established church, but at the national level, the jealousy and distrust among the various denominations led them all to support a policy that none should be established.

3. The Application of the Religion Clauses to the States: An Introduction to "Incorporation." The discussion in note 2 about federalism and protecting state establishments has implications for whether the modern Court has acted properly in applying the Religion Clauses to state and local government actions. (Much of the Court's religion docket involves such actions: public school policies, criminal laws, state programs of aid for private schools, etc.) Because the First Amendment limits only Congress, it (like the rest of the Bill of Rights) applies to states and their subdivisions only through "incorporation" into the

Due Process Clause of the Fourteenth Amendment. See Cantwell v. Connecticut, 310 U.S. 296 (1940) (free exercise); Everson v. Board of Education, 330 U.S. 1 (1947) (nonestablishment). Section II-D-3 discusses incorporation in more detail, including the debate whether the ratifiers of the Fourteenth Amendment meant to incorporate the Bill of Rights.

But for now, consider this question: If the sources in note 2 are correct, and the Establishment Clause reflected a purpose to *protect* state establishments from federal action, how can it be incorporated to *restrict* states' power (often through the means of a federal court)? Isn't that turning the clause on its head? Justice Thomas made this argument in his concurring opinion in *Newdow* (p. 74). One possible answer is that the clause reflected not only a states' rights principle, but also a personal liberty: The prohibition on a national established church not only prevented interference with state arrangements, but also protected individuals and groups from (federal) impositions in matters of religion. See, e.g., Abington School Dist. v. Schempp, 374 U.S. 203 (Brennan, J., concurring) (see p. 76). Moreover, even if the clause was originally a states' rights provision, it may have come to be understood as a personal liberty by the time the Fourteenth Amendment was enacted in 1868. The next section explores these arguments in more detail.

Does this "federalism" aspect also raise questions about whether it was proper to incorporate the Free Exercise Clause?

The historical debate over incorporation is a serious one, with respectable arguments on both sides. Keep in mind, though, that the debate is now almost entirely among scholars: The Supreme Court has taken incorporation as a given for decades, and there is little prospect that it will ever change its mind. When a federal district judge in 1982 wrote a detailed, scholarly opinion holding that the Establishment Clause did not apply to states, he was swiftly reversed by the court of appeals and the Supreme Court. Wallace v. Jaffree, 472 U.S. 38, 48-49 (1985) (disapproving of the district court's "remarkable conclusion" and calling incorporation an "elementary proposition of law").

4. "No Preference Among Religions." The Senate debates were not recorded, but judging by the successive drafts the central establishment issue there was whether to confine the prohibition to establishment of "one religious society in preference to others." Had this proposal been accepted, it would have reflected what is called the "non-preferentialist" interpretation of establishment, under which the government is permitted to aid religion in general, so long as it does not discriminate among denominations. Justice Rehnquist proposed this approach in his dissenting opinion in Wallace v. Jaffree, 472 U.S. at 91-114. According to his reading of the historical background, the framers "saw the Amendment as designed to prohibit the establishment of a national religion, and perhaps to prevent discrimination among sects. They did not see it as requiring neutrality on the part of government between religion and irreligion." *Id.* at 98. Based on the debates and the votes, do you agree with Rehnquist? For competing assessments of the historical evidence, see Robert Cord, Separation of Church and State: Historical Fact and Current Fiction (1982) (supporting nonpreferentialism); Douglas Laycock, "Nonpreferential" Aid to Religion: A False Claim About Original Intent, 27 Wm. & Mary L. Rev. 875 (1986) (relying on the rejected drafts, among other things, to argue against nonpreferentialism); see also Part V-A-2.

b. Issues Concerning Free Exercise

1. "Conscience" and "Religion." Madison's original proposal would have protected "the full and equal rights of conscience." This is somewhat surprising, since three of the states, including his own Virginia, had proposed language protecting "the free exercise of religion, according to the dictates of conscience," borrowing language Madison himself had crafted for the Virginia Declaration of Rights. At the close of the House debate, this was replaced by Fisher Ames's proposal, which read: "Congress shall make no law establishing religion, or to prevent the free exercise thereof, or to infringe the rights of conscience." In the Senate, the drafts wavered back and forth between "rights of conscience" and "free exercise of religion." Ultimately, the language selected was "free exercise of religion."

What difference might this make? As we will see, in recent years the Supreme Court has considered claims that free exercise rights extend beyond traditional religious views to encompass other deeply held conscientious beliefs. See, e.g., United States v. Seeger (p. 712). Did the founders address that question?

Historian William Lee Miller writes:

> In some other respects Madison's proposal of 1789 did go beyond the First Amendment as eventually adopted. In the clause quoted above he sought to protect "the full and equal rights of conscience." If "conscience" should be taken, as we do today, to mean not only belief but also principled moral conviction, and not only religious but also non-religious belief and conviction, then Madison's proposal would have been an "advance" (if you regard the direction as forward) over even what twentieth-century courts have come to hold.
>
> *Conscience* is one of the many large and important words—*virtue, luxury, corruption,* and perhaps even *liberty* are others—that have undergone a considerable change in meaning across the centuries, and that had at the very least a different nuance in the ideological frame of eighteenth-century Americans from what they mean today. *Conscience* in that century and earlier—as in Roger Williams's attack on persecution for cause of conscience—meant belief or conviction about religious matters, including, to be sure, convictions that stood against this and that orthodoxy, but the word did not ordinarily move outside the realm of religion altogether, nor did it apply to any and all serious moral convictions.

William Lee Miller, The First Liberty: Religion and the American Republic 112-123 (1985). Does this imply that it made no difference whether the Amendment referred to "conscience" or to "religion"? If that is so, then why did the various proposals shift back and forth? Was this purely for aesthetic reasons? And why did the Ames proposal (adopted at one point by the House) protect *both* "conscience" *and* "religion"? Was the proposal redundant?

In the end, it may make no difference whether the selection of the term "religion" over "conscience" was meaningful, since the ultimate result was "religion." If "conscience" was understood to be limited to religious convictions, as Miller maintains, then both versions of the Amendment were limited to religious belief. If "conscience" was understood to be broader than "religion" (as it is today) then the substitution of the phrase "free exercise of religion" for Madison's original proposal protecting "conscience" reflects a deliberate decision to confine the protections of the Amendment to "religion."

But perhaps the difference between "conscience" and "religion" lies elsewhere. John Witte writes: "Liberty of conscience was a guarantee to be left alone to choose, to entertain, and to change one's religious beliefs. Free exercise of religion was the right to act publicly on the choices of conscience once made, without intruding on or obstructing the rights of others or the general peace of the community." Witte, 71 Notre Dame L. Rev. at 394. In this reading, the difference between "conscience" and "religion" is not that the former extends to nonreligious moral convictions, but that the latter extends to acts as well as beliefs. This relates to the next point of interest.

2. The "Exercise" of Religion.   Recall that Jefferson's Letter to the Danbury Baptists stated that "the legislative powers of government reach actions only, and not opinions." Later, in reliance on this statement, the Supreme Court adopted what is known as the belief-conduct distinction, holding that the free exercise clause protects belief, but not (at least not fully) action. Reynolds v. United States, 98 U.S. 145, 164 (1879) (see p. 113). This position is difficult to square with the language of the Amendment. As one of your editors has written:

> As defined by dictionaries at the time of the framing, the word "exercise" strongly connoted action. The American edition of Samuel Johnson's *Dictionary of the English Language*, published in Philadelphia in 1805, used the following terms to define "exercise": "Labour of the body," "Use; actual application of any thing," "Task; that which one is appointed to perform," and "act of divine worship, whether public or private." Noah Webster's American dictionary defined "exercise" as "employment." James Buchanan's 1757 dictionary defined "exercise" as "[t]o use or practice."

McConnell, 103 Harv. L. Rev. at 1489. John Witte has written that "the phrase [free exercise of religion] generally connoted various forms of free public religious action—religious speech, religious worship, religious assembly, religious publication, religious education, among others." Witte, 71 Notre Dame L. Rev. at 395.

3. "Prohibiting" Free Exercise.   Another potentially significant word in the amendment is "prohibiting." The Amendment forbids laws "respecting" establishment, laws "prohibiting" free exercise, and laws "abridging" the freedom of speech, press, or assembly. Does this mean that it is permissible for the government to "abridge" the right of free exercise, so long as it is not "prohibited"? How would this accord with the observation of Charles Carroll (the only Roman Catholic in the First Congress) that "the rights of conscience are, in their nature, of peculiar delicacy, and will little bear the gentlest touch of governmental hand"? Note that the word "prohibiting" crept into the draft amendment after final House consideration and before Senate consideration, without any recorded vote. No one seemed to notice the difference.

Ten years later, John Marshall argued that Congress had greater power over the press than over establishment of religion, because the term "abridging" was less encompassing than the term "respecting." Madison, in response, stated that "the liberty of conscience and the freedom of the press were *equally* and *completely* exempted from all authority whatever of the United States." He went on to argue:

> [I]f Congress may regulate the freedom of the press, provided they do not abridge it, because it is said only "they shall not abridge it," and is not said "they shall make no law respecting it," the analogy of reasoning is conclusive that Congress may

regulate and even *abridge* the free exercise of religion, provided they do not *prohibit* it; because it is said only "they shall not prohibit it," and is *not* said "they shall make not law *respecting* it, or no law *abridging* it."

James Madison, Report on the Virginia Resolutions (January 18, 1800). How much weight do you give to this argument by Madison?

2. Perspectives and Developments in the Early Republic

DETACHED MEMORANDUM
James Madison (ca. 1820)

[The United States] have the noble merit of first unshackling the conscience from persecuting laws, and of establishing among religious Sects a legal equality. If some of the States have not embraced this just and this truly Xn principle in its proper latitude, all of them present examples by which the most enlightened States of the old world may be instructed; and there is one State at least, Virginia, where religious liberty is placed on its true foundation and is defined in its full latitude [in Jefferson's religious freedom bill]. Here the separation between the authority of human laws, and the natural rights of Man excepted from the grant on which all political authority is founded, is traced as distinctly as words can admit. . . . Every provision for [rights of conscience] short of this principle, will be found to leave crevices at least thro' which bigotry may introduce persecution; a monster, that feeding & thriving on its own venom, gradually swells to a size and strength overwhelming all laws divine & human. . . .

Strongly guarded as is the separation between Religion & Govt in the Constitution of the United States[,] the danger of encroachment by Ecclesiastical Bodies may be illustrated by precedents already furnished in their short history. (See the cases in which negatives were put by J.M. on two bills passd by Congs and his signature withheld from another. . . .)

But besides the danger of a direct mixture of Religion & civil Government, there is an evil which ought to be guarded agst in the indefinite accumulation of property from the capacity of holding it in perpetuity by ecclesiastical corporations. The power of all corporations, ought to be limited in this respect. The growing wealth acquired by them never fails to be a source of abuses. . . .

Are the U.S. duly awake to the tendency of the precedents they are establishing, in the multiplied incorporations of Religious Congregations with the faculty of acquiring & holding property real as well as personal? Do not many of these acts give this faculty, without limit either as to time or as to amount? And must not bodies, perpetual in their existence, and which may be always gaining without ever losing, speedily gain more than is useful, and in time more than is safe? . . .

Is the appointment of Chaplains to the two Houses of Congress consistent with the Constitution, and with the pure principle of religious freedom?

In strictness the answer on both points must be in the negative. The Constitution of the U.S. forbids everything like an establishment of a national religion. The law appointing Chaplains establishes a religious worship for the national representatives, to be performed by Ministers of religion, elected by a majority of them; and these are to be paid out of the national taxes. Does not this involve the principle of a national establishment, applicable to a provision for a religious worship for the Constituent as well as of the representative Body, approved by the majority, and conducted by Ministers of religion paid by the entire nation.

The establishment of the chaplainship to Congs is a palpable violation of equal rights, as well as of Constitutional principles: The tenets of the chaplains elected [by the majority] shut the door of worship agst the members whose creeds & consciences forbid a participation in that of the majority. To say nothing of other sects, this is the case with that of Roman Catholics & Quakers who have always had members in one or both of the Legislative branches. Could a Catholic clergyman ever hope to be appointed a Chaplain? To say that his religious principles are obnoxious or that his sect is small, is to lift the evil at once and exhibit in its naked deformity the doctrine that religious truth is to be tested by numbers, or that the major sects have a right to govern the minor. . . .

Were the establishment to be tried by its fruits, are not the daily devotions conducted by these legal Ecclesiastics, already degenerating into a scanty attendance, and a tiresome formality?

Rather than let this step beyond the landmarks of power have the effect of a legitimate precedent, it will be better to apply to it the legal aphorism de minimis non curat lex. . . .

Better also to disarm in the same way, the precedent of Chaplainships for the army and navy, than erect them into a political authority in matters of religion. The object of this establishment is seducing; the motive to it is laudable. But is it not safer to adhere to a right principle, and trust to its consequences, than confide in the reasoning however specious in favor of a wrong one. Look thro' the armies & navies of the world, and say whether in the appointment of their ministers of religion, the spiritual interest of the flocks or the temporal interest of the Shepherds, be most in view: whether here, as elsewhere the political care of religion is not a nominal more than a real aid. If the spirit of armies be devout, the spirit out of the armies will never be less so; and a failure of religious instruction & exhortation from a voluntary source within or without, will rarely happen: and if such be not the spirit of armies, the official services of their Teachers are not likely to produce it. . . .

The case of navies with insulated crews may be less within the scope of these reflections. But it is not entirely so. The chance of a devout officer, might be of as much worth to religion, as the service of an ordinary chaplain (were it admitted that religion has a real interest in the latter). . . .

Religious proclamations by the Executive recommending thanksgivings & fasts are shoots from the same root with the legislative acts reviewed.

Altho' recommendations only, they imply a religious agency, making no part of the trust delegated to political rulers.

NOTES AND QUESTIONS

1. The Background of the Detached Memorandum. The Detached Memorandum concerning religion and government is an undated document in Madison's handwriting, written sometime between 1817 and 1832. It was discovered in 1946 in the papers of his biographer, along with similar memoranda on other subjects, and was published later that year. See Elizabeth Fleet, Madison's "Detached Memoranda," 3 Wm. & Mary Q. 534, 558 (1946), reprinted in 5 The Founders' Constitution 103 (Philip B. Kurland & Ralph Lerner eds., 1987). The authenticity of the document has not been seriously questioned, but its relevance to constitutional interpretation has been.

2. The Memorandum and Constitutional Meaning. How much weight should the Detached Memorandum receive as evidence of the original meaning of the Religion Clauses? Should Madison's views be taken as central, since he was such a prime mover behind the clauses? Did Madison's views as of around 1820, after he had retired from public life, correspond to the views he espoused during the 1789 debates (pp. 58-62)?

Madison argues that religious bodies should not be able to incorporate and should have their property holdings limited in duration or amount. Was he advocating special restrictions on religious organizations? Compare the Detached Memorandum with his 1811 message vetoing an act of Congress that incorporated an Episcopal congregation in the District of Columbia (see p. 288)—one of the two "negatives . . . by J.M." referred to in the memorandum. If he favored a special rule against religious corporations, would that be a historically accurate understanding of the Religion Clauses? A proper one?

The memorandum also opposes the appointment and payment of official chaplains for the House and Senate and for soldiers and sailors. The congressional chaplaincies were instituted by the first Congress in 1789, three days before it reached agreement on the language of the Religion Clauses. See Marsh v. Chambers, 463 U.S. 783 (1983) (p. 494). (Madison wrote in an 1822 letter that he had opposed the measure at the time.) Does this show that on this question, Madison was out of step with the original understanding of the clauses? The military chaplaincies have been upheld on the ground that they preserve the ability of military personnel to exercise their faith in confined conditions. For discussion, Part III-C-4 below. Does this undercut the value of Madison's view as an indicator of the original meaning? Is Madison convincing when he argues that the precedent set by military chaplaincies, or any of these other practices, is too dangerous?

Finally, the memorandum opposes proclamations by presidents of days of thanksgiving and prayer. While in the White House, Madison himself first refused to issue such proclamations, but later he did so on four occasions during the War of 1812. (In the 1822 letter mentioned above, he said he had been mistaken to issue them.) What does this course of events show about the original meaning of the Religion Clauses? What does it show more generally about looking to particular government actions as evidence of the original meaning of a constitutional provision?

3. Disestablishment and Religious "Voluntaryism" in the Early Republic. As we have already noted (p. 63), at the time of the First Amendment Massachusetts and two other New England states still retained "establishments" in the sense of tax assessments (however liberalized) to support clergy and churches. These practices were terminated in the early 1800s: in New Hampshire and Connecticut by 1820, and in Massachusetts in 1833. See p. 26 above. Professor Carl Esbeck summarizes the causes:

In the early national period, religious voluntaryism was on the ascendance. Church membership was soaring in the populist, nonhierarchical churches often staffed by clergy without formal credentials. These churches embodied a more accessible and personal religion, often planted by revivals and circuit riders. American religion was undergoing a major transformation, one abandoning many remaining vestiges of the European Reformation past and moving on toward norms shaped by an altogether new American ethos that was caught up in individualism, progress, and frontier expansion. Under those influences, then, and factors such as the leveling of social classes in society and the disintegration wrought by large-scale immigration, the American theory of religious freedom pushed for the decoupling of formal ties between religious institutions and government institutions. To use a more modern descriptor, the church and its ecclesiastical affairs were deregulated. Henceforth, the civil state had no legal authority, and its courts thus had no subject matter jurisdiction over those topics that were inherently religious and thus within the sole province of the church.

Carl H. Esbeck, Dissent and Disestablishment: The Church-State Settlement in the Early Republic, 2004 B.Y.U. L. Rev. 1385, 1395-1396. Should any of these developments that occurred after 1791—such as the demise of the New England religious taxes—figure in understanding the original meaning of the Religion Clauses?

4. The Sunday Mail Controversy. The major Religion Clause debate in the early Republic involved the fervent efforts—reflected in thousands of citizen petitions—to stop the Post Office's practice of delivering mail on Sundays, which had begun in 1810 and was reauthorized in 1825. Andrew J. King, Sunday Law in the Nineteenth Century, 64 Albany L. Rev. 675, 684-685 (2000).

Opponents of Sunday mail argued that it profaned the Sabbath and "prevented postal employees from 'enjoy[ing] the same opportunities of attending to moral and religious instruction or intellectual improvement on that day which is enjoyed by the rest of their fellow citizens.'" Kurt T. Lash, Power and the Subject of Religion, 59 Ohio St. L.J. 1069, 1130-1131 (1998) (quotation omitted). A Senate committee chaired by future vice president Richard M. Johnson issued a report recommending against stopping Sunday mails:

> The transportation of the mail on the first day of the week, it is believed, does not interfere with the rights of conscience. The petitioners for its discontinuance appear to be actuated from a religious zeal, which may be commendable if confined to its proper sphere; but they assume a position better suited to an ecclesiastical than to a civil institution. They appear, in many instances, to lay it down as an axiom, that the practice is a violation of the law of God. Should Congress, in their legislative capacity, adopt the sentiment, it would establish the principle, that the Legislature is a proper tribunal to determine what are the laws of God. . . . [T]he only method [of] avoiding [a slippery slope to religious establishments], with their attendant train of evils, is to adhere strictly to the spirit of the constitution, which regards the General Government in no other light than that of a civil institution, wholly destitute of religious authority.

5 Register of Debates in Congress, App. 24-25 (Gales & Seaton eds., 1829). What does the debate indicate about the understanding of the Religion Clauses in the early Republic? Did this passage in the report adequately deal with the argument that Sunday mails should be discontinued to protect postal employees who worship on that day? Was there another remedy for that problem?

3. Incorporation in the Fourteenth Amendment

The Bill of Rights added to the Constitution in 1791 was designed to limit the power of the federal government that the Constitution had created. That is why the First Amendment begins with the phrase "Congress shall make no law . . ." Before the Civil War, there were a few unsuccessful efforts to argue that these rights were also good against the states. Chief Justice Marshall rejected one in Barron v. Mayor and City Council of City of Baltimore, 32 U.S. (7 Pet.) 243 (1833), where the owner of a wharf destroyed by the city made a claim under the Fifth Amendment for just compensation. In the following case, the Supreme Court rejected the claim that the Free Exercise Clause applied to acts of state government:

PERMOLI v. NEW ORLEANS
44 U.S. (3 How.) 589 (1845)

[On October 31, 1842, the First Municipality of New Orleans enacted this ordinance:

[I]t shall be unlawful to carry to, and expose in, any of the Catholic churches of this municipality, any corpse . . . [A]ny priest who may celebrate any funeral at any of the aforesaid churches [shall be subject to a fine of $50. All] corpses shall be brought to the obituary chapel, situated in Rampart street, wherein all funeral rites shall be performed as heretofore.

On November 11 the city issued a warrant against Permoli, a Catholic priest, for having said funeral prayers over the body of Louis LeRoy in St. Augustin's Catholic Church. The City Court entered judgment for the city and imposed a fine of $50. Permoli sought review in the Supreme Court.]

Mr. Justice CATRON delivered the opinion of the Court.

As this case comes here on a writ of error to bring up the proceedings of a state court, before proceeding to examine the merits of the controversy, it is our duty to determine whether this court has jurisdiction of the matter.

The ordinances complained of, must violate the Constitution or laws of the United States, or some authority exercised under them; if they do not, we have no power by the 25th section of the Judiciary Act to interfere. The Constitution makes no provision for protecting the citizens of the respective states in their religious liberties; this is left to the state constitutions and laws: nor is there any inhibition imposed by the Constitution of the United States in this respect on the states. We must therefore look beyond the Constitution for the laws that are supposed to be violated, and on which our jurisdiction can be founded . . .

[Here the Court rejected (among others) the argument that Permoli was protected by the first article of the Northwest Ordinance, which Congress had extended to the territory of Orleans in 1805. It forbade molesting any person "on account of his mode of worship or religious sentiments." See 1 Stat. 50, 51-53 (1789). But that law had been displaced in 1812 when Louisiana was admitted to the Union with her own constitution, "on an equal footing with the original states in all respects whatever."] In our judgment, the question presented by the record is exclusively of state cognizance, and equally so in the old states and the new ones; and that the writ of error must be dismissed.

NOTES AND QUESTIONS

1. The Background of *Permoli*. Things were not quite as they seemed in *Permoli*. The First Municipality—bounded by the levee, Esplanade, Rampart, and Canal Streets—was the city proper, and it was largely populated by Catholics. Most (sometimes all) members of the municipal council that adopted the ordinance were Catholics. There was only one Protestant church in the entire municipality, at the very edge, on Canal Street. And it was the practice of Catholics, but not Protestants, to hold funeral services with the corpse exposed before the congregation. New Orleans had annual problems with yellow fever. The ordinance was defended as an effort to prevent the spread of the disease. As the city's lawyer argued, "If Catholics are wronged, Catholics have wronged them. This circumstance . . . may not lessen the injury, but it weakens the wrong." 44 U.S. (3 How.) at 602. Is this so?

A likely explanation for the course of events is that the municipal authorities were siding with the lay leaders of the congregation in a conflict with the bishop by cutting off a source of revenue under the guise of a health regulation. The case appears to be at the center of a fascinating tale of ecclesiastical and political intrigue. See the entry on *Permoli* in Religion and American Law: An Encyclopedia 358-360 (Paul Finkelman ed., 2000). These questions are, of course, beside the point because the Court held that Father Permoli could only look to Louisiana law for protection.

2. The Fourteenth Amendment and Incorporation. The Civil War changed the balance of state and federal power. Slavery was an institution embodied in state law, with recognition—if not outright protection—in the federal Constitution. It took a national effort to abolish it, and the Reconstruction amendments created rights against the states designed to root it out. For our purposes the question is whether they did more, and if so, how much? Section one of the Fourteenth Amendment states in part:

> No State shall make or enforce any law which shall abridge the privileges or immunities of citizens of the United States; nor shall any State deprive any person of life, liberty, or property, without due process of law; nor deny to any person within its jurisdiction the equal protection of the laws.

Many scholars argue that the individual freedoms protected against federal encroachment by the Bill of Rights were intended to be protected against the states as "privileges or immunities of citizens of the United States." See Michael Kent Curtis, No State Shall Abridge (1986); Akhil Reed Amar, The Bill of Rights (1998). They point out that the principal author of the Amendment, as well as the floor leaders who presented the proposed Amendment in both the House and the Senate, refer to the Privileges or Immunities Clause as including the protections of the first eight amendments. John A. Bingham, the author of

Section One of the Amendment, referred to it as a "grant of power to enforce the Bill of Rights." Cong. Globe, 39th Cong., 1st Sess. 1034 (1866). Jacob Howard, floor manager of the Fourteenth Amendment in the Senate, explained that the Privileges or Immunities Clause comprehended "the personal rights guaranteed and secured by the first eight Amendments of the Constitution; such as the freedom of speech and of the press; the right of the people peaceably to assemble and petition the Government for a redress of grievances," and so on. *Id.* at 2765. Application of the Bill of Rights to the states remains controversial, however, at least as a matter of theory. See Daniel O. Conkle, Toward a General Theory of the Establishment Clause, 82 Nw. U. L. Rev. 1113, 1136 (1988).

One piece of historical evidence may seem to cut against the claim that the Fourteenth Amendment was intended to incorporate the Religion Clauses. In 1875, Representative James G. Blaine of Maine introduced this proposed constitutional Amendment:

> No State shall make any law respecting an establishment of religion or prohibiting the free exercise thereof; and no money raised by taxation in any State for the support of public schools, or derived from any public fund therefor, nor any public lands devoted thereto, shall ever be under the control of any religious sect, nor shall any money so raised or lands so devoted be divided between religious sects or denominations.

4 Cong. Rec. 205 (1875). The House approved the amendment by a wide margin, but in the Senate it failed to get the required two-thirds majority (28-16, with 27 abstentions). F. William O'Brien, The Blaine Amendment 1875-1876, 41 U. Det. L.J. 137 (1963).

Wouldn't it have been odd for Congress to consider the first clause of the Blaine Amendment if the Fourteenth Amendment had already made the religion clauses applicable to the states? Why do that job twice? It is possible that the 44th Congress (that of 1875) misunderstood the work of the 39th Congress (of 1868). On the other hand it is conceivable that the Blaine Amendment failed in the Senate because it was deemed unnecessary. But the 39th and 44th Congresses had several dozen members in common, including Blaine himself. If incorporation were already a fait accompli, it would have been natural for someone to point that out; nobody did.

Michael Kent Curtis has suggested a third possibility. Suppose the Fourteenth Amendment *was* intended to incorporate the Bill of Rights in 1868. The Slaughter-House Cases, 83 U.S. 36, nullified that work in 1873 by giving a narrow reading to the Privileges or Immunities Clause. The Blaine Amendment would have put things to right in 1876 by *re*-incorporating the religion clauses. No State Shall Abridge, at 169-170. The legislative history of the Blaine Amendment does not discuss this possibility. Conkle, 82 Nw. U. L. Rev. at 1139 n.125. Is Curtis's a realistic interpretation? If Congress thought the *Slaughter-House Cases* were a mistake, why limit their correction to this part of the First Amendment? For more on the Blaine Amendment, see pp. 362-366.

3. Incorporating the Two Clauses.   Over a period of many decades, the Supreme Court gradually "incorporated" most of the Bill of Rights freedoms through the Due Process Clause, including both parts of the Religion Clause. This greatly multiplied the scope of these provisions. When they applied only to the federal government, and the federal government's activity was essentially limited to foreign affairs and the regulation of commerce, the occasions for conflict between church and state were few. With incorporation, all that would change.

(a) **Free exercise.**   The first step was the conclusion—building through the end of the nineteenth century and confirmed in Lochner v. New York, 198 U.S. 45 (1905)—that the Due Process Clause contained a substantive prohibition against certain legislative encroachments on personal liberty. At first the liberty at stake was the freedom to work and make contracts. Then it was extended to the education of one's children, Pierce v. Society of Sisters (p. 366), and to the freedom of speech. Gitlow v. New York, 268 U.S. 652 (1925). In 1940 the Court held that the fundamental concept of liberty embodied in the Due Process Clause also embraced the free exercise of religion. Cantwell v. Connecticut (p. 124). Conceptually, this raises few difficulties: The free exercise of religion is a quintessential individual right, and had been recognized at the state level from the beginning.

(b) **Nonestablishment.**   Seven years after *Cantwell* the Supreme Court decided that the Establishment Clause also applied to the states. Everson v. Board of Education (p. 339). This is a trickier proposition, for several reasons. First, under the Supreme Court's theory of selective incorporation, not all provisions of the Bill of Rights, but only those "implicit in the concept of ordered liberty," such as freedom of speech, are incorporated. Palko v. Connecticut, 302 U.S. 319, 326 (1937); Adamson v. California, 332 U.S. 46, 67 (1947). Does the Establishment Clause meet this test? By 1791 every state had granted liberty of worship and conscience in some significant form, but about half the states still had some form of religious establishment, such as tax assessments to support clergy. Likewise, today several European countries, including England, maintain established churches (albeit in minimal form). None of these governments appears illiberal or oppressive. As long as free exercise rights are guaranteed, are the added requirements of the Establishment Clause fundamental to "ordered liberty" or "decency and fairness"?

Second, it is arguable that the Establishment Clause, at least in many of its applications, does not protect any personal "liberty." To the extent that the Establishment Clause protects individuals against religious coercion, it is conceptually similar to other liberties. But to the extent that the clause embodies a broader notion of "separation," it more closely resembles the separation of powers, or perhaps the enumeration of power in Art. I, § 8. Whose "liberty" is at stake in cases of this sort? For discussion, see Carl H. Esbeck, The Establishment Clause as a Structural Restraint on Governmental Power, 84 Iowa L. Rev. 1, 25-32 (1998).

To compound the difficulty, the original meaning of the Establishment Clause had a "federalism" component. Consider, for example, the following argument by Justice Thomas:

ELK GROVE UNIFIED SCHOOL DISTRICT v. NEWDOW
542 U.S. 1 (2004)

[*Newdow* involved an Establishment Clause challenge to the recitation in public schools of the Pledge of Allegiance with the phrase "under God" coming after "one nation." The Court held that the plaintiff, the noncustodial father of a schoolchild, lacked legal standing to sue in federal court. Several justices wrote separately to say that they would have upheld the "under God" phrase on the merits, including Justice Thomas, who wrote the following lone opinion.]

Justice THOMAS, concurring in the judgment.

. . . I would take this opportunity to begin the process of rethinking the Establishment Clause. I would acknowledge that the Establishment Clause is a federalism provision, which, for this reason, resists incorporation. Moreover, as I will explain, the Pledge policy is not implicated by any sensible incorporation of the Establishment Clause, which would probably cover little more than the Free Exercise Clause. . . .

II

I accept that the Free Exercise Clause, which clearly protects an individual right, applies against the States through the Fourteenth Amendment. But the Establishment Clause is another matter. The text and history of the Establishment Clause strongly suggest that it is a federalism provision intended to prevent Congress from interfering with state establishments. . . .

A

The Establishment Clause provides that "Congress shall make no law respecting an establishment of religion." As a textual matter, this Clause probably prohibits Congress from establishing a national religion. Perhaps more importantly, the Clause made clear that Congress could not interfere with state establishments, notwithstanding any argument that could be made based on Congress' power under the Necessary and Proper Clause. See A. Amar, The Bill of Rights 36-39 (1998).

Nothing in the text of the Clause suggests that it reaches any further. The Establishment Clause does not purport to protect individual rights. By contrast, the Free Exercise Clause plainly protects individuals against congressional interference with the right to exercise their religion, and the remaining Clauses within the First Amendment expressly disable Congress from "abridging [particular] *freedom[s]*." (Emphasis added.) This textual analysis is consistent with the prevailing view that the Constitution left religion to the States. See, e.g., 2 J. Story, Commentaries on the Constitution of the United States § 1873 (5th ed. 1891); see also Amar, The Bill of Rights, at 32-42; *id.*, at 246-257. History also supports this understanding: At the founding, at least six States had established religions, see McConnell, The Origins and Historical Understanding of Free Exercise of Religion, 103 Harv. L. Rev. 1409, 1437 (1990). . . .

Quite simply, the Establishment Clause is best understood as a federalism provision—it protects state establishments from federal interference but does not protect any individual right. These two features independently make incorporation of the Clause difficult to understand. The best argument in favor of incorporation would be that, by disabling Congress from establishing a national religion, the Clause protected an individual right, enforceable against the Federal Government, to be free from coercive federal establishments. Incorporation of this individual right, the argument goes, makes sense. . . .

But even assuming that the Establishment Clause precludes the Federal Government from establishing a national religion, it does not follow that the Clause created or protects any individual right. For the reasons discussed above, it is more likely that States and only States were the direct beneficiaries. Moreover, incorporation of this putative individual right leads to a peculiar outcome: It would prohibit precisely what the Establishment Clause was intended to protect—*state* establishments of religion. . . . Nevertheless, the potential right against federal establishments is the only candidate for incorporation.

I would welcome the opportunity to consider more fully the difficult questions whether and how the Establishment Clause applies against the States[1]. . . .

C

Through the Pledge policy, the State has not created or maintained any religious establishment, and neither has it granted government authority to an existing religion. The Pledge policy does not expose anyone to the legal coercion associated with an established religion. Further, no other free-exercise rights are at issue. It follows that religious liberty rights are not in question and that the Pledge policy fully comports with the Constitution.

For further presentations of the "federalism" argument against incorporating the Establishment Clause, see, e.g., Steven D. Smith, Foreordained Failure: The Quest for a Constitutional Principle of Religious Freedom ch. 2 (1995);William K. Lietzau, Rediscovering the Establishment Clause: Federalism and the Rollback of Incorporation, 39 DePaul L. Rev. 1191 (1990).

But for argument in favor of incorporation, see Steven K. Green, Federalism and the Establishment Clause: A Reassessment, 38 Creighton L. Rev. 761 (2005). And consider Justice Brennan's solution to the problem:

SCHOOL DISTRICT OF ABINGTON TOWNSHIP v. SCHEMPP
374 U.S. 203 (1963)

Mr. Justice BRENNAN, concurring.

[The Court in this and a companion case held that the defendants—public school districts in Pennsylvania and Maryland—had violated the Establishment Clause by conducting prayer exercises at the opening of each school day. The exercises consisted of readings from the Bible and recitation of the Lord's Prayer. Justice Brennan joined the opinion of the Court (see p. 486), but added this discussion about the application of the Religion Clauses to state and local defendants.]

1. [Relocated footnote.] It may well be the case that anything that would violate the incorporated Establishment Clause would actually violate the Free Exercise Clause, further calling into doubt the utility of incorporating the Establishment Clause. See, e.g., A. Amar, The Bill of Rights 253-254 (1998). Lee v. Weisman (1992) [p. 12] (striking down a school-initiated prayer at public school graduation ceremony) could be thought of this way to the extent that anyone might have been "coerced" into a religious exercise. . . .

No one questions that the Framers of the First Amendment intended to restrict exclusively the powers of the Federal Government. Whatever limitations that Amendment now imposes upon the States derive from the Fourteenth Amendment. The process of absorption of the religious guarantees of the First Amendment as protections against the States under the Fourteenth Amendment began with the Free Exercise Clause. In 1923 the Court held that the protections of the Fourteenth included at least a person's freedom "to worship God according to the dictates of his own conscience. . . . " Meyer v. Nebraska. Cantwell v. Connecticut completed in 1940 the process of absorption of the Free Exercise Clause and recognized its dual aspect: the Court affirmed freedom of belief as an absolute liberty, but recognized that conduct, while it may also be comprehended by the Free Exercise Clause, "remains subject to regulation for the protection of society."

The absorption of the Establishment Clause has, however, come later and by a route less easily charted. It has been suggested, with some support in history, that absorption of the First Amendment's ban against congressional legislation "respecting an establishment of religion" is conceptually impossible because the Framers meant the Establishment Clause also to foreclose any attempt by Congress to disestablish the existing official state churches. Whether or not such was the understanding of the Framers and whether such a purpose would have inhibited the absorption of the Establishment Clause at the threshold of the Nineteenth Century are questions not dispositive of our present inquiry. For it is clear on the record of history that the last of the formal state establishments was dissolved more than three decades before the Fourteenth Amendment was ratified, and thus the problem of protecting official state churches from federal encroachments could hardly have been any concern of those who framed the post—Civil War Amendments. Any such objective of the First Amendment, having become historical anachronism by 1868, cannot be thought to have deterred the absorption of the Establishment Clause to any greater degree than it would, for example, have deterred the absorption of the Free Exercise Clause. That no organ of the Federal Government possessed in 1791 any power to restrain the interference of the States in religious matters is indisputable. See Permoli v. New Orleans. It is equally plain, on the other hand, that the Fourteenth Amendment created a panoply of new federal rights for the protection of citizens of the various States. And among those rights was freedom from such state governmental involvement in the affairs of religion as the Establishment Clause had originally foreclosed on the part of Congress.

It has also been suggested that the "liberty" guaranteed by the Fourteenth Amendment logically cannot absorb the Establishment Clause because that clause is not one of the provisions of the Bill of Rights which in terms protects a "freedom" of the individual. The fallacy in this contention, I think, is that it underestimates the role of the Establishment Clause as a coguarantor, with the Free Exercise Clause, of religious liberty. The Framers did not entrust the liberty of religious beliefs to either clause alone. The Free Exercise Clause "was not to be the full extent of the Amendment's guarantee of freedom from governmental intrusion in matters of faith." [Citation omitted.]

Finally, it has been contended that absorption of the Establishment Clause is precluded by the absence of any intention on the part of the Framers of the Fourteenth Amendment to circumscribe the residual powers of the States to aid religious activities and institutions in ways which fell short of formal establishments. That argument relies in part upon the express terms of the abortive Blaine Amendment—proposed several years after the adoption of the Fourteenth Amendment—which would have added to the First Amendment a provision that "[n]o State shall make any law respecting an establishment of religion. . . . " Such a restriction would have been superfluous, it is said, if the Fourteenth Amendment had already made the Establishment Clause binding upon the States.

The argument proves too much, for the Fourteenth Amendment's protection of the free exercise of religion can hardly be questioned; yet the Blaine Amendment would also have added an explicit protection against state laws abridging that liberty. Even if we assume that the draftsmen of the Fourteenth Amendment saw no immediate connection between its protections against state action infringing personal liberty and the guarantees of the First Amendment, it is certainly too late in the day to suggest that their assumed inattention to the question dilutes the force of these constitutional guarantees in their application to the States. It is enough to conclude that the religious liberty embodied in the Fourteenth Amendment would not be viable if the Constitution were interpreted to forbid only establishments ordained by Congress.

NOTES AND QUESTIONS

1. The Basis for Incorporation. Justice Brennan concedes for the sake of argument that the Establishment Clause may have had a federalist purpose in 1791. But, he argues, it no longer served that function by 1868; the last of the state establishments was dissolved in 1833. What work did it do, then, in the mid-nineteenth century? Kurt Lash argues that it came to stand for a "nonestablishment principle" which could be implemented at the state no less than the federal level. Indeed some states—Iowa in 1857 for example—put establishment clauses in their constitutions, using the precise language of the First Amendment, strongly suggesting that the language had lost its original "state's rights" meaning. The Second Adoption of the Establishment Clause: The Rise of the Nonestablishment Principle, 27 Ariz. St. L.J. 1085, 1133 (1995).

Suppose Lash's account is historically accurate. Would it help the case for incorporation of the Establishment Clause? What he calls the nonestablishment principle is one that is *capable* of being applied to the states. Does Lash's argument bear on whether the framers of the Fourteenth Amendment *intended* to apply the Establishment Clause to the states? If they did, can we safely assume that they meant to import the contemporary version and leave behind the original meaning?

Does Lash's argument help us with the textual problem of *where* in the Fourteenth Amendment to attach the Establishment Clause? Justice Brennan proposes that we understand it as "a coguarantor, with the Free Exercise Clause, of religious liberty." If that were so we could attach it, as we do free exercise, to the Due Process Clause. Does the Establishment Clause do nothing more than prevent religious coercion? Are its further requirements of church-state separation (if any) incorporated against the states? For discussion of a variety of such questions, see Esbeck, 84 Iowa L. Rev. 1. Justice Brennan also stresses the connection between the two clauses when he comes to assess the significance of the Blaine Amendment. Some say it casts doubt on the incorporation of the Establishment Clause. But that argument, Brennan says, "proves too much," for it would cast equal doubt on the incorporation of free exercise. Does that simply mean that free exercise should not be incorporated either? See also, e.g., Smith, Foreordained Failure (arguing that the framers meant to leave questions of free exercise as well as establishment to the states).

2. Why Allow Local Establishments? Is there any normative argument for permitting religious establishments within small units of government? Consider that some religions are more communal than individualistic in nature: To such believers, their own spiritual welfare is affected by the conduct of others. A familiar example might be an Israeli kibbutz, or the utopian community of New Harmony, Indiana. Perhaps they believe in communal Sabbath observance; or in the sharing of property, like the early Christian believers; or in avoidance of modern technology; or in the prohibition of alcohol, tobacco, or pornography. (Maybe the very idea that our spiritual welfare is purely a product of our individual relationships to God is a sectarian premise, rooted in Protestantism.) Under a system that forbids religious establishments at all levels of government, such believers are not able to live their religiously grounded way of life, because the only communities permitted under the Establishment Clause are diverse, pluralistic regimes with no official religion. Might it be desirable to allow people to establish explicitly religious communities—provided that no one is forced to join, everyone is free to leave, and basic human rights are respected?

Philosopher Robert Nozick has argued for what he calls a "utopia of utopias," in which people are allowed to establish nonliberal subcommunities within a broader framework of a liberal society:

ANARCHY, STATE, AND UTOPIA
Robert Nozick (1974)

[T]though there is great liberty to choose among communities, many particular communities internally may have many restrictions unjustifiable on libertarian grounds: that is, restrictions which libertarians would condemn if they were enforced by a central state apparatus. For example, paternalistic intervention into people's lives, restrictions on the range of books which may circulate in the community, limitation on the kinds of sexual behavior, and so on. But this is merely another way of pointing out that in a free society people may contract into various restrictions which the government may not legitimately impose upon them. Though the framework is libertarian and laissez-faire, *individual communities within it need not be*, and perhaps no community within it will choose to be so. Thus, the characteristics of the framework need not pervade the individual communities. In *this* laissez-faire system it could turn out that though they are permitted, there are no actually functioning "capitalist" institutions; or that some communities have them and others don't or some communities have some of them, or what you will. . . .

The difference seems to me to reside in the difference between a face-to-face community and a nation. In a nation, one knows that there are nonconforming individuals, but one need not be directly confronted by these individuals or by the fact of their nonconformity. Even if one finds it offensive that others do not conform, even if the knowledge that there exist nonconformists rankles and makes one very unhappy, this does not constitute being harmed by the others or having one's rights violated. Whereas in a face-to-face community one cannot avoid being directly confronted with what one finds to be offensive. How one lives in one's immediate environment is affected.

NOTES AND QUESTIONS

1. Federalism and Local Establishments of Religion.   Might Nozick's "utopia of utopias" be achievable through a creative use of federalism, where establishment of religion is forbidden at higher levels (the federal government, perhaps even states) but permitted in local communities, where citizens are free to enter or exit in accordance with their preferences? Would this be a good idea? Would it increase the overall level of religious freedom, by enabling believers with a communal conception of religious exercise to live according to their beliefs? Whose religious liberty would be diminished? What would be the practical problems with such a system?

2. Federalism and Colonial Establishments.   Could the Massachusetts Bay Colony—with all its seeming intolerance to heretics and unbelievers—be defended in Nozickean terms? After all, the Pilgrims and Puritans traveled across the ocean to what was then a wilderness, and did not force (or ask) anyone to join them against their will. Persons of other beliefs were free to form their own colonies. Nathaniel Ward, minister of the church at Ipswich and a principal coauthor (with John Cotton) of the Massachusetts Body of Liberties (1641), wrote the following defense of the Massachusetts system:

> First, such as have given or taken any unfriendly reports of us New-English, should doe well to recollect themselves. We have been reputed a Colluvies of wild Opinionists, swarmed into a remote wildernes to find elbow-roome for our phanatick Doctrines and practices: I trust our diligence past, and constant sedulity against such persons and courses, will plead better things for us. I dare take upon me . . . to proclaime to the world, in the name of our Colony, that all Familists, Antinomians, Anabaptists, and other Enthusiasts, shall have free Liberty to keep away from us, and such as wiell come to be gone as fast as they can, the sooner the better.

Nathaniel Ward, The Simple Cobbler of Aggawam in America 3 (1647).

3. Federalism Concerning Free Exercise Too?   Do the arguments for local discretion concerning religious establishments also imply that localities should be able to decide how much to permit or restrict the free exercise of religion? After all, communal values are also reflected in how much religious dissent the community permits—and again, dissenters can simply exit. Consider the argument that

> local government—and more generally the decentralization of power—is a robust structural component of religious liberty. First, the dispersal of political authority

prevents the amassing of power to benefit or burden religion in any one institution, thus guarding against governmental overreaching. Second, the dispersal of political authority gives local governments the ability to serve as counterweights to private religious power, thus preventing religious overreaching.

Richard C. Schragger, The Role of the Local in the Doctrine and Discourse of Religious Liberty, 117 Harv. L. Rev. 1810, 1815 (2004).

4. The City of Rajneeshpuram.   In the early 1980s, followers of the Bhagwan Rajneesh, a charismatic Indian guru, purchased the Big Muddy ranch, in a remote eastern Oregon valley 12 miles from the town of Antelope. They transformed it into a thriving town of 4,000 residents, with a 4,500-foot paved airstrip, a 44-acre reservoir, an 88,000-square-foot meeting hall, and a thriving restaurant, called the Zorba-the-Buddha Rajneesh Restaurant. The Bhagwan himself was reported to own 93 Rolls Royce automobiles. When they encountered resistance from the townspeople of Antelope, the newcomers outvoted them and took over the town government. The group disintegrated in 1985, amid charges of corruption, immigration fraud, and conspiracy to commit murder—on which several members were convicted. The Bhagwan Rajneesh died in 1990, after conviction for immigration fraud and deportation to India. At the height of their success, the residents of Rajneeshpuram sought legal recognition as a municipality. The state of Oregon opposed this on the ground that it would constitute an establishment of religion:

STATE OF OREGON v. CITY OF RAJNEESHPURAM

598 F. Supp. 1208 (D. Ore. 1984)

FRYE, Judge:

[The court accepts the following allegations as true, for purposes of the motion to dismiss.]

The City of Rajneeshpuram is a municipal corporation located in Wasco County, Oregon. The City was incorporated by a Proclamation of Incorporation on May 26, 1982, following a unanimous vote of 154 electors. Later a city council was elected, a city government organized, and a city charter enacted. The City is comprised of three separate parcels of land and a county road connecting the parcels. The City is located entirely within the confines of Rancho Rajneesh, a 64,229 acre parcel controlled by Rajneesh Foundation International (RFI). The only public thoroughfare and the only publicly owned property within Rancho Rajneesh and the City is a county road. RFI is a nonprofit religious corporation organized to advance the teachings of the Bhagwan Shree Rajneesh. The followers of the Bhagwan assert that he is an enlightened religious master. RFI is a part of the organizational structure through which the followers of the Bhagwan practice their religion. The Rajneesh Neo-Sannyas International Commune ("the Commune") is a corporation organized under Oregon's Co-operative Corporations Act and does not issue stock. The purpose of the Commune, according to its articles of incorporation, is "... to be a religious community where life is, in every respect, guided by the religious teachings of Bhagwan Shree Rajneesh and whose members live a communal life with a common treasury...." Because of the Commune's control over all real property in and around the City, no person may reside in Rajneeshpuram without the consent of the Commune and Ma Anand Sheela [personal secretary to the Bhagwan]. All residents of Rajneeshpuram are either members or invitees of the Commune. The Commune possesses and has exercised substantial and direct control over visitor access to Rajneeshpuram. Only a small portion of Rajneeshpuram is accessible by the county road. Most of the City, including City Hall, is accessible only by means of roads controlled by the Commune. Visitors to the City are asked to check in at a visitor's center and have been required to obtain a visitor's pass as a condition to access to facilities (other than City Hall) not located directly on the county road right-of-way. Some visitors have been searched as a condition of entry to the City. The followers of the Bhagwan assert that the development of Rajneeshpuram is the fulfillment of a religious vision. The primary purpose for establishing the City of Rajneeshpuram was to advance the religion of Rajneeshism. The City was founded to fulfil a religious vision. The City was designed and functions as a spiritual mecca for followers of the Bhagwan worldwide. It serves as a monument to and the residence of the Bhagwan, and as a gathering place for followers at institutions of religious training and at three annual religious festivals.

DISCUSSION AND ANALYSIS

The issue which this court will address is whether, assuming the allegations of the complaint are true, the Establishment Clause of the First Amendment to the United States Constitution is violated by the operation and existence of the City of Rajneeshpuram as a sovereign municipal government, validated and supported by the State of Oregon as otherwise required by state law. [The court cites the three-part test of Lemon v. Kurtzman (see p. 11).]

The State of Oregon's main argument is that it is unconstitutional to give municipal power and status to a city (1) in which all land is subject to the control of a religious corporation, (2) in which residency is controlled by a religious corporation and limited to followers of that religion or their guests, and (3) whose *raison d'etre* is the practice and advancement of a particular religion. Under such facts, the State of Oregon argues, giving the City of Rajneeshpuram municipal status and power is the same as giving municipal status and power to a religion, and that a clearer example of establishment of religion could not be imagined.

Defendants counter that the only alleged factual difference between a city composed entirely of adherents of one religion, such as the German Benedictines of Mount Angel, and the Rajneeshees of the City of Rajneeshpuram, is the form of land ownership and the concomitant restriction on residency in the city. Defendants argue that to find the existence and operation of the City of Rajneeshpuram unconstitutional would be to penalize defendants because they believe in communal rather than private ownership of land. As stated in defendants' memoranda in support of their motion to dismiss the State of Oregon's complaint:

> According to the state's allegations, if 150 Rajneeshees or Catholics had lived at Rancho Rajneesh without a commune and without a single land owner, their petition for incorporation would have been acceptable. The state failed to give any reason why membership in the Commune or the nature of property ownership requires that the right to municipal incorporation be taken away. Defendant asserts that such a denial would be unconstitutional in its infringement upon each individual's right to vote, right to associate and right to own property.

But the State of Oregon argues that denying municipal status to the City of Rajneeshpuram would not interfere with defendants' rights to practice religion, or to associate freely, or to have access to public services. If the City of Rajneeshpuram did not exist, the State of Oregon argues, defendants could still practice their religion and freely associate; the only difference would be that public services would be provided by Wasco County rather than by the City of Rajneeshpuram.

The State relies heavily on Larkin v. Grendel's Den (1982) (see p. 704). There, the Supreme Court held unconstitutional a Massachusetts statute giving churches a discretionary power to veto liquor license applications of premises within five hundred feet of the church. The court held that the statute failed both the "primary effect" and "excessive entanglement" tests of *Lemon*:

> We can assume that the churches would act in good faith in their exercise of the statutory power, yet [the statute] does not by its terms require that churches' power be used in a religiously neutral way. "[T]he potential for conflict inheres in the situation," and appellants have not suggested any "effective means of guaranteeing" that the delegated power "will be used exclusively for secular, neutral, and nonideological purposes." In addition, the mere appearance of a joint exercise of legislative authority by Church and State provides a significant symbolic benefit to religion in the minds of some by reason of the power conferred. . . . Turning to the third phase of the inquiry called for by *Lemon v. Kurtzman*, we see that we have not previously had occasion to consider the entanglement implications of a statute vesting significant governmental authority in churches. This statute enmeshes churches in the exercise of substantial governmental powers contrary to our consistent interpretation of the Establishment Clause; "[t]he objective is to prevent, as far as possible, the intrusion of either [Church or State] into the precincts of the other." *Lemon*. We went on in that case to state: "Under our system the choice has been made that government is to be entirely excluded from the area of religious instruction *and churches excluded from the affairs of government*. The Constitution decrees that religion must be a private matter for the individual, the family, and the institutions of private choice, and that while some involvement and entanglement are inevitable, lines must be drawn."

In the present case, assuming as true the facts alleged by the State of Oregon, the existence and operation of the City of Rajneeshpuram impacts a number of the *Grendel's Den* concerns. The existence of the City of Rajneeshpuram gives the appearance of a joint exercise of legislative authority by church and state. Religious organizations control or own all real property within the City of Rajneeshpuram. The potential for religious-secular conflict with respect to actions of the City is inherent. Finally, the nature and extent of potential or actual control by religion over the government of the City raises serious entanglement problems.

CONCLUSIONS AND RULING

If the facts alleged in the State of Oregon's complaint are true, the court concludes that the potential injury to the anti-establishment principle of the First Amendment by the existence and the operation of the City of Rajneeshpuram clearly outweighs the potential harm to defendants' free exercise of religion rights. To deny defendants the right to operate a city is the only means of achieving a compelling state and federal interest—that of avoiding an establishment of religion. If the City of Rajneeshpuram were to cease to exist, defendants would not be precluded from practicing their religion nor from associating with whom they choose in order to do so. Defendants would not be denied access to public services. Public services would be provided by Wasco County. In short, although defendants' freedom to freely practice their religion would be burdened if the City of Rajneeshpuram were no longer recognized as a city, the burden upon them is small and indirect compared to the harm to be done to the Establishment Clause by allowing the City of Rajneeshpuram to operate as a city.

[T]here is a difference between the effect on and benefit to religion of the provision of ordinary municipal services to a city of private landowners of one religion and to the City of Rajneeshpuram, where the land is communally owned and controlled by religious organizations. The provision of services by a municipal government in a city whose residents are private landowners of one religious faith has the direct and primary effect of aiding the individual landowners and residents living in the city. The effect on the religion of those private landowners is remote, indirect, and incidental. In contrast, if, as alleged, all of the real property in the City of Rajneeshpuram is owned or controlled by religious organizations, the provision of municipal services by the City of Rajneeshpuram necessarily has the effect of aiding not only the individual residents of the City of Rajneeshpuram, but also of directly, obviously, and immediately benefitting the religious organizations themselves.

Given the facts as alleged by the State of Oregon, the court could conclude that the acts of the State of Oregon and Wasco County in recognizing the existence and operation of the City of Rajneeshpuram have as a principal and primary effect the advancement of the religion of Rajneeshism. Finally, given the alleged power and control of religious organizations and leaders over all real property and residency within the City of Rajneeshpuram, the court could conclude that the existence and operation of the City of Rajneeshpuram would represent "an excessive government entanglement with religion." *Lemon.*

IT IS ORDERED that defendants' motion to dismiss is DENIED.

NOTE AND QUESTIONS

Do you agree with this decision as an interpretation of the Establishment Clause? As a matter of first principles? Whose liberty is being protected here? Is it the right of non-Rajneesh adherents to move into the community? Is that right restricted because of the municipal status of the city, or because of private property ownership? In considering these questions, is the unsavory experience of this group relevant? Would your reaction be different if the religious group involved were one you considered more admirable? For another example of litigation over a local government made up of one religious community, see Bd. of Ed., Kiryas Joel Village School Dist. v. Grumet, 512 U.S. 687 (1994) (p. 252) (striking down special school district created by state legislature along lines of Hasidic Jewish settlement).

What would be the result if a group devoted to a secular belief system—for example, a feminist commune—were to purchase property, build housing, create a community, and seek municipal status?

III

RELIGION IN THE REGULATORY STATE

It is customary to divide the subject of religion and law along doctrinal lines—first the Establishment Clause, then the Free Exercise Clause. We introduced the two clauses in a general way in Part I, and provided a sketch of the historical and theoretical background of both clauses in Part II. In Parts III, IV, and V we consider a variety of legal problems with religious implications in the United States today. We group them in functional, not doctrinal, ways. Part III takes as its point of departure this fact: In the modern world the government plays a more active role in our everyday lives than it did a century or two ago. Consider, as a crude measure of the extent of government regulation, the growth in size of the Federal Register. A hundred years ago it did not exist. In 1936, its first year, it covered 2,599 pages. In 2004 the number exceeded 75,600. The cases that follow in this Part arise from efforts by federal and state governments to provide welfare and unemployment benefits; to regulate health, education, labor relations, and the environment; to promote civil rights; to control fraud; and to administer a variety of tax programs. Virtually all of these laws were enacted in the last century.

In a society that is pervasively regulated, as ours now is, there are many more occasions for conflict between the government and religious actors. How, if at all, should the law take account of this concern? Can legislatures and agencies draft exemptions that excuse religious objectors from compliance with rules that other people have to follow—as they have long done in the case of military service? If lawmakers draft laws that are neutral and generally applicable (that take no account of religion), does the First Amendment empower the courts to make exemptions? In other words, is an "accommodation"—a special provision exempting religious conduct from regulation—sometimes constitutionally required?

This counterpoint of regulation and accommodation has created an odd sort of doctrinal difficulty. If there is a constitutional requirement for accommodation of religious conduct, it will most likely be found in the Free Exercise Clause. Some say, though, that it is a violation of the Establishment Clause for the government to give any special benefit or recognition to religion. In that case, we have a First Amendment in conflict with itself—the Establishment

Clause forbidding what the Free Exercise Clause requires. This supposed conflict has seemed more serious in some decades than in others. In the 1960s, the
Free Exercise Clause was understood to lean toward accommodation and the
Establishment Clause away from it. This was the period of maximum tension.
And because the law was fixed at both ends by constitutional boundaries, it was
controlled by judges. Since the early 1990s, the Free Exercise Clause has been
read to require less accommodation, and the Establishment Clause to permit
more. This greatly reduces the conflict between the clauses, and gives lawmakers
an increased measure of discretion. What is the best solution to this problem?
Which gives the most protection to religious liberty? Are the goals of the Establishment Clause at odds with the freedom of religious exercise?

Part III is divided into four sections. In section A we review the rise and fall of
the idea that the Free Exercise Clause requires religious accommodation. In
section B we look in more detail at free exercise litigation under the chief
standards. In section C we ask whether and when the Establishment Clause
permits accommodation. This has an obvious bearing on how courts should
answer the first question. But legislators will also want to know how far they
can go in cases where they are not compelled by the Constitution—how
much room (if any) there is between the floor of free exercise and the ceiling
of nonestablishment. In section D we sample some of the regulatory issues that
confront religious institutions (churches, synagogues, colleges, etc.).

A. FREE EXERCISE: IS ACCOMMODATION REQUIRED?

In this section we review the rise and fall of the idea that free exercise requires
religious accommodation. As shown by People v. Philips (p. 103), the idea has
a long history in American law. As a federal constitutional principle, however, it
is relatively recent, and relatively short-lived. The Supreme Court first formally
embraced the idea in 1963, in Sherbert v. Verner (p. 124). Employment Division v.
Smith (p. 137) put an end to it in 1990. The Court held instead that a neutral,
generally applicable law was consistent with the Free Exercise Clause no matter
how seriously it might conflict with religious norms. Efforts since then to
reinstate the *Sherbert* rule (judicially or legislatively) have met with only limited
success: Congress's effort was struck down in part by the Court (City of Boerne v.
Flores, p. 150), although a number of states have retained the more protective
rule by legislation or court decision, and Congress's effort still applies at the
federal level. Did the more protective rule lose ground because judges simply do
not give enough weight to religious freedom? Or is it because the more protective rule is inherently unworkable—a recipe for anarchy if we enforce it consistently, and for religious discrimination or hypocrisy if we don't?

1. The Historical Debate

In recent years, there has been a lively debate among historians and constitutional scholars over what the Free Exercise Clause was probably understood to

mean at the time of its framing. In a section of City of Boerne v. Flores not reprinted, Justices O'Connor and Scalia take up the debate. This issue is of great importance to "originalists," who believe that the Constitution should be interpreted according to its original understanding. Even non-originalist judges and theorists, moreover, usually use the original understanding at least as a starting point for analysis—whether because the framers are considered to have been wise constitutional statesmen, or because constitutional interpretation requires a mix of historical and other arguments. Consider for yourself how powerful these historical arguments are. The following are samples of academic writing on both sides of the controversy:

THE ORIGINS AND HISTORICAL UNDERSTANDING OF FREE EXERCISE OF RELIGION

Michael W. McConnell
103 Harv. L. Rev. 1409 (1990)

Although often linked with Jefferson's "Enlightenment-deist-rationalist" stance toward religious freedom, Madison's views on the religion-state question should be distinguished from those of his fellow Virginian, and hence from [John] Locke. . . . Madison advocated a jurisdictional division between religion and government based on the demands of religion rather than solely on the interests of society. In his *Memorial and Remonstrance*, he wrote:

> The Religion then of every man must be left to the conviction and conscience of every man; and it is the right of every man to exercise it as these may dictate. . . . It is the duty of every man to render to the Creator such homage, and such only, as he believes to be acceptable to him.

Moreover, Madison claimed that this duty to the Creator is "precedent both in order of time and degree of obligation, to the claims of Civil Society," and "therefore that in matters of Religion, no man's right is abridged by the institution of Civil Society."

This striking passage illuminates the radical foundations of Madison's writings on religious liberty. While it does not prove that Madison supported free exercise exemptions, it suggests an approach toward religious liberty consonant with them. If the scope of religious liberty is defined by religious duty (man must render to God "such homage . . . as he believes to be acceptable to him"), and if the claims of civil society are subordinate to the claims of religious freedom, it would seem to follow that the dictates of religious faith must take precedence over the laws of the state, even if they are secular and generally applicable. . . .

[Washington, too, expressed support for religious accommodations, writing to a group of Quakers in 1789:

> [I]n my opinion the conscientious scruples of all men should be treated with great delicacy and tenderness; and it is my wish and desire, that the laws may always be as extensively accommodated to them, as a due regard to the protection and essential interests of the nation may justify and permit. . . .]

D. Legal Protections After Independence

The Revolution inspired a wave of constitution-writing in the new states. Eleven of the thirteen states (plus Vermont) adopted new constitutions between 1776 and 1780. Of those eleven, six (plus Vermont) included an explicit bill of rights; three more states adopted a bill of rights between 1781 and 1790. With the exception of Connecticut, every state, with or without an establishment, had a constitutional provision protecting religious freedom by 1789, although two states confined their protections to Christians and five other states confined their protections to theists. There was no discernible difference between the free exercise provisions adopted by the states with an establishment and those without. The free exercise clauses of Massachusetts and New Hampshire were almost identical to those of New Jersey, Pennsylvania, and Delaware. Freedom of religion was universally said to be an unalienable right; the status of other rights commonly found in state bills of rights, such as property or trial by jury, was more disputed and often considered derivative of civil society.

These state constitutions provide the most direct evidence of the original understanding, for it is reasonable to infer that those who drafted and adopted the first amendment assumed the term "free exercise of religion" meant what it had meant in their states. The wording of the state provisions thus casts light on the meaning of the first amendment.

New York's 1777 Constitution was typical:

> [T]he free exercise and enjoyment of religious profession and worship, without discrimination or preference, shall forever hereafter be allowed, within this State, to all mankind: Provided, That the liberty of conscience, hereby granted, shall not be so construed as to excuse acts of licentiousness, or justify practices inconsistent with the peace or safety of this State.

Likewise, New Hampshire's provision stated:

> Every individual has a natural and unalienable right to worship GOD according to the dictates of his own conscience, and reason; and no subject shall be hurt, molested, or restrained in his person, liberty or estate for worshipping GOD, in the manner and season most agreeable to the dictates of his own conscience, . . . provided he doth not disturb the public peace, or disturb others, in their religious worship.

As a final example, Georgia's religious liberty clause read: "All persons whatever shall have the free exercise of their religion; provided it be not repugnant to the peace and safety of the State." Other state provisions were similar. In addition to these state provisions, article I of the Northwest Ordinance of 1787, enacted contemporaneously with the drafting of the Constitution and re-enacted by the First Congress, provided: "No person, demeaning himself in a peaceable and orderly manner, shall ever be molested on account of his mode of worship, or religious sentiments, in the said territory."

While differing in their particulars, these constitutional provisions [were similar] both in the scope of the liberty and in its limitations. Each of these elements warrants attention.

1. *Scope of the Liberty.*—Each of the state constitutions first defined the scope of the free exercise right in terms of the conscience of the individual believer and the actions that flow from that conscience. None of the provisions confined the protection to beliefs and opinions, as did Jefferson, nor to expression of beliefs and opinions, as some recent scholars have suggested. Indeed, the language appears to have been drafted precisely to refute those interpretations. Maryland, for example, prohibited punishment of any person "on account of his religious persuasion *or* profession, *or* for his religious practice." Opinion, expression of opinion, and practice were all expressly protected. The key word "exercise," found in six of the constitutions, was defined in dictionaries of the day to mean "action." Two of the other constitutions used terms as broad or broader— Maryland referred to religious "practice," Rhode Island to matters of "religious concernment."

Nor did these constitutions [define] the scope of free exercise negatively, as a sphere of otherworldly concern that does not affect the public interest. The free exercise provisions defined the free exercise right affirmatively, based on the scope of duties to God perceived by the believer. The New Hampshire formulation defined the believer's right by "the dictates of his own conscience, and reason"; it extended to all "matters of religious concernment," according to Rhode Island. These could, and often would, include matters of concern to the public. This is consistent with the proposition, reflected in Madison's Memorial and Remonstrance, that the right of free exercise precedes and is superior to the social contract.

Although the free exercise right plainly extends to some forms of conduct, the scope of protected conduct in these clauses is less clear. The provisions fall into two categories. Four states—Virginia, Georgia, Maryland, and Rhode Island—protected all actions stemming from religious conviction, subject to certain limitations. The Virginia Bill of Rights, the model for three of the state proposals for the first amendment and presumably the greatest influence on Madison, is especially clear on this point. It provides that "all men are equally entitled to the free exercise of religion, according to the dictates of conscience" and defined "religion" as "the duty which we owe to our Creator, and the manner of discharging it." In the biblical tradition, "duties" to God included actions, perhaps all of life, and not just speech and opinion. So according to Virginia, the right of free exercise extended to all of a believer's duties to God and included a choice of means as well as ends.

By contrast, eight states—New York, New Hampshire, Delaware, Massachusetts, New Jersey, North Carolina, Pennsylvania, and South Carolina—plus the Northwest Ordinance, confined their protection of conduct to acts of "worship." The word "worship" usually signifies the rituals or ceremonial acts of religion, such as the administration of sacraments or the singing of hymns, and thus would indicate a more restrictive scope for the free exercise provisions.

The limitation to "worship" was not carried over into the federal free exercise clause, which in this respect most closely resembles the Georgia provision. No direct evidence suggests whether the adoption of the broader formulation was deliberate, but this seems consistent with the general theological currents of Protestant America, which were "low church" and anti-ritualistic. One of the main elements of the Great Awakening was the insistence that duties to God extend beyond the four walls of the church and the partaking of the sacraments. . . . The federal free exercise clause seems in every respect to have followed the most expansive models among the states. . . .

2. *Limits on the Liberty.*—The second common element in state free exercise provisions is that the provisions limit the right by particular, defined state interests. Nine of the states limited the free exercise right to actions that were "peaceable" or that would not disturb the "peace" or "safety" of the state. Four of these also expressly disallowed acts of licentiousness or immorality; two forbade acts that would interfere with the religious practices of others; one forbade the "civil injury or outward disturbance of others"; one added acts contrary to "good order"; and one disallowed acts contrary to the "happiness," as well as the peace and safety, of society.

These provisos are the most revealing and important feature of the state constitutions. They . . . make sense only if free exercise envisions religiously compelled exemptions from at least some generally applicable laws. Since even according to the Lockean no-exemptions view religious persons cannot be prohibited from engaging in otherwise legal activities, the provisos would only have effect if religiously motivated conduct violated the general laws in some way. The "peace and safety" clauses identify a narrower subcategory of the general laws; the free exercise provisions would exempt religiously motivated conduct from these laws up to the point that such conduct breached public peace or safety.[a]

The language of these provisos cannot be dismissed as boilerplate, synonymous with "an assertion of interest on the part of the public." The debates surrounding the drafting of these provisos suggest that they served as independent criteria for evaluating assertions of legislative power. The debate over the free exercise provision of the Virginia Bill of Rights of 1776 most clearly demonstrates the understanding of the states that passed these provisos. George Mason, chief architect of the religious liberty clause of the Declaration, proposed "that all men should enjoy the fullest toleration in the exercise of religion, according to the dictates of conscience, unpunished and unrestrained by the magistrate, unless under color of religion any man disturb the peace, the happiness, or safety of society." Madison . . . criticized the breadth of Mason's proposed state interest limitation. Madison proposed instead that free exercise be protected "unless under color of religion the preservation of equal liberty and the existence of the State are manifestly endangered." This is obviously a much narrower state interest exception than Mason's. While "peace" and "safety" refer to the fundamental peacekeeping functions of government, "happiness" is a term as compendious as all of public policy. The "peace, happiness, or safety of society" is therefore a standard that would encompass virtually all legitimate forms of legislation. The "preservation of equal liberty" and "manifest endangerment of the existence of the State," on the other hand, is a standard that only the most critical acts of government can satisfy.

The Virginia legislature ultimately passed a religious liberty guarantee that did not spell out the nature of the state interest that could outweigh a free

---

a. The New York Constitution empowered the legislature to pass laws pertaining to the "good government, welfare, and prosperity" of the State (N.Y. Const. of 1777, art. XIX); yet it limited the free exercise right only with respect to "licentiousness" and the "peace and safety" of the state, which appears to be a more limited subset of the laws. [EDITORS' NOTE.]

exercise claim. Apparently, the legislature could not decide between the Mason and Madison formulations and compromised through silence. . . . In any event, the dispute between Madison and Mason would not have mattered if the proviso were of no legal significance, and the proviso would have been of no legal significance if the "full and free exercise of religion" did not include the right of exemption from generally applicable laws that conflict with religious conscience.

The wording of the state constitutions also provides some guidance regarding when the government's interest is sufficiently strong to override an admitted free exercise claim. The modern Supreme Court has stated only that the government's interest must be "compelling," "of the highest order," "overriding," or "unusually important." These formulations are unnecessarily open-ended, leading to grudging and inconsistent results. The historical sources suggest that the government's interest can be more precisely delimited in a few specific areas, although other cases will remain difficult to resolve.

The most common feature of the state provisions was the government's right to protect public peace and safety. As Madison expressed it late in life, the free exercise right should prevail "in every case where it does not trespass on private rights or the public peace." This indicates that a believer has no license to invade the private rights of others or to disturb public peace and order, no matter how conscientious the belief or how trivial the private right on the other side. There is no free exercise right to kidnap another person for the purpose of proselytizing, or to trespass on private property—whether it be an abortion clinic or a defense contracting plant—to protest immoral activity. Conduct on public property must be peaceable and orderly, so that the rights of others are not disturbed.

Where the rights of others are not involved, however, the free exercise right prevails. The state constitutional provisions give no warrant to paternalistic legislation touching on religious concerns. They protect the "public" peace and safety but respect the right of the believer to weigh spiritual costs without governmental interference. Thus, some modern free exercise controversies, such as the refusal by Jehovah's Witnesses to receive blood transfusions or the enforcement of minimum wage laws in a religious community, should be easy to resolve and require no subjective judicial judgments about the importance of public policy. Moreover, the early free exercise clauses seem to allow churches and other religious institutions to define their own doctrine, membership, organization, and internal requirements without state interference. As Jefferson wrote to the Reverend Samuel Miller, "the government of the United States [is] interdicted by the Constitution from intermeddling with religious institutions, their doctrines, discipline, or exercises." That their internal practices may seem unjust or repugnant to the majority should be of no moment. Only a handful of states allowed laws against "licentiousness" or immorality to override free exercise claims, and those provisions may well have referred to public displays of immoral behavior. . . .

E. ACTUAL FREE EXERCISE CONTROVERSIES

An examination of actual free exercise controversies in the preconstitutional period bears out these conclusions. To be sure, the issue of exemptions did not often arise. The American colonies were peopled almost entirely by adherents of various strains of Protestant Christianity. The Protestant moral code and mode of worship was, for the most part, harmonious with the mores of the larger society. Even denominations like the Quakers, whose theology and religious practice differed sharply from the others, entertained similar beliefs about public decorum. Moreover, the governments of that era were far less intrusive than the governments of today. Thus, the occasions when religious conscience came into conflict with generally applicable secular legislation were few.

Nonetheless, the issue of exemptions did arise, primarily centered around three issues: oath requirements, military conscription, and religious assessments. The resolution of these conflicts suggests that exemptions were seen as a natural and legitimate response to the tension between law and religious convictions.

1. *Oaths.*—By far the most common source of friction was the issue of oaths. The oath requirement was the principal means of ensuring honest testimony and of solemnizing obligations. At a time when perjury prosecutions were unusual, extratemporal sanctions for telling falsehoods or reneging on commitments were thought indispensable to civil society. Quakers and certain other Protestant sects, however, conscientiously refused to take oaths, producing more serious consequences than it might at first seem. A regime requiring oaths prior to court testimony effectively precluded these groups from using the court system to protect themselves and left them vulnerable to their adversaries, "who could sue them for property and never doubt the result." There are three possible responses. First, the government could eliminate the oath-taking requirement for everyone, making oath-taking purely voluntary. Second, the government could continue to insist on the oath requirement, making it impossible for dissenters to give evidence in court or participate in any civic activity involving an oath. Third, the government could continue the oath requirement for the majority, allowing those with religious scruples to comply by an alternative procedure. According to the no-exemption view, only the first two possibilities are available. But the first possibility is disruptive of the entire judicial system and the second is unnecessarily harsh to the dissenters.

The third alternative—to create a religious exception to the oath requirement—was in fact adopted in most of the colonies. As early as the seventeenth century the proprietors of the Carolina colony permitted Quakers to enter pledges in a book in lieu of swearing an oath. Similarly, New York passed a law in 1691 permitting Quakers to testify by affirmation in civil cases, and in 1734 passed a law permitting Quakers to qualify for the vote by affirmation instead of oath. Jews in Georgia received dispensation to omit the words "on the faith of a Christian" from the naturalization oath required in 1740. In 1743, Massachusetts, one of the states with a strong established church tradition, substituted an affirmation requirement for " 'Quakers [who] profess to be in their consciences scrupulous of taking oaths.' " By 1789, virtually all of the states had enacted oath exemptions.

2. *Military Conscription.*—The exemption issue also arose in connection with military conscription. Exemption from conscription provides a particularly telling example due to the entirely secular nature of conscription, its importance to preservation of the state in times of war, and the high costs the granting of exemptions imposes on others. Several denominations in colonial America, most prominently the Quakers and Mennonites, refused on religious grounds to bear arms. As early as 1670-80, Quakers in several states asserted that liberty of conscience

exempted them from bearing arms. Rhode Island, North Carolina, and Maryland granted the exemptions; New York refused. It is presumably not coincidental that Rhode Island, North Carolina, and Maryland had explicit free exercise or liberty of conscience clauses in the seventeenth century, while New York did not.

In Georgia, the Moravians claimed a right to be exempt from military service during the troubles with Spanish Florida, and when they were denied, the entire Moravian community departed Georgia between 1737 and 1740 and moved to Pennsylvania. Pennsylvania, where Quakers were most numerous and influential, went without a militia until 1755, when one was organized on a voluntary basis. The issue arose in New York again in 1734, and again the Quakers were denied exemption from penalties imposed for refusal to train for military service. The colony finally relented in 1755, provided the objector would pay a commutation fee or send a substitute. Massachusetts and Virginia soon adopted similar policies. New Hampshire exempted Quakers from conscription in 1759. Later, the Continental Congress was to grant exemptions in these words:

> As there are some people, who, from religious principles, cannot bear arms in any case, this Congress intend no violence to their consciences, but earnestly recommend it to them, to contribute liberally in this time of universal calamity, to the relief of their distressed brethren in the several colonies, and to do all other services to their oppressed Country, which they can consistently with their religious principles.

The language as well as the substance of this policy is particularly significant, since it recognizes the superior claim of religious "conscience" over civil obligation, even at a time of "universal calamity," and leaves the appropriate accommodation to the judgment of the religious objectors.

3. *Religious Assessments.*—A third example of a religious exception recognized under the preconstitutional free exercise provisions is found only in states with established churches. Such states often required the citizens to make payments for the support of ministers either of the established church or of their own denomination. Not uncommonly, however, these states accommodated the objection of members of sects conscientiously opposed to compelled tithes. For example, from 1727 on, Massachusetts and Connecticut exempted Baptists and Quakers from ministerial taxes. This exception was expressly, if grudgingly, made in recognition of the "alleged scruple of conscience" of these sects. . . .

It might be objected that the example of exemptions from religious assessments is inapt, because the generally applicable law is itself religious, not secular, and would be unconstitutional under the establishment clause today. . . . The decisive question, however, is whether the people at the time of adoption of the first amendment would likely have considered exemptions, whether legislative or judicial, an appropriate remedy when law and conscience conflict. Those states with established churches had free exercise provisions which were almost identical to the provisions in states without establishment; and the establishment states understood the principle of free exercise to entail exemption from religious assessments, solely for the benefit of those with religious scruples. . . .

4. *Other Religious Exemptions.*—Other colonies and states responded to particular conflicts between religious convictions and generally applicable laws by exempting those faced with the conflict. The Trustees of Georgia, for example, allowed certain groups of Protestant refugees from the European Continent

virtual rights of self-government, a form of wholesale exemption that enabled these dissenters from the Church of England to organize themselves in accordance with their own faith. A group from Salzburg formed the town of Ebenezer, described by one historian as "a state within a state, a sort of theocracy under the direction of their ministers with daily conferences of the entire congregation in which God's guidance was invoked at the beginning and end."

In 1764, the colonial legislature of Rhode Island passed a statute waiving the laws governing marriage ceremonies for "any persons possessing [professing] the Jewish religion who may be joined in marriage, according to their own usages and rites." In 1798, the state legislature exempted Jewish residents from the operation of state incest law, "within the degrees of affinity or consanguinity allowed by their religion." This was important because Jewish law was understood to encourage the marriage between uncle and niece, a relationship illegal under Rhode Island law.

Similarly, both North Carolina and Maryland exempted Quakers from the requirement of removing their hats in court, which they considered a form of obeisance to secular authority forbidden by their religion. This exemption may seem trivial today, but it was an issue of historical and emotional importance to the Quakers of that day. One of the most notorious courtroom cases of religious intolerance in England involved William Penn's refusal to remove his hat when he appeared in court to face an indictment for speaking to an unlawful assembly. . . . Although acquitted on the charge on which he was tried, Penn was held in contempt and imprisoned for refusing to doff his hat. This case became a cause celebre in America, and the North Carolina and Maryland exemptions were no doubt passed as a result.

The history of oath requirements, military conscription, religious assessments, and other sources of conflict between religious convictions and general legislation demonstrates that religion-specific exemptions were familiar and accepted means of accommodating these conflicts. Rather than make oaths, military service, and tithes voluntary for everyone, which would undercut important public programs and objectives, and rather than coerce the consciences of otherwise loyal and law-abiding citizens who were bound by religious duty not to comply, the colonies and states wrote special exemptions into their laws. Lest the exemptions be extended too broadly, they confined the exemptions to denominations or categories known or proven to be "conscientiously" opposed. This aspect of the historical practice parallels in its purposes the requirement of "sincerity" under current law, although the tendency to recognize only those beliefs that are a formal part of the religious dogma of the claimant's denomination has been superseded by a more individualistic view of religious conscience.

A CONSTITUTIONAL RIGHT OF RELIGIOUS EXEMPTION: AN HISTORICAL PERSPECTIVE

Philip A. Hamburger
60 Geo. Wash. L. Rev. 915 (1992)

Did late eighteenth-century Americans understand the Free Exercise Clause of the United States Constitution to provide individuals a right of exemption from civil laws to which they had religious objections? Claims of exemption based on the Free Exercise Clause have prompted some of the Supreme Court's most prominent free exercise decisions, and therefore this historical inquiry about a right of exemption may have implications for our constitutional jurisprudence. . . .

In fact, late eighteenth-century Americans tended to assume that the Free Exercise Clause did not provide a constitutional right of religious exemption from civil laws. The first part of this Article examines and calls into question [Professor] McConnell's arguments that the Free Exercise Clause may have created such a right. The second part of this Article then considers more generally the history of a right of religious exemption and shows the extent to which Americans did not seek and even rejected such a right. Among other things, the second part also suggests how Americans reconciled their distaste for a right of exemption with their support for religious freedom. Of course, many Americans sympathized with their neighbors who had pious scruples about oaths, military service, and a few other legal requirements, and, therefore, in various statutes and even state constitutions, Americans expressly granted religious exemptions from some specified civil obligations. Americans did not, however, authorize or acknowledge a general constitutional right of religious exemption from civil laws.

I. MCCONNELL'S EVIDENCE

Eighteenth-century Americans spoke and wrote extensively about religious freedom and about government. Yet Professor McConnell apparently cites no instance in which a late eighteenth-century American explicitly and unambiguously said that an individual's right to the free exercise of religion included a general right of peaceable, religious exemption from civil laws—that is, from the otherwise secular laws of secular government. . . .

A. STATE CONSTITUTIONS

McConnell finds support for his position in the religion clauses of certain state constitutions . . . that acknowledged an individual's right to the free exercise of religion or to freedom of worship but that added a caveat, such as, "provided he doth not disturb the public peace." According to McConnell, these caveats indicate that the right of free exercise was understood to include a right of exemption from religiously objectionable civil laws, except with regard to nonpeaceable behavior. . . .

[However, t]he behavior described by the caveats included more than just nonpeaceful behavior. A caveat that required persons to avoid disturbing the "good order," "safety," or "happiness" of society or of the state appears to have demanded a greater degree of obedience than just peaceful behavior. Indeed, in Maryland, the caveat expressly mentioned persons who "shall infringe the laws of morality, or injure others in their natural, civil or religious rights," and, in New York and South Carolina, the caveats dealt with, among other things, "acts of licentiousness." Even those caveats that mentioned only disturbances of the peace did not exclusively concern acts of violence or force. According to long tradition, the criminal offenses over which common law courts had jurisdiction were said to be "contra pacem." Consequently, the phrase "contra pacem" became associated with the notion of violation of law. Whereas McConnell assumes that a disturbance of the peace was simply nonpeaceful behavior, eighteenth-century lawyers made clear that "every breach of law is against the peace."[15] Thus, the disturb-the-peace caveats apparently permitted government to deny religious freedom, not merely in the event of violence or force, but, more generally, upon the occurrence of illegal actions.

The caveats, moreover, described the availability rather than the extent of the guaranteed religious freedom; instead of implying that the right of free exercise was very extensive—that it permitted peaceable departure from civil law—the caveats stated the conditions upon which religious liberty could be denied. This point can be illustrated with particular clarity by the Revolutionary constitutions of New Jersey, Delaware, and South Carolina. In these constitutions, the caveats about peaceable behavior clearly related to guarantees of equality or nondiscrimination rather than to the free exercise or freedom of worship clauses. In New Jersey, article XVIII of the constitution concerned freedom of worship, and article XIX stated that:

> no Protestant inhabitant of this Colony shall be denied the enjoyment of any civil right, merely on account of his religious principles; but that all persons, professing a belief in the faith of any Protestant sect, who shall demean themselves peaceably under the government, as hereby established, . . . shall fully and freely enjoy every privilege and immunity, enjoyed by others their fellow subjects.

In Delaware, section 2 of the Declaration of Rights spoke of freedom of worship, and section 3 provided that Christians "ought . . . to enjoy equal Rights and Privileges in this State, unless, under Colour of Religion, any Man disturb the Peace, Happiness or Safety of Society." The South Carolina Constitution declared:

> That all persons and religious societies who acknowledge that there is one God, and a future state of rewards and punishments, and that God is publicly to be worshipped, shall be freely tolerated. The Christian Protestant religion shall be deemed, and is hereby constituted and declared to be, the established religion of this State. That all denominations of Christian Protestants in this State, demeaning themselves peaceably and faithfully, shall enjoy equal religious and civil privileges.

Thus, in New Jersey, Delaware, and South Carolina, the caveats related to language concerning equality and nondiscrimination, not to the language about free exercise, freedom of worship, or toleration. The caveats stated the

---

15. Incidentally, this definition of a breach of the peace was recognized by Baptists who pleaded for an expanded religious freedom. Dissenting ministers who opposed most legislation with respect to religion and who insisted that individuals not be treated differently on account of their religions frequently were accused of opposing the regulation of morality. In responding to such charges, dissenters pointed out that the state could punish immoralities—peaceful and nonpeaceful—as breaches of the peace. For example, after setting forth his strong stand on religious freedom, a Baptist, Caleb Blood, explained:

> This however, by no means prohibits the civil magistrate from enacting those laws that shall enforce the observance of those precepts in the christian religion, the violation of which is a breach of the civil peace; viz. such as forbid murder, theft, adultery, false witness, and injuring our neighbor, either in person, name, or estate. . . .

conditions under which government could deny the religious freedom otherwise guaranteed.

Although not as clear as the New Jersey, Delaware, and South Carolina constitutions, other state constitutions with disturb-the-peace caveats are susceptible of similar interpretation. . . . For example, Georgia's constitution said that "[a]ll persons whatever shall have the free exercise of their religion; provided it be not repugnant to the peace and safety of the State." The second clause could have been a condition of the availability of a relatively narrow right of free exercise rather than a limitation on an otherwise very extensive right. In short, the theory that the disturb-the-peace caveats evince a right of religious exemption fails to explain the Delaware, New Jersey, and South Carolina constitutions; in contrast, the theory that the caveats permitted government to deny an otherwise guaranteed religious freedom explains the words of all early state constitutions. . . .

This interpretation—thus far based largely on the words of the caveats—can be verified by the context in which the caveats were written. Like Englishmen before them, Americans disagreed about the circumstances in which government should be able to deny the religious liberty otherwise guaranteed. It will be seen that Americans took at least three broadly different positions on the availability of religious freedom and that their variously formulated religion clauses more or less reflected those three positions.

The first approach made use of the ideas of John Locke. Some Americans, drawing upon Locke, argued that government should be able to discourage dangerous beliefs—that it should be able to deny religious liberty not only to persons whose religious opinions prompted actual violations of law but also to persons whose opinions merely tended to have this effect. In the words of a Vermont minister,

> every one has an undoubted right to choose that religion and mode of worship which to him appears most agreeable to the word of God, unless it be such as evidently tends to destroy civil peace and government; in that case no one ought to be tolerated—self-preservation forbids it.

In accord with this approach, Georgia's constitution permitted Georgia to deny religious freedom to persons whose religion was "repugnant" to the peace and safety of the state. Such was the position Jefferson denounced in the preamble to his Act for Establishing Religious Freedom:

> [T]o suffer the civil magistrate to intrude his powers into the field of opinion, and to restrain the profession or propagation of principles on supposition of their ill tendency, is a dangerous fallacy. . . . [I]t is time enough for the rightful purposes of civil government, for its officers to interfere when principles break out into overt acts against peace and good order.

As Jefferson understood, some Americans still assumed that government had a right to restrain religious opinions it considered potentially dangerous.

Many Americans repudiated the idea that a religious opinion could be restrained merely on account of its bad tendency and adopted, instead, a second approach: that government should be able to deny religious liberty only to individuals who disturbed the peace—who actually violated civil law. Taking a version of this approach, the Northwest Ordinance declared that "[n]o person demeaning himself in a peaceable and orderly manner shall ever be molested on account of his mode of worship or religious sentiments in the said territory." Yet even this ameliorated type of caveat still specified circumstances in which government could deny a person the religious freedom he otherwise was guaranteed. . . . If a person was not a good and peaceable citizen, he could be penalized on account of his religion.

In contrast was a third position—taken by those constitutions that did not qualify their guarantees of religious liberty. Some of the constitutions that took this third approach not only omitted caveats from their religion clauses but also included provisions condemning the punishment of individuals "on account" of their religious beliefs. Similar to these constitutions was Jefferson's Act for Establishing Religious Freedom. As seen above, the preamble to the Act condemned at least the first approach; in addition, the body of the Act stated that no man shall "suffer on account of his religious opinions or belief." Thus, the Americans who abandoned the caveats apparently recognized that the caveats were designed to allow the punishment of individuals on account of their religion. Whereas McConnell asserts that the caveats reveal an expansive notion of free exercise—including a right of exemption—in fact, the caveats permitted discriminatory restrictions on the availability of religious freedom and, for this reason, were condemned as intolerant. . . .

C. EXEMPTIONS FROM PARTICULAR CIVIL OBLIGATIONS

Both before and after the adoption of constitutions guaranteeing the free exercise of religion, legislative and constitutional documents (including charters) granted exemptions from particular obligations, such as oaths, conscription, and assessments. McConnell suggests that when legislatures and other bodies created these exemptions they were attempting to reflect a free exercise right of exemption. Yet legislators equally may have been showing their sympathy for Quakers and others whose piety prevented their conformity to law. As McConnell concedes, the issue whether an individual was understood to have a general constitutional right of religious exemption from civil laws is hardly the same issue as whether statutes or, occasionally, constitutions granted exemptions with respect to a few specific matters. . . .

II. A CONSTITUTIONAL RIGHT OF RELIGIOUS EXEMPTION IN THE
    EIGHTEENTH CENTURY?

A review of McConnell's evidence has suggested reasons to doubt whether Americans thought the First Amendment provided a constitutional right of religious exemption from civil laws. It remains necessary, however, to examine more generally Americans' attitudes toward such a right. Although Americans frequently said religious freedom was based on an authority higher than the civil government and that the exercise of religion could not be submitted to civil authority, does this mean that they sought a religious or constitutional right of exemption from civil laws? . . . [The evidence] suggest[s], first, that the free exercise of religion tended not to be considered a particularly extensive or radical claim of religious liberty—indeed, it was a freedom espoused not only by dissenters but also by establishments. Second, when advocating religious freedom—even a religious freedom broader than mere free exercise—dissenters who were politically active and influential in lobbying for expanded religious liberty did not seek a constitutional right of exemption from objectionable civil laws. Third, a right of exemption may have been considered a "law respecting religion" and may have been understood to create "unequal civil rights"—precisely what many dissenters considered attributes of establishment and sought to abolish. . . .

B. EXEMPTION

Whether claiming free exercise or a broader religious liberty, dissenters—particularly politically active and influential dissenters—tended not to ask for a right of exemption from religiously objectionable civil laws. Just as establishment writers could acknowledge that religion was based on an authority higher than the civil government, so too dissenters typically could admit that natural liberty was protected only through submission to civil government and its laws. According to vast numbers of Americans, individuals in the state of nature had a liberty that was free from civil restraints but was insecure; therefore, said these Americans, individuals sought protection for their natural liberty by establishing civil government. Liberty could only be obtained by submission to the civil laws of civil government.

One reason late eighteenth-century ideas about religious freedom did not seem to require a general religious exemption is that the jurisdiction of civil government and the authority of religion were frequently considered distinguishable. It should not be assumed that late eighteenth-century Americans viewed religion as being necessarily in tension with civil authority. In fact, many Americans, especially dissenters seeking an expansion of religious liberty, repeatedly spoke of civil authority as if it could be differentiated from the scope of religion or religious freedom. This assumption is apparent in the language of the First Amendment, which begins, "Congress shall make no law." Rather than suppose that civil laws will in some respects prohibit the free exercise of religion and that exemptions will be necessary, the First Amendment assumes Congress can avoid enacting laws that prohibit free exercise. So too, it assumes Congress can avoid making laws respecting the establishment of religion.

In explaining the difference between religious and civil matters, Americans of the last half of the eighteenth century employed several different formulations. Locke had argued that individuals entrusted civil government with the security of "temporal goods" and "the things of this life" but that "the care of each man's soul, and the things of heaven . . . is left entirely to every man's self." Similarly, many Americans differentiated between the temporal and the spiritual, between "this world" and "the Kingdom of Christ." Americans also sometimes listed the things that civil authority could not establish or determine. Typically, they mentioned religious belief and doctrine—what Locke had called "speculative opinions." Occasionally, they also specified the internal governance of a sect and its mode or form of worship. . . .

The assumption that religious liberty would not, or at least should not, affect civil authority over civil matters was so widely held that a general right of religious exemption rarely became the basis for serious controversy. Of course, some dissenters did broadly claim religious exemption from objectionable civil laws, on grounds of freedom of conscience or even divine command.

Their claims, however, illustrate the marginal character of the support for a general right of religious exemption. For example, John Bolles—a Rogerene [member of a small New England Baptist sect]—apparently claimed some religious exemption from civil laws. In defense of two Quaker women who "went naked . . . one into a Meeting, the other . . . through the Streets of Salem," Bolles wrote that "they did it in Submission to a divine Power . . . as a Sign." For precedent, he cited the Bible, saying simply: "Isaiah went Naked." This was not, however, the sort of analysis that most late eighteenth-century Americans found persuasive with respect to constitutional law.

Although other dissenters, less extreme than Bolles, did seek exemption from civil laws, they typically asked, not for a general right of exemption, but merely for exemptions from a small number of specified civil obligations. Of these limited exemptions, moreover, only those relating to military service frequently were granted in constitutions. Even constitutional military exemptions, however, often appear to have been given largely for reasons of compassion and politics.

Indeed, the idea that individuals had a general right to be exempted from civil laws contrary to their consciences was so unpopular that establishment writers attempted to use it to smear their opponents. By citing lurid stories about the sixteenth-century Anabaptists of Munster and by attributing the enthusiasms of extremists to dissenters as a whole, establishment writers could accuse dissenters of attempting to subvert all civil liberty. For example, in support of Connecticut's religious establishment, Elihu Hall said that persons objecting to that establishment on grounds of conscience were making arguments that would justify nonpayment of civil taxes or breach of contract: "Thus a man may plead Conscience for the support or excuse of all the moral Dishonesty and Promise & Covenant-breaking in the World. But men have no Right to be their own Judges in their own Case in moral Matters, and where their neighbors Interest is equally concerned with their own."

To defend themselves from such accusations, dissenters who sought an expanded religious liberty disavowed a right of exemption from civil laws. Writing against the Connecticut establishment, Ebenezer Frothingham argued that no "hurt" would be done to "any man's civil interest, by different sects worshipping God in different places in the same town." Eight different sects might live together in one community, but none, he observed, would be exempt: "If any person of . . . these professions breaks the law, he lies open to punishment, equally so, as if there was but one profession in the town." Frothingham was not alone. Other influential dissenters also rejected a right of exemption.[111]

---

111. [John] Leland, [leader of Virginia's Baptists,] explicitly opposed exemptions from civil laws. Although Baptists had religious objections to contracts between a minister and his flock, Leland nonetheless argued that such contracts, if made, were enforceable. Moreover, "To indulge [ministers] with an exemption from taxes and bearing arms is a tempting emolument. The law should be silent about them; protect them as citizens, not as sacred officers, for the civil law knows no sacred religious officers." For Leland, conscience provided no legal objection to law that was silent about religion. . . .

In 1780, [Massachusetts Baptist leader Isaac] Backus noted that his opponents "have raked up the German Anabaptists whom they represent as 'pleading conscience for lying with each other's wives, and for murdering their peaceable neighbors.'" He went on to say: "And all this without producing so much as a single word from all our writings to prove their charges against us." After complaining about the new Massachusetts establishment, Backus said: "I challenge all our opponents to prove, if they can, that we have ever desired any other religious liberty, than to have this partiality entirely removed." Backus wrote "the state is armed with the sword to guard the peace and the civil rights of all persons and societies and to punish those who violate the same." . . .

... Although some dissenters asked for grants of exemption from a few specified civil obligations, such as military service, dissenters typically did not demand a general exemption from objectionable civil laws, let alone a constitutional right to such an exemption. If the myriad and voluble dissenters who sought an expansion of religious freedom were advocating a general constitutional right of religious exemption from civil laws, it is remarkable that they tended not to claim such a right and that some of their leading publicists disavowed it.

C. ESTABLISHMENT

In the late eighteenth century, the overwhelming majority of dissenters sought, not a constitutional right of exemption, but an end to establishments. ... In the last half of the eighteenth century, many Americans had unequal civil rights on account of their religious opinions; others had equal civil rights but thought this equality precarious. Therefore, many of these Americans wanted guarantees of equal civil rights. Of course, some wanted equality only for Protestants or Christians. Yet a form of equal civil rights was, increasingly, the minimum dissenters believed was theirs by right and what they believed they could get. Indeed, some—anxious that religion not be dependent upon civil government—demanded that government avoid legislating with respect to religion. If civil government was established for exclusively civil purposes, they argued, then it had no authority to make any law concerning religion. These anti-establishment claims—and, to a lesser degree, the grants of exemption from a few, specified obligations—were the goals pursued by large numbers of dissenters. For these Americans, the possibility of a general right of exemption was, at most, a distraction from the real issues at stake.

What dissenters said about establishments, moreover, had implications for exemption. Of course, the anti-establishment demands for equal civil rights and for the absence of laws respecting religion were made in response to legislative or constitutional provisions that benefitted particular denominations or, more broadly, a particular religion rather than in response to claims of exemption for the religiously scrupulous. Nonetheless, the dissenters' positions on establishment were suggestive of their position on exemption. A right of exemption for the religiously scrupulous could be considered a law respecting religion. It even could create unequal civil rights; in the words of the Virginia Act for Establishing Religious Freedom, men's "opinions in matters of religion" shall "in no wise diminish, enlarge, or affect their civil capacities." The sweeping language with which so many Americans attacked establishments was not the language of persons seeking a constitutional right of exemption.

[Hamburger also cites official statements of several denominations:] In its confession of faith, the Presbyterian Church in the United States declared: "Infidelity or difference in religion, doth not make void the magistrate's just and legal authority, nor free the people from their due obedience to him." The Rules of Church Government of the Dutch Reformed Church began its section "of Christian Discipline" by warning that "christian discipline is spiritual, and exempts no person from the judgement and punishment of the civil power." When the Methodist Episcopal Church met in Baltimore in 1784 it required members of that sect to liberate their slaves, but added: "These rules are to affect the members of our Society no further than as they are consistent with the laws of the States in which they reside." ...

NOTES AND QUESTIONS

1. The Meaning of the "Peace and Safety" Limitations.   Do you understand why Professors McConnell and Hamburger focus so extensively on the "peace and safety" provisos or caveats of the early state constitutions? McConnell argues that they are evidence that "free exercise" was understood to entail at least some exemptions from civil laws, because otherwise the provisos would be meaningless. Hamburger disagrees with McConnell on two grounds. First, he argues that the caveats are not limitations on the free exercise right otherwise granted, but authorize the state to restrict or abrogate the free exercise right of any group or sect that violates the provisos: "[The caveats] described the availability rather than the extent of the guaranteed religious freedom; instead of implying that the right of free exercise was very extensive—that it permitted peaceable departure from civil law—the caveats stated the conditions upon which religious liberty could be denied." Second, he argues that terms such as the "peace and safety" of society did not refer to a particular subset of the laws, but rather to the entire body of the law. If he is correct on these two points, then what was the extent of religious freedom in these states?

2. Did Religious Freedom Advocates Disavow Exemptions? Professor Hamburger quotes extensively from advocates of religious freedom who seemingly disavow any broad claim of religious exemptions. See also Marci A. Hamilton, Religion, the Rule of Law, and the Good of the Whole: A View from the Clergy, 18 J. L. & Pol. 387 (2002) (offering a similar interpretation of founding-era religious views). In a later article, Professor McConnell provides a different interpretation of this evidence:

The question naturally arose, however: What if, under claim of conscience, a religious adherent asserts a right to do some terrible thing? The question is found, in some form, in virtually every tract against liberty of conscience, and most of the writings advocating religious toleration offer some variant of the same answer. Pierre Bayle, for example, noted that critics claim that if freedom of religion were adopted, "magistrates would not be able to punish a man who robs or kills, after being persuaded of the lawfulness [meaning lawfulness according to religious law] of these actions." The answer, he said, is that the magistrate "is not obliged to have any regard for conscience except in matters which do not affect the public peace." The magistrate "is obliged to maintain society and punish all those who destroy the foundations, as murderers and robbers do." William Penn described one of the objections to liberty of conscience as follows: "at this Rate ye may pretend to Cut our Throats, and do all Manner of Savage Acts." Penn's response was to deny that believers sought exemptions from any laws "that tend to Sober, Just, and Industrious Living." John Leland, the leader of the Virginia Baptists during the assessment controversy, and constituent of Madison's, stated that should a man "disturb the peace and good order of the civil police, he should be punished according to his crime, let his religion be what it will; but when a man is a peaceable subject of state, he should be protected in worshipping the Deity according to the dictates of his own conscience."

The example of Roger Williams is also significant. He went to some lengths to deny that freedom of conscience would lead to anarchy, and his comments sometimes have been interpreted to mean that believers are compelled to comply with all generally applicable laws. A leading modern scholar of Roger Williams disagrees with this interpretation:

Williams did not simply define an inviolate area of conscience and then leave the government free to act in any manner outside this narrowly prescribed area. Rather, for him, both conscience and government had limits. The civil government was limited to its responsibility for preserving peace and civility. The conscience was limited by its obligation to submit itself to the government as God's ordinance for preserving peace and civility. Thus, neither Williams' letter to Providence concerning taxes nor his famous Ship of State letter may be read as subjecting the claims of conscience to any generally applicable law so long as it does not deliberately infringe upon religious belief or act. Rather, in both cases Williams saw conscience subjected to particular laws, and he viewed these laws as within the specific scope of the government's ordained responsibilities.[46]

Two points about these exchanges are significant. First, the argument would not arise if the freedom of religion were generally understood as not embracing exemptions from generally applicable laws; the law already forbade "robbing," "killing," and "savage acts." Thus, the very existence—indeed ubiquity—of the controversy shows that the freedom-protective interpretation was a real possibility in the eighteenth century, and not (as some suggest) a modern Warren Court–style innovation. Second, the typical response was to concede that conscience had to give way to laws necessary for the public peace. Precisely what sorts of laws may fall within this category was often left vague, but it is this issue—what public purposes are sufficiently important that they justify limiting the rights of conscience—that framed the debate.

Michael W. McConnell, Freedom from Persecution or Protection of the Rights of Conscience?: A Critique of Justice Scalia's Historical Arguments in *City of Boerne v. Flores*, 39 Wm. & Mary L. Rev. 819 (1998).

As you now begin reading cases involving particular free exercise disputes, consider how they would be resolved under Professor McConnell's view of the historical evidence and by contrast under Professor Hamburger's. You can start by applying the historical evidence to a very early case, decided less than a generation after the enactment of the First Amendment.

2. The First Free Exercise Cases

The following case, People v. Philips, is the first whose written opinion has come down to us, decided on the basis of the free exercise provision of a state constitution. The judge was DeWitt Clinton, one of the most prominent legal-political figures of the time: mayor of New York, sometime senator and presidential candidate.

PEOPLE v. PHILIPS
New York Court of General Sessions (June 14, 1813)*

[In 1813, one James Cating, a resident of New York City, was the victim of theft. Shortly after, he received his property back from his pastor, the Rev. Mr. Anthony Kohlmann, Rector of St. Peter's, then the only Roman catholic church in the city. Upon questioning, Rev. Kohlmann refused to divulge the

---

46. Timothy L. Hall, Roger Williams and the Foundations of Religious Liberty, 71 B.U. L. Rev. 455, 486 (1991).
* This decision was privately reported and was reprinted in 1 Western L.J. (1843) and in W. Sampson, ed., The Catholic Question in America (1813, reprint 1974). See also Privileged Communications to Clergymen, The Catholic Lawyer 199 (July 1955).

identity of the person or persons from whom he had received the goods, explaining that the information came to him in the course of a penitent's confession. On the basis of other information, Daniel Philips and his wife were indicted for receipt of the stolen goods, and the priest was summoned to give evidence in court.]

... Mr. Kohlmann was then called and sworn, and examined by Mr. Gardinier. He begged leave of the Court to state his reasons for declining to answer, which he did in the following terms:

... [I]f called upon to testify in quality of a minister of a sacrament, in which my God himself has enjoined on me a perpetual and inviolable secrecy, I must declare to this honorable Court, that I cannot, I must not answer any question that has a bearing upon the restitution in question; and that it would be my duty to prefer instantaneous death or any temporal misfortune, rather than disclose the name of the penitent in question. For, were I to act otherwise, I should become a traitor to my church, to my sacred ministry and to my God. In fine, I should render myself guilty of eternal damnation. ...

Mr. Gardinier, the District Attorney:

... The true principle, it is apprehended, in our happy state of religious equality is this: every man shall be allowed to reconcile himself to his maker in the way he may think most effectual; and seeing that none can pretend to greater certainty than his neighbour, so, to no one of the various sects shall be given the privilege of dictating to others their course of religious worship. Thus, all stand equal; no one pretending to the right of dictating to the others. But whenever any one shall claim to do what may justly offend the others, he claims an unequal, and so an unconstitutional *"preference."* Thus, the jew may keep his own sabbath, but he shall not violate that of the christian. Under a religious tenet, no sect would be permitted to indulge in what society deems cruelty, dishonesty, or public indecency, for it would offend the rest, though the worshippers might deem themselves engaged in a holy rite. Nor ought any be allowed to conceal, when called upon in courts of justice, matters pertaining to the safety of the rest—for if they are so allowed, they make for themselves a rule of evidence, contrary to a pre-existing principle of law, involving the safety of the whole community. If they say, our religion teaches us this, society replies all religions are equal—none shall be disturbed—each one may seek heaven as seems fit to its votaries, this is the toleration society has *"granted"* to all—but still society is superior to them all, and not, nor ever could be supposed to have granted to any, the right of silence, when its own interest and safety may be jeopardized by that silence. The common safety, is the common right—and any pretension, whether of a religious or social institution, which claims the right to withhold from society the knowledge of matters, relating to its safety, soars above the level of the common equality, and demands such an unreasonable "preference," as society would be false to itself to allow.

Finally the constitution has granted, religious *"profession and worship,"* to all denominations, *"without discrimination or preference"* but it has not granted exemption from previous legal duties. It has expelled the demon of persecution from our land: but it has not weakened the arm of public justice. Its equal and steady impartiality has soothed all the contending sects into the most harmonious equality, but to none of them has it yielded any of the rights of a well organized government.

On Monday, the 14th of June, the Jury were called, and all appeared; the Honorable DE WITT CLINTON, *Mayor*, then proceeded to deliver the DECISION OF THE COURT, premising, that the Bench were unanimous in their opinion, but had left him to pronounce the reasons of that opinion, and that responsibility he had taken upon himself.

In order to criminate the defendants, the reverend Anthony Kohlmann, a minister of the Roman catholic church of this city, has been called upon as a witness, to declare what he knows on the subject of this prosecution. To this question he has declined answering, and has stated in the most respectful manner the reasons which govern his conduct. That all his knowledge respecting this investigation, is derived from his functions as a minister of the Roman catholic church, in the administration of penance, one of their seven sacraments; and that he is bound by the canons of his church, and by the obligations of his clerical office, to the most inviolable secrecy—which he cannot infringe, without exposing himself to degradation from office—to the violation of his own conscience, and to the contempt of the catholic world. . . .

The question then is, whether a Roman catholic priest shall be compelled to disclose what he has received in confession—in violation of his conscience, of his clerical engagements, and of the canons of his church, and with a certainty of being stripped of his sacred functions, and cut off from religious communion and social intercourse with the denomination to which he belongs.

This is an important enquiry; It is important to the church upon which it has a particular bearing. It is important to all religious denominations, because it involves a principle which may in its practical operation affect them all; we have therefore, devoted the few moments we could spare, to an exposition of the reasons that have governed our unanimous opinion: But before we enter upon this investigation, we think it but an act of justice to all concerned in it, to state, that it has been managed with fairness, candour, and a liberal spirit, and that the counsel on both sides have displayed great learning and ability; and it is due particularly to the public prosecutors, to say, that neither in the initiation nor conducting of this prosecution, has there been manifested the least disposition to trespass upon the rights of conscience—and it is equally due to the reverend Mr. Kohlmann to mention, that the articles stolen, were delivered by him to police, for the benefit of the owners, in consequence of the efficacy of his admonitions to the offenders, when they would otherwise, in all probability, have been retained, and that his conduct has been marked by a laudable regard for the laws of the country, and the duties of his holy office.

It is a general rule, that every man when legally called upon to testify as a witness, must relate all he knows. This is essential to the administration of civil and criminal justice.

But to this rule there are several exceptions—a husband and wife cannot testify against each other, except for personal aggressions—nor can an attorney or counsellor, be forced to reveal the communications of his client—nor is a man obliged to answer any question, the answering of which may oblige him to accuse himself of a crime, or subject him to penalties of punishment. . . .

There can be no doubt but that the witness does consider, that his answering on this occasion, would be such a high handed offence against religion, that it would expose him to punishment in a future state—and it must be conceded by all, that it would subject him to privations and disgrace in this world. It is true, that he would not be obnoxious to criminal punishment, but the reason why he is excused where he would be liable to such punishment, applies with greater force to this case, where his sufferings would be aggravated by the compunctious visitings of a wounded conscience, and the gloomy perspective of a dreadful *hereafter*; although he would not lose an estate, or compromit a civil right, yet he would be deprived of his only means of support and subsistence—and although he would not confess a crime, or acknowledge his infamy, yet he would act an offence against high heaven, and seal his disgrace in the presence of his assembled friends, and to the affliction of a bereaved church and a weeping congregation.

It cannot therefore, for a moment he believed, that the mild and just principles of the common Law would place the witness in such a dreadful predicament; in such a horrible dilemma, between perjury and false swearing: If he tells the truth he violates his ecclesiastical oath—If he prevaricates he violates his judicial oath—Whether he lies, or whether he testifies the truth he is wicked, and it is impossible for him to act without acting against the laws of rectitude and the light of conscience.

The only course is, for the court to declare that he shall not testify or act at all. And a court prescribing a different course must be governed by feelings and views very different from those which enter into the composition of a just and enlightened tribunal, that looks with a propitious eye upon the religious feelings of mankind, and which dispenses with an equal hand the universal and immutable elements of justice. . . .

There are no express adjudications in the British courts applied to similar or analogous cases, which contradict the inferences to be drawn from the general principles which have been discussed and established in the course of this investigation: Two only have been pointed out as in any respect analogous, which we shall now proceed to consider. [Discussion of British precedents omitted.]

But this is a great constitutional question, which must not be solely decided by the maxims of the common law, but by the principles of our government: We have considered it in a restricted shape, let us now look at it upon more elevated ground; upon the ground of the constitution, of the social compact, and of civil and religious liberty.

Religion is an affair between God and man, and not between man and man. The laws which regulate it must emanate from the Supreme Being, not from human institutions. Established religions, deriving their authority from man, oppressing other denominations, prescribing creeds of orthodoxy, and punishing non-conformity, are repugnant to the first principles of civil and political liberty, and in direct collision with the divine spirit of christianity. Although no human legislator has a right to meddle with religion, yet the history of the world, is a history of oppression and tyranny over the consciences of men. And the sages who formed our constitution, with this instructive lesson before their eyes, perceived the indispensable necessity of applying a preventitive, that would forever exclude the introduction of calamities, that have deluged the world with tears and with blood, and the following section was accordingly engrafted in our state constitution:

> "And whereas we are required by the benevolent principles of rational liberty, not only to expel civil tyranny, but also to guard against that spiritual oppression

and intolerance, wherewith the bigotry and ambition of weak and wicked princes have scourged mankind, This convention doth further in the name, and by the authority of the good people of this state, ordain, determine, and declare, that the free exercise and enjoyment of religious profession and worship, without discrimination or preference, shall forever hereafter be allowed within this state, to all mankind. Provided, that the liberty of conscience, hereby granted, shall not be so construed as to excuse acts of licentiousness, or justify practices inconsistent with the peace or safety of this state."

Considering that we had just emerged from a colonial state, and were infected with the narrow views and bigotted feelings, which prevailed at that time so strongly against the Roman Catholics, that a priest was liable to the punishment of death if he came into the colony, this declaration of religious freedom, is a wonderful monument of the wisdom, liberality, and philanthropy of its authors. Next to William Penn, the framers of our constitution were the first legislators who had just views of the nature of religious liberty, and who established it upon the broad and imperishable basis of justice, truth, and charity. . . .

A provision conceived in a spirit of the most profound wisdom, and the most exalted charity, ought to receive the most liberal construction. Although by the constitution of the United States, the powers of congress do not extend beyond certain enumerated objects; yet to prevent the danger of constructive assumptions, the following amendment was adopted: "Congress shall make no law respecting an establishment of religion, or prohibiting the free exercise thereof." In this country there is no alliance between church and state; no established religion; no tolerated religion—for toleration results from establishment—but religious freedom guaranteed by the constitution, and consecrated by the social compact.

It is essential to the free exercise of a religion, that its ordinances should be administered—that its ceremonies as well as its essentials should be protected. The sacraments of a religion are its most important elements. We have but two in the Protestant Church—Baptism and the Lord's Supper—and they are considered the seals of the covenant of grace. Suppose that a decision of this court, or a law of the state should prevent the administration of one or both of these sacraments, would not the constitution be violated, and the freedom of religion be infringed? Every man who hears me will answer in the affirmative. Will not the same result follow, if we deprive the Roman catholic of one of his ordinances? Secrecy is of the essence of penance. The sinner will not confess, nor will the priest receive his confession, if the veil of secrecy is removed: To decide that the minister shall promulgate what he receives in confession, is to declare that there shall be no penance; and this important branch of the Roman catholic religion would be thus annihilated.

It has been contended that the provision of the constitution which speaks of practices inconsistent with the peace or safety of the state, excludes this case from the protection of the constitution, and authorizes the interference of this tribunal to coerce the witness. In order to sustain this position, it must be clearly made out that the concealment observed in the sacrament of penance, is a practice inconsistent with the peace or safety of the state.

The Roman catholic religion has existed from an early period of christianity—at one time it embraced almost all Christendom, and it now covers the greater part. The objections which have been made to penance, have been theological, not political. The apprehensions which have been entertained of this religion, have reference to the supremacy, and dispensing power, attributed to the bishop of Rome, as head of the catholic church—but we are yet to learn, that the confession of sins has ever been considered as of pernicious tendency, in any other respect than its being a theological error—or its having been sometimes in the hands of bad men, perverted to the purposes of peculation, an abuse inseparable from all human agencies.

The doctrine contended for, by putting hypothetical cases, in which the concealment of a crime communicated in penance, might have a pernicious effect, is founded on false reasoning, if not on false assumptions: To attempt to establish a general rule, or to lay down a general proposition from accidental circumstances, which occur but rarely, or from extreme cases, which may sometimes happen in the infinite variety of human actions, is totally repugnant to the rules of logic and the maxims of law. The question is not, whether penance may sometimes communicate the existence of an offence to a priest, which he is bound by his religion to conceal, and the concealment of which, may be a public injury, but whether the natural tendency of it is to produce practices inconsistent with the public safety or tranquillity. There is in fact, no secret known to the priest, which would be communicated otherwise, than by confession—and no evil results from this communication—on the contrary, it may be made the instrument of great good. The sinner may be admonished and converted from the evil of his ways: Whereas if his offence was locked up in his own bosom, there would be no friendly voice to recall him from his sins, and no paternal hand to point out to him the road to virtue.

The language of the constitution is emphatic and striking, it speaks of *acts of licentiousness*, of *practices inconsistent* with the *tranquillity* and *safety of the state*, it has reference to something actually, not negatively injurious. To acts committed, not to acts omitted—offences of a deep dye, and of an extensively injurious nature: It would be stretching it on the rack [to] say, that it can possibly contemplate the forbearance of a Roman catholic priest, to testify what he has received in confession, or that it could ever consider the safety of the community involved in this question. To assert this as the genuine meaning of the constitution, would be to mock the understanding, and to render the liberty of conscience a mere illusion. It would be to destroy the enacting clause of the proviso—and to render the exception broader than the rule, to subvert all the principles of sound reasoning, and overthrow all the convictions of common sense.

If a religious sect should rise up and violate the decencies of life, by practicing their religious rites, in a state of nakedness; by following incest, and a community of wives. If the Hindoo should attempt to introduce the burning of widows on the funeral piles of their deceased husbands, or the Mahometan his plurality of wives, or the Pagan his bacchanalian orgies or human sacrifices. If a fanatical sect should spring up, as formerly in the city of Munster, and pull up the pillars of society, or if any attempt should be made to establish the inquisition, then the licentious acts and dangerous practices, contemplated by the constitution, would exist, and the hand of the magistrate would be rightfully raised to chastise the guilty agents.

But until men under pretence of religion, act counter to the fundamental principles of morality, and endanger the well being of the state, they are to be protected in the free exercise of their religion. If they are in error, or if they are wicked, they are to answer to the *Supreme Being*, not to the unhallowed intrusion of frail fallible mortals.

We speak of this question, not in a theological sense, but in its legal and constitutional bearings. Although we differ from the witness and his brethren, in our religious creed, yet we have no reason to question the purity of their motives, or to impeach their good conduct as citizens. They are protected by the laws and constitution of this country, in the full and free exercise of their religion, and this court can never countenance or authorize the application of insult to their faith, or of torture to their consciences.

There being no evidence against the Defendants, they were acquitted.

With this decision, compare:

SIMON'S EXECUTORS v. GRATZ
2 Pen. & W. 412 (Pa. 1831)

[A civil trial affecting the estate of one Simon, deceased, was scheduled for Saturday, May 7, 1831. The executor of the estate, Levi Philips, a Jew, was an essential witness. The plaintiffs moved for a continuance on the ground that Philips "had scruples of conscience against appearing in court to-day, and attending to any secular business." The trial proceeded, and plaintiff's counsel took a nonsuit and appealed to the Pennsylvania Supreme Court. Plaintiffs argued that they were entitled to a continuance under the free exercise provisions of the Pennsylvania Constitution. Counsel distinguished Stansbury v. Marks (p. 3) on the ground that the case had been settled without appellate argument or decision. Counsel relied on People v. Philips and on the "recent" congressional decision regarding the Sunday mails (see p. 70).]

GIBSON, C.J.—The religious scruples of persons concerned with the administration of justice, will receive all the indulgence that is compatible with the business of government; and had circumstances permitted it, this cause would not have been ordered for trial on the Jewish Sabbath. But when a continuance for conscience' sake, is claimed as a right, and at the expense of a term's delay, the matter assumes a different aspect.

It never has been held except in a single instance, that the course of justice may be obstructed by any scruple or obligation whatever. The sacrifice that ensues from an opposition of conscientious objection to the performance of a civil duty, ought, one would think, to be on the part of him whose moral or religious idios[y]ncrasy, makes it necessary; else a denial of the lawfulness of capital punishment would exempt a witness from testifying to facts that might serve to convict a prisoner of murder, or to say nothing of the other functionaries of the law, excuse the sheriff, for refusing to execute one capitally convicted. That is an exemption which none would pretend to claim; yet it would inevitably follow from the principle insisted on here. Indeed a more apposite instance of conflict betwixt religious obligation and social duty, can hardly be imagined. Rightly considered, there are no duties half so sacred as those which the citizen owes to the laws. In the judicial investigation of facts, the secrets of no man will be wantonly exposed, nor will his principles be wantonly violated; but a respect for these must not be suffered to interfere with the operations of that organ of the government which has more immediately to do with the protection of person and property: the safety of the citizen, and the very existence of society require that it should not. That every other obligation shall yield to that of the laws, as to a superior moral force, is a tacit condition of membership in every society, whether lay or secular, temporal or spiritual, because no citizen can lawfully hold communion with those who have associated on any other terms; and this ought, in all cases of collision, to be accounted a sufficient dispensation to the conscience. I therefore entirely dissent from the opinion of the Mayor's Court of New York, in the case which has been cited. No one is more sensible than I, of the benefit derived by society from the offices of the Catholic clergy, or of the policy of protecting the secrets of auricular confession. But considerations of policy address themselves with propriety to the legislature, and not to a magistrate whose course is prescribed not by discretion, but rules already established.

NOTES AND QUESTIONS

1. Exemptions in the Nineteenth Century.   For a full discussion of the background of People v. Philips, see Walter J. Walsh, The First Free Exercise Case, 73 Geo. Wash. L. Rev. 1 (2004).

The courts of five states decided claims for exemptions from generally applicable laws during the years between ratification of the Bill of Rights and the Civil War. In two states, exemptions were required under state constitutions. People v. Philips; Commonwealth v. Cronin, 1 Q.L.J. 128 (Va. Richmond Cir. Ct. 1856). In two states, exemptions were rejected. Simon's Executors v. Gratz; State v. Willson, 13 S.C.L. (2 McCord) 393 (1823). In one state, the exemption was denied on the facts without clear statement of legal principle. Commonwealth v. Drake, 15 Mass. (14 Tyng) 161 (1818).

In the federal courts, only one case asserting a free exercise exemption has been found. Permoli v. New Orleans, 44 U.S. (3 How.) 588 (1845) (p. 71). The question presented was the constitutionality of a city ordinance forbidding open casket funerals within certain boundaries, which encompassed the Roman Catholic cathedral. Lawyers for both sides in *Permoli* seemed to assume that the Free Exercise Clause required exemptions in at least some circumstances; the argument hinged in large part on whether the ordinance was a legitimate health regulation. The case went to the Supreme Court, where the exemptions issue was not addressed because of the Court's conclusion that the First Amendment was inapplicable to actions of state and local governments.

Members of Congress also seemed to assume that the Free Exercise Clause applied even to acts of general applicability. When proponents of legislation that would become the Civil Rights Act of 1875 proposed extending the Act's prohibition of racial nondiscrimination to churches (in addition to schools, inns, railroad, steamships, places of public amusement, and other places of public accommodation), several senators protested that this would violate the First Amendment, and the bill was amended to exclude them. See Cong. Globe,

42 Cong., 2d Sess. 759 (1872) (Sen. Carpenter); *id.* at 847-848, 896 (Sen. Frelinghuysen); *id.* at 898 (Sen. Morton); *id.* at 899 (vote on amendment); but see *id.* at 823-826 (Sen. Sumner defending application of the bill to churches, stating "Here is nothing of religion—it is the political law, the law of justice, the law of equal rights"). Professor Kurt Lash has argued that by the time of adoption of the Fourteenth Amendment, the Free Exercise Clause was generally understood as a substantive liberty rather than merely a protection from discriminatory legislation. Kurt T. Lash, The Second Adoption of the Free Exercise Clause: Religious Exemptions Under the Fourteenth Amendment, 88 Nw. U. L. Rev. 1106 (1994).

2. Exemptions and Judicial Review.   Justice John Bannister Gibson, author of the *Simon's Executors* opinion, was one of the most highly regarded jurists of his era, most famous for his dissenting opinion in Eakin v. Raub, 12 Serg. & Rawle 155 (Pa. 1828), rebutting the arguments for judicial review of unconstitutional legislation. His interpretation of constitutional free exercise may be related to his narrow view of the proper authority of the courts in constitutional matters.

One of the most striking passages of his opinion was the statement: "Rightly considered, there are no duties half so sacred as those which the citizen owes to the laws." Compare that statement to Madison's Memorial and Remonstrance Against Religious Assessments (p. 49).

3. Belief and Conduct: The Mormon Cases

Possibly the most dramatic conflict between the governments of the United States and the institutions of a religion involved the Church of Jesus Christ of Latter-Day Saints, commonly known as the "Mormons." For a concise description, see Sydney Ahlstrom, A Religious History of the American People 501-509 (1972). In 1827, during a time of religious ferment and revival, a young farmer named Joseph Smith, Jr., reported that he had received a revelation. The angel Moroni, he said, appeared to him in a vision and led him to a set of golden plates written in a then-undeciphered language ("reformed Egyptian" hieroglyphics), which Smith translated through miraculous means. This became The Book of Mormon—the story of three groups of early migrants to the American continent, their travails, and a visit to them by the resurrected Jesus. Soon, Smith began to baptize followers and formed a new church. As Smith's biographer observed: This "was no mere dissenting sect. It was a religious creation, one intended to be to Christianity what Christianity was to Judaism: that is, a reform and a consummation." Fawn Brodie, No Man Knows My History (1945).

The Mormon Church gathered converts, but also faced fierce opposition. The new church was both socially and theologically radical: It challenged many cherished American beliefs, including the importance of individual private property, the traditional family, the separation of church and state, and the sufficiency of the Bible as a source of revelation. Most controversially, Smith announced (first privately, later publicly) a revelation requiring the practice of polygamy—the marriage of Mormon men to multiple wives. The background and consequences of the polygamy revelation are discussed fully in Sarah Barringer Gordon, The Mormon Question: Polygamy and Constitutional Conflict in Nineteenth Century America (2002). The Mormons were chased from the location of their first temple in Kirtland, Ohio, to Missouri. Again they clashed with the locals. Smith proclaimed vengeance on their oppressors, and claimed "I will be a second Mohammed." Soon, however, they were driven from the state. Missouri's governor issued an order interpreted to authorize the "extermination" of the Mormons, and the Mormons appealed in vain to President Buchanan for protection. Buchanan, who later concluded the federal government lacked power to prevent secession, thought it likewise lacked power to prevent Mormon extermination.

The Mormons fled across the Mississippi River to Nauvoo, Illinois, where they built a remarkable town of 15,000 residents, the largest and fastest growing city in the Prairie State. Nauvoo was given a charter that made it almost an autonomous theocratic principality. Converts poured in from other lands, especially from the urban poor of England. Smith, who added the title "King of the Kingdom of God" to his previous titles as prophet and apostle, declared his candidacy for President of the United States. Alas, after he ordered the destruction of an opposition newspaper in Nauvoo without due process, he was seized by the Illinois militia and, on June 27, 1844, killed while awaiting trial in nearby Carthage.

Under the leadership of Brigham Young, the Latter-Day Saints moved again—this time to an area outside the jurisdiction of the United States, in the valley of the Great Salt Lake, arriving in July 1847. They formed the autonomous state of Deseret, encompassing most of what is now Utah and southern Idaho, and stretching as far southwest as San Bernardino, California. In 1850, as a result of the Mexican War, Utah became a territory of the United States, and Young was appointed territorial governor. By this time, however, the Mormon practice of polygamy had become a national political issue. The 1856 Republican Party Platform denounced polygamy and slavery as "twin relics of barbarism." Cong. Globe 1410 (1860). Young was replaced as governor in 1857, and the region prepared for war. The nation's largest military encampment perched on the edge of Salt Lake City, prepared for attack, and the Mormons abandoned their home city and moved to the more defensible redoubts of rugged southern Utah. The outbreak of the Civil War postponed the conflict. But in 1862 Congress passed the Morrill Act, 12 Stat. 501, the first of a series of statutes designed to bring the Mormon practice of polygamy to a halt.

There is some debate about how widespread polygamy was. According to one estimate it involved only 7 to 8 percent of Mormon men, mostly those higher up in the church. Thomas O'Dea, The Mormons 246 (1957). Others put the numbers considerably higher. Richard S. Van Wagoner, Mormon Polygamy: A History 91 (2d ed. 1989). In any case, it proved surprisingly difficult to enforce the laws. It was hard to prove the fact of multiple marriages in court: The territory kept no marriage records, weddings took place in the temple before witnesses unwilling to talk, and under territorial law a wife could not testify against her husband even if she was willing. Moreover, the laws setting up the territory left the summoning of juries and the prosecution of most crimes in the hands of local rather than federal officials, and they were naturally more sympathetic to plural marriage than outsiders would be. Snow v. United States, 85 U.S. (18 Wall.) 317 (1873); Clinton v. Englebrecht, 80 U.S. (13 Wall.) 434 (1872). Congress corrected the last two difficulties in the Poland Act of 1874, 18 Stat. 253. That same year George Reynolds, private secretary to Brigham Young, was indicted.

REYNOLDS v. UNITED STATES

98 U.S. 145 (1878)

This is an indictment found in the District Court for the third judicial district of the Territory of Utah, charging George Reynolds with bigamy, in violation of sect. 5352 of the Revised Statutes, which [states]:

> Every person having a husband or wife living, who marries another, whether married or single, in a Territory, or other place over which the United States have exclusive jurisdiction, is guilty of bigamy, and shall be punished by a fine of not more than $500, and by imprisonment for a term of not more than five years.

Mr. Chief Justice WAITE delivered the opinion of the court.

[At trial Reynolds] proved that at the time of his alleged second marriage he was, and for many years before had been, a member of the Church of Jesus Christ of Latter-Day Saints, commonly called the Mormon Church, and a believer in its doctrines; that it was an accepted doctrine of that church "that it was the duty of male members of said church, circumstances permitting, to practise polygamy; . . . that this duty was enjoined by different books which the members of said church believed to be of divine origin, and among others the Holy Bible, and also that the members of the church believed that the practice of polygamy was directly enjoined upon the male members thereof by the Almighty God, in a revelation to Joseph Smith, the founder and prophet of said church; that the failing or refusing to practise polygamy by such male members of said church, when circumstances would admit, would be punished, and that the penalty for such failure and refusal would be damnation in the life to come." He also proved "that he had received permission from the recognized authorities in said church to enter into polygamous marriage; . . . that Daniel H. Wells, onc having authority in said church to perform the marriage ceremony, married the said defendant on or about the time the crime is alleged to have been committed, to some woman by the name of Schofield, and that such marriage ceremony was performed under and pursuant to the doctrines of said church."

Upon [the refusal to charge that these facts negate criminal intent] the question is raised, whether religious belief can be accepted as a justification of an overt act made criminal by the law of the land. The inquiry is not as to the power of Congress to prescribe criminal laws for the Territories, but as to the guilt of one who knowingly violates a law which has been properly enacted, if he entertains a religious belief that the law is wrong.

Congress cannot pass a law for the government of the Territories which shall prohibit the free exercise of religion. The first amendment to the Constitution expressly forbids such legislation. Religious freedom is guaranteed everywhere throughout the United States, so far as congressional interference is concerned. The question to be determined is, whether the law now under consideration comes within this prohibition.

The word "religion" is not defined in the Constitution. We must go elsewhere, therefore, to ascertain its meaning, and nowhere more appropriately, we think, than to the history of the times in the midst of which the provision was adopted. The precise point of the inquiry is, what is the religious freedom which has been guaranteed.

[We can learn much about the meaning of our federal constitutional guarantee, by examining the Bill for Establishment of Religious Freedom drafted by Thomas Jefferson in 1777 and finally enacted in Virginia in 1786.] In the preamble of this act religious freedom is defined; and after a recital "that to suffer the civil magistrate to intrude his powers into the field of opinion, and to restrain the profession or propagation of principles on supposition of their ill tendency, is a dangerous fallacy which at once destroys all religious liberty," it is declared "that it is time enough for the rightful purposes of civil government for its officers to interfere when principles break out into overt acts against peace and good order." In these two sentences is found the true distinction between what properly belongs to the church and what to the State.

In a little more than a year after the passage of this statute the convention met which prepared the Constitution of the United States. Of this convention Mr. Jefferson was not a member, he being then absent as minister to France. As soon as he saw the draft of the Constitution proposed for adoption, he, in a letter to a friend, expressed his disappointment at the absence of an express declaration insuring the freedom of religion. [And] at the first session of the first Congress the amendment now under consideration was proposed with others by Mr. Madison. It met the views of the advocates of religious freedom, and was adopted. Mr. Jefferson afterwards, in reply to an address to him by a committee of the Danbury Baptist Association, took occasion to say:

> Believing with you that religion is a matter which lies solely between man and his God; that he owes account to none other for his faith or his worship; that the legislative powers of the government reach actions only, and not opinions,— I contemplate with sovereign reverence that act of the whole American people which declared that their legislature should "make no law respecting an establishment of religion or prohibiting the free exercise thereof," thus building a wall of separation between church and State. Adhering to this expression of the supreme will of the nation in behalf of the rights of conscience, I shall see with sincere satisfaction the progress of those sentiments which tend to restore man to all his natural rights, convinced he has no natural right in opposition to his social duties.

Coming as this does from an acknowledged leader of the advocates of the measure, it may be accepted almost as an authoritative declaration of the scope and effect of the amendment thus secured. Congress was deprived of all legislative power over mere opinion, but was left free to reach actions which were in violation of social duties or subversive of good order.

Polygamy has always been odious among the northern and western nations of Europe, and, until the establishment of the Mormon Church, was almost exclusively a feature of the life of Asiatic and of African people. At common law, the second marriage was always void, and from the earliest history of England polygamy has been treated as an offence against society. After the establishment of the ecclesiastical courts, and until the time of James I, it was punished through the instrumentality of those tribunals. . . . By the statute of 1 James I (c. 11), the offence . . . was made punishable in the civil courts, and the penalty was death. As this statute was limited in its operation to England and Wales, it was at a very early period re-enacted, generally with some modifications, in all the colonies. In connection with the case we are now considering, it is a significant fact that on the 8th of December, 1788, after the passage of the act establishing religious freedom, and after the convention of Virginia had recommended as an amendment to the Constitution of the United States the declaration in a bill of rights that "all men have an equal, natural, and unalienable right to the free exercise of religion, according to the dictates of conscience," the legislature of that State substantially enacted the statute of James I, death penalty included, because, as recited in the preamble, "it hath been doubted whether bigamy or poligamy be punishable by the laws of this Commonwealth." From that day to this we think it may safely be said there never has been a time in any State of the Union when polygamy has not been an offence against society, cognizable by the civil courts and punishable with more or less severity. In the face of all this evidence, it is impossible to believe that the constitutional guaranty of religious freedom was intended to prohibit legislation in respect to this most important feature of social life. Marriage, while from its very nature a sacred obligation, is nevertheless, in most civilized nations, a civil contract, and usually regulated by law. Upon it society may be said to be built, and out of its fruits spring social relations and social obligations and duties, with which government is necessarily required to deal. In fact, according as monogamous or polygamous marriages are allowed, do we find the principles on which the government of the people, to a greater or less extent, rests. Professor Lieber says, polygamy leads to the patriarchal principle, and which, when applied to large communities, fetters the people in stationary despotism, while that principle cannot long exist in connection with monogamy. Chancellor Kent observes that this remark is equally striking and profound. 2 Kent, Com. 81, note (e). An exceptional colony of polygamists under an exceptional leadership may sometimes exist for a time without appearing to disturb the social condition of the people who surround it; but there cannot be a doubt that, unless restricted by some form of constitution, it is within the legitimate scope of the power of every civil government to determine whether polygamy or monogamy shall be the law of social life under its dominion.

In our opinion, the statute immediately under consideration is within the legislative power of Congress. [T]he only question which remains is, whether those who make polygamy a part of their religion are excepted from the operation of the statute. If they are, then those who do not make polygamy a part of their religious belief may be found guilty and punished, while those who do, must be acquitted and go free. This would be introducing a new element into criminal law. Laws are made for the government of actions, and while they cannot interfere with mere religious belief and opinions, they may with practices. Suppose one believed that human sacrifices were a necessary part of religious worship, would it be seriously contended that the civil government under which he lived could not interfere to prevent a sacrifice? Or if a wife religiously believed it was her duty to burn herself upon the funeral pile of her dead husband, would it be beyond the power of the civil government to prevent her carrying her belief into practice?

So here, as a law of the organization of society under the exclusive dominion of the United States, it is provided that plural marriages shall not be allowed. Can a man excuse his practices to the contrary because of his religious belief? To permit this would be to make the professed doctrines of religious belief superior to the law of the land, and in effect to permit every citizen to become a law unto himself. Government could exist only in name under such circumstances.

A criminal intent is generally an element of crime, but every man is presumed to intend the necessary and legitimate consequences of what he knowingly does. Here the accused knew he had been once married, and that his first wife was living. He also knew that his second marriage was forbidden by law. When, therefore, he married the second time, he is presumed to have intended to break the law. And the breaking of the law is the crime. Every act necessary to constitute the crime was knowingly done, and the crime was therefore knowingly committed. Ignorance of a fact may sometimes be taken as evidence of a want of criminal intent, but not ignorance of the law. The only defence of the accused in this case is his belief that the law ought not to have been enacted. It matters not that his belief was a part of his professed religion: it was still belief, and belief only.

In Regina v. Wagstaff, the parents of a sick child, who omitted to call in medical attendance because of their religious belief that what they did for its cure would be effective, were held not to be guilty of manslaughter, while it was said the contrary would have been the result if the child had actually been starved to death by the parents, under the notion that it was their religious duty to abstain from giving it food. But when the offence consists of a positive act which is knowingly done, it would be dangerous to hold that the offender might escape punishment because he religiously believed the law which he had broken ought never to have been made. No case, we believe, can be found that has gone so far.

NOTES AND QUESTIONS

1. The Proper Domains of Law and Religion.   Chief Justice Waite begins his opinion by acknowledging that Congress cannot (ever?) pass a law prohibiting the free exercise of religion. The question in *Reynolds*, as he sees it, is whether polygamy is an "exercise of religion."

(a) **Belief and conduct.**   Waite invokes Thomas Jefferson's help in separating the portion of human endeavor that is religious from the portion that is not. In the Bill for Establishment of Religious Freedom Jefferson distinguished between "opinion" (or "principles") and "overt acts." In his letter to the Danbury Baptists he distinguished between "faith or . . . worship" ("opinions") and "actions." Later in his opinion Chief Justice Waite contrasts "mere religious belief and opinions" with "practices." What do these terms signify? Consider first belief (faith, opinion). At a minimum, this might embrace one's conviction that certain propositions or writings were true—the New Testament, the Book of Mormon, the Westminster Confession, the Koran, etc. Does it just refer to a kind of interior assent? If so, do we need a First Amendment to protect our right to believe? How would the government prohibit mere belief unaccompanied by action? Consider Davis v. Beason, below (upholding an oath required of potential voters). Why was the government there concerned with what voters believed?

Jefferson associated faith with worship. Worship might include prayer and other liturgical practices—attendance at church or synagogue, masses and sacraments, and so on. Is this something the government would want to control? Is *Permoli* an instance of this? Mormon weddings, as we have observed, take place in the temple. They have a sacramental character that distinguishes them from other marriage ceremonies. Rex E. Lee, What Do Mormons Believe? 33-34 (1992). If marriage is a sacrament, why is the issue in *Reynolds* a matter of "conduct" rather than "worship"? Are there some activities that are both belief (or worship) *and* conduct? If there are, can the government regulate them or not? How do we decide?

What did the Court mean by "actions" or "practices"—what we have been calling conduct? Does this category include everything that is *not* interior assent to a creed, or prayer, or liturgy? Anything that has an outward manifestation or public impact? This would include many activities that are required or recommended by the moral codes of various religions.

(b) The "two kingdoms": civil and religious. There are actually two dichotomies in Waite's opinion. The first concerns the activities of religious people (belief and conduct). The second concerns the division of jurisdiction between civil and religious authorities. This one is more fundamental. Jefferson's Bill talks about where "the civil magistrate" may intrude his powers. His letter to the Danbury Baptists envisions "a wall of separation between church and State." Eighteenth century writers often pictured separate and non-overlapping spheres of influence for religious and civil authorities. Recall what Madison said in his Memorial and Remonstrance ¶1: "Before any man can be considered as a member of Civil Society, he must be considered as a subject of the Governor of the Universe[.]" We owe duties to each, but duties to God come first in order of precedence. (See p. 49.) This idea that we find in Madison and Jefferson is religious in origin. The theology of two kingdoms can be found in Augustine's City of God. It was carried forward in different ways by Martin Luther and John Calvin (the forerunner of the Reformed tradition to which our Puritan and Presbyterian forebears adhered). Michael W. McConnell, "God Is Dead and We Have Killed Him!": Freedom of Religion in the Post-Modern Age, 1993 B.Y.U. L. Rev. 163, 167-168; Harold J. Berman and John Witte, Jr., The Transformation of Western Legal Philosophy in Lutheran Germany, 62 S. Cal. L. Rev. 1573, 1585-1595 (1989). The distinction between belief and conduct is a way of defining the territory our constitution allocates to each kingdom.

The theory of two kingdoms, a legacy of the Protestant Reformation, had important and liberating political implications. It meant that the government was not omnipotent, and if it could be limited in one respect it could be limited in others. McConnell, 1993 B.Y.U. L. Rev. at 169. But it does not work very well for Reynolds. Why not? In modern terms we would say that Reynolds wanted an exemption from the statute. Is this consistent with the two kingdoms theory? Can X fall within God's jurisdiction (a matter of belief or worship) for Reynolds and within Congress's jurisdiction (a matter of conduct) for others? (Could we say that there are marriages and there are marriages—some are sacramental and some are not?) If X falls within God's jurisdiction, does the two kingdoms theory ever allow the government to *refuse* an exemption? On what grounds?

2. Marriage and Religious Exercise. Chief Justice Waite offers analogies to explain why this practice cannot be left up to the Mormons—that would be like allowing suttee or human sacrifice, he says. Would it? Might we argue that the victims of human sacrifice (and maybe suttee, too) do not choose their fate, but polygamous partners do? Why should that matter? Is this a modern variant of the two kingdoms theory—self-regarding acts are beyond the government's power, other-regarding acts are within it? Is it true that marriage is a self-regarding act? Reread the Court's citation of Professor Lieber and Chancellor Kent. What is the meaning of these observations? Does the first wife consent to her husband's marrying a second? Does polygamy have some effect on the children of the marriage partners? For better or worse? May the government take account of this in deciding whether to regulate polygamy? See Maura Strassberg, Distinctions of Form or Substance: Monogamy, Polygamy and Same-Sex Marriage, 75 N.C. L. Rev. 1501 (1997).

Should *Reynolds* be decided the same way today? See State v. Holm, 2006 WL 1319595 (Ut. 2006) (rejecting polygamy claims under both federal and state constitutions); but see *id.* (Durham, C.J., dissenting) (both excerpted at http://www.bc.edu/ReligionAndTheConstitution).

3. Further Antipolygamy Legislation.

(a) The Edmunds Act.   The government's success against Reynolds established that the Morrill Act was constitutional, but it had little practical effect on polygamy prosecutions. There remained the difficulty of proving multiple marriages. Congress solved this problem by creating a new offense (unlawful cohabitation) in the Edmunds Act, 22 Stat. 30 (1882); it required no proof of marriage, nor even of sexual intercourse. It was enough that a man lived in the same house with two women. Cannon v. United States, 116 U.S. 55 (1885). The Act also disqualified from jury service those who approved of the practice of polygamy (effectively, all faithful church members). This approach worked. Over the next 11 years the government secured more than 1,000 convictions for unlawful cohabitation. For a clear and careful account of the Mormons' legal travails during this period, see Edwin B. Firmage and Richard C. Mangrum, Zion in the Courts (1988).

The Edmunds Act did more than attack the practice of polygamy. It took aim at the political power of Mormons in the territory. Congress created a commission to oversee future elections, and disqualified polygamists and those unlawfully cohabiting from voting or holding office. See Murphy v. Ramsey, 114 U.S. 15 (1885). The effect of this was more serious than might appear: "[B]y and large, the polygamists were also the Mormons' leaders," because the practice was limited to males of moral worth and financial ability. Firmage and Mangrum, Zion in the Courts at 168. Within a few years the commission had disenfranchised and swept these people from office.

(b) The Edmunds-Tucker Act.   Still Congress was not satisfied. Mormon voters still predominated in the territory. To wrest power from their hands and bring the church to its knees, Congress in 1887 enacted the Edmunds-Tucker Act, 24 Stat. 635. Several of its provisions cleared up outstanding difficulties with polygamy prosecutions: Section 1 allowed wives to testify against their husbands; §9 required all marriages to be registered with the probate court. Other provisions further rearranged political power in the Utah territory. Women were disenfranchised—perhaps on the theory that Mormon women were too submissive to their husbands (§20). (The Utah territory had been the second jurisdiction in the nation to give women the right to vote.) And voters and public officials were required to swear that they would not commit polygamy nor "aid or abet, counsel or advise, any other person to" do so (§24). Davis v. Beason, the next case, deals with a similar provision in the Idaho territorial law.

DAVIS v. BEASON
133 U.S. 333 (1890)

[Davis, a member of the Church of Jesus Christ of Latter-Day Saints, was indicted for conspiring with others to register to vote in the Idaho Territory, as it then was, in violation of territorial law. The law required registrants to take an oath as follows:

> I do swear . . . that I am not a bigamist or polygamist; that I am not a member of any order, organization or association which teaches, advises, counsels or encourages its members . . . to commit the crime of bigamy or polygamy, . . . or which practises . . . celestial marriage as a doctrinal rite of such organization; that I do not, and will not, . . . teach, advise, counsel, or encourage any person to commit the crime of bigamy or polygamy, . . . either as a religious duty or otherwise[.]

He was found guilty, fined $500, and remanded to custody until the judgment was satisfied. Davis filed a petition for habeas corpus, which the district court denied. He appealed.]

Mr. Justice FIELD . . . delivered the opinion of the Court.

On this appeal our only inquiry is whether . . . an offense was committed of which the territorial court had jurisdiction to try the defendant. And on this point there can be no serious discussion or difference of opinion. Bigamy and polygamy are crimes by the laws of all civilized and Christian countries. They are crimes by the laws of the United States, and they are crimes by the laws of Idaho. They tend to destroy the purity of the marriage relation, to disturb the peace of families, to degrade woman, and to debase man. Few crimes are more pernicious to the best interests of society, and receive more general or more deserved punishment. To extend exemption from punishment for such crimes would be to shock the moral judgment of the community. To call their advocacy a tenet of religion is to offend the common sense of mankind. If they are crimes, then to teach, advise, and counsel their practice is to aid in their commission, and such teaching and counseling are themselves criminal, and proper subjects of punishment, as aiding and abetting crime are in all other cases. The term "religion" has reference to one's views of his relations to his Creator, and to the obligations they impose of reverence for his being and character, and of obedience to his will. It is often confounded with the cultus or form of worship of a particular sect, but is distinguishable from the latter. The first amendment to the constitution, in declaring that congress shall make no law respecting the establishment of religion or forbidding the free exercise thereof, was intended to allow every one under the jurisdiction of the United States to entertain such notions respecting his relations to his Maker and the duties they impose as may be approved by his judgment and conscience, and to exhibit his sentiments in such form of worship as he may think proper, not injurious to the equal rights of others, and to prohibit legislation for the support of any religious tenets, or the modes of worship of any sect. . . . It was never intended or supposed that the amendment could be invoked as a protection against legislation for the punishment of acts inimical to the peace, good order, and morals of society. With man's relations to his Maker and the obligations he may think they impose, and the manner in which an expression shall be made by him of his belief on those subjects, no interference can be permitted, provided always the laws of society, designed to secure its peace and prosperity, and the morals of its people, are not interfered with. However free the exercise of religion may be, it must be subordinate to the criminal laws of the country, passed with reference to actions regarded by general consent as properly the subjects of punitive legislation. There have been sects which denied as a part of their religious tenets that there should be any marriage tie, and advocated promiscuous intercourse of the sexes, as prompted by the passions of its members. And history discloses the fact that the necessity of human sacrifices, on special occasions, has been a tenet of many sects. Should a sect of either of these kinds ever find its way into this country, swift punishment would follow the carrying into effect of its doctrines, and no heed would be given to the pretense that, as religious beliefs, their supporters could be protected in their exercise by the constitution of the United States. Probably never before in the history of this country has it been seriously contended that the whole punitive power of the government for acts, recognized by the general consent of the Christian world in modern times as proper matters for prohibitory legislation, must be suspended in order that the tenets of a religious sect encouraging crime may be carried out without hindrance. . . .

It is assumed by counsel of the petitioner that, because no mode of worship can be established, or religious tenets enforced, in this country, therefore any form of worship may be followed, and any tenets, however destructive of society, may be held and advocated, if asserted to be a part of the religious doctrines of those advocating and practicing them. But nothing is further from the truth. While legislation for the establishment of a religion is forbidden, and its free exercise permitted, it does not follow that everything which may be so called can be tolerated. Crime is not the less odious because sanctioned by what any particular sect may designate as "religion." . . .

The judgment of the court below is therefore affirmed.

NOTES AND QUESTIONS

1. Belief, Conduct, and Expression.   Justice Field restates and elaborates on the belief/action distinction proposed by Chief Justice Waite in *Reynolds*. He says that "religion" is often confused with "the cultus or form of worship of a particular sect," but it is more than that. How much more? Field speaks at one point of "obedience to his [creator's] will." Why does this not include the practice of polygamy, if God requires it? Like Waite, Field seems to exclude "acts" from the coverage of "religion"—at least acts "recognized . . . as proper matters for prohibitory legislation."

The law in *Davis* forbade more than acts. It also required citizens to take a kind of test oath—to forswear certain associations and beliefs—before they could register to vote. Consider whether this kind of requirement is consistent with the distinction between belief and conduct that Chief Justice Waite announced in *Reynolds*, and that Justice Field repeats here. The law made it a crime to teach another that celestial marriage was a religious duty. Is that belief or conduct? Does the First Amendment give no protection to speaking one's beliefs out loud? What about belonging to an organization that teaches . . . , etc.? Does Field mean to say that membership in the Mormon church is conduct, and therefore not protected by the Free Exercise Clause?

2. The Dissolution of the Mormon Church.   As a practical matter the most significant sanctions in the Edmunds-Tucker Act dealt not with polygamy prosecutions or the franchise, but with the Mormon Church itself. Section 17 annulled the territorial act incorporating the Church and directed the Attorney General to wind up its affairs; section 13 ordered him to collect most of the Church's real property, which was to be applied to the use and benefit of the common schools of the territory.* This was a serious blow, and not just in financial terms. The institutional Church played an indispensable role in the religious lives of its members—regulating marriages, building temples, conducting missionary work and welfare activities, counseling, punishing and forgiving offenses, and so on. The Church had acquired property with a value of perhaps $3 million. In accordance with its beliefs about communal ownership, the Church owned capital stock in community herds, general stores, and irrigation projects, and businesses like the Deseret News Company, the Zion's Savings Bank, mines and quarries, ranches, and other vital parts of the economic infrastructure. Leonard J. Arrington, Great Basin Kingdom: An Economic History of the Latter-Day Saints 362-363 (1958). The Act had an exemption for parsonages, and for buildings and grounds used exclusively for worship, but that would not leave the Church with much. Within a few months of the Act's passage, the United States filed for a decree dissolving the corporation and an order forfeiting its property, except for the Temple block in Salt Lake City. The territorial supreme court granted the decree. The United States Supreme Court affirmed.

THE LATE CORPORATION OF THE CHURCH OF JESUS CHRIST OF LATTER-DAY SAINTS v. UNITED STATES

136 U.S. 1 (1890)

BRADLEY, J.

. . . The principal questions raised are—First, as to the power of Congress to repeal the charter of the Church of Jesus Christ of Latter-Day Saints; and, secondly, as to the power of Congress and the courts to seize the property of said corporation, and to hold the same for the purposes mentioned in the decree.

[The church originally received its charter in 1851 from the State of Deseret, the provisional government set up by Brigham Young when the Mormons arrived at the Great Salt Lake. When Utah was made a territory, the territorial legislature confirmed the charter. Because of this, the church argued that its charter was a contract which the government was forbidden to impair under the doctrine of Dartmouth College v. Woodward, 17 U.S. (4 Wheat.) 518 (1819). The Court responded:] In the sixth section of the act establishing a territorial government in Utah, approved September 9, 1850, it is declared [that] "All the laws passed by the legislative assembly and governor shall be submitted to the Congress of the United States, and, if disapproved, shall be null and of no effect." [I]t is too plain for argument that this charter or enactment was subject to revocation and repeal by Congress whenever it should see fit to exercise its

---

*The Morrill Act had in theory lifted the church's charter 15 years before, and forbidden it to acquire more than $50,000 worth of real property. 12 Stat. 501. But this provision had not been enforced. The Edmunds-Tucker Act was designed to make it effective.

power for that purpose. Like any other act of the territorial legislature, it was subject to this condition. . . . Congress, for good and sufficient reasons of its own, . . . had a full and perfect right to repeal its charter and abrogate its corporate existence, which, of course, depended upon its charter.

The next question is, whether Congress or the court had the power to cause the property of the said corporation to be seized and taken possession of, as was done in this case.

[We hold that they did, for three reasons. First, when] a business corporation, instituted for the purposes of gain or private interest, is dissolved, the modern doctrine is that its property, after payment of its debts, equitably belongs to its stockholders. But this doctrine has never been extended to public or charitable corporations. As to these, the ancient and established rule prevails, namely, that when a corporation is dissolved, its personal property, like that of a man dying without heirs, ceases to be the subject of private ownership, and becomes subject to the disposal of the sovereign authority; while its real estate reverts or escheats to the grantor or donor. . . . But the grantor of all, or the principal part, of the real estate of the Church of Jesus Christ of Latter-Day Saints was really the United States, from whom the property was derived by the church, or its trustees, through the operation of the town-site act. [Second, the Morrill Act in 1862] prohibited the acquiring or holding of real estate of greater value than $50,000 in a Territory, and no legal title had vested in any of the lands in Salt Lake City at that time, as the town site act was not passed until March 2, 1867. There can be no doubt, therefore, that the real estate of the corporation in question could not, on its dissolution, revert or pass to any other person or persons than the United States.

[Third, where] a charitable corporation is dissolved, and no private donor, or founder, appears to be entitled to its real estate (its personal property not being subject to such reclamation), the government, or sovereign authority, as the chief and common guardian of the State, either through its judicial tribunals or otherwise, necessarily has the disposition of the funds of such corporation, to be exercised, however, with due regard to the objects and purposes of the charitable uses to which the property was originally devoted, so far as they are lawful and not repugnant to public policy.

[The Court went on to hold that the original religious purpose of the property, support of the Mormon Church, was repugnant to public policy because the Church promoted polygamy]—a crime against the laws, and abhorrent to the sentiments and feelings of the civilized world. . . . The organization of a community for the spread and practice of polygamy is, in a measure, a return to barbarism. It is contrary to the spirit of Christianity, and of the civilization which Christianity has produced in the western world. [Congress certainly] had power to direct proceedings to be instituted for the forfeiture and escheat of the real estate of the corporation; and, if a judgment should be rendered in favor of the government in these proceedings, the power to dispose of the proceeds of the lands thus forfeited and escheated, for the use and benefit of common schools in the territory, is beyond dispute. It would probably have power to make such a disposition of the proceeds if the question were merely one of charitable uses, and not of forfeiture. . . .

[Chief Justice FULLER, joined by Justices FIELD and LAMAR, dissented.]
    . . . Congress has the power to extirpate polygamy in any of the territories, by the enactment of a criminal code directed to that end; but it is not authorized,

under the cover of that power, to seize and confiscate the property of persons, individuals, or corporations, without office found, because they may have been guilty of criminal practices.

NOTES AND QUESTIONS

1. The Mormon Dissolution and the First Amendment. Does it seem odd that the Church makes no First Amendment claim in *The Late Corporation?* The Edmunds-Tucker Act put the Church (in its corporate form) out of existence, took nearly all its property, and handed it out to the public schools. Why was this not a violation of religious freedom? One possible historical analogy is Henry VIII's break from the Roman Catholic Church in the 1530s, during which the monarchy dissolved England's monasteries, confiscated their treasures, vandalized the buildings, and sold off their libraries of books, distributing much of the proceeds as patronage to various gentry. See Richard Rex, Henry VIII and the English Reformation 71 (1993) ("The expropriations . . . made the nature and extent of [royal] supremacy [over religion] clear."). Was the Act dissolving the Mormon Church constitutional because the Church—some 100,000 members (136 U.S. at 14) and hierarchy—still existed as an ecclesiastical polity? Note, too, that the Act exempted from seizure parsonages and buildings and grounds used exclusively for worship. Could we say that the Act was constitutional because it regulated only the secular affairs of the Church, and left its purely religious affairs untouched?

Could we say that the First Amendment does not come into play in this case because it is concerned only with individual rights? Recall Jefferson's reply to the Danbury Baptists, quoted in *Reynolds* : "[R]eligion is a matter which lies solely between man and his God." And recall the decision in *Davis* upholding a law that penalized membership in the Mormon Church. We deal with the question of free exercise claims by *institutions* at more length in section III-D below.

2. The Mormon Capitulation. The decision in *The Late Corporation* was the coup de grace in the Mormons' battle with the federal government. Wilford Woodruff, the President of the Church, issued a Manifesto on September 24, 1890, announcing that it had been revealed to him that the Church must cease the practice of polygamy. Relations with the federal government improved. President Harrison granted amnesty to Mormons who complied with the law from 1890 on. What was left of the Church's property was returned. In 1896 Utah was granted statehood. And the Mormons were on their way toward being recognized as a mainstream American religion. For a thoughtful reflection on the episode, see Frederick Mark Gedicks, The Integrity of Survival: A Mormon Response to Stanley Hauerwas, 42 DePaul L. Rev. 167 (1992).

4. Modern Exemptions

In the view reflected in Reynolds v. United States, there was little or no room for constitutionally mandated religious exemptions. As a theoretical matter religion and civil authority occupied separate, nonintersecting spheres. They should not come into conflict. As a practical matter religious exemptions would "permit every citizen to become a law unto himself." Suppose, though, that the sphere of civil authority became very large, as it has done in the century since *Reynolds*. And suppose that religion embraces more than mere belief as *Reynolds* presupposed. There would be many more conflicts. Under a no accommodation rule, the government would always get its way. What is left of religious liberty in this regime? What is left of the rule of law if courts can grant exemptions whenever there is a conflict?

Around the mid-twentieth century, the Court began to change its approach toward religiously motivated conduct and civil law. Cantwell v. Connecticut, 310 U.S. 296 (1940), was the first decision to apply the Free Exercise Clause to state and local laws through incorporation in the Fourteenth Amendment. The Court overturned the conviction of Cantwell, a Jehovah's Witness, for committing a breach of the piece by playing an anti-Catholic record to passersby on the streets of New Haven, Connecticut. Citing *Reynolds*, the Court reasserted a distinction between "freedom to believe and freedom to act": "The first is absolute but, in the nature of things, the second cannot be. Conduct remains subject to regulation for the protection of society." But it went on to indicate that even cases concerning action called for "the weighing of conflicting interests"—the freedom to preach against the interest in "peace and good order"—and that the government restriction must not "unduly . . . infringe the protected interest." The Court found that Cantwell had made no assault or threat of bodily harm and engaged in no profanity or "personal abuse," but had only "aroused animosity" with his unpopular religious views. Therefore he had raised no "clear and present menace to public peace and order," and his conviction was unconstitutional.

Where *Reynolds* had given no protection to "action," *Cantwell* applied a balancing test. Is that because the "action" in this case was speech and expression (while polygamy was not)? *Cantwell* was one of a host of decisions in the 1940s and 1950s in which the Court extended First Amendment protection to the Jehovah's Witnesses, a group whose aggressive street preaching and solicitation often provoked hostile or violent reactions. In these decisions, the Court began to establish free exercise of religion, along with freedom of speech, as a "preferred freedom" that could only be restricted on a strong showing by the government. Free exercise seemed to reach this preferred status fully in Sherbert v. Verner.

SHERBERT v. VERNER
374 U.S. 398 (1963)

Mr. Justice BRENNAN delivered the opinion of the Court.

Appellant, a member of the Seventh-Day Adventist Church, was discharged by her South Carolina employer because she would not work on Saturday, the Sabbath Day of her faith.[1] When she was unable to obtain other employment because from conscientious scruples she would not take Saturday work, she filed a claim for unemployment compensation benefits under the South Carolina Unemployment Compensation Act. That law provides that, to be eligible for

1. Appellant became a member of the Seventh-Day Adventist Church in 1957, at a time when her employer, a textile-mill operator, permitted her to work a five-day week. It was not until 1959 that the work week was changed to six days, including Saturday, for all three shifts in the employer's mill. . . .

benefits, a claimant must be "able to work and . . . is available for work"; and, further, that a claimant is ineligible for benefits "[i]f . . . he has failed, without good cause . . . to accept available suitable work when offered him by the employment office or the employer." The appellee Employment Security Commission, in administrative proceedings under the statute, found that appellant's restriction upon her availability for Saturday work brought her within the provision disqualifying for benefits insured workers who fail, without good cause, to accept "suitable work when offered . . . by the employment office or the employer. . . ." The Commission's finding was sustained by the [trial court and the state supreme court].

The door of the Free Exercise Clause stands tightly closed against any governmental regulation of religious *beliefs* as such, Cantwell v. Connecticut. Government may neither compel affirmation of a repugnant belief; nor penalize or discriminate against individuals or groups because they hold religious views abhorrent to the authorities; nor employ the taxing power to inhibit the dissemination of particular religious views. On the other hand, the Court has rejected challenges under the Free Exercise Clause to governmental regulation of certain overt acts prompted by religious beliefs or principles, for "even when the action is in accord with one's religious convictions, [it] is not totally free from legislative restrictions." Braunfeld v. Brown (1961). . . . Plainly enough, appellant's conscientious objection to Saturday work constitutes no conduct prompted by religious principles of a kind within the reach of state legislation. If, therefore, the decision of the South Carolina Supreme Court is to withstand appellant's constitutional challenge, it must be either because her disqualification as a beneficiary represents no infringement by the State of her constitutional rights of free exercise, or because any incidental burden on the free exercise of appellant's religion may be justified by a "compelling state interest in the regulation of a subject within the State's constitutional power to regulate[.]"

We turn first to the question whether the disqualification for benefits imposes any burden on the free exercise of appellant's religion. We think it is clear that it does. In a sense the consequences of such a disqualification to religious principles and practices may be only an indirect result of welfare legislation within the State's general competence to enact; it is true that no criminal sanctions directly compel appellant to work a six-day week. But this is only the beginning, not the end, of our inquiry. For "[i]f the purpose or effect of a law is to impede the observance of one or all religions or is to discriminate invidiously between religions, that law is constitutionally invalid even though the burden may be characterized as being only indirect." *Braunfeld.* Here not only is it apparent that appellant's declared ineligibility for benefits derives solely from the practice of her religion, but the pressure upon her to forego that practice is unmistakable. The ruling forces her to choose between following the precepts of her religion and forfeiting benefits, on the one hand, and abandoning one of the precepts of her religion in order to accept work, on the other hand. Governmental imposition of such a choice puts the same kind of burden upon the free exercise of religion as would a fine imposed against appellant for her Saturday worship.

Nor may the South Carolina court's construction of the statute be saved from constitutional infirmity on the ground that unemployment compensation benefits are not appellant's "right" but merely a "privilege." It is too late in the day to doubt that the liberties of religion and expression may be infringed by the denial of or placing of conditions upon a benefit or privilege. . . . In Speiser v. Randall (1958), we emphasized that conditions upon public benefits cannot be sustained if they so operate, whatever their purpose, as to inhibit or deter the exercise of First Amendment freedoms. We there struck down a condition which limited the availability of a tax exemption to those members of the exempted class who affirmed their loyalty to the state government granting the exemption. While the State was surely under no obligation to afford such an exemption, we held that the imposition of such a condition upon even a gratuitous benefit inevitably deterred or discouraged the exercise of First Amendment rights of expression and thereby threatened to "produce a result which the State could not command directly." "To deny an exemption to claimants who engage in certain forms of speech is in effect to penalize them for such speech." Likewise, to condition the availability of benefits upon this appellant's willingness to violate a cardinal principle of her religious faith effectively penalizes the free exercise of her constitutional liberties.

Significantly South Carolina expressly saves the Sunday worshiper from having to make the kind of choice which we here hold infringes the Sabbatarian's religious liberty. When in times of "national emergency" the textile plants are authorized by the State Commissioner of Labor to operate on Sunday, "no employee shall be required to work on Sunday . . . who is conscientiously opposed to Sunday work; and if any employee should refuse to work on Sunday on account of conscientious . . . objections he or she shall not jeopardize his or her seniority by such refusal or be discriminated against in any other manner." No question of the disqualification of a Sunday worshiper for benefits is likely to arise, since we cannot suppose that an employer will discharge him in violation of this statute. The unconstitutionality of the disqualification of the Sabbatarian is thus compounded by the religious discrimination which South Carolina's general statutory scheme necessarily effects.

We must next consider whether some compelling state interest enforced in the eligibility provisions of the South Carolina statute justifies the substantial infringement of appellant's First Amendment right. It is basic that no showing merely of a rational relationship to some colorable state interest would suffice; in this highly sensitive constitutional area, "[o]nly the gravest abuses, endangering paramount interest, give occasion for permissible limitation." No such abuse or danger has been advanced in the present case. The appellees suggest no more than a possibility that the filing of fraudulent claims by unscrupulous claimants feigning religious objections to Saturday work might not only dilute the unemployment compensation fund but also hinder the scheduling by employers of necessary Saturday work. But that possibility is not apposite here because no such objection appears to have been made before the South Carolina Supreme Court, and we are unwilling to assess the importance of an asserted state interest without the views of the state court. Nor, if the contention had been made below, would the record appear to sustain it; there is no proof whatever to warrant such fears of malingering or deceit as those which the respondents now advance. Even if consideration of such evidence is not foreclosed by the prohibition against judicial inquiry into the truth or falsity of religious beliefs, United States v. Ballard (1944)—a question as to which we intimate no view since it is not before us—it is highly doubtful whether such evidence would be sufficient to warrant a substantial infringement of religious liberties. For even if the possibility of spurious claims did threaten to dilute the fund and disrupt the scheduling of work, it would plainly be incumbent upon the appellees to demonstrate that no alternative forms of regulation would combat such abuses without infringing First Amendment rights. . . .

In holding as we do, plainly we are not fostering the "establishment" of the Seventh-day Adventist religion in South Carolina, for the extension of unemployment benefits to Sabbatarians in common with Sunday worshipers reflects nothing more than the governmental obligation of neutrality in the face of religious differences, and does not represent that involvement of religious with secular institutions which it is the object of the Establishment Clause to forestall. Nor does the recognition of the appellant's right to unemployment benefits under the state statute serve to abridge any other person's religious liberties. Nor do we, by our decision today, declare the existence of a constitutional right to unemployment benefits on the part of all persons whose religious convictions are the cause of their unemployment. This is not a case in which an employee's religious convictions serve to make him a nonproductive member of society. Finally, nothing we say today constrains the States to adopt any particular form or scheme of unemployment compensation. Our holding today is only that South Carolina may not constitutionally apply the eligibility provisions so as to constrain a worker to abandon his religious convictions respecting the day of rest. This holding but reaffirms a principle that we announced a decade and a half ago, namely that no State may "exclude individual Catholics, Lutherans, Mohammedans, Baptists, Jews, Methodists, Non-believers, Presbyterians, or the members of any other faith, because of their faith, or lack of it, from receiving the benefits of public welfare legislation." Everson v. Board of Education (1947).

Mr. Justice STEWART, concurring in the result.

. . . Because the appellant refuses to accept available jobs which would require her to work on Saturdays, South Carolina has declined to pay unemployment compensation benefits to her. Her refusal to work on Saturdays is based on the tenets of her religious faith. The Court says that South Carolina cannot under these circumstances declare her to be not "available for work" within the meaning of its statute because to do so would violate her constitutional right to the free exercise of her religion.

Yet what this Court has said about the Establishment Clause must inevitably lead to a diametrically opposite result. If the appellant's refusal to work on Saturdays were based on indolence, or on a compulsive desire to watch the Saturday television programs, no one would say that South Carolina could not hold that she was not "available for work" within the meaning of its statute. That being so, the Establishment Clause as construed by this Court not only permits but affirmatively requires South Carolina equally to deny the appellant's claim for unemployment compensation when her refusal to work on Saturdays is based upon her religious creed. For, as said in Everson v. Board of Education, the Establishment Clause bespeaks "a government . . . stripped of all power . . . to support, or otherwise to assist any or all religions . . . ," and no State "can pass laws which aid one religion. . . ." In Mr. Justice Rutledge's words, . . . the Establishment Clause forbids "every form of public aid or support for religion." *Id.* . . .

To require South Carolina to so administer its laws as to pay public money to the appellant under the circumstances of this case is thus clearly to require the

State to violate the Establishment Clause as construed by this Court. This poses no problem for me, because I think the Court's mechanistic concept of the Establishment Clause is historically unsound and constitutionally wrong. I think the process of constitutional decision in the area of the relationships between government and religion demands considerably more than the invocation of broad-brushed rhetoric of the kind I have quoted. And I think that the guarantee of religious liberty embodied in the Free Exercise Clause affirmatively requires government to create an atmosphere of hospitality and accommodation to individual belief or disbelief. In short, I think our Constitution commands the positive protection by government of religious freedom—not only for a minority, however small—not only for the majority, however large—but for each of us.

South Carolina would deny unemployment benefits to a mother unavailable for work on Saturdays because she was unable to get a babysitter. Thus, we do not have before us a situation where a State provides unemployment compensation generally, and singles out for disqualification only those persons who are unavailable for work on religious grounds. This is not, in short, a scheme which operates so as to discriminate against religion as such. But the Court nevertheless holds that the State must prefer a religious over a secular ground for being unavailable for work—that state financial support of the appellant's religion is constitutionally required to carry out "the governmental obligation of neutrality in the face of religious differences. . . ."

Yet in cases decided under the Establishment Clause the Court has decreed otherwise. It has decreed that government must blind itself to the differing religious beliefs and traditions of the people. With all respect, I think it is the Court's duty to face up to the dilemma posed by the conflict between the Free Exercise Clause of the Constitution and the Establishment Clause as interpreted by the Court. . . .

Mr. Justice HARLAN, whom Mr. Justice WHITE joins, dissenting.

[T]he implications of the present decision are far more troublesome than its apparently narrow dimensions would indicate at first glance. The meaning of today's holding . . . is that the State must furnish unemployment benefits to one who is unavailable for work if the unavailability stems from the exercise of religious convictions. The State, in other words, must single out for financial assistance those whose behavior is religiously motivated, even though it denies such assistance to others whose identical behavior (in this case, inability to work on Saturdays) is not religiously motivated.

It has been suggested that such singling out of religious conduct for special treatment may violate the constitutional limitations on state action. See Kurland, *Of Church and State and The Supreme Court*, 29 U. Chi. L. Rev. 1. My own view, however, is that at least under the circumstances of this case it would be a permissible accommodation of religion for the State, if it *chose* to do so, to create an exception to its eligibility requirements for persons like the appellant. The constitutional obligation of "neutrality" is not so narrow a channel that the slightest deviation from an absolutely straight course leads to condemnation. There are too many instances in which no such course can be charted, too many areas in which the pervasive activities of the State justify some special provision for religion to prevent it from being submerged by an all-embracing secularism. The State violates its obligation of neutrality when, for example, it mandates a daily religious exercise in its public schools, with all the attendant pressures on the school children that such an exercise entails. But there is, I believe, enough flexibility in the Constitution to permit a legislative judgment accommodating an unemployment compensation law to the exercise of religious beliefs such as appellant's.

For very much the same reasons, however, I cannot subscribe to the conclusion that the State is constitutionally *compelled* to carve out an exception to its general rule of eligibility in the present case. Those situations in which the Constitution may require special treatment on account of religion are, in my view, few and far between, and this view is amply supported by the course of constitutional litigation in this area. See, e.g., Reynolds v. United States. Such compulsion in the present case is particularly inappropriate in light of the indirect, remote, and insubstantial effect of the decision below on the exercise of appellant's religion and in light of the direct financial assistance to religion that today's decision requires.

[The concurring opinion of Justice Douglas is omitted.]

NOTES AND QUESTIONS

1. **Strict Scrutiny.** *Sherbert*, like Cantwell v. Connecticut, distinguishes between the regulation of belief and the regulation of conduct. With respect to the latter it proposes a new test (*Cantwell*'s was limited to speech). In deciding on a claim for exemption a court should first ask whether the government has imposed a burden on the claimant's free exercise right. If so, the government must show a compelling state interest in the regulation being attacked. And it must show that there are "no alternative forms of regulation" less restrictive of First Amendment rights.

(a) **Burden on religious exercise.** We will examine the subject of burdens in more detail in section B-2-a below. For present purposes, let us simply accept the Court's characterization of the "suitable work" requirement as functionally equivalent to "a fine imposed against appellant for her Saturday worship."

(b) **Compelling interest, and no less restrictive means of regulating.** We will take up the notion of a compelling state interest in section B-2-c below. What justification did South Carolina offer for denying benefits to sabbatarians? How could a state prove that the danger of malingering was substantial? How much malingering would suffice to outweigh a sincere claim of exemption?

2. **Formal Neutrality.** Justice Harlan claims that the decision to give Sherbert "special treatment on account of religion" is inconsistent with (or at least not compelled by) the principle of neutrality that should govern Religion Clause cases. In his view, the government does not violate the First Amendment if it treats religion like other personal reasons (child care, indolence) for declining work. The government can steer a safe course if it simply avoids religious classifications. This is like the theory that the government should be "color blind" with respect to race. Douglas Laycock calls it "formal neutrality" to emphasize this point; it looks at statutory drafting, not at a law's effects on religious behavior. Formal, Substantive, and Disaggregated Neutrality Toward

Religion, 39 DePaul L. Rev. 993 (1990). It is the chief competitor to the theory that free exercise requires some kind of accommodation. The strongest version appears in Philip Kurland's article, which Justice Harlan cites. Kurland maintains that legislatures no less than courts are bound by formal neutrality; religious exemptions are forbidden. (Harlan says they are permitted, but not required.) For a position similar to Kurland's, see Mark V. Tushnet, "Of Church and State and the Supreme Court": Kurland Revisited, 1989 Sup. Ct. Rev. 373.

(a) **Formal neutrality in general.**   Formal neutrality is a more anemic version of free exercise than is *Sherbert*'s strict scrutiny test. What does it protect us against? Would it save Jonas Phillips in Stansbury v. Marks? Would it apply in *Cantwell* ? What about *Permoli*, where the ordinance forbade exposing corpses "in any of the Catholic churches of this municipality"? What about the territorial law in Davis v. Beason, which spoke about "celestial marriage"?

A rule of formal neutrality would afford pretty good protection against persecution or overt discrimination against religious minorities. It would, however, allow a state to forbid all consumption of alcoholic beverages, even at Catholic masses and Jewish seders. What is the attraction of this kind of rule? Kurland says that exemptions are subsidies. 29 U. Chi. L. Rev. at 46. If so, they may give us more religion than a free market would support. Was this the effect of South Carolina's payment to Sherbert? Which would have the greater impact on the practice of Catholicism—a strict regime of prohibition or an exemption allowing wine at mass?

Is the formal neutrality rule justified because allowing courts to grant exemptions poses a danger of unfairness? *Sherbert* requires courts to investigate the content of religious belief, because only "religious" claims qualify for exemption. This "places an official imprimatur on certain types of belief systems to the exclusion of others." William Marshall, In Defense of *Smith* and Free Exercise Revisionism, 58 U. Chi. L. Rev. 309, 310-311 (1991). Is there an Establishment Clause problem with allowing judges to decide what counts as religion? *Sherbert* also requires courts to investigate the sincerity of belief; otherwise the indolent could get Saturdays off by feigning a religious objection. Will courts making these inquiries see more familiar claimants as more sympathetic? Reviewing the cases after *Sherbert*, Mark Tushnet observed that the results were "troubling because, put bluntly, the pattern is that sometimes Christians win but non-Christians never do." 1989 Sup. Ct. Rev. at 381. Is this true? Formal neutrality forces us to trade some degree of religious liberty for interdenominational fairness. Is this the best solution?

(b) **Can *Sherbert* be defended on grounds of formal neutrality or equality?**   So far, we have assumed that *Sherbert*'s result is in tension with the idea of formal neutrality or equality between religion and other activities—that instead *Sherbert* promotes some other ideal, such as accommodation of religiously motivated choices. But perhaps *Sherbert* is consistent even with formal neutrality.

First, was the law in *Sherbert* indeed formally neutral? Title 68 of the South Carolina Code made no mention of religion. But as Justice Brennan noted, Title 64 saved Sunday worshippers from Sherbert's predicament when plants were open on that day. (One might add that general Sunday-closing laws, still widespread in 1963, likely meant that Sunday worshippers seldom faced the problem in the first place.) Note that this argument necessitates looking at the entire corpus of state law. Is that how we should judge "neutrality"?

Second, Justice Stevens, who advocates a "facial neutrality" interpretation of the Free Exercise Clause, defends the *Sherbert* rule on a different equality-based ground:

> The State . . . provides unemployment benefits to those persons who become "unemployed through no fault of their own," . . . but singles out the religiously-motivated choice that subjected [this applicant] to dismissal as her fault and indeed as "misconduct connected with . . . work." The State thus regards her "religious claims less favorably than other claims." In such an instance, granting unemployment benefits is necessary to protect religious observers against unequal treatment.

Hobbie v. Unemployment Appeals Commission, 480 U.S. 136, 146-147 (1987) (Stevens, J., concurring).

Similarly, Professors Eisgruber and Sager have argued that *Sherbert* reflects not a principle of autonomy or special accommodation for religious conscience, but rather a principle of "equal regard": the state must "treat the deep, religiously inspired concerns of minority religious believers with the same regard as that enjoyed by the deep concerns of citizens generally." Christopher L. Eisgruber and Lawrence G. Sager, The Vulnerability of Conscience: The Constitutional Basis for Protecting Religious Conduct, 61 U. Chi. L. Rev. 1245, 1285 (1994). Persons such as Mrs. Sherbert

> fit the general profile of persons who would be approved for benefits[:] they were generally available for work, they had powerful reasons to decline particular jobs, and the range of employment opportunities they had to decline was comparatively narrow. Under these circumstances, . . . it seems perfectly appropriate to worry that ad hoc administrative refusals to treat such religiously motivated applicants as entitled to unemployment benefits represent a failure of equal regard. It also seems appropriate to protect against such failures by applying the compelling state interest test.

Id. at 1287.

Is it true that, as Justice Stevens claims, the unemployment rules that were used against Mrs. Sherbert "single[d] out" religiously motivated choices? In fact, the state seems to provide unemployment benefits notwithstanding some "personal" reasons for refusing available work (if the work is not in the worker's profession, if it is too far away, if the pay is not up to the worker's past standards, etc.). Unemployed physicists are not required to take "available" work as grocery store baggers. But the state refuses to provide benefits for unemployment attributable to other "personal reasons" (ideological objection to the work, the need to care for a child or elderly dependent, etc.). Should religious reasons be classified along with the "good reasons" or with the bad? If the standard is neutrality, what is the benchmark or baseline for neutrality? Eisgruber and Sager suggest comparing the treatment of religious reasons with that of "deep" or "powerful" secular reasons. Is that a satisfactory standard? An administrable one?

Compare *Sherbert* with Wimberly v. Labor and Industrial Relations Commission, 479 U.S. 511 (1987). In *Wimberly*, the Court unanimously rejected a claim for unemployment compensation by a worker who left her job on account of pregnancy. The federal Unemployment Tax Act provides that "no person shall be denied compensation under . . . State law solely on the basis of pregnancy or termination of pregnancy." 26 U.S.C. § 3304(a)(12). The Court held that "Congress intended only to prohibit States from singling out pregnancy for unfavorable treatment." 479 U.S. at 516. Since under the state law in question, "*all* persons who leave work for reasons not causally connected to the work or the employer are disqualified from receiving benefits," the Court held that "pregnancy was not the 'sole basis' for the decision" to deny her unemployment benefits." *Id.* at 517. The Court did not cite or distinguish the *Sherbert* line of cases. Are they reconcilable?

The Court in *Wimberly* relied on legislative history to support its conclusion, and the claimant made no constitutional argument. Could Wimberly have made a constitutional argument, based on the right to privacy in matters of procreation? Consider the following argument: Denial of benefits "burdens" the right in both cases, but the outcome should be different because the Free Exercise Clause "singles out" religion and protects it from the inhibiting effect of government action, while the privacy right is satisfied when the government policy makes no reference, overt or implicit, to procreational choice. Does this distinction make sense as a matter of constitutional theory? Does it matter that the free exercise of religion is an explicit constitutional right, while procreational freedom is considered to be implicit in this nation's traditions of autonomy and ordered liberty? Is there any other basis for distinction?

3. Does *Sherbert* Conflict with the Establishment Clause? Justice Stewart argues that the result in *Sherbert* is at odds with the way the Court, in 1963, interpreted the Establishment Clause. He refers to two doctrines: (1) a "no aid" principle sometimes traced to Everson v. Board of Education, 330 U.S. 1 (1947); and (2) a neutrality principle much like Professor Kurland's ("the government must blind itself to . . . differing religious beliefs"). Note that these are not the same. A law giving aid to all private schools is neutral in Kurland's sense, but insofar as it covered parochial schools it would violate the "no aid" principle

Let us suppose for the moment that there *is* a "no aid" principle—a subject we will take up in Part IV. Does it forbid payment of unemployment compensation? The money does not (so far as we know) go to Sherbert's church. The government does not pay her *for* her religious observance. Her sabbatarianism is, as it were, a kind of disability that renders certain job offers unsuitable, and leaves her among the ranks of the deserving unemployed. Should a "no aid" principle forbid aid of this kind? Why? Because such aid moves people to become Seventh-Day Adventists? Because it makes Sherbert a more faithful sabbatarian? Should it matter that in order to qualify a person has to give up more (a steady job) than she gets (22 weeks of benefits)?

Justice Harlan argued that accommodation was inconsistent with the principle of free exercise neutrality. Justice Stewart argued that it was forbidden by the principle of Establishment Clause neutrality. If Stewart was right, there is a real tension between the two clauses: Exemptions are both required and forbidden. See Suzanna Sherry, Lee v. Weisman: Paradox Redux, 1992 Sup. Ct. Rev. 123; John H. Garvey, Freedom and Equality in the Religion Clauses, 1981 Sup. Ct. Rev. 193. How did Stewart propose resolving this tension? There is an appealing symmetry about making neutrality the interpretive key to both clauses. Would they be consistent if we did? Would this offer more or less protection to religious liberty than Justice Stewart's solution?

The decision in *Sherbert* imposes a new drain on the South Carolina unemployment compensation fund. Suppose that the state, to reduce that expense, enacts a law requiring employers to give sabbatarians their sabbath off. (Adele Sherbert could then keep her job.) Employers might be indifferent to the change. They fund the unemployment system, and when an employer lays off an employee like Sherbert his contribution rate goes up. Thus, either solution—pay unemployment or give sabbath relief—costs him money. Sherbert would naturally prefer to keep her job. Could South Carolina take this approach? See Estate of Thornton v. Caldor, Inc. (p. 7). Why might it be more objectionable than *Sherbert?* Because coworkers bear some of the burden of accommodation? (They shift to cover for absent sabbatarians.) Does it matter, for Establishment Clause purposes, who bears the burden?

4. Later Unemployment Decisions.   After *Sherbert* the Court repeatedly reaffirmed its holding that workers discharged or unable to obtain replacement work on account of religious scruples are constitutionally entitled to unemployment compensation. Thomas v. Review Board, 450 U.S. 707 (1981); Hobbie v. Unemployment Appeals Commission, 480 U.S. 136 (1987); Frazee v. Illinois Dept. of Employment Security, 489 U.S. 829 (1989). As we will see, even after the Court substantially changed its interpretation of the Free Exercise Clause, the unemployment cases were reaffirmed, and they remain good law.

WISCONSIN v. YODER
406 U.S. 205 (1972)

Mr. Chief Justice BURGER delivered the opinion of the Court.

[Members of the Old Order Amish religion reject, on religious grounds, many aspects of the modern world. Three Amish families in rural Wisconsin refused to send their children, ages 14 and 15, to school and thereby violated the state's law requiring attendance at a public or private school until age 16. The Amish argued that the secondary school would be "an impermissible exposure of their children to a 'worldly' influence"—including an emphasis on intellectualism, competitiveness, success, and conformity with peers—"in conflict with their beliefs." Instead, the Amish believed that their children, once they had learned basic language and math skills in school through eighth grade, should in their crucial adolescent years focus on "acquir[ing] Amish attitudes favoring manual work and self-reliance and the specific skills needed to perform the adult role of an Amish farmer or housewife." The Amish parents were convicted of violating the law and were fined $5 apiece.]

I

. . . There is no doubt as to the power of a State, having a high responsibility for education of its citizens, to impose reasonable regulations for the control and duration of basic education. See, e.g., Pierce v. Society of Sisters (1925). Providing public schools ranks at the very apex of the function of a State. Yet even this paramount responsibility was, in *Pierce,* made to yield to the right of parents to provide an equivalent education in a privately operated system. . . . Thus, a State's interest in universal education, however highly we rank it, is not totally free from a balancing process when it impinges on fundamental rights and interests, such as those specifically protected by the Free Exercise Clause of the First Amendment, and the traditional interest of parents with respect to the religious upbringing of their children so long as they, in the words of *Pierce*, "prepare [them] for additional obligations."

It follows that in order for Wisconsin to compel school attendance beyond the eighth grade against a claim that such attendance interferes with the practice of a legitimate religious belief, it must appear either that the State does not deny the free exercise of religious belief by its requirement, or that there is a state interest of sufficient magnitude to override the interest claiming protection under the Free Exercise Clause. . . .

The essence of all that has been said and written on the subject is that only those interests of the highest order and those not otherwise served can overbalance legitimate claims to the free exercise of religion. We can accept it as settled, therefore, that, however strong the State's interest in universal compulsory education, it is by no means absolute to the exclusion or subordination of all other interests. E.g., Sherbert v. Verner.

II

We come then to the quality of the claims of the respondents concerning the alleged encroachment of Wisconsin's compulsory school-attendance statute on their rights and the rights of their children to the free exercise of the religious beliefs they and their forbears have adhered to for almost three centuries. . . . A way of life, however virtuous and admirable, may not be interposed as a barrier to reasonable state regulation of education if it is based on purely secular considerations; to have the protection of the Religion Clauses, the claims must be rooted in religious belief. Although a determination of what is a "religious" belief or practice entitled to constitutional protection may present a most delicate question, the very concept of ordered liberty precludes allowing every person to make his own standards on matters of conduct in which society as a whole has important interests. Thus, if the Amish asserted their claims because of their subjective evaluation and rejection of the contemporary secular values accepted by the majority, much as Thoreau rejected the social values of his time and isolated himself at Walden Pond, their claims would not rest on a religious basis. Thoreau's choice was philosophical and personal rather than religious, and such belief does not rise to the demands of the Religion Clauses.

III

. . . Wisconsin concedes that under the Religion Clauses religious beliefs are absolutely free from the State's control, but it argues that "actions," even though religiously grounded, are outside the protection of the First Amendment. But our decisions have rejected the idea that religiously grounded conduct is always outside the protection of the Free Exercise Clause. It is true that activities of individuals, even when religiously based, are often subject to regulation by the States in the exercise of their undoubted power to promote the health, safety, and general welfare, or the Federal Government in the exercise of its delegated powers. But to agree that religiously grounded conduct must often be subject to the broad police power of the State is not to deny that there are areas of conduct protected by the Free Exercise Clause of the First Amendment and thus beyond the power of the State to control, even under regulations of general applicability. This case, therefore, does not become easier because respondents were convicted for their "actions" in refusing to send their children to the public high school; in this context belief and action cannot be neatly confined in logic-tight compartments.

Nor can this case be disposed of on the grounds that Wisconsin's requirement for school attendance to age 16 applies uniformly to all citizens of the State and does not, on its face, discriminate against religions or a particular religion, or that it is motivated by legitimate secular concerns. A regulation neutral on its face may, in its application, nonetheless offend the constitutional requirement for governmental neutrality if it unduly burdens the free exercise of religion. *Sherbert.* The Court must not ignore the danger that an exception from a general obligation of citizenship on religious grounds may run afoul of the Establishment Clause, but that danger cannot be allowed to prevent any exception no matter how vital it may be to the protection of values promoted by the right of free exercise. . . .

We turn, then, to the State's broader contention that its interest in its system of compulsory education is so compelling that even the established religious practices of the Amish must give way. Where fundamental claims of religious freedom are at stake, however, we cannot accept such a sweeping claim; despite its admitted validity in the generality of cases, we must searchingly examine the interests that the State seeks to promote by its requirement for compulsory education to age 16, and the impediment to those objectives that would flow from recognizing the claimed Amish exemption.

[The Court rejected the claim that forcing Amish teenagers to attend school was necessary to prepare them "to be self-reliant and self-sufficient participants in society:] Whatever their idiosyncracies as seen by the majority, this record shows that the Amish community has been a highly successful social unit within our society, even if apart from the conventional" mainstream." Its members are productive and very law-abiding members of society; they reject public welfare in any of its usual forms. . . .

There is nothing in this record to suggest that the Amish qualities of reliability, self-reliance, and dedication to work would fail to find ready markets in today's society. Absent some contrary evidence supporting the State's position, we are unwilling to assume that persons possessing such valuable vocational skills and habits are doomed to become burdens on society should they determine to leave the Amish faith, nor is there any basis in the record to warrant a finding that an additional one or two years of formal school education beyond the eighth grade would serve to eliminate any such problem that might exist.

Insofar as the State's claim rests on the view that a brief additional period of formal education is imperative to enable the Amish to participate effectively and intelligently in our democratic process, it must fail. The Amish alternative to formal secondary education has enabled them to function effectively in their day-to-day life under self-imposed limitations on relations with the world, and to survive and prosper in contemporary society as a separate, sharply identifiable and highly self-sufficient community for more than 200 years in this country. . . . Indeed, the Amish communities singularly parallel and reflect many of the virtues of Jefferson's ideal of the "sturdy yeoman" who would form the basis of what he considered as the ideal of a democratic society. . . .

V

. . . [T]he Amish in this case have . . . demonstrate[d] the adequacy of their alternative mode of continuing informal vocational education in terms of precisely those overall interests that the State advances in support of its program of compulsory high school education. In light of this convincing showing, one that probably few other religious groups or sects could make, and weighing the minimal difference between what the State would require and what the Amish already accept, it was incumbent on the State to show with more particularity how its admittedly strong interest in compulsory education would be adversely affected by granting an exemption to the Amish.

NOTES AND QUESTIONS

1. The Free Exercise Exemption in *Yoder*. *Yoder* stands for the proposition that the Free Exercise Clause bars enforcement even of laws that are "neutral on their face," if they conflict with religious exercise and fail to serve a sufficiently important governmental interest. Note that, unlike *Sherbert*, the law at issue was truly generally applicable, in the sense that it did not brook exceptions. The full merits of the *Yoder* decision are interesting and controversial, and will be considered below in Part V-A (p. 580). For present purposes, it is important as the Court's clearest statement of the view that some accommodations are mandatory under the Free Exercise Clause.

But what does it mean to say that "some" accommodations are mandatory? Do you think *Yoder* suggests that accommodations for religious conduct must be granted readily, or only sparingly?

2. Improperly Evaluating a Religion? *Yoder* focused quite a bit on the disciplined and self-reliant nature of the Amish. Is such a focus inappropriate, because it puts judges in the place of deciding which religions are socially productive and which are not? Or is it perfectly appropriate (and indeed necessary) for the *Sherbert* exemptions analysis, in order to determine whether regulating the religious conduct is essential to a compelling state interest?

3. Free Exercise Exemptions and "Higher Duties." Suppose that the idea of legal exemptions for religiously motivated conduct depends on the proposition stated in Madison's Memorial and Remonstrance—that duties to God are "precedent, both in order of time and in degree of obligation, to the claims of civil society." (See p. 49.) Is this proposition too dangerous to be acceptable—a recipe for violence and other impositions on other persons in the name of religion? Does the role that religious fervor apparently played in motivating the terrorist attacks of September 11, 2001 simply dramatize the danger? Or are these objections answered fully by the principle that religiously motivated conduct may be prohibited in order to protect a compelling governmental interest?

4. Free Exercise Exemptions After *Yoder*. *Yoder* turned out to be the high-water mark for mandatory free exercise exemptions. As noted above (p. 133), the Court continued to rule that unemployment benefits must be provided to religiously conscientious claimants in circumstances similar to *Sherbert*. Otherwise, however, the Court never again ordered a free exercise exemption.

Several decisions held that the "compelling interest" standard of *Sherbert* and *Yoder* was not triggered, either because the government action did not significantly "burden" religion or because it took place in a context in which government should have broad discretion to act. See, e.g., Lyng v. Northwest Indian

Cemetery Protective Assn., 485 U.S. 439 (1988) (no burden from government's construction of road that disturbed Native Americans' pilgrimage to sacred sites); Jimmy Swaggart Ministries v. Bd. of Equalization, 493 U.S. 378 (1990) (no burden from applying sales tax to sale of Bibles and religious literature); Goldman v. Weinberger, 475 U.S. 534 (1986) (under highly deferential judicial review, no free exercise exemption for religiously conscientious military personnel from general military regulation limiting the wearing of headgear); O'Lone v. Estate of Shabazz, 482 U.S. 342 (1987) (prisoners' free exercise challenges to prison regulations also evaluated under highly deferential "rational basis" standard). Other decisions held that even under the compelling interest standard or something like it, the government's restriction on free exercise was justified. United States v. Lee, 455 U.S. 252 (1982) (requirement of paying social security taxes could be applied to Amish employers despite their conscientious objection, because of overriding interest in preserving social security system); Bob Jones University v. United States, 461 U.S. 574 (1983) (government could remove tax exemption from racially discriminatory private college, even though the discrimination was based on religious doctrine, because of the compelling interest in preventing government support for racial discrimination in education). We will consider several of these decisions in later sections of Part III.

5. The Demise of Exemptions

The "compelling interest" standard of *Sherbert* looked highly protective (from the individual's point of view), or highly intrusive (from the government's point of view), but in fact free exercise claimants rarely prevailed in court. Perhaps the greatest practical significance of the doctrine lay in the argument it afforded religious people in legislatures or in front of administrative bodies. Other than *Yoder* and cases involving unemployment compensation, parties asserting a claim for free exercise exemptions in the Supreme Court always lost. The Court always ruled either that they had shown no burden on their exercise of religion or that the governmental interest was compelling. At the same time, some Justices (including Stevens and Rehnquist) wrote separate opinions worrying about the fact that the *Sherbert-Yoder* interpretation forced the government to evaluate the strength and sincerity of religious claims, that it created the potential for unfairly giving religious claimants an advantage, and that it empowered the courts to second-guess legislatures through an essentially subjective balancing test. In 1990, the Court made it official: Free exercise exemptions are no longer required—at least usually not.

EMPLOYMENT DIVISION v. SMITH
494 U.S. 872 (1990)

Justice SCALIA delivered the opinion of the Court.

[Oregon law prohibits the possession of a "controlled substance" unless it is prescribed by a doctor. Violation is a Class B felony. Peyote, a hallucinogenic drug, is classified as a controlled substance. Respondents Alfred Smith and

Galen Black were fired from their jobs with a private drug rehabilitation organization because they ingested peyote for sacramental purposes at a ceremony of the Native American Church. The Employment Division denied their request for unemployment compensation because they had been discharged for work-related "misconduct." Smith and Black sued in state court, claiming that the denial of benefits violated their free exercise rights under the First Amendment. The Oregon Supreme Court ruled in their favor.]

II

. . . The Free Exercise Clause of the First Amendment, which has been made applicable to the States by incorporation into the Fourteenth Amendment, provides that "Congress shall make no law respecting an establishment of religion, or prohibiting the free exercise thereof. . . ." The free exercise of religion means, first and foremost, the right to believe and profess whatever religious doctrine one desires. Thus, the First Amendment obviously excludes all "governmental regulation of religious *beliefs* as such." The government may not compel affirmation of religious belief, punish the expression of religious doctrines it believes to be false, impose special disabilities on the basis of religious views or religious status, or lend its power to one or the other side in controversies over religious authority or dogma.

But the "exercise of religion" often involves not only belief and profession but the performance of (or abstention from) physical acts: assembling with others for a worship service, participating in sacramental use of bread and wine, proselytizing, abstaining from certain foods or certain modes of transportation. It would be true, we think (though no case of ours has involved the point), that a State would be "prohibiting the free exercise [of religion]" if it sought to ban such acts or abstentions only when they are engaged in for religious reasons, or only because of the religious belief that they display. It would doubtless be unconstitutional, for example, to ban the casting of "statues that are to be used for worship purposes," or to prohibit bowing down before a golden calf.

Respondents in the present case, however, seek to carry the meaning of "prohibiting the free exercise [of religion]" one large step further. They contend that their religious motivation for using peyote places them beyond the reach of a criminal law that is not specifically directed at their religious practice, and that is concededly constitutional as applied to those who use the drug for other reasons. They assert, in other words, that "prohibiting the free exercise [of religion]" includes requiring any individual to observe a generally applicable law that requires (or forbids) the performance of an act that his religious belief forbids (or requires). As a textual matter, we do not think the words must be given that meaning. It is no more necessary to regard the collection of a general tax, for example, as "prohibiting the free exercise [of religion]" by those citizens who believe support of organized government to be sinful, than it is to regard the same tax as "abridging the freedom . . . of the press" of those publishing companies that must pay the tax as a condition of staying in business. It is a permissible reading of the text, in the one case as in the other, to say that if prohibiting the exercise of religion (or burdening the activity of printing) is not the object of the tax but merely the incidental effect of a generally applicable and otherwise valid provision, the First Amendment has not been offended.

Our decisions reveal that the latter reading is the correct one. We have never held that an individual's religious beliefs excuse him from compliance with an otherwise valid law prohibiting conduct that the State is free to regulate. On the contrary, the record of more than a century of our free exercise jurisprudence contradicts that proposition. As described succinctly by Justice Frankfurter in Minersville School Dist. v. Gobitis (1940): "Conscientious scruples have not, in the course of the long struggle for religious toleration, relieved the individual from obedience to a general law not aimed at the promotion or restriction of religious beliefs." [I]n Reynolds v. United States, . . . we rejected the claim that criminal laws against polygamy could not be constitutionally applied to those whose religion commanded the practice. "Laws," we said, "are made for the government of actions, and while they cannot interfere with mere religious belief and opinions, they may with practices. . . . Can a man excuse his practices to the contrary because of his religious belief? To permit this would be to make the professed doctrines of religious belief superior to the law of the land, and in effect to permit every citizen to become a law unto himself."

Subsequent decisions have consistently held that the right of free exercise does not relieve an individual of the obligation to comply with a "valid and neutral law of general applicability on the ground that the law proscribes (or prescribes) conduct that his religion prescribes (or proscribes)." . . .

The only decisions in which we have held that the First Amendment bars application of a neutral, generally applicable law to religiously motivated action have involved not the Free Exercise Clause alone, but the Free Exercise Clause in conjunction with other constitutional protections, such as freedom of speech and of the press, see[, e.g.,] Cantwell v. Connecticut; or the right of parents to direct the education of their children, see Wisconsin v. Yoder. . . .

The present case does not present such a hybrid situation, but a free exercise claim unconnected with any communicative activity or parental right. Respondents urge us to hold, quite simply, that when otherwise prohibitable conduct is accompanied by religious convictions, not only the convictions but the conduct itself must be free from governmental regulation. We have never held that, and decline to do so now. There being no contention that Oregon's drug law represents an attempt to regulate religious beliefs, the communication of religious beliefs, or the raising of one's children in those beliefs, the rule to which we have adhered ever since *Reynolds* plainly controls. . . .

Respondents argue that even though exemption from generally applicable criminal laws need not automatically be extended to religiously motivated actors, at least the claim for a religious exemption must be evaluated under the balancing test set forth in Sherbert v. Verner. Under the *Sherbert* test, governmental actions that substantially burden a religious practice must be justified by a compelling governmental interest. Applying that test we have, on three occasions, invalidated state unemployment compensation rules that conditioned the availability of benefits upon an applicant's willingness to work under conditions forbidden by his religion. See *Sherbert*; Thomas v. Review Bd. (1981); Hobbie v. Unemployment Appeals Comm'n (1987). We have never invalidated any governmental action on the basis of the *Sherbert* test except the denial of unemployment compensation. Although we have sometimes purported to apply the *Sherbert* test in contexts other than that, we have always found the test satisfied.

The *Sherbert* test, it must be recalled, was developed in a context that lent itself to individualized governmental assessment of the reasons for the relevant conduct. [A] distinctive feature of unemployment compensation programs is that their eligibility criteria invite consideration of the particular circumstances behind an applicant's unemployment: "The . . . 'good cause' standard [for refusing available work, set out in the unemployment statutes in *Sherbert*,] created a mechanism for individualized exemptions." Bowen v. Roy (1986). [O]ur decisions in the unemployment cases stand for the proposition that where the State has in place a system of individual exemptions, it may not refuse to extend that system to cases of "religious hardship" without compelling reason.

Whether or not the decisions are that limited, they at least have nothing to do with an across-the-board criminal prohibition on a particular form of conduct. Although, as noted earlier, we have sometimes used the *Sherbert* test to analyze free exercise challenges to such laws, we have never applied the test to invalidate one. We conclude today that the sounder approach, and the approach in accord with the vast majority of our precedents, is to hold the test inapplicable to such challenges. The government's ability to enforce generally applicable prohibitions of socially harmful conduct, like its ability to carry out other aspects of public policy, "cannot depend on measuring the effects of a governmental action on a religious objector's spiritual development." To make an individual's obligation to obey such a law contingent upon the law's coincidence with his religious beliefs, except where the State's interest is "compelling"—permitting him, by virtue of his beliefs, "to become a law unto himself," Reynolds v. United States—contradicts both constitutional tradition and common sense.

The "compelling government interest" requirement seems benign, because it is familiar from other fields. But using it as the standard that must be met before the government may accord different treatment on the basis of race, or before the government may regulate the content of speech, is not remotely comparable to using it for the purpose asserted here. What it produces in those other fields—equality of treatment and an unrestricted flow of contending speech—are constitutional norms; what it would produce here—a private right to ignore generally applicable laws—is a constitutional anomaly.[3]

Nor is it possible to limit the impact of respondents' proposal by requiring a "compelling state interest" only when the conduct prohibited is "central" to the individual's religion. It is no more appropriate for judges to determine the "centrality" of religious beliefs before applying a "compelling interest" test in the free exercise field, than it would be for them to determine the "importance" of ideas before applying the "compelling interest" test in the free speech field. What principle of law or logic can be brought to bear to contradict a believer's assertion that a particular act is "central" to his personal faith? Judging the

---

3. [W]e have held that race-neutral laws that have the effect of disproportionately disadvantaging a particular racial group do not thereby become subject to compelling-interest analysis under the Equal Protection Clause, see Washington v. Davis (1976); and we have held that generally applicable laws unconcerned with regulating speech that have the effect of interfering with speech do not thereby become subject to compelling-interest analysis under the First Amendment, see Citizen Publishing Co. v. United States (1969) (antitrust laws). Our conclusion that generally applicable, religion-neutral laws that have the effect of burdening a particular religious practice need not be justified by a compelling governmental interest is the only approach compatible with these precedents.

centrality of different religious practices is akin to the unacceptable "business of evaluating the relative merits of differing religious claims." . . .

If the "compelling interest" test is to be applied at all, then, it must be applied across the board, to all actions thought to be religiously commanded. Moreover, if "compelling interest" really means what it says (and watering it down here would subvert its rigor in the other fields where it is applied), many laws will not meet the test. Any society adopting such a system would be courting anarchy, but that danger increases in direct proportion to the society's diversity of religious beliefs, and its determination to coerce or suppress none of them. Precisely because "we are a cosmopolitan nation made up of people of almost every conceivable religious preference," Braunfeld v. Brown (1961), and precisely because we value and protect that religious divergence, we cannot afford the luxury of deeming presumptively invalid, as applied to the religious objector, every regulation of conduct that does not protect an interest of the highest order. The rule respondents favor would open the prospect of constitutionally required religious exemptions from civic obligations of almost every conceivable kind—ranging from compulsory military service, to the payment of taxes, to health and safety regulation such as manslaughter and child neglect laws, compulsory vaccination laws, drug laws, and traffic laws; to social welfare legislation such as minimum wage laws, child labor laws, animal cruelty laws, and laws providing for equality of opportunity for the races. The First Amendment's protection of religious liberty does not require this.[5]

Values that are protected against government interference through enshrinement in the Bill of Rights are not thereby banished from the political process. Just as a society that believes in the negative protection accorded to the press by the First Amendment is likely to enact laws that affirmatively foster the dissemination of the printed word, so also a society that believes in the negative protection accorded to religious belief can be expected to be solicitous of that value in its legislation as well. It is therefore not surprising that a number of States have made an exception to their drug laws for sacramental peyote use. But to say that a nondiscriminatory religious-practice exemption is permitted, or even that it is desirable, is not to say that it is constitutionally required, and that the appropriate occasions for its creation can be discerned by the courts. It may fairly be said that leaving accommodation to the political process will place at a relative disadvantage those religious practices that are not widely engaged in; but that unavoidable consequence of democratic government must be preferred to a system in which each conscience is a law unto itself or in which judges weigh the social importance of all laws against the centrality of all religious beliefs. . . .

5. Justice O'Connor contends that the "parade of horribles" in the text only "demonstrates . . . that courts have been quite capable of . . . strik[ing] sensible balances between religious liberty and competing state interests." But the cases we cite have struck "sensible balances" only because they have all applied the general laws, despite the claims for religious exemption. In any event, Justice O'Connor mistakes the purpose of our parade: it is not to suggest that courts would necessarily permit harmful exemptions from these laws (though they might), but to suggest that courts would constantly be in the business of determining whether the "severe impact" of various laws on religious practice . . . suffices to permit us to confer an exemption. It is a parade of horribles because it is horrible to contemplate that federal judges will regularly balance against the importance of general laws the significance of religious practice.

Because respondents' ingestion of peyote was prohibited under Oregon law, and because that prohibition is constitutional, Oregon may, consistent with the Free Exercise Clause, deny respondents unemployment compensation when their dismissal results from use of the drug. The decision of the Oregon Supreme Court is accordingly reversed.

Justice O'CONNOR, with whom Justice BRENNAN, Justice MARSHALL, and Justice BLACKMUN join as to [this excerpt] concurring in the judgment.

Although I agree with the result the Court reaches in this case, I cannot join its opinion. In my view, today's holding dramatically departs from well-settled First Amendment jurisprudence, appears unnecessary to resolve the question presented, and is incompatible with our Nation's fundamental commitment to individual religious liberty. . . .

As the Court recognizes, . . . the "free *exercise*" of religion often, if not invariably, requires the performance of (or abstention from) certain acts. . . . Because the First Amendment does not distinguish between religious belief and religious conduct, conduct motivated by sincere religious belief, like the belief itself, must be at least presumptively protected by the Free Exercise Clause.

The Court today, however, interprets the Clause to permit the government to prohibit, without justification, conduct mandated by an individual's religious beliefs, so long as that prohibition is generally applicable. But a law that prohibits certain conduct—conduct that happens to be an act of worship for someone—manifestly does prohibit that person's free exercise of his religion. A person who is barred from engaging in religiously motivated conduct is barred from freely exercising his religion. Moreover, that person is barred from freely exercising his religion regardless of whether the law prohibits the conduct only when engaged in for religious reasons, only by members of that religion, or by all persons. It is difficult to deny that a law that prohibits religiously motivated conduct, even if the law is generally applicable, does not at least implicate First Amendment concerns.

The Court responds that generally applicable laws are "one large step" removed from laws aimed at specific religious practices. The First Amendment, however, does not distinguish between laws that are generally applicable and laws that target particular religious practices. Indeed, few States would be so naive as to enact a law directly prohibiting or burdening a religious practice as such. Our free exercise cases have all concerned generally applicable laws that had the effect of significantly burdening a religious practice. . . .

To say that a person's right to free exercise has been burdened, of course, does not mean that he has an absolute right to engage in the conduct. Under our established First Amendment jurisprudence, we have recognized that the freedom to act, unlike the freedom to believe, cannot be absolute. Instead, we have respected both the First Amendment's express textual mandate and the governmental interest in regulation of conduct by requiring the government to justify any substantial burden on religiously motivated conduct by a compelling state interest and by means narrowly tailored to achieve that interest. . . .

Although the Court suggests that the compelling interest test, as applied to generally applicable laws, would result in a "constitutional anomaly," the First Amendment unequivocally makes freedom of religion, like freedom from race discrimination and freedom of speech, a "constitutional nor[m]," not an "anomaly." . . . As the language of the Clause itself makes clear, an individual's free exercise of religion is a preferred constitutional activity. A law that makes criminal such an activity therefore triggers constitutional concern—and heightened judicial scrutiny—even if it does not target the particular religious conduct at issue. . . . The Court's parade of horribles not only fails as a reason for discarding the compelling interest test, it instead demonstrates just the opposite: that courts have been quite capable of applying our free exercise jurisprudence to strike sensible balances between religious liberty and competing state interests.

Finally, the Court today suggests that the disfavoring of minority religions is an "unavoidable consequence" under our system of government and that accommodation of such religions must be left to the political process. In my view, however, the First Amendment was enacted precisely to protect the rights of those whose religious practices are not shared by the majority and may be viewed with hostility. The history of our free exercise doctrine amply demonstrates the harsh impact majoritarian rule has had on unpopular or emerging religious groups such as the Jehovah's Witnesses and the Amish. Indeed, the words of Justice Jackson in Board of Education v. Barnette (1943) (overruling *Gobitis* [on which the majority relies]) are apt:

> The very purpose of a Bill of Rights was to withdraw certain subjects from the vicissitudes of political controversy, to place them beyond the reach of majorities and officials and to establish them as legal principles to be applied by the courts. One's right to life, liberty, and property, to free speech, a free press, freedom of worship and assembly, and other fundamental rights may not be submitted to vote; they depend on the outcome of no elections.

The compelling interest test reflects the First Amendment's mandate of preserving religious liberty to the fullest extent possible in a pluralistic society. For the Court to deem this command a "luxury" is to denigrate "[t]he very purpose of a Bill of Rights."

[Justice O'Connor concluded, however, that Oregon did have a compelling interest in regulating peyote use by its citizens, and that it could not grant exemptions without undermining the program. The remaining three justices dissented, concluding that there was no compelling interest in prohibiting peyote use in Native American worship.]

NOTES AND QUESTIONS

1. The Facts in *Smith*. The Court's broad holding in *Smith* means that the decision has little relation to the specific facts of the case. But there is an interesting story behind the *Smith* case, which is told in Garrett Epps, To an Unknown God: Religious Freedom on Trial (2001).

2. *Smith* and Precedent. Apart from whether *Smith*'s holding is justified, what do you think of the Court's treatment of the chief precedents on the other side, *Sherbert* and *Yoder*? How did the Court distinguish those decisions? Are the distinctions convincing? Do they create significant loopholes in *Smith*'s general rule that exemptions are not mandated?

The majority also employed language from Minersville School Dist. v. Gobitis, 310 U.S. 596 (1940), which held that public schools did not have to excuse Jehovah's Witness schoolchildren from a daily ceremony of saluting the flag and reciting the Pledge of Allegiance (to which the children and their families objected on religious grounds). But as Justice O'Connor's opinion indicates, *Gobitis* was overruled just three years later in Board of Education v. Barnette, 319 U.S. 624 (1943), on the ground that the schoolchildren could not be coerced to express a majority view of patriotism with which they disagreed. (*Barnette* is discussed fully in Part V-A (p. 479).) *Gobitis* came widely to be viewed as one of the Court's great constitutional mistakes, and *Barnette* as one of its great successes. Thus, "[r]elying on *Gobitis* without mentioning *Barnette* is like relying on *Plessy v. Ferguson* without mentioning *Brown v. Board of Education.*" Michael W. McConnell, Free Exercise Revisionism and the *Smith* Decision, 57 U. Chi. L. Rev. 1109, 1124 (1990).

3. Values Underlying the *Smith* Holding.   Earlier we discussed three concerns that lie behind the Religion Clauses: noncoercion, neutrality, and separation. In *Smith*, the conflict is between noncoercion and a certain version of neutrality (formal neutrality). If you do not recall what these terms mean, review pp. 4-7, 28-29, 129-130 above. How did the Court choose between these purposes? Was it on the basis of the constitutional text? The historical understanding? The Court's judgment regarding how to achieve the purposes of the First Amendment? Does the *Smith* rule contravene some other concept of neutrality besides formal neutrality?

Does the concept of church-state separation play any part in this controversy? If so, which way does it cut? Does it separate church and state to exempt ceremonies of the Native American Church from the surveillance and interference entailed by enforcement of the criminal law? Or would accommodation entangle the government with religion by forcing the authorities to distinguish between sincerely motivated religious uses of peyote and recreational drug use?

4. Judicial Restraint: Deference to Political Officials.   The *Smith* decision can be understood as introducing a fourth concern: the concern that democratically accountable officials should be given latitude to make practical accommodations between religious interests and governmental interests. This concern we will call "judicial restraint." Note that the Court did not *require* the State of Oregon to exempt the sacramental use of peyote from its drug laws; nor did it suggest that an exemption for religious uses only would violate the Establishment Clause. Rather, the Court stated that a religious accommodation would be "desirable" in the discretion of the legislature. This adopts neither the position of pure "formal neutrality" (treating religion just the same as any other activity), nor the position of pure "substantive neutrality" (taking account of religion in order to minimize negative or positive effects on it). *Smith* suggests that "formal neutrality" is the constitutional minimum (i.e., any law that targets religion for unfavorable treatment is subject to strict scrutiny), but that legislatures may adopt a policy of "substantive neutrality" (i.e., exempting religion in order to avoid negative effects on it).

Why might that be desirable (or not)? Is a robust policy of substantive neutrality judicially manageable? Are courts more responsive to minority religious concerns than legislatures? What is the basis for choosing between decision-making institutions? Cf., e.g., Marci A. Hamilton, Religious Institutions, the

No-Harm Doctrine, and the Public Good, 2004 B.Y.U. L. Rev. 1099, 1215 ("The courts do not have the tools or the resources to investigate the larger public good and therefore are in no position to determine whether an exemption should be carved out of a particular law. The exemption decision properly belongs to the body entrusted with ensuring the public good—the legislature—which is situated through its many contacts with the people and its access to wide-ranging, independent investigation to determine how particular religious practices will impact and therefore potentially harm citizens."); with Brief Amicus Curiae of the Baptist Joint Committee *et al.*, in Gonzales v. O Centro Espirita Beneficente Uniao do Vegetal, 126 S. Ct. 1211 (2006) (see p. 202), at 11 ("Under [the pre-*Smith*] approach, a court need not question the general [f]indings underlying a given [l]aw," but can "merely ask whether the findings apply strongly to the circumstances of the religious claimant—a fact-based inquiry that falls well within judges' competence and experience.") (available at 2005 WL 2237539). Cf. Joanne C. Brant, Taking the Supreme Court at Its Word: The Implications for RFRA and Separation of Powers, 56 Mont. L. Rev. 5 (1995) (arguing that *Smith* is supported by concerns of institutional competence of judges); with Gregory P. Magarian, How to Apply the Religious Freedom Restoration Act to Federal Law Without Violating the Constitution, 99 Mich. L. Rev. 1903, 1945-1960 (2001) (rejecting the argument).

5. Judicial Restraint: Reducing Judges' Discretion. *Smith* also has the virtue of advancing another kind of "judicial restraint": It appears to reduce the degree of judicial discretion in this sensitive area. Under the *Sherbert-Yoder* "compelling interest" test, any government policy that substantially burdens the exercise of religion (potentially a very large category) is subjected to a balancing test, with the results seemingly dependent on the attitude and ideology of the particular judge. Under *Smith*, legislatures and lower courts have a more objective and predictable standard to apply: whether the law is formally neutral toward religion. But how objective and how predictable is that standard? Was the policy at issue in Stansbury v. Marks (p. 3) neutral and generally applicable? In *Sherbert*? How should courts handle cases of that sort? We return to the issues of "neutrality" and "general applicability" in section B-1.

6. The Application of *Smith* to Institutional Free Exercise Claims. *Smith* involved claims of religious exercise by individual adherents. But a common potential application of the decision is to claims by congregations and other religious institutions that they should enjoy some degree of constitutional autonomy from government regulation. For example, should a church be able to hire a minister, or a religious school a teacher or principal, without regard to the general law against sex discrimination in employment? We will consider such questions in detail in section D below. For now, can you think of any reason why an institution's free exercise claim should be treated any differently than an individual's—either under the language of *Smith*, or under general considerations about the government-religion relationships?

7. Commentary on *Smith*. Smith was one of the most heavily criticized constitutional decisions of recent times. See, e.g., Douglas Laycock, The Remnants of Free Exercise, 1990 Sup. Ct. Rev. 1; Michael W. McConnell, Free Exercise Revisionism and the Smith Decision, 57 U. Chi. L. Rev. 1109; Stephen L. Carter, The Resurrection of Religious Freedom?, 107 Harv. L. Rev. 118 (1993); David E. Steinberg, Rejecting the Case Against the Free Exercise Exemption: A Critical

Assessment, 75 B.U. L. Rev. 241 (1995). But it was not without its defenders. See, e.g., Gerard Bradley, Beguiled: Free Exercise Exemptions and the Siren Song of Liberalism, 20 Hofstra L. Rev. 245 (1991); Mark Tushnet, The Rhetoric of Free Exercise Discourse, 1993 B.Y.U. L. Rev. 117; Hamilton, 2004 B.Y.U. L. Rev. 1099 (defending *Smith* on both historical and "rule of law" grounds).

We will consider some further constitutional arguments for and against religious accommodations in section C-1 below. For now, consider this exchange between Professors William Marshall and Michael McConnell:

IN DEFENSE OF *SMITH* AND FREE EXERCISE REVISIONISM

William P. Marshall
58 U. Chi. L. Rev. 308 (1991)

In Employment Division v. Smith, the Supreme Court held that the Free Exercise Clause does not compel courts to grant exemptions from generally applicable criminal laws to individuals whose religious beliefs conflict with those laws. The *Smith* opinion itself . . . cannot be readily defended. The decision, as written, is neither persuasive nor well-crafted. It exhibits only a shallow understanding of free exercise jurisprudence and its use of precedent borders on fiction. The opinion is also a paradigmatic example of judicial overreaching. The holding extends beyond the facts of the case, the lower court's decision on the issue, and even the briefs of the parties. In fact, it appears that the Court framed the free exercise issue in virtually the broadest terms possible in order to allow it to reach its landmark result. My task is then to defend *Smith*'s rejection of constitutionally compelled free exercise exemptions without defending *Smith* itself. In so doing, I concentrate on the two critical theoretical concerns: (1) the cogency of exemption analysis; and (2) the role of equality in free exercise theory. Both concerns lead to a rejection of the free exercise exemption claim.

I. THE TROUBLE WITH EXEMPTIONS

A. THE INHERENT DIFFICULTIES

[A] particular analysis should be rejected when it undermines the constitutional values it purports to protect, is inherently arbitrary, forces courts to engage in a balancing process that systematically underestimates the state interest, and threatens other constitutional values. Such is the case with free exercise exemption analysis.

First, exemption analysis threatens free exercise values because it requires courts to consider the legitimacy of the religious claim of the party seeking the exemption. Under the exemption analysis, the court must first determine, at a definitional level, whether the belief at issue is "religious." Then it must determine whether the belief is sincerely held. [B]oth inquiries are not only awkward and counterproductive; they also threaten the values of religious freedom. Moreover, the judicial definition of religion does more than simply limit religion; it places an official imprimatur on certain types of belief systems to the exclusion of others. At the very least, as Justice Stevens has argued, this power of approval or disapproval raises Establishment Clause problems.

... Minority belief systems—not majority belief systems—will bear the brunt of the definition and the sincerity inquiries. A court is more likely to find against a claimant on definitional grounds when the religion is bizarre, relative to the cultural norm, and is more likely to find that a religious belief is insincere when the belief in question is, by cultural norms, incredulous. The religious claims most likely to be recognized, therefore, are those that closely parallel or directly relate to the culture's predominant religious traditions. To put it in concrete terms, Mrs. Sherbert's claim that she is forbidden to work on Saturdays is likely to be accepted as legitimate; Mr. Hodges's claim that he must dress like a chicken when going to court is not.

Second, the exemption analysis requires courts to engage in a highly problematic form of constitutional balancing. In other doctrinal areas, the Court balances the state interest in the regulation at issue against the interests of the regulated class taken as a whole. Exemption analysis, however, requires a court to weigh the state interest against the interest of the narrower class comprised only of those seeking exemption. This leads to both unpredictability in the process and potential inconsistency in result as each regulation may be subject to limitless challenges based upon the peculiar identity of the challenger.

Third, the exemption balancing process necessarily leads to underestimating the strength of the countervailing state interest. The state interest in a challenged regulation will seldom be seriously threatened if only a few persons seek exemption from it. A legitimate state interest is often "compelling" only in relation to cumulative concerns. If, for example, one factory is exempt from anti-pollution requirements, the state's interest in protecting air quality will not be seriously disturbed. When many factories pollute, on the other hand, the state interest is seriously threatened. Weighing the state interest against a narrow class seeking exemption is similar to asking whether this particular straw is the one that breaks the camel's back.

Finally, in some circumstances, free exercise exemption analysis may result in a troublesome interplay with the Speech Clause that threatens both speech and free exercise interests. Many activities that raise only speech concerns when undertaken by a secular group—literature distribution, for example—will raise both speech and free exercise concerns when undertaken by a religious group. The problem is that allowing only free exercise exemptions from governmental restrictions on those activities would mean that only religious groups could engage in the expressive activity. Such a result offends the central Speech Clause principle of content neutrality; it creates, in effect, a content-based distinction in favor of religious expression. . . .

II. EXEMPTIONS AND THE TWO FACES OF EQUALITY

A. DENOMINATIONAL EQUALITY

[The critics'] most sympathetic argument is that the denial of exemptions would have a disproportionate impact on minority groups. [They are] correct in noting that neutral restrictions have disproportionate impacts. . . . [C]ultural traditions and social mores generally reflect majoritarian religious beliefs. Legislators are more likely to be aware of majoritarian religious practices (their own) when they fashion general regulations, and thus are unlikely to place disabilities on those practices. Similarly, they are less likely to be concerned with religious practices outside their religious tradition and accordingly are more likely to place burdens on those practices inadvertently. [The critics] thus plausibly argue[ ] that concerns of denominational neutrality might support allowing exemptions in those cases where the challenged regulation results in de facto inequality for a minority religious practice.

On the other hand, the free exercise exemption "cure" is arguably worse than the "disease"—i.e., the harm to religious exercise created by neutral laws. After all, even without the free exercise exemption, the constitutional protection for religion is extensive and stringent. The Free Exercise Clause itself prohibits any direct attempt to single out religion for adverse treatment, and the Free Speech Clause includes the protection of prayer, proselytizing, preaching, and aspects of religious conscience in its ambit. Moreover, the incidental de facto inequality created by neutral laws is just that—incidental. It occurs only randomly and haphazardly. Some minority religious beliefs will be aligned with majority beliefs, while other minority beliefs will not. The Amish, unlike Jews, are not disadvantaged by Sunday closing laws. In other circumstances this pattern will be reversed. Jews, unlike the Amish, are not disadvantaged by social security laws. One need not fully accept Professor Mark Tushnet's claim that in a complex society "the overall distribution of burdens and benefits is likely to be reasonably fair" to acknowledge that minority religions will be on both sides of neutral laws.

B. EQUALITY OF BELIEF

The free exercise exemption, however, raises another serious concern. Granting exemptions only to religious claimants promotes its own form of inequality: a constitutional preference for religious over non-religious belief systems.

Case law readily illustrates this problem. In Wisconsin v. Yoder, the Court explicitly stated that constitutional exemption from compulsory education requirements was available only to the Amish on religious grounds and would not be available to a non-religious group seeking exemption because of adherence to, for example, the philosophical precepts of Henry David Thoreau. Similarly, in Thomas v. Review Board, the Court held that exemption from unemployment insurance requirements would be available to an individual whose religious tenets prevent him from working in an armaments factory, but would not be available to one whose claim was based upon "personal philosophical choice."

This favoritism for religious belief over other beliefs itself raises serious constitutional concerns. Most obviously, a constitutional preference for religious belief cuts at the heart of the central principle of the Free Speech Clause—that every idea is of equal dignity and status in the marketplace of ideas.

The free exercise exemption also offends Establishment Clause principles. Special treatment for religion connotes sponsorship and endorsement; providing relative benefits for religion over non-religion may have the impermissible effect of advancing religion. In fact, the type of discrimination created by the free exercise exemption is arguably worse than the de facto inequality purportedly redressed by the exemption analysis because it is intentional, a matter of critical concern in equal protection analysis. The explicit assertion in the free exercise claim that religious belief is uniquely entitled to constitutional protection is also troublesome from another equal protection vantage. As the Court has noted, explicit endorsement of inequality is particularly egregious because it sends a clear message of second-class status. Thus, the explicit inequality required by the free exercise exemption analysis more directly and powerfully harms equality interests than does the inadvertent de facto discrimination caused by generally applicable laws.

A RESPONSE TO PROFESSOR MARSHALL
Michael W. McConnell
58 U. Chi. L. Rev. 329 (1991)

The heart of Marshall's position is that free exercise exemptions are a form of "favoritism for religious belief over other beliefs." He can say this, however, only by ignoring the symmetrical character of the free exercise and establishment principles. Both "single out" religion for special treatment, but sometimes this is an advantage and sometimes a disadvantage. When a Jehovah's Witness refuses to work in an armaments factory, he is constitutionally entitled to unemployment benefits, while a secular antiwar activist in the same position is not. In this context, it may appear that religion is "favored." But if a public school football coach (or even a member of the team) offers a prayer or other religious inspiration before the game, he will be stopped; a girls' tennis coach who offers feminist words of inspiration before the game engages in protected speech. When the Reverend Jerry Falwell's Liberty University applied recently for public bonds, it was turned down because of its religious teaching; no one would consider turning down Antioch College because of its secular ideology. In these contexts, religion seems "disfavored." It is simply not accurate to describe the pre-*Smith* constitutional scheme, taken as a whole, as "favoritism" for religion.

It would be possible to accept Marshall's position on free exercise of religion (no "singling out") and still maintain consistency with the Establishment Clause. This would mean that religion cannot be "singled out" under either clause. If a public school teacher wants to tell his class about the importance of a personal relationship with Jesus Christ, that would be no different from holding forth about the importance of Martin Luther King or of protecting the environment. But that is not Marshall's position. As he says, "the Establishment Clause uniquely singles out government advancement of religion as a matter to be avoided. . . . [T]here is no comparable limitation on other types of belief systems." Having embraced the "singling out" position with reference to establishment, why is Marshall so reluctant to extend it to free exercise?

Marshall's admonitions about the difficulty of defining and identifying religion . . . are, of course, no less pertinent under the Establishment Clause than under the Free Exercise Clause. . . . Apparently, in Marshall's world, religion can be "singled out" only for the purpose of exclusion from government benefits. When government interference is at issue, religion must be accorded protection no greater than that given secular beliefs. This combination—"singling out" under the Establishment Clause, "equal treatment" under the Free Exercise Clause—is a powerful instrument for the secularization of society. It is hard to see anything "neutral" about it.

Marshall suggests at one point that his view of the Establishment Clause might not preclude statutory religious exemptions. But his explanation for why the free exercise exemption "offends Establishment Clause principles" is equally applicable to statutory exemptions: "Special treatment for religion connotes sponsorship and endorsement; providing relative benefits for religion over non-religion may have the impermissible effect of advancing religion." If Marshall is right about free exercise exemptions, he must be wrong about statutory exemptions; "special treatment" is special treatment, whether judicial or statutory. But if he admits that under his reasoning statutory exemptions are unconstitutional, Marshall forfeits any possible support for his position in precedent, history, or a jurisprudence of judicial restraint.

Those who claim that religion may not be "singled out" must grapple with the very text of the First Amendment, which refers specifically to "religion." Why religion is distinguished from other forms of belief is open to many interpretations, but that it was distinguished seems undeniable. My position is not "that the Constitution prefers religious belief." Rather, I contend that the Constitution treats religious belief differently—sometimes better, sometimes worse, depending on whether the context is one of interference or advancement. The unifying principle is that the religious life of the people should be insulated, to the maximum possible degree, from the effect of governmental action, whether favorable or unfavorable. To extend this principle to all other beliefs and activities would be impossible.

6. Responses After Smith: Federal Religious Freedom Legislation, State Legislation, and State Constitutional Rulings

The *Smith* decision galvanized opposition from religious and civil liberties groups from all corners of the ideological-theological spectrum. The ACLU and Americans United joined the American Center For Law and Justice and the Christian Legal Society, the American Jewish Congress joined the National Association of Evangelicals, and Republicans joined Democrats in enacting legislation, the Religious Freedom Restoration Act of 1993 (RFRA), designed to return to the *Sherbert-Yoder* standard.[*] The Court was not amused:

CITY OF BOERNE v. FLORES
521 U.S. 507 (1997)

Justice KENNEDY delivered the opinion of the Court.

A decision by local zoning authorities to deny a church a building permit was challenged under the Religious Freedom Restoration Act of 1993 (RFRA).

---

[*] For review of the background of RFRA, see, e.g., Bradley P. Jacob, Free Exercise in the "Lobbying Nineties," 84 Neb. L. Rev. 795 (2006); Thomas C. Berg, What Hath Congress Wrought? An Interpretive Guide to the Religious Freedom Restoration Act, 39 Vill. L. Rev. 1 (1994); Douglas Laycock and Oliver Thomas, Interpreting the Religious Freedom Restoration Act, 73 Tex. L. Rev. 210 (1994); Scott C. Idleman, The Religious Freedom Restoration Act: Pushing the Limits of Legislative Power, 73 Tex. L. Rev. 247 (1994).

The case calls into question the authority of Congress to enact RFRA. We conclude the statute exceeds Congress' power.

I

Situated on a hill in the city of Boerne, Texas, some 28 miles northwest of San Antonio, is St. Peter Catholic Church. Built in 1923, the church's structure replicates the mission style of the region's earlier history. The church seats about 230 worshippers, a number too small for its growing parish. Some 40 to 60 parishioners cannot be accommodated at some Sunday masses. In order to meet the needs of the congregation the Archbishop of San Antonio gave permission to the parish to plan alterations to enlarge the building.

A few months later, the Boerne City Council passed an ordinance authorizing the city's Historic Landmark Commission to prepare a preservation plan with proposed historic landmarks and districts. Under the ordinance, the Commission must preapprove construction affecting historic landmarks or buildings in a historic district.

Soon afterwards, the Archbishop applied for a building permit so construction to enlarge the church could proceed. City authorities, relying on the ordinance and the designation of a historic district (which, they argued, included the church), denied the application. The Archbishop brought this suit challenging the permit denial in the United States District Court for the Western District of Texas.

The complaint contained various claims, but to this point the litigation has centered on RFRA and the question of its constitutionality. The Archbishop relied upon RFRA as one basis for relief from the refusal to issue the permit. The District Court concluded that by enacting RFRA Congress exceeded the scope of its enforcement power under § 5 of the Fourteenth Amendment. The court certified its order for interlocutory appeal and the Fifth Circuit reversed, finding RFRA to be constitutional. We granted certiorari, and now reverse.

II

Congress enacted RFRA in direct response to the Court's decision in Employment Div. v. Smith. [Unhappy with the holding of *Smith*,] Congress announced:

1. [T]he framers of the Constitution, recognizing free exercise of religion as an unalienable right, secured its protection in the First Amendment to the Constitution;
2. laws "neutral" toward religion may burden religious exercise as surely as laws intended to interfere with religious exercise;
3. governments should not substantially burden religious exercise without compelling justification;
4. in Employment Division v. Smith the Supreme Court virtually eliminated the requirement that the government justify burdens on religious exercise imposed by laws neutral toward religion; and
5. the compelling interest test as set forth in prior Federal court rulings is a workable test for striking sensible balances between religious liberty and competing prior governmental interests.

The Act's stated purposes are:

1. to restore the compelling interest test as set forth in Sherbert v. Verner and Wisconsin v. Yoder, and to guarantee its application in all cases where free exercise of religion is substantially burdened; and
2. to provide a claim or defense to persons whose religious exercise is substantially burdened by government.

RFRA prohibits "[g]overnment" from "substantially burden[ing]" a person's exercise of religion even if the burden results from a rule of general applicability unless the government can demonstrate the burden "(1) is in furtherance of a compelling governmental interest; and (2) is the least restrictive means of furthering that compelling governmental interest." The Act's mandate applies to any "branch, department, agency, instrumentality, and official (or other person acting under color of law) of the United States," as well as to any "State, or . . . subdivision of a State." The Act's universal coverage is confirmed in § 2000bb-3(a), under which RFRA "applies to all Federal and State law, and the implementation of that law, whether statutory or otherwise, and whether adopted before or after [RFRA's enactment]." In accordance with RFRA's usage of the term, we shall use "state law" to include local and municipal ordinances.

III

A

Under our Constitution, the Federal Government is one of enumerated powers. The judicial authority to determine the constitutionality of laws, in cases and controversies, is based on the premise that the "powers of the legislature are defined and limited; and that those limits may not be mistaken, or forgotten, the constitution is written." Marbury v. Madison (1803).

Congress relied on its Fourteenth Amendment enforcement power in enacting the most far reaching and substantial of RFRA's provisions, those which impose its requirements on the States. The Fourteenth Amendment provides, in relevant part:

Section 1. . . . No State shall make or enforce any law which shall abridge the privileges or immunities of citizens of the United States; nor shall any State deprive any person of life, liberty, or property, without due process of law; nor deny to any person within its jurisdiction the equal protection of the laws. . . .

Section 5. The Congress shall have power to enforce, by appropriate legislation, the provisions of this article.

The parties disagree over whether RFRA is a proper exercise of Congress' § 5 power "to enforce" by "appropriate legislation" the constitutional guarantee that no State shall deprive any person of "life, liberty, or property, without due process of law" nor deny any person "equal protection of the laws."

In defense of the Act respondent contends, with support from the United States as amicus, that RFRA is permissible enforcement legislation. Congress, it is said, is only protecting by legislation one of the liberties guaranteed by the Fourteenth Amendment's Due Process Clause, the free exercise of religion, beyond what is necessary under Smith. It is said the congressional decision to dispense with proof of deliberate or overt discrimination and instead concentrate on a law's effects accords with the settled understanding that §5 includes the power to enact legislation designed to prevent as well as remedy constitutional violations. It is further contended that Congress' §5 power is not limited to remedial or preventive legislation.

All must acknowledge that §5 is "a positive grant of legislative power" to Congress. . . . Legislation which deters or remedies constitutional violations can fall within the sweep of Congress' enforcement power even if in the process it prohibits conduct which is not itself unconstitutional and intrudes into "legislative spheres of autonomy previously reserved to the States." For example, the Court upheld a suspension of literacy tests . . . under Congress' parallel power to enforce the provisions of the Fifteenth Amendment, as a measure to combat racial discrimination in voting, South Carolina v. Katzenbach (1966), despite the facial constitutionality of the tests under Lassiter v. Northampton County Bd. of Elections (1959).

It is also true, however, that "[a]s broad as the congressional enforcement power is, it is not unlimited." In assessing the breadth of §5's enforcement power, we begin with its text. Congress has been given the power "to enforce" the "provisions of this article." We agree with respondent, of course, that Congress can enact legislation under §5 enforcing the constitutional right to the free exercise of religion. The "provisions of this article," to which §5 refers, include the Due Process Clause of the Fourteenth Amendment. Congress' power to enforce the Free Exercise Clause follows from our holding in Cantwell v. Connecticut that the "fundamental concept of liberty embodied in [the Fourteenth Amendment's Due Process Clause] embraces the liberties guaranteed by the First Amendment."

Congress' power under §5, however, extends only to "enforc[ing]" the provisions of the Fourteenth Amendment. The Court has described this power as "remedial." The design of the Amendment and the text of §5 are inconsistent with the suggestion that Congress has the power to decree the substance of the Fourteenth Amendment's restrictions on the States. Legislation which alters the meaning of the Free Exercise Clause cannot be said to be enforcing the Clause. Congress does not enforce a constitutional right by changing what the right is. It has been given the power "to enforce," not the power to determine what constitutes a constitutional violation. . . . While the line between measures that remedy or prevent unconstitutional actions and measures that make a substantive change in the governing law is not easy to discern, and Congress must have wide latitude in determining where it lies, the distinction exists and must be observed. There must be a congruence and proportionality between the injury to be prevented or remedied and the means adopted to that end. Lacking such a connection, legislation may become substantive in operation and effect. History and our case law support drawing the distinction, one apparent from the text of the Amendment.

[The Court's discussion of Fourteenth Amendment history and case law is omitted.]

B

Respondent contends that RFRA is a proper exercise of Congress' remedial or preventive power. The Act, it is said, is a reasonable means of protecting the free exercise of religion as defined by *Smith*. It prevents and remedies laws which are enacted with the unconstitutional object of targeting religious beliefs and practices. To avoid the difficulty of proving such violations, it is said, Congress can simply invalidate any law which imposes a substantial burden on a religious practice unless it is justified by a compelling interest and is the least restrictive means of accomplishing that interest. If Congress can prohibit laws with discriminatory effects in order to prevent racial discrimination in violation of the Equal Protection Clause, then it can do the same, respondent argues, to promote religious liberty.

While preventive rules are sometimes appropriate remedial measures, there must be a congruence between the means used and the ends to be achieved. The appropriateness of remedial measures must be considered in light of the evil presented. Strong measures appropriate to address one harm may be an unwarranted response to another, lesser one.

. . . RFRA's legislative record lacks examples of modern instances of generally applicable laws passed because of religious bigotry. The history of persecution in this country detailed in the hearings mentions no episodes occurring in the past 40 years. The absence of more recent episodes stems from the fact that, as one witness testified, "deliberate persecution is not the usual problem in this country." House Hearings (statement of Douglas Laycock). Rather, the emphasis of the hearings was on laws of general applicability which place incidental burdens on religion. Much of the discussion centered upon anecdotal evidence of autopsies performed on Jewish individuals and Hmong immigrants in violation of their religious beliefs, and on zoning regulations and historic preservation laws (like the one at issue here), which as an incident of their normal operation, have adverse effects on churches and synagogues. It is difficult to maintain that they are examples of legislation enacted or enforced due to animus or hostility to the burdened religious practices or that they indicate some widespread pattern of religious discrimination in this country. Congress' concern was with the incidental burdens imposed, not the object or purpose of the legislation. . . .

Regardless of the state of the legislative record, RFRA cannot be considered remedial, preventive legislation, if those terms are to have any meaning. RFRA is so out of proportion to a supposed remedial or preventive object that it cannot be understood as responsive to, or designed to prevent, unconstitutional behavior. It appears, instead, to attempt a substantive change in constitutional protections. . . . Sweeping coverage ensures its intrusion at every level of government, displacing laws and prohibiting official actions of almost every description and regardless of subject matter. RFRA's restrictions apply to every agency and official of the Federal, State, and local Governments. RFRA applies to all federal and state law, statutory or otherwise, whether adopted before or after its enactment. RFRA has no termination date or termination mechanism. Any law is subject to challenge at any time by any individual who alleges a substantial burden on his or her free exercise of religion. . . .

The stringent test RFRA demands of state laws reflects a lack of proportionality or congruence between the means adopted and the legitimate end to be achieved. If an objector can show a substantial burden on his free exercise, the State must demonstrate a compelling governmental interest and show that the law is the least restrictive means of furthering its interest. Claims that a law substantially burdens someone's exercise of religion will often be difficult to contest. Requiring a State to demonstrate a compelling interest and show that it has adopted the least restrictive means of achieving that interest is the most demanding test known to constitutional law. If " 'compelling interest' really means what it says . . . many laws will not meet the test. . . . [The test] would open the prospect of constitutionally required religious exemptions from civic obligations of almost every conceivable kind." *Smith.* Laws valid under *Smith* would fall under RFRA without regard to whether they had the object of stifling or punishing free exercise. We make these observations not to reargue the position of the majority in *Smith* but to illustrate the substantive alteration of its holding attempted by RFRA. Even assuming RFRA would be interpreted in effect to mandate some lesser test, say one equivalent to intermediate scrutiny, the statute nevertheless would require searching judicial scrutiny of state law with the attendant likelihood of invalidation. This is a considerable congressional intrusion into the States' traditional prerogatives and general authority to regulate for the health and welfare of their citizens.

The substantial costs RFRA exacts, both in practical terms of imposing a heavy litigation burden on the States and in terms of curtailing their traditional general regulatory power, far exceed any pattern or practice of unconstitutional conduct under the Free Exercise Clause as interpreted in *Smith.* Simply put, RFRA is not designed to identify and counteract state laws likely to be unconstitutional because of their treatment of religion. In most cases, the state laws to which RFRA applies are not ones which will have been motivated by religious bigotry. If a state law disproportionately burdened a particular class of religious observers, this circumstance might be evidence of an impermissible legislative motive. RFRA's substantial burden test, however, is not even a discriminatory effects or disparate impact test. It is a reality of the modern regulatory state that numerous state laws, such as the zoning regulations at issue here, impose a substantial burden on a large class of individuals. When the exercise of religion has been burdened in an incidental way by a law of general application, it does not follow that the persons affected have been burdened any more than other citizens, let alone burdened because of their religious beliefs. In addition, the Act imposes in every case a least restrictive means requirement—a requirement that was not used in the pre-*Smith* jurisprudence RFRA purported to codify—which also indicates that the legislation is broader than is appropriate if the goal is to prevent and remedy constitutional violations.

When Congress acts within its sphere of power and responsibilities, it has not just the right but the duty to make its own informed judgment on the meaning and force of the Constitution. . . . Our national experience teaches that the Constitution is preserved best when each part of the Government respects both the Constitution and the proper actions and determinations of the other branches. When the Court has interpreted the Constitution, it has acted within the province of the Judicial Branch, which embraces the duty to say what the law is. *Marbury.* When the political branches of the Government act against the background of a judicial interpretation of the Constitution already issued, it must be understood that in later cases and controversies the Court will treat its precedents with the respect due them under settled principles, including *stare decisis,* and contrary expectations must be disappointed. RFRA was designed to control cases and controversies, such as the one before us; but as the provisions of the federal statute here invoked are beyond congressional authority, it is this Court's precedent, not RFRA, which must control.

* * *

It is for Congress in the first instance to "determin[e] whether and what legislation is needed to secure the guarantees of the Fourteenth Amendment," and its conclusions are entitled to much deference. Katzenbach v. Morgan. Congress' discretion is not unlimited, however, and the courts retain the power, as they have since *Marbury v. Madison,* to determine if Congress has exceeded its authority under the Constitution. Broad as the power of Congress is under the Enforcement Clause of the Fourteenth Amendment, RFRA contradicts vital principles necessary to maintain separation of powers and the federal balance. The judgment of the Court of Appeals sustaining the Act's constitutionality is reversed.

Justice STEVENS, concurring.

In my opinion, the Religious Freedom Restoration Act of 1993 (RFRA) is a "law respecting an establishment of religion" that violates the First Amendment to the Constitution.

If the historic landmark on the hill in Boerne happened to be a museum or an art gallery owned by an atheist, it would not be eligible for an exemption from the city ordinances that forbid an enlargement of the structure. Because the landmark is owned by the Catholic Church, it is claimed that RFRA gives its owner a federal statutory entitlement to an exemption from a generally applicable, neutral civil law. Whether the Church would actually prevail under the statute or not, the statute has provided the Church with a legal weapon that no atheist or agnostic can obtain. This governmental preference for religion, as opposed to irreligion, is forbidden by the First Amendment.

Justice O'CONNOR, with whom Justice BREYER joins except as to a portion of Part I, dissenting.

I dissent from the Court's disposition of this case. I agree with the Court that the issue before us is whether the Religious Freedom Restoration Act (RFRA) is a proper exercise of Congress' power to enforce § 5 of the Fourteenth Amendment. But as a yardstick for measuring the constitutionality of RFRA, the Court uses its holding in Employment Div. v. Smith, the decision that prompted Congress to enact RFRA as a means of more rigorously enforcing the Free Exercise Clause. I remain of the view that *Smith* was wrongly decided, and I would use this case to reexamine the Court's holding there. Therefore, I would direct the parties to brief the question whether *Smith* represents the correct understanding of the Free Exercise Clause and set the case for reargument. If the Court were to correct the misinterpretation of the Free Exercise Clause set forth in *Smith,* it would simultaneously put our First Amendment jurisprudence back on course and allay the legitimate concerns of a majority in Congress who believed that *Smith* improperly restricted religious liberty. We would then be in a position to review RFRA in light of a proper interpretation of the Free Exercise Clause.

I agree with much of the reasoning set forth in Part III-A of the Court's opinion. Indeed, if I agreed with the Court's standard in *Smith,* I would join the opinion. [The historical portion of Justice O'Connor's opinion is omitted.]

NOTES AND QUESTIONS

1. RFRA's Application to Federal Laws. After *Boerne*, what about the application of RFRA to prevent federal laws and regulations from burdening religion? Is *Boerne* solely a case about the rights of states as against federal legislation? What is the significance, if any, of the Court's statements that RFRA violated principles of "separation of powers" and that "the Court will treat its precedents with the respect due them under settled principles"? Do these statements suggest that Congress violates the constitutional separation of powers by legislating contrary to *Smith*'s understanding of religious freedom, even as applied to federal laws? Or are these statements still limited to the context of Congress overriding state laws through the Fourteenth Amendment?

The Supreme Court has not directly ruled on this question (although in Gonzales v. O Centro Espirita Beneficente Uniao do Vegetal, 126 S. Ct. 1211 (2006), it applied RFRA to a federal drug law without questioning constitutionality). The courts of appeals that have considered the question have all upheld congressional power to enact RFRA as applied to other federal laws. The leading case, In re Young, 141 F.3d 854 (8th Cir. 1998), upheld the statute's application to limit the federal bankruptcy laws—in that case, to prevent the trustee of a bankrupt couple from seeking to recover against a church tithes that the couple had made in good faith to the church during the year before their bankruptcy. The court said (*id.* at 860-861):

> While Congress cannot, through ordinary legislation, amend the Court's authoritative interpretation of the Constitution, "congressional disapproval of a Supreme Court decision does not impair the power of Congress to legislate a different result, as long as Congress had that power in the first place." See also *Boerne* ("When Congress acts within its sphere of power and responsibilities, it has not just the right but the duty to make its own informed judgment on the meaning and force of the Constitution. . . ."). Congress has often provided statutory protection of individual liberties that exceed the Supreme Court's interpretation of constitutional protection. See, e.g., Privacy Protection Act of 1980 (reacting to Zurcher v. Stanford Daily (1978), and providing journalists with greater protection against searches and seizures); National Defense Authorization Act for Fiscal Years 1988 and 1989 (reacting to Goldman v. Weinberger (1986), and providing that members of military were entitled to wear religious headgear); cf. Pregnancy Discrimination Act (reacting to Geduldig v. Aiello (1974), and equating employment discrimination based on pregnancy with employment discrimination based on gender). Because Congress need not agree with everything the Supreme Court does in order for its legislation to pass constitutional muster, we conclude that RFRA is not contrary to the Constitution merely because Congress disagreed with the *Smith* Court's interpretation of the Free Exercise Clause.
>
> The key to the separation of powers issue in this case is thus not whether Congress disagreed with the Supreme Court's constitutional analysis, but whether Congress acted beyond the scope of its constitutional authority in applying RFRA to federal law. . . .
>
> We conclude that RFRA is an appropriate means by Congress to modify the United States bankruptcy laws [passed under its Article I power]. . . . [RFRA] has effectively amended the Bankruptcy Code, and has engrafted the additional clause to §548(a)(2)(A) that a recovery that places a substantial burden on a debtor's exercise of religion will not be allowed unless it is the least restrictive means to

satisfy a compelling governmental interest. The Trustee has not contended, and we can conceive of no argument to support the contention, that Congress is incapable of amending the legislation that it has passed.

For elaboration of the arguments supporting congressional power to apply RFRA to the federal government, see, e.g., Gregory P. Margarian, How to Apply the Religious Freedom Restoration Act to Federal Law Without Violating the Constitution, 99 Mich. L. Rev. 1903, 1923-1944 (2001); Thomas C. Berg, The New Attacks on Religious Freedom Legislation, and Why They Are Wrong, 21 Cardozo L. Rev. 415, 444-451 (1999); Michael Stokes Paulsen, A RFRA Runs Through It: The Religious Freedom Restoration Act and the U.S. Code, 56 Montana L. Rev. 249 (1995). For elaboration of the attack on RFRA's federal applications, see, e.g., Eugene Gressman and Angela C. Carmella, The RFRA Revision of the Free Exercise, 57 Ohio St. L.J. 65 (1996); Marci N. Hamilton, The Religious Freedom Restoration Act Is Unconstitutional, Period, 1 U. Pa. J. Const. L. 1 (1998); Edward J. Blatnik, Note, No RFRAF Allowed: The Status of the Religious Freedom Restoration Act's Federal Applications in the Wake of *City of Boerne v. Flores*, 98 Colum. L. Rev. 1410 (1998).

These arguments concerning congressional power to enact RFRA are separate from arguments about whether RFRA or other accommodation statutes violate the Establishment Clause by favoring religious claims for exemption from law—an issue we take up in section III-C below.

Assuming that RFRA remains valid as applied to federal law, questions will arise concerning its scope—in particular, the meaning of the requirement that the government justify "substantial burdens" on religion by showing a "compelling governmental interest." These questions are addressed in section III-B below.

2. New Federal Legislation Affecting State and Local Laws: RLUIPA.   After *Boerne*, Congress sought again to apply the compelling interest test to state and local government activities, this time by relying on other constitutional powers: to regulate interstate commerce and to place conditions on federal spending. The proposed Religious Liberty Protection Act, introduced in 1998, would have applied RFRA's "compelling interest/least restrictive means" requirement to state and local laws substantially burdening religion if (1) "the substantial burden is imposed in a program or activity that receives Federal financial assistance," or if (2) "the substantial burden affects, or removal of that substantial burden would affect, commerce with foreign nations, among the several States, or with Indian tribes." This bill failed for a number of reasons, among them opposition from civil rights groups who claimed that the law would authorize discrimination in housing and employment on the basis of race, sex, or sexual orientation. Do you think that such fears were realistic?

Eventually Congress settled for passing narrower, "targeted" legislation. The Religious Land Use and Institutionalized Persons Act (RLUIPA), enacted in 2000, applies the "substantial burden/compelling interest" test in the contexts of federally assisted programs and of activities affecting interstate commerce—but only in two areas. The first is substantial burdens on religious exercise imposed by "land use regulations," such as zoning laws or the landmark preservation law at issue in *Boerne*. The second is substantial burdens "on the religious exercise of a person residing in or confined to an institution," primarily a prison or a mental institution.

RLUIPA's prison provision was upheld against a challenged based on the Establishment Clause in Cutter v. Wilkinson, 544 U.S. 709 (2005). *Cutter* did not address possible challenges that RLUIPA exceeds the scope of Congress's authority to legislate under its powers (1) to regulate interstate commerce and (2) to place conditions on federal spending. For discussion of these issues, see, e.g., Thomas C. Berg, The Constitutional Future of Religious Freedom Legislation, 20 U. Ark. Little Rock L. Rev. 715 (1998); H. Rep. No. 106-219, Religious Liberty Protection Act of 1999, 106th Cong., 1st Sess. 14-16 (1999) (both supporting congressional power); Daniel O. Conkle, Congressional Alternatives in the Wake of *City of Boerne v. Flores*: The (Limited) Role of Congress in Protecting Religious Liberty from State and Local Infringement, 20 U. Ark. Little Rock L. Rev. 633 (1998) (questioning congressional power).

The following excerpt from a joint statement by RLUIPA's cosponsoring senators summarizes the constitutional arguments under these powers:

SPENDING CLAUSE

The Spending Clause provisions are modeled directly on similar provisions in other civil rights laws. Congressional power to attach germane conditions to federal spending has long been upheld. *South Dakota v. Dole* (1987); *Steward Machine Co. v. Davis* (1937). The bill's protections are properly confined to each federally assisted "program or activity," which is defined by incorporating a subset of the definition of the same phrase in Title VI of the Civil Rights Act of 1964. In most applications, this means the department that administers the challenged land use regulation or the department that administers the institution in which the claimant is housed.

COMMERCE CLAUSE

The Commerce Clause provisions require proof of a "jurisdictional element which would ensure, through case-by-case inquiry, that the [burden on religious exercise] in question affects interstate commerce." The Gun Free Schools Act, struck down in [*United States v.*] *Lopez* [(1995)], and the Violence Against Women Act, struck down in *United States v. Morrison* (2000), were invalid because they regulated non-economic activity and required no proof of such a jurisdictional element. But the Court assumes that if such a "jurisdictional element" is proved in each case, the aggregate of all such effects in individual cases will be a substantial effect on commerce. *Camps Newfound/Owatonna, Inc. v. Town of Harrison* (U.S. 1997) ("although the summer camp involved in this case may have a relatively insignificant impact on the commerce of the entire Nation, the interstate commercial activities of nonprofit entities as a class are unquestionably significant"); *Lopez* (explaining how small volumes of home-grown wheat could, in the aggregate, substantially affect commerce).

The jurisdictional element in this bill is that, in each case, the burden on religious exercise, or removal of that burden, will affect interstate commerce. This will most commonly be proved by showing that the burden prevents a specific economic transaction in commerce, such as a construction project, purchase or rental of a building, or an interstate shipment of religious goods. The aggregate of all such transactions is obviously substantial, and this is confirmed by data presented to the House Subcommittee on the Constitution.

Joint Statement of Sens. Hatch and Kennedy, 146 Cong. Rec. S7774, S7775 (July 27, 2000). Is this use of the Commerce Power inappropriate because "commerce" is just a pretext for protecting the noncommercial human right of religious freedom? Consider Berg, 20 U. Ark. Little Rock L. Rev. at 758 ("Congress used this method in the Civil Rights Act of 1964 to reach the moral evil of discrimination. Now, as then, the fact that Congress is addressing a civil or moral right does not mean it cannot rely on the Commerce Power.").

Other sections of RLUIPA further protect religious activity against land use regulation. The government must satisfy the compelling interest test if it imposes a burden through a regulation or system of regulations "that permit the government to make individualized assessments of the proposed uses for the property involved." Moreover, a regulation or action is absolutely forbidden if it "treats a religious assembly or institution on less than equal terms with a non-religious assembly or institution," "discriminates against any assembly or institution on the basis of religion or religious denomination," "totally excludes religious assemblies from a jurisdiction," or "unreasonably limits religious assemblies, institutions, or structures within a jurisdiction." These provisions are predicated on Congress's power under section 5 of the Fourteenth Amendment. Do they comply with the limits that *Boerne* set on that power? Consider this excerpt from the sponsors' statement:

> The land use sections of the bill . . . enforce the Free Exercise and Free Speech Clauses as interpreted by the Supreme Court. Congress may act to enforce the Constitution when it has "reason to believe that many of the laws affected by the congressional enactment have a significant likelihood of being unconstitutional." *Boerne*. The standard is not certainty, but "reason to believe" and "significant likelihood." This Act more than satisfies that standard—in two independent ways.
>
> First, the bill satisfies the constitutional standard factually. The hearing record demonstrates a widespread practice of individualized decisions to grant or refuse permission to use property for religious purposes. These individualized assessments readily lend themselves to discrimination, and they also make it difficult to prove discrimination in any individual case. But the committees in each house have examined large numbers of cases, and the hearing record reveals a widespread pattern of discrimination against churches as compared to secular places of assembly, and of discrimination against small and unfamiliar denominations as compared to larger and more familiar ones. This factual record is itself sufficient to support prophylactic rules to simplify the enforcement of constitutional standards in land use regulation of churches. . . .
>
> Second, and without regard to the factual record, the land use provisions of this bill satisfy the constitutional standard legally. Each subsection closely tracks the legal standards in one or more Supreme Court opinions, codifying those standards for greater visibility and easier enforceability.
>
> [The statement first refers to the section] requiring that substantial burdens on religious exercise be justified by a compelling interest . . . where government has authority to make individualized assessments of the proposed uses to which the property will be put. Where government makes such individualized assessments, permitting some uses and excluding others, it cannot exclude religious uses without compelling justification. See *Church of Lukumi Babalu Aye v. City of Hialeah* (1993); *Employment Division v. Smith*.
>
> Sections 2(b)(1) and (2) [, the "less than equal terms" and "discrimination" sections mentioned above,] prohibit various forms of discrimination against or among religious land uses. These sections enforce the Free Exercise Clause rule [*Smith*] against laws that burden religion and are not neutral and generally applicable.

146 Cong. Rec. at S7775-S7776. For amplification of these arguments, see Douglas Laycock, State RFRAs and Land Use Regulation, 32 U.C. Davis L. Rev. 755 (1999). You may want to consider again your analysis of RLUIPA after you read the decisions on how to define "neutrality" and "general applicability," in section B-1 (pp. 162-173).

3. State Religious Freedom Statutes.   With RFRA struck down as to state and local laws, defenders of broad free exercise rights turned to the individual states. As of this writing, 12 states have passed "mini-RFRAs" applying the *Sherbert/Yoder* compelling interest test to their own laws burdening religion.* For discussion of these provisions, see, e.g., the articles in Symposium: Restoring Religious Freedom in the States, 32 U.C. Davis L. Rev., no. 3 (Spring 1999); Gary S. Gildin, A Blessing in Disguise: Protecting Minority Faiths Through State Religious Freedom Non-Restoration Acts, 28 Harv. J.L. & Pub. Pol'y 411 (2000).

4. State Constitutional Rulings.   In addition, a number of state courts interpret their states' existing constitutional provisions to apply the compelling interest standard or something like it.[†] See generally Daniel A. Crane, Beyond RFRA: Free Exercise of Religion Comes of Age in the State Courts, 10 St. Thomas. L. Rev. 235 (1998); Angela C. Carmella, State Constitutional Protection of Religious Exercise: An Emerging Post-*Smith* Jurisprudence, 1993 B.Y.U. L. Rev. 275. State provisions can raise their own distinctive issues. For example, the Washington Supreme Court interpreted the state constitution to require exemption of a church's building exterior from application of a local historic-preservation ordinance. First Covenant Church v. City of Seattle, 120 Wash.2d 203, 840 P.2d 174 (1992). The court adopted a "compelling interest" test requiring exemptions, instead of a *Smith*-like test of formal neutrality, on the basis of a provision stating:

> Absolute freedom of conscience in all matters of religious sentiment, belief, and worship, shall be guaranteed to every individual, and no one shall be molested or disturbed in person or property on account of religion; but the liberty of conscience hereby secured shall not be so construed as to excuse acts of licentiousness or justify practices inconsistent with the peace and safety of the state.

Wash. Const. art. I, § 11. The court explained, among other things, that

> The language of our state constitution is significantly different and stronger than the federal constitution. The First Amendment limits government action that "prohibits" free exercise. Our state provision "absolutely" protects freedom of worship and bars conduct that merely "disturbs" another on the basis of religion.

---

*Alabama Religious Freedom Amendment, Ala. Const., amend. No. 622 (enacted 1998); Arizona Religious Freedom Restoration Act, Ariz. Rev. Stat. §§ 41-1493 to 41-1493.01 (1998); Connecticut Religious Freedom Restoration Act, Conn. Gen Stat. § 52-571b (1993); Florida Religious Freedom Restoration Act, Fla. Stat. §§ 761.01-761.05 (1998); Idaho Religious Freedom Restoration Act, Id. Stat. § 73-4 (1999); Illinois Religious Freedom Restoration Act, 775 Ill. Comp. Stat. § 35 (1998); Missouri Religious Freedom Restoration Act, Mo. Rev. Stat. § 1.302 (2003); New Mexico Religious Freedom Restoration Act, N.M.S.A. §§ 28-22-1 to 28-22-5 (2000); Oklahoma Religious Freedom Act, 51 Okl. St. Ann. §§ 251 to 258 (2000); Rhode Island Religious Freedom Restoration Act, R.I. Gen. Laws § 42-80 (1993); South Carolina Religious Freedom Act, So. Car. Stat. §§ 1-32-30 to 1-32-60 (1999); Texas Religious Freedom Restoration Act, Tex. Civ. Prac. & Rem. §§ 110.001-110.012 (1999).

[†] See, e.g., Attorney General v. Desilets, 418 Mass. 316, 636 N.E.2d 233 (1994). People v. deJonge, 442 Mich. 266, 501 N.W.127 (1993); State v. Hershberger, 462 N.W.2d 393 (Minn. 1990); Humphrey v. Lane, 89 Ohio St. 3d 62, 728 N.E.2d 1039 (2000); First Covenant Church v. City of Seattle, 120 Wash. 2d 203, 840 P.2d 174 (1992); State v. Miller, 202 Wis. 2d 56, 549 N.W.2d 235 (1996).

Any action that is not licentious or inconsistent with the "peace and safety" of the state is "guaranteed" protection. . . .

Finally, the majority in *Smith II* accepts the fact that its rule places minority religions at a disadvantage. Our court, conversely, has rejected the idea that a political majority may control a minority's right of free exercise through the political process.

The court then held that the governmental interest in "preservation of significant structures" was not sufficiently compelling to outweigh the church's freedom to make alterations to its building for theological or other reasons. A concurring opinion was more specific, calling for "more attention to the rich language of Const. art. 1, § 11":

[The section] expressly limits the governmental interests that may outweigh the otherwise absolute right to religious liberty. Only the government's interest in peace and safety or in preventing licentious acts can excuse an imposition on religious liberty. . . .

. . . Historic preservation does not prevent licentious behavior, or ensure peace or safety. While the Ordinance has a very noble aim, it simply does not further one of the limited governmental interests that the drafters of our state constitution thought important enough to infringe on religious liberty. Under Const. art. 1, § 11, we need not even reach the issue of whether Seattle's interest in landmark preservation is significant.

Why did the Washington court apply the compelling interest approach, rather than the *Smith* approach, under its own constitution? Because the state provision had different language than the First Amendment? Because in the court's view, *Smith* is simply a bad decision?

B. CURRENT FREE EXERCISE LITIGATION

After *Smith*, free exercise litigation can go in one of two directions. If *Smith* itself governs, then litigation is likely to focus on whether the law in question is "neutral" and "generally applicable," and perhaps on whether the case involves a "hybrid" of free exercise and some other constitutional right. However, in some legal contexts there is stronger protection for free exercise than under *Smith*: This is the case for federal laws (where RFRA presumably still applies) and laws in states with "mini-RFRAs" or with stronger constitutional free exercise protections. In this section we will consider both areas. These issues, however, are often intertwined with other free exercise questions, such as the burden on the claimant and the strength of the governmental justification. Observe how those issues are treated as well.

1. *Free Exercise Under* Smith: *Neutrality and General Applicability*

CHURCH OF THE LUKUMI BABALU AYE v. CITY OF HIALEAH
508 U.S. 520 (1993)

Justice KENNEDY delivered the opinion of the Court, except as to Part II-A-2.

[Santeria, an Afro-Cuban religion with a significant number of adherents in southern Florida, practices animal sacrifice in birth, marriage, and death rites, for the cure of the sick, for the initiation of new members and priests, and during an annual celebration. Animals sacrificed include pigeons, chickens, goats, and sheep. The animals are killed by cutting the carotid arteries in the neck. The sacrificed animal is cooked and eaten, except after healing and death rituals. When the Church of the Lukumi Babalu Aye announced its plan to open a Santeria church in Hialeah, the city council held an emergency public session and passed a series of ordinances outlawing animal sacrifice, defined as killing an animal in a "public or private ritual or ceremony not for the primary purpose of food consumption." The effect of the ordinances was to prohibit the killing of animals for religious purposes while continuing to permit (equally painful) animal killing for other purposes, including food, scientific experimentation, pest control, clothing, and sport. The district court and the court of appeals upheld the ordinances.]

II

. . . In addressing the constitutional protection for free exercise of religion, our cases establish the general proposition that a law that is neutral and of general applicability need not be justified by a compelling governmental interest even if the law has the incidental effect of burdening a particular religious practice. Employment Division v. Smith. Neutrality and general applicability are interrelated, and, as becomes apparent in this case, failure to satisfy one requirement is a likely indication that the other has not been satisfied. A law failing to satisfy these requirements must be justified by a compelling governmental interest and must be narrowly tailored to advance that interest. These ordinances fail to satisfy the *Smith* requirements. We begin by discussing neutrality.

A
1

[The Church argued that the ordinances were not facially neutral because they specifically targeted "sacrifice" and "ritual." The Court did not find this fact dispositive, since both words had secular as well as religious meanings. But, the Court continued, the Free Exercise Clause protects against governmental hostility which is masked as well as overt, and in this case the record showed that suppression of Santeria sacrifice was the object of the ordinances. The text, though not dispositive, was one indication. A second was the "impact" of the ordinances, which in practice applied only to Santeria. A third was the fact that the "legitimate governmental interests in protecting the public health and preventing cruelty to animals could be addressed by restrictions stopping far short of a flat prohibition of all Santeria sacrificial practice." The city could have protected health by enacting "a general regulation on the disposal of organic garbage," and could have prevented cruelty by regulating "the method of slaughter itself, not a religious classification that is said to bear some general relation to it."

One of the ordinances, No. 87-40, was broader on its face. It was simply an incorporation of the Florida animal cruelty statute, punishing anyone who "unnecessarily . . . kills any animal."] The problem, however, is the interpretation given to the ordinance by respondent and the Florida attorney general.

Killings for religious reasons are deemed unnecessary, whereas most other killings fall outside the prohibition. The city, on what seems to be a per se basis, deems hunting, slaughter of animals for food, eradication of insects and pests, and euthanasia as necessary. There is no indication in the record that respondent has concluded that hunting or fishing for sport is unnecessary. Indeed, one of the few reported Florida cases [holds] that the use of live rabbits to train greyhounds is not unnecessary. Further, because it requires an evaluation of the particular justification for the killing, this ordinance represents a system of "individualized governmental assessment of the reasons for the relevant conduct." As we noted in *Smith*, in circumstances in which individualized exemptions from a general requirement are available, the government "may not refuse to extend that system to cases of 'religious hardship' without compelling reason." Respondent's application of the ordinance's test of necessity devalues religious reasons for killing by judging them to be of lesser import than nonreligious reasons. Thus, religious practice is being singled out for discriminatory treatment.

2

In determining if the object of a law is a neutral one under the Free Exercise Clause, we can also find guidance in our equal protection cases. . . . Here, as in equal protection cases, we may determine the city council's object from both direct and circumstantial evidence. Relevant evidence includes, among other things, the historical background of the decision under challenge, the specific series of events leading to the enactment or official policy in question, as well as the legislative or administrative history, including contemporaneous statements made by members of the decisionmaking body. These objective factors bear on the question of discriminatory object.

That the ordinances were enacted " 'because of,' not merely 'in spite of,' " their suppression of Santeria religious practice, is revealed by the events preceding enactment of the ordinances. . . . The minutes and taped excerpts of the June 9 session, both of which are in the record, evidence significant hostility exhibited by residents, members of the city council, and other city officials toward the Santeria religion and its practice of animal sacrifice. The public crowd that attended the June 9 meetings interrupted statements by council members critical of Santeria with cheers[.] When Councilman Martinez, a supporter of the ordinances, stated that in prerevolution Cuba "people were put in jail for practicing this religion," the audience applauded. [Other statements by members of the city council were in a similar vein.]

B

We turn next to a second requirement of the Free Exercise Clause, the rule that laws burdening religious practice must be of general applicability. [I]nequality results when a legislature decides that the governmental interests it seeks to advance are worthy of being pursued only against conduct with a religious motivation.

. . . In this case we need not define with precision the standard used to evaluate whether a prohibition is of general application, for these ordinances fall well below the minimum standard necessary to protect First Amendment rights. . . .

[The City's ostensible interests are] protecting the public health and preventing cruelty to animals. The ordinances are underinclusive for those ends. They fail to prohibit nonreligious conduct that endangers these interests in a similar or greater degree than Santeria sacrifice does. The underinclusion is substantial, not inconsequential. [T]he ordinances are drafted with care to forbid few killings but those occasioned by religious sacrifice. [The Court listed numerous practices not forbidden: hunting, extermination of mice and rats, euthanasia of stray animals, the infliction of pain for medical experiments, etc.]

III

A law burdening religious practice that is not neutral or not of general application must undergo the most rigorous of scrutiny. . . .

[Here, e]ven were the governmental interests compelling, the ordinances are not drawn in narrow terms to accomplish those interests. As we have discussed, all four ordinances are overbroad or underinclusive in substantial respects. The proffered objectives are not pursued with respect to analogous non-religious conduct, and those interests could be achieved by narrower ordinances that burdened religion to a far lesser degree. . . .

[Moreover, the underinclusiveness of the ordinances shows that the interests they serve are not compelling.] "[A] law cannot be regarded as protecting an interest 'of the highest order' . . . when it leaves appreciable damage to that supposedly vital interest unprohibited." [Quotation omitted.] As we show above, the ordinances are underinclusive to a substantial extent with respect to each of the interests that respondent has asserted, and it is only conduct motivated by religious conviction that bears the weight of the governmental restrictions. There can be no serious claim that those interests justify the ordinances. . . .

Justice SCALIA, with whom THE CHIEF JUSTICE joins, concurring in part and concurring in the judgment.

The Court analyzes the "neutrality" and the "general applicability" of the Hialeah ordinances in separate sections[,] and allocates various invalidating factors to one or the other of those sections. If it were necessary to make a clear distinction between the two terms, I would draw a line somewhat different from the Court's. But I think it is not necessary, and would frankly acknowledge that the terms are not only "interrelated," but substantially overlap. . . .

[I decline to join in section II.A.2 of the Court's opinion] because it departs from the opinion's general focus on the object of the laws at issue to consider the subjective motivation of the lawmakers, i.e., whether the Hialeah City Council actually intended to disfavor the religion of Santeria. As I have noted elsewhere, it is virtually impossible to determine the singular "motive" of a collective legislative body, and this Court has a long tradition of refraining from such inquiries.

Perhaps there are contexts in which determination of legislative motive must be undertaken. But I do not think that is true of analysis under the First Amendment (or the Fourteenth, to the extent it incorporates the First). The First Amendment does not refer to the purposes for which legislators enact laws, but to the effects of the laws enacted: "Congress shall make no law . . . prohibiting the free exercise [of religion]. . . ." This does not put us in the business of invalidating laws by reason of the evil motives of their authors. Had the Hialeah City Council set out resolutely to suppress the practices of Santeria, but ineptly adopted ordinances that failed to do so, I do not see how those laws could be said to "prohibi[t] the free exercise" of religion. Nor, in my view, does it matter that a legislature consists entirely of the pure-hearted, if the law it enacts in fact singles out a religious practice for special burdens. Had the ordinances here been passed with no motive on the part of any councilman except the ardent desire to prevent cruelty to animals (as might in fact have been the case), they would nonetheless be invalid.

What is "neutrality"? Is it different from "general applicability"? How neutral and how generally applicable must a law or policy be to be exempt from further scrutiny under *Smith*? Consider the following cases, decided after *Lukumi* :

RADER v. JOHNSTON, 924 F. Supp. 1540 (D. Neb. 1996): Douglas Rader, a freshman at the University of Nebraska-Kearney (UNK), challenged UNK's requirement that full-time students live on campus during their freshmen year. Rader, a devout Christian, wished to live in the Christian Student Fellowship (CSF) house, across the street from campus, in order to "share a lifestyle which glorifies Christ." He asserted that "the obnoxious alcohol parties in the [university] dormitories, the immoral atmosphere, and the intolerance towards those who profess to be Christians would severely hinder my free exercise of religion and be a definite hardship for me." He specifically pointed to the policy allowing 24-hour visitation in dorm rooms by members of the opposite sex, and the availability of condoms in dormitory vending machines.

The freshman-dorm policy included three exceptions in its text: married students, students age 19 or older on the first class day of the fall semester, and students living with their parents or legal guardians in the local community. The policy also allowed case-by-case exceptions for "significant and truly exceptional circumstances." Under this rubric, the district court found, UNK had allowed exceptions for

> cases of serious medical need and single parent pregnancies; a student, living outside the "Kearney community," who wished to drive his pregnant sister to classes at UNK; a student who was depressed and experienced headaches; a student with learning disabilities; a student who was mourning the death of a parent and a close friend; a student who wished to help care for her great-grandmother; and a student who was a non-custodial parent entitled to visitation with his son on alternating weekends. . . . When all of the exceptions to the freshman housing policy— published, unenumerated, or created at the discretion of administrators—are taken into account, only 1,600 of the 2,500 freshmen attending UNK are required by the University to comply with the parietal rule.

The district court concluded that "UNK administrators grant exceptions to the policy, at their discretion, in a broad range of circumstances not enumerated in the rule and not well defined or limited. While defendants grant petitions for exceptions to the parietal rule in circumstances such as medical need and single parent pregnancies that would likely impose a harsh burden on the petitioner, they also grant exceptions in a variety of other less onerous circumstances . . . [but] refuse to extend exceptions to students, such as Douglas Rader, who wish to live at CSF. [I]n order to meet the general applicability requirement, at a minimum 'government, in pursuit of legitimate interests, cannot in a selective manner impose burdens only on conduct motivated by religious belief.' *Lukumi*."

The court also found that the freshman-housing rule was not "being enforced in a neutral manner," in part for the same reason: that so many other students were exempted from it. In addition, the court pointed to testimony that the administrator who denied Rader's request had done so "without conducting any investigation into the circumstances of the petition as was his ordinary custom before denying requests for exemptions [on nonreligious grounds]." Instead, the court found that the administrator, a Baptist minister, had rejected the petition based on his own judgment that there was " 'nothing in the residence hall environment which would prohibit the free exercise of [Rader's], or any other person[']s, faith' "—thereby "judg[ing] Rader's petition in terms of his own religious experiences." The court also found "antipathy toward members of CSF" among UNK administrators. One administrator expressed the "opinion [that] students who do not wish to live in the residence halls for religious reasons should not attend UNK." Another testified that she would not grant any freshman requests to live at CSF because the group did not promote the goal of diversity of thought, and claimed that she "would differ with [Rader and CSF]. Diversity of thought is positive." Finally, a study that UNK relied on to support its policy "indicates that living in the residential halls [versus at home] increases the likelihood that a student will exhibit no religious preference by the time he or she is a senior in college."

The court therefore applied the compelling interest test even under Employment Division v. Smith, and it rejected UNK's arguments that the on-campus policy served the purposes of improving academic performance, fostering diversity and tolerance among students, and ensuring full occupancy of the residence halls. The court again noted the large number of students already exempted and added: " '[A] law cannot be regarded as protecting an interest' of the highest order ". . . when it leaves appreciable damage to that supposedly vital interest unprohibited.' *Lukumi*." In particular, the exemptions for students living locally with their parents and for those 19 or older undercut the asserted interests in promoting diversity. Moreover, "[i]f UNK's goals in enforcement of the parietal rule were of such great importance, one would expect the University to enact and enforce the policy in the same manner on all its campuses[. It did not]." Finally, the court concluded that residence at CSF would "to a large extent" satisfy the asserted interests in academics and diversity, since CSF had housed foreign students while 90 percent of UNK students were white and from Nebraska; the disciplined atmosphere at CSF would be "much more conducive" than the residence halls to studying; and Rader would interact with other students in his classes, at his job, and in sports activities.

FRATERNAL ORDER OF POLICE v. CITY OF NEWARK
170 F.3d 359 (3d Cir. 1999)

ALITO, Circuit Judge:
This appeal presents the question whether the policy of the Newark (N.J.) Police Department regarding the wearing of beards by officers violates the Free Exercise Clause of the First Amendment. Under that policy, . . . exemptions are

made for medical reasons (typically because of a skin condition called pseudo folliculitis barbae), but the Department refuses to make exemptions for officers whose religious beliefs prohibit them from shaving their beards. Because the Department makes exemptions from its policy for secular reasons and has not offered any substantial justification for refusing to provide similar treatment for officers who are required to wear beards for religious reasons, we conclude that the Department's policy violates the First Amendment. . . .

I

Since 1971, male officers in the Newark Police Department have been subject to an internal order that requires them to shave their beards. In relevant part, the order provides: "Full beards, goatees or other growths of hair below the lower lip, on the chin, or lower jaw bone area are prohibited." ("Order 71-15"). The order permits officers to wear mustaches and sideburns, and it allows exemptions from the "no-beard" rule for undercover officers whose "assignments or duties permit a departure from the requirements."

Officers Faruq Abdul-Aziz and Shakoor Mustafa are both devout Sunni Muslims who assert that they believe that they are under a religious obligation to grow their beards. According to the affidavit of an imam, "it is an obligation for men who can grow a beard, to do so" and not to shave. The affidavit continues:

> . . . The Quran commands the wearing of a beard implicitly. The Sunnah is the detailed explanation of the general injunctions contained in the Quran. The Sunnah says in too many verses to recount[:] "Grow the beard, trim the mustache."
> . . . I teach as the Prophet Mohammed taught that the Sunnah must be followed as well as the Quran. This is the unequivocal teaching for the past 1,418 years, by the one billion living Sunni Muslims world wide.
> . . . The refusal by a Sunni Muslim male who can grow a beard, to wear one is a major sin. I teach based upon the way I was taught and it is understood in my faith that the non-wearing of a beard by the male who can, for any reason is as [serious] a sin as eating pork.
> . . . This is not a discretionary instruction; it is a commandment. A Sunni Muslim male will not be saved from this major sin because of an instruction of another, even an employer, to shave his beard and the penalties will be meted out by Allah.

The defendants have not disputed the sincerity of the plaintiffs' beliefs. . . .

II

[Summary of *Smith* and *Lukumi* omitted.]

The *Smith* Court, however, did not overrule its prior free exercise decisions, but rather distinguished them. In this case, the plaintiffs contend that their Free Exercise claim is not governed by the generally applicable *Smith* rule but is instead governed by the Court's pre-*Smith* decisions. In this connection, the plaintiffs make three arguments. First, they contend that the *Smith* decision should be limited to cases involving criminal prohibitions. Second, they argue that the *Smith* analysis does not apply to government rules that, like the "no-beard" policy, already make secular exemptions for certain individuals. Finally, they maintain that the *Smith* rule does not bar their exemption claim because they are relying on both the Free Exercise Clause and the Free Speech Clause.

The District Court accepted the plaintiffs' first argument, applied the Court's pre-*Smith* jurisprudence, and concluded that the Free Exercise Clause prohibits the Department from enforcing its "no-beard" policy against Aziz and Mustafa. While we disagree with the District Court's conclusion that *Smith* is limited to the criminal context, we believe that the plaintiffs are entitled to a religious exemption since the Department already makes secular exemptions. As a result, we need not reach the plaintiffs' "hybrid" free speech/free exercise argument.

III

B

. . . Aziz and Mustafa contend that, since the Department provides medical— but not religious—exemptions from its "no-beard" policy, it has unconstitutionally devalued their religious reasons for wearing beards by judging them to be of lesser import than medical reasons. The Department, on the other hand, maintains that its distinction between medical exemptions and religious exemptions does not represent an impermissible value judgment because medical exemptions are made only so as to comply with the Americans with Disabilities Act ("ADA"). While this argument initially appears persuasive, it ultimately cannot be sustained.

It is true that the ADA requires employers to make "reasonable accommodations" for individuals with disabilities. However, Title VII of the Civil Rights Act of 1964 imposes an identical obligation on employers with respect to accommodating religion. 42 U.S.C. § 2000e(j). This parallel requirement undermines the Department's contention that it provides a medical exception, but not a religious exception, because it believes that "the law may require" a medical exception. Furthermore, it is noteworthy that the Department has clearly been put on notice of Title VII's religious accommodation requirements. In light of these circumstances, we cannot accept the Department's position that its differential treatment of medical exemptions and religious exemptions is premised on a good-faith belief that the former may be required by law while the latter are not.

We also reject the argument that, because the medical exemption is not an "individualized exemption," the *Smith/Lukumi* rule does not apply. While the Supreme Court did speak in terms of "individualized exemptions" in *Smith* and *Lukumi*, it is clear from those decisions that the Court's concern was the prospect of the government's deciding that secular motivations are more important than religious motivations. If anything, this concern is only further implicated when the government does not merely create a mechanism for individualized exemptions, but instead, actually creates a categorical exemption for individuals with a secular objection but not for individuals with a religious objection. See generally *Lukumi* ("All laws are selective to some extent, but categories of selection are of paramount concern when a law has the incidental effect of burdening religious practice."). Therefore, we conclude that the Department's decision to provide medical exemptions while refusing religious exemptions is sufficiently suggestive of discriminatory intent so as to trigger heightened scrutiny under *Smith* and *Lukumi*.

Contrary to the Department's contention, our decision to apply heightened scrutiny is entirely consistent with the result in *Smith*. In *Smith*, the Court upheld an Oregon law that prohibited the "knowing or intentional possession of a 'controlled substance' unless the substance has been prescribed by a medical practitioner." The Department argues that, since the prescription exception did not prompt the *Smith* Court to apply heightened scrutiny to the Oregon law, we should not apply heightened scrutiny in the instant case based on the Department's allowance of medical exemptions. This argument, however, overlooks a critical difference between the prescription exception in the Oregon law and the medical exemption in this case.

The Department's decision to allow officers to wear beards for medical reasons undoubtedly undermines the Department's interest in fostering a uniform appearance through its "no-beard" policy. By contrast, the prescription exception to Oregon's drug law does not necessarily undermine Oregon's interest in curbing the unregulated use of dangerous drugs. Rather, the prescription exception is more akin to the Department's undercover exception, which does not undermine the Department's interest in uniformity because undercover officers "obviously are not held out to the public as law enforcement person[nel]." The prescription exception and the undercover exception do not trigger heightened scrutiny because the Free Exercise Clause does not require the government to apply its laws to activities that it does not have an interest in preventing. However, the medical exemption raises concern because it indicates that the Department has made a value judgment that secular (i.e., medical) motivations for wearing a beard are important enough to overcome its general interest in uniformity but that religious motivations are not. As discussed above, when the government makes a value judgment in favor of secular motivations, but not religious motivations, the government's actions must survive heightened scrutiny.

C

The Department has not offered any interest in defense of its policy that is able to withstand any form of heightened scrutiny. The Department contends that it wants to convey the image of a " 'monolithic, highly disciplined force' " and that "[u]niformity [of appearance] not only benefits the men and women that risk their lives on a daily basis, but offers the public a sense of security in having readily identifiable and trusted public servants." We will address separately all of the interests that we can discern in this passage.

The Department hints that other officers and citizens might have difficulty identifying a bearded officer as a genuine Newark police officer and that this might undermine safety. But while safety is undoubtedly an interest of the greatest importance, the Department's partial no-beard policy is not tailored to serve that interest. Uniformed officers, whether bearded or clean-shaven, should be readily identifiable. Officers who wear plain clothes are not supposed to stand out to the same degree as uniformed officers, and in any event the Department permits such officers to wear beards for medical reasons. The Department does not contend that these medical exemptions pose a serious threat to the safety of the members of the force or to the general public, and there is no apparent reason why permitting officers to wear beards for religious reasons should create any greater difficulties in this regard.

The Department also suggests that permitting officers to wear beards for religious reasons would undermine the force's morale and esprit de corps. However, the Department has provided no legitimate explanation as to why the presence of officers who wear beards for medical reasons does not have this effect but the presence of officers who wear beards for religious reasons would. And the same is true with respect to the Department's suggestion that the presence of officers who wear beards for religious reasons would undermine public confidence in the force. We are at a loss to understand why religious exemptions threaten important city interests but medical exemptions do not. Conceivably, the Department may think that permitting officers to wear beards for religious reasons would present a greater threat to the sense of uniformity that it wishes to foster because the difference that this practice highlights—namely, a difference in religious belief and practice—is not superficial (like the presence of pseudo folliculitis barbae) and thus may cause divisions in the ranks and among the public. (There is no doubt that religious differences have been a cause of dissension throughout much of human history.) But if this is the Department's thinking—and we emphasize that the Department has not spelled out this argument in so many words—what it means is that Sunni Muslim officers who share the plaintiffs' religious beliefs are prohibited from wearing beards precisely for the purpose of obscuring the fact that they hold those beliefs and that they differ in this respect from most of the other members of the force. In other words, if this is the real reason for the distinction that is drawn between medical and religious exemptions, we have before us a policy the very purpose of which is to suppress manifestations of the religious diversity that the First Amendment safeguards. Before sanctioning such a policy, we would require a far more substantial showing than the Department has made in this case. We thus conclude that the Department's policy cannot survive any degree of heightened scrutiny and thus cannot be sustained.

NOTES AND QUESTIONS

1. Neutrality, General Applicability, and Exceptions to a Law. How many exceptions must there be to a policy to make it less than neutral and generally applicable? One? (Note that the Third Circuit did not treat the exception for undercover officers as an exception to the rule, since it does not undermine the purposes of the rule. Is that a coherent distinction?) In *Rader*, the exceptions amounted to about a third of the cases. How should courts analyze laws that make a few secular exceptions, but refuse to make religious exceptions?

How should we define the full scope of the law for purposes of this analysis? Every law applies to some subset of the human race; no law applies to absolutely everything. How can we tell the difference between an exception and a lack of coverage? For an argument that these are equivalent, see Frederick Schauer, Exceptions, 58 U. Chi. L. Rev. 871 (1991). Would it make any difference if the laws were framed in terms of who is included rather than in terms of a general rule with an exception? For example: "All unmarried freshman students under the age of 19 not living within the Kearney community in their parents' home must live in a dormitory. No exceptions." The Third Circuit suggests that the issue is not whether the law makes exceptions per se, but whether it is underinclusive: whether it applies to less than the entire universe of cases that pose the problem the law seeks to solve. This is a familiar idea from equal protection jurisprudence—but it is no more clearly defined here than there. Was the drug law upheld in *Smith* nongenerally applicable because it did not apply to alcohol, which is functionally similar to the drugs on the forbidden list? Was the rule in *Rader* nongenerally applicable because it did not apply to sophomores, juniors, and seniors?

One commentator has argued, in the light of *Rader* and *Fraternal Order of Police*, that "religious liberty will often prevail against burdens imposed by underinclusive (and thus nongenerally applicable) laws and governmental policies." Richard A. Duncan, Free Exercise Is Dead, Long Live Free Exercise: *Smith, Lukumi,* and the General Applicability Requirement, 3 U. Pa. J. Const. L. 850, 884 (2001). Nearly all laws have exceptions, many of them at some cost to the goals underlying the law. If Professor Duncan is correct, what is left of the *Smith* rule, and its concern for deferring to democratically enacted laws?

2. The Narrower Interpretation: "Singling Out" Religion.   What is the alternative interpretation? In Thomas v. Anchorage Equal Rights Comm'n, 165 F.3d 692 (9th Cir. 1999), vacated on ripeness grounds, 220 F.3d 1134 (9th Cir. 2000) (en banc), a Ninth Circuit panel rejected the argument that Alaska's prohibition on discrimination by landlords on the basis of marital status is underinclusive. The court reasoned (165 F.3d at 701-702):

> The underinclusiveness at play in *Lukumi* . . . was of a different constitutional order altogether from that at issue here. There, "the underinclusion [was] substantial, not inconsequential." *Lukumi.* There, the ordinances were "drafted with care to forbid few killings but those occasioned by religious sacrifice." Here, in contrast to the situation in *Lukumi,* the "underinclusion"—which consists of only a single exception per challenged provision—is relatively inconsequential. Boiled down, in *Lukumi,* the ordinances applied essentially only to the Santeria; here, the challenged laws apply essentially to all landlords.
>
> Underinclusiveness is not in and of itself a talisman of constitutional infirmity; rather, it is significant only insofar as it indicates something more sinister. In *Lukumi,* the Court considered the ordinances' lack of neutrality and general applicability as a proxy of the Hialeah lawmakers' illicit intention to single out the Santeria religion for unfavorable treatment. The Court observed that the pattern of exemptions present in the Hialeah ordinances betrayed their object as one of suppressing religious exercise. Because the ordinances were "designed to persecute or oppress a religion or its practices," the Court concluded that the permissive *Smith* standard did not apply.
>
> There is no hint that the Alaska laws were "drafted with care to forbid few [instances of marital status discrimination] but those occasioned by religious [conviction]." Nor do the laws "in a selective manner impose burdens only on conduct motivated by religious belief." There is, in sum, no indication that Alaska lawmakers were impelled by a desire to target or suppress religious exercise. The housing laws, we think, have the purpose of preventing discrimination on the basis of marital status; any burden on religiously motivated conduct, even if substantial, is incidental. Consequently, absent some other exception, *Smith,* not *Lukumi,* governs the landlords' claims.

If we apply this standard to the facts of *Rader* and *Fraternal Order of Police*, how would those cases have come out? Under the Ninth Circuit's standard, what is left of the requirement of general applicability? How does it differ from neutrality?

3. Problems. Consider the following situations.

(a) A small religious group believes that the divine being they worship visits the earth one night a month in a local cornfield, and that it is spiritually necessary to view this visitation. When the owner of the field (who is not a member of the sect) refuses permission, the members meet in the field anyway, and they are arrested and charged with trespass to private property. In their defense, they point out that the law of trespass contains exceptions allowing entry on land in cases of adverse possession, law-enforcement needs, and private or public necessity (i.e., to escape harm to oneself or prevent harm to others). What result under the above decisions? Cf. Eugene Volokh, Intermediate Questions of Religious Exemptions—A Research Agenda with Test Suites, 21 Cardozo L. Rev. 595, 634 (1999) (raising an analogous hypothetical).

(b) Consider the following case from the late 1800s: Ho Ah Kow, a Chinese alien, was confined in the county jail in San Francisco. The sheriff cut off his "queue" (a braided tail of hair with sacred meaning in Chinese religion), pursuant to a county ordinance requiring that all inmates' hair be cut to no more one inch from the scalp. It was widely accepted that the city adopted this ordinance knowing that cutting the queue would cause religious distress to Chinese prisoners, so that the threat of cutting would pressure the Chinese to pay municipal fines rather than remain in the jail. The large majority of the inmates affected by the ordinance were Chinese. Ho Ah Kow sued the sheriff and the city for damages. If the case arose today, and Ho Ah Kow's cause of action was based on the Free Exercise Clause, what would be the governing standard, and what result? See Ho Ah Kow v. Nunan, 12 F. Cas. 252 (C.C.D. Cal. 1879) (ruling for plaintiff under, among other things, the Equal Protection Clause).

(c) Suppose that in response to the connection between terrorism and some forms of radical Islam, the federal government undertakes a surveillance program of mosques and Islamic centers throughout the United States. The actions include wiretapping and calling leaders in for questioning. Some of these actions may raise questions under the Fourth Amendment to the Constitution, which prohibits "unreasonable" searches and seizures. Would these actions also violate the Free Exercise Clause?

(d) Remember that several provisions of the latest federal religious freedom statute, RLUIPA, claim to be enforcing the Free Exercise Clause in a way consistent with *Smith* and *Lukumi*, and thus to be within Congress's power to enforce the Fourteenth Amendment. (See p. 160.) One section prohibits any zoning regulation that "treats a religious assembly or institution on less than equal terms with a nonreligious assembly or institution." Did Congress have power to pass this section?

NOTES ON "HYBRID" CLAIMS

1. Hybrid Claims in General. The other chief recurring free exercise issue under Employment Division v. Smith stems from the Court's reference to cases that involve "the Free Exercise Clause in conjunction with other constitutional protections, such as freedom of speech." The Court suggested that heightened scrutiny should continue to apply to such "hybrid" claims. That is how *Smith* distinguished Wisconsin v. Yoder—which it said involved a hybrid of free exercise and parental rights over children's education—as well as several previous decisions involving religious speech or association.

The hybrid-rights doctrine seems to say that two constitutional claims, each of which would be insufficient on its own, require strict or at least heightened scrutiny when combined in a single action. Does this doctrine make any sense? Is it anything more than a clever way to distinguish previous decisions? In his concurring opinion in *Lukumi*, Justice Souter criticized the hybrid-rights concept as "ultimately untenable" (508 U.S. at 567):

> If a hybrid claim is simply one in which another constitutional right is implicated, then the hybrid exception would probably be so vast as to swallow the *Smith* rule, and, indeed, the hybrid exception would cover the situation exemplified by *Smith*, since free speech and associational rights are implicated in the peyote smoking ritual. But if a hybrid claim is one in which a litigant would actually obtain an exemption from a formally neutral, generally applicable law under another constitutional provision, then there would have been no reason for the Court in what *Smith* calls the hybrid cases to have mentioned the Free Exercise Clause at all.

At least one court has reacted to the difficulties in the concept by simply refusing to apply it. See Kissinger v. Board of Trustees, 5 F.3d 177, 180 (6th Cir. 1993) (holding that because the hybrid-rights exception is "completely illogical," "we will not use a stricter test than that used in *Smith*" until the Court requires so more clearly). Other courts have effectively ignored the doctrine by analyzing whether the nonfree-exercise claim is viable on its own. See, e.g., Brown v. Hot, Sexy, and Safer Productions, 68 F.3d 525, 539 (1st Cir. 1995) (rejecting students' and parents' hybrid-rights objection to a compulsory, sexually explicit school assembly, on the basis that the parents had not shown that their right to control their children's education was violated). If the hybrid-rights doctrine only applies when the nonfree-exercise claim would justify relief (or at least heightened scrutiny) on its own, then as Justice Souter points out, there is "no reason [to] mention[ ] the Free Exercise Clause at all."

No court has ever adopted the other polar approach mentioned by Justice Souter: triggering strict or heightened scrutiny whenever another constitutional right is even "implicated" or "invoked" in the pleadings. That would, in effect, overrule Employment Division v. Smith by triggering strict scrutiny in virtually any case.

Several courts have settled on a middle ground: A hybrid claim triggers stricter review if, but only if, the non-free-exercise claim is "colorable." See, e.g., Thomas v. Anchorage Equal Rights Comm., 165 F.3d at 703-704; Swanson v. Guthrie Ind. School Dist., 135 F.3d 694, 700 (10th Cir. 1998); Axson-Flynn v. Johnson, 356 F.3d 1277, 1295-96 (10th Cir. 2004). But does this standard shed any more light on the problem? What does it mean to say that a claim is "colorable" if it would not prevail? In the *Axson-Flynn* case, the court of appeals defined a colorable claim as one with "a fair probability, or likelihood," of success (analogous to the standard for granting a preliminary injunction). But the district court had opined that a claim is colorable if it is not "wholly insubstantial or frivolous." 151 F. Supp. 1326, 1338 (D. Utah 2001). Which standard is a better interpretation of *Smith*? Of the Free Exercise Clause?

2. The Religion/Speech Hybrid. Because religious activity often takes the form of speech or other expression, the most common hybrid of constitutional claims is of free speech and free exercise. See, e.g., Chalifoux v. New Caney Ind. School Dist., 976 F. Supp. 659 (S.D. Tex. 1997) (school ban on students wearing gang symbols, as applied to Catholic rosaries, violated hybrid of free speech and free exercise). But the relationship of free speech and free exercise raises complications. The logic of the hybrid-rights doctrine would suggest that the religious content or motivation of speech would add to its constitutional protection; but as we will see in section V-B, a central theme in the law of freedom of speech is that the government must not favor the expression of one viewpoint over others. We examine this question in detail in Part V-B-2 (p. 611).

3. Problems: Other Hybrid-Right Cases. In the following situations, what hybrid rights should the free exercise claimant pursue? This is not a course on constitutional rights in general; but what is the claimant's likelihood of success in these cases?

(a) Landlords and unmarried couples. In Thomas v. Anchorage Equal Rights Commission (see note 1), two landlords, Thomas and Baker, who each owned a small number of apartments, refused to rent the apartments to unmarried couples who planned to live together. Thomas and Baker, devout Christians, believed that renting to an unmarried couple sleeping together would be facilitating the sin of fornication. Laws of the city of Anchorage and the state of Alaska make it unlawful to refuse to rent to others on the basis of marital status (which has been construed to cover unmarried cohabitation). The laws also make it unlawful for a landlord to "represent to a person" that rental of a property will be refused based on marital status, and for a landlord to "make, print, or publish" any statement indicating any discrimination in rental on the basis of marital status. Thomas and Baker objected to the provisions, stating that if they were forced to rent to unmarried cohabiting couples, they would have to leave the business and sell their property.

Thomas is one of several recent cases involving small landlords refusing to rent to unmarried couples. These disputes raise interesting questions not only about the hybrid-rights doctrine, but also about what constitutes a significant "burden" on religious exercise and when the government has a "compelling" interest that justifies the burden. Accordingly, we will return to the landlord cases in those sections below (section B-2, p. 182 and p. 210).

(b) Clergy employment. Suppose that the First Community Church fires the Rev. Janet Jones, who has been an associate minister at the church for three years with responsibilities for teaching Sunday school classes, counseling parishioners, and sometimes preaching at worship services. Jones sues the church alleging employment discrimination based on sex under Title VII of the federal Civil Rights Act. The church, which has no doctrinal objection to women serving as clergy, asserts in response that Jones was terminated because her performance in the job was not acceptable. What constitutional defenses should the church raise to her lawsuit? Which hybrid-rights defenses? Cf. EEOC v. Catholic Univ. of America, 83 F.3d 455 (D.C. Cir. 1996) (dismissing sex discrimination suit by canon law professor, in part on basis of hybrid-rights analysis). (We look at clergy employment disputes in more detail in section D-3 (p. 310).)

One possible hybrid constitutional claim in this context is the right of association for expressive purposes that the Court has found implicit in the First

Amendment's free speech provision. In Boy Scouts of America v. Dale, 530 U.S. 640 (2000), the Court held that a state law forbidding discrimination based on sexual orientation in public accommodations could not be applied to prevent the Boy Scouts from removing an openly gay assistant scoutmaster. The Court held that application of the anti-discrimination law would "force the organization to send a message . . . that the Boy Scouts accepts homosexual conduct as a legitimate form of behavior," contrary to the Scouts' goal of promoting "morally straight" and "clean" behavior as it understood those terms. *Id.* at 653, 650. Does *Dale* provide the basis for a hybrid-right defense to the claim by the Rev. Jones?

In connection with the right of association, does it matter that the church has no tenet objecting to women serving as clergy? The Boy Scouts had argued for a broader right than the *Dale* Court recognized: the right of any noncommercial expressive association to choose its own leaders and spokesmen, whether or not the leader contravenes any particular message or tenet of the organization. Might that claim be "colorable" enough to support a hybrid claim? Should religious associations have any greater right than secular expressive associations to choose their leaders?

2. Issues Under Heightened Free Exercise Scrutiny

When a case involves federal action governed by RFRA, state action governed by RLUIPA or a state constitutional or statutory provision, or a matter of internal church governance or other issue subject to a higher standard of review under the Free Exercise Clause, or a variety of other issues, litigation will still take the pre-*Smith* form. In these cases the plaintiff bears the obligation of demonstrating a constitutionally cognizable burden on her sincere exercise of religion. The obligation then shifts to the government to establish that its conduct is the least restrictive means of achieving a compelling governmental interest—or some functionally equivalent test. In the next two sets of materials, we examine the concepts of burden, sincerity, and compelling interest.

a. What Is a "Burden"?

Whether government action "burdens" religious exercise is often a difficult question. If a law imposes a criminal sanction for following a tenet of one's faith, the burden may seem clear. But what if, as a result of government action, the practice of religion becomes more expensive, more inconvenient, or (as a practical matter) impossible? What if, as a result of religious exercise, the claimant forfeits a right to an otherwise available benefit? We take up these questions in this section.

BRAUNFELD v. BROWN
366 U.S. 599 (1961)

Mr. Chief Justice WARREN announced the judgment of the Court and an opinion in which Mr. Justice BLACK, Mr. Justice CLARK, and Mr. Justice WHITTAKER concur.

This case concerns the constitutional validity of the application to appellants of the Pennsylvania criminal statute, enacted in 1959, which proscribes the Sunday retail sale of certain enumerated commodities. [In a companion case, McGowan v. Maryland, the Court held that the Sunday closing law did not violate the Establishment Clause.] Thus the only question for consideration is whether the statute interferes with the free exercise of appellants' religion.

Appellants are merchants in Philadelphia who engage in the retail sale of clothing and home furnishings within the proscription of the statute in issue. Each of the appellants is a member of the Orthodox Jewish faith, which requires the closing of their places of business and a total abstention from all manner of work from nightfall each Friday until nightfall each Saturday. [The complaint, which sought an injunction against application of the statute,] alleged that appellants had previously kept their places of business open on Sunday; that each of appellants had done a substantial amount of business on Sunday, compensating somewhat for their closing on Saturday; that Sunday closing will result in impairing the ability of all appellants to earn a livelihood and will render appellant Braunfeld unable to continue in his business. . . .

Appellants contend that the enforcement against them of the Pennsylvania statute will prohibit the free exercise of their religion because, due to the statute's compulsion to close on Sunday, appellants will suffer substantial economic loss, to the benefit of their non-Sabbatarian competitors, if appellants also continue their Sabbath observance by closing their businesses on Saturday; that this result will either compel appellants to give up their Sabbath observance, a basic tenet of the Orthodox Jewish faith, or will put appellants at a serious economic disadvantage if they continue to adhere to their Sabbath. . . .

In *McGowan*, . . . we took cognizance of the evolution of Sunday Closing Laws from wholly religious sanctions to legislation concerned with the establishment of a day of community tranquillity, respite and recreation, a day when the atmosphere is one of calm and relaxation rather than one of commercialism, as it is during the other six days of the week. We reviewed the still growing state preoccupation with improving the health, safety, morals and general well-being of our citizens.

[T]he freedom to act, even when the action is in accord with one's religious convictions, is not totally free from legislative restrictions. As pointed out in Reynolds v. United States, legislative power over mere opinion is forbidden but it may reach people's actions when they are found to be in violation of important social duties or subversive of good order, even when the actions are demanded by one's religion.

It is to be noted that, in [*Reynolds*], the religious practices themselves conflicted with the public interest. In such cases, to make accommodation between the religious action and an exercise of state authority is a particularly delicate task, because resolution in favor of the State results in the choice to the individual of either abandoning his religious principle or facing criminal prosecution.

But, again, this is not the case before us because the statute at bar does not make unlawful any religious practices of appellants; the Sunday law simply regulates a secular activity and, as applied to appellants, operates so as to make the practice of their religious beliefs more expensive. Furthermore, the law's effect does not inconvenience all members of the Orthodox Jewish faith but only those who believe it necessary to work on Sunday. And even these are not faced with as serious a choice as forsaking their religious practices or subjecting themselves to criminal prosecution. Fully recognizing that the alternatives open to appellants and others similarly situated—retaining their present occupations and incurring economic disadvantage or engaging in some other commercial activity which does not call for either Saturday or Sunday labor—may well result in some financial sacrifice in order to observe their religious beliefs, still the option is wholly different than when the legislation attempts to make a religious practice itself unlawful.

To strike down, without the most critical scrutiny, legislation which imposes only an indirect burden on the exercise of religion, i.e., legislation which does not make unlawful the religious practice itself, would radically restrict the operating latitude of the legislature. Statutes which tax income and limit the amount which may be deducted for religious contributions impose an indirect economic burden on the observance of the religion of the citizen whose religion requires him to donate a greater amount to his church; statutes which require the courts to be closed on Saturday and Sunday impose a similar indirect burden on the observance of the religion of the trial lawyer whose religion requires him to rest on a weekday. The list of legislation of this nature is nearly limitless. . . .

Of course, to hold unassailable all legislation regulating conduct which imposes solely an indirect burden on the observance of religion would be a gross oversimplification. If the purpose or effect of a law is to impede the observance of one or all religions or is to discriminate invidiously between religions, that law is constitutionally invalid even though the burden may be characterized as being only indirect. But if the State regulates conduct by enacting a general law within its power, the purpose and effect of which is to advance the State's secular goals, the statute is valid despite its indirect burden on religious observance unless the State may accomplish its purpose by means which do not impose such a burden.

Mr. Justice BRENNAN, concurring and dissenting. . . .

Admittedly, these laws do not compel overt affirmation of a repugnant belief, nor do they prohibit outright any of appellants' religious practices, as did the federal law upheld in *Reynolds.* That is, the laws do not say that appellants must work on Saturday. But their effect is that appellants may not simultaneously practice their religion and their trade, without being hampered by a substantial competitive disadvantage. Their effect is that no one may at one and the same time be an Orthodox Jew and compete effectively with his Sunday-observing fellow tradesmen. This clog upon the exercise of religion, this state-imposed burden on Orthodox Judaism, has exactly the same economic effect as a tax levied upon the sale of religious literature. . . .

In fine, the Court, in my view, has exalted administrative convenience to a constitutional level high enough to justify making one religion economically disadvantageous. The Court would justify this result on the ground that the effect on religion, though substantial, is indirect. The Court forgets, I think, a warning uttered during the congressional discussion of the First Amendment itself: ". . . the rights of conscience are, in their nature, of peculiar delicacy, and will little bear the gentlest touch of governmental hand. . . ." Annals of Cong. 730 (remarks of Representative Daniel Carroll of Maryland, August 15, 1789).

Mr. Justice STEWART, dissenting.

I agree with substantially all that Mr. Justice BRENNAN has written. Pennsylvania has passed a law which compels an Orthodox Jew to choose between his religious faith and his economic survival. That is a cruel choice. It is a choice which I think no State can constitutionally demand. For me this is not something that can be swept under the rug and forgotten in the interest of enforced Sunday togetherness. I think the impact of this law upon these appellants grossly violates their constitutional right to the free exercise of their religion.

NOTES AND QUESTIONS

1. Are Sunday Closing Laws Neutral and "Secular"? Note that the Court treats the Sunday closing law, despite its close connection to Christian beliefs, as promoting "community tranquillity, respite and recreation, a day when the atmosphere is one of calm and relaxation rather than one of commercialism, as it is during the other six days of the week." In McGowan v. Maryland, 366 U.S. 420 (1961), and other cases in the same Term as *Braunfeld*, the Court rejected Establishment Clause challenges to these laws. That ruling may be questionable, but because of it, for doctrinal purposes we treat Braunfeld's free exercise claim as a claim for exemption from a secular enactment.

2. Categories of Burdens on Religion. The Chief Justice asserts that "the statute at bar does not make unlawful any religious practices of appellants; [it] simply regulates a secular activity and [thereby makes] the practice . . . of religious beliefs more expensive." This has an air of common sense about it. Executing Saturday observers surely is a greater constraint than forcing them (along with everyone else) to close on Sunday. So maybe we should have categories of constraints as we have categories of protected acts—and with greater constitutional protection for more serious or substantial constraints. See John H. Garvey, What Are Freedoms For? 157-173 (1996). But what should the categories be?

(a) Direct versus indirect burdens. The *Braunfeld* opinion proposes that we distinguish between direct and indirect constraints. A direct constraint imposes some sort of sanction on a religious activity *x*. If you practice polygamy you will be thrown in jail; if you discriminate against unmarried cohabitants you will be forced from the rental market. Your legal status changes, in some way, as a result of your religious activity. An indirect constraint is one regulates some *other* activity, and has spillover effects on *x*. You must close your shop on Sunday; this makes it difficult to observe Saturday sabbath and still keep in business. (Note that an indirect regulation is not the same as a "neutral" regulation under *Smith*. The law against peyote use in *Smith* was neutral toward religion (since it prohibited nonreligious peyote use as well), but it directly criminalized the Native Americans' religious practices.)

(b) Is economic cost a "burden"? In what sense does the Sunday closing law burden the religious exercise of Jewish merchants? To be sure, it means that they cannot do business on Sunday, which is an economic loss, but the same is true for all other merchants, including faceless corporations that know no God. They, too, might wish to be open on Sunday. Why are the Jewish merchant's losses any greater or more significant?

Certainly burdens on religion often take the form of economic losses—a money fine, tort liability against a church, the denial of benefits in *Sherbert*. And Braunfeld feels the economic loss more acutely because his religious convictions cause him also to be closed on Saturday, which puts him at a disadvantage vis-à-vis his non-Jewish competitors (who can stay open six days a week instead of Braunfeld's five). But why is that cost attributable to the Sunday closing law? Even if there were no such law, and most businesses stayed open all week, the observant Jewish merchant would be at an economic disadvantage (opening only six days instead of the competitors' seven). The ratio of five-sixths of the available business is less than six-sevenths, but not by much. And for the most part, we say that believers should bear the costs and consequences of their own beliefs. Is that a sufficient answer to the plaintiffs in *Braunfeld*?

Do Justices Brennan and Stewart believe that any law making the exercise of religion substantially more difficult or expensive is subject to strict scrutiny? What if the 35 m.p.h. speed limit makes me late to church? What if parking regulations make it more expensive to build a synagogue building? What if high rates of property tax leave an individual unable to make contributions to his religion?

Is the only answer to these hypotheticals that the Sunday closing law is not truly secular and religiously neutral (see note 1)?

(c) The denial of benefits as a burden: *Sherbert* revisited. Compare the burden on free exercise in *Braunfeld* with that in Sherbert v. Verner (p. 129), decided just two years later:

> Here not only is it apparent that appellant's declared ineligibility for benefits derives solely from the practice of her religion, but the pressure upon her to forego that practice is unmistakable. The ruling forces her to choose between following the precepts of her religion and forfeiting benefits, on the one hand, and abandoning one of the precepts of her religion in order to accept work, on the other hand. Governmental imposition of such a choice puts the same kind of burden upon the free exercise of religion as would a fine imposed against appellant for her Saturday worship.
>
> [T]o condition the availability of benefits upon this appellant's willingness to violate a cardinal principle of her religious faith effectively penalizes the free exercise of her constitutional liberties.

(i) How does the constraint found insufficient in *Braunfeld* differ from the constraint in *Sherbert*? Adele Sherbert also observed the sabbath on Saturday. And the law there didn't make this unlawful—it simply made it more expensive by withholding unemployment compensation benefits from people who declined Saturday work. But note that Sherbert's refusal to be available for Saturday work directly affected her rights—she was therefore ineligible for unemployment compensation. *Sherbert* held that the work availability requirement imposed "the same kind of burden upon the free exercise of religion as would a fine imposed . . . for her Saturday worship." By contrast, whether the *Braunfeld* plaintiffs observed the sabbath or not would have no effect on their legal rights: No one was permitted to open shop on Sunday.

(ii) Although the effect of the provision in *Sherbert* was more direct, nonetheless many observers—even those generally sympathetic to *Sherbert*'s "compelling interest" test—have found the test's application in this context troubling. In what sense did the denial of unemployment compensation burden the exercise of Adele Sherbert's religion? In the absence of an unemployment compensation scheme, she would bear the economic consequences of her inability to work on Saturday. Did the existence of the program make her any worse off? Garvey, 1981 Sup. Ct. Rev. 193. Perhaps it did: she had to pay contributions to the fund during her employment but then was denied benefits from the program when she needed them. Michael W. McConnell and Richard A. Posner, An Economic Approach to Issues of Religious Freedom, 56 U. Chi. L. Rev. 1, 40 (1989). On the other hand, granting her benefits would mean that although she paid the same contributions as other workers, she was insured against an extra risk—namely, the risk that job requirements would conflict with her religious tenets. *Id.* at 41 ("Requiring the state to pay benefits to Mrs. Sherbert is a bit like requiring an insurer to include smokers in a health insurance program at no additional premium."). Is being a smoker a good analogy to being a Saturday worshiper? If the difference is that the government must be "neutral" toward the religious worshiper, what does neutrality require?

(iii)   Putting aside the intricacies of the unemployment compensation context, *Sherbert* seems to stand for one extremely important principle: Denial of eligibility for an otherwise available governmental benefit on account of the exercise of religion is constitutionally equivalent to a fine or a penalty on the exercise of the constitutional right. Under *Smith*, that may or may not be sufficient to win a free exercise case, but denials of benefits are treated the same as penalties for purposes of constitutional analysis. This idea has come to be known as the doctrine of unconstitutional conditions.

There is an extensive literature on this subject. See, e.g., Richard A. Epstein, The Supreme Court, 1987 Term—Foreword: Unconstitutional Conditions, State Power, and the Limits of Consent, 102 Harv. L. Rev. 4 (1988); Kathleen M. Sullivan, Unconstitutional Conditions, 102 Harv. L. Rev. 1413 (1989); Seth F. Kreimer, Allocational Sanctions: The Problem of Negative Rights in a Positive State, 132 U. Pa. L. Rev. 1293 (1984). The basic idea is that the government is (generally) not required to pay for the costs of exercising a constitutional right—the government need not provide a printing press so an individual can engage in free speech—but the government may not deny a benefit the individual otherwise would receive on account of his own exercise of that right. The classic case, Speiser v. Randall, 357 U.S. 513 (1958), cited in *Sherbert*, involved a state law granting veterans a property tax exemption, but only if they signed a loyalty oath. To be sure, the government was under no obligation to provide this benefit to anyone, but once it did so, it could not deny the benefit to those who exercised their constitutional right not to take a loyalty oath.

The unconstitutional conditions doctrine can be seen as a response to changes in governmental authority that have come in the past century. In a time when the government—especially the federal government, the original subject of the Bill of Rights' restrictions—mostly engaged in the function of keeping the public peace through criminal law and foreign relations, the only evident threats to constitutional freedoms came from exercise of that kind of power. With the advent of the welfare state, when the livelihoods of millions of Americans are dependent on government grants and employment, the threats to constitutional freedom now frequently come through the attachment of conditions to benefits. In the earlier era, Justice Holmes famously rejected the argument of a policeman who had been fired for making a political speech: "The petitioner may have a constitutional right to talk politics, but he has no constitutional right to be a policeman." McAuliffe v. Mayor of New Bedford, 155 Mass. 216, 220 (1892). Gradually, over the past 100 years, the Court has come to adopt the idea of unconstitutional conditions in a variety of constitutional contexts. See William Van Alstyne, The Demise of the Right-Privilege Distinction in Constitutional Law, 81 Harv. L. Rev. 1439 (1968).

Sherbert was the case in which the Court adopted the unconstitutional conditions argument under the Free Exercise Clause. Although the scope of the clause is greatly diminished as a result of *Smith*, the Court has never repudiated that teaching of *Sherbert*.

3. Problems: Compelled Support for Objectionable Conduct.   In an increasing number of cases, individuals or entities involved somehow in the marketplace object to being compelled by law to provide direct or indirect support for behavior they regard as sinful. When do such requirements "substantially burden" religion, possibly triggering strict free exercise scrutiny?

(a) Landlords and unmarried tenants.   Return to Thomas v. Anchorage Equal Rights Commission (p. 175), the case about landlords who refused to rent to unmarried cohabiting couples. The landlords said that if they were forced by state law to rent to such couples, they would have to leave the business and sell their property. Would that impose a substantial burden on their religious conscience? Is this situation more like *Braunfeld*, or like *Sherbert*?

Judges have disagreed on this issue. Cf. *Thomas*, 165 F.3d at 712-714 (finding a substantial burden on landlords from a "Hobson's choice" of renting against their conscience or giving up their livelihood); with Smith v. Fair Employment & Housing Comm., 12 Cal. 4th 1143, 1170-1176, 913 P.2d 909, 925-929 (1996) (plurality opinion) (finding no substantial burden). The "burden" issue raises at least two questions:

First, is it a sufficient penalty on the landlord's exercise of religion to require him to get out of the landlord business? If rental property is an investment, just like anything else, why is it a substantial burden for him to have to shift investments from residential rental property to commercial rental property, or stocks and bonds? Does it matter whether the landlord is actively engaged in the management of the property?

Second, what precisely is the nature of the landlords' religious exercise here? They asserted that "facilitating cohabitation [between unmarried persons] in any way is tantamount to facilitating sin [fornication]." Does that mean that, if they were grocery store clerks, they would refuse to sell groceries to the cohabiting couple? That they would decline to employ either one of the couple, since the pay would help support the cohabiting household? What if the mail carrier declined to deliver their mail? Or the recorder of deeds at the courthouse refused to process their papers for purchase of a home? Are there limits to the notion of "facilitation"? On the other hand, if "facilitation" is a question of degree, then the connection here is fairly close. The landlords are not being asked to contract with the cohabiting couple in some unrelated aspect of the latter's lives: They are being asked to provide the bedroom. For analysis of this issue in another context, see John H. Garvey and Amy V. Coney, Catholic Judges in Capital Cases, 81 Marq. L. Rev. 303, 317-331 (1998) (discussing Catholic moral theology on "cooperation with evil").

Again, does it matter whether the landlord manages a small or large number of units, and whether he personally manages the property? Note that antidiscrimination laws in many jurisdictions exempt small landlords or employers—those who rent only a few units or employ only a few workers. Why?

(b) Payment for contraceptives. To help ensure citizens' ability to obtain contraceptives, the legislature has required that any employer who provides insurance coverage to employees for prescriptions must include prescription contraceptives as well. A Catholic social services organization objects to paying for contraceptive use, which the Catholic Church regards as a sin. The organization also objects to avoiding the requirement by ending all prescription benefits for employees, on the ground that "the Gospel message of justice and charity" requires it to pay "just wages and benefits to employees." See Catholic Charities of Sacramento v. Superior Court, 32 Cal. 4th 527, 85 P.3d 67 (2004) (raising the question "whether Catholic Charities' beliefs about the requirements of 'justice and charity' are necessarily equivalent to *religious* beliefs"). Does the compelled payment for contraceptives impose a constitutionally significant burden on the religious employer? Couldn't Catholic Charities just discontinue prescription benefits and pay its employees higher wages so they could afford their own insurance?

LYNG v. NORTHWEST INDIAN CEMETERY PROTECTIVE ASSOCIATION

485 U.S. 439 (1988)

Justice O'CONNOR delivered the opinion of the Court.

This case requires us to consider whether the First Amendment's Free Exercise Clause prohibits the Government from permitting timber harvesting in, or constructing a road through, a portion of a National Forest that has traditionally been used for religious purposes by members of three American Indian tribes in northwestern California. We conclude that it does not.

[As part of a road-building project linking the towns of Gasquet and Orleans, California ("the G-O road"), the United States Forest Service proposed to pave a 6-mile segment through the Chimney Rock section of the Six Rivers National Forest. The Hoopa Valley Indian Reservation adjoins the Forest, and the Chimney Rock area is used for religious purposes by Yurok, Karok, and Tolowa Indians. A study commissioned by the Forest Service in preparation of its environmental impact statement concluded that the Indian religious rituals required "privacy, silence, and an undisturbed natural setting." The study, completed in 1979, concluded that constructing a road along any of the available routes "would cause serious and irreparable damage to the sacred areas which are an integral and necessary part of the belief systems and lifeway of Northwest California Indian peoples." In 1982 the Forest Service decided to build the road anyway, though it chose a route that went as far as possible from the Indian spiritual sites. The alternative routes that would have avoided the Chimney Rock area altogether were rejected because they would have required the acquisition of private land, had serious soil stability problems, and would in any event have traversed areas having ritualistic value to American Indians.

[The primary purpose of the G-O road was to haul timber harvested under a management plan adopted at about this time by the Forest Service.] The management plan provided for one-half-mile protective zones around all the religious sites identified in the report that had been commissioned in connection with the G-O road.

[Respondents (an Indian organization, individual Indians, and others) sued for injunctive relief claiming, among other things, that the road-building and timber-harvesting decisions violated their rights under the Free Exercise Clause. The district court agreed, and the Ninth Circuit affirmed.]

III

A

[R]espondents contend that the burden on their religious practices is heavy enough to violate the Free Exercise Clause unless the Government can demonstrate a compelling need to complete the G-O road or to engage in timber harvesting in the Chimney Rock area. We disagree.

In Bowen v. Roy (1986), we considered a challenge to a federal statute that required the States to use Social Security numbers in administering certain welfare programs. Two applicants for benefits under these programs contended that their religious beliefs prevented them from acceding to the use of a Social Security number for their 2-year-old daughter because the use of a numerical identifier would "'rob the spirit' of [their] daughter and prevent her from attaining greater spiritual power." Similarly, in this case, it is said that disruption of the natural environment caused by the G-O road will diminish the sacredness of the area in question and create distractions that will interfere with "training and ongoing religious experience of individuals using [sites within] the area for personal medicine and growth . . . and as integrated parts of a system of religious belief and practice which correlates ascending degrees of personal power with a geographic hierarchy of power." The Court rejected this kind of challenge in *Roy*:

> The Free Exercise Clause simply cannot be understood to require the Government to conduct its own internal affairs in ways that comport with the religious beliefs of particular citizens. Just as the Government may not insist that [the Roys] engage in any set form of religious observance, so [they] may not demand that the Government join in their chosen religious practices by refraining from using a number to identify their daughter. . . .
> . . . The Free Exercise Clause affords an individual protection from certain forms of governmental compulsion; it does not afford an individual a right to dictate the conduct of the Government's internal procedures.

The building of a road or the harvesting of timber on publicly owned land cannot meaningfully be distinguished from the use of a Social Security number in *Roy*. In both cases, the challenged Government action would interfere significantly with private persons' ability to pursue spiritual fulfillment according to their own religious beliefs. In neither case, however, would the affected individuals be coerced by the Government's action into violating their religious beliefs; nor would either governmental action penalize religious activity by denying any person an equal share of the rights, benefits, and privileges enjoyed by other citizens.

We are asked to distinguish this case from *Roy* on the ground that the infringement on religious liberty here is "significantly greater," or on the ground that the Government practice in *Roy* was "purely mechanical" whereas this case involves "a case-by-case substantive determination as to how a particular unit of land will be managed." Similarly, we are told that this case can be distinguished from *Roy* because "the government action is not at some physically removed location where it places no restriction on what a practitioner may do." The State suggests that the Social Security number in *Roy* "could be characterized as interfering with Roy's religious tenets from a subjective point of view, where the government's conduct of 'its own internal affairs' was known to him only secondhand and did not interfere with his ability to practice his religion." In this case, however, it is said that the proposed road will "physically destro[y] the environmental conditions and the privacy without which the [religious] practices cannot be conducted."

These efforts to distinguish *Roy* are unavailing. This Court cannot determine the truth of the underlying beliefs that led to the religious objections here or in *Roy*, and accordingly cannot weigh the adverse effects on the appellees in *Roy* and compare them with the adverse effects on the Indian respondents. Without the ability to make such comparisons, we cannot say that the one form of incidental interference with an individual's spiritual activities should be subjected to a different constitutional analysis than the other.

. . . It is true that this Court has repeatedly held that indirect coercion or penalties on the free exercise of religion, not just outright prohibitions, are subject to scrutiny under the First Amendment. Thus, for example, ineligibility for unemployment benefits, based solely on a refusal to violate the Sabbath, has been analogized to a fine imposed on Sabbath worship. *Sherbert.* This does not and cannot imply that incidental effects of government programs, which may make it more difficult to practice certain religions but which have no tendency to coerce individuals into acting contrary to their religious beliefs, require government to bring forward a compelling justification for its otherwise lawful actions. The crucial word in the constitutional text is "prohibit": "For the Free Exercise Clause is written in terms of what the government cannot do to the individual, not in terms of what the individual can exact from the government." *Sherbert* (Douglas, J., concurring).

Whatever may be the exact line between unconstitutional prohibitions on the free exercise of religion and the legitimate conduct by government of its own affairs, the location of the line cannot depend on measuring the effects of a governmental action on a religious objector's spiritual development. The Government does not dispute, and we have no reason to doubt, that the logging and road-building projects at issue in this case could have devastating effects on traditional Indian religious practices. [But even if we] accept the Ninth Circuit's prediction, according to which the G-O road will "virtually destroy the . . . Indians' ability to practice their religion," the Constitution simply does not provide a principle that could justify upholding respondents' legal claims. However much we might wish that it were otherwise, government simply could not operate if it were required to satisfy every citizen's religious needs and desires. A broad range of government activities—from social welfare programs to foreign aid to conservation projects—will always be considered essential to the spiritual well-being of some citizens, often on the basis of sincerely held religious beliefs.

Others will find the very same activities deeply offensive, and perhaps incompatible with their own search for spiritual fulfillment and with the tenets of their religion. The First Amendment must apply to all citizens alike, and it can give to none of them a veto over public programs that do not prohibit the free exercise of religion. The Constitution does not, and courts cannot, offer to reconcile the various competing demands on government, many of them rooted in sincere religious belief, that inevitably arise in so diverse a society as ours. That task, to the extent that it is feasible, is for the legislatures and other institutions. Cf. The Federalist No. 10 (suggesting that the effects of religious factionalism are best restrained through competition among a multiplicity of religious sects).

. . . Respondents attempt to stress the limits of the religious servitude that they are now seeking to impose on the Chimney Rock area of the Six Rivers National Forest. While defending an injunction against logging operations and the construction of a road, they apparently do not *at present* object to the area's being used by recreational visitors, other Indians, or forest rangers. Nothing in the principle for which they contend, however, would distinguish this case from another lawsuit in which they (or similarly situated religious objectors) might seek to exclude all human activity but their own from sacred areas of the public lands. . . . No disrespect for these practices is implied when one notes that such beliefs could easily require de facto beneficial ownership of some rather spacious tracts of public property. Even without anticipating future cases, the diminution of the Government's property rights, and the concomitant subsidy of the Indian religion, would in this case be far from trivial: the District Court's order permanently forbade commercial timber harvesting, or the construction of a two-lane road, anywhere within an area covering a full 27 sections (i.e. more than 17,000 acres) of public land.

The Constitution does not permit government to discriminate against religions that treat particular physical sites as sacred, and a law prohibiting the Indian respondents from visiting the Chimney Rock area would raise a different set of constitutional questions. Whatever rights the Indians may have to the use of the area, however, those rights do not divest the Government of its right to use what is, after all, its land.

B

Nothing in our opinion should be read to encourage governmental insensitivity to the religious needs of any citizen. The Government's rights to the use of its own land, for example, need not and should not discourage it from accommodating religious practices like those engaged in by the Indian respondents. It is worth emphasizing, therefore, that the Government has taken numerous steps in this very case to minimize the impact that construction of the G-O road will have on the Indians' religious activities. . . . No sites where specific rituals take place were to be disturbed. In fact, a major factor in choosing among alternative routes for the road was the relation of the various routes to religious sites: the route selected by the Regional Forester is, he noted, "the farthest removed from contemporary spiritual sites; thus, the adverse audible intrusions associated with the road would be less than all other alternatives." . . .

Except for abandoning its project entirely, and thereby leaving the two existing segments of road to dead-end in the middle of a National Forest, it is difficult to see how the Government could have been more solicitous. . . .

Justice BRENNAN, with whom Justice MARSHALL and Justice BLACKMUN join, dissenting.

"'[T]he Free Exercise Clause,'" the Court explains today, "'is written in terms of what the government cannot do to the individual, not in terms of what the individual can exact from the government.'" Pledging fidelity to this unremarkable constitutional principle, the Court nevertheless concludes that even where the Government uses federal land in a manner that threatens the very existence of a Native American religion, the Government is simply not "*doing*" anything to the practitioners of that faith. Instead, the Court believes that Native Americans who request that the Government refrain from destroying their religion effectively seek to exact from the Government *de facto* beneficial ownership of federal property. These two astonishing conclusions follow naturally from the Court's determination that federal land-use decisions that render the practice of a given religion impossible do not burden that religion in a manner cognizable under the Free Exercise Clause, because such decisions neither coerce conduct inconsistent with religious belief nor penalize religious activity. The constitutional guarantee we interpret today, however, draws no such fine distinctions between types of restraints on religious exercise, but rather is directed against any form of governmental action that frustrates or inhibits religious practice. Because the Court today refuses even to acknowledge the constitutional injury respondents will suffer, and because this refusal essentially leaves Native Americans with absolutely no constitutional protection against perhaps the gravest threat to their religious practices, I dissent. . . .

I cannot accept the Court's premise that the form of the government's restraint on religious practice, rather than its effect, controls our constitutional analysis. Respondents here have demonstrated that construction of the G-O road will completely frustrate the practice of their religion, for as the lower courts found, the proposed logging and construction activities will virtually destroy respondents' religion, and will therefore necessarily force them into abandoning those practices altogether. Indeed, the Government's proposed activities will restrain religious practice to a far greater degree here than in any of the cases cited by the Court today. None of the religious adherents in Thomas v. Review Board or Sherbert v. Verner, for example, claimed or could have claimed that the denial of unemployment benefits rendered the practice of their religions impossible; at most, the challenged laws made those practices more expensive. Here, in stark contrast, respondents have claimed—and proved—that the desecration of the high country will prevent religious leaders from attaining the religious power or medicine indispensable to the success of virtually all their rituals and ceremonies. Similarly, in *Yoder* the compulsory school law threatened to "undermin[e] the Amish community and religious practice," and thus to force adherents to "abandon belief . . . or . . . to migrate to some other and more tolerant region." Here the threat posed by the desecration of sacred lands that are indisputably essential to respondents' religious practices is both more direct and more substantial than that raised by a compulsory school law that simply exposed Amish children to an alien value system. And of course respondents here do not even have the option, however unattractive it might be, of migrating to more hospitable locales; the site-specific nature of their belief system renders it nontransportable.

Ultimately, the Court's coercion test turns on a distinction between governmental actions that compel affirmative conduct inconsistent with religious belief, and those governmental actions that prevent conduct consistent with religious belief. In my view, such a distinction is without constitutional significance. The crucial word in the constitutional text, as the Court itself acknowledges, is "prohibit," a comprehensive term that in no way suggests that the intended protection is aimed only at governmental actions that coerce affirmative conduct.[4] Nor does the Court's distinction comport with the principles animating the constitutional guarantee: religious freedom is threatened no less by governmental action that makes the practice of one's chosen faith impossible than by governmental programs that pressure one to engage in conduct inconsistent with religious beliefs. The Court attempts to explain the line it draws by arguing that the protections of the Free Exercise Clause "cannot depend on measuring the effects of a governmental action on a religious objector's spiritual development," for in a society as diverse as ours, the Government cannot help but offend the "religious needs and desires" of some citizens. While I agree that governmental action that simply offends religious sensibilities may not be challenged under the Clause, we have recognized that laws that affect spiritual development by impeding the integration of children into the religious community or by increasing the expense of adherence to religious principles— in short, laws that frustrate or inhibit religious practice—trigger the protections of the constitutional guarantee. Both common sense and our prior cases teach us, therefore, that governmental action that makes the practice of a given faith more difficult necessarily penalizes that practice and thereby tends to prevent adherence to religious belief. The harm to the practitioners is the same regardless of the manner in which the government restrains their religious expression, and the Court's fear that an "effects" test will permit religious adherents to challenge governmental actions they merely find "offensive" in no way justifies its refusal to recognize the constitutional injury citizens suffer when governmental action not only offends but actually restrains their religious practices. Here, respondents have demonstrated that the Government's proposed activities will completely prevent them from practicing their religion, and such a showing, no less than those made out in *Hobbie, Thomas, Sherbert,* and *Yoder,* entitles them to the protections of the Free Exercise Clause. . . .

In the final analysis, the Court's refusal to recognize the constitutional dimension of respondents' injuries stems from its concern that acceptance of respondents' claim could potentially strip the Government of its ability to manage and use vast tracts of federal property. In addition, the nature of respondents' site-specific religious practices raises the specter of future suits in which Native Americans seek to exclude all human activity from such areas. These concededly legitimate concerns lie at the very heart of this case, which represents yet another

4. The Court is apparently of the view that the term "prohibit" in the Free Exercise Clause somehow limits the constitutional protection such that it cannot possibly be understood to reach " 'any form of government action that frustrates or inhibits religious practice.' " Although the dictionary is hardly the final word on the meaning of constitutional language, it is noteworthy that Webster's includes, as one of the two accepted definitions of "prohibit," "to prevent from doing something." Webster's Ninth New Collegiate Dictionary (1983). Government action that frustrates or inhibits religious practice fits far more comfortably within this definition than does the Court's affirmative compulsion test.

stress point in the longstanding conflict between two disparate cultures—the dominant Western culture, which views land in terms of ownership and use, and that of Native Americans, in which concepts of private property are not only alien, but contrary to a belief system that holds land sacred. Rather than address this conflict in any meaningful fashion, however, the Court disclaims all responsibility for balancing these competing and potentially irreconcilable interests, choosing instead to turn this difficult task over to the Federal Legislature. Such an abdication is more than merely indefensible as an institutional matter: by defining respondents' injury as "nonconstitutional," the Court has effectively bestowed on one party to this conflict the unilateral authority to resolve all future disputes in its favor, subject only to the Court's toothless exhortation to be "sensitive" to affected religions. In my view, however, Native Americans deserve—and the Constitution demands—more than this.

Prior to today's decision, several Courts of Appeals had attempted to fashion a test that accommodates the competing "demands" placed on federal property by the two cultures. Recognizing that the Government normally enjoys plenary authority over federal lands, the Courts of Appeals required Native Americans to demonstrate that any land-use decisions they challenged involved lands that were "central" or "indispensable" to their religious practices. Although this requirement limits the potential number of free exercise claims that might be brought to federal land management decisions, and thus forestalls the possibility that the Government will find itself ensnared in a host of Lilliputian lawsuits, it has been criticized as inherently ethnocentric, for it incorrectly assumes that Native American belief systems ascribe religious significance to land in a traditionally Western hierarchical manner. It is frequently the case in constitutional litigation, however, that courts are called upon to balance interests that are not readily translated into rough equivalents. At their most absolute, the competing claims that both the Government and Native Americans assert in federal land are fundamentally incompatible, and unless they are tempered by compromise, mutual accommodation will remain impossible.

I believe it appropriate, therefore, to require some showing of "centrality" before the Government can be required either to come forward with a compelling justification for its proposed use of federal land or to forego that use altogether. "Centrality," however, should not be equated with the survival or extinction of the religion itself. In *Yoder*, for example, we treated the objection to the compulsory school attendance of adolescents as "central" to the Amish faith even though such attendance did not prevent or otherwise render the practice of that religion impossible, and instead simply threatened to "undermine" that faith. Because of their perceptions of and relationship with the natural world, Native Americans consider all land sacred. Nevertheless, the [Forest Service] Report reveals that respondents here deemed certain lands more powerful and more directly related to their religious practices than others. Thus, in my view, while Native Americans need not demonstrate, as respondents did here, that the Government's land-use decision will assuredly eradicate their faith, I do not think it is enough to allege simply that the land in question is held sacred. Rather, adherents challenging a proposed use of federal land should be required to show that the decision poses a substantial and realistic threat of frustrating their religious practices. Once such a showing is made, the burden should shift to the Government to come forward with a compelling state interest sufficient to justify the infringement of those practices. [The courts need not be the ones who decide the question of centrality]: Native Americans would be the arbiters of which practices are central to their faith, subject only to the normal requirement that their claims be genuine and sincere.

NOTES AND QUESTIONS

1. The "Substantiality" or "Centrality" of a Burden. What is the majority's definition of "burden"? What is Justice Brennan's? How would these standards work? Note that the burden in *Lyng* is "indirect" in the sense used in *Braunfeld*: no penalty is attached to the Indians' acts exercising their religion. Should that be dispositive? Professor Michael Dorf argues that in the case of incidental burdens on the exercise of fundamental rights, the claimant should be required to show "substantiality." Incidental Burdens on Fundamental Rights, 109 Harv. L. Rev. 1175 (1996). That seems similar to Justice Brennan's view that the claimants must show "centrality." But what is the answer to the majority's argument:

> This Court cannot determine the truth of the underlying beliefs that led to the religious objections, . . . and accordingly cannot weigh the adverse effects on the [government] and compare them with the adverse effects on the Indian respondents. Without the ability to make such comparisons, we cannot say that the one form of incidental interference with an individual's spiritual activities should be subjected to a different constitutional analysis than the other.

Are the courts supposed to second-guess the claimant's assertion that a particular practice (or a particular location) is "central" to their religious beliefs? How can a court do that? (Justice Brennan closes his opinion by stating that "Native Americans would be the arbiters of which practices are central to their faith, subject only to the normal requirement that their claims be genuine and sincere." How is that consistent with his advocacy of a "centrality" threshold?) What if only a few Indians consider a particular location "central"? Do numbers matter?

2. Theological Outlooks and the Definition of "Burden." It has been argued that *Lyng* and the decision it cites, Bowen v. Roy, 476 U.S. 693 (1986), reflect a lack of understanding or sympathy for Native American religious concepts. See David C. Williams and Susan Williams, Volitionalism and Religious Liberty, 76 Cornell L. Rev. 769 (1991). Protestant Christianity, the religion with the most pervasive historical influence on American culture, tends to view religion as a matter of the individual's will ("volition") and conduct, and therefore not to regard government action as a "burden" on believers unless it coerces their volitional acts in some way. For Native Americans, however, the state of the physical world—the state of particular places like Chimney Rock, or the existence of a social security number somewhere—has spiritual significance; it has an effect on the state of people's souls. By rejecting these claims, is the Court limiting the Free Exercise Clause to what fits with Christian theology?

But perhaps the narrower definition of burden is the only one possible in a society with many different faiths. If the spiritual damage from government's action elsewhere is a cognizable burden, can I object on free exercise grounds to the government prosecuting a war that deeply disturbs me for theological reasons? Going back to *Lyng* itself: Since Indians tend to invest their ancestral homelands with spiritual significance, and since virtually the entire United States was once the ancestral homeland of one or more tribes, what would be the consequence of finding a cognizable burden in *Lyng*? Recently, some Native Americans objected to the plan of NASA, the U.S. space agency, to place the cremated remains of a former employee on an unmanned lunar craft; the agency had meant to honor the employee's wish to land on the moon, but the objectors said this desecrated the moon, a sacred place in many Native American beliefs. "NASA Apologizes to Navajos for Plans to Put Remains on Moon," Salt Lake Trib., Jan. 14, 1998.

On the other hand, if the destruction of a religious way of life as in *Lyng* does not constitute a burden of the exercise of religion, what does? And Professor Ira Lupu has suggested a ground for finding a cognizable burden in *Lyng* even in individualist, Western legal terms: Through their long use of the land, the Native Americans had obtained an easement by prescription. Ira C. Lupu, Where Rights Begin: The Problem of Burdens on the Free Exercise of Religion, 102 Harv. L. Rev. 933, 973-974 (1989). Does that solve the problem?

3. Establishment Clause Issues. Another way to think about the effects of the Native Americans' claim is to consider the Establishment Clause dimensions of this case, which no Justice mentions. Justice Brennan maintains that the government must protect the land for the Indians' religious use, and Justice O'Connor maintains that they may do so. But is the government permitted, under the Establishment Clause, to allow the beliefs of one particular religious group to govern federal land use policy? Is it permitted, in effect, to maintain open air places of worship at public expense, and to maintain those places in accordance with sectarian beliefs? Consider the *Lemon* trilogy of purpose, effect, and entanglement. If secular considerations militate in favor of building a road, what secular purpose is to be served by not doing so? Can the perceived sacredness of the land be a secular reason? Does preservation of the land have the effect of advancing the Indians' religion? Does determining the Indians' religious requirements, and setting federal land use policy in accordance with them, amount to "excessive entanglement"? If the answer to any of these questions is "yes," does this mean that accommodating the Indians would be unconstitutional, or does it suggest that the *Lemon* test is flawed?

4. Effects on Nonmandatory Religious Conduct. In Jimmy Swaggart Ministries v. Bd. of Equalization, 493 U.S. 378 (1990), the Court unanimously refused to find a "constitutionally significant" burden from applying a state sales tax to the sales of Bibles and evangelistic materials. The Court reasoned that there was "no evidence in this case that collection and payment of the tax violates [Swaggart's] sincere religious beliefs"; the state had not "condition[ed] receipt of an important benefit upon conduct proscribed by a religious faith, or . . . denie[d] such a benefit because of conduct mandated by religious belief." Rather the tax merely "decrease[d] the amount of money [Swaggart] has to spend on its religious activities." *Id.* at 391-392.

Does *Swaggart* announce a further limitation on cognizable burdens—not only that the government's action must prohibit the religious practice (as opposed to just making it more difficult), but that the practice prohibited must be *mandated* by the faith (as opposed to, say, merely motivated by it)? If so, is that determination any easier or more appropriate for a court to make than whether the practice is "central" to the faith?

Consider the following problem: Suppose a Muslim inmate in a state prison asserts that he must take meals in a room where he can face Mecca while eating and must have running water available to purify himself while eating. Should a court reject these claims if it determines that the practices are not "obligatory" for Muslims? See Mack v. O'Leary, 80 F.3d 1175 (7th Cir. 1996) (Posner, J.) (answering no, and defining a substantial burden as "one that forces adherents of a religion to refrain from religiously *motivated* conduct, inhibits or constrains conduct or expression that manifests a central tenet of a person's religious beliefs, or compels conduct or expression that is contrary to those beliefs") (emphasis in original).

In one provision of the RLUIPA statute of 2000, Congress made clear that the religious exercise protected against substantial burdens includes "any exercise of religion, whether or not compelled by, or central to, a system of religious belief"; the provision also inserts the same standard into RFRA. 42 U.S.C. § 2000cc-5(7)(A), incorporated into 42 U.S.C. § 2000bb-2(4). If this standard had been applied in *Swaggart*, would it have changed the result? In Henderson v. Kennedy, 265 F.3d 1072 (D.C. Cir. 2001), the court, on a rehearing petition, held that the new provision "did not alter the propriety of inquiring into the importance of a religious practice when assessing whether a substantial burden exists." It therefore reaffirmed its prior decision that a federal regulation prohibiting the sale of T-shirts on the National Mall did not impose a substantial burden on the plaintiffs under RFRA, because there was still a "multitude of means" by which they could "engage in their vocation to spread the gospel," including "distribut[ing] t-shirts for free on the Mall, or sell[ing] them on streets surrounding the Mall." *Id.* at 1073.

5. Burdens from Discriminatory Laws. Suppose a state passes a law that imposes a $5 annual license surcharge on each school bus operated by religious elementary schools, but not on buses operated by secular private schools. A religious school that owns several buses challenges the statute. Can the state get the lawsuit dismissed on the ground that $5 per bus imposes only a minimal marginal economic cost on the activity of operating the school? See Church of the Lukumi Babalu Aye v. City of Hialeah, p. 162 (Blackmun, J., dissenting) (stating that "a law that targets religious practice for disfavored treatment . . . burdens the free exercise of religion" and "automatically will fail strict scrutiny").

Does your answer suggest that such claims of "discrimination" are analytically distinct from claims of a "burden"? If so, then should that lead to different kinds of review—and does that suggest that RFRA was wrong to bring all free exercise claims under one standard?

b. Sincerity and Consistency

To warrant accommodation under free exercise principles, it is not sufficient that the claimant merely say he or she has a religious belief that would be burdened by the government action. The claim must be sincere. But courts cannot look into the hearts of men. How can sincerity be judged? Can it be done without invading the very freedom of conscience that the First Amendment is meant to protect?

UNITED STATES v. BALLARD
322 U.S. 78 (1944)

Mr. Justice DOUGLAS delivered the opinion of the Court.

Respondents were indicted and convicted for using, and conspiring to use, the mails to defraud. The indictment was in twelve counts. It charged a scheme to defraud by organizing and promoting the I Am movement through the use of the mails. The charge was that certain designated corporations were formed, literature distributed and sold, funds solicited, and memberships in the I Am movement sought "by means of false and fraudulent representations, pretenses and promises." The false representations charged were eighteen in number. It is sufficient at this point to say that they covered respondents' alleged religious doctrines or beliefs. They were all set forth in the first count.

[Respondents, Edna W. Ballard and Donald Ballard, claimed to be divine messengers for the "ascended masters"—Saint Germain, Jesus, George Washington, and Godfre Ray King. By virtue of their alleged supernatural contacts, principally with Saint Germain, respondents boasted of extraordinary healing powers and represented that they had in fact healed hundreds of individuals of curable and incurable diseases. The gravamen of the complaint was that such representations were knowingly and falsely made with an intent to defraud people of money and property through the mails.

Respondents moved to quash the indictment, asserting that it attacked and restricted their religious beliefs in violation of the free exercise clause of the federal Constitution. The district court denied the motion, but agreed to limit the jury inquiry to the good faith of respondents. In relevant part the jury charge stated: "The jury will be called upon to pass on the question of whether or not the defendants honestly and in good faith believed the representations which are set forth in the indictment . . . or whether these representations were mere pretenses without honest belief on the part of the defendants . . . made for the purpose of procuring money. . . ." The jury rendered a guilty verdict from which the Ballards appealed, principally on the grounds that it was error to overrule the demurrer to the indictment and the motion to quash, and, in the alternative, to disallow proof of the truth of respondents' religious doctrines or beliefs.]

The Circuit Court of Appeals reversed the judgment of conviction and granted a new trial, one judge dissenting. In its view the restriction of the issue in question to that of good faith was error. Its reason was that the scheme to defraud alleged in the indictment was that respondents made the eighteen alleged false representations; and that to prove that defendants devised the scheme described in the indictment "it was necessary to prove that they schemed to make some, at least, of the (eighteen) representations . . . and that some, at least, of the representations which they schemed to make were false." One judge thought that the ruling of the District Court was also error because it was "as prejudicial to the issue of honest belief as to the issue of purposeful misrepresentation."

The case is here on a petition for a writ of certiorari which we granted because of the importance of the question presented.

... [W]e do not agree that the truth or verity of respondents' religious doctrines or beliefs should have been submitted to the jury. Whatever this particular indictment might require, the First Amendment precludes such a course, as the United States seems to concede. "The law knows no heresy, and is committed to the support of no dogma, the establishment of no sect." The First Amendment has a dual aspect. It not only "forestalls compulsion by law of the acceptance of any creed or the practice of any form of worship" but also "safeguards the free exercise of the chosen form of religion." Cantwell v. Connecticut. "Thus the Amendment embraces two concepts,—freedom to believe and freedom to act. The first is absolute but, in the nature of things, the second cannot be." *Id.* Freedom of thought, which includes freedom of religious belief, is basic in a society of free men. It embraces the right to maintain theories of life and of death and of the hereafter which are rank heresy to followers of the orthodox faiths. Heresy trials are foreign to our Constitution. Men may believe what they cannot prove. They may not be put to the proof of their religious doctrines or beliefs. Religious experiences which are as real as life to some may be incomprehensible to others. Yet the fact that they may be beyond the ken of mortals does not mean that they can be made suspect before the law. Many take their gospel from the New Testament. But it would hardly be supposed that they could be tried before a jury charged with the duty of determining whether those teachings contained false representations. The miracles of the New Testament, the Divinity of Christ, life after death, the power of prayer are deep in the religious convictions of many. If one could be sent to jail because a jury in a hostile environment found those teachings false, little indeed would be left of religious freedom. The Fathers of the Constitution were not unaware of the varied and extreme views of religious sects, of the violence of disagreement among them, and of the lack of any one religious creed on which all men would agree. They fashioned a charter of government which envisaged the widest possible toleration of conflicting views. Man's relation to his God was made no concern of the state. He was granted the right to worship as he pleased and to answer to no man for the verity of his religious views. The religious views espoused by respondents might seem incredible, if not preposterous, to most people. But if those doctrines are subject to trial before a jury charged with finding their truth or falsity, then the same can be done with the religious beliefs of any sect. When the triers of fact undertake that task, they enter a forbidden domain. The First Amendment does not select any one group or any one type of religion for preferred treatment. It puts them all in that position. As stated in Davis v. Beason, "With man's relations to his Maker and the obligations he may think they impose, and the manner in which an expression shall be made by him of his belief on those subjects, no interference can be permitted, provided always the laws of society, designed to secure its peace and prosperity, and the morals of its people, are not interfered with." So we conclude that the District Court ruled properly when it withheld from the jury all questions concerning the truth or falsity of the religious beliefs or doctrines of respondents.

The judgment is reversed and the cause is remanded to the Circuit Court of Appeals for further proceedings in conformity to this opinion.

Mr. CHIEF JUSTICE STONE, with whom Mr. Justice ROBERTS and Mr. Justice FRANKFURTER agree, dissenting.

I am not prepared to say that the constitutional guaranty of freedom of religion affords immunity from criminal prosecution for the fraudulent procurement of money by false statements as to one's religious experiences, more than it renders polygamy or libel immune from criminal prosecution. I cannot say that freedom of thought and worship includes freedom to procure money by making knowingly false statements about one's religious experiences. To go no further, if it were shown that a defendant in this case had asserted as a part of the alleged fraudulent scheme, that he had physically shaken hands with St. Germain in San Francisco on a day named, or that, as the indictment here alleges, by the exertion of his spiritual power he "had in fact cured . . . hundreds of persons afflicted with diseases and ailments," I should not doubt that it would be open to the Government to submit to the jury proof that he had never been in San Francisco and that no such cures had ever been effected. In any event I see no occasion for making any pronouncement on this subject in the present case.

The indictment charges respondents' use of the mails to defraud and a conspiracy to commit that offense by false statements of their religious experiences which had not in fact occurred. But it also charged that the representations were "falsely and fraudulently" made, that respondents "well knew" that these representations were untrue, and that they were made by respondents with the intent to cheat and defraud those to whom they were made. With the assent of the prosecution and the defense the trial judge withdrew from the consideration of the jury the question whether the alleged religious experiences had in fact occurred, but submitted to the jury the single issue whether petitioners honestly believed that they had occurred, with the instruction that if the jury did not so find, then it should return a verdict of guilty. On this issue the jury, on ample evidence that respondents were without belief in the statements which they had made to their victims, found a verdict of guilty. The state of one's mind is a fact as capable of fraudulent misrepresentation as is one's physical condition or the state of his bodily health. There are no exceptions to the charge and no contention that the trial court rejected any relevant evidence which petitioners sought to offer. Since the indictment and the evidence support the conviction, it is irrelevant whether the religious experiences alleged did or did not in fact occur or whether that issue could or could not, for constitutional reasons, have been rightly submitted to the jury. Certainly none of respondents' constitutional rights are violated if they are prosecuted for the fraudulent procurement of money by false representations as to their beliefs, religious or otherwise. . . .

On the issue submitted to the jury in this case it properly rendered a verdict of guilty. As no legally sufficient reason for disturbing it appears, I think the judgment below should be reversed and that of the District Court reinstated.

Mr. Justice JACKSON, dissenting.

I should say the defendants have done just that for which they are indicted. If I might agree to their conviction without creating a precedent, I cheerfully would do so. I can see in their teachings nothing but humbug, untainted by any trace of truth. But that does not dispose of the constitutional question whether misrepresentation of religious experience or belief is prosecutable; it rather emphasizes the danger of such prosecutions. . . .

In the first place, as a matter of either practice or philosophy I do not see how we can separate an issue as to what is believed from considerations as to what is believable. The most convincing proof that one believes his statements is to show that they have been true in his experience. Likewise, that one knowingly falsified is best proved by showing that what he said happened never did happen. How can the Government prove these persons knew something to be false which it cannot prove to be false? If we try religious sincerity severed from religious verity, we isolate the dispute from the very considerations which in common experience provide its most reliable answer.

In the second place, any inquiry into intellectual honesty in religion raises profound psychological problems. William James, who wrote on these matters as a scientist, reminds us that it is not theology and ceremonies which keep religion going. Its vitality is in the religious experiences of many people. "If you ask what these experiences are, they are conversations with the unseen, voices and visions, responses to prayer, changes of heart, deliverances from fear, inflowings of help, assurances of support, whenever certain persons set their own internal attitude in certain appropriate ways." If religious liberty includes, as it must, the right to communicate such experiences to others, it seems to me an impossible task for juries to separate fancied ones from real ones, dreams from happenings, and hallucinations from true clairvoyance. Such experiences, like some tones and colors, have existence for one, but none at all for another. They cannot be verified to the minds of those whose field of consciousness does not include religious insight. When one comes to trial which turns on any aspect of religious belief or representation, unbelievers among his judges are likely not to understand and are almost certain not to believe him.

And then I do not know what degree of skepticism or disbelief in a religious representation amounts to actionable fraud. James points out that "Faith means belief in something concerning which doubt is theoretically possible." Belief in what one may demonstrate to the senses is not faith. All schools of religious thought make enormous assumptions, generally on the basis of revelations authenticated by some sign or miracle. The appeal in such matters is to a very different plane of credulity than is invoked by representations of secular fact in commerce. Some who profess belief in the Bible read literally what others read as allegory or metaphor, as they read Aesop's fables. Religious symbolism is even used by some with the same mental reservations one has in teaching of Santa Claus or Uncle Sam or Easter bunnies or dispassionate judges. It is hard in matters so mystical to say how literally one is bound to believe the doctrine he teaches and even more difficult to say how far it is reliance upon a teacher's literal belief which induces followers to give him money. . . .

The chief wrong which false prophets do to their following is not financial. The collections aggregate a tempting total, but individual payments are not ruinous. I doubt if the vigilance of the law is equal to making money stick by over-credulous people. But the real harm is on the mental and spiritual plane. There are those who hunger and thirst after higher values which they feel wanting in their humdrum lives. They live in mental confusion or moral anarchy and seek vaguely for truth and beauty and moral support. When they are deluded and then disillusioned, cynicism and confusion follow. The wrong of these things, as I see it, is not in the money the victims part with half so much as in the mental and spiritual poison they get. But that is precisely the thing the Constitution put beyond the reach of the prosecutor, for the price of freedom of religion or of speech or of the press is that we must put up with, and even pay for, a good deal of rubbish.

Prosecutions of this character easily could degenerate into religious persecution. I do not doubt that religious leaders may be convicted of fraud for making false representations on matters other than faith or experience, as for example if one represents that funds are being used to construct a church when in fact they are being used for personal purposes. But that is not this case, which reaches into wholly dangerous ground. When does less than full belief in a professed credo become actionable fraud if one is soliciting gifts or legacies? Such inquiries may discomfort orthodox as well as unconventional religious teachers, for even the most regular of them are sometimes accused of taking their orthodoxy with a grain of salt.

I would dismiss the indictment and have done with this business of judicially examining other people's faiths.

NOTES AND QUESTIONS

1. Sincerity and the Problem of Exemptions.   The difficulties of determining whether an asserted religious belief is "sincere" may have a good deal to do with the courts' narrow interpretations of what "burdens" warrant a free exercise exemption. If it is easy to show a cognizable burden at the threshold, then heightened scrutiny of the government's action will be triggered frequently, including in some cases where the claimant is feigning a religious belief in order to get the benefits of exemption. But since courts cannot easily dismiss religious claims as insincere, that puts pressure on the other part of the threshold inquiry: whether there is a significant burden on the religious belief.

2. How to Determine Sincerity?   How can courts tell whether a person's claim regarding the exercise of religion is sincere?

(a) Consistency?   One possible approach is to examine the claimant's practices to determine whether he is consistent. If a worker claims unemployment benefits on account of discharge for refusal to work on Saturday, his stated day of Sabbath observance, it would be relevant to determine whether he typically observes the Sabbath (or whether he plays golf or works around the house). But an insistence on consistency can have its difficulties: Believers may be completely sincere about tenets of their faith even if they sometimes fail to live up to them, or there may be reasons not apparent to an outsider that explain the supposed inconsistencies. Consider the following cases:

In Thomas v. Review Board, 450 U.S. 707 (1981), a Jehovah's Witness resigned from employment in a steel fabricating plant when he was transferred to a department that made turrets for military tanks. He testified that "contributing to the production of arms violated his religion," but further examination revealed that he would be willing to work on production of materials, such as steel, that would be used "ultimately" to manufacture arms. He also stated that he was "struggling" with his beliefs and was unable to "articulate" them with precision. The lower court found Thomas's willingness to work in the production of steel used for armaments inconsistent with his supposed religious tenet. The Supreme Court disagreed:

> We see, therefore, that Thomas drew a line, and it is not for us to say that the line he drew was an unreasonable one. Courts should not undertake to dissect religious beliefs because the believer admits that he is "struggling" with his position or because his beliefs are not articulated with the clarity and precision that a more sophisticated person might employ.

The "determination of what is a 'religious' belief or practice," the Court noted, "is more often than not a difficult and delicate task," which must not "turn upon a judicial perception of the particular belief or practice in question; religious beliefs need not be acceptable, logical, consistent, or comprehensible to others in order to merit First Amendment protection."

In Bowen v. Roy, 476 U.S. 693 (1986), a Native American descended from the Abenaki tribe challenged the requirement that he obtain a social security number for his two-year-old daughter (named Little Bird of the Snow) as a precondition to applying for welfare benefits. He testified that obtaining a social security number would " 'rob the spirit' of his daughter and prevent her from attaining greater spiritual power." Apparently this belief was predicated on "recent conversations with an Abenaki chief," who taught that "technology is 'robbing the spirit of man.' " At trial it was revealed that father and mother as well as an older sibling had social security numbers. More surprisingly, on the last day of trial a federal officer discovered that the family had already obtained a social security number for Little Bird of the Snow. The father then took the stand and explained that the spiritual injury would be caused by using, not by obtaining, the number. Although much of the litigation focused on these events (with four justices concluding that the case was either moot or unripe), neither the government nor any of the justices suggested that there was any reason to doubt the sincerity of the claim. Should they have done so?

(b) Denominational tenets? Another approach is to inquire whether the claimant's religion espouses the tenet on which he bases his claim. If a person claims that as a Roman Catholic he must refrain from work on Wednesday, there may be some reason to doubt his sincerity. But here again there are pitfalls. In Thomas v. Review Board the lower court also gave "significant weight" to evidence that other Jehovah's Witnesses at the claimant's place of employment professed to find the work "scripturally acceptable." The Supreme Court responded that

> [i]ntrafaith differences of that kind are not uncommon among followers of a particular creed, and the judicial process is singularly ill equipped to resolve such differences in relation to the Religion Clauses. One can, of course, imagine an asserted claim so bizarre, so clearly nonreligious in motivation, as not to be entitled to protection under the Free Exercise Clause; but that is not the case here, and the guarantee of free exercise is not limited to beliefs which are shared by all of the members of a religious sect. Particularly in this sensitive area, it is not within the

judicial function and judicial competence to inquire whether the petitioner or his fellow worker more correctly perceived the commands of their common faith. Courts are not arbiters of scriptural interpretation.

Similarly, in Frazee v. Illinois Employment Security Dept. 489 U.S. 229 (1989), the Court upheld a free exercise claim for unemployment compensation by a person who claimed to be a Christian, but of no particular denomination, who concluded as a matter of personal religious conviction that he must not work on Sunday. The Court stated that "[u]ndoubtedly, membership in an organized religious denomination, especially one with a specific tenet forbidding members to work on Sunday, would simplify the problem of identifying sincerely held religious beliefs," but it held that a sincerely held religious belief is protected even if the individual is not "responding to the commands of a particular religious organization."

c. Governmental Justifications

i. General Methodology

Assuming that a law that burdens religious practice must be supported by a significant justification—e.g., the "least restrictive means" to a "compelling governmental interest"—how does a court determine whether that standard is met? The court must decide what reasons are constitutionally weighty enough to limit religious freedom. It also has to consider the possibility that while one free exercise accommodation would raise little difficulty, others might follow from it and together produce a serious problem.

UNITED STATES v. LEE
455 U.S. 252 (1982)

[*Lee* was a suit by a member of the Old Order Amish who employed several other Amish on his farm and in his carpentry shop. He objected to the federal government's requirement that he pay the employer's share of social security taxes based on his employee's wages, and that he withhold the employees' share from their wages. His objection to participating in the social security system was based on the Amish belief that they should provide for their own elderly and needy. The scriptural basis was I Timothy 5:8: "But if any provide not . . . for those of his own house, he hath denied the faith, and is worse than an infidel." Based on this same tenet, Lee and other Old Order Amish also refused to accept social security benefits for which they were eligible. The social security statute, § 1402(g), exempts "self-employed" religious believers, including Amish, from paying the tax if they have a religious objection to it; but the exemption itself did not cover employment of other Amish, and therefore Lee's objection was based on the Free Exercise Clause.

Lee sued for a refund of taxes that he had been required to pay. The district court upheld his constitutional claim. On appeal, the Supreme Court, in an opinion by Chief Justice Burger, accepted Lee's claim that the social security law conflicted with his sincere religious tenets. But the Court still reversed and ruled for the government, reasoning as follows:]

[II]

A

. . . The conclusion that there is a conflict between the Amish faith and the obligations imposed by the social security system is only the beginning, however, and not the end of the inquiry. Not all burdens on religion are unconstitutional. The state may justify a limitation on religious liberty by showing that it is essential to accomplish an overriding governmental interest.

B

Because the social security system is nationwide, the governmental interest is apparent. The social security system in the United States serves the public interest by providing a comprehensive insurance system with a variety of benefits available to all participants, with costs shared by employers and employees. The social security system is by far the largest domestic governmental program in the United States today, distributing approximately $11 billion monthly to 36 million Americans. The design of the system requires support by mandatory contributions from covered employers and employees. This mandatory participation is indispensable to the fiscal vitality of the social security system. "[W]idespread individual voluntary coverage under social security . . . would undermine the soundness of the social security program." Senate Report (1965). Moreover, a comprehensive national social security system providing for voluntary participation would be almost a contradiction in terms and difficult, if not impossible, to administer. Thus, the Government's interest in assuring mandatory and continuous participation in and contribution to the social security system is very high.

C

The remaining inquiry is whether accommodating the Amish belief will unduly interfere with fulfillment of the governmental interest. In Braunfeld v. Brown, this Court noted that "to make accommodation between the religious action and an exercise of state authority is a particularly delicate task . . . because resolution in favor of the State results in the choice to the individual of either abandoning his religious principle or facing . . . prosecution." The difficulty in attempting to accommodate religious beliefs in the area of taxation is that "we are a cosmopolitan nation made up of people of almost every conceivable religious preference." The Court has long recognized that balance must be struck between the values of the comprehensive social security system, which rests on a complex of actuarial factors, and the consequences of allowing religiously based exemptions. To maintain an organized society that guarantees religious freedom to a great variety of faiths requires that some religious practices yield to the common good. Religious beliefs can be accommodated, see, e.g., Thomas v. Review Board; *Sherbert*, but there is a point at which accommodation would "radically restrict the operating latitude of the legislature." *Braunfeld*.

Unlike the situation presented in Wisconsin v. Yoder, it would be difficult to accommodate the comprehensive social security system with myriad exceptions flowing from a wide variety of religious beliefs. The obligation to pay the social security tax initially is not fundamentally different from the obligation to pay income taxes; the difference—in theory at least—is that the social security tax revenues are segregated for use only in furtherance of the statutory program. There is no principled way, however, for purposes of this case, to distinguish between general taxes and those imposed under the Social Security Act. If, for example, a religious adherent believes war is a sin, and if a certain percentage of the federal budget can be identified as devoted to war-related activities, such individuals would have a similarly valid claim to be exempt from paying that percentage of the income tax. The tax system could not function if denominations were allowed to challenge the tax system because tax payments were spent in a manner that violates their religious belief. Because the broad public interest in maintaining a sound tax system is of such a high order, religious belief in conflict with the payment of taxes affords no basis for resisting the tax.

III

Congress has accommodated, to the extent compatible with a comprehensive national program, the practices of those who believe it a violation of their faith to participate in the social security system. In § 1402(g) Congress granted an exemption, on religious grounds, to self-employed Amish and others. Confining the § 1402(g) exemption to the self-employed provided for a narrow category which was readily identifiable. Self-employed persons in a religious community having its own "welfare" system are distinguishable from the generality of wage earners employed by others.

Congress and the courts have been sensitive to the needs flowing from the Free Exercise Clause, but every person cannot be shielded from all the burdens incident to exercising every aspect of the right to practice religious beliefs. When followers of a particular sect enter into commercial activity as a matter of choice, the limits they accept on their own conduct as a matter of conscience and faith are not to be superimposed on the statutory schemes which are binding on others in that activity. Granting an exemption from social security taxes to an employer operates to impose the employer's religious faith on the employees. . . . The tax imposed on employers to support the social security system must be uniformly applicable to all, except as Congress provides explicitly otherwise.

Justice STEVENS, concurring in the judgment.

. . . Congress already has granted the Amish a limited exemption from social security taxes. See § 1402(g). As a matter of administration, it would be a relatively simple matter to extend the exemption to the taxes involved in this case. As a matter of fiscal policy, an enlarged exemption probably would benefit the social security system because the nonpayment of these taxes by the Amish would be more than offset by the elimination of their right to collect benefits. In view of the fact that the Amish have demonstrated their capacity to care for their own, the social cost of eliminating this relatively small group of dedicated believers would be minimal. Thus, if we confine the analysis to the Government's interest in rejecting the particular claim to an exemption at stake in this case, the constitutional standard as formulated by the Court has not been met.

The Court rejects the particular claim of this appellee, not because it presents any special problems, but rather because of the risk that a myriad of other claims would be too difficult to process. The Court overstates the magnitude of this risk because the Amish claim applies only to a small religious community with an established welfare system of its own. Nevertheless, I agree with the Court's conclusion that the difficulties associated with processing other claims to tax exemption on religious grounds justify a rejection of this claim.[2] I believe, however, that this reasoning supports the adoption of a different constitutional standard than the Court purports to apply.

The Court's analysis supports a holding that there is virtually no room for a "constitutionally required exemption" on religious grounds from a valid tax law that is entirely neutral in its general application.[3] Because I agree with that holding, I concur in the judgment.

GONZALES v. O CENTRO ESPIRITA BENEFICENTE UNIAO DO VEGETAL

126 S. Ct. 1211 (2006)

Chief Justice ROBERTS delivered the opinion of the Court.

A religious sect with origins in the Amazon Rainforest receives communion by drinking a sacramental tea, brewed from plants unique to the region, that contains a hallucinogen regulated under the Controlled Substances Act by the Federal Government. The Government concedes that this practice is a sincere exercise of religion, but nonetheless sought to prohibit the small American branch of the sect from engaging in the practice, on the ground that the Controlled Substances Act bars all use of the hallucinogen. The sect sued to block

---

2. In my opinion, the principal reason for adopting a strong presumption against such claims is not a matter of administrative convenience. It is the overriding interest in keeping the government—whether it be the legislature or the courts—out of the business of evaluating the relative merits of differing religious claims. The risk that governmental approval of some and disapproval of others will be perceived as favoring one religion over another is an important risk the Establishment Clause was designed to preclude.

3. Today's holding is limited to a claim to a tax exemption. I believe, however, that a standard that places an almost insurmountable burden on any individual who objects to a valid and neutral law of general applicability on the ground that the law proscribes (or prescribes) conduct that his religion prescribes (or proscribes) better explains most of this Court's holdings than does the standard articulated by the Court today. See, e.g., *Braunfeld*; *Reynolds*; [other decisions rejecting exemptions.] The principal exception is Wisconsin v. Yoder. . . . The Court's attempt to distinguish *Yoder* is unconvincing because precisely the same religious interest is implicated in both cases, and Wisconsin's interest in requiring its children to attend school until they reach the age of 16 is surely not inferior to the federal interest in collecting these social security taxes.

[Justice Stevens distinguished Lee's claim from Thomas v. Review Board and Sherbert v. Verner as follows:] A tax exemption entails no cost to the claimant; if tax exemptions were dispensed on religious grounds, every citizen would have an economic motivation to join the favored sects. No comparable economic motivation could explain the conduct of the employees in *Sherbert* and *Thomas*. In both of those cases changes in work requirements dictated by the employer forced the employees to surrender jobs that they would have preferred to retain rather than accept unemployment compensation. In each case the treatment of the religious objection to the new job requirements as though it were tantamount to a physical impairment that made it impossible for the employee to continue to work under changed circumstances could be viewed as a protection against unequal treatment rather than a grant of favored treatment for the members of the religious sect.

enforcement against it of the ban on the sacramental tea, and [obtained] a preliminary injunction.

It relied on the Religious Freedom Restoration Act of 1993 [p. 151]. . . . We conclude that the Government has not carried the burden expressly placed on it by Congress in the Religious Freedom Restoration Act, and affirm the grant of the preliminary injunction.

I

[The Court discussed Employment Division v. Smith (p. 137) and RFRA,] which adopts a statutory rule comparable to the constitutional rule rejected in *Smith*. Under RFRA, the Federal Government may not, as a statutory matter, substantially burden a person's exercise of religion, "even if the burden results from a rule of general applicability." The only exception recognized by the statute requires the Government to satisfy the compelling interest test—to "demonstrat[e] that application of the burden to the person—(1) is in further-ance of a compelling government interest; and (2) is the least restrictive means of furthering that compelling governmental interest." . . . [3]

The Controlled Substances Act, 21 U. S. C. § 801 *et seq.*, regulates the importa-tion, manufacture, distribution, and use of psychotropic substances. The Act classifies substances into five schedules based on their potential for abuse, the extent to which they have an accepted medical use, and their safety. Substances listed in Schedule I of the Act are subject to the most comprehensive restrictions, including an outright ban on all importation and use. . . .

O Centro Espírita Beneficente União do Vegetal (UDV) is a Christian Spiritist sect based in Brazil, with an American branch of approximately 130 individuals. Central to the UDV's faith is receiving communion through hoasca (pro-nounced "wass-ca"), a sacramental tea made from two plants unique to the Amazon region. One of the plants [contains dimethyltryptamine (DMT), a hal-lucinogen that] is listed in Schedule I. . . .

[U.S. Customs inspectors seized a shipment of hoasca to the American UDV and threatened the group with prosecution. The UDV sued federal officials and sought a preliminary injunction. The government claimed three compelling interests:] protecting the health and safety of UDV members, preventing the diversion of hoasca from the church to recreational users, and complying with the 1971 United Nations Convention on Psychotropic Substances, a treaty signed by the United States. . . .

[As to health risks, the] Government presented evidence to the effect that use of hoasca, or DMT more generally, can cause psychotic reactions, cardiac irre-gularities, and adverse drug interactions. The UDV countered by citing studies documenting the safety of its sacramental use of hoasca and presenting evidence that minimized the likelihood of the health risks raised by the Government. With respect to diversion, the Government pointed to a general rise in the illicit use of hallucinogens, and cited interest in the illegal use of DMT and hoasca in particular; the UDV emphasized the thinness of any market for hoasca, the

---

3. In City of Boerne v. Flores [p. 150], we held [RFRA's] application to States to be beyond Congress' legislative authority under § 5 of the 14th Amendment.

relatively small amounts of the substance imported by the church, and the absence of any diversion problem in the past.

The District Court concluded that the evidence on health risks was "in equipoise," and similarly that the evidence on diversion was "virtually balanced." In the face of such an even showing, the court reasoned that the Government had failed to demonstrate a compelling interest justifying what it acknowledged was a substantial burden on the UDV's sincere religious exercise. The court also rejected the asserted interest in complying with the [treaty].

[The preliminary injunction entered by the court] requires the church to import the tea pursuant to federal permits, to restrict control over the tea to persons of church authority, and to warn particularly susceptible UDV members of the dangers of hoasca. [The court of appeals affirmed the injunction.]

III

[T]he Government contends that the Act's description of Schedule I substances as having "a high potential for abuse," "no currently accepted medical use in treatment in the United States," and "a lack of accepted safety for use ... under medical supervision," by itself precludes any consideration of individualized exceptions such as that sought by the UDV.... According to the Government, there would be no way to cabin religious exceptions once recognized, and "the public will misread" such exceptions as signaling that the substance at issue is not harmful after all. Under the Government's view, there is no need to assess the particulars of the UDV's use or weigh the impact of an exemption for that specific use, because the Controlled Substances Act serves a compelling purpose and simply admits of no exceptions.

A

RFRA, and the strict scrutiny test it adopted, contemplate an inquiry more focused than the Government's categorical approach. RFRA requires the Government to demonstrate that the compelling interest test is satisfied through application of the challenged law "to the person"—the particular claimant whose sincere exercise of religion is being substantially burdened. RFRA expressly adopted the compelling interest test "as set forth in Sherbert v. Verner and Wisconsin v. Yoder." In each of those cases, this Court looked beyond broadly formulated interests justifying the general applicability of government mandates and scrutinized the asserted harm of granting specific exemptions to particular religious claimants. In *Yoder*, for example, we permitted an exemption for Amish children from a compulsory school attendance law. We recognized that the State had a "paramount" interest in education, but held that "despite its admitted validity in the generality of cases, we must searchingly examine the interests that the State seeks to promote ... and the impediment to those objectives that would flow from recognizing the claimed Amish exemption." The Court explained that the State needed "to show with more particularity how its admittedly strong interest ... would be adversely affected by granting an exemption to the Amish."

In *Sherbert*, the Court upheld a particular claim to a religious exemption from a state law denying unemployment benefits to those who would not work on Saturdays, but explained that it was not announcing a constitutional right to unemployment benefits for "all persons whose religious convictions are the cause of their unemployment." The Court distinguished the case "in which an employee's religious convictions serve to make him a nonproductive member of society." *Ibid.*; see also *Smith* (O'Connor, J., concurring in judgment) (strict scrutiny "at least requires a case-by-case determination of the question, sensitive to the facts of each particular claim"). . . .

B

Under the more focused inquiry required by RFRA and the compelling interest test, the Government's mere invocation of the general characteristics of Schedule I substances [c]annot carry the day. It is true, of course, that Schedule I substances such as DMT are exceptionally dangerous. Nevertheless, there is no indication that Congress, in classifying DMT, considered the harms posed by the particular use at issue here—the circumscribed, sacramental use of hoasca by the UDV. . . . Congress' determination that DMT should be listed under Schedule I simply does not provide a categorical answer that relieves the Government of the obligation to shoulder its burden under RFRA.

This conclusion is reinforced by the Controlled Substances Act itself. The Act contains a provision authorizing the Attorney General to "waive the requirement for registration of certain manufacturers, distributors, or dispensers if he finds it consistent with the public health and safety." 21 U.S.C. § 822(d). The fact that the Act itself contemplates that exempting certain people from its requirements would be "consistent with the public health and safety" indicates that congressional findings with respect to Schedule I substances should not carry the determinative weight, for RFRA purposes, that the Government would ascribe to them.

And in fact an exception has been made to the Schedule I ban for religious use. For the past 35 years, there has been a regulatory exemption for use of peyote—a Schedule I substance—by the Native American Church. See 21 CFR § 1307.31. In 1994, Congress extended that exemption to all members of every recognized Indian Tribe. See 42 U.S.C. § 1996a(b)(1). . . . If such use is permitted in the face of the congressional findings [f]or hundreds of thousands of Native Americans practicing their faith, it is difficult to see how those same findings alone can preclude any consideration of a similar exception for the 130 or so American members of the UDV who want to practice theirs. See Church of Lukumi v. Hialeah ("It is established in our strict scrutiny jurisprudence that 'a law cannot be regarded as protecting an interest 'of the highest order' . . . when it leaves appreciable damage to that supposedly vital interest unprohibited.' ").

The Government responds that there is a "unique relationship" between the United States and the Tribes. . . . [But n]othing about the unique political status of the Tribes makes their members immune from the health risks the Government asserts accompany any use of a Schedule I substance, nor insulates the Schedule I substance the Tribes use in religious exercise from the alleged risk of diversion.

The Government argues that the existence of a congressional exemption for peyote does not indicate that the Controlled Substances Act is amenable to judicially crafted exceptions. RFRA, however, plainly contemplates that courts would recognize exceptions—that is how the law works. . . .

C

... The Government points to some pre-*Smith* cases relying on a need for uniformity in rejecting claims for religious exemptions under the Free Exercise Clause, but those cases strike us as quite different from the present one. Those cases did not embrace the notion that a general interest in uniformity justified a substantial burden on religious exercise; they instead scrutinized the asserted need and explained why the denied exemptions could not be accommodated. In United States v. Lee, for example, the Court rejected a claimed exception to the obligation to pay Social Security taxes, noting that "mandatory participation is indispensable to the fiscal vitality of the social security system" and that the "tax system could not function if denominations were allowed to challenge the tax system because tax payments were spent in a manner that violates their religious belief." [Such] cases show that the Government can demonstrate a compelling interest in uniform application of a particular program by offering evidence that granting the requested religious accommodations would seriously compromise its ability to administer the program.

Here the Government's argument for uniformity is different; it rests not so much on the particular statutory program at issue as on slippery-slope concerns that could be invoked in response to any RFRA claim for an exception to a generally applicable law. The Government's argument echoes the classic rejoinder of bureaucrats throughout history: If I make an exception for you, I'll have to make one for everybody, so no exceptions. But RFRA operates by mandating consideration, under the compelling interest test, of exceptions to "rule[s] of general applicability." Congress determined that the legislated test "is a workable test for striking sensible balances between religious liberty and competing prior governmental interests." This determination finds support in our cases; in *Sherbert*, for example, we rejected a slippery-slope argument similar to the one offered in this case, dismissing as "no more than a possibility" the State's speculation "that the filing of fraudulent claims by unscrupulous claimants feigning religious objections to Saturday work" would drain the unemployment benefits fund. ...

We do not doubt that there may be instances in which a need for uniformity precludes the recognition of exceptions to generally applicable laws under RFRA. But it would have been surprising to find that this was such a case, given the longstanding exemption from the Controlled Substances Act for religious use of peyote, and the fact that the very reason Congress enacted RFRA was to respond to a decision [*Smith*] denying a claimed right to sacramental use of a controlled substance. And in fact the Government has not offered evidence demonstrating that granting the UDV an exemption would cause the kind of administrative harm recognized as a compelling interest in *Lee* [and similar cases]. The Government failed to convince the District Court at the preliminary injunction hearing that health or diversion concerns provide a compelling interest in banning the UDV's sacramental use of hoasca. It cannot compensate for that failure now with the bold argument that there can be no RFRA exceptions at all to the Controlled Substances Act. See Tr. of Oral Arg. 17 (Deputy Solicitor General statement that exception could not be made even for "rigorously policed" use of "one drop" of substance "once a year").

IV

[The Court then turned to the 1971 Convention, which] calls on signatories to prohibit the use of hallucinogens, including DMT. The Government argues that it has a compelling interest in meeting its international obligations by complying with the Convention. [The Court found that the Convention covered the hoasca mixture.]

The fact that hoasca is covered by the Convention, however, does not automatically mean that the Government has demonstrated a compelling interest in applying the Controlled Substances Act, which implements the Convention, to the UDV's sacramental use of the tea. At the present stage, it suffices to observe that the Government did not even submit evidence addressing the international consequences of granting an exemption for the UDV. The Government simply submitted two affidavits by State Department officials attesting to the general importance of honoring international obligations and of maintaining the leadership position of the United States in the international war on drugs. We do not doubt the validity of these interests, any more than we doubt the general interest in promoting public health and safety by enforcing the Controlled Substances Act, but under RFRA invocation of such general interests, standing alone, is not enough. . . .

The Government repeatedly invokes Congress' findings and purposes underlying the Controlled Substances Act, but Congress had a reason for enacting RFRA, too. Congress recognized that "laws 'neutral' toward religion may burden religious exercise as surely as laws intended to interfere with religious exercise," and legislated "the compelling interest test" as the means for the courts to "strik[e] sensible balances between religious liberty and competing prior governmental interests." We have no cause to pretend that the task assigned by Congress to the courts under RFRA is an easy one. Indeed, the very sort of difficulties highlighted by the Government here were cited by this Court in deciding that the approach later mandated by Congress under RFRA was not required as a matter of constitutional law under the Free Exercise Clause. See *Smith*. But Congress has determined that courts should strike sensible balances, pursuant to a compelling interest test that requires the Government to address the particular practice at issue. Applying that test, we conclude that the courts below did not err in determining that the Government failed to demonstrate, at the preliminary injunction stage, a compelling interest in barring the UDV's sacramental use of hoasca.

NOTES AND QUESTIONS

1. Measuring the Government's Interest: One Exemption or Many? As the *Lee* and *Uniao do Vegetal* (*UDV*) cases show, a crucial question under the compelling interest or heightened scrutiny approach is whether the government's interest is measured by the consequences of granting one exemption or many. The state interest in denying the particular exemption is usually weaker than the interest underlying the law as a whole (which would not be threatened unless there were many exemptions).

If the opinion in *Lee* had looked at the marginal cost of exempting only the Amish, it likely would have ruled against the government, since the Amish are a small group and (as Justice Stevens pointed out) their refusal of benefits means that the overall fiscal effect of leaving them out of the system might be positive. The Court instead warned of the "myriad exceptions flowing from a wide variety of religious beliefs." Why did it worry about that in *Lee* and not in *Yoder*? Both the Court and Justice Stevens mention that *Lee* involved an objection to taxes. Why would that make a difference? Because taxes are only money? Because many people want to avoid paying taxes? What if evidence were presented in *Yoder* that some parents want to avoid the chore of getting their children off to school in the morning?

Although the *Uniao do Vegetal* case involves the Religious Freedom Restoration Act (which the Court assumed governs federal laws, see pp. 157-158) rather than the pre-*Smith* Free Exercise Clause doctrine, it still raises the same issue: Is uniform enforcement of the drug laws, without any exceptions, necessary to serve the government's compelling interests? The Court rejects the necessity for uniform coverage. But why isn't there just as much concern with "myriad exceptions" in drug cases? Does the *UDV* opinion answer that question? Consider a couple of possible answers:

First, perhaps *Lee* is factually distinguishable from *UDV*. What factors might cause a greater risk of multiple exceptions in the former case than in the latter? The nature of taxes versus drugs? The particular tax versus the particular drug? The presence of other exemptions that do, or do not, undercut the government's interest?

Second, perhaps *Lee* applied a less demanding legal standard than did *UDV* (and *Yoder*). Did *Lee* follow the "compelling interest/least restrictive means" test that RFRA reinstated? If *Lee* applied a weaker test, doesn't that undermine Congress's assertion in RFRA that it was merely "restoring" a compelling interest test that had governed up until Employment Division v. Smith? Compare two sections of RFRA (p. 151): 42 U.S.C. § 2000bb(a)(5) (approving of "the compelling interest test as set forth in prior Federal court rulings"), and *id.* § 2000bb(b)(2) (stating that RFRA's purpose is "to restore the compelling interest test as set forth in Sherbert v. Verner and Wisconsin v. Yoder"). If *Lee* and *Yoder* embody different tests, which one does RFRA "restore"?

2. Differentiating Between Religious Claims.   Focusing only on the costs of exempting the UDV requires distinguishing the group's conduct from other religiously motivated drug use. In the court of appeals, Judge McConnell distinguished prior cases that had rejected claims for exemption from drug laws: "[T]he fact that *hoasca* is a relatively uncommon substance used almost exclusively as part of a well-defined religious service makes an exemption for bona fide religious purposes less subject to abuse than if the religion required its constant consumption, or if the drug were a more widely used substance like marijuana or methamphetamine." O Centro Espirita Beneficente Uniao do Vegetal v. Ashcroft, 389 F.3d 973, 1023 (10th Cir. 2004) (en banc) (McConnell, J., concurring). Does having courts differentiate between "well-defined" and "constant" or uncontrolled religious uses raise any constitutional concerns? Does it put authorities in the position of declaring "good" and "bad" religions? In a dissent in *Smith* itself, Justice Blackmun argued: "Though the State must treat all religions equally, and not favor one over another, this obligation is fulfilled by the uniform application of the 'compelling interest' test to all free exercise claims, not by reaching uniform results as to all claims." 494 U.S. at 918. Is this answer satisfactory?

Will such differentiation between free exercise claims tend to produce discrimination against minority religions? One might expect that when judges draw these fine lines, they will tend to see the conduct of more familiar faiths as less threatening. A recent empirical survey, however, has found that in a decade of cases involving claims for religious exemptions, minority religions lost no greater a share of cases than did larger faiths, and the groups with the lowest success rate were the quite familiar Catholics and Baptists. Gregory C. Sisk, How Traditional and Minority Religions Fare in the Courts: Empirical Evidence from Religious Liberty Cases, 76 Colo. L. Rev. 1021 (2005). What might explain these counterintuitive statistics?

3. Policing to Prevent Harms: Entanglement?   To ensure that the UDV's use remained controlled, the preliminary injunction "required that the church, upon demand by the [Drug Enforcement Administration], identify its members who handle *hoasca* outside of ceremonies, allow for on-site inspections and inventories, provide samples, identify times and locations of ceremonies, and designate a liaison to the DEA." Do those provisions entangle the government with the UDV and make the injunction constitutionally improper?

4. "Least Restrictive Alternative" and Exemptions.   The idea that a restriction on religion must not only serve a compelling interest, but be the least restrictive means of doing so, appeared in *Sherbert*, 374 U.S. at 407, and was codified in RFRA. If the particular claimant's practice does not threaten the state's interest at all, then exemption is a less restrictive alternative. Often, however, exemption will frustrate the law's purpose partially but not entirely. How much frustration of the state's interest is too much? Consider Braunfeld v. Brown (p. 176), where exempting Saturday worshipers would, in Justice Brennan's words, "make Sundays a little noisier, and the task of police and prosecutor a little more difficult." Are these sufficient reason to reject an exemption?

5. Commercial Activity and "Imposing on Others."   For another possible distinction explaining United States v. Lee, consider the Court's statement that Amish employers enter commercial activity "as a matter of choice" and that granting an exemption from social security taxes would "impose [their] faith on their employees." Do you agree? Could the Amish employer argue just the opposite: that his employees work for him "as a matter of choice" and the government is "imposing" on him by trying to force him to pay taxes he regards as evil? Did Adele Sherbert, the claimant in Sherbert v. Verner, engage in commercial work "as a matter of choice" and "impose" her tenets on her employer by refusing to work on Saturdays? In other words, the determination of who is imposing on whom depends on setting a baseline of rights. Is the baseline the common law, which generally allows an owner of a business or property to refuse to deal with others based on her moral objections? On the other hand, consider the fact that a number of federal and state civil rights laws prohibit commercial businesses from discriminating on the basis of race, sex, marital status, and other factors in employing workers, serving customers, and renting out housing. Do those laws reflect a different baseline, under which the commercial enterprise that discriminates is indeed "imposing" on employees or customers?

If religious exemptions are not available to those engaged in commercial activity, does this inappropriately force employers to separate their faith from their work?

Lee was followed in St. Agnes Hospital v. Riddick, 748 F. Supp. 319 (D. Md. 1990), where a government-sanctioned accreditation agency required all medical residency programs in obstetrics and gynecology to provide clinical training in elective abortions, sterilizations, and artificial contraception. The agency withdrew the certification of St. Agnes, a Catholic hospital. The district court rejected St. Agnes's free exercise challenge, quoting the language above from *Lee* about employers imposing on their employees. Was the court right to follow *Lee*? In one sense, the imposition on others in *St. Agnes* seems even clearer: While the employees in *Lee* were themselves Amish and could be said to have accepted Amish norms, many residents at the hospital came from outside the Catholic faith and probably did not agree with Catholic norms on abortion or contraception. But consider the following questions:

First, it seems a serious matter for a hospital to have to provide training in a procedure it regards as murder. Is that an argument for distinguishing *Lee*?

Second, St. Agnes Hospital was not "commercial" in the familiar sense of operating for profit, so strictly speaking the passage from *Lee* does not apply. But nonprofit programs can also have effects on society. Does it make sense to treat for-profit entities as per se ineligible for exemptions, but nonprofits as eligible?

Finally, the accreditation rules in *St. Agnes* exempted individual residents from having to participate in procedures they conscientiously opposed. Such "conscience clauses" are common, and they sometimes extend to health care institutions as well as individuals. See, e.g., 42 U.S.C. § 300a-7 (providing that individuals or entities supported by various federal funding programs may not be required to perform, assist in, or provide facilities or support for abortions or sterilization procedures "contrary to [their] religious beliefs or moral convictions"). What justification is there for protecting the conscientious tenets of individuals but not of entities or communities? The *St. Agnes* court answered:

> An individual resident who declines, for moral or religious reasons, to participate in a particular procedure offers strong assurance that she/he will not employ that procedure in post-graduation practice. St. Agnes requires its residents, who are of different moral and religious beliefs, to abstain from participating in and refuse clinical training in certain proscribed procedures while under contract with St. Agnes. Such an arrangement does not offer any assurances that once St. Agnes' residents finish their training they will not perform those procedures as practicing physicians.

Would it be a "less restrictive alternative," under the *Sherbert/Yoder* test, to require that the residents get family-planning training elsewhere, or to limit their license in some way?

6. Problems.

(a) Landlords and unmarried tenants, revisited. Return to the facts of Thomas v. Anchorage Equal Rights Commission (p. 175). Assuming that the city must come up with a "compelling" (or at least strong) reason for forbidding the landlords, Thomas and Baker, to discriminate against unmarried couples, what facts would be relevant to that determination? What result under the approaches in *Lee* and *UDV*?

A landlord who refused to rent to an African-American couple, or an inter-racial couple, as a matter of religious conscience (say, a religious belief in racial segregation) might lose on a free exercise claim to be exempt from an antidis-crimination law. See Bob Jones Univ. v. United States, 461 U.S. 574, 603-604 (1983) (upholding withdrawal of tax exemption from racially discriminatory college on basis of "compelling interest" in, and "firm national policy" of, avoiding government support for racial discrimination in education). What factors would you raise or investigate to argue that a refusal to rent to a couple because they are unmarried is different? See *Thomas*, 165 F.3d at 714-717 (finding no "firm national policy" because federal constitutional law allows marital-status discrimination, other states permit it, and Alaska laws favor mar-ried over unmarried relationships in welfare benefits, inheritance of property, testimonial privileges, and other ways). If you argue that how the city of Ancho-rage or the state of Alaska treats marriage in other contexts is relevant to the compelling interest test, what Supreme Court authority would you cite for that argument? Why are federal and other state laws relevant—can't Anchorage and Alaska decide that discrimination against unmarried couples is a serious prob-lem, even if the federal government and other states disagree? For a sensitive discussion of some of these issues, and the various interests at stake in the landlord-tenant cases, see Marie Failinger, Remembering Mrs. Murphy: A Reme-dies Approach to the Conflict Between Gay/Lesbian Renters and Religious Landlords, 29 Cap. U. L. Rev. 383 (2001).

(b) **Zoning regulations.** As we have indicated, religious entities frequently run up against state and local zoning laws or architectural preservation regula-tions. Under the new federal religious freedom statute, RLUIPA (see p. 158), many such land use restrictions are subject to the standard of compelling interest/least restrictive means if they impose a "substantial burden" on religious exercise. Under that standard, or some other form of "heightened" scrutiny, what result in the following situations?

(i) A small congregation of Orthodox Jews conducts services twice daily in the home of its elderly rabbi, whose physical condition limits his ability to travel. The services involve 10 or 20 people typically, but as many as 50 on Saturdays and holidays. The property and the neighborhood are (and were at the time the rabbi purchased the property) zoned for single-family residential use only, which prohibits its use for organized religious services as well as for many other purposes (apartment buildings, commercial uses, etc.). The city does not forbid residents from hosting small groups of friends and neighbors infor-mally in their home for religious meetings, including regular meetings such as midweek Bible study groups in local Christian churches. The daily services usu-ally cause no substantial disturbance to the neighborhood, but the larger holi-day and Saturday services have occasionally disturbed neighbors for several reasons: chanting and singing during the services, a few visiting congregants from out of town asking for directions to the services, and groups of 20 to 30 people standing on the sidewalk before and after services (pursuant to Jewish law, the worshipers do not drive cars on these days). The city forbids the services, and the rabbi and other worshipers sue to enjoin application of the zoning law.

What result and why? Cf. Grosz v. City of Miami Beach, 721 F.2d 729 (5th Cir. 1983) (rejecting free exercise claim in these circumstances under a test "balancing" city's interest against burden on religion).

(ii)   For ten years, Western Presbyterian Church operated a program feeding breakfast to homeless people at its church building in an office/university neighborhood of Washington, D.C. There were no incidents of harm or assault to neighbors from the kitchen's operation, and eventually neighbors became accustomed to the operation. However, the Church moved to new property a few blocks away, in an area of apartment buildings, and it proposed to continue the feeding program at the new site. The neighbors at the new site objected strongly and offered to help support an alternative location in a nonresidential area several blocks away. The District's zoning board ruled that the Church's use was prima facie prohibited in this zone and the Church must seek a zoning variance, a process that would require several months during which the program would be discontinued. The Church sued to enjoin the application of this decision. What result and why? See Western Presbyterian Church v. Bd. of Zoning Adjustment, 849 F. Supp. 77 (D.D.C. 1994).

ii. Paternalistic Justifications

So far, the governmental justifications have all related to the interests of other people, or of the government as an institution. But some laws are designed to protect individuals from hurting themselves. Is there any special problem with laws of this sort, when they interfere with religious exercise? Religious practice often entails sacrifice. When should the government step in to say that the sacrifice is too great?

BAUMGARTNER v. FIRST CHURCH OF CHRIST, SCIENTIST
141 Ill. App. 3d 898, 490 N.E.2d 1319 (1986)

Presiding Judge BUCKLEY delivered the opinion of the court:

Plaintiff, Mary Baumgartner, as executor of the estate of John Baumgartner, deceased, brought an action for wrongful death against the First Church of Christ, Scientist ("Mother Church"), Ruth L. Tanner, and the Northern Trust Company, as executor of the estate of Paul A. Erickson, deceased. Plaintiff's action arises out of Christian Science treatment rendered to decedent by Tanner and Erickson. . . .

Initially, we observe that Christian Science is a widely known religion and courts will take judicial notice of its general teachings. Its basic premise, as plaintiff acknowledges in her pleading, is that physical disease can be healed by spiritual means alone. As stated in an article on Christian Science from the Encyclopedia Britannica (15th ed., 1984):

Christian Science is a religious denomination founded in the United States in 1879 by Mary Baker Eddy (1821-1910), author of the book that contains the definitive statement of its teaching, Science and Health with Key to the Scriptures. About one-third of its nearly 3,000 congregations are located in 56 countries outside the

United States, with membership concentrated in areas with strong Protestant traditions. It is widely known for its practice of spiritual healing, an emphasis best understood in relation to its historical background and teaching. . . .

The cure of disease through prayer is seen as a necessary element in a full redemption from the flesh. Church historian Karl Holl summarizes the concept of treatment, or prayer, in Christian Science as "a silent yielding of self to God, an ever closer relationship to God, until His omnipresence and love are felt effectively by man," and he distinguishes this decisively from willpower or mental suggestion.

. . . Plaintiff's fourth amended complaint alleged that on October 13, 1974, the decedent, plaintiff's husband, contracted acute prostatitis. The illness manifested itself through severe pain in the groin area and the inability to urinate. Decedent immediately contacted Paul Erickson and advised him of his illness. Decedent requested that Erickson provide him with Christian Science treatment. Erickson, a Christian Science practitioner, had provided decedent with Christian Science healing on several prior occasions. He was also plaintiff's teacher and advisor on Christian Science. Erickson had been instructed by the Mother Church in the methods of Christian Science healing and was listed in The Christian Science Journal, a publication of the organization. By listing practitioners in the journal, the Mother Church certifies their training and competence.

Erickson came to decedent's home shortly after being contacted and administered hot baths and Christian Science treatment. Erickson also "massaged and manipulated" decedent's prostate gland. For the next several days, decedent's condition remained unchanged. Erickson therefore contacted defendant Ruth Tanner and directed her to go to decedent's home to assist in rendering Christian Science healing. Tanner was a Christian Science nurse certified by the Department of Care of the Mother Church and was also listed in its journal. Tanner proceeded to provide Christian Science treatment to decedent. Erickson called daily to check on decedent's condition and he visited frequently to provide healing.

Decedent's condition began to deteriorate. Plaintiff alleges that decedent decided he wanted medical treatment for his illness and that he no longer wished to be treated by Tanner and Erickson. She further alleges that when Erickson was advised of this request, he told decedent that he would die if a medical doctor was called and assured decedent that he was being cured by Christian Science healing. Decedent and plaintiff did not call in a medical doctor and instead continued with the Christian Science healing provided by Tanner and Erickson. Decedent's condition further deteriorated and he died on October 23, 1974, 10 days after he became ill.

At the time of his death, decedent had been a wealthy inventor and industrialist. He was survived by plaintiff and his two minor children. The complaint alleges that prior to his death, decedent changed his will at the insistence of Erickson and made the Mother Church a residual beneficiary of approximately one-half of his multi-million dollar estate.

[The district court dismissed the action on First Amendment grounds, and this appeal followed.]

I

We first address the propriety of the trial court's dismissal of the count in plaintiff's complaint seeking recovery for medical malpractice. This claim is based on the premise that Erickson and Tanner were under a legal duty to comply with the standards of diagnosis and care that are imposed upon members of the medical profession even though they had been retained by decedent for Christian Science treatment. We find no merit to plaintiff's claim. Legislative and judicial distinctions between medical and spiritual treatment belie the existence of any such duty.

Our state legislature recognized the fundamental difference between spiritual treatment of human ailments and medical treatment when it enacted the Medical Practice Act. This Act exempts religious treatment from licensing, testing and other regulation. Specifically, section 4474 provides that the Act does not apply to "persons treating human ailments by prayer or spiritual means as an exercise or enjoyment of religious freedom." Similarly, nurses who provide "care of the sick where treatment is by prayer or spiritual means" are expressly exempt from the requirement that all nurses be licensed. It follows that persons in these categories, exempt as a matter of public policy from the statutory framework which sets up standards for the medical profession, may not be held liable for failing to comply with medical standards to which they are not subject.

The argument that Christian Science practitioners should be held to medical standards has been expressly rejected by the New Hampshire Supreme Court. (Spead v. Tomlinson (1904).) There, the court affirmed a directed verdict for a Christian Science practitioner where the plaintiff sought to recover for medical malpractice. In so holding, the court noted that the plaintiff knew that the defendant was not a member of the regular school of physicians and did not practice according to its methods, but instead was a Christian Scientist and practiced according to the methods recognized by such healers. The *Spead* court reasoned:

> As is said in Story's Bailments, § 435: "If a person will knowingly employ a common matmaker to weave or embroider a fine carpet, he must impute the bad workmanship to his own folly. So, if a man who has a disorder of his eye should employ a farrier to cure the disease, and he should lose his sight by using the remedy prescribed in such cases for horses, he would certainly have no legal ground of complaint." And in cases involving the liability of medical practitioners courts have held that, "If there are distinct and differing schools of practice, as allopathic, or old school, homeopathic, Thompsonian, hydropathic, or water cure, and a physician of one of those schools is called in, his treatment is to be tested by the general doctrines of his school, and not by those of other schools."

Our supreme court has adopted the key principle upon which the *Spead* decision was predicated: that a plaintiff may not successfully establish a standard of care for one health care specialty by offering the testimony of someone who practices a different specialty. (Dolan v. Galluzzo (Ill. 1979).) In *Dolan*, it was held that the standard of care for a podiatrist may not be established through a physician or surgeon.

Here, plaintiff does not allege that Erickson or Tanner held themselves out to decedent as medical practitioners, nor that decedent expected or asked them to render medical treatment. As plaintiff concedes in her complaint, followers of Christian Science do not use medical aid to treat illness, but instead rely solely upon spiritual means. Decedent specifically requested Christian Science treatment when he became ill and could not have reasonably expected anything other than spiritual healing from Tanner and Erickson. There is no allegation that decedent was incompetent prior to his death. Viewing these facts and circumstances in light of the authorities cited above, we find that plaintiff cannot state a cause of action for medical malpractice.

II

We next consider plaintiff's count based on a theory of Christian Science malpractice. Specifically, plaintiff alleges that Erickson and Tanner deviated from the standard of care of an ordinary Christian Science practitioner and nurse when they treated decedent. We find no basis for recovery under such a theory.

The United States Constitution dictates that the only entity with the authority and power to determine whether there has been a deviation from "true" Christian Science practice is the Christian Science Church itself. As the United States Supreme Court has held, the first amendment bars the judiciary from considering whether certain religious conduct conforms to the standards of a particular religious group. (Thomas v. Review Board.) In *Thomas*, it was held that probing the proper interpretation of religious beliefs "is not within the judicial function and judicial competence" and that "[c]ourts are not arbiters of scriptural interpretation." Similarly, in [Serbian Orthodox Diocese] v. Milivojevich (1976), the United States Supreme Court reversed a decision by the Illinois Supreme Court, holding that the court improperly inquired into the propriety of the removal of a bishop from his post and the reorganization of the church diocese. . . .

As in each of the above mentioned cases, adjudication of the present case would require the court to extensively investigate and evaluate religious tenets and doctrines: first, to establish the standard of care of an "ordinary" Christian Science practitioner; and second, to determine whether Erickson and Tanner deviated from those standards. We believe that the first amendment precludes such an intrusive inquiry by the civil courts into religious matters. . . .

Plaintiff in her brief relies on Prince v. Massachusetts (1944), Cox v. New Hampshire (1941), and Reynolds v. United States. In *Prince*, it was held that the use of children to sell church literature violated a statute prohibiting child labor. In *Cox*, the court held that parades for religious purposes did not excuse a church group from obtaining a permit. *Reynolds* held that the religious practice of polygamy violated state law.

We find each of the above cases distinguishable from the present case. In each instance, the wrongful conduct, although religiously motivated, could be analyzed without first evaluating the tenets of a particular religion. Moreover, the polygamous marriage bans were upheld in *Reynolds* because the practice consisted of overt acts determined to be deleterious to public morals and welfare. No such overt, immoral activity is involved in this case.

Plaintiff also cites Jacobson v. Massachusetts (1905), where an individual's claim of exemption from compulsory small pox vaccination was denied because the state's interest in public health was superior. We find this case to be inapposite since society can protect itself from the danger of loathsome and contagious disease, an issue which is not now before us.

We find none of the above authorities cited by plaintiff to be persuasive analogy. The question of whether or not defendants deviated from the standard of care of an ordinary Christian Scientist is not a justiciable controversy. Accordingly, the trial court properly dismissed plaintiff's count seeking recovery for Christian Science malpractice.

III

Next, we consider whether the trial court correctly dismissed plaintiff's count based on ordinary negligence. Plaintiff alleged that Erickson and Tanner were negligent because they failed to withdraw from treating decedent when requested to do so; failed to withdraw when they knew or should have known Christian Science treatment was not curing decedent; failed to consult a medical doctor when they knew or should have known Christian Science treatment was not curing decedent's illness; failed to consult a medical doctor when requested to do so and when they knew decedent was going to die without medical treatment; advised decedent not to obtain medical care; coerced decedent into not calling in a medical doctor; misrepresented to decedent that the Christian Science treatment was working; and breached a fiduciary relationship.

To set forth a cause of action sounding in negligence, a plaintiff must allege the existence of a duty of reasonable care owed plaintiff by defendant, breach of that duty and injury proximately resulting from the breach. . . .

Applying these principles to the case at hand, we find that plaintiff's negligence claim must fail. For the court to determine whether defendants breached any duty owed to decedent would require a searching inquiry into Christian Science beliefs and the validity of such beliefs. As established above, such an inquiry is precluded by the first amendment.

We recognize that plaintiff alleges in her complaint that Erickson and Tanner persuaded decedent and his family not to call in a medical doctor through "coercion" and "intimidation." Such allegations, however, are merely conclusionary. Plaintiff does not allege that decedent was not rational or mentally incompetent. Nor does she allege that decedent or herself was physically imprisoned by defendants and thus unable to contact a physician. The facts as alleged by plaintiff fail to show that the Christian Science treatment provided to decedent, a competent adult, was not a matter of his own choice and free will at all times prior to his death. Our supreme court has made it clear that a competent adult has the right under the first amendment to refuse medical treatment when it conflicts with his religious beliefs.

Accordingly, we conclude that plaintiff has failed to state a cause of action for negligence and that the trial court properly dismissed plaintiff's negligence count.

IV

We next consider plaintiff's count alleging that defendants acted with intentional or reckless disregard for decedent's health and safety. The allegations in this count are virtually identical to those in the count premised on ordinary negligence. Plaintiff merely added the words "acted intentionally or with reckless disregard." We believe that the same rationale which caused plaintiff's negligence count to fail also causes the intentional/reckless disregard count to fail. Whether or not defendants negligently or intentionally applied church doctrine is not a justiciable controversy. . . .

For the foregoing reasons, the judgment of the circuit court of Cook County is affirmed.

SWANN v. PACK

527 S.W.2d 99 (Tenn. 1975)

HENRY, Justice.

We granted certiorari in this case to determine whether the State of Tennessee may enjoin a religious group from handling snakes as a part of its religious service and in accordance with its Articles of Faith, on the basis of such action constituting a public nuisance.

The Circuit Court at Newport permanently enjoined the defendant, Pack, Pastor of The Holiness Church of God in Jesus Name, of Newport, and one of his Elders from "handling, displaying or exhibiting dangerous and poisonous snakes", predicating its action primarily upon a finding that "the handling of said dangerous and poisonous snakes is in violation of T.C.A. § 39-2208[1] and that said practice is done in the presence of children and other people attending church services. . . ."

The Court of Appeals, in a split decision, found the injunction to be overbroad and modified it to read that the respondents

> are permanently enjoined from handling, displaying or exhibiting dangerous and poisonous snakes in such manner as will endanger the life or health of persons who do not consent to exposure to such danger. . . .

I

To place this controversy in proper perspective, we note the pleadings and trial proceedings.

On April 14, 1973, the District Attorney General of the Second Judicial Circuit filed his petition in the Circuit Court at Newport charging that respondents Pack and certain designated Elders, including Albert Ball, had been handling snakes as a part of their church service "for the last two years"; that this was one of the rituals of the church to test the faith and sincerity of belief of church members; that Pastor Pack "has become anointed", along with other members of the church and has "advanced" to using deadly drugs, to wit, strychnine; that at a

---

1. Section 39-2208 reads as follows:

HANDLING SNAKES SO AS TO ENDANGER LIFE—PENALTY
It shall be unlawful for any person, or persons, to display, exhibit, handle or use any poisonous or dangerous snake or reptile in such a manner as to endanger the life or health of any person.

Any person violating the provisions of this section shall be guilty of a misdemeanor and punished by a fine of not less than fifty dollars ($50.00) nor more than one hundred and fifty dollars ($150), or by confinement in jail not exceeding six (6) months, or by both such fine and imprisonment, in the discretion of the court.

church service on April 7, 1973, snakes were handled and an "Indian boy was bitten and his arm became swollen"; that two named church members drank strychnine and died as a result; that, at the funeral of one of these, Pastor Pack, and others, handled snakes; and that Pastor Pack has proclaimed his intentions to continue these practices. The prayer was for an injunction enjoining respondents "from handling, displaying, or exhibiting poisonous snakes or taking or using strychnine or other poisonous medicines." In the alternative, and upon failure of the named defendants to cease and desist, petitioner prayed that the church be padlocked as a public nuisance.

By order entered April 21, 1973, the trial court found these facts to be true; that § 39-2208 had been violated and ordered that the defendants be

> [e]njoined from handling poisonous snakes or using deadly poisons in any church service being conducted in said church or at *any other place in Cocke County, Tennessee*, until further orders of the Court. (Emphasis supplied). . . .

. . . [T]he record reflects that immediately following the above quoted language the trial judge added, in his own handwriting, the following:

> However, any person who wishes to swallow strychnine or other poison may do so if he does not make it available to any other persons.

The further result of this order was that defendants could not practice snake handling, from which death *might* ensue[2] but could drink strychnine, a highly poisonous drug.

The record reflects no explanation for this incongruity.

Thereafter, the District Attorney General filed a second petition alleging stepped up activity, at the Holiness Church. On July 1, 1973, "a national convention for the snake handlers' cult of the United States" was held and "many dangerous and poisonous snakes were displayed" and one of the handlers had been bitten and was in a Chattanooga hospital recuperating. Services were conducted on July 3 and July 7, 1973, and again snakes were handled. All this led the District Attorney General to conclude and charge that Cocke County was in imminent danger and likely to "become the snake handling capital of the world". . . .

It was stipulated that various witnesses would testify that they had never seen anyone other than designated representatives of this particular church handle snakes; that they never saw any person who was either a parishioner or a non-member present at the church services who had ever been placed in immediate danger.

It was further stipulated that an anthropologist would testify that snake handling is a legitimate part of their religious service; that she had never seen anyone endangered by handling snakes; that proper precautions were always taken;

---

2. The most common question that arises regarding ritual snake handling is the surprisingly small number of fatalities. L. M. Klauner, "the undoubted authority on the rattlesnake," writes that the fatalities from this cause (rattlesnake bite) for the entire United States, with a population of over 160 million, seldom exceed 30 per year. Of every 100 people bitten by rattlesnakes, only about 3 will die. W. LaBarre, They Shall Take up Serpents, pp. 13-14 (University of Minnesota Press 1962) (hereinafter referred to as LaBarre).

and that handling snakes is a legitimate and historic part of the church service. Two other witnesses would verify this testimony.

It was further stipulated that the "Indian boy", bitten at one of the services, was thirty years old.

It was further stipulated that the Holiness Church of God in Jesus Name is located about a half mile from the nearest paved road, and at the end of a dead-end, dirt, private, mountain road and on property owned by the church.

The issues were not fully developed and the record is meager.

The State made no contention that this is not an organized religious group nor did it question that the practice of handling snakes was a recognized part of its Articles of Faith, nor did it question the sincerity of the conviction of the respondents.

By final decree the trial judge made the injunction permanent, directing that defendants "be perpetually enjoined from handling, displaying or exhibiting dangerous and poisonous snakes at the said Holiness Church of God in Jesus Name, *or at any other place in Cocke County, Tennessee.*"

II

The history and development of the Holiness Church is relevant.

The Mother Church[5] was founded in 1909 at Sale Creek in Grasshopper Valley, Tennessee, approximately thirty-five miles northeast of Chattanooga, by George Went Hensley. Hensley was motivated by a dramatic experience which occurred atop White Oak Mountain on the eastern rim of the valley during which he confronted and seized a rattlesnake which he took back to the valley and admonished the people to "take up or be doomed to eternal hell."

Hensley, and his followers, based their beliefs and practices on Mark 16, verses 17 and 18, which in the Authorized or King James version, read as follows:

> And these signs shall follow them that believe; in my name shall they cast out devils; and shall *speak with new tongues; They shall take up serpents;* and if they *drink any deadly thing*, it shall not hurt them, they shall lay hands on the sick, and they shall recover. (Italics ours)[7]

The church Hensley[8] founded spread throughout the south and southeast and continues to exist today, primarily in rural and relatively isolated regions throughout this area. The Holiness Church of God in Jesus Name, in Cocke County, is a part of this movement. LaBarre, in They Shall Take Up Serpents, asserts that "[t]he roots of the movement lie deep in American religious history"

5. Dolly Pond Church of God with Signs Following. Collins, Tennessee Snake Handlers, page 1 (1947) (hereinafter referred to as Collins).
7. Both the Old and New Testaments, however, contain language which would appear to be injunctions against snake handling and speaking in tongues. In Ecclesiastes (King James version) 10:11, it is said: "Surely the serpent will bite without enchantment, and a babbler is no better." St. Paul warns the Corinthians, in his First Epistle (Ch. 10, Verse 9) "Neither let us tempt Christ, as some of them also tempted, and were destroyed of serpents."
8. Hensley remained active in the ministry of the church for some forty-six years. He said he had been bitten four hundred times "till I'm speckled all over like a guinea hen." (LaBarre, page 45) This founder and prophet of the church died, refusing medical attention, as a result of being bitten by a diamondback rattlesnake during a prayer meeting at Lester's Shed near Altha, Florida, on Sunday night, July 24, 1955 (*Ibid.*, page 48).

and asserts that it is one of the "offshoots of Methodism." Writers seem to be in general agreement that it is a "charismatic sect, or cult, or group of the Pentecostal variety."

To say that this is not a conventional movement would be a masterpiece of understatement. Its beliefs and practices are, to say the least, unconventional and out of harmony with contemporary customs, mores and notions of morality. They oppose drinking (to include carbonated beverages, tea and coffee), smoking, dancing, the use of cosmetics, jewelry or other adornment. They regard the use of medicine as a sure sign of lack of faith in God's ability to cure the sick and look upon medical doctors as being for the use of those who do not trust God. When greeting each other, the men use the "holy kiss", a mouth-to-mouth osculation "accompanied by a vigorous, if not passionate hug." The "holy kiss" is not exchanged between members of the opposite sexes.

But it is their belief in handling serpents that has catapulted them into the limelight and has produced their legal difficulties.

There is some apparent confusion with respect to their purpose in the use of serpents as a central practice in their religious beliefs. Harden et al. v. State (Tenn. 1948) treated snake handling as being "the test and proof of the sincerity of their belief." In this record it is asserted that the use of serpents is designed as a test of the faith and sincerity of church members. Our research indicates that this is not precisely correct. Their basic reason is compliance with the scripture as they interpret it, and as required by their Articles of Faith. But the practice of snake handling is not a test of faith, nor proof of godliness. Its sole purpose is to "confirm the word". . . .

Lastly, it should be pointed out that snakes are only handled when the member or handler has become "anointed". As we understand this phenomenon and the emotional reaction it produces, it is something akin to saying that a member doesn't handle snakes until the "spirit moves him." Unquestionably this is an emotional stimulus produced by extreme faith and generating great courage. Perhaps the whole belief in "anointment" can best be summed up by the defendant, Liston Pack:

> When I become anointed to handle serpents, my hands get real numb. It is a tremendous feeling. Maybe symbolic to an electric shock, only an electric shock could hurt you. This'll be pure joy. . . .
>
> It comes from inside . . . If you've got the Holy Ghost in you, it'll come out and nothing can hurt you. Faith brings contact with God and then you're anointed. It is not tempting God. You can't tempt God by doing what He says do. You can have faith, but if you never feel the anointing, you had better leave the serpent alone.

Such is the nature of the religious group with which we deal. . . .

IV

. . . We hold that under the First Amendment to the Constitution of the United States and under the substantially stronger provisions of Article 1, Section 3 of the Constitution of Tennessee,[*] a religious practice may be limited,

---

* "That all men have a natural and indefeasible right to worship Almighty God according to the dictates of their own conscience; that no man can of right be compelled to attend, erect, or support

curtailed or restrained to the point of outright prohibition, where it involves a clear and present danger to the interests of society; but the action of the state must be reasonable and reasonably dictated by the needs and demands of society as determined by the nature of the activity as balanced against societal interests. Essentially, therefore, the problem becomes one of a balancing of the interests between religious freedom and the preservation of the health, safety and morals of society. The scales must be weighed in favor of religious freedom, and yet the balance is delicate.

The right to the free exercise of religion is not absolute and unconditional. Nor is its sweep susceptible of discrete and concrete compartmentalization. It is perforce, of necessity, a vague and nebulous notion, defying the certainties of definition and the niceties of description. At some point the freedom of the individual must wane and the power, duty and interest of the state becomes compelling and dominant.

Certain guidelines do, however, emerge under both constitutions.

Free exercise of religion does not include the right to violate statutory law.

It does not include the right to commit or maintain a nuisance.

The fact that one acts from the promptings of religious beliefs does not immunize against lawless conduct.

But, again, the scales are always weighted in favor of free exercise and the state's interest must be compelling; it must be substantial; the danger must be clear and present and so grave as to endanger paramount public interests.

We decide this controversy in the light of these objectives. In doing so we have not lost sight of the fact that snake handling is central to respondents' faith. We recognize that to forbid snake handling is to remove the theological heart of the Holiness Church and this has prompted this Court to investigate and research this matter with meticulous care and to announce its decision through an unusually extensive opinion. . . .

VI

. . . Under this record, showing as it does, the handling of snakes in a crowded church sanctuary, with virtually no safeguards, with children roaming about unattended, with the handlers so enraptured and entranced that they are in a virtual state of hysteria and acting under the compulsion of "anointment," we would be derelict in our duty if we did not hold that respondents and their confederates have combined and conspired to commit a public nuisance and plan to continue to do so. The human misery and loss of life at their "Homecoming" of April 7, 1973, is proof positive.

. . . Tennessee has the right to guard against the unnecessary creation of widows and orphans. Our state and nation have an interest in having a strong, healthy, robust, taxpaying citizenry capable of self-support and of bearing arms and adding to the resources and reserves of manpower. We, therefore, have a substantial and compelling state interest in the face of a clear and present danger so grave as to endanger paramount state interests.

---

any place of worship, or to maintain any minister against his consent; that no human authority can, in any case whatever, control or interfere with the rights of conscience; and that no preference shall ever be given, by law, to any religious establishment or mode of worship." [Relocated text—Eds.]

It has been held that a state may compel polio shots; may regulate child labor; may require compulsory chest x-rays; may decree compulsory water fluoridation; may mandate vaccinations as a condition of school attendance; and may compel medical care to a dying patient. [Citations omitted.]

This holding is in no sense dependent upon the way or manner in which snakes are handled since it is not based upon the snake handling statute. Irrespective of its import, we hold that those who publicly handle snakes in the presence of other persons and those who are present aiding and abetting are guilty of creating and maintaining a public nuisance. Yes, the state has a right to protect a person from himself and to demand that he protect his own life.

Suicide is not specifically denounced as a crime under our statutes but was a crime at the common law. Tennessee adopted the Common Law as it existed at the time of the separation of the colonies. An attempt to commit suicide is probably not an indictable offense under Tennessee law; however, such an attempt would constitute a grave public wrong, and we hold that the state has a compelling interest in protecting the life and promoting the health of its citizens.

Most assuredly the handling of poisonous snakes by untrained persons and the drinking of strychnine are not calculated to increase one's lifespan.

VIII

The trial judge enjoined the respondents from handling poisonous snakes or using deadly poisons in any church service in Cocke County but authorized the consumption of strychnine.

He erred.

The Court of Appeals modified the injunction so as to enjoin respondents from handling, displaying or exhibiting dangerous and poisonous snakes in such manner as will endanger the life or health of persons who do not consent to exposure to such danger.

There is no reason to restrict the injunction to the terms of the statute, nor is there any occasion for applying a "consenting adult" criterion.

On remand the trial judge will enter an injunction perpetually enjoining and restraining all parties respondent from handling, displaying or exhibiting dangerous and poisonous snakes or from consuming strychnine or any other poisonous substances, within the confines of the State of Tennessee. . . .

We fully appreciate the fact that the decision we reach imposes stringent limitations upon the pursuit of a religious practice, a result we endeavored to avoid. After long and careful analysis of alternatives and lengthy deliberations on all aspects of this problem we reached the conclusion that paramount considerations of public policy precluded less stringent solutions. We gave consideration to limiting the prohibition to handling snakes in the presence of children, but rejected this approach because it conflicts with the parental right and duty to direct the religious training of his children. We considered the adoption of a "consenting adult" standard but, again, this practice is too fraught with danger to permit its pursuit in the frenzied atmosphere of an emotional church service, regardless of age or consent. We considered restricting attendance to members only, but this would destroy the evangelical mission of the church. We considered permitting only the handlers themselves to be present, but this frustrates the purpose of confirming the faith to non-believers and separates the pastor and leaders from the congregation. We could find no rational basis for limiting or restricting the practice, and could conceive of no alternative plan or procedure which would be palatable to the membership or permissible from a standpoint of compelling state interest. The very considerations which impel us to outright prohibition, would preclude fragmentation of the religious services or the pursuit of this practice on a limited basis.

NOTES AND QUESTIONS

There is considerable appeal in the idea that the government may not override a believer's religious exercise purely for paternalistic reasons. The Free Exercise Clause seems to rest on a theory that government should leave religion to individual choice, and thus it would seem to be a good instance to apply John Stuart Mill's famous libertarian definition of the powers of government: "That the only purpose for which power can be rightfully exercised over any member of a civilized community, against his will, is to prevent harm to others. His own good, either physical or moral, is not a sufficient warrant." John Stuart Mill, On Liberty, in John Stuart Mill, Three Essays 15 (Oxford ed. 1975). (Consider also the religious freedom provisions of state constitutions enacted around the time of the First Amendment, most of which provided that religious freedom could be limited to protect the "peace and safety" of the "public" or "the state." See section A-1.) But there are complications.

1. Children and Medical Care. *Baumgartner* involved an adult who was presumably capable of making informed decisions for himself regarding spiritual and medical matters. But paternalism is a stronger justification for governmental intervention when the protected parties are children, even if the children themselves are believers.

Consider the following case: A ten-year-old girl, who with her parents is a devout adherent of Christian Science, falls sick with flulike symptoms and a stiff neck. Her parents, consistent with the family's faith, call an accredited Christian Science practitioner for several sessions of prayer and spiritual treatment. However, the girl's symptoms worsen, and ten days later she dies of acute meningitis. The parents are criminally prosecuted for manslaughter and felony child neglect for failing to seek medical treatment. What result? Cf. Walker v. Superior Court, 47 Cal. 3d 112, 763 P.2d 852 (1988) (upholding conviction, rejecting free exercise claim).

Walker is one of several recent cases in which parents have been prosecuted after they failed to obtain medical treatment for their children on religious grounds and their children died. Although more than 40 states have passed legislation exempting those who use religious in lieu of medical treatment from such laws, the exemptions have been narrowly construed by the courts. See also Lundman v. McKown, 530 N.W.2d 807 (Minn. App. 1995) (upholding $1.5 million damage award for noncustodial father against mother and stepfather in similar circumstances, but reversing punitive damage award against Church).

State courts that have upheld criminal convictions in these cases over free exercise challenges have quoted the Supreme Court's dictum in Prince v. Massachusetts, 321 U.S. 158, 170 (1944): "Parents may be free to become martyrs themselves. But it does not follow they are free, in identical circumstances, to make martyrs of their children before they have reached the age of full and legal discretion when they can make that choice for themselves." *Prince* involved a Jehovah's Witness who was convicted for violating child labor laws by bringing her niece with her to distribute religious literature on street corners. The Court upheld the aunt's conviction even though the child had begged to accompany her on the mission; that is, the child was protected on paternalistic grounds even against her expressed wishes.

Yet in Pierce v. Society of Sisters, Wisconsin v. Yoder, Employment Division v. Smith, and other decisions, the Court has recognized that parents have a constitutional right to control the religious upbringing of their children, even when the state believes it is not in the child's best interests. Where do the parents' rights end and the state's right to intervene begin? When do children become old enough to make such decisions for themselves?

Assuming that paternalism to protect children is justified, the judgment that the state must intervene in these cases seems necessarily to be predicated on the premise that the religious belief in the efficacy of nonmedical care is "false." How can this premise be justified? Should the parents be permitted to introduce evidence of the efficacy of spiritual treatment? (Christian Science publications are filled with first-person accounts of remarkable cures.) How could such evidence be evaluated? Which alternative does greater harm to free exercise: to reject the religious claims without allowing proof, or to subject those claims to the review of civil authorities? Cf. United States v. Ballard (p. 193).

Suppose it could be shown that following the Christian Science way of life, coupled with the avoidance of medicine (which often makes mistakes), is *on average* healthier than the typical American way of life, even if in a particular case medical care would be efficacious. How would that affect the state's justification for intervention? If the state does not intervene to prevent other parental practices that have an adverse effect on the children's health and well being—such as allowing them to eat large amounts of fatty and sugared food without getting much exercise—should the state be permitted to intervene in these cases?

2. Problems: Distinguishing Paternalism from Harm to Others.   Ever since Mill's treatise, critics have responded that there is no conduct that is completely without effects on others, or at least that the distinction between the two categories is too unclear to serve as the basis for legal rules. See, e.g., James Fitzjames Stephen, Liberty, Equality, Fraternity 66 (1873) ("by far the most important part of our conduct regards both ourselves and others"). For a somewhat similar argument, see Eugene Volokh, A Common Law Model for Religious Exemptions, 46 UCLA Rev. 1465, 1515 (1999) ("The difficulty is that what constitutes 'invading the rights of others' and 'imposing improper externalities on others' are hotly contested questions.").

If the Free Exercise Clause only permits government to intervene on the basis of harm to others, how would you evaluate the following situations and arguments:

(a) The argument in *Pack* itself that deaths or injuries among snake handlers deprive the state of a "strong, healthy, robust, taxpaying citizenry capable of self-support and of bearing arms and adding to the resources and reserves of manpower."

(b) Suppose that in *Pack* no children are present at the services, but one of the snake-handling believers is a parent of minor-age children. Can she be prohibited from handling snakes?

(c) How would you analyze the facts in the *Uniao do Vegetal* case (p. 202), involving sacramental consumption of a tea containing a hallucinogenic substance at a worship service? Does it involve harm to the believer only or harm to others?

(d) Jehovah's Witnesses refuse to receive blood transfusions, on the basis of various biblical passages forbidding "eating the blood" (Leviticus 17:10). A Jehovah's Witness woman incurs serious injuries in a car accident and is brought to a municipally owned hospital. Although she is unconscious, she wears a card (as is common) stating that she is a Jehovah's Witness and wishes not to receive a transfusion. Can the doctor override that expressed wish? See John F. Kennedy Mem. Hospital v. Heston, 279 A.2d 670 (N.J. 1971) (yes, on basis of doctor's and hospital's interests in following professional norms and avoiding potential malpractice claim).

(e) In the preceding situation, suppose the patient dies after explicitly refusing a transfusion that would have prevented the death. Her husband, as executor of her estate, brings a wrongful death suit against the driver who caused the accident (and who was unquestionably negligent). The defendant answers that the victim failed to reasonably mitigate her damages (in tort law terms, the death was an "avoidable consequence" of the accident). What result? See Munn v. Algee, 924 F.2d 568 (5th Cir. 1991) (ruling for defendant under Employment Division v. Smith).

(f) Members of a religious sect, who are competent adults, work in a sect-owned commercial business making widgets, which are also made by a number of competing businesses. The members work as unpaid or lowly paid volunteers on the basis of religious motivation. The sect is prosecuted by the federal government for failing to pay the minimum wages required by statute. What result? See Tony & Susan Alamo Foundation v. Sec'y of Labor, 471 U.S. 290 (1985) (rejecting free exercise defense).

C. THE ESTABLISHMENT CLAUSE: IS ACCOMMODATION PERMITTED?

The cases thus far have involved claims that the government *must* accommodate religious exercise. But there are numerous cases in which government officials—either the legislature or various executive officers—choose to accommodate religion as a matter of policy. As one commentator has summarized:

> Religious exemptions . . . exist in over 2,000 [federal and state] statutes. . . . In the United States Code, for example, exemptions exist in food inspection laws for the ritual slaughter of animals, and for the preparation of food in accordance with religious practices. The tax laws contain numerous exemptions for religious groups and allow deductions for contributions to religious organizations. Federal copyright laws contain an exemption for materials that are to be used for religious purposes. Antidiscrimination laws, including Title VII, the Fair Housing Act, and

the Aid to the Disabled Act, contain exemptions for religious organizations. Ministers are automatically exempt from compulsory military training and service. Aliens seeking asylum can do so on the grounds that they will suffer religious persecution if returned to their home countries and gambling laws contain an exemption for religious organizations. Those in the military may wear religious apparel while wearing their uniforms, subject to limitations imposed by the Secretary of Defense. And . . . federal drug laws contain an exemption for the religious use of peyote by members of the Native American Church.

James E. Ryan, *Smith* and the Religious Freedom Restoration Act: An Iconoclastic Assessment, 78 Va. L. Rev. 1407, 1445-1447 (1992).

Some people have argued that this "permissible accommodation" represents a special benefit or favoritism for religion, and is unconstitutional under the Establishment Clause. This presents a conundrum: How can religious accommodation sometimes be *required* under the Free Exercise Clause, but *forbidden* under the Establishment Clause? As you will see, the Supreme Court has never accepted the proposition that religious accommodations are per se violations of the Establishment Clause, but it has constrained the power of the government to accommodate religion in several ways.

1. Introduction: The "Clash" Between the Clauses

It is often said that there is a "tension" between the Free Exercise and Establishment Clauses. This manifests itself most clearly in two doctrinal areas: accommodation of religion and funding of religious activities. In the accommodation context, the Free Exercise Clause is said to require, or at least permit, exceptions from generally applicable laws that conflict with religious exercise. But some say that such exceptions are an unconstitutional benefit to religion, forbidden under the Establishment Clause. In this subpart, we will explore that argument from three perspectives: first, judicial doctrine, particularly the Court's Establishment Clause test set forth in Lemon v. Kurtzman; second, the history behind the First Amendment; and finally, other important considerations.

a. The "Clash" and the Lemon v. Kurtzman Test

THOMAS v. REVIEW BOARD
450 U.S. 707 (1981)

[This was an unemployment compensation case, similar to Sherbert v. Verner (p. 124). The majority (eight Justices) held that the state must provide unemployment compensation to a worker who left his job because of religious objections to the work.]

Justice REHNQUIST, dissenting.

The Court today holds that the State of Indiana is constitutionally required to provide direct financial assistance to a person solely on the basis of his religious beliefs. Because I believe that the decision today adds mud to the already muddied waters of First Amendment jurisprudence, I dissent.

I

The Court correctly acknowledges that there is a "tension" between the Free Exercise and Establishment Clauses of the First Amendment of the United States Constitution. Although the relationship of the two Clauses has been the subject of much commentary, the "tension" is a fairly recent vintage, unknown at the time of the framing and adoption of the First Amendment. The causes of the tension, it seems to me, are threefold. First, the growth of social welfare legislation during the latter part of the 20th century has greatly magnified the potential for conflict between the two Clauses, since such legislation touches the individual at so many points in his life. Second, the decision by this Court that the First Amendment was "incorporated" into the Fourteenth Amendment and thereby made applicable against the States similarly multiplied the number of instances in which the "tension" might arise. The third, and perhaps most important, cause of the tension is our overly expansive interpretation of both Clauses. By broadly construing both Clauses, the Court has constantly narrowed the channel between the Scylla and Charybdis through which any state or federal action must pass in order to survive constitutional scrutiny.

None of these developments could have been foreseen by those who framed and adopted the First Amendment. The First Amendment was adopted well before the growth of much social welfare legislation and at a time when the Federal Government was in a real sense considered a government of limited delegated powers. Indeed, the principal argument against adopting the Constitution without a "Bill of Rights" was not that such an enactment would be undesirable but that it was unnecessary because of the limited nature of the Federal Government. So long as the Government enacts little social welfare legislation, as was the case in 1791, there are few occasions in which the two Clauses may conflict. Moreover, as originally enacted, the First Amendment applied only to the Federal Government, not the government of the States. Barron v. Baltimore (1833). The Framers could hardly anticipate *Barron* being superseded by the "selective incorporation" doctrine adopted by the Court, a decision which greatly expanded the number of statutes which would be subject to challenge under the First Amendment. . . .

II

The decision today illustrates how far astray the Court has gone in interpreting the Free Exercise and Establishment Clauses of the First Amendment. Although the Court holds that a State is constitutionally required to provide direct financial assistance to persons solely on the basis of their religious beliefs and recognizes the "tension" between the two Clauses, it does little to help resolve that tension or to offer meaningful guidance to other courts which must decide cases like this on a day-by-day basis. Instead, it simply asserts that there is no Establishment Clause violation here and leaves the tension between the two Religion Clauses to be resolved on a case-by-case basis. As suggested above, however, I believe that the "tension" is largely of this Court's own making, and would diminish almost to the vanishing point if the Clauses were properly interpreted.

Just as it did in Sherbert v. Verner, the Court today reads the Free Exercise Clause more broadly than is warranted. As to the proper interpretation of the

Free Exercise Clause, I would accept the decision of Braunfeld v. Brown and the dissent in *Sherbert*. In *Braunfeld*, we held that Sunday closing laws do not violate the First Amendment rights of Sabbatarians. . . . Likewise in this case, it cannot be said that the State discriminated against Thomas on the basis of his religious beliefs or that he was denied benefits *because* he was a Jehovah's Witness. Where, as here, a State has enacted a general statute, the purpose and effect of which is to advance the State's secular goals, the Free Exercise Clause does not in my view require the State to conform that statute to the dictates of religious conscience of any group. As Justice Harlan recognized in his dissent in Sherbert v. Verner, supra: "Those situations in which the Constitution may require special treatment on account of religion are . . . few and far between." Like him I believe that although a State could choose to grant exemptions to religious persons from state unemployment regulations, a State is not constitutionally compelled to do so.[2]

The Court's treatment of the Establishment Clause issue is equally unsatisfying. Although today's decision requires a State to provide direct financial assistance to persons solely on the basis of their religious beliefs, the Court nonetheless blandly assures us, just as it did in *Sherbert*, that its decision "plainly" does not foster the "establishment" of religion. I would agree that the Establishment Clause, properly interpreted, would not be violated if Indiana voluntarily chose to grant unemployment benefits to those persons who left their jobs for religious reasons. But I also believe that the decision below is inconsistent with many of our prior Establishment Clause cases. Those cases, if faithfully applied, would require us to hold that such voluntary action by a State did violate the Establishment Clause.

Justice Stewart noted this point in his concurring opinion in *Sherbert*. He observed that decisions like *Sherbert*, and the one rendered today, squarely conflict with the more extreme language of many of our prior Establishment Clause cases. In Everson v. Board of Education (1947), the Court stated that the Establishment Clause bespeaks a "government . . . stripped of all power . . . to support, or otherwise to assist any or all religions . . . ," and no State "can pass laws which aid one religion . . . [or] all religions." In Torcaso v. Watkins (1961), the Court asserted that the government cannot "constitutionally pass laws or impose requirements which aid all religions as against non-believers." And in Abington School District v. Schempp (1963), the Court adopted Justice Rutledge's words in *Everson* that the Establishment Clause forbids " 'every form of public aid or support for religion.' "

In recent years the Court . . . has stated a three-part test to determine the constitutionality of governmental aid to religion. See Lemon v. Kurtzman (1971). First, the statute must serve a secular legislative purpose. Second, it must have a "primary effect" that neither advances nor inhibits religion. And third, the State and its administration must avoid excessive entanglement with religion.

2. To the extent *Sherbert* was correctly decided, it might be argued that cases [forbidding government aid to religiously affiliated schools] were wrongly decided. The "aid" rendered to religion in these latter cases may not be significantly different, in kind or degree, than the "aid" afforded Mrs. Sherbert or Thomas. For example, if the State in *Sherbert* could not deny compensation to one refusing work for religious reasons, it might be argued that a State may not deny reimbursement to students who choose for religious reasons to attend parochial schools. . . .

It is not surprising that the Court today makes no attempt to apply those principles to the facts of this case. If Indiana were to legislate what the Court today requires—an unemployment compensation law which permitted benefits to be granted to those persons who quit their jobs for religious reasons—the statute would "plainly" violate the Establishment Clause as interpreted in such cases as *Lemon*[.] First, although the unemployment statute as a whole would be enacted to serve a secular legislative purpose, the proviso would clearly serve only a religious purpose. It would grant financial benefits for the sole purpose of accommodating religious beliefs. Second, there can be little doubt that the primary effect of the proviso would be to "advance" religion by facilitating the exercise of religious belief. Third, any statute including such a proviso would surely "entangle" the State in religion far more than the mere grant of tax exemptions, as in Walz v. Tax Commission (1970), or the award of tuition grants and tax credits, as in Committee for Public Education v. Nyquist (1973). By granting financial benefits to persons solely on the basis of their religious beliefs, the State must necessarily inquire whether the claimant's belief is "religious" and whether it is sincerely held. Otherwise any dissatisfied employee may leave his job without cause and claim that he did so because his own particular beliefs required it.

It is unclear from the Court's opinion whether it has temporarily retreated from its expansive view of the Establishment Clause, or wholly abandoned it. I would welcome the latter. Just as I think that Justice Harlan in *Sherbert* correctly stated the proper approach to free exercise questions, I believe that Justice Stewart, dissenting in Abington School District v. Schempp, *supra*, accurately stated the reach of the Establishment Clause. He explained that the Establishment Clause is limited to "government support of proselytizing activities of religious sects by throwing the weight of secular authorit[ies] behind the dissemination of religious tenets." See McCollum v. Board of Education (1948) (Reed, J., dissenting) (impermissible aid is only "purposeful assistance directly to the church itself or to some religious group . . . performing ecclesiastical functions"). Conversely, governmental assistance which does not have the effect of "inducing" religious belief, but instead merely "accommodates" or implements an independent religious choice does not impermissibly involve the government in religious choices and therefore does not violate the Establishment Clause of the First Amendment. I would think that in this case, as in *Sherbert*, had the State voluntarily chosen to pay unemployment compensation benefits to persons who left their jobs for religious reasons, such aid would be constitutionally permissible because it redounds directly to the benefit of the individual.

In sum, my difficulty with today's decision is that it reads the Free Exercise Clause too broadly and it fails to squarely acknowledge that such a reading conflicts with many of our Establishment Clause cases. As such, the decision simply exacerbates the "tension" between the two Clauses. If the Court were to construe the Free Exercise Clause as it did in *Braunfeld* and the Establishment Clause as Justice Stewart did in *Schempp*, the circumstances in which there would be a conflict between the two Clauses would be few and far between. Although I heartily agree with the Court's tacit abandonment of much of our rhetoric about the Establishment Clause, I regret that the Court cannot see its way clear to restore what was surely intended to have been a greater degree of flexibility to the Federal and State Governments in legislating consistently with the Free

Exercise Clause. Accordingly, I would affirm the judgment of the Indiana Supreme Court.

NOTES AND QUESTIONS

1. **The Clash Between the Clauses.** Justice Rehnquist identifies a clash between required accommodations under the Free Exercise Clause (as in *Sherbert* and *Yoder*) and the Establishment Clause test of Lemon v. Kurtzman, 403 U.S. 602 (1971), under which government action must have a secular purpose and primarily secular effect (both of which may be inconsistent with special protection for religious exercise). If there is such a clash, it could be resolved in one of three ways. First, as Rehnquist recommends, the Court could alter both its free exercise doctrine (eliminating the mandatory accommodation doctrine of *Sherbert*) and its establishment doctrine (eliminating the hostility toward accommodations implicit in the *Lemon* test). This would give legislators the latitude, but not the obligation, to accommodate religion, and would drastically reduce the judicial role. This corresponds to the position we have been calling "judicial restraint." Second, the Court could keep its (pre-*Smith*) free exercise doctrine unchanged, and alter its Establishment Clause doctrine to be more hospitable toward religious accommodations. This would allow the legislatures to enact exemptions, and also allow courts to require them. This corresponds to the position we have been calling "accommodation." Third, the Court could eliminate the pre-*Smith* doctrine of mandatory free exercise exemptions, and keep its Establishment Clause test unchanged—essentially eliminating judicial accommodations and making legislative accommodations constitutionally suspect if not per se unconstitutional. This corresponds to the "secularist" or "no-aid separationist" view. Under it, "formal equality" between religion and nonreligion would be not only permitted but constitutionally required. Of course, the Court could leave the "tension" in place, which is the "activist" position. This allows the courts to decide in each individual case, whether accommodation is required, permitted, or forbidden. What might be the virtue in that?

In general terms, since Thomas v. Review Board, the Supreme Court has moved in the direction Rehnquist recommended, toward greater judicial restraint. We have already seen the demise of mandatory free exercise exemptions in the *Smith* decision. Now we will see the Court's efforts to deal with legislative accommodations. This effort remains in considerable flux and confusion.

2. **The Secular Purpose Prong of Lemon v. Kurtzman.** As Justice Rehnquist notes in his *Thomas* opinion, one part of the Establishment Clause test of *Lemon* is that laws must have a "secular purpose." A dictionary definition of "secular purpose" would seem to mean a purpose unrelated to religion. Since the purpose of accommodations is to facilitate the free exercise of religion, such provisions would seem vulnerable to constitutional challenge under the *Lemon* test. But cf. Wallace v. Jaffree, 472 U.S. 38 (1985) (O'Connor, J., concurring) ("It is disingenuous to look for a purely secular purpose when the manifest objective of a statute is to facilitate the free exercise of religion by lifting a government-imposed burden. Instead, the Court should simply acknowledge that the

religious purpose of such a statute is legitimated by the Free Exercise Clause."). Does this solve the problem? Couldn't it still be argued that accommodations of the free exercise of religion necessarily "favor" religion over nonreligion, in violation of the "secular effect" prong of *Lemon*? Such tensions are what led critics to claim that the *Lemon* test was at war with free exercise protections.

b. The Historical Understanding

History provides support for the proposition that the framers thought that exemptions from generally applicable laws were permissible, even if not constitutionally compelled. As explained in the McConnell excerpt, section A-1 (p. 87), colonial and state governments not infrequently exempted religious believers from general laws such as military conscription, and there were no voiced complaints that these practices were a vestige of establishment. (Indeed, since exemptions protected minority religions, such as Quakers, and since establishment was associated with religious majoritarianism, it would have been unlikely for a person of that age to think of exemptions as establishments.) Washington and Madison both supported draft exemptions, and the Continental Congress passed a resolution to that effect.

Constitutional historians who oppose the idea that free exercise *compelled* exemptions dismiss these accommodations as matters of legislative grace. But that suggests that they were not deemed unconstitutional. Moreover, those who argued against constitutionally mandatory exemptions in the early period, such as Justice Gibson in Simon's Executors v. Gratz (see p. 109), did so on the ground that they should be a matter of legislative discretion. McConnell writes that the historical record shows

> that exemptions on account of religious scruple should have been familiar to the framers and ratifiers of the free exercise clause. There is no substantial evidence that such exemptions were considered constitutionally questionable, whether as a form of establishment or as an invasion of liberty of conscience. Even opponents of exemptions did not make that claim. The modern argument against religious exemptions, based on the establishment clause, is thus historically unsupportable.

McConnell, 103 Harv. L. Rev. at 1511-1512.

On the other hand, Philip Hamburger writes: "A right of exemption for the religiously scrupulous could be considered a law respecting religion. It even could create unequal civil rights; in the words of the Virginia Act For Establishing Religious Freedom, men's 'opinions in matters of religion' shall 'in no wise diminish, enlarge, or affect their civil capacities.'" See Hamburger, 60 Geo. Wash. L. Rev. at 947 (p. 101).

The accommodation issue arose during deliberations over the Bill of Rights, in connection with what would become the second amendment. Three states (North Carolina, Virginia, and Rhode Island) had proposed that "any person religiously scrupulous of bearing arms ought to be exempted, upon payment of an equivalent to employ another to bear arms in his stead." Madison's draft of a proposed Bill of Rights contained a similar provision, appended to what is now the Second Amendment, though it left the requirement of a substitute to legislative discretion. The Select Committee proposed and the House of Representatives debated a more generous exemption:

ANNALS OF CONGRESS
Aug. 17, 20, 1789
House of Representatives

[17 AUG.]

The House again resolved itself into a committee, MR. BOUDINOT in the chair, on the proposed amendments to the constitution. The third clause of the fourth proposition in the report was taken into consideration, being as follows: "A well regulated militia, composed of the body of the people, being the best security of a free state, the right of the people to keep and bear arms shall not be infringed; but no person religiously scrupulous shall be compelled to bear arms."

MR. GERRY.—This declaration of rights, I take it, is intended to secure the people against the mal-administration of the Government; if we could suppose that, in all cases, the rights of the people would be attended to, the occasion for guards of this kind would be removed. Now, I am apprehensive, sir, that this clause would give an opportunity to the people in power to destroy the constitution itself. They can declare who are those religiously scrupulous, and prevent them from bearing arms.

. . . For this reason, he wished the words to be altered so as to be confined to persons belonging to a religious sect scrupulous of bearing arms.

MR. JACKSON did not expect that all the people of the United States would turn Quakers or Moravians; consequently, one part would have to defend the other in case of invasion. Now this, in his opinion, was unjust, unless the constitution secured an equivalent: for this reason he moved to amend the clause, by inserting at the end of it, "upon paying an equivalent, to be established by law."

MR. SMITH, of South Carolina, inquired what were the words used by the conventions respecting this amendment. If the gentleman would conform to what was proposed by Virginia and Carolina, he would second him. He thought they were to be excused provided they found a substitute.

MR. JACKSON was willing to accommodate. He thought the expression was, "No one, religiously scrupulous of bearing arms, shall be compelled to render military service, in person, upon paying an equivalent."

MR. SHERMAN conceived it difficult to modify the clause and make it better. It is well known that those who are religiously scrupulous of bearing arms, are equally scrupulous of getting substitutes or paying an equivalent. Many of them would rather die than do either one or the other; but he did not see an absolute necessity for a clause of this kind. We do not live under an arbitrary Government, said he, and the States, respectively, will have the government of the militia, unless when called into actual service; besides, it would not do to alter it so as to exclude the whole of any sect, because there are men amongst the Quakers who will turn out, notwithstanding the religious principles of the society, and defend the cause of their country. Certainly it will be improper to prevent the exercise of such favorable dispositions, at least whilst it is the practice of nations to determine their contests by the slaughter of their citizens and subjects.

MR. VINING hoped the clause would be suffered to remain as it stood, because he saw no use in it if it was amended so as to compel a man to find a substitute, which, with respect to the Government, was the same as if the person himself turned out to fight.

MR. STONE inquired what the words "religiously scrupulous" had reference to: was it of bearing arms? If it was, it ought so to be expressed.

MR. BENSON moved to have the words "but no person religiously scrupulous shall be compelled to bear arms," struck out. He would always leave it to the benevolence of the Legislature, for, modify it as you please, it will be impossible to express it in such a manner as to clear it from ambiguity. No man can claim this indulgence of right. It may be a religious persuasion, but it is no natural right, and therefore ought to be left to the discretion of the Government. If this stands part of the constitution, it will be a question before the Judiciary on every regulation you make with respect to the organization of the militia, whether it comports with this declaration or not. It is extremely injudicious to intermix matters of doubt with fundamentals.

I have no reason to believe but the Legislature will always possess humanity enough to indulge this class of citizens in a matter they are so desirous of; but they ought to be left to their discretion.

The motion for striking out the whole clause being seconded, was put, and decided in the negative—22 members voting for it, and 24 against it. . . .

[20 AUG.]

MR. SCOTT objected to the clause in the sixth amendment, "No person religiously scrupulous shall be compelled to bear arms." He observed that if this becomes part of the constitution, such persons can neither be called upon for their services, nor can an equivalent be demanded; it is also attended with still further difficulties, for a militia can never be depended upon. This would lead to the violation of another article in the constitution, which secures to the people the right of keeping arms, and in this case recourse must be had to a standing army. I conceive it, said he, to be a legislative right altogether. There are many sects I know, who are religiously scrupulous in this respect; I do not mean to deprive them of any indulgence the law affords; my design is to guard against those who are of no religion. It has been urged that religion is on the decline; if so, the argument is more strong in my favor, for when the time comes that religion shall be discarded, the generality of persons will have recourse to these pretexts to get excused from bearing arms.

MR. BOUDINOT thought the provision in the clause, or something similar to it, was necessary. Can any dependence, said he, be placed in men who are conscientious in this respect? or what justice can there be in compelling them to bear arms, when, according to their religious principles, they would rather die than use them? He adverted to several instances of oppression on this point, that occurred during the war. In forming a militia, an effectual defence ought to be calculated, and no characters of this religious description ought to be compelled to take up arms. I hope that in establishing this Government, we may show the world that proper care is taken that the Government may not interfere with the religious sentiments of any person. Now, by striking out the clause, people may be led to believe that there is an intention in the General Government to compel all its citizens to bear arms.

NOTES AND QUESTIONS

The proposal to exempt religious conscientious objectors in the Constitution passed the House, but by a mere 24-22 vote, and it was rejected by the Senate. Note that there were three positions in the House debate. First, the majority (led by Boudinot) advocated the mandatory accommodation. Second, a significant group (led by Benson) said that draft exemptions, while desirable, should be left to legislative discretion. Third, some members (such as Jackson) took the view that draft exemptions were "unjust." The latter view may not translate into a categorical opposition to all religious accommodations, however, since at least some of these members (including Jackson) favored a draft exemption on the condition that the exempted citizen pay for an equivalent.

The proposal and debate are highly ambiguous with respect to whether the First Amendment *compels* religious accommodations. No one suggested that this might be the case, and one might surmise that the express militia draft exemption was necessary only if there were no such protections under the Free Exercise Clause. This assumption may be faulty for two reasons, however. First, the militias are arms of the state governments except when in actual federal service; thus, the First Amendment, which applied only to Congress, would not have applied. Second, members of Congress who deemed draft exemptions important might have thought it useful to spell this out, and not trust to the more generally worded Free Exercise Clause. For an argument that military draft exemptions do not support the claim of free exercise exemptions, see Ellis West, The Right to Religion-Based Exemptions in Early America: The Case of Conscientious Objectors to Conscription, 10 J.L. & Rel. 367, 376-377 (1994).

What, though, do the proposal and debate tell us about the constitutional *permissibility* of legislative exemptions?

c. Other General Questions About Accommodation

Before we study the Court's recent decisions, consider a few other general issues concerning religious accommodations:

1. The Problem of Secular Conscience: The Draft-Exemption Cases. What is the reason for permitting (or even requiring) distinctive protection for religiously motivated conduct? There are some people who hold deeply felt conscientious views that affect their actions but are secular in nature. Is it fair for a legislature not to accommodate them when it accommodates a similar objection by a religious citizen?

This question was posed sharply during the late 1960s, when some young men drafted for the Vietnam War objected to combat training and service on the basis of conscientious tenets that were not religious in any traditional sense. The federal conscription statute contained an exemption, 50 U.S.C. App. § 456(g), for persons "who by reason of their religious training and belief are conscientiously opposed to participation in war in any form." The statute defined religious training and belief as belief "in relation to a Supreme Being involving duties superior to those arising from any human relation." Seeger claimed status as a conscientious objector on "religious" grounds but added that he was skeptical about the existence of God and that his was "a belief in and devotion to goodness and virtue for their own sakes, and a religious faith in a purely ethical creed." In United States v. Seeger, 380 U.S. 163 (1965), the Supreme Court broadly construed the statutory exemption to cover Seeger, because he had "[a] sincere and meaningful belief which occupies in [his] life . . . a place parallel to that filled by the God of those admittedly qualifying for the exemption." *Id.* at 176.

Seeger is formally a case about defining the term "religion" (in a statute in that instance, but with implications for defining it in the First Amendment). It will therefore be considered in full in Part VI, "What is 'Religion'?" But behind the decision lies the question whether it would be wrong to accommodate conscientious objections grounded in religion but not those grounded in other deeply held belief systems. The Court referred to "the diverse manners in which beliefs, equally paramount in the lives of their possessors, may be articulated." 380 U.S. at 183.

Welsh v. United States, 398 U.S. 333 (1970), posed the problem even more sharply. Like Seeger, Welsh objected to military service on conscientious grounds. But he "was far more insistent and explicit . . . in denying that his views were religious"; he struck the word "religious" entirely from his conscientious objector application; he said that his beliefs had come "by reading in the fields of history and sociology"; and he said that his duty not to kill another person "is not 'superior to those arising from any human relation.' On the contrary. *it is essential to every human relation." Id.* at 341, 343 (emphasis in original). The Court again extended the exemption. The plurality held that the provision covered "all those whose consciences, spurred by deeply held moral, ethical, or religious beliefs, would give them no rest or peace if they allowed themselves to become a part of an instrument of war." *Id.* at 344.

Justice Harlan objected to this interpretation, arguing that it "completely transformed the statute by reading out of it any distinction between religiously acquired beliefs and those deriving from 'essentially political, sociological, or philosophical views or a personal moral code.' " *Id.* at 351 (Harlan, J., concurring in the result). Since the statute could not fairly be read to cover Welsh, Harlan said, the constitutional question had to be confronted:

> The "radius" of this legislation is the conscientiousness with which an individual opposes war in general, yet the statute, as I think it must be construed, excludes from its "scope" individuals motivated by teachings of non-theistic religions, and individuals guided by an inner voice that bespeaks secular and not "religious" reflection. . . . This in my view offends the Establishment Clause and is that kind of classification that this Court has condemned.

Id. at 357-358. Harlan concurred in the result only because he believed that the better judicial remedy for the unconstitutional favoring of religion was to extend the exemption to secular objectors like Welsh.

Why should one person who is deeply opposed to killing be exempted from going to war because the source of his belief is religious, while another is compelled to go because his source is secular? If it is troubling to make such a distinction, is that because of particular features of the draft-exemption issue? Or does it show a problem with religious accommodation in general? See, e.g., Frederick M. Gedicks, An Unfirm Foundation: The Regrettable Indefensibility of Free Exercise Exemptions, 20 U. Ark. Little Rock L.J. 555, 574 (1998) ("There no longer exists a plausible explanation of why religious believers—and only believers—are constitutionally entitled to be excused from complying with otherwise legitimate laws that burden practices motivated by moral belief.")

Perhaps, on the other hand, special concern for religious liberty is not troubling. Recall the arguments you have already read in favor of religious accommodations. The text of the Free Exercise Clause singles out religious freedom for protection from government interference; this is perfectly justifiable because the Establishment Clause places a parallel restriction on the affirmative sponsorship of religion; and for the generation that framed the Constitution, accommodations were viewed as at least permissible and perhaps (in some cases) mandated. Cf. Nelson Tebbe, Free Exercise and the Problem of Symmetery, 56 Hast. L. Rev. 699 (2005) (arguing that religious exemptions can be justified on the basis of religious liberty, but not on the basis of any kind of "neutrality").

2. Accommodations as a "Quid Pro Quo" for Establishment Clause Limits. Consider in more depth the idea that special accommodation of private religious conduct—whether mandated by courts or simply enacted by legislatures— is justified because it is balanced by special restrictions on religion in other constitutional contexts. One variation of this argument has been advanced by Professor Abner Greene:

> Under the Establishment Clause, [l]aw may not be enacted for the express purpose of advancing the values believed to be commanded by religion. For religion involves a reference to an extrahuman source of value, which can be shared only by believers in the same faith, not by citizens as citizens. Enacting religious faith into law excludes nonbelievers from the legislative process in a real and significant way. But if we construe the Establishment Clause to prohibit legislation enacted for the express purpose of advancing religious values, then the predicate for universal obedience to law has been removed. A religious conscientious objector may legitimately claim that because she was thwarted from offering her values for majority acceptance as law, she should have at least a prima facie right of exemption from law that conflicts with her religion. The Free Exercise Clause works as a counterweight to the Establishment Clause; it gives back what the Establishment Clause takes away.

Abner S. Greene, The Political Balance of the Religion Clauses, 102 Yale L.J. 1611, 1643-1644 (1993). Do religious accommodations reflect the notion that religious values should be separate from, or excluded from influencing, law and legislation? Or do they reflect, as a matter of history or logic, the notion that religion should be left free precisely so that it *can* influence politics? Greene essentially answers that if religion is simply another actor in the public square, then to give it special protection from general legal norms is unwarranted and unfair. Is there any good answer to this point?

As we will see in Part V-D, the Court does not interpret the Establishment Clause to place significant restrictions on the role of religion in politics. However, the case law has read the clause to raise significant barriers to (i) government conducting religious exercises or displaying religious symbols (see Part V-A) and (ii) government providing financial aid to religiously grounded education or social services (see Part IV). Do either of these special limits on government action concerning religion provide a better "quid pro quo" to balance and justify special accommodation of religious conduct?

3. The "Religious" Justification for Religious Accommodation. Why precisely did the founding generation think that special concern for religious conscience was legitimate? To a significant extent, we have seen, the idea of religious accommodation rested on a *theological* justification, one held by dissenting evangelical Protestants in particular but by others in the founding generation as well. See McConnell, 103 Harv. L. Rev. 1409. The idea is that duties to God are prior to duties to society, but that trying to coerce worship or obedience to the true God is theologically ineffective since true faith must be voluntary. Professor Steven Smith calls this pair of propositions "the religious justification" for religious freedom. Steven D. Smith, The Rise and Fall of Religious Freedom in Constitutional Discourse, 140 U. Pa. L. Rev. 149, 154-156 (1991). He suggests that it was "central" to the founding generation's commitment to religious freedom, and also that is the only argument that can distinguish religious ideas and conscientious beliefs from their secular counterparts and thereby explain special protection for the former. *Id.* at 157-166, 197-218. Similarly, one of your casebook editors argues that

> [t]he best reasons for protecting religious freedom rest on the assumption that religion is a good thing. Our Constitution guarantees religious freedom because religious people want to practice their faith. . . .
>
> [This] is the most convincing explanation for why our society adopted the right to religious freedom in the first place. It is possible to imagine a society of skeptics insisting on a free exercise clause, but the idea is far-fetched.
>
> The religious justification is also the reason why many, perhaps most, religious believers claim the right to freedom today. It enables them to perform their religious duties, and to avoid religious sanctions. It allows them to pursue the truth, as God gives them to know the truth.

John H. Garvey, What Are Freedoms For? 49, 57 (1996). In particular, Dean Garvey argues that "[f]rom a religious point of view," "believers face a special kind of suffering" when a law conflicts with their faith: The believer "might have to choose between violating the law and risking damnation," and at the very least "she has to disappoint [God] in order to comply with the law." *Id.* at 52-54.

Is there something flawed with a "religious" justification for religious freedom? Professor Smith argues that the religious justification has come to have a "self-canceling" quality. The modern understanding of religious freedom and "neutrality" toward religion includes the idea that government may not base policy on one particular theological rationale—including, unfortunately, the theological justification that supports religious freedom in the first place. Smith, 140 U. Pa. L. Rev. at 181-196. To dramatize the paradox, Smith suggests that Thomas Jefferson's Bill for Establishing Religious Freedom (see p. 54)— one of America's landmark advances in religious freedom—would violate modern Establishment Clause tests because of its language ("Almighty God hath created the mind free," and government coercion in religious matters "is a departure from the plan of the Holy author of our religion"). Smith, 140 U. Pa. L. Rev. at 194-195 ("it is hard to see how [an observer] could fail to find an endorsement of religion in Jefferson's statute"). Does this indeed show that there is a self-canceling quality to religious freedom? Or does it instead show that the Establishment Clause cannot possibly require the kind of neutrality (no government reliance on religious premises) that Smith identifies?

In a different vein, Garvey's thesis about "religious duties" and "religious sanctions" has been attacked on the ground that a religious justification cannot support exemptions for any religion other than the one on whose theology the justification is based:

> [I]f extra-temporal consequences are what justify exemptions, then Protestants would reject all claims for exemptions not founded on duties to God that they recognize, for only the breach of those duties would in fact produce the extra-temporal consequences. Religious believers do not view compliance with imagined duties as a good. Rather, they view compliance with actual duties as a good. [The religious justification] should seek freedom from man's laws only for those following God's laws—those laws that God has actually laid down, not those that someone might believe He has laid down.

Larry Alexander, Good God, Garvey! The Inevitability and Impossibility of a Religious Justification of Free Exercise Exemptions, 47 Drake L. Rev. 35, 40 (1998).

What is the answer to this challenge? Garvey argues that exemptions only for religious exercise are justified by "transcendent consequences" that the religious believer faces, harms that are both "more serious . . . more lasting" than temporal, or secular, harms. What are Freedoms For? at 53. But he also asserts that some of the "religious justifications" for religious freedom apply to all beliefs about God, including *non* belief. "Coercion [of belief] is futile no less for atheists than for Catholics and Jews. God may give them faith or he may not, but the government can't help him out. So too with the discovery of truth. It's no use letting only right-thinking Christians search, because we're talking about revelation and God can reveal himself to anyone." *Id.* at 53-54. For this reason, atheists too can object to laws that require them to engage in worship (e.g., school prayers) or that limit the pursuit of knowledge on questions of religion. Do these other religious arguments—"coercion of belief is futile" and "God can speak to anyone"—explain why a religious believer could support exemptions for other religions' practices, even though he thinks those practices are not divinely required?

2. Current Doctrine

Now we turn to the Court's decisions, especially recent ones. The question of religious accommodation arose in a few early cases. In Zorach v. Clauson, 343 U.S. 306 (1952), for example, the Court upheld public school "release time" programs, in which students were allowed to attend religious classes sponsored by the denomination of their choice for specified hours during the school week. After noting that the program involved no coercion of unwilling students, the Court stated that striking down the law would "press the concept of separation of Church and State to [e]xtremes":

> We are a religious people whose institutions presuppose a Supreme Being. We guarantee the freedom to worship as one chooses. We make room for as wide a

variety of beliefs and creeds as the spiritual needs of man deem necessary. We sponsor an attitude on the part of government that shows no partiality to any one group and that lets each flourish according to the zeal of its adherents and the appeal of its dogma. When the state encourages religious instruction or cooperates with religious authorities by adjusting the schedule of public events to sectarian needs, it follows the best of our traditions. For it then respects the religious nature of our people and accommodates the public service to their spiritual needs. To hold that it may not would be to find in the Constitution a requirement that the government show a callous indifference to religious groups.

The Court also upheld legislative exemptions from general laws in Gillette v. United States, 401 U.S. 437 (1971) (military draft exemptions), and Arlan's Department Store v. Kentucky, 371 U.S. 218 (1962) (exemption from Sunday Closing laws for persons who observe a sabbath on a different day). The Court also presupposed the legitimacy of accommodations in its free exercise cases. On the other hand, in several decisions the Court struck down government actions that, even though they were not all exemptions as such, still might colorably be called accommodations of religion. See, e.g., McCollum v. Bd. of Education, 333 U.S. 203 (1948) (release time program for religious classes on school premises); Wallace v. Jaffree, 472 U.S. 38 (1985) (moment of silence); and Estate of Thornton v. Caldor, Inc. (p. 7) (exemption for employees from Saturday work). While these decisions could be distinguished, the underlying constitutional theory of religious accommodations was uncertain, and the Court did not grapple seriously with the doctrinal issues involved. However, the approach to legislative accommodations has been partly clarified by two decisions in the late 1980s and one very recently.

CUTTER v. WILKINSON
544 U.S. 709 (2005)

Justice GINSBURG delivered the opinion of the Court.

Section 3 of the Religious Land Use and Institutionalized Persons Act of 2000 (RLUIPA) [42 U.S.C. § 2000cc], provides in part: "No government shall impose a substantial burden on the religious exercise of a person residing in or confined to an institution," unless the burden furthers "a compelling governmental interest," and does so by "the least restrictive means." Plaintiffs below, petitioners here, are current and former inmates of institutions operated by the Ohio Department of Rehabilitation and Correction and assert that they are adherents of "nonmainstream" religions: the Satanist, Wicca, and Asatru religions, and the Church of Jesus Christ Christian. They complain that Ohio prison officials (respondents here), in violation of RLUIPA, have failed to accommodate their religious exercise "in a variety of different ways, including [refusing to allow them to receive religious literature, engage in group worship, or follow dress and appearance mandates of their faiths]."

In response to petitioners' complaints, respondent prison officials have mounted a facial challenge to the institutionalized-persons provision of RLUIPA; respondents contend, *inter alia*, that the Act improperly advances religion in violation of the First Amendment's Establishment Clause. We [reject this argument and uphold the Act.]

I

A

RLUIPA is the latest of long-running congressional efforts to accord religious exercise heightened protection from government-imposed burdens, consistent with this Court's precedents. [The Court's review of *Smith*, RFRA, and *Boerne* is omitted.]

Before enacting §3, Congress documented, in hearings spanning three years, that "frivolous or arbitrary" barriers impeded institutionalized persons' religious exercise. See [J]oint Statement of Senator Hatch and Senator Kennedy on RLUIPA ("Whether from indifference, ignorance, bigotry, or lack of resources, some institutions restrict religious liberty in egregious and unnecessary ways."). . . .

II

B

[T]he first of the two [Religion] Clauses, commonly called the Establishment Clause, commands a separation of church and state. The second, the Free Exercise Clause, requires government respect for, and noninterference with, the religious beliefs and practices of our Nation's people. While the two Clauses express complementary values, they often exert conflicting pressures.

Our decisions recognize that "there is room for play in the joints" between the Clauses, some space for legislative action neither compelled by the Free Exercise Clause nor prohibited by the Establishment Clause. See, e.g., Employment Division v. Smith ("[A] society that believes in the negative protection accorded to religious belief can be expected to be solicitous of that value in its legislation"); Corporation of Presiding Bishop v. Amos (1987) (Federal Government may exempt secular nonprofit activities of religious organizations from Title VII's prohibition on religious discrimination in employment).

. . . [W]e hold that §3 of RLUIPA fits within the corridor between the Religion Clauses: On its face, the Act qualifies as a permissible legislative accommodation of religion that is not barred by the Establishment Clause.

Foremost, we find RLUIPA's institutionalized-persons provision compatible with the Establishment Clause because it alleviates exceptional government-created burdens on private religious exercise.[6] Furthermore, the Act on its face does not founder on shoals our prior decisions have identified: Properly applying RLUIPA, courts must take adequate account of the burdens a requested accommodation may impose on nonbeneficiaries, see Estate of Thornton v. Caldor [p. 7]; and they must be satisfied that the Act's prescriptions are and will be administered neutrally among different faiths, see Kiryas Joel School Dist. v. Grumet [p. 253].[8]

---

6. [Relocated footnote: The Court noted that the court of appeals, in striking down RLUIPA, had relied on the *Lemon* test of secular purpose, secular effect, and non-entanglement.] We resolve this case on other grounds.

8. Directed at obstructions institutional arrangements place on religious observances, RLUIPA does not require a State to pay for an inmate's devotional accessories. See, e.g., Charles v. Verhagen (7th Cir. 2003) (overturning prohibition on possession of Islamic prayer oil but leaving inmate-plaintiff with responsibility for purchasing the oil).

. . . Section 3 covers state-run institutions—mental hospitals, prisons, and the like—in which the government exerts a degree of control unparalleled in civilian society and severely disabling to private religious exercise.[9] RLUIPA thus protects institutionalized persons who are unable freely to attend to their religious needs and are therefore dependent on the government's permission and accommodation for exercise of their religion.[10]

We note in this regard the Federal Government's accommodation of religious practice by members of the military. See, e.g., Katcoff v. Marsh (2d Cir. 1985) [p. 268] (describing the Army chaplaincy program). In Goldman v. Weinberger (1986), we held that the Free Exercise Clause did not require the Air Force to exempt an Orthodox Jewish officer from uniform dress regulations so that he could wear a yarmulke indoors. In a military community, the Court observed, "there is simply not the same [individual] autonomy as there is in the larger civilian community." *Id.* Congress responded to *Goldman* by prescribing that "a member of the armed forces may wear an item of religious apparel while wearing the uniform," unless "the wearing of the item would interfere with the performance [of] military duties [or] the item of apparel is not neat and conservative." 10 U.S.C. § 774(a)-(b).

We do not read RLUIPA to elevate accommodation of religious observances over an institution's need to maintain order and safety. Our decisions indicate that an accommodation must be measured so that it does not override other significant interests. In *Caldor*, the Court struck down a Connecticut law that "arm[ed] Sabbath observers with an absolute and unqualified right not to work on whatever day they designate[d] as their Sabbath." We held the law invalid under the Establishment Clause because it "unyielding[ly] weigh[ted]" the interests of Sabbatarians "over all other interests."

We have no cause to believe that RLUIPA would not be applied in an appropriately balanced way, with particular sensitivity to security concerns. While the Act adopts a "compelling governmental interest" standard, "[c]ontext matters" in the application of that standard.[11] Lawmakers supporting RLUIPA were

9. See, e.g., *id.* (prison's regulation prohibited Muslim prisoner from possessing ritual cleansing oil); Young v. Lane (7th Cir. 1991) (prison's regulation restricted wearing of yarmulkes); Hunafa v. Murphy (7th Cir. 1990) (noting instances in which Jewish and Muslim prisoners were served pork, with no substitute available).

10. Respondents argue, in line with the Sixth Circuit, that RLUIPA goes beyond permissible reduction of impediments to free exercise. The Act, they project, advances religion by encouraging prisoners to "get religion," and thereby gain accommodations afforded under RLUIPA. While some accommodations of religious observance, notably the opportunity to assemble in worship services, might attract joiners seeking a break in their closely guarded day, we doubt that all accommodations would be perceived as "benefits." For example, congressional hearings on RLUIPA revealed that one state corrections system served as its kosher diet "a fruit, a vegetable, a granola bar, and a liquid nutritional supplement—each and every meal."

The argument, in any event, founders on the fact that Ohio already facilitates religious services for mainstream faiths. The State provides chaplains, allows inmates to possess religious items, and permits assembly for worship.

11. The Sixth Circuit posited that an irreligious prisoner and member of the Aryan Nation who challenges prison officials' confiscation of his white supremacist literature as a violation of his free association and expression rights would have his claims evaluated under the deferential rational-relationship standard [while a] member of the Church of Jesus Christ Christian challenging a similar withholding . . . would have a stronger prospect of success because a court would review his claim under RLUIPA's compelling-interest standard. Courts, however, may be expected to recognize the government's countervailing compelling interest in not facilitating inflammatory racist activity that could imperil prison security and order.

mindful of the urgency of discipline, order, safety, and security in penal institutions. They anticipated that courts would apply the Act's standard with "due deference to the experience and expertise of prison and jail administrators in establishing necessary regulations and procedures to maintain good order, security and discipline, consistent with consideration of costs and limited resources." Joint Statement.

Finally, RLUIPA does not differentiate among bona fide faiths. In *Kiryas Joel*, we invalidated a state law that carved out a separate school district to serve exclusively a community of highly religious Jews, the Satmar Hasidim. We held that the law violated the Establishment Clause, in part because it "single[d] out a particular religious sect for special treatment." RLUIPA presents no such defect. It confers no privileged status on any particular religious sect, and singles out no bona fide faith for disadvantageous treatment.

B

The Sixth Circuit misread our precedents to require invalidation of RLUIPA as "impermissibly advancing religion by giving greater protection to religious rights than to other constitutionally protected rights." Our decision in *Amos* counsels otherwise. There, we upheld against an Establishment Clause challenge a provision exempting "religious organizations from Title VII's prohibition against discrimination in employment on the basis of religion." The District Court in *Amos*, reasoning in part that the exemption improperly "single[d] out religious entities for a benefit," had [struck it down, but we reversed]. Religious accommodations, we held, need not "come packaged with benefits to secular entities."

Were the Court of Appeals' view the correct reading of our decisions, all manner of religious accommodations would fall. Congressional permission for members of the military to wear religious apparel while in uniform would fail, as would accommodations Ohio itself makes. Ohio could not, as it now does, accommodate "traditionally recognized" religions: The State provides inmates with chaplains "but not with publicists or political consultants," and allows "prisoners to assemble for worship, but not for political rallies." Reply Brief for United States 5.

In upholding RLUIPA's institutionalized-persons provision, we emphasize that respondents "have raised a facial challenge to [the Act's] constitutionality, and have not contended that under the facts of any of [petitioners'] specific cases ... applying RLUIPA would produce unconstitutional results."[13] ...

"For more than a decade, the federal Bureau of Prisons has managed the largest correctional system in the Nation under the same heightened scrutiny standard as RLUIPA without compromising prison security, public safety, or the constitutional rights of other prisoners." Brief for United States. We see no reason to anticipate that abusive prisoner litigation will overburden the operations of state and local institutions. ... Should inmate requests for religious accommodations become excessive, impose unjustified burdens on other

---

13. Respondents argue that prison gangs use religious activity to cloak their illicit and often violent conduct. ... It bears repetition, however, that prison security is a compelling state interest, and that deference is due to institutional officials' expertise in this area. Further, prison officials may appropriately question whether a prisoner's religiosity, asserted as the basis for a requested accommodation, is authentic. ...

institutionalized persons, or jeopardize the effective functioning of an institution, the facility would be free to resist the imposition. In that event, adjudication in as-applied challenges would be in order.

Cutter was decided 15 years after the following case in which a legislative accommodation of religion was struck down under the Establishment Clause. Can the two be reconciled?

TEXAS MONTHLY v. BULLOCK, 489 U.S. 1 (1989): The Court struck down an exemption in the sales-tax laws for Texas for "[p]eriodicals that are published or distributed by a religious faith and that consist wholly of writings promulgating the teaching of the faith and books that consist wholly of writings sacred to a religious faith." In an opinion joined by two other members of the Court, Justice Brennan wrote that the exemption violated the Establishment Clause:

"In proscribing all laws 'respecting an establishment of religion,' the Constitution prohibits, at the very least, legislation that constitutes an endorsement of one or another set of religious beliefs or of religion generally. . . . The core notion animating the requirement that a statute possess 'a secular legislative purpose' and that 'its principal or primary effect . . . be one that neither advances nor inhibits religion,' Lemon v. Kurtzman, is [that government] may not place its prestige, coercive authority, or resources behind a single religious faith or behind religious belief in general, compelling nonadherents to support the practices or proselytizing of favored religious organizations and conveying the message that those who do not contribute gladly are less than full members of the community.

"It does not follow, of course, that government policies with secular objectives may not incidentally benefit religion. The nonsectarian aims of government and the interests of religious groups often overlap, and this Court has never required that public authorities refrain from implementing reasonable measures to advance legitimate secular goals merely because they would thereby relieve religious groups of costs they would otherwise incur. Nor have we required that legislative categories make no explicit reference to religion."

Justice Brennan cited Court decisions requiring that religious student groups receive equal access to state university facilities, and upholding an income tax deduction for families' schooling costs at any school including religious schools. "And in the case most nearly on point, Walz v. Tax Comm'n [(1970)], we sustained a property tax exemption that applied to religious properties no less than to real estate owned by a wide array of nonprofit organizations, despite the sizable tax savings it accorded religious groups.

"In all of these cases, however, we emphasized that the benefits derived by religious organizations flowed to a large number of nonreligious groups as well. Indeed, were those benefits confined to religious organizations, they could not have appeared other than as state sponsorship of religion; if that were so, we would not have hesitated to strike them down for lacking a secular purpose and effect. See, e.g., Thornton v. Caldor.

"Texas' sales tax exemption for periodicals published or distributed by a religious faith and consisting wholly of writings promulgating the teaching of the faith lacks sufficient breadth to pass scrutiny under the Establishment

Clause. Every tax exemption constitutes a subsidy that affects nonqualifying taxpayers, forcing them to become 'indirect and vicarious donors.' ' [Citations omitted.] Insofar as that subsidy is conferred upon a wide array of nonsectarian groups as well as religious organizations in pursuit of some legitimate secular end, the fact that religious groups benefit incidentally does not deprive the subsidy of the secular purpose and primary effect mandated by the Establishment Clause. However, when government directs a subsidy exclusively to religious organizations that is not required by the Free Exercise Clause and that either burdens nonbeneficiaries markedly or cannot reasonably be seen as removing a significant state-imposed deterrent to the free exercise of religion, as Texas has done, it 'provide[s] unjustifiable awards of assistance to religious organizations' and cannot but 'conve[y] a message of endorsement' to slighted members of the community. This is particularly true where, as here, the subsidy is targeted at writings that promulgate the teachings of religious faiths. . . .

"How expansive the class of exempt organizations or activities must be to withstand constitutional assault depends upon the State's secular aim in granting a tax exemption. [For example,] if Texas sought to promote reflection and discussion about questions of ultimate value and the contours of a good or meaningful life, then a tax exemption would have to be available to an extended range of associations whose publications were substantially devoted to such matters; the exemption could not be reserved for publications dealing solely with religious issues, let alone restricted to publications advocating rather than criticizing religious belief or activity, without signaling an endorsement of religion that is offensive to the principles informing the Establishment Clause."

Justice Brennan's opinion also rejected the state's argument that "[w]ithout such an exemption, [the] sales tax might trammel free exercise rights, as did the flat license tax this Court struck down as applied to proselytizing by Jehovah's Witnesses" in Murdock v. Pennsylvania, 319 U.S. 105 (1943). "[T]he State has adduced no evidence that the payment of a sales tax by subscribers to religious periodicals or purchasers of religious books would offend their religious beliefs or inhibit religious activity. The State therefore cannot claim persuasively that its tax exemption is compelled by the Free Exercise Clause in even a single instance, let alone in every case. No concrete need to accommodate religious activity has been shown.

"Moreover, even if members of some religious group succeeded in demonstrating that payment of a sales tax . . . would violate their religious tenets, it is by no means obvious that the State would be required by the Free Exercise Clause to make individualized exceptions for them. In United States v. Lee [p. 199], we ruled unanimously that the Federal Government need not exempt an Amish employer from the payment of Social Security taxes, notwithstanding our recognition that compliance would offend his religious beliefs."

The plurality distinguished *Murdock* and Follett v. McCormick, 321 U.S. 573 (1944), which also invalidated a flat license or occupational tax as applied to itinerant Jehovah's Witness preachers. In those cases, "[t]he Court acknowledged that imposing an income or property tax on preachers would not be unconstitutional. It emphasized, however, that a flat license or occupation tax poses a greater threat to the free exercise of religion than do those other taxes, because it is 'levied and collected as a condition to the pursuit of activities whose enjoyment is guaranteed by the First Amendment' and thus 'restrains in advance those constitutional liberties ... and inevitably tends to suppress their exercise.' ... [I]t is questionable whether, consistent with the Free Exercise Clause, government may exact a facially neutral license fee designed for commercial salesmen from religious missionaries whose principal work is preaching and who only occasionally sell religious tracts for small sums. ...[10]

"The sales tax that Texas imposes is not ... a flat tax that 'restrains in advance' the free exercise of religion. On the contrary, because the tax is equal to a small fraction of the value of each sale and payable by the buyer, it poses little danger of stamping out missionary work involving the sale of religious publications, and in view of its generality it can hardly be viewed as a covert attempt to curtail religious activity."

Justice Blackmun, joined by Justice O'Connor, concurred in the judgment: "I would like to decide the present case without necessarily sacrificing either the Free Exercise Clause value or the Establishment Clause value. It is possible for a State to write a tax-exemption statute consistent with both values: for example, a state statute might exempt the sale not only of religious literature distributed by a religious organization but also of philosophical literature distributed by non-religious organizations devoted to such matters of conscience as life and death, good and evil, being and nonbeing, right and wrong. ...

"In this case, by confining the tax exemption exclusively to the sale of religious publications, Texas engaged in preferential support for the communication of religious messages. Although some forms of accommodating religion are constitutionally permissible, see *Amos*, this one surely is not. A statutory preference for the dissemination of religious ideas offends our most basic understanding of what the Establishment Clause is all about and hence is constitutionally intolerable. ...

"At oral argument, appellees suggested that the statute at issue here exempted from taxation the sale of atheistic literature distributed by an atheistic organization. If true, this statute might survive Establishment Clause scrutiny, as well as Free Exercise and Press Clause scrutiny. But, as appellees were quick to concede at argument, the record contains nothing to support this facially implausible interpretation of the statute."

Justice White also concurred in the judgment: "The Texas law at issue here discriminates on the basis of the content of publications: it provides that '[p]eriodicals ... that consist wholly of writings promulgating the teaching of (a religious faith) ... are exempted' from the burdens of the sales tax law. Thus, the content of a publication determines whether its publisher is exempt or nonexempt. Appellant is subject to the tax, but other publications are not because of the message they carry. This is plainly forbidden by the Press Clause

10. "In *Murdock*, the Court noted that Seventh-day Adventist missionaries, who sold religious literature while proselytizing door to door in a manner akin to Jehovah's Witnesses, earned on average only $65 per month in 1941, half of which they were permitted to keep in order to pay their traveling and living expenses. The license fee whose application was challenged in *Murdock* amounted to $1.50 for one day, $7 for one week, $12 for two weeks, and $20 for three weeks. If towns were permitted to levy such fees from itinerant preachers whose average earnings totaled only $32.50 per month before income taxes because their sales of religious literature were merely incidental to their primary evangelical mission, then they could easily throttle such missionary work. A Seventh-day Adventist who spent each day in a different town would have to pay $45 in fees over the course of a 30-day month; if his income were only $32.50, he could not even afford the necessary licenses, let alone support himself once he had met his legal obligations."

of the First Amendment. [That] is the proper basis for reversing the judgment below."

Justice Scalia, joined by two other justices, dissented: "It is not always easy to determine when accommodation slides over into promotion, and neutrality into favoritism, but the withholding of a tax upon the dissemination of religious materials is not even a close case. The subjects of the exemption before us consist exclusively of 'writings promulgating the teaching of the faith' and 'writings sacred to a religious faith.' If there is any close question, it is not whether the exemption is permitted, but whether it is constitutionally compelled in order to avoid 'interference with the dissemination of religious ideas.' [*Murdock* and *Follett*] are not as readily distinguishable as Justice Brennan suggests. I doubt whether it would have made any difference (as he contends) if the municipalities had attempted to achieve the same result of burdening the religious activity through a sales tax rather than a license tax; surely such a distinction trivializes the holdings."

NOTES AND QUESTIONS

As *Cutter* and *Texas Monthly* exemplify, the Court has upheld some legislative accommodations—provisions that single out religious conduct for protection—but has struck down others as establishments of religion. Consider what factors may distinguish the two cases, as you also take account of other recent decisions and arguments concerning accommodations.

1. Across-the-Board vs. Specific Accommodations? Was the RLUIPA accommodation more justifiable because it potentially protected a wide range of religious practices by prisoners of many denominations? By contrast, the *Texas Monthly* exemption operated only in one statutory context, sales taxes. Many other legislative exemptions are similarly "retail" in nature—applying only to a particular conflict between law and conscience, such as draft exemptions for religious pacifists—as opposed to authorizing exemptions at "wholesale" under a general standard such as RFRA's and RLUIPA's compelling interest test. Which method of accommodation, general or specific, is more consistent with the purposes of the Establishment Clause? Cf. Ira C. Lupu, Reconstructing the Establishment Clause: The Case Against Discretionary Accommodation of Religion, 140 U. Pa. L. Rev. 555 (1991) (criticizing context-specific exemptions for favoring religions with political power); with Marci A. Hamilton, The Religious Freedom Restoration Act Is Unconstitutional, Period, 1 U. Pa. J. Const. L. 1, 10-11 (1998) (criticizing general legislation and preferring specific "legislative exemptions urged by those religions actually burdened").

2. Burdens Removed from Religion vs. Burdens Imposed on Others? *Cutter* found it important that RLUIPA (a) "alleviates exceptional government-created burdens on private religious exercise" and (b) is "measured so that it does not override other significant interests" or "impose [unacceptable burdens] on nonbeneficiaries." These factors also figured in *Texas Monthly*; you should be able to state exactly how. Is this sort of test, involving the burdens removed from religion and the burdens imposed on others, the "holding" of *Texas Monthly*?

(a) **What exactly is the test?**   Justice Brennan wrote in *Texas Monthly* that an accommodation law is unconstitutional if it "either burdens nonbeneficiaries markedly or cannot reasonably be seen as removing a significant state-imposed deterrent to the free exercise of religion." In a footnote elsewhere in his opinion, he restated the "test" as follows: legislative accommodations have been approved "that did not, or would not, impose substantial burdens on nonbeneficiaries . . . or that were designed to alleviate government intrusions that might significantly deter adherents of a particular faith from conduct protected by the Free Exercise Clause." 489 U.S. at 18 n.8. Are these two statements of the criteria equal? Suppose that an accommodation removes a significant state-imposed burden from religion but also imposes a significant burden on others. Is it valid or invalid? Think about that question as you review the problems in note 5 posing examples of accommodations. Does an accommodation have to satisfy both criteria? Are the two criteria to be weighed against each other, and if so how can that be done?

(b) **Burdens removed from religion.**   Justice Brennan's opinion in *Texas Monthly* states that imposing a generally applicable sales tax on each sale of a religious publication would not significantly inhibit religion so as to justify a legislative exemption. Perhaps the burden would be insufficiently "substantial" to justify a constitutionally mandated exemption (see part B-2-a above). But shouldn't the legislature have discretion to accommodate religion on is own initiative even if it is not required to do so—and don't *Cutter* and other decisions suggest that this discretion exists? You should be aware that the year after *Texas Monthly*, the Court unanimously confirmed that imposing a general sales tax on the sale of Bibles, sermon tapes, and devotional aids created no "constitutionally significant burden" on the free exercise of religion, again because it was "not a flat tax" and it "represent[ed] only a small fraction of any retail sale." Jimmy Swaggart Ministries v. Board of Equalization, 493 U.S. 378 (1990). But why isn't it sufficient that a tax of this sort, in addition to decreasing the amount of money the Ministries has available, imposes a marginal cost on its evangelistic activity and thus, on the margin, will discourage that activity? The *Swaggart* Court left open the possibility that "a more onerous tax rate, even if generally applicable, might effectively choke off an adherent's religious practices." Can a court draw that line—either in deciding whether to mandate an exception or in reviewing an exemption made by the legislature?

(c) **Burdens imposed on others: *Cutter*.**   The Court in *Cutter* found that RLUIPA's prison provisions did not "override other significant interests," because the legislative history indicated an intent that the Act be interpreted with "due deference to the experience and expertise of prison and jail administrators in establishing necessary regulations and procedures to maintain good order, security and discipline, consistent with consideration of costs and limited resources." Does this uphold RLUIPA's prison provisions by taking all of the teeth out of them? Does it make any sense to demand that the government show a "compelling" need for regulation and then turn around and give "deference" to the government concerning that asserted need? In the *Uniao do Vegetal* case on the meaning of RLUIPA's predecessor RFRA (see p. 202), the Court adopted a more vigorous interpretation of the compelling interest standard. If the more vigorous version governed RLUIPA's prison provisions, would they—should they—have been struck down as establishments?

(d) Burdens imposed on others: workplace accommodations. Questions concerning the extent to which a religious accommodation harms other persons, or other interests, arise in many contexts. For a review, see Jonathan C. Lipson, On Balance: Religious Liberty and Third-Party Harms, 84 Minn. L. Rev. 589 (2000). One common question is whether an employer can be required to accommodate an employee whose sabbath falls on a work day, or whose religious duties in some other way conflict with the employer's requirements. In Estate of Thornton v. Caldor, 472 U.S. 703 (1985)—cited in *Cutter* and reprinted in Part I of this book (p. 7)—the Court held that a state law that imposed an absolute requirement on employers to give their employees time off on their Sabbath violated the Establishment Clause because of the "unyielding weighting" it gave to the interests of Sabbath observers over other concerns, such as the possible "substantial economic burdens on employers" or the "significant burdens on other employees required to work in place of the Sabbath observers."

Compare the law in *Caldor* with § 701(j) of Title VII of the 1964 Civil Rights Act. That title prohibits discrimination in employment based on religion, and the section defines "religion" to include "all aspects of religious observance and practice, as well as belief, unless an employer demonstrates that he is unable to reasonably accommodate to an employee's religious observances without undue hardship on the conduct of the employer's business." In other words, the statute seems to say, an employer must accommodate an employee's conflict with a workplace rule—even, presumably, a facially religion-neutral rule—unless the accommodation would be unreasonable or would impose an undue hardship.

However, in Trans World Airlines v. Hardison, 432 U.S. 63 (1977), the Court interpreted the Title VII religious accommodation provision narrowly. Hardison, a clerk at a TWA maintenance facility, joined the Worldwide Church of God, which required that he refrain from work from sunset Friday through sunset Saturday. He was asked to work Saturdays when a fellow employee went on vacation. The union refused to seek a "swap" between Hardison and another employee because, under the terms of the collective-bargaining agreement, Hardison had insufficient seniority to bid for a shift having Saturdays off. The company refused to allow him to work longer daily hours over a four-day week, because this would have left his position unfilled on Saturdays or involved a transfer of another employee that would have "undermanned another operation" or required TWA to pay overtime wages. Hardison refused to work on Saturdays and was fired.

The Court held that TWA had not violated the statute. It stated first that because "[c]ollective bargaining, aimed at effecting workable and enforceable agreements between management and labor, lies at the core of our national labor policy," the statute should not be read to require that "an agreed-upon seniority system must give way when necessary to accommodate religious observances." It also argued that "to give Hardison Saturdays off, TWA would have had to deprive another employee of his shift preference at least in part because he did not adhere to a religion that observed the Saturday Sabbath." Because Title VII was aimed at "eliminating discrimination in employment," it should not be read "to contemplate such unequal treatment" of other employees. Finally, the Court held that "[t]o require TWA to bear more than a de minimis cost in order to give Hardison Saturdays off is an undue hardship."

Justice Marshall dissented: "[I]f an accommodation [under §701(j)] can be rejected simply because it involves preferential treatment, then the regulation and the statute, while brimming with 'sound and fury,' ultimately 'signif[y] nothing.' . . . The accommodation issue by definition arises only when a neutral rule of general applicability conflicts with the religious practices of a particular employee." He added that "while important [Establishment Clause] questions would be posed by interpreting the law to compel employers (or fellow employees) to incur substantial costs to aid the religious observer, not all accommodations are costly," and little attempt had been made to accommodate Hardison's sabbath observance.

Was Justice Marshall right that *Hardison* effectively nullified Title VII's reasonable accommodation provision? Was *Hardison*'s interpretation required by the Establishment Clause—or is there some middle ground between absolute and minimal accommodation? The Workplace Religious Freedom Act, a bill introduced in several recent sessions of Congress, would strengthen the Title VII provision by providing, among other things, that "undue hardship" on an employer means more than just the "de minimis cost" of *Hardison*, but rather "significant difficulty or expense." See, e.g., S.1124, §2(a)(2), 105th Cong., 2d Sess. (1997). If the bill passed, would it be constitutionally objectionable?

Why is it ever legitimate for government to shift the cost of religious exercise from the believer to someone else? Thornton (the employee involved in *Caldor*) and Hardison are adherents to religions that make costly demands on believers. No one ever promised that keeping the sabbath would be easy. Why is it legitimate for the government to extend "reasonable" accommodation to protect employees from bearing the economic consequences of their religious beliefs? On the other hand, the government shifts the burdens of personal decisions from workers to employers in a variety of contexts, including pregnancy, family emergencies, jury duty, military reserve duty, and physical and mental handicap. From the employer's point of view these duties to accommodate cost only money, and given the weak state of "economic liberty rights," economic burdens on employers are not of constitutional magnitude. Why should the Establishment Clause be interpreted to prefer merely economic concerns?

Recall that in Thomas v. Anchorage Equal Rights Comm'n, 165 F.3d 692 (9th Cir. 1999) (p. 175), a Ninth Circuit panel held that a landlord with a religious conviction against facilitating fornication was constitutionally entitled to an exemption from Alaska's law forbidding discrimination on the basis of marital status. In responding to the argument that granting such an exemption would violate the Establishment Clause because it "would result in direct injury to other identifiable persons," the court responded that "Establishment Clause jurisprudence concerns itself with only one kind of 'harm': the stigmatization of religious minorities." Since the "harm" inflicted by the religious exemption was "economic, not religious" (the court described the harm as "the marginal reduction in the number of apartment units available for rent"), it was "beyond the pale of the Establishment Clause." Is this a correct interpretation of Supreme Court precedent? Is it correct as a matter of first principles?

For discussion of the problem of accommodating religious conduct in the light of the interests of other employees, see, e.g., Vikram David Amar, State RFRAs and the Workplace, 32 U.C. Davis L. Rev. 513 (1999).

3. Religious Speech and Accommodation. Another distinctive factor in *Texas Monthly* may be Justice White's concurring argument (echoed implicitly by Justice Blackmun) that the Texas sales-tax exemption violated the Free Press Clause by "discriminat[ing] on the basis of the content of publications." The Free Speech Clause likewise presumptively prohibits different treatment on the basis of the content of speech, particularly the viewpoint reflected in the speech. Does the First Amendment in some aspect (free speech, nonestablishment) prohibit accommodation of religious activity when that activity takes the form of speech? If a religiously motivated antiabortion activist is prosecuted for protesting outside (or impeding access to) an abortion clinic, and the state in question has enacted a version of RFRA, can that statute apply and require the state to show a compelling interest in restricting the protesters' activity? Can such a principle about equal treatment of religious speech distinguish *Texas Monthly* from *Cutter*? This issue is considered in detail in Part V-B.

4. Underlying Values in Accommodation Cases.   The power of legislatures to make special accommodation for religious conduct raises questions about which values underlying the Religion Clauses are most fundamental. As we already have suggested in connection with constitutionally mandated accommodation (see pp. 4-7, 129-131), the issue may pose a conflict in values between an emphasis on equal treatment of religion (what we have called "formal neutrality") and an emphasis on liberty and private choice in religious matters.

Does *Texas Monthly*, by striking down an accommodation limited to religious publications, uphold equal treatment between religion and other ideas, at the expense of any special concern for liberty and choice in religious matters?

Does *Cutter*, by allowing Congress to strengthen prisoners' religion-based claims but not other civil rights claims, make religious liberty fundamental, though at the expense of equality between religious and nonreligious beliefs?

Corporation of Presiding Bishop v. Amos, 483 U.S. 327 (1987), discussed in both *Cutter* and *Texas Monthly*, upheld the exemption in Title VII allowing religious organizations to discriminate based on religion in hiring any of their employees, not just those engaged in "religious" activities. The majority reasoned that without the broader exemption, it would be a "significant burden on a religious organization to require it, on pain of substantial liability, to predict which of its activities a secular court will consider religious. The line is hardly a bright one, and an organization might understandably be concerned that a judge would not understand its religious tenets and sense of mission." Moreover, the exemption did not impermissibly advance religion under the second part of the Lemon v. Kurtzman test:

> Undoubtedly, religious organizations are better able now to advance their purposes than they were prior to the 1972 amendment to § 702. But . . . [a] law is not unconstitutional simply because it *allows* churches to advance religion, which is their very purpose. For a law to have forbidden "effects" under *Lemon*, it must be fair to say that the *government itself* has advanced religion through its own activities and influence.

By emphasizing that the religious organization was the one advancing religion, and the governmental exemption merely allowed it to do so, *Amos* seemed to focus on the underlying value of respecting the choices of private religious groups. But suppose that equality between religion and other ideas or activities ("formal neutrality") is the fundamental principle of the Religion Clauses. Can you construct an argument that the exemption upheld in *Amos* was consistent with that value? See, e.g., Christopher L. Eisgruber and Lawrence G. Sager, Congressional Power and Religious Liberty After *City of Boerne v. Flores*, 1997 Sup. Ct. Rev. 79, 134-135. Could the employment exemption be seen as necessary to ensuring that religious organizations have the same right as other ideological organizations—say, the Sierra Club—to demand loyalty from their employees?

Amos also said that exempting religious organizations from the religious-discrimination law "effectuates a more complete separation" between church and state "and avoids [an] intrusive inquiry" into whether an activity is religious or secular. Does the value of church-state separation always cut in favor of religious accommodations, or are there any ways in which such accommodations are in tension with separation?

5. Problems on Legislative Accommodations. Try to apply the analysis of *Cutter* and *Texas Monthly* to some other accommodation cases, for example:

(a) Draft exemptions. Return to the facts of Welsh v. United States (see p. 235). Suppose that the court had interpreted "religious training and belief" in the draft-exemption provision *not* to extend to Welsh, who held "deep conscientious scruples" that he said were based on "readings in the field of history and sociology" rather than on "religious training." Would exempting a devout Quaker while refusing to exempt Welsh be unconstitutional under *Texas Monthly*?

(b) Tithing and RFRA. What about the facts of *In re Young* (p. 157): a bankruptcy trustee, acting on behalf of the Youngs' creditors, sued the Youngs' church to recover tithes paid by the Youngs in good faith during the months preceding their bankruptcy. The church raised the Religious Freedom Restoration Act in defense, arguing that the recovery of good-faith contributions on which it had relied would seriously burden its ministry. Would applying RFRA to block the recovery of tithes violate the Establishment Clause?

3. Denominational Neutrality

One danger of legislative or executive accommodations is that government officials will favor some religions over others. Politically influential religions will win accommodations; others will not. The majority in Employment Division v. Smith was willing to call this an "unavoidable consequence of democratic government." But in other cases it has been a matter of judicial concern. How should this problem be handled? Consider the following cases.

LARSON v. VALENTE, 456 U.S. 228 (1982): A Minnesota statute required charitable organizations soliciting donations to register with the state and to file an extensive annual report detailing their income and its sources, their costs of various sorts, and their transfers of property or funds out of the state. A charity's registration could be withdrawn if it is engaged in fraudulent or deceptive practices or if it spent an "unreasonable" amount of its revenue on management or fundraising costs. At first the statute exempted all religious organizations from the registration and reporting requirements, but in 1978 the legislature adopted a "50 percent rule" stating that only those religious organizations that received more than half of their total contributions from members or affiliated organizations would remain exempt. The Unification Church (sometimes known as "Moonies" after its leader the Rev. Sun Myung Moon) engaged in extensive door-to-door solicitation and was not eligible for the amended exemption. The Church sued, alleging that the statute violated rights of free exercise, free speech, equal protection, and nonestablishment.

The Supreme Court began its opinion by stating the principle of "denominational neutrality":

> The clearest command of the Establishment Clause is that one religious denomination cannot be officially preferred over another. Before the Revolution, religious establishments of differing denominations were common throughout the Colonies. But the Revolutionary generation emphatically disclaimed that European legacy, and "applied the logic of secular liberty to the condition of religion and the churches": If Parliament had lacked the authority to tax unrepresented colonists, then by the same token the newly independent States should be powerless to tax their citizens for the support of a denomination to which they did not belong. The force of this reasoning led to the abolition of most denominational establishments at the state level by the 1780's, and led ultimately to the inclusion of the Establishment Clause in the First Amendment in 1791.
>
> This constitutional prohibition of denominational preferences is inextricably connected with the continuing vitality of the Free Exercise Clause. Madison once noted: "Security for civil rights must be the same as that for religious rights. It consists in the one case in the multiplicity of interests and in the other in the multiplicity of sects." Madison's vision—freedom for all religion being guaranteed by free competition between religions—naturally assumed that every denomination would be equally at liberty to exercise and propagate its beliefs. But such equality would be impossible in an atmosphere of official denominational preference. Free exercise thus can be guaranteed only when legislators—and voters—are required to accord to their own religions the very same treatment given to small, new, or unpopular denominations. As Justice Jackson noted in another context, "there is no more effective practical guaranty against arbitrary and unreasonable government than to require that the principles of law which officials would impose upon a minority must be imposed generally."

The Court found that the 50 percent rule "clearly grants denominational preference" and therefore had to satisfy strict constitutional scrutiny. It found that the rule was not "closely fitted" to serve any compelling interest that the state had in preventing abuses in charitable solicitation. The majority reasoned that there was no showing that members would control an organization or safeguard against abusive fundraising practices simply because they contributed more than half the organization's income. The majority also found that the statute was ill-fitted because "the need for public disclosure more plausibly rises in proportion with the *absolute amount*, rather than with the *percentage*, of non-member contributions" (emphasis in original). Justice White dissented.

BOARD OF EDUCATION, KIRYAS JOEL VILLAGE SCHOOL DISTRICT v. GRUMET
512 U.S. 687 (1994)

Justice SOUTER delivered the opinion of the Court [except as to Part II-Introduction and Part II-A].

The village of Kiryas Joel in Orange County, New York, is a religious enclave of Satmar Hasidim, practitioners of a strict form of Judaism. [A] special state statute passed in 1989 carved out a separate [school] district, following village lines, to serve this distinctive population. . . . Because this unusual Act is tantamount to an allocation of political power on a religious criterion and neither presupposes nor requires governmental impartiality toward religion, we hold that it violates the [Establishment Clause].

I

The Satmar Hasidic sect takes its name from the town near the Hungarian and Romanian border where, in the early years of this century, Grand Rebbe Joel Teitelbaum molded the group into a distinct community. After World War II and the destruction of much of European Jewry, the Grand Rebbe and most of his surviving followers moved to the Williamsburg section of Brooklyn, New York. Then, 20 years ago, the Satmars purchased an approved but undeveloped subdivision in the town of Monroe and began assembling the community that has since become the village of Kiryas Joel. When a zoning dispute arose in the course of settlement, the Satmars presented the Town Board of Monroe with a petition to form a new village within the town, a right that New York's Village Law gives almost any group of residents who satisfy certain procedural niceties. Neighbors who did not wish to secede with the Satmars objected strenuously, and after arduous negotiations the proposed boundaries of the village of Kiryas Joel were drawn to include just the 320 acres owned and inhabited entirely by Satmars. The village, incorporated in 1977, has a population of about 8,500 today. Rabbi Aaron Teitelbaum, eldest son of the current Grand Rebbe, serves as the village rov (chief rabbi) and rosh yeshivah (chief authority in the parochial schools).

The residents of Kiryas Joel are vigorously religious people who make few concessions to the modern world and go to great lengths to avoid assimilation into it. They interpret the Torah strictly; segregate the sexes outside the home; speak Yiddish as their primary language; eschew television, radio, and English-language publications; and dress in distinctive ways that include headcoverings and special garments for boys and modest dresses for girls. Children are educated in private religious schools, most boys at the United Talmudic Academy where they receive a thorough grounding in the Torah and limited exposure to secular subjects, and most girls at Bais Rochel, an affiliated school with a curriculum designed to prepare girls for their roles as wives and mothers.

These schools do not, however, offer any distinctive services to handicapped children, who are entitled under state and federal law to special education services even when enrolled in private schools. Starting in 1984 the Monroe-Woodbury Central School District provided such services for the children of Kiryas Joel at an annex to Bais Rochel, but a year later ended that arrangement in response to our decisions in Aguilar v. Felton (1985) and School Dist. of Grand Rapids v. Ball (1985) [holding such programs unconstitutional]. Children from Kiryas Joel who needed special education (including the deaf, the mentally retarded, and others suffering from a range of physical, mental, or emotional disorders) were then forced to attend public schools outside the village, which their families found highly unsatisfactory. Parents of most of these children withdrew them from the Monroe-Woodbury secular schools, citing "the panic, fear and trauma [the children] suffered in leaving their own community and being with people whose ways were so different," and some sought administrative review of the public-school placements.

... By 1989, only one child from Kiryas Joel was attending Monroe-Woodbury's public schools; the village's other handicapped children received privately funded special services or went without. It was then that the New York Legislature passed the statute at issue in this litigation, which provided that the village of Kiryas Joel "is constituted a separate school district, ... and shall have and enjoy all the powers and duties of a union free school district." ... In signing the bill into law, Governor Cuomo recognized that the residents of the new school district were "all members of the same religious sect," but said that the bill was "a good faith effort to solve th[e] unique problem" associated with providing special education services to handicapped children in the village.

Although it enjoys plenary legal authority over the elementary and secondary education of all school-aged children in the village, the Kiryas Joel Village School District currently runs only a special education program for handicapped children. The other village children have stayed in their parochial schools, relying on the new school district only for transportation, remedial education, and health and welfare services. If any child without a handicap in Kiryas Joel were to seek a public-school education, the district would pay tuition to send the child into Monroe-Woodbury or another school district nearby. Under like arrangements, several of the neighboring districts send their handicapped Hasidic children into Kiryas Joel, so that two thirds of the full-time students in the village's public school come from outside. In all, the new district serves just over 40 full-time students, and two or three times that many parochial school students on a part-time basis.

Several months before the new district began operations, the [plaintiffs, who included officers of the state school board association,] brought this action ... challenging Chapter 748 under [the Establishment Clause].

II

"A proper respect for both the Free Exercise and the Establishment Clauses compels the State to pursue a course of 'neutrality' toward religion," favoring neither one religion over others nor religious adherents collectively over non-adherents. Chapter 748, the statute creating the Kiryas Joel Village School District, departs from this constitutional command by delegating the State's discretionary authority over public schools to a group defined by its character as a religious community, in a legal and historical context that gives no assurance that governmental power has been or will be exercised neutrally. ...

A

... It is undisputed that those who negotiated the village boundaries when applying the general village incorporation statute drew them so as to exclude all but Satmars, and that the New York Legislature was well aware that the village remained exclusively Satmar in 1989 when it adopted Chapter 748. The significance of this fact to the state legislature is indicated by the further fact that carving out the village school district ran counter to customary districting practices in the State. Indeed, the trend in New York is not toward dividing school districts but toward consolidating them. The thousands of small common school districts laid out in the early 19th century have been combined and recombined, first into union free school districts and then into larger central school districts, until only a tenth as many remain today. Most of these cover several towns, many of them cross county boundaries, and only one remains precisely coterminous with an incorporated village. The object of the State's practice of consolidation is the creation of districts large enough to provide a comprehensive education at affordable cost, which is thought to require at least 500 pupils for a combined junior-senior high school. The Kiryas Joel Village School District, in contrast, has only 13 local, full-time students in all (even including out-of-area and part-time students leaves the number under 200), and in offering only special education and remedial programs it makes no pretense to be a full-service district.

The origin of the district in a special Act of the legislature, rather than the State's general laws governing school district reorganization, is likewise anomalous. Although the legislature has established some 20 existing school districts by special Act, all but one of these are districts in name only, having been designed to be run by private organizations serving institutionalized children. They have neither tax bases nor student populations of their own but serve children placed by other school districts or public agencies. . . . Thus the Kiryas Joel Village School District is exceptional to the point of singularity, as the only district coming to our notice that the legislature carved from a single existing district to serve local residents.

Because the district's creation ran uniquely counter to state practice, following the lines of a religious community where the customary and neutral principles would not have dictated the same result, we have good reasons to treat this district as the reflection of a religious criterion for identifying the recipients of civil authority. Not even the special needs of the children in this community can explain the legislature's unusual Act, for the State could have responded to the concerns of the Satmar parents without implicating the Establishment Clause, as we explain in some detail further on. We therefore find the legislature's Act to be substantially equivalent to defining a political subdivision and hence the qualification for its franchise by a religious test, resulting in a purposeful and forbidden "fusion of governmental and religious functions." Larkin v. Grendel's Den (1982) [p. 704].[6]

B

The fact that this school district was created by a special and unusual Act of the legislature also gives reason for concern whether the benefit received by the Satmar community is one that the legislature will provide equally to other religious (and nonreligious) groups. This is the second malady the *Larkin* Court

---

6. Because it is the unusual circumstances of this district's creation that persuade us the State has employed a religious criterion for delegating political power, this conclusion does not imply that any political subdivision that is coterminous with the boundaries of a religiously homogeneous community suffers the same constitutional infirmity. The district in these cases is distinguishable from one whose boundaries are derived according to neutral historical and geographic criteria, but whose population happens to comprise coreligionists.

identified in the law before it, the absence of an "effective means of guarantee-ing" that governmental power will be and has been neutrally employed." . . .

The fundamental source of constitutional concern here is that the legislature itself may fail to exercise governmental authority in a religiously neutral way. The anomalously case-specific nature of the legislature's exercise of state author-ity in creating this district for a religious community leaves the Court without any direct way to review such state action for the purpose of safeguarding a principle at the heart of the Establishment Clause, that government should not prefer one religion to another, or religion to irreligion. Because the religious community of Kiryas Joel did not receive its new governmental authority simply as one of many communities eligible for equal treatment under a general law,[11] we have no assurance that the next similarly situated group seeking a school district of its own will receive one; unlike an administrative agency's denial of an exemption from a generally applicable law, which "would be entitled to a judicial audi-ence," a legislature's failure to enact a special law is itself unreviewable. Nor can the historical context in these cases furnish us with any reason to suppose that the Satmars are merely one in a series of communities receiving the benefit of special school district laws. Early on in the development of public education in New York, the State rejected highly localized school districts for New York City when they were promoted as a way to allow separate schooling for Roman Cath-olic children. And in more recent history, the special Act in these cases stands alone.

C

In finding that Chapter 748 violates the requirement of governmental neu-trality by extending the benefit of a special franchise, we do not deny that the Constitution allows the State to accommodate religious needs by alleviating special burdens. Our cases leave no doubt that in commanding neutrality the Religion Clauses do not require the government to be oblivious to impositions that legitimate exercises of state power may place on religious belief and prac-tice. Rather, there is "ample room under the Establishment Clause for 'benevo-lent neutrality which will permit religious exercise to exist without sponsorship and without interference"; "government may (and sometimes must) accommo-date religious practices and . . . may do so without violating the Establishment Clause." . . .

But accommodation is not a principle without limits, and what petitioners seek is an adjustment to the Satmars' religiously grounded preferences that our cases do not countenance. . . . Petitioners' proposed accommodation singles out a particular religious sect for special treatment, and whatever the limits of permissible legislative accommodations may be, it is clear that neutrality as among religions must be honored. See Larson v. Valente [p. 251].

III

. . . The dissent protests it is novel to insist " 'up front' " that a statute not tailor its benefits to apply only to one religious group. . . . Indeed, under the

---

11. This contrasts with the process by which the village of Kiryas Joel itself was created, involving, as it did, the application of a neutral state law designed to give almost any group of residents the right to incorporate.

dissent's theory, if New York were to pass a law providing school buses only for children attending Christian day schools, we would be constrained to uphold the statute against Establishment Clause attack until faced by a request from a non-Christian family for equal treatment under the patently unequal law. Cf. Everson v. Board of Education (upholding school bus service provided all pupils). And . . . the license [that Justice Scalia] takes in suggesting that the Court holds the Satmar sect to be New York's established church is only one symptom of his inability to accept the fact that this Court has long held that the First Amendment reaches more than classic, 18th-century establishments.

In these cases we are clearly constrained to conclude that the statute before us fails the test of neutrality. It delegates a power this Court has said "ranks at the very apex of the function of a State," to an electorate defined by common religious belief and practice, in a manner that fails to foreclose religious favoritism. It therefore crosses the line from permissible accommodation to impermissible establishment.

[Justice O'Connor's concurring opinion, joining in Parts II-B, II-C, and III of the primary opinion, is omitted.]

Justice STEVENS, with whom Justice BLACKMUN and Justice GINSBURG join, concurring.

New York created a special school district for the members of the Satmar religious sect in response to parental concern that children suffered " 'panic, fear and trauma' " when " 'leaving their own community and being with people whose ways were so different.' " To meet those concerns, the State could have taken steps to alleviate the children's fear by teaching their schoolmates to be tolerant and respectful of Satmar customs. Action of that kind would raise no constitutional concerns and would further the strong public interest in promoting diversity and understanding in the public schools.

Instead, the State responded with a solution that affirmatively supports a religious sect's interest in segregating itself and preventing its children from associating with their neighbors. The isolation of these children, while it may protect them from "panic, fear and trauma," also unquestionably increased the likelihood that they would remain within the fold, faithful adherents of their parents' religious faith. By creating a school district that is specifically intended to shield children from contact with others who have "different ways," the State provided official support to cement the attachment of young adherents to a particular faith. It is telling, in this regard, that two-thirds of the school's full-time students are Hasidic handicapped children from outside the village; the Kiryas Joel school thus serves a population far wider than the village—one defined less by geography than by religion.

Affirmative state action in aid of segregation of this character is unlike the evenhanded distribution of a public benefit or service, a "release time" program for public school students involving no public premises or funds, or a decision to grant an exemption from a burdensome general rule. It is, I believe, fairly characterized as establishing, rather than merely accommodating, religion.

Justice KENNEDY, concurring in the judgment.

The Court's ruling that the Kiryas Joel Village School District violates the Establishment Clause is in my view correct, but my reservations about what the Court's reasoning implies for religious accommodations in general are sufficient to require a separate writing. . . .

. . . I agree that a religious accommodation demands careful scrutiny to ensure that it does not so burden nonadherents or discriminate against other religions as to become an establishment. I disagree, however, with the suggestion that the Kiryas Joel Village School District contravenes these basic constitutional commands. . . .

New York's object in creating the Kiryas Joel Village School District—to accommodate the religious practices of the handicapped Satmar children—is validated by the principles that emerge from [our] precedents. E.g., *Texas Monthly.* First, by creating the district, New York sought to alleviate a specific and identifiable burden on the Satmars' religious practice. The Satmars' way of life, which springs out of their strict religious beliefs, conflicts in many respects with mainstream American culture. . . . Attending the Monroe-Woodbury public schools, where they were exposed to much different ways of life, caused the handicapped Satmar children understandable anxiety and distress. New York was entitled to relieve these significant burdens. . . .

Second, by creating the district, New York did not impose or increase any burden on non-Satmars, compared to the burden it lifted from the Satmars. . . . There is a point, to be sure, at which an accommodation may impose a burden on nonadherents so great that it becomes an establishment. See, e.g., Estate of Thornton v. Caldor. This action has not been argued, however, on the theory that non-Satmars suffer any special burdens from the existence of the [d]istrict.

Third, the creation of the school district to alleviate the special burdens borne by the handicapped Satmar children cannot be said, for that reason alone, to favor the Satmar religion to the exclusion of any other. . . . The Court insists that religious favoritism is a danger here, because . . . "we have no assurance that the next similarly situated group seeking a school district of its own will receive one; . . . a legislature's failure to enact a special law is itself unreviewable."

This reasoning reverses the usual presumption that a statute is constitutional and, in essence, adjudges the New York Legislature guilty until it proves itself innocent. No party has adduced any evidence that the legislature has denied another religious community like the Satmars its own school district under analogous circumstances. The legislature, like the judiciary, is sworn to uphold the Constitution, and we have no reason to presume that the New York Legislature would not grant the same accommodation in a similar future case. The fact that New York singled out the Satmars for this special treatment indicates nothing other than the uniqueness of the handicapped Satmar children's plight. It is normal for legislatures to respond to problems as they arise—no less so when the issue is religious accommodation. Most accommodations cover particular religious practices. [Justice Kennedy cited statutes and regulations exempting the use or transport of peyote for Native American worship services; exempting religious headgear worn by military personnel, including, "[f]or example, Jewish yarmulkes . . . if they do not exceed 6 inches in diameter"; and exempting from Prohibition laws the making, transport, or use of "wine for sacramental purposes."]

Nor is it true that New York's failure to accommodate another religious community facing similar burdens would be insulated from challenge in the courts. The burdened community could sue the State of New York, contending that

New York's discriminatory treatment of the two religious communities violated the Establishment Clause. To resolve this claim, the court would have only to determine whether the community does indeed bear the same burden on its religious practice as did the Satmars in Kiryas Joel. While a finding of discrimination would then raise a difficult question of relief, the discrimination itself would not be beyond judicial remedy.

[Justice Kennedy joined in invalidating the district only because its boundaries had been drawn on the basis of religious affiliation.]

Justice SCALIA, with whom THE CHIEF JUSTICE and Justice THOMAS join, dissenting.

The Court today finds that the Powers That Be, up in Albany, have conspired to effect an establishment of the Satmar Hasidim. I do not know who would be more surprised at this discovery: the Founders of our Nation or Grand Rebbe Joel Teitelbaum, founder of the Satmar. The Grand Rebbe would be astounded to learn that after escaping brutal persecution and coming to America with the modest hope of religious toleration for their ascetic form of Judaism, the Satmar had become so powerful, so closely allied with Mammon, as to have become an "establishment" of the Empire State. And the Founding Fathers would be astonished to find that the Establishment Clause—which they designed "to insure that no one powerful sect or combination of sects could use political or governmental power to punish dissenters," Zorach (Black, J., dissenting)—has been employed to prohibit characteristically and admirably American accommodation of the religious practices (or more precisely, cultural peculiarities) of a tiny minority sect. . . .

II

[In this section, Justice Scalia argued that the principle of Larkin v. Grendel's Den prohibiting certain delegations of governmental power—must be confined to delegations of power to religious institutions, and not extended to the exercise of governmental power by groups of citizens who happen to belong to one religion.]

III

I turn, next, to Justice Souter's second justification for finding an establishment of religion: his facile conclusion that the New York Legislature's creation of the Kiryas Joel school district was religiously motivated. But in the Land of the Free, democratically adopted laws are not so easily impeached by unelected judges. To establish the unconstitutionality of a facially neutral law on the mere basis of its asserted religiously preferential (or discriminatory) effects[,] Justice Souter "must be able to show the absence of a neutral, secular basis" for the law.

There is of course no possible doubt of a secular basis here. The New York Legislature faced a unique problem in Kiryas Joel: a community in which all the nonhandicapped children attend private schools, and the physically and mentally disabled children who attend public school suffer the additional handicap of cultural distinctiveness. It would be troublesome enough if these peculiarly dressed, handicapped students were sent to the next town, accompanied by their similarly clad but unimpaired classmates. But all the unimpaired children of Kiryas Joel attend private school. The handicapped children suffered sufficient emotional trauma from their predicament that their parents kept them home from school. Surely the legislature could target this problem, and provide a public education for these students, in the same way it addressed, by a similar law, the unique needs of children institutionalized in a hospital. [Citation omitted.]

Since the obvious presence of a neutral, secular basis renders the asserted preferential effect of this law inadequate to invalidate it, Justice Souter is required to come forward with direct evidence that religious preference was the objective. [He argues that legislators] created the [d]istrict in order to further the Satmar religion, rather than for any proper secular purpose, because (1) they created the district in an extraordinary manner—by special Act of the legislature, rather than under the State's general laws governing school-district reorganization; (2) the creation of the district ran counter to a state trend toward consolidation of school districts; and (3) the district includes only adherents of the Satmar religion. On this indictment, no jury would convict.

One difficulty with the first point is that it is not true. There was really nothing so "special" about the formation of a school district by an Act of the New York Legislature. The State has created both large school districts and small specialized school districts for institutionalized children through these special Acts. [Citing statutes.] But in any event all that the first point proves, and the second point as well (countering the trend toward consolidation), is that New York regarded Kiryas Joel as a special case, requiring special measures. . . .

Justice Souter's case against the statute comes down to nothing more, therefore, than his third point: the fact that all the residents of the Kiryas Joel Village School District are Satmars. But all its residents also wear unusual dress, have unusual civic customs, and have not much to do with people who are culturally different from them. On what basis does Justice Souter conclude that it is the theological distinctiveness rather than the cultural distinctiveness that was the basis for New York State's decision? The normal assumption would be that it was the latter, since it was not theology but dress, language, and cultural alienation that posed the educational problem for the children. . . .

. . . In order to invalidate a facially neutral law, Justice Souter would have to show not only that legislators were aware that religion caused the problems addressed, but also that the legislature's proposed solution was motivated by a desire to disadvantage or benefit a religious group (i.e., to disadvantage or benefit them because of their religion). . . . Here a facially neutral statute extends an educational benefit to the one area where it was not effectively distributed. Whether or not the reason for the ineffective distribution had anything to do with religion, it is a remarkable stretch to say that the Act was motivated by a desire to favor or disfavor a particular religious group. The proper analogy to Chapter 748 is not the Court's hypothetical law providing school buses only to Christian students, but a law providing extra buses to rural school districts (which happen to be predominantly Southern Baptist). . . .

IV

But even if Chapter 748 were intended to create a special arrangement for the Satmars because of their religion . . . , it would be a permissible accommodation. . . .

At bottom, the Court's "no guarantee of neutrality" argument is an assertion of this Court's inability to control the New York Legislature's future denial of comparable accommodation. [Justice Scalia, like Justice Kennedy, argued that if a comparable exemption were later denied, the aggrieved group could sue for denominational discrimination.]

The Court's demand for "up front" assurances of a neutral system is at war with both traditional accommodation doctrine and the judicial role. [M]ost efforts at accommodation seek to solve a problem that applies to members of only one or a few religions. Not every religion uses wine in its sacraments, but that does not make an exemption from Prohibition for sacramental wine use impermissible, nor does it require the State granting such an exemption to explain in advance how it will treat every other claim for dispensation from its controlled-substances laws. Likewise, not every religion uses peyote in its services, but we have suggested [in Employment Division v. Smith] that legislation which exempts the sacramental use of peyote from generally applicable drug laws is not only permissible, but desirable, without any suggestion that some "up front" legislative guarantee of equal treatment for sacramental substances used by other sects must be provided. The record is clear that the necessary guarantee can and will be provided, after the fact, by the courts.

Contrary to the Court's suggestion, I do not think that the Establishment Clause prohibits formally established "state" churches and nothing more. I have always believed, and all my opinions are consistent with the view, that the Establishment Clause prohibits the favoring of one religion over others. . . . What I attack is the Court's imposition of novel "up front" procedural requirements on state legislatures. Making law (and making exceptions) one case at a time, whether through adjudication or through highly particularized rulemaking or legislation, violates, ex ante, no principle of fairness, equal protection, or neutrality simply because it does not announce in advance how all future cases (and all future exceptions) will be disposed of. If it did, the manner of proceeding of this Court itself would be unconstitutional.

NOTES AND QUESTIONS

1. Denominational Neutrality and the First Amendment.   As you think about the problem of "denominational neutrality" in accommodations, first consider *Larson v. Valente*, which provides precedent for *Kiryas Joel*. The *Larson* Court's conclusion that equality among religions was one of the most important principles of the Founding is confirmed repeatedly in both statements and constitutional enactments of that period. Baptist leader John Leland proposed an amendment to the Massachusetts Constitution forbidding the legislature to "establish any religion by law, [or] give any one sect a preference to another." In a similar vein, Jonas Phillips (of *Stansbury v. Marks* (p. 3)) drafted a petition to the Constitutional Convention stating that American Jews desired a provision that "all Religious societies are on an Equal footing." Rhode Island proposed an amendment to the federal Constitution that "no particular sect or society ought to be favored or established by law." Madison's initial draft of the Free Exercise Clause provided that "the full and equal rights of conscience [shall not] be in any manner, nor on any pretext, infringed." Every one of the 12 state

constitutional provisions protecting religious liberty contained language referring to denominational equality (though in two states this equality was extended
only to Christian denominations). New York and South Carolina both specified
that the right of free exercise was to be "without discrimination or preference,"
and Virginia provided that "all men are equally entitled to the free exercise of
religion." Other states used words like "every," "all," "no," "equal," or "equally"
to make the same point.

2. What Constitutes a Denominational Preference?   But what makes the Minnesota law in *Larson* unequal? Accommodations need not apply to all religious
denominations: That would render unconstitutional all accommodations for
specific practices in specific statutory contexts. In Gillette v. United States,
401 U.S. 437 (1971), the Court upheld a federal law exempting religious conscientious objectors who objected to all wars, but not objectors to particular wars.
This had the effect of excusing adherents to the traditional "peace churches,"
such as Quakers and Mennonites, but not adherents to religions, such as Roman
Catholicism, that espouse "just war" doctrine. The Court stated that accommodations need not be equal if there are "neutral, secular reasons," not based on
religious favoritism, for distinguishing among religious practices.

What makes *Larson* different from *Gillette*? Why is the legislature's view that an
organization whose members contribute a majority of its funds is less likely to
abuse its trust not a "neutral, secular reason"? The *Larson* Court stated that the
Minnesota provision

> is not simply a facially neutral statute, the provisions of which happen to have a
> "disparate impact" upon different religious organizations. On the contrary, [it]
> makes explicit and deliberate distinctions between different religious organiza-
> tions. We agree with the Court of Appeals' observation that the provision effectively
> distinguishes between "well-established churches" that have "achieved strong but
> not total financial support from their members," on the one hand, and "churches
> which are new and lacking in a constituency, or which, as a matter of policy, may
> favor public solicitation over general reliance on financial support from mem-
> bers," on the other hand.
>
> [Moreover,] *Gillette* is readily distinguishable from the present case. Section 6(j)
> "focused on individual conscientious belief, not on sectarian affiliation." Under
> § 6(j), conscientious objector status was available on an equal basis to both the
> Quaker and the Roman Catholic, despite the distinction drawn by the latter's
> church between "just" and "unjust" wars. As we noted in *Gillette*, the "critical
> weakness of petitioners' establishment claim" arose "from the fact that § 6(j),
> on its face, simply [did] not discriminate on the basis of religious affiliation." In
> contrast, the statute challenged in the case before us focuses precisely and solely
> upon religious organizations.

Is this distinction sound? Consider also the following passage from *Larson*:

> The legislative history discloses that the legislators perceived that the italicized
> language would bring a Roman Catholic Archdiocese within the Act, that the
> legislators did not want the amendment to have that effect, and that an amend-
> ment deleting the italicized clause was passed in committee for the sole purpose of
> exempting the Archdiocese from the provisions of the Act. On the other hand,
> there were certain religious organizations that the legislators did not want to

exempt from the Act. One State Senator explained that the fifty per cent rule was "an attempt to deal with the religious organizations which are soliciting on the street and soliciting by direct mail, but who are not substantial religious institutions in . . . our state." Another Senator said, "what you're trying to get at here is the people that are running around airports and running around streets and soliciting people and you're trying to remove them from the exemption that normally applies to religious organizations." Still another Senator, who apparently had mixed feelings about the proposed provision, stated, "I'm not sure why we're so hot to regulate the Moonies anyway."

Perhaps *Larson* should be understood as applying strict scrutiny only to laws that have a discriminatory purpose.

3. The Remedy for Denominational Discrimination.   Note that the remedy in *Larson* was to extend the accommodation to all religions. Was that correct? If the Minnesota statute was an "establishment of religion," why wasn't the proper remedy to hold the statute unconstitutional—with the result that all religions would be subject to the solicitation regulations? Does this suggest that *Larson* should not have been analyzed as an establishment case? The Unification Church could have argued that the solicitation regulations imposed a burden on its exercise of religion. If the case arose today, the discriminatory nature of the statute would then be relevant to show that the statute was not "neutral and generally applicable" under *Smith*, and thus was subject to strict scrutiny, and also to impeach the state's claim that its interest was compelling. Then it would be obvious that the correct remedy is to extend the accommodation. What was the point of describing the case as arising under the Establishment Clause?

4. *Kiryas Joel* and the Requirement of "Up Front" Neutrality.   Now turn to *Kiryas Joel*. Does the Court there really hold that it is unconstitutional for a state actor to accommodate the needs of a particular religion if it does not adopt an "up front" general rule to govern all such needs in the future? What is the justification for that? Why, as Justices Kennedy and Scalia argue, is it not sufficient for members of a future group to sue if they are denied a comparable accommodation? Isn't that what happened in Larson v. Valente?

5. Standing in Denominational Equality Cases.   Note that in *Larson*, the plaintiffs were members of the group that had been denied the accommodation extended to other religious groups. The plaintiffs in *Kiryas Joel* were school board officials from other districts, suing in their capacity as taxpayers. They sued in state court in New York, where the standing rules are less restrictive than in federal court. Should they have had standing to sue? If the gravamen of their complaint is that the legislature might not extend a comparable accommodation to a similarly situated group, why not wait for a member of such a group to challenge the statute? Note that the state defended the statute on the ground that the situation facing the Village of Kiryas Joel was unique, and thus warranted a unique solution. One way to test that proposition is to see whether another group appears and claims to be similarly situated. If there is no such group, then the state's defense gains in plausibility.

6. Problems.   Apply your understanding of denominational neutrality to the following situations:

(a) An earlier section (p. 183) presented the problem of Catholic Charities, a religious social service organization, being required by state law to pay for contraceptive prescriptions for its employees whenever it pays for other prescriptions. The law contains an exemption for a "religious employer" conscientiously opposed to contraception, where "religious employer" is defined as meeting, among other things, all of the following criteria: (1) "the inculcation of religious values is the purpose of the entity"; (2) "the entity primarily employs persons who share [its] religious tenets"; and (3) "the entity serves primarily persons who share [its] religious tenets." The Catholic Church pushed for adding an exemption to the law in the first place; the sponsor of the law opposed any broader exemption on the ground that "[t]he intention of the exemption [is] to provide for exemption for what is religious activity. The more secular the activity gets, the less religiously based it is, and the more we believe that they should be required to cover prescription drug benefits for contraception." Catholic Charities, who employs and serves non-Catholics, challenged the statute on the ground, among others, that it constituted denominational discrimination. How would you analyze this question?

(b) Members of the Christian Science Church, who conscientiously refuse medical treatment and seek spiritual treatment for illness, sometimes go to Church-owned facilities called "sanitoria" to receive prayer and other spiritual treatment. While in the sanitoria they receive basic nursing care such as changing of bedpans and assistance with eating and dressing. The federal Medicare and Medicaid statutes provide reimbursement for various costs of medical and nursing care that patients with medical conditions receive in a hospital or nursing home. Congress extended these statutes and budgeted additional funds to provide reimbursement for the nursing care given to a patient by a "religious nonmedical health care institution" (RNHCI), in cases where the patient would be eligible for Medicare or Medicaid but rejects medical care for reasons of religious conscience. The statute allows RNHCIs to qualify for reimbursement as hospitals or nursing homes, but it also exempts RNHCIs from several forms of medical-related regulation applicable to hospitals and nursing homes. An RNHCI is defined as an institution that provides *only* nonmedical services and treats *only* patients who rely on religious healing. Christian Science sanitoria are the only institutions that have received reimbursements, and much of the testimony in favor of allowing the payments came from Christian Science officials and individuals. Does the statute authorizing payments to RNHCIs and exempting them from regulation violate the principle of "denominational neutrality"? See Children's Healthcare Is a Legal Duty v. Min de Parle, 212 F.3d 1084 (8th Cir. 2000).

(c) Imagine you are legal counsel to a school board. A Hindu girl in gym class asks to be allowed to wear a long-sleeved shirt and leg coverings in lieu of the mandatory uniform, in order to accommodate sincere religious beliefs regarding female modesty. The gym teacher is willing to make the exception, but is worried that she is unable to anticipate all the possible requests for exceptions from gym class rules that might arise. Is it constitutional to accommodate the Hindu student and leave future cases to future decision?

One possible difference between this hypothetical and the facts of *Kiryas Joel* is that *Kiryas Joel* involved an act of the legislature and the hypothetical involved the decision of an administrative official. Can (should?) the principle of *Kiryas Joel* be confined to statutes? Recall the following passage from Zorach v. Clauson (p. 238):

A Catholic student applies to his teacher for permission to leave the school during hours on a Holy Day of Obligation to attend a mass. A Jewish student asks his teacher for permission to be excused for Yom Kippur. A Protestant wants the afternoon off for a family baptismal ceremony. . . . The teacher in other words cooperates in a religious program to the extent of making it possible for her students to participate in it. Whether she does it occasionally for a few students, regularly for one, or pursuant to a systematized program designed to further the religious needs of all the students does not alter the character of the act.

7. Religious Freedom and Religious "Segregation." What do you think of Justice Stevens's argument that the Kiryas Joel law was problematic because it "affirmatively support[ed] a religious sect's interest in segregating itself and preventing its children from associating with their neighbors," and "provided official support to cement the attachment of young adherents to a particular faith"? Does the right of free exercise include the right of a religious minority to separate itself from the wider society? To bring up children in the faith? Does the Establishment Clause contain an inherent bias toward assimilation? See, e.g., Christopher L. Eisgruber, The Constitutional Value of Assimilation, 96 Colum. L. Rev. 87 (1996) (arguing that it does). Or does it leave the degree of desired assimilation to decision by each group? Compare Justice Stevens's opinion with Wisconsin v. Yoder. How are the two cases different? Abner Greene, *Kiryas Joel* and Two Mistakes about Equality, 96 Colum. L. Rev. 1 (1996), defends the constitutional value of "decentralized nomic communities" that are "constituted by people who share a comprehensive world view that extends to creating law for the community. Such communities check the centralized government's lawmaking and create separate normative cultures." *Id.* at 4. See also Robert M. Cover, The Supreme Court, 1982 Term—Foreword: Nomos and Narrative, 97 Harv. L. Rev. 4 (1983).

Do the arguments for the autonomy of such communities extend to situations where they exercise governmental power over a jurisdiction? Greene defends such an extension as long as the citizens have chosen to live in the community and the governmental body does not behave in an independently unconstitutional way, for example by explicitly teaching religious doctrines in its schools. Did the Kiryas Joel district satisfy these two criteria?

At about the same time the Court decided *Kiryas Joel* it also held, under the Equal Protection Clause, that states could not draw legislative district lines on the basis of race in order to create majority-black or majority-Hispanic districts. See, e.g., Shaw v. Reno, 509 U.S. 630 (1993); Miller v. Johnson, 515 U.S. 900 (1995). The two sets of decisions appear consistent, forbidding the drawing of lines to "sort" voters into districts by race or religion; but the consistency is only on the surface, since most of the justices who approved of racially conscious districting disapproved of the Kiryas Joel district, and vice versa. The exception was Justice Kennedy, whose concurrence in *Kiryas Joel* emphasized that the state had "draw[n] political boundaries on the basis of religion." Assuming that it is constitutionally wrong to treat racial makeup as an overriding consideration in drawing political boundaries, is there a constitutional reason to treat religion differently? Cf. Thomas C. Berg, Religion, Race, Segregation, and Districting: Comparing *Kiryas Joel* with *Shaw/Miller*, 26 Cumb.

L. Rev. 365, 375-381 (1996) (distinguishing religious line-drawing from racial line-drawing on the ground of religious freedom interests); with Christopher L. Eisgruber, Ethnic Segregation by Religion and Race: Reflections on *Kiryas Joel* and *Shaw v. Reno*, 26 Cumb. L. Rev. 515 (1996) (arguing that race-conscious districting counteracts segregation by facilitating election of minority legislators, while the Satmar-only district promoted segregation).

4. Pervasive Governmental Presence

Most church-state cases presuppose the division between a public sphere, in which the government must be neutral (in some sense) regarding religion, and a private sphere, in which religious free exercise may flourish. The "separation between church and state" is thus a variant on the idea of the "public-private distinction." What happens when the government is so pervasive and dominant a presence that there is little "private" space left for free exercise? Consider these cases:

CRUZ v. BETO
405 U.S. 319 (1972)

PER CURIAM.

The complaint, alleging a cause of action under 42 U.S.C. § 1983, states that Cruz is a Buddhist, who is in a Texas prison. While prisoners who are members of other religious sects are allowed to use the prison chapel, Cruz is not. He shared his Buddhist religious material with other prisoners and, according to the allegations, in retaliation was placed in solitary confinement on a diet of bread and water for two weeks, without access to newspapers, magazines, or other sources of news. He also alleged that he was prohibited from corresponding with his religious advisor in the Buddhist sect. Those in the isolation unit spend 22 hours a day in total idleness.

Again, according to the allegations, Texas encourages inmates to participate in other religious programs; providing at state expense chaplains of the Catholic, Jewish, and Protestant faiths, providing also at state expense copies of the Jewish and Christian Bibles, conducting weekly Sunday school classes and religious services. According to the allegations, points of good merit are given prisoners as a reward for attending orthodox religious services, those points enhancing a prisoner's eligibility for desirable job assignments and early parole consideration. Respondent answered, denying the allegations and moving to dismiss.

The Federal District Court denied relief without a hearing or any findings, saying the complaint was in an area that should be left "to the sound discretion of prison administrators." It went on to say, "Valid disciplinary and security reasons not known to this court may prevent the 'equality' of exercise of religious practices in prison." The Court of Appeals affirmed.

Federal courts sit not to supervise prisons but to enforce the constitutional rights of all "persons," including prisoners. We are not unmindful that prison officials must be accorded latitude in the administration of prison affairs, and that prisoners necessarily are subject to appropriate rules and regulations. But persons in prison, like other individuals, have the right to petition the Government for redress of grievances which, of course, includes "access of prisoners to the courts for the purpose of presenting their complaints." . . .

If Cruz was a Buddhist and if he was denied a reasonable opportunity of pursuing his faith comparable to the opportunity afforded fellow prisoners who adhere to conventional religious precepts, then there was palpable discrimination by the State against the Buddhist religion, established 600 B.C., long before the Christian era.[2] The First Amendment, applicable to the States by reason of the Fourteenth Amendment, prohibits government from making a law "prohibiting the free exercise" of religion. If the allegations of this complaint are assumed to be true, as they must be on the motion to dismiss, Texas has violated the First and Fourteenth Amendments.

The motion for leave to proceed in forma pauperis is granted. The petition for certiorari is granted, the judgment is vacated, and the cause remanded for a hearing and appropriate findings.

Mr. Chief Justice BURGER, concurring in the result.

I concur in the result reached even though the allegations of the complaint are on the borderline necessary to compel an evidentiary hearing. Some of the claims alleged are frivolous; others do not present justiciable issues. There cannot possibly be any constitutional or legal requirement that the government provide materials for every religion and sect practiced in this diverse country. At most, Buddhist materials cannot be denied to prisoners if someone offers to supply them.

Mr. Justice REHNQUIST, dissenting.

Unlike the Court, I am not persuaded that petitioner's complaint states a claim under the First Amendment, or that if the opinion of the Court of Appeals is vacated the trial court must necessarily conduct a trial upon the complaint.

Under the First Amendment, of course, Texas may neither "establish a religion" nor may it "impair the free exercise" thereof. Petitioner alleges that voluntary services are made available at prison facilities so that Protestants, Catholics, and Jews may attend church services of their choice. None of our prior holdings indicates that such a program on the part of prison officials amounts to the establishment of a religion. . . .

None of our holdings under the First Amendment requires that, in addition to being allowed freedom of religious belief, prisoners be allowed freely to evangelize their views among other prisoners. There is no indication in petitioner's complaint that the prison officials have dealt more strictly with his efforts to convert other convicts to Buddhism than with efforts of communicants of other faiths to make similar conversions.

---

2. We do not suggest, of course, that every religious sect or group within a prison—however few in number—must have identical facilities or personnel. A special chapel or place of worship need not be provided for every faith regardless of size; nor must a chaplain, priest, or minister be provided without regard to the extent of the demand. But reasonable opportunities must be afforded to all prisoners to exercise the religious freedom guaranteed by the First and Fourteenth Amendment without fear of penalty.

By reason of his status, petitioner is obviously limited in the extent to which he may practice his religion. He is assuredly not free to attend the church of his choice outside the prison walls. But the fact that the Texas prison system offers no Buddhist services at this particular prison does not, under the circumstances pleaded in his complaint, demonstrate that his religious freedom is being impaired. Presumably prison officials are not obligated to provide facilities for any particular denominational services within a prison, although once they undertake to provide them for some they must make only such reasonable distinctions as may survive analysis under the Equal Protection Clause.

What petitioner's basic claim amounts to is that because prison facilities are provided for denominational services for religions with more numerous followers, the failure to provide prison facilities for Buddhist services amounts to a denial of the equal protection of the laws. There is no indication from petitioner's complaint how many practicing Buddhists there are in the particular prison facility in which he is incarcerated, nor is there any indication of the demand upon available facilities for other prisoner activities. . . . Absent a complaint alleging facts showing that the difference in treatment between petitioner and his fellow Buddhists and practitioners of denominations with more numerous adherents could not reasonably be justified under any rational hypothesis, I would leave the matter in the hands of the prison officials.

KATCOFF v. MARSH
755 F.2d 223 (2d Cir. 1985)

MANSFIELD, Circuit Judge.

This appeal raises the question of whether Congress and the United States Army ("Army"), in furnishing chaplains as part of our armed forces to enable soldiers to practice the religions of their choice, violate the Constitution. We hold that, except in a few respects that require further consideration, they do not.

Appellants, two practicing attorneys who were Harvard Law School students when they commenced the action, appeal from [a district court] order granting summary judgment dismissing their complaint, which seeks declaratory and injunctive relief against continuation of the Army's chaplaincy program as violative of the Establishment Clause. . . .

In providing our armed forces with a military chaplaincy Congress has perpetuated a facility that began during Revolutionary days before the adoption of our Constitution, and that has continued ever since then, with the size of the chaplaincy growing larger in proportion to the increase in the size of our Army. When the Continental Army was formed those chaplains attached to the militia of the 13 colonies became part of our country's first national army. On July 29, 1775, the Continental Congress authorized that a Continental Army chaplain be paid, and within a year General George Washington directed that regimental Continental Army chaplains be procured.

Upon the adoption of the Constitution and before the December 1791 ratification of the First Amendment Congress authorized the appointment of a commissioned Army chaplain. Since then, as the Army has increased in size the military chaplaincy has been extended and Congress has increased the number of Army chaplains. . . .

In 1981 the Army had approximately 1,427 active-duty commissioned chaplains, 10 auxiliary chaplains, 1,383 chaplain's assistants, and 48 Directors of Religious Education. These chaplains are appointed as commissioned officers with rank and uniform but without command. Before an applicant may be appointed to the position of chaplain he must receive endorsement from an ecclesiastical endorsing agency recognized by the Armed Forces Chaplains Board, of which there are 47 in the United States, representing 120 denominations. In addition to meeting the theological standards of the endorsing agency the applicant must also meet minimum educational requirements established by the Department of Defense, which are more stringent than those of some religious denominations having endorsing agencies and are designed to insure the applicant's ability to communicate with soldiers of all ranks and to administer religious programs. In deciding upon the denominations of chaplains to be appointed the Office of the Chief of Chaplains establishes quotas based on the denominational distribution of the population of the United States as a whole. The entire civilian church population rather than the current military religious population is used in order to assure that in the event of war or total mobilization the denominational breakdown will accurately reflect that of the larger-sized Army.

Upon his appointment the chaplain, except for a number of civilian clerics provided voluntarily or by contract, is subject to the same discipline and training as that given to other officers and soldiers. He is trained in such subjects as Army organization, command relationships, supply, planning, teaching, map-reading, types of warfare, security, battlefield survival, and military administration. When ordered with troops into any area, including a combat zone under fire, he must obey. He must be prepared to meet problems inherent in Army life, including how to handle trauma, death or serious injury of soldiers on the field of battle, marital and family stresses of military personnel, tending the wounded or dying, and psychological treatment of soldiers' drug or alcohol abuse, as well as the alleviation of tensions between soldiers and their commanders. On the other hand, the chaplain is not required to bear arms or receive training in weapons. Under Articles 33 and 35 of the Geneva Conventions Relative to Treatment of Prisoners of War "chaplains" are accorded a non-combatant status, which means that they are not to be considered prisoners of war and they may exercise their ministry among prisoners of war. Promotion of a chaplain within the military ranks is based solely on his military performance and not on his effectiveness as a cleric.

The primary function of the military chaplain is to engage in activities designed to meet the religious needs of a pluralistic military community, including military personnel and their dependents. In view of the Army's huge size (some 788,000 soldiers and 1,300,000 dependents in 1981) and its far-flung distribution (291,000 soldiers stationed abroad and many in remote areas of the United States) the task is an important and formidable one. The Army consists of a wide spectrum of persons of different ethnic, racial and religious backgrounds who go into military service from varied social, economic and educational environments. The great majority of the soldiers in the Army express religious preferences. About 80% are under 30 years of age and a large number are married. As a result it has become necessary to provide religious facilities for soldiers of some 86 different denominations.

A sample survey of military personnel made by the Army in 1979 revealed the following religious preferences among enlisted personnel:

Protestant	38.5%
Catholic	22.5%
Mormon	2.5%
Eastern Orthodox	0.5%
Moslem	1.0%
Jewish	0.7%
Buddhist	0.7%
Other religions not listed	19.3%
No religious preference	14.3%

Aside from the problems arising out of the sheer size and pluralistic nature of the Army, its members experience increased needs for religion as the result of being uprooted from their home environments, transported often thousands of miles to territories entirely strange to them, and confronted there with new stresses that would not otherwise have been encountered if they had remained at home. In 1981 approximately 37% of the Army's active duty soldiers, amounting to 293,000 persons, were stationed overseas in locations such as Turkey, Sinai, Greece, or Korea. In most of these areas the Judeo-Christian faiths of most American soldiers are hardly represented at all by local clergy and the average soldier is separated from the local populace by a linguistic and cultural wall. Within the United States the same problem exists in a somewhat different way in that, although the linguistic or cultural barrier may be absent, local civilian clergy in the rural areas where most military camps are centered are inadequate to satisfy the soldiers' religious needs because they are too few in number for the task and are usually of different religious denominations from those of most of the nearby troops.

The problem of meeting the religious needs of Army personnel is compounded by the mobile, deployable nature of our armed forces, who must be ready on extremely short notice to be transported from bases (whether or not in the United States) to distant parts of the world for combat duty in fulfillment of our nation's international defense commitments. Unless there were chaplains ready to move simultaneously with the troops and to tend to their spiritual needs as they face possible death, the soldiers would be left in the lurch, religiously speaking. In the opinion of top generals of the Army and those presently in the chaplaincy, unless chaplains were made available in such circumstances the motivation, morale and willingness of soldiers to face combat would suffer immeasurable harm and our national defense would be weakened accordingly.

Many soldiers in the Army also suffer serious stresses from other causes attributable largely to their military service, which can be alleviated by counseling and spiritual assistance from a leader of their respective faiths. Among these are tensions created by separation from their homes, loneliness when on duty in strange surroundings involving people whose language or customs they do not share, fear of facing combat or new assignments, financial hardships, personality conflicts, and drug, alcohol or family problems. The soldier faced with any of these problems at home would usually be able to consult his spiritual adviser. The Army seeks to furnish the same services through military chaplains. In doing so the Army has proceeded on the premise that having uprooted the soldiers from their natural habitats it owes them a duty to satisfy their Free Exercise rights, especially since the failure to do so would diminish morale, thereby weakening our national defense.

To meet the religious needs of our armed forces Army chaplains and their assistants engage in a wide variety of services to military personnel and their families who wish to use them. No chaplain is authorized to proselytize soldiers or their families. The chaplain's principal duties are to conduct religious services (including periodic worship, baptisms, marriages, funerals and the like), to furnish religious education to soldiers and their families, and to counsel soldiers with respect to a wide variety of personal problems. In addition the chaplain, because of his close relationship with the soldiers in his unit, often serves as a liaison between the soldiers and their commanders, advising the latter of racial unrest, drug or alcohol abuse, and other problems affecting the morale and efficiency of the unit, and helps to find solutions. In some areas the Army also makes available religious retreats, in which soldiers voluntarily withdraw for a short period from the routine activities of daily living to another location for spiritual reflection and renewal. . . . Over the years the Army has built or acquired more than 500 chapels which are used for the conduct of religious services of many different denominations. In addition it has built more than 100 Religious Educational Facilities, which are used for religious services and classes in religious education for soldiers and members of their families of all ages (including children). The Army has purchased and made available for voluntary use by various denominations numerous chaplain's kits, vocational kits, communion sets and vestments, and religious publications (including Holy Scriptures and Prayer Books for Jewish Personnel, the New Testament of our Lord and Savior Jesus Christ, and a Book of Worship), and has developed a Cooperative Curriculum for Religious Education of the Armed Forces. Professional education and training has also been furnished to Army chaplains. . . .

The great majority of the chaplaincy's services, facilities, and supplies are procured by the Army through funds appropriated by Congress, which amounted to over $85 million for the fiscal year 1981, of which more than $62 million was used to pay the salaries and other compensation of chaplains, chaplain's assistants and auxiliary chaplains. Much smaller amounts were paid for the services of contract chaplains ($332,000), directors of religious education ($221,000), and organists and choir directors ($412,000). Some $7.7 million of non-appropriated funds, representing voluntary contributions or designated offerings from soldiers and their dependents, were also used in the fiscal year 1981 to provide for the needs of the Army's chaplaincy program. Generally speaking, non-appropriated funds are used for denominational activities such as the purchase of sacred items and literature and the salaries of organists and the choir directors.

Appellants' complaint, filed on November 23, 1979, seeks a declaratory judgment that the foregoing program violates the Establishment Clause and injunctive relief. The complaint alleges that the "constitutional rights of Army personnel and their dependents to freely exercise their religion can better be served by an alternative Chaplaincy program which is privately funded and controlled." In the district court and here appellants have not questioned the need to satisfy the Free Exercise rights of military personnel but have claimed that government funding of the chaplaincy program is unnecessary. . . .

Turning to the merits, the Establishment Clause of the First Amendment, which provides that "Congress shall make no law respecting an establishment of religion," was designed by our Founding Fathers to insure religious liberty for our country's citizens by precluding a government from imposing, sponsoring, or supporting religion or forcing a person to remain away from the practice of religion. Everson v. Board of Education (1947).

> The "establishment of religion" clause of the First Amendment means at least this: Neither a state nor the Federal Government can set up a church. Neither can pass laws which aid one religion, aid all religions, or prefer one religion over another. Neither can force nor influence a person to go to or to remain away from church against his will or force him to profess a belief or disbelief in any religion. No person can be punished for entertaining or professing religious beliefs or disbeliefs, for church attendance or non-attendance.

The Army chaplaincy does not seek to "establish" a religion according to this simple formula. It observes the basic prohibition expressed by the Court in Zorach v. Clauson:

> The government must be neutral when it comes to competition between sects. It may not thrust any sect on any person. It may not make a religious observance compulsory. It may not coerce anyone to attend church, to observe a religious holiday, or to take religious instruction.

Since the program meets the requirement of voluntariness by leaving the practice of religion solely to the individual soldier, who is free to worship or not as he chooses without fear of any discipline or stigma, it might be viewed as not proscribed by the Establishment Clause. Indeed, if the Army prevented soldiers from worshiping in their own communities by removing them to areas where religious leaders of their persuasion and facilities were not available it could be accused of violating the Establishment Clause unless it provided them with a chaplaincy since its conduct would amount to inhibiting religion.

Congress' authorization of a military chaplaincy before and contemporaneous with the adoption of the Establishment Clause is also "weighty evidence" that it did not intend that Clause to apply to such a chaplaincy. . . . In interpreting the Bill of Rights such "an unbroken practice . . . is not something to be lightly cast aside." Walz v. Tax Commission. . . .

If the current Army chaplaincy were viewed in isolation, there could be little doubt that it would fail to meet the Lemon v. Kurtzman conditions. Although the ultimate objective of the chaplaincy may be secular in the sense that it seeks to maintain the efficiency of the Army by improving the morale of our military personnel, its immediate purpose is to promote religion by making it available, albeit on a voluntary basis, to our armed forces. The effect of the program, moreover, is to advance the practice of religion. Administration of the program, involving arrangements with many church organizations of different denominations, entangles the government with religious accrediting bodies.

However, neither the Establishment Clause nor statutes creating and maintaining the Army chaplaincy may be interpreted as if they existed in a sterile vacuum. They must be viewed in the light of the historical background of their enactment to the extent that it sheds light on the purpose of the Framers of the Constitution. [T]he Establishment Clause must in any event be interpreted to accommodate other equally valid provisions of the Constitution, including the Free Exercise Clause, when they are implicated.

The present case involves two other provisions of our Constitution, which must not only be respected but, to the extent possible, interpreted compatibly with the Establishment Clause. The first of these is the War Power Clause of Art. I, §8, which provides in pertinent part that Congress shall have the power to "provide for the common Defence," "to raise and support Armies," and to "make Rules for the Government and Regulation of the land and naval Forces." Although military conduct is not immune from judicial review when challenged as violative of the Bill of Rights, the Supreme Court has recognized that:

> [J]udges are not given the task of running the Army. . . . The military constitutes a specialized community governed by a separate discipline from that of the civilian. Orderly government requires that the judiciary be as scrupulous not to interfere with legitimate Army matters as the Army must be scrupulous not to intervene in judicial matters. . . .

The second provision of the Constitution which plays a vital role in our interpretation of the Establishment Clause is the Free Exercise Clause of the same Amendment. It is readily apparent that this Clause, like the Establishment Clause, obligates Congress, upon creating an Army, to make religion available to soldiers who have been moved by the Army to areas of the world where religion of their own denominations is not available to them. Otherwise the effect of compulsory military service could be to violate their rights under both Religion Clauses of the First Amendment. Unless the Army provided a chaplaincy it would deprive the soldier of his right under the Establishment Clause not to have religion inhibited and of his right under the Free Exercise Clause to practice his freely chosen religion. . . .

Applying these principles to the present case, we start with plaintiffs' concession that some chaplaincy is essential. Except for peripheral claims that a few practices of the government's military chaplaincy amount to "religious proselytism," their lawsuit hinges entirely on their contention that a privately funded chaplaincy, patterned on the present military program, would fully and fairly meet the government's needs under the War Power Clause and the free-exercise needs of military personnel. For the most part, we disagree.

To begin with, defendants have described in detail the various functions performed by the Army's chaplains and the inability of local civilian clergy or special organizations of civilian clergy to meet the religious needs of the many different denominations in the armed forces. They note that among the inadequacies of a civilian clergy would be the questionable ability of many denominations, particularly the smaller ones, to fund a civilian chaplaincy and the lack of training in the military subjects needed to enable the civilian chaplain to function effectively in the field.

[P]laintiffs have not come forward with any evidence or offer through discovery or depositions to establish that the many religious denominations involved, including the principal Catholic, Protestant and Jewish organizations in the United States, would support and be willing to pay their respective shares of the $85 million required to operate a civilian chaplaincy and to provide such additional sums as may be required in case of war or national emergency. Nor have plaintiffs come forward with assurances from the numerous religious organizations involved that they would seek to agree upon each denomination's proportionate share of the overall financial obligation and that they would be able and willing to honor their respective obligations in the years ahead. It is obvious from the evidence offered by the defendants that without enforceable commitments on the part of these various denominations the Army would be unable to maintain a functioning civilian chaplaincy. Assuming hypothetically that such a program could be launched, it would constantly be teetering on the brink of disaster. An impractical alternative is no alternative at all. . . .

Aside from the obvious financial infeasibility of appellants' alternative proposal, plaintiffs offer no evidence that civilian chaplains would accept military discipline, which is essential to the efficient operation of our armed forces. This discipline demands willingness to undergo thorough military training except in the use of firearms, to remain with an Army unit for a specified period of time, to obey orders to move overnight with that unit to other locations, which might be thousands of miles away, and to advance as ordered on the battlefield and risk their lives in order to minister to the wounded and dying. Thus, since plaintiffs' suggested alternative of a civilian chaplaincy amounts to nothing more than speculation, unsupported by some showing of practical feasibility, it fails to survive the evidentiary showing advanced by the defendants. . . .

Lastly, even if plaintiffs' proposal were feasible it would, assuming the *Lemon* standard advanced by the plaintiffs were held applicable, violate the Establishment Clause. The Army, financed by Congress, would to at least some extent still be commanding the civilian chaplains and supporting them with taxpayer-provided "logistical support, coordination and training in military affairs" (Appellants' Reply Br. 18), including transport, food and facilities.

We find that the more appropriate standard of relevancy to our national defense and reasonable necessity is met by the great majority of the Army's existing chaplaincy activities. The purpose and effect of the program is to make religion, religious education, counseling and religious facilities available to military personnel and their families under circumstances where the practice of religion would otherwise be denied as a practical matter to all or a substantial number. As a result, the morale of our soldiers, their willingness to serve, and the efficiency of the Army as an instrument for our national defense rests in substantial part on the military chaplaincy, which is vital to our Army's functioning.

In a few areas, however, the reasonable necessity for certain activities of the military chaplaincy is not readily apparent. For instance, it appears that in some large urban centers, such as at the Pentagon in Washington, D.C., in New York City and San Francisco, government funds may be used to provide military chaplains, facilities and retreats to "armchair" military personnel who, like other government civil servants, commute daily to their homes and spend their free hours (including weekends) in locations where civilian clergy and facilities are just as available to them as to other non-military citizens. Plaintiffs also assert that government-financed Army chaplains and facilities are provided to retired military personnel and their families. If the ability of such personnel to worship in their own communities is not inhibited by their military service and funds for these chaplains and facilities would not otherwise be expended, the justification for a governmental program of religious support for them is questionable and, notwithstanding our deference to Congress in military matters, requires a showing that they are relevant to and reasonably necessary for the conduct of our national defense by the Army. A remand therefore becomes necessary to determine whether, according to the standard we have outlined, government financing of a military chaplaincy in these limited areas for the purposes indicated is constitutionally permissible.

NOTES AND QUESTIONS

1. Pervasive Governmental Presence. *Cruz* and *Katcoff* both involve environments where active (even controlling) participation by government is necessary if religious exercise is to be possible at all. It thus casts the "wall of separation" in a different light. In John Locke's philosophy (see p. 38), the scope of government is strictly limited, and church and state are strictly separated. If government is not limited, that formula becomes problematic. Imagine a pure socialist system where the government owns all real property, all places of employment, and the entire means of production, but is nonetheless committed to freedom of religion. What would free exercise of religion look like? What would nonestablishment look like? Is it not clear that the government would own the churches and employ the ministers? Is it not clear that the government would have to find some method of allocating resources among religious faiths? (What was that method in *Katcoff*?)

Our system is far from the socialist regime described above, but it is also far from the minimalist state envisioned by Locke. What are the implications for religious freedom of an enlarged welfare-regulatory state?

In the ordinary civilian context, a chaplaincy program like that in *Katcoff* would violate both establishment and free exercise principles in numerous ways. Try to identify every feature of the military chaplaincy program that would violate the Constitution under civilian conditions. Do you agree that the military context requires a different result? Why or why not?

2. Other Religious Accommodations in Prison Settings. Chaplaincy programs are one example of accommodations of religion in highly institutionalized settings like prisons or the military. Consider two other examples:

(a) RLUIPA. Recall that in Cutter v. Wilkinson (p. 239), the Court upheld the constitutionality of section 3 of the Religious Land Use and Institutionalized Persons Act (RLUIPA), which requires state prisons to refrain from imposing substantial burdens on prisoners' religious exercise unless the burden is supported by a compelling interest such as order or security. The Court noted that the statute "does not require a State to pay for an inmate's devotional accessories," giving Islamic prayer oil as an example. But as *Katcoff* notes, the military pays for chaplains and religious buildings. And prisons that provide kosher diets may incur extra expense for doing so. Why are "devotional accessories" different, and what is the line between the two situations?

(b) Religious programs in prisons. Relying on some studies indicating the value of religion in rehabilitating people, a few states have experimented with "faith-based" wings of prisons, where inmates who volunteer for such a program participate in Bible studies and other Christian religious activities. See, e.g., Daniel Brook, When God Goes to Prison, Legal Affairs, May-June, 2003, at 28-29 (available at WL 2003-JUN LEGAFF 22). Is such a program supported by the analysis in *Katcoff*?

3. Problem: Determinations Concerning Child Custody or Adoption. Another situation in which the government's role is pervasive—in decision making if not in physical control—is determining where to place a child in a parental custody dispute or in an adoption. In these contexts the overwhelming consideration is the welfare or "best interests" of the child. To what extent does that standard override religious interests (of parents, for example) under the Free Exercise Clause? To what extent does it permit consideration of religion in ways that the Establishment Clause might otherwise forbid?

Barbara and Jeffrey Kendall were married for six years before their divorce proceedings, and had three children. When they were married, Barbara was Jewish and Jeffrey Roman Catholic; they agreed that their children would be raised Jewish, and the children attended Jewish schools. After a few years, Barbara became committed to Orthodox Judaism in particular, and Jeffrey converted to a fundamentalist Protestant church that teaches that those who do not believe the church's particular Christian beliefs are "damned to go to hell where there will be 'weeping and gnashing of teeth.'" Jeffrey stated these beliefs regularly to the children, took them to church services at which the doctrine was taught, and on one or two occasions ordered the oldest child (age eight) not to wear Jewish clothing or long sideburns. Based on this evidence, the trial court, after awarding joint custody, placed restrictions on both parents sharing religious beliefs with the children in a manner that "substantially promotes . . . their alienation from either parent." The court specifically prohibited Jeffrey from taking the children to church "if it promotes rejection rather than acceptance of their mother and their own Jewish self-identity," or if the services include the message that people "who do not accept Jesus Christ as their lord and savior are destined to burn in hell." Are these restrictions consistent with the Free Exercise Clause? See Kendall v. Kendall, 426 Mass. 238, 687 N.E.2d 1228 (1997) (yes, under a standard of "clear evidence of substantial harm".)

4. Restrictions on Government-Supported Clergy. Return to the case of military or prison chaplains. Where the clergy are employees of the government, how much freedom do they have to determine for themselves how to carry on their religious functions? Is it constitutional to forbid government-paid chaplains to proselytize? What other restrictions on their ability to preach might be permissible? Consider the following case.

RIGDON v. PERRY

962 F. Supp. 150 (D.D.C. 1997)

SPORKIN, District Judge. . . .

II

UNDISPUTED FACTS

This lawsuit was precipitated by events surrounding the so-called "Project Life Postcard Campaign," in which the Catholic Church in the United States sought to speak with a unified voice urging Congress to override the President's veto of HR 1833, also known as the Partial Birth Abortion Ban Act. The campaign began on June 29, 1996 and was set to last "at least until the Congress votes on whether to override the President's veto." The Campaign consisted of Catholic priests throughout the country preaching to their parishioners against an abortion procedure known medically as intact dilation and evacuation, and colloquially as "partial birth abortion." Priests were encouraged to "ask their parishioners to sign postcards urging their U.S. Senators and Representatives to vote to override the President's veto."

On or about May 29, 1996, the Archdiocese for the Military Services sent a letter informing Catholic chaplains in the U.S. military of the Post Card Campaign. Among other things, the letter stated, "You might well consider asking your parishioners to be a part of this joint effort. I am sending you information and addresses of the appropriate legislators as well as a copy of the project postcard that you could copy and give to your parishioners to enlist their cooperation in these efforts on behalf of human life."

Apparently in response to a request by the Office of the Chief Chaplain, on June 5, 1996, an Air Force Judge Advocate General ("JAG") issued an opinion letter regarding participation in the Post Card Campaign by Air Force chaplains. The JAG stated, "We believe that the applicable directives prohibit you from participating in this campaign or encouraging other Air Force chaplains or members to participate in it." The JAG's stated reasons were three-fold. First, he cited a Department of Defense Directive and an Air Force regulation prohibiting a member on active duty from using "his official authority or influence for soliciting votes for a particular issue." Second, the memorandum cited an Air Force regulation that prohibits a member on active duty from participating in partisan political activity, defined to include "supporting issues identified with national political parties or ancillary organizations." Third, the memorandum cited a DoD Instruction which provides that an "Air Force member may not participate in political activities while on duty; while wearing a uniform, badge insignia or other similar item that identifies his position; or while in any building occupied in the discharge of official duties by an individual employed by the United States Government."

On June 21, 1996, a memorandum from Navy Deputy Chief of Chaplains A. B. Holderby, Jr. to staff chaplains stated that members on active duty may not use "their official position to solicit votes for a particular candidate or issue." It further stated that "[a]nti-lobbying laws prohibit government employees from using appropriated funds to directly or indirectly influence congressional action on pending legislation." Therefore, the memorandum instructed, Navy personnel may not "officially participate or urge others to participate in" the Post Card Campaign. The memorandum specifically instructed that "[n]o one acting in an official capacity may distribute post-cards or use government resources such as congregation newsletters to publicize the campaign." However, these restrictions would not preclude chaplains from "discuss[ing] the morality of current issues in their sermons or religious teachings pursuant to their religion." Additionally, members were not restricted from communicating with members of Congress in their "personal or private capacities." . . .

B. The Plaintiffs

Plaintiff Father Rigdon holds the rank of Lieutenant Colonel in the Air Force. He is a Roman Catholic chaplain in the Ready Reserve who provides Catholic Coverage at Andrews Air Force Base, which means that he is available to fill in for the regular chaplain on short notice to say mass, hear confession, or provide counseling. He provides such coverage at least twenty days per year. Upon receiving the May 29 letter regarding the "Project Life Postcard Campaign" from the Military Archdiocese, Father Rigdon "considered [it] to be a directive from [his] bishop concerning the content of [his] preaching," a directive that his conscience as well as Canon 768 of the Catholic Code of Canon Law required him to follow. According to Father Rigdon's declaration submitted on November 8, 1996, the "Air Force memorandum issued in June created a conflict of conscience between the demands of [his] faith and [his] desire to conform to military directives."

The military directives prevailed in Father Rigdon's mind. While on active duty during the last three days of the Post Card campaign in September, Father Rigdon did not feel "free . . . to preach[ ] in favor of overriding the President's veto and distribute[ ] postcards." Further, he interpreted and continues to interpret the "encourage other[s] to participate" language contained in the Judge Advocate General opinion as prohibiting him from encouraging others to write to Congress "in all contexts, including private counseling of Air Force members as well as urging them to write their members of Congress in a homily." He further interprets the opinion as barring him from urging Air Force personnel [to] contac[t] Congress about any legislative issue, not just the Partial Birth Abortion Bar Act. Consequently, Father Rigdon was and continues to be "wary of addressing moral issues that intersect with legislation in homilies or counseling for fear of disciplinary action" against him. Father Rigdon notes that the Project Life Postcard Campaign was not the first such campaign sponsored by the Roman Catholic Church and "surely will not be the last."

In his declaration submitted on March 25, 1997 in support of his motion for preliminary injunction, Father Rigdon states that the Partial Birth Abortion Ban Act, which failed to become law in the 104th Congress, has been reintroduced in the 105th Congress and has already passed the House of Representatives. He further notes,

> If called upon to say Mass at Andrews Air Force Base, I would like to encourage my congregation to call or write their Senators in support of this bill. Because of the Memoranda issued by the Air Force last June, and the position articulated by the Defendants since then, I am afraid to speak to my congregation about the Partial Birth Abortion Ban Act for fear of prosecution or other action against me.

Plaintiff Rabbi Kaye is an active duty Air Force chaplain stationed at Offutt Air Force Base in Nebraska and currently holds the rank of Captain. According to Rabbi Kaye, "it is impossible, indeed incoherent, to separate moral teachings from Judaism. And when a law is immoral [he] believe[s] that as a Rabbi [he] must not remain silent." Thus, Rabbi Kaye believes that he must be able to speak out against or in favor of legislation concerning what he considers to be immoral practices, including "partial birth" abortion, euthanasia, and "various forms of sexual immorality."[5]

There is no dispute that the military continues to prohibit military chaplains from encouraging their military congregants to contact Congress in favor of the Partial Birth Abortion Ban Act. There also is no dispute that the existence of the military chaplaincy is critical to fulfilling the free exercise rights of service men and women and their families, and that service members are forced to rely exclusively on chaplains when stationed in parts of the country in regions where clergy of their faith are not available, in countries overseas where religious freedom is not recognized or their religion not prevalent, and when deployed in conflicts. The defendants merely contend that the anti-lobbying restrictions on preaching and counseling by military chaplains (which also apply to all other service members) advance the compelling interests of a politically disinterested military establishment, the good order and discipline of service members essential to military readiness and national defense, and the protection of the political rights of individual service members.

III

DISCUSSION

[The case arose under the Religious Freedom Restoration Act.] The next question is whether the substantial burden on the plaintiffs' free exercise rights is the least restrictive means of furthering a compelling governmental interest. The defendants argue that the anti-lobbying restriction is "meant to maintain a politically disinterested military establishment under civilian control . . . serv[ing] both the stability of our democratic political system and the ability of the military to focus on its mission of military readiness and national defense." Also, these restrictions purportedly prevent "attempts to influence

---

5. There are several other plaintiffs in this lawsuit. Plaintiff Muslim American Military Association ("MAMA") consists of service members in all the branches of the Armed Services. Ghayth Nur Kashif is Imam of the MAMA. He claims that the Quran requires a Muslim to give alms to the poor. According to him, if Congress "is considering welfare reform, as it did this [past] summer, a Muslim Chaplain should be free to tell his Congregants how this command of the Quran should affect their view of welfare reform, and he should be free to tell them if they have an obligation to contact their Congressman." Other than this hypothetical situation, the Imam does not indicate that he or any other Muslim chaplain in the military ever desired to tell his congregants to urge Congress to vote in favor of the Partial Birth Abortion Ban Act, but did not do so due to the military regulations at issue herein. Because at least one of the plaintiffs' claims are justiciable (Rabbi Kaye's), the Court need not address the justiciability of the MAMA's claims.

The two other plaintiffs are Liam Downes, a Third Class Petty Officer in the Navy, and his wife, Karen, both of whom are Roman Catholics and who are parishioners of the Naval Academy Chapel. They assert that the defendants' actions interfere with their right to receive information pertaining to moral issues during religious services and individual counseling from their priest. . . . As noted above, the Court need not address the justiciability of these plaintiffs' claims, because Rabbi Kaye's claims are justiciable. Therefore, the plaintiffs' motion to amend shall be denied as moot.

the political activities of others ... [and] undue interference in individual service members' rights to participate in their personal capacities in the political process." According to the defendants, these ends would not be served "if each chaplain were permitted to turn his or her ministry into a political action forum. Political conflicts within the service ranks could easily arise from different religions or denominations instructing their members to lobby differently from one another on particular political issues."

A politically-disinterested military, good order and discipline, and the protection of service members' rights to participate in the political process are compelling governmental interests, but the defendants have not shown how these interests are in any way furthered by the restriction on the speech of military chaplains. Relying on nothing more than what they claim is "common sense," the defendants assert that if service people receive different religious counsel on lobbying, "[p]olitical conflicts" will result. They further assert that "[c]onflicts of this nature could severely undermine military discipline, cohesion, and readiness to the serious detriment of the National Security."

It is difficult to understand why the defendants have singled out for proscription a seemingly innocuous request to congregants to write to Congress. There is no suggestion that Rabbi Kaye or Father Rigdon wish to have their congregants "proselytize" their fellow soldiers on the morality of a piece of abortion legislation or encourage their fellow troops to contact Congress. While this Court should be deferential to what the defendants "perceive[ ] to be a clear danger to the loyalty, discipline, or morale of troops," the defendants have failed to submit any evidence showing how Rabbi Kaye's or Father Rigdon's contemplated speech would in any way enhance a potential for "political conflicts" that the defendants already tolerate, let alone create a clear danger to the loyalty, discipline or morale of the troops.

Recently, this Circuit held under the RFRA that the federal government's interest in eradicating sex discrimination—a compelling governmental interest—was outweighed by a religious university's right to autonomy in its employment of ministers. See EEOC v. Catholic Univ. (D.C. Cir. 1996). Here, the compelling interests advanced by the military are outweighed by the military chaplains' right to autonomy in determining the religious content of their sermons, especially because the defendants have failed to show how the speech restriction as applied to chaplains advances these interests.

IV

CONCLUSION

What we have here is the government's attempt to override the Constitution and the laws of the land by a directive that clearly interferes with military chaplains' free exercise and free speech rights, as well as those of their congregants. On its face, this is a drastic act and can be sanctioned only by compelling circumstances. The government clearly has not met its burden. The "speech" that the plaintiffs intend to employ to inform their congregants of their religious obligations has nothing to do with their role in the military. They are neither being disrespectful to the Armed Forces nor in any way urging their congregants to defy military orders. The chaplains in this case seek to preach only what they would tell their non-military congregants. There is no need for heavy-handed censorship, and any attempt to impinge on the plaintiffs' constitutional and legal rights is not acceptable.

NOTES AND QUESTIONS

1. Problems: Restrictions on Chaplains.   What is the scope of the ruling in *Rigdon*? To what extent can "military morale" or "prison security" be the basis for restricting chaplains' religious speech and exercise?

(a) What if a military chaplain begins preaching that killing, even in warfare, is sinful? According to a 2001 press report, a Muslim chaplain in the Army sought a *fatwa* (legal opinion) from Islamic clerics in the Arab world on whether Muslim soldiers could participate in the U.S. war against the Taliban. Ultimately the clerics answered that Muslim soldiers could not participate. Can the chaplain be disciplined as a result of this set of facts? Could he be disciplined simply for making the request of these clerics, even if they had authorized participation?

(b) What if a prison or military chaplain begins preaching race hatred? What if an evangelical Christian chaplain preaches that non-believers will go to hell when they die? Are these issues legally analogous? Recently an evangelical Protestant Navy chaplain, preaching a funeral sermon for a deceased sailor, told the audience that he had led the sailor to a "born-again experience" before the latter's death; the chaplain stated "that the sailor was certainly in heaven and 'mentioned in passing' that according to John 3:36, those who do not accept Jesus are doomed for eternity." Alan Cooperman, Military Wrestles With Disharmony Among Chaplains, Wash. Post, Aug. 30, 2005, at A01. The chaplain was reprimanded for his sermon. Was that discipline required by the Establishment Clause? Was it forbidden by RFRA or the Free Exercise or Free Speech clauses?

A number of evangelical chaplains in the military claim that they have been discouraged from, or threatened with discipline for, praying in the name of Jesus in settings where soldiers of other faiths may be present. See e.g., Julia Duin, Military Chaplains Told to Shy from Jesus, Wash. Times, Dec. 21, 2005. Would such a restriction be required—or permissible? If chaplains are required to be "ecumenical" and not "proselytize," how is the line between acceptable and unacceptable activity to be drawn and enforced?

(c) How far can prison or military officials go in ensuring that chaplains do not threaten order or security with their sermons? The issue has arisen recently concerning chaplains allegedly inciting rebellion by preaching radical Islamic ideas to prisoners and servicemen. Can prison or military officials conduct surveillance of religious services? Can they conduct surveillance of a chaplain's sermons off-base or outside the prisons? Can they refuse ahead of time to accept for service any chaplain with a suspected tie to a radical group? See, e.g., Shannon McMahon, U.S. Defense Officials Seek Other Groups to Certify Chaplains, Chi. Trib., Oct. 15, 2003.

2. Chaplaincies and the Purposes of Disestablishment.   How can religious autonomy be reconciled to government employment? Recall the Baptists' argument against governmental financial support for clergy (p. 28):

> If, therefore, the State provide a Support for Preachers of the Gospel, and they receive it in Consideration of their Services, they must certainly when they Preach act as Officers of the State, and ought to be Accountable thereto for their Conduct, not only as Members of civil Society, but also *as Preachers*. The Consequence of this is, that those whom the State employs in its Service it has a Right to *regulate* and *dictate to*; it may judge and determine *who* shall preach; *when* and *where* they shall preach; and *what* they must preach.

Declaration of the Virginia Association of Baptists (Dec. 25, 1776), in 1 The Papers of Thomas Jefferson 660-661 (J. Boyd ed., 1950) (emphases in original). Does Judge Sporkin's opinion demonstrate that the Baptists were wrong? Do the various controversies involving chaplains demonstrate that the Baptists were right?

D. INSTITUTIONAL RELIGION

"Religion," Justice Douglas once observed, "is an individual experience." Wisconsin v. Yoder, 406 U.S. 205, 243 (1972) (Douglas, J., dissenting). Not everyone sees it this way. For many people religion is a group activity. People form communities of faith, worship God together, agree on creeds, instruct and correct each other, recruit new members, and so on. This is not just a matter of sociability; it is often built into the structure of their beliefs. Jewish law requires the presence of ten men (a minyan) for the conduct of prayer services. Roman Catholic canon law provides that unless there is a good reason a priest must not celebrate Mass without the participation of at least one of the faithful. As Justice Brennan once wrote:

> "Religion includes important communal elements for most believers. They exercise their religion through religious organizations, and these organizations must be protected by the [Free Exercise] [C]lause." For many individuals, religious activity derives meaning in large measure from participation in a larger religious community. Such a community represents an ongoing tradition of shared beliefs, an organic entity not reducible to a mere aggregation of individuals.

Corporation of Presiding Bishop v. Amos, 483 U.S. 327, 341-342 (1987) (concurring in the judgment) (quoting Douglas Laycock, Towards a General Theory of the Religion Clauses: The Case of Church Labor Relations and the Right to Church Autonomy, 81 Colum. L. Rev. 1373, 1389 (1981)).

Of course we may think of religious groups as associations of individuals. Part of the individual experience Justice Douglas spoke of may be the freedom of religious association—voluntarily joining with like-minded believers. This approach fits well with some Protestant forms of ecclesiology. Others maintain that the religious congregation is *not* just an association of individuals. It is instead an irreducible whole—the basic unit of religious life. Consider the Christian theologian Rudolf Bultmann's description of the church's role in the process of salvation: "Not the individual but the 'church' is called, to it belongs the promise. [T]he individual . . . finds deliverance, but only because he belongs to the . . . community, not because of his personality." Jesus and the Word 47 (1958).

Religious groups are organized in many different ways. The Church of Jesus Christ of Latter Day Saints has a well articulated structure drawn from scriptural models. In setting up this structure the Church is guided by rules internal to the practice of religion: There are apostles, bishops, and so on. (Just as, in setting up a baseball team, the Chicago Cubs are guided by rules internal to the game of baseball: They have a pitcher, shortstop, etc.) But if the Church wants to own property, make contracts, receive gifts, run hospitals and schools, and so on, it may have to organize in a different way under state law. A local church might, for example, have to become a corporation because state law does not permit unincorporated associations to own land.

There is a scene in the movie *Mrs. Doubtfire* where Robin Williams, playing two different characters, has dinner at two tables in the same restaurant. At one table he sits with his ex-wife and children in the guise of Mrs. Doubtfire; at another he negotiates a TV contract in propria persona. As you might suppose, he gets confused running back and forth, with unhappy consequences at both tables. Religious groups that have to operate in two different organizational forms can face problems of this sort.

1. Formation of Churches

a. Religious Structures

Let us begin by looking at the kinds of groups that religious actors may create. Speaking mainly of Christian churches, the Supreme Court has suggested that they may be divided into two categories: congregational and hierarchical.

Congregational churches are autonomous local units subject to no higher ecclesiastical authority. Decisions within such churches are made by a majority of the members of the congregation, or else by some local organism set up for the purpose. Watson v. Jones, 80 U.S. (13 Wall.) 679, 722-727 (1872). Baptists, Disciples of Christ, Quakers, Unitarians, and some Lutheran churches are good examples. Baptists maintain, for example, that local churches have final authority on matters of church doctrine and law. Though local churches may join together in regional and national organizations like the Southern Baptist Convention, the association is a loose one. Churches send "messengers," not "delegates." Within local churches power rests with the members—those who have been baptized. And in cases where members cannot all agree, the majority rules.

These principles of organization are closely tied to religious beliefs. The small, self-governing local church has a parallel in the first century Christian community at Corinth to which Paul addressed two of his letters. Authority resides with the local church members because Baptists believe that Jesus speaks to all the faithful, without the need for an intermediary. Majority rule is religiously sensible because "[d]iscerning the leading of the Spirit takes time and sensitivity, and a group may fail to reach agreement." In that case the sentiment of the majority is the best approximation to God's will. Normal H. Maring and Winthrop S. Hudson, A Baptist Manual of Polity and Practice chs. 3-5 (rev. ed. 1991).

The Supreme Court has defined hierarchical churches "as those organized as a body with other churches having similar faith and doctrine with a common ruling convocation or ecclesiastical head." Kedroff v. St. Nicholas Cathedral, 344 U.S. 94, 110 (1952). We might gain a little clarity by subdividing this group into episcopal and presbyterial forms. In hierarchical churches that are episcopal in form, local congregations are under the control of higher church authorities, and clerical superiors play a significant role. The Russian Orthodox Church involved in *Kedroff* is an example. So are the other Orthodox churches, Roman Catholics, Episcopalians, and some Lutheran and Brethren churches. The episcopal form, like others, is typically tied to religious beliefs. The Roman Catholic Church, for example, affirms that "[w]hen Christ instituted the Twelve, 'he constituted them in the form of a college or permanent assembly, at the head of which he placed Peter, chosen from among them.' . . . [S]o in like fashion the Roman Pontiff, Peter's successor, and the bishops, the successors of the apostles, are related with and united to one another." Catechism of the Catholic Church ¶880, at 233 (1994) (quotations omitted). "The bishops, as vicars and legates of Christ, govern the particular Churches assigned to them," but "[t]heir authority must be exercised in communion with the whole Church under the guidance of the Pope." *Id.* ¶¶894-895, at 236-237.

The presbyterial form of government (sometimes called associational, connectional, or synodal) also has hierarchical features, but it lies somewhere between the congregational and episcopal forms. Local congregations have more autonomy than, say, Catholic or Episcopalian parishes. But above them is an array of offices with more or less authority over matters of doctrine and discipline, to which local churches elect representatives both lay and clerical. The Presbyterian Church (U.S.A.) is a good example. The local church is governed by the session, which consists of the pastor (the minister) and the ruling elders (elected by the laity of the congregation). Above the session in authority is the presbytery, made up of ministers and ruling elders from each church in a geographic area. This is, practically speaking, the principal governing body in the Presbyterian Church. Presbyteries in turn are united into synods. At the highest level is the General Assembly, a national body made up of equal delegations of pastors and elders from each presbytery. See The Constitution of the Presbyterian Church (U.S.A.), Part II: Book of Order §§ G-9.0000-G13.0200. There are no worldwide authorities. Other churches organized along these lines are the Assemblies of God and some Reformed churches.

b. Secular Structures

The organizational forms we have described have religious origins and objectives. The Third Street Baptist Church is organized as it is because, the congregation believes, that is how Jesus set up his church and it is the most effective way to do God's work. The church's religious structure is governed by religious rules drawn from sources like the Bible. But a loose group of several hundred people (the number changing every year) is not the best organization for holding title to real estate, making contracts, suing and being sued, limiting liability, and so on. How do religious groups organize to accomplish these objectives? Here the church must look to civil rules found in state law.

1. Unincorporated Association.   One approach is to form an unincorporated association, like a labor union or a political club. There used to be real disadvantages to this form. At common law an unincorporated association could not take title to real estate nor bring suit as an entity. About half of the 50 states now have statutes recognizing unincorporated religious associations. Members of a congregation adopt articles of association and bylaws, and elect a board of directors (or trustees) to manage the association's affairs. The trustees hold property for the benefit of the association. Paul G. Kauper and Stephen C. Ellis, Religious Corporations and the Law, 71 Mich. L. Rev. 1499, 1541-1542 (1973). There are also provisions, like those in the Federal Rules of Civil Procedure (Rule 17(b)), authorizing associations to sue and be sued in their common name.

2. Trustee Corporation.   The earliest statutory form of ecclesiastical corporation in the United States was the trustee corporation, an approach now used sparingly. See generally Carl Zollman, American Church Law §§ 105-116, 233-261 (1917). The trustees in such a corporation are an entity unto themselves and may make contracts and otherwise bind the corporation. This may work well in a hierarchical church where the bishop is himself a trustee. But it creates problems for hierarchical churches with lay trustees, and for congregational churches where the trustees are separate from the congregation. For example, the trusteeship form led to conflicts in a number of states between Roman Catholic lay trustees and their bishops over control of church property and the right to choose priests or vicars. See Patrick W. Carey, People, Priests, and Prelates: Ecclesiastical Democracy and the Tensions of Trusteeism (U. Notre Dame Press 1987). For a three-year period, the Bishop of New Orleans and the lay trustees of the Cathedral Church of St. Louis could not agree on the appointment of a vicar for the church. The trustees, who controlled the property, refused to allow the bishop's appointee to serve, and the bishop, in retaliation, ordered the priests not to conduct services in the church. The Louisiana Supreme Court declined to intervene, and ultimately the bishop prevailed. Wardens of the Church of St. Louis v. Blanc, 8 Rob. 51, 1844 WL 1490, *1 (La. 1844). Similar controversies broke out in New York, Philadelphia, Norfolk, Charleston, and Buffalo. Can you see why American property law, shaped by the predominant American Protestant model, encouraged the trustees in these controversies?

3. Membership Corporation.   The solution to such difficulties that has proven most popular is the creation of a membership corporation. It is a form of organization available in 43 jurisdictions. The membership of the corporation is defined by the constitution or bylaws, and usually consists of the congregation itself. There is a board of directors, and they are sometimes called trustees, but property is owned by the corporation itself; the trustees are managers rather than owners. The Model Nonprofit Corporation Act provides a relatively familiar procedure that can be specifically adapted to religious corporations. See MNPCA § 1.40(30) (1988). This rather democratic form is well suited for congregational polities. Kauper and Ellis, 71 Mich. L. Rev. at 1539-1540, 1554-1557.

It may be adapted for hierarchical churches, though, by limiting membership rights to a few people who exercise ecclesiastical authority. Adam J. Maida and Nicholas P. Cafardi, Church Property, Church Finances, and Church-Related Corporations 129 (1983).

4. Corporation Sole.   A different kind of solution more plainly adapted for hierarchical churches is the formation of a corporation sole. As its name suggests, this is a one-person operation. It incorporates an office and vests power in the individual holding the office, for example, the Corporation of the Presiding Bishop of The Church of Jesus Christ of Latter-Day Saints, or the Catholic Bishop of Chicago. Corporation of Presiding Bishop v. Amos, 483 U.S. 327, 330 & n.3 (1987); NLRB v. Catholic Bishop of Chicago, 440 U.S. 490, 492 (1979).

c. First Amendment Concerns

A corporate charter is a grant of authority from the state that confers certain powers on the entity it creates. Nowadays it is a relatively easy thing to secure. One simply files papers with the secretary of state and pays a modest fee. A charter was harder to get when the First Amendment was adopted. It required an act of the legislature. Does the act of incorporation pose constitutional difficulties? Consider the opinions of Joseph Story and James Madison.

TERRETT v. TAYLOR
13 U.S. (9 Cranch) 43 (1815)

STORY, J. delivered the opinion of the Court as follows:

At a very early period the religious establishment of England seems to have been adopted in the colony of Virginia; and, of course, the common law upon that subject, so far as it was applicable to the circumstances of that colony. The local division into parishes for ecclesiastical purposes can be very early traced; and the subsequent laws enacted for religious purposes evidently presuppose the existence of the Episcopal church with its general rights and authorities growing out of the common law. What those rights and authorities are, need not be minutely stated. It is sufficient that, among other things, the church was capable of receiving endowments of land, and that the minister of the parish was, during his incumbency, seized of the freehold of its inheritable property, as emphatically persona ecclesiae, and capable, as a sole corporation, of transmitting that inheritance to his successors. The church wardens, also, were a corporate body clothed with authority and guardianship over the repairs of the church and its personal property; and the other temporal concerns of the parish were submitted to a vestry composed of persons selected for that purpose. In order more effectually to cherish and support religious institutions, and to define the authorities and rights of the Episcopal officers, the legislature, from time to time, enacted laws on this subject. . . .

Such were some of the rights and powers of the Episcopal church at the time of the American revolution; and under the authority thereof the purchase of the lands stated in the bill before the Court, was undoubtedly made. And the property so acquired by the church remained unimpaired, notwithstanding the revolution; for the statute of 1776, ch. 2, completely confirmed and established the rights of the church to all its lands and other property.

The stat. 1784, ch. 88, proceeded yet further. It expressly made the minister and vestry, and, in case of a vacancy, the vestry of each parish respectively, and their successors forever, a corporation by the name of the Protestant Episcopal church in the parish where they respectively resided, to have, hold, use and enjoy all the glebes, churches and chapels, burying-grounds, books, plate and ornaments appropriated to the use of, and every other thing the property of the late Episcopal church, to the sole use and benefit of the corporation. The same statute also provided for the choice of new vestries, and repealed all former laws relating to vestries and church wardens, and to the support of the clergy, &c. and dissolved all former vestries; and gave the corporation extensive powers as to the purchasing, holding, aliening, repairing and regulating [of] the church property. This statute was repealed by the statute of 1786, ch. 12, with a proviso saving to all religious societies the property to them respectively belonging, and authorizing them to appoint, from time to time, according to the rules of their sect, trustees who should be capable of managing and applying such property to the religious use of such societies; and the statute of 1788, ch. 47, declared that the trustees appointed in the several parishes to take care of and manage the property of the Protestant Episcopal church, and their successors, should, to all intents and purposes, be considered as the successors to the former vestries, with the same powers of holding and managing all the property formerly vested in them. All these statutes, from that of 1776, ch. 2, to that of 1788, ch. 47, and several others, were repealed by the statute of 1798, ch. 9, as inconsistent with the principles of the constitution and of religious freedom; and by the statute of 1801, ch. 5 (which was passed after the district of Columbia was finally separated from the states of Maryland and Virginia), the legislature asserted their right to all the property of the Episcopal churches in the respective parishes of the state; and, among other things, directed and authorized the overseers of the poor, and their successors in each parish wherein any glebe land was vacant or should become so, to sell the same and appropriate the proceeds to the use of the poor of the parish.

It is under this last statute that the bill charges the Defendants (who are overseers of the poor of the parish of Fairfax) with claiming a title to dispose of the land in controversy.

This summary view of so much of the Virginia statutes as bears directly on the subject in controversy, presents not only a most extraordinary diversity of opinion in the legislature as to the nature and property of aid in the temporal concerns of religion, but the more embarrassing considerations of the constitutional character and efficacy of those laws touching the rights and property of the Episcopal church.

It is conceded on all sides that, at the revolution, the Episcopal church no longer retained its character as an exclusive religious establishment. And there can be no doubt that it was competent to the people and to the legislature to deprive it of its superiority over other religious sects, and to withhold from it any support by public taxation. But, although it may be true that "religion can be directed only by reason and conviction, not by force or violence," and that "all men are equally entitled to the free exercise of religion according to the dictates of conscience," as the bill of rights of Virginia declares, yet it is difficult to perceive how it follows as a consequence that the legislature may not enact laws more effectually to enable all sects to accomplish the great objects of religion by giving them corporate rights for the management of their property, and the regulation of their temporal as well as spiritual concerns. Consistent with the constitution of Virginia the legislature could not create or continue a religious establishment which should have exclusive rights and prerogatives, or compel the citizens to worship under a stipulated form or discipline, or to pay taxes to those whose creed they could not conscientiously believe. But the free exercise of religion cannot be justly deemed to be restrained by aiding with equal attention the votaries of every sect to perform their own religious duties, or by establishing funds for the support of ministers, for public charities, for the endowment of churches, or for the sepulture of the dead. And that these purposes could be better secured and cherished by corporate powers, cannot be doubted by any person who has attended to the difficulties which surround all voluntary associations. While, therefore, the legislature might exempt the citizens from a compulsive attendance and payment of taxes in support of any particular sect, it is not perceived that either public or constitutional principles required the abolition of all religious corporations. . . .

How far the statute of 1786, ch. 12, repealing the statute of 1784, ch. 88, incorporating the Episcopal churches, and the subsequent statutes in furtherance thereof of 1788, ch. 47, and ch. 53, were consistent with the principles of civil right or the constitution of Virginia, is a subject of much delicacy, and perhaps not without difficulty. It is observable, however, that they reserve to the churches all their corporate property, and authorize the appointment of trustees to manage the same. . . . In respect . . . to public corporations which exist only for public purposes, such as counties, towns, cities, &c. the legislature may, under proper limitations, have a right to change, modify, enlarge or restrain them, securing however, the property for the uses of those for whom and at whose expense it was originally purchased. But that the legislature can repeal statutes creating private corporations, or confirming to them property already acquired under the faith of previous laws, and by such repeal can vest the property of such corporations exclusively in the state, or dispose of the same to such purposes as they may please, without the consent or default of the corporators, we are not prepared to admit; and we think ourselves standing upon the principles of natural justice, upon the fundamental laws of every free government, upon the spirit and the letter of the constitution of the United States, and upon the decisions of most respectable judicial tribunals, in resisting such a doctrine. The statutes of 1798 Ch. 9, and of 1801, ch. 5, are not, therefore in our judgment, operative so far as to divest the Episcopal church of the property acquired, previous to the revolution, by purchase or by donation. In respect to the latter statute, there is this farther objection, that it passed after the district of Columbia was taken under the exclusive jurisdiction of congress, and as to the corporations and property within that district, the right of Virginia to legislate no longer existed.

In 1811 Congress passed a bill incorporating the Protestant Episcopal Church in the Town of Alexandria in the District of Columbia. President Madison vetoed the bill. Here is the message that accompanied his veto.

MADISON'S VETO MESSAGE
22 Annals of Congress 982-983 (1811)

To the House of Representatives of the United States:

Having examined and considered the bill, entitled "An Act Incorporating the Protestant Episcopal Church in the town of Alexandria, in the District of Columbia," I now return the bill to the House of Representatives, in which it originated, with the following objections:

Because the bill exceeds the rightful authority to which Governments are limited, by the essential distinction between civil and religious functions, and violates, in particular, the article of the Constitution of the United States, which declares, that "Congress shall make no law respecting a religious establishment." The bill enacts into, and establishes by law, sundry rules and proceedings relative purely to the organization and polity of the church incorporated, and comprehending even the election and removal of the Minister of the same; so that no change could be made therein by the particular society, or by the general church of which it is a member, and whose authority it recognises. This particular church, therefore, would so far be a religious establishment by law; a legal force and sanction being given to certain articles in its constitution and administration. Nor can it be considered, that the articles thus established are to be taken as the descriptive criteria only of the corporate identity of the society, inasmuch as this identity must depend on other characteristics; as the regulations established are generally unessential, and alterable according to the principles and canons, by which churches of that denomination govern themselves; and as the injunctions and prohibitions contained in the regulations, would be enforced by the penal consequences applicable to a violation of them according to the local law.

Because the bill vests in the said incorporated church an authority to provide for the support of the poor, and the education of poor children of the same; an authority which being altogether superfluous, if the provision is to be the result of pious charity, would be a precedent for giving to religious societies, as such, a legal agency in carrying into effect a public and civil duty.

[The House was unable to muster a two-thirds majority to override Madison's veto.]

NOTES AND QUESTIONS

1. Incorporation: Special Benefit or Baseline Right? In Madison's and Story's time a church generally needed the help of the legislature—a special act—to incorporate. Nowadays it can be done with the help of an executive or administrative agency—the office of the secretary of state. Does this have any bearing on whether incorporation violates the Establishment Clause? Does it matter that under the modern system it is so cheap and easy to get a charter that almost any religious (or nonreligious) group can have one? Does the constitutionality of incorporation practices turn on the kind of power a charter gives a church?

Madison asserts that it would be unconstitutional for Congress to authorize the incorporation of the Episcopal Church. Might we assert just the opposite today—that it would be a violation of religious freedom not to let a church incorporate, when businesses and nonprofit organizations are routinely allowed to? The Constitution of Virginia, art. IV, §14, says that "The General Assembly shall not grant a charter of incorporation to any church or religious denomination, but may secure the title to church property to an extent to be limited by law." Is that a forbidden discrimination against churches? Does the answer depend on how Virginia law otherwise treats churches—how it permits them to hold property, whether it provides any limitation on their liability, whether its tax laws treat them as advantageously as nonprofit corporations, and so on?

2. Corporate Forms Specifically for Religion.   A number of states have laws that create specific corporate forms for specific religious denominations. New York's Religious Corporations Law has separate provisions for several dozen denominations. Thus there are separate statutory sections for the Protestant Episcopal Church, the Orthodox Church, the Presbyterian Church, the Roman Catholic Church, the Rutherran Greek Catholic Church, the Dutch Reformed Church, Baptist churches, the Christian Science Church, the Church of the Nazarene—not to mention "Spiritualist Churches connected with the National Spiritualist Association." McKinney's Consol. Laws of N.Y., Book 50. Here is one of the provisions regarding Jewish congregations (§207):

> A congregation of the Jewish faith may at any general or special corporate meeting thereof change the number of its trustees to not more than seventy-two and classify them so that the terms of one-third shall expire each year and the trustees elected shall hold office for three years. . . . The right of the members of such congregation to vote at meetings thereof shall be fixed by its by-laws, but every member of such congregation entitled to vote at any meeting thereof may vote by proxy on any proposition to sell, mortgage or lease any of its property. . . .

Suppose that a state may constitutionally apply its general nonprofit corporation law to religious corporations. Do the Establishment Clause limits on accommodation (section III-C above) prevent the state from providing separately for religious corporations? For specific denominations? Why might a state want to do so? Suppose a particular Jewish congregation decides for religious reasons that members must be present to vote. Does §207 override that determination?

3. Corporate Law Restrictions.   Suppose that the First Amendment permits, if it does not require, a state to provide for the incorporation of churches. Are there further constraints on the type of corporation a state can authorize or require? Consider the following case, which enforces a Pennsylvania law requiring that church property be controlled by lay members of the congregation.

MAZAIKA v. KRAUCZUNAS
233 Pa. 138 (1911)

STEWART, J. Either the deliverances of this court, as reported in 221 Pa. 213 and 229 Pa. 476, with respect to the ownership of church property and congregational power in connection therewith, have been seriously misapprehended, or the present proceeding is a clear attempt to circumvent the law as we have there declared it. In the first of the cases referred to (Krauczunas v. Hoban), the effort was on the part of the 10 lay members of the congregation, duly chosen trustees of the legal title to the church property, to compel a reconveyance to them of the title by Bishop Hoban, who had previously been designated trustee of the title for a special purpose, which had been fully accomplished. The effort of these trustees was resisted, not on the ground that the congregation was without statutory right to choose its own trustee or trustees for the purpose indicated, or that the election of these particular trustees was in any way irregular, but distinctly on the ground that any such election, except as it resulted in the choice of the bishop of the diocese in which the property was located, offended against the rules and regulations of the Catholic Church. To make this clear, it is only necessary to quote a single finding of fact, and the conclusion derived therefrom, on which the lower court rested its dismissal of the plaintiffs' bill. The finding was as follows: "The canons of the Roman Catholic Church provide and require that the title to the property of the Roman Catholic Congregation which is under the jurisdiction of the Roman Catholic bishop of the diocese in which the congregation has its place of worship, must be in the ordinary, or, in the present case, in the bishop of the diocese." This was the conclusion derived: "If a congregation is formed for the purpose of religious worship according to the faith and rites of the Catholic Church, and has accepted the pastor assigned to it by the bishop of the diocese, has placed itself under the authority of the bishop and submitted itself to his authority in all ecclesiastical matters, the title to its property must be taken and held as provided by the canons of the Catholic Church. The property acquired by the congregation under such circumstances is the property of the church, and is subject to its control, and must be held in the manner directed by its laws. . . . The title to the real estate described in plaintiffs' bill is properly and legally vested in the defendant, Rt. Rev. Michael J. Hoban, Bishop of Scranton, as trustee for St. Joseph's Lithuanian Catholic Congregation, in accordance with the laws and usages of the Catholic Church." . . .

Nothing is asserted in this connection but ecclesiastical rules and regulations, which, except as they are aided by legal conveyance, are ineffectual to divest any owner of his property.

But more than this, the position taken by the defendant and sustained by the court is in direct opposition to the law, whose supremacy over all ecclesiastical rules and regulations, when rights of property are concerned, is not to be questioned. The act of April 26, 1855 § 7, provides that: "Whensoever any property, real or personal, shall hereafter be bequeathed, devised or conveyed to any ecclesiastical corporation, bishop, ecclesiastic, or other person, for the use of any church, congregation, or religious society, for religious worship or sepulture, or the maintenance of either, the same shall not be otherwise taken and held, or enure, than subject to the control and disposition of the lay members of such church, congregation, or religious society, or such constituted officers or representatives thereof," etc. We accordingly sustained the appeal, and ordered that Bishop Hoban reconvey the church property to the plaintiffs as trustees. It is to be remarked in this connection that these trustees, because of their attempt to vindicate their right under the law, had been excommunicated by the bishop.

Nevertheless, the bishop complied with the decree of the court, and made conveyance of the title; he followed it up, however, with an episcopal interdict which closed the doors of the church against the congregation. This interdict reads as follows: "The Members of St. Joseph's Congregation—Greeting: The court has decided that the Catholic bishop of Scranton must hand over to a band of excommunicated apostates the deed of the Catholic Church of St. Joseph's. As the church cannot be used for any other worship than Catholic worship, and as it is intolerable to hold Catholic services in a church controlled by members who despise the church and her laws, and who have lost their Catholic faith, I am exceedingly pained to be obliged to place the Lithuanian Catholic Church of St. Joseph's under interdict until the members of the congregation shall turn these faithless men out and place the church once more under the care of the bishop of the diocese of Scranton, according to the laws of the Catholic Church. I now declare that the Lithuanian Catholic Church of St. Joseph's, North Main avenue, in this city of Scranton, is hereby placed under interdiction from midnight of Sunday, May 31-June 1, 1908, and that no Catholic services of any kind shall be held therein, nor shall any Catholic enter therein without incurring ecclesiastical censure, until the interdict shall be removed. [Signed] Michael John Hoban, Bishop of Scranton."

Simultaneously with the proclamation of this edict, a meeting of the congregation was called, elsewhere than in the church, to determine how the title to the property was to be held. We are not now concerned with the factional differences which disturbed that meeting, and resulted in a separate meeting of the dissentients, except to say that the latter repudiated the action attempted at the meeting regularly called, and declined to reconvey the title to the bishop. The present bill was filed to enforce compliance. . . .

The resolution embodying the action of the meeting was as follows: "Whereas, it is deemed advisable and proper, and it is also the desire of the members of St. Joseph's Lithuanian Catholic Congregation of the city of Scranton, Pennsylvania, to vest the title to all the property of said St. Joseph's Lithuanian Catholic Congregation of the city of Scranton, Pennsylvania, in Rt. Rev. Michael J. Hoban, Bishop of Scranton, as trustee for said St. Joseph's Lithuanian Catholic Congregation, in accordance with the laws, rules and usages of the Catholic Church in the diocese of Scranton and state of Pennsylvania: Now, therefore, be it resolved, that all the property of said St. Joseph's Lithuanian Catholic Congregation is, and is hereby declared, subject to the jurisdiction of the Catholic Church and the Catholic bishop of Scranton; and be it further resolved, that Rt. Rev. Michael J. Hoban, Bishop of Scranton, be, and is hereby, chosen and designated trustee for said St. Joseph's Lithuanian Catholic Congregation of the city of Scranton, Pennsylvania, to hold as such trustee all the property of said congregation, and the title thereto in accordance with the laws, rules and usages of the Catholic Church in the diocese of Scranton and state of Pennsylvania."

The significance of the language here employed can be fully understood only as we recall what was said by this court in Krauczunas v. Hoban, *supra*, the language of the interdict of the bishop closely following upon our decision, and the rules and regulations of the Catholic Church with respect to the property of the congregation, as defined by Bishop Hoban in his testimony in the case. In the case referred to, we distinctly held that the case was one involving the right of property, and that the law governing was not to be found in the rules and regulations of the general ecclesiastical system, but in the statute of April 26, 1855[.] The contention of the bishop there was that he had a right to hold the title to the property under the Catholic system, virtute officii. This view having prevailed with the court below, we sustained the appeal, and expressly held that the position taken "is in direct opposition to the law whose supremacy over all ecclesiastical rules and regulations, when the rights of property are concerned, is not to be questioned."

We further held that the conveyance to the appellees in that case constituted an executed legal estate in the congregation, and created a dry, passive trust, which gave the trustees neither interest in the estate, nor power to control it or direct its management in any way; that trustees in such case become simply the depository of the legal title and nothing more. We refer in this connection to only so much of the interdict as decreed that it shall continue in force "until the members of the congregation shall turn out these faithless men [the acting trustees] and place the church once more under the care of the bishop of the diocese of Scranton according to the laws of the Catholic Church." We make no question here of the authority of the bishop under the rules of the church for this coercive decree. It was nevertheless a manifest attempt to deny to the congregation freedom of action with respect to property of which, under the law of the land, it was sole owner; notwithstanding, the bishop, as he himself asserts, was acting strictly in line with his episcopal duty and prerogative. He had testified that as bishop of the diocese he had control and disposition of the church property under the general laws of the church. He was asked: "Whether, under the ecclesiastical law of the Catholic Church, the lay members had the right of control and disposition of the property, or whether the bishop had the right." His answer was as follows: "Under the general law of the church, the lay people have not the right to control." He was again asked: "Under the law of the church, the ecclesiastical law, have the members of the church the right to hold the property as trustee for the congregation?" His answer was: "No; they have not." In this reflected light, we may see the real significance of the language used in the resolution declaring for the election of Rt. Rev. Bishop Hoban, "to hold as trustee all the property of said congregation and the title thereto in accordance with the laws, rules, and usages of the Catholic Church in the diocese of Scranton;" that is to say, even to a denial to the congregation of the chief incident of its ownership—control of the property which is its own under the laws of the state of Pennsylvania. In the case above cited, we took occasion to explain, in the hope that it would end this prolonged controversy, that a trust in such cases gives to the trustee neither interest in the estate, nor power to control it or direct its management in any way; that it creates no duty for the trustee to perform, and leaves nothing to his discretion; that he is simply the passive, silent depository of the legal title, and nothing more.

In view of the plain words of the statute thus called to their attention as to the exclusive right of property in the congregation, the unquestioned sovereignty of the law where rights of property are involved, the legal inhibition against the bishop, qua bishop, exercising control of the church property, the positive conflict in this respect between the rules and regulations of the Catholic Church and the statute laws of the state, what other conclusion can be reached than that the action of the meeting of the congregation, as expressed in the resolution we have referred to, and at which it is claimed Bishop Hoban was elected trustee, was a clear attempt to invest that particular ecclesiastic with an authority over the congregational property which the law expressly forbids? . . .

Let us make this plain, even though it be only to repeat: What the law does not expressly allow to such trustee, it forbids. The office of trustee simply of legal title is not created by ecclesiastical authority, but created by the law; such trustee can exercise no control whatever over the property held in trust; being an officer created by law, and answerable only to the law, he can derive neither authority nor power from any other source. His duties, privileges, authority and responsibility qua trustee can neither be enlarged nor impaired by ecclesiastical interference, and any attempt to so interfere would be quite as illegal as though forbidden in express terms. . . .

The decree of the court requiring the defendants to execute, acknowledge, and deliver a proper deed of the premises described in the plaintiff's bill held in trust by them for St. Joseph's Lithuanian Catholic Congregation of the city of Scranton to Rt. Rev. Michael J. Hoban, Bishop of Scranton, as trustee for St. Joseph's Lithuanian Catholic Congregation of the city of Scranton, is reversed, and it is ordered that the appellees pay the costs of this proceeding.

NOTES AND QUESTIONS

1. The History of the Dispute. The fight over control of St. Joseph's Church was prolonged. In 1892 the Lithuanian congregation organized as an unincorporated religious association. It bought some land in Scranton and took title in the names of several members of the association as trustees. In 1901 the congregation resolved, over some dissent, to convey the property to Bishop Hoban as trustee. In 1906 it decided, again over some dissent, to take it back and give it to ten lay trustees. The bishop objected that Roman Catholic canon law required him to hold title in his own name. The Pennsylvania Supreme Court, relying on the 1855 act, sided with the congregation. Krauczunas v. Hoban, 221 Pa. 213 (1908). The bishop then forbade Catholics to enter the church or to use it for Catholic services. In 1908 the pro-bishop faction tried again to wrest title from the trustees and convey it to the bishop. They held a meeting of the congregation, voted to give the bishop title, and sued to enforce that result. They lost again, after two more trips to the Supreme Court. The first was Mazaika v. Krauczunas, 229 Pa. 47 (1910). The second was this case.

The faction in control of the church then began inviting non-Catholic ministers to hold services there. The pro-bishop faction sued to enjoin this activity and lost again. It was, the court said, an effort "to accomplish indirectly that which we have repeatedly declared may not be done." Novickas v. Krauczunas, 240 Pa. 248, 255 (1913). The bishop finally gave in, rescinded his interdiction of the church, dropped his insistence that title be put in his name, and appointed a pastor. The opposition (preferring to keep the minister they had chosen in the interim) locked him out. The loyal faction sued again, and this time the Pennsylvania Supreme Court held in their favor. The 1855 law gave the congregation control of the property, but the congregation had no power to divert it from its original use. They held the property subject to an implied trust in favor of the Catholic Church. Novicky v. Krauczunas, 245 Pa. 86 (1914).

2. Which Law Governs: the Church's or the State's? The bishop claimed in the first three cases that under church (canon) law, once a parish accepted a priest and submitted itself to the bishop's authority, its property became the church's property, and title had to be held by the bishop. The court held that under Pennsylvania law the congregation retained control, and that church law was subordinate to state law. Why is this so? Why not treat Roman Catholic canon law like New York law, and *Mazaika* as a case about choice of law?

3. First Amendment Issues. The 1855 Pennsylvania law may require church property to be held by lay members, but can it survive under the First Amendment (once the amendment applies to the states)? What if any burden does the statute place on religious exercise by the Catholic Church? After the last decision in the series, Novicky v. Krauczunas, the party controlling the property can't do whatever it wants; it is subject to a trust in favor of the Catholic Church. But suppose instead that the faction opposing the bishop had won in *Novicky*. What leverage would this give other Catholic congregations in disagreements with their bishops? When might congregations want to use it? Now think about the situation after *Novicky*. Suppose St. Joseph's wanted the bishop to send A and not B as its priest. Does it have more bargaining power than it would if the bishop held title to the church? See Peter Guilday, The Catholic Church in Virginia (1815-1822) 5-7 (1924).

But perhaps this only looks at half of the equation: What about the religious exercise of the lay faction opposing the bishop? Would a ruling against them have interfered with their free exercise? Or would it simply, and appropriately, have left them subject to the rules of the Church of which they chose to be members?

Does the First Amendment have anything to say about state interference with the distribution of power within churches? Is there a free exercise problem even after Employment Division v. Smith?

The 1855 Pennsylvania statute was similar to laws passed in New York and Michigan the same year. The influx of Catholic immigrants to eastern cities in the 1840s had encouraged the growth of the Know Nothings, a nativist movement opposed to "foreign" influences. In 1854 the Know Nothings gained control of Massachusetts and Delaware, and had a fair degree of electoral success in New York and Pennsylvania. Their platform was openly anti-Catholic. Patrick J. Dignan, A History of the Legal Incorporation of Catholic Church Property in the United States (1784-1932) ch. 6 (1933). Should their influence have any bearing on the constitutionality of the 1855 act?

2. *Internal Church Disputes: Principles of Institutional Autonomy*

Let us now turn from problems attending the creation of churches to problems arising from disputes within churches. The most common legal questions have stemmed from church divisions—either a local parish breaking from its larger body, or a local congregation itself splitting into factions—and resulting disputes over who gets the church building and other property that the group once held in common. In a series of such cases, the Supreme Court has suggested two different ways of deciding who gets the property. The first is the rule of deference, articulated in the first case below, Watson v. Jones. The second is the rule of neutral principles, which we will explain later on.

The cases on church property disputes also declare some general principles concerning the constitutional autonomy of religious institutions. We therefore use this section to examine the foundations of institutional religious freedom. The idea of institutional religious autonomy also appears in cases involving another kind of "internal" dispute: that between a church and its clergy. We take a quick look at clergy disputes in this section, before examining them in more detail in section C-3, "Churches as Employers."

a. Church Property Disputes

WATSON v. JONES
80 U.S. 679 (1872)

[During the Civil War the General Assembly (the national body) of the Presbyterian Church steadfastly opposed the institution of slavery. In May 1865 the General Assembly instructed church Sessions, Presbyteries, and Synods that Southerners could not join the church or become ministers if they had fought in the war or approved of slavery, unless they first repented of these sins. This caused a division within the Walnut Street Presbyterian Church in Louisville, Kentucky, and in the Presbytery and Synod (the local and regional bodies) to which it belonged. Watson, a member of the Walnut Street Church Session (the governing body of a congregation), was a leader of the proslavery faction. His sentiments were shared by a majority of the Session; most of the congregation, by contrast, supported the action of the General Assembly. In 1867 the General Assembly held that the antislavery party were the true representatives of the Walnut Street church. It dropped Watson and another Session member who shared his views from the roll of elders. Watson disputed this action, claiming that the General Assembly had acted beyond its authority under the church constitution in cutting him off. Jones, an antislavery member of the Walnut Street church, brought this diversity action to enjoin Watson and his party from taking possession of the church. The circuit court held for Jones, and the Supreme Court affirmed.]

Mr. Justice MILLER now delivered the opinion of the court.

[The] questions which have come before the civil courts concerning the rights to property held by ecclesiastical bodies, may, so far as we have been able to examine them, be profitably classified under three general heads, which of course do not include cases governed by considerations applicable to a church established and supported by law as the religion of the state.

1. The first of these is when the property which is the subject of controversy has been, by the deed or will of the donor, or other instrument by which the property is held, by the express terms of the instrument devoted to the teaching, support, or spread of some specific form of religious doctrine or belief.

2. The second is when the property is held by a religious congregation which, by the nature of its organization, is strictly independent of other ecclesiastical associations, and so far as church government is concerned, owes no fealty or obligation to any higher authority.

3. The third is where the religious congregation or ecclesiastical body holding the property is but a subordinate member of some general church organization in which there are superior ecclesiastical tribunals with a general and ultimate power of control more or less complete, in some supreme judicatory over the whole membership of that general organization.

In regard to the first of these classes it seems hardly to admit of a rational doubt that an individual or an association of individuals may dedicate property by way of trust to the purpose of sustaining, supporting, and propagating definite religious doctrines or principles, provided that in doing so they violate no law of morality, and give to the instrument by which their purpose is evidenced, the formalities which the laws require. And it would seem also to be the obvious duty of the court, in a case properly made, to see that the property so dedicated is not diverted from the trust which is thus attached to its use. . . . This is the general doctrine of courts of equity as to charities, and it seems equally applicable to ecclesiastical matters.

. . . [T]hough the task may be a delicate one and a difficult one, it will be the duty of the court in such cases, when the doctrine to be taught or the form of worship to be used is definitely and clearly laid down, to inquire whether the party accused of violating the trust is holding or teaching a different doctrine, or using a form of worship which is so far variant as to defeat the declared objects of the trust. . . .

The second class of cases which we have described has reference to the case of a church of a strictly congregational or independent organization, governed solely within itself, either by a majority of its members or by such other local organism as it may have instituted for the purpose of ecclesiastical government; and to property held by such a church, either by way of purchase or donation, with no other specific trust attached to it in the hands of the church than that it is for the use of that congregation as a religious society.

In such cases where there is a schism which leads to a separation into distinct and conflicting bodies, the rights of such bodies to the use of the property must be determined by the ordinary principles which govern voluntary associations. If the principle of government in such cases is that the majority rules, then the numerical majority of members must control the right to the use of the property. If there be within the congregation officers in whom are vested the powers of such control, then those who adhere to the acknowledged organism by which the body is governed are entitled to the use of the property. . . . There being no [t]rust imposed upon the property when purchased or given, the court will not imply one for the purpose of expelling from its use those who by regular succession and order constitute the church, because they may have changed in some respect their views of religious truth. . . .

[The third class of cases involves] property acquired in any of the usual modes for the general use of a religious congregation which is itself part of a large and general organization of some religious denomination, with which it is more or less intimately connected by religious views and ecclesiastical government.

The case before us is one of this class, growing out of a schism which has divided the congregation and its officers, and the presbytery and synod, and which appeals to the courts to determine the right to the use of the property so acquired. Here is no case of property devoted forever by the instrument which conveyed it, or by any specific declaration of its owner, to the support of any special religious dogmas, or any peculiar form of worship, but of property purchased for the use of a religious congregation, and so long as any existing religious congregation can be ascertained to be that congregation, or its regular and legitimate successor, it is entitled to the use of the property. In the case of an independent congregation we have pointed out how this identity, or succession, is to be ascertained, but in cases of this character we are bound to look at the fact that the local congregation is itself but a member of a much larger and more important religious organization, and is under its government and control, and is bound by its orders and judgments. There are in the Presbyterian system of ecclesiastical government, in regular succession, the presbytery over the session or local church, the synod over the presbytery, and the General Assembly over all. These are called, in the language of the church organs, "judicatories," and they entertain appeals from the decisions of those below, and prescribe corrective measures in other cases.

In this class of cases we think the rule of action which should govern the civil courts, founded in a broad and sound view of the relations of church and state under our system of laws, and supported by a preponderating weight of judicial authority is, that, whenever the questions of discipline, or of faith, or ecclesiastical rule, custom, or law have been decided by the highest of these church judicatories to which the matter has been carried, the legal tribunals must accept such decisions as final, and as binding on them, in their application to the case before them.

[In this country the] right to organize voluntary religious associations to assist in the expression and dissemination of any religious doctrine, and to create tribunals for the decision of controverted questions of faith within the association, and for the ecclesiastical government of all the individual members, congregations, and officers within the general association, is unquestioned. All who unite themselves to such a body do so with an implied consent to this government, and are bound to submit to it. But it would be a vain consent and would lead to the total subversion of such religious bodies, if any one aggrieved by one of their decisions could appeal to the secular courts and have them reversed. It is of the essence of these religious unions, and of their right to establish tribunals for the decision of questions arising among themselves, that those decisions should be binding in all cases of ecclesiastical cognizance, subject only to such appeals as the organism itself provides for.

Nor do we see that justice would be likely to be promoted by submitting those decisions to review in the ordinary judicial tribunals. Each of these large and influential bodies (to mention no others, let reference be had to the Protestant Episcopal, the Methodist Episcopal, and the Presbyterian churches), has a body of constitutional and ecclesiastical law of its own, to be found in their written organic laws, their books of discipline, in their collections of precedents, in their usage and customs, which as to each constitute a system of ecclesiastical law and religious faith that tasks the ablest minds to become familiar with. It is not to be supposed that the judges of the civil courts can be as competent in the ecclesiastical law and religious faith of all these bodies as the ablest men in each are in reference to their own. It would therefore be an appeal from the more learned tribunal in the law which should decide the case, to one which is less so.

NOTES AND QUESTIONS

1. The First Amendment and Internal Church Disputes. *Watson* was decided in 1872, four years after ratification of the Fourteenth Amendment. The Supreme Court had not yet "incorporated" the First Amendment in the Fourteenth, so it did not apply to the states. Nor had the Court yet decided Erie Railroad Co. v. Tompkins, 304 U.S. 64 (1938)—it still felt free to apply general rules of federal common law in diversity cases. That is what it did in *Watson*. But in Kedroff v. St. Nicholas Cathedral, 344 U.S. 94 (1952), the Court suggested that the rule of deference might have a foundation in the Free Exercise Clause.

It is easy to see how these cases implicate First Amendment principles—the court is asked to turn a church over to one religious faction and prevent another from using it. But it seems as though a resolution either way limits someone's religious freedom. A decision in Watson's favor keeps Jones out; a decision in Jones's favor keeps Watson out. Why should the Free Exercise Clause require the latter result? Why doesn't the Establishment Clause forbid it? Arlin M. Adams and William R. Hanlon, Jones v. Wolf: Church Autonomy and the Religion Clauses of the First Amendment, 128 U. Pa. L. Rev. 1211, 1297 (1980). Is it because members of the Presbyterian Church have consented to abide by decisions of the General Assembly (as parties to a contract may agree to have their disputes resolved by an arbitrator)? How do members signify this consent? The Presbyterian Church practices infant baptism, so one can become a member without really meaning to. Does this undercut the contract theory?

In *Kedroff*, too, the Court held that the general church should prevail over a local dissident. By way of explanation it spoke of "freedom for religious organizations." The Court's meaning seemed to be "that the Church as a spiritual body has liberties [that] differ from those possessed by the members of the Church." Mark DeWolfe Howe, Foreword: Political Theory and the Nature of Liberty, 67 Harv. L. Rev. 91, 92 (1953). Does it make sense to think of a church as something more than the sum of its members? How can it have its own rights? Recall the religious perspectives on this question mentioned at the beginning of this section (p. 282).

2. The Limits of Deference. Should a court defer to *whatever* decision is handed down by the highest authority in the church? Suppose Watson offered to prove that the General Assembly had ignored its own rules of procedure in reaching its decision to drop him from the roll of elders. Suppose he offered to prove that Jones had lied to the General Assembly about Watson's beliefs concerning slavery. Suppose that Watson sold his minister a horse and the minister refused to pay, claiming the horse was lame. Would a court have to accept as binding a church tribunal's resolution of that dispute?

3. Difficulties with the Deference Approach. The Court in *Watson* divided the universe of churches into congregational and hierarchical. Each type had its own rule of deference—local majority rule in the first, rule by the highest church authority in the second. This is a rough but useful first approximation. But must we fit all church polities into these two forms, or are there structures for which we must invent still other rules? Suppose the Serbian Orthodox Church (a hierarchical organization) decided, during the chaos attending the partition of the former Yugoslavia, to grant a good deal of autonomy to its American dioceses, and that one of these then tried to pull away. Cf. *Serbian Eastern Orthodox Diocese v. Milivojevich* (p. 307). Or suppose that the Episcopal Church (another hierarchical church) wanted to experiment with a "traditional" parish, and so set up a congregation outside its usual lines of authority. *Watson* argues that the rule of deference keeps courts from deciding theological questions. But here the court must answer a theological question in order to decide which rule of deference to apply. How else might it proceed? Consider the following case.

JONES v. WOLF
443 U.S. 595 (1979)

[The Vineville Presbyterian Church of Macon, Georgia, was a member of the Presbyterian Church in the United States (PCUS), the Southern Presbyterian denomination. Like the northern Presbyterian body in Watson v. Jones, the PCUS had a generally hierarchical or connectional form of government, with actions of congregations subject to review and control by higher church courts—presbytery, synod, and General Assembly—set forth in the PCUS constitution.

In 1973, a majority of the congregation, together with their pastor, voted to separate from the PCUS over theological and social issues and to join a more conservative Presbyterian denomination. The vote was 164 to 94. The lawsuit was over who had the right to the church property, the majority or the minority.]

Mr. Justice BLACKMUN delivered the opinion of the Court. . . .

I

. . . The property at issue and on which the church is located . . . evidenced by conveyances to the "Trustees of [or 'for'] Vineville Presbyterian Church and their successors in office," or simply to the "Vineville Presbyterian Church." The funds used to acquire the property were contributed entirely by local church members. Pursuant to resolutions adopted by the congregation, the church repeatedly has borrowed money on the property. This indebtedness is evidenced by security deeds variously issued in the name of the "Trustees of the Vineville Presbyterian Church," or, again, simply the "Vineville Presbyterian Church."

. . . In response to the schism within the Vineville congregation, the Augusta-Macon Presbytery appointed a commission to investigate the dispute and, if possible, to resolve it. The commission eventually issued a written ruling declaring that the minority faction constituted "the true congregation of Vineville Presbyterian Church," and withdrawing from the majority faction "all authority to exercise office derived from the [PCUS]." The majority took no part in the commission's inquiry, and did not appeal its ruling to a higher PCUS tribunal.

Representatives of the minority faction . . . brought this class action in state court, seeking declaratory and injunctive orders establishing their right to exclusive possession and use of the Vineville church property as a member congregation of the PCUS. [The Georgia courts, purporting to apply "neutral principles of law" to the dispute, ruled for the majority.]

II

Georgia's approach to church property litigation has evolved in response to Presbyterian Church v. Hull Church (1969) (*Presbyterian Church I*). That case was a property dispute between the PCUS and two local Georgia churches that had withdrawn from the PCUS. The Georgia Supreme Court resolved the controversy by applying a theory of implied trust, whereby the property of a local church affiliated with a hierarchical church organization was deemed to be held in trust for the general church, provided the general church had not "substantially abandoned" the tenets of faith and practice as they existed at the time of affiliation. This Court reversed, holding that Georgia would have to find some other way of resolving church property disputes that did not draw the state courts into religious controversies. . . .

On remand, the Georgia Supreme Court concluded that, without the departure-from-doctrine element, the implied trust theory would have to be abandoned in its entirety. (*Presbyterian Church II.*) In its place, the court adopted what is now known as the "neutral principles of law" method for resolving church property disputes. The court examined the deeds to the properties, the state statutes dealing with implied trusts, and the Book of Church Order to determine whether there was any basis for a trust in favor of the general church. Finding nothing that would give rise to a trust in any of these documents, the court awarded the property on the basis of legal title, which was in the local church, or in the names of trustees for the local church. Review was again sought in this Court, but was denied.

The neutral-principles analysis was further refined by the Georgia Supreme Court in Carnes v. Smith (Ga. 1976). That case concerned a property dispute between The United Methodist Church and a local congregation that had withdrawn from that church. As in *Presbyterian Church II*, the court found no basis for a trust in favor of the general church in the deeds, the corporate charter, or the state statutes dealing with implied trusts. The court observed, however, that the constitution of The United Methodist Church, its Book of Discipline, contained an express trust provision in favor of the general church.[2] On this basis, the church property was awarded to the denominational church.

In the present case, the Georgia courts sought to apply the neutral-principles analysis of *Presbyterian Church II* and *Carnes* to the facts presented by the Vineville church controversy. Here, as in those two earlier cases, the deeds conveyed the property to the local church. Here, as in the earlier cases, neither the state statutes dealing with implied trusts, nor the corporate charter of the Vineville church, indicated that the general church had any interest in the property. And here, as in *Presbyterian Church II,* but in contrast to *Carnes*, the provisions of the constitution of the general church, the Book of Church Order, concerning the ownership and control of property failed to reveal any language of trust

---

2. The Book of Discipline of The United Methodist Church (1968) requires that

> title to all real property now owned or hereafter acquired by an unincorporated local church . . . shall be held by and/or conveyed and transferred to its duly elected trustees . . . and their successors in office . . . in trust, nevertheless, for the use and benefit of such local church *and of The United Methodist Church.* Every instrument of conveyance of real estate shall contain the appropriate trust clause as set forth in the Discipline (¶1503) (emphasis added). . . .

in favor of the general church. The courts accordingly held that legal title to the property of the Vineville church was vested in the local congregation. Without further analysis or elaboration, they further decreed that the local congregation was represented by the majority faction, respondents herein.

III

[The] primary advantages of the neutral-principles approach are that it is completely secular in operation, and yet flexible enough to accommodate all forms of religious organization and polity. The method relies exclusively on objective, well-established concepts of trust and property law familiar to lawyers and judges. It thereby promises to free civil courts completely from entanglement in questions of religious doctrine, polity, and practice. Furthermore, the neutral-principles analysis shares the peculiar genius of private-law systems in general—flexibility in ordering private rights and obligations to reflect the intentions of the parties. Through appropriate reversionary clauses and trust provisions, religious societies can specify what is to happen to church property in the event of a particular contingency, or what religious body will determine the ownership in the event of a schism or doctrinal controversy. In this manner, a religious organization can ensure that a dispute over the ownership of church property will be resolved in accord with the desires of the members.

This is not to say that the application of the neutral-principles approach is wholly free of difficulty. The neutral-principles method, at least as it has evolved in Georgia, requires a civil court to examine certain religious documents, such as a church constitution, for language of trust in favor of the general church. In undertaking such an examination, a civil court must take special care to scrutinize the document in purely secular terms, and not to rely on religious precepts in determining whether the document indicates that the parties have intended to create a trust. In addition, there may be cases where the deed, the corporate charter, or the constitution of the general church incorporates religious concepts in the provisions relating to the ownership of property. If in such a case the interpretation of the instruments of ownership would require the civil court to resolve a religious controversy, then the court must defer to the resolution of the doctrinal issue by the authoritative ecclesiastical body. . . .

IV

It remains to be determined whether the Georgia neutral-principles analysis was constitutionally applied on the facts of this case. Although both the trial court and the Supreme Court of Georgia viewed the case as involving nothing more than an application of the principles developed in *Presbyterian Church II* and in *Carnes*, the present case contains a significant complicating factor absent in each of those earlier cases. *Presbyterian Church II* and *Carnes* each involved a church property dispute between the general church and the entire local congregation. Here, the local congregation was itself divided between a majority of 164 members who sought to withdraw from the PCUS, and a minority of 94 members who wished to maintain the affiliation. Neither of the state courts alluded to this problem, however; each concluded without discussion or analysis that the title to the property was in the local church and that the local church was represented by the majority rather than the minority.

Petitioners earnestly submit that the question of which faction is the true representative of the Vineville church is an ecclesiastical question that cannot be answered by a civil court. At least, it is said, it cannot be answered by a civil court in a case involving a hierarchical church, like the PCUS, where a duly appointed church commission has determined which of the two factions represents the "true congregation." Respondents, in opposition, argue in effect that the Georgia courts did no more than apply the ordinary presumption that, absent some indication to the contrary, a voluntary religious association is represented by a majority of its members.

If in fact Georgia has adopted a presumptive rule of majority representation, defeasible upon a showing that the identity of the local church is to be determined by some other means, we think this would be consistent with both the neutral-principles analysis and the First Amendment. Majority rule is generally employed in the governance of religious societies. Furthermore, the majority faction generally can be identified without resolving any question of religious doctrine or polity. . . . Most importantly, any rule of majority representation can always be overcome, under the neutral-principles approach, either by providing, in the corporate charter or the constitution of the general church, that the identity of the local church is to be established in some other way, or by providing that the church property is held in trust for the general church and those who remain loyal to it. Indeed, the State may adopt any method of overcoming the majoritarian presumption, so long as the use of that method does not impair free-exercise rights or entangle the civil courts in matters of religious controversy.

Neither the trial court nor the Supreme Court of Georgia, however, explicitly stated that it was adopting a presumptive rule of majority representation. [The Court remanded for a determination of that question.]

Mr. Justice POWELL, with whom THE CHIEF JUSTICE, Mr. Justice STEWART, and Mr. Justice WHITE join, dissenting.

 . . . The first stage in the "neutral principles of law" approach [approved by the Court] operates as a restrictive rule of evidence. A court is required to examine the deeds to the church property, the charter of the local church (if there is one), the book of order or discipline of the general church organization, and the state statutes governing the holding of church property. The object of the inquiry, where the title to the property is in the local church, is "to determine whether there [is] any basis for a trust in favor of the general church." The court's investigation is to be "completely secular," "rel[ying] exclusively on objective, well-established concepts of trust and property law familiar to lawyers and judges." [But the] constitutional documents of churches tend to be drawn in terms of religious precepts. Attempting to read them "in purely secular terms" is more likely to promote confusion than understanding. Moreover, whenever religious polity has not been expressed in specific statements referring to the property of a church, there will be no evidence of that polity cognizable under the neutral-principles rule. Lacking such evidence, presumably a court will impose some rule of church government derived from state law. In the present case, for example, the general and unqualified authority of the Presbytery over the actions of the Vineville church had not been expressed in secular terms of control of its property. As a consequence, the Georgia courts could find no acceptable evidence of this authoritative relationship, and they imposed instead a congregational form of government determined from state law.

[The] Georgia courts, as a matter of state law, granted control to the schismatic faction, and thereby effectively reversed the doctrinal decision of the church courts. This indirect interference by the civil courts with the resolution of religious disputes within the church is no less proscribed by the First Amendment than is the direct decision of questions of doctrine and practice.[2]

When civil courts step in to resolve intrachurch disputes over control of church property, they will either support or overturn the authoritative resolution of the dispute within the church itself. The new analysis, under the attractive banner of "neutral principles," actually invites the civil courts to do the latter. The proper rule of decision, that I thought had been settled until today [by Watson v. Jones], requires a court to give effect in all cases to the decisions of the church government agreed upon by the members before the dispute arose.

[The neutral principles approach is no more helpful in resolving the second question in this case.] Where, as here, the neutral-principles inquiry reveals no trust in favor of the general church, and the local congregation is split into factions, the basic question remains unresolved: which faction should have control of the local church?

The Court acknowledges that the church law of the Presbyterian Church in the United States (PCUS), of which the Vineville church is a part, provides for the authoritative resolution of this question by the Presbytery. Indeed, the Court indicates that Georgia, consistently with the First Amendment, may adopt the Watson v. Jones rule of adherence to the resolution of the dispute according to church law—a rule that would necessitate reversal of the judgment for the respondents. But instead of requiring the state courts to take this approach, the Court approves as well an alternative rule of state law: the Georgia courts are said to be free to "adop[t] a presumptive rule of majority representation, defeasible upon a showing that the identity of the local church is to be determined by some other means." This showing may be made by proving that the church has "provid[ed], in the corporate charter or the constitution of the general church, that the identity of the local church is to be established in some other way."

On its face, this rebuttable presumption also requires reversal of the state court's judgment in favor of the schismatic faction. The polity of the PCUS commits to the Presbytery the resolution of the dispute within the local church. Having shown this structure of church government for the determination of the identity of the local congregation, the petitioners have rebutted any presumption that this question has been left to a majority vote of the local congregation.

---

2. . . . The neutral principles approach creates other difficulties. It imposes on the organization of churches additional legal requirements which in some cases might inhibit their formation by forcing the organizers to confront issues that otherwise might never arise. It could also precipitate church property disputes, for existing churches may deem it necessary, in light of today's decision, to revise their constitutional documents, characters, and deeds to include a specific statement of church polity in the language of property and trust law.

NOTES AND QUESTIONS

1. The Unconstitutional Approach: "Departure from Doctrine."   Let us first consider the approach Georgia took before 1969—the same approach long used by English courts (see, e.g., Attorney General v. Pearson, 3 Mer. 353, 36 Eng. Rep. 135 (Ch. 1817) (Lord Eldon)). Georgia assumed that when people gave property to churches, they wanted it to be used to support the dogmas they and their church believed in at the time of the gift. Church property was, then, subject to an implied trust. If the general church changed its doctrine and a local church objected, it could spin off in order to be faithful to the terms of the trust. This was what happened with the Hull Memorial Presbyterian Church in Savannah when the general church decided to ordain women and make some other changes. But in Presbyterian Church v. Hull Church, 393 U.S. 440 (1969) (discussed in Jones v. Wolf), the Supreme Court held that the departure-from-doctrine rule violated the First Amendment, because it ran the risk "of inhibiting the free development of religious doctrine and of implicating secular interests in matters of purely ecclesiastical concern." If Georgia wanted to decide the case, it had to find a way to do it without getting involved in the resolution of religious questions.

That may seem to be the right answer in many cases under a system of disestablishment of religion. Why should the state prevent churches from changing their doctrines? But suppose the original donors of the property expressly provide that the property be used for the propagation of a particular doctrine—predestination, for example. Now, suppose that the majority faction in the congregation has ceased to believe in predestination, and is using the property to advocate a different view. Under Jones v. Wolf, can the courts enforce the terms of the trust? If not, why not? What did the Court say about this issue in *Watson*? To put the point another way, why is it constitutional for the state to *refuse* to enforce the terms of a trust merely because the donors' instructions were religious in nature, when it stands ready to enforce trusts devoted to the propagation of secular doctrines and ideologies?

2. The Constitutional Alternatives: Deference and Neutral Principles.   One way to avoid such questions is to apply the rule of deference—do what the church authorities say. In Jones v. Wolf the Presbytery said that the minority should get control of the Vineville Church. Would the Constitution permit Georgia to adopt this rule? The rule of neutral principles gives control to the local majority in Vineville. Can both of these conflicting rules be consistent with the First Amendment? If you were an official with a national religious denomination, would you be happy that states are free to choose either rule? See William G. Ross, The Need for an Exclusive and Uniform Application of "Neutral Principles" in the Adjudication of Church Property Disputes, 32 St. Louis U. L.J. 263, 305 (1987) (arguing for a uniform approach so that "[n]ational churches [can] better evaluate the consequences of controversial pronouncements on social and doctrinal issues").

3. Questions About "Neutral Principles."   In what sense are Georgia's new principles neutral? In one sense they are anything but. The default rule, which now applies unless the parties make some other provision, is that local churches can split off from hierarchical churches and take their property with them. The general church can prevent this outcome by getting its name on the deed, or having the local church create a trust in its corporate charter, or (like the United Methodist Church in *Carnes*) putting an express trust provision in its own constitution. But unless it takes one of these precautions, it will lose.

To be more precise, it will then go to step two of the *Jones* default rule: Within the local church, the majority rules. If the majority favors the general church (as it did in Watson v. Jones), the general church will win. But if the majority favors secession (as it did in Jones v. Wolf), the local church will win. The combination of these two rules—the local church can do as it wishes, and within the local church the majority rules—results in treating hierarchical churches just like congregational churches unless the church has made explicit provision otherwise. John H. Garvey, Churches and the Free Exercise of Religion, 4 Notre Dame J.L. Ethics & Pub. Pol'y 567 (1990).

Why should congregationalism be the norm to which churches are expected to conform unless they specify otherwise? The Court points out, correctly, that under the rule of neutral principles any group creating a church has "flexibility in ordering private rights and obligations to reflect the intentions of the parties." Can it be an unconstitutional burden to require hierarchical religious groups to engage in this kind of advance planning? Are there reasons, other than laziness or lack of imagination, why they might wish not to? Will the legal steps required by the neutral-principles approach affect all religious groups equally?

The "neutral principles" approach for intra-church disputes recalls the rule of Employment Division v. Smith (p. 137) that "neutral and generally applicable laws" do not violate the Free Exercise Clause. If you think that the *Smith* rule gives free exercise too little protection against the government, isn't the same rule also inappropriate for internal church disputes?

What if the "neutral" state law does not allow the church flexibility? Suppose, for example, that the law in *Mazaika* (p. 291) had not singled out churches, but had required that the boards of all corporations have at least five voting members, and that no entity could provide otherwise in its by-laws. As applied to a Catholic church or diocese, does this violate the First Amendment?

4. Applying Neutral Principles.   Exactly what evidence does the rule of neutral principles permit a court to consider, in deciding whether there has been a trust in favor of the general church? The Court mentions deeds, the corporate charter of the local church, the constitution of the general church, and state statutes dealing with trusts. What other documents are relevant? Minutes of church meetings? Letters? Some courts avoid these difficulties by adopting a doctrine of formal title—they will award the property to the entity whose name is on the deed, with no further questions asked. Palace Hills Church v. International Church, 467 F. Supp. 357, 362 (D. Ariz. 1979); Ira Mark Ellman, Driven from the Tribunal: Judicial Resolution of Internal Church Disputes, 69 Calif. L. Rev. 1378, 1409 (1981).

The Court in *Jones* states that any examination of documents must be done "in purely secular terms." What does this mean? Suppose a donor leaves money to "the Roman Catholic Archbishop of Chicago." The words "Roman Catholic" obviously have a religious significance. So too the word "Archbishop." If there were two claimants to that title, we would have to consult the law of the Catholic Church to determine the true one. If we subtract the religious aspect of these words, what is the secular residue? Congregation Beth Yitzhok v. Briskman, 566

F. Supp. 555 (E.D.N.Y. 1983); John H. Mansfield, The Religion Clauses of the First Amendment and the Philosophy of the Constitution, 72 Calif. L. Rev. 847, 866-867 (1984).

b. Other Principles of Church Autonomy: Clergy Disputes

1. The *Serbian Orthodox* Case. The approval of "neutral principles" in Jones v. Wolf came only three years after Serbian Eastern Orthodox Diocese v. Milivojevich, 426 U.S. 696 (1976). In that case, the governing body of the Serbian Orthodox Church, a hierarchical organization, suspended Milivojevich, the bishop of its American-Canadian Diocese, while it investigated various complaints against him. The Church also split the diocese into three smaller ones and appointed two additional bishops. When Milivojevich refused to accept his suspension or the reorganization of dioceses (claiming that the Church was "pro-Communist" among other things), the Church removed him as bishop. Milivojevich sued in Illinois state court for a declaration that he was the true bishop and an injunction preventing the Church from interfering with his control over the diocese and its property. The Illinois Supreme Court ultimately held that the removal of Milivojevich was "arbitrary" and invalid because it violated the Church's constitution and codes (including a requirement that he be tried within one year of the indictment against him). The court also held that the reorganization into three dioceses "clear[ly]" exceeded the Church's jurisdiction and was invalid, basing its ruling on what it found to be "neutral principles" in the constitutions of the Church and the diocese.

The U.S. Supreme Court reversed, holding on both issues that the state court had unconstitutionally "substituted its interpretation of the Diocesan and Mother Church Constitutions for that of the highest ecclesiastical tribunals in which church law vests authority to make that interpretation." In effect, the Court held that the state courts were not allowed to interpret the Church's legal documents; the only constitutionally permissible approach in this case was deference to the Church tribunal under Watson v. Jones. How can this be squared with the acceptance of "neutral principles of law" in Jones v. Wolf?

2. The "Ministerial Exemption" from Antidiscrimination Laws. Numerous decisions have held that clergy members fired or disciplined by their religious employers may not sue for race or sex discrimination under Title VII of the Civil Rights Act, even though the statute's text contains no exception barring such claims. The first case recognizing the "ministerial exception," and resting it on constitutional grounds, was McClure v. Salvation Army, 460 F.2d 553 (5th Cir. 1972). Significantly, the ministerial exemption from antidiscrimination laws has been repeatedly reaffirmed in lower courts even after Employment Division v. Smith did away with most constitutionally mandated exemptions from "neutral laws of general applicability." See, e.g., Combs v. Central Texas Ann. Conf., United Methodist Church, 173 F.3d 343 (5th Cir. 1999) (p. 310).

The ministerial exemption is discussed in detail in the next section (D-3). But for now, consider some possible reasons why the laws against race and sex discrimination, which appear to be generally applicable to employers and facially neutral toward religion, should not be applied to cases of alleged discrimination against clergy.

3. Religious Institutional Autonomy: Its Grounds and Scope. Put differently, what grounds are there for giving religious institutions a distinctive constitutional autonomy in cases such as *Serbian Orthodox* and discrimination claims by clergy? There might be both broad and narrow reasons.

(a) Inquiry into religious doctrine. In *Serbian Orthodox*, the Court noted that the state courts that had overturned the church's defrocking of Bishop Milivojevich had done so on the basis of "a searching and therefore impermissible inquiry into church polity." 426 U.S. at 723. Similarly, one reason courts give for rejecting clergy members' discrimination suits is that determining whether a church's reasons for firing a minister were legitimate, as opposed to discriminatory, would require a court to evaluate religious questions—"to review a church's determination of God's appointed." Rayburn v. Gen. Conf. of Seventh-Day Adventists, 772 F.2d 1164, (4th Cir. 1985). Can you explain how this might be inconsistent with Jones v. Wolf?

(b) Non-entanglement under the Establishment Clause. Judicial inquiry into religious doctrines may be one example of a broader problem: too much contact between the institutions of the state and the church. As we have seen, established churches typically were regulated by civil authorities (see, e.g., p. 15); and one component of the Lemon v. Kurtzman test for Establishment Clause violations (see p. 11) is "excessive entanglement between church and state." It has been argued that the Establishment Clause declares the state incompetent to regulate or otherwise act on religious matters such as "ecclesiastical governance, the resolution of doctrine, the composing of prayers, and the teaching of religion." Carl H. Esbeck, The Establishment Clause as a Structural Restraint on Government Power, 84 Iowa L. Rev. 1, 10-11 (1998). Does this rationale extend beyond cases involving ministers, to other employees?

(c) Rights of speech and association. Recall that even after Employment Division v. Smith, strict free exercise scutiny may continue for "hybrid" claims of free exercise with other rights, such as rights of speech and association. Recall also that in Boy Scouts of America v. Dole, 530 U.S. 640 (2000) (p. 176), the Court held that the state would violate the Boy Scouts' right to associate for expressive purposes if it forbade them to remove an openly gay assistant scoutmaster, whose presence as a leader would contradict the Scouts' organizational message of promoting "morally straight" and "clean" behavior as it understood those terms. Does the right recognized in *Dale* support the ministerial exemption from antidiscrimination laws? Does it protect a religious institution's employment decisions concerning positions other than clergy?

(d) The distinctive value of institutions. Do institutional free exercise claims have a distinctive value compared with the claims of individuals such as the adherents in *Smith*? Professor Kathleen Brady notes that although *Smith* permitted regulation of religiously motivated conduct, it gave absolute protection to religious beliefs; she argues that because "religious groups play an essential role in shaping individual religious belief and, indeed, in the very formulation of religious ideas, the freedom of belief that *Smith* envisions requires protections for religious organizations." Kathleen A. Brady, Religious Organizations and Free Exercise: The Surprising Lessons of *Smith*, 2004 B.Y.U. L. Rev. 1633, 1676-77. Couldn't one say the same about regulation of religious conduct by individuals: that prohibition of the conduct will inevitably damage the individuals' underlying belief?

Is the distinctive constitutional value of religion—the feature that warrants giving it special constitutional status compared with other beliefs—the fact that it is typically exercised communally rather than individually? But cf. Ira C. Lupu, Free Exercise Exemption and Religious Institutions: The Case of Employment Discrimination, 67 B.U. L. Rev. 391 (1987) (arguing that religious exemption doctrine rests on the value of sincere, voluntary religious choices, and that only individuals, not institutions, fit this model).

Do free exercise claims by institutions pose less of a threat of societal "anarchy," of the kind that worried the Court in *Smith*, than the potentially limitless realm of claims by individuals? See Brady, 2004 B.Y.U. L. Rev. at 1677-78 ("Permitting religious groups to shape community practice according to shared norms may have a great impact upon the lives of members and employees, but any direct effect on the larger society will usually be minimal.") Doesn't this argument depend on differentiating which practices are classified as "internal" and which "direct[ly a]ffect" society?

3. Churches as Employers

Churches are nonprofit institutions, and to a great extent they rely on the voluntary and uncompensated services of their members to do their work. In some faiths full-time religious workers—Trappist and Dominican monks, for example—take vows of poverty. There are nonetheless many people who work for churches and church-related institutions for a living. These include most obviously rabbis, ministers, priests, and mullahs; temple administrators, sextons, directors of choirs and of youth ministries; secretaries, janitors, and maintenance people—in short, all those who work directly for the church as a legal entity. In March 1995, religious organizations employed a total of 1,296,500 full-time and part-time workers. This number does not include people working for educational institutions, hospitals, publishing houses, social services, second-hand stores, radio or television stations, etc., operated by religious organizations. Bureau of Labor Statistics, 43 Employment and Earnings no.6, p.20 (June 1996). Hundreds of thousands more work for church-related institutions that are separately incorporated or at least legally distinct: teachers in parochial schools and at religiously affiliated colleges and universities, social workers at organizations like Catholic Social Services, doctors, nurses, and staff at religiously affiliated hospitals, and so on. In its relations with these people the religious institution often behaves like any other employer. It may sign an employment contract. For nonministerial employees it will withhold income tax, and sometimes social security and medicare taxes. It will issue a paycheck drawn on a bank where it maintains an account.

And yet this is not an ordinary sort of work, calling for ordinary kinds of credentials. The Roman Catholic Code of Canon Law asks for this kind of resume (canon 521):

§ 1 To be validly appointed a parish priest, one must be in the sacred order of priesthood.

§2 He is also to be outstanding in sound doctrine and uprightness of character, endowed with zeal for souls and other virtues, and possessed of those qualities which by universal or particular law are required for the care of the parish in question.

And this is the job description (canon 528):

§1 The parish priest has the obligation of ensuring that the word of God is proclaimed in its entirety to those living in the parish. He is therefore to see to it that the lay members of Christ's faithful are instructed in the truths of faith[.] He is to foster works which promote the spirit of the Gospel, including its relevance to social justice.
§2 The parish priest is to take care that the blessed Eucharist is the centre of the parish assembly of the faithful.

Disputes over hiring, firing, performance, and compensation arise as frequently within churches as elsewhere. But when they arise in churches, the traditional rule has been that secular courts will defer to the decision of church authorities. Here is how the Court put the deference rule in Gonzalez v. Archbishop of Manila, 280 U.S. 1 (1929), a case from the Philippine Islands where the petitioner sued the archbishop for refusing to appoint him as a chaplain (he was not qualified under canon law because he was not a clergyman and lacked the requisite knowledge of Christian doctrine):

Because the appointment is a canonical act, it is the function of the church authorities to determine what the essential qualifications of a chaplain are and whether the candidate possesses them. In the absence of fraud, collusion, or arbitrariness, the decisions of the proper church tribunals on matters purely ecclesiastical, although affecting civil rights, are accepted in litigation before the secular courts as conclusive, because the parties in interest made them so by contract or otherwise.

The rule of deference in contract cases is like the rule of deference for property cases that was announced in Watson v. Jones (p. 296). In fact, the First Amendment problems are often identical. In a dispute over property both parties may agree that the bishop holds title; the question may be who is the lawful bishop. See, e.g., Serbian Eastern Orthodox Diocese v. Milivojevich; Kedroff v. St. Nicholas Cathedral (pp. 299, 307).

In *Milivojevich*, the Court applied the rule of deference and held that civil courts could not review whether the Serbian Orthodox Church's defrocking of a bishop was lawful under the Church's substantive and procedural rules. But remember that *Milivojevich* was decided only three years before Jones v. Wolf (p. 300), in which the Court held that "neutral principles of law" could be used to resolve internal church disputes over property. As you saw from the property cases, the application of "neutral principles" frequently produces a different result than if the court simply deferred to the church's internal tribunals. In this section, we investigate in more detail why the courts have been less willing to apply so-called neutral principles to disputes involving clergy than to those purely over property.

But even in clergy employment cases, there is some sentiment for the contending rule of neutral principles. Moreover, remember that in Employment Division v. Smith, the Court held that applying "neutral and generally applicable laws" to religious claims will almost always be constitutional. Has *Smith* strengthened even further the argument for neutral principles over deference?

We consider this question in the context of Title VII and other laws against discrimination by race, sex, age, handicap, or other characteristics—laws that could be considered neutral in the sense that they apply to religious and non-religious employers alike. Religious organizations are exempt by statute from the religious nondiscrimination requirements. See Corporation of Presiding Bishop v. Amos (p. 250). But they are not explicitly exempted from the race and sex nondiscrimination rules. Does the First Amendment allow the government to enforce this rule against churches in their employment of clergy? What about other positions in religious organizations?

COMBS v. CENTRAL TEXAS ANNUAL CONFERENCE OF THE UNITED METHODIST CHURCH
173 F.3d 343 (5th Cir. 1999)

W. Eugene DAVIS, Circuit Judge:

Reverend Pamela Combs appeals the dismissal of her Title VII sex and pregnancy discrimination suit against the First United Methodist Church of Hurst ("First United") and the Central Texas Annual Conference of the United Methodist Church ("Central Texas Conference"). The sole question presented in this appeal is whether the district court correctly determined that the Free Exercise Clause of the First Amendment precluded it from considering Reverend Combs's employment discrimination case. For the reasons that follow, we conclude that the district court was correct and affirm.

I

. . . Reverend Combs is a graduate of the New Orleans Theological Seminary. In 1988, she was ordained as a Baptist minister. In 1993, she was hired as First United's Singles Minister. In late 1994, she was appointed First United's Associate Minister. In this new position, she served communion, assisted in baptisms, performed marriages, and led funerals. . . .

In October 1995, Reverend Combs, who was—and still is—married, announced that she was pregnant. She requested and was granted maternity leave for the expected childbirth. In March 1996, she had her annual interview with the United Methodist Board of Ordained Ministry. The board again recommended unanimously that Reverend Combs continue with the process of having her ordination recognized within the Methodist Church.

Around this time, Reverend Combs questioned why her pay was substantially lower than that of the male ministers she had replaced. She also requested a housing allowance because she and her family had moved out of the parsonage to free up space for other church use. In response, the Staff Parish Relations Committee made several adjustments to her compensation package.

In April 1996, Reverend Combs took some accrued vacation time and began her eight-week maternity leave, as provided for clergy by the rules of the United Methodist Church Book of Discipline. On April 17, 1996, she gave birth. Unfortunately, however, Reverend Combs suffered serious post-partum complications, which required hospitalization, surgery, heavy medication, and extensive rest.

During this period of incapacitation, Reverend Combs's position within First United was questioned by her pastor and immediate supervisor, Dr. John Fielder. He challenged her competence, performance, and honesty. . . . The church then denied her the maternity benefits she had been granted and demanded she repay those benefits that had already been paid to her.

Nevertheless, in June 1996, the Bishop of the Central Texas Conference reappointed Reverend Combs as an Associate Minister for First United. However, when Reverend Combs returned to work on June 17, 1996, she was told by Dr. Fielder that she had been terminated and that she was required to leave the premises immediately. The next day, Reverend Combs went to the Staff Parish Relations Committee. The committee stated that Dr. Fielder said she had resigned and that the committee had accepted her resignation. Reverend Combs protested that she had not resigned, but to no avail. Reverend Combs then brought the matter to the attention of the Central Texas Conference. However, she found no support from that organization either.

. . . Reverend Combs sued both the Central Texas Conference and First United, alleging discrimination on the basis of her sex and her pregnancy in violation of Title VII. She alleged that the deprivation of her benefits and her termination were the conclusion of a practice of discrimination that included disparate salary and treatment while she was employed. [The defendants moved for summary judgment based on, among other things, the First Amendment. The district court granted the motion, and Combs appealed.]

All parties agree that, at least for the purposes of this appeal, the following facts are true: Reverend Combs was a member of the clergy performing traditional clerical functions; both Defendants are churches and at least one of them employed Reverend Combs; and Reverend Combs's claims are based purely on sex and pregnancy and do not directly involve matters of religious dogma or ecclesiastical law. In addition, for the purposes of this appeal, we assume that Reverend Combs's allegations are sufficient to support a finding of discrimination. [Paragraph relocated from footnote.]

II

The question before us is whether the Free Exercise Clause of the First Amendment deprives a federal court of jurisdiction to hear a Title VII employment discrimination suit brought against a church by a member of its clergy, even when the church's challenged actions are not based on religious doctrine.

All parties agree that prior to 1990, the district court decision would have been correct. In McClure v. Salvation Army (5th Cir. 1972), this Court established a church-minister exception to the coverage of Title VII. In this appeal, however, Reverend Combs questions whether *McClure* and its church minister exception still stand in light of the Supreme Court's decision in Employment Division v. Smith. To resolve this question, we start by reviewing *McClure* and move from that case forward.

A

In 1972, this Court was asked whether Mrs. Billie McClure, a Salvation Army officer alleging discrimination on the basis of her sex, could state a claim against the Salvation Army under Title VII of the Civil Rights Act of 1964. Relying in part upon the findings of the district court, this Court determined that the Salvation Army was an "employer" under Title VII, and that the Salvation Army was engaged in interstate commerce. Therefore, the Court determined that the Salvation Army fell within the general coverage of Title VII.

The Court also determined that the Salvation Army was a church and that Mrs. McClure was an ordained minister within that church. These findings required the Court to address two further questions: Was the Salvation Army exempt from Title VII under Section 702's religious exemption? If not, did the First Amendment exempt the Salvation Army's treatment of Mrs. McClure from federal review under Title VII?

In answering the first question, the Court concluded that although Section 702 exempts religious organizations from Title VII's coverage for religious discrimination, it does not provide a blanket exemption for all discrimination. Title VII still prohibits a religious organization from discriminating on the basis of race, color, sex, or national origin. Because Mrs. McClure was alleging discrimination on the basis of her sex, this Court held that her claim did not fall within the Section 702 exemption.

After determining that Mrs. McClure's claim fell within the statutory coverage of Title VII, the Court addressed whether the Free Exercise Clause of the First Amendment permitted such a claim by a minister against her church. The Court began by noting that the First Amendment has built a "wall of separation" between church and state. After describing this wall, the Court stated:

> Only in rare instances where a "compelling state interest in the regulation of a subject within the State's constitutional power to regulate" is shown can a court uphold state action which imposes even an "incidental burden" on the free exercise of religion. In this highly sensitive constitutional area " '[o]nly the gravest abuses, endangering paramount interests, give occasion for permissible limitation.' " Sherbert v. Verner.

This Court then emphasized the importance of the relationship between an organized church and its ministers, describing it as the church's "lifeblood." The Court reviewed a series of cases in which the Supreme Court had placed matters of church government and administration beyond the regulation of civil authorities. *McClure* (citing and describing Watson v. Jones (affirming state court decision not to become involved in factional dispute within church); Gonzalez v. Archbishop of Manila (declining, absent fraud, collusion, or arbitrariness, to involve secular courts in matters purely ecclesiastical); Kedroff v. St. Nicholas Cathedral (holding that legislation transferring control of Russian Orthodox churches from Patriarch of Moscow to convention of North American churches is unconstitutional interference with the free exercise of religion); Kreshik v. St. Nicholas Cathedral (overturning, as unconstitutional involvement in matters of church administration, state court ruling that Patriarch of Moscow did not control Russian Orthodox churches within North America); Presbyterian Church v. Hull Church (warning against civil court involvement in church property litigation)).

After reviewing this Supreme Court precedent, the *McClure* Court determined that applying Title VII to the employment relationship between the Salvation Army and Mrs. McClure "would involve an investigation and review . . . [that] would . . . cause the State to intrude upon matters of church administration and government which have so many times before been proclaimed to be matters of a singular ecclesiastical concern." Thus, the Court held that applying Title VII to the relationship under consideration "would result in an encroachment by the State into an area of religious freedom which it is forbidden to enter by the principles of the free exercise clause of the First Amendment." The Court therefore affirmed the district court's dismissal of Mrs. McClure's claim.

Most of our sister circuits adopted the church-minister exception articulated in *McClure*. See, e.g., Natal v. Christian and Missionary Alliance (1st Cir. 1989); Rayburn v. General Conf. of Seventh-day Adventists (4th Cir. 1985); Hutchison v. Thomas (6th Cir. 1986); Young v. Northern Illinois Conf. of United Methodist Church (7th Cir. 1994); Scharon v. St. Luke's Episcopal Presbyterian Hosp. (8th Cir. 1991); Minker v. Baltimore Annual Conf. of United Methodist Church (D.C. Cir. 1990). Although the Supreme Court itself has never adopted the *McClure* exception, it is the law of this circuit and much of the rest of the country.

B

Reverend Combs contends in this appeal that the *McClure* church-minister exception cannot stand in light of the Supreme Court's decision in . . . *Smith* and City of Boerne v. Flores.

[Her argument] is relatively straightforward: First, in *Smith* and *Boerne*, the Supreme Court held that the First Amendment does not bar the application of facially neutral laws even when these laws burden the exercise of religion. Second, *McClure* was based on the now-rejected "compelling interest" test. For these reasons, Reverend Combs argues that *McClure* no longer controls and therefore she should be permitted to pursue her Title VII discrimination claim against First United and the Central Texas Conference.

1

A well-reasoned opinion from the D.C. Circuit recently considered the precise question presented to us. In E.E.O.C. v. Catholic University (D.C. Cir. 1996), that court was asked whether, in light of *Smith*, a professor who was also a Catholic nun could sue Catholic University for sex discrimination in the denial of her application for tenure. In resolving this issue, the D.C. Circuit addressed the post-*Smith* validity of the ministerial exception.

The D.C. Circuit began its analysis by making the important distinction between two different strands of free exercise law. The court stated, "government action may burden the free exercise of religion, in violation of the First Amendment, in two quite different ways: by interfering with a believer's ability to observe the commands or practices of his faith, . . . and by encroaching on the ability of a church to manage its internal affairs." The court emphasized that the Supreme Court has shown a particular reluctance to interfere with a church's selection of its own clergy.

The court concluded that *Smith* did not address the Free Exercise Clause's protection to a church against government encroachment into the church's internal management. Rather, *Smith* only addressed the strand of Free Exercise Clause protection afforded an individual to practice his faith. Thus, the *Catholic University* court determined that the language in *Smith* that the plaintiff relied on—"the right of free exercise does not relieve an individual of the obligation to comply with a valid and neutral law of general applicability"—did not mean that a church, as opposed to an individual, is never entitled to relief from a neutral law of general application.

The D.C. Circuit provided two main reasons for its conclusion. First, the court stated that:

> [T]he burden on free exercise that is addressed by the ministerial exception is of a fundamentally different character from that at issue in *Smith* and in the cases cited by the [Supreme] Court in support of its holding. The ministerial exception is not invoked to protect the freedom of an individual to observe a particular command or practice of his church. Rather it is designed to protect the freedom of the church to select those who will carry out its religious mission. Moreover, the ministerial exception does not present the dangers warned of in *Smith*. Protecting the authority of a church to select its own ministers free of government interference does not empower a member of that church, by virtue of his beliefs, to become a law unto himself. Nor does the exception require judges to determine the centrality of religious beliefs before applying a "compelling interest" test in the free exercise field.

Second, the D.C. Circuit acknowledged that the Supreme Court had rejected the "compelling interest" test cited by some courts (including *McClure*) when invoking the ministerial exception. The court observed, however, that many courts applying the exception rely on a long line of Supreme Court cases standing for the fundamental proposition that churches should be able to "decide for themselves, free from state interference, matters of church government as well as those of faith and doctrine." The D.C. Circuit concluded, "we cannot believe that the Supreme Court in *Smith* intended to qualify this century-old affirmation of a church's sovereignty over its own affairs."

2

We agree with both the reasoning and the conclusion of the D.C. Circuit. Especially important is that court's distinction between the two strands of free exercise cases—restrictions on an individual's actions that are based on religious beliefs and encroachments on the ability of a church to manage its internal affairs. Reverend Combs acknowledges this distinction, but argues that it does not determine the outcome of this case. Instead, Reverend Combs contends that *Smith* and *Boerne* indicate that the constitutional protection for religious freedom is impermissibly broadened when it grants churches immunity from employment actions by clergy when such actions are not based on questions of religious dogma or ecclesiastical law. We disagree.

Smith's language is clearly directed at the first strand of free exercise law, where an individual contends that, because of his religious beliefs, he should not be required to conform with generally applicable laws. The concerns raised in *Smith* are quite different from the concerns raised by Reverend Combs's case, which pertains to interference in internal church government. We concur wholeheartedly with the D.C. Circuit's conclusion that *Smith*, which concerned individual free exercise, did not purport to overturn a century of precedent protecting the church against governmental interference in selecting its ministers.

We also disagree with Reverend Combs's argument that *McClure* is no longer good law because it relied on the "compelling state interest" test rejected by the Supreme Court in *Smith*. Our review of *McClure* reveals that although this Court presented the "compelling state interest" test in its general discussion of First Amendment law, the test is never applied or even mentioned later in the opinion. Thus, it is unclear how much this Court was actually relying on this test. Moreover, even if the *McClure* panel was relying on the *Sherbert* test, we hold that the church-minister exception survives *Sherbert*'s demise. As the D.C. Circuit observed in *Catholic University*, the primary doctrinal underpinning of the church-minister exception is not the *Sherbert* test, but the principle that churches must be free "to decide for themselves, free from state interference, matters of church government as well as those of faith and doctrine." *Kedroff.* This fundamental right of churches to be free from government interference in their internal management and administration has not been affected by the Supreme Court's decision in *Smith* and the demise of *Sherbert*.

3

The final point to address is Reverend Combs's argument that *Catholic University* is distinguishable from this case because a resolution of Sister McDonough's claim in *Catholic University* would have required an evaluation of church doctrine, while there would be no such need in this case.

Sister McDonough was denied tenure at Catholic University at least in part because the reviewing committees decided that her teaching and scholarship failed to meet the standards required of a tenured member of Catholic University's Canon Law Faculty. Indeed at trial, the parties introduced an "extensive body of conflicting testimony" concerning the quality of Sister McDonough's publications. We agree that the district court would have been placed in an untenable position had it been required to evaluate the merits of Sister McDonough's canon law scholarship. Having a civil court determine the merits of canon law scholarship would be in violent opposition to the constitutional principle of the separation of church and state. See Presbyterian Church v. Hull Church (civil courts are not permitted to determine ecclesiastical questions). Reverend Combs argues that because the resolution of her claim, in contrast to that of Sister McDonough, requires no evaluation or interpretation of religious doctrine, her claim should be allowed to proceed.

Not long after our decision in *McClure*, this Court rejected a similar argument in Simpson v. Wells Lamont Corp. (5th Cir. 1974).[7] As this Court observed in *Simpson*, the First Amendment concerns are twofold. The first concern is that secular authorities would be involved in evaluating or interpreting religious doctrine. The second quite independent concern is that in investigating employment discrimination claims by ministers against their church, secular authorities

---

7. In *Simpson*, the plaintiff argued that the *McClure* exception should not apply to his racial discrimination claim because it was unrelated to church dogma. This Court disagreed, however, and determined that the First Amendment protection relative to the relationship between a church and a minister extended beyond purely dogmatic issues.

would necessarily intrude into church governance in a manner that would be inherently coercive, even if the alleged discrimination were purely nondoctrinal. This second concern is the one present here. This second concern alone is enough to bar the involvement of the civil courts.

In short, we cannot conceive how the federal judiciary could determine whether an employment decision concerning a minister was based on legitimate or illegitimate grounds without inserting ourselves into a realm where the Constitution forbids us to tread, the internal management of a church.

CONCLUSION

This case involves the interrelationship between two important governmental directives—the congressional mandate to eliminate discrimination in the workplace and the constitutional mandate to preserve the separation of church and state. As this Court previously observed in *McClure*, both of these mandates cannot always be followed. In such circumstances, the constitutional mandate must override the mandate that is merely congressional. Thus, we are persuaded that the First Amendment continues to give the church the right to select its ministers free from Title VII's restrictions.

NOTES AND QUESTIONS

1. Free Exercise and Clergy Employment. *Combs* raises a number of questions about the Free Exercise Clause as applied to alleged discrimination in the employment of clergy.

(a) First, why is Title VII unlike other generally applicable laws (which Employment Division v. Smith says can be applied to religious actors)? Is it because the authority of a church to hire clergy is so extraordinarily important to its independence and its ability to minister to its flock? (If so, consider whether *Smith* should have given an exemption for the use of peyote, which after all was a central sacrament of the Native American Church's worship service.) Is Title VII different (as *Combs* suggests) because the religious freedom claimant is an institution, not an individual, and the *Smith* opinion speaks of individuals? (If so, is that explanation consistent with City of Boerne v. Flores?) Do decisions regarding clergy employment implicate "hybrid rights" (see p. 173), and if so which other constitutional rights are involved? See Joanne C. Brant, "Our Shield Belongs to the Lord": Religious Employers and a Constitutional Right to Discriminate, 21 Hast. Const. L.Q. 275, 311-320 (1994).[*]

The *Combs* court suggests that there is a "fundamental right of churches to be free from government interference in their internal management and administration." We will explore the contours of that right in a moment.

---

[*] For two further, divergent analyses of free exercise rights in the church employment context, see Douglas Laycock, Towards a General Theory of the Religion Clauses: The Case of Church Labor Relations and the Right to Church Autonomy, 81 Colum. L. Rev. 1373 (1981) (advocating a broad right of church autonomy); and Ira C. Lupu, Free Exercise Exemption and Religious Institutions: The Case of Employment Discrimination, 67 B.U. L. Rev. 391 (1987) (advocating narrow church autonomy rights).

(b) Before you go further, though, notice that the right of clergy hiring extends beyond even pre-*Smith* exemptions law: The right is virtually absolute. For one thing, neither *Combs* nor the other decisions applying the ministerial exception inquire seriously into whether there is a "compelling governmental interest" in overriding the church's choice of minister. Yet in other cases, the eradication of discrimination has been held to be a compelling interest, sufficient to override free exercise claims. See Bob Jones University v. United States, 461 U.S. 574, 604 (1983) (upholding withdrawal of tax exemption from college that forbade interracial dating between students). See also Boy Scouts of America v. Dale (p. 176) (holding that an organization's right to discriminate concerning leadership positions as a matter of expressive association "is not absolute" and can be overridden "by regulations adopted to serve compelling state interests"). Why shouldn't the ministerial exemption be overridden by "compelling interests" too?

In particular, consider whether there is a compelling interest in protecting the religious exercise of *the clergy member*: after all, Pamela Combs likely felt a call to be a Methodist minister, and the Fifth Circuit's decision closes that door to her. Why should the religious concerns of the church prevail over the religious concerns of the member?

Consider one possible reason for ruling for the church. In Gonzalez v. Archbishop of Manila (p. 310), the Court said that civil courts accept the decisions of church tribunals "because the parties in interest made them so by contract or otherwise." Is that why the court favors the church over the Reverend Combs? Is it likely that Combs signed something like a contract when she joined the staff at First Methodist Church, and if so did that document say she would never challenge any actions of the church against her in court?

By contrast, consider the arguments for applying the antidiscrimination laws in Jane Rutherford, Equality as the Primary Constitutional Value: The Case for Applying Employment Discrimination Laws to Religion, 81 Cornell L. Rev. 1049, 1126-1128 (1996):

> The problems of discrimination persist because they are deeply imbedded in our common culture. Law, alone, has been unable to eradicate bias. The only hope is broad scale change in social and cultural values. One part of that culture is a religious heritage that is pervasively discriminatory. Section 702 of Title VII of the Civil Rights Act allows religious groups to discriminate on religious grounds, and courts sometimes permit religious institutions to discriminate on the basis of race, sex, age, or disability. Such Congressional or judicial exceptions to civil rights laws violate the Free Exercise Clause because they limit the rights of minorities, women, the aged, and the disabled to practice their religious beliefs on the same terms as the dominant groups. . . .
>
> Courts faced with these decisions are caught in a dilemma. Any decision intrudes on a free exercise right, either of the religious groups or those excluded. The only solution to the dilemma is to look outside the religion clauses for a principled way to decide. That principle may be found in the primacy of equality. Equality is the most important constitutional value for three reasons: (1) history reveals that equality is the unifying force that defines us as a nation; (2) equality is necessary to provide legitimacy for democratic government; and (3) the primacy of equality assures that other constitutional values will be protected.

Do you agree that religious doctrine limiting certain roles to members of a particular sex or religion violate the free exercise rights of the members? Do you agree that, in the event of conflict, "equality" trumps free exercise?

(c) Most of the cases, *Combs* included, also appear to treat the clergy exemption as absolute on the other side of the free exercise ledger: the "burden on religion." By contrast, even under the *Smith* regime, free exercise exemptions were usually limited to conduct motivated by religious belief. Likewise, when a secular organization claims that being forced to retain a certain leader would interfere with its right of "expressive association," the Court inquires whether "the presence of that person affects in a significant way the group's ability to advocate public or private viewpoints." Boy Scouts of America v. Dale, 530 U.S. at 648. In *Combs*, the plaintiff would have liked to depose her former boss and ask him why he fired her. It is possible that the reason had nothing whatever to do with religious issues; indeed, under oath, he might (hypothetically) have admitted that he was prejudiced against women. Since this prejudice is condemned by the doctrines of his church no less than by the law, see The Book of Discipline of the United Methodist Church 93-95 (1992), how can enforcing the antidiscrimination laws interfere with the exercise of religion? Why not limit the free exercise protection to cases where the relevant officials assert sincere claims of a religious motivation for the hiring decision (e.g., a Catholic parish or Orthodox Jewish congregation refusing to hire a woman as clergy)?

Some recent decisions have followed this suggestion. The Third Circuit refused to dismiss a former Catholic university chaplain's complaint alleging that her demotion was motivated by sex discrimination not based in any religious tenets. The court reasoned: "[E]mployment discrimination unconnected to religious belief, religious doctrine, or the internal regulations of a church is simply the exercise of intolerance, not the free exercise of religion that the Constitution protects." Petruska v. Gannon University, ____ F.3d ____, 2006 WL 1410038 (3d Cir. 2006). See also Bollard v. Cal. Province, Society of Jesus, 196 F.3d 940 (9th Cir. 1999) (refusing to dismiss complaint filed by former Jesuit novice who sought damages for alleged sexual harassment that forced him to withdraw from training for priesthood).

2. Entanglement and the Establishment Clause. Perhaps the ministerial exception rests not only on grounds of free exercise and noncoercion, but on the value of separation. Several decisions hold that Title VII, as applied to clergy employment, runs afoul of the Establishment Clause rule proposed in Lemon v. Kurtzman, 403 U.S. 602 (1971), because it fosters an excessive government entanglement with religion. One such ruling is Rayburn v. General Conference of Seventh-Day Adventists, 772 F.2d 1164 (4th Cir. 1985), which dismissed a sex discrimination suit against the Adventist Church by a pastoral associate:

> The application of Title VII to employment decisions of this nature would result in an intolerably close relationship between church and state both on a substantive and procedural level. On a substantive level, the unrefuted evidence from [the Church] emphasized the importance of "spirituality" as an attribute of an associate in pastoral care and stated that in making an appointment, "The guidance of the Holy Spirit is always sought so that the one chosen can be God's appointed, as well as the one who has the support of his/her fellow churchmembers." It is axiomatic that the guidance of the state cannot substitute for that of the Holy

Spirit and that a courtroom is not the place to review a church's determination of "God's appointed."

Moreover, the goals of a church in the selection of its spiritual leaders and of a governmental agency in the performance of its statutory mandate may not be the same. . . . Bureaucratic suggestion in employment decisions of a pastoral character, in contravention of a church's own perception of its needs and purposes, would constitute unprecedented entanglement with religious authority and compromise the premise "that both religion and government can best work to achieve their lofty aims if each is left free of the other within its respective sphere."

On a procedural level, entanglement might also result from a protracted legal process pitting church and state as adversaries. . . . A Title VII action is potentially a lengthy proceeding, involving state agencies and commissions, the EEOC, the federal trial courts and courts of appeal. Church personnel and records would inevitably become subject to subpoena, discovery, cross-examination, the full panoply of legal process designed to probe the mind of the church in the selection of its ministers. . . . There is the danger that churches, wary of EEOC or judicial review of their decisions, might make them with an eye to avoiding litigation or bureaucratic entanglement rather than upon the basis of their own personal and doctrinal assessments of who would best serve the pastoral needs of their members.

The "excessive entanglement" rationale may explain why in many cases the clergy exemption has protected even churches that do not claim a religious motivation for discrimination. Whatever the church's motivation, to impose liability under Title VII sanctions the church for its choice of clergy and pressures it to keep a clergy member it has decided to reject. Moreover, because Title VII and similar laws generally allow the defendant to rebut a charge of discrimination by showing some other, nondiscriminatory reason for discharging the plaintiff, ministerial suits might often end up focusing on whether the minister was performing the job well, an inquiry that may involve the court in theological judgments. (Remember that Pamela Combs's senior pastor questioned her "competence, performance, and honesty.") Finally, *Rayburn* suggests that the very process of investigating a clergy suit may impermissibly entangle church and state. In light of these considerations, are decisions such as *Petruska* and *Bollard* (see note 1(c), pp. 318-319) incorrect in allowing suits by clergy against their religious institutions to proceed?

Is deference to the organization's self-definition concerning leaders indeed unique to religious organizations? In Boy Scouts v. Dale, the Court said that "we give deference to an association's assertions regarding the nature of its expression [and] also give deference to an association's view [that accepting a certain leader] would impair its expression." 530 U.S. at 653. That sounds parallel to the idea of nonentanglement in the religious context. How different should freedom of association be for religious and secular expressive associations?

3. Employment in Other Jobs and Other Activities.   To what extent do the above rationales—free exercise and nonentanglement—apply to jobs other than clergy in a religious congregation? In NLRB v. Catholic Bishop of Chicago, 440 U.S. 490 (1979), the Supreme Court held that the National Labor Relations Act, which requires employers to bargain collectively with employees, did not apply to lay teachers in church-related schools (the particular case involved Catholic high schools). The Court said that applying the Act "present[ed] a serious risk that the First Amendment will be infringed," and therefore, the Act should not be applied unless that was "the affirmative intention of Congress clearly expressed." The Court explained why there was a serious risk of constitutional violations:

> In recent decisions involving aid to parochial schools we have recognized the critical and unique role of the teacher in fulfilling the mission of a church-operated school. What was said of the schools in Lemon v. Kurtzman is true of the schools in this case: "Religious authority necessarily pervades the school system." The key role played by teachers in such a school system has been the predicate for our conclusions that governmental aid channeled through teachers creates an impermissible risk of excessive governmental entanglement in the affairs of the church-operated schools. . . .
>
> The Court of Appeals' opinion refers to charges of unfair labor practices filed against religious schools. The court observed that in those cases the schools had responded that their challenged actions were mandated by their religious creeds. The resolution of such charges by the Board, in many instances, will necessarily involve inquiry into the good faith of the position asserted by the clergy-administrators and its relationship to the school's religious mission. It is not only the conclusions that may be reached by the Board which may impinge on rights guaranteed by the Religion Clauses, but also the very process of inquiry leading to findings and conclusions.
>
> The Board's exercise of jurisdiction will have at least one other impact on church-operated schools. The Board will be called upon to decide what are "terms and conditions of employment" and therefore mandatory subjects of bargaining. . . . Inevitably the Board's inquiry will implicate sensitive issues that open the door to conflicts between clergy-administrators and the Board, or conflicts with negotiators for unions[.]

After a brief examination of the legislative history, the Court concluded that Congress had not clearly expressed an "affirmative intention" to bring church-operated schools within the Act. The dissent disagreed on the question of statutory construction and did not reach the constitutional question.

Catholic Bishop, together with *Combs* and *Rayburn*, suggests several considerations in deciding how far a religious organization's right to autonomy in employment extends.

(a) **The nature of the plaintiff's job.** Should the exemption concerning clergy extend to all positions involved in religious worship and sacraments—say, a church organist who is not ordained? (If your answer is yes, consider whether that can be squared with *Smith*, which involved a sacrament of the Native American Church.) If there is a "fundamental right of churches to be free from government interference in their internal management and administration" (as *Combs* puts it), does that mean that no race or sex discrimination claim can be brought by a church's bookkeeper, or secretary? If lay teachers at parochial schools are exempt (*Catholic Bishop*), should school doctors and nurses be? Decisions extending the employment exemption include EEOC v. Catholic University of America, 83 F.3d 455 (D.C. Cir. 1996) (teacher of canon law); Little v. Wuerl, 929 F.2d 944 (3rd Cir. 1991) (high school teacher); EEOC v. Pacific Press Publishing Ass'n, 676 F.2d 1272 (9th Cir. 1982) (secretary); Assemany v. Archdiocese of Detroit, 434 N.W.2d 233 (Mich. App. 1988) (organist). But cf., e.g., EEOC v. Mississippi College, 626 F.2d 477 (5th Cir. 1980) (Title VII clergy exception does not extend to claims involving non-theology faculty at sectarian college).

What if the right of "expressive association" under Boy Scouts v. Dale is added to the picture? As to what jobs does it shield a religious organization's employment decisions?

(b) The nature of the defendant institution and its activity. Just as the employment exemptions may not extend to some jobs (even in a church) that are religiously insignificant, the exemption may not extend to some institutions that are too peripheral to the church's real mission to warrant exemption. But how should a court decide when a separately incorporated institution is "too peripheral"? NLRB v. Catholic Bishop exempts parochial schools from the Wagner Act. Why treat them like churches? What about hospitals? Scharon v. St. Luke's Episcopal Presbyterian Hospitals, 929 F.2d 360 (8th Cir. 1991) (exemption extends to claims by hospital chaplain). What about church-related or church-run social service agencies—retirement homes, adoption agencies, drug and pregnancy counseling centers, soup kitchens, etc.? NLRB v. Hanna Boys Center, 940 F.2d 1295 (9th Cir. 1991), refused to apply *Catholic Bishop* to a residential school for orphaned boys, requiring the school to bargain not only with cooks and maintenance workers, but even with child-care workers who counseled the boys. And in Tony & Susan Alamo Foundation v. Secretary of Labor, 471 U.S. 290 (1985), the Court applied the Fair Labor Standards Act to businesses run by a nonprofit religious organization. The Foundation objected that it would violate the Free Exercise Clause to pay workers the minimum wage when they wanted to forego salaries for religious reasons; and that enforcing the Act's recordkeeping requirements would create a forbidden entanglement. The Court rejected both claims. Does this suggest that such businesses are also not entitled to the ministerial exemption from Title VII?

(c) The nature of the plaintiff's claim. Sometimes the plaintiff's particular legal claim is crucial. Some courts have held that church-related schools can be forced to bargain with their teachers under state labor laws, unlike under the federal law. See, e.g., Hill-Murray Federation of Teachers v. Hill-Murray Catholic School, 487 N.W.2d 857 (Minn. 1992). How can that be squared with *Catholic Bishop?*

(d) The statutory Title VII exemption: *Amos.* If the decisions involving non-clergy employment require the court to inquire how "religious" is the job or institution in question, doesn't that inquiry itself create entanglement? Recall the case of Corporation of Presiding Bishop v. Amos (p. 250). Title VII, the federal law against employment discrimination, originally contained an exemption permitting religious organizations to discriminate based on religion in jobs involving "religious activities." Later, however, Congress added an exemption allowing religious organizations to discriminate on the basis of religion in all their activities (secular as well as religious). In *Amos*, the Court upheld the exemption against an Establishment Clause challenge, in part because without the broadened exemption it would be "a significant burden on a religious organization to require it, on pain of substantial liability, to predict which of its activities a secular court will consider religious." If this is the rationale for the statutory exemption, then how could it be permissible for the courts, in the cases listed earlier in this note, to distinguish between jobs in a religious institution—for example, to bar sex discrimination claims against a church concerning clergy positions but not other positions?

Several justices in *Amos* noted that the religious organization in question there—a gymnasium operated by the Mormon Church—was a nonprofit entity; they suggested that it might be unconstitutional to extend the broad exemption for religious discrimination to for-profit commercial entities. Does the nonprofit/ for-profit line make any sense? Aren't there commercial businesses that make or sell religious products, or that seek to operate on religious principles?

4. Torts by Churches

In this section we look at the liability of churches and synagogues for torts. The constitutional implications of these lawsuits are sometimes overlooked. It is easier to see the hand of the government—and the role of the First Amendment—when the legislature passes a law, or an agency enforces a regulation, against religious groups. But the common law is also law, and judges and juries represent the government just as authoritatively as the other two branches. The Supreme Court has held that tort rules can abridge the freedom of speech. New York Times v. Sullivan, 376 U.S. 254 (1964). This is true, too, for the freedom of religion. Cf. Kreshik v. St. Nicholas Cathedral, 363 U.S. 190 (1960).

In terms of their financial impact on religious institutions, tort rules may be the most significant of all. For example, by June 2005, it was reported, settlements in cases alleging sexual abuse by priests had cost the Roman Catholic Church in America $1.06 billion; a $120 million compensation fund created by the diocese of Covington, Kentucky, pushed the total past the billion-dollar mark. Associated Press, June 10, 2005 (available on Westlaw at 6/10/05 APWIRES 08:17:10).

In this section we will consider two aspects of tort suits that present First Amendment difficulties. One is the standard of conduct that gives rise to liability. The other is the problem of ascending liability within religious institutions.

NALLY v. GRACE COMMUNITY CHURCH OF THE VALLEY
47 Cal. 3d 278, 763 P.2d 948 (1988)

[Kenneth Nally began attending the Grace Church, the largest Protestant church in Los Angeles, while he was a student at UCLA in 1974. The church offered pastoral counseling to members on matters of faith and the application of Christian principles to everyday problems. These counselors taught that the Bible contains truths that govern Christians in their relations with God and in their personal lives. Nally suffered from depression and visited with one of the church's counselors (Rea) five times in 1978. In March of 1979 Nally took an overdose of an antidepressant drug and was hospitalized for six days. Upon his release he stayed for a while with the church pastor (MacArthur). Both the hospital psychiatrist, and a physician whom he saw at MacArthur's prompting, urged Nally to commit himself to a psychiatric hospital, but Nally declined and his parents rejected the idea of involuntary commitment. Nally did meet with another church counselor (Thomson), and during their session asked whether Christians who commit suicide would still be saved. Thomson answered that "a person who is once saved is always saved," but told Nally that "it would be wrong to be thinking in such terms." Several days later Nally moved back home.

During the last week of his life Nally saw several physicians, visited two psychologists' offices, and had an unhappy meeting with a former girlfriend. On April 1, 1979 he killed himself with a shotgun.

Nally's parents sued the church, MacArthur, Rea, Thomson, and the pastor of the church's college department (Cory) for wrongful death. They made three claims: (1) Clergy malpractice. They charged that MacArthur—because he had not referred Nally for professional psychiatric or psychological care—had failed to exercise the standard of care for a clergyman of his sect and training in the community. (2) Negligence. They charged that MacArthur and the church were negligent in not requiring their counselors to have psychological training; and that the counselors were negligent in not referring Nally for professional help when they became aware of his suicidal tendencies. (3) Intentional infliction of emotional distress. They also charged that the defendants had taught certain Protestant religious doctrines that conflicted with Nally's Catholic upbringing and exacerbated his preexisting feelings of guilt and depression. In the same vein they complained that Thomson had suggested to Nally that if he "accepted Jesus Christ as his personal savior, [he] would still be accepted into heaven if he committed suicide."

The trial court granted summary judgment for the defendants. The Court of Appeal reversed and allowed the case to go to trial, igniting a controversy about the propriety of an action for clergy malpractice. At the conclusion of the plaintiffs' evidence the trial court again dismissed the case, on the basis of insufficient evidence. The Court of Appeal again reversed, but in this opinion it would have allowed only counts (2) and (3) to go to the jury. The California Supreme Court reversed. The Court first rejected the cause of action for negligent failure to prevent suicide.]

Under traditional tort law principles, one is ordinarily not liable for the actions of another and is under no duty to protect another from harm, in the absence of a special relationship of custody or control. [T]wo cases imposed such a duty in wrongful death actions after plaintiffs proved that the deceased committed suicide in a hospital or other in-patient facility that had accepted the responsibility to care for and attend to the needs of the suicidal patient. [But neither] case suggested extending the duty of care to personal or religious counseling relationships in which one person provided nonprofessional guidance to another seeking advice and the counselor had no control over the environment of the individual being counseled.

[T]he indeterminate nature of liability the Court of Appeal imposes on nontherapist counselors could deter those most in need of help from seeking treatment out of fear that their private disclosures could subject them to involuntary commitment to psychiatric facilities. . . .

We also note that the Legislature has exempted the clergy from the licensing requirements applicable to marriage, family, child and domestic counselors, and from the operation of statutes regulating psychologists. In so doing, the Legislature has recognized that access to the clergy for counseling should be free from state imposed counseling standards, and that "the secular state is not equipped to ascertain the competence of counseling when performed by those affiliated with religious organizations." . . .

Even assuming that workable standards of care could be established in the present case, an additional difficulty arises in attempting to identify with precision those to whom the duty should apply. Because of the differing theological views espoused by the myriad of religions in our state and practiced by church members, it would certainly be impractical, and quite possibly unconstitutional, to impose a duty of care on pastoral counselors. Such a duty would necessarily be intertwined with the religious philosophy of the particular denomination or ecclesiastical teachings of the religious entity.

[With respect to the claim for intentional infliction of emotional distress, the court observed, we] have found only one California case . . . allowing a cause of action for wrongful death based on defendant's outrageous conduct in causing a suicide. In Tate v. Canonica (Cal. App. 1960), the court allowed a widow to state a cause of action for wrongful death based on intentional infliction of emotional distress after she alleged that defendant intentionally made threats and accusations against her husband and such conduct was a substantial factor in bringing about the husband's suicide. The *Tate* court rejected as inapplicable to intentional torts, the defenses of supervening cause and contributory negligence. Thus, under *Tate*, a plaintiff may resist a demurrer to a wrongful death action for intentional conduct leading to suicide if he can allege facts sufficient to show that defendant's conduct was outrageous and a substantial factor in the decedent's suicide.

[The Court of Appeal had held that the trial court should have admitted a tape recording made by Pastor Thomson in 1980 (after Nally's death), and that with this tape there was enough evidence on this count to go to the jury. On the tape—a recording of lectures to seminary students—Thomson was asked whether a person who commits suicide can be saved. Thomson replied, in a manner consistent with Reformation Protestant views about sin and grace, that a person neither acquires salvation by his own works nor forfeits it by the commission of subsequent sins. He went on to say that "suicide for a believer is the Lord saying, 'Okay, come on home.'" The California Supreme Court held that the trial court had properly excluded the tape, because it proved little about what Thomson might have said months before in different circumstances to Nally. Without this evidence, the claim was properly dismissed.]

NOTES AND QUESTIONS

1. Charitable Immunity.   There was a time when the Nallys could not have sued the church, for reasons rooted in the common law rather than in the Constitution. The doctrine of charitable immunity took hold in America in the latter half of the nineteenth century. There were a number of ideas behind it. One was that exposing charities to tort liability would discourage people from making gifts to them. Another was that people like Nally who get benefits from charities assume the risk of negligence, and impliedly waive any claims against their benefactors. Still another was that charities should not be held liable for the torts of their servants because they derived no gain from their employment. American Law Institute, Restatement (Second) of Torts §895E, comment c (1979). During this period, charities (including religious enterprises) were immune from suit in much the same way as local governments and public officials were. By the middle of the twentieth century these arguments had lost force, due in part to the widespread availability of liability insurance. Today the notion of charitable immunity affords only spotty protection to religious institutions. See Note, The Quality of Mercy: "Charitable Torts" and Their Continuing Immunity, 100 Harv. L. Rev. 1382 (1987).

2. Tort Liability and the First Amendment.   In New York Times v. Sullivan, mentioned above, the U.S. Supreme Court overturned a $500,000 libel judgment against the *Times*. The Court held that the common law of libel was inconsistent with the Free Speech Clause insofar as it allowed public officials to sue for negligently false statements. Newspapers could say what they liked about public officials, provided it was not maliciously or recklessly false. *Nally* presents a parallel under the Free Exercise Clause. Suppose the common law of negligence (or whatever) allowed people to collect damages from a church and its ministers for what they counseled their patrons. Would the Free Exercise Clause permit this? The Free Speech Clause?

It seems clear, does it not, that the First Amendment precludes the tort of clergy malpractice. Imagine a legal rule requiring a minister to adhere to a standard of care typical for clergy of that sect and training in the community. Would we have one standard for Jews and another for Christian Scientists? How would a court decide what counted as the substandard practice of Christian Science?

Consider now the tort of intentional infliction of emotional distress. The plaintiffs claimed that the defendants had contributed to Nally's depression by criticizing the Catholic faith he was raised in. The Court of Appeal suggested that Pastor Thomson might have been liable for making suicide more alluring to Nally. (On the tape he said that "suicide for a believer is the Lord saying, 'Okay, come on home.'") Thomson made that statement while he was explaining certain Protestant views about faith, sin, grace, and salvation. Defendants' instruction *could* have had one or both of these effects. Should a court therefore hold them liable? Is there a difference between these statements and the threats in Tate v. Canonica, the case cited in *Nally*? Defamation may contribute to a plaintiff's depression, but the First Amendment nevertheless protects it. Why? Do the same reasons apply to religious instruction?

The other claim the Nallys made was that the defendants had acted negligently in not referring their son for professional help when they became aware of his suicidal tendencies. This claim, unlike the other two, is not necessarily tied to the religious nature of the defendants' counseling. It might also be made against nonprofessional secular counselors—people who work in college dormitories, pregnancy counseling centers, shelters for homeless people or battered women, etc. The legal rule it enforces would nevertheless have effects on religious counseling. Some people believe we find God in our deepest moments of despair. Suppose a minister views psychotherapy as the wrong way out of that despair. Can the government, under the First Amendment, require him to point his parishoners in that direction? Unlike clergy malpractice, the tort of negligence does not set a specific standard for religious behavior. It may therefore be less susceptible to Establishment Clause challenge. As for the Free Exercise Clause, Employment Division v. Smith allows the state to regulate religious behavior by means of neutral, generally applicable laws. Do negligence laws fit within any of *Smith*'s exceptions to this general rule?

3. Belief and Truth. Recall that in United States v. Ballard, 322 U.S. 78 (1944) (p. 193), the Court held that a jury could not inquire into the truth or falsity of religious claims.

In *Nally*, the plaintiffs asserted that professional psychiatric help cures depression better than the Bible does. The defendants may have thought otherwise. (It's not clear that they opposed professional treatment.) Can the law impose liability for acting on the latter assumption without judging it to be false? If *Ballard* precludes a tort action in *Nally*, does it enforce the Free Exercise Clause more strictly than Employment Division v. Smith now allows? It has been argued that churches' First Amendment protection against tort actions has rested largely on the constitutional bar against evaluating religious doctrines—such as whether a clergy counselor's advice was "fraudulent" or "unreasonable"—but that for various reasons, including the *Smith* decision, this protection may be eroding. Scott C. Idleman, Tort Liability, Religious Entities, and the Decline of Constitutional Protection, 75 Ind. L.J. 219 (2000).

4. Two Kinds of Torts. All tort actions against churches make the practice of religion more expensive. But some torts impose liability for religious actions and some do not. *Nally* involved claims of the first kind. So do cases where a plaintiff complains that she has been subjected to church discipline. Jehovah's Witnesses and some Anabaptist churches and Orthodox Jewish congregations subject members who have been expelled to "shunning," i.e., social and economic ostracizing. See Paul v. Watchtower Bible Society, 819 F.2d 875 (9th Cir.), cert. denied, 484 U.S. 926 (1987); Bear v. Reformed Mennonite Church, 341 A.2d 105 (Pa. 1975). The Church of Scientology engages in a kind of discipline known as "fair game" against defecting members. Wollersheim v. Church of Scientology, 260 Cal. Rptr. 331 (Cal. 2d App. Dist. 1989), cert. denied, 495 U.S. 910 (1990). Should we react differently to these cases when a church member wishes to sever her connection with the church? What if the church physically (or mentally) prevents her from doing so? See generally Carl H. Esbeck, Tort Claims Against Church and Ecclesiastical Officers: The First Amendment Considerations, 89 W. Va. L. Rev. 1 (1986); Richard R. Hammar, Pastor, Church & Law ch. 4 (1996).

In cases of the second kind the law imposes liability on churches for nonreligious actions. There is no religious justification for letting a sidewalk deteriorate, driving too fast, or sexually abusing one's parishioners. Imposition of liability on the primary actor in cases like these presents no real First Amendment question. But the issue gets more complicated when plaintiffs try to extend liability to other people.

MOSES v. DIOCESE OF COLORADO

863 P.2d 310 (Colo. 1993)

Justice ERICKSON delivered the Opinion of the Court.

[In 1984 Mary Moses Tenantry was a parishioner at St. Philip and St. James Episcopal Church in Denver. She sought counseling from Father Paul Robinson, an assistant priest at the parish, and their sessions eventually led to a sexual affair.

Tenantry's sister learned of the affair in 1985 and informed Father Vernon Myers, the rector of the parish. Myers told the bishop, William Frey. The diocese took no action until 1986 when Tenantry's husband, Geoffrey Moses, learned of the affair and met with Fathers Robinson and Myers and Bishop Frey.

At the meeting Moses agreed to allow the bishop to supervise "whatever needed to happen." The bishop had Father Robinson reassigned to a parish in Colorado Springs and advised him to seek counseling. He also met with Tenantry, who told him that she feared for the loss of her salvation because of her affair with Father Robinson. Bishop Frey gave her absolution for her sins. Tenantry told the bishop that she still loved Robinson. He advised her to forget about him, and told her (in response to her inquiry) not to speak of the matter except to her husband or a counselor.

In 1990 Tenantry and Moses divorced and her mental health deteriorated. She filed this action against the Diocese, Bishop Frey, and Father Robinson. Robinson filed for bankruptcy, and the claims against him were severed. The jury held the Bishop and the Diocese liable for breach of fiduciary duty and negligent hiring and supervision and awarded Tenantry damages of $728,100; it also held them vicariously liable for Father Robinson's breach of fiduciary duty and awarded $488,400.]

We affirm the judgment of the trial court on the issues of breach of fiduciary duty and negligent hiring and supervision. We reverse the judgment on vicarious liability.

II

The [case of] Watson v. Jones established the doctrine of judicial abstention in matters involving court interpretation of ecclesiastical law. [See also, e.g.,] Kedroff v. St. Nicholas Cathedral; Presbyterian Church v. Hull Church; Serbian E. Orthodox Diocese v. Milivojevich.

The principle of these cases, as this court has recognized, is that courts must not become embroiled in disputes involving a religious organization if the court would be required to interpret or weigh church doctrine. [The "neutral principles" doctrine] allows a court to apply the neutral laws of the state to religious organizations but forbids a court from resolving disputed issues of religious doctrine and practice. In Jones v. Wolf, the Supreme Court of the United States explained, "[t]he neutral-principles approach cannot be said to 'inhibit' the free exercise of religion, any more than do other neutral provisions of state law governing the manner in which churches own property, hire employees, or purchase goods." . . .

Application of a secular standard to secular conduct that is tortious is not prohibited by the Constitution. See Employment Division v. Smith. The Supreme Court has not granted churches broad immunity against being sued in civil courts. Civil actions against clergy members and their superiors that involve claims of a breach of fiduciary duty, negligent hiring and supervision, and vicarious liability are actionable if they are supported by competent evidence in the record.

The facts of Tenantry's case indicate that an organization, confronted with the misdeeds of one of its agents, assumed control of the matter and in the process of protecting itself injured a vulnerable individual. The defendants have not argued that Bishop Frey's decision to assume control and resolve the problems created by Father Robinson and Tenantry's relationship was a matter of purely ecclesiastical concern. Tenantry's claims in this case do not involve disputes within the church and are not based solely on ecclesiastical or disciplinary matters which would call into question the trial court's power to render a judgment against the defendants. Our decision does not require a reading of the Constitution and Canons of the Protestant Episcopal Church or any other documents of church governance. Because the facts of this case do not require interpreting or weighing church doctrine and neutral principles of law can be applied, the First Amendment is not a defense against Tenantry's claims.

III

[A] prerequisite to finding a fiduciary duty is the existence of a fiduciary relationship. "A fiduciary relation exists between two persons when one of them is under a duty to act for or to give advice for the benefit of another upon matters within the scope of the relation." Restatement (Second) of Torts § 874 cmt. a. [The] existence of the fiduciary relationship is a question of fact for the jury. In this case, the jury was properly instructed on the requisite elements of a fiduciary relationship and determined a fiduciary relationship existed between Bishop Frey and Tenantry. The jury's determination of a factual issue will not be reversed if the record reveals a reasonable basis to support it.

In the meeting between Bishop Frey and Tenantry the parties did not occupy equal positions. Bishop Frey held a position of authority in the church and had the power to resolve conflicts in the church. In addition, Bishop Frey's role during the meeting was as a counselor to Tenantry, not as a representative of the Diocese or Father Robinson. If Bishop Frey was acting only for the Diocese and Father Robinson, he failed to convey that fact to Tenantry and led her to believe he was acting in her interest.

Bishop Frey had ordered a meeting with Tenantry and Tenantry believed he had the power to decide if she would lose her salvation. Tenantry was mentally unstable and Bishop Frey recognized that she was fragile and had a pathological sense of guilt. The superior position of Bishop Frey and the power he had over Tenantry is evinced by Tenantry's request for permission to talk to people in her family and for special permission to speak to her husband. The record supports the jury's finding that Bishop Frey was in a superior position and was able to exert substantial influence over Tenantry.

An unequal relationship does not automatically create a fiduciary duty. In order to be liable the superior party must assume a duty to act in the dependent party's best interest. The defendants assert they are not liable because Bishop Frey and the Diocese did not take any action that would allow the jury to conclude they assumed a duty to Tenantry. There is sufficient evidence that the defendants assumed a duty to Tenantry when they acted to resolve the problems that were the result of the relationship between Father Robinson and Tenantry.

Father Myers informed the Diocese of the relationship between Tenantry and Father Robinson as early as August of 1985. Father Myers stated he took no action after informing the Diocese because the Diocese had assumed control of the matter. The fact the Diocese had assumed control was reinforced by

Bishop Frey's assumption of personal responsibility for the resolution of the matter. Bishop Frey asked Moses to rely on him to take care of "whatever needed to happen" to resolve the issues created by the sexual relationship between Tenantry and Father Robinson. Bishop Frey asked to speak to Tenantry to resolve the problem. The record supports the jury's finding that Bishop Frey and the Diocese assumed a duty on behalf of Tenantry. One of the fiduciary's duties is the duty to deal "with utmost good faith and solely for the benefit" of the dependent party. Once a member of the clergy accepts the parishioner's trust and accepts the role of counselor, a duty exists to act with the utmost good faith for the benefit of the parishioner. The breach of the duty which the Diocese and Bishop Frey assumed is evinced by Bishop Frey's actions.

[Acting] as the representative for the Diocese, Bishop Frey failed to assist Tenantry in understanding that she was not the only person responsible for her sexual relationship with Father Robinson. He did not recommend counseling for Tenantry but did recommend counseling for Father Robinson and ordered Father Robinson to make progress reports on the counseling. Bishop Frey's only action in regard to Tenantry was to bind her to secrecy. Thus, Bishop Frey assumed control of a situation that demanded he consider Tenantry's interests and then used Tenantry's trust to her detriment.

The record supports the jury's finding that a fiduciary relationship existed between Bishop Frey and Tenantry, that the Diocese and Bishop Frey assumed a duty toward Tenantry, and that the Diocese and Bishop Frey breached their duty.

IV

Bishop Frey and the Diocese contend that the jury erred in finding the Diocese negligent in hiring and supervising Father Robinson and that the alleged negligence caused Tenantry's injuries. Bishop Frey and the Diocese maintain that there was no employment relationship between the Diocese and Father Robinson and even if there was, there was insufficient evidence in the record to support these negligence claims.[15]

A

An employer may be liable for harm to others for negligently employing an improper person for a task which may involve a risk to others. It is axiomatic that a prerequisite to establishing negligent hiring is an employment or agency relationship. The existence of an agency relationship is ordinarily a question of fact to be determined by the fact finder.

[The] evidence presented at trial shows that the structure of the Episcopal Church is basically hierarchal. A pamphlet distributed by the Episcopalian Church titled "About Being an Episcopalian" contains a chart of the "Structure

---

15. Frey and the Diocese also contend that the First Amendment of the United States Constitution was violated by the trial court when it admitted into evidence two pamphlets which helped establish the employment relationship between the Diocese and Robinson. As discussed *supra* Part II, Tenantry's claims for negligent hiring and supervision are not barred by the First Amendment of the United States Constitution because neutral principles of law can be applied. In order to determine if an employer-employee relationship exists, we do not have to interpret or weigh church doctrine.

of the Episcopal Church." The chart graphically shows that the bishop presides over the Diocese and the priests. A priest presides over the parish "subject to the bishop's approval." In "The Episcopal Church: Essential Facts," another pamphlet admitted during the trial, the Episcopal Church defines the role of priests: "Priests (also known as presbyters) are ordained and consecrated to assist the bishop in overseeing the Church." The pamphlet sets forth that the diocese "is governed by its bishop and a diocesan convention composed of clergy of the diocese and lay persons elected by the parishes." Vestries call rectors to serve only after consultation with the bishop. Additionally, the bishop signs a letter promoting a priest to a pastor of a parish.

Other evidence presented at trial establishes the relationship among the rector, the bishop, the diocese, and the assistant priest. The rector supervises an assistant priest's counseling duties which are specifically prescribed by regulations promulgated by the Diocese. In addition, the rector in this case stated that he reported to the bishop and that the bishop made final decisions on discipline. Father Robinson testified that when a priest needs pastoral care, the priest looks to the bishop. The Diocese has independent responsibility for the employment of priests. [The priest's education is monitored by the bishop; he is put through a screening for hire by the Diocese which includes psychological evaluation.] The bishop oversees ordination, discipline, counseling, the maintenance of personnel files and the provision of information with respect to hiring. Vestries rely on the Diocese to prepare and educate candidates, to obtain psychological evaluations of candidates for ordination, and provide information about individuals who are being considered for clergy positions in the parish. While the individual priests and parishes may be independently responsible for their day-to-day activities, the Diocese exercises an employment option in the hiring of its pastors. . . .

Because an agency or employment relationship existed between the Diocese and Father Robinson, and Father Robinson's duties included a close relationship with parishioners, the Diocese could be liable for negligent hiring and supervision. Liability of the employer is predicated on the employer's antecedent ability to recognize a potential employee's "attribute[s] of character or prior conduct" which would create an undue risk of harm to those with whom the employee came in contact in executing his employment responsibilities. . . .

The duty is increased in this case because the Diocese placed Father Robinson in a position that required not only frequent contact with others, but induced reliance and trust through the counseling process. [Father] Robinson's duties included counseling and close association with parishioners at the church. The Diocese was in possession of a psychological report which concluded that Father Robinson has a "sexual identification ambiguity."[23] Another psychological

---

23. At trial a clinical psychologist testified:

> Dr. Dolby[, the psychologist filing the report on Father Robinson,] makes a statement [that Father Robinson] has a history of sexual identification ambiguity. Although he says that [Father Robinson] functions exclusively as a heterosexual both physically and in fantasy. His marriage is apparently satisfying. I don't understand what that means. Obviously, it would be of some concern to know if he is having any sort of struggle in the area of sexual identity. That is something that I think a reasonably prudent bishop or anyone else reading this would want to know what that meant, what is the issue that has been found here.

report indicated that Father Robinson had a problem with depression and suffered from low self-esteem. An expert testified that a large number of clergy who have sexual relationships with their parishioners do so partially as a result of suffering from depression and low self-esteem. Father Robinson's struggle with his sexual identity and his problems with depression and low self-esteem put the Diocese on notice to inquire further whether Father Robinson was capable of counseling parishioners. These reports gave the Diocese a reason to believe Father Robinson should not be put in a position to counsel vulnerable individuals and that he might be unable to handle the transference phenomenon. The failure to communicate this knowledge to the vestry and subsequent placement of Father Robinson in the role of counselor breached the Diocese's duty of care to Tenantry.

B

The jury also found the Diocese was negligent in its supervision of Father Robinson. The Restatement (Second) of Agency section 213 [comment d] states:

> The principal may be negligent because he has reason to know that the servant or other agent, because of his qualities, is likely to harm others in view of the work or instrumentalities entrusted to him. If the dangerous quality of the agent causes harm, the principal may be liable under the rule that one initiating conduct having undue tendency to cause harm is liable therefor.

[Both] the Diocese and Bishop Frey had previous exposure to the problem of sexual relationships developing between priests and parishioners because the problem had arisen seven times before. The psychological reports gave notice that further supervision may be required. The reports indicate problems of sexual identification ambiguity, depression and low self-esteem. Father Robinson's file also indicated he had problems with authority. Father Robinson had an inability to respond to superior authority. A reasonable person would have inquired further into Father Robinson's known difficulty in dealing with superior authority, and would have assumed a greater degree of care in monitoring his conduct. In light of its knowledge, it was reasonable for the jury to determine the defendants should have been alert to the possibility of problems with Father Robinson and taken adequate steps to insure Father Robinson was not in a position where he could abuse the trust he enjoys as a priest conducting counseling.

V

The jury determined that the Diocese and Bishop Frey were vicariously liable for Father Robinson's tortious conduct. Father Robinson, however, was not acting within the scope and course of his employment and therefore the Diocese and Bishop Frey are not vicariously liable. The agency doctrine of vicarious liability is based on the theory of respondeat superior which postulates that a master may be liable for the acts of an agent acting on the master's behalf. An employer may be held vicariously liable for an employee's tort only when the tort is committed within the course and scope of employment. An employee is acting within the scope of his employment if he is doing the work assigned to him by his employer, or what is necessarily incidental to that work, or customary in the employer's business.

[But Father Robinson was not acting in the scope of his employment when he had sex with Tenantry.] Bishop Frey testified that Father Robinson's conduct was a "serious breach of [his] ordination vows." Father Robinson testified that his physical relationship was not within the scope of his employment with the church. Even Tenantry's own experts testified that Father Robinson's sexual conduct was outside the scope of his priestly duties. [We therefore order the trial court to vacate the portion of its judgment holding the Diocese and Bishop Frey vicariously liable for Father Robinson's acts.]

Chief Justice ROVIRA, concurring in part and dissenting in part:

The majority holds that sufficient evidence was presented at trial to create a question for the jury regarding whether an employment or agency relationship existed between the Diocese of Colorado (diocese) and Father Paul Robinson and therefore, the diocese may be liable for the negligent hiring and supervision of Robinson. [I disagree.]

The uncontradicted evidence presented at trial established that the diocese neither had the right of continuous control over Father Robinson nor exercised that "right." Indeed, no evidence was presented which created even the inference that the diocese was vested with such power over Father Robinson. Canon 14(a) of the Episcopal Church provides that "[a]ll assistant Clergy . . . shall be selected by the rector . . . and shall serve under the authority and direction of the Rector." Numerous witnesses testified that it was the rector at St. Philip and St. James Parish who gave Father Robinson his assignments and who instructed him as to how to carry out his day-to-day duties. Those same witnesses testified that those day-to-day activities would be supervised and controlled by the rector, and not the diocese or the bishop.

[The court also] concludes that "the Diocese exercises an employment option in the hiring of its pastors." Like continuous control in the context of agency, the power of continuous control is a critical element, or prerequisite, to finding an employer-employee relationship. Other particularly probative indicators of an employment relationship include the power to hire and terminate, and whether the purported employer pays the salary of or otherwise compensates the alleged employee.

[T]he undisputed evidence reveals that the diocese neither had nor exercised the right to control Father Robinson's day-to-day activities. Similarly, the undisputed evidence established that the diocese did not have the power or authority to either hire or terminate Father Robinson. Canon 14(a) provides that "[a]ny assistant selected shall serve at the discretion of the Rector." . . .

The diocese did not have the power to control Father Robinson's day-to-day activities. Nor did it have the power or authority to initiate or terminate Robinson's employment with the parish. Finally, it was the parish of St. Philip and St. James that was responsible for compensating Robinson, not the diocese.

Thus, I am of the opinion that the uncontradicted evidence precludes, as a matter of law, a finding that the diocese and Father Robinson occupied an employer-employee relationship.

334 III. Religion in the Regulatory State

NOTES AND QUESTIONS

The jury in *Moses* held the bishop and the diocese liable on three grounds: vicarious liability (respondeat superior), negligent hiring and supervision, and breach of fiduciary duty.

1. Vicarious Liability.   Under the first theory, the church hierarchy (Bishop Frey and the Diocese of Colorado) is automatically liable for the tort of its agent (Father Robinson) when he is acting within the scope of his authority. But the Colorado Supreme Court, like most other courts to address the issue of clergy sex abuse—reversed on this claim on the ground that Robinson was acting outside the scope of his employment when he engaged in sex with Tenantry. Typically, the stronger legal claims against the church hierarchy are directly for its own actions, such as negligence in supervising the clergy member or breach of fiduciary duty.

2. Who Is the Clergy Member's Employer (Under Vicarious Liability or Negligence)?   It may be crucial to decide whether the clergy member was an employee of the defendant not only for vicarious liability, but also for negligence, since a defendant only has responsibility to supervise its agents or employees. Was the *Moses* court correct that Father Robinson was an agent or employee not just of the local parish but of the diocese? In the Episcopal Church, the bishop, the diocesan head, exercises several supervisory roles: evaluating candidates' suitability for the priesthood, monitoring their education, ultimately ordaining them, and even thereafter maintaining some oversight. On the other hand Father Robinson was actually hired by the parish vestry, acting on the recommendation of the parish rector. The parish paid Father Robinson's salary; and the rector gave him his assignments and supervised his performance on a day-to-day basis. Consider the analogy of a young associate in a law firm. He is licensed by the state bar, which must approve his education and his character and fitness. In case of egregious misconduct it may revoke his license. But he is hired and paid by his firm. Is this how we should think about Episcopal priests?

Other Christian churches have more simple polities than the Episcopalians. In the Roman Catholic Church, the epitome of a "hierarchical" church, the bishop not only ordains priests but assigns them to parishes. Code of Canon Law, cans. 523, 547 (1983). Does that mean we can say with confidence that the Catholic diocese is the priest's employer?

In Baptist churches, whose polity is "congregational," the local church plays the central role. Affiliations like the American Baptist Churches may agree on minimum educational requirements and furnish names of available ministers. But ordination is done on the local level. It does not signify a belief in apostolic succession. It is rather like the commissioning of Paul and Barnabas by the church at Antioch (Acts 13:3)—a laying-on-of-hands by various other ministers. Pastors are hired by the congregation, typically by a vote of three-fourths of the members present and voting. Norman H. Maring & Winthrop S. Hudson, A Baptist Manual of Polity and Practice 69-70, 115-117, 269 (1991). This suggests that the local church is the Baptist pastor's employer; but who precisely should do the supervision? The board of deacons? The congregation?

Compared to a diocese or higher body, the local church typically has fewer assets to compensate a plaintiff (which is why plaintiffs sue higher bodies) and is less likely to have insurance against this kind of liability. Moreover, often the local congregation (church, synagogue) is an unincorporated association. The common law did not recognize such a group as a legal entity, so it couldn't sue or be sued in its own name. Many states today have changed this rule by statute. See, e.g., Cal. Civ. Proc. Code § 388 (West 1973). But if the association has no insurance, how would it satisfy a judgment? Can church members be sued as a class and held collectively liable to pay the judgment out of their own assets? Hutchins v. Grace Tabernacle United Pentecostal Church, 804 S.W.2d 598 (Tex. App. 1991).

Can employer liability (negligent supervision or respondeat superior) reach reach beyond the diocese to even higher religious bodies such as regional conferences of bishops? The U.S. Conference of Catholic Bishops (USCCB) issues pronouncements on matters of concern to the Church (economic justice, war, abortion), makes recommendations to churches and its own member bishops, and occasionally makes authoritative rules. On such bodies, see Decree on the Bishops' Pastoral Office in the Church (Christus Dominus) ¶¶4-5, in Walter M. Abbott, S.J., The Documents of Vatican II 398-400 (1966). Could a plaintiff alleging sexual abuse by a parish priest sue the USCCB on a theory that the U.S. bishops failed to respond to a known problem of abuse? Could a plaintiff sue the pope?

3. Constitutional Issues Concerning Negligence Claims. *Moses* held that imposing liability on the bishop and diocese for negligent supervision of the priest did not raise any First Amendment problems. Was this correct? Consider these possible constitutional difficulties:

First, in *Moses* the court admitted into evidence two pamphlets issued by the Episcopal Church ("About Being an Episcopalian," and "The Episcopal Church: Essential Facts") to help it form a picture of the relation between bishop and priest and determine whether the priest was the diocese's agent. What constitutional problems might be created when a court or jury needs to read and interpret such documents? What cases would you cite to argue that there is a constitutional problem? Can the question who is the clergyman's "employer" be determined on the basis of neutral, secular principles of law?

Second, suppose you are the lawyer for the Episcopal Diocese of Denver and the bishop, who has just paid out $728,100 to Ms. Tenantry, asks you how the diocese can avoid such exposure in the future. There are two directions to take. One is for the diocese to become more "Catholic" in its employment practices— it might wrest authority to appoint assistant pastors away from vestries and rectors, and make sure that no one went into a local parish who posed a risk of misbehaving. The other is for the diocese to become more "Baptist"—it could have much *less* to do with priestly appointments, so that when it was sued the next time it could safely disclaim responsibility for the choice of Father Robinson. The rules about ascending liability for torts thus push churches toward the extremes of hierarchicalism and congregationalism, and away from moderate or mixed forms of polity. Is this an establishment of the safer forms of polity? Is it a restriction of the religious freedom of Episcopalians? Remember that a church's choice of how to organize itself can have theological implications and is part of the free exercise of religion (see, e.g., Kedroff v. St. Nicholas Cathedral (p. 299 above)). Is the free exercise claim defeated by the fact that the common law rule of agency applies not just to churches as such, but to all sorts of institutions?

Finally, in a negligence case the jury must decide whether the bishop was "reasonable" in acting or failing to act: for example, in ordering counseling for a priest rather than suspending him upon receiving word of a complaint. Is there a problem with a jury deciding how a reasonable bishop would act? Is this another attempt to sue for clergy malpractice as in *Nally*?

Because of concerns such as these, some courts have reached the opposite result from *Moses* and cases like it, and have concluded that holding a higher body liable for negligence in hiring or supervising clergy violates the Religion Clauses. See, e.g., Swanson v. Roman Catholic Bishop of Portland, 692 A.2d 441, 444-45 (Me. 1997) (rejecting such claims because they call on court to "examine church doctrine governing the church's authority over [the priest]" and would "infringe upon [the church's] right to determine the standards governing the relationship between the church, its bishop, and the parish priest"). For discussion of these issues, see, e.g., Ira C. Lupu and Robert W. Tuttle, Sexual Misconduct and Ecclesiastical Immunity, 2004 B.Y.U. L. Rev. 1789.

Is there a middle way between liability as in *Moses* and immunity as in *Swanson*? Lupu and Tuttle suggest a solution by analogy to the Supreme Court's ruling on defamation suits, New York Times v. Sullivan (see p. 326 above): a religious body with authority over the clergy member should be liable only on a showing of "actual malice," that is, that it had knowledge of a risk of sexual misconduct and intentionally or recklessly failed to act. See also, e.g., Gibson v. Brewer, 952 S.W.2d 239 (Mo. 1997) (recognizing tort for intentional, but not for negligent, failure to supervise clergy). But would such a standard encourage religious bodies to remain ignorant of their clergy's activities so as to avoid liability?

4. Breach of Fiduciary Duty. The *Moses* court held that the bishop had a fiduciary duty to Tenantry—a stringent duty to act "solely for [her] benefit"—in part because he "held a position of authority in the church" and "Tenantry believed he had the power to decide if she would lose her salvation." The bishop breached his duty, the court said, because he failed "to assist Tenantry in understanding that she was not the only person responsible for her sexual relationship with Father Robinson" and "did not recommend counseling for [her]." Instead he heard Tenantry's confession and gave her absolution for her sins. Is imposing liability on these grounds consistent with *Nally*'s rejection of clergy malpractice claims? Is it consistent with the First Amendment? Lupu and Tuttle criticize decisions like *Moses* on the ground that

> religious institutions have their own set of interests, some religious and some material, which may conflict with the interests of individuals. Accordingly, members of the religious community do not have any legitimate expectations that organizations will respond to assertions of sexual misconduct by clergy with actions taken for the sole benefit of the accuser.

This argument may show why no fiduciary duty was assumed: can you also use it to construct an argument (or arguments) that imposing such a duty violates the Religion Clauses? Is the fiduciary-duty tort more, or less, problematic on constitutional grounds than the negligent-supervision tort?

Suppose that the bishop did not engage in direct counseling of the parishioner; is there still a basis for finding a fiduciary duty? Is it enough that the bishop or diocese expressed concern for the parishioner's welfare through a letter? See Winkler v. Rocky Mountain Conference, 923 P.2d 152 (Colo. App.

1995) (imposing fiduciary-duty liability in part on this ground). In several notorious recent cases involving serial child abusers in the priesthood, the bishop had received complaints about the priest. If the bishop failed to investigate, is the diocese liable to all later victims of the priest's abuse based on breach of fiduciary duty (as opposed to, say, negligent supervision)? See, e.g., Martinelli v. Bridgeport Roman Catholic Diocesan Corp., 196 F.3d 409 (2d Cir. 1999) (holding diocese liable as fiduciary to other boys who had been part of same group to whom priest had acted as advisor). Is it enough that the diocese generally states that its member churches provide counseling to parishioners, even if the diocese does not itself provide the counseling? See Doe v. Evans, 814 So.2d 370 (Fla. 2002) (holding diocese liable).

5. Misconduct with Children. Although *Moses* involved a relationship between a clergyman and an adult parishioner, with no claims of assault or other criminal acts, the most widely publicized and tragic cases of sexual misconduct have involved clergy abusing children. The difference certainly may affect the validity of the underlying tort claim (for example, there may be no tort when an adult parishioner consents to a relationship), as well as the amount of damages. But should it affect First Amendment defenses? An appellate court rejecting a claim by an adult parishioner wrote: "Those courts that find no First Amendment bar to claims of negligent hiring, retention, and supervision generally do so in the context of allegations involving sexual assault on a child. . . . [T]he instant case presents a less compelling factual scenario." Doe v. Evans, 718 So. 2d 286 (Fla. App.1 Dist. 1998). That court was reversed on appeal (see 814 So. 2d 370 (Fla. 2002)), but was it correct?

6. Punitive Damages. The largest monetary awards in cases of ascending liability often come as a result not of compensatory damages, but of punitive damages added on for malicious or reckless conduct. In City of Newport v. Fact Concerts, Inc., 453 U.S. 247 (1981), the Supreme Court rejected punitive damages against cities and towns under 42 U.S.C. § 1983, a leading civil rights statute, in part because such an award "'punishes' only the [municipal] taxpayers, who took no part in the commission of the tort"; is unpredictable in its size; and can place "strain on local treasuries and therefore on services available to the public at large." See also Gertz v. Welch, 418 U.S. 323 (1974) (First Amendment prohibits punitive damages in defamation cases absent showing of reckless disregard for truth because juries can "assess punitive damages in wholly unpredictable amounts bearing no necessary relation to the actual harm caused" and can "selectively punish expressions of unpopular views"). In the light of these precedents, should the First Amendment bar the imposition of punitive damages on a congregation or higher religious body for wrongs done by its clergy?

7. Church Bankruptcies. The overwhelming actual or threatened liability for numerous sexual-abuse claims has led several Catholic dioceses to follow the lead of business corporations facing mass tort liability and file for reorganization under Chapter 11 of the federal bankruptcy law. Such a filing raises numerous questions, starting with the moral and theological: isn't the Church contradicting its own teaching of care for those in need by seeking to avoid responsibility to compensate those who have been harmed? See David A. Skeel, Jr., Avoiding Moral Bankruptcy, 44 B.C. L. Rev. 1181 (2003) (acknowledging the moral objection but arguing that bankruptcy may be justified as a means of coordinating compensation payments to multiple victims).

Among the numerous legal issues in an ecclesiastical bankruptcy, consider two with First Amendment implications. First, what is the property of the diocese that is subject to the claims of creditors; for example, does it include individual parishes and schools? Suppose that canon law, the Catholic Church's own legal code, makes church buildings and schools the property of the parish—either outright or because the bishop holds them in trust for the parish—but that civil law would designate them the property of the diocese (and thus within creditors' reach). Should the bankruptcy court ignore the Church's own rules concerning ecclesiastical properties? If the court does so and sells churches and schools to pay victims, would that violate the Religious Freedom Restoration Act (which still applies to federal laws, see p. 157)? Are bankruptcy laws different from other federal laws governed by RFRA? See, e.g., In re Catholic Bishop of Spokane, 329 B.R. 304 (Bkrt. E.D. Wash. 2005).

Second, Chapter 11, in order to ensure the preservation of assets for creditors, "calls for extensive oversight of nearly every significant decision made by the debtor" after it declares bankruptcy. Skeel, 44 B.C. L. Rev. at 1193. If United Airlines while in Chapter 11 decided to buy a host of new planes to expand its routes, it would have to get the bankruptcy judge's approval. If a diocese in Chapter 11 sees a need to start a new church or school in an impoverished neighborhood, must it likewise get court approval?

For discussion of a wide range of issues concerning church bankruptcies, see the articles in Symposium, Bankruptcy in the Religious Non-Profit Context, 29 Seton Hall Legis. J. 341-557 (Spring 2005).

IV

THE POWER OF THE PURSE

One of the most potent of governmental powers is the power to tax and spend—to tax all of the people, and to spend on certain activities approved by the legislature. One of the historic features of an established church is that the government would compel taxpayers to support the favored church either through mandatory tithes or through use of general tax revenues. Perhaps more than any other church-state issue, the use of tax funds for support of religious education has been a battleground throughout American history, both in legislatures and in the courts. In this Part, we explore the constitutional limits on the power of the purse, with special reference to the question of private religious schools.

A. INTRODUCTION: GOVERNMENT AID IN MODERN TIMES AND IN THE FOUNDING GENERATION

Only after World War II did the Supreme Court begin to confront the issue of whether government funding could extend to religious education. The issue arose then for several reasons: the dramatically expanded role of government during the New Deal in providing public welfare benefits, an increased effort by Catholic schools to obtain equal funding, and finally the Court's own decision to apply the Establishment Clause to state laws (in Everson v. Board of Education, which follows). But in deciding *Everson*, the Court turned for guidance to history: in particular, to the controversy over religious assessments in Virginia in the 1780s. Materials on that dispute, and the similar controversy in Massachusetts, are found in Part II-C. Here we first look at *Everson* itself and its implications, and then we consider the role that history has played in *Everson* and other modern controversies over government funding.

EVERSON v. BOARD OF EDUCATION
330 U.S. 1 (1947)

Mr. Justice BLACK delivered the opinion of the Court.

A New Jersey statute authorizes its local school districts to make rules and contracts for the transportation of children to and from schools.[1] The appellee, a township board of education, acting pursuant to this statute authorized reimbursement to parents of money expended by them for the bus transportation of their children on regular busses operated by the public transportation system. Part of this money was for the payment of transportation of some children in the community to Catholic parochial schools. These church schools give their students, in addition to secular education, regular religious instruction conforming to the religious tenets and modes of worship of the Catholic Faith. The superintendent of these schools is a Catholic priest.

The appellant, in his capacity as a district taxpayer, filed suit in a State court challenging the right of the Board to reimburse parents of parochial school students. He contended that the statute and the resolution passed pursuant to it violated both the State and the Federal Constitutions. . . .

The New Jersey statute is challenged as a "law respecting an establishment of religion." The First Amendment, as made applicable to the states by the Fourteenth, commands that a state "shall make no law respecting an establishment of religion, or prohibiting the free exercise thereof. . . ." These words of the First Amendment reflected in the minds of early Americans a vivid mental picture of conditions and practices which they fervently wished to stamp out in order to preserve liberty for themselves and for their posterity. Doubtless their goal has not been entirely reached; but so far has the Nation moved toward it that the expression "law respecting an establishment of religion," probably does not so vividly remind present-day Americans of the evils, fears, and political problems that caused that expression to be written into our Bill of Rights. Whether this New Jersey law is one respecting the "establishment of religion" requires an understanding of the meaning of that language, particularly with respect to the imposition of taxes. Once again, therefore, it is not inappropriate briefly to review the background and environment of the period in which that constitutional language was fashioned and adopted.

A large proportion of the early settlers of this country came here from Europe to escape the bondage of laws which compelled them to support and attend government favored churches. The centuries immediately before and contemporaneous with the colonization of America had been filled with turmoil, civil strife, and persecutions, generated in large part by established sects determined to maintain their absolute political and religious supremacy. With the power of government supporting them, at various times and places, Catholics had

1. "Whenever in any district there are children living remote from any schoolhouse, the board of education of the district may make rules and contracts for the transportation of such children to and from school, including the transportation of school children to and from school other than a public school, except such school as is operated for profit in whole or in part.

"When any school district provides any transportation for public school children to and from school, transportation from any point in such established school route to any other point in such established school route shall be supplied to school children residing in such school district in going to and from school other than a public school, except such school as is operated for profit in whole or in part." New Jersey Laws 1941.

persecuted Protestants, Protestants had persecuted Catholics, Protestant sects had persecuted other Protestant sects, Catholics of one shade of belief had persecuted Catholics of another shade of belief, and all of these had from time to time persecuted Jews. In efforts to force loyalty to whatever religious group happened to be on top and in league with the government of a particular time and place, men and women had been fined, cast in jail, cruelly tortured, and killed. Among the offenses for which these punishments had been inflicted were such things as speaking disrespectfully of the views of ministers of government-established churches, nonattendance at those churches, expressions of non-belief in their doctrines, and failure to pay taxes and tithes to support them.

These practices of the old world were transplanted to and began to thrive in the soil of the new America. The very charters granted by the English Crown to the individuals and companies designated to make the laws which would control the destinies of the colonials authorized these individuals and companies to erect religious establishments which all, whether believers or non-believers, would be required to support and attend. An exercise of this authority was accompanied by a repetition of many of the old world practices and persecutions. Catholics found themselves hounded and proscribed because of their faith; Quakers who followed their conscience went to jail; Baptists were peculiarly obnoxious to certain dominant Protestant sects; men and women of varied faiths who happened to be in a minority in a particular locality were persecuted because they steadfastly persisted in worshipping God only as their own consciences dictated. And all of these dissenters were compelled to pay tithes and taxes to support government-sponsored churches whose ministers preached inflammatory sermons designed to strengthen and consolidate the established faith by generating a burning hatred against dissenters.

These practices became so commonplace as to shock the freedom-loving colonials into a feeling of abhorrence. The imposition of taxes to pay ministers' salaries and to build and maintain churches and church property aroused their indignation. It was these feelings which found expression in the First Amendment. No one locality and no one group throughout the Colonies can rightly be given entire credit for having aroused the sentiment that culminated in adoption of the Bill of Rights' provisions embracing religious liberty. But Virginia, where the established church had achieved a dominant influence in political affairs and where many excesses attracted wide public attention, provided a great stimulus and able leadership for the movement. The people there, as elsewhere, reached the conviction that individual religious liberty could be achieved best under a government which was stripped of all power to tax, to support, or otherwise to assist any or all religions, or to interfere with the beliefs of any religious individual or group.

The movement toward this end reached its dramatic climax in Virginia in 1785-86 when the Virginia legislative body was about to renew Virginia's tax levy for the support of the established church. Thomas Jefferson and James Madison led the fight against this tax. Madison wrote his great Memorial and Remonstrance against the law. [See p. 49.] In it, he eloquently argued that a true religion did not need the support of law; that no person, either believer or non-believer, should be taxed to support a religious institution of any kind; that the best interest of a society required that the minds of men always be wholly free; and that cruel persecutions were the inevitable result of government-established religions. Madison's Remonstrance received strong support throughout Virginia, and the Assembly postponed consideration of the proposed tax measure until its next session. When the proposal came up for consideration at that session, it not only died in committee, but the Assembly enacted the famous "Virginia Bill for Religious Liberty" [see p. 54] originally written by Thomas Jefferson. The preamble to that Bill stated among other things that

> Almighty God hath created the mind free; that all attempts to influence it by temporal punishments, or burthens, or by civil incapacitations, tend only to beget habits of hypocrisy and meanness, and are a departure from the plan of the Holy author of our religion who being Lord both of body and mind, yet chose not to propagate it by coercions on either . . . ; that to compel a man to furnish contributions of money for the propagation of opinions which he disbelieves, is sinful and tyrannical; that even the forcing him to support this or that teacher of his own religious persuasion, is depriving him of the comfortable liberty of giving his contributions to the particular pastor, whose morals he would make his pattern. . . .

And the statute itself enacted

> That no man shall be compelled to frequent or support any religious worship, place, or ministry whatsoever, nor shall be enforced, restrained, molested, or burthened, in his body or goods, nor shall otherwise suffer on account of his religious opinions or belief. . . .

This Court has previously recognized that the provisions of the First Amendment, in the drafting and adoption of which Madison and Jefferson played such leading roles, had the same objective and were intended to provide the same protection against governmental intrusion on religious liberty as the Virginia statute. Prior to the adoption of the Fourteenth Amendment, the First Amendment did not apply as a restraint against the states. Most of them did soon provide similar constitutional protections for religious liberty. But some states persisted for about half a century in imposing restraints upon the free exercise of religion and in discriminating against particular religious groups. . . .

The "establishment of religion" clause of the First Amendment means at least this: Neither a state nor the Federal Government can set up a church. Neither can pass laws which aid one religion, aid all religions, or prefer one religion over another. Neither can force nor influence a person to go to or to remain away from church against his will or force him to profess a belief or disbelief in any religion. No person can be punished for entertaining or professing religious beliefs or disbeliefs, for church attendance or non-attendance. No tax in any amount, large or small, can be levied to support any religious activities or institutions, whatever they may be called, or whatever form they may adopt to teach or practice religion. Neither a state nor the Federal Government can, openly or secretly, participate in the affairs of any religious organizations or groups and vice versa. In the words of Jefferson, the clause against establishment of religion by law was intended to erect "a wall of separation between Church and State." Reynolds v. United States.

We must consider the New Jersey statute in accordance with the foregoing limitations imposed by the First Amendment. But we must not strike that state statute down if it is within the state's constitutional power even though it approaches the verge of that power. New Jersey cannot consistently with the "establishment of religion" clause of the First Amendment contribute tax-raised funds to the support of an institution which teaches the tenets and faith of any church. On the other hand, other language of the amendment commands that New Jersey cannot hamper its citizens in the free exercise of their own religion. Consequently, it cannot exclude individual Catholics, Lutherans, Mohammedans, Baptists, Jews, Methodists, Non-believers, Presbyterians, or the members of any other faith, *because of their faith, or lack of it,* from receiving the benefits of public welfare legislation. While we do not mean to intimate that a state could not provide transportation only to children attending public schools, we must be careful, in protecting the citizens of New Jersey against state-established churches, to be sure that we do not inadvertently prohibit New Jersey from extending its general State law benefits to all its citizens without regard to their religious belief.

Measured by these standards, we cannot say that the First Amendment prohibits New Jersey from spending tax-raised funds to pay the bus fares of parochial school pupils as a part of a general program under which it pays the fares of pupils attending public and other schools. It is undoubtedly true that children are helped to get to church schools. There is even a possibility that some of the children might not be sent to the church schools if the parents were compelled to pay their children's bus fares out of their own pockets when transportation to a public school would have been paid for by the State. The same possibility exists where the state requires a local transit company to provide reduced fares to school children including those attending parochial schools, or where a municipally owned transportation system undertakes to carry all school children free of charge. Moreover, state-paid policemen, detailed to protect children going to and from church schools from the very real hazards of traffic, would serve much the same purpose and accomplish much the same result as state provisions intended to guarantee free transportation of a kind which the state deems to be best for the school children's welfare. And parents might refuse to risk their children to the serious danger of traffic accidents going to and from parochial schools, the approaches to which were not protected by policemen. Similarly, parents might be reluctant to permit their children to attend schools which the state had cut off from such general government services as ordinary police and fire protection, connections for sewage disposal, public highways and sidewalks. Of course, cutting off church schools from these services, so separate and so indisputably marked off from the religious function, would make it far more difficult for the schools to operate. But such is obviously not the purpose of the First Amendment. That Amendment requires the state to be a neutral in its relations with groups of religious believers and non-believers; it does not require the state to be their adversary. State power is no more to be used so as to handicap religions, than it is to favor them.

This Court has said that parents may, in the discharge of their duty under state compulsory education laws, send their children to a religious rather than a public school if the school meets the secular educational requirements which the state has power to impose. See Pierce v. Society of Sisters (1925). It appears that these parochial schools meet New Jersey's requirements. The State contributes no money to the schools. It does not support them. Its legislation, as applied, does no more than provide a general program to help parents get their children, regardless of their religion, safely and expeditiously to and from accredited schools.

The First Amendment has erected a wall between church and state. That wall must be kept high and impregnable. We could not approve the slightest breach. New Jersey has not breached it here.

Mr. Justice RUTLEDGE, with whom Mr. Justice FRANKFURTER, Mr. Justice JACKSON and Mr. Justice BURTON agree, dissenting.

"Congress shall make no law respecting an establishment of religion, or prohibiting the free exercise thereof." U.S. Const. Am. I.

"Well aware that Almighty God hath created the mind free; . . . that to compel a man to furnish contributions of money for the propagation of opinions which he disbelieves, is sinful and tyrannical; . . . .

"*We, the General Assembly, do enact,* That no man shall be compelled to frequent or support any religious worship, place, or ministry whatsoever, nor shall be enforced, restrained, molested, or burthened in his body or goods, nor shall otherwise suffer on account of his religious opinions or belief." [Virginia Religious Liberty Bill.]

I cannot believe that the great author of those words, or the men who made them law, could have joined in this decision. Neither so high nor so impregnable today as yesterday is the wall raised between church and state by Virginia's great statute of religious freedom and the First Amendment, now made applicable to all the states by the Fourteenth. New Jersey's statute sustained is the first, if indeed it is not the second breach to be made by this Court's action. That a third, and a fourth, and still others will be attempted, we may be sure. . . . Thus with time the most solid freedom steadily gives way before continuing corrosive decision. . . .

I

Not simply an established church, but any law respecting an establishment of religion is forbidden. The Amendment was broadly but not loosely phrased. It is the compact and exact summation of its author's views formed during his long struggle for religious freedom. In Madison's own words characterizing Jefferson's Bill for Establishing Religious Freedom, the guaranty he put in our national charter, like the bill he piloted through the Virginia Assembly, was "a Model of technical precision, and perspicuous brevity." Madison could not have confused "church" and "religion," or "an established church" and "an establishment of religion."

The Amendment's purpose was not to strike merely at the official establishment of a single sect, creed or religion, outlawing only a formal relation such as had prevailed in England and some of the colonies. Necessarily it was to uproot all such relationships. But the object was broader than separating church and state in this narrow sense. It was to create a complete and permanent separation of the spheres of religious activity and civil authority by comprehensively forbidding every form of public aid or support for religion. In proof the Amendment's wording and history unite with this Court's consistent utterances whenever attention has been fixed directly upon the question. . . .

No one would claim today that the Amendment is constricted, in "prohibiting the free exercise" of religion, to securing the free exercise of some formal or creedal observance, of one sect or of many. It secures all forms of religious expression, creedal, sectarian or nonsectarian wherever and however taking place, except conduct which trenches upon the like freedoms of others or clearly and presently endangers the community's good order and security. . . .

"Religion" has the same broad significance in the twin prohibition concerning "an establishment." The Amendment was not duplicitous. "Religion" and "establishment" were not used in any formal or technical sense. The prohibition broadly forbids state support, financial or other, of religion in any guise, form or degree. It outlaws all use of public funds for religious purposes.

II

No provision of the Constitution is more closely tied to or given content by its generating history than the religious clause of the First Amendment. It is at once the refined product and the terse summation of that history. The history includes not only Madison's authorship and the proceedings before the First Congress, but also the long and intensive struggle for religious freedom in America, more especially in Virginia, of which the Amendment was the direct culmination. [Lengthy discussion of the Virginia assessment controversy omitted.]

All the great instruments of the Virginia struggle for religious liberty thus became warp and woof of our constitutional tradition, not simply by the course of history, but by the common unifying force of Madison's life, thought and sponsorship. He epitomized the whole of that tradition in the Amendment's compact, but nonetheless comprehensive, phrasing.

As the Remonstrance discloses throughout, Madison opposed every form and degree of official relation between religion and civil authority. For him religion was a wholly private matter beyond the scope of civil power either to restrain or to support. Denial or abridgment of religious freedom was a violation of rights both of conscience and of natural equality. State aid was no less obnoxious or destructive to freedom and to religion itself than other forms of state interference. "Establishment" and "free exercise" were correlative and coextensive ideas, representing only different facets of the single great and fundamental freedom. . . .

In no phase was he more unrelentingly absolute than in opposing state support or aid by taxation. Not even "three pence" contribution was thus to be exacted from any citizen for such a purpose. Remonstrance, Par. 3. Tithes had been the life blood of establishment before and after other compulsions disappeared. Madison and his coworkers made no exceptions or abridgments to the complete separation they created. Their objection was not to small tithes. It was to any tithes whatsoever. "If it were lawful to impose a small tax for religion the admission would pave the way for oppressive levies." Not the amount but "the principle of assessment was wrong." And the principle was as much to prevent "the interference of law in religion" as to restrain religious intervention in political matters. In this field the authors of our freedom would not tolerate "the first experiment on our liberties" or "wait till usurped power had strengthened itself by exercise, and entangled the question in precedents." Remonstrance, Par. 3. Nor should we.

In view of this history no further proof is needed that the Amendment forbids any appropriation, large or small, from public funds to aid or support any and all religious exercises. . . .

Does New Jersey's action furnish support for religion by use of the taxing power? Certainly it does, if the test remains undiluted as Jefferson and Madison made it, that money taken by taxation from one is not to be used or given to support another's religious training or belief, or indeed one's own. Today as then the furnishing of "contributions of money for the propagation of opinions which he disbelieves" is the forbidden exaction; and the prohibition is absolute for whatever measure brings that consequence and whatever amount may be sought or given to that end.

The funds used here were raised by taxation. The Court does not dispute nor could it that their use does in fact give aid and encouragement to religious instruction. It only concludes that this aid is not "support" in law. But Madison and Jefferson were concerned with aid and support in fact not as a legal conclusion "entangled in precedents." Remonstrance, Par. 3. Here parents pay money to send their children to parochial schools and funds raised by taxation are used to reimburse them. This not only helps the children to get to school and the parents to send them. It aids them in a substantial way to get the very thing which they are sent to the particular school to secure, namely, religious training and teaching.

Believers of all faiths, and others who do not express their feeling toward ultimate issues of existence in any creedal form, pay the New Jersey tax. When the money so raised is used to pay for transportation to religious schools, the Catholic taxpayer to the extent of his proportionate share pays for the transportation of Lutheran, Jewish and otherwise religiously affiliated children to receive their non-Catholic religious instruction. Their parents likewise pay proportionately for the transportation of Catholic children to receive Catholic instruction. Each thus contributes to "the propagation of opinions which he disbelieves" in so far as their religions differ, as do others who accept no creed without regard to those differences. Each thus pays taxes also to support the teaching of his own religion, an exaction equally forbidden since it denies "the comfortable liberty" of giving one's contribution to the particular agency of instruction he approves.

New Jersey's action therefore exactly fits the type of exaction and the kind of evil at which Madison and Jefferson struck. Under the test they framed it cannot be said that the cost of transportation is no part of the cost of education or of the religious instruction given. That it is a substantial and a necessary element is shown most plainly by the continuing and increasing demand for the state to assume it. Nor is there pretense that it relates only to the secular instruction given in religious schools or that any attempt is or could be made toward allocating proportional shares as between the secular and the religious instruction. It is precisely because the instruction is religious and relates to a particular faith, whether one or another, that parents send their children to religious schools under the *Pierce* doctrine. And the very purpose of the state's contribution is to defray the cost of conveying the pupil to the place where he will receive not simply secular, but also and primarily religious, teaching and guidance.

Finally, transportation, where it is needed, is as essential to education as any other element. Its cost is as much a part of the total expense, except at times in amount, as the cost of textbooks, of school lunches, of athletic equipment, of writing and other materials; indeed of all other items composing the total burden. Now as always the core of the educational process is the teacher-pupil relationship. Without this the richest equipment and facilities would go for naught. . . . Without buildings, without equipment, without library, textbooks and other materials, and without transportation to bring teacher and pupil together in such an effective teaching environment, there can be not even the skeleton of what our times require. Hardly can it be maintained that transportation is the least essential of these items, or that it does not in fact aid, encourage, sustain and support, just as they do, the very process which is its purpose to accomplish. No less essential is it, or the payment of its cost, than the very teaching in the classroom or payment of the teacher's sustenance. Many types of equipment, now considered essential, better could be done without.

For me, therefore, the feat is impossible to select so indispensable an item from the composite of total costs, and characterize it as not aiding, contributing to, promoting or sustaining the propagation of beliefs which it is the very end of all to bring about. Unless this can be maintained, and the Court does not maintain it, the aid thus given is outlawed. . . . No rational line can be drawn between payment for such larger, but not more necessary, items [as buildings, books, or teachers] and payment for transportation. The only line that can be so drawn is one between more dollars and less. Certainly in this realm such a line can be no valid constitutional measure.

IV

But we are told that the New Jersey statute is valid in its present application because the appropriation is for a public, not a private purpose, namely, the promotion of education, and the majority accept this idea in the conclusion that all we have here is "public welfare legislation." If that is true and the Amendment's force can be thus destroyed, what has been said becomes all the more pertinent. For then there could be no possible objection to more extensive support of religious education by New Jersey.

If the fact alone be determinative that religious schools are engaged in education, thus promoting the general and individual welfare, together with the legislature's decision that the payment of public moneys for their aid makes their work a public function, then I can see no possible basis, except one of dubious legislative policy, for the state's refusal to make full appropriation for support of private, religious schools, just as is done for public instruction. There could not be, on that basis, valid constitutional objection.

Our constitutional policy does not deny the value or the necessity for religious training, teaching or observance. Rather it secures their free exercise. But to that end it does deny that the state can undertake or sustain them in any form or degree. For this reason the sphere of religious activity, as distinguished from the secular intellectual liberties, has been given the twofold protection and, as the state cannot forbid, neither can it perform or aid in performing the religious function. The dual prohibition makes that function altogether private. It cannot be made a public one by legislative act. This was the very heart of Madison's Remonstrance, as it is of the Amendment itself.

[The majority adds two further arguments:] one that the aid extended partakes of the nature of a safety measure, the other that failure to provide it would make the state unneutral in religious matters, discriminating against or hampering such children concerning public benefits all others receive.

[The majority's] approach, if valid, supplies a ready method for nullifying the Amendment's guaranty, not only for this case and others involving small grants in aid for religious education, but equally for larger ones. The only thing needed will be for the Court again to transplant the "public welfare-public function" view from its proper nonreligious due process bearing to First Amendment application, holding that religious education is not "supported" though it may be aided by the appropriation, and that the cause of education generally is furthered by helping the pupil to secure that type of training. . . .

VI

Short treatment will dispose of what remains. Whatever might be said of some other application of New Jersey's statute, the one made here has no semblance of bearing as a safety measure or, indeed, for securing expeditious conveyance. The transportation supplied is by public conveyance, subject to all the hazards and delays of the highway and the streets incurred by the public generally in going about its multifarious business.

Nor is the case comparable to one of furnishing fire or police protection, or access to public highways. These things are matters of common right, part of the general need for safety.[56] Certainly the fire department must not stand idly by while the church burns. Nor is this reason why the state should pay the expense of transportation or other items of the cost of religious education.[57] . . .

Two great drives are constantly in motion to abridge, in the name of education, the complete division of religion and civil authority which our forefathers made. One is to introduce religious education and observances into the public schools. The other, to obtain public funds for the aid and support of various private religious schools. In my opinion both avenues were closed by the Constitution. Neither should be opened by this Court. The matter is not one of quantity, to be measured by the amount of money expended. Now as in Madison's day it is one of principle, to keep separate the separate spheres as the First Amendment drew them; to prevent the first experiment upon our liberties; and to keep the question from becoming entangled in corrosive precedents. We should not be less strict to keep strong and untarnished the one side of the shield of religious freedom than we have been of the other.

---

56. The protections are of a nature which does not require appropriations specially made from the public treasury and earmarked, as is New Jersey's here, particularly for religious institutions or uses. The First Amendment does not exclude religious property or activities from protection against disorder or the ordinary accidental incidents of community life. It forbids support, not protection from interference or destruction.

57. Neither do we have here a case of rate-making by which a public utility extends reduced fares to all school children, including patrons of religious schools. Whether or not legislative compulsion upon a private utility to extend such an advantage would be valid, or its extension by a municipally owned system, we are not required to consider. In the former instance, at any rate, and generally if not always in the latter, the vice of using the taxing power to raise funds for the support of religion would not be present.

NOTES AND QUESTIONS

1. Strict Separation Versus Neutrality. In the *Everson* opinions, two theories of the relations between government and religion seem to be in conflict. Under one theory, often called "strict separation," the government may not "contribute tax-raised funds to the support of an institution which teaches the tenets and faith of any church" no matter what form the subsidy may take. Under the other theory, often called "neutrality," the government may subsidize any institution that is providing a public service, and need not (or may not) discriminate either in favor of religious institutions or against them. The two theories are not reconcilable, since the refusal to grant funds to an otherwise eligible institution performing a public service on the ground that it teaches the tenets and faith of a church necessarily discriminates against religious institutions.

This can be understood as a choice between two baselines for determining whether religion is aided or advanced. The separationists' implicit baseline is that of government inaction. Compared to government inaction, religion is "aided" when religious schools or other institutions that teach or inculcate religion receive government money. The neutrality baseline is determined by the government's treatment of analogous nonreligious activities or institutions. Thus, if *all* nonprofit groups receive a subsidy in the form of tax-deductible contributions, or if *all* schools receive a particular form of assistance, and if religious institutions and schools are treated neither better nor worse than their nonreligious counterparts, then religion is not "aided" or "advanced" beyond this baseline; it is simply treated neutrally.

Justice Black's majority opinion enunciates both theories, but in the end applies the neutrality approach. Since transportation subsidies serve a public purpose, and since they are extended to students attending any accredited nonprofit school in the district, the Court holds that it does not favor religion to include religious school students in the program. But the opinion strongly suggests that the Court would not carry the neutrality theory to its logical conclusion; indeed, the Court says that the *Everson* program may go to the "verge" of constitutional limits. Under the neutrality theory, what are those limits?

Justice Rutledge espouses the theory of strict separation. But here again, it is questionable whether he was willing to take the theory to its logical extreme. Does Justice Rutledge believe that the state should not provide police, fire, or mail service to churches? Could churchgoers use a subsidized transit service? What about tax exemptions? Justice Rutledge responds that police and fire protection are matters of "common right." What does that mean? Who determines what services will be provided as a matter of "common right"? Why can't a state decide to make transportation to school a matter of "common right"? What are the limits on the theory of "strict separation"?

This conflict between proponents of neutrality and proponents of strict separation bears some resemblance to the argument regarding free exercise accommodations. Both involve a conflict between formal neutrality (treating all institutions and activities alike, without regard for religion) and special treatment for religion—except that the special treatment in the aid context would work to the disadvantage of the religious. Why isn't the "strict separation" position a form of discrimination against religion, and thus unconstitutional under *Smith* and *Lukumi* (see pp. 137, 162)? Alternatively, why isn't religious accommodation a form of discrimination in favor of religion and thus a violation of the Establishment Clause?

2. Denominational Neutrality in *Everson*. There is some confusion in the opinions over whether the program in *Everson* was open to students at schools other than the public schools and the Catholic schools. The state statute authorized transportation subsidies for pupils at all nonprofit schools. (Is the exclusion of for-profit schools constitutionally troublesome?) But the local school board enacted a resolution that mentioned only the public school and the Catholic school, apparently because there were no other schools in the township. We have omitted the sections of the opinions discussing this point, because it is almost universally agreed that it would be unconstitutional to single out Catholic schools for a special benefit if there were other nonprofit private schools in the area. But even if there are no other such schools, does the *Kiryas Joel* decision (p. 253) invalidate an ordinance that mentions only the schools of one denomination?

3. Financial Aid and the Noncoercion Principle. Another principle that we have mentioned in connection with both religion clauses is that of noncoercion, or leaving decisions about religious matters to the choices of individuals or private groups. See pp. 4-5. Which way does that principle point in cases like *Everson?* Who are the persons being coerced by government, and in what way(s)? Should we be principally concerned about coercing taxpayers to support the propagation of opinion of which they disapprove, or with ensuring that parents and children have a full range of choices about educational philosophy? Is there any reason to be concerned about the effect of the aid on the autonomy of the religious schools themselves?

NOTE ON THE USES OF HISTORY: RELIGIOUS ASSESSMENTS AND THE ESTABLISHMENT CLAUSE

In *Everson,* the majority and the dissenting Justices agree that the program should be evaluated in light of the Virginia Assessment Controversy of the 1780s. You should now read (or review) those materials (section II-C). Your instructor may also have you read or review the materials on religious assessments in Massachusetts (pp. 17-29) and on the drafting of the Establishment Clause (pp. 56-64).

1. The Virginia Assessment Controversy. To Justice Rutledge, the transportation subsidy in *Everson* "exactly fits the type of exaction and the kind of evil at which Madison and Jefferson struck." Transportation is part of the cost of education; education at religious schools includes inculcation in the principles of the faith (that is a principal reason why parents choose religious schools); therefore, to use tax funds for transportation is to compel taxpayers to support religious instruction.

Is Justice Rutledge right? Is a program of compulsory taxation for churches constitutionally identical to a program of tax support for transportation to religious and secular schools? Consider the possible grounds of distinction:

(a) Secular purpose? The Virginia bill proposed a tax for the purpose of reinvigorating religion, on the rationale that "the general diffusion of Christian knowledge hath a natural tendency to correct the morals of men, restrain their vices, and preserve the peace of society." (Was that a "secular purpose"?) The purpose of the New Jersey bill was to provide safe transportation, or perhaps to subsidize education.

(b) Neutral criteria? The Virginia bill allocated the money to religious bodies only, unless the taxpayer objected, in which case it went into the general treasury, to be used for education. No money went to private nonreligious bodies. The New Jersey bill was neutral between religious and secular recipients.

(c) Direct versus indirect aid? The proceeds of the Virginia tax would be paid directly to the religious organizations; the funds appropriated by the New Jersey bill were paid to parents.

(d) Religious uses or content? The Virginia payments were earmarked for religious uses—the minister's salary and upkeep of houses of worship. The New Jersey payments were earmarked for use for safe transportation, which does not in itself have religious content.

In the cases that follow, consider the relevance of each of those distinctions to the issue at hand: (a) Is the purpose secular? (b) Are the funds allocated neutrally between religious and nonreligious entities, or are they skewed in favor of the religious? (c) Do the funds go directly to a religious organization, or do they pass through the hands of an independent third party, such as parents? (d) Are the funds used for materials or activities with religious content? In your opinion, which—if any—of these distinctions should make a difference?

2. The Massachusetts Assessment Controversy. *Everson* focuses on the Virginia history, but of course that was only one state. What does the Massachusetts history show about government funding and the Establishment Clause? Consider the following points:

(a) Massachusetts (and two other New England states, Connecticut and New Hampshire) still had tax assessments for supporting clergy and churches at the time the First Amendment was ratified. If the Establishment Clause reflects a strict prohibition on government funding, would these states have supported the clause? Might they have supported the Clause, but solely on the ground that it left the funding issue to the states and indeed even protected state establishments (the so-called "federalism" interpretation of the Clause)? If that is the case, does it make any sense to apply the "no funding" principle to state laws, as *Everson* did? (See pp. 62-64.)

(b) On the other hand, the Massachusetts assessment system was seriously breaking down by 1791. Although it was ostensibly neutral between denominations, like the proposed Virginia assessment, dissenters were constantly complaining that it was administered unequally and had an unequal impact on them. Does this show that by the time of the First Amendment, tax support for religious teaching (even for all religions) was basically coming to be viewed as inconsistent with religious freedom?

3. The Drafting of the Establishment Clause. What do the debates and votes on the drafts of the First Amendment indicate about the issue in *Everson*? A central issue at the time, reflected in the drafts, was whether aid to religion that was "nonpreferential" between denominations was consistent with religious liberty. Suppose that the drafting history shows that the First Amendment ratifiers, like the voters in Virginia, rejected even "nonpreferential" aid. See pp. 64-65. What does that say for the bus payments in *Everson*?

BOARD OF EDUCATION v. ALLEN, 392 U.S. 236 (1968):   Pursuant to a New York law, local school districts lent free textbooks to students in grades 7 through 12, including nonpublic-school students. The textbooks loaned were those approved by the public schools for the same, secular subjects. The Court upheld the program on the basis of *Everson*: "Of course books are different from buses. . . . [But] we cannot agree with appellants either that all teaching in a sectarian school is religious or that the processes of secular and religious training are so intertwined that secular textbooks furnished to students by the public are in fact instrumental in the teaching of religion." The Court said that it had "long recognized that religious schools pursue two goals, religious instruction and secular education":

> [T]he continued willingness to rely on private school systems, including parochial systems, strongly suggests that a wide segment of informed opinion, legislative and otherwise, has found that those schools do an acceptable job of providing secular education to their students. This judgment is further evidence that parochial schools are performing, in addition to their sectarian function, the task of secular education.

Justice Black, who had written the opinion in *Everson* upholding bus reimbursements, dissented sharply in *Allen*: "[I]t is not difficult to distinguish books, which are the heart of any school, from bus fares, which provide a convenient and helpful general public transportation service. With respect to the former, state financial support actively and directly assists the teaching and propagation of sectarian religious viewpoints in clear conflict with the First Amendment's establishment bar; with respect to the latter, the State merely provides a general and nondiscriminatory transportation service in no way related to substantive religious views and beliefs."

Justice Black went on to describe the purposes of the Establishment Clause as follows:

> To authorize a State to tax its residents for such church purposes is to put the State squarely in the religious activities of certain religious groups that happen to be strong enough politically to write their own religious preferences and prejudices into the laws. This links state and churches together in controlling the lives and destinies of our citizenship—a citizenship composed of people of myriad religious faiths, some of them bitterly hostile to and completely intolerant of the others. . . .
>
>   . . . The same powerful sectarian religious propagandists who have succeeded in securing passage of the present law to help religious schools carry on their sectarian religious purposes can and doubtless will continue their propaganda, looking toward complete domination and supremacy of their particular brand of religion. And it nearly always is by insidious approaches that the citadels of liberty are most successfully attacked. . . .
>
>   . . . The Court's affirmance here bodes nothing but evil to religious peace in this country.

NOTES AND QUESTIONS

1. **Allen and Everson.** What is the constitutional theory under which the textbook loan program is sustained? Is it sufficient that the program provides the same, or an equivalent, benefit to all schoolchildren, whether they attend religious or secular schools? Or is it essential to the holding that the textbooks involved are secular in content, like the bus rides in *Everson*? Can't secular textbooks be used to teach religious doctrine? To test the difference between these rationales, ask yourself whether it would have been constitutional for New York to pay (equally) for textbooks in both public and private schools, without limiting private schools to secular books.

In a footnote, the Court noted that textbooks had previously been paid for by parents, not by the schools. It could be argued, therefore, that the textbook subsidy (like the transportation subsidy in *Everson*) benefited the parents, and not the religious schools. Was this an essential element in the Court's holding? Would a similar principle allow the state to defray some or all of the tuition paid by the parents?

2. **The Dangers of Government Aid: School Autonomy.** There is one potentially significant difference between transportation reimbursements (*Everson*) and providing secular textbooks (*Allen*): Provision of the textbooks could undermine the religious character of the school curriculum. If the private schools pay for their own textbooks, they will select them in accord with their own values and educational judgments. Under the program in *Allen*, however, they get free textbooks if and only if they use the same ones that were approved for use in the public schools. These, presumably, are entirely secular, and reflect the values and educational judgments of the elected school board. The program thus has the tendency to secularize the private school curriculum and bring it into conformity with majoritarian preferences. In effect, the private schools were bribed (to use a stark term) to conform to the public schools' secular curricular choices instead of their own religious ones. Indeed, in the years after *Allen*, Catholic textbook publishing went into a serious decline, and the curriculum in Catholic schools (other than in religion classes) began much more closely to resemble that in public schools. Part of the explanation was no doubt cultural, but the spread of programs like that in *Allen* may have contributed.

Is this a good thing? Does it advance religious liberty? Whose? Should these considerations have affected the constitutional analysis in *Allen*? If so, how would you articulate the constitutional doctrine? Conversely, is there any argument that it was unconstitutional to limit the private schools' textbook choices to secular books?

3. **The Dangers of Government Aid: Divisiveness.** Justice Black argues that "religious peace" is endangered by aid to private religious schools. Is this true? Consider the following counterargument: If all, or most, children attend the same set of schools, parents who care about the ideological content of the curriculum will be driven to disputes over the common curriculum. Some may favor progressive education, some the basics. Some may want extensive sex education emphasizing personal autonomy; others desire an abstinence program. Some may be multiculturalists or feminists, others traditionalists. If families are able to choose their own schools (consistent with objective accreditation standards), then different schools can pursue different approaches, and there will be no

need for a struggle to determine one common curricular stance. In this sense, common schools can be compared to an established church: If everyone is forced to participate in the same institution, the result is a struggle for supremacy. But if different people are allowed to select their own institutions, on equal terms, then they can live together in relative harmony.

When Justice Black speaks so sharply of "powerful sectarian religious propagandists [seeking] domination and supremacy," to whom is he referring? Recall Justice Black's rhetoric when you read, in the next section, about the origins of this controversy in the Catholic-Protestant struggles of the nineteenth century.

4. Standing to Sue in Financial Aid Cases.   Most suits challenging government financial aid to religious schools are brought by taxpayers. But the general rule is that federal taxpayers lack standing to sue to challenge a federal expenditure of funds on the basis that it exceeds congressional powers and incrementally increases the plaintiff's tax burden. Frothingham v. Mellon, 262 U.S. 447 (1923). The same limit generally bars a federal court from hearing claims by state taxpayers challenging state expenditures. An example of the restriction on taxpayer standing is Miller v. California Commission on the Status of Women, 469 U.S. 806 (1984), where the Court dismissed a case in which taxpayers challenged the expenditure of funds for ideological advocacy with which they disagreed. If that principle were applicable to Establishment Clause claims, federal courts would lack jurisdiction to hear constitutional challenges to expenditures of funds for religious activities.

However, in 1968, on the same day as *Allen*, the Court concluded that Establishment Clause challenges are an exception to the *Frothingham* rule. Flast v. Cohen, 392 U.S. 83 (1968). The Court held that a taxpayer could sue to challenge governmental expenditures if he (1) challenged an "exercis[e] of congressional power under the taxing and spending clause of Art. I, § 8, of the Constitution" and (2) asserted that "the challenged enactment exceeds specific constitutional limitations imposed upon the exercise of the [t]axing and spending power and not simply that the enactment is generally beyond the powers delegated to Congress." *Id.* at 102-103. The Establishment Clause was such a specific limitation, the Court said, because "one of the specific evils feared by those who drafted [it] was that the taxing and spending power would be used to favor one religion over another or to support religion in general." *Id.* at 103.

Is *Flast*'s distinction a logical one? If the taxpayers were correct on the merits in *Frothingham* and *Miller*, wouldn't that imply that the government had similarly "exceed[ed] specific constitutional limits"? Why are cases in which "the enactment is generally beyond the powers delegated to Congress" different from cases under the Bill of Rights? Is it because individuals do not suffer the requisite "injury" from violations of government structure? Note that *Flast* implies that the relevant Establishment Clause "injury" is the coercion of the taxpayer to support religious teaching. Does this further imply that taxpayers lack standing to bring claims that do not implicate such a personal injury, but rather concern the "structural" implications (if any) of the separation of church and state? For example, in the *Kiryas Joel* case (see p. 253), the plaintiff challenging the Kiryas Joel district was a school board official elsewhere in the state. Because the suit was brought in state court, where federal standing principles do not apply, the issue of standing did not arise. Would this plaintiff have had standing in federal court to object to (1) drawing district lines along religious lines, where he did not live in the district, or (2) accommodating only the Satmar Hasidim, where he was not a member of a comparable group that requested and was denied equal treatment?*

B. THE HISTORICAL STRUGGLE OVER NONPUBLIC EDUCATION: SUBSIDY OR SUPPRESSION?

The *Everson* opinions contain much discussion of the Virginia Assessment Controversy of 1785, but no reference to the history of public schools or of private school funding in the years between the Founding and 1947. In fact, long before the federal courts were involved in the issue, religious school funding was the subject of extensive controversy during several periods of our history. Many of the ideas reflected in modern constitutional debate had their origins in nineteenth-century political argument.

1. Before the Civil War

Public education—that is, a system of free schools, open to all, and financed and controlled by the government—was essentially unknown to the Framers of the First Amendment. Prior to 1830 most schools were private. Almost all (even those organized by towns) were conducted under religious auspices. Families able to pay for the education of their young did so; the poor were educated, if at all, through a combination of private philanthropy and governmental grants. Governmental financial support for education (especially in the more religiously diverse big cities) typically took the form of grants to private schools for the education of the poor. Many of these schools were religious. Between 1800 and 1830, New York provided public funds to Presbyterian, Episcopalian, Methodist, Quaker, Dutch Reformed, Baptist, Lutheran, and Jewish schools, to an African Free School, and to the "Free School Society," a nonsectarian charitable school that was the forerunner of the public school system. These arrangements were not challenged as "establishments" under either state or federal constitutions. For detailed historical accounts of the pluralistic educational system of this period, see Carl F. Kaestle, Pillars of the Republic: Common Schools and American Society, 1780-1860, at 57, 166-167 (1983); Lloyd P. Jorgenson, The State and the Non-Public School, 1825-1925, at 1-19 (1987); Diane Ravitch, The Great School Wars, New York City, 1805-1973: A History of the Public Schools as

---

* In Valley Forge Christian College v. Americans United for Separation of Church & State, 454 U.S. 464 (1982), the Court held that taxpayers did not have standing to challenge the transfer of certain unused government property to a religious college. The Court offered two reasons to distinguish *Flast*: (1) that the challenge was to an agency action rather than an Act of Congress, and (2) that the action was pursuant to the government's power to dispose of federal property (art. IV, § 3) rather than (as in *Flast*) "an exercise of authority conferred by the taxing and spending clause of Art. I, § 8." *Id.* at 479-480. Should either of those differences have mattered? At the time, many observers predicted that *Valley Forge* was the beginning of a more fundamental reconsideration of *Flast*, but in the ensuing years, it has had little effect outside its own narrow compass.

Battlefield of Social Change 6-7 (1974); Richard J. Gabel, Public Funds for Church and Private Schools 147-470 (1937).

Early federal aid, which typically took the form of land grants, went to private as well as public schools, including religious schools. In Washington, D.C., where the Establishment Clause then applied, education was provided entirely through private and semipublic institutions—including denominational schools—partially at public expense until 1848. Gabel, Public Funds at 173-179.

By the Civil War, however, most northern and western states had established public school systems—often called "common schools"—and most ceased to support nonpublic education. The idea that government financial support should go only to government-run schools was the product of a bitter political and religious conflict that began in the 1830s and continued through most of the nineteenth century. John Jeffries and James Ryan describe the conflict:

A POLITICAL HISTORY OF THE ESTABLISHMENT CLAUSE
John C. Jeffries, Jr., and James E. Ryan
100 Mich. L. Rev. 279 (2001)

For most of its history, public education in America had been unabashedly patriotic and unmistakably Protestant. Whatever the state of faith at the time of the Framing, by the middle third of the nineteenth century, when the common-school movement took hold, the nation had experienced a massive evangelical resurgence. Protestant ministers and churchmen led the common-school movement and took for granted "a congruence of purpose between the common school and the Protestant churches." Civic leaders assumed "that Americanism and Protestantism were synonyms and that education and Protestantism were allies." Early common schools featured Bible reading, prayer, hymns, and holiday observances, all reinforced by the exhortations of the teacher and the pervasive Protestantism of the texts.

The problem was that Protestantism was not one religion but many. In an age when genuinely secular public education was "simply inconceivable," common-school advocates had to find a way to keep religion in the public schools but keep controversy out. They did so by promoting least-common-denominator Protestantism and rejecting particularistic influences. The architect of this strategy was Horace Mann, secretary of the nation's first board of education (in Massachusetts) from 1837-1849 and the leading figure in the common-school movement. Mann himself was a Unitarian, and hence personally liberal and latitudinal, but in Massachusetts, he had to contend with orthodox Congregationalists, Baptists, Methodists, and other Christian sects. Mann waged fierce battle with conservative critics, deriding their demands for more pronounced religious content as "sectarian." Under that label, he banned doctrines "peculiar to specific denominations but not common to all." Charges of "godlessness" were answered with a strategy described as "a stroke of genius." Mann insisted on Bible reading, *without commentary*, as the foundation of moral education. In his own words, "our system earnestly inculcates all Christian morals; it founds its morals on the basis of religion; it welcomes the religion of the Bible; and, in receiving the Bible, it allows it to do what it is allowed to do in no other system—*to speak for itself.*"

Though Protestants clashed on many questions, they agreed on the Bible. Bible reading in public school became the basis for a pan-Protestant compromise, a vague and inclusive Protestantism that, when augmented by specific doctrinal instruction at Sunday school, proved acceptable to all. Consequently, "most Protestant churches declared a truce with each other at the doors of the common school." The instruction behind those doors was nondenominational but emphatically not secular. A generalized Protestantism became the common religion of the common school. From its inception, therefore, American public education was religious but nonsectarian. Both characteristics were essential to the consensus of support for the common school.

Of course, that consensus did not include Catholics. At the time of the Revolution, 30,000 Catholics lived in the new United States, barely one percent of the population. By 1830, that number had increased to 600,000. By 1850, there were 1.5 million U.S. Catholics, and twice that many ten years later. The number quadrupled to twelve million in 1900, and doubled again by 1930. This population was mostly immigrant, in the early days mostly Irish, and mostly poor. They found the public schools unfriendly and inhospitable. Unaccompanied Bible reading, which was the cornerstone of the Protestant consensus, was to Catholics an affront. Public school students read from the King James Version, which the Catholic Church did not recognize. Indeed, the very fact of a direct and unmediated approach to God contradicted Catholic doctrine. The Douay Bible provided not only the officially approved English translation of the Scriptures, but also authoritative annotation and comment. Reading the unadorned text invited the error of private interpretation. As one cleric put the point in 1840: "The Catholic church tells her children that they must be taught their religion by AUTHORITY—the Sects say, read the bible, judge for yourselves."

Religious conflict over Bible reading grew intense. In Maine and Massachusetts, Catholic students suffered beatings or expulsions for refusing to read from the Protestant Bible, and crowds in Philadelphia rioted over whether Catholic children could be released from the classroom during Bible reading. Above the level of the street, the most important consequence of Protestant religiosity in the public schools was to confirm the determination of Catholics to go elsewhere. If the public schools were Protestant, the Catholics wanted their own schools, and for that, they needed money.

The earliest confrontation over public funding came in New York, where by 1840 Catholics had considerable sway. Bishop John Hughes argued that if the State planned to educate all children under one roof, then it should exclude religion "in every shape and form." Knowing that was impossible, however, he campaigned instead for state support of church schools. The Bishop's efforts so outraged Protestant and nativist opinion that in 1842 the New York legislature prohibited funding of any school where "any religious sectarian doctrine or tenet shall be taught, inculcated, or practiced." This episode united Protestants in defense of public education and against government funding for Catholic schools. The two sides refought the funding battle several times, until a state constitutional amendment in 1894 squashed a temporary Catholic victory in New York City by banning any public money for church-related schools.

For the remainder of the nineteenth century and into the twentieth, the Protestant position was that public schools must be "nonsectarian" (which was usually understood to allow Bible reading and other Protestant observances) and public money must not support "sectarian" schools (which in practical terms meant Catholic). The self-interested underside of these propositions surfaced repeatedly. The Know-Nothing Party arose in the 1850s to fight immigration and Catholic influence. Their 1856 platform demanded public education free from denominational influence, but simultaneously declared the Bible "the depository and fountain of all civil and religious freedom" and condemned any effort to remove it from the classroom. In 1869 the National Teachers Association (forerunner of today's National Education Association) resolved both that "the appropriation of public funds for the support of sectarian schools is a violation of the fundamental principles of our American system of education" *and* that "the Bible should not only be studied, venerated, and honored . . . but devotionally read, and its precepts inculcated in all the common schools of the land."

The divide between Protestants and Catholics was not merely theological; it was also political, cultural, and in some sense racial. American Protestants saw their faith as allied with republicanism and feared Catholicism as inimical to democracy. As Stephen Macedo noted, Americans "could see that the still-young republic's core principles of individual freedom and democratic equality were at odds with the church's authoritarian institutional structure, its long-standing association with feudal or monarchial governments, its insistence on close ties between church and state, its endorsement of censorship, and its rejection of individual rights to freedom of conscience and worship. . . ."[10] Rome hampered attempts by American Catholics to abandon the Church's legacy by issuing reactionary pronouncements ideally suited to confirm the rankest prejudice. The Vatican "rejected, proscribed, and condemned" the possibility of genuinely secular public education. Gregory XVI "greatly deplore[d] the fact that, where the ravings of human reason extend, there is somebody who studies new things and strives to know more than is necessary, against the advice of the apostle." And Pius IX ridiculed freedom of conscience as the "liberty of perdition."

The perception of Catholics as somehow un-American was fortified by the fact that they were overwhelmingly immigrant, urban, and poor. All three characteristics threatened defenders of Protestant, rural America. For example, Josiah Strong, a prominent evangelical and author of *Our Country*, a best-seller of the 1880s, freely mixed religious and social issues in his list of seven perils facing the nation. They were, in order: immigration, Catholicism, Mormonism, intemperance, socialism, wealth, and the city.

All these swirling sentiments came to a point in controversies over the public schools. Catholic educational separatism challenged the Protestant vision of a Christian America. Protestants responded by trying to keep Bible reading in the public schools and to interdict funding of sectarian education.

NOTES AND QUESTIONS

1. What Makes a School "Nonsectarian" or "Neutral"? In this controversy, the common school supporters claimed that their schools were "nonsectarian,"

10. Stephen Macedo, Diversity and Distrust: Civic Education in a Multicultural Democracy 61 (2000).

while the Catholics claimed, with some justice, that the schools were effectively Protestant.

How could common school supporters defend Bible reading in the schools while opposing funding for schools teaching Catholic doctrine? They argued that "[t]he presence of the Bible was demanded by many sects and, indeed, by individuals rather than by any one sect. It therefore seemed that Protestants did not act as a church and did not violate the separation of church and state when they formed a majority and placed the Bible in their publicly funded schools." Philip Hamburger, Separation of Church and State 228 (2002). Is this defense convincing?

If the common school position was not convincing, what was wrong with it? There are two possible ways of looking at the problem, with two quite different solutions:

First, the problem with the public schools might be that they were not non-sectarian enough. The solution therefore was to eliminate prayer, Bible reading, and moral-religious instruction from the schools. This solution presupposes that secular education is neutral toward religion.

Second, the problem might be that any school—or at least, any school that seeks to accomplish its objective of molding future citizens—necessarily imparts teachings that have moral and religious significance and cannot, therefore, be "neutral." What would follow from this way of understanding the problem?

2. Were the Common Schools Themselves an "Establishment of Religion"? Modern constitutional debates are framed in terms of whether assistance to nonpublic schools is an establishment of religion. Can the question be turned around? In his book, The Great Tradition of the American Churches (1953), religious historian Winthrop Hudson calls the early common schools the "new Protestant establishment." Is that an accurate description? Political theorist Stephen Macedo defends the common school movement on these grounds:

> Without minimizing the racialist element in nineteenth-century Americanism, we should also not let it obscure other factors that were at work, including the clear opposition between the American political creed and the doctrines of the nineteenth-century Roman Catholic Church. Many Americans, including many Catholic Americans, feared institutional Catholicism's hostility to free self-government, and not without reason. They could see that the still young republic's core principles of individual freedom and democratic equality were at odds with the church's authoritarian institutional structure, its long-standing association with feudal or monarchical governments, its insistence on close ties between church and state, its endorsement of censorship, and its rejection of individual rights to freedom of conscience and worship.
>
> [T]o grant [Catholic schools] public money would have defeated the dominant public purpose: to cast the public's weight behind a publicly controlled institution that could be trusted to bring together children of many faiths and to inculcate a common political, moral, and religious perspective.

Macedo, Diversity and Distrust at 61, 75. Macedo argues that common schools contributed to the "transformation" of American Catholicism into something closer to American political ideals. "All of this will seem to many like the height of illiberality," he observes. But the "fact is that many 'private' communities in mid-nineteenth-century America—including some religious ones—*did* need to be transformed in order to generate greater support for liberal democratic principles." *Id.* at 85-86.

What kind of an argument is this? Does Macedo claim that the common schools were neutral among religious denominations? He argues that the government should "inculcate" a "common . . . religious perspective." Is that suggestion consistent with the Establishment Clause?

2. After the Civil War

a. Reconstruction

After the northern victory in the Civil War, Congress began to appropriate large sums of money to provide schooling for the newly emancipated freedmen of the South. In the same year that it passed the Fourteenth Amendment, Congress enacted a statute instructing the Freedmen's Bureau to work through private benevolent associations whenever the latter provided suitable teachers. Act of July 16, 1866, § 13. Most of these associations were missionary societies from the North, some interdenominational and some affiliated with particular religious denominations. Public funds went to Presbyterian, Methodist, Baptist, Congregationalist, and other religious educational societies. See Ronald E. Butchart, Northern Schools, Southern Blacks, and Reconstruction: Freedmen's Education, 1862-1875, at 4-9, 33-52 (1980); Ward M. McAfee, Religion, Race, and Reconstruction: The Public Schools in the Politics of the 1870s (1998). The work of the Freedmen's Bureau ended by about 1870. Although some educators were critical of the missionary focus of these schools, the issue was never framed in terms of church-state separation, and the experience had little effect on the debate over aid to nonpublic (mostly Catholic) schools in the rest of the country.

b. The Blaine Amendment

Within a few years that debate resumed, and for the first time it moved to the national political stage. The debate took place against a background of increasing concerns about immigration and a rising tide of anti-Catholicism. Horace Bushnell, a prominent advocate of common schools in Connecticut, told an audience that "We are still, as Americans, a Protestant people." He declared the common school to be "a fundamental institution from the first—in our view a Protestant institution—associated with all our religious convictions, opinions, and the public sentiment of our Protestant society." He warned that the Catholic clergy were "preparing for an assault upon the common school system." If funds were provided to Catholic schools, their children

> will be shut up in schools that do not teach them what, as Americans, they most of all need to know, the political geography and political history of the world, the rights of humanity, the struggles by which those rights are vindicated, and the glorious rewards of liberty and social advancement that follow. They will be instructed mainly into the foreign prejudices and superstitions of their fathers, and the state, which proposes to be clear of all sectarian affinities in religion, will pay the bills!

Charles Glenn, The Myth of the Common School 227-229 (1987). "If the children of Papists are really in danger of being corrupted in the Protestant schools of enlightened, free and happy America," a Baptist publication editorialized, "it may be well for their conscientious parents and still more conscientious priests, to return them to the privileges of their ancestral homes." Jorgenson, The State and the Non-Public School at 107.

These anti-Catholic sentiments had long been a part of American popular culture. John Jay, for example, had led an effort to amend the New York Constitution of 1777 to exclude Catholics from the state. See Charles Lincoln, The Constitutional History of New York 541 (1906). But anti-Catholic feeling received a boost from the Vatican's 1864 publication of the *Syllabus of Errors* and the 1870 encyclical on papal infallibility in matters of faith and morals. The *Syllabus of Errors* was a list, issued by Pope Pius IX, of 80 propositions that the Roman Catholic Church deemed erroneous (at least in their extreme form). Among them were:

15. Every man is free to embrace and profess that religion which, guided by the light of reason, he shall consider true.

55. The Church ought to be separated from the State and the State from the Church.

In the United States as well as in parts of Europe, these documents were much criticized by opponents of the Catholic Church and treated as confirmation that Catholic teaching was antithetical to liberal democratic government. Theodore Roosevelt, for example, commented: "The Church is in no way suited to this country and can never have any great permanent growth except through immigration, for its thought is Latin and entirely at variance with the dominant thought of our country and institutions." Jorgenson, The State and the Nonpublic School at 130.

As legal historian Philip Hamburger has noted, opposition to parochial school funding also rose at this time among "liberals" who were skeptical of traditional Christianity altogether. But this group "had little hope of prevailing in national party politics," so the anti-funding campaign at this time relied additionally—even predominantly—on "a Protestant, anti-Catholic [concept of church-state] separation." Separation of Church and State at 328.

In 1875, President Ulysses S. Grant brought the issue of parochial school funding to the national political stage in a speech to the Army of Tennessee. He stated that "[i]f we are to have another contest in the near future of our national existence I predict that the dividing line will not be Mason and Dixon's but between patriotism and intelligence on the one side and superstition, ambition and ignorance on the other." He urged his listeners to "[e]ncourage free schools and resolve that not one dollar of money appropriated for their support no matter how raised, shall be appropriated to the support of any sectarian school. Resolve that neither the State nor the Nation, nor both combined, shall support institutions of learning other than those sufficient to afford to every child growing up in the land the opportunity of a good common school education, [u]nmixed with sectarian, pagan or atheistical tenets. . . . Keep the church and state forever separate." Quoted in Anson Phelps Stokes and Leo Pfeffer, Church and State in the United States 272 (rev. one-vol. ed. 1964).

Republican presidential aspirant James G. Blaine introduced a constitutional amendment:

> No State shall make any law respecting an establishment of religion, or prohibiting the free exercise thereof; and no money raised by taxation in any State for the support of public schools, or derived from any public fund therefor, nor any public lands devoted thereto, shall ever be under the control of any religious sect; nor shall any money so raised or lands so devoted be divided between religious sects or denominations.

With minor changes, this proposal was approved by the House of Representatives on August 4, 1876, by a vote of 180 to 7, with 98 representatives not voting. Evidently, the Democrats, who held a majority in the House, determined not to oppose the amendment so shortly before a hard-fought presidential election. Moreover, they apparently realized that the wording of this amendment was so narrow that it would be essentially meaningless.

In the Senate, Republicans criticized the version of the amendment passed by the House as a "fraud and a sham," on the ground that it would permit any state or the federal government to raise money by taxation or through land grants for the support of sectarian or denominational schools, so long as the money were not taken from the public schools fund. Accordingly, they introduced a more sweeping amendment, which prohibited any form of state financial support to any "school, educational or other institution, under the control of any religious or anti-religious sect, organization, or denomination, or wherein the particular creed or tenets of any religious or anti-religious sect, organization, or denomination shall be taught." Like the House version, the amendment affirmed that "[t]his article shall not be construed to prohibit the reading of the Bible in any school or institution." After lively debate, this proposal failed to receive the requisite two-thirds vote, though it attained a 28-16 majority, largely on partisan lines, with 27 senators not voting. The debate had a number of interesting and revealing features:

1. Applicability of the Bill of Rights to the States. The first clauses of both versions of the Blaine Amendment would have applied the Free Exercise and Establishment Clauses to the states. Since the debate took place less than a decade after ratification of the Fourteenth Amendment, this is often cited as evidence that the Fourteenth Amendment was not understood at the time to "incorporate" these provisions of the Bill of Rights against the states. See, e.g., F. William O'Brien, The Blaine Amendment 1875-1876, 41 U. Det. L. Rev. 137 (1963). (On the incorporation controversy, see pp. 71-79.) Indeed, no participant in the debates, pro or con, made any suggestion that application of the Free Exercise and Establishment Clauses to the states had already been accomplished.

A contrary interpretation is offered by legal historian Richard Aynes:

> The difficulty with that argument [against incorporation] is that intervening decisions in *The Slaughter-House Cases*, 83 U.S. (16 Wall.) 36 (1873), *United States v. Cruikshank*, 92 U.S. 542 (1876), and *Walker v. Sauvinet*, 92 U.S. 90 (1876), had indicated that the Supreme Court would not interpret the Fourteenth Amendment to enforce the Bill of Rights against the states. Indiana Senator Oliver

Morton, who had been a member of the 39th Congress, supported the Blaine Amendment while lamenting that the Fourteenth and Fifteenth Amendments "have, I fear, been very much impaired by construction, and one of them in some respects, almost destroyed by construction." 4 Cong. Rec. 5585 (1876). . . .

. . . [S]upporters of the Blaine Amendment may have accepted the decisions of the Supreme Court as binding and sought to achieve at least a part of their initial Fourteenth Amendment objectives in Blaine.

Richard L. Aynes, The Blaine Amendment, in Religion and Law: An Encyclopedia 39-41 (Paul Finkelman ed., 2000).

2. The Debate over Whether Nonsectarian Education Is Possible. Proponents of the amendment distinguished between teaching "religion" and teaching "the particular tenets or creed of some denomination." 4 Cong. Rec. 5588 (1876) (Sen. Edmunds). That is how the same amendment could forbid publicly supported schools from teaching the "particular creeds or tenets" of any religion while at the same time allow Bible reading in the schools. Senator Edmunds of Vermont, chair of the Judiciary Committee and an Episcopalian, explained that the "good of the young" would not be advanced by "being compelled to decide between contending priests whether the true theory and doctrine of the gospel is that of a trinity or a unitarian doctrine, or whether in the holy sacrament the elements show the real presence or only the symbolic and the memorial one," but that they "can still be taught the homely virtues and the right-minded truth and purity that belong to the personal teaching of all creeds." *Id.* He drew an analogy to the daily prayer of the congressional chaplain, which he described as "not the prayer of creed but the prayer of man imploring the beneficent protection of his Creator." *Id.*

Opponents responded that this supposed nonsectarianism was simply Protestantism in disguise. They explained that Catholics were opposed to "free schools" for "the reason that they were sectarian. Even the very Bible which was used in the schools was a sectarian book." 4 Cong. Rec. 5590 (Sen. Bogy). Senator Bogy, a Catholic Democrat from Missouri, commented (*id.*):

What is, strictly and logically speaking, sectarian teaching, I am not able to tell. What is religious teaching, it is very hard to say. To tell a child that there is a God is religion. To tell him that the Son of God was born and, as God, was crucified for the redemption of a fallen world, is religious. Yet the Unitarian would tell you that it is not true, as he does not believe in the Trinity. We have prayer here every morning; and no one listens to it with more reverence than I do; for I believe in prayer. . . . But is that sectarian teaching or not? Who can draw the distinction?

At no point did any participant in the debate advocate secular schools. Such an idea would have been opposed by Protestants and Catholics alike. By common consent, a principal purpose of schools was to inculcate the moral virtue necessary for citizens of a republic, and morality and religion were deemed inseparable. The debate, rather, was between those who believed that "nonsectarian" education was possible and those who believed that "nonsectarianism" was equivalent to nondenominational Protestantism.

3. The Debate over Catholicism. The controversy over the compatibility of Catholicism and liberal institutions, and the corresponding accusation of anti-Catholic bigotry, played a major role in the debates. The principal spokesmen for the Blaine Amendment, Senator Edmunds and Senator Oliver Morton of Indiana, both quoted at length from the 1864 encyclical of Pope Pius IX containing the *Syllabus of Errors*, implying that it was the anti-republican character of Catholic doctrine that made the amendment necessary. 4 Cong. Rec. 5587-5588, 5591. Indeed, Edmunds prefaced his quotations from the encyclical with the remark that this would convince his listeners "that I am right in what precisely this issue is." This was a vulnerable point for the opposition, as is evident in this exchange between Edmunds and Senator Whyte, a Protestant from Maryland who attempted to defend Catholic interests:

> *Mr. Whyte.* . . . In my judgment the danger is not present which this article, proposed in response to an ephemeral popular demand, is designed to avert; and it seems to me, to use plain words, nearly an accusation against a large body of fellow-citizens as loyal to republican liberty as we proclaim ourselves to be.
> *Mr. Edmunds.* Will the Senator allow me to ask him a question? . . . The question I wished to ask was precisely in point to what the Senator was saying, that there was no present danger of the kind to which he alludes, whether he had read the mandate ordinarily called the encyclical letter and the syllabus of errors promulgated by the holy Pontiff in 1864 on this very subject?
> *Mr. Whyte.* Yes; but 1864 is not 1876 by a long shot.
> *Mr. Edmunds.* It lacks twelve years of it.
> *Mr. Whyte.* And a good many things which people did in 1864 they do not do to-day, I am happy to add.
> *Mr. Edmunds.* Does the Senator mean to say that he understands that the principles or declarations of this letter have been changed, or withdrawn, or modified?
> *Mr. Whyte.* Yes, sir.
> *Mr. Edmunds.* I should like to see the proof of it.

Id. at 5583. This inspired Senator Bogy to declare:

> [T]his discussion is much to be deplored. I think I know the motive, and the animus which have prompted all this thing. I do not believe it is because of a great devotion to the principles of religious liberty. That great idea which is now moving the modern world is used merely as a cloak from the most unworthy partisan motive. [Now that] "the bloody shirt" can no longer call out the mad bull, another animal has to be brought forth by these matadores to engage the attention of the people in this great arena in which we are soon all to be combatants. The Pope, the old Pope of Rome, is to be the great bull that we are all to attack.

Id. at 5589. Other Democrats likewise accused proponents of the amendment of anti-Catholic bigotry. To this, Senator Morton responded: "if anybody has attacked the Catholic religion here to-night I have not heard it." *Id.* at 5593. Cf. Marc D. Stern, Blaine Amendments, Anti-Catholicism, and Anti-Catholic Dogma, 2 First Am. L. Rev. 153 (2003), which argues that the *Syllabus of Errors* and other Vatican statements created a reasonable, even if ultimately erroneous, "fear of an anti-democratic, autocratic Catholic Church which was seeking political power everywhere." *Id.* at 176.

4. Two Theories of Religious Liberty.　　Participants in the debate articulated two distinct theories of religious liberty, which remain prominent to this day. Opponents of the measure argued that families should have an equal right to obtain an education in accordance with their conscience and convictions, and that no particular form of education—religious or secular—should be favored. Senator Kernan, a Catholic Democrat from New York, speaking for "those people who believe that it is their duty either in the family or in the school to have their secular education accompanied with instruction in their faith," explained:

> All [we] say is if our Protestant friends prefer to have schools where there is no religion taught, it is their right; we concede it to them; we would not take it from them; but we feel it our duty to bring our children up in our own faith. I state it as clearly and as fairly as I can, and I assure my friend that when he expresses the idea that those to whom he alludes would take from Protestants the right to have their children educated just as they see fit, he does them great wrong. We hold it to be their right and their duty to have their children educated in the way they think right and the way they think best, and we only ask that we should be allowed to educate ours as we think best.

Id. at 5585-5586. He insisted that this could be accomplished without "favoring one sect rather than another" by funding each institution "*pro rata* according to the number they supported or cut them all off." *Id.* at 5584.

Supporters of the amendment did not view public schools as one choice among many, let alone as sectarian institutions. To them, the public schools were an essential institution of republican government. Indeed, some Republican legislators maintained that the federal government could require states to maintain a common school system under the clause of the Constitution stating that "the United States shall guarantee to every State in this Union a Republican Form of Government." U.S. Const. art. IV, § 4. To them, financial support for religious education was the same as financial support for the church itself. Senator Morton explained:

> The support of a school by public taxation is the same thing in principle as an established church. If we can appropriate money to establish, if you please, a Catholic school, it involves the whole principle of supporting the Catholic Church at public expense, or if you please a Protestant school and the support of a Protestant Church at public expense. . . . Now, sir, that there should be perfect freedom of religious opinion in our country is essential to our life as a nation, and we cannot have that and we cannot have perfect equality except upon the condition that religion shall not be maintained at public expense and that denominational schools of religion shall not be maintained at public expense. Every sect is left free. The Catholics may have as many schools as they see proper and teach their religion, and so may Protestants—no abridgement of their freedom. They have the largest liberty; but when it is done at public expense and all are taxed for their support, then the principle of equality is gone.

4 Cong. Rec. 5585.

It is evident that the two sides in the debate were talking past one another. To the proponents, the common schools were seen as neutral and broadly acceptable to everyone; to the extent that any parents preferred a sectarian education, all religious denominations have an equal right to build their own schools at their own expense. To the opponents, the common schools were seen as inculcating a particular version of Christianity, which was acceptable to most Protestants but not to Catholics or others. Indeed, they did not believe that a "neutral" form of education was possible. To them, equality could not be achieved unless all families had an equal right to choose education in accordance with their own beliefs.

5. "Little Blaine Amendments" in the States.   Although the Blaine Amendment never achieved the necessary two-thirds vote in both houses of Congress, it served as the model for so-called "little Blaine Amendments" in the states. Indeed, Congress demanded the inclusion of such provisions as a condition to statehood in the Dakotas, Montana, Washington, and New Mexico. By 1890, some 29 states had enacted some form of limitation on private school funding in their state constitutions. We consider the effect of these provisions on current issues in section E below.

For discussion and analysis of both the Blaine Amendment and its state offspring, from varying perspectives, see, e.g., Ward M. McAfee, The Historical Context of the Failed Blaine Amendment of 1876, 2 First Am. L. Rev. 1 (2003); Kyle Duncan, Secularism's Laws: State Blaine Amendments and Religious Persecution, 72 Fordham L. Rev. 493 (2003); Richard M. Garnett, The Theology of the Blaine Amendments, 2 First Am. L. Rev. 45 (2003); Steven K. Green, "Blaming Blaine": Understanding the Blaine Amendment and the "No-Funding" Principle, 2 First Am. L. Rev. 107 (2003); Toby J. Heytens, Note, School Choice and State Constitutions, 86 Va. L. Rev. 117 (2000); Joseph Viteritti, Blaine's Wake: School Choice, the First Amendment, and State Constitutional Law, 21 Harv. J.L. & Pub. Pol'y 657, 673 (1998); Frank Kemerer, State Constitutions and School Vouchers, 120 Educ. L. Rep. 1 (1997); Steven K. Green, The Blaine Amendment Reconsidered, 36 Am. J. Legal Hist. 38 (1992).

c. Continued Conflict

In the late 1880s, controversy over nonpublic schools intensified as efforts were made in a number of states—most notably Massachusetts, Illinois, and Wisconsin—to enact compulsory education laws, which threatened the existence of parochial schools. In 1922, the voters of Oregon approved a referendum, backed by the Ku Klux Klan, that required all school-age children to attend public schools. See generally William G. Ross, Forging New Freedoms: Nativism, Education, and the Constitution, 1917-1927 (1994). This was the Supreme Court's response:

PIERCE v. SOCIETY OF SISTERS
268 U.S. 510 (1925)

Mr. Justice McREYNOLDS delivered the opinion of the Court.

. . . The challenged act, effective September 1, 1926, requires every parent, guardian, or other person having control or charge or custody of a child between 8 and 16 years to send him "to a public school for the period of time a public school shall be held during the current year" in the district where the child resides; and failure so to do is declared a misdemeanor. . . . The manifest purpose is to compel general attendance at public schools by normal children, between 8 and 16, who have not completed the eighth grade. . . .

[T]he Society's bill alleges that the enactment conflicts with the right of parents to choose schools where their children will receive appropriate mental and religious training, the right of the child to influence the parents' choice of a school, the right of schools and teachers therein to engage in a useful business or profession, and is accordingly repugnant to the Constitution and void. And, further, that unless enforcement of the measure is enjoined the corporation's business and property will suffer irreparable injury.

No question is raised concerning the power of the state reasonably to regulate all schools, to inspect, supervise and examine them, their teachers and pupils; to require that all children of proper age attend some school, that teachers shall be of good moral character and patriotic disposition, that certain studies plainly essential to good citizenship must be taught, and that nothing be taught which is manifestly inimical to the public welfare.

The inevitable practical result of enforcing the act under consideration would be destruction of appellees' primary schools, and perhaps all other private primary schools for normal children within the state of Oregon. Appellees are engaged in a kind of undertaking not inherently harmful, but long regarded as useful and meritorious. Certainly there is nothing in the present records to indicate that they have failed to discharge their obligations to patrons, students, or the state. And there are no peculiar circumstances or present emergencies which demand extraordinary measures relative to primary education.

[W]e think it entirely plain that the Act of 1922 unreasonably interferes with the liberty of parents and guardians to direct the upbringing and education of children under their control. As often heretofore pointed out, rights guaranteed by the Constitution may not be abridged by legislation which has no reasonable relation to some purpose within the competency of the state. The fundamental theory of liberty upon which all governments in this Union repose excludes any general power of the state to standardize its children by forcing them to accept instruction from public teachers only. The child is not the mere creature of the state; those who nurture him and direct his destiny have the right, coupled with the high duty, to recognize and prepare him for additional obligations.

NOTES AND QUESTIONS

1. The Source of the Right: Substantive Due Process or Religious Freedom? Note that *Pierce* was decided under the doctrine of "substantive due process," the controversial idea that courts may invalidate laws that impinge on human freedoms (including economic liberty) without sufficient justification in the public interest. This, presumably, was because the Court had not yet held that the First Amendment applied to the states through the Fourteenth Amendment. Later the Court described the right of parents to send their children to religious schools as arising under the Free Exercise Clause. Committee for Public Education & Religious Liberty v. Nyquist, 413 U.S. 756, 788 (1973). Is *Pierce* correctly decided as a free exercise case after Employment Division v. Smith? (Recall the so-called hybrid-rights exception to *Smith*.) In addition, *Pierce* is frequently cited as an illustration of the Court's "privacy" doctrine, a modern version of substantive due process that is the foundation for abortion rights and contraceptive rights, among others. See Roe v. Wade, 410 U.S. 113 (1973).

2. A Common Democratic Education. Do you think *Pierce* was correctly decided? Why doesn't the state have a legitimate interest in ensuring that all children, for both their own good and the good of society, receive an education in common with other children, under a curriculum designed to impart democratic values? See Amy Gutmann, Democratic Education 116 (1987) ("a primary purpose of [public] schools is to cultivate common democratic values among all children, regardless of their academic ability, class, race, religion, or sex"). To be sure, some private schools might have an adequate curriculum, but some will not—and regulation of the curriculum might be far more difficult and more divisive than simply requiring all children to attend public schools. Moreover, allowing children to attend private schools might exacerbate differences along religious, racial, and socioeconomic lines. Consider the argument made by attorneys for the governor of Oregon in support of the law:

BRIEF FOR THE GOVERNOR OF OREGON IN PIERCE v. SOCIETY OF SISTERS

Brief at 38-40, reprinted in 23 Landmark Briefs and
Arguments of the Supreme Court of the United States 3, 45-47
(Philip B. Kurland and Gerhard Casper eds., 1975)

Under all governments, even those which are the most free and democratic in their character, the citizen must always owe duties to the state; and it necessarily follows that the state has an interest in making it certain (which can only be done by appropriate legislation) that the citizen is fitted, both in mind and body, to perform these duties. . . .

The discretionary powers of a State are broad enough to permit it to decide that compulsory attendance at public schools is a proper "precautionary measure against the moral pestilence of paupers, vagabonds, and possibly convicts."

The voters of Oregon who adopted [the law] had the right to base their action on the belief that the fact that the great increase in juvenile crime in the United States followed so closely after the great increase in the number of children in the United States who were not attending public schools, was more than a coincidence.

The voters in Oregon might also have based their action in adopting this law upon the alarm which they felt at the rising tide of religious suspicions in this country, and upon their belief that the basic cause of such religious feelings was the separation of children along religious lines during the most susceptible years of their lives, with the inevitable awakening of a consciousness of separation, and a distrust and suspicion of those from whom they were so carefully guarded. The voters of Oregon might have felt that the mingling together, during a portion of their education, of the children of all races and sects might be the best safeguard against future internal dissensions with the consequent weakening of the community against foreign dangers.

[T]he Supreme Court [is aware of] the evil effects upon a State of the immigration of ignorant foreigners, unacquainted with and lacking sympathy with, American institutions and ideals. In this connection, it should be remembered that the vast majority of children not now attending the Public Schools of Oregon who will be compelled to do so by the new statute, are either themselves immigrants or the children of immigrants.

Surely a State can require of all immigrants admitted to all the advantages and opportunities of life in the United States, that their children may be taught by the State the English language, and the character of American institutions and government.

NOTES AND QUESTIONS

1. **Education, Democracy, and Pluralism.**

(a) **Do common schools promote tolerance?**   The argument that private, religious schools create a sense of "separation, distrust, and suspicion" along religious lines in children of a susceptible age, and that a policy of "mingling together" children of "all races and sects" is a safeguard against such animosity, has a modern ring to it. Indeed, this is one of the principal arguments today against a system of educational choice, or "vouchers." Is there anything wrong with this argument? Why shouldn't the government be able to foster racial and religious tolerance and understanding by insisting on universal education in common schools? How would you vote if *Pierce* were decided today?

(b) **Or do common schools reflect intolerance of difference?**   Does it affect your answer to know that the principal advocates for the Oregon law were members of the Ku Klux Klan, and that the argument above was their argument? Why might the Ku Klux Klan—not ordinarily considered an organization committed to the mutual toleration of "all races and sects"—advocate such a measure? In its historical context, the intolerance of this proposal is transparent: The public schools were intended to be an instrument for "Americanizing" immigrant children, especially Catholics. As Stephen Monsma has written, "[A]nti-Catholicism and the common school ideal worked to reinforce each other. Catholics, to the extent they rejected the common schools, proved the worst suspicions of nativist Americans. They, it was held, were determined to hold onto their allegiance to a foreign potentate [the Pope] and to resist the democratizing, character-building, Americanizing efforts of the common schools of their adopted land." Stephen V. Monsma, When Sacred and Secular Mix 139 (1998). Stripped of its nativist and anti-Catholic bias, however, is this a constitutionally acceptable purpose? *Can* the argument be stripped of bias against whatever groups would form and patronize nonpublic schools?

Pierce brings into focus a conflict between a democratic ideal of education, in which the community as a whole decides what values to impart to the next generation, and a pluralistic ideal of education, in which different values will be imparted to different children. Which of these ideals is most consistent with the principle of nonestablishment?

2. Educational Rights and Government Aid.   If the Supreme Court was correct in *Pierce* that "[t]he fundamental theory of liberty upon which all governments in this Union repose excludes any general power of the state to standardize its children by forcing them to accept instruction from public teachers only," why is it permissible for the state to provide free education only to those willing to "accept instruction from public teachers only"?

It is easy to see the argument for requiring all students to attend common schools (the ideal of democratic control over education), and it is easy to see the argument for allowing families to choose what kind of school to use without economic discrimination or penalty (the pluralistic ideal), but what is the argument for allowing nonpublic schools to exist, while devoting all public funds to a single set of schools run by the government? Doesn't that amount to educational freedom only for the rich?

Are restrictions on private or religious school aid in conflict with this century's emphasis, since the New Deal, that government may promote (or restrict) freedom through its provision of positive benefits? See Thomas C. Berg, Anti-Catholicism and Modern Church-State Relations, 33 Loy. U. Chi. L.J. 121, 131 (2001):

> Prohibitions on aid to private education had rested partly on a "negative conception of the state," widely accepted in 19th-century America, under which tax-supported aid to a private entity or activity was a departure from the state's proper role of simply preserving liberty. But the New Deal emphasized that active government, through subsidies and regulation, could and should promote liberty in a positive way. The New Jersey law in *Everson* authorizing bus reimbursements, introduced in 1937 and passed in 1941, was a Depression-era welfare measure, and many other forms of parochial school aid such as textbook loans and hot lunch programs stemmed from the New Deal or the Progressive era programs. As theologian John Bennett, one of the few liberal Protestant clergy who actively supported some form of parochial aid, stated, the availability of equal aid affected "the opportunity of citizens to exercise their religious liberty in positive ways . . . [W]hat if positive free exercise of these rights depends upon 'cooperation' between Church and state?"
>
> Despite these arguments, . . . [o]n this issue many New Deal liberals reverted to laissez-faire premises that they would otherwise reject; they invoked a negative conception of the state under which aid to Catholic schools was positive favoritism for them rather than an attempt to equalize them with the aid already given to state-run schools.

3. Anti-Catholic Stereotyping and the First Amendment.   Even in recent times, the question of school funding has been affected by the antagonism many Americans have felt toward Roman Catholicism. See Michael Schwartz, The Persistent Prejudice: Anti-Catholicism in America (1984). Recall Justice Hugo Black's reference to parochial aid supporters as "powerful sectarian religious propagandists" seeking "complete domination and supremacy of their particular brand of religion." Board of Education v. Allen (p. 352). Now you can see the origins and background of that rhetoric. In 1947, the same year that *Everson* was decided, John Dewey, America's foremost philosopher of education, wrote an essay that declared:

> One of the basic ideas which made possible the creation of a homogeneous society out of the welter of heterogeneous peoples in this New World was that the power of the State came to be irrevocably divorced from the power of any Church and that all of the children of all of the people were permitted and encouraged to gain knowledge in an institution that was free from the control of any sect or class or individual or even of the Federal government.
>
> [Now] more treacherously and boldly than ever before is suggested the idea that schools sponsored by organizations of various sectarian persuasions should be supported by the public treasury. . . . The Roman Catholic hierarchy, for example, has attempted for many years to gain public fiscal aid and its program has been advanced through active lobbying for school lunches, health programs and school transportation facilities for Catholic schools. . . . It is essential that this basic issue be seen for what it is, namely, as the encouragement of a powerful reactionary world organization in the most vital realm of democratic life with the resulting promulgation of principles inimical to democracy.

John Dewey, 15 The Later Works, 1925-1953, at 284-285 (Jo Ann Boydston ed., 1989). It is curious that Dewey would credit the separation of church and state with the "creation of a homogeneous society out of the welter of heterogeneous peoples in this New World," and that an advocate of church-state separation would base government policy on the characterization of a religious denomination as a "powerful reactionary world organization." Isn't the purpose of the Establishment Clause to protect diversity of opinion, rather than to produce homogeneity? For a fascinating study of anti-Catholic attitudes among mid-twentieth-century American intellectuals, see John T. McGreevy, Thinking on One's Own: Catholicism in the American Intellectual Imagination, 1928-1960, 97 J. Am. Hist. (June 1997). See also Hamburger, Separation of Church and State at 391-478 (tracing continuing anti-Catholic elements in opposition to parochial school aid in mid 1900s).

4. International Comparisons. The United States is virtually the only Western democracy to reserve public funding to a government-run secular school system. Most such nations—including Canada, Great Britain, France, West Germany, the Netherlands, and Belgium—provide funding for private religious schools as well as public schools. For a detailed description of the experience in these nations, see Charles Glenn, Choice of Schools in Six Nations (U.S. Dept. of Education, 1989).

5. Secular Public Schools and Aid to Religious Schools. As you can see, one problem with the denial of aid to "sectarian" schools was that the early public schools themselves had a religious cast: their official programs "featured Bible reading, prayer, hymns, and holiday observances," usually of the mainline Protestant variety. Ryan and Jeffries (p. 356). However, by the second half of the 20th century, many official religious observances were eliminated from public schools, whether by administrative policies or by judicial decisions, state or federal. Most dramatically, the Supreme Court in two 1960s decisions struck down the practices of teacher-led prayer and official Bible readings in the classroom at the beginning of the school day. Engel v. Vitale, 370 U.S. 421 (1962); Abington School Dist. v. Schempp, 374 U.S. 203 (1963). We will examine *Engel* and *Schempp* later in the book (pp. 484, 486).

Soon after those decisions, the Court turned its attention closely to the question of aid to private religious schools, as the next section discusses. Do you think that the elimination of official religious elements from public schools (a) strengthened the case for denying aid to private religious schools? One can argue that when public schools no longer favor one religion, such as generic Protestantism, then people of other faiths have a less pressing need to opt out and attend a school of their own faith. Or does the secularization of the public school (b) strengthen the case for *providing* aid to religious schools—on the ground that without such aid, the state's preferential funding of public schools disfavors those parents who want some religious elements in their children's education? Think about those questions as you turn to the Court's modern decisions on government aid.

C. THE *LEMON* APPROACH: NO AID TO RELIGIOUS TEACHING

1. *The Basic Decisions*

LEMON v. KURTZMAN
403 U.S. 602 (1971)

Mr. Chief Justice BURGER delivered the opinion of the Court.

These two appeals raise questions as to Pennsylvania and Rhode Island statutes providing state aid to church-related elementary and secondary schools. . . .

I

THE RHODE ISLAND STATUTE

The Rhode Island Salary Supplement Act was enacted in 1969. It rests on the legislative finding that the quality of education available in nonpublic elementary schools has been jeopardized by the rapidly rising salaries needed to attract competent and dedicated teachers. The Act authorizes state officials to supplement the salaries of teachers of secular subjects in nonpublic elementary schools by paying directly to a teacher an amount not in excess of 15% of his current annual salary. As supplemented, however, a nonpublic school teacher's salary cannot exceed the maximum paid to teachers in the State's public schools, and the recipient must be certified by the state board of education in substantially the same manner as public school teachers.

In order to be eligible for the Rhode Island salary supplement, the recipient must teach in a nonpublic school at which the average per-pupil expenditure on secular education is less than the average in the State's public schools during a specified period. . . .

The Act also requires that teachers eligible for salary supplements must teach only those subjects that are offered in the State's public schools. They must use "only teaching materials which are used in the public schools." Finally, any teacher applying for a salary supplement must first agree in writing "not to teach a course in religion for so long as or during such time as he or she receives any salary supplements" under the Act. . . .

THE PENNSYLVANIA STATUTE

. . . The Pennsylvania [statute] was passed in 1968 in response to a crisis that the Pennsylvania Legislature found existed in the State's nonpublic schools due to rapidly rising costs. . . .

The statute authorizes appellee state Superintendent of Public Instruction to "purchase" specified "secular educational services" from nonpublic schools. Under the "contracts" authorized by the statute, the State directly reimburses nonpublic schools solely for their actual expenditures for teachers' salaries, textbooks, and instructional materials. A school seeking reimbursement must maintain prescribed accounting procedures that identify the "separate" cost of the "secular educational service." These accounts are subject to state audit. The funds for this program were originally derived from a new tax on horse and harness racing, but the Act is now financed by a portion of the state tax on cigarettes.

There are several significant statutory restrictions on state aid. Reimbursement is limited to courses "presented in the curricula of the public schools." It is further limited "solely" to courses in the following "secular" subjects: mathematics, modern foreign languages,[4] physical science, and physical education. Textbooks and instructional materials included in the program must be approved by the state Superintendent of Public Instruction. Finally, the statute prohibits reimbursement for any course that contains "any subject matter expressing religious teaching, or the morals or forms of worship of any sect."

. . . It appears that some $5 million has been expended annually under the Act. The State has now entered into contracts with some 1,181 nonpublic elementary and secondary schools [enrolling] more than 20% of the total number of students in the State. More than 96% of these pupils attend church-related schools, and most of these schools are affiliated with the Roman Catholic church. . . .

II

In Everson v. Board of Education, this Court upheld a state statute that reimbursed the parents of parochial school children for bus transportation expenses. There Mr. Justice Black, writing for the majority, suggested that the decision carried to "the verge" of forbidden territory under the Religion Clauses. Candor compels acknowledgment, moreover, that we can only dimly perceive the lines of demarcation in this extraordinarily sensitive area of constitutional law.

[The First Amendment's] authors did not simply prohibit the establishment of a state church or a state religion, an area history shows they regarded as very important and fraught with great dangers. Instead they commanded that there should be "no law respecting an establishment of religion." A law may be one "respecting" the forbidden objective while falling short of its total realization. A law "respecting" the proscribed result, that is, the establishment of religion, is

4. Latin, Hebrew, and classical Greek are excluded.

not always easily identifiable as one violative of the Clause. A given law might not establish a state religion but nevertheless be one "respecting" that end in the sense of being a step that could lead to such establishment and hence offend the First Amendment.

In the absence of precisely stated constitutional prohibitions, we must draw lines with reference to the three main evils against which the Establishment Clause was intended to afford protection: "sponsorship, financial support, and active involvement of the sovereign in religious activity." Walz v. Tax Commission (1970).

Every analysis in this area must begin with consideration of the cumulative criteria developed by the Court over many years. Three such tests may be gleaned from our cases. First, the statute must have a secular legislative purpose; second, its principal or primary effect must be one that neither advances nor inhibits religion; finally, the statute must not foster "an excessive government entanglement with religion."

Inquiry into the legislative purposes of the Pennsylvania and Rhode Island statutes affords no basis for a conclusion that the legislative intent was to advance religion. On the contrary, the statutes themselves clearly state that they are intended to enhance the quality of the secular education in all schools covered by the compulsory attendance laws. There is no reason to believe the legislatures meant anything else. A State always has a legitimate concern for maintaining minimum standards in all schools it allows to operate. . . .

In *Allen* the Court acknowledged that secular and religious teachings were not necessarily so intertwined that secular textbooks furnished to students by the State were in fact instrumental in the teaching of religion. The legislatures of Rhode Island and Pennsylvania have concluded that secular and religious education are identifiable and separable. In the abstract we have no quarrel with this conclusion.

The two legislatures, however, have also recognized that church-related elementary and secondary schools have a significant religious mission and that a substantial portion of their activities is religiously oriented. They have therefore sought to create statutory restrictions designed to guarantee the separation between secular and religious educational functions and to ensure that State financial aid supports only the former. All these provisions are precautions taken in candid recognition that these programs approached, even if they did not intrude upon, the forbidden areas under the Religion Clauses. We need not decide whether these legislative precautions restrict the principal or primary effect of the programs to the point where they do not offend the Religion Clauses, for we conclude that the cumulative impact of the entire relationship arising under the statutes in each State involves excessive entanglement between government and religion.

III

. . . Our prior holdings do not call for total separation between church and state; total separation is not possible in an absolute sense. Some relationship between government and religious organizations is inevitable. Fire inspections, building and zoning regulations, and state requirements under compulsory school-attendance laws are examples of necessary and permissible contacts.

Judicial caveats against entanglement must recognize that the line of separation, far from being a "wall," is a blurred, indistinct, and variable barrier depending on all the circumstances of a particular relationship. . . .

In order to determine whether the government entanglement with religion is excessive, we must examine the character and purposes of the institutions that are benefited, the nature of the aid that the State provides, and the resulting relationship between the government and the religious authority. . . .

(A) RHODE ISLAND PROGRAM

The District Court made extensive findings on the grave potential for excessive entanglement that inheres in the religious character and purpose of the Roman Catholic elementary schools of Rhode Island, to date the sole beneficiaries of the Rhode Island Salary Supplement Act.

The church schools involved in the program are located close to parish churches. This understandably permits convenient access for religious exercises since instruction in faith and morals is part of the total educational process. The school buildings contain identifying religious symbols such as crosses on the exterior and crucifixes, and religious paintings and statutes either in the classrooms or hallways. Although only approximately 30 minutes a day are devoted to direct religious instruction, there are religiously oriented extracurricular activities. Approximately two-thirds of the teachers in these schools are nuns of various religious orders. Their dedicated efforts provide an atmosphere in which religious instruction and religious vocations are natural and proper parts of life in such schools. Indeed, as the District Court found, the role of teaching nuns in enhancing the religious atmosphere has led the parochial school authorities to attempt to maintain a one-to-one ratio between nuns and lay teachers in all schools rather than to permit some to be staffed almost entirely by lay teachers.

On the basis of these findings the District Court concluded that the parochial schools constituted "an integral part of the religious mission of the Catholic Church." The various characteristics of the schools make them "a powerful vehicle for transmitting the Catholic faith to the next generation." This process of inculcating religious doctrine is, of course, enhanced by the impressionable age of the pupils, in primary schools particularly. In short, parochial schools involve substantial religious activity and purpose.

The substantial religious character of these church-related schools gives rise to entangling church-state relationships of the kind the Religion Clauses sought to avoid. Although the District Court found that concern for religious values did not inevitably or necessarily intrude into the content of secular subjects, the considerable religious activities of these schools led the legislature to provide for careful governmental controls and surveillance by state authorities in order to ensure that state aid supports only secular education.

The dangers and corresponding entanglements are enhanced by the particular form of aid that the Rhode Island Act provides. Our decisions from *Everson* to *Allen* have permitted the States to provide church-related schools with secular, neutral, or nonideological services, facilities, or materials [such as b]us transportation, school lunches, public health services, and secular textbooks. . . .

In *Allen* the Court refused to make assumptions, on a meager record, about the religious content of the textbooks that the State would be asked to provide.

We cannot, however, refuse here to recognize that teachers have a substantially different ideological character from books. In terms of potential for involving some aspect of faith or morals in secular subjects, a textbook's content is ascertainable, but a teacher's handling of a subject is not. We cannot ignore the danger that a teacher under religious control and discipline poses to the separation of the religious from the purely secular aspects of precollege education. The conflict of functions inheres in the situation.

In our view the record shows these dangers are present to a substantial degree. The Rhode Island Roman Catholic elementary schools are under the general supervision of the Bishop of Providence and his appointed representative, the Diocesan Superintendent of Schools. In most cases, each individual parish, however, assumes the ultimate financial responsibility for the school, with the parish priest authorizing the allocation of parish funds. With only two exceptions, school principals are nuns appointed either by the Superintendent or the Mother Provincial of the order whose members staff the school. By 1969 lay teachers constituted more than a third of all teachers in the parochial elementary schools, and their number is growing. They are first interviewed by the superintendent's office and then by the school principal. The contracts are signed by the parish priest, and he retains some discretion in negotiating salary levels. Religious authority necessarily pervades the school system.

The schools are governed by the standards set forth in a "Handbook of School Regulations," which has the force of synodal law in the diocese. It emphasizes the role and importance of the teacher in parochial schools: "The prime factor for the success or the failure of the school is the spirit and personality, as well as the professional competency, of the teacher. . . ." The Handbook also states that: "Religious formation is not confined to formal courses; nor is it restricted to a single subject area." Finally, the Handbook advises teachers to stimulate interest in religious vocations and missionary work. Given the mission of the church school, these instructions are consistent and logical.

Several teachers testified, however, that they did not inject religion into their secular classes. And the District Court found that religious values did not necessarily affect the content of the secular instruction. But what has been recounted suggests the potential if not actual hazards of this form of state aid. The teacher is employed by a religious organization, subject to the direction and discipline of religious authorities, and works in a system dedicated to rearing children in a particular faith. These controls are not lessened by the fact that most of the lay teachers are of the Catholic faith. Inevitably some of a teacher's responsibilities hover on the border between secular and religious orientation.

We need not and do not assume that teachers in parochial schools will be guilty of bad faith or any conscious design to evade the limitations imposed by the statute and the First Amendment. We simply recognize that a dedicated religious person, teaching in a school affiliated with his or her faith and operated to inculcate its tenets, will inevitably experience great difficulty in remaining religiously neutral. Doctrines and faith are not inculcated or advanced by neutrals. With the best of intentions such a teacher would find it hard to make a total separation between secular teaching and religious doctrine. What would appear to some to be essential to good citizenship might well for others border on or constitute instruction in religion. Further difficulties are inherent in the combination of religious discipline and the possibility of disagreement between teacher and religious authorities over the meaning of the statutory restrictions.

We do not assume, however, that parochial school teachers will be unsuccessful in their attempts to segregate their religious beliefs from their secular educational responsibilities. But the potential for impermissible fostering of religion is present. The Rhode Island Legislature has not, and could not, provide state aid on the basis of a mere assumption that secular teachers under religious discipline can avoid conflicts. The State must be certain, given the Religion Clauses, that subsidized teachers do not inculcate religion—indeed the State here has undertaken to do so. To ensure that no trespass occurs, the State has therefore carefully conditioned its aid with pervasive restrictions. An eligible recipient must teach only those courses that are offered in the public schools and use only those texts and materials that are found in the public schools. In addition the teacher must not engage in teaching any course in religion.

A comprehensive, discriminating, and continuing state surveillance will inevitably be required to ensure that these restrictions are obeyed and the First Amendment otherwise respected. Unlike a book, a teacher cannot be inspected once so as to determine the extent and intent of his or her personal beliefs and subjective acceptance of the limitations imposed by the First Amendment. These prophylactic contacts will involve excessive and enduring entanglement between state and church. . . .

[The Court's analysis of the Pennsylvania program is similar.]

V

. . . Finally, nothing we have said can be construed to disparage the role of church-related elementary and secondary schools in our national life. Their contribution has been and is enormous. Nor do we ignore their economic plight in a period of rising costs and expanding need. Taxpayers generally have been spared vast sums by the maintenance of these educational institutions by religious organizations, largely by the gifts of faithful adherents.

The merit and benefits of these schools, however, are not the issue before us in these cases. The sole question is whether state aid to these schools can be squared with the dictates of the Religion Clauses. Under our system the choice has been made that government is to be entirely excluded from the area of religious instruction and churches excluded from the affairs of government. The Constitution decrees that religion must be a private matter for the individual, the family, and the institutions of private choice, and that while some involvement and entanglement are inevitable, lines must be drawn.

Mr. Justice WHITE, dissenting:

No one in these cases questions the constitutional right of parents to satisfy their state-imposed obligation to educate their children by sending them to private schools, sectarian or otherwise, as long as those schools meet minimum standards established for secular instruction. The States are not only permitted, but required by the Constitution, to free students attending private schools from any public school attendance obligation. Pierce v. Society of Sisters. The States may also furnish transportation for students, *Everson*, and books for teaching secular subjects to students attending parochial and other private as well as public schools, *Allen.* . . .

Our prior cases have recognized the dual role of parochial schools in American society: they perform both religious and secular functions. Our cases also recognize that legislation having a secular purpose and extending governmental assistance to sectarian schools in the performance of their secular functions does not constitute "law[s] respecting an establishment of religion" forbidden by the First Amendment merely because a secular program may incidentally benefit a church in fulfilling its religious mission. That religion may indirectly benefit from governmental aid to the secular activities of churches does not convert that aid into an impermissible establishment of religion. . . .

It is enough for me that the States and the Federal Government are financing a separable secular function of overriding importance in order to sustain the legislation here challenged. That religion and private interests other than education may substantially benefit does not convert these laws into impermissible establishments of religion.

It is unnecessary, therefore, to urge that the Free Exercise Clause of the First Amendment at least permits government in some respects to modify and mold its secular programs out of express concern for free-exercise values. The Establishment Clause, however, coexists in the First Amendment with the Free Exercise Clause and the latter is surely relevant in cases such as these. Where a state program seeks to ensure the proper education of its young, in private as well as public schools, free exercise considerations at least counsel against refusing support for students attending parochial schools simply because in that setting they are also being instructed in the tenets of the faith they are constitutionally free to practice.

NOTES AND QUESTIONS

1. The Catch-22 in *Lemon*: Effect and Entanglement. Be sure you understand the logic of the *Lemon* opinion. It sets up what the Court has elsewhere called a " 'Catch-22' argument: The very supervision of the aid to assure that it does not further religion [under the effect prong] renders the statute invalid [under the entanglement prong]." Bowen v. Kendrick, 487 U.S. 589, 615 (1988). For aid to be valid, the state must be "certain" that it is not subsidizing religious instruction; but to be "certain" would require "intrusive" surveillance and supervision of private school classrooms, which is independently unconstitutional. Thus, if governments enforce "secular use" restrictions, they violate the "entanglement" prong, and if they don't, they violate the "effects" prong. Catch-22.

2. Criticisms of *Lemon*. *Lemon*'s underlying premise has been criticized on two major grounds. Some object to the Court's assumption that teachers in nonpublic schools cannot be relied on to obey the strictures against religious indoctrination without constant monitoring and surveillance. Especially in subject areas such as mathematics, physics, or remedial English, these critics maintain that there is little risk that government funds would be used for religious purposes, and no need for entangling methods of enforcement.

Others have a more fundamental objection: that there is no justification for requiring state-funded teachers to refrain from religious instruction, so long as funds are allocated on a neutral basis neither favoring nor disfavoring religion. According to these critics, the sole governmental interest is in ensuring that education provided at government expense is of high quality, and the government should be neutral (i.e., indifferent) about religious or philosophical content. Indeed, they contend that it violates the First Amendment for the government to give money to private institutions on the condition that they forgo their constitutional right to engage in religious instruction.

3. Anti-Catholic Stereotypes?   In his concurring opinion (not reproduced above), Justice Douglas commented that "[w]e deal not with evil teachers but with zealous ones who may use any opportunity to indoctrinate a class." He included a footnote from Loraine Boettner's book, Roman Catholicism 360 (1962):

> In the parochial schools Roman Catholic indoctrination is included in every subject. History, literature, geography, civics, and science are given a Roman Catholic slant. The whole education of the child is filled with propaganda. That, of course, is the very purpose of such schools, the very reason for going to all of the work and expense of maintaining a dual school system. Their purpose is not so much to educate, but to indoctrinate and train, not to teach Scripture truths and Americanism, but to make loyal Roman Catholics. The children are regimented, and are told what to wear, what to do, and what to think.

Is this just a throwback to the anti-Catholic stereotypes of the nineteenth century, discussed in section B above? To what extent were the Court's school aid decisions driven by a notion that Catholic schools are engaged in "indoctrination" rather than "education"? See McGreevy, Thinking on One's Own (p. 371). Ira C. Lupu, The Increasingly Anachronistic Case Against School Vouchers, 13 Notre Dame J.L. Ethics & Pub. Pol'y 375, 385 (1999), describes *Lemon* and other opinions as "open and conspicuous tracts about the pervasive religious indoctrination thought to accompany the system of Catholic education."

On the other hand, there have been many studies of the educational quality of Catholic primary and secondary schools. See Anthony S. Bryk et al., Catholic Schools and the Common Good (1993); James S. Coleman et al., High School Achievement: Public, Catholic, and Private Schools Compared (1983); James S. Coleman et al., Public and Private High Schools: The Impact of Communities (1987); Andrew M. Greeley & Peter H. Rossi, The Education of Catholic Americans (1966). These studies show that Catholic schools, in comparison with public schools, tend on average to produce higher cognitive achievement, are less racially segregated, produce results less reflective of differences across family backgrounds, and are particularly effective in educating children from poor and minority backgrounds. See Bryk, Catholic Schools and the Common Good at 57-58 (summary). There is also some literature criticizing these studies, primarily based on the argument that Catholic schools benefit from their ability to be more selective than public schools. See *id.* at 58-59.

Should such evidence (or contradictory evidence) be relevant to the First Amendment issue? For an account of the societal attitudes toward Catholic schools from the 1940s through the present, see Berg, 33 Loy. U. Chi. L.J. 121 (p. 370).

4. Entanglement: Government Surveillance.   Because the schools in *Lemon* were willing to enforce restrictions on religious uses of aid, the Court's decision ultimately rested on the "entanglement" that such surveillance would cause. Consider the following arguments about this rationale:

(a) Entanglement is an inappropriate ground for striking down aid. After all, whose rights are infringed when the state engages in close surveillance of a religious school? Presumably only the rights of the school, its faculty, and its students—can you think of anyone else? But if the school is willing to accept aid with restrictions, why should someone else—a taxpayer, usually—be able to sue to block the aid? See Douglas Laycock, The Right to Church Autonomy as Part of the Free Exercise of Religion, in 2 Government Intervention in Religious Affairs 28, 38 (Dean Kelley ed., 1986) ("An atheist plaintiff asserting a church's right to be left alone even at the cost of losing government aid is the best possible illustration of why there are rules on standing."). Doesn't *Lemon* reflect a paternalistic second-guessing of the school about its best interests?

(b) On the other hand, the Establishment Clause itself may reflect such a paternalistic judgment. It seeks, at least in part, to protect the established church from being "corrupted" by the state. Remember Madison's argument in the Memorial and Remonstrance (p. 49) that establishments, "instead of maintaining the purity and efficacy of religion, have had a contrary operation," creating "pride and indolence in the clergy, [and] ignorance and servility in the laity." Memorial and Remonstrance ¶7. Since the state-supported religion itself will often fail to take such a long-range view, perhaps others (taxpayers and the courts) should be permitted to argue it. In this respect, consider Justice Brennan's concurrence in *Lemon*:

> The Rhode Island statute requires Roman Catholic teachers to surrender their right to teach religion courses and to promise not to "inject" religious teaching into their secular courses. This has led at least one teacher to stop praying with his classes, a concrete testimonial to the self-censorship that inevitably accompanies state regulation of delicate First Amendment freedoms. [This case] surely raises more than an imagined specter of governmental "secularization of a creed."

403 U.S. at 650. As a result, some advocates of religious education believe that *Lemon* was a blessing in disguise. If anyone set out to devise a public policy that would have the effect of destroying religiously distinctive education, they say, he should enact laws similar to those at issue in *Allen* and *Lemon*. In *Allen*, religious schools are given free textbooks so long as they adopt the same textbooks that are approved for use in the public schools, which means strictly secular textbooks. In *Lemon*, a portion of the salary costs of teachers in religious schools is paid by the state if the teachers promise not to allow any religious content to slip into their teaching. Both programs give financial rewards for secularization. Would financially pressed schools have been able to resist this? Do all forms of aid to religious schools have this consequence? Does the denial of aid also have secularizing effects?

5. The *Lemon* Test in General.   The three-part *Lemon* test has been extended well beyond its original school aid context, and has been treated as a general test for Establishment Clause violations. (See p. 11.) It has been much criticized in the Supreme Court, but it has not been overruled. Often the Supreme

Court ignores it, but the lower courts cannot do so. Recall the three prongs of the *Lemon* test: Government action must have a secular purpose, must not have a "primary" effect of advancing or inhibiting religion, and must not create "excessive" church-state entanglement. Do you know what each of these prongs forbids?

6. The Continuing Controversy over Aid. *Lemon* did not settle the question of aid to nonpublic education: Throughout the early 1970s, state legislatures, especially in the Northeast, experimented with aid programs. This happened for two reasons. First, with the decline of anti-Catholicism, the political resistance to these schemes diminished. Second, aid to nonpublic education was seen as a practical response to the surge in school-age populations, which sorely taxed the resources and facilities of the public schools. Meanwhile, costs for Catholic schools were rapidly increasing at this time (partly because of the decline in the number of members of religious orders available to teach and the attendant need to hire lay teachers), and many Catholic schools, especially in the large cities, were forced to close. Many legislatures realized that it would be cheaper to provide modest subsidies to nonpublic schools than to bear the burden of large numbers of former nonpublic students entering the public system at a time when it was already overburdened. Following the lead of *Everson* and *Allen*, legislatures attempted to find other ways to assist the secular functions of nonpublic schools.

COMMITTEE FOR PUBLIC EDUCATION v. NYQUIST, 413 U.S. 756 (1973): In 1972, New York state enacted three programs designed to assist nonpublic elementary and secondary education. The first provided direct money grants to nonpublic schools for the "maintenance and repair of . . . facilities and equipment to ensure [pupils'] health, welfare and safety." The grants, made to schools with large numbers of low-income students, were on a per-pupil basis but could not exceed either the school's maintenance/repair costs for the previous year or 50 percent of the average per-student cost for public schools.

The second and third programs were for families using nonpublic schools. Families with incomes below $5,000 were eligible for a tuition grant of $50 for each grade school child and $100 for each high school child, but not to exceed half of the child's tuition. There were no restrictions on the use of the grants. Families with incomes above that, but less than $25,000, were eligible for a tuition tax credit for each child, which diminished as the taxable income increased.

The Court's opinion described a "profile" of the "sectarian, nonpublic schools" that could qualify under the law: schools that

(a) impose religious restrictions on admissions; (b) require attendance of pupils at religious activities; (c) require obedience by students to the doctrines and dogmas of a particular faith; (d) require pupils to attend instruction in the theology or doctrine of a particular faith; (e) are an integral part of the religious mission of the church sponsoring [them]; (f) have as a substantial purpose the inculcation of religious values; (g) impose religious restrictions on faculty appointments; and (h) impose religious restrictions on what or how the faculty may teach.

The Court invalidated all three programs under the "effects" part of the *Lemon* test. With respect to the maintenance and repair grants, a unanimous Court objected that "[n]o attempt is made to restrict payments to those expenditures related to the upkeep of facilities used exclusively for secular purposes. . . . Nothing in the statute . . . bars a qualifying school from paying out of state funds the salaries of employees who maintain the school chapel, or the cost of renovating classrooms in which religion is taught . . . , or the cost of heating and lighting those same facilities. Absent [such] restrictions . . . , this section has a primary effect that advances religion in that it subsidizes directly the religious activities of sectarian elementary and secondary schools." *Everson* (bus transportation) and *Allen* (secular textbooks) were distinguished on the ground that they involved secular functions.

The Court also rejected the argument that the statute aided only secular functions because it provided only 50 percent of the amount expended for comparable maintenance in public schools. Pointing to *Lemon*, where the Rhode Island salary supplement was struck down although it provided only 15 percent of a teacher's annual salary, the Court said that "a mere statistical judgment will not suffice as a guarantee that state funds will not be used to finance religious education. . . . [The state was not permitted to assume that a teacher] would surely devote at least 15% of his efforts to purely secular education, thus exhausting the state grant. It takes little imagination to perceive the extent to which States might openly subsidize parochial schools under such a loose standard of scrutiny."

By a 6-3 vote, the Court also invalidated the tuition grants and tax credits. The majority reasoned that the tuition grants could not be given directly to sectarian schools without "an effective means of guaranteeing that the state aid . . . will be used exclusively for secular, neutral, and nonideological purposes." It found that the fact that the grants went to parents was "only one among many factors to be considered," and again it distinguished the bus payments and textbook loans to families in *Everson* and *Allen* on the ground that those were secular in nature. In a footnote (number 39), the Court rejected the argument that the aid to secular education outweighed the aid to religious instruction and was therefore the "primary" effect of the program under *Lemon*: "We do not think that such metaphysical judgments are either possible or necessary. Our cases simply do not support the notion that a law found to have a 'primary' effect to promote some legitimate end under the State's police power is immune from further examination to ascertain whether it also has the direct and immediate effect of advancing religion."

In another footnote (number 38), the Court also said it was "important" that the tuition grants went only to private-school families, while in *Everson* and *Allen* the "beneficiaries included all schoolchildren, those in public as well as those in private schools." The Court rejected the argument that the tuition grants sought to ensure "comparable benefits to all parents of schoolchildren":

> The grants to parents of private schoolchildren are given in addition to the right that they have to send their children to public schools "totally at state expense." And in any event, the argument proves too much, for it would also provide a basis for approving through tuition grants the complete subsidization of all religious schools on the ground that such action is necessary if the State is fully to equalize

the position of parents who elect such schools—a result wholly at variance with the Establishment Clause. [W]e need not decide whether the significantly religious character of the statute's beneficiaries might differentiate the present cases from a case involving some form of public assistance (e.g., scholarships) made available generally without regard to the sectarian-nonsectarian, or public-nonpublic nature of the institution benefited. Thus, our decision today does not compel [the invalidation of] the educational assistance provisions of the "G. I. Bill" [which provided scholarships to veterans for use at public or private colleges including religious ones].

The state defended the tuition grants on the ground that, because they were *reimbursements,* parents need not pay the money to the religious school. The Court found this irrelevant: "[I]f the grants are offered as an incentive to parents to send their children to sectarian schools by making unrestricted cash payments to them, the Establishment Clause is violated whether or not the actual dollars given eventually find their way into the sectarian institutions. . . . [The] substantive impact is still the same." The argument that the grants funded only secular services because they were limited to 50 percent of tuition was also rejected, for the same reasons as the maintenance-repair grants were. Finally, the Court rejected the argument that the tuition grants were "designed to promote the free exercise of religion [of] 'low-income parents'" who "without state assistance [would have difficulty exercising] their right to have their children educated in a religious environment." The Court said.

> [T]ension inevitably exists between the Free Exercise and the Establishment Clauses, and . . . it may often not be possible to promote the former without offending the latter. As a result of this tension, our cases require the State to maintain an attitude of "neutrality," neither "advancing" nor "inhibiting" religion. In its attempt to enhance the opportunities of the poor to choose between public and nonpublic education, the State has taken a step which can only be regarded as one "advancing" religion. However great our sympathy for the burdens experienced by those who must pay public school taxes at the same time that they support other schools because of the constraints of "conscience and discipline," [this may not] justify an eroding of the limitations of the Establishment Clause.

The Court also invalidated the tuition tax credit as indistinguishable from the tuition grant: "[I]n both instances the money involved represents a charge made upon the state for the purpose of religious education." In Walz v. Tax Commission, 397 U.S. 664 (1970), the Court had upheld New York's system of exempting religious organizations from property taxes. *Nyquist* distinguished the school tax credits from the *Walz* exemption on several grounds. First, "[t]ax exemptions for church property [unlike aid for religious schools] enjoyed an apparently universal approval in this country both before and after the adoption of the First Amendment. . . . [By contrast,] tax benefits for parents whose children attend parochial schools are a recent innovation, occasioned by the growing financial plight of such nonpublic institutions." Second, tax exemptions "constitute[d] a reasonable and balanced attempt to guard against [the] dangers" of government oppressing religion by taxation; while "[s]pecial tax benefits . . . render assistance to parents who send their children to sectarian schools, [and thus] aid and advance those religious institutions." They also "tend to increase rather than limit [church-state] involvement." Finally, the Court noted that "[t]he exemption challenged in *Walz* . . . covered all property devoted to religious, educational, or charitable purposes," while the tuition tax credits "flow primarily to the parents of children attending sectarian, nonpublic schools. . . . [I]n terms of the potential divisiveness of any legislative measure the narrowness of the benefitted class [is] an important factor."

NOTES AND QUESTIONS

1. *Nyquist*'s Arguments. *Nyquist* mounts an array of arguments against the New York program. Are the arguments sound?

(a) Channeling aid to secular uses. The Court says that public buses and secular textbooks are inherently neutral and nonideological in nature. Why isn't the same thing true of light, heating, and building maintenance? To be sure, the facilities for which maintenance grants were provided could be used for classes in which religious teaching took place. But by the same token, in *Everson* there was no attempt to ensure that the students receiving transportation attended only secular classes, and in *Allen* there was no attempt to require that the textbooks be used only for secular instruction. Each of the cases involves a necessary input to education. Is there really a difference between *Everson/Allen* and *Nyquist?*

(b) Partial aid as a "statistical guarantee" of secular effect. Why is the Court unwilling to accept a "statistical guarantee" that aid covering only part of educational costs will support the secular component of the education? Suppose the state offered to pay for half of the maintenance and repair costs for academic buildings (excluding chapels and other places reserved for worship), on the theory that at least half of what goes on in parochial schools is education of secular value. Would that be constitutional? In *Lemon*, the state paid for only 15 percent of the salaries of teachers of secular subjects, but the aid was still invalidated. Is the Court there going beyond forbidding the funding of religion, and in fact penalizing religious schools by denying them support even for the secular value they provide? See Michael W. McConnell, The Selective Funding Problem: Abortions and Religious Schools, 104 Harv. L. Rev. 989, 1046-1047 (1991). Is the Court saying that the secular value of parochial schools is nonexistent or minimal?

How can the state calculate what the secular value of parochial schools is? Consider, for example Jesse H. Choper, The Establishment Clause and Aid to Parochial Schools, 56 Cal. L. Rev. 260, 288, 342 (1968):

> Government aid to parochial schools is constitutional to the extent that it does not exceed the value of [secular] services [provided by the schools]. . . .
>   Payment to a parochial school of the same amount that such education costs in the public schools should be immune from establishment clause challenge.

Suppose, as is often the case, that a parochial school's per-student costs are less than that of the public school's—say, $5,000 per student versus $7,000 for the public school. If the parochial school receives only that lesser amount, should a taxpayer be barred from complaining, even if the aid pays the cost of providing religious as well as secular education? Isn't the taxpayer getting full secular value (as measured by public-school costs)? Under Dean Choper's test, could the state actually pay the parochial school $7,000 per student—the full public-school cost—even if this exceeded the parochial school's own costs?

(c) **Special incentive, or just equalizing with public schools?** *Nyquist* objects that the tuition grants "are offered as an incentive to parents to send their children to sectarian schools." By the same reasoning, could the provision of free public education be described as "an incentive to parents to send their children to secular schools"? Prior to the 1840s, parents generally had to pay for the cost of their children's education, and the choice between secular and sectarian education was essentially uninfluenced by government. *Nyquist* says that the state should remain neutral toward religion, and the *Lemon* test says that the state should neither advance nor inhibit religion. If so, is it legitimate for the state to give children a free education if they are willing to attend a secular school, but require them to pay the cost (on top of taxes for the support of public education) if they wish to attend a religious school?

The dissenters in *Nyquist* argue that the grants and tax credits to parents simply equalized benefits, in light of the provision of a free public (secular) education. The majority disagrees, explaining that the grants were "in addition to the right that [parents] have to send their children to public schools 'totally at state expense.'" Which side is correct on this? What are the underlying assumptions of each side?

(d) **Problem: Aid to college students.** Government grants and loans to college students, such as G.I. Bill benefits and Pell grants, are typically available for students attending religious colleges—even "pervasively religious" colleges—as well as public and other secular universities. These programs were common in 1973. But after *Nyquist*, would it be unconstitutional to use a Pell grant at a religious college?

If *Nyquist* means that even "indirect" aid (aid to students and families rather than to the school) must be confined to strictly secular uses, then using a grant at a religious college would be impermissible. But that is not how *Nyquist* has usually been read. Footnote 38 suggests that these forms of aid may be constitutional because all university-level students pay tuition—thus it is "neutral" for the government to provide scholarships to all students. By contrast, since primary and secondary education in public schools is free, tuition vouchers or tax credits benefit only students attending nonpublic schools. In other words, this is another distinction that rests, at least partly, on whether the aid can be used only at private schools, or at public as well as private schools. But does the tuition grant for private schools merely equalize things, since the state already provides free tuition in public schools? If higher-education aid cannot be distinguished on this basis, can it be distinguished because of the age and impressionability of students?

2. Tax Exemptions and Tax Credits. *Nyquist*'s invalidation of the tuition tax credits may be particularly open to objection in the light of Walz v. Tax Commission (see p. 383), which upheld the inclusion of churches in property tax exemptions. *Walz* sounded two themes in upholding the exemptions. One was a difference between tax exemptions and affirmative government aid: "The grant of a tax exemption is not sponsorship since the government does not transfer part of its revenue to churches but simply abstains from demanding that the church support the state." 397 U.S. at 675. The other was the fact that churches were exempted as part of "a broad class of property owned by non-profit, quasi-public corporations which include hospitals, libraries, playgrounds, scientific, professional, historical and patriotic groups." *Id.* at 673.

Is the first assertion—that tax relief is not a subsidy—true? Don't tax exemptions and subsidies have the same economic effect? Consider the following answer:

> The reflexive invocation of the "subsidy" label [for a tax exemption] assumes away the key issue, i.e., whether tax exemption is a constitutionally proper acknowledgment of the sovereignty of sectarian institutions. If so, the resulting tax benefits are not subsidies because they implement, rather than deviate from, a normative tax base. . . .
>
> The first [reason for treating an exemption as the proper baseline rather than as a "subsidy"] is historical: . . . the founding generation proclaimed the separation of church and state while simultaneously confirming and extending tax exemption for churches. [The Founders] thought of exemption as a form of separationism. . . .
>
> The second reason [for treating an exemption as the baseline] is the illusory nature of the promise that conflict will be avoided by taxing churches. [T]axing sectarian actors and activity is as litigation-engendering as granting them exemption.

Edward A. Zelinsky, Are Tax "Benefits" for Religious Institutions Constitutionally Dependent on Benefits for Secular Entities?, 42 B.C. L. Rev. 805, 837, 839-840 (2001). Assume that tax exemption for churches is not a subsidy, and that this is the key to *Walz.* How then can the *Nyquist* Court treat the tax credit for parents as an establishment? Does Professor Zelinsky's argument apply to *individual* tax credits or deductions as well as to *institutional* tax exemptions?

If the second theme above—equal treatment with other organizations—is the key to Establishment Clause validity, is *Nyquist* any more defensible? The tax credit there applied to all private schools, secular as well as religious. Are you convinced by the arguments the Court made to distinguish *Walz*?

3. The Free Exercise Dimension of Aid. The *Nyquist* majority distinguished *Walz*, in part, on the ground that taxation of churches could be a form of hostility toward religion, in violation of free exercise values. Does the denial of assistance to private education, solely on the ground that it has a religious content, exhibit hostility toward religion (or at least toward the religions that tend to operate primary and secondary schools)? Are you satisfied with the Court's treatment of the free exercise dimension of the issue?

On the other hand, is the provision of affirmative aid required by free exercise values? Federal, state, and local governments provide a system of public parks, at taxpayers' expense, in accordance with the tastes and wishes of the public. Does fairness require that Americans who do not like the public parks should be given a share of the parks' budget to purchase access to private parks more to their liking? Suppose your answer is "no." Why is the issue in *Nyquist* any different?

4. Whom Is the "No Aid" Principle Meant to Protect? Perhaps these cases should be analyzed according to whose rights are being protected. There are three plausible candidates: (1) taxpayers are protected from having their tax dollars used for the propagation of religious doctrine; (2) schoolchildren are protected from religious indoctrination by the government; and (3) religious schools are protected from interference with their autonomy and religious mission.

(a) Taxpayers. If the purpose of the doctrine is taxpayer protection, the distinctions drawn among the cases are highly formalistic. To be sure, it may be possible to guarantee that taxpayers' dollars are not spent for items that are themselves religious in nature, such as religious symbols, chapels, or teaching. But any aid to the secular aspects of education will inevitably aid the entire enterprise. As a matter of economic reality, it doesn't much matter whether the state pays for chalk or for chasubles; both are items in a single budget. The effect on the institution is the same. On the other hand, to the extent that aid to nonpublic schools achieves the public purpose of education more cheaply—or at least at no greater cost—than paying for those children to attend public schools, then perhaps taxpayers have no legitimate objection to any of the programs. If it is legitimate for taxpayers to be compelled to pay for education (which no one doubts), and if religious schools educate children at least as well at no greater cost (as they do), then how can it be said that taxpayers are being taxed for the support of religion?

(b) Children. Perhaps the purpose of the doctrine is to protect children from government-funded religious indoctrination. If the government itself engaged in religious teaching, or if it offered additional benefits to those who attend religious instruction, this concern would be paramount. But it is not obvious that any of the programs yet considered would implicate that concern. As long as the government provides transportation to *all* schools, textbooks for *all* schools, salaries to teachers at *all* schools, and facility maintenance at *all* schools, on an equal basis, the child's decision to attend one school rather than another cannot be attributed to the government. In other contexts, the receipt of government financial aid is not deemed sufficient to render the actions of a private recipient attributable to the government. See Rendell-Baker v. Kohn, 457 U.S. 830 (1982); Blum v. Yaretsky, 457 U.S. 991 (1982). Realistically, it is hard to see how the doctrine can be said to protect students at religious schools. They (or their parents) chose to attend religious schools, and government aid does not make the school any more religious.

(c) Religious schools. If the purpose of the doctrine is to protect religious schools against interference with their autonomy, the cases seem to have been randomly decided. The concern (as voiced by Justice Brennan in the quotation at p. 380) is that religious schools will be induced to secularize aspects of their operations to receive government money. If that is the concern, the Court was correct to strike down the program in *Lemon*, which would have required teachers to agree not to include religious perspectives in their teaching, and correct to uphold the program in *Everson*, since there was no danger that the public buses at issue there could be secularized. But there was no justification for striking the maintenance and repair grants in *Nyquist;* heat, light, and facility maintenance have no more ideological content than buses. And the Court should have struck down the textbook program in *Allen*, since the offer to pay for only secular textbooks was a clear inducement for the schools to secularize their curriculum.

2. Lemon *Applied: Different Forms of Aid, Different Institutions*

The Court of the 1970s used the *Lemon* approach to decide the constitutionality not only of various legislative programs assisting nonpublic schools but also of programs assisting other nonpublic institutions. It followed *Lemon* and *Nyquist* in rejecting most forms of aid for religious elementary and secondary schools, with a few exceptions. But it was more willing to countenance aid to other institutions, such as colleges and universities and social service organizations. Some of the distinctions the Court made provoked sharp criticism from both supporters and opponents of aid. For a review, see John Garvey, Another Way of Looking at School Aid, 1985 Sup. Ct. Rev. 61.

a. *Forms of Aid to Nonpublic Schools*

1. Fine Distinctions.

(a) Instructional materials (versus books?).   In Meek v. Pittenger, 421 U.S. 349 (1975), the Court held it unconstitutional for states to provide instructional materials such as periodicals, photographs, maps, charts, sound recordings, and films to religious schools. The Court reasoned:

> [A]s part of general legislation made available to all students, a State may include church-related schools in programs providing bus transportation, school lunches, and public health facilities—secular and nonideological services unrelated to the primary, religion-oriented educational function of the sectarian school. The indirect and incidental benefits to church-related schools from those programs do not offend the constitutional prohibition against establishment. But the massive aid provided the church-related nonpublic schools of Pennsylvania by Act 195 is neither indirect or incidental.
>
> For the 1972-1973 school year the Commonwealth authorized just under $12 million of direct aid to the predominantly church-related nonpublic schools of Pennsylvania through the loan of instructional material and equipment. . . . To be sure, the material and equipment that are the subjects of the loan—maps, charts, and laboratory equipment, for example—are "self-polic[ing], in that starting as secular, nonideological and neutral, they will not change in use." But faced with the substantial amounts of direct support authorized by Act 195, it would simply ignore reality to attempt to separate secular educational functions from the predominantly religious role performed by many of [the] schools. . . . Even though earmarked for secular purposes, "when it flows to an institution in which religion is so pervasive that a substantial portion of its functions are subsumed in the religious mission," state aid has the impermissible primary effect of advancing religion.

At the same time, however, *Meek* reaffirmed the holding of *Allen* that the state could lend (secular) textbooks to religious-school students. Is there any principled difference between lending textbooks and lending other instructional materials? The textbooks were lent to the students, while the instructional materials were lent to the schools. But is that a real difference? Justice Brennan commented in *Meek* that it was "pure fantasy to treat the textbook program as a loan to students," since the books were provided at the request of the school officials and stored on school premises when not being used by the students. In Wolman v. Walter, 433 U.S. 229 (1977), the state, attempting to comply with

Meek, authorized lending similar instructional materials and equipment (films, maps, etc.) to students, storing the materials on school premises. The Court struck this down, saying that to distinguish between loans to schools and loans to students would "exalt form over substance." *Id.* at 250. Why isn't the same true of books? The ruling that the state could provide textbooks but not maps inspired Senator Daniel Patrick Moynihan to ask: "What will they do with atlases, which are maps in books?"

(b) Auxiliary instruction and services. The *Meek* Court also held it unconstitutional for the state to provide "auxiliary services"—remedial and therapeutic services, speech and hearing services, English as a second language, and the like—through its own public school personnel on the premises of religious schools. Although the services were provided by public school personnel to individual students, the Court reasoned that any form of educational instruction within a religious school carried an unacceptable risk that religious content would be interjected into the teaching, which could be prevented only by an unacceptably entangling enforcement mechanism. But then in *Wolman*, the Court held that such services could be provided in temporary classrooms or other neutral sites away from the religious schools—thus implicitly rejecting the theory that any aid to the educational enterprise of the religious school is unconstitutional. Are public-school remedial teachers substantially more likely to impart religious doctrine in a classroom within the religious school (or, as the Court expressed it, "in the pervasively sectarian atmosphere of a religious institution") than in a mobile unit parked across the street?

Wolman also approved state provision of speech, hearing, and psychological *diagnostic* services by public personnel on the premises of the schools, distinguishing these from *therapeutic* services (struck down in *Meek*) on the ground that the contact with the students is likely to be briefer, and less likely to have religious content.

(c) Test administration costs. In Levitt v. Committee for Public Education, 413 U.S. 472 (1973), the Court invalidated a statute reimbursing religious schools for the cost of administering state-mandated tests, where the tests were prepared by teachers at the school. The Court explained that there is a "substantial risk that these examinations, prepared by teachers under the authority of religious institutions, will be drafted with an eye, unconsciously or otherwise, to inculcate students in the religious precepts of the sponsoring church." *Id.* at 481. But in *Wolman*, the Court approved state provision of services for *standardized* tests, which religious-school teachers had no hand in drafting.

(d) Bus transportation revisited: field trips. The *Wolman* Court also held it unconstitutional for the state to provide transportation for religious school students on field trips to "governmental, industrial, cultural, and scientific centers designed to enrich the secular studies of students." Transportation *to* schools for religious instruction was therefore constitutional (*Everson*), but transportation *from* school to secular sites was unconstitutional.

2. The Strictest No-Aid Decisions: Remedial Classes by Public School Teachers. The no-aid position reached its high-water mark in 1985 in two cases involving programs, one local and one federal, where public school teachers were sent into K-12 religious schools after hours to teach remedial and other classes in math, English, and other subjects. By 5-4 votes the Court struck down both programs, with Justice Brennan writing the opinions. Grand Rapids

School Dist. v. Ball, 473 U.S. 373 (1985); Aguilar v. Felton, 473 U.S. 402 (1985). The decisions illustrated again the "Catch 22" to which aid programs could be subject under *Lemon*. In *Ball*, the city of Grand Rapids's program used public school teachers without explicitly restricting religious content in the classes they taught; the Court struck down the program under the effects prong of *Lemon* on the ground that it would "advance" religion. In *Aguilar*, which involved a federal program (Title I) providing teachers to students in low-income schools, there were restrictions on religious content in the classes. The Court ruled, as it had in *Lemon*, that enforcing those restrictions would require a "comprehensive surveillance" that would create excessive church-state entanglement.

Ball identified three ways in which the classes in the religious schools might impermissibly advance religion:

> First, the teachers participating in the programs may become involved in intentionally or inadvertently inculcating particular religious tenets or beliefs. Second, the programs may provide a crucial symbolic link between government and religion, thereby enlisting—at least in the eyes of impressionable youngsters—the powers of government to the support of the religious denomination operating the school. Third, the programs may have the effect of directly promoting religion by impermissibly providing a subsidy to the primary religious mission of the institutions affected.

Are these rationales at all convincing? Consider the first. How serious is the risk that public school teachers will engage in religious teaching as a result of their presence on the premises of religious schools? Justice O'Connor, dissenting in *Aguilar*, called the risk "greatly exaggerated." 473 U.S. at 428.

Turn now to the second and third rationales. If they are valid, should any of the forms of aid to religious schools in the Court's previous cases have been upheld? Why was there no "symbolic union" between the state and religious schools from the transportation reimbursements in *Everson*? As for the "subsidy" argument, it made no difference to the *Ball* Court that the subsidized courses merely supplemented the basic curriculum with courses that had not previously been offered. But if the provision of supplemental courses is a benefit to the school whether or not the school had previously provided those courses, why isn't the same true of textbooks, school lunches, diagnostic services, and transportation? Aren't these all services that the religious schools *could* pay for? Did *Ball* and *Aguilar* augur the end of any serious attempt to determine whether the economic benefit of an aid program went to the school or to the child?

Turn now to the entanglement holding of *Aguilar*. Since the teachers whose activities had to be monitored were public school employees, who were state-regulated on a daily basis, why did monitoring them in the context of Title I present an entanglement problem?

We will return to *Ball* and *Aguilar* in section D-2 below (p. 417). They were the first decisions to be overruled when the Court moved away from the "no aid" approach.

3. Confusion. The cases applying *Lemon* to aid for K-12 schools involved close votes and fine distinctions because the Court was fractured over the issue. Three Justices voted to uphold almost all of the aid programs; three

Justices voted to strike almost all of them down; and the three Justices in the middle often could not agree. Consider the voting lineup in *Wolman*:

> BLACKMUN, J. announced the judgment of the Court and delivered the opinion of the Court with respect to Parts I, V, VI, VII, and VIII, in which STEWART and STEVENS, JJ., joined; in which as to Part I, BURGER, C.J., and BRENNAN, MARSHALL, and POWELL, JJ., also joined; in which as to Part V, BURGER, C.J., and MARSHALL and POWELL, JJ., also joined; in which as to Part VI, BURGER, C.J., and POWELL, J., also joined; in which as to Parts VII and VIII, BRENNAN and MARSHALL, JJ., also joined; and an opinion with respect to Parts II, III, and IV, in which BURGER, C.J., and STEWART and POWELL, JJ., joined. BURGER, C.J., dissented in part. BRENNAN, J., MARSHALL, J., and STEVENS, J., filed opinions concurring in part and dissenting in part. POWELL, J., filed an opinion concurring in part, concurring in the judgment in part, and dissenting in part. WHITE and REHNQUIST, JJ., filed a statement concurring in the judgment in part and dissenting in part.

Justice Stevens, representing the wing of the Court most opposed to aid, argued in *Wolman* that the Establishment Clause

> should not differentiate between direct and indirect subsidies, or between instructional materials like globes and maps on the one hand and instructional materials like textbooks on the other. . . . [A] state subsidy of sectarian schools is invalid regardless of the form it takes. The financing of buildings, field trips, instructional materials, educational tests, and schoolbooks are all equally invalid. For all give aid to the school's educational mission, which at heart is religious.

433 U.S. at 265. But even Stevens's position was not absolute: "The State can plainly provide public health services to children attending nonpublic schools. The diagnostic and therapeutic services [in the *Wolman* case] may fall into this category."

At the other end of the ideological spectrum, Justices Rehnquist and White dissented from virtually every holding striking down forms of aid. In *Meek*, 421 U.S. at 395 (quotations omitted), Rehnquist explained:

> "[I]t should be wholly acceptable for the State to contribute to the secular education of children going to sectarian schools rather than to insist that if parents want to provide their children with religious as well as secular education, the State will refuse to contribute anything to their secular training." . . . The Court apparently believes that the Establishment Clause of the First Amendment not only mandates religious neutrality on the part of government but also requires that this Court go further and throw its weight on the side of those who believe that our society as a whole should be a purely secular one. Nothing in the First Amendment or in the cases interpreting it requires such an extreme approach to this difficult question, and "[a]ny interpretation of [the Establishment Clause] and the constitutional values it serves must also take account of the free exercise clause and the values it serves."

Finally, one of the "swing" votes in *Wolman*, Justice Powell, defended the Court's results against the charges of inconsistency and incoherence (433 U.S. at 262-263):

> Our decisions in this troubling area draw lines that often must seem arbitrary. No doubt we could achieve greater analytical tidiness if we were to accept the broadest implications of the observation in *Meek*, that "[s]ubstantial aid to the

educational function of [sectarian] schools . . . necessarily results in aid to the sectarian enterprise as a whole." If we took that course, it would become impossible to sustain state aid of any kind even if the aid is wholly secular in character and is supplied to the pupils rather than the institutions. . . . This Court has not yet thought that such a harsh result is required by the Establishment Clause. Certainly few would consider it in the public interest. Parochial schools, quite apart from their sectarian purpose, have provided an educational alternative for millions of young Americans; they often afford wholesome competition with our public schools; and in some States they relieve substantially the tax burden incident to the operation of public schools. The State has, moreover, a legitimate interest in facilitating education of the highest quality for all children within its boundaries, whatever school their parents have chosen for them.

. . . Our decisions have sought to establish principles that preserve the cherished safeguard of the Establishment Clause without resort to blind absolutism. If this endeavor means a loss of some analytical tidiness, then that too is entirely tolerable.

Do you agree that the sometimes fine distinctions in these cases were justified as an effort to balance conflicting values?

b. Distinctions Among Institutions

Although one might think that the same constitutional limitations would apply to funding of *all* religious institutions, in fact there was, until recently, relatively little controversy over funding issues other than those connected with schools. Federal and state funds routinely go to religiously affiliated organizations in the fields of health, social welfare, rehabilitation, disaster relief, child care, and higher education. See Stephen V. Monsma, When Sacred and Secular Mix: Religious Nonprofit Organizations and Public Money (1996). Why?

i. Hospitals

At the other end of the spectrum from religious elementary schools, in the Supreme Court's view, are religiously affiliated hospitals. There is a long tradition of religious hospitals participating in government funding programs. Under the Hill-Burton Hospital Construction Act of 1946 (Pub. L. No. 88-443, codified at 42 U.S.C. § 291), nearly 40 percent of Jewish and Christian hospitals in the nation by 1965 had received direct government grants for constructing facilities. Timothy W. Burgess, Note, Government Aid to Religious Social Service Providers, 75 Va. L. Rev. 1077, 1084-1085 (1989). Moreover, Medicare and Medicaid fund large shares of patient costs in religious hospitals (in one survey of Catholic hospitals, 44.7 percent of inpatient days by Medicare and 9.3 percent by Medicaid). Edward S. Mally, Jr., Health Care Handbook 16-18 (1986). And Medicare has traditionally reimbursed hospitals even for the services of chaplains because of the "beneficial therapeutic effect on the medical condition of the patient."[7]

7. Baylor Univ. Med. Ctr. v. Blue Cross Ass'n, Provider Reimbursement Review Board (PRRB) Dec. No. 82-D59, Medicare & Medicaid Guide (CCH) ¶31,871 at 9314 (Feb. 25, 1982), aff'd, Medicare & Medicaid Guide (CCH) ¶31,971 (Apr. 21, 1982) (HCFA Deputy Adm'r Dec'n) (App. M). See also American Hospital Ass'n, Statement on Hospital Chaplaincy (1967) and related technical advisory bulletin (App. O).

Yet there is little suggestion that such support violates the Establishment Clause. Long ago, in Bradfield v. Roberts, 175 U.S. 291 (1899), the Court held that Congress could appropriate funds for construction of a new building at a Catholic hospital in the District of Columbia, owned and operated by an order of nuns:

> The [Catholic ties] do not change the legal character of the corporation or render it on that account a religious or sectarian body. Whether the individuals who compose the [hospital's] corporation under its charter happen to be all Roman Catholics, or all Methodists, or Presbyterians, or Unitarians, or members of any other religious organization, or of no organization at all, is of not the slightest consequence with reference to the law of its incorporation, nor can the individual beliefs upon religious matters of the various incorporators be inquired into. Nor is it material that the hospital may be conducted under the auspices of the Roman Catholic Church. . . . That fact does not alter the legal character of the corporation, which is incorporated under an act of Congress, and its powers, duties, and character are to be solely measured by the charter under which it alone has any legal existence. There is no allegation that its hospital work is confined to members of that church or that in its management the hospital has been conducted so as to violate its charter in the smallest degree. It is simply the case of a secular corporation being managed by people who hold to the doctrines of the Roman Catholic Church, but who nevertheless are managing the corporation according to the law under which it exists.

Consider some questions about *Bradfield.*

1. Does It Matter if a Hospital Is "Sectarian"?   Under what legal principle was this case decided? The Court did not apparently think it relevant to inquire whether the operations of the hospital included religious teaching or ritual. Nothing in the legislation prohibited the use of the funds for religious purposes (such as construction of a chapel as part of the hospital complex). The Court expressly stated that the religious character of the organization running the hospital "is of not the slightest consequence." One interpretation is that it relies on a purely formal distinction between grants to a religious denomination or church and grants to separately incorporated institutions (even if owned by a church). Is that an appropriate constitutional principle?

Problem: Could a separately incorporated religious medical facility ever be "religious" or "sectarian" enough in its practices to be disqualified from aid? Consider the following: Members of the Christian Science Church believe in healing through prayer and other spiritual means and reject medical care. The Church operates "sanitoria," facilities where seriously ill citizens can come to receive Christian Science spiritual treatment while receiving nonmedical nursing care such as bathing, dressing, bandaging wounds, and feeding. Patients in hospitals who have sufficiently serious conditions to qualify for federal Medicare benefits can receive benefits for such nursing care as well. The Medicare statute includes Christian Science sanitoria in the general definition of eligible "health care institutions" and thus allows reimbursement for nursing services at sanitoria. Are such reimbursements constitutional? See, e.g., Children's Healthcare Is a Legal Duty v. Min de Parle, 212 F.3d 1084 (8th Cir. 2000).

2. Schools Versus Other Institutions.

(a) History.   The distinction between funding religious primary and secondary schools and funding other religious institutions goes back well into the nineteenth century. The House version of the failed Blaine Amendment applied only to public schools, a term that did not include institutions of higher education, orphanages, prisons, or other institutions where religious instruction was common. Perhaps that is one reason it passed without significant controversy. The Senate version, however, applied to "any institution" where religious tenets might be taught. The Democratic opponents of the amendment made effective use of this point, for while only Catholics and some Lutherans maintained systems of schools, it was common practice for other religious denominations to provide higher education and social services.

Senator Kernan of New York, for example, explained that he was reluctantly willing to support the House version of the amendment because the common school system "is regarded with great interest by a large portion of our people" and "sectarian dissensions would arise" if the common school moneys were divided among the religious denominations. 4 Cong. Rec. 5580-5581. But he pointed out that the Senate version of the amendment would interfere with widely accepted practices. The amendment would, he said, prevent a veteran in a soldiers' home from obtaining "religious ministrations" in an hour of need, and inmates of juvenile reformatories from hearing Christian teaching. "Take your State hospitals and prisons," he said.

> They are institutions of the State, supported entirely by the public money, and in every one that I ever heard of in our State, in every jail, every reformatory, and every prison, the keep that would not send for the minister of the gospel of that religious persuasion which the inmate wished and allow him to teach him and read to him and have him unite with him in the religious service to which the person was attached, or instruct him in that which he wished to be instructed in, would be denounced, and there would be a cry of indignation at such a violation of the rights of conscience by people of every creed. But this amendment forbids the reading or teaching of any creed or tenet of religion in any such institution.

4 Cong. Rec. 5581-5582. Senator Eaton added that his city of Hartford, Connecticut, gave $1,000 a year to two orphan asylums, one Catholic and one Protestant, and that it would be "absurd" to prevent the practice.

Republicans preferred not to address the implications of the amendment for institutions other than schools. Senator Morton: "I do not intend, so far as I am concerned, to be diverted from this great question by what is said in regard to orphan asylums and hospitals. There is a great principle underlying this amendment." 4 Cong. Rec. 5585.

(b) Does the distinction make sense? As you will see, the distinction between the funding of primary and secondary religious education and the funding of other services provided by religious groups—including higher education—persists to this day. State funding for religious primary or secondary schools is largely limited to a few programs concerning "failing" public schools in a few cities such as Milwaukee and Cleveland, and any new programs of this sort will continue to face challenges under state constitutions. But public funds are commonly provided for child care, higher education, sex education, health care, elder care, and numerous other social services by religious organizations. This distinction has a history. But does it have a rationale?

ii. Universities

Recall that the second and third "prongs" of the *Lemon* test—effects and entanglement—work in tandem. The "effects" test requires the government to ensure that its aid will not be used for religious indoctrination. The "entanglement" test holds the aid program unconstitutional if the measures taken to enforce the "effects" test intrude on the autonomy of the religious school. Together they create what Justice White called "an insoluble paradox": The state "cannot finance secular instruction if it permits religion to be taught in the same classroom; but if it exacts a promise that religion not be so taught—a promise the school and its teachers are quite willing and on this record able to give—and enforces it, it is then entangled in the 'no entanglement' aspect." *Lemon*, 403 U.S. at 668.

But the force of this doctrinal pincers may be a matter of degree. *Lemon* and *Ball* said that the government must be "certain" that publicly funded teachers do not inculcate religion. But how certain must it be? Can the government be certain that teachers in *public* schools do not inculcate religion? (It is widely reported that in many parts of the country, teachers continue to lead classes in prayer.) How much risk can we tolerate, consistent with the First Amendment? By the same token, every interaction between government and religious schools intrudes, to some degree, on the autonomy of the schools. How much entanglement is too much?

The practical impact of these questions of degree became apparent when the Court decided Tilton v. Richardson, 403 U.S. 672 (1971), on the same day as *Lemon*. Although the Court struck down down aid to religious primary and secondary schools in *Lemon*, it upheld a federal program of aid to colleges and universities, including religious colleges and universities, in *Tilton*. The program provided grants for construction and repair of academic buildings on condition that the buildings not "be used for sectarian instruction or as a place for religious worship." Chief Justice Burger, in a plurality opinion, distinguished between aid to religious higher education and aid to religious elementary and secondary education:

> There are generally significant differences between the religious aspects of church-related institutions of higher learning and parochial elementary and secondary schools. The "affirmative if not dominant policy" of the instruction in pre-college church schools is "to assure future adherents to a particular faith by having control of their total education at an early age." There is substance to the contention that college students are less impressionable and less susceptible to religious indoctrination. . . . The skepticism of the college student is not an inconsiderable barrier to any attempt or tendency to subvert the congressional objectives and limitations. Furthermore, by their very nature, college and postgraduate courses tend to limit the opportunities for sectarian influence by virtue of their own internal disciplines. Many church-related colleges and universities are characterized by a high degree of academic freedom and seek to evoke free and critical responses from their students. . . .
>
> Since religious indoctrination is not a substantial purpose or activity of these church-related colleges and universities, there is less likelihood than in primary and secondary schools that religion will permeate the area of secular education. This reduces the risk that government aid will in fact serve to support religious

activities. Correspondingly, the necessity for intensive government surveillance is diminished and the resulting entanglements between government and religion lessened. Such inspection as may be necessary to ascertain that the facilities are devoted to secular education is minimal and indeed hardly more than the inspections that States impose over all private schools within the reach of compulsory education laws.

The Court did unanimously strike down a provision of the statute that limited the no-religious-use restriction to 20 years. *Tilton* held that the restriction had to continue indefinitely.

Justice Brennan dissented in part:

> [A] sectarian university is the equivalent in the realm of higher education of the Catholic elementary schools in Rhode Island; it is an educational institution in which the propagation and advancement of a particular religion are a primary function of the institution. [The] institution is dedicated to two goals, secular education and religious instruction. When aid flows directly to the institution, both functions benefit. . . . The "religious enterprise" aided by the construction grants involves the maintenance of an educational environment—which includes high-quality, purely secular educational courses—within which religious instruction occurs in a variety of ways.
>
> The plurality also argues that no impermissible entanglement exists here. . . . I do not see any significant difference in the Federal Government's telling the sectarian university not to teach any nonsecular subjects in a certain building, and Rhode Island's telling the Catholic school teacher not to teach religion. The vice is the creation through subsidy of a relationship in which the government polices the teaching practices of a religious school or university.

Are you persuaded by the distinction between religious high schools and religious colleges? A majority of the Court was not. Four Justices voted that aid to either high schools or colleges was unconstitutional, and one Justice voted that aid to either was permissible. Indeed, the one point that they agreed on was that the distinction drawn by the plurality was unpersuasive. Nonetheless, the distinction remained good law for years and may still be so today.

In Hunt v. McNair, 413 U.S. 734 (1973), and Roemer v. Board of Public Works, 426 U.S. 736 (1976), the Court upheld operating and construction subsidies to qualifying colleges and universities, including religiously affiliated institutions, on the ground that the religious institutions, unlike religious primary and secondary schools, were not "pervasively sectarian." Thus under *Lemon*, if a government grant recipient was "pervasively sectarian," the courts presumed that there was an unacceptable risk that aid (if not inherently neutral and non-ideological in character, such as transportation, textbooks, or school lunches) would benefit religion, and that this could not be prevented without excessive entanglement.

If the grant recipients were not "pervasively sectarian," however, the courts presumed that they would "exercise their delegated control over use of the funds in compliance with the statutory, and therefore the constitutional mandate [that the funds be used only for secular purposes]." *Roemer*, 426 U.S. at 760. In such a case, there would be no need for invasive monitoring and surveillance, and hence no excessive entanglement. The grants would be constitutional unless it could be proven that the funds were used for "specifically religious activities."

Under this approach, the outcome of the case depends almost entirely on whether the recipient institution is "pervasively sectarian." What does this phrase mean? Is this a proper inquiry? Is it neutral among religious denominations? The Supreme Court has consistently held that religious primary and secondary schools are "pervasively sectarian" (despite evidence presented in some lower courts that urban parochial school systems have religiously mixed faculty and student body and little in the way of formal religious instruction). It may be presumed that churches themselves are "pervasively sectarian." But the Court has never held that any other religiously affiliated institution falls within this category. The doctrine therefore had the effect consequence of forbidding most aid to private elementary and secondary schools, while allowing substantial government aid to religious colleges and social service activities. See Frederick M. Gedicks, The Rhetoric of Church and State: A Critical Analysis of Religion Clause Jurisprudence 85-88 (1995).

Why is it necessary to be certain that government-funded teachers in primary and secondary schools not inculcate religion (as *Ball* and *Aguilar* held (pp. 389-390)), but acceptable to presume that teachers and employees of other religious institutions will obey the strictures against religious indoctrination? And if the requirement that religious primary and secondary schools secularize themselves as a condition to receiving aid is unconstitutional (which is one interpretation of the entanglement doctrine), why is it constitutional to force other religious institutions to secularize themselves as a condition of receiving aid?

iii. Social Service Organizations

The Court has distinguished hospitals and many universities from lower-level schools for purposes of eligibility for government aid. What about the vast range of nonmedical social services—feeding programs, homeless shelters, child care, drug and alcohol rehabilitation, job retraining—that government might support? Aid to private social service agencies, many of them religious, is also extensive: More than 350 federal programs by the early 1980s provided nearly $50 billion, 7 percent of federal outlays for the year. Note, 75 Va. L. Rev. at 1080-1087. But the nature of such programs and agencies varies widely. Some, such as food pantries, provide nonideological services in a generally nonideological setting. In Bowen v. Kendrick, 487 U.S. 589 (1988), however, the Supreme Court reviewed a social service program coming much closer to the sort of moral education provided in elementary and secondary schools. In an effort to combat teenage pregnancy, Congress authorized grants to public and nonpublic organizations, including religious organizations, to conduct research, counsel teens, and provide other services. The statute was challenged as a violation of the Establishment Clause both on its face and as applied. The plaintiffs presented evidence that some grantees were "pervasively sectarian" organizations and that some grants had been used specifically to fund religious moral instruction.

The Supreme Court, applying the *Lemon* test, refused to strike down the statute on its face. It analogized the social services to universities rather than elementary schools, finding no indication "that a significant proportion of the federal funds will be disbursed to 'pervasively sectarian' institutions." Thus it "refused to presume that aid would be used in a way that would have the primary effect of advancing religion." The Court did remand the case for the taking of evidence on whether particular grants violated the Establishment Clause. It said that the plaintiffs could prove this by showing either that a grantee was "pervasively sectarian" or that a grant had been "used to fund 'specifically religious activities.'" Justice Blackmun dissented, saying that "[t]he risk of advancing religion at public expense . . . is much greater when the religious organization is directly engaged in pedagogy [as here] than where it is neutrally dispensing medication, food, or shelter."

In terms of its doctrine, Bowen v. Kendrick was no real break from the *Lemon* approach. It continued a tradition of distinguishing social services from primary and secondary schools, but simultaneously reaffirmed that "pervasively sectarian" institutions could not receive funds. But its practical effect on the teenage-pregnancy program was great: It was drastically more expensive for the plaintiffs to litigate over the facts of hundreds of individual grants to religious organizations than to bring one facial challenge wiping the statute off the books, as had been done with aid to K–12th-grade schools.

Does the combination of results in *Ball* and *Aguilar* (see pp. 389-390 above) and *Kendrick* make any sense? According to the Court, it is unconstitutional for public school specialists to assist poor children with remedial reading and math on the premises of inner city Catholic schools, with beneficiaries chosen on an objective basis, but constitutional to give grants to religiously affiliated groups on a subjective, competitive basis to encourage sexual responsibility. To what theory of religious freedom do these results conform? How can you account for these results as a matter of the Court's Establishment Clause doctrine?

Dissatisfaction with such results soon generated a very different approach toward cases involving aid to religious institutions.

D. THE NEW APPROACH: THE PERMISSIBILITY OF "NEUTRAL" AID

Beginning in the mid-1980s the Court adopted a much different—and more permissive—approach to government aid to religious institutions, based on the idea that the government must be neutral in its allocation of funds, rather than the idea that it must support only secular activities. The new approach appeared first in cases involving tax benefits, where churches and other religious institutions had long been included among the charitable nonprofit groups that receive the benefit of tax exemptions and tax deductions. As you have read, in 1970 the Court, with only one dissent, rejected the claim that property tax exemptions for houses of worship are an impermissible subsidy (Walz v. Tax Commission, p. 385). Later the Court upheld a statute giving a tax deduction for educational expenses, including tuition at religious schools (Mueller v. Allen, 463 U.S. 388 (1983)). The neutrality principle also prevailed in cases involving access by religious speakers to government property for activities involving religious speech. In 1981, over one dissent, the Court rejected a state's claim that allowing a student group to use public university facilities for prayer and Bible study would violate the separation of church and state (Widmar v. Vincent, p. 622).

In the following series of decisions, the "neutrality" principle was extended, step by step, to cover affirmative aid for study at religious institutions. The first decision, *Witters*, involved a cash grant to an individual rather than directly to a religious school. But its implications were broader: It set forth clearly the premises of the neutrality approach, which were then extended, at least in part, to programs of "direct" aid as well.

1. The Rise of Neutrality: "Private Choice" Programs of Aid

WITTERS v. WASHINGTON DEPT. OF SERVICES FOR THE BLIND
474 U.S. 481 (1986)

Justice MARSHALL delivered the opinion of the Court.

The Washington Supreme Court ruled that the First Amendment precludes the State of Washington from extending assistance under a state vocational rehabilitation assistance program to a blind person studying at a Christian college and seeking to become a pastor, missionary, or youth director. Finding no such federal constitutional barrier on the record presented to us, we reverse and remand.

Petitioner Larry Witters applied in 1979 to the Washington Commission for the Blind for vocational rehabilitation services pursuant to Wash. Rev. Code § 74.16.181. That statute authorized the Commission, inter alia, to "[p]rovide for special education and/or training in the professions, business or trades" so as to "assist visually handicapped persons to overcome vocational handicaps and to obtain the maximum degree of self-support and self-care." Petitioner, suffering from a progressive eye condition, was eligible for vocational rehabilitation assistance under the terms of the statute. He was at the time attending Inland Empire School of the Bible, a private Christian college in Spokane, Washington, and studying the Bible, ethics, speech, and church administration in order to equip himself for a career as a pastor, missionary, or youth director.

The Commission denied petitioner aid. It relied on an earlier determination embodied in a Commission policy statement that "[t]he Washington State constitution forbids the use of public funds to assist an individual in the pursuit of a career or degree in theology or related areas," and on its conclusion that petitioner's training was "religious instruction" subject to that ban. . . .

Petitioner then instituted an action in State Superior Court for review of the administrative decision; the court affirmed on the same state-law grounds cited by the agency. The State Supreme Court affirmed as well [but under the Establishment Clause].

II

. . . We are guided, as was the court below, by the three-part test set out by this Court in *Lemon*. Our analysis relating to the first prong of that test is simple: all parties concede the unmistakably secular purpose of the Washington program.

That program was designed to promote the well-being of the visually handicapped through the provision of vocational rehabilitation services, and no
more than a minuscule amount of the aid awarded under the program is likely
to flow to religious education. No party suggests that the State's "actual purpose" in creating the program was to endorse religion, or that the secular purpose articulated by the legislature is merely "sham."

The answer to the question posed by the second prong of the *Lemon* test is
more difficult. We conclude, however, that extension of aid to petitioner is not
barred on that ground either. It is well settled that the Establishment Clause is
not violated every time money previously in the possession of a State is conveyed
to a religious institution. For example, a State may issue a paycheck to one of its
employees, who may then donate all or part of that paycheck to a religious
institution, all without constitutional barrier; and the State may do so even knowing that the employee so intends to dispose of his salary. It is equally well-settled,
on the other hand, that the State may not grant aid to a religious school, whether
cash or in-kind, where the effect of the aid is "that of a direct subsidy to the
religious school" from the State. Grand Rapids v. Ball. Aid may have that effect
even though it takes the form of aid to students or parents. *Id.*; see, e.g., *Nyquist.*
The question presented is whether, on the facts as they appear in the record
before us, extension of aid to petitioner and the use of that aid by petitioner to
support his religious education is a permissible transfer similar to the hypothetical salary donation described above, or is an impermissible "direct subsidy."

Certain aspects of Washington's program are central to our inquiry. As far as
the record shows, vocational assistance provided under the Washington program is paid directly to the student, who transmits it to the educational institution of his or her choice. Any aid provided under Washington's program that
ultimately flows to religious institutions does so only as a result of the genuinely
independent and private choices of aid recipients. Washington's program is
"made available generally without regard to the sectarian-nonsectarian, or public-nonpublic nature of the institution benefitted," and is in no way skewed
towards religion. It is not one of "the ingenious plans for channeling state
aid to sectarian schools that periodically reach this Court," *Nyquist.* It creates
no financial incentive for students to undertake sectarian education. It does not
tend to provide greater or broader benefits for recipients who apply their aid to
religious education, nor are the full benefits of the program limited, in large
part or in whole, to students at sectarian institutions. On the contrary, aid recipients have full opportunity to expend vocational rehabilitation aid on wholly
secular education, and as a practical matter have rather greater prospects to do
so. Aid recipients' choices are made among a huge variety of possible careers, of
which only a small handful are sectarian. In this case, the fact that aid goes to
individuals means that the decision to support religious education is made by
the individual, not by the State.

Further, and importantly, nothing in the record indicates that, if petitioner
succeeds, any significant portion of the aid expended under the Washington program as a whole will end up flowing to religious education. The function of the
Washington program is hardly "to provide desired financial support for nonpublic,
sectarian institutions." The program, providing vocational assistance to the visually
handicapped, does not seem well suited to serve as the vehicle for such a subsidy.
No evidence has been presented indicating that any other person has ever sought

to finance religious education or activity pursuant to the State's program. The combination of these factors, we think, makes the link between the State and the school petitioner wishes to attend a highly attenuated one. . . .

Justice POWELL, with whom THE CHIEF JUSTICE and Justice REHNQUIST join, concurring.

. . . I write separately to emphasize that Mueller v. Allen (1983) strongly supports the result we reach today.

As the Court states, the central question in this case is whether Washington's provision of aid to handicapped students has the "principal or primary effect" of advancing religion. *Mueller* makes the answer clear: state programs that are wholly neutral in offering educational assistance to a class defined without reference to religion do not violate the second part of the Lemon v. Kurtzman test, because any aid to religion results from the private choices of individual beneficiaries. Thus, in *Mueller*, we sustained a tax deduction for certain educational expenses, even though the great majority of beneficiaries were parents of children attending sectarian schools. We noted the State's traditionally broad taxing authority, but the decision rested principally on two other factors. First, the deduction was equally available to parents of public school children and parents of children attending private schools. Second, any benefit to religion resulted from the "numerous private choices of individual parents of school-age children."

The state program at issue here provides aid to handicapped students when their studies are likely to lead to employment. Aid does not depend on whether the student wishes to attend a public university or a private college, nor does it turn on whether the student seeks training for a religious or a secular career. It follows that under *Mueller* the State's program does not have the "principal or primary effect" of advancing religion.[3]

The Washington Supreme Court reached a different conclusion because it found that the program had the practical effect of aiding religion in this particular case. In effect, the court analyzed the case as if the Washington Legislature had passed a private bill that awarded respondent free tuition to pursue religious studies.

Such an analysis conflicts with both common sense and established precedent. Nowhere in *Mueller* did we analyze the effect of Minnesota's tax deduction on the parents who were parties to the case; rather, we looked to the nature and consequences of the program viewed as a whole. This is the appropriate perspective for this case as well. Viewed in the proper light, the Washington program easily satisfies the second prong of the *Lemon* test.

[Justice White and Justice O'Connor also wrote concurring opinions endorsing Justice Powell's approach and his reliance on Mueller v. Allen.]

------

3. Contrary to the Court's suggestion, this conclusion does not depend on the fact that petitioner appears to be the only handicapped student who has sought to use his assistance to pursue religious training. Over 90% of the tax benefits in *Mueller* ultimately flowed to religious institutions. Nevertheless, the aid was thus channeled by individual parents and not by the State, making the tax deduction permissible under the "primary effect" test of *Lemon*.

NOTES AND QUESTIONS

1. *Witters* **Versus** *Lemon.*   *Witters* purports to follow the *Lemon* approach, but does it really? Does the Court ask whether the Inland Empire School of the Bible is "pervasively sectarian"? Does the Court demand that the state be certain that government funded teachers avoid religious instruction? Does the Court require any policing that might in turn create entanglement? If the Court does not focus on these issues, on what does it focus?

Witters was a unanimous decision—the first one in a long string of cases involving aid to religious institutions. This was so notwithstanding the fact that the money was used for explicitly religious courses at a highly sectarian school, for the purpose of training for the ministry. What sense does it make to say that the state may pay for ministerial training at the Inland Empire School of the Bible but not for state-mandated courses in math, English, reading, science, music, and so forth at a nonpublic high school (Aguilar v. Felton)? Consider some possibilities:

(a) **Higher education?**   *Witters* could be an example of the Court's willingness to allow aid to many colleges and universities (see section C-1 above). But does that line of decisions explain why the aid could be used at a pervasively religious Bible college to train for the ministry?

(b) **The percentage of religious beneficiaries?**   Despite the designation of Justice Marshall's opinion as a majority, five of the Justices expressed agreement with Justice Powell that the case should be decided on the broader ground that "state programs that are wholly neutral in offering educational assistance to a class defined without reference to religion do not violate the second part of the Lemon v. Kurtzman test, because any aid to religion results from the private choices of individual beneficiaries." To support this broader rationale, Justice Powell cited—and criticized Justice Marshall for failing to cite—Mueller v. Allen, the 1983 decision that had upheld a statute allowing taxpayers to take state income tax deductions for expenses incurred for their children's education. By far the largest deductible expense, tuition, was applicable only to taxpayers using nonpublic schools, 96 percent of which were religious. Nevertheless the Court upheld the statute: "We would be loath to adopt a rule grounding the constitutionality of a facially neutral law on annual reports reciting the extent to which various classes of citizens claimed benefits under the law." 463 U.S. at 401.

In *Witters,* Justice Marshall's opinion found it important that only a small part of the overall vocational rehabilitation fund (unlike the large share of the deductions in *Mueller*) would be used at religious schools. But the opinions of the five justices who endorsed *Mueller* can be read as saying this factor should not matter. Which side was the law after *Witters*? Which side is right?

(c) **Aid channeled to an individual?**   The Court stated that "[a]s far as the record shows, vocational assistance provided under the Washington program is paid directly to the student, who transmits it to the educational institution of his or her choice." As we will see in future decisions, this feature—the fact that an individual has made the choice to use the aid in a religious setting—has assumed great significance for the Court. But does this feature distinguish the tuition grants and credits struck down in *Nyquist?* And why does channeling aid in this way make it more permissible? For discussion and evaluation of this factor, see Laura S. Underkuffler, Vouchers and Beyond: The Individual as Causative Agent in Establishment Clause Jurisprudence, 75 Ind. L.J. 167 (2000).

2. The Incremental Extension of the "Neutrality" and "Choice" Approach:
Zobrest **and** *Rosenberger.*   *Witters* focused on the neutrality of the aid and the individual's choice of where to use it. This approach was extended, modestly, in two later decisions that approved aid but hedged the approval with qualifications. In Zobrest v. Catalina Foothills School Dist., 509 U.S. 1 (1993), the Court upheld the provision, under federal disability law, of a sign-language interpreter to a deaf student in a Catholic high school. Although the interpreter would act as a conduit for religious messages in classes and chapel services, the Court upheld the aid on the ground that it was part of an overall statute that "distribute[d] benefits neutrally" to students in public, private, and religious schools and simply allowed the family to choose a school, thereby "ensur[ing] that a government-paid interpreter will be present in a sectarian school only as a result of the private decision of individual parents." The Court also distinguished earlier no-aid cases, and thus narrowed its ruling, on several grounds: the provision of the interpreter did not relieve the school of an expense it otherwise would have assumed, the program did not put any money into the coffers of the school, and the interpreter would not interject any more religious content than was always present in the messages he was relaying.

In Rosenberger v. Rector and Visitors of Univ. of Virginia, 515 U.S. 819 (1995), the Court held, 5-4, that when the University set up a program for paying the bills for printing costs of a wide variety of student groups including student publications, the Establishment Clause did not require or authorize the University to withhold payments for religious publications, that is, those that "primarily promot[e] or manifes[t]" a belief "about a deity or an ultimate reality." (The Court went further and held that the denial of assistance to a student religious magazine violated the Free Speech Clause, a ruling that we discuss in section E below (p. 435).) On the Establishment Clause issue, the majority again emphasized that the overall aid program was "neutral toward religion," supporting publications with a wide range of viewpoints. Again, however, the emphasis on neutrality was hedged with qualifications. The Court noted several grounds on which to distinguish the assistance for religious publications from the kind of "direct money payments to sectarian institutions" that historically have presented "special Establishment Clause dangers." First, the University's payments came out of a limited fund drawn from student activity fees, rather than from "a general tax fund." Second, the University paid the outside printing contractors directly, rather than reimbursing the student publication for its outlays, meaning that "no public funds flow directly to [a religious publication's] coffers."

Do the qualifications in these two decisions—for example, that no money flowed into religious schools' coffers—make sense? They appear to have been superseded by the following major decision:

ZELMAN v. SIMMONS-HARRIS
536 U.S. 639 (2002)

Chief Justice REHNQUIST delivered the opinion of the Court.

The State of Ohio has established a pilot program designed to provide educational choices to families with children who reside in the Cleveland City School District. The question presented is whether this program offends the

Establishment Clause of the United States Constitution. We hold that it does not.

There are more than 75,000 children enrolled in the Cleveland City School District. The majority of these children are from low-income and minority families. Few of these families enjoy the means to send their children to any school other than an inner-city public school. For more than a generation, however, Cleveland's public schools have been among the worst performing public schools in the Nation. In 1995, a Federal District Court declared a "crisis of magnitude" and placed the entire Cleveland school district under state control. Shortly thereafter, the state auditor found that Cleveland's public schools were in the midst of a "crisis that is perhaps unprecedented in the history of American education." The district had failed to meet any of the 18 state standards for minimal acceptable performance. Only 1 in 10 ninth graders could pass a basic proficiency examination, and students at all levels performed at a dismal rate compared with students in other Ohio public schools. More than two-thirds of high school students either dropped or failed out before graduation. Of those students who managed to reach their senior year, one of every four still failed to graduate. Of those students who did graduate, few could read, write, or compute at levels comparable to their counterparts in other cities.

It is against this backdrop that Ohio enacted, among other initiatives, its Pilot Project Scholarship Program. The program provides financial assistance to families in any Ohio school district that is or has been "under federal court order requiring supervision and operational management of the district by the state superintendent." Cleveland is the only Ohio school district to fall within that category.

The program provides two basic kinds of assistance to parents of children in a covered district. First, the program provides tuition aid for students in kindergarten through third grade, expanding each year through eighth grade, to attend a participating public or private school of their parent's choosing. Second, the program provides tutorial aid for students who choose to remain enrolled in public school. The tuition aid portion of the program is designed to provide educational choices to parents who reside in a covered district. Any private school, whether religious or nonreligious, may participate in the Program and accept program students so long as the school is located within the boundaries of a covered district and meets statewide educational standards. Participating private schools must agree not to discriminate on the basis of race, religion, or ethnic background, or to "advocate or foster unlawful behavior or teach hatred of any person or group on the basis of race, ethnicity, national origin, or religion." Any public school located in a school district adjacent to the covered district may also participate in the program. Adjacent public schools are eligible to receive a $2,250 tuition grant for each program student accepted in addition to the full amount of per-pupil state funding attributable to each additional student. All participating schools, whether public or private, are required to accept students in accordance with rules and procedures established by the state superintendent.

Tuition aid is distributed to parents according to financial need. Families with incomes below 200% of the poverty line are given priority and are eligible to receive 90% of private school tuition up to $2,250. For these lowest-income families, participating private schools may not charge a parental co-payment greater than $250. For all other families, the program pays 75% of tuition costs, up to $1,875, with no co-payment cap. These families receive tuition aid only if the number of available scholarships exceeds the number of low-income children who choose to participate. Where tuition aid is spent depends solely upon where parents who receive tuition aid choose to enroll their child. If parents choose a private school, checks are made payable to the parents who then endorse the checks over to the chosen school. . . .

The program has been in operation within the Cleveland City School District since the 1996-1997 school year. In the 1999-2000 school year, 56 private schools participated in the program, 46 (or 82%) of which had a religious affiliation. None of the public schools in districts adjacent to Cleveland have elected to participate. More than 3,700 students participated in the scholarship program, most of whom (96%) enrolled in religiously affiliated schools. Sixty percent of these students were from families at or below the poverty line. In the 1998-1999 school year, approximately 1,400 Cleveland public school students received tutorial aid. This number was expected to double during the 1999-2000 school year.

The program is part of a broader undertaking by the State to enhance the educational options of Cleveland's schoolchildren in response to the 1995 takeover. That undertaking includes programs governing community and magnet schools. Community schools are funded under state law but are run by their own school boards, not by local school districts. These schools enjoy academic independence to hire their own teachers and to determine their own curriculum. They can have no religious affiliation and are required to accept students by lottery. During the 1999-2000 school year, there were 10 start-up community schools in the Cleveland City School District with more than 1,900 students enrolled. For each child enrolled in a community school, the school receives state funding of $4,518, twice the funding a participating program school may receive.

Magnet schools are public schools operated by a local school board that emphasize a particular subject area, teaching method, or service to students. For each student enrolled in a magnet school, the school district receives $7,746, including state funding of $4,167, the same amount received per student enrolled at a traditional public school. As of 1999, parents in Cleveland were able to choose from among 23 magnet schools, which together enrolled more than 13,000 students in kindergarten through eighth grade. . . .

In July 1999, respondents filed this action in United States District Court, seeking to enjoin the . . . program on the ground that it violated the Establishment Clause of the United States Constitution. [The District Court granted summary judgment for respondents. A divided panel of the Court of Appeals affirmed.] We granted certiorari, and now reverse the Court of Appeals.

The Establishment Clause of the First Amendment, applied to the States through the Fourteenth Amendment, prevents a State from enacting laws that have the "purpose" or "effect" of advancing or inhibiting religion. Agostini v. Felton (1997). There is no dispute that the program challenged here was enacted for the valid secular purpose of providing educational assistance to poor children in a demonstrably failing public school system. Thus, the question presented is whether the Ohio program nonetheless has the forbidden "effect" of advancing or inhibiting religion.

To answer that question, our decisions have drawn a consistent distinction between government programs that provide aid directly to religious schools,

Mitchell v. Helms (2000); *Agostini*; *Rosenberger*, and programs of true private choice, in which government aid reaches religious schools only as a result of the genuine and independent choices of private individuals, Mueller v. Allen (1983); *Witters*; *Zobrest*. While our jurisprudence with respect to the constitutionality of direct aid programs has "changed significantly" over the past two decades, our jurisprudence with respect to true private choice programs has remained consistent and unbroken. Three times we have confronted Establishment Clause challenges to neutral government programs that provide aid directly to a broad class of individuals, who, in turn, direct the aid to religious schools or institutions of their own choosing. Three times we have rejected such challenges. [*Mueller, Witters, Zobrest.*]

Mueller, Witters, and *Zobrest* . . . make clear that where a government aid program is neutral with respect to religion, and provides assistance directly to a broad class of citizens who, in turn, direct government aid to religious schools wholly as a result of their own genuine and independent private choice, the program is not readily subject to challenge under the Establishment Clause. A program that shares these features permits government aid to reach religious institutions only by way of the deliberate choices of numerous individual recipients. The incidental advancement of a religious mission, or the perceived endorsement of a religious message, is reasonably attributable to the individual recipient, not to the government, whose role ends with the disbursement of benefits. . . .

We believe that the program challenged here is a program of true private choice, consistent with *Mueller, Witters,* and *Zobrest,* and thus constitutional. As was true in those cases, the Ohio program is neutral in all respects toward religion. It is part of a general and multifaceted undertaking by the State of Ohio to provide educational opportunities to the children of a failed school district. It confers educational assistance directly to a broad class of individuals defined without reference to religion, i.e., any parent of a school-age child who resides in the Cleveland City School District. The program permits the participation of *all* schools within the district, religious or nonreligious. Adjacent public schools also may participate and have a financial incentive to do so. Program benefits are available to participating families on neutral terms, with no reference to religion. The only preference stated anywhere in the program is a preference for low-income families, who receive greater assistance and are given priority for admission at participating schools.

There are no "financial incentive[s]" that "ske[w]" the program toward religious schools. Such incentives "[are] not present . . . where the aid is allocated on the basis of neutral, secular criteria that neither favor nor disfavor religion, and is made available to both religious and secular beneficiaries on a nondiscriminatory basis." *Agostini.* The program here in fact creates financial *dis*incentives for religious schools, with private schools receiving only half the government assistance given to community schools and one-third the assistance given to magnet schools. Adjacent public schools, should any choose to accept program students, are also eligible to receive two to three times the state funding of a private religious school. Families too have a financial disincentive to choose a private religious school over other schools. Parents that choose to participate in the scholarship program and then to enroll their children in a private school (religious or nonreligious) must copay a portion of the school's tuition. Families that choose a community school, magnet school, or traditional public school pay nothing. Although such features of the program are not necessary to its constitutionality, they clearly dispel the claim that the program "creates . . . financial incentive[s] for parents to choose a sectarian school." *Zobrest*.[3]

Respondents suggest that even without a financial incentive for parents to choose a religious school, the program creates a "public perception that the State is endorsing religious practices and beliefs." But we have repeatedly recognized that no reasonable observer would think a neutral program of private choice, where state aid reaches religious schools solely as a result of the numerous independent decisions of private individuals, carries with it the *imprimatur* of government endorsement. *Mueller; Zobrest; Mitchell.* The argument is particularly misplaced here since "the reasonable observer in the endorsement inquiry must be deemed aware" of the "history and context" underlying a challenged program. Good News Club v. Milford Central School (2001). Any objective observer familiar with the full history and context of the Ohio program would reasonably view it as one aspect of a broader undertaking to assist poor children in failed schools, not as an endorsement of religious schooling in general.

There also is no evidence that the program fails to provide genuine opportunities for Cleveland parents to select secular educational options for their school-age children. Cleveland schoolchildren enjoy a range of educational choices: They may remain in public school as before, remain in public school with publicly funded tutoring aid, obtain a scholarship and choose a religious school, obtain a scholarship and choose a nonreligious private school, enroll in a community school, or enroll in a magnet school. That 46 of the 56 private schools now participating in the program are religious schools does not condemn it as a violation of the Establishment Clause. The Establishment Clause question is whether Ohio is coercing parents into sending their children to religious schools, and that question must be answered by evaluating *all* options Ohio provides Cleveland schoolchildren, only one of which is to obtain a program scholarship and then choose a religious school.

Justice Souter speculates that because more private religious schools currently participate in the program, the program itself must somehow discourage the participation of private nonreligious schools.[4] But Cleveland's preponderance of religiously affiliated private schools certainly did not arise as a result of the program; it is a phenomenon common to many American cities. Indeed, by all accounts the program has captured a remarkable cross-section of private schools, religious and nonreligious. It is true that 82% of Cleveland's participating private schools are religious schools, but it is also true that 81% of private schools in Ohio are religious schools. To attribute constitutional significance

---

3. Justice Souter suggests the program is not "neutral" because program students cannot spend scholarship vouchers at traditional public schools. This objection is mistaken: Public schools in Cleveland already receive $7,097 in public funding per pupil–$4,167 of which is attributable to the State. Program students who receive tutoring aid and remain enrolled in traditional public schools therefore direct almost twice as much state funding to their chosen school as do program students who receive a scholarship and attend a private school. Justice Souter does not seriously claim that the program differentiates based on the religious status of beneficiaries or providers of services, the touchstone of neutrality under the Establishment Clause.

4. Justice Souter appears to base this claim on the unfounded assumption that capping the amount of tuition charged to low-income students (at $2,500) favors participation by religious schools. But elsewhere he claims that the program spends *too much* money on private schools and chides the state legislature for even proposing to raise the scholarship amount for low-income recipients. . . .

to this figure, moreover, would lead to the absurd result that a neutral school-choice program might be permissible in some parts of Ohio, such as Columbus, where a lower percentage of private schools are religious schools, but not in inner-city Cleveland, where Ohio has deemed such programs most sorely needed, but where the preponderance of religious schools happens to be greater. Likewise, an identical private choice program might be constitutional in some States, such as Maine or Utah, where less than 45% of private schools are religious schools, but not in other States, such as Nebraska or Kansas, where over 90% of private schools are religious schools.

Respondents and Justice Souter claim that even if we do not focus on the number of participating schools that are religious schools, we should attach constitutional significance to the fact that 96% of scholarship recipients have enrolled in religious schools. They claim that this alone proves parents lack genuine choice, even if no parent has ever said so. We need not consider this argument in detail, since it was flatly rejected in *Mueller*, where we found it irrelevant that 96% of parents taking deductions for tuition expenses paid tuition at religious schools. Indeed, we have recently found it irrelevant even to the constitutionality of a direct aid program that a vast majority of program benefits went to religious schools. See *Agostini; Mitchell.* The constitutionality of a neutral educational aid program simply does not turn on whether and why, in a particular area, at a particular time, most private schools are run by religious organizations, or most recipients choose to use the aid at a religious school. As we said in *Mueller*, "[s]uch an approach would scarcely provide the certainty that this field stands in need of, nor can we perceive principled standards by which such statistical evidence might be evaluated."

This point is aptly illustrated here. The 96% figure upon which respondents and Justice Souter rely discounts entirely (1) the more than 1,900 Cleveland children enrolled in alternative community schools, (2) the more than 13,000 children enrolled in alternative magnet schools, and (3) the more than 1,400 children enrolled in traditional public schools with tutorial assistance. Including some or all of these children in the denominator of children enrolled in nontraditional schools during the 1999-2000 school year drops the percentage enrolled in religious schools from 96% to under 20%. The 96% figure also represents but a snapshot of one particular school year. In the 1997-1998 school year, by contrast, only 78% of scholarship recipients attended religious schools. ... [6]

Respondents finally claim that we should look to Committee for Public Ed. & Religious Liberty v. Nyquist [p. 381] to decide these cases. We disagree for two reasons. First, the program in *Nyquist* was quite different from the program challenged here. *Nyquist* involved a New York program that gave a package of benefits exclusively to private schools and the parents of private school enrollees.

---

6. Justice Souter and Justice Stevens claim that community schools and magnet schools are separate and distinct from program schools, simply because the program itself does not include community and magnet school options. But none of the dissenting opinions explain how there is any perceptible difference between scholarship schools, community schools, or magnet schools from the perspective of Cleveland parents looking to choose the best educational option for their school-age children. Parents who choose a program school in fact receive from the State precisely what parents who choose a community or magnet school receive—the opportunity to send their children largely at state expense to schools they prefer to their local public school.

Although the program was enacted for ostensibly secular purposes, we found that its "function" was "*unmistakably* to provide desired financial support for non-public, sectarian institutions" (emphasis added). Its genesis, we said, was that private religious schools faced "increasingly grave fiscal problems." The program thus provided direct money grants to religious schools. It provided tax benefits "unrelated to the amount of money actually expended by any parent on tuition," ensuring a windfall to parents of children in religious schools. It similarly provided tuition reimbursements designed explicitly to "offe[r] . . . an incentive to parents to send their children to sectarian schools." Indeed, the program flatly prohibited the participation of any public school, or parent of any public school enrollee. Ohio's program shares none of these features. Second, were there any doubt that the program challenged in *Nyquist* is far removed from the program challenged here, we expressly reserved judgment with respect to "a case involving some form of public assistance (e.g., scholarships) made available generally without regard to the sectarian-nonsectarian, or public-nonpublic nature of the institution benefited." That, of course, is the very question now before us, and it has since been answered, first in *Mueller,* then in *Witters,* and again in *Zobrest.* To the extent the scope of *Nyquist* has remained an open question in light of these later decisions, we now hold that *Nyquist* does not govern neutral educational assistance programs that, like the program here, offer aid directly to a broad class of individual recipients defined without regard to religion.[7]

In sum, the Ohio program is entirely neutral with respect to religion. It provides benefits directly to a wide spectrum of individuals, defined only by financial need and residence in a particular school district. It permits such individuals to exercise genuine choice among options public and private, secular and religious. The program is therefore a program of true private choice. In keeping with an unbroken line of decisions rejecting challenges to similar programs, we hold that the program does not offend the Establishment Clause.

The judgment of the Court of Appeals is reversed.

[Concurring opinions by Justices O'Connor and Thomas, and a dissenting opinion by Justice Stevens, are omitted.]

Justice SOUTER, with whom Justice STEVENS, Justice GINSBURG, and Justice BREYER join, dissenting.

. . . The majority's statements of Establishment Clause doctrine cannot be appreciated without some historical perspective on the Court's announced limitations on government aid to religious education, and its repeated repudiation of limits previously set. [T]he cases can be categorized in three groups. In the period from 1947 to 1968, the basic principle of no aid to religion through school benefits was unquestioned. [*Everson.*] Thereafter for some 15 years, the Court termed its efforts as attempts to draw a line against aid that would

---

7. Justice Breyer would raise the invisible specters of "divisiveness" and "religious strife" to find the program unconstitutional. It is unclear exactly what sort of principle Justice Breyer has in mind, considering that the program has ignited no "divisiveness" or "strife" other than this litigation. Nor is it clear where Justice Breyer would locate this presumed authority to deprive Cleveland residents of a program that they have chosen but that we subjectively find "divisive." We quite rightly have rejected the claim that some speculative potential for divisiveness bears on the constitutionality of educational aid programs. Mitchell v. Helms.

be divertible to support the religious, as distinct from the secular, activity of an institutional beneficiary. [*Lemon*; *Nyquist*.]

Then, starting in 1983, concern with divertibility was gradually lost in favor of approving aid in amounts unlikely to afford substantial benefits to religious schools, when offered evenhandedly without regard to a recipient's religious character, and when channeled to a religious institution only by the genuinely free choice of some private individual. [*Mueller*; *Witters*; *Zobrest*] Now, the three stages are succeeded by a fourth, in which the substantial character of government aid is held to have no constitutional significance, and the espoused criteria of neutrality in offering aid, and private choice in directing it, are shown to be nothing but examples of verbal formalism. . . .

II

Although it has taken half a century since *Everson* to reach the majority's twin standards of neutrality and free choice, the facts show that, in the majority's hands, even these criteria cannot convincingly legitimize the Ohio scheme.

A

Consider first the criterion of neutrality. [In applying this criterion,] it makes sense to focus on a category of aid that may be directed to religious as well as secular schools, and ask whether the scheme favors a religious direction. Here, one would ask whether the voucher provisions, allowing for as much as $2,250 toward private school tuition (or a grant to a public school in an adjacent district), were written in a way that skewed the scheme toward benefiting religious schools.

This, however, is not what the majority asks. The majority looks not to the provisions for tuition vouchers, but to every provision for educational opportunity: "The program permits the participation of *all* schools within the district, [as well as public schools in adjacent districts], religious or nonreligious." The majority then finds confirmation that "participation of *all* schools" satisfies neutrality by noting that the better part of total state educational expenditure goes to public schools, thus showing there is no favor of religion.

The illogic is patent. If regular, public schools (which can get no voucher payments) "participate" in a voucher scheme with schools that can, and public expenditure is still predominantly on public schools, then the majority's reasoning would find neutrality in a scheme of vouchers available for private tuition in districts with no secular private schools at all. . . .

B

The majority addresses the issue of choice the same way it addresses neutrality, by asking whether recipients or potential recipients of voucher aid have a choice of public schools among secular alternatives to religious schools. Again, however, the majority asks the wrong question and misapplies the criterion. The majority has confused choice in spending scholarships with choice from the entire menu of possible educational placements, most of them open to anyone willing to attend a public school. . . . If "choice" is present whenever there is any educational alternative to the religious school to which vouchers can be endorsed, then there will always be a choice and the voucher can always be constitutional, even in a system in which there is not a single private secular school as an alternative to the religious school. . . .

It is not, of course, that I think even a genuine choice criterion is up to the task of the Establishment Clause when substantial state funds go to religious teaching; the discussion in Part III, infra, shows that it is not. The point is simply that if the majority wishes to claim that choice is a criterion, it must define choice in a way that can function as a criterion with a practical capacity to screen something out.

If, contrary to the majority, we ask the right question about genuine choice to use the vouchers, the answer shows that something is influencing choices in a way that aims the money in a religious direction: of 56 private schools in the district participating in the voucher program (only 53 of which accepted voucher students in 1999-2000), 46 of them are religious; 96.6% of all voucher recipients go to religious schools, only 3.4% to nonreligious ones. [Two-thirds of these families sent their children to schools run by another faith.]

[Even *this*] might be consistent with true choice if the students "chose" their religious schools over a wide array of private nonreligious options, or if it could be shown generally that Ohio's program had no effect on educational choices and thus no impermissible effect of advancing religious education. But both possibilities are contrary to fact. First, even if all existing nonreligious private schools in Cleveland were willing to accept large numbers of voucher students, only a few more than the 120 currently enrolled in such schools would be able to attend, as the total enrollment at all nonreligious private schools in Cleveland for kindergarten through eighth grade is only 510 children, and there is no indication that these schools have many open seats. Second, the $2,500 cap that the program places on tuition for participating low-income pupils has the effect of curtailing the participation of nonreligious schools: "nonreligious schools with higher tuition (about $4,000) stated that they could afford to accommodate just a few voucher students." By comparison, the average tuition at participating Catholic schools in Cleveland in 1999-2000 was $1,592, almost $1,000 below the cap. . . . [16]

[Nor does it matter] that the State did not deliberately design the network of private schools for the sake of channeling money into religious institutions. The criterion is one of genuinely free choice on the part of the private individuals who choose, and a Hobson's choice is not a choice, whatever the reason for being Hobsonian.

III

I do not dissent merely because the majority has misapplied its own law, for even if I assumed *arguendo* that the majority's formal criteria were satisfied on the facts, today's conclusion would be profoundly at odds with the Constitution. Proof of this is clear on two levels. The first is circumstantial, in the now

16. The majority notes that I argue both that the Ohio program is unconstitutional because the voucher amount is too low to create real private choice and that any greater expenditure would be unconstitutional as well. The majority is dead right about this, and there is no inconsistency here: any voucher program that satisfied the majority's requirement of "true private choice" would be even more egregiously unconstitutional than the current scheme due to the substantial amount of aid to religious teaching that would be required.

discarded symptom of violation, the substantial dimension of the aid. The second is direct, in the defiance of every objective supposed to be served by the bar against establishment.

A

The scale of the aid to religious schools approved today is unprecedented, both in the number of dollars and in the proportion of systemic school expenditure supported. Each measure has received attention in previous cases. On one hand, the sheer quantity of aid, when delivered to a class of religious primary and secondary schools, was suspect on the theory that the greater the aid, the greater its proportion to a religious school's existing expenditures, and the greater the likelihood that public money was supporting religious as well as secular instruction. . . .

On the other hand, the Court has found the gross amount unhelpful for Establishment Clause analysis when the aid afforded a benefit solely to one individual, however substantial as to him, but only an incidental benefit to the religious school at which the individual chose to spend the State's money. See *Witters, Zobrest.* When neither the design nor the implementation of an aid scheme channels a series of individual students' subsidies toward religious recipients, the relevant beneficiaries for establishment purposes, the Establishment Clause is unlikely to be implicated. . . .

The Cleveland voucher program has cost Ohio taxpayers $33 million since its implementation in 1996 ($28 million in voucher payments, $5 million in administrative costs), and its cost was expected to exceed $8 million in the 2001-2002 school year. . . . The gross amounts of public money contributed are symptomatic of the scope of what the taxpayers' money buys for a broad class of religious-school students. In paying for practically the full amount of tuition for thousands of qualifying students, the scholarships purchase everything that tuition purchases, be it instruction in math or indoctrination in faith. . . .

B

[This program threatens a variety of harms that the Establishment Clause is designed to protect us against. First, it impinges on the freedom of conscience that Jefferson spoke of in his Bill for Establishing Religious Freedom—the idea that no one "shall be compelled to . . . support any religious worship, place, or ministry whatsoever." Second, it creates a danger of corrosive secularism in religious schools. This] risk is already being realized. In Ohio, for example, a condition of receiving government money under the program is that participating religious schools may not "discriminate on the basis of . . . religion," Ohio Rev.Code Ann. § 3313.976(A)(4) (West Supp.2002), which means the school may not give admission preferences to children who are members of the patron faith; children of a parish are generally consigned to the same admission lotteries as non-believers, §§ 3313.977(A)(1)(c)-(d). . . . Nor is the State's religious antidiscrimination restriction limited to student admission policies: by its terms, a participating religious school may well be forbidden to choose a member of its own clergy to serve as teacher or principal over a layperson of a different religion claiming equal qualification for the job. Indeed, a separate condition that "[t]he school . . . not . . . teach hatred of any person or group on the basis of . . . religion," § 3313.976(A)(6), could be understood (or subsequently broadened) to prohibit religions from teaching traditionally legitimate articles of faith as to the error, sinfulness, or ignorance of others, if they want government money for their schools. . . .

Justice BREYER, with whom Justice STEVENS and Justice SOUTER join, dissenting.

I

[The Religion] Clauses embody an understanding, reached in the 17th century after decades of religious war, that liberty and social stability demand a religious tolerance that respects the religious views of all citizens, permits those citizens to "worship God in their own way," and allows all families to "teach their children and to form their characters" as they wish. C. Radcliffe, The Law & Its Compass 71 (1960). The Clauses reflect the Framers' vision of an American Nation free of the religious strife that had long plagued the nations of Europe. Whatever the Framers might have thought about particular 18th-century school funding practices, they undeniably intended an interpretation of the Religion Clauses that would implement this basic First Amendment objective.

In part for this reason, the Court's 20th-century Establishment Clause cases—both those limiting the practice of religion in public schools and those limiting the public funding of private religious education—focused directly upon social conflict, potentially created when government becomes involved in religious education. . . .

[A]n earlier American society might have found a less clear-cut church/state separation compatible with social tranquility. . . . The 20th-century Court was fully aware, however, that immigration and growth had changed American society dramatically since its early years.

[The Court] understood the Establishment Clause to prohibit . . . favoritism [for one or some religions]. Yet *how* did the Clause achieve that objective? Did it simply require the government to give each religion an equal chance to introduce religion into the primary schools—a kind of "equal opportunity" approach to the interpretation of the Establishment Clause? Or, did that Clause avoid government favoritism of some religions by insisting upon "separation"—that the government achieve equal treatment by removing itself from the business of providing religious education for children? . . .

[T]he Court concluded that the Establishment Clause required "separation," in part because an "equal opportunity" approach was not workable. . . . With respect to government aid to private education, did not history show that efforts to obtain equivalent funding for the private education of children whose parents did not hold popular religious beliefs only exacerbated religious strife?

The upshot is the development of constitutional doctrine that reads the Establishment Clause as avoiding religious strife, *not* by providing every religion with an *equal opportunity* (say, to secure state funding or to pray in the public schools), but by drawing fairly clear lines of *separation* between church and state—at least where the heartland of religious belief, such as primary religious education, is at issue.

II

The principle underlying these cases—avoiding religiously based social conflict—remains of great concern. As religiously diverse as America had become when the Court decided its major 20th-century Establishment Clause cases, we are exponentially more diverse today. America boasts more than 55 different religious groups and subgroups with a significant number of members.

Under these modern-day circumstances, how is the "equal opportunity" principle to work—without risking the "struggle of sect against sec[t"]? School voucher programs finance the religious education of the young. And, if widely adopted, they may well provide billions of dollars that will do so. Why will different religions not become concerned about, and seek to influence, the criteria used to channel this money to religious schools? Why will they not want to examine the implementation of the programs that provide this money—to determine, for example, whether implementation has biased a program toward or against particular sects, or whether recipient religious schools are adequately fulfilling a program's criteria? If so, just how is the State to resolve the resulting controversies without provoking legitimate fears of the kinds of religious favoritism that, in so religiously diverse a Nation, threaten social dissension?

Consider the voucher program here at issue. That program insists that the religious school accept students of all religions. Does that criterion treat fairly groups whose religion forbids them to do so? The program also insists that no participating school "advocate or foster unlawful behavior or teach hatred of any person or group on the basis of race, ethnicity, national origin, or religion." And it requires the State to "revoke the registration of any school if, after a hearing, the superintendent determines that the school is in violation" of the program's rules. As one *amicus* argues, "it is difficult to imagine a more divisive activity" than the appointment of state officials as referees to determine whether a particular religious doctrine "teaches hatred or advocates lawlessness."

. . . How will the public react to government funding for schools that take controversial religious positions on topics that are of current popular interest—say, the conflict in the Middle East or the war on terrorism? Yet any major funding program for primary religious education will require criteria. And the selection of those criteria, as well as their application, inevitably pose problems that are divisive. . . .

IV

I do not believe that the "parental choice" aspect of the voucher program sufficiently offsets the concerns I have mentioned. Parental choice cannot help the taxpayer who does not want to finance the religious education of children. It will not always help the parent who may see little real choice between inadequate nonsectarian public education and adequate education at a school whose religious teachings are contrary to his own. It will not satisfy religious minorities unable to participate because they are too few in number to support the creation of their own private schools. It will not satisfy groups whose religious beliefs preclude them from participating in a government sponsored program, and who may well feel ignored as government funds primarily support the education of children in the doctrines of the dominant religions. And it does little to ameliorate the entanglement problems or the related problems of social division that Part II, *supra,* describes.

_____

NOTES AND QUESTIONS

1. **Neutrality and Private Choice.** The Court in *Zelman* emphasized that Ohio had created a program of "true private choice" in which parents had "genuine opportunities" to select secular educational options. What makes a secular option genuine? Suppose the average test scores at community (charter) and magnet schools were poor—only slightly higher than the Cleveland district overall? Would the educational inadequacy of the schools keep them from counting as a genuine option? Would that mean that a voucher program is unconstitutional if the voucher schools are significantly superior to the public school alternatives? From the point of view of educational reform and improvement, isn't that perverse?

It has been argued that without further safeguards, the Cleveland voucher program "steer[ed] students into religious training" because the regular public schools were inadequate and religious schools constituted a large percentage of the voucher schools. Ira C. Lupu and Robert W. Tuttle, Sites of Redemption: A Wide-Angle Look at Vouchers and Sectarian Service Providers, 18 J.L. & Pol. 539, 596-597 (2002). See also Steve K. Green, Does the majority offer an answer to this criticism? In the absence of a voucher program, does the state steer students away from religious training by funding only public schools, which must be secular? See, e.g., Thomas C. Berg, Vouchers and Religious Schools: The New Constitutional Questions, 72 U. Cin. L. Rev. 151, 158-159 (2003); Eugene Volokh, Equal Treatment Is Not Establishment, 13 Notre Dame J.L. Eth. & Pub. Pol'y 341, 348 (1999). Which form of "steering" is more objectionable, in its nature or its degree?

What if a state offers vouchers for private schools for all parents, not just low-income parents, simply as the alternative to the public schools rather than as part of a menu including public-school choice options. Would that be constitutional?

The private schools, including religious ones, received substantially less per pupil in Cleveland than public schools. What if they receive the same amount as public schools? What if that exceeds the per-pupil cost for a given religious school? The Court says that the fact that they receive less shows that the program is not skewed toward religion; does it show that it is skewed against religion, so that a religious school could demand the same per-pupil amount?

Suppose that, instead of providing aid in the form of a voucher, a state provided aid in the form of a per-student payment to the schools. Would that make a constitutional difference under *Zelman*? Should it make a difference?

2. **Vouchers and Minority Religions.** Do voucher programs tend to worsen the status of minority religions? See Steven K. Green, The Illusionary Aspect of "Private Choice" for Constitutional Analysis, 38 Willamette L. Rev. 549, 559 (2002) ("vouchers will benefit those faiths with established private schools and existing support structures," while "other faiths desiring to establish private schools will find themselves at a distinct competitive disadvantage, particularly

considering the start-up costs associated with creating new schools"); see also Alan Brownstein, Evaluating School Voucher Programs Through a Liberty, Equality, and Free Speech Matrix, 31 Conn. L. Rev. 871, 920-923 (1999). But see Thomas C. Berg, Minority Religions and the Religion Clauses, 82 Wash. U. L.Q. 919, 994 (2004) ("If small religious groups find it difficult to create schools with the help of government benefits, they must find it even more difficult to do so without such aid."). Is the issue here the effect that vouchers will have on public schools? What is the connection between public schools and the status of minority religions?

3. Vouchers and Religious Division. Do you agree with Justice Breyer that vouchers for religious schools pose constitutionally unacceptable risks of religious divisiveness? The fears might be of (a) fights over which schools should be eligible to receive vouchers and (b) the separation of school-age children into different schools, so that they fail to mix and understand each other. Are these both legitimate constitutional concerns? Should the risk of division from any given program be the criterion for evaluating its constitutionality? There is undoubtedly also some divisiveness caused by excluding religious schools from programs open to their secular counterparts. And if more parents who want religion in their children's education could send them to religious schools, won't there be fewer divisive efforts to "impose" religion in the public schools (the subject of Part V of this book)?

For further explication of the concern that vouchers would cause divisiveness, see, e.g., Laura S. Underkuffler, The "Blaine" Debate: Must States Fund Religious Schools, 2 First Am. L. Rev. 179, 186-94 (2003). For a criticism of considering "religious division" as a factor in Religion Clause adjudication, see Richard W. Garnett, Religion, Division, and the First Amendment, 94 Georgetown L. J. _____ (forthcoming 2006).

4. Vouchers and School Autonomy. Cleveland's program required private schools to agree not to discriminate on the basis of race, religion, or ethnic background. Private schools also had to promise that they would not "advocate or foster unlawful behavior or teach hatred of any person or group on the basis of race, ethnicity, national origin, or religion." Political scientist Stephen Macedo has praised the nondiscrimination requirement. This, he says, will induce the schools to become less sectarian—"more attuned to public values." Stephen Macedo, Constituting Civil Society: School Vouchers, Religious Nonprofit Organizations, and Liberal Public Values, 75 Chi.-Kent L. Rev. 417 (2000). Is that a good thing? Why might the government have an interest in making religious schools less religious? Is such an interest legitimate?

At pages 353, 380, and 387, we discussed the danger that aid to religious schools could have a secularizing effect on those schools. This was particularly evident in the requirement in the program in *Lemon* that teachers agree not to include religious or moral elements in their classroom teaching, and in the requirement in the program in Board of Education v. Allen (p. 352) that the state-subsidized textbooks be the same as those used in the public schools. Preventing government pressure to secularize was one possible interpretation of the constitutional value underlying the "entanglement" prong of *Lemon*. Are the requirements of nondiscrimination and not teaching hatred subject to the same critique? Is it possible to have neutral education funding without introducing a government incentive for religious schools to secularize?

May religious schools object to these conditions and claim constitutional exemption from them? If Cleveland wanted to exempt religious schools from those conditions, would it be forbidden to do so?

2. "Direct" Aid: The First (?) Overrulings

Zelman indicates that the Court will uphold most if not all aid programs involving "true private choice." But *Zelman* distinguishes and suggests a different analysis for "programs that provide aid directly to religious schools." What is the current status of the *Lemon*-era decisions forbidding direct aid to pervasively sectarian schools?

The Court has retreated from a no-aid position in these cases too. Recently it has twice overruled earlier decisions forbidding direct aid. Agostini v. Felton, 521 U.S. 203 (1997), arose on a motion to vacate the injunction in Aguilar v. Felton (p. 390). The program was unchanged except for the location of classes: public school employees, paid with federal funds, offered remedial instruction to low-income children in schools, including private schools, in low-income neighborhoods. Following *Aguilar*, such instruction had been offered off the premises of religious schools, most commonly in trailers parked just outside the property line.

Agostini overruled *Aguilar*. It also overruled Grand Rapids School Dist. v. Ball (p. 389) with respect to the Shared Time program in that case—the program of remedial and enrichment courses taught by public school employees. *Agostini* did not overrule *Ball* with respect to the Community Education program, in which the courses were often taught by religious-school employees temporarily hired by the public schools.

The majority in *Agostini* emphasized that the instruction was delivered by public school employees on religiously neutral terms to all qualifying low-income children; it abandoned the presumption that any teacher on the premises of religious schools was likely to teach religion. It also abandoned the "symbolic union" of church and state as an independent criterion, and the presumption that any aid to the educational function of a religious school necessarily aids religion. It merged the entanglement prong of the *Lemon* test into the effects test; entanglement is relevant now only if it advances or inhibits religion.

How far has the Court moved toward permitting direct aid on an equal basis to religious schools? Here is its latest word on the subject.

MITCHELL v. HELMS
530 U.S. 793 (2000)

Justice THOMAS announced the judgment of the Court and delivered an opinion, in which THE CHIEF JUSTICE, Justice SCALIA, and Justice KENNEDY join. . . .

I

A

[The case involved Chapter 2 of the Education Consolidation and Improvement Act of 1981.] Like the provision at issue in Agostini [v. Felton], Chapter 2 channels federal funds to local educational agencies (LEA's), which are usually public school districts, via state educational agencies (SEA's), to implement programs to assist children in elementary and secondary schools. Among other things, Chapter 2 provides aid

> for the acquisition and use of instructional and educational materials, including library services and materials (including media materials), assessments, reference materials, computer software and hardware for instructional use, and other curricular materials.

LEA's and SEA's must offer assistance to both public and private schools (although any private school must be nonprofit). Participating private schools receive Chapter 2 aid based on the number of children enrolled in each school, and allocations of Chapter 2 funds for those schools must generally be "equal (consistent with the number of children to be served) to expenditures for programs . . . for children enrolled in the public schools of the [LEA]." . . . Chapter 2 funds may only "supplement and, to the extent practical, increase the level of funds that would . . . be made available from non-Federal sources." LEA's and SEA's may not operate their programs "so as to supplant funds from non-Federal sources." . . .

[T]he "services, materials, and equipment" provided to private schools must be "secular, neutral, and nonideological." . . . [P]rivate schools may not acquire control of Chapter 2 funds or title to Chapter 2 materials, equipment, or property. . . .

[A]bout 30% of Chapter 2 funds spent in Jefferson Parish are allocated for private schools. [In 1986-1987, 46 private schools participated, of which] 34 were Roman Catholic; 7 were otherwise religiously affiliated; and 5 were not religiously affiliated.

[The Fifth Circuit struck down the provision of materials to religious schools based on Meek v. Pittenger (1975; p. 388) and Wolman v. Walter (1977; p. 388), although it noted that the Court's subsequent case law was changing toward permitting more aid.]

II

[I]n *Agostini*, . . . we brought some clarity to our case law, by overruling two anomalous precedents (one in whole, the other in part) and by consolidating some of our previously disparate considerations under a revised test[:]

> To summarize, New York City's Title I program does not run afoul of any of three primary criteria we currently use to evaluate whether government aid has the effect of advancing religion: It does not result in governmental indoctrination; define its recipients by reference to religion; or create an excessive entanglement.

. . . We conclude that [Chapter 2] neither results in religious indoctrination by the government nor defines its recipients by reference to religion. . . . *Meek* and *Wolman* are anomalies in our case law. We therefore conclude that they are no longer good law.

A

As we indicated in *Agostini*, . . . the question whether governmental aid to religious schools results in governmental indoctrination is ultimately a question whether any religious indoctrination that occurs in those schools could reasonably be attributed to governmental action. We have also indicated that the answer to the question of indoctrination will resolve the question whether a program of educational aid "subsidizes" religion, as our religion cases use that term.

In distinguishing between indoctrination that is attributable to the State and indoctrination that is not, we have consistently turned to the principle of neutrality, upholding aid that is offered to a broad range of groups or persons without regard to their religion. If the religious, irreligious, and areligious are all alike eligible for governmental aid, no one would conclude that any indoctrination that any particular recipient conducts has been done at the behest of the government. . . . To put the point differently, if the government, seeking to further some legitimate secular purpose, offers aid on the same terms, without regard to religion, to all who adequately further that purpose, then it is fair to say that any aid going to a religious recipient only has the effect of furthering that secular purpose. The government, in crafting such an aid program, has had to conclude that a given level of aid is necessary to further that purpose among secular recipients and has provided no more than that same level to religious recipients.

As a way of assuring neutrality, we have repeatedly considered whether any governmental aid that goes to a religious institution does so "only as a result of the genuinely independent and private choices of individuals." *Agostini*. We have viewed as significant whether the "private choices of individual parents," as opposed to the "unmediated" will of government, Grand Rapids v. Ball, determine what schools ultimately benefit from the governmental aid, and how much. For if numerous private choices, rather than the single choice of a government, determine the distribution of aid pursuant to neutral eligibility criteria, then a government cannot, or at least cannot easily, grant special favors that might lead to a religious establishment. Private choice also helps guarantee neutrality by mitigating the preference for pre-existing recipients that is arguably inherent in any governmental aid program, and that could lead to a program inadvertently favoring one religion or favoring religious private schools in general over nonreligious ones. . . .

Agostini's second primary criterion for determining the effect of governmental aid is closely related to the first. The second criterion requires a court to consider whether an aid program "define[s] its recipients by reference to religion." . . . [T]his second criterion looks to the same set of facts as does our focus, under the first criterion, on neutrality, but the second criterion uses those facts to answer a somewhat different question—whether the criteria for allocating the aid "creat[e] a financial incentive to undertake religious indoctrination." In *Agostini* we set out the following rule for answering this question:

> This incentive is not present, however, where the aid is allocated on the basis of neutral, secular criteria that neither favor nor disfavor religion, and is made available to both religious and secular beneficiaries on a nondiscriminatory basis. . . .

[There is a] close relationship between this rule, incentives, and private choice. For to say that a program does not create an incentive to choose religious schools is to say that the private choice is truly "independent," *Witters*. . . .

B

[D]ismissing *Agostini* as factually distinguishable, [the plaintiffs/respondents] offer two rules that they contend should govern our determination of whether Chapter 2 has the effect of advancing religion. They argue first, and chiefly, that "direct, nonincidental" aid to the primary educational mission of religious schools is always impermissible. Second, they argue that provision to religious schools of aid that is divertible to religious use is similarly impermissible. Respondents' arguments are inconsistent with our more recent case law, . . . and we therefore reject them.

1

Although some of our earlier cases did emphasize the distinction between direct and indirect aid, the purpose of this distinction was merely to prevent "subsidization" of religion. As even the dissent all but admits, our more recent cases address this purpose not through the direct/indirect distinction but rather through the principle of private choice. . . . If aid to schools, even "direct aid," is neutrally available and, before reaching or benefiting any religious school, first passes through the hands (literally or figuratively) of numerous private citizens who are free to direct the aid elsewhere, the government has not provided any "support of religion," *Witters*. Although the presence of private choice is easier to see when aid literally passes through the hands of individuals[,] there is no reason why the Establishment Clause requires such a form. . . .

Of course, we have seen "special Establishment Clause dangers," *Rosenberger*, when *money* is given to religious schools or entities directly rather than, as in *Witters* and Mueller v. Allen, indirectly.[8] But direct payments of money are not at issue in this case, and we refuse to allow a "special" case to create a rule for all cases.

2

Respondents also contend that the Establishment Clause requires that aid to religious schools not be impermissibly religious in nature or be divertible to religious use. We agree with the first part of this argument but not the second. Respondents' "no divertibility" rule is inconsistent with our more recent case law and is unworkable. So long as the governmental aid is not itself "unsuitable for use in the public schools because of religious content," *Allen*, and eligibility for aid is determined in a constitutionally permissible manner, any use of that aid to indoctrinate cannot be attributed to the government and is thus not of constitutional concern. . . .

The issue is not divertibility of aid but rather whether the aid itself has an impermissible content. Where the aid would be suitable for use in a public

8. The reason for such concern is not that the form *per se* is bad, but that such a form creates special risks that governmental aid will have the effect of advancing religion (or, even more, a purpose of doing so). An indirect form of payment reduces these risks. It is arguable, however, at least after *Witters*, that the principles of neutrality and private choice would be adequate to address those special risks, for it is hard to see the basis for deciding *Witters* differently simply if the State had sent the tuition check directly to whichever school Witters chose to attend. Similarly, we doubt it would be unconstitutional if . . . a government employer directly sent a portion of an employee's paycheck to a religious institution designated by that employee pursuant to a neutral charitable program. [T]he Federal Government appears to have long had such a [payroll deduction] program [for federal employees].

school, it is also suitable for use in any private school. . . . [J]ust as [in *Zobrest*] a government interpreter does not herself inculcate a religious message—even when she is conveying one—so also a government computer or overhead projector does not itself inculcate a religious message, even when it is conveying one. . . .

A concern for divertibility, as opposed to improper content, is [also] misplaced . . . because it is boundless—enveloping all aid, no matter how trivial—and thus has only the most attenuated (if any) link to any realistic concern for preventing an "establishment of religion." Presumably, for example, government-provided lecterns, chalk, crayons, pens, paper, and paintbrushes would have to be excluded from religious schools under respondents' proposed rule. . . .

C

The dissent serves up a smorgasbord of 11 factors that, depending on the facts of each case "in all its particularity," could be relevant to the constitutionality of a school-aid program. . . . While the dissent delights in the perverse chaos that all these factors produce, the Constitution becomes unnecessarily clouded, and legislators, litigants, and lower courts groan. . . .

One of the dissent's factors deserves special mention: whether a school that receives aid (or whose students receive aid) is pervasively sectarian. . . . [T]here was a period when this factor mattered, particularly if the pervasively sectarian school was a primary or secondary school. But that period is one that the Court should regret, and it is thankfully long past.

There are numerous reasons to formally dispense with this factor. First, its relevance in our precedents is in sharp decline. [For example, in] *Witters* . . . we did not ask whether the Inland Empire School of the Bible was pervasively sectarian. . . .

Second, the religious nature of a recipient should not matter to the constitutional analysis, so long as the recipient adequately furthers the government's secular purpose. . . . [I]t is most bizarre [to] reserve special hostility for those who take their religion seriously, who think that their religion should affect the whole of their lives, or who make the mistake of being effective in transmitting their views to children.

Third, the inquiry into the recipient's religious views required by a focus on whether a school is pervasively sectarian is not only unnecessary but also offensive. It is well established . . . that courts should refrain from trolling through a person's or institution's religious beliefs. See Employment Division v. Smith.

Finally, hostility to aid to pervasively sectarian schools has a shameful pedigree that we do not hesitate to disavow. Although the dissent professes concern for "the implied exclusion of the less favored," the exclusion of pervasively sectarian schools from government-aid programs is just that, particularly given the history of such exclusion. Opposition to aid to "sectarian" schools acquired prominence in the 1870's with Congress's consideration (and near passage) of the Blaine Amendment, which would have amended the Constitution to bar any aid to sectarian institutions. Consideration of the amendment arose at a time of pervasive hostility to the Catholic Church and to Catholics in general, and it was an open secret that "sectarian" was code for "Catholic." Notwithstanding its history, of course, "sectarian" could, on its face, describe the school of any religious sect, but the Court eliminated this possibility of confusion when, in Hunt v. McNair (1973), it coined the term "pervasively sectarian"—a term which, at that time, could be applied almost exclusively to Catholic parochial schools and which even today's dissent exemplifies chiefly by reference to such schools. . . .

This doctrine, born of bigotry, should be buried now.

III

Applying the two relevant *Agostini* criteria, we see no basis for concluding that Jefferson Parish's Chapter 2 program "has the effect of advancing religion." . . .

Taking the second criterion first, it is clear that Chapter 2 aid "is allocated on the basis of neutral, secular criteria that neither favor nor disfavor religion, and is made available to both religious and secular beneficiaries on a nondiscriminatory basis." *Agostini.* Aid is allocated based on enrollment . . . , and allocations to private schools must "be equal (consistent with the number of children to be served) to expenditures for programs under this subchapter for children enrolled in the public schools of the [LEA]." . . . The allocation criteria therefore create no improper incentive.

[For the same reasons,] Chapter 2 also satisfies the first *Agostini* criterion. . . . Private decisionmaking controls because of the per capita allocation scheme, and those decisions are independent because of the program's neutrality. It is the students and their parents—not the government—who, through their choice of school, determine who receives Chapter 2 funds. The aid follows the child.

Because Chapter 2 aid is provided pursuant to private choices, it is not problematic that one could fairly describe Chapter 2 as providing "direct" aid. . . . The ultimate beneficiaries of Chapter 2 aid are the students who attend the schools that receive that aid, and this is so regardless of whether individual students lug computers to school each day or, as Jefferson Parish has more sensibly provided, the schools receive the computers. . . .

Finally, Chapter 2 satisfies the first *Agostini* criterion because it does not provide to religious schools aid that has an impermissible content. The statute explicitly bars anything of the sort, providing that all Chapter 2 aid for the benefit of children in private schools shall be "secular, neutral, and nonideological," and the record indicates that the Louisiana SEA and the Jefferson Parish LEA have faithfully enforced this requirement insofar as relevant to this case. . . .

There is evidence that equipment has been, or at least easily could be, diverted for use in religious classes. Justice O'Connor, however, finds the safeguards against diversion adequate to prevent and detect actual diversion. [But the safeguards are minimal.] In addition, we agree with the dissent that there is evidence of actual diversion and that, were the safeguards anything other than anemic, there would almost certainly be more such evidence. In any event, for reasons we discussed in Part II-B-2, the evidence of actual diversion and the weakness of the safeguards against actual diversion are not relevant to the constitutional inquiry, whatever relevance they may have under the statute and regulations. . . .

IV

[I]n short, . . . Jefferson Parish need not exclude religious schools from its Chapter 2 program.[19] To the extent that Meek v. Pittenger and Wolman v. Walter conflict with this holding, we overrule them.

Justice O'CONNOR, with whom Justice BREYER joins, concurring in the judgment. . . .

Agostini . . . controls [this case]. To the extent our decisions in *Meek* and *Wolman* are inconsistent with the Court's judgment today, I agree that those decisions should be overruled. . . .

I

I write separately because, in my view, the plurality announces a rule of unprecedented breadth for the evaluation of Establishment Clause challenges to government school-aid programs. Reduced to its essentials, the plurality's rule states that government aid to religious schools does not have the effect of advancing religion so long as the aid is offered on a neutral basis and the aid is secular in content. The plurality also rejects the distinction between direct and indirect aid, and holds that the actual diversion of secular aid by a religious school to the advancement of its religious mission is permissible. . . .

[N]eutrality is an important reason for upholding government-aid programs against Establishment Clause challenges. . . . Nevertheless, we have never held that a government-aid program passes constitutional muster *solely* because of the neutral criteria it employs as a basis for distributing aid. . . .

I also disagree with the plurality's conclusion that actual diversion of government aid to religious indoctrination is consistent with the Establishment Clause. Although "[o]ur cases have permitted some government funding of secular functions performed by sectarian organizations," our decisions "provide no precedent for the use of public funds to finance religious activities." *Rosenberger* (O'Connor, J., concurring). . . . In both *Agostini* [and] Board of Educ. v. Allen, we rested our approval of the relevant programs in part on the fact that the aid had not been used to advance the religious missions of the recipient schools. . . .

The plurality bases its holding that actual diversion is permissible on *Witters* and *Zobrest*. . . . [W]e decided *Witters* and *Zobrest* on the understanding that the aid was provided directly to the individual student who, in turn, made the choice of where to put that aid to use. . . . This characteristic of both programs made them less like a direct subsidy, which would be impermissible under the Establishment Clause, and more akin to the government issuing a paycheck to an employee who, in turn, donates a portion of that check to a religious institution. . . .

Like Justice Souter, I do not believe that we should treat a per-capita-aid program the same as the true private-choice programs considered in *Witters*

19. Indeed, as petitioners observe, to require exclusion of religious schools from such a program would raise serious questions under the Free Exercise Clause. See, e.g., Church of Lukumi Babalu Aye, Inc. v. Hialeah ("At a minimum, the protections of the Free Exercise Clause pertain if the law at issue discriminates against some or all religious beliefs."); cf. *Rosenberger* (holding that Free Speech Clause bars exclusion of religious viewpoints from limited public forum).

and *Zobrest*. First, when the government provides aid directly to the student beneficiary, that student can attend a religious school and yet retain control over whether the secular government aid will be applied toward the religious education. The fact that aid flows to the religious school and is used for the advancement of religion is therefore *wholly* dependent on the student's private decision. . . .

Second, I believe the distinction between a per-capita school-aid program and a true private-choice program is significant for purposes of endorsement. In terms of public perception, a government program of direct aid to religious schools based on the number of students attending each school differs meaningfully from the government distributing aid directly to individual students who, in turn, decide to use the aid at the same religious schools. In the former example, if the religious school uses the aid to inculcate religion in its students, it is reasonable to say that the government has communicated a message of endorsement. Because the religious indoctrination is supported by government assistance, the reasonable observer would naturally perceive the aid program as *government* support for the advancement of religion.

That the amount of aid received by the school is based on the school's enrollment does not separate the government from the endorsement of the religious message. The aid formula does not—and could not—indicate to a reasonable observer that the inculcation of religion is endorsed only by the individuals attending the religious school, who each affirmatively choose to direct the secular government aid to the school and its religious mission. No such choices have been made. In contrast, when government aid supports a school's religious mission only because of independent decisions made by numerous individuals to guide their secular aid to that school, . . . endorsement of the religious message is reasonably attributed to the individuals who select the path of the aid.

Finally, the distinction between a per-capita-aid program and a true private-choice program is important when considering aid that consists of direct monetary subsidies. . . . If, as the plurality contends, a per-capita-aid program is identical in relevant constitutional respects to a true private-choice program, then there is no reason that, under the plurality's reasoning, the government should be precluded from providing direct money payments to religious organizations (including churches) based on the number of persons belonging to each organization. And, because actual diversion is permissible under the plurality's holding, the participating religious organizations (including churches) could use that aid to support religious indoctrination. To be sure, the plurality does not actually hold that its theory extends to direct money payments. That omission, however, is of little comfort. In its logic—as well as its specific advisory language, see n.8—the plurality opinion foreshadows the approval of direct monetary subsidies to religious organizations, even when they use the money to advance their religious objectives. . . .

II

[Justice O'Connor evaluated the program under the *Agostini* criteria, finding first that it "d[id] not define aid recipients by reference to religion" and therefore "create[d] no financial incentive to undertake religious indoctrination," and second that it did not "result in governmental indoctrination."]

The Chapter 2 program at issue here bears the same hallmarks . . . that we found important in *Agostini*. First, . . . Chapter 2 aid is distributed on the basis of neutral, secular criteria. . . . Second, the statute requires participating SEA's and LEA's to use and allocate Chapter 2 funds only to supplement the funds otherwise available to a religious school. Chapter 2 funds must in no case be used to supplant funds from non-Federal sources. Third, no Chapter 2 funds ever reach the coffers of a religious school. Like the Title I program considered in *Agostini*, all Chapter 2 funds are controlled by public agencies—the SEA's and LEA's. The LEA's purchase instructional and educational materials and then lend those materials to public and private schools. With respect to lending to private schools under Chapter 2, the statute specifically provides that the relevant public agency must retain title to the materials and equipment. Together with the supplantation restriction, this provision ensures that religious schools reap no financial benefit by virtue of receiving loans of materials and equipment. Finally, the statute provides that all Chapter 2 materials and equipment must be "secular, neutral, and nonideological." That restriction is reinforced by a further statutory prohibition on "the making of any payment . . . for religious worship or instruction." Although respondents claim that Chapter 2 aid has been diverted to religious instruction, that evidence is *de minimis*, as I explain at greater length below.

III

[I]n *Meek* and *Wolman*, we adhered to *Allen*, holding that the textbook lending programs at issue in each case did not violate the Establishment Clause. At the same time, however, we held in both cases that the lending of instructional materials and equipment to religious schools was unconstitutional. . . .

[T]echnology's advance . . . has only made the distinction between textbooks and instructional materials and equipment more suspect. . . . That *Allen*, *Meek*, and *Wolman* would permit the constitutionality of a school-aid program to turn on whether the aid took the form of a computer rather than a book further reveals the inconsistency inherent in their logic.

Respondents insist that . . . materials and equipment, unlike textbooks, are reasonably divertible to religious uses. . . . [But the "divertibility"] theory does not provide a logical distinction. . . . An educator can use virtually any instructional tool, whether it has ascertainable content or not, to teach a religious message. . . . [E]ven a publicly financed lunch would apparently be unconstitutional under a divertibility rationale because religious-school officials conceivably could use the lunch to lead the students in a blessing over the bread. . . .

IV

[I] would adhere to the rule that we have applied in the context of textbook lending programs: To establish a First Amendment violation, plaintiffs must prove that the aid in question actually is, or has been, used for religious purposes. . . . In *Agostini*, we repeatedly emphasized that it would be inappropriate to presume inculcation of religion[.]

V

[Justice O'Connor found that the program adequately protected against actual diversion to religious uses. She first described the safeguards against diversion, which included signed assurances by recipient schools, monitoring visits by officials, and random review of requests for materials.] Respondents, the plurality, and Justice SOUTER all fault the above-described safeguards primarily because they depend on the good faith of participating religious school officials. . . . [But] it is entirely proper to presume that these school officials will act in good faith. That presumption is especially appropriate in this case, since there is no proof that religious school officials have breached their schools' assurances or failed to tell government officials the truth.

The evidence proffered by respondents, and relied on by the plurality and Justice Souter, concerning actual diversion of Chapter 2 aid in Jefferson Parish is *de minimis*. [Justice O'Connor noted cases in which Chapter 2 materials had been used in theology classes and connected by networks to non-Chapter 2 computers.] [N]either piece of evidence demonstrates that Chapter 2 aid actually was diverted to religious education. At most, it proves the possibility. . . .

I know of no case in which we have declared an entire aid program unconstitutional on Establishment Clause grounds solely because of violations on the miniscule scale of those at issue here. . . . While extensive violations might require a remedy along the lines asked for by respondents, no such evidence has been presented here. . . .

. . . As in *Agostini*, the Chapter 2 aid is allocated on the basis of neutral, secular criteria; the aid must be supplementary and cannot supplant non-Federal funds; no Chapter 2 funds ever reach the coffers of religious schools; the aid must be secular; any evidence of actual diversion is *de minimis*; and the program includes adequate safeguards. Regardless of whether these factors are constitutional requirements, they are surely sufficient to find that the program at issue here does not have the impermissible effect of advancing religion. . . . Accordingly, I concur in the judgment.

Justice SOUTER, with whom Justice STEVENS and Justice GINSBURG join, dissenting. . . .

. . . [The] majority today mistakes the significance of facts that have led to conclusions of unconstitutionality in earlier cases. . . . [Moreover, the] plurality position breaks fundamentally with Establishment Clause principle. . . .

[I]

[A]fter *Everson* and *Allen*, the state of the law applying the Establishment Clause to public expenditures producing some benefit to religious schools was this:

1. Government aid to religion is forbidden, and tax revenue may not be used to support a religious school or religious teaching.

2. Government provision of such paradigms of universally general welfare benefits as police and fire protection does not count as aid to religion.

3. Whether a law's benefit is sufficiently close to universally general welfare paradigms to be classified with them, as distinct from religious aid, is a function of the purpose and effect of the challenged law in all its particularity. The judgment is not reducible to the application of any formula. Evenhandedness of distribution as between religious and secular beneficiaries is a relevant factor, but not a sufficiency test of constitutionality. There is no rule of religious equal protection to the effect that any expenditure for the benefit of religious school

students is necessarily constitutional so long as public school pupils are favored on ostensibly identical terms. . . .

II

A

The most deceptively familiar of [Establishment Clause] considerations is "neutrality."

. . . [*Allen*] used "neutrality" to describe an adequate state of balance between government as ally and as adversary to religion. The term was not further defined, and a few subsequent school cases used "neutrality" simply to designate the required relationship to religion, without explaining how to attain it. . . .

[*Lemon* shifted] the use of the word "neutral" from labeling the required position of the government to describing a benefit that was nonreligious. . . . [T]hereafter, we regularly used "neutral" in this second sense of "secular" or "nonreligious." . . .

[T]he Court again transformed the sense of "neutrality" in the 1980's. Reexamining and reinterpreting *Everson* and *Allen*, we began to use the word "neutral" to mean "evenhanded," in the sense of allocating aid on some common basis to religious and secular recipients. . . .

[The "evenhandedness"] kind of neutrality is relevant in judging whether a benefit scheme so characterized should be seen as aiding a sectarian school's religious mission, but this neutrality is not alone sufficient to qualify the aid as constitutional. . . . [T]he basic principle of establishment scrutiny of aid remains the principle as stated in *Everson*, that there may be no public aid to religion or support for the religious mission of any institution.

B

[E]venhandedness in distributing a benefit approaches the equivalence of constitutionality in this area only when the term refers to such universality of distribution that it makes no sense to think of the benefit as going to any discrete group. Conversely, when evenhandedness refers to distribution to limited groups within society, like groups of schools or schoolchildren, it does make sense to regard the benefit as aid to the recipients.

Hence, if we looked no further than evenhandedness, and failed to ask what activities the aid might support, or in fact did support, religious schools could be blessed with government funding as massive as expenditures made for the benefit of their public school counterparts, and religious missions would thrive on public money.

At least three main lines of enquiry addressed particularly to school aid have emerged to complement evenhandedness neutrality. First, we have noted that two types of aid recipients heighten Establishment Clause concern: pervasively religious schools and primary and secondary religious schools. Second, we have identified two important characteristics of the method of distributing aid: directness or indirectness of distribution and distribution by genuinely independent choice. Third, we have found relevance in at least five characteristics of the aid itself: its religious content; its cash form; its divertibility or actually diversion to religious support; its supplantation of traditional items of religious school expense; and its substantiality. . . .

III

A

... [T]he plurality's new criterion ... appears to take evenhandedness neutrality and in practical terms promote it to a single and sufficient test for the establishment constitutionality of school aid. ... [T]he plurality's proposal would replace the principle of no aid with a formula for generous religious support.

First, the plurality treats an external observer's attribution of religious support to the government as the sole impermissible effect of a government aid scheme. ... State aid not attributed to the government would still violate a taxpayer's liberty of conscience, threaten to corrupt religion, and generate disputes over aid. ...

Second, the plurality apparently assumes as a fact that equal amounts of aid to religious and nonreligious schools will have exclusively secular and equal effects, on both external perception and on incentives to attend different schools. But there is no reason to believe that this will be the case; ... we have long recognized that unrestricted aid to religious schools will support religious teaching in addition to secular education. ...

Third, the plurality assumes that per capita distribution rules safeguard the same principles as independent, private choices. But that is clearly not so. ... Not the least of the significant differences between per capita aid and aid individually determined and directed is the right and genuine opportunity of the recipient to choose not to give the aid. To hold otherwise would be to license the government to donate funds to churches based on the number of their members. ...

B

The plurality's conception of evenhandedness does not, however, control the case[; Justice O'Connor's crucial concurrence] turns on the misapplication of accepted categories of school aid analysis. The facts most obviously relevant to the Chapter 2 scheme in Jefferson Parish are those showing divertibility and actual diversion in the circumstance of pervasively sectarian religious schools. The type of aid, the structure of the program, and the lack of effective safeguards clearly demonstrate the divertibility of the aid. While little is known about its use, owing to the anemic enforcement system in the parish, even the thin record before us reveals that actual diversion occurred. ... [28]

IV ...

The ... plurality's notion of evenhandedness neutrality as a practical guarantee of the validity of aid to sectarian schools would be the end of the principle of no aid to the schools' religious mission. ...

---

28. ... [U]nconstitutional supplantation [likely] occurred as well. ... Chapter 2 aid impermissibly relieved religious schools of some costs that they otherwise would have borne. ... Chapter 2 aid was significant in the development of teaching curriculums, the introduction of new programs, and the support of old ones. The ... concept of supplementing instead of supplanting was poorly understood by the sole government official administering the program, who apparently believed that the bar on supplanting was nothing more than a prohibition on paying for replacements of equipment that religious schools had previously purchased. ... [O]fficials of at least one religious school admitted that the government aid was used to create the library. ...

[T]he point is nailed down in the plurality's attack on the legitimacy of considering a school's pervasively sectarian character when judging whether aid to the school is likely to aid its religious mission. The relevance of this consideration is simply a matter of common sense: where religious indoctrination pervades school activities of children and adolescents, it takes great care to be able to aid the school without supporting the doctrinal effort. . . . The plurality nonetheless condemns any enquiry into the pervasiveness of doctrinal content as a remnant of anti-Catholic bigotry (as if evangelical Protestant schools and Orthodox Jewish yeshivas were never pervasively sectarian), and it equates a refusal to aid religious schools with hostility to religion (as if aid to religious teaching were not opposed in this very case by at least one religious respondent and numerous religious *amici curiae* in a tradition claiming descent from Roger Williams).

NOTES AND QUESTIONS

1. What Is the Holding in *Mitchell*?   *Mitchell* presents a bit of a puzzle. Five Justices take the view that proven use of direct government aid for religious purposes is unconstitutional. (The four-Justice plurality disagrees.) Seven Justices conclude that some of the Chapter 2 materials in *Mitchell* have, in fact, been used for religious purposes. (The two concurring Justices disagree, holding that any violations were, at worst, *de minimis*.) How, then, is the program upheld? The judgment upholding the program is based on a combination of two inconsistent theories, each rejected by a majority of the Court: four Justices hold that religious use of neutrally provided materials is not unconstitutional, and two Justices hold that there was no substantial religious use. This kind of voting paradox is not unusual in the Supreme Court, but it does seem odd.

Because Justice O'Connor's concurrence rests on a narrower rationale, it is the controlling opinion—even though Justice Thomas's opinion got more votes. Foreshadowing the majority opinion in *Zelman*, which she joined, Justice O'Connor states that a "genuine private choice program" is constitutional even if some, or many, of the beneficiaries use their share of funds for education with a religious component. But she treats direct aid to the school programs differently. They must have safeguards to prevent "diversion" of public funds to expressly religious uses—even if the direct aid is provided on a per-student basis.

This distinction could have significant effects on schools that incorporate religious elements in all of their programs. These schools would still be able to receive vouchers after *Zelman*, but they might have to change their programs in order to receive direct aid.

2. Direct Aid vs. Private Choice.   Why should a program of direct aid be constitutionally different from a program of private choice? Some direct-aid programs involve the legislature determining the amount of aid to a school on a discretionary basis, which may create too great a potential for government favoritism on religious matters. But if the aid a school receives is determined by a per-capita or per-student formula, doesn't it reflect the "genuine and independent choices of numerous beneficiaries" just as in *Zelman*? Justice O'Connor offers reasons why a per-capita direct aid program should still be more restricted. What do you think of her argument that direct aid just *looks* more like government endorsement? What about her argument that with per-capita direct aid, unlike a voucher system, the family using a religious school cannot refuse the share of aid attributable to them? Does it make sense to premise a major doctrinal distinction on the possibility of beneficiaries declining the benefits?

How does one tell a direct-aid program from a private-choice program? Suppose that in *Zelman*, the state of Ohio had sent voucher checks directly to the school, and parents then had to go to the school to endorse the check. Would that make the program one of direct aid?

In Rosenberger v. Rector and Visitors of the University of Virginia (p. 403), the Court approved including an evangelical Christian student magazine in the University's aid program because the University would make payments to third-party printers rather than to the magazine itself. Is that because this feature would make the aid "indirect" rather than direct? Why should this method of payment be more constitutionally acceptable than simply reimbursing the magazine for the printing bills it paid?

3. The End of the "Pervasively Sectarian" Category?   After Mitchell v. Helms, exactly how much is left of the Lemon v. Kurtzman approach? It seems that if a direct aid program that includes religious schools contains no safeguards against the use of the aid for religious teaching, such aid will be struck down.

But if a direct-aid program contains such safeguards, is it still subject to the objection that in a "pervasively sectarian" school, enforcement of the safeguards would create unconstitutional entanglement between church and state? Does Mitchell v. Helms do away with the "pervasively sectarian" category from *Lemon*? Justice Thomas's plurality opinion clearly would bury the doctrine. But Justices O'Connor and Breyer provide the key fifth and sixth votes; does their opinion join in the burial?

In Columbia Union College v. Oliver, 254 F.3d 496 (4th Cir. 2001) (hereafter *Columbia Union II*), the question was whether a college affiliated with the Seventh-Day Adventist Church could receive direct cash grants from the state of Maryland (the same grants that had been approved for Catholic colleges in Roemer v. Board of Public Works; see p. 396). The size of the grants was determined by a per-student formula (excluding theology students), and the funds could not be used for "sectarian" purposes. The state denied Columbia Union's application for $800,000 for math, computer, nursing, and lab programs on the ground that the college was pervasively sectarian. After several rounds of litigation, the court of appeals finally ruled for the college. The court held first that *Mitchell* had "replaced the pervasively sectarian test with a principle of 'neutrality plus' ": A neutral aid program should be approved if aid under it had not been diverted to religious uses and there were adequate safeguards against future diversion. The court found that aid to the college satisfied these factors; it added that aid to colleges should be evaluated "more leniently than aid to primary and secondary schools." *Columbia Union II*, 254 F.3d at 503-507.

This was not the only ground for the court's decision, however; as an independent holding, it affirmed the district court's ruling that the college was not pervasively sectarian. *Id.* at 508. The inquiry that the district court had to undertake on this issue may exemplify how awkward the "pervasively sectarian" inquiry could be. An earlier court of appeals opinion in the protracted litigation had directed the district court to consider four factors: "mandatory student worship services; an express preference for hiring and admissions for members of the affiliated church . . . ; academic courses implemented with the primary goal of religious indoctrination; and church dominance over college affairs as illustrated by its control over the board of trustees and financial expenditures." Columbia Union College v. Clarke, 159 F.3d 151, 163 (4th Cir. 1998) (hereafter *Columbia Union I*).

The facts under these standards were ambiguous. The college required attendance at prayer services, but excused more than half the student body for a variety of reasons. The catalog stated that "Christian principles should characterize every phase of college life," but it also included "a wide variety of traditional liberal arts courses" that could expose students "to a wide variety of academic disciplines." Although 36 of 40 full-time faculty members were Adventists, this need not have resulted from an actual policy of preferring church members. And although 90 percent of the board members were required to be Adventist members, the college inevitably had some day-to-day autonomy from the church. *Id.* at 164-167. In *Columbia Union I*, the court of appeals stated that the existing record would permit a reasonable fact-finder to conclude either way on the "pervasively sectarian" question, and it remanded for a trial to develop a fuller record. *Id.* at 164-165. The district court then concluded, based on thousands of pages of evidence, that the college was not pervasively sectarian, and in *Columbia Union II* the court of appeals affirmed, stating that the district court's finding on this "heavily fact intensive" question was "not clearly erroneous." 254 F.3d at 508, 510.

In *Columbia Union I*, Judge Wilkinson wrote a dissent from the decision to remand, arguing against a trial on the "pervasively sectarian" issue for two reasons. First,

> [t]he majority sends the clear message that these Establishment Clause questions can only be satisfactorily resolved upon a voluminous record that requires a court to scrutinize a religious institution's sectarian character with laser-like precision. . . .
>
> [R]eligious institutions will be without clear guidance as to when they may become too sectarian. [For example, m]ay Mount Saint Mary's [one of the Catholic colleges receiving aid] raise its requirement [for priests on the trustee board] to one-half [from one-fourth]? How are these colleges to know?

159 F.3d at 175-176 (Wilkinson, J., dissenting). Second, "a lengthy trial on Columbia Union's sectarian character denigrates the very values underlying our Constitution's religion clauses. . . . The scrutiny the majority now demands will encourage [institutions] to disown their own religious character in order to gain funding." The dissent noted that "[i]n a final plea to [state regulators] for funding[,] the president of Columbia Union College asked, 'If we recant, would we qualify?' Those words capture what this case is about." *Id.* at 175, 177.

Were the dissent's two objections to the pervasively sectarian doctrine—its lack of clear lines and its discrimination against religion—validated by the Supreme Court in *Mitchell*? Are the objections well founded?

4. Problems.

(a) **Disaster relief for churches.** Suppose that in the wake of the devastation left by Hurricane Katrina, property owners in the Gulf Coast area are eligible for federal disaster relief, under which they can have their dwellings or businesses rebuilt and submit invoices or receipts for the repairs (up to a certain limit) to the government. May a church apply for this relief to rebuild its sanctuary?

(b) **University radio station.** Fordham University is a large Catholic-affiliated university that probably would not be considered "pervasively sectarian" under the *Lemon* analysis. Fordham operates a noncommercial radio station that broadcasts 24 hours a day, seven days a week, providing news, music, and information. For an hour each week, at 11 A.M. on Sundays, it broadcasts a Roman Catholic Mass live from the university chapel. The U.S. Commerce Department provides funds for the construction of new facilities for radio stations. Fordham applied for funds to install a new antenna and rebuild its production room. It was denied on the basis that the weekly mass broadcast would contravene a Commerce Department regulation prohibiting "the use of federally funded equipment for purposes the essential thrust of which are sectarian."

Fordham challenged the denial, and the government responded that the restriction implements the Establishment Clause. What result under the approach from *Lemon* through *Aguilar* and *Ball*? See Fordham University v. Brown, 856 F. Supp. 684 (D.D.C. 1994) (upholding the denial as a reasonable attempt "to implement the Constitution's jurisprudence"). What result under current law, including *Rosenberger* and Mitchell v. Helms? Is the broadcast of the mass clear "actual diversion" of the aid to religious purposes? Does it matter that the vast majority of the station's programming is secular?

Note that the claim in the *Fordham* case was that the denial of the aid was not just not required by, but actually violated, the First Amendment. We will explore this issue in more detail in section E below. If the legislature cut off funds to a college radio station because of a weekly program that the legislature deemed "indecent," would there be a First Amendment problem? Is an exclusion based on religious programming different?

5. **Why the Shift in Aid Doctrine?**   Obviously, Establishment Clause doctrine regarding aid to education—whether indirect or direct—has changed significantly since the *Lemon* approach of the 1970s. What larger historical context explains this shift? Consider three hypotheses:

(a) **Racial desegregation.**   One of the principal issues facing the Court and the nation in the early 1970s was the racial desegregation of the schools. Swann v. Charlotte-Mecklenburg Board of Ed., 402 U.S. 1, the first Supreme Court decision to order mandatory busing for desegregation purposes, was decided in 1971, the same year as Lemon v. Kurtzman. This policy was soon extended to northern schools. Keyes v. School District No. 1, 413 U.S. 189 (1973); see also Dayton Bd. of Education v. Brinkman, 443 U.S. 526 (1979). These decisions met with massive resistance, including "white flight" to suburban school districts and to private schools. Thus, in the 1970s, private schools were often seen as vehicles for avoidance of the Court's desegregation efforts, and government aid to private schools was seen as an obstacle to integration rather than as a means of ensuring pluralism and diversity in education. In Norwood v. Harrison, 413 U.S. 455 (1973)—decided on the same day as *Nyquist* (see p. 381)—the Court invalidated a Mississippi program in which the state lent textbooks to students in racially segregated private schools, on the ground that this is "a form of financial assistance inuring to the benefit of the private schools themselves." This was in considerable tension with the earlier holding in *Allen*, upholding a textbook loan program partly on theory that it benefited students, not religious schools. Perhaps it is no surprise that some of the Justices most committed to desegregation—such as Justices Marshall and Brennan—urged overruling *Allen*. More generally, the Court may have been using Establishment Clause doctrine as a convenient doctrinal peg for an effort to protect the desegregation program from the escape hatch of private education. See Douglas Laycock, The Underlying Unity of Separation and Neutrality, 46 Emory L.J. 43, 61-62 (1997); Berg, 33 Loy. U. Chi. L.J. at 158-160.

By the time of *Agostini*, mandatory busing for desegregation was being abandoned in many quarters. See Oklahoma City Public Schools v. Dowell, 498 U.S. 237 (1991) (allowing a school district with a prior policy of intentional segregation to dismantle a busing plan and institute neighborhood school assignments). The public schools of most large cities in the United States were more racially segregated than ever, and many provided education of deplorable quality. Moreover, inner-city private (especially Catholic) schools were increasingly seen as among the most successfully integrated schools in many cities and as effective providers of quality education to the underprivileged. See p. 379 above. See also Nicole Stelle Garnett and Richard W. Garnett, School Choice, The First Amendment, and Social Justice, 4 Tex. Rev. L. & Pol'y 301, 341-347 (2000). Perhaps it is not surprising that the Court now takes a different view of these schools. But for a warning that increased resort to religious schools may increase segregation, see Robert K. Vischer, Racial Segregation in American Churches and Its Implications for School Vouchers, 53 Fla. L. Rev. 193 (2001).

(b) State action. In the 1960s the Supreme Court adopted an expansive understanding of state action doctrine under the Fourteenth Amendment. See, e.g., Burton v. Wilmington Parking Auth., 365 U.S. 715 (1961). The impetus behind this movement, most would agree, was to apply the nondiscrimination norms of the Equal Protection Clause to important nongovernmental institutions. Although the Court never said so, some Justices took the view that receipt of government funding was sufficient to turn a school into a state actor. The combination of Engel v. Vitale, 370 U.S. 421 (1962), which outlawed religious exercises in public schools, and this view of state action leads to the conclusion that public aid may not go to schools that engage in religious exercises. See, for example, Justice Douglas's concurrence in *Lemon*, 403 U.S. at 632-633:

> Public financial support of parochial schools puts those schools under disabilities with which they were not previously burdened. For, as we held in Cooper v. Aaron [358 U.S. 1 (1958)], governmental activities relating to schools "must be exercised consistent with federal constitutional requirements." There we were concerned with equal protection; here we are faced with issues of Establishment of religion and its Free Exercise as those concepts are used in the First Amendment.
>
> Where the governmental activity is the financing of the private school, the various limitations or restraints imposed by the Constitution on state governments come into play. . . . [O]nce one of the States finances a private school, it is duty-bound to make certain that the school stays within secular bounds. . . .

By the 1980s, the pressure to expand state action doctrine had subsided, in part because Congress extended equal protection by statute—Title VI of the Civil Rights Act of 1964 and similar legislation attaching nondiscrimination requirements to the receipt of federal funds, as a statutory matter. In Rendell-Baker v. Kohn, 457 U.S. 830 (1982), and Blum v. Yaretsky, 457 U.S. 991 (1982), the Court held that the receipt of governmental grants is not sufficient to make the recipient organization a state actor. Rather, "constitutional standards are invoked only when it can be said that the State is *responsible* for the specific conduct of which the plaintiff complains. . . . [A] State normally can be held responsible for a private decision only when it has exercised coercive power or has provided such significant encouragement, either overt or covert, that the choice must in law be deemed to be that of the State." *Blum*, 457 U.S. at 1004. Applied in the context of aid to private schools, this understanding of state action doctrine supports the result in *Agostini* and *Mitchell*: The religious exercises in private schools cannot be attributed to the state if the funding was neutrally provided and the government itself plays no part in the decision to include a religious element in the education.

(c) **Attitudes toward religion.** Some commentators have suggested that the Court's aid-to-education opinions during the 1970s evinced a hostility, or at least an indifference, toward religion, and particularly toward Catholicism. See Michael W. McConnell, Religious Freedom at a Crossroads, 59 U. Chi. L. Rev. 115, 120-127 (1992). In part, this may have reflected a scientific or rationalist perspective, which understands religion as inherently subjective and nonrational. In part, as we have discussed above (pp. 370, 379), it may have been a reflection of common perceptions of pre-Vatican II Catholicism as doctrinaire and opposed to free thought.

More recently, postmodern currents in American intellectual life have cast doubt on the distinction between "objective reason" and "subjective opinion," thus restoring the legitimacy of religious worldviews in the competition of ideas. See Frederick M. Gedicks, Public Life and Hostility to Religion, 78 Va. L. Rev. 671 (1992); Larry Alexander, Liberalism, Religion, and the Unity of Epistemology, 30 San Diego L. Rev. 763 (1993) (disputing claim that religion is epistemologically distinct from other normative positions). The idea that religious perspectives have a legitimate place to play in education (as opposed to being "interjected" into the curriculum, as the Court's opinions earlier suggested) has accordingly gained in respectability. See Warren A. Nord, Religion and American Education: Rethinking a National Dilemma (1995).

Moreover, attitudes toward Catholicism have dramatically changed, especially in the wake of the election of President John F. Kennedy and the changes of the Second Vatican Council. Today, four products of Catholic education sit as Justices of the Supreme Court (Roberts, Scalia, Kennedy, and Thomas).[*] Finally, while the vast majority of religious schools still were Catholic in the early 1970s, religious schools are now operated or used by large numbers of non-Catholics as well. See Ira C. Lupu, The Increasingly Anachronistic Case Against School Vouchers, 13 Notre Dame J.L. Ethics & Pub. Pol'y 375, 386-387 (1999). These wider changes in American cultural attitudes may have influenced the Court's thinking about religion and education.

---

[*] The fifth member of the new Catholic majority on the Court, Samuel Alito, was the son of a public school teacher and attended public schools—perhaps symbolizing the fact that even as Catholic education came to be viewed as more "mainstream," an increasing percentage of Catholics used public schools.

E. STATE RESTRICTIONS ON AID TO RELIGION: IS NEUTRALITY CONSTITUTIONALLY REQUIRED?

ROSENBERGER v. RECTOR AND VISITORS OF UNIV. OF VIRGINIA, 515 U.S. 819 (1995): As already discussed (p. 403), *Rosenberger* involved a program under which the University used a student-activity-fee fund to pay the bills of student organizations reflecting a wide variety of interests and perspectives—in one year, 118 student groups including 15 publications. The program denied funding to religious publications, that is, those that "primarily promot[e] or manifes[t]" a belief "about a deity or an ultimate reality." *Wide Awake*, a student magazine addressing a variety of issues, religious and social, from an evangelical Christian perspective, was denied funding and challenged the denial on the ground that it violated its rights under the Free Speech Clause. It asserted, and the Court accepted, that by its program for assisting student organizations the University had created a "limited public forum," making its facilities available for student expression. The Court ruled, 5-4, that the exclusion of *Wide Awake* from this forum was unconstitutional:

"It is axiomatic that the government may not regulate speech based on its substantive content or the message it conveys. . . . In the realm of private speech or expression, government regulation may not favor one speaker over another. Discrimination against speech because of its message is presumed to be unconstitutional. . . . When the government targets not subject matter but particular views taken by speakers on a subject, the violation of the First Amendment is all the more blatant. Viewpoint discrimination is thus an egregious form of content discrimination. The government must abstain from regulating speech when the specific motivating ideology or the opinion or perspective of the speaker is the rationale for the restriction. . . .

"The [student-activity funding program] is a forum more in a metaphysical than in a spatial or geographic sense, but the same principles are applicable. [I]n Lamb's Chapel [v. Center Moriches School Dist. (1993)], a school district had opened school facilities for use after school hours by community groups for a wide variety of social, civic, and recreational purposes. The district, however, had enacted a formal policy against opening facilities to groups for religious purposes. Invoking its policy, the district rejected a request from a group desiring to show a film series addressing various child-rearing questions from a 'Christian perspective.' . . . Our conclusion was unanimous: '[I]t discriminates on the basis of viewpoint to permit school property to be used for the presentation of all views about family issues and child-rearing except those dealing with the subject matter from a religious standpoint.'

"The University does acknowledge . . . that 'ideologically driven attempts to suppress a particular point of view are presumptively unconstitutional in funding, as in other contexts,' but insists that this case does not present that issue because the Guidelines draw lines based on content, not viewpoint. . . . We conclude, nonetheless, that here, as in *Lamb's Chapel*, viewpoint discrimination is the proper way to interpret the University's objections to Wide Awake. By the very terms of the SAF prohibition, the University does not exclude religion as a subject matter but selects for disfavored treatment those student journalistic efforts with religious editorial viewpoints. Religion may be a vast area of inquiry, but it also provides, as it did here, a specific premise, a perspective, a standpoint from which a variety of subjects may be discussed and considered. The prohibited perspective, not the general subject matter, resulted in the refusal to make third-party payments, for the subjects discussed were otherwise within the approved category of publications."

Justice Souter's dissent argued that the University's exclusion covered atheistic as well as theistic publications and therefore did not discriminate against a particular viewpoint. The majority answered that this argument "reflects an insupportable assumption that all debate is bipolar and that anti-religious speech is the only response to religious speech. Our understanding of the complex and multifaceted nature of public discourse has not embraced such a contrived description of the marketplace of ideas. If the topic of debate is, for example, racism, then exclusion of several views on that problem is just as offensive to the First Amendment as exclusion of only one. It is as objectionable to exclude both a theistic and an atheistic perspective on the debate as it is to exclude one, the other, or yet another political, economic, or social viewpoint. The dissent's declaration that debate is not skewed so long as multiple voices are silenced is simply wrong; the debate is skewed in multiple ways. . . .

". . . [W]hen the State is the speaker, it may make content-based choices. When the University determines the content of the education it provides, it is the University speaking, and we have permitted the government to regulate the content of what is or is not expressed when it is the speaker or when it enlists private entities to convey its own message. In the same vein, . . . [w]hen the government disburses public funds to private entities to convey a governmental message, it may take legitimate and appropriate steps to ensure that its message is neither garbled nor distorted by the grantee.

"It does not follow, however, . . . that viewpoint-based restrictions are proper when the University does not itself speak or subsidize transmittal of a message it favors but instead expends funds to encourage a diversity of views from private speakers. . . .

"The University urges that, from a constitutional standpoint, funding of speech differs from provision of access to facilities [as in *Lamb's Chapel*] because money is scarce and physical facilities are not. [But the] government cannot justify viewpoint discrimination among private speakers on the economic fact of scarcity. Had the meeting rooms in *Lamb's Chapel* been scarce, had the demand been greater than the supply, our decision would have been no different. It would have been incumbent on the State, of course, to ration or allocate the scarce resources on some acceptable neutral principle; but nothing in our decision indicated that scarcity would give the State the right to exercise viewpoint discrimination that is otherwise impermissible."

NOTES AND QUESTIONS

1. Funding Denials and Viewpoint Discrimination. *Rosenberger* appeared to be an especially sharp break because it held that sometimes a religious activity or organization is not just *permitted* to receive financial assistance on the same terms as other activities, but is *constitutionally entitled* to equal assistance.

The Court reasoned that the University's exclusion of "religious activities" (defined as an activity "which primarily promotes or manifests a particular belief in or about a deity or an absolute reality") constituted viewpoint discrimination. This category of restriction is the most suspect under the Free Speech Clause because by discriminating against a viewpoint the government skews the public debate on whatever topic is being debated. We will examine free speech law in more detail below (Part V-B). But basically, if the government creates opportunities for private persons to speak on its property, it is almost always forbidden to restrict or disfavor one viewpoint, as opposed to others, on a given topic. On the other hand, the government might create a forum for expression in a government setting and limit it to certain persons or to certain subject matter: for example, an electronic listserve for public university students to discuss school-related matters. The school could exclude discussion of national politics from the listserve, but it likely could not exclude a message concerning a university-related matter because of the view expressed in it (e.g., excluding a student's message about the content of the curriculum simply because the message was critical of the existing curriculum). These are simple examples, however, and many cases, including *Rosenberger* itself, are more complex.

In a portion of the excerpt above, the majority responds to Justice Souter's argument that the University had not excluded any viewpoint, but had merely excluded the "subject matter" of religion, and therefore had not "skewed debate by funding one religion but not its competitors." Implicit in this argument is the idea that the only "competitors" to a particular religious worldview are other religions, atheism, and agnosticism. Does this approach make sense? For example, could a state university exclude "feminist publications" so long as it also excluded "anti-feminist" publications—all publications "primarily promoting or manifesting a view about the relation between gender and power"? Could a feminist publication argue that this skews the debate by implying that gender oppression is not a pressing public concern? Could the same argument be made concerning the exclusion of "religious" publications?

In a subsequent case, Justice Souter—again in dissent—argued that a statute requiring the National Endowment for the Arts (NEA), in making grants to artists, to take into consideration "general standards of decency and respect for the diverse beliefs and values of the American public" was viewpoint discriminatory. National Endowment for the Arts v. Finley, 524 U.S. 569, 605-606 (1998) (Souter, J., dissenting):

> [R]estrictions turning on decency, especially those couched in terms of "general standards of decency," are quintessentially viewpoint based: they require discrimination on the basis of conformity with mainstream mores. . . . Just as self-evidently, a statute disfavoring speech that fails to respect America's "diverse beliefs and values" is the very model of viewpoint discrimination; it penalizes any view disrespectful to any belief or value espoused by someone in the American populace.

Do you agree? Can you think of any point of view that cannot be expressed "decently" and with "respect" for other views? Under Justice Souter's view, would it be constitutional to prohibit the NEA from funding "religious" art (that is, art "manifesting a belief in or about a deity")? Would this restriction be constitutionally required? Is Justice Souter's understanding of viewpoint discrimination consistent in the two cases?

2. How Far Are Funding Exclusions Prohibited?   Did *Rosenberger* stand for the principle that activities reflecting religious viewpoints may not be excluded from any program of government benefits? Such a principle could strike down many restrictions on funding of religious activities. Recall, for example, that during the late 1800s and early 1900s the large majority of states adopted prohibitions on the funding of religious K-12 schools or the religious teaching in them (see section B above, pp. 362-366). Do such restrictions violate the First Amendment? Consider the following decision.

LOCKE v. DAVEY
540 U.S. 712 (2004)

Chief Justice REHNQUIST delivered the opinion of the Court.

The State of Washington established the Promise Scholarship Program to assist academically gifted students with postsecondary education expenses. In accordance with the State Constitution, students may not use the scholarship at an institution where they are pursuing a degree in devotional theology. We hold that such an exclusion from an otherwise inclusive aid program does not violate the Free Exercise Clause of the First Amendment.

The Washington State Legislature found that "[s]tudents who work hard . . . and successfully complete high school with high academic marks may not have the financial ability to attend college because they cannot obtain financial aid or the financial aid is insufficient." Wash. Rev. Code § 28B.119.005. In 1999, to assist these high-achieving students, the legislature created the Promise Scholarship Program, which provides a scholarship, renewable for one year, to eligible students for postsecondary education expenses. Students may spend their funds on any education-related expense, including room and board. The scholarships are funded through the State's general fund, and their amount varies each year depending on the annual appropriation, which is evenly prorated among the eligible students. The scholarship was worth $1,125 for academic year 1999-2000 and $1,542 for 2000-2001.

To be eligible for the scholarship, a student must meet academic, income, and enrollment requirements. A student must graduate from a Washington public or private high school and either graduate in the top 15% of his graduating class, or attain on the first attempt a cumulative score of 1,200 or better on the Scholastic Assessment Test I or a score of 27 or better on the American College Test. The student's family income must be less than 135% of the State's median. Finally, the student must enroll "at least half time in an eligible postsecondary institution in the state of Washington," and may not pursue a degree in theology at that institution while receiving the scholarship. Private institutions, including those religiously affiliated, qualify as "eligible postsecondary institution[s]" if they are accredited by a nationally recognized accrediting body. A "degree in theology" is not defined in the statute, but, as both parties concede, the statute simply codifies the State's constitutional prohibition on providing funds to students to pursue degrees that are "devotional in nature or designed to induce religious faith." [Citing parties' briefs.]

Respondent, Joshua Davey, was awarded a Promise Scholarship, and chose to attend Northwest College. Northwest is a private, Christian college affiliated with the Assemblies of God denomination, and is an eligible institution under the Promise Scholarship Program. Davey had "planned for many years to attend a Bible college and to prepare [himself] through that college training for a lifetime of ministry, specifically as a church pastor." To that end, when he enrolled in Northwest College, he decided to pursue a double major in pastoral ministries and business management/administration. There is no dispute that the pastoral ministries degree is devotional and therefore excluded under the Promise Scholarship Program.

At the beginning of the 1999-2000 academic year, Davey met with Northwest's director of financial aid. He learned for the first time at this meeting that he could not use his scholarship to pursue a devotional theology degree. He was informed that to receive the funds appropriated for his use, he must certify in writing that he was not pursuing such a degree at Northwest. He refused to sign the form and did not receive any scholarship funds. Davey then [sued state officials in federal court] to enjoin the State from refusing to award the scholarship solely because a student is pursuing a devotional theology degree, and for damages. He argued the denial of his scholarship based on his decision to pursue a theology degree violated, *inter alia,* the Free Exercise, Establishment, and Free Speech Clauses of the First Amendment, as incorporated by the Fourteenth Amendment, and the Equal Protection Clause of the Fourteenth Amendment. [The district court granted summary judgment for the state, but the court of appeals reversed and ordered judgment for Davey.]

[The two Religion] Clauses, the Establishment Clause and the Free Exercise Clause, are frequently in tension. Yet we have long said that "there is room for play in the joints" between them. In other words, there are some state actions permitted by the Establishment Clause but not required by the Free Exercise Clause. This case involves that "play in the joints" described above. Under our Establishment Clause precedent, the link between government funds and religious training is broken by the independent and private choice of recipients. See Zelman v. Simmons-Harris [p. 403]. As such, there is no doubt that the State could, consistent with the Federal Constitution, permit Promise Scholars to pursue a degree in devotional theology, see Witters v. Dept. of Services [p. 399], and the State does not contend otherwise. The question before us, however, is whether Washington, pursuant to its own constitution,[1] which has been authoritatively interpreted as prohibiting even indirectly funding religious instruction that will prepare students for the ministry, see Witters v. State Comm'n for the Blind (Wash. 1989), can deny them such funding without violating the Free Exercise Clause.

Davey urges us to answer that question in the negative. He contends that under the rule we enunciated in Church of Lukumi Babalu Aye v. Hialeah [p. 162], the program is presumptively unconstitutional because it is not facially

---

1. The relevant provision of the Washington Constitution, Art. I, § 11, states:

"Religious Freedom. Absolute freedom of conscience in all matters of religious sentiment, belief and worship, shall be guaranteed to every individual, and no one shall be molested or disturbed in person or property on account of religion; but the liberty of conscience hereby secured shall not be so construed as to excuse acts of licentiousness or justify practices inconsistent with the peace and safety of the state. No public money or property shall be appropriated for or applied to any religious worship, exercise or instruction, or the support of any religious establishment."

neutral with respect to religion.[2] We reject his claim of presumptive unconstitutionality, however; to do otherwise would extend the *Lukumi* line of cases well beyond not only their facts but their reasoning. In *Lukumi*, the city of Hialeah made it a crime to engage in certain kinds of animal slaughter. We found that the law sought to suppress ritualistic animal sacrifices of the Santeria religion. In the present case, the State's disfavor of religion (if it can be called that) is of a far milder kind. It imposes neither criminal nor civil sanctions on any type of religious service or rite. It does not deny to ministers the right to participate in the political affairs of the community. See McDaniel v. Paty [p. 666]. And it does not require students to choose between their religious beliefs and receiving a government benefit.[3] See Sherbert v. Verner [p. 124]. The State has merely chosen not to fund a distinct category of instruction.

Justice Scalia argues, however, that generally available benefits are part of the "baseline against which burdens on religion are measured." Because the Promise Scholarship Program funds training for all secular professions, Justice Scalia contends the State must also fund training for religious professions. But training for religious professions and training for secular professions are not fungible. Training someone to lead a congregation is an essentially religious endeavor. Indeed, majoring in devotional theology is akin to a religious calling as well as an academic pursuit. And the subject of religion is one in which both the United States and state constitutions embody distinct views—in favor of free exercise, but opposed to establishment—that find no counterpart with respect to other callings or professions. That a State would deal differently with religious education for the ministry than with education for other callings is a product of these views, not evidence of hostility toward religion.

Even though the differently worded Washington Constitution draws a more stringent line than that drawn by the United States Constitution, the interest it seeks to further is scarcely novel. In fact, we can think of few areas in which a State's antiestablishment interests come more into play.[4] Since the founding of our country, there have been popular uprisings against procuring taxpayer funds to support church leaders, which was one of the hallmarks of an "established" religion.[5] [See, e.g.,] J. Madison, Memorial and Remonstrance Against

2. Davey, relying on Rosenberger v. Rector and Visitors of Univ. of Va. [p. 435], contends that the Promise Scholarship Program is an unconstitutional viewpoint restriction on speech. But the Promise Scholarship Program is not a forum for speech. The purpose of the Promise Scholarship Program is to assist students from low- and middle-income families with the cost of postsecondary education, not to " 'encourage a diversity of views from private speakers' " [Quoting *Rosenberger.*] Our cases dealing with speech forums are simply inapplicable. Davey also argues that the Equal Protection Clause protects against discrimination on the basis of religion. Because we hold that the program is not a violation of the Free Exercise Clause, however, we apply rational-basis scrutiny to his equal protection claims.
3. Promise Scholars may still use their scholarship to pursue a secular degree at a different institution from where they are studying devotional theology.
4. Justice Scalia notes that the State's "philosophical preference" to protect individual conscience is potentially without limit; however, the only interest at issue here is the State's interest in not funding the religious training of clergy. Nothing in our opinion suggests that the State may justify any interest that its "philosophical preference" commands.
5. Perhaps the most famous example of public backlash is the defeat of "A Bill Establishing A Provision for Teachers of the Christian Religion" [p. 48] in the Virginia Legislature. The bill sought to assess a tax for "Christian teachers," and was rejected after a public outcry. In its stead, the "Virginia Bill for Religious Liberty," which was originally written by Thomas Jefferson, was enacted. This bill [p. 54] guaranteed "that no man shall be compelled to frequent or support any religious worship, place, or ministry whatsoever."

Religious Assessments [p. 49] (noting the dangers to civil liberties from supporting clergy with public funds).

Most States that sought to avoid an establishment of religion around the time of the founding placed in their constitutions formal prohibitions against using tax funds to support the ministry. *E.g.*, Ga. Const., Art. IV, §5 (1789), reprinted in 2 Federal and State Constitutions, Colonial Charters and Other Organic Laws 789 (F. Thorpe ed., 1909) (reprinted 1993) ("All persons shall have the free exercise of religion, without being obliged to contribute to the support of any religious profession but their own"); Pa. Const., Art. II (1776) in *id.* ("[N]o man ought or of right can be compelled to attend any religious worship, or erect or support any place of worship, or maintain any ministry, contrary to, or against, his own free will and consent"); [also six other state constitutional provisions from this period]. The plain text of these constitutional provisions prohibited *any* tax dollars from supporting the clergy.

We have found nothing to indicate, as Justice Scalia contends, that these provisions would not have applied so long as the State equally supported other professions or if the amount at stake was *de minimis*. That early state constitutions saw no problem in explicitly excluding *only* the ministry from receiving state dollars reinforces our conclusion that religious instruction is of a different ilk.[6]

Far from evincing the hostility toward religion which was manifest in *Lukumi*, we believe that the entirety of the Promise Scholarship Program goes a long way toward including religion in its benefits.[7] The program permits students to attend pervasively religious schools, so long as they are accredited. As Northwest advertises, its "concept of education is distinctly Christian in the evangelical sense." It prepares *all* of its students, "through instruction, through modeling, [and] through [its] classes, to use . . . the Bible as their guide, as the truth," no matter their chosen profession. And under the Promise Scholarship Program's current guidelines, students are still eligible to take devotional theology courses. Davey notes all students at Northwest are required to take at least four devotional courses, "Exploring the Bible," "Principles of Spiritual Development," "Evangelism in the Christian Life," and "Christian Doctrine," and some students may have additional religious requirements as part of their majors.

In short, we find neither in the history or text of Article I, §11 of the Washington Constitution, nor in the operation of the Promise Scholarship Program, anything

6. The *amici* contend that Washington's Constitution was born of religious bigotry because it contains a so-called "Blaine Amendment," which has been linked with anti-Catholicism. [See, e.g.,] Mitchell v. Helms (plurality opinion) [p. 417]. As the State notes and Davey does not dispute, however, the provision in question is not a Blaine Amendment. The enabling Act of 1889, which authorized the drafting of the Washington Constitution, required the state constitution to include a provision "for the establishment and maintenance of systems of public schools, which shall be . . . free from sectarian control." This provision was included in Article IX, §§ 4, of the Washington Constitution ("All schools maintained and supported wholly or in part by the public funds shall be forever free from sectarian control or influence"), and is not at issue in this case. Neither Davey nor *amici* have established a credible connection between the Blaine Amendment and Article I, § 11, the relevant constitutional provision. Accordingly, the Blaine Amendment's history is simply not before us.

7. Washington has also been solicitous in ensuring that its constitution is not hostile towards religion, and at least in some respects, its constitution provides greater protection of religious liberties than the Free Exercise Clause, see First Covenant Church of Seattle v. Seattle [p. 161] (rejecting standard in Employment Division v. Smith in favor of more protective rule). We have found nothing in Washington's overall approach that indicates it "single[s] out" anyone "for special burdens on the basis of . . . religious callings" as Justice Scalia contends.

that suggests animus towards religion. Given the historic and substantial state interest at issue, we therefore cannot conclude that the denial of funding for vocational religious instruction alone is inherently constitutionally suspect.

Without a presumption of unconstitutionality, Davey's claim must fail. The State's interest in not funding the pursuit of devotional degrees is substantial and the exclusion of such funding places a relatively minor burden on Promise Scholars. If any room exists between the two Religion Clauses, it must be here. We need not venture further into this difficult area in order to uphold the Promise Scholarship Program as currently operated by the State of Washington.

Justice Scalia, with whom Justice Thomas joins, dissenting.

In *Lukumi*, the majority opinion held that "[a] law burdening religious practice that is not neutral . . . must undergo the most rigorous of scrutiny," and that "the minimum requirement of neutrality is that a law not discriminate on its face." The concurrence of two Justices stated that "[w]hen a law discriminates against religion as such, . . . it automatically will fail strict scrutiny." *Id.* (Blackmun, J., joined by O'Connor, J., concurring in judgment). . . . These opinions are irreconcilable with today's decision, which sustains a public benefits program that facially discriminates against religion.

I

We articulated the principle that governs this case more than 50 years ago in Everson v. Board of Education [p. 339]:

> New Jersey cannot hamper its citizens in the free exercise of their own religion. Consequently, it cannot exclude individual Catholics, Lutherans, Mohammedans, Baptists, Jews, Methodists, Non-believers, Presbyterians, or the members of any other faith, because of their faith, or lack of it, from receiving the benefits of public welfare legislation.

When the State makes a public benefit generally available, that benefit becomes part of the baseline against which burdens on religion are measured; and when the State withholds that benefit from some individuals solely on the basis of religion, it violates the Free Exercise Clause no less than if it had imposed a special tax.

That is precisely what the State of Washington has done here. It has created a generally available public benefit, whose receipt is conditioned only on academic performance, income, and attendance at an accredited school. It has then carved out a solitary course of study for exclusion: theology. No field of study but religion is singled out for disfavor in this fashion. Davey is not asking for a special benefit to which others are not entitled. He seeks only *equal* treatment—the right to direct his scholarship to his chosen course of study, a right every other Promise Scholar enjoys.

The Court's reference to historical "popular uprisings against procuring taxpayer funds to support church leaders" is therefore quite misplaced. That history involved not the inclusion of religious ministers in public benefits programs like the one at issue here, but laws that singled them out for financial aid. For example, the Virginia bill at which Madison's Remonstrance was directed provided: "[F]or the support of Christian teachers . . . [a] sum payable for tax on the property within this Commonwealth, is hereby assessed." Laws supporting the clergy in other States operated in a similar fashion. See S. Cobb, The Rise of Religious Liberty in America 131, 169, 270, 295, 304, 386 (1902). One can concede the Framers' hostility to funding the clergy *specifically*, but that says nothing about whether the clergy had to be excluded from benefits the State made available to all. No one would seriously contend, for example, that the Framers would have barred ministers from using public roads on their way to church.[1]

The Court does not dispute that the Free Exercise Clause places some constraints on public benefits programs, but finds none here, based on a principle of "play in the joints." I use the term "principle" loosely, for that is not so much a legal principle as a refusal to apply *any* principle when faced with competing constitutional directives. There is nothing anomalous about constitutional commands that abut. A municipality hiring public contractors may not discriminate *against* blacks or *in favor of* them; it cannot discriminate a little bit each way and then plead "play in the joints" when haled into court. If the Religion Clauses demand neutrality, we must enforce them, in hard cases as well as easy ones. Even if "play in the joints" were a valid legal principle, surely it would apply only when it was a close call whether complying with one of the Religion Clauses would violate the other. But that is not the case here. It is not just that "the State could, consistent with the Federal Constitution, permit Promise Scholars to pursue a degree in devotional theology." The establishment question *would not even be close*, as is evident from the fact that this Court's decision in *Witters* was unanimous. Perhaps some formally neutral public benefits programs are so gerrymandered and devoid of plausible secular purpose that they might raise specters of state aid to religion, but an evenhanded Promise Scholarship Program is not among them.

In any case, the State already has all the play in the joints it needs. There are any number of ways it could respect both its unusually sensitive concern for the conscience of its taxpayers *and* the Federal Free Exercise Clause. It could make the scholarships redeemable only at public universities (where it sets the curriculum), or only for select courses of study. Either option would replace a program that facially discriminates against religion with one that just happens not to subsidize it. The State could also simply abandon the scholarship program altogether. If that seems a dear price to pay for freedom of conscience, it is only because the State has defined that freedom so broadly that it would be offended by a program with such an incidental, indirect religious effect.

What is the nature of the State's asserted interest here? It cannot be protecting the pocketbooks of its citizens; given the tiny fraction of Promise Scholars who would pursue theology degrees, the amount of any citizen's tax bill at stake is *de minimis*. It cannot be preventing mistaken appearance of endorsement;

---

1. Equally misplaced is the Court's reliance on founding-era state constitutional provisions that prohibited the use of tax funds to support the ministry. There is no doubt what these provisions were directed against: measures of the sort discussed earlier in text, singling out the clergy for public support. The Court offers no historical support for the proposition that they were meant to exclude clergymen from general benefits available to all citizens. In choosing to interpret them in that fashion, the Court needlessly gives them a meaning that not only is contrary to our Religion Clause jurisprudence, but has no logical stopping-point short of the absurd. No State with such a constitutional provision has, so far as I know, ever prohibited the hiring of public employees who use their salary to conduct ministries, or excluded ministers from generally available disability or unemployment benefits.

where a State merely declines to penalize students for selecting a religious major, "[n]o reasonable observer is likely to draw . . . an inference that the State itself is endorsing a religious practice or belief." *Witters* (O'Connor, J., concurring). Nor can Washington's exclusion be defended as a means of assuring that the State will neither favor nor disfavor Davey in his religious calling. Davey will throughout his life contribute to the public fisc through sales taxes on personal purchases, property taxes on his home, and so on; and nothing in the Court's opinion turns on whether Davey winds up a net winner or loser in the State's tax-and-spend scheme.

No, the interest to which the Court defers is not fear of a conceivable Establishment Clause violation, budget constraints, avoidance of endorsement, or substantive neutrality—none of these. It is a pure philosophical preference: the State's opinion that it would violate taxpayers' freedom of conscience *not* to discriminate against candidates for the ministry. This sort of protection of "freedom of conscience" has no logical limit and can justify the singling out of religion for exclusion from public programs in virtually any context. The Court never says whether it deems this interest compelling (the opinion is devoid of any mention of standard of review) but, self-evidently, it is not.[2]

II

The Court makes no serious attempt to defend the program's neutrality, and instead identifies two features thought to render its discrimination less offensive. The first is the lightness of Davey's burden. The Court offers no authority for approving facial discrimination against religion simply because its material consequences are not severe. I might understand such a test if we were still in the business of reviewing facially neutral laws that merely happen to burden some individual's religious exercise, but we are not. See Employment Division v. Smith. Discrimination *on the face of a statute* is something else. The indignity of being singled out for special burdens on the basis of one's religious calling is so profound that the concrete harm produced can never be dismissed as insubstantial. The Court has not required proof of "substantial" concrete harm with other forms of discrimination, see, e.g., Brown v. Board of Education—and it should not do so here.

Even if there were some threshold quantum-of-harm requirement, surely Davey has satisfied it. The First Amendment, after all, guarantees *free* exercise

---

2. The Court argues that those pursuing theology majors are not comparable to other Promise Scholars because "training for religious professions and training for secular professions are not fungible." That may well be, but all it proves is that the State has a r*ational basis* for treating religion differently. [But i]f religious discrimination required only a rational basis, the Free Exercise Clause would impose no constraints other than those the Constitution already imposes on all government action. The question is not whether theology majors are different, but whether the differences are substantial enough to justify a discriminatory financial penalty that the State inflicts on no other major. Plainly they are not.

Equally unpersuasive is the Court's argument that the State may discriminate against theology majors in distributing public benefits because the Establishment Clause and its state counterparts are themselves discriminatory. The Court's premise is true at some level of abstraction—the Establishment Clause discriminates against religion by singling it out as the one thing a State may not establish. All this proves is that a State has a compelling interest in not committing *actual* Establishment Clause violations. Cf. Widmar v. Vincent [p. 622]. We have never inferred from this principle that a State has a constitutionally sufficient interest in discriminating against religion in whatever other context it pleases, so long as it claims some connection, however attenuated, to establishment concerns.

of religion, and when the State exacts a financial penalty of almost $3,000 for religious exercise—whether by tax or by forfeiture of an otherwise available benefit—religious practice is anything *but* free. The Court's only response is that "Promise Scholars may still use their scholarship to pursue a secular degree at a different institution from where they are studying devotional theology." But part of what makes a Promise Scholarship attractive is that the recipient can apply it to his *preferred* course of study at his *preferred* accredited institution. That is part of the "benefit" the State confers. The Court distinguishes our precedents only by swapping the benefit to which Davey was actually entitled (a scholarship for his chosen course of study) with another, less valuable one (a scholarship for any course of study *but* his chosen one). On such reasoning, any facially discriminatory benefits program can be redeemed simply by redefining what it guarantees.

The other reason the Court thinks this particular facial discrimination less offensive is that the scholarship program was not motivated by animus toward religion. The Court does not explain why the legislature's motive matters, and I fail to see why it should. If a State deprives a citizen of trial by jury or passes an *ex post facto* law, we do not pause to investigate whether it was actually trying to accomplish the evil the Constitution prohibits. It is sufficient that the citizen's rights have been infringed. . . .

The Court has not approached other forms of discrimination this way. When we declared racial segregation unconstitutional, we did not ask whether the State had originally adopted the regime, not out of "animus" against blacks, but because of a well-meaning but misguided belief that the races would be better off apart. It was sufficient to note the current effect of segregation on racial minorities. See *Brown*. . . . We do sometimes look to legislative intent to smoke out more subtle instances of discrimination, but we do so as a *supplement* to the core guarantee of facially equal treatment, not as a replacement for it.

[W]e have rejected the Court's methodology in this very context. In McDaniel v. Paty, . . . the State defended the statute [excluding clergy from the legislature] as an attempt to be faithful to its constitutional separation of church and state, and we accepted that claimed benevolent purpose as bona fide. Nonetheless, because it did not justify facial discrimination against religion, we invalidated the restriction.

It may be that Washington's original purpose in excluding the clergy from public benefits was benign, and the same might be true of its purpose in maintaining the exclusion today. But those singled out for disfavor can be forgiven for suspecting more invidious forces at work. Let there be no doubt: This case is about discrimination against a religious minority. Most citizens of this country identify themselves as professing some religious belief, but the State's policy poses no obstacle to practitioners of only a tepid, civic version of faith. Those the statutory exclusion actually affects—those whose belief in their religion is so strong that they dedicate their study and their lives to its ministry—are a far narrower set. One need not delve too far into modern popular culture to perceive a trendy disdain for deep religious conviction. In an era when the Court is so quick to come to the aid of other disfavored groups, see, e.g., Romer v. Evans (1996) [striking down state constitutional provision forbidding enactment of laws against sexual-orientation discrimination], its indifference in this case, which involves a form of discrimination to which the Constitution actually speaks, is exceptional.

* * *

Today's holding is limited to training the clergy, but its logic is readily extendible, and there are plenty of directions to go. What next? Will we deny priests and nuns their prescription-drug benefits on the ground that taxpayers' freedom of conscience forbids medicating the clergy at public expense? This may seem fanciful, but recall that France has proposed banning religious attire from schools, invoking interests in secularism no less benign than those the Court embraces today. When the public's freedom of conscience is invoked to justify denial of equal treatment, benevolent motives shade into indifference and ultimately into repression. Having accepted the justification in this case, the Court is less well equipped to fend it off in the future. I respectfully dissent.

Justice THOMAS, dissenting.

Because the parties agree that a "degree in theology" means a degree that is "devotional in nature or designed to induce religious faith," I assume that this is so for purposes of deciding this case. With this understanding, I join Justice Scalia's dissenting opinion. [However, definitions of "theology" can] include the study of theology from a secular perspective as well as from a religious one.

Assuming that the State denies Promise Scholarships only to students who pursue a degree in devotional theology, I believe that Justice Scalia's application of our precedents is correct. . . .

NOTES AND QUESTIONS

1. The Free Exercise Rationale in Locke v. Davey. The Court says that Washington's disfavoring of religion is only of a "mil[d] kind." Consider the hypothetical on p. 192, in which a state imposes a $5 surcharge on a license fee for a private-school bus when the school operating the bus is religious. Is this mild disfavoring of religion constitutional after *Davey*?

(a) No animus? Even though the Washington rule by its terms discriminates according to a religion-based criterion (theology, or theology "from a devotional perspective"), the Court rejects heightened scrutiny and emphasizes that the state rule did not reflect "hostility" or "animus" to religion. Does a free exercise litigant now have to show not just non-neutrality, but also animus toward religion? If so, is that consistent with *Lukumi* (p. 162)? What would an "animus" standard say about the viability of decisions like Rader v. Johnston (p. 166) or Fraternal Order of Police v. Newark (p. 167), which held that religious exercise must receive protection when other, non-religious interests are exempted from a law?

(b) No burden on free exercise? The majority says that the denial of funding does not burden religion. It also says that the Washington condition "does not require students to choose between their religious beliefs and receiving a government benefit" because "Promise Scholars may still use their scholarship to pursue a secular degree at a different institution from where they are studying devotional theology." Are these conclusions convincing? What is the interest in forcing students like Davey to go to an entirely different college if they want to take another degree?

Suppose that there is no other evangelical Protestant college within 100 miles of Northwest College. Suppose that the state's requirement effectively meant that Davey had to take eight years of college to finish his two degrees. Would either of these facts matter?

(c) **State discretion?** An important theme in the majority opinion is that the state should have "play in the joints" to pursue church-state separation beyond the extent required by the Establishment Clause. One question, raised in Justice Scalia's dissent, is why there must be such a "space" between the two Religion Clauses. Why isn't equal treatment, or neutrality, toward religion a joint command of both the Free Exercise and Establishment clauses? Does the Court's approach rest on the assumption that the two clauses have opposing purposes?

Assume that the state should have room to pursue greater separation than the Establishment Clause requires. Did the Court have to rule for the state in *Davey* in order to preserve that discretion? If Joshua Davey had won the case, would there be *any* situation in which the state had discretion to bar funding for religious uses even though it was not required to do so?

For a critique of *Davey*'s arguments and an assessment of its application to future cases, see Douglas Laycock, Theology Scholarships, the Pledge of Allegiance, and Religious Liberty: Avoiding the Extremes But Missing the Liberty, 118 Harv. L. Rev. 155, 162-218 (2004).

2. Viewpoint Discrimination. Why does the Court reject Davey's claim that the Washington rule constitutes viewpoint discrimination violating the Free Speech Clause? How did this case differ from *Rosenberger*? Perhaps it is obviously true that a state can discriminate based on viewpoint in funding college scholarships. For example, Washington might have wanted to exclude from its program all degrees in astrology, or all science degrees that taught that the world was created in seven days 6,000 years ago. Does this show that viewpoint discrimination in a scholarship program must be permissible? Does it show that the restriction in *Davey* was permissible?

3. State Blaine Amendments and Anti-Catholic Animus? The majority dodges the argument that Washington's article I, § 11 reflects an anti-Catholic animus associated with the federal Blaine Amendment (see pp. 361-366). The opinion leaves open the possibility of challenging other state provisions more closely modelled on the Blaine Amendment—for example, Washington's provision that bars state aid to any school that is "sectarian" or "under sectarian control or influence" (Wash. Const. art. IX, § 4; cf. the language of the Blaine Amendment, p. 362). If the latter sort of provision is at issue, should its roots in the Blaine Amendment color the constitutional analysis of it today? Under current conditions, a significant number of the schools affected by state no-aid provisions are non-Catholic, such as the evangelical college Davey attended. Does that remove whatever "taint" there might be from nineteenth century anti-Catholicism? Consider also the fact that the states that passed no-aid provisions in the 1800s often mandated or allowed official prayers and Bible readings in public schools, but that those practices no longer are followed today. Does that make the restrictions on aid to private religious education more defensible today? Why or why not?

Can the particular language of a state restriction make it more objectionable or less so? For example, some provisions, such as Washington's article IX, § 4, bar aid to a school as an entity if it is "sectarian" or "under sectarian control." Others, such as Washington's article I, § 11, bar aid to religious teaching or instruction. What difference might this make? Is it relevant to the Court's free exercise ruling in *Davey*?

4. State Restrictions and Elementary and Secondary-School Vouchers. The major issue after *Davey* concerns programs of vouchers for students in grades K-12 and whether, under various state restrictions, religious schools may participate in such programs. Lower courts have divided on whether state restrictions should be interpreted to exclude religious schools from a voucher programs. For example, Chittenden Town School Dist. v. Vermont Dept. of Educ., 169 Vt. 310, 738 A.2d 539 (1999), held that including religious schools in a state program paying tuition for certain students at public or private high schools violated Vermont's provision against "compelled support" of religious instruction. But the Wisconsin Supreme Court upheld a voucher program for Milwaukee students against a challenge based on a similar provision and also based on a provision prohibiting the use of state money "for the benefit of" religious schools. Jackson v. Benson, 218 Wis. 835, 578 N.W.2d 602 (1998). One argument under such provisions is that vouchers "support" or "benefit" students and families, not the schools or their religious instruction.

Problem: Vouchers after *Davey*. Suppose that a state enacts a program under which K-12 students in failing public schools (those with especially low test scores and graduation rates) may receive vouchers to pay tuition at a nearby public school or a secular private school—but the program excludes religiously affiliated private schools because of a state constitutional provision barring such assistance. Parents who wish, on religious grounds, to send their children to religious schools sue claiming that the exclusion violates the Free Exercise and Free Speech clauses. Does Locke v. Davey eliminate their claims? What are the arguments on both sides?

F. ONGOING CONTROVERSIES OVER GOVERNMENT AID

1. *"Strings" on Government Aid*

When religious organizations accept funding, do they forfeit the constitutional and statutory protections they have from governmental interference? Do they forfeit free exercise rights? Do they forfeit statutory rights? Does it matter what form the government assistance may take? Those are the issues raised in the following materials:

DODGE v. THE SALVATION ARMY
1989 WL 53857 (S.D. Miss. 1989)

Dan M. RUSSELL, JR., District Judge:

FACTS

The plaintiff Jamie Kellam Dodge was employed by the defendant Salvation Army in its Domestic Violence Shelter as the Victims' Assistance Coordinator.

When initially employed by the Salvation Army, the plaintiff filled out an employment application which listed her church affiliation as "Catholic." Furthermore, on a yearly basis the plaintiff executed a statement indicating that she understood and would adhere to the personnel policies and procedures of the Salvation Army.

[According to a letter signed by defendant, the position filled by the plaintiff was] "made possible by a grant from the Criminal Justice Department.". . . . An examination of the Subgrant Application Packet submitted to the office of Criminal Justice Planning in Jackson, Mississippi, indicates that the Salvation Army requested a total of $30,241.00 to fund the "Salvation Army's Assistance Program." Of the $30,241.00 requested, $22,680.75 was to come from the federal government and $7,560.25 from state and local government. An examination of the submitted budget indicates that a total of $20,139.00 was allotted for personnel. This included $14,353.00 to fully fund the position of Victims' Assistance Coordinator. [Paragraph relocated.]

On August 27, 1987, after being seen using the Salvation Army's copy machine and after being confronted, the plaintiff admitted to Sylvia Fisher, the Director of the Domestic Violence Shelter, that she used the copy machine to copy manuals and information on Satanic/Wiccan rituals. The plaintiff was terminated shortly after being discovered and after making the admissions. Thereafter, on August 28, 1987, the plaintiff was sent a letter by Sylvia Fisher confirming her termination, which stated in part that "[t]his letter is to confirm your dismissal from employment as Victims' Assistance Coordinator for the Salvation Army Domestic Violence Shelter. On yesterday you admitted to charges of copying and compiling information related to occult practices that are inconsistent with the religious purposes of the Salvation Army."

LAW

A. THE RELIGIOUS EXEMPTION

The Salvation Army is a "church" operating as a religious corporation, and therefore is entitled to rely on Section 702 of the Civil Rights Act of 1964, which exempts religious organizations from Title VII's prohibition against discrimination in employment on the basis of religion.[5]

[I]n Corporation of Presiding Bishop v. Amos [p. 250], the United States Supreme Court held that the application of Section 702 to the secular non-profit activities of a religious organization does not violate the Establishment Clause of the First Amendment. Therefore, it appears that regardless of whether an employee's duties within the non-profit organization are secular or not, the religious exemption can be used as a basis for termination. In the case sub judice this Court must no longer delineate between religious and non-religious activities in considering whether the plaintiff's job was one in which the Salvation Army could justifiably apply the exemption. In light of Amos it appears that the Salvation Army can appropriately terminate any of its employees that do not adhere to its religious purposes.

---

5. This subchapter [i.e., Title VII of the Civil Rights Act of 1964, 42 U.S.C. § 2000e et seq.] shall not apply . . . to a religious corporation, association, educational institution, or society with respect to the employment of individuals of a particular religion to perform work connected with the carrying on by such corporation, association, educational institution, or society of activities.

However, even though the religious exemption does permit the Salvation Army to terminate an employee based on religious grounds, the fact that the plaintiff's position as Victims' Assistance Coordinator was funded substantially, if not entirely, by federal, state and local government, gives rise to constitutional considerations which effectively prohibit the application of the exemption to the facts in this case.

B. THE APPLICATION OF SECTION 702

[A]lthough the plaintiff received her paycheck and supervision from the Salvation Army, her employment was made possible by the combined funds of federal, state and local government. Based upon the fact that the plaintiff's position was funded substantially, if not exclusively by government sources, the Court must consider if the application of the Section 702 exemption to this situation is constitutional. [The Court's summary of the *Lemon* test is omitted.]

This Court is of the opinion that the first requirement in *Lemon*, that Section 702 serve a secular purpose, is satisfied. However, the second requirement that the statute in question have a principal or primary effect that neither advances nor inhibits religion, fails under the facts of this case. As was stated in *Amos* :

> For a law to have forbidden "effects" under *Lemon*, it must be fair to say that the government itself has advanced religion through its own activities and influence. As the Court observed in *Walz*, "[F]or the men who wrote the Religion Clauses of the First Amendment, the 'establishment' of a religion connoted sponsorship, financial support, and active involvement of the sovereign and religious activity."

Based on the facts in the present case, the effect of the government substantially, if not exclusively, funding a position such as the Victims' Assistance Coordinator and then allowing the Salvation Army to choose the person to fill or maintain the position based on religious preference clearly has the effect of advancing religion and is unconstitutional.

This Court is of the opinion that although *Amos* does not specifically address the issue of funding, the Supreme Court went to great lengths to distinguish *Amos* from *Lemon* on the questions of financial support and active involvement by the sovereign. As the record reveals, the Salvation Army receives substantial and direct funding from governmental grants for the position of Victims' Assistance Coordinator. It is clear from the inferences derived from the references made by the Supreme Court in *Amos* to financial support and direct funding which were in issue in *Lemon*, that *Lemon* and not *Amos* really controls the issues in this case.

Regarding the final element of *Lemon*, it is clear that Section 702, under the facts of the case sub judice, creates an excessive government entanglement with religion. . . . This Court is of the opinion that in the present case excessive government entanglements exist with the religious purpose of the Salvation Army when said purpose permeates the application for and the supervision of a government grant which substantially, if not exclusively, funded the Victims' Assistance Coordinator position held by the plaintiff. The benefits received by the Salvation Army were not indirect or incidental. The grants constituted direct financial support in the form of a substantial subsidy, and therefore to allow the Salvation Army to discriminate on the basis of religion, concerning the employment of the Victims' Assistance Coordinator, would violate the Establishment Clause of the First Amendment in that it has a primary effect of advancing religion and creating excessive government entanglement. For these reasons Section 702 as applied to the facts in the case sub judice is unconstitutional and therefore the plaintiff's Cross-Motion for Summary Judgment must be granted.

NOTES AND QUESTIONS

1. Government Aid and Religion-Based Hiring. Is the *Dodge* case rightly decided? Several other decisions have held that a religious institution did not "waive[ ] the Title VII exemption for [religion-based hiring] because . . . it received federal funds." Hall v. Baptist Memorial Health Care Corp., 215 F.3d 618, 625 (6th Cir. 2000); Siegel v. Truett-McConnell College, 13 F. Supp. 2d 1335, 1344 (N.D. Ga. 1994) ("a student's use of his or her [Pell] grant money [at a college does not] support the argument that the government itself is advancing religion through its own activities"); Saucier v. Employment Sec. Dept., 90 Wash. App. 461, 954 P.2d 285 (1998) (upholding Salvation Army's exemption from paying unemployment taxes even though position of former employee seeking unemployment benefits had been funded by federal and state grants). Are these decisions correct? Are they distinguishable from *Dodge?*

Recall the reasons why a religious organization might consider it important to favor members of its own faith in employment, even for positions that other people might not see as obviously "religious":

> Many faith-based organizations believe that they cannot maintain their religious vision over a sustained time period without the ability to replenish their staff with individuals who share the tenets and doctrines of the association. They prefer working with those of the same faith, not out of animus toward others, but out of a desire to surround themselves with those who reinforce their faith. This guaranteed ability is central to each organization's freedom to define its own mission according to the dictates of its faith. It was for this reason that Congress wrote an exemption from religious discrimination by religious employers into Title VII of the Civil Rights Act of 1964.

Community Solutions Act of 2001, H.R. Rep. No. 107-138. Do these rationales apply just as fully when the religious organization is receiving federal funds for the activity? Does the district court in *Dodge* offer a good reason to limit the exemption approved in *Amos* when the activity is government funded?

Professor Alan Brownstein has argued that government-funded activities are different from the *Amos* situation:

> Because it is clear as a matter of constitutional law and statutory mandate that state funds cannot be used for religious purposes or to advance religion, there is no ambiguity here as there was in *Amos* as to the secular or religious nature of the job functions that are at issue. [Thus] there can be no chilling effect created by uncertainty as to how these jobs would be characterized by a reviewing court. Indeed, it is hard to identify any legitimate secular purpose [in allowing religious discrimination for] job functions that the law requires to be secular.

> [Moreover,] the argument in *Amos* that religious discrimination in hiring should be tolerated because it allows churches to advance religion makes little sense in the context of [government-funded] programs. Here, employees will be engaged in federally funded functions. [The exemption] provides religious organizations coercive economic power that would otherwise be unavailable to them were it not for the state's assistance.

Alan Brownstein, Constitutional Questions About Charitable Choice, in Welfare Reform and Faith-Based Organizations 219, 235 (Derek Davis & Barry Hankins eds., 1999).

Does Professor Brownstein adequately distinguish *Amos*? Does he take sufficient account of the organization's various interests in hiring members of its own faith? Consider the following testimony in support of the "Charitable Choice" program, which allows religious social services to compete equally for government funds without having to give up their religious character or their ability to employ members of their own faith. (Charitable Choice is discussed more fully in section IV-F-2.)

> Occasionally, the charge is made that charitable choice is Government-funded job discrimination. This is untrue. The purpose of charitable choice funding is not to create jobs, or to fill the coffers of faith-based organizations ["FBOs"], but to fund social services for those in need. It is the faith-based organization, of course, that is making staffing decisions on the basis of religion, not the Government.

H.R. Rep. No. 107-138, at 33. It has also been claimed that Professor Brownstein's argument

> fail[s] to account for the FBO's perspective. From the government's perspective, to feed the hungry or house the destitute is secular work. But from the perspective of the FBO, to operate a soup kitchen or open a shelter for the homeless are acts of mercy and thus spiritual service. . . . [E]ven when not engaged in "religious indoctrination" such as proselytizing or worship, FBOs view what they are doing as religiously motivated and thus may desire that such acts of mercy and love be performed by those of like-minded creed.

Testimony of Carl H. Esbeck, Senior Counsel to the Deputy Attorney General, before the Subcommittee on Human Resources, House Ways and Means Committee, June 14, 2001 (available at http://www.house.gov/ways=means/ humres/107cong/6-14-01/record/usdoj.htm).

2. Problems: The Scope of *Dodge*. Now assume that the *Dodge* ruling is correct, and consider the following situations:

(a) Suppose the next case involves a domestic violence shelter that is not "pervasively sectarian": In that case, why would it be unconstitutional for the agency to discriminate on the basis of religion in hiring?

(b) If, as is the case in *Dodge*, the employee's job does not include any religious teaching, does that deprive the employer of the right to enforce any religious standards of expression or behavior? Suppose that Z is a secretary at an anti-abortion, religiously affiliated adoption agency; her work is "secular" and is funded by a government grant. If Z publicly states that the Bible does not forbid abortion, may her employer dismiss her? (Could a government-funded *secular* domestic violence shelter fire an employee for using the copying machine to reproduce materials taking a position that the leaders of the organization disapprove of, such as pro-life pamphlets? Is there any difference between the two situations?)

(c) Does the court's decision apply to all employees of the organization, or only to those whose funding is "substantially, if not exclusively" provided by the government? Could the domestic violence shelter in this case insist that its executive director hold religious beliefs compatible with the Salvation Army?

GROVE CITY COLLEGE v. BELL
465 U.S. 555 (1984)

Justice WHITE delivered the opinion of the Court.

Section 901(a) of Title IX of the Education Amendments of 1972, 20 U.S.C. § 1681(a), prohibits sex discrimination in "any education program or activity receiving Federal financial assistance," and § 902 directs agencies awarding most types of assistance to promulgate regulations to ensure that recipients adhere to that prohibition. Compliance with departmental regulations may be secured by termination of assistance "to the particular program, or part thereof, in which . . . noncompliance has been . . . found" or by "any other means authorized by law."

This case presents several questions concerning the scope and operation of these provisions and the regulations established by the Department of Education. We must decide, first, whether Title IX applies at all to Grove City College, which accepts no direct assistance but enrolls students who receive federal grants that must be used for educational purposes. If so, we must identify the "education program or activity" at Grove City that is "receiving Federal financial assistance" and determine whether federal assistance to that program may be terminated solely because the College violates the Department's regulations by refusing to execute an Assurance of Compliance with Title IX. Finally, we must consider whether the application of Title IX to Grove City infringes the First Amendment rights of the College or its students.

I

Petitioner Grove City College is a private, coeducational, liberal arts college that has sought to preserve its institutional autonomy by consistently refusing state and federal financial assistance. Grove City's desire to avoid federal oversight has led it to decline to participate, not only in direct institutional aid programs, but also in federal student assistance programs under which the College would be required to assess students' eligibility and to determine the amounts of loans, work-study funds, or grants they should receive. Grove City has, however, enrolled a large number of students who receive Basic Educational Opportunity Grants (BEOGs), 20 U.S.C. § 1070a, under the Department of Education's Alternate Disbursement System (ADS).[5]

5. The Secretary, in his discretion, has established two procedures for computing and disbursing BEOGs. Under the Regular Disbursement System (RDS), the Secretary estimates the amount that an institution will need for grants and advances that sum to the institution, which itself selects eligible students, calculates awards, and distributes the grants by either crediting students' accounts or issuing checks. 34 CFR §§ 690.71-.85 (1982). Most institutions whose students receive BEOGs

II

In defending its refusal to execute the Assurance of Compliance required by the Department's regulations, Grove City first contends that neither it nor any "education program or activity" of the College receives any federal financial assistance within the meaning of Title IX by virtue of the fact that some of its students receive BEOGs and use them to pay for their education. We disagree.

[T]he language of § 901(a) contains no hint that Congress perceived a substantive difference between direct institutional assistance and aid received by a school through its students. The linchpin of Grove City's argument that none of its programs receives any federal assistance is a perceived distinction between direct and indirect aid, a distinction that finds no support in the text of § 901(a). Nothing in § 901(a) suggests that Congress elevated form over substance by making the application of the nondiscrimination principle dependent on the manner in which a program or activity receives federal assistance. There is no basis in the statute for the view that only institutions that themselves apply for federal aid or receive checks directly from the federal government are subject to regulation. We have recognized the need to " 'accord [Title IX] a sweep as broad as its language,' " and we are reluctant to read into § 901(a) a limitation not apparent on its face.

Our reluctance grows when we pause to consider the available evidence of Congress' intent. The legislative history of the amendments is replete with statements evincing Congress' awareness that the student assistance programs established by the amendments would significantly aid colleges and universities. [The Court's summary of this evidence is omitted.]

V

Grove City's final challenge to the Court of Appeals' decision—that conditioning federal assistance on compliance with Title IX infringes First Amendment rights of the College and its students—warrants only brief consideration. Congress is free to attach reasonable and unambiguous conditions to federal financial assistance that educational institutions are not obligated to accept. Grove City may terminate its participation in the BEOG program and thus avoid the requirements of § 901(a). Students affected by the Department's action may either take their BEOGs elsewhere or attend Grove City without federal financial assistance. Requiring Grove City to comply with Title IX's prohibition of discrimination as a condition for its continued eligibility to participate in the BEOG program infringes no First Amendment rights of the College or its students.

Justice POWELL, with whom Chief Justice BURGER and Justice O'CONNOR join, concurring.

As I agree that the holding in this case is dictated by the language and legislative history of Title IX, and the Regulations of the Department of Education, I join the Court's decision. I do so reluctantly and write briefly to record my view

---

participate in the RDS, but the ADS is an option made available by the Secretary to schools that wish to minimize their involvement in the administration of the BEOG program. Institutions participating in the program through the ADS must make appropriate certifications to the Secretary, but the Secretary calculates awards and makes disbursements directly to eligible students. 34 CFR §§ 690.91-.96 (1982).

that the case is an unedifying example of overzealousness on the part of the Federal Government.

Grove City College (Grove City) may be unique among colleges in our country; certainly there are few others like it. Founded more than a century ago in 1876, Grove City is an independent, coeducational liberal arts college. It describes itself as having "both a Christian world view and a freedom philosophy," perceiving these as "interrelated." At the time of this suit, it had about 2,200 students and tuition was surprisingly low for a private college. Some 140 of the College's students were receiving Basic Educational Opportunity Grants (BEOGs), and 342 had obtained Guaranteed Student Loans (GSLs). The grants were made directly to the students through the Department of Education, and the student loans were guaranteed by the federal government. Apart from this indirect assistance, Grove City has followed an unbending policy of refusing all forms of government assistance, whether federal, state or local. It was and is the policy of this small college to remain wholly independent of government assistance, recognizing—as this case well illustrates—that with acceptance of such assistance one surrenders a certain measure of the freedom that Americans always have cherished.

This case involves a Regulation adopted by the Department to implement § 901(a) of Title IX. It is well to bear in mind what § 901(a) provides:

> No person in the United States shall, on the basis of sex, be excluded from participation in, be denied the benefits of, or be subjected to discrimination under any education program or activity receiving federal financial assistance. . . .

The sole purpose of the statute is to make unlawful "discrimination" by recipients of federal financial assistance on the "basis of sex." The undisputed fact is that Grove City does not discriminate—and so far as the record in this case shows—never has discriminated against anyone on account of sex, race, or national origin. This case has nothing whatever to do with discrimination past or present. The College therefore has complied to the letter with the sole purpose of § 901(a).

On the basis of the evidence, which included the formal published statement of Grove City's strong "non-discrimination policy," [the Administrative Law Judge] stated:

> It should also be noted that there is not the slightest hint of any failure to comply with Title IX, save the refusal to submit an executed Assurance of Compliance with Title IX. This refusal is obviously a matter of conscience and belief.

NOTES AND QUESTIONS

1. Constitutional Limits on Funding Conditions. Does the First Amendment place any limits on the ability of the government to attach conditions to the receipt of government funds?

2. Direct Versus Indirect Aid. In *Grove City*, the Court disregarded any possible difference between direct and indirect aid. Is that consistent with the Establishment Clause case law?

3. The Reach of the "Strings."   In a portion of the opinion not reproduced here, the Supreme Court held that the antidiscrimination provisions of Title IX applied only to the specific "program or activity, or part thereof" receiving federal funds, and not to the entire institution. In the case of student grants and loans, the Court held that the "program or activity" was confined to admissions and financial aid. See John H. Garvey, The "Program or Activity" Rule in Antidiscrimination Law, 23 Harv. J. Legis. 445 (1986). In response, Congress enacted the Civil Rights Restoration Act of 1987, Pub. L. No. 100-259, which defined "program or activity" broadly to include the entire institution to which funds are distributed (e.g., the entire college or university). In response to concerns expressed by religious organizations, however, Congress attached a proviso: that the definition does not apply to an entity "controlled by a religious organization if the application of [this section] would not be consistent with the religious tenets of such organization." 20 U.S.C. § 1681(a)(3).

Is the proviso constitutionally required? In other words, does the First Amendment compel Congress to exempt grantees controlled by religious organizations from the antidiscrimination laws to the extent that those laws are inconsistent with the organization's religious tenets?

Is the proviso broad enough? What about grantees that are religious in inspiration or motivation but not "controlled by" a religious denomination? And what if the antidiscrimination laws are not inconsistent with the tenets of the organization, but enforcement of those laws would interfere with the autonomy of the organization?

Is the proviso unconstitutional? Is it unwise?

BOB JONES UNIVERSITY v. UNITED STATES
461 U.S. 574 (1983)

[Until 1970 the Internal Revenue Service granted tax-exempt status to all private schools, even those that discriminated in admissions on the basis of race. It also allowed charitable deductions for contributions to such schools. In that year the IRS changed its policy, and announced that it would no longer allow exemptions or deductions for private schools that practice racial discrimination. It then revoked the tax-exempt status of Bob Jones University. The University paid a token tax and filed for a refund.

[Bob Jones University is not affiliated with any religious denomination, but is dedicated to teaching fundamentalist Christian religious beliefs. The corporation runs a school with an enrollment of about 5,000 students, from kindergarten through college and graduate school. Teachers must be devout Christians. Students are screened as to their religious beliefs, and their public and private conduct is strictly regulated by the school. The University's sponsors believe that the Bible forbids interracial dating and marriage. At one time it refused to admit African Americans—a policy it changed in 1971. In 1975 it adopted a rule forbidding interracial dating or marriage. Students who violate the rule are expelled. The University continues to deny admission to applicants engaged in an interracial marriage or known to advocate interracial marriage or dating.

[The principal issue in the case was whether the IRS had interpreted the statute correctly in 1970. The IRS maintained, and the Court eventually agreed, that an institution could not qualify for an exemption unless it was charitable in the common law sense—that is, unless it served a public purpose and was not contrary to public policy. Racial discrimination in education is obviously contrary to public policy. It is forbidden in public schools by Brown v. Board of Education, 347 U.S. 483 (1954), and discouraged in private schools by laws such as the 1964 Civil Rights Act. The Court was a little troubled by the fact that this was a new reading of the tax code (and one the IRS had rejected for a long time), but in the end it decided to go along with the IRS on the issue of interpretation.

[The Court then turned to a constitutional question. The district court had held that the 1970 interpretation "violated the University's rights under the Religion Clauses of the First Amendment." The court of appeals reversed on this point.]

III

Petitioners contend that, even if the Commissioner's policy is valid as to nonreligious private schools, that policy cannot constitutionally be applied to schools that engage in racial discrimination on the basis of sincerely held religious beliefs. As to such schools, it is argued that the IRS construction of § 170 and § 501(c)(3) violates their free exercise rights under the Religion Clauses of the First Amendment. This contention presents claims not heretofore considered by this Court in precisely this context.

This Court has long held the Free Exercise Clause of the First Amendment an absolute prohibition against governmental regulation of religious beliefs. As interpreted by this Court, moreover, the Free Exercise Clause provides substantial protection for lawful conduct grounded in religious belief. However, "[n]ot all burdens on religion are unconstitutional. . . . The state may justify a limitation on religious liberty by showing that it is essential to accomplish an overriding governmental interest."

On occasion this Court has found certain governmental interests so compelling as to allow even regulations prohibiting religiously based conduct. In Prince v. Massachusetts (1944), for example, the Court held that neutrally cast child labor laws prohibiting sale of printed materials on public streets could be applied to prohibit children from dispensing religious literature. The Court found no constitutional infirmity in "excluding [Jehovah's Witness children] from doing there what no other children may do." Denial of tax benefits will inevitably have a substantial impact on the operation of private religious schools, but will not prevent those schools from observing their religious tenets.

The governmental interest at stake here is compelling. [T]he Government has a fundamental, overriding interest in eradicating racial discrimination in education[29]—discrimination that prevailed, with official approval, for the first 165 years of this Nation's history. That governmental interest substantially

29. We deal here only with religious schools—not with churches or other purely religious institutions; here, the governmental interest is in denying public support to racial discrimination in education. [R]acially discriminatory schools "exer[t] a pervasive influence on the entire educational process," outweighing any public benefit that they might otherwise provide, Norwood v. Harrison (1973).

outweighs whatever burden denial of tax benefits places on petitioners' exercise of their religious beliefs. The interests asserted by petitioners cannot be accommodated with that compelling governmental interest, and no "less restrictive means" are available to achieve the governmental interest.[30]

NOTES AND QUESTIONS

1. *Bob Jones* Versus Clergy Employment. In *Bob Jones*, in contrast to Combs v. United Methodist Church (see p. 310), the Court enforced a nondiscrimination rule against a religious defendant. What explains the difference in the two cases? One possibility is that *Bob Jones* is about race and *Combs* is about sex. As a constitutional matter, our society is more strongly committed to racial than to sexual equality. Courts look at race cases with strict scrutiny; in sex cases they use intermediate scrutiny. Korematsu v. United States, 323 U.S. 214 (1944); United States v. Virginia, 518 U.S. 515 (1996). So perhaps we could say that in race cases the government has a compelling interest that outweighs a church's First Amendment right. Could the Equal Employment Opportunity Commission order a denomination to ordain more Hispanics, if that group was underrepresented in the ranks of the clergy?

If the real difference between the two cases lies in the nature of the claim, how might courts deal with other forms of discrimination? Many churches have rules forbidding homosexual conduct. Does this mean that claims of discrimination on the basis of sexual orientation should fail? Cf. Gay Rights Coalition v. Georgetown Univ., 536 A.2d 1 (D.C. 1987). Few churches have religious reasons for preferring young people over old people. Does this mean that courts should have a freer hand in enforcing the Age Discrimination in Employment Act? Gargano v. Diocese of Rockville Centre, 80 F.3d 87 (2d Cir. 1996); Weissman v. Congregation Shaare Emeth, 38 F.3d 1038 (8th Cir. 1994); Geary v. Visitation of the Blessed Virgin Mary Parish School, 7 F.3d 324 (3d Cir. 1993); Minker v. Baltimore Annual Conference of United Methodist Church, 894 F.2d 1354 (D.C. Cir. 1990). What about disabilities? EEOC v. St. Francis Xavier Parochial Sch., 928 F. Supp. 29 (D.D.C. 1996).

Does it matter that *Bob Jones* involves tax exemption, while *Combs* involves outright regulation? Notice the Court's observation in *Bob Jones* that "[d]enial of tax benefits . . . will not prevent those schools from observing their religious tenets." What exactly does the Court mean by "prevent"? Suppose Congress withdrew the income tax exemption from churches that maintain a male-only

---

30. Bob Jones University also contends that denial of tax exemption violates the Establishment Clause by preferring religions whose tenets do not require racial discrimination over those which believe racial intermixing is forbidden. It is well settled that neither a State nor the Federal Government may pass laws which "prefer one religion over another," Everson v. Board of Education, but "[i]t is equally true" that a regulation does not violate the Establishment Clause merely because it "happens to coincide or harmonize with the tenets of some or all religions." McGowan v. Maryland (1961). See Harris v. McRae (1980). The IRS policy at issue here is founded on a "neutral, secular basis," and does not violate the Establishment Clause. In addition, as the Court of Appeals noted, "the uniform application of the rule to all religiously operated schools avoids the necessity for a potentially entangling inquiry into whether a racially restrictive practice is the result of sincere religious belief."

clergy, such as the Catholic Church and many evangelical Protestant groups. Would this "prevent" them from observing their religious tenets? See Mary E. Becker, The Politics of Women's Wrongs and the Bill of "Rights": A Bicentennial Perspective, 53 U. Chi. L. Rev. 453, 485-486 (1992) (advocating such a withdrawal).

Does it matter that *Bob Jones* involves a school rather than a church? Look at footnote 29. Is the real difference between *Bob Jones* and *Combs* the identity of the defendants (or the plaintiffs)? The Court suggests that the eradication of discrimination in education is an especially important governmental interest. If that is true, why can't the Court identify a statute that Bob Jones University had violated?

2. Tax Exemptions Versus Other Forms of Aid. Consider the differences among *Dodge, Grove City,* and *Bob Jones. Dodge* involved a direct grant; *Grove City* involved indirect aid through grants and loans to students; *Bob Jones* involved tax exemption. Does the form of the aid matter? Could the government attach conditions to the use of the mails or the roads? At what point does the attachment of conditions become equivalent to regulation?

3. Government Aid and Religious Autonomy. On the whole, is it more of a threat to the independence and vitality of religious institutions to exclude them from generally available public benefits, or to subject them to the conditions that are attached to those benefits? Should this decision be made collectively, as a matter of constitutional law, or should the institutions be permitted to decide whether and when the aid is worth the conditions? Should the Free Exercise Clause protect against "strings" on aid to the same extent that it protects against direct regulation? Why should these forms of government power be treated differently?

2. Religious Social Services and the "Faith-Based Initiative" Debate: Issues of Government Aid and Religious Autonomy

We close this Part of the casebook with a set of materials on a subject that has been of great interest in recent years: the participation of religiously based organizations in government-funded social service programs. This topic serves as a convenient review of government aid to religion, for it raises questions concerning not only the rights of taxpayers to object to supporting religion, but also the rights of religious social service organizations to preserve their autonomy if they receive government funds.

As we noted earlier (section C-1, p. 397), the provision of social services, and the government's role in such services, has become an increasingly important topic over the decades. The share of the gross domestic product that flows through the federal government and goes to pay for health care, research, education, job training, and other human services has increased from less than 0.4 percent in 1960 to just under 3 percent in 1980 and to nearly 4.5 percent in 1997. See "Historical Tables" in the Budget of the United States Government, Fiscal Year 1999, at 50-64. Perhaps two-thirds of this money flows to private nonprofit organizations, through vouchers, grants, contracts, and related instruments.

The nonprofit organizations receiving government aid to provide social services have for decades included religiously affiliated organizations such as

Catholic Charities, Lutheran Social Services, and various Jewish charities. But often the government provider arrangements (contracts, grant conditions, etc.) have required that the provider take steps to separate itself from religious elements—for example, form a corporation separate from its sponsoring church, refrain from explicit religious teaching in its programs, remove religious symbols from places where services are provided, and refrain from religious considerations in hiring employees. As a result, the religious organizations that receive aid have been, for the most part, those that are relatively comfortable with making their religion implicit rather than explicit—treating it as the motivation underlying their work rather than an obvious feature on its surface. Organizations that see explicit religious teaching and preaching as inseparable from their charitable actions—in other words, organizations that the Supreme Court might have called "pervasively sectarian"—often could not meet the criteria for aid. For discussion of this background, see Welfare Reform and Faith-Based Organizations (Derek Davis & Barry Hankins eds., 1999) (hereafter "Davis and Hankins") (chapters by Julie A. Segal and Stanley Carlson-Thies).

In recent years many people have grown dissatisfied with these limits on the participation of religious social service providers. Much of the dissatisfaction has come from the increasing belief that seriously religious organizations do a better job than secular bureaucracies of serving their clients, especially where reformation of behavior is at issue. For presentations of this case, see Marvin Olasky, The Tragedy of American Compassion (1992); Ronald J. Sider and Heidi Rolland Unruh, An (Ana)Baptist Theological Perspective on Church-State Cooperation: Evaluating Charitable Choice, in Davis and Hankins at 94-95. (Several studies, however, have found insufficient evidence to support this belief. See, e.g., Mark Ragan, Faith-Based vs. Secular: Using Administrative Data to Compare the Performance of Faith-Affiliated and Other Social Service Providers, Roundtable on Religion and Social Welfare Policy (December 2004), available at http://www.religionandsocialpolicy.org/docs/research.)

As part of the welfare reform legislation passed in 1996, Congress sought to promote wider cooperation with religious social services by enacting what are commonly called the "Charitable Choice" provisions. These provisions, which are applicable only to certain federal welfare programs involving block grants from the federal government to the states, forbid discrimination against religious organizations as grantees. They also aim, as one section of the statute below puts it, to permit religious organizations to receive funds "without impairing the[ir] religious character," but also "without diminishing the religious freedom of beneficiaries of assistance funded under such program." Whether these goals can be achieved at the same time is the fundamental question posed by Charitable Choice.

Charitable Choice received dramatically increased attention in early 2001 when President George W. Bush, in one of his first domestic initiatives, proposed to expand it to many other federal welfare programs and created an Office for Faith-Based Programs in each of several federal agencies. The so-called Faith-Based Initiative passed the House, see Community Solutions Act of 2001, H.R. 7, 107th Cong., 1st Sess. (passed by House on July 19, 2001), but stalled in the Senate because of constitutional and policy objections, primarily to the funding of entities that discriminated in employment on the basis of religious commitment or sexual orientation. In the meantime, however, the Bush administration has implemented a number of the proposals through executive orders. For a summary and comprehensive analysis of the Bush administration's steps, see Ira C. Lupu and Robert W. Tuttle, The Faith-Based Initiative and the Constitution, 55 DePaul L. Rev. 1 (2005).

The Faith-Based Initiative, or Charitable Choice, raises in an illuminating way the two fundamental constitutional issues concerning government aid to religious entities. First, is extending aid on equal terms to religious entities that engage in substantial religious teaching a violation of the rights of taxpayers, or of ultimate beneficiaries who are uncomfortable with such teaching? Or is such aid necessary to prevent unfair (or even unconstitutional) discrimination against religious providers and the beneficiaries who desire religious services? Second, does the provision of aid on equal terms actually harm the organization that receives it because the "strings" attached to the aid (see section IV-F-1) undermine the organization's autonomy and independence? Does the organization have any legal right to receive aid free of the "strings"?

We analyze these questions by first reprinting the basic Charitable Choice provision from the 1996 legislation, and then offering some materials with which to assess the constitutionality of this approach.

PERSONAL RESPONSIBILITY AND WORK OPPORTUNITY RECONCILIATION ACT OF 1996

Pub. L. No. 104-93

§ 104 (42 U.S.C. § 604A). SERVICES PROVIDED BY CHARITABLE, RELIGIOUS, OR PRIVATE ORGANIZATIONS

(a) In general

(1) State options

A State may—

(A) administer and provide services under the programs described [in subsection (a)(2)] through contracts with charitable, religious, or private organizations; and

(B) provide beneficiaries of assistance under the [same] programs . . . with certificates, vouchers, or other forms of disbursement which are redeemable with such organizations.

(2) Programs described [omitted]

(b) Religious organizations

The purpose of this section is to allow States to contract with religious organizations, or to allow religious organizations to accept certificates, vouchers, or other forms of disbursement under any program described in subsection (a)(2) of this section, on the same basis as any other nongovernmental provider without impairing the religious character of such organizations, and without diminishing the religious freedom of beneficiaries of assistance funded under such program.

(c) Nondiscrimination against religious organizations

In the event a State exercises its authority under subsection (a) of this section, religious organizations are eligible, on the same basis as any other private organization, as contractors to provide assistance, or to accept certificates, vouchers, or other forms of disbursement, under any program described in subsection (a)(2) of this section so long as the programs are implemented consistent with the Establishment Clause of the United States Constitution. Except as provided in subsection (k) of this section, neither the Federal Government nor a State receiving funds under such programs shall discriminate against an organization which is or applies to be a contractor to provide assistance, or which accepts certificates, vouchers, or other forms of disbursement, on the basis that the organization has a religious character.

(d) Religious character and freedom

(1) Religious organizations

A religious organization with a contract described in subsection (a)(1)(A) of this section, or which accepts certificates, vouchers, or other forms of disbursement under subsection (a)(1)(B) of this section, shall retain its independence from Federal, State, and local governments, including such organization's control over the definition, development, practice, and expression of its religious beliefs.

(2) Additional safeguards

Neither the Federal Government nor a State shall require a religious organization to—

(A) alter its form of internal governance; or

(B) remove religious art, icons, scripture, or other symbols;

in order to be eligible to contract to provide assistance, or to accept certificates, vouchers, or other forms of disbursement, funded under a program described in subsection (a)(2) of this section.

(e) Rights of beneficiaries of assistance

(1) In general

If an individual described in paragraph (2) has an objection to the religious character of the organization or institution from which the individual receives, or would receive, assistance funded under any program described in subsection (a)(2) of this section, the State in which the individual resides shall provide such individual (if otherwise eligible for such assistance) within a reasonable period of time after the date of such objection with assistance from an alternative provider that is accessible to the individual and the value of which is not less than the value of the assistance which the individual would have received from such organization.

(2) Individual described

An individual described in this paragraph is an individual who receives, applies for, or requests to apply for, assistance under a program described in subsection (a)(2) of this section.

(f) Employment practices

A religious organization's exemption provided under section 2000e-1 of this title regarding employment practices shall not be affected by its participation in, or receipt of funds from, programs described in subsection (a)(2) of this section.

(g) Nondiscrimination against beneficiaries

Except as otherwise provided in law, a religious organization shall not discriminate against an individual in regard to rendering assistance funded under any program described in subsection (a)(2) of this section on the basis of religion, a religious belief, or refusal to actively participate in a religious practice.

(h) Fiscal accountability

(1) In general

Except as provided in paragraph (2), any religious organization contracting to provide assistance funded under any program described in subsection (a)(2) of this section shall be subject to the same regulations as other contractors to account in accord with generally accepted auditing principles for the use of such funds provided under such programs. . . .

(j) Limitations on use of funds for certain purposes

No funds provided directly to institutions or organizations to provide services and administer programs under subsection (a)(1)(A) of this section shall be expended for sectarian worship, instruction, or proselytization.

(k) Preemption

Nothing in this section shall be construed to preempt any provision of a State constitution or State statute that prohibits or restricts the expenditure of State funds in or by religious organizations.

a. Does Aid to Faith-Based Charities Violate the Establishment Clause?

The statute allows religious social service organizations receiving federal funds to maintain religious symbols in their buildings (subsection (d)(2)) and to favor persons of their own faith in employment (subsection (f)). Does permitting aid under those circumstances violate the Establishment Clause? In answering that question, you should consider not only the Supreme Court decisions on aid that you have already read but also the Court's decision in Bowen v. Kendrick (p. 397), Dodge v. Salvation Army (p. 448), and the line of decisions that appear to disagree with *Dodge* (p. 451).

1. Is Charitable Choice "Neutral"? To a significant extent, the debate over the constitutionality of Charitable Choice tracks the general debate over whether the primary Religion Clause principle is "neutrality," which would tend to approve equal aid to religious providers, or some version of "separation," which would tend to reject such church-state interaction. But there is also a debate over whether Charitable Choice is "neutral." Professor Carl Esbeck argues:

> Rightly interpreted, the Establishment Clause does not require that faith-based providers censor their religious expression and secularize their identity as conditions of participation in a governmental program. So long as the welfare program has as its object the public purpose of society's betterment—that is, help for the poor and needy—and so long as the program is equally open to all providers, religious and secular, then the First Amendment requirement that the law be neutral as to religion is fully satisfied.

Carl Esbeck, A Constitutional Case for Governmental Cooperation with Faith-Based Social Service Providers, 46 Emory L.J. 1, 40 (1997). Professor Alan Brownstein responds:

> State funding of religious organizations is problematic and controversial because of legitimate concerns about the fairness of allocation arrangements and the fear that politically powerful groups will aggrandize state resources. The risk that funding mechanisms may disproportionately favor certain religions and exclude others raises serious issues about the incentives created by such apportionments. Given the diversity of religious faiths in the United States, a constitutional guarantee that only requires that subsidies must be distributed according to formally neutral criteria does not come close to adequately addressing this problem.

Alan Brownstein, Interpreting the Religion Clauses in Terms of Liberty, Equality, and Free Speech Values—A Critical Analysis of "Neutrality Theory" and Charitable Choice, 13 Notre Dame J.L. Ethics & Pub. Pol'y 243, 283 (1999).

2. Religion-Based Hiring by Charitable Choice Providers. As the previous section (IV-F-1) noted, the Charitable Choice statute has been criticized for permitting religious agencies receiving funds to discriminate on the basis of religion in hiring. Review those arguments and the case of Dodge v. Salvation Army (pp. 448-452) now. Is it unconstitutional for government to fund a program and allow the organization to engage in religion-based hiring with respect to that program?

3. Religious Accommodations in Charitable Choice. The statute protects a religious provider in "the definition [and] expression of its religious beliefs" and in its display of "religious art, icons, scripture, or other symbols" on its premises. Professor Brownstein argues that these provisions are unconstitutional because they do not give "religious and secular speech and speakers an equal playing field. Religious organizations are provided a powerful advantage that is unavailable to their secular counterparts because they are immunized from state regulation." *Id.* at 244. What authority would you cite for this argument? What authority against it? What would be the equivalent of religious symbols for a secular organization receiving funds? Political posters? Could a state deny aid to an otherwise eligible secular social service provider on the ground that it displays political posters or engages in political speech?

4. Vouchers Versus Contracts for Services. Subsection (a)(1) of the statute lists two ways in which states may involve religious social service organizations: contracting directly with the organization to provide services, or giving vouchers to beneficiaries for use at any eligible (including religious) organization. Which of the two methods is more vulnerable to Establishment Clause objections? Professor Brownstein, a leading critic of Charitable Choice, directs his criticisms "primarily to direct grants of aid" and says that vouchers "raise different questions." Brownstein, Constitutional Questions, *in* Davis and Hankins at 256 n.37. Why might contracts for services be more vulnerable to challenge than vouchers are?

As we saw in earlier materials (p. 429), the line between "direct aid" and "private choice" programs such as vouchers is not always clear. Consider this case:

FREEDOM FROM RELIGION FOUNDATION v. McCALLUM

324 F.3d 880 (7th Cir. 2003)

Posner, Circuit Judge.

This is a taxpayer suit to enjoin Wisconsin correctional authorities from funding Faith Works, a halfway house that, like Alcoholics Anonymous, incorporates Christianity into its treatment program. The plaintiffs argue that this funding constitutes an establishment of religion, in violation of the Constitution. The district judge rejected the argument after a bench trial.

If a convicted criminal is out on parole (or probation, but we need not discuss that separately) and living in Milwaukee and he violates the terms of the parole, his parole officer may offer him, as an alternative to being sent back to prison, enrollment in one of several halfway houses with which the state has contracts. The officer can recommend a specific halfway house—the one he thinks best for the particular offender—but the offender is free to choose one of the others. One of the authorized halfway houses, Faith Works, which focuses on employment needs, drug and alcohol addiction, and parental responsibility, has a religious theme: it encourages the offender to establish a personal relationship with God through the mediation of Jesus Christ. Parole officers have recommended Faith Works to some parolees, but have been careful to explain that it is a nonbinding recommendation and that Faith Works is a Christian institution and its program of rehabilitation has a significant Christian element. Parole officers who recommend Faith Works are required to offer the offender a secular halfway house as an alternative. And although Faith Works will enroll an offender even if he is not a Christian, a parole officer will not recommend Faith Works to an offender who has no Christian identity and religious interest and will not advise anyone to convert to Christianity in order to get the most out of Faith Works.

There is no evidence that in recommending Faith Works a parole officer will be influenced by his own religious beliefs. His end is secular, the rehabilitation of a criminal, though the means include religion when the offender chooses Faith Works. Because the Supreme Court will not allow a public agency to force religion on people even if the agency honestly and indeed correctly believes that it is the best way of achieving a secular end that is within government's constitutional authority to promote, the state may not require offenders to enroll in Faith Works even if it is the best halfway house in Milwaukee for any or even all offenders. The choice must be private, to provide insulating material between government and religion. It is private; it is the offender's choice.

The success of Alcoholics Anonymous is evidence that Christianity can be a valuable element in a program for treating addiction. And alone among the approved halfway houses in Milwaukee, Faith Works offers a nine-month residential program; the secular programs are only three months. The longer term makes Faith Works uniquely attractive to the correctional authorities because they believe that many offenders need the longer period of supervised residence in order to succeed in becoming reintegrated into civil society. So the state waived the usual bidding requirements when it contracted with Faith Works, which it had not done with the other halfway houses in Milwaukee. A similar program has operated in New York, reportedly successfully.

If an offender enrolls in Faith Works, the state reimburses a part of the cost in accordance with the terms of the contract, just as it does in the case of offenders who enroll in secular halfway houses. Pending the final outcome of this litigation, however, the parole and probation officers have stopped referring offenders to Faith Works, and the halfway house is empty.

The district judge was right to dismiss the suit. A city does not violate the establishment clause by giving parents vouchers that they can use to purchase private school education for their children, even if most of the private schools in the city are parochial schools—provided, of course, that the parents are not required to use the vouchers to attend a parochial school rather than a secular school. Zelman v. Simmons-Harris. The practice challenged in the present case is similar. The state in effect gives eligible offenders "vouchers" that they can use to purchase a place in a halfway house, whether the halfway house is "parochial" or secular. We have put "vouchers" in scare quotes because the state has dispensed with the intermediate step by which the recipient of the publicly funded private service hands his voucher to the service provider. But so far as the policy of the establishment clause is concerned, there is no difference between giving the voucher recipient a piece of paper that directs the public agency to pay the service provider and the agency's asking the recipient to indicate his preference and paying the provider whose service he prefers.

Nor does it make a difference that the state, rather than accrediting halfway houses, enters into contracts with them. Obviously it has not refused to enter into contracts with halfway houses that are secular—all but one of its contracts are with secular houses. The only evidence of favoritism, the bid waiver, is unpersuasive; it was granted because Faith Works' program has such attractive features from a purely secular standpoint, such as the length of the program, that the state was eager to have it on its menu of halfway-house choices. That most of the halfway houses with which the state has contracts are secular makes this an easier case than the school voucher case. Most private schools in this country are parochial schools, so that a voucher system, at least in the short run (in the long run the existence of such a system is likely to stimulate the creation of new secular private schools), will give a definite boost to religion. Most halfway houses are secular.

The plaintiffs argue that by recommending Faith Works to some offenders, parole officers steer the offenders to a religious program and by doing so provide governmental support to religion. The implications of the argument are unacceptable. If recommending a religious institution constituted an establishment of religion, a public school guidance counselor could not recommend that a student apply to a Catholic college even if the counselor thought that the particular college would be the best choice for the particular student. And, coming closer to home, a parole officer could not recommend to a parolee who had a serious drinking problem that he enroll in Alcoholics Anonymous, even if the officer believed that this was the only alcoholic-treatment program that would keep the parolee from committing further crimes. To suppose such recommendations unlawful would be to adopt a doctrinaire interpretation of the establishment clause remote from its underlying purpose and historical understanding. Suggestion is not a synonym for coercion.

The plaintiffs' lawyer acknowledged at argument that it would be lawful for a public agency to rate public and private, including parochial, schools and publish the rating, even if it put a Catholic school at the top. That would be tantamount to recommending that school. He argued that the difference between that case and this one is that there are no objective criteria for rating halfway houses and therefore ratings or, what are equivalent, recommendations would involve discretionary judgments possibly influenced by the religious preferences of the agency or public employees doing the rating or making the recommendations. That is a danger, though the district court found, not clearly erroneously, that it has not materialized. A school year has a standard length, so that a school that announced it was shortening its school year to three months would quickly be stripped of its accreditation. There is no standard halfway-house treatment program that would enable an "objective" comparison to be made between a three-month secular halfway-house program and Faith Works' nine-month program. Lack of uniform intake criteria would defeat efforts to use the recidivism rate as a test of quality. In short, it is easier to establish accreditation criteria for schools than for halfway houses.

If religiously oriented halfway houses were obviously of little value from a correctional standpoint, the danger of seepage of religious preferences or aversions into the process of rating or recommendation might tip the scale against allowing such halfway houses to receive public funding even as mediated by private choice. But on the contrary—and quite apart from the evidence, confirmed by long experience with the parallel case of Alcoholics Anonymous, that for some substance abusers religion is an effective treatment—there is the fact that Faith Works offers a program that lasts three times as long as that of any of its secular competitors. To exclude Faith Works from this competition on the basis of a speculative fear that parole or probation officers might recommend its program because of their own Christian faith would involve the sacrifice of a real good to avoid a conjectured bad. It would be perverse if the Constitution required this result.

The plaintiffs try to turn the real good of Faith Works' program in their favor by arguing that because it is indeed the best program, offenders who are advised to enroll in it—perhaps all offenders who are eligible for a halfway house—have no real choice. But quality cannot be coercion. That would amount to saying that a city cannot adopt a school voucher system if the parochial schools in the city are better than the public or secular private schools. Faith Works, penalized because its secular competitors were unwilling to invest as much in the rehabilitation of offenders, would have an incentive to reduce the quality of its program, while those competitors would have an incentive to reduce the quality of their own programs in order to make Faith Works' "violation" of the establishment clause more perspicuous and encourage it to curtail its program. There would be a race to the bottom.

It is a misunderstanding of freedom (another paradox, given the name of the principal plaintiff) to suppose that choice is not free when the objects between which the chooser must choose are not equally attractive to him. It would mean that a person was not exercising his free will when in response to the question whether he preferred vanilla or chocolate ice cream he said vanilla, because it was the only honest answer that he could have given and therefore "he had no choice."

NOTES AND QUESTIONS

Under the Charitable Choice statute as well as Supreme Court precedent, funds provided directly to a religious organization may not be used for religious teaching ("sectarian worship, instruction, or proselytizing," the statute puts it), but funds reaching the organization through the choices of individual beneficiaries are not so restricted. For social services that incorporate explicit religious teaching throughout their programs, this distinction is crucial.

1. What Is and Is Not "Direct Aid?" In *McCallum* Judge Posner comments that "so far as the policy of the establishment clause is concerned, there is no difference between giving the voucher recipient a piece of paper that directs the public agency to pay the service provider and the agency's asking the recipient to indicate his preference and paying the provider whose service he prefers." Is that true? Is it consistent with Supreme Court precedent?

2. Genuine Choice and Options. Judge Posner reasons that an individual receiving aid does not lack free choice in where to use it simply because one service provider is more attractive than another. Is this consistent with *Zelman*, which required that for a program to be one of "true private choice," it must offer "genuine" secular options? Recall that in *Zelman*, the Cleveland public schools had been declared educationally inadequate—that was the very motivation for enacting the voucher program. If Judge Posner's approach were followed in *Zelman*, would the unreformed, failing public schools count as a "genuine" option?

3. Problems: What Can an Entity Receiving Direct Grants Do? What exactly is the "sectarian worship, instruction, or proselytization" on which funds provided directly to religious organizations may not be spent? Consider some examples under the Adolescent and Family Life (AFL) Act, which provides grants to social services organizations, religious and nonreligious, to combat teenage pregnancy. In Bowen v. Kendrick, 487 U.S. 589 (1988) (p. 397), the Court upheld the Act against a facial Establishment Clause challenge but noted that both the Act itself and the Constitution forbade direct grants to be used to promote religion or teach particular religious doctrines. After *Kendrick*, a booklet published by the agency implementing the AFL program, the Department of Health and Human Services, offered the following hypotheticals concerning the restrictions on religious teaching. How would you analyze these situations, under the Charitable Choice statute and under the Establishment Clause?

(1) An AFL project is invited to present a prevention program to adolescents attending a church-affiliated summer camp. Does this present a problem? . . .

(4) May services be provided in settings which contain religious symbols? . . .

(6) A project runs a residential care program which provides shelter and a variety of services for pregnant teens. The organization which sponsors the project makes religious counselors available for AFL clients and others at the shelter. The counselors are not paid for with AFL funds. They do not see AFL clients unless clients specifically request spiritual counseling. Does this present any problem? . . .

(7) A grantee has produced informational material of a sectarian nature with non-project funds. It is available in an office utilized by both non-AFL clients and AFL clients. Is this appropriate?

b. Do "Strings on Aid" Violate Religious Autonomy?

1. Restrictions on Religious Activity.   Subsection (j) of the Charitable Choice statute prohibits the use of direct aid "for sectarian worship, instruction, or proselytization." And subsection (g) says that a religious organization may not discriminate against a beneficiary in a government-funded program "on the basis of religion, a religious belief, or refusal to actively participate in a religious practice." Are these subsections constitutionally required? Or are they constitutionally objectionable?

What if a religious organization believes—as many do—that the only way to solve an individual's problem of addiction or mental illness is for the individual to attend worship, hear a religious message, and experience a conversion in his soul? Does subsection (g) prevent the organization from demanding such attendance? If so, does the provision effectively disqualify the very organizations, the "seriously religious" ones, that it was meant to include? On this ground Professor Olasky, an early proponent of the charitable choice idea whose book is cited above, later announced his opposition. Note that subsection (e)(1) of the Charitable Choice provision guarantees beneficiaries a nonreligious alternative. Why is that not sufficient protection?

2. Restrictions on Discrimination in Hiring.   Under the Charitable Choice statute, the religious organization receiving funds is typically free to continue to discriminate in hiring on the basis of religion. Suppose that the statute were amended to apply religious nondiscrimination laws applicable to the organization; would that be unconstitutional? What if the religious nondiscrimination requirement applied only to jobs directly funded by the government?

Under the statute, the organization remains subject to federal laws prohibiting discrimination in employment on the basis of race, sex, or ethnicity. There is no federal law prohibiting employment discrimination on the basis of sexual orientation. But suppose that a state that includes religious agencies in its social service funding also has a rule that organizations receiving funds may not discriminate in employment on the basis of sexual orientation. As applied to a religious agency with doctrinal objections to homosexual behavior, would applying such a rule violate the agency's religious freedom? Would it depend on the governing standard for free exercise claims? Or would *exempting* the religious agency from the rule be the unconstitutional course?

V

RELIGION AND THE GOVERNMENT'S INFLUENCE ON CULTURE

This Part examines the various ways governments act to create and shape the culture. These include both affirmative efforts to promote ideas and practices thought to be worthy and negative efforts to repress ideas and practices at odds with the public ethos. This is something all governments do. The flag, the national anthem, the Smithsonian Museum, public schools and libraries, and national holidays (Veterans Day, Martin Luther King Day) are all artifacts of this kind of statecraft. So too are anticommunist propaganda, obscenity laws, and regulation of hate speech. The government is necessarily a major influence on the culture insofar as it controls key institutions for the development and dissemination of ideas, such as schools, universities, museums, public squares, historical sites, artistic and scientific grants, and media of communications. This Part is devoted to the treatment of religion within those government-controlled institutions. If religious messages are conveyed, is that an endorsement? If religious messages are eliminated, is that hostility? Is there a neutral course?

Historically, religion has almost always been part of national identity—a source of legitimacy, pride, and national unity. Religion is called upon to give meaning to a nation's history, to stiffen its resolve in crises, and to confirm ideas about its destiny. When the Puritans who settled Massachusetts Bay Colony arrived in 1630 their leader, John Winthrop, announced that "the Lord will be our God and delight to dwell among us, as his own people [so] that men shall say of succeeding plantations: the lord make it like that of New England: for we must consider that we shall be as a City upon a Hill [Mt. 5.14] the eyes of all people are upon us[.]" John Winthrop, 2 Papers 294 (1931). When Abraham Lincoln was elected to a second term, he offered a more sober reflection on the civil war in which the country was then engaged. "American slavery is one of those offenses which, in the providence of God, must needs come, but which, having continued through His appointed time, He now wills to remove, and . . . He gives to both North and South, this terrible war, as the woe due to

471

those by whom the offense came[.]" Abraham Lincoln, Second Inaugural Address, in 8 Collected Works of Abraham Lincoln 333 (1953). During times of national crisis, American political leaders often turn to prayer and religious imagery. After the destruction of the World Trade Center, banners proclaiming "God Bless America" blossomed throughout the land, on government buildings as well as on private homes and offices.

To what extent does the Constitution limit the government's ability to enlist religious themes and institutions in shaping our social self-consciousness? Some maintain that it strictly forbids any such effort. Others argue that the First Amendment applies only when there would be a coercive or proselytizing effect; or that the permissibility of government religious expression depends on tradition, divisiveness, degree of sectarianism, or other factors; or that it is a question of balance. Whether we can and must separate religion completely from our public life, or whether we should adopt some other policy—one of neutrality, for example—is the principal concern of this Part.

We begin, in section A, by looking at familiar practices with religious overtones where the government has played the role of speaker (or impresario): test oaths, school prayers and curriculum, "blue" (Sunday closing) laws, and the publication of speech and symbols at government expense. The bulk of this material concerns religion in public schools, which are the most obvious place where government speaks and tries to create a common culture. In these cases, we most often look to the Establishment Clause for guidance.

Section B examines in detail government efforts to control the communication of ideas by private speakers. In these cases the most prominent constitutional provisions are the Free Speech and Free Exercise clauses. We begin with some basic rules of free speech law, and then ask whether those rules change toward greater constitutional protection or toward a greater governmental power to restrict when the speech is religious in content.

The Court has held, with a few exceptions, that the government may not engage in religious speech itself but also may not restrict private speech on the basis that it is religious. But while government and private speech are distinct categories, some cases fall near the line between them, and we examine these in section C. Finally, section D takes up the role that religion may play in government, not in terms of explicitly religious government actions (such as official prayers or religious exercises) but as the basis for government action in secular political matters of justice and the common good. The most prominent area in which religion and politics mix currently is abortion and other matters of sexuality, but the constitutional and moral questions extend to many other political matters.

A. EFFORTS TO CREATE A PUBLIC CULTURE

In the law of the First Amendment dealing with freedom of speech, we draw a distinction between cases where the government acts as a speaker and cases where the government regulates private speech. Mark Yudof, When Government Speaks (1983); Steven H. Shiffrin and Jesse H. Choper, The First Amendment ch. 7 (2d ed. 1996). This section looks at cases that fall in the first of these categories. For example, when public schools teach creation science or when a city puts up a crèche at Christmas time, the government makes a statement that has religious content.

It may be tempting to say of these cases what John Locke did in his Letter Concerning Toleration (see p. 38):

> It may indeed be alleged that the magistrate may make use of arguments, and thereby draw the heterodox into the way of truth, and procure their salvation. I grant it; but this is common to him with other men. In teaching, instructing, and redressing the erroneous by reason, he may certainly do what becomes any good man to do. Magistracy does not oblige him to put off either humanity or Christianity; but it is one thing to persuade, another to command; one thing to press with arguments, another with penalties.

This remains the rule for most speech. Government may speak against tobacco and in favor of families. The Free Speech Clause stops the government from restricting citizens' speech, but it does not usually prevent the government itself from speaking. But contrary to Locke, today it is usually thought that religion is an *exception* to the general rule permitting the government to express and argue for ideas. What accounts for the difference?

1. Compelled Statements of Belief: Test Oaths and Others

We begin with a practice that, by most lights, is more constitutionally objectionable than the garden variety case of government speech. A *test oath* is a statement that the government requires a person to affirm in order to maintain his liberty or citizenship, or more commonly as a condition ("test") of the person's right to hold a government office, vote, or engage in some other civic activity. When the oath is religious, such a case involves both of the asserted wrongs mentioned above: (1) coercion and (2) government expression of a religious position. The government not only composes the oath but also pressures private parties to join in—raising questions of freedom (speech, religion) as well as nonestablishment. Test oaths were a central feature of the British establishment of religion (see p. 16).

TORCASO v. WATKINS, 367 U.S. 488 (1961): Article 37 of the Declaration of Rights of Maryland's Constitution provided that "[n]o religious test ought ever to be required as a qualification for any office of profit or trust in this State, other than a declaration of belief in the existence of God." Torcaso was barred from serving as a notary public because he would not declare a belief in God. The Court struck down the requirement under the First Amendment on the ground that it put "[t]he power and authority of the [state] on the side of one particular sort of believers—those who are willing to say they believe in 'the existence of God'":

"It is true that there is much historical precedent for such laws. [In fact,] many of those who had fled [Europe] to escape religious test oaths turned out to be perfectly willing, when they had the power to do so, to force dissenters from their faith to take test oaths in conformity with that faith. . . . The effect of all this was the formal or practical 'establishment' of particular religious faiths in most of the Colonies, with consequent burdens imposed on the free exercise of the faiths of non-favored believers.

"There were, however, wise and farseeing men in the Colonies—too many to mention—who spoke out against test oaths and all the philosophy of intolerance behind them. . . .

"When our Constitution was adopted, the desire to put the people 'securely beyond the reach' of religious test oaths brought about the inclusion in Article VI of that document of a provision that 'no religious Test shall ever be required as a Qualification to any Office or public Trust under the United States.' Article VI [shows] that '[t]he test oath is abhorrent to our tradition.' Not satisfied, however, with Article VI and other guarantees in the original Constitution, the First Congress proposed and the States very shortly thereafter adopted our Bill of Rights, including the First Amendment."

The Court held that test oaths for state office violated the principle of Everson v. Board of Education [p. 339] that "[n]either a State nor the Federal Government can constitutionally force a person 'to profess a belief or disbelief in any religion.' Neither can constitutionally pass laws or impose requirements which aid all religions as against non-believers, and neither can aid those religions based on a belief in the existence of God as against those religions founded on different beliefs." (In a footnote, number 11, the Court added: "Among religions in this country which do not teach what would generally be considered a belief in the existence of God are Buddhism, Taoism, Ethical Culture, Secular Humanism and others[.]")

The Court concluded that the fact "that a person is not compelled to hold public office cannot possibly be an excuse for barring him from office by state-imposed criteria forbidden by the Constitution," and that the Maryland test oath "unconstitutionally invades the appellant's freedom of belief and religion."

NOTES AND QUESTIONS

1. The "No Religious Test" Clause. As *Torcaso* points out, the original U.S. Constitution includes a provision forbidding the federal government to do what Maryland did here. The Religious Test Clause appears at the end of the Oath Clause (art. VI, cl. 3):

> The Senators and Representatives before mentioned, and the Members of the several State Legislatures, and all executive and judicial Officers, both of the United States and of the several States, shall be bound by Oath or Affirmation, to support this Constitution; but no religious Test shall ever be required as a Qualification to any office or public Trust under the United States.

The background of the clause is thoroughly discussed in Gerald V. Bradley, The No Religious Test Clause and the Constitution of Religious Liberty: A Machine That Has Gone of Itself, 37 Case W. Res. L. Rev. 674 (1987).

Note that the Constitution itself requires public officials to take one kind of oath—to support the Constitution—and a belief in God is implicit in the very idea of an oath. The alternative of an affirmation was added as an accommodation because, as Justice Story observed, "there are known denominations of men, who are conscientiously scrupulous of taking oaths (among which is that pure and distinguished sect of Christians, commonly called Friends, or Quakers)" and the Framers wished "to prevent any unjustifiable exclusion from office." A Familiar Exposition of the Constitution of the United States § 426 (1840).

2. Religious Test Oaths and the First Amendment. What part of the First Amendment does Article 37 violate? The Court concludes by saying that it invades Torcaso's "freedom of belief and religion." This suggests that the relevant part of the First Amendment is the Free Exercise Clause. The free exercise violation may be clear as applied to followers of Buddhism or the other religions mentioned in footnote 11 that do not teach a belief in the existence of God. But what if the potential officeholder is an atheist: Does his position amount to the "exercise of religion"? What if the potential officeholder objects to the oath simply because he has no particular belief about a deity (for or against): Can that position be the exercise of religion?

On the other hand, in striking down the oath the Court cited Everson v. Board of Education, an Establishment Clause decision. What features of the oath would make it an Establishment Clause violation? The affirmation required was not of any particular church, but only of a very general belief in God. Does that save it from being an establishment?

Perhaps this is a case in which the two clauses easily work together.

3. Can Belief Be Compelled? Can requirements like a test oath really affect religious belief? One might suppose not: If religious faith is an internal matter, there seems little danger that the government can affect it by compelling outward compliance.

One answer to this question comes from the Baptist religious leader Roger Williams. Williams objected to compulsion not because it would affect belief, but because it forced the faithful into "hypocrisy"—they were made "to act and practice in matters of religion and worship against the doubts and checks of their consciences," praying with "their bodies . . . when their souls are far off." The Bloody Tenent of Persecution for Cause of of Conscience, in Irwin H. Polishook, Roger Williams, John Cotton, and Religious Freedom 84, 89 (1967). Another possible answer comes from the English statesman Edmund Burke, who wrote: "Strange it is, but so it is, that men, driven by force from their habits in one mode of religion, have, by contrary habits, under the same force, often quietly settled in another. They suborn their reason to declare in favor of their necessity." Letter to Richard Burke on the Protestant Ascendancy in Ireland (1793), in 6 Works of the Rt. Hon. Edmund Burke 285, 395 (Little, Brown, 9th ed., 1889). Burke's point is that coercion may be effective over time, as individuals' consciences conform to their outward professions.

4. Justifications for Religious Test Oaths. Let us not simply ignore the reasons that societies had for imposing religious test oaths.

(a) Preventing subversion or violence. One historical reason was to prevent political subversion, since the state and its enemies were often defined by antagonistic religious beliefs. For example, Queen Elizabeth I required her ministers to take an oath of supremacy and allegiance acknowledging her as head of church and state, and renouncing all foreign (i.e., Catholic) spiritual jurisdiction. 1 Eliz. c.1 (1558). After the failed Gunpowder Plot of 1605 (an alleged sabotage conspiracy among Catholics), Parliament passed an "Act for the better discovering and repressing of popish recusants," which required a long oath saying that one sided with King James I and against the Pope. 3 Jac. I. c.4 (1606). John Locke supported withholding toleration from Catholics as well as atheists: "That Church can have no right to be tolerated by the magistrate which is constituted upon such a bottom that all those who enter into it do thereby ipso facto deliver themselves up to the protection and service of another prince." We saw similar views about Catholic allegiances to the Pope displayed in nineteenth-century America (see pp. 356-365).

It is difficult to see how the "preventing subversion" rationale can justify an oath about religion in America, where the government—unlike the English crown is not defined as officially religious? But religious beliefs sometimes are intimately connected with dangerous behavior, as we were reminded on September 11, 2001. Could the federal government require that any Muslim seeking federal employment forswear a belief in the necessity of armed *jihad* against Western nations?

(b) Good conduct and honesty.   When the federal Convention adopted the Article VI clause against test oaths, Luther Martin of Maryland noted that "there were some members *so unfashionable* as to think, that a *belief of the existence of a Deity*, and of a *state of future rewards and punishments* would be some security for the good conduct of our rulers." The Records of the Federal Convention 227 n.100 (Max Farrand ed. 1966) (italics in original). Likewise, John Locke, in his Letter on Toleration (p. 38), would have denied toleration to atheists on the ground that they did not have the fear of eternal punishment that would keep them honest: "Promises, covenants, and oaths, which are the bonds of human society, can have no hold upon an atheist." Suppose there were empirical support for the proposition that those who declare a belief in God behave better or more honestly in office—say they are convicted of official misconduct (embezzlement, extortion, mail fraud, etc.) 15 percent less often—than nondeclarants. Would that justify an oath requirement?

5. Secular Oaths and the First Amendment.   Might the oath in *Torcaso* be unconstitutional quite apart from the Religion Clauses? Think again about the Court's closing statement that the oath "invades the appellant's freedom of belief and religion." Is freedom of belief protected (perhaps by the Free Speech Clause) in cases where the affirmation required has no religious significance?

When does an oath have religious significance? Recall Davis v. Beason, 133 U.S. 333 (1890) (p. 119), in which the Idaho Territory did not let people vote unless they swore that they did not belong to any organization that taught its members to commit bigamy or practiced "plural or celestial marriage as a doctrinal or celestial rite" and that they did not advocate committing polygamy "either as a religious duty or otherwise." Is this constitutional after *Torcaso*? Does it survive free exercise scrutiny because it is aimed at polygamy committed for whatever reason? Cf. Employment Division v. Smith (p. 137). Does it violate the Free Exercise Clause because, as we know from evidence outside the text of the oath, its point was to disenfranchise Mormons? Cf. Church of Lukumi Babalu Aye v. City of Hialeah (p. 162).

What about an oath that effectively excludes persons with particular religious views? Could a public university decline to hire a professor who would not sign a declaration that he does not regard homosexual relations as sinful? Could it ask whether a prospective faculty member belongs to any organizations that teach or advocate inequality between the sexes?

COMMONWEALTH v. COOKE

7 Am. L. Reg. 417 (Police Ct. 1859)

MAINE, J.—[Cooke, a public school teacher in Boston, Massachusetts, was charged with assaulting Thomas Wall, an 11-year-old student. Pursuant to state law, the Bible in the common English version was read in the school, and scholars sufficiently advanced were required to read or commit to memory the Lord's Prayer and the Ten Commandments. On Sunday, March 13, Wall's parish priest, addressing nine hundred children of St. Mary's Church, told them not to be cowards to their religion, and not to read or repeat the Commandments in school. If they did, he said, he would read their names from the altar.]

It further appeared, from the evidence, that there was a concerted plan of action on Monday, the 14th, between many of the boys to refuse to obey the orders of the school, if required to read or repeat the Lord's Prayer or the Commandments, and that two-thirds of the scholars composing the school where Wall attended, and numbering about sixty, declared their intention not to comply with the rules of the school in that particular. And from all the evidence it was manifest that Wall was one of, if not the principal actor. He . . . was punished by the defendant with a rattan stick, some three feet in length, and three-eighths of an inch thick, by whipping upon his hands. From the time when the punishment commenced to the time when it ended, repeated inquiries were made of Wall if he would comply with the requirements of the school. Some thirty minutes' time was occupied in the whole. During this time there were several intervals, at two of which the defendant was absent from the room some little time. The blows were not given in quick succession, but with deliberation. During the chastisement Wall was encouraged by others, who told him not to give up. This was while defendant was absent from the room. The master ceased to punish, when Wall submitted to the requirements of the school.

From the effect of the punishment Wall's hands were swollen, he was taken to the sink by the defendant twice, and his hands held in water. The physician who saw his hands in the afternoon of Monday, and prescribed for them, after describing their appearance, says that he did not think the injury very severe; that at the time he thought he would recover from it in twenty-four hours.

Now, was the punishment so inflicted without justification, and in violation of the constitutional rights of Wall? [The constitution of Massachusetts provides:]

> That it is the right as well as the duty of all men in society publicly and at stated seasons to worship the Supreme Being, the great Creator and Preserver of the universe. And no subject shall be hurt, molested, or restrained in his person, liberty, or estate, for worshiping God in the manner and seasons most agreeably to the dictates of his own conscience, or for his religious professions or sentiments, provided he doth not disturb the public peace, or obstruct others in their religious worship.

[This passage] was intended to prevent persecution by punishing for religious opinions. The Bible has long been in our common schools. It was placed there by our fathers, not for the purpose of teaching sectarian religion, but a knowledge of God and of his will, whose practice is religion. . . . But, in doing this, no scholar is requested to believe it, none to receive it as the only true version of the laws of God. The teacher enters into no argument to prove its correctness, and gives no instructions in theology from it. To read the Bible in school for these and like purposes, or to require it to be read without sectarian explanations, is no interference with religious liberty. . . .

By this the court is not to be understood as justifying the inflicting of punishment upon a scholar so long as he holds out against the commands of the school. The punishment must not be extended beyond the limits of sound discretion, and this every master must decide at his peril. In this case the punishment inflicted, when compared with the offence committed, and all the attendant circumstances as they appeared upon the trial, was neither excessive, nor inflicted through malice by the defendant.

The defendant is discharged.

NOTES AND QUESTIONS

1. Affirmations Versus Mere Statements.   *Cooke* predates the Fourteenth Amendment (1868), so the constitutional rights it speaks of stem from under the state constitution. How would we decide the case today? Is Massachusetts's rule like the oath in *Torcaso*? Notice the court's comment that "no scholar is requested to believe it, none to receive it as the only true version of the laws of God." Is there no free exercise violation if the student need not affirm what he recites? Why would Thomas Wall's priest urge him to resist? Recall Burke's argument (p. 475) that outward compliance will eventually tend to affect inward belief. Was there a danger of that in Thomas Wall's case?

2. Religious Content and Purpose.   If the practice in *Cooke* was less troublesome than a religious test oath because no "affirmation" was required, was it nevertheless still invalid because the recitations it required were religious—indeed, of a particular Christian outlook? Massachusetts probably did not adopt its practice of Bible reading and pious recitations with the goal of disfavoring Catholics; but could it violate the Free Exercise Clause by leaving that rule in place once Catholics began to arrive in large numbers? In the Catholic Church, particularly in the nineteenth century, the teaching authority of the church played a much greater role in its members' collective understanding of scripture than was true among Protestants. A requirement that the Bible be read "without comment" would thus have been understood to inculcate the Protestant view that revelation was available to each individual through the scripture, without the need for ecclesiastical mediation. Could the state violate the Free Exercise Clause by enforcing its rule with the kind of enthusiasm Cooke displayed?

Let us now return to a variation that we explored in connection with test oaths. What about compelled recitations that are not so overtly religious in content: What does the First Amendment say about them? That is the issue next, in the famous "flag salute" case.

BOARD OF EDUCATION v. BARNETTE
319 U.S. 624 (1943)

Mr. Justice JACKSON delivered the opinion of the Court.

The [West Virginia] Board of Education on January 9, 1942, adopted a resolution . . . ordering that the salute to the flag become "a regular part of the program of activities in the public schools," that all teachers and pupils "shall be required to participate in the salute honoring the Nation represented by the Flag; provided, however, that refusal to salute the Flag be regarded as an Act of insubordination, and shall be dealt with accordingly." . . .

Failure to conform is "insubordination" dealt with by expulsion. Readmission is denied by statute until compliance. Meanwhile the expelled child is "unlawfully absent" and may be proceeded against as a delinquent. His parents or guardians are liable to prosecution, and if convicted are subject to fine not exceeding $50 and jail term not exceeding thirty days.

Appellees [sued in federal court] for themselves and others similarly situated asking its injunction to restrain enforcement of these laws and regulations against Jehovah's Witnesses. The Witnesses are an unincorporated body teaching that the obligation imposed by law of God is superior to that of laws enacted by temporal government. Their religious beliefs include a literal version of Exodus, Chapter 20, verses 4 and 5, which says: "Thou shalt not make unto thee any graven image, or any likeness of anything that is in heaven above, or that is in the earth beneath, or that is in the water under the earth; thou shalt not bow down thyself to them nor serve them." They consider that the flag is an "image" within this command. For this reason they refuse to salute it[. A three-judge court enjoined enforcement of the statute, and the state appealed.]

[T]he compulsory flag salute and pledge requires affirmation of a belief and an attitude of mind. It is not clear whether the regulation contemplates that pupils forego any contrary convictions of their own and become unwilling converts to the prescribed ceremony or whether it will be acceptable if they simulate assent by words without belief and by a gesture barren of meaning. It is now a commonplace that censorship or suppression of expression of opinion is tolerated by our Constitution only when the expression presents a clear and present danger of action of a kind the State is empowered to prevent and punish. It would seem that involuntary affirmation could be commanded only on even more immediate and urgent grounds than silence. But here the power of compulsion is invoked without any allegation that remaining passive during a flag salute ritual creates a clear and present danger that would justify an effort even to muffle expression. To sustain the compulsory flag salute we are required to say that a Bill of Rights which guards the individual's right to speak his own mind, left it open to public authorities to compel him to utter what is not in his mind.

[The issue does not] as we see it turn on one's possession of particular religious views or the sincerity with which they are held. While religion supplies appellees' motive for enduring the discomforts of making the issue in this case, many citizens who do not share these religious views hold such a compulsory rite to infringe constitutional liberty of the individual. It is not necessary to inquire whether non-conformist beliefs will exempt from the duty to salute unless we first find power to make the salute a legal duty.

[In Minersville School District v. Gobitis (1940),] we upheld the practice challenged here today. We reasoned] that "National unity is the basis of national security," that the authorities have "the right to select appropriate means for its attainment," and hence . . . that such compulsory measures toward "national unity" are constitutional. Upon the verity of this assumption depends our answer in this case.

National unity as an end which officials may foster by persuasion and example is not in question. The problem is whether under our Constitution compulsion as here employed is a permissible means for its achievement.

Struggles to coerce uniformity of sentiment in support of some end thought essential to their time and country have been waged by many good as well as by evil men. Nationalism is a relatively recent phenomenon but at other times and places the ends have been racial or territorial security, support of a dynasty or regime, and particular plans for saving souls. As first and moderate methods to attain unity have failed, those bent on its accomplishment must resort to an ever-increasing severity. As governmental pressure toward unity becomes greater, so strife becomes more bitter as to whose unity it shall be. Probably no deeper division of our people could proceed from any provocation than from finding it necessary to choose what doctrine and whose program public educational officials shall compel youth to unite in embracing. Ultimate futility of such attempts to compel coherence is the lesson of every such effort from the Roman drive to stamp out Christianity as a disturber of its pagan unity, the Inquisition as a means to religious and dynastic unity, the Siberian exiles as a means to Russian unity, down to the fast failing efforts of our present totalitarian enemies. Those who begin coercive elimination of dissent soon find themselves exterminating dissenters. Compulsory unification of opinion achieves only the unanimity of the graveyard.

It seems trite but necessary to say that the First Amendment to our Constitution was designed to avoid these ends by avoiding these beginnings. There is no mysticism in the American concept of the State or of the nature or origin of its authority. We set up government by consent of the governed, and the Bill of Rights denies those in power any legal opportunity to coerce that consent. Authority here is to be controlled by public opinion, not public opinion by authority. . . .

If there is any fixed star in our constitutional constellation, it is that no official, high or petty, can prescribe what shall be orthodox in politics, nationalism, religion, or other matters of opinion or force citizens to confess by word or act their faith therein. If there are any circumstances which permit an exception, they do not now occur to us.

We think the action of the local authorities in compelling the flag salute and pledge transcends constitutional limitations on their power and invades the sphere of intellect and spirit which it is the purpose of the First Amendment to our Constitution to reserve from all official control.

The decision of this Court in Minersville School District v. Gobitis [is] overruled, and the judgment enjoining enforcement of the West Virginia Regulation is affirmed.

Mr. Justice FRANKFURTER, dissenting.

One who belongs to the most vilified and persecuted minority in history is not likely to be insensible to the freedoms guaranteed by our Constitution. Were my

purely personal attitude relevant I should whole-heartedly associate myself with
the general libertarian views in the Court's opinion, representing as they do the
thought and action of a lifetime. But as judges we are neither Jew nor Gentile,
neither Catholic nor agnostic. We owe equal attachment to the Constitution and
are equally bound by our judicial obligations whether we derive our citizenship
from the earliest or the latest immigrants to these shores. As a member of this
Court I am not justified in writing my private notions of policy into the Constitution, no matter how deeply I may cherish them or how mischievous I may
deem their disregard. The duty of a judge who must decide which of two claims
before the Court shall prevail, that of a State to enact and enforce laws within its
general competence or that of an individual to refuse obedience because of the
demands of his conscience, is not that of the ordinary person. It can never be
emphasized too much that one's own opinion about the wisdom or evil of a law
should be excluded altogether when one is doing one's duty on the bench. The
only opinion of our own even looking in that direction that is material is our
opinion whether legislators could in reason have enacted such a law. In the light
of all the circumstances, including the history of this question in this Court, it
would require more daring than I possess to deny that reasonable legislators
could have taken the action which is before us for review. Most unwillingly,
therefore, I must differ from my brethren with regard to legislation like this.
I cannot bring my mind to believe that the "liberty" secured by the Due Process
Clause gives this Court authority to deny to the State of West Virginia the attainment of that which we all recognize as a legitimate legislative end, namely, the
promotion of good citizenship, by employment of the means here chosen[.]

Under our constitutional system the legislature is charged solely with civil
concerns of society. If the avowed or intrinsic legislative purpose is either to
promote or to discourage some religious community or creed, it is clearly within
the constitutional restrictions imposed on legislatures and cannot stand. But it
by no means follows that legislative power is wanting whenever a general nondiscriminatory civil regulation in fact touches conscientious scruples or religious
beliefs of an individual or a group. Regard for such scruples or beliefs undoubtedly presents one of the most reasonable claims for the exertion of legislative
accommodation. It is, of course, beyond our power to rewrite the state's requirement, by providing exemptions for those who do not wish to participate in the
flag salute or by making some other accommodations to meet their scruples.
That wisdom might suggest the making of such accommodations and that
school administration would not find it too difficult to make them and yet
maintain the ceremony for those not refusing to conform, is outside our province to suggest. . . .

What one can say with assurance is that the history out of which grew
constitutional provisions for religious equality and the writings of the great
exponents of religious freedom—Jefferson, Madison, John Adams, Benjamin
Franklin—are totally wanting in justification for a claim by dissidents of exceptional immunity from civic measures of general applicability, measures not in
fact disguised assaults upon such dissident views. The great leaders of the
American Revolution were determined to remove political support from every
religious establishment. They put on an equality the different religious sects—
Episcopalians, Presbyterians, Catholics, Baptists, Methodists, Quakers, Hugue-
nots—which, as dissenters, had been under the heel of the various orthodoxies

that prevailed in different colonies. So far as the state was concerned, there was to be neither orthodoxy nor heterodoxy. And so Jefferson and those who followed him wrote guaranties of religious freedom into our constitutions. Religious minorities as well as religious majorities were to be equal in the eyes of the political state. But Jefferson and the others also knew that minorities may disrupt society. It never would have occurred to them to write into the Constitution the subordination of the general civil authority of the state to sectarian scruples.

The constitutional protection of religious freedom terminated disabilities, it did not create new privileges. It gave religious equality, not civil immunity. Its essence is freedom from conformity to religious dogma, not freedom from conformity to law because of religious dogma.

NOTES AND QUESTIONS

1. Religious Creed Versus Secular Creed.   Note that the flag salute at this time did not contain the words "under God." These were added by an act of Congress in 1954. Would their presence in the pledge make a difference? The majority opinion states that "no official, high or petty, can prescribe what shall be orthodox in politics, nationalism, religion, or other matters of opinion." This does not appear to distinguish between religious and other forms of orthodoxy. Would it make a difference to Justice Frankfurter? Note that he distinguishes between government action with the purpose "either to promote or to discourage some religious community or creed" and government action with a secular civic purpose. The First Amendment prohibits an "establishment of religion"— not an establishment of secular ideology or patriotism. As we will discuss shortly (p. 507), the constitutionality of including "under God" in the Pledge has recently been challenged. See Newdow v. U.S. Congress, 328 F.3d 466 (9th Cir. 2003), rev'd on standing grounds, Elk Grove Unified School Dist. v. Newdow, 542 U.S. 1 (2004). If this were held to be an establishment violation, the remedy would be to remove the offending religious language, leaving the Pledge again a purely secular creed—from which objecting students must be excused under *Barnette.*

2. The Persecution of Jehovah's Witnesses.   The historical background of this case warrants notice. In 1940 the Supreme Court upheld the expulsion of two Jehovah's Witness children from public school in Pennsylvania for refusing to salute the flag. Minersville School Dist. v. Gobitis, 310 U.S. 586 (1940) (majority opinion by Frankfurter, J.). The West Virginia State Board of Education adopted its compulsory flag salute 19 months later, in a resolution containing recitals from the *Gobitis* opinion. By then, the United States had entered World War II. Jehovah's Witnesses were suspected of a lack of patriotism, and even of sabotage, because they refused to salute the flag and because many of them opposed military training and service. Their children were expelled from schools in nearly every state. See generally Shawn F. Peters, Judging Jehovah's Witnesses: Religious Persecution and the Dawn of the Rights Revolution (2000). In 1942, Mississippi and Louisiana passed laws making it a criminal offense to distribute literature explaining why Jehovah's Witnesses could not salute the flag. No. 591 Appellees' Br. 72 (O.T. 1942). In January of 1943, the Fourth

Circuit upheld the conviction of a group of public officials and American Legionnaires in Richwood, West Virginia, for forcing several Witnesses to drink large doses of castor oil and then dragging them by rope through the streets. Catlette v. United States, 132 F.2d 902 (4th Cir. 1943). *Barnette* may have been a reaction to this violence.

3. Constitutionally Required Oaths. What exactly is the constitutional violation here? Article VI, cl. 3 of the U.S. Constitution, as we observed above, requires public officials to pledge allegiance to the Constitution. Article II, §1 requires the President to take this oath: "I do solemnly swear (or affirm) that I will faithfully execute the Office of President of the United States, and will to the best of my Ability, preserve, protect and defend the Constitution of the United States." Suppose that the Witnesses' religious scruples cover pledging allegiance to the Constitution as well as the flag. If elected to office must they be excused from the requirements of Articles II and VI? Does the First Amendment partially repeal the Oath Clauses? If not, how is West Virginia's law different?

4. Problems: Compulsory Pledges. Is the rule against compulsory pledges absolute? Can you imagine a case where the government would be justified in making it a crime to refuse to utter a statutorily prescribed formula?

(a) What about requiring employers to make a pledge of nondiscrimination on their letterhead? Or landlords to announce that they will rent to unmarried couples—even if they have religious objections to cohabitation before marriage? See Thomas v. Anchorage Equal Rights Comm'n, 165 F.3d 692 (9th Cir. 1999) (p. 175).

(b) What about compelling fundamentalist Protestant students to affirm the truth of Darwinian evolution in response to questions on a biology test?

2. *Official Prayers and Religious Exercises in Public Schools: The Modern Decisions*

Not so long ago it was a common practice for public schoolchildren to begin each day with prayer and Bible reading as well as the Pledge of Allegiance. Horace Mann, secretary of the Massachusetts Board of Education from 1837 to 1849, promoted reading the Bible without comment as a way of fostering a common religion and morality in public schools. Whatever else might divide them, he thought, Christians (and most Americans were Christians) could unite in their devotion to the word of God. Denominations differed over what the scriptures meant, but people could avoid interpretive disputes by reading them without comment. Commonwealth v. Cooke, in the previous section, arose under that regime.

When the issue of school prayer reached the U.S. Supreme Court in the 1960s, this regime was still in place. But the series of decisions that follow dismantled it. The Pennsylvania law in Abington School District v. Schempp (p. 486), like the Massachusetts law in Commonwealth v. Cooke, directed children to read the Bible without comment and to recite the Lord's Prayer. But Pennsylvania made participation voluntary. In Engel v. Vitale (p. 484) and Lee v. Weisman (p. 498) we see a further relaxation: Prayers evolve from Christian to merely theistic. This is an adaptation that Mann would probably have endorsed. It is a way of pursuing his goal (a common religion and morality) in a more diverse society. In Wallace v. Jaffree (p. 496), decided before *Weisman*, the state went a step further. State law still encouraged prayer, but it was silent prayer. The Court struck down all these practices.

a. The Basic Decisions

ENGEL v. VITALE
370 U.S. 421 (1962)

Mr. Justice BLACK delivered the opinion of the Court.

The respondent Board of Education of Union Free School District No. 9, New Hyde Park, New York, acting in its official capacity under state law, directed the School District's principal to cause the following prayer to be said aloud by each class in the presence of a teacher at the beginning of each school day: "Almighty God, we acknowledge our dependence upon Thee, and we beg Thy blessings upon us, our parents, our teachers and our Country." This daily procedure was adopted on the recommendation of the State Board of Regents [which oversees public school systems].

Shortly after the practice of reciting the Regents' prayer was adopted by the School District, the parents of ten pupils brought this action in a New York State Court insisting that use of this official prayer in the public schools was contrary to the beliefs, religions, or religious practices of both themselves and their children[.] The New York Court of Appeals [upheld the practice] so long as the schools did not compel any pupil to join in the prayer over his or his parents' objection. . . .

It is a matter of history that this very practice of establishing governmentally composed prayers for religious services was one of the reasons which caused many of our early colonists to leave England and seek religious freedom in America. The Book of Common Prayer, which was created under governmental direction and which was approved by Acts of Parliament in 1548 and 1549, set out in minute detail the accepted form and content of prayer and other religious ceremonies to be used in the established, tax-supported Church of England. The controversies over the Book and what should be its content repeatedly threatened to disrupt the peace of that country as the accepted forms of prayer in the established church changed with the views of the particular ruler that happened to be in control at the time.[7] Powerful groups representing some of the varying religious views of the people struggled among themselves to impress their particular views upon the Government and obtain amendments of the Book more suitable to their respective notions of how religious services should

---

7. The first major revision of the Book of Common Prayer was made in 1552 during the reign of Edward VI. In 1553, Edward VI died and was succeeded by Mary who abolished the Book of Common Prayer entirely. But upon the accession of Elizabeth, in 1558, the Book was restored with important alterations from the form it had been given by Edward VI. The resentment to this amended form of the Book was kept firmly under control during the reign of Elizabeth but, upon her death in 1603, a petition signed by more than 1,000 Puritan ministers was presented to King James I asking for further alterations in the Book. Some alterations were made and the Book retained substantially this form until it was completely suppressed again in 1645 as a result of the successful Puritan Revolution. Shortly after the restoration in 1660 of Charles II, the Book was again reintroduced, and again with alterations. Rather than accept this form of the Book some 2,000 Puritan ministers vacated their benefices.

be conducted in order that the official religious establishment would advance their particular religious beliefs. Other groups, lacking the necessary political power to influence the Government on the matter, decided to leave England and its established church and seek freedom in America from England's governmentally ordained and supported religion. . . .

By the time of the adoption of the Constitution, our history shows that there was a widespread awareness among many Americans of the dangers of a union of Church and State. [Under the First] Amendment's prohibition against governmental establishment of religion, as reinforced by the provisions of the Fourteenth Amendment, government in this country, be it state or federal, is without power to prescribe by law any particular form of prayer which is to be used as an official prayer in carrying on any program of governmentally sponsored religious activity. . . .

Neither the fact that the prayer may be denominationally neutral nor the fact that its observance on the part of the students is voluntary can serve to free it from the limitations of the Establishment Clause, as it might from the Free Exercise Clause. . . . Although these two clauses may in certain instances overlap, they forbid two quite different kinds of governmental encroachment upon religious freedom. The Establishment Clause, unlike the Free Exercise Clause, does not depend upon any showing of direct governmental compulsion and is violated by the enactment of laws which establish an official religion whether those laws operate directly to coerce non-observing individuals or not. This is not to say, of course, that laws officially prescribing a particular form of religious worship do not involve coercion of such individuals. When the power, prestige and financial support of government is placed behind a particular religious belief, the indirect coercive pressure upon religious minorities to conform to the prevailing officially approved religion is plain. But the purposes underlying the Establishment Clause go much further than that. Its first and most immediate purpose rested on the belief that a union of government and religion tends to destroy government and to degrade religion. The history of governmentally established religion, both in England and in this country, showed that whenever government had allied itself with one particular form of religion, the inevitable result had been that it had incurred the hatred, disrespect and even contempt of those who held contrary beliefs. That same history showed that many people had lost their respect for any religion that had relied upon the support of government to spread its faith. The Establishment Clause thus stands as an expression of principle on the part of the Founders of our Constitution that religion is too personal, too sacred, too holy, to permit its "unhallowed perversion" by a civil magistrate. Another purpose of the Establishment Clause rested upon an awareness of the historical fact that governmentally established religions and religious persecutions go hand in hand. The Founders knew that only a few years after the Book of Common Prayer became the only accepted form of religious services in the established Church of England, an Act of Uniformity was passed to compel all Englishmen to attend those services and to make it a criminal offense to conduct or attend religious gatherings of any other kind—a law which was consistently flouted by dissenting religious groups in England and which contributed to widespread persecutions of people like John Bunyan who persisted in holding "unlawful (religious) meetings . . . to the great disturbance and distraction of the good subjects of this kingdom. . . ." And they knew that similar persecutions had received the sanction of law in several of the colonies in this country soon after the establishment of official religions in those colonies. It was in large part to get completely away from this sort of systematic religious persecution that the Founders brought into being our Nation, our Constitution, and our Bill of Rights with its prohibition against any governmental establishment of religion. The New York laws officially prescribing the Regents' prayer are inconsistent both with the purposes of the Establishment Clause and with the Establishment Clause itself. . . .

It is true that New York's establishment of its Regents' prayer as an officially approved religious doctrine of that State does not amount to a total establishment of one particular religious sect to the exclusion of all others—that, indeed, the governmental endorsement of that prayer seems relatively insignificant when compared to the governmental encroachments upon religion which were commonplace 200 years ago. To those who may subscribe to the view that because the Regents' official prayer is so brief and general there can be no danger to religious freedom in its governmental establishment, however, it may be appropriate to say in the words of James Madison, the author of the First Amendment:

> It is proper to take alarm at the first experiment on our liberties. . . . Who does not see that the same authority which can establish Christianity, in exclusion of all other Religions, may establish with the same ease any particular sect of Christians, in exclusion of all other Sects? That the same authority which can force a citizen to contribute three pence only of his property for the support of any one establishment, may force him to conform to any other establishment in all cases whatsoever?

ABINGTON SCHOOL DISTRICT v. SCHEMPP
374 U.S. 203 (1963)

Mr. Justice CLARK delivered the opinion of the Court.

The Commonwealth of Pennsylvania by law requires that "At least ten verses from the Holy Bible shall be read, without comment, at the opening of each public school on each school day. Any child shall be excused from such Bible reading, or attending such Bible reading, upon the written request of his parent or guardian." The Schempp family, husband and wife and two of their three children, brought suit to enjoin enforcement of the statute, contending that [the law violated] the First Amendment. A three-judge statutory District Court for the Eastern District of Pennsylvania [agreed.]

The [Schempps] are of the Unitarian faith. . . . [The] children attend the Abington Senior High School, which is a public school operated by appellant district.

On each school day at the Abington Senior High School between 8:15 and 8:30 A.M., while the pupils are attending their home rooms or advisory sections, opening exercises are conducted pursuant to the statute. The exercises are broadcast into each room in the school building through an intercommunications system and are conducted under the supervision of a teacher by students attending the school's radio and television workshop. Selected students from this course gather each morning in the school's workshop studio for the exercises, which include readings by one of the students of 10 verses of the Holy Bible, broadcast to each room in the building. This is followed by the recitation of the Lord's Prayer, likewise over the intercommunications system, but also by the students in the various classrooms, who are asked to stand and join in repeating the prayer in unison. The exercises are closed with the flag salute and such pertinent announcements as are of interest to the students. Participation in the opening exercises, as directed by the statute, is voluntary. The student reading the verses from the Bible may select the passages and read from any version he chooses, although the only copies furnished by the school are the King James version, copies of which were circulated to each teacher by the school district. During the period in which the exercises have been conducted the King James, the Douay and the Revised Standard versions of the Bible have been used, as well as the Jewish Holy Scriptures. There are no prefatory statements, no questions asked or solicited, no comments or explanations made and no interpretations given at or during the exercises. The students and parents are advised that the student may absent himself from the classroom or, should he elect to remain, not participate in the exercises. [At trial Edward Schempp testified] that he had considered having Roger and Donna excused from attendance at the exercises but decided against it for several reasons, including his belief that the children's relationships with their teachers and classmates would be adversely affected.[3]

The wholesome "neutrality" of which this Court's cases speak . . . stems from a recognition of the teachings of history that powerful sects or groups might bring about a fusion of governmental and religious functions or a concert or dependency of one upon the other to the end that official support of the State or Federal Government would be placed behind the tenets of one or of all orthodoxies. This the Establishment Clause prohibits. And a further reason for neutrality is found in the Free Exercise Clause, which recognizes the value of religious training, teaching and observance and, more particularly, the right of every person to freely choose his own course with reference thereto, free of any compulsion from the state. This the Free Exercise Clause guarantees. Thus . . . the two clauses may overlap. [The Establishment Clause] withdrew all legislative power respecting religious belief or the expression thereof. The test may be stated as follows: what are the purpose and the primary effect of the enactment? If either is the advancement or inhibition of religion then the enactment exceeds the scope of legislative power as circumscribed by the Constitution. That is to say that to withstand the strictures of the Establishment Clause

---

3. The trial court summarized his testimony as follows:

> Edward Schempp, the children's father, testified that after careful consideration he had decided that he should not have Roger or Donna excused from attendance at these morning ceremonies. Among his reasons were the following. He said that he thought his children would be "labeled as 'odd balls'" before their teachers and classmates every school day; that children, like Roger's and Donna's classmates, were liable "to lump all particular religious difference(s) or religious objections (together) as 'atheism'" and that today the word "atheism" is often connected with "atheistic communism," and has "very bad" connotations, such as "un-American" or "anti-Red," with overtones of possible immorality. Mr. Schempp pointed out that due to the events of the morning exercises following in rapid succession, the Bible reading, the Lord's Prayer, the Flag Salute, and the announcements, excusing his children from the Bible reading would mean that probably they would miss hearing the announcements so important to children. He testified also that if Roger and Donna were excused from Bible reading they would have to stand in the hall outside their "homeroom" and that this carried with it the imputation of punishment for bad conduct.

there must be a secular legislative purpose and a primary effect that neither advances nor inhibits religion. The Free Exercise Clause . . . withdraws from legislative power, state and federal, the exertion of any restraint on the free exercise of religion. Its purpose is to secure religious liberty in the individual by prohibiting any invasions thereof by civil authority. Hence it is necessary in a free exercise case for one to show the coercive effect of the enactment as it operates against him in the practice of his religion. The distinction between the two clauses is apparent—a violation of the Free Exercise Clause is predicated on coercion while the Establishment Clause violation need not be so attended.

Applying the Establishment Clause principles to the cases at bar we find that the States are requiring the selection and reading at the opening of the school day of verses from the Holy Bible and the recitation of the Lord's Prayer by the students in unison. These exercises are prescribed as part of the curricular activities of students who are required by law to attend school. They are held in the school buildings under the supervision and with the participation of teachers employed in those schools. [The trial court] found that such an opening exercise is a religious ceremony and was intended by the State to be so. We agree[.] Given that finding, the exercises and the law requiring them are in violation of the Establishment Clause.[9] . . .

It is insisted that unless these religious exercises are permitted a "religion of secularism" is established in the schools. We agree of course that the State may not establish a "religion of secularism" in the sense of affirmatively opposing or showing hostility to religion, thus "preferring those who believe in no religion over those who do believe." We do not agree, however, that this decision in any sense has that effect. In addition, it might well be said that one's education is not complete without a study of comparative religion or the history of religion and its relationship to the advancement of civilization. It certainly may be said that the Bible is worthy of study for its literary and historic qualities. Nothing we have said here indicates that such study of the Bible or of religion, when presented objectively as part of a secular program of education, may not be effected consistently with the First Amendment. But the exercises here do not fall into those categories. They are religious exercises, required by the States in violation of the command of the First Amendment that the Government maintain strict neutrality, neither aiding nor opposing religion.

Mr. Justice STEWART, dissenting.

[T]he cases before us [are] difficult ones for me. For there is involved in these cases a substantial free exercise claim on the part of those who affirmatively desire to have their children's school day open with the reading of passages from the Bible.

It might be argued here that parents who wanted their children to be exposed to religious influences in school could, under Pierce [v. Society of

---

9. It goes without saying that the laws and practices involved here can be challenged only by persons having standing to complain. But the requirements for standing to challenge state action under the Establishment Clause, unlike those relating to the Free Exercise Clause, do not include proof that particular religious freedoms are infringed. The parties here are school children and their parents, who are directly affected by the laws and practices against which their complaints are directed. These interests surely suffice to give the parties standing to complain. See Engel v. Vitale. [Relocated footnote—EDS.]

Sisters (1925) (p. 366)], send their children to private or parochial schools. But the consideration which renders this contention too facile to be determinative has already been recognized by the Court: "Freedom of speech, freedom of the press, freedom of religion are available to all, not merely to those who can pay their own way." Murdock v. Pennsylvania (1943).

It might also be argued that parents who want their children exposed to religious influences can adequately fulfill that wish off school property and outside school time. [But] a compulsory state educational system so structures a child's life that if religious exercises are held to be an impermissible activity in schools, religion is placed at an artificial and state-created disadvantage. Viewed in this light, permission of such exercises for those who want them is necessary if the schools are truly to be neutral in the matter of religion. And a refusal to permit religious exercises thus is seen, not as the realization of state neutrality, but rather as the establishment of a religion of secularism, or at the least, as government support of the beliefs of those who think that religious exercises should be conducted only in private.

What seems to me to be of paramount importance, then, is recognition of the fact that the claim advanced here in favor of Bible reading is sufficiently substantial to make simple reference to the constitutional phrase "establishment of religion" as inadequate an analysis of the cases before us as the ritualistic invocation of the non-constitutional phrase "separation of church and state." What these cases compel, rather, is an analysis of just what the "neutrality" is which is required by the interplay of the Establishment and Free Exercise Clauses of the First Amendment, as imbedded in the Fourteenth.

[This is not a case] like Brown v. Board of Education (1954), in which this Court held that, in the sphere of public education, the Fourteenth Amendment's guarantee of equal protection of the laws required that race not be treated as a relevant factor. A segregated school system is not invalid because its operation is coercive; it is invalid simply because our Constitution presupposes that men are created equal, and that therefore racial differences cannot provide a valid basis for governmental action. Accommodation of religious differences on the part of the State, however, is not only permitted but required by that same Constitution.

The governmental neutrality which the First and Fourteenth Amendments require in the cases before us, in other words, is the extension of evenhanded treatment to all who believe, doubt, or disbelieve—a refusal on the part of the State to weight the scales of private choice. In these cases, therefore, what is involved is not state action based on impermissible categories, but rather an attempt by the State to accommodate those differences which the existence in our society of a variety of religious beliefs makes inevitable. The Constitution requires that such efforts be struck down only if they are proven to entail the use of the secular authority of government to coerce a preference among such beliefs.

[I]t seems to me clear that certain types of exercises would present situations in which no possibility of coercion on the part of secular officials could be claimed to exist. Thus, if such exercises were held either before or after the official school day, or if the school schedule were such that participation were merely one among a number of desirable alternatives, it could hardly be contended that the exercises did anything more than to provide an opportunity for the voluntary expression of religious belief. On the other hand, a law which provided for religious exercises during the school day and which contained no excusal provision would obviously be unconstitutionally coercive upon those who did not wish to participate. And even under a law containing an excusal provision, if the exercises were held during the school day, and no equally desirable alternative were provided by the school authorities, the likelihood that children might be under at least some psychological compulsion to participate would be great. In a case such as the latter, however, I think we would err if we *assumed* such coercion in the absence of any evidence.

[I would remand] for further hearings.

NOTES AND QUESTIONS

Engel and *Schempp* together reject two narrower readings of the Establishment Clause, and adopt a broader reading. Is the broader reading supportable?

1. "No Preference Among Religions." The Regents' prayer, like Horace Mann's plan for reading the Bible without comment, was a kind of religious least common denominator. It actually went a step better: Unlike the Bible, whose appeal is limited to Jews and Christians, the Regents' prayer could appeal to all theists. But *Engel* says that "the fact that the prayer may be denominationally neutral" does not "free it from . . . the Establishment Clause." Is there such a thing as a "denominationally neutral" prayer? Won't a least common denominator prayer clash with the views of those who want more specific references to Jesus or Allah? (We will consider historical arguments concerning the nonpreferentialism position shortly.)

2. "No Coercion." The other argument New York made in defense of its prayer was that students could opt out; no child was penalized for refusing to join in the exercise. This seems to be an important distinction between this case and cases such as *Cooke* and *Barnette*. The Court responded to this argument by saying first, in *Engel*, that students were "indirectly" coerced to participate, and second, in *Engel* and *Schempp*, that in any event an Establishment Clause plaintiff did not have to prove coercion. What does it mean to say that the students were subject to "indirect coercive pressure"? Who applied the pressure? What was the penalty for resisting?

(a) The basis for the "no coercion" test. Is the Court's statement that Establishment Clause plaintiffs need not prove coercion dictum? Where did the Court get this idea? Justice Black did not cite any authority. He did say that historically establishments have led to hatred, disrespect, contempt, and persecution of nonbelievers, but this sounds like coercion. Is there any other historical evidence for the claim that the Establishment Clause forbids noncoercive practices? Compare Michael W. McConnell, Coercion: The Lost Element of Establishment, 27 Wm. & Mary L. Rev. 933 (1986), with Douglas Laycock, "Non-Coercive" Support for Religion: Another False Claim About the Establishment Clause, 26 Val. U. L. Rev. 37 (1991).

In Part I-A we examined a variety of individual and institutional harms that the Free Exercise Clause and the Establishment Clause are designed to prevent. Which of these harms does the government cause when it sponsors voluntary nondenominational prayer? Is an endorsement of prayer sufficient harm in itself to justify a holding of unconstitutionality?

(b) Questions about the "no coercion" test. Suppose we were to require a showing of coercion in Establishment Clause cases. How much would our First Amendment jurisprudence change? The Regents' prayer might still be forbidden. (The Court found it indirectly coercive.) Would we have more municipal decorations at Christmas? Easter? More public displays of piety by politicians? Suppose the Kentucky legislature passed a resolution making Presbyterianism the official religion of the commonwealth, as the cardinal is the official bird. Would that be constitutional? Is financial support for parochial schools coercive?

Some commentators argue that if coercion were a necessary element in any Establishment Clause violation, the clause would be redundant—it would not do any work that the Free Exercise Clause does not also do. Is that true? Consider again the various harms that the First Amendment addresses. And see Michael S. Paulsen, *Lemon* Is Dead, 43 Case W. Res. L. Rev. 795, 843-845 n.171 (1993).

3. "Neutrality" Toward Religion. *Schempp* holds that the practices of Bible reading and prayer are unconstitutional because they violate a rule of "neutrality" toward religion. This is obviously a stricter test than nonpreferentialism. It forbids "official support . . . of one *or of all* orthodoxies." *Schempp* also makes clear that even noncoercive religious exercises in schools violate the Establishment Clause. In rejecting both the nonpreferentialism and coercion tests, *Schempp* follows *Engel*. But it adds something to *Engel* by adding the term "neutrality." What does the rule of neutrality mean, and what is the foundation for it?

(a) Equal treatment ("formal" neutrality)? As you know, in cases under the Free Exercise Clause, the Court now says that the government may regulate religious exercise as long as it does so through "neutral, generally applicable laws." Employment Division v. Smith (p. 137). In the *Smith* formulation, neutrality appears to be what Professor Laycock calls "formal" neutrality: Government treats religion the same as it treats other beliefs and activities (at least other comparable ones). Douglas Laycock, Formal, Substantive, and Disaggregated Neutrality Toward Religion, 39 DePaul L. Rev. 993, 999-1000 (1990). What would be the Establishment Clause counterpart to this rule? That official prayers are invalid because there is no accompanying secular message in the prayer? Or does one have to consider what messages the school sends at other times; for example, could the school sponsor prayers on some mornings as long as it sponsored other forms of private devotion, like yoga and transcendental meditation, on other mornings? Can the sponsorship of prayers be defended on the ground that the school conveys secular messages through its curriculum the rest of the day?

(b) "No encouraging" of religion ("substantive" neutrality)? When *Schempp* refers to the Free Exercise Clause, it actually speaks of "the right of every person to freely choose his own course with reference [to religion], free of any compulsion from the state." And *Schempp* was decided the same day as Sherbert v. Verner, 374 U.S. 398 (1963), which interpreted the Free Exercise Clause to apply strict scrutiny to government programs that unduly burdened private religious exercises, even pursuant to a facially religion-neutral law. Professor Laycock calls this "substantive" neutrality: It focuses not on the form of the law, but on its impact on religious practice. Laycock, 39 DePaul L. Rev. 993. What would be the Establishment Clause counterpart to this rule? That government programs that *promote or encourage* religious exercises should also be subject to strict scrutiny?

That the government should do nothing to interfere with voluntary religious practices under either clause?

(c) **"No advancement or inhibition of religion" (the *Lemon* test)?**   Finally, *Schempp* states that "the purpose and the primary effect of the enactment" must not be "the advancement or inhibition of religion." This was the source of the first two "prongs" of the three-part Establishment Clause test of Lemon v. Kurtzman. As you have seen before (Part IV-C), the three-part *Lemon* test applied by the Supreme Court between 1971 and 1985 produced a fairly strict separation between government and religion. To what extent can we attribute this result to the first two prongs of the test? Notice the repeated statement that a law must "neither advance *nor inhibit* religion" (emphasis added). The Court says that Pennsylvania's law advanced religion and that forbidding the Bible readings would not inhibit religion. Sometimes, however, the law will affect religion no matter which way it is framed. Should the school district make Christmas a holiday (thereby advancing religion), or should it hold classes (thereby inhibiting students whose religion would lead them to be absent)? In such a case, perhaps the best the law can aim for is the minimum possible effect. But which is the lesser effect?

(d) **Accommodation and neutrality in *Schempp*.**   Justice Stewart made a similar argument about inhibition in *Schempp*: He said that forbidding prayers at the beginning of the school day could be said to discourage religion. Because the school day occupies so large a part of the pupils' time, Justice Stewart argued, to exclude any religious element from the school day would have a secularizing effect on the students' lives. He thus argued that as long as the prayers were entirely voluntary, the practice of providing an opportunity for prayer at school merely accommodated voluntary religious choice. Are noncoercive prayers a permissible accommodation under the standards you studied in Section III-C above? Under the "best" theory of accommodations?

Shortly after *Engel* and *Schempp*, a federal district court in Michigan explored the following compromise: Before the beginning of the school day, a classroom would be set aside for students who wished to participate in a prayer. (As many classrooms could be used as there were different modes of prayer.) The prayer would have to be completed and the classroom emptied before the bell instructing students to go to their homeroom. This would make it difficult for anyone to tell which students chose to participate. Reed v. Van Hoven, 237 F. Supp. 48 (D. Mich. 1965). The plan apparently was never put into effect. Would it be constitutional?

NOTE ON OFFICIAL RELIGIOUS EXERCISES AND HISTORY

Do *Engel* and *Schempp* adequately deal with the history of government-sponsored religious exercises in America? There is a long record of such exercises. On October 3, 1789, President George Washington issued a proclamation:

> Whereas it is the duty of all nations to acknowledge the providence of Almighty God, to obey His will, to be grateful for His benefits, and humbly to implore His protection and favor; and

> Whereas both Houses of Congress have, by their joint committee, requested me "to recommend to the people of the United States a day of public thanksgiving and prayer, to be observed by acknowledging with grateful hearts the many and signal favors of Almighty God, especially by affording them an opportunity peaceably to establish a form of government for their safety and happiness":
>
> Now, therefore, I do recommend and assign Thursday, the 26th day of November next, to be devoted by the people of these States to the service of that great and glorious Being who is the beneficent author of all the good that was, that is, or that will be; that we may then all unite in rendering unto Him our sincere and humble thanks for His kind care and protection of the people of this country. . . .

Most Presidents since then have done the same. Thomas Jefferson, and Madison later expressed constitutional regrets for having done so. Are these proclamations unconstitutional? If they are constitutional, why is that so?

1. Noncoercive? Some might argue that Thanksgiving proclamations are distinguishable from school prayers because they are much more clearly voluntary. But does that suggest that nonvoluntariness—coercion—is an essential element of an establishment (in contradiction to *Engel* and *Schempp*)?

2. Nonpreferential Between Religions? Dissenting in Wallace v. Jaffree (p. 496), then-Justice Rehnquist relied on the record of Thanksgiving proclamations, among other practices, to argue that the Establishment Clause was intended not to require neutrality toward religion or separation of church and state, but to forbid "preference among religious sects or denominations." Rehnquist noted that Madison's original proposal for what became the Religion Clauses was: "The civil rights of none shall be abridged on account of religious worship, nor shall any national religion be established, nor shall the full and equal rights of conscience be . . . infringed." In response to questions on the floor of the House about similar language, Madison explained that he "believed that the people feared one sect might obtain a pre-eminence, or two combine together, and establish a religion to which they would compel others to conform." Rehnquist wrote:

> It seems indisputable from these glimpses of Madison's thinking . . . that he saw the amendment as designed to prohibit the establishment of a national religion, and perhaps to prohibit discrimination among sects. . . .
>
> The actions of the First Congress . . . confirm the view that Congress did not mean that the Government should be neutral between religion and irreligion. . . . The Northwest Ordinance [of 1789, reenacting an earlier version] provided that "[r]eligion, morality, and knowledge, being necessary to good government and the happiness of mankind, schools and the means of education shall forever be encouraged."

Justice Rehnquist also quoted Justice Joseph Story's leading 1845 treatise on the Constitution, which stated:

> The real object of the [F]irst Amendment was not to countenance, much less to advance, Mahometanism, or Judaism, or infidelity, by prostrating Christianity; but to exclude all rivalry among Christian sects, and to prevent any national ecclesiastical establishment which should give to a hierarchy the exclusive patronage of the national government.

Finally, Rehnquist quoted Thomas Cooley's leading nineteenth-century treatise Constitutional Limitations (1868):

> [T]he American constitutions contain no provisions which prohibit the authorities from such solemn recognition of a superintending Providence in public transactions and exercises as the general religious sentiment of mankind inspires. . . . Undoubtedly, the spirit of the Constitution will require, in all these cases, that care be taken to avoid discrimination in favor of or against any one religious denomination or sect; but the power to do any of these things does not become unconstitutional simply because of its susceptibility to abuse.

Is there an argument, against Rehnquist's position, that the original understanding is not limited to preferences between religious sects? See p. 64.

Suppose that "no preference between sects" is the correct interpretation of the original understanding. Does that cover only preferences between Christian sects, as Justice Story said? Is a prayer or expression of thanks to "Almighty God" or the "Supreme Being" nonpreferential?

3. An Unbroken Specific Practice: *Marsh v. Chambers*. In Marsh v. Chambers, 463 U.S. 783 (1983), the Nebraska legislature opened each session with a prayer offered by a chaplain who was selected by a council of legislators and paid out of public funds. The same Presbyterian minister had served as chaplain for 16 years. Chambers, a legislator and taxpayer, challenged the practice as an establishment of religion, but the Supreme Court upheld it.

The Court noted that "[t]he opening of sessions of legislative and other deliberative public bodies with prayer is deeply embedded in the history and tradition of this country." Specifically, the first Congress approved payment of funds for House and Senate chaplains, in 1789, only three days before it reached agreement on the language of the First Amendment. "Clearly the men who wrote the [Amendment] did not view paid legislative chaplains and opening prayers as a violation of [it], for the practice . . . has continued without interruption ever since." The Court said that "[s]tanding alone, historical patterns cannot justify contemporary violations of constitutional guarantees, but there is far more here than historical patterns." This "unique history" showed that the amendment's framers "saw no real threat to the Establishment Clause" from legislative prayer.

Justice Brennan dissented: "I have no doubt that, if any group of law students were asked to apply the principles of *Lemon* to the question of legislative prayer, they would nearly unanimously find the practice to be unconstitutional." He argued that it was "self-evident" that the purpose of legislative prayer was "preeminently religious"; that the chaplaincy had a primarily religious effect by "explicitly link[ing] religious beliefs and observance to the power and prestige of the State"; and that the practice of the legislature selecting a chaplain and requiring "suitable" prayers "involves precisely the sort of [entangling] supervision that agencies of government should if at all possible avoid."

The majority in *Marsh* treated the historical approval of legislative prayer as conclusive; it did not even purport to apply the *Lemon* test. Would *Engel* and *Schempp* have been decided differently under the *Marsh* approach? What makes the history of legislative prayer "unique" and especially powerful is, in large part, that the first Congress approved the specific practice, on almost the same day it approved the First Amendment. This cannot be said of public school prayers, because public schools did not exist in any substantial form until the 1800s—although the broader practice of public prayer of course goes back further.

Should the specificity of the historical precedent play as important a role as it did in *Marsh*? Suppose that the reason congressional chaplaincies (or any other particular practice) received easy approval is that one especially powerful legislator vigorously supported them. Would an emphasis on each specific practice undercut the task of drawing consistent legal *principles* from the history? The early Congresses approved payments for missionaries to give religious education to Indians; under *Marsh*, could Congress now fund missionaries as long as they are educating Native Americans? Does the approach in *Marsh* avoid these difficulties?

Is legislative prayer coercive? Why is it different in this regard from the Regents' prayer? Does the opinion suggest that the government may sponsor voluntary prayers so long as the audience is made up of adults? Suppose the prayer in *Marsh* was not coercive. Does the Court's approval of the practice suggest that Establishment Clause plaintiffs must show coercion in order to win?

Beyond the fact of history, is there any coherent theory that would justify the legislative prayer upheld in *Marsh*? One possibility is that it lies outside the ambit of the First Amendment altogether; neither the appointment of a chaplain nor the saying of a prayer is a "law" within the meaning of the first five words of the Amendment. Is that persuasive?

Marsh had noted that the Nebraska chaplain had removed references to Christ from his prayers (at the request of a Jewish legislator) and that there was "no indication that the prayer opportunity has been exploited to proselytize or advance any one, or to disparage any other, faith or belief." 463 U.S. at 794-795. In the light of these passages, should a court order that any clergy member giving an official legislative prayer must keep the prayer "nonsectarian" or "nonproselytizing"? See Hinrichs v. Bosma, 410 F. Supp. 2d 745 (S.D. Ind. 2006) (entering such an order).

4. Problems: Government-Sponsored Voluntary Prayer. Is it possible (or desirable) to adopt a hard-and-fast rule regarding government sponsorship of prayer—either that this is always unconstitutional or that it is constitutional whenever there is no coercion involved? Consider these contexts, taken from actual incidents:

(a) Suppose the administrator of a national park invites local clergy to conduct worship services on weekends at the campfire ring of the park campground.

(b) Suppose a municipal airport maintains a chapel, with worship services conducted by clergy volunteers of any denomination that wishes to do so. These services are announced over the airport public address system.

(c) Suppose that after the September 11 attack, the mayor and city council announce a "prayer vigil" to be held on the steps of the city hall.

(d) Suppose that before public school sporting events, and after his final speech to the team, the coach asks if any team members have anything they would like to share with the group—knowing that the team captain, a member of the Fellowship of Christian Athletes, is likely to offer a prayer.

Are all of these scenarios unconstitutional? All of them constitutional? Are there relevant differences? Are there additional facts you need to know to answer the question? If so, what are they?

b. The Reaffirmation (Extension?) of the School-Prayer Decisions

WALLACE v. JAFFREE, 472 U.S. 38 (1985): *Jaffree* involved a challenge to a 1981 Alabama statute that authorized a period of silence in public school classrooms at the beginning of the day "for meditation or voluntary prayer." A 1978 statute had already required a moment of silence "for meditation." (A third statute, authorizing teachers to lead willing students in a prescribed prayer to "Almighty God . . . the Creator and Supreme Judge of the world," was declared unconstitutional in the lower courts and the state did not seek Supreme Court review on that issue.)

Applying the three-part Lemon v. Kurtzman test, the Court stated that a law violates the first prong "if it is entirely motivated by a purpose to advance religion." The statute authorizing "meditation or voluntary prayer" violated that prong because it was motivated by no purpose other than encouraging students to pray during the silent period. The Court noted that the sponsor of the provision had said it was an "effort to return voluntary prayer to our public schools" and, testifying as a witness during the lawsuit, had said that he had "no other purpose in mind." This purpose was "confirmed," the majority said, by the fact that although students have a right to choose to pray during a moment of silence, "the 1978 statute already protected that right, containing nothing that prevented any student from engaging in voluntary prayer during a silent minute of meditation"; thus the sole purpose of adding "or voluntary prayer" in the 1981 statute was "to characterize prayer as a favored practice." Given this purpose, the majority said, it did not need to assess "the practical significance" of the added words under the "effects" prong of the *Lemon* test.

Justice O'Connor concurred in the judgment, explaining that although this statute had the purpose and effect of endorsing prayer, other moment of silence statutes would pass constitutional muster:

> [A] state-sponsored moment of silence in the public schools is different from state-sponsored vocal prayer or Bible reading. First, a moment of silence is not inherently religious. Silence, unlike prayer or Bible reading, need not be associated with a religious exercise. Second, a pupil who participates in a moment of silence need not compromise his or her beliefs. During a moment of silence, a student who objects to prayer is left to his or her own thoughts, and is not compelled to listen to the prayers or thoughts of others. . . .
>
> The analysis above suggests that moment of silence laws in many States should pass Establishment Clause scrutiny because they do not favor the child who chooses to pray during a moment of silence over the child who chooses to meditate or reflect. [But the 1981 Alabama law] does not stand on the same footing. However deferentially one examines its text and legislative history, however objectively one views the message attempted to be conveyed to the public, the conclusion is unavoidable[, for the reasons the majority gives,] that the purpose of the statute is to endorse prayer in public schools.

Chief Justice Burger, dissenting, noted that the sponsor's legislative statements had been added to the record after the debate and his courtroom testimony came well after the statute was enacted: "[T]here is not a shred of evidence that the legislature as a whole shared the sponsor's motive." Burger also noted that the sponsor had testified he had an additional purpose of "clear[ing] up a widespread misunderstanding that a schoolchild is legally prohibited from engaging in silent, individual prayer once he steps inside a public school building." Justice White dissented on a similar ground.

NOTES AND QUESTIONS

1. Moment of Silence Laws. It seems clear that the Court would be willing to uphold a properly drafted moment-of-silence law. The majority did not question the validity of the 1978 law requiring a one-minute period "for meditation." A number of states have such laws. The leading court of appeals decision since *Jaffree* upheld Georgia's version, which provided for a "moment of silent reflection" and added that it was "not intended to be and shall not be conducted as a religious service or exercise." Bown v. Gwinnett County Schools, 112 F.3d 1464 (11th Cir. 1997).

Setting aside a moment "for meditation" at the beginning of school likely leads to some increase in prayer, since students otherwise would be occupied throughout the school day. And perhaps most legislators are motivated to support such laws in order to accommodate students who want to pray. In what sense, therefore, are such laws "neutral" under the standards of *Schempp* or *Lemon*? Suppose a state enacts a moment of silence for "meditation or voluntary prayer," without the kind of history—and previous statute "for mediation"—that Alabama had. Is such a law unconstitutional?

2. The Controversy Over the *Lemon* Test. Decisions such as *Engel, Schempp*, and *Jaffree*—and the *Lemon* analysis underlying them—were criticized for striking down traditional practices of public religion and for allegedly being hostile to religion. Critics advocated the various alternative Establishment Clause tests, including nonpreferentialism and noncoercion. Reflecting this controversy, the Court in several decisions from the 1980s on did not employ the three-part test. For example, Marsh v. Chambers (p. 494) judged the constitutionality of legislative prayers by a historical test, looking solely at the actions of the First Congress. In other cases, however, the Court turned to the *Lemon* factors. One such case was Lamb's Chapel v. Center Moriches School Dist., 508 U.S. 384 (1993), where the Court's reliance on *Lemon* prompted this concurring statement from Justice Scalia:

> I join the Court's conclusion [but not its invocation of the *Lemon* test.] Like some ghoul in a late-night horror movie that repeatedly sits up in its grave and shuffles abroad, after being repeatedly killed and buried, *Lemon* stalks our Establishment Clause jurisprudence once again, frightening the little children and school attorneys of Center Moriches Union Free School District. Its most recent burial, only last Term, was, to be sure, not fully six-feet under: our decision in Lee v. Weisman, conspicuously avoided using the supposed "test" but also declined the invitation to repudiate it. Over the years, however, no fewer than five of the currently sitting Justices have, in their own opinions, personally driven pencils through the creature's heart[,] and a sixth has joined an opinion doing so. . . .
>
> The secret of the *Lemon* test's survival, I think, is that it is so easy to kill. It is there to scare us (and our audience) when we wish it to do so, but we can command it to

return to the tomb at will. When we wish to strike down a practice it forbids, we invoke it, see, e.g., Aguilar v. Felton; when we wish to uphold a practice it forbids, we ignore it entirely, see Marsh v. Chambers. Sometimes, we take a middle course, calling its three prongs "no more than helpful signposts." Such a docile and useful monster is worth keeping around, at least in a somnolent state; one never knows when one might need him.

In the early 1990s, however, many people expected that the school-prayer decisions and the *Lemon* test would be overturned, or at least limited, by the "conservative" justices appointed in the 1980s by President Ronald Reagan. The following decision, in 1992, came as something of a surprise. Does it extend *Engel* and *Schempp*, or limit them?

LEE v. WEISMAN
505 U.S. 577 (1992)

Justice KENNEDY delivered the opinion of the Court. . . .

I

Deborah Weisman graduated from Nathan Bishop Middle School, a public school in Providence, [Rhode Island,] at a formal ceremony in June 1989. She was about 14 years old. For many years it has been the policy of the Providence School Committee and the Superintendent of Schools to permit principals to invite members of the clergy to give invocations and benedictions at middle school and high school graduations. Many, but not all, of the principals elected to include prayers as part of the graduation ceremonies. Acting for himself and his daughter, Deborah's father, Daniel Weisman, objected to any prayers at Deborah's middle school graduation, but to no avail. The school principal, petitioner Robert E. Lee, invited a rabbi to deliver prayers at the graduation exercises for Deborah's class. Rabbi Leslie Gutterman, of the Temple Beth El in Providence, accepted.

It has been the custom of Providence school officials to provide invited clergy with a pamphlet entitled "Guidelines for Civic Occasions," prepared by the National Conference of Christians and Jews. The Guidelines recommend that public prayers at nonsectarian civic ceremonies be composed with "inclusiveness and sensitivity," though they acknowledge that "[p]rayer of any kind may be inappropriate on some civic occasions." The principal gave Rabbi Gutterman the pamphlet before the graduation and advised him the invocation and benediction should be nonsectarian.

Rabbi Gutterman's prayers were as follows:

INVOCATION

God of the Free, Hope of the Brave: For the legacy of America where diversity is celebrated and the rights of minorities are protected, we thank You. May these young men and women grow up to enrich it. For the liberty of America, we thank You. May these new graduates grow up to guard it. For the political process of America in which all its citizens may participate, for its court system where all may seek justice we thank You. May those we honor this morning always turn to it in trust. For the destiny of America we thank You. May the graduates of Nathan

Bishop Middle School so live that they might help to share it. May our aspirations for our country and for these young people, who are our hope for the future, be richly fulfilled. Amen.

BENEDICTION

O God, we are grateful to You for having endowed us with the capacity for learning which we have celebrated on this joyous commencement. Happy families give thanks for seeing their children achieve an important milestone. Send Your blessings upon the teachers and administrators who helped prepare them. The graduates now need strength and guidance for the future, help them to understand that we are not complete with academic knowledge alone. We must each strive to fulfill what You require of us all: To do justly, to love mercy, to walk humbly. We give thanks to You, Lord, for keeping us alive, sustaining us and allowing us to reach this special, happy occasion. Amen.

[The] parties stipulate that attendance at graduation ceremonies is voluntary. The graduating students enter as a group in a processional, subject to the direction of teachers and school officials, and sit together, apart from their families. . . . There the students stood for the Pledge of Allegiance and remained standing during the Rabbi's prayers. Even on the assumption that there was a respectful moment of silence both before and after the prayers, the Rabbi's two presentations must not have extended much beyond a minute each, if that. . .

II

These dominant facts mark and control the confines of our decision: State officials direct the performance of a formal religious exercise at promotional and graduation ceremonies for secondary schools. Even for those students who object to the religious exercise, their attendance and participation in the state-sponsored religious activity are in a fair and real sense obligatory, though the school district does not require attendance as a condition for receipt of the diploma.

This case does not require us to revisit the difficult questions dividing us in recent [Establishment Clause] cases. . . . We can decide the case without reconsidering the general constitutional framework by which public schools' efforts to accommodate religion are measured. Thus we do not accept the invitation of petitioners and *amicus* the United States to reconsider [the test of] Lemon v. Kurtzman. . . .

. . . It is beyond dispute that, at a minimum, the Constitution guarantees that government may not coerce anyone to support or participate in religion or its exercise, or otherwise act in a way which "establishes a [state] religion or religious faith, or tends to do so." Lynch [v. Donnelly (1984).] The State's involvement in the school prayers challenged today violates these central principles.

That involvement is as troubling as it is undenied. A school official, the principal, decided that an invocation and a benediction should be given; this is a choice attributable to the State, and from a constitutional perspective it is as if a state statute decreed that the prayers must occur. The principal chose the religious participant, here a rabbi, and that choice is also attributable to the State. The reason for the choice of a rabbi is not disclosed by the record, but the potential for divisiveness over the choice of a particular member of the clergy to conduct the ceremony is apparent. . . .

. . . Principal Lee [also] provided Rabbi Gutterman with a copy of the "Guidelines for Civic Occasions," and advised him that his prayers should be nonsectarian. Through these means the principal directed and controlled the content of the prayer. Even if the only sanction for ignoring the instructions were that the rabbi would not be invited back, we think no religious representative who valued his or her continued reputation and effectiveness in the community would incur the State's displeasure in this regard. It is a cornerstone principle of our Establishment Clause jurisprudence that "it is no part of the business of government to compose official prayers for any group of the American people to recite as a part of a religious program carried on by government," Engel v. Vitale, and that is what the school officials attempted to do. . . .

The degree of school involvement here made it clear that the graduation prayers bore the imprint of the State and thus put school-age children who objected in an untenable position. We turn our attention now to consider the position of the students, both those who desired the prayer and she who did not.

To endure the speech of false ideas or offensive content and then to counter it is part of learning how to live in a pluralistic society, a society which insists upon open discourse towards the end of a tolerant citizenry. . . . It is argued that our constitutional vision of a free society requires confidence in our own ability to accept or reject ideas of which we do not approve, and that prayer at a high school graduation does nothing more than offer a choice. By the time they are seniors, high school students no doubt have been required to attend classes and assemblies and to complete assignments exposing them to ideas they find distasteful or immoral or absurd or all of these. Against this background, students may consider it an odd measure of justice to be subjected during the course of their educations to ideas deemed offensive and irreligious, but to be denied a brief, formal prayer ceremony that the school offers in return. This argument cannot prevail, however. It overlooks a fundamental dynamic of the Constitution.

The First Amendment protects speech and religion by quite different mechanisms. Speech is protected by insuring its full expression even when the government participates, for the very object of some of our most important speech is to persuade the government to adopt an idea as its own. The method for protecting freedom of worship and freedom of conscience in religious matters is quite the reverse. In religious debate or expression the government is not a prime participant, for the Framers deemed religious establishment antithetical to the freedom of all. The Free Exercise Clause embraces a freedom of conscience and worship that has close parallels in the speech provisions of the First Amendment, but the Establishment Clause is a specific prohibition on forms of state intervention in religious affairs with no precise counterpart in the speech provisions. The explanation lies in the lesson of history that was and is the inspiration for the Establishment Clause, the lesson that in the hands of government what might begin as a tolerant expression of religious views may end in a policy to indoctrinate and coerce. A state-created orthodoxy puts at grave risk that freedom of belief and conscience which are the sole assurance that religious faith is real, not imposed. . . .

As we have observed before, there are heightened concerns with protecting freedom of conscience from subtle coercive pressure in the elementary and secondary public schools. . . . What to most believers may seem nothing more than a reasonable request that the nonbeliever respect their religious practices, in a school context may appear to the nonbeliever or dissenter to be an attempt to employ the machinery of the State to enforce a religious orthodoxy.

. . . The undeniable fact is that the school district's supervision and control of a high school graduation ceremony places public pressure, as well as peer pressure, on attending students to stand as a group or, at least, maintain respectful silence during the Invocation and Benediction. This pressure, though subtle and indirect, can be as real as any overt compulsion. Of course, in our culture standing or remaining silent can signify adherence to a view or simple respect for the views of others. . . . [But t]here can be no doubt that for many, if not most, of the students at the graduation, the act of standing or remaining silent was an expression of participation in the Rabbi's prayer. That was the very point of the religious exercise. It is of little comfort to a dissenter, then, to be told that for her the act of standing or remaining in silence signifies mere respect, rather than participation. What matters is that, given our social conventions, a reasonable dissenter in this milieu could believe that the group exercise signified her own participation or approval of it.

Finding no violation under these circumstances would place objectors in the dilemma of participating, with all that implies, or protesting. We do not address whether that choice is acceptable if the affected citizens are mature adults, but we think the State may not, consistent with the Establishment Clause, place primary and secondary school children in this position. Research in psychology supports the common assumption that adolescents are often susceptible to pressure from their peers towards conformity, and that the influence is strongest in matters of social convention. To recognize that the choice imposed by the State constitutes an unacceptable constraint only acknowledges that the government may no more use social pressure to enforce orthodoxy than it may use more direct means.

The injury caused by the government's action . . . is that the State, in a school setting, in effect required participation in a religious exercise. It is, we concede, a brief exercise during which the individual can concentrate on joining its message, meditate on her own religion, or let her mind wander. But the embarrassment and the intrusion of the religious exercise cannot be refuted by arguing that these prayers, and similar ones to be said in the future, are of a de minimis character. To do so would be an affront to the Rabbi who offered them and to all those for whom the prayers were an essential and profound recognition of divine authority. . . .

[P]etitioners . . . argu[e] that the option of not attending the graduation excuses any inducement or coercion in the ceremony itself. The argument lacks all persuasion. Law reaches past formalism. . . . Everyone knows that in our society and in our culture high school graduation is one of life's most significant occasions. . . .

[T]he Constitution forbids the State to exact religious conformity from a student as the price of attending her own high school graduation[.]

Justice BLACKMUN, with whom Justice STEVENS and Justice O'CONNOR join, concurring. . . .

I join the Court's opinion today because I find nothing in it inconsistent with the essential precepts of the Establishment Clause developed in our precedents.

The Court holds that the graduation prayer is unconstitutional because the State "in effect required participation in a religious exercise." Although our precedents make clear that proof of government coercion is not necessary to prove an Establishment Clause violation, it is sufficient. . . .

The mixing of government and religion can be a threat to free government, even if no one is forced to participate. When the government puts its imprimatur on a particular religion, it conveys a message of exclusion to all those who do not adhere to the favored beliefs. A government cannot be premised on the belief that all persons are created equal when it asserts that God prefers some. Only "[a]nguish, hardship and bitter strife" result "when zealous religious groups struggl[e] with one another to obtain the Government's stamp of approval." *Engel.*

When the government arrogates to itself a role in religious affairs, it abandons its obligation as guarantor of democracy. Democracy requires the nourishment of dialogue and dissent, while religious faith puts its trust in an ultimate divine authority above all human deliberation. When the government appropriates religious truth, it "transforms rational debate into theological decree." Those who disagree no longer are questioning the policy judgment of the elected but the rules of a higher authority who is beyond reproach. . . . Democratic government will not last long when proclamation replaces persuasion as the medium of political exchange.

Likewise, we have recognized that "[r]eligion flourishes in greater purity, without than with the aid of Gov[ernment]." . . . When the government favors a particular religion or sect, the disadvantage to all others is obvious, but even the favored religion may fear being "taint[ed] . . . with a corrosive secularism." Grand Rapids v. Ball. The favored religion may be compromised as political figures reshape the religion's beliefs for their own purposes; it may be reformed as government largesse brings government regulation. Keeping religion in the hands of private groups minimizes state intrusion on religious choice and best enables each religion to "flourish according to the zeal of its adherents and the appeal of its dogma." Zorach v. Clauson.

Justice SOUTER, with whom Justice STEVENS and Justice O'CONNOR join, concurring.

I join the whole of the Court's opinion, and fully agree that prayers at public school graduation ceremonies indirectly coerce religious observance. [But] state coercion of religious conformity [is not] a necessary element of an Establishment Clause violation. . . .

While petitioners insist that the prohibition extends only to the "coercive" features and incidents of establishment, they cannot easily square that claim with the constitutional text. The First Amendment forbids not just laws "respecting an establishment of religion," but also those "prohibiting the free exercise thereof." Yet laws that coerce non-adherents to "support or participate in any religion or its exercise," would virtually by definition violate their right to religious free exercise. Thus, a literal application of the coercion test would render the Establishment Clause a virtual nullity. . . .

Petitioners argue from the political setting in which the Establishment Clause was framed, and from the Framers' own political practices following ratification, that government may constitutionally endorse religion so long as it does not coerce religious conformity. The setting and the practices . . . yield some evidence for petitioners' argument, [but] they do not reveal the degree of consensus in early constitutional thought that would raise a threat to stare decisis. . . .

The Framers adopted the Religion Clauses in response to a long tradition of coercive state support for religion, particularly in the form of tax assessments, but their special antipathy to religious coercion did not exhaust their hostility to the features and incidents of establishment. Indeed, Jefferson and Madison opposed any political appropriation of religion, and, even when challenging the hated assessments, they did not always temper their rhetoric with distinctions between coercive and non-coercive state action. When, for example, Madison criticized Virginia's general assessment bill, he invoked principles antithetical to all state efforts to promote religion. An assessment, he wrote, is improper not simply because it forces people to donate "three pence" to religion, but, more broadly, because "it is itself a signal of persecution. It degrades from the equal rank of Citizens all those whose opinions in Religion do not bend to those of the Legislative authority." Memorial and Remonstrance. Madison saw that, even without the tax collector's participation, an official endorsement of religion can impair religious liberty.

Petitioners contend that because the early Presidents included religious messages in their inaugural and Thanksgiving Day addresses, the Framers could not have meant the Establishment Clause to forbid non-coercive state endorsement of religion. The argument ignores the fact, however, that Americans today find such proclamations less controversial than did the founding generation, whose published thoughts on the matter belie petitioners' claim. President Jefferson, for example, steadfastly refused to issue Thanksgiving proclamations of any kind, in part because he thought they violated the Religion Clauses. Letter from Thomas Jefferson to Rev. S. Miller (Jan. 23, 1808), in 5 The Founders' Constitution. In explaining his views to the Reverend Samuel Miller, Jefferson effectively anticipated, and rejected, petitioners' position: "[I]t is only proposed that I should recommend, not prescribe a day of fasting & prayer. That is, that I should indirectly assume to the U.S. an authority over religious exercises which the Constitution has directly precluded from them. It must be meant too that this recommendation is to carry some authority, and to be sanctioned by some penalty on those who disregard it; not indeed of fine and imprisonment, but of some degree of proscription perhaps in public opinion." By condemning such non-coercive state practices that, in "recommending" the majority faith, demean religious dissenters "in public opinion," Jefferson necessarily . . . construed the Establishment Clause to forbid not simply state coercion, but also state endorsement, of religious belief and observance. And if he opposed impersonal presidential addresses for inflicting "proscription in public opinion," all the more would he have condemned less diffuse expressions of official endorsement.

During his first three years in office, James Madison also refused to call for days of thanksgiving and prayer, though later, amid the political turmoil of the War of 1812, he did so on four separate occasions. Upon retirement, in an essay condemning as an unconstitutional "establishment" the use of public money to support congressional and military chaplains, he concluded that "[r]eligious proclamations by the Executive recommending thanksgivings & fasts are shoots from the same root with the legislative acts reviewed. Altho' recommendations only, they imply a religious agency, making no part of the trust delegated to political rulers." [Citing Madison's "Detached Memorandum" (p. 67).]

To be sure, the leaders of the young Republic engaged in some of the practices that separationists like Jefferson and Madison criticized. The First Congress did hire institutional chaplains, and Presidents Washington and Adams unapologetically marked days of "public thanksgiving and prayer." Yet in the face of the separationist dissent, those practices prove, at best, that the Framers simply did not share a common understanding of the Establishment Clause, and, at worst, that they, like other politicians, could raise constitutional ideals one day and turn their backs on them the next. . . .

Justice SCALIA, with whom THE CHIEF JUSTICE, Justice WHITE, and Justice THOMAS join, dissenting. . . .

I

. . . From our Nation's origin, prayer has been a prominent part of governmental ceremonies and proclamations. The Declaration of Independence, the document marking our birth as a separate people, "appeal[ed] to the Supreme Judge of the world for the rectitude of our intentions" and avowed "a firm reliance on the protection of divine Providence." In his first inaugural address, after swearing his oath of office on a Bible, George Washington deliberately made a prayer a part of his first official act as President: "it would be peculiarly improper to omit in this first official act my fervent supplications to that Almighty Being who rules over the universe, who presides in the councils of nations, and whose providential aids can supply every human defect, that His benediction may consecrate to the liberties and happiness of the people of the United States a Government instituted by themselves for these essential purposes." Inaugural Addresses of the Presidents of the United States 2 (1989). Such supplications have been a characteristic feature of inaugural addresses ever since. . . .

Our national celebration of Thanksgiving likewise dates back to President Washington. [Justice Scalia quoted Washington's 1789 proclamation of thanksgiving and prayer (p. 492).] This tradition of Thanksgiving Proclamations—with their religious theme of prayerful gratitude to God—has been adhered to by almost every President.

The other two branches of the Federal Government also have a long-established practice of prayer at public events. As we detailed in Marsh [v. Chambers], Congressional sessions have opened with a chaplain's prayer ever since the First Congress. And this Court's own sessions have opened with the invocation "God save the United States and this Honorable Court" since the days of Chief Justice Marshall. . . .

II

The Court presumably would separate graduation invocations and benedictions from other instances of public "preservation and transmission of religious beliefs" on the ground that they involve "psychological coercion." . . . The Court's argument that state officials have "coerced" students to take part in the invocation and benediction at graduation ceremonies is, not to put too fine a point on it, incoherent. . . .

. . . According to the Court, students at graduation who want "to avoid the fact or appearance of participation" in the invocation and benediction are psychologically obligated by "public pressure, as well as peer pressure, . . . to stand as a group or, at least, maintain respectful silence" during those prayers. . . . The Court acknowledges that "in our culture standing . . . can signify adherence to a view or simple respect for the views of others." (Much more often the latter than the former, I think, except perhaps in the proverbial town meeting, where one votes by standing.) But if it is a permissible inference that one who is standing is doing so simply out of respect for the prayers of others that are in progress, then how can it possibly be said that a "reasonable dissenter . . . could believe that the group exercise signified her own participation or approval"? Quite obviously, it cannot. I may add, moreover, that maintaining respect for the religious observances of others is a fundamental civic virtue that government (including the public schools) can and should cultivate—so that even if it were the case that the displaying of such respect might be mistaken for taking part in the prayer, I would deny that the dissenter's interest in avoiding even the false appearance of participation constitutionally trumps the government's interest in fostering respect for religion generally. . . .

III

The deeper flaw in the Court's opinion does not lie in its wrong answer to the question whether there was state-induced "peer-pressure" coercion; it lies, rather, in the Court's making violation of the Establishment Clause hinge on such a precious question. The coercion that was a hallmark of historical establishments of religion was coercion of religious orthodoxy and of financial support by force of law and threat of penalty. Typically, attendance at the state church was required; only clergy of the official church could lawfully perform sacraments; and dissenters, if tolerated, faced an array of civil disabilities. Thus, for example, in the colony of Virginia, where the Church of England had been established, ministers were required by law to conform to the doctrine and rites of the Church of England; and all persons were required to attend church and observe the Sabbath, were tithed for the public support of Anglican ministers, and were taxed for the costs of building and repairing churches.

The Establishment Clause was adopted to prohibit such an establishment of religion at the federal level (and to protect state establishments of religion from federal interference). I will further acknowledge for the sake of argument that, as some scholars have argued, by 1790 the term "establishment" had acquired an additional meaning—"financial support of religion generally, by public taxation"—that reflected the development of "general or multiple" establishments, not limited to a single church. But that would still be an establishment coerced by force of law. And I will further concede that our constitutional tradition, from the Declaration of Independence and the first inaugural address of Washington, quoted earlier, down to the present day, has, with a few aberrations, ruled out of order government-sponsored endorsement of religion—even when no legal coercion is present, and indeed even when no ersatz, "peer-pressure" psycho-coercion is present—where the endorsement is sectarian, in the sense of specifying details upon which men and women who believe in a benevolent, omnipotent Creator and Ruler of the world, are known to differ (for example, the divinity of Christ). But there is simply no support for the proposition that the officially sponsored nondenominational invocation and benediction read by Rabbi Gutterman—with no one legally coerced to recite them—violated the Constitution of the United States. To the contrary, they are so characteristically American they could have come from the pen of George Washington or Abraham Lincoln himself. . . .

The reader has been told much in this case about the personal interest of Mr. Weisman and his daughter, and very little about the personal interests on the other side. They are not inconsequential. Church and state would not be such a difficult subject if religion were, as the Court apparently thinks it to be, some purely personal avocation that can be indulged entirely in secret, like pornography, in the privacy of one's room. For most believers it is *not* that, and has never been. Religious men and women of almost all denominations have felt it necessary to acknowledge and beseech the blessing of God as a people, and not just as individuals, because they believe in the "protection of divine Providence," as the Declaration of Independence put it; not just for individuals but for societies; because they believe God to be, as Washington's first Thanksgiving Proclamation put it, the "Great Lord and Ruler of Nations." One can believe in the effectiveness of such public worship, or one can deprecate and deride it. But the long-standing American tradition of prayer at official ceremonies displays with unmistakable clarity that the Establishment Clause does not forbid the government to accommodate it. . . .

I must add one final observation: The founders of our Republic knew the fearsome potential of sectarian religious belief to generate civil dissension and civil strife. And they also knew that nothing, absolutely nothing, is so inclined to foster among religious believers of various faiths a toleration—no, an affection—for one another than voluntarily joining in prayer together, to the God whom they all worship and seek. Needless to say, no one should be compelled to do that, but it is a shame to deprive our public culture of the opportunity, and indeed the encouragement, for people to do it voluntarily. The Baptist or Catholic who heard and joined in the simple and inspiring prayers of Rabbi Gutterman on this official and patriotic occasion was inoculated from religious bigotry and prejudice in a manner that cannot be replicated. To deprive our society of that important unifying mechanism, in order to spare the nonbeliever what seems to me the minimal inconvenience of standing or even sitting in respectful nonparticipation, is as senseless in policy as it is unsupported in law.

NOTES AND QUESTIONS

1. Establishment Clause Tests: "No Coercion" Versus *Lemon*. Recall that *Weisman* came in the midst of great controversy over whether the Court should narrow its interpretation of the Establishment Clause to prohibit government only from coercing people to participate in religious activity, or whether it should retain the holding (or dictum) of *Engel* and *Schempp* that even noncoercive official religious exercises were forbidden. Which option does *Weisman* take? Given the finding of coercion in *Weisman*, is any inference about other cases (where coercion cannot be shown) dictum?

Justice Souter in *Weisman* responds to those who argue that the founding generation did not mean to prohibit non-coercive acknowledgments of religion. Are you convinced by his response?

2. The Meaning of Coercion. *Weisman* relies on the concept of coercion, but does it stretch the concept so much as to make it meaningless? First, the Court finds sufficient pressure to attend the graduation ceremony even though no school rule requires it. Given the peer-oriented nature of adolescents, is there any official school event that would lack that aspect of coercion? What about a football game? A dance? A baccalaureate service the night before graduation? What about prayers at other state activities, like the start of the legislative day?

Second, the Court treats pressure to stand silently during the prayer as sufficient. Since the school will almost always require decorum from the audience during an official event, does this again mean that any religious exercise during such an event will be invalid? Would it be more honest for the Court to say that even noncoercive official prayers are forbidden in public schools?

Abner Greene, The Pledge of Allegiance Problem, 64 Fordham L. Rev. 451 (1995), suggests that under *Weisman*'s definition of coercion, a school may not conduct the Pledge of Allegiance in classrooms—even if the Pledge does not contain the phrase "under God" and even if, in obedience to Board of Education v. Barnette (p. 479), the school lets objecting students refrain from reciting it. Picking up on a suggestion from Justice Scalia's dissent, Greene argues that (a) under *Barnette* and other decisions, the school may not coerce participation in statements of a secular creed either, and (b) *Weisman* treats a public ceremony as "coercive" even when the student is allowed to stand silently through it. *Id.* at 451-452. Doesn't this show again that *Weisman* really finds an establishment violation based on something less than coercion? Or is there some other constitutional difference between religious and secular creeds that distinguishes the two cases?

3. "No Preference Among Religions" Revisited. Another alternative to *Lemon* is "nonpreferentialism," which Justices Rehnquist and Scalia advocate on historical grounds (in *Jaffree* and *Weisman* respectively) and Justice Souter attacks in his *Weisman* concurrence. Who has the better of the historical argument there?

Whatever the answer to the historical question, the majority of the Court has shown no interest in the nonpreferentialism approach. In another passage from *Weisman* (omitted above), the majority reaffirmed *Engel*'s rejection of "nonpreferential" prayers:

> We are asked to recognize the existence of a practice of nonsectarian prayer, prayer within the embrace of what is known as the Judeo-Christian tradition, . . . more acceptable than one which, for example, makes explicit references to the God of Israel, or to Jesus Christ. . . . [It may be] that there has emerged in this country a civic religion, one which is tolerated when sectarian exercises are not. . . .
>
> [But] the central meaning of the Religion Clauses . . . is that all creeds must be tolerated and none favored. The suggestion that government may establish an official or civic religion as a means of avoiding the establishment of . . . more specific creeds strikes us as a contradiction.

4. "Under God" in the Pledge of Allegiance. Eleven years after Board of Education v. Barnette, the words "under God" were added to the Pledge of Allegiance between "one nation" and "indivisible." Act of June 14, 1954, ch. 297, § 7, 68 Stat. 249, codified at 4 U.S.C. § 4. May a public school conduct recitations of the

Pledge with this phrase in school classrooms? After *Engel* and *Weisman*, it is difficult to claim that classroom exercises do not have a coercive effect. But is the Pledge with "under God" in it like an official prayer—in which case the religious language must be eliminated as those prayers were—or does it remain a secular exercise, which the state may still conduct as long as it exempts dissenters as *Barnette* requires? In a controversial decision, the Ninth Circuit held that the "under God" language turned the Pledge into a "religious act" or "religious exercise" that the school therefore could not impose in a classroom setting:

> In the context of the Pledge, the statement that the United States is a nation "under God" is a profession of a religious belief, namely, a belief in monotheism. The recitation that ours is a nation "under God" is not a mere acknowledgment that many Americans believe in a deity. Nor is it merely descriptive of the undeniable historical significance of religion in the founding of the Republic. Rather, the phrase "one nation under God" in the context of the Pledge is normative. To recite the Pledge is not to describe the United States; instead, it is to swear allegiance to the values for which the flag stands: unity, indivisibility, liberty, justice, and—since 1954—monotheism. A profession that we are a nation "under God" is identical, for Establishment Clause purposes, to a profession that we are a nation "under Jesus," a nation "under Vishnu," a nation "under Zeus," or a nation "under no god," because none of these professions can be neutral with respect to religion. The school district's practice of teacher-led recitation of the Pledge aims to inculcate in students a respect for the ideals set forth in the Pledge, including the religious values it incorporates.

Newdow v. U.S. Congress, 328 F.3d 466, 487 (9th Cir. 2003).

The Supreme Court, however, reversed on the ground that the plaintiff, Michael Newdow, lacked standing to object to a religious exercise in his daughter's classroom, because he did not have legal custody of her (the girl's mother, who had custody, did not object to the pledge). Elk Grove Unified School Dist. v. Newdow, 542 U.S. 1 (2004). Three justices would have upheld the Pledge on its merits and therefore concurred in the judgment. Chief Justice Rehnquist argued:

> I do not believe that the phrase "under God" in the Pledge converts its recital into a "religious exercise" of the sort described in *Lee*. Instead, it is a declaration of belief in allegiance and loyalty to the United States flag and the Republic that it represents. The phrase "under God" is in no sense a prayer, nor an endorsement of any religion, but a simple recognition of the fact noted in H.R.Rep. No. 1693, at 2: "From the time of our earliest history our peoples and our institutions have reflected the traditional concept that our Nation was founded on a fundamental belief in God." Reciting the Pledge, or listening to others recite it, is a patriotic exercise, not a religious one; participants promise fidelity to our flag and our Nation, not to any particular God, faith, or church. . . .
>
> When courts extend constitutional prohibitions beyond their previously recognized limit, they may restrict democratic choices made by public bodies. Here, Congress prescribed a Pledge of Allegiance, the State of California required patriotic observances in its schools, and the School District chose to comply by requiring teacher-led recital of the Pledge of Allegiance by willing students. Thus, we have three levels of popular government—the national, the state, and the local—collaborating to produce the Elk Grove ceremony. The Constitution only requires that schoolchildren be entitled to abstain from the ceremony if they chose to do so. To give the parent of such a child a sort of "heckler's veto" over a patriotic

ceremony willingly participated in by other students, simply because the Pledge of Allegiance contains the descriptive phrase "under God," is an unwarranted extension of the Establishment Clause, an extension which would have the unfortunate effect of prohibiting a commendable patriotic observance.

Justice O'Connor's separate opinion concluded that the Pledge with "under God" was an instance of permissible "ceremonial deism"—"references to God and invocations of divine assistance" that "can serve to solemnize an occasion instead of to invoke divine provenance." This category "most clearly encompasses such things as the national motto ('In God We Trust'), religious references in traditional patriotic songs such as the Star-Spangled Banner, and the words with which the Marshal of this Court opens each of its sessions ('God save the United States and this honorable Court')." Justice O'Connor wrote that a "reasonable observer . . . , fully aware of our national history and the origins of such practices, would not perceive these acknowledgments as signifying a government endorsement of any specific religion, or even of religion over non-religion." And she concluded that "under God" in the Pledge was such a permissible acknowledgment because of four factors:

History and ubiquity

The constitutional value of ceremonial deism turns on a shared understanding of its legitimate nonreligious purposes, That sort of understanding can exist only when a given practice has been in place for a significant portion of the Nation's history, and when it is observed by enough persons that it can fairly be called ubiquitous. By contrast, novel or uncommon references to religion can more easily be perceived as government endorsements because the reasonable observer cannot be presumed to be fully familiar with their origins.

Absence of worship or prayer

"[O]ne of the greatest dangers to the freedom of the individual to worship in his own way [lies] in the Government's placing its official stamp of approval upon one particular kind of prayer or one particular form of religious services." Because of this principle, only in the most extraordinary circumstances could actual worship or prayer be defended as ceremonial deism. We have upheld only one such prayer against Establishment Clause challenge, and it was supported by an extremely long and unambiguous history. See *Marsh*. Any statement that has as its purpose placing the speaker or listener in a penitent state of mind, or that is intended to create a spiritual communion or invoke divine aid, strays from the legitimate secular purposes of solemnizing an event and recognizing a shared religious history. . . .

Absence of reference to particular religion

"The clearest command of the Establishment Clause is that one religious denomination cannot be officially preferred over another." Larson v. Valente. While general acknowledgments of religion need not be viewed by reasonable observers as denigrating the nonreligious, the same cannot be said of instances "where the endorsement is sectarian, in the sense of specifying details upon which men and women who believe in a benevolent, omnipotent Creator and Ruler of the world are known to differ." *Weisman* (Scalia, J., dissenting). As a result, no religious acknowledgment could claim to be an instance of ceremonial deism if it explicitly favored one particular religious belief system over another.

Minimal religious content

A final factor that makes the Pledge an instance of ceremonial deism, in my view, is its highly circumscribed reference to God. In most of the cases in which we have struck down government speech or displays under the Establishment Clause, the offending religious content has been much more pervasive. . . . [T]he brevity of a reference to religion or to God in a ceremonial exercise can be important for several reasons. First, it tends to confirm that the reference is being used to acknowledge religion or to solemnize an event rather than to endorse religion in any way. Second, it makes it easier for those participants who wish to "opt out" of language they find offensive to do so without having to reject the ceremony entirely. And third, it tends to limit the ability of government to express a preference for one religious sect over another.

If reciting "under God" in the Pledge is unconstitutional, what about other brief references such "In God We Trust" on coins? Indeed, what about reciting the Declaration of Independence, which states that "inalienable rights" come from "the Creator"—how is that different from stating that the nation is "under God"? Or is the recitation of the Pledge of special concern because it explicitly calls for the person to affirm the statements in it ("I pledge allegiance to . . .")? If a court determines that "under God" in the Pledge is simply an instance of ceremonial deism— "solemniz[ing] an occasion instead of invoking divine provenance"—has the court thereby secularized religious language and degraded religion, just as opponents of establishment have warned? See generally, e.g., Steven B. Epstein, Rethinking the Constitutionality of Ceremonial Deism, 96 Colum. L. Rev. 2083 (1996).

3. Public Religious Displays

As we will see, the large majority of Establishment Clause cases have involved education because that is the most important way in which government shapes public opinion and influences the culture. But the government controls other cultural resources, such as public space. This too can be used to advance or inhibit religion. Do the following materials indicate that the Court is more lenient toward religious elements in government programs outside the public schools? Should it be more lenient?

a. Crèches (and Other Holiday Symbols)

LYNCH v. DONNELLY
465 U.S. 668 (1984)

THE CHIEF JUSTICE delivered the opinion of the Court.

We granted certiorari to decide whether the Establishment Clause of the First Amendment prohibits a municipality from including a crèche, or Nativity scene, in its annual Christmas display.

I

Each year, in cooperation with the downtown retail merchants' association, the City of Pawtucket, Rhode Island, erects a Christmas display as part of its observance of the Christmas holiday season. The display is situated in a park owned by a nonprofit organization and located in the heart of the shopping district. The display is essentially like those to be found in hundreds of towns or cities across the Nation—often on public grounds—during the Christmas season. The Pawtucket display comprises many of the figures and decorations traditionally associated with Christmas, including, among other things, a Santa Claus house, reindeer pulling Santa's sleigh, candy-striped poles, a Christmas tree, carolers, cutout figures representing such characters as a clown, an elephant, and a teddy bear, hundreds of colored lights, a large banner that reads "SEASONS GREETINGS," and the crèche at issue here. All components of this display are owned by the City.

The crèche, which has been included in the display for 40 or more years, consists of the traditional figures, including the Infant Jesus, Mary and Joseph, angels, shepherds, kings, and animals, all ranging in height from 5" to 5'. In 1973, when the present crèche was acquired, it cost the City $1365; it now is valued at $200. The erection and dismantling of the crèche costs the City about $20 per year; nominal expenses are incurred in lighting the crèche. No money has been expended on its maintenance for the past 10 years.

Respondents, Pawtucket residents and individual members of the Rhode Island affiliate of the American Civil Liberties Union, and the affiliate itself, brought this action in the United States District Court for Rhode Island, challenging the City's inclusion of the crèche in the annual display. [The lower courts held that including the crèche in the display violated the Establishment Clause.]

II

Our history is replete with official references to the value and invocation of Divine guidance in deliberations and pronouncements of the Founding Fathers and contemporary leaders. Beginning in the early colonial period long before Independence, a day of Thanksgiving was celebrated as a religious holiday to give thanks for the bounties of Nature as gifts from God. President Washington and his successors proclaimed Thanksgiving, with all its religious overtones, a day of national celebration and Congress made it a National Holiday more than a century ago. That holiday has not lost its theme of expressing thanks for Divine aid any more than has Christmas lost its religious significance.

Executive Orders and other official announcements of Presidents and of the Congress have proclaimed both Christmas and Thanksgiving National Holidays in religious terms. And, by Acts of Congress, it has long been the practice that federal employees are released from duties on these National Holidays, while being paid from the same public revenues that provide the compensation of the Chaplains of the Senate and the House and the military services. Thus, it is clear that Government has long recognized—indeed it has subsidized—holidays with religious significance.

Other examples of reference to our religious heritage are found in the statutorily prescribed national motto "In God We Trust," which Congress and the

President mandated for our currency, and in the language "One nation under God," as part of the Pledge of Allegiance to the American flag. . . .

Art galleries supported by public revenues display religious paintings of the 15th and 16th centuries, predominantly inspired by one religious faith. The National Gallery in Washington, maintained with Government support, for example, has long exhibited masterpieces with religious messages, notably the Last Supper, and paintings depicting the Birth of Christ, the Crucifixion, and the Resurrection, among many others with explicit Christian themes and messages. The very chamber in which oral arguments on this case were heard is decorated with a notable and permanent—not seasonal—symbol of religion: Moses with Ten Commandments. Congress has long provided chapels in the Capitol for religious worship and meditation.

There are countless other illustrations of the Government's acknowledgment of our religious heritage and governmental sponsorship of graphic manifestations of that heritage. Congress has directed the President to proclaim a National Day of Prayer each year "on which [day] the people of the United States may turn to God in prayer and meditation at churches, in groups, and as individuals." Our Presidents have repeatedly issued such Proclamations. Presidential proclamations and messages have also issued to commemorate Jewish Heritage Week and the Jewish High Holy Days. One cannot look at even this brief résumé without finding that our history is pervaded by expressions of religious beliefs[.]

III

[In deciding Establishment Clause cases] we have often found it useful to inquire whether the challenged law or conduct has a secular purpose, whether its principal or primary effect is to advance or inhibit religion, and whether it creates an excessive entanglement of government with religion. Lemon v. Kurtzman. But, we have repeatedly emphasized our unwillingness to be confined to any single test or criterion in this sensitive area. . . .

The Court has invalidated legislation or governmental action on the ground that a secular purpose was lacking, but only when it has concluded there was no question that the statute or activity was motivated wholly by religious considerations. [T]here is insufficient evidence to establish that the inclusion of the crèche is a purposeful or surreptitious effort to express some kind of subtle governmental advocacy of a particular religious message. In a pluralistic society a variety of motives and purposes are implicated. The City, like the Congresses and Presidents, however, has principally taken note of a significant historical religious event long celebrated in the Western World. The crèche in the display depicts the historical origins of this traditional event long recognized as a National Holiday.

[T]he display is sponsored by the City to celebrate the Holiday and to depict the origins of that Holiday. These are legitimate secular purposes.[6] The District Court's inference, drawn from the religious nature of the crèche, that the City has no secular purpose was, on this record, clearly erroneous.

---

6. The City contends that the purposes of the display are "exclusively secular." We hold only that Pawtucket has a secular purpose for its display, which is all that Lemon v. Kurtzman requires. Were the test that the government must have "exclusively secular" objectives, much of the conduct and legislation this Court has approved in the past would have been invalidated.

The District Court found that the primary effect of including the crèche is to confer a substantial and impermissible benefit on religion in general and on the Christian faith in particular. Comparisons of the relative benefits to religion of different forms of governmental support are elusive and difficult to make. But to conclude that the primary effect of including the crèche is to advance religion in violation of the Establishment Clause would require that we view it as more beneficial to and more an endorsement of religion, for example, than expenditure of large sums of public money for [textbooks, bus transportation, and college building grants provided to religious schools and their students, which the Court has upheld.] It would also require that we view it as more of an endorsement of religion than the Sunday Closing Laws upheld in McGowan v. Maryland (1961); the release time program for religious training in Zorach v. Clauson; and the legislative prayers upheld in Marsh v. Chambers. . . .

The dissent asserts some observers may perceive that the City has aligned itself with the Christian faith by including a Christian symbol in its display and that this serves to advance religion. We can assume, arguendo, that the display advances religion in a sense; but our precedents plainly contemplate that on occasion some advancement of religion will result from governmental action. . . . Here, whatever benefit to one faith or religion or to all religions, is indirect, remote and incidental; display of the crèche is no more an advancement or endorsement of religion than the Congressional and Executive recognition of the origins of the Holiday itself as "Christ's Mass," or the exhibition of literally hundreds of religious paintings in governmentally supported museums.

[The Court then turned to the entanglement prong, first holding that the crèche created no "administrative entanglement" between the city and religious institutions.] There is no evidence of contact with church authorities concerning the content or design of the exhibit prior to or since Pawtucket's purchase of the crèche. No expenditures for maintenance of the crèche have been necessary; and since the City owns the crèche, now valued at $200, the tangible material it contributes is de minimis. In many respects the display requires far less ongoing, day-to-day interaction between church and state than religious paintings in public galleries. There is nothing here, of course, like the "comprehensive, discriminating, and continuing state surveillance" or the "enduring entanglement" present in *Lemon.*

[This] Court has not held that political divisiveness alone can serve to invalidate otherwise permissible conduct. And we decline to so hold today. [A]part from this litigation there is no evidence of political friction or divisiveness over the crèche in the 40-year history of Pawtucket's Christmas celebration. The District Court stated that the inclusion of the crèche for the 40 years has been "marked by no apparent dissension" and that the display has had a "calm history." Curiously, it went on to hold that the political divisiveness engendered by this lawsuit was evidence of excessive entanglement. A litigant cannot, by the very act of commencing a lawsuit, however, create the appearance of divisiveness and then exploit it as evidence of entanglement. . . .

IV

Justice Brennan describes the crèche as a "re-creation of an event that lies at the heart of Christian faith." The crèche, like a painting, is passive; admittedly it is a reminder of the origins of Christmas. Even the traditional, purely secular displays extant at Christmas, with or without a crèche, would inevitably recall the religious nature of the Holiday. The display engenders a friendly community spirit of good will in keeping with the season. The crèche may well have special meaning to those whose faith includes the celebration of religious masses, but none who sense the origins of the Christmas celebration would fail to be aware of its religious implications. That the display brings people into the central city, and serves commercial interests and benefits merchants and their employees, does not, as the dissent points out, determine the character of the display.[12]

Of course the crèche is identified with one religious faith but no more so than the examples we have set out from prior cases in which we found no conflict with the Establishment Clause. It would be ironic, however, if the inclusion of a single symbol of a particular historic religious event, as part of a celebration acknowledged in the Western World for 20 centuries, and in this country by the people, by the Executive Branch, by the Congress, and the courts for two centuries, would so "taint" the City's exhibit as to render it violative of the Establishment Clause. To forbid the use of this one passive symbol—the crèche—at the very time people are taking note of the season with Christmas hymns and carols in public schools and other public places, and while the Congress and Legislatures open sessions with prayers by paid chaplains would be a stilted over-reaction contrary to our history and to our holdings. If the presence of the crèche in this display violates the Establishment Clause, a host of other forms of taking official note of Christmas, and of our religious heritage, are equally offensive to the Constitution.

The Court has acknowledged that the "fears and political problems" that gave rise to the Religion Clauses in the 18th century are of far less concern today. We are unable to perceive the Archbishop of Canterbury, the Vicar of Rome, or other powerful religious leaders behind every public acknowledgment of the religious heritage long officially recognized by the three constitutional branches of government. Any notion that these symbols pose a real danger of establishment of a state church is far-fetched indeed.

Justice O'CONNOR, concurring.

I concur in the opinion of the Court. I write separately to suggest a clarification of our Establishment Clause doctrine. The suggested approach leads to the same result in this case as that taken by the Court, and the Court's opinion, as I read it, is consistent with my analysis.

I

The Establishment Clause prohibits government from making adherence to a religion relevant in any way to a person's standing in the political community. Government can run afoul of that prohibition in two principal ways. One is excessive entanglement with religious institutions, which may interfere with the independence of the institutions, give the institutions access to government or governmental powers not fully shared by non-adherents of the religion, and foster the creation of political constituencies defined along religious lines. The

12. Justice Brennan states that "by focusing on the holiday 'context' in which the crèche appear[s]," the Court seeks to "explain away the clear religious import of the crèche," and that it has equated the crèche with a Santa's house or a talking wishing well. Of course this is not true.

second and more direct infringement is government endorsement or disapproval of religion. Endorsement sends a message to non-adherents that they are outsiders, not full members of the political community, and an accompanying message to adherents that they are insiders, favored members of the political community. Disapproval sends the opposite message.

Our prior cases have used the three-part test articulated in Lemon v. Kurtzman as a guide to detecting these two forms of unconstitutional government action. It has never been entirely clear, however, how the three parts of the test relate to the principles enshrined in the Establishment Clause. Focusing on institutional entanglement and on endorsement or disapproval of religion clarifies the *Lemon* test as an analytical device. . . .

The central issue in this case is whether Pawtucket has endorsed Christianity by its display of the crèche. To answer that question, we must examine both what Pawtucket intended to communicate in displaying the crèche and what message the City's display actually conveyed. . . .

The meaning of a statement to its audience depends both on the intention of the speaker and on the "objective" meaning of the statement in the community. . . . If the audience is large, as it always is when government "speaks" by word or deed, some portion of the audience will inevitably receive a message determined by the "objective" content of the statement, and some portion will inevitably receive the intended message. . . .

The purpose prong of the *Lemon* test asks whether government's actual purpose is to endorse or disapprove of religion. The effect prong asks whether, irrespective of government's actual purpose, the practice under review in fact conveys a message of endorsement or disapproval. An affirmative answer to either question should render the challenged practice invalid.

A

The purpose prong of the *Lemon* test requires that a government activity have a secular purpose. That requirement is not satisfied, however, by the mere existence of some secular purpose, however dominated by religious purposes. . . . The proper inquiry . . . is whether the government intends to convey a message of endorsement or disapproval of religion.

Applying that formulation to this case, I would find that Pawtucket did not intend to convey any message of endorsement of Christianity or disapproval of non-Christian religions. The evident purpose of including the crèche in the larger display was not promotion of the religious content of the crèche but celebration of the public holiday through its traditional symbols. Celebration of public holidays, which have cultural significance even if they also have religious aspects, is a legitimate secular purpose. . . .

B

Focusing on the evil of government endorsement or disapproval of religion makes clear that the effect prong of the *Lemon* test is properly interpreted not to require invalidation of a government practice merely because it in fact causes, even as a primary effect, advancement or inhibition of religion. The laws upheld in *Walz* (tax exemption for religious, educational, and charitable organizations), in *McGowan* (mandatory Sunday closing law), and in *Zorach* (released time from school for off-campus religious instruction) had such effects, but they did not violate the Establishment Clause. What is crucial is that a government practice not have the effect of communicating a message of government endorsement or disapproval of religion. It is only practices having that effect, whether intentionally or unintentionally, that make religion relevant, in reality or public perception, to status in the political community.

Pawtucket's display of its crèche, I believe, does not communicate a message that the government intends to endorse the Christian beliefs represented by the crèche. Although the religious and indeed sectarian significance of the crèche, as the district court found, is not neutralized by the setting, the overall holiday setting changes what viewers may fairly understand to be the purpose of the display—as a typical museum setting, though not neutralizing the religious content of a religious painting, negates any message of endorsement of that content. The display celebrates a public holiday, and no one contends that declaration of that holiday is understood to be an endorsement of religion. The holiday itself has very strong secular components and traditions. Government celebration of the holiday, which is extremely common, generally is not understood to endorse the religious content of the holiday, just as government celebration of Thanksgiving is not so understood. The crèche is a traditional symbol of the holiday that is very commonly displayed along with purely secular symbols, as it was in Pawtucket.

These features combine to make the government's display of the crèche in this particular physical setting no more an endorsement of religion than such governmental "acknowledgments" of religion as legislative prayers of the type approved in Marsh v. Chambers, government declaration of Thanksgiving as a public holiday, printing of "In God We Trust" on coins, and opening court sessions with "God save the United States and this honorable court." Those government acknowledgments of religion serve, in the only ways reasonably possible in our culture, the legitimate secular purposes of solemnizing public occasions, expressing confidence in the future, and encouraging the recognition of what is worthy of appreciation in society. For that reason, and because of their history and ubiquity, those practices are not understood as conveying government approval of particular religious beliefs. . . . It is significant in this regard that the crèche display apparently caused no political divisiveness prior to the filing of this lawsuit, although Pawtucket had incorporated the crèche in its annual Christmas display for some years. . . .

Justice BRENNAN, with whom Justice MARSHALL, Justice BLACKMUN, and Justice STEVENS join, dissenting. . . .

The Court advances two principal arguments to support its conclusion that the Pawtucket crèche satisfies the *Lemon* test. Neither is persuasive.

First. The Court, by focusing on the holiday "context" in which the nativity scene appeared, seeks to explain away the clear religious import of the crèche and the findings of the District Court that most observers understood the crèche as both a symbol of Christian beliefs and a symbol of the City's support for those beliefs. . . . But it blinks reality to claim, as the Court does, that by including such a distinctively religious object as the crèche in its Christmas display, Pawtucket has done no more than make use of a "traditional" symbol of the holiday, and has thereby purged the crèche of its religious content and conferred only an "incidental and indirect" benefit on religion.

[E]ven in the context of Pawtucket's seasonal celebration, the crèche retains a specifically Christian religious meaning. I refuse to accept the notion implicit in today's decision that non-Christians would find that the religious content of the crèche is eliminated by the fact that it appears as part of the City's otherwise secular celebration of the Christmas holiday. The nativity scene is clearly distinct in its purpose and effect from the rest of the Hodgson Park display for the simple reason that it is the only one rooted in a biblical account of Christ's birth. It is the chief symbol of the characteristically Christian belief that a divine Savior was brought into the world and that the purpose of this miraculous birth was to illuminate a path toward salvation and redemption. For Christians, that path is exclusive, precious and holy. But for those who do not share these beliefs, the symbolic re-enactment of the birth of a divine being who has been miraculously incarnated as a man stands as a dramatic reminder of their differences with Christian faith. . . . To be so excluded on religious grounds by one's elected government is an insult and an injury that, until today, could not be countenanced by the Establishment Clause.

Second. . . . The Court apparently believes that once it finds that the designation of Christmas as a public holiday is constitutionally acceptable, it is then free to conclude that virtually every form of governmental association with the celebration of the holiday is also constitutional. The vice of this dangerously superficial argument is that it overlooks the fact that the Christmas holiday in our national culture contains both secular and sectarian elements. To say that government may recognize the holiday's traditional, secular elements of gift-giving, public festivities and community spirit, does not mean that government may indiscriminately embrace the distinctively sectarian aspects of the holiday.

When government decides to recognize Christmas day as a public holiday, it does no more than accommodate the calendar of public activities to the plain fact that many Americans will expect on that day to spend time visiting with their families, attending religious services, and perhaps enjoying some respite from pre-holiday activities. The Free Exercise Clause, of course, does not necessarily compel the government to provide this accommodation, but neither is the Establishment Clause offended by such a step. Because it is clear that the celebration of Christmas has both secular and sectarian elements, it may well be that by taking note of the holiday, the government is simply seeking to serve the same kinds of wholly secular goals—for instance, promoting goodwill and a common day of rest—that were found to justify Sunday Closing laws in *McGowan*. If public officials go further and participate in the secular celebration of Christmas—by, for example, decorating public places with such secular images as wreaths, garlands or Santa Claus figures—they move closer to the limits of their constitutional power but nevertheless remain within the boundaries set by the Establishment Clause. But when those officials participate in or appear to endorse the distinctively religious elements of this otherwise secular event, they encroach upon First Amendment freedoms. For it is at that point that the government brings to the forefront the theological content of the holiday, and places the prestige, power and financial support of a civil authority in the service of a particular faith.

The inclusion of a crèche in Pawtucket's otherwise secular celebration of Christmas clearly violates these principles. Unlike such secular figures as

Santa Claus, reindeer and carolers, a nativity scene represents far more than a mere "traditional" symbol of Christmas. The essence of the crèche's symbolic purpose and effect is to prompt the observer to experience a sense of simple awe and wonder appropriate to the contemplation of one of the central elements of Christian dogma—that God sent His son into the world to be a Messiah. Contrary to the Court's suggestion, the crèche is far from a mere representation of a "particular historic religious event." It is, instead, best understood as a mystical re-creation of an event that lies at the heart of Christian faith. To suggest, as the Court does, that such a symbol is merely "traditional" and therefore no different from Santa's house or reindeer is not only offensive to those for whom the crèche has profound significance, but insulting to those who insist for religious or personal reasons that the story of Christ is in no sense a part of "history" nor an unavoidable element of our national "heritage."

II

[I]ntuition tells us that some official "acknowledgment" is inevitable in a religious society if government is not to adopt a stilted indifference to the religious life of the people. It is equally true, however, that if government is to remain scrupulously neutral in matters of religious conscience, as our Constitution requires, then it must avoid those overly broad acknowledgments of religious practices that may imply governmental favoritism toward one set of religious beliefs. This does not mean, of course, that public officials may not take account, when necessary, of the separate existence and significance of the religious institutions and practices in the society they govern. Should government choose to incorporate some arguably religious element into its public ceremonies, that acknowledgment must be impartial; it must not tend to promote one faith or handicap another; and it should not sponsor religion generally over non-religion.

[W]e have noted that government cannot be completely prohibited from recognizing in its public actions the religious beliefs and practices of the American people as an aspect of our national history and culture. While I remain uncertain about these questions, I would suggest that such practices as the designation of "In God We Trust" as our national motto, or the references to God contained in the Pledge of Allegiance can best be understood, in Dean Rostow's apt phrase, as a form of "ceremonial deism," protected from Establishment Clause scrutiny chiefly because they have lost through rote repetition any significant religious content. Moreover, these references are uniquely suited to serve such wholly secular purposes as solemnizing public occasions, or inspiring commitment to meet some national challenge in a manner that simply could not be fully served in our culture if government were limited to purely non-religious phrases. [T]hat necessity, coupled with their long history, gives those practices an essentially secular meaning.

Under our constitutional scheme, the role of safeguarding our "religious heritage" and of promoting religious beliefs is reserved as the exclusive prerogative of our nation's churches, religious institutions and spiritual leaders. Because the Framers of the Establishment Clause understood that "religion is too personal, too sacred, too holy to permit its 'unhallowed perversion' by civil [authorities]," Engel v. Vitale, the clause demands that government play no role in this effort. . . . [T]he City's action should be recognized for what it is: a coercive, though perhaps small, step toward establishing the sectarian preferences of the majority at the expense of the minority, accomplished by placing public facilities and funds in support of the religious symbolism and theological tidings that the crèche conveys.

Justice BLACKMUN, with whom Justice STEVENS joins, dissenting.

. . . [T]he majority does an injustice to the crèche and the message it manifests. While certain persons, including the Mayor of Pawtucket, undertook a crusade to "keep Christ in Christmas," the Court today has declared that presence virtually irrelevant. The majority urges that the display, "with or without a crèche," "recall[s] the religious nature of the Holiday," and "engenders a friendly community spirit of good will in keeping with the season." Before the District Court, an expert witness for the city made a similar, though perhaps more candid, point, stating that Pawtucket's display invites people "to participate in the Christmas spirit, brotherhood, peace, and let loose with their money." The crèche has been relegated to the role of a neutral harbinger of the holiday season, useful for commercial purposes, but devoid of any inherent meaning and incapable of enhancing the religious tenor of a display of which it is an integral part. The city has its victory—but it is a Pyrrhic one indeed.

The import of the Court's decision is to encourage use of the crèche in a municipally sponsored display, a setting where Christians feel constrained in acknowledging its symbolic meaning and non-Christians feel alienated by its presence. Surely, this is a misuse of a sacred symbol.

Five years later, the Court returned to the holiday-display issue. Are the two decisions consistent?

COUNTY OF ALLEGHENY v. ACLU, 492 U.S. 573 (1989): This litigation concerned two recurring holiday displays on public property in downtown Pittsburgh. The first, a crèche depicting the Christian Nativity scene, was placed on the Grand Staircase of the Allegheny County Courthouse. The crèche was donated by the Holy Name Society, a Roman Catholic group, and bore a sign to that effect. Over the manger was an angel bearing a banner proclaiming "Gloria in Excelsis Deo." The second display was an 18-foot Hanukkah menorah, installed just outside the City-County Building next to the city's 45-foot decorated Christmas tree. At the foot of the tree was a sign bearing the mayor's name and declaring the city's "salute to liberty." The menorah was owned by Chabad, a Jewish group, but was stored, erected, and removed each year by the city. The American Civil Liberties Union (ACLU) and seven local residents sued to enjoin both displays.

A splintered Court held that the first display violated the Establishment Clause, but the second did not. Justice Blackmun wrote the opinion of the Court on the first point; he wrote for himself alone on the second. He applied the "endorsement" test proposed by Justice O'Connor in Lynch v. Donnelly: "We turn first to the county's crèche display. There is no doubt, of course, that the crèche itself is capable of communicating a religious message. Indeed, the crèche in this lawsuit uses words, as well as the picture of the Nativity scene, to make its religious meaning unmistakably clear. 'Glory to God in the Highest!' says the angel in the crèche—Glory to God because of the birth of Jesus. This praise to God in Christian terms is indisputably religious—indeed sectarian— just as it is when said in the Gospel or in a church service.

"Under the Court's holding in *Lynch*, the effect of a crèche display turns on its setting. Here, unlike in *Lynch*, nothing in the context of the display detracts from the crèche's religious message. The *Lynch* display composed a series of figures and objects, each group of which had its own focal point. Santa's house and his reindeer were objects of attention separate from the crèche, and had their specific visual story to tell. Similarly, whatever a 'talking' wishing well may be, it obviously was a center of attention separate from the crèche. Here, in contrast, the crèche stands alone: it is the single element of the display on the Grand Staircase. . . .

"The fact that the crèche bears a sign disclosing its ownership by a Roman Catholic organization does not alter this conclusion. On the contrary, the sign simply demonstrates that the government is endorsing the religious message of that organization, rather than communicating a message of its own. But the Establishment Clause does not limit only the religious content of the government's own communications. It also prohibits the government's support and promotion of religious communications by religious organizations. Indeed, the very concept of 'endorsement' conveys the sense of promoting someone else's message."

With regard to the menorah Justice Blackmun, writing now for himself, said: "[T]he relevant question for Establishment Clause purposes is whether the combined display of the tree, the sign, and the menorah has the effect of endorsing both Christian and Jewish faiths, or rather simply recognizes that both Christmas and Chanukah are part of the same winter-holiday season, which has attained a secular status in our society. [The Christmas tree, unlike the menorah, is not a religious symbol (though it once was).] The tree, moreover, is clearly the predominant element in the city's display. The 45-foot tree occupies the central position beneath the middle archway in front of the Grant Street entrance to the City-County Building; the 18-foot menorah is positioned to one side. Given this configuration, it is much more sensible to interpret the meaning of the menorah in light of the tree, rather than vice versa. . . . The mayor's sign further diminishes the possibility that the tree and the menorah will be interpreted as a dual endorsement of Christianity and Judaism. The sign states that during the holiday season the city salutes liberty. Moreover, the sign draws upon the theme of light, common to both Chanukah and Christmas as winter festivals, and links that theme with this Nation's legacy of freedom, which allows an American to celebrate the holiday season in whatever way he wishes, religiously or otherwise. . . . Given all these considerations, it is not 'sufficiently likely' that residents of Pittsburgh will perceive the combined display of the tree, the sign, and the menorah as an 'endorsement' or 'disapproval . . . of their individual religious choices.'"

Justice O'Connor concurred in the judgment as to both the crèche and the menorah. Three justices would have held both displays unconstitutional. Justice Kennedy, joined by three others, would have upheld both displays. Justice Kennedy objected to the majority's reliance on the "endorsement" test. Here is what he had to say: "[Under the endorsement] test, the touchstone of an Establishment Clause violation is whether non-adherents would be made to feel like 'outsiders' by government recognition or accommodation of religion. Few of our traditional practices recognizing the part religion plays in our society can withstand scrutiny under a faithful application of this formula.

"Some examples suffice to make plain my concerns. [Justice Kennedy cited Thanksgiving proclamations, Congress's employment of a chaplain, the National Day of Prayer, our national motto, the Pledge of Allegiance, and the Court beginning its sessions with 'God save the United States and this honorable Court.'] Either the endorsement test must invalidate scores of traditional practices recognizing the place religion holds in our culture, or it must be twisted and stretched to avoid inconsistency with practices we know to have been permitted in the past, while condemning similar practices with no greater endorsement effect simply by reason of their lack of historical antecedent. Neither result is acceptable.

"In addition to disregarding precedent and historical fact, the majority's approach to government use of religious symbolism threatens to trivialize constitutional adjudication. [The endorsement test adopted by] Justice Blackmun embraces a jurisprudence of minutiae. A reviewing court must consider whether the city has included Santas, talking wishing wells, reindeer, or other secular symbols as 'a center of attention separate from the crèche.' [Then it must consider] the prominence of the setting in which the display is placed. In this case, the Grand Staircase of the county courthouse proved too resplendent. [A test like this] could provide workable guidance to the lower courts, if ever, only after this Court has decided a long series of holiday display cases, using little more than intuition and a tape measure. Deciding cases on the basis of such an unguided examination of marginalia is irreconcilable with the imperative of applying neutral principles in constitutional adjudication."

NOTES AND QUESTIONS

1. **Distinguishing** *Lynch* **and** *Allegheny*: **The Three Plastic Animals Rule.** Why is the crèche constitutional in *Lynch* and not in *Allegheny*? What is the distinction between the two cases under the endorsement test, proposed by Justice O'Connor in *Lynch* and followed by the majority in *Allegheny*? Did Pittsburgh (but not Pawtucket) intend to endorse Christianity? The Court suggests that the Allegheny County display had a different perceived meaning because the crèche stood alone. In Pawtucket it was flanked by Santa's house, reindeer, and a talking wishing well. Why should that matter? Because plastic animals dilute the religious value of the display enough to make it innocuous? Five members of the Court in *Allegheny County* voted to uphold the menorah display, apparently because it was accompanied by a tree and a sign saluting liberty. Does the Court's rule have it backward? A legal requirement that the government may not exhibit religious symbols unless it surrounds them with cartoon characters should offend some religious believers. If the government is going to display religious symbols, why shouldn't it treat them with respect?

2. **Civil Religion.** What is it about a Christmas crèche that makes this case unique? We have seen in our examination of test oaths, school prayer, and school curriculum the Court's repeated insistence that the government may not proclaim a religious message. Even Sunday closing laws, as Justice Brennan

points out, have been spared only because they are "continued today solely for secular reasons." One could make a similar argument for Christmas scenes. The display in *Lynch* was put on by Pawtucket in cooperation with the downtown retail merchants' association, and they sponsored it because it was good for business. But there remains this difference between the two cases: The merchants in *Lynch* used indisputably religious means to accomplish their secular purpose. Under the Establishment Clause, we have not distinguished between religion as a means and religion as an end in itself. In late-eighteenth-century Virginia, Patrick Henry advocated support for teachers of the Christian religion not because they would advance the cause of salvation but because "the general diffusion of Christian knowledge hath a natural tendency to correct the morals of men, restrain their vices, and preserve the peace of society" (p. 47). The proposal is nonetheless viewed as an establishment of religion.

The Court in *Lynch* did not defend the crèche as commercial advertising. It said that "[t]he display is sponsored by the City to celebrate the Holiday and to depict the origins of that Holiday." This sounds like an innocent and familiar idea. Cities celebrate Mothers' Day, Groundhog Day, and St. Patrick's Day and hold ethnic heritage festivals. Can they endorse religion as one among many traditions that (some) citizens hold on to? The City of San Jose has a 20-foot-high sculpture of the Aztec god Quetzalcoatl that celebrates Mexican and Spanish contributions to the city's culture. Alvarado v. San Jose, 94 F.3d 1223 (9th Cir. 1996). Should we distinguish in our thinking about this problem between majority and minority religions?

3. History and Crèches. The *Lynch* Court makes a similar historical argument about crèches, but its analogies are not as close. Early Puritan communities forbade Christmas celebrations, believing them to be "Popish." Christmas was observed in a variety of ways in eighteenth-century America: feasting, revelry, games, mummery, church devotions, and so forth. There was public celebration, but perhaps not the civic and commercial direction we see today. The first community Christmas tree was put up in New York City in 1912. Penne L. Restad, Christmas in America (1995); Stephen Nissenbaum, The Battle for Christmas (1996). Perhaps municipal crèches are no older. Lacking evidence of eighteenth-century manger scenes, the Court falls back on Thanksgiving proclamations, our national motto, our public collections of religious art, the chaplain's prayer in Marsh v. Chambers (p. 494), and similar practices. Is such historical evidence specific enough to be conclusive as it was in *Marsh*? Is the point that crèches are less objectionable than these practices, and must be constitutional if they are? What is the measure of objectionability?

4. The Endorsement Test. The endorsement test proposed by Justice O'Connor in *Lynch* and applied in *Allegheny* has had an important, though uneven, influence over the last 20 years. She suggests that we understand the *Lemon* test as a prohibition on government endorsement (or disapproval) of religion. The purpose prong forbids the government to intentionally convey such a message. The effects prong forbids government action whose "objective" meaning, intended or not, is one of endorsement or disapproval. We have seen the Court, or some of its members, adopt this approach not only in *Allegheny*, but in other cases, such as Texas Monthly v. Bullock (plurality opinion) (p. 243), Edwards v. Aguillard (p. 555), and Wallace v. Jaffree (p. 496). Is this a comprehensive "test" for church-state conflicts?

The endorsement test might be appropriate for cases about government speech on religious topics, like *Lynch*, without necessarily being useful for cases about accommodations for religious groups, or aid to parochial schools, or church property disputes, or delegations of power to religious bodies. Can you see why? The endorsement test asks what message the government communicates by its action. But with many government actions, the primary purpose and effect are something else than communicating a message. Would the issue of aid to parochial schools be different if appropriations were made covertly, the way Congress funds the CIA? Steven D. Smith, Symbols, Perceptions, and Doctrinal Illusions: Establishment Neutrality and the "No Endorsement" Test, 86 Mich. L. Rev. 266, 288 (1987).

How useful is the endorsement test within its proper domain? Consider several difficulties suggested by Smith, 86 Mich. L. Rev. 266.

(a) What does the term "endorsement" mean? Does Wisconsin endorse the Amish by exempting them from compulsory school attendance laws? Would the city of Madison endorse the Amish if it held an Amish festival? Could the mayor adopt plain dress and speak German while at the festival? Could he join in the Amish grace before meals? How is the problem in *Lynch* different?

(b) According to the endorsement test, the effects prong of *Lemon* forbids practices that create a perception that the government has endorsed (or disapproved of) religion. But whose perceptions count? Justice O'Connor implies in *Lynch* that we should ask the citizens of Pawtucket. Any citizen? That would make life easy for plaintiffs. And we can foresee objections to almost every action the government takes. Suppose we ask for the perception of a majority of Pawtucket's citizens. Would this test serve Justice O'Connor's objective of protecting religious minorities and outsiders? In Wallace v. Jaffree, 472 U.S. at 76 (O'Connor, J., concurring), Justice O'Connor decided that the relevant perceptions were those of "an objective observer, acquainted with the text, legislative history, and implementation of the statute." If this is so, how do we distinguish between actual intent and perceived intent (between parts one and two of the endorsement test)? A hypothetical observer familiar with the law's legislative history will know (as best one can) the lawmaker's true intent. Can he have a perception at variance with that?

(c) What is the point of this restatement of *Lemon*? It rests on the premise that endorsement "mak[es] adherence to a religion relevant . . . to a person's standing in the political community," and "sends a message to non-adherents that they are outsiders [and] to adherents that they are insiders." Is it true that witnessing government endorsement of ideas we do not share or symbols that we do not value makes us less than full members of the political community? Does a city sponsoring a St. Patrick's Day parade send a message that non-Irish are "excluded"? Most of us disagree with a lot of what the government says and does, but as long as we have as much right as anyone to participate in the decisions, we do not think our citizenship is devalued. Why are religious symbols different?

For further discussion of the endorsement test, see Jessie Hill, Putting Religious Symbolism in Context: A Linguistic Critique of the Endorsement Test, 104 Mich. L. Rev. 491 (2005); Jesse H. Choper, The Endorsement Test: Its Status and

Desirability, 18 J.L. & Pol. 499 (2002); Shari Seidman Diamond and Andrew Koppelman, Measured Endorsement, 60 Md. L. Rev. 713 (2001); Donald L. Beschle, The Conservative as Liberal: The Religion Clauses, Liberal Neutrality, and the Approach of Justice O'Connor, 62 Notre Dame L. Rev. 151 (1987); Arnold Loewy, Rethinking Government Neutrality Towards Religion Under the Establishment Clause: The Untapped Potential of Justice O'Connor's Insight, 64 N.C. L. Rev. 1049 (1986); William P. Marshall, "We Know It When We See It": The Supreme Court and Establishment, 59 S. Cal. L. Rev. 495 (1986).

5. Religious Displays and Freedom of Speech. In Capitol Square Review & Advisory Bd. v. Pinette, 515 U.S. 753 (1995), the Court held that the state of Ohio could not refuse the Ku Klux Klan permission to erect a freestanding cross in a public plaza, directly in front of the state capitol, where other groups had been permitted to erect displays. (Interestingly, the Klan was denied a permit not because its expression was racist but because it was religious.) The Court held that the square was a traditional public forum for citizen expression and so a group could not be excluded because of the content of its speech without a compelling reason; it also held that the Establishment Clause did not justify excluding the Klan.

Pinette and other cases of religious speech in the public forum are examined in more detail in section B-3 below. For now, consider whether *Pinette* is consistent with *Allegheny*'s ruling against the Pittsburgh crèche, where the Court held that the sign showing ownership of the crèche by the Catholic society "simply demonstrates that the government is [unconstitutionally] endorsing the religious message of that organization."

b. Ten Commandments Displays, and History Revisited

The most recent major dispute over governmental religious symbols has concerned the Ten Commandments. Just as the Court allowed some but not all religious holiday displays in *Lynch* and *Allegheny*, the following two decisions allow some but not all Decalogue displays. See if you can tell where the decisions draw the line. Also pay attention to the historical arguments in the opinions of Justice Stevens and Scalia.

McCREARY COUNTY v. AMERICAN CIVIL LIBERTIES UNION
125 S. Ct. 2722 (2005)

Justice SOUTER delivered the opinion of the Court. . . .

I

In the summer of 1999, petitioners McCreary County and Pulaski County, Kentucky (hereinafter Counties), put up in their respective courthouses large, gold-framed copies of an abridged text of the King James version of the Ten Commandments. . . . In Pulaski County, amidst reported controversy over the propriety of the display, the Commandments were hung in a ceremony presided over by the county Judge-Executive, who called them "good rules to live by" and who recounted the story of an astronaut who became convinced "there must be a divine

God" after viewing the Earth from the moon. The Judge-Executive was accompanied by the pastor of his church, who called the Commandments "a creed of ethics" and told the press after the ceremony that displaying the Commandments was "one of the greatest things the judge could have done to close out the millennium." In both counties, this was the version of the Commandments posted:

"Thou shalt have no other gods before me.
"Thou shalt not make unto thee any graven images.
"Thou shalt not take the name of the Lord thy God in vain.
"Remember the sabbath day, to keep it holy.
"Honor thy father and thy mother.
"Thou shalt not kill.
"Thou shalt not commit adultery.
"Thou shalt not steal.
"Thou shalt not bear false witness.
"Thou shalt not covet.
"Exodus 20:3-17."

In each county, the hallway display was "readily visible to . . . county citizens who use the courthouse to conduct their civic business, to obtain or renew driver's licenses and permits, to register cars, to pay local taxes, and to register to vote.".

[The ACLU sued in federal court for] a preliminary injunction against maintaining the displays. . . . Within a month, and before the District Court had responded to the request for injunction, the legislative body of each County authorized a second, expanded display, by nearly identical resolutions reciting that the Ten Commandments are "the precedent legal code upon which the civil and criminal codes of . . . Kentucky are founded," and stating several grounds for taking that position: that "the Ten Commandments are codified in Kentucky's civil and criminal laws"; that the Kentucky House of Representatives had in 1999 "voted unanimously . . to adjourn . . . 'in remembrance and honor of Jesus Christ, the Prince of Ethics'"; that the "County Judge and . . . magistrates agree with the arguments set out by Judge [Roy] Moore" in defense of his "display [of] the Ten Commandments in his courtroom";[*] and that the "Founding Father[s] [had an] explicit understanding of the duty of elected officials to publicly acknowledge God as the source of America's strength and direction."

As directed by the resolutions, the Counties expanded the displays of the Ten Commandments in their locations, [to add] eight other documents in smaller frames, each either having a religious theme or excerpted to highlight a religious element. The documents were the "endowed by their Creator" passage from the Declaration of Independence; the Preamble to the Constitution of Kentucky; the national motto, "In God We Trust"; a page from the Congressional Record of February 2, 1983, proclaiming the Year of the Bible and

---

* [Moore gained nationwide attention—and support—when, as an Alabama trial judge, he posted a Ten Commandments plaque behind his courtroom bench and later, as the state's chief justice, erected a large granite monument of the Commandments in the rotunda of the state supreme court building. Moore refused to obey a federal court decision ordering the removal of the monument, Glassroth v. Moore, 335 F.3d 1282 (11th Cir. 2003); he argued that the order was unlawful and that requiring its removal would force him to deny God. For his refusal, Moore was disciplined by being removed from office. Moore v. Judicial Inquiry Com'n, 891 So. 2d 848 (Ala. 2004).—EDS.]

including a statement of the Ten Commandments; a proclamation by President Abraham Lincoln designating April 30, 1863, a National Day of Prayer and Humiliation; an excerpt from President Lincoln's "Reply to Loyal Colored People of Baltimore upon Presentation of a Bible," reading that "[t]he Bible is the best gift God has ever given to man"; a proclamation by President Reagan marking 1983 the Year of the Bible; and the Mayflower Compact.

[The district court entered a preliminary injunction against both the first and second displays. The court found that the original display lacked any secular purpose under *Lemon*] because the Commandments "are a distinctly religious document, believed by many Christians and Jews to be the direct and revealed word of God." . . . The court found that the second version also "clearly lack[ed] a secular purpose" because the "Count[ies] narrowly tailored [their] selection of foundational documents to incorporate only those with specific references to Christianity."

[The Counties did not appeal the preliminary injunction but instead erected a new, third display consisting of the Commandments and] framed copies of the Magna Carta, the Declaration of Independence, the Bill of Rights, the lyrics of the Star Spangled Banner, the Mayflower Compact, the National Motto, the Preamble to the Kentucky Constitution, and a picture of Lady Justice. The collection is entitled "The Foundations of American Law and Government Display" and each document comes with a statement about its historical and legal significance. The comment on the Ten Commandments reads:

> The Ten Commandments have profoundly influenced the formation of Western legal thought and the formation of our country. That influence is clearly seen in the Declaration of Independence, which declared that 'We hold these truths to be self-evident, that all men are created equal, that they are endowed by their Creator with certain unalienable Rights, that among these are Life, Liberty, and the pursuit of Happiness.' The Ten Commandments provide the moral background of the Declaration of Independence and the foundation of our legal tradition.

The ACLU moved to supplement the preliminary injunction to enjoin the Counties' third display, [and the district court granted the motion. The court of appeals affirmed. The Supreme Court affirmed as well.]

II

Twenty-five years ago in a case prompted by posting the Ten Commandments in Kentucky's public schools, this Court recognized that the Commandments "are undeniably a sacred text in the Jewish and Christian faiths" and held that their display in public classrooms violated the First Amendment's bar against establishment of religion. Stone v. Graham (1980). *Stone* found a predominantly religious purpose in the government's posting of the Commandments. . . . The Counties ask for a different approach here by arguing that official purpose is unknowable and the search for it inherently vain. In the alternative, the Counties would avoid the District Court's conclusion by having us limit the scope of the purpose enquiry so severely that any trivial rationalization would suffice, under a standard oblivious to the history of religious government action like the progression of exhibits in this case.

A

Ever since Lemon v. Kurtzman summarized the three familiar considerations for evaluating Establishment Clause claims, looking to whether government action has "a secular legislative purpose" has been a common, albeit seldom dispositive, element of our cases. . . .

The touchstone for our analysis is the principle that the "First Amendment mandates governmental neutrality between religion and religion, and between religion and nonreligion." [Citations omitted.] When the government acts with the ostensible and predominant purpose of advancing religion, it violates that central Establishment Clause value of official religious neutrality, there being no neutrality when the government's ostensible object is to take sides. Manifesting a purpose to favor one faith over another, or adherence to religion generally, clashes with the "understanding, reached . . . after decades of religious war, that liberty and social stability demand a religious tolerance that respects the religious views of all citizens." Zelman v. Simmons-Harris [p. 403] (Breyer, J., dissenting). By showing a purpose to favor religion, the government "sends the . . . message to . . . nonadherents 'that they are outsiders, not full members of the political community, and an accompanying message to adherents that they are insiders, favored members.' " [Quoting Lynch (O'Connor, J., concurring).]

B

Despite the intuitive importance of official purpose to the realization of Establishment Clause values, the Counties ask us to abandon Lemon's purpose test, or at least to truncate any enquiry into purpose here. Their first argument is that the very consideration of purpose is deceptive: according to them, true "purpose" is unknowable, and its search merely an excuse for courts to act selectively and unpredictably in picking out evidence of subjective intent. The assertions are as seismic as they are unconvincing.

Examination of purpose is a staple of statutory interpretation that makes up the daily fare of every appellate court in the country. [Citations omitted.] With enquiries into purpose this common, if they were nothing but hunts for mares' nests deflecting attention from bare judicial will, the whole notion of purpose in law would have dropped into disrepute long ago.

But scrutinizing purpose does make practical sense, as in Establishment Clause analysis, where an understanding of official objective emerges from readily discoverable fact, without any judicial psychoanalysis of a drafter's heart of hearts. The eyes that look to purpose belong to an "'objective observer,'" one who takes account of the traditional external signs that show up in the " 'text, legislative history, and implementation of the statute,' " or comparable official act. [Citations omitted.] There is, then, nothing hinting at an unpredictable or disingenuous exercise when a court enquires into purpose after a claim is raised under the Establishment Clause.

The cases with findings of a predominantly religious purpose point to the straightforward nature of the test. In [Wallace v. Jaffree (p. 496)], for example, we inferred purpose from a change of wording from an earlier statute to a later one, each dealing with prayer in schools. . . .

Nor is there any indication that the enquiry is rigged in practice to finding a religious purpose dominant every time a case is filed. In the past, the test has not been fatal very often, presumably because government does not generally act unconstitutionally, with the predominant purpose of advancing religion. . . .

C . . .

1

[A]lthough a legislature's stated reasons will generally get deference, the secular purpose required has to be genuine, not a sham, and not merely secondary to a religious objective. . . .

Even the Counties' own cited authority confirms that we have not made the purpose test a pushover for any secular claim. True, Wallace v. Jaffree said government action is tainted by its object "if it is entirely motivated by a purpose to advance religion," a remark that suggests, in isolation, a fairly complaisant attitude. But in that very case the Court declined to credit Alabama's stated secular rationale of "accommodation" for legislation authorizing a period of silence in school for meditation or voluntary prayer, given the implausibility of that explanation in light of another statute already accommodating children wishing to pray. . . . [13]

2

The Counties' second proffered limitation can be dispatched quickly. They argue that purpose in a case like this one should be inferred, if at all, only from the latest news about the last in a series of governmental actions, however close they may all be in time and subject. But the world is not made brand new every morning, and the Counties are simply asking us to ignore perfectly probative evidence; they want an absentminded objective observer, not one presumed to be familiar with the history of the government's actions and competent to learn what history has to show. The Counties' position just bucks common sense: reasonable observers have reasonable memories, and our precedents sensibly forbid an observer "to turn a blind eye to the context in which [the] policy arose."[14]

III

[The Court then turned to the display and its two predecessors, emphasizing that "under the Establishment Clause context is key" in determining "what viewers may fairly understand to be the purpose of the display."]

A

The display rejected in Stone v. Graham had two obvious similarities to the first one in the sequence here: both set out a text of the Commandments as distinct from any traditionally symbolic representation, and each stood alone, not part of an arguably secular display. *Stone* stressed the significance of integrating the Commandments into a secular scheme to forestall the broadcast of

---

13. [To allow a government religious action] so long as any secular purpose for the government action is apparen[t] would leave the purpose test with no real bite, given the ease of finding some secular purpose for almost any government action. . . .

14. One consequence of taking account of the purpose underlying past actions is that the same government action may be constitutional if taken in the first instance and unconstitutional if it has a sectarian heritage. This presents no incongruity, however, because purpose matters. Just as Holmes's dog could tell the difference between being kicked and being stumbled over, it will matter to objective observers whether posting the Commandments follows on the heels of displays motivated by sectarianism, or whether it lacks a history demonstrating that purpose . . .

an otherwise clearly religious message, and for good reason, the Commandments being a central point of reference in the religious and moral history of Jews and Christians. They proclaim the existence of a monotheistic god (no other gods). They regulate details of religious obligation (no graven images, no sabbath breaking, no vain oath swearing). And they unmistakably rest even the universally accepted prohibitions (as against murder, theft, and the like) on the sanction of the divinity proclaimed at the beginning of the text. Displaying that text is thus different from a symbolic depiction, like tablets with 10 roman numerals, which could be seen as alluding to a general notion of law, not a sectarian conception of faith. Where the text is set out, the insistence of the religious message is hard to avoid in the absence of a context plausibly suggesting a message going beyond an excuse to promote the religious point of view. [T]he Counties' solo exhibit here did nothing more to counter the sectarian implication than the postings at issue in *Stone*. What is more, at the ceremony for posting the framed Commandments in Pulaski County, the county executive was accompanied by his pastor, who testified to the certainty of the existence of God. The reasonable observer could only think that the Counties meant to emphasize and celebrate the Commandments' religious message.

B

[The Court also agreed that the second display—the Commandments accompanied by other documents making theistic and Christian references—was unconstitutional.] Together, the display and [its authorizing] resolution presented an indisputable, and undisputed, showing of an impermissible purpose.

Today, the Counties make no attempt to defend their undeniable objective, but instead hopefully describe version two as "dead and buried." Their refusal to defend the second display is understandable, but the reasonable observer could not forget it.

C

1

After the Counties changed lawyers, they mounted a third display, without a new resolution or repeal of the old one. The result was the "Foundations of American Law and Government" exhibit, which placed the Commandments in the company of other documents the Counties thought especially significant in the historical foundation of American government. In trying to persuade the District Court to lift the preliminary injunction, the Counties cited several new purposes for the third version, including a desire "to educate the citizens of the county regarding some of the documents that played a significant role in the foundation of our system of law and government." [But the lower courts were right to reject these arguments.]

[A]lthough repeal of the earlier county authorizations would not have erased them from the record of evidence bearing on current purpose, the extraordinary resolutions for the second display passed just months earlier were not repealed or otherwise repudiated. Indeed, the sectarian spirit of the common resolution found enhanced expression in the third display, which quoted more of the purely religious language of the Commandments than the first two displays had done; for additions, see App. to Pet. for Cert. 189a ("I the LORD thy God am a jealous God") (text of Second Commandment in third display); ("the

LORD will not hold him guiltless that taketh his name in vain") (from text of Third Commandment); and ("that thy days may be long upon the land which the LORD thy God giveth thee") (text of Fifth Commandment). No reasonable observer could swallow the claim that the Counties had cast off the objective so unmistakable in the earlier displays.

Nor did the selection of posted material suggest a clear theme that might prevail over evidence of the continuing religious object. In a collection of documents said to be "foundational" to American government, it is at least odd to include a patriotic anthem, but to omit the Fourteenth Amendment, the most significant structural provision adopted since the original Framing. And it is no less baffling to leave out the original Constitution of 1787 while quoting the 1215 Magna Carta even to the point of its declaration that "fish-weirs shall be removed from the Thames." If an observer found these choices and omissions perplexing in isolation, he would be puzzled for a different reason when he read the Declaration of Independence seeking confirmation for the Counties' posted explanation that the "Ten Commandments' . . . influence is clearly seen in the Declaration"; in fact the observer would find that the Commandments are sanctioned as divine imperatives, while the Declaration of Independence holds that the authority of government to enforce the law derives "from the consent of the governed." If the observer had not thrown up his hands, he would probably suspect that the Counties were simply reaching for any way to keep a religious document on the walls of courthouses constitutionally required to embody religious neutrality.

2

In holding the preliminary injunction adequately supported by evidence that the Counties' purpose had not changed at the third stage, we do not decide that the Counties' past actions forever taint any effort on their part to deal with the subject matter. We hold only that purpose needs to be taken seriously under the Establishment Clause and needs to be understood in light of context; an implausible claim that governmental purpose has changed should not carry the day in a court of law any more than in a head with common sense. It is enough to say here that district courts are fully capable of adjusting preliminary relief to take account of genuine changes in constitutionally significant conditions.

Nor do we have occasion here to hold that a sacred text can never be integrated constitutionally into a governmental display on the subject of law, or American history. We do not forget, and in this litigation have frequently been reminded, that our own courtroom frieze was deliberately designed in the exercise of governmental authority so as to include the figure of Moses holding tablets exhibiting a portion of the Hebrew text of the later, secularly phrased Commandments; in the company of 17 other lawgivers, most of them secular figures, there is no risk that Moses would strike an observer as evidence that the National Government was violating neutrality in religion.

IV

The importance of neutrality as an interpretive guide is no less true now than it was when the Court broached the principle in Everson v. Board of Education [p. 339], We all agree, of course, on the need for some interpretative help. The

First Amendment contains no textual definition of "establishment," and the term is certainly not self-defining. . . .

Given the variety of interpretative problems, the principle of neutrality has provided a good sense of direction: the government may not favor one religion over another, or religion over irreligion, religious choice being the prerogative of individuals under the Free Exercise Clause. The principle has been helpful simply because it responds to one of the major concerns that prompted adoption of the Religion Clauses. The Framers and the citizens of their time intended not only to protect the integrity of individual conscience in religious matters, but to guard against the civic divisiveness that follows when the Government weighs in on one side of religious debate; nothing does a better job of roiling society, a point that needed no explanation to the descendants of English Puritans and Cavaliers (or Massachusetts Puritans and Baptists). A sense of the past thus points to governmental neutrality as an objective of the Establishment Clause, and a sensible standard for applying it. To be sure, given its generality as a principle, an appeal to neutrality alone cannot possibly lay every issue to rest, or tell us what issues on the margins are substantial enough for constitutional significance. . . .

[P]ublic discourse at the present time certainly raises no doubt about the value of the interpretative approach invoked for 60 years now. We are centuries away from the St. Bartholomew's Day massacre and the treatment of heretics in early Massachusetts, but the divisiveness of religion in current public life is inescapable. This is no time to deny the prudence of understanding the Establishment Clause to require the Government to stay neutral on religious belief, which is reserved for the conscience of the individual.

Justice O'CONNOR, concurring. . . .

Reasonable minds can disagree about how to apply the Religion Clauses in a given case. But the goal of the Clauses is clear: to carry out the Founders' plan of preserving religious liberty to the fullest extent possible in a pluralistic society. By enforcing the Clauses, we have kept religion a matter for the individual conscience, not for the prosecutor or bureaucrat. At a time when we see around the world the violent consequences of the assumption of religious authority by government, Americans may count themselves fortunate: Our regard for constitutional boundaries has protected us from similar travails, while allowing private religious exercise to flourish. The well-known statement that "[w]e are a religious people," Zorach v. Clauson (1952), has proved true. Americans attend their places of worship more often than do citizens of other developed nations, and describe religion as playing an especially important role in their lives. Those who would renegotiate the boundaries between church and state must therefore answer a difficult question: Why would we trade a system that has served us so well for one that has served others so poorly? . . .

[The Framers] may not have foreseen the variety of religions for which this Nation would eventually provide a home. . . . But they did know that line-drawing between religions is an enterprise that, once begun, has no logical stopping point. They worried that "the same authority which can establish Christianity, in exclusion of all other Religions, may establish with the same ease any particular sect of Christians, in exclusion of all other Sects." [Memorial and Remonstrance (p. 49).]

Justice SCALIA, with whom THE CHIEF JUSTICE and Justice THOMAS join, and with whom Justice KENNEDY joins as to Parts II and III, dissenting.

I would uphold McCreary County and Pulaski County, Kentucky's (hereinafter Counties) displays of the Ten Commandments. I shall discuss first, why the Court's oft repeated assertion that the government cannot favor religious practice is false; second, why today's opinion extends the scope of that falsehood even beyond prior cases; and third, why even on the basis of the Court's false assumptions the judgment here is wrong.

I

A

On September 11, 2001 I was attending in Rome, Italy an international conference of judges and lawyers, principally from Europe and the United States. That night and the next morning virtually all of the participants watched, in their hotel rooms, the address to the Nation by the President of the United States concerning the murderous attacks upon the Twin Towers and the Pentagon, in which thousands of Americans had been killed. The address ended, as Presidential addresses often do, with the prayer "God bless America." The next afternoon I was approached by one of the judges from a European country, who, after extending his profound condolences for my country's loss, sadly observed "How I wish that the Head of State of my country, at a similar time of national tragedy and distress, could conclude his address 'God bless _____.' It is of course absolutely forbidden."

That is one model of the relationship between church and state—a model spread across Europe by the armies of Napoleon, and reflected in the Constitution of France, which begins "France is [a] . . . secular . . . Republic." France Const., Art. 1. Religion is to be strictly excluded from the public forum. This is not, and never was, the model adopted by America. George Washington added to the form of Presidential oath prescribed by Art. II, § 1, cl. 8, of the Constitution, the concluding words "so help me God." The Supreme Court under John Marshall opened its sessions with the prayer, "God save the United States and this Honorable Court." The First Congress instituted the practice of beginning its legislative sessions with a prayer. The same week that Congress submitted the Establishment Clause as part of the Bill of Rights for ratification by the States, it enacted legislation providing for paid chaplains in the House and Senate. Marsh v. Chambers. The day after the First Amendment was proposed, the same Congress that had proposed it requested the President to proclaim "a day of public thanksgiving and prayer, to be observed, by acknowledging, with grateful hearts, the many and signal favours of Almighty God." President Washington offered the first Thanksgiving Proclamation [p. 492] shortly thereafter. . . . [1]

---

1. These actions of our First President and Congress and the Marshall Court were not idiosyncratic; they reflected the beliefs of the period. Those who wrote the Constitution believed that morality was essential to the well-being of society and that encouragement of religion was the best way to foster morality. . . . President Washington opened his Presidency with a prayer, and reminded his fellow citizens at the conclusion of it that "reason and experience both forbid us to expect that National morality can prevail in exclusion of religious principle." Farewell Address (1796) [p. 41]. President John Adams wrote to the Massachusetts Militia, "we have no government armed with power capable of contending with human passions unbridled by morality and religion. . . . Our Constitution was made only for a moral and religious people. It is wholly inadequate to the government of any other."

The same Congress also reenacted the Northwest Territory Ordinance of 1787, Article III of which provided: "Religion, morality, and knowledge, being necessary to good government and the happiness of mankind, schools and the means of education shall forever be encouraged." . . .

Nor have the views of our people on this matter significantly changed. Presidents continue to conclude the Presidential oath with the words "so help me God." Our legislatures, state and national, continue to open their sessions with prayer led by official chaplains. The sessions of this Court continue to open with the prayer "God save the United States and this Honorable Court." Invocation of the Almighty by our public figures, at all levels of government, remains commonplace. Our coinage bears the motto "IN GOD WE TRUST." And our Pledge of Allegiance contains the acknowledgment that we are a Nation "under God." As one of our Supreme Court opinions rightly observed, "We are a religious people whose institutions presuppose a Supreme Being." *Zorach*.

With all of this reality (and much more) staring it in the face, how can the Court *possibly* assert that "'the First Amendment mandates governmental neutrality between . . . religion and nonreligion,'" and that "[m]anifesting a purpose to favor . . . adherence to religion generally" is unconstitutional? Who says so? Surely not the words of the Constitution. Surely not the history and traditions that reflect our society's constant understanding of those words. Surely not even the current sense of our society, recently reflected in an Act of Congress adopted *unanimously* by the Senate and with only 5 nays in the House of Representatives, criticizing a Court of Appeals opinion that had held "under God" in the Pledge of Allegiance unconstitutional. See Act of Nov. 13, 2002.

Nothing stands behind the Court's assertion that governmental affirmation of the society's belief in God is unconstitutional except the Court's own say-so, citing as support only the unsubstantiated say-so of earlier Courts going back no farther than the mid-20th century. . . . [And this say-so] is discredited because the Court has not had the courage (or the foolhardiness) to apply the neutrality principle consistently.

What distinguishes the rule of law from the dictatorship of a shifting Supreme Court majority is the absolutely indispensable requirement that judicial opinions be grounded in consistently applied principle. That is what prevents judges from ruling now this way, now that—thumbs up or thumbs down—as their personal preferences dictate. . . . [Yet s]ometimes the Court chooses

---

Letter (Oct. 11, 1798), reprinted in 9 Works of John Adams 229 (C. Adams ed.1971). Thomas Jefferson concluded his second inaugural address by inviting his audience to pray:

> I shall need, too, the favor of that Being in whose hands we are, who led our fathers, as Israel of old, from their native land and planted them in a country flowing with all the necessaries and comforts of life; who has covered our infancy with His providence and our riper years with His wisdom and power and to whose goodness I ask you to join in supplications with me that He will so enlighten the minds of your servants, guide their councils, and prosper their measures that whatsoever they do shall result in your good, and shall secure to you the peace, friendship, and approbation of all nations.

James Madison, in his first inaugural address, likewise placed his confidence "in the guardianship and guidance of that Almighty Being whose power regulates the destiny of nations, whose blessings have been so conspicuously dispensed to this rising Republic, and to whom we are bound to address our devout gratitude for the past, as well as our fervent supplications and best hopes for the future."

to decide cases on the principle that government cannot favor religion, and sometimes it does not. . . . [I]ndeed, we have even approved (post-*Lemon*) government-led prayer to God. [*Marsh.*] . . .

Besides appealing to the demonstrably false principle that the government cannot favor religion over irreligion, today's opinion suggests that the posting of the Ten Commandments violates the principle that the government cannot favor one religion over another. That is indeed a valid principle where public aid or assistance to religion is concerned, Zelman v. Simmons-Harris, or where the free exercise of religion is at issue, Church of the Lukumi v. Hialeah [p. 162], but it necessarily applies in a more limited sense to public acknowledgment of the Creator. If religion in the public forum had to be entirely nondenominational, there could be no religion in the public forum at all. One cannot say the word "God," or "the Almighty," one cannot offer public supplication or thanksgiving, without contradicting the beliefs of some people that there are many gods, or that God or the gods pay no attention to human affairs. With respect to public acknowledgment of religious belief, it is entirely clear from our Nation's historical practices that the Establishment Clause permits this disregard of polytheists and believers in unconcerned deities, just as it permits the disregard of devout atheists. The Thanksgiving Proclamation issued by George Washington at the instance of the First Congress was scrupulously nondenominational—but it was monotheistic. . . .

Historical practices thus demonstrate that there is a distance between the acknowledgment of a single Creator and the establishment of a religion. The former is, as Marsh v. Chambers put it, "a tolerable acknowledgment of beliefs widely held among the people of this country." The three most popular religions in the United States, Christianity, Judaism, and Islam—which combined account for 97.7% of all believers—are monotheistic. All of them, moreover (Islam included), believe that the Ten Commandments were given by God to Moses, and are divine prescriptions for a virtuous life. Publicly honoring the Ten Commandments is thus indistinguishable, insofar as discriminating against other religions is concerned, from publicly honoring God. Both practices are recognized across such a broad and diverse range of the population—from Christians to Muslims—that they cannot be reasonably understood as a government endorsement of a particular religious viewpoint.[4]

B

A few remarks are necessary in response to the criticism of this dissent by the Court, as well as Justice Stevens' criticism in the related case of Van Orden v. Perry [see p. 537 below]. . . .

[T]here were doubtless some who thought [that the Establishment Clause] should have a broader meaning [than just "no statements of preference between monotheistic religions,"], but those views were plainly rejected. Justice Stevens says that reliance on [historical acknowledgments of religion] is "bound

---

4. This is not to say that a display of the Ten Commandments could never constitute an impermissible endorsement of a particular religious view. The Establishment Clause would prohibit, for example, governmental endorsement of a particular version of the Decalogue as authoritative. Here the display of the Ten Commandments alongside eight secular documents, and the plaque's explanation for their inclusion, make clear that they were not posted to take sides in a theological dispute.

to paint a misleading picture," but it is hard to see why. What is more probative of the meaning of the Establishment Clause than the actions of the very Congress that proposed it, and of the first President charged with observing it?

Justice Stevens also appeals to the undoubted fact that some in the founding generation thought that the Religion Clauses of the First Amendment should have a *narrower* meaning, protecting only the Christian religion or perhaps only Protestantism. I am at a loss to see how this helps his case, except by providing a cloud of obfuscating smoke. (Since most thought the Clause permitted government invocation of monotheism, and some others thought it permitted government invocation of Christianity, he proposes that it be construed not to permit any government invocation of religion at all.) At any rate, those narrower views of the Establishment Clause were as clearly rejected as the more expansive ones. Washington's First Thanksgiving Proclamation is merely an example. *All* of the actions of Washington and the First Congress upon which I have relied, virtually all Thanksgiving Proclamations throughout our history, and *all* the other examples of our Government's favoring religion that I have cited, have invoked God, but not Jesus Christ. . . .

Justice Stevens [also] says that if one is serious about following the original understanding of the Establishment Clause, he must repudiate its incorporation into the Fourteenth Amendment, and hold that it does not apply against the States. This is more smoke. . . . The notion that incorporation empties the incorporated provisions of their original meaning has no support in either reason or precedent.

Justice Stevens argues that original meaning should not be the touchstone anyway, but that we should rather "expoun[d] the meaning of constitutional provisions with one eye towards our Nation's history and the other fixed on its democratic aspirations." . . . Even assuming, however, that the meaning of the Constitution ought to change according to "democratic aspirations," why are those aspirations to be found in Justices' notions of what the Establishment Clause ought to mean, rather than in the democratically adopted dispositions of our current society? As I have observed above, numerous provisions of our laws and numerous continuing practices of our people demonstrate that the government's invocation of God (and hence the government's invocation of the Ten Commandments) is unobjectionable. . . . To ignore all this is not to give effect to "democratic aspirations" but to frustrate them.

Finally, I must respond to Justice Stevens' assertion that I would "marginaliz[e] the belief systems of more than 7 million Americans" who adhere to religions that are not monotheistic. Surely that is a gross exaggeration. The beliefs of those citizens are entirely protected by the Free Exercise Clause, and by those aspects of the Establishment Clause that do not relate to government acknowledgment of the Creator. Invocation of God despite their beliefs is permitted not because nonmonotheistic religions cease to be religions recognized by the religion clauses of the First Amendment, but because governmental invocation of God is not an establishment. Justice Stevens fails to recognize that in the context of public acknowledgments of God there are legitimate *competing* interests: On the one hand, the interest of that minority in not feeling "excluded"; but on the other, the interest of the overwhelming majority of religious believers in being able to give God thanks and supplication *as a people,* and with respect to our national endeavors. Our national tradition has resolved that conflict in favor of the majority. . . .

II

[Even accepting the *Lemon* test, Justice Scalia argued, the Court's approach] modifies *Lemon* to ratchet up the Court's hostility to religion. First, the Court justifies inquiry into legislative purpose, not as an end itself, but as a means to ascertain the appearance of the government action to an "'objective observer.'" Under this approach, even if a government could show that its actual purpose was not to advance religion, it would presumably violate the Constitution as long as the Court's objective observer would [mistakenly] think otherwise. . . .

Second, the Court replaces *Lemon's* requirement that the government have "*a* secular . . . purpose" (emphasis added) with the heightened requirement that the secular purpose "predominate" over any purpose to advance religion. The Court treats this extension as a natural outgrowth of the longstanding requirement that the government's secular purpose not be a sham, but simple logic shows the two to be unrelated. If the government's proffered secular purpose is not genuine, then the government has no secular purpose at all. The new demand that secular purpose predominate contradicts *Lemon*'s more limited requirement. . . .

By shifting the focus of *Lemon*'s purpose prong from the search for a genuine, secular motivation to the hunt for a predominantly religious purpose, the Court converts what has in the past been a fairly limited inquiry into a rigorous review of the full record. Those responsible for the adoption of the Religion Clauses would surely regard it as a bitter irony that the religious values they designed those Clauses to *protect* have now become so distasteful to this Court that if they constitute anything more than a subordinate motive for government action they will invalidate it.

III

Even accepting the Court's *Lemon*-based premises, the displays at issue here were constitutional. . . .

B

On its face, the Foundations Displays manifested the purely secular purpose that the Counties asserted before the District Court: "to display documents that played a significant role in the foundation of our system of law and government." That the Displays included the Ten Commandments did not transform their apparent secular purpose into one of impermissible advocacy for Judeo-Christian beliefs. . . . [W]hen the Ten Commandments appear alongside other documents of secular significance in a display devoted to the foundations of American law and government, the context communicates that the Ten Commandments are included, not to teach their binding nature as a religious text, but to show their unique contribution to the development of the legal system. This is doubly true when the display is introduced by a document that informs passersby that it "contains documents that played a significant role in the foundation of our system of law and government." . . .

Perhaps in recognition of the centrality of the Ten Commandments as a widely recognized symbol of religion in public life, the Court is at pains to dispel the impression that its decision will require governments across the country to sandblast the Ten Commandments from the public square. The constitutional problem, the Court says, is with the Counties' *purpose* in erecting the Foundations Displays, not the displays themselves. The Court adds in a footnote: "One consequence of taking account of the purpose underlying past actions is that the same government action may be constitutional if taken in the first instance and unconstitutional if it has a sectarian heritage."

This inconsistency may be explicable in theory, but I suspect that the "objective observer" with whom the Court is so concerned will recognize its absurdity in practice. By virtue of details familiar only to the parties to litigation and their lawyers, [these counties] have been ordered to remove the same display that appears in courthouses from Mercer County, Kentucky to Elkhart County, Indiana. Displays erected in silence (and under the direction of good legal advice) are permissible, while those hung after discussion and debate are deemed unconstitutional. Reduction of the Establishment Clause to such minutiae trivializes the Clause's protection against religious establishment; indeed, it may inflame religious passions by making the passing comments of every government official the subject of endless litigation.

C

In any event, the Court's conclusion that the Counties exhibited the Foundations Displays with the purpose of promoting religion is doubtful. . . .

[T]he Court faults the Counties for not *repealing* the resolution expressing what the Court believes to be an impermissible intent. Under these circumstances, the Court says, "no reasonable observer could swallow the claim that the Counties had cast off the objective so unmistakable in the earlier displays," . . The Court implies that the Counties may have been able to remedy the "taint" from the old resolutions by enacting a new one. But that action would have been wholly unnecessary in light of the explanation that the Counties included *with the displays themselves*: A plaque next to the documents informed all who passed by that each display "contains documents that played a significant role in the foundation of our system of law and government." . . .

[There is] no basis for attributing whatever intent motivated the first and second displays to the third. Given the presumption of regularity that always accompanies our review of official action, the Court has identified no evidence of a purpose to advance religion in a way that is inconsistent with our cases. The Court may well be correct in identifying the third displays as the fruit of a desire to display the Ten Commandments, but neither our cases nor our history support its assertion that such a desire renders the fruit poisonous.

VAN ORDEN v. PERRY
125 S. Ct. 2854 (2005)

Chief Justice REHNQUIST announced the judgment of the Court and delivered an opinion, in which Justice SCALIA, Justice KENNEDY, and Justice THOMAS join. . . .

The 22 acres surrounding the Texas State Capitol contain 17 monuments and 21 historical markers commemorating the "people, ideals, and events that compose Texan identity." Tex. H. Con. Res. 38, 77th Leg. (2001).[1] The monolith

1. The monuments are: Heroes of the Alamo, Hood's Brigade, Confederate Soldiers, Volunteer Fireman, Terry's Texas Rangers, Texas Cowboy, Spanish-American War, Texas National Guard, Ten Commandments, Tribute to Texas School Children, Texas Pioneer Woman, The Boy Scouts'

challenged here stands 6 feet high and 3-½ feet wide. It is located to the north of the Capitol building, between the Capitol and the Supreme Court building. Its primary content is the text of the Ten Commandments. . . . The bottom of the monument bears the inscription "PRESENTED TO THE PEOPLE AND YOUTH OF TEXAS BY THE FRATERNAL ORDER OF EAGLES OF TEXAS 1961." [The monument was challenged in a federal court suit by Van Orden, a lawyer who frequently visited the capitol grounds to use the state law library nearby.]

Whatever may be the fate of the *Lemon* test in the larger scheme of Establishment Clause jurisprudence, we think it not useful in dealing with the sort of passive monument that Texas has erected on its Capitol grounds. Instead, our analysis is driven both by the nature of the monument and by our Nation's history.

As we explained in Lynch v. Donnelly [p. 510]: "There is an unbroken history of official acknowledgment by all three branches of government of the role of religion in American life from at least 1789." [Review of such acknowledgments, beginning with presidential thanksgiving proclamations, omitted.]

[Moreover, a]cknowledgments of the role played by the Ten Commandments in our Nation's heritage are common throughout America. We need only look within our own Courtroom. Since 1935, Moses has stood, holding two tablets that reveal portions of the Ten Commandments written in Hebrew, among other lawgivers in the south frieze. Representations of the Ten Commandments adorn the metal gates lining the north and south sides of the Courtroom as well as the doors leading into the Courtroom. Moses also sits on the exterior east facade of the building holding the Ten Commandments tablets.

Similar acknowledgments can be seen throughout a visitor's tour of our Nation's Capital. For example, a large statue of Moses holding the Ten Commandments, alongside a statue of the Apostle Paul, has overlooked the rotunda of the Library of Congress' Jefferson Building since 1897. And the Jefferson Building's Great Reading Room contains a sculpture of a woman beside the Ten Commandments with a quote above her from the Old Testament (Micah 6:8). A medallion with two tablets depicting the Ten Commandments decorates the floor of the National Archives. Inside the Department of Justice, a statue entitled "The Spirit of Law" has two tablets representing the Ten Commandments lying at its feet. In front of the Ronald Reagan Building is another sculpture that includes a depiction of the Ten Commandments. So too a 24-foot-tall sculpture, depicting, among other things, the Ten Commandments and a cross, stands outside the federal courthouse that houses both the Court of Appeals and the District Court for the District of Columbia. Moses is also prominently featured in the Chamber of the United States House of Representatives.[9] . . .

There are, of course, limits to the display of religious messages or symbols. For example, [i]n the classroom context [involved in Stone v. Graham], we found that [posting the Commandments] had an improper and plainly religious purpose. As evidenced by *Stone*'s almost exclusive reliance upon two of our school

_____

Statue of Liberty Replica, Pearl Harbor Veterans, Korean War Veterans, Soldiers of World War I, Disabled Veterans, and Texas Peace Officers.
9. Other examples of monuments and buildings reflecting the prominent role of religion abound. For example, the Washington, Jefferson, and Lincoln Memorials all contain explicit invocations of God's importance. . . .

prayer cases, it stands as an example of the fact that we have "been particularly vigilant in monitoring compliance with the Establishment Clause in elementary and secondary schools." . . .

The placement of the Ten Commandments monument on the Texas State Capitol grounds is a far more passive use of those texts than was the case in *Stone*, where the text confronted elementary school students every day. . . . The monument is therefore also quite different from the prayers involved in *Schempp* and Lee v. Weisman. Texas has treated her Capitol grounds monuments as representing the several strands in the State's political and legal history. The inclusion of the Ten Commandments monument in this group has a dual significance, partaking of both religion and government.

Justice BREYER, concurring in the judgment.

In Abington School Dist. v. Schempp [p. 486], Justice Goldberg, joined by Justice Harlan, wrote, in respect to the First Amendment's Religion Clauses, that there is "no simple and clear measure which by precise application can readily and invariably demark the permissible from the impermissible." *Id.* (concurring opinion). One must refer instead to the basic purposes of those Clauses. They seek to "assure the fullest possible scope of religious liberty and tolerance for all." They seek to avoid that divisiveness based upon religion that promotes social conflict, sapping the strength of government and religion alike. *Zelman* (Breyer, J., dissenting). They seek to maintain that "separation of church and state" that has long been critical to the "peaceful dominion that religion exercises in [this] country," where the "spirit of religion" and the "spirit of freedom" are productively "united," "reign[ing] together" but in separate spheres "on the same soil." A. de Tocqueville, Democracy in America (1835). . . .

The Court has made clear, as Justices Goldberg and Harlan noted, that the realization of these goals means that government must "neither engage in nor compel religious practices," that it must "effect no favoritism among sects or between religion and nonreligion," and that it must "work deterrence of no religious belief." *Schempp* (concurring opinion). The government must avoid excessive interference with, or promotion of, religion. But the Establishment Clause does not compel the government to purge from the public sphere all that in any way partakes of the religious. See, e.g., Marsh v. Chambers. Such absolutism is not only inconsistent with our national traditions, but would also tend to promote the kind of social conflict the Establishment Clause seeks to avoid.

[None of the Court's tests, such as "neutrality" or *Lemon*, can] readily explain the Establishment Clause's tolerance, for example, of the prayers that open legislative meetings, see *Marsh*; certain references to, and invocations of, the Deity in the public words of public officials; the public references to God on coins, decrees, and buildings; or the attention paid to the religious objectives of certain holidays, including Thanksgiving.

If the relation between government and religion is one of separation, but not of mutual hostility and suspicion, one will inevitably find difficult borderline cases. And in such cases, I see no test-related substitute for the exercise of legal judgment. That judgment is not a personal judgment. Rather, as in all constitutional cases, it must reflect and remain faithful to the underlying purposes of the Clauses, and it must take account of context and consequences measured in light of those purposes. While the Court's prior tests provide useful guideposts—and might well lead to the same result the Court reaches today—no exact formula can dictate a resolution to such fact-intensive cases.

The case before us is a borderline case. . . . In certain contexts, a display of the tablets of the Ten Commandments can convey not simply a religious message but also a secular moral message (about proper standards of social conduct). And in certain contexts, a display of the tablets can also convey a historical message (about a historic relation between those standards and the law)—a fact that helps to explain the display of those tablets in dozens of courthouses throughout the Nation, including the Supreme Court of the United States.

Here the tablets have been used as part of a display that communicates not simply a religious message, but a secular message as well. The circumstances surrounding the display's placement on the capitol grounds and its physical setting suggest that the State itself intended the latter, nonreligious aspects of the tablets' message to predominate. And the monument's 40-year history on the Texas state grounds indicates that that has been its effect.

The group that donated the monument, the Fraternal Order of Eagles, a private civic (and primarily secular) organization, while interested in the religious aspect of the Ten Commandments, sought to highlight the Commandments' role in shaping civic morality as part of that organization's efforts to combat juvenile delinquency. The Eagles' consultation with a committee composed of members of several faiths in order to find a nonsectarian text underscores the group's ethics-based motives. The tablets, as displayed on the monument, prominently acknowledge that the Eagles donated the display, a factor which, though not sufficient, thereby further distances the State itself from the religious aspect of the Commandments' message.

The physical setting of the monument, moreover, suggests little or nothing of the sacred. The monument sits in a large park containing 17 monuments and 21 historical markers, all designed to illustrate the "ideals" of those who settled in Texas and of those who have lived there since that time. The setting does not readily lend itself to meditation or any other religious activity. But it does provide a context of history and moral ideals. It (together with the display's inscription about its origin) communicates to visitors that the State sought to reflect moral principles, illustrating a relation between ethics and law that the State's citizens, historically speaking, have endorsed. That is to say, the context suggests that the State intended the display's moral message—an illustrative message reflecting the historical "ideals" of Texans—to predominate.

[A] further factor is determinative here. As far as I can tell, 40 years passed in which the presence of this monument, legally speaking, went unchallenged (until the single legal objection raised by petitioner). And I am not aware of any evidence suggesting that this was due to a climate of intimidation. Hence, those 40 years suggest more strongly than can any set of formulaic tests that few individuals, whatever their system of beliefs, are likely to have understood the monument as amounting, in any significantly detrimental way, to a government effort to favor [religion or a particular religious view].

This case, moreover, is distinguishable from instances where the Court has found Ten Commandments displays impermissible. The display is not on the grounds of a public school, where, given the impressionability of the young, government must exercise particular care in separating church and state. See, e.g., *Weisman*; *Stone*. This case also differs from *McCreary County*, where the short (and stormy) history of the courthouse Commandments' displays demonstrates the substantially religious objectives of those who mounted them, and the effect of this readily apparent objective upon those who view them. [I]n today's world, in a Nation of so many different religious and comparable nonreligious fundamental beliefs, a more contemporary state effort to focus attention upon a religious text is certainly likely to prove divisive in a way that this longstanding, pre-existing monument has not.

For these reasons, I believe that the Texas display . . . might satisfy this Court's more formal Establishment Clause tests [such as "no advancement" or "no endorsement" of religion]. But, as I have said, in reaching the conclusion that the Texas display falls on the permissible side of the constitutional line, I rely less upon a literal application of any particular test than upon consideration of the basic purposes of the First Amendment's Religion Clauses themselves. . . .

At the same time, to reach a contrary conclusion here, based primarily upon the religious nature of the tablets' text would, I fear, lead the law to exhibit a hostility toward religion that has no place in our Establishment Clause traditions. Such a holding might well encourage disputes concerning the removal of longstanding depictions of the Ten Commandments from public buildings across the Nation. And it could thereby create the very kind of religiously based divisiveness that the Establishment Clause seeks to avoid.

In light of these considerations, I [would approve the Texas display but] cannot agree with today's plurality's analysis,

Justice STEVENS, with whom Justice GINSBURG joins, dissenting.

The plurality [and Justice Scalia's *McCreary* dissent] rel[y] heavily on the fact that our Republic was founded, and has been governed since its nascence, by leaders who spoke then (and speak still) in plainly religious rhetoric. . . .

[But] the presentation of these religious statements as a unified historical narrative is bound to paint a misleading picture[, and it fails] to account for the acts and publicly espoused views of other influential leaders of that time. Notably absent from their historical snapshot is the fact that Thomas Jefferson refused to issue the Thanksgiving proclamations that Washington had so readily embraced based on the argument that to do so would violate the Establishment Clause. [The plurality and Justice Scalia] disregard the substantial debates that took place regarding the constitutionality of the early proclamations and acts they cite, see, e.g., Letter from James Madison to Edward Livingston (July 10, 1822) (arguing that Congress' appointment of Chaplains to be paid from the National Treasury was "not with my approbation" and was a "deviation" from the principle of "immunity of Religion from civil jurisdiction"), and paper over the fact that Madison more than once repudiated the views attributed to him by many [quoting, e.g., the Detached Memorandum (p. 67)].

[T]here is another critical nuance lost in the plurality's portrayal of history. Simply put, many of the Founders who are often cited as authoritative expositors of the Constitution's original meaning understood the Establishment Clause to stand for a *narrower* proposition than the plurality, for whatever reason, is willing to accept. Namely, many of the Framers understood the word "religion" in the Establishment Clause to encompass only the various sects of Christianity.

[P]rior to the Philadelphia Convention, the States had begun to protect "religious freedom" in their various constitutions. Many of those provisions, however, restricted "equal protection" and "free exercise" to Christians, and invocations of the divine were commonly understood to refer to Christ. That historical background likely informed the Framers' understanding of the First Amendment. [For example,] Justice Story adopted [this view] in his famous Commentaries [on the Constitution (1835)], in which he wrote that the "real object" of the Clause was:

> not to countenance, much less to advance Mahometanism, or Judaism, or infidelity, by prostrating Christianity; but to exclude all rivalry among Christian sects, and to prevent any national ecclesiastical establishment, which should give to an hierarchy the exclusive patronage of the national government[.]

Along these lines, for nearly a century after the Founding, many accepted the idea that America was not just a *religious* nation, but "a Christian nation." Church of Holy Trinity v. United States (1892).

The original understanding of the type of "religion" that qualified for constitutional protection under the Establishment Clause likely did not include those followers of Judaism and Islam who are among the preferred "monotheistic" religions Justice Scalia has embraced in his *McCreary County* opinion. The inclusion of Jews and Muslims inside the category of constitutionally favored religions surely would have shocked Chief Justice Marshall and Justice Story. . . . Justice Scalia's inclusion of Judaism and Islam is a laudable act of religious tolerance, but it is one that is unmoored from the Constitution's history and text, and moreover one that is patently arbitrary in its inclusion of some, but exclusion of other (e.g., Buddhism), widely practiced non-Christian religions. . . .

Indeed, to constrict narrowly the reach of the Establishment Clause to the views of the Founders would lead to more than this unpalatable result; it would also leave us with an unincorporated constitutional provision—in other words, one that limits only the *federal* establishment of "a national religion." See Elk Grove Unified School Dist. v. Newdow (Thomas, J., concurring in judgment) [p. 74]. Under this view, not only could a State constitutionally adorn all of its public spaces with crucifixes or passages from the New Testament, it would also have full authority to prescribe the teachings of Martin Luther or Joseph Smith as *the* official state religion. Only the Federal Government would be prohibited from taking sides, (and only then as between Christian sects).

A reading of the First Amendment dependent on either of the purported original meanings expressed above would eviscerate the heart of the Establishment Clause. It would replace Jefferson's "wall of separation" with a perverse wall of exclusion—Christians inside, non-Christians out. It would permit States to construct walls of their own choosing—Baptists inside, Mormons out; Jewish Orthodox inside, Jewish Reform out. A Clause so understood might be faithful to the expectations of some of our Founders, but it is plainly not worthy of a society whose enviable hallmark over the course of two centuries has been the continuing expansion of religious pluralism and tolerance.

Unless one is willing to renounce over 65 years of Establishment Clause jurisprudence and cross back over the incorporation bridge, appeals to the religiosity of the Framers ring hollow. . . .

It is our duty, therefore, to interpret the First Amendment's command that "Congress shall make no law respecting an establishment of religion" not by merely asking what those words meant to observers at the time of the founding, but instead by deriving from the Clause's text and history the broad principles that remain valid today. As we have said in the context of statutory interpretation, legislation "often [goes] beyond the principal evil [at which the statute was aimed] to cover reasonably comparable evils, and it is ultimately the provisions of our laws rather than the principal concerns of our legislators by which we are governed." [Citation omitted.] In similar fashion, we have construed the Equal Protection Clause of the Fourteenth Amendment to prohibit segregated schools, see Brown v. Board of Education, even though those who drafted that Amendment evidently thought that separate was not unequal. . . .

To reason from the broad principles contained in the Constitution does not, as Justice Scalia suggests, require us to abandon our heritage in favor of unprincipled expressions of personal preference. The task of applying the broad principles that the Framers wrote into the text of the First Amendment is, in any event, no more a matter of personal preference than is one's selection between two (or more) sides in a heated historical debate. We serve our constitutional mandate by expounding the meaning of constitutional provisions with one eye towards our Nation's history and the other fixed on its democratic aspirations. See McCulloch v. Maryland (1819) ("[W]e must never forget, that it is *a constitution* we are expounding" that is intended to "endure for ages to come, and, consequently, to be adapted to the various *crises* of human affairs"). . . .

The principle that guides my analysis is neutrality.[35] The basis for that principle is firmly rooted in our Nation's history and our Constitution's text. I recognize that the requirement that government must remain neutral between religion and irreligion would have seemed foreign to some of the Framers; so too would a requirement of neutrality between Jews and Christians. Fortunately, we are not bound by the Framers' expectations—we are bound by the legal principles they enshrined in our Constitution. Story's vision that States should not discriminate between Christian sects has as its foundation the principle that government must remain neutral between valid systems of belief. As religious pluralism has expanded, so has our acceptance of what constitutes valid belief systems. The evil of discriminating today against atheists, "polytheists[,] and believers in unconcerned deities," *McCreary County* (Scalia, J., dissenting), is in my view a direct descendent of the evil of discriminating among Christian sects. The Establishment Clause thus forbids it and, in turn, forbids Texas from displaying the Ten Commandments monument the plurality so casually affirms.

NOTES AND QUESTIONS

1. No Secular Purpose. Should the Constitution invalidate a government action solely because of its purpose, without inquiring into its effect? Such a rule

---

35. Justice Thomas contends that the Establishment Clause cannot include such a neutrality principle because the Clause reaches only the governmental coercion of individual belief or disbelief. . . . A Clause so interpreted would not prohibit explicit state endorsements of religious orthodoxies of particular sects, actions that lie at the heart of what the Clause was meant to regulate. The government could, for example, take out television advertisements lauding Catholicism as the only pure religion. . . .

is very unusual—even unique—in constitutional law. There are also questions about whether a multimember body, such as a legislature or county commission, can have single "purpose," in light of the multiple motives and goals of various members. We consider some of these questions in greater detail in the next section, A-4. For a defense of the secular purpose requirement of *Lemon*, see Andrew Koppelman, Secular Purpose, 88 Va. L. Rev. 87 (2002) (arguing that the requirement "follows directly from a principle at the core of the Establishment Clause: that government may not declare religious truths").

Why doesn't the Court take the third display in *McCreary County* at its face value—a collection of documents historically relevant to American law, including the Ten Commandments? The majority in effect holds that the previous displays tainted the final one. When would that taint dissipate? Does the Court give enough guidance on that question? The majority also criticizes the display for omitting the original Constitution and the Fourteenth Amendment and including the national anthem and Magna Carta. Why is that relevant to whether the display endorses the religious message of the Ten Commandments? Finally, the majority takes the expansion of the Commandments' text in the third display as an indication of religious purpose. Is the Court saying that religious documents cannot appear in a historical display unless their texts are bowdlerized? What theory of the First Amendment would support that view?

2. Justice Breyer's Decisive Vote: Pragmatism and Quelling Division. Justice Breyer's decisive opinion in *Van Orden* is notable for taking a highly pragmatic approach to these issues. First, it suggests that some religious symbols should be upheld because litigation against them breeds more social division than do the symbols themselves. See also William P. Marshall, The Concept of Offensiveness in First Amendment Jurisprudence, 66 Ind. L. J. 351, 376 (1991). If the government's religious practice has not caused conflict in the past, does this merely show that the dissenting minority is too small or powerless to make its voice heard?

Second, Breyer treats social division over religious issues as more than just a harm that the Constitution seeks generally to prevent by disestablishing religion. He treats the existence of division over a particular practice as itself a criterion (*the* criterion?) for whether the practice is unconstitutional. Does this offer a sufficiently clear constitutional standard? Are courts capable of assessing whether particular practices create unacceptable social conflict? How much conflict is too much? For a critique of the emphasis on "divisiveness" in Establishment Clause jurisprudence, see Richard W. Garnett, Religion, Division, and the First Amendment, 94 Georgetown L.J. _____ (forthcoming 2006).

Finally, Breyer suggests that no single test can adequately analyze all Establishment Clause issues. The Court's other "swing" vote, Justice O'Connor, had offered endorsement as an overarching test for establishment. Does Breyer's position jettison the endorsement test? If so, does it replace it with any clear standard?

3. Features of the Ten Commandments.

(a) Are they nonsectarian? Do the Ten Commandments really function as a common text for monotheists? Various versions of the Decalogue have different organizational and numbering schemes, reflecting theological differences:

For Jews the First Commandment is [a stand-alone] affirmative statement: "I the LORD am your God who brought you out of the land of Egypt, the house of bondage." . . . It is a statement of faith that in itself is a Commandment. It is a statement, of course, that can only apply to Jews[.] Most Protestants do not consider this to be part of the Ten Commandments. Rather, it is for them simply a prefatory statement. Roman Catholics and Lutherans incorporate this sentence into their First Commandment, but it does not stand alone. Thus, there are actually three versions of "the First Commandment"—Jewish, Protestant, and Catholic/Lutheran.

The Second Commandment is equally complicated. . . . The most obvious substantive difference in [its] numbering schemes concerns the emphasis on sculpture or graven images. The prohibition on "graven images" stands alone as the Second Commandment for Protestants, which reflects ideological and theological aspects of the Protestant reformation in most of Europe. Jews, Catholics, and Lutherans do not make this provision a separate commandment.

Paul Finkelman, The Ten Commandments on the Courthouse Lawn and Elsewhere, 73 Fordham L. Rev. 1477, 1486-1487 (2005). In his *McCreary County* dissent, Justice Scalia responded to this point: "I doubt that most religious adherents are even aware that there are competing versions with doctrinal consequences (I certainly was not). In any event, the context of the display here could not conceivably cause the viewer to believe that the government was taking sides in a doctrinal controversy." 125 S. Ct. at 2762 n.12. Does Finkelman imbue the differences in various texts of the Commandments with significance that only a theologian would recognize? Or does Justice Scalia's response, in seeking to save government posting of the Commandments, strip their texts of important theological meaning?

(b) Are they a foundation of American law? Professor Finkelman argues:

Rarely have American lawmakers turned to the Commandments for guidance. Those laws that dovetail with the Commandments, such as prohibitions on stealing or perjury, are found in virtually all cultures. However, most of the other provisions of the Commandments have never been part of our law, at least since independence. . . . The framers [v]alued freedom of expression, freedom of thought, and freedom of belief and worship—they thus rejected as a source of law a set of precepts or "commandments" that would have limited the right of people to believe what they want and worship as they wish.

73 Fordham L. Rev. at 1516. And the majority notes that the Declaration of Independence identifies the source of government authority as the consent of the governed, not the mandate of God. Is that an adequate analysis of the Declaration—which, after all, states that the inalienable rights to life, liberty, and the pursuit of happiness come from "the Creator"? Does the Declaration ultimately conclude that people should have power over their government because this is a God-given right?

4. The Original Understanding Revisited. You can use the opinions of Justices Scalia and Stevens as summations of the historical arguments for and against allowing the government to make expressive or symbolic "acknowledgments" of religion.

The Court in *McCreary County* and Justice Stevens in *Van Orden* argue that neutrality as an Establishment Clause requirement is "firmly rooted in our Nation's history" and responds to "the major concerns that prompted the [clause's]adoption." Can these arguments be said to rely on the original understanding of the clause—albeit at a more general level? Or does this kind of approach allow judges to take whatever general values they think are important and read those into the Constitution in the guise of enforcing the "original" meaning? Can you explain the various situations in which the courts allow government action that departs from neutrality concerning religion: legislative prayers, presidential thanksgiving proclamations and inaugural addresses, affirmations of God on coins and in the Pledge of Allegiance? Does Justice O'Connor's notion of "ceremonial deism" (see p. 509 above) justify these practices?

Should Justice Scalia's view in *McCreary County* be seen as a variation on Establishment Clause nonpreferentialism? Nonpreferentialism is generally an "equal footing" doctrine for religious denominations. For example, voucher advocates say that religious schools of all denominations should be permitted to participate on an equal basis. But Justice Scalia advocates a nonpreferentialism of a different sort: a single message that is broad enough, or nonsectarian enough, to satisfy the wishes of nearly all religious believers. Is this the same? Is it a persuasive account of the original understanding? What are Justice Stevens's responses to it, and are they persuasive? Is Justice Scalia's position undercut by the fact that it leaves out some religious believers—for example, polytheists and perhaps Buddhists?

Recall that in the 1980s, Justice Rehnquist unsuccessfully advocated limiting the Establishment Clause to prohibiting preferences among religious sects (see p. 493). That proposal went nowhere in part because it seemed contradicted by the actions of the first Congress, which rejected drafts of the First Amendment that would have prohibited preferences for "one religious sect or society" and instead substituted the broader ban on any establishment "of religion." Does Scalia's proposal differ from Rehnquist's? Does it avoid the objections aimed at Rehnquist's proposal?

Suppose that pursuant to Marsh v. Chambers (p. 494), a legislature invites clergy of various faiths to give prayers at the beginning of legislative days. Does Scalia's position in *McCreary* imply that a Christian cleric should be forbidden from praying in the name of Jesus? See Hinrichs v. Bosma (p. 495). That if a priest of a pagan group proposes to give a prayer to a number of gods, he could be excluded from the clergy rotation? Cf. Simpson v. Chesterfield County Bd. of Supervisors, 404 F.3d 276 (4th Cir. 2005) (upholding board's rejection of Wiccan prayer as falling outside board's Judeo-Christian or monotheistic tradition, even though Wiccan leader described her beliefs and prayer as monotheistic rather than polytheistic).

4. School Curriculum Issues: Evolution and Creationism

We now return to Establishment Clause issues in the public schools. Although prayers at school events or at the beginning of the school day can have great symbolic meaning, schools affect children more pervasively through the classroom teaching that takes up several hours each day. Does this pervasive effect make it all the more important that the curriculum be free of explicit religious teaching? Or does the exclusion of religious teaching from the curriculum make the public schools an agent of secularizing pressure on students? From a constitutional perspective, is secularizing pressure any less objectionable than pro-religious pressure?

One of the most contentious and recurring issues in the public school curriculum involves the teaching of evolution. In 1859, the year Commonwealth v. Cooke (p. 477) was decided, Charles Darwin published *The Origin of Species*, in which he argued that existing forms of life evolved from common origins by a process of natural selection (a process Herbert Spencer later termed "survival of the fittest"). Like young Thomas Wall, Darwin represented a challenge to the generic Christian orthodoxy accepted in the public schools. The leading high school botany text of the time, Asa Gray's First Lessons in Botany and Vegetable Physiology (1857), taught students that "the Creator established a definite number of species at the beginning, which have continued by propagation, each after its kind." Darwin's work implied that the Creator—if there was one—had a different role than the one described in the Bible.

Darwin's theory found its way into the public high schools within two generations without much controversy. But not many children went to high school then (fewer than 4% in 1890). By 1920 that number had increased dramatically. At the same time there had arisen within evangelical Protestantism a movement militantly opposed to secular, liberal trends in modern culture. The movement was called "fundamentalism" after a set of small books, The Fundamentals: A Testimony of the Truth (1910-1915), purporting to state the few essential points of Christian doctrine. One of these was the inerrancy of scripture.

By the early 1920s these two ways of looking at the world began to collide, and several states passed laws against teaching evolution in the public schools. Tennessee was one. Its 1925 Anti-Evolution Act made it unlawful for a public school teacher "to teach any theory that denies the story of the divine creation of man as taught in the bible, and to teach instead that man has descended from a lower order of animals." The Tennessee Supreme Court upheld the law in Scopes v. State, 289 S.W. 363 (1927), against the charge that it violated the state's constitutional prohibition against giving preference to any religious establishment:

> [The Act] requires the teaching of nothing. It only forbids the teaching of the evolution of man from a lower order of animals. . . . As the law thus stands, while the theory of evolution of man may not be taught in the schools of the state, nothing contrary to that theory is required to be taught. . . .
>
> Much has been said in argument about the motives of the Legislature in passing this act. But the validity of a statute must be determined by its natural and legal effect, rather than proclaimed motives.

Though Scopes was convicted in court of teaching evolution, he got a more approving judgment from the press. Popular accounts of the trial, especially those of H.L. Mencken, made Clarence Darrow (Scopes's lawyer) the winner and William Jennings Bryan (appearing as a special prosecutor) the loser. *Inherit the Wind*, a popular movie from 1960, takes the same point of view.

In fact, however, the characters and the sequel were more complicated. Bryan was not the bigoted ignoramus the movie portrayed. He had run three times as the Democratic candidate for president on a progressive platform; he had served as Wilson's Secretary of State, resigning in protest over Wilson's drift toward war. The same year he began his campaign against evolution, he proposed creating a federal Department of Education. Bryan certainly believed that Darwinism was wrong for theological reasons, but he was just as concerned about its social

implications: A belief in the survival of the fittest, he feared, could cause exploit-
ation of labor, military aggression, and racial injustice (he pointed out the
"scientific racism" in many pro-evolution texts). See Michael Kazin, A Godly
Hero: The Life of William Jennings Bryan (2006).

As for the sequel of the trial, conventional wisdom has it that evolution quickly
took over high school science everywhere outside a few remote corners of the
Appalachians and the Ozarks. In reality, most textbooks avoided the word "evolution" and omitted discussion of the origins of life and the evolution of man.
This situation prevailed until the late 1950s, when the Soviet launching of *Sput-
nik* (1957), the National Defense Education Act (1958), and the National
Science Foundation's Biological Science Curriculum Study (1959) led to a massive revision of high school science curriculums. For splendid discussions of
these matters, see two books by Edward J. Larson, Summer for the Gods: The
Scopes Trial and America's Continuing Debate Over Science and Religion
(1997), and Trial and Error (1985).

The new wave of biology textbooks arrived in 1965 at Little Rock Central High
School—the same school where in 1957 Governor Orval Faubus had deployed
the National Guard to prevent the admission of nine black students. See Cooper
v. Aaron, 358 U.S. 1 (1958).

EPPERSON v. ARKANSAS
393 U.S. 97 (1968)

Mr. Justice FORTAS delivered the opinion of the Court.

This appeal challenges the constitutionality of the "anti-evolution" statute
which the State of Arkansas adopted in 1928 to prohibit the teaching in its public
schools and universities of the theory that man evolved from other species of life.
The statute was a product of the upsurge of "fundamentalist" religious fervor of
the twenties. The Arkansas statute was an adaption of the famous Tennessee
"monkey law" which that State adopted in 1925. The constitutionality of the
Tennessee law was upheld by the Tennessee Supreme Court in the celebrated
Scopes case in 1927.

The Arkansas law makes it unlawful for a teacher in any state-supported
school or university "to teach the theory or doctrine that mankind ascended
or descended from a lower order of animals," or "to adopt or use in any such
institution a textbook that teaches" this theory. Violation is a misdemeanor and
subjects the violator to dismissal from his position.

The present case concerns the teaching of biology in a high school in
Little Rock. According to the testimony, until the events here in litigation, the
official textbook furnished for the high school biology course did not have a
section on the Darwinian Theory. Then, for the academic year 1965–1966, the
school administration, on recommendation of the teachers of biology in the
school system, adopted and prescribed a textbook which contained a chapter
setting forth "the theory about the origin . . . of man from a lower form of animal."

Susan Epperson, a young woman who graduated from Arkansas' school system and then obtained her master's degree in zoology at the University of
Illinois, was employed by the Little Rock school system in the fall of 1964 to
teach 10th grade biology at Central High School. At the start of the next academic year, 1965, she was confronted by the new textbook (which one surmises

from the record was not unwelcome to her). She faced at least a literal dilemma because she was supposed to use the new textbook for classroom instruction and presumably to teach the statutorily condemned chapter; but to do so would be a criminal offense and subject her to dismissal. [The Arkansas Supreme Court, reversing a judgment of the chancery court, upheld the law.]

Government in our democracy, state and national, must be neutral in matters of religious theory, doctrine, and practice. It may not be hostile to any religion or to the advocacy of no religion; and it may not aid, foster, or promote one religion or religious theory against another or even against the militant opposite. The First Amendment mandates governmental neutrality between religion and religion, and between religion and non-religion.

[Epperson argued that the law was unconstitutionally vague because it was not clear whether it forbade "explanation" of the theory of evolution or merely "teaching that the theory is true." But the Court held that under either interpretation, the law violated the Religion Clauses.]

There is and can be no doubt that the First Amendment does not permit the State to require that teaching and learning must be tailored to the principles or prohibitions of any religious sect or dogma. In Everson v. Board of Education, this Court, in upholding a state law to provide free bus service to school children, including those attending parochial schools, said: "Neither [a state nor the federal government] can pass laws which aid one religion, aid all religions, or prefer one religion over another."

. . . While study of religions and of the Bible from a literary and historic viewpoint, presented objectively as part of a secular program of education, need not collide with the First Amendment's prohibition, the State may not adopt programs or practices in its public schools or colleges which "aid or oppose" any religion. This prohibition is absolute. It forbids alike the preference of a religious doctrine or the prohibition of theory which is deemed antagonistic to a particular dogma. . . . The test was stated as follows in Abington School District v. Schempp: "[W]hat are the purpose and the primary effect of the enactment? If either is the advancement or inhibition of religion then the enactment [is unconstitutional]." . . .

In the present case, there can be no doubt that Arkansas has sought to prevent its teachers from discussing the theory of evolution because it is contrary to the belief of some that the Book of Genesis must be the exclusive source of doctrine as to the origin of man. No suggestion has been made that Arkansas' law may be justified by considerations of state policy other than the religious views of some of its citizens. It is clear that fundamentalist sectarian conviction was and is the law's reason for existence.[16] Its antecedent,

---

16. The following advertisement is typical of the public appeal which was used in the campaign to secure adoption of the statute:

THE BIBLE OR ATHEISM, WHICH?

All atheists favor evolution. If you agree with atheism vote against Act No. 1. If you agree with the Bible vote for Act No. 1. . . . Shall conscientious church members be forced to pay taxes to support teachers to teach evolution which will undermine the faith of their children? The Gazette said Russian Bolshevists laughed at Tennessee. True, and that sort will laugh at Arkansas. Who cares? Vote FOR ACT NO. 1.

The Arkansas Gazette, Little Rock, Nov. 4, 1928, p.12, cols. 4-5.

Tennessee's "monkey law," candidly stated its purpose: to make it unlawful "to teach any theory that denies the story of the Divine Creation of man as taught in the Bible, and to teach instead that man has descended from a lower order of animals." Perhaps the sensational publicity attendant upon the Scopes trial induced Arkansas to adopt less explicit language. It eliminated Tennessee's reference to "the story of the Divine Creation of man" as taught in the Bible, but there is no doubt that the motivation for the law was the same: to suppress the teaching of a theory which, it was thought, "denied" the divine creation of man.

Arkansas' law cannot be defended as an act of religious neutrality. Arkansas did not seek to excise from the curricula of its schools and universities all discussion of the origin of man. The law's effort was confined to an attempt to blot out a particular theory because of its supposed conflict with the Biblical account, literally read.

Mr. Justice BLACK, concurring.

[The] Court, not content to strike down this Arkansas Act on the unchallengeable ground of its plain vagueness, chooses rather to invalidate it as a violation of the Establishment of Religion Clause of the First Amendment. I would not decide this case on such a sweeping ground for the following reasons, among others.

1. In the first place I find it difficult to agree with the Court's statement that "there can be no doubt that Arkansas has sought to prevent its teachers from discussing the theory of evolution because it is contrary to the belief of some that the Book of Genesis must be the exclusive source of doctrine as to the origin of man." It may be instead that the people's motive was merely that it would be best to remove this controversial subject from its schools; there is no reason I can imagine why a State is without power to withdraw from its curriculum any subject deemed too emotional and controversial for its public schools. And this Court has consistently held that it is not for us to invalidate a statute because of our views that the "motives" behind its passage were improper; it is simply too difficult to determine what those motives were.

2. A second question that arises for me is whether this Court's decision forbidding a State to exclude the subject of evolution from its schools infringes the religious freedom of those who consider evolution an anti-religious doctrine. If the theory is considered anti-religious, as the Court indicates, how can the State be bound by the Federal Constitution to permit its teachers to advocate such an "anti-religious" doctrine to schoolchildren? The very cases cited by the Court as supporting its conclusion hold that the State must be neutral, not favoring one religious or anti-religious view over another. The Darwinian theory is said to challenge the Bible's story of creation; so too have some of those who believe in the Bible, along with many others, challenged the

---

Letters from the public expressed the fear that teaching of evolution would be "subversive of Christianity," and that it would cause school children "to disrespect the Bible[.]" One letter read: "The cosmogony taught by [evolution] runs contrary to that of Moses and Jesus, and as such is nothing, if anything at all, but atheism. . . . Now let the mothers and fathers of our state that are trying to raise their children in the Christian faith arise in their might and vote for this anti-evolution bill that will take it out of our tax supported schools. When they have saved the children, they have saved the state."

Darwinian theory. Since there is no indication that the literal Biblical doctrine of the origin of man is included in the curriculum of Arkansas schools, does not the removal of the subject of evolution leave the State in a neutral position toward these supposedly competing religious and anti-religious doctrines? Unless this Court is prepared simply to write off as pure nonsense the views of those who consider evolution an anti-religious doctrine, then this issue presents problems under the Establishment Clause far more troublesome than are discussed in the Court's opinion.

NOTES AND QUESTIONS

1. **Why Is Evolution so Controversial?**   How can we explain the antipathy that fundamentalist Christians (and a few others) feel toward the teaching of evolution?

First, it is important to distinguish between two camps of anti-Darwinians, which may be called "young earth creationism" and "intelligent design" theory. Young earth creationists accept the biblical account of creation literally. In their view, the process of creation took place over a period of six 24-hour days and happened relatively recently (less than 10,000 years ago). God created each species individually, and no species evolved from another. This position appears to be at odds with the geologic evidence (unless you believe, as some do, that God deliberately made the world with misleading carbon 14 dating and other misclues), and thus presents a direct clash between science and revelation.

Intelligent design theorists generally accept the geologic dating of the earth and agree that the evidence supports microevolution (change within species and in the composition of population). They maintain, however, that it is scientifically impossible for living things as they now exist to have evolved by chance through large numbers of random mutations. In particular, they argue that many biological systems exhibit the quality of "irreducible complexity," meaning that a system consists of two or more interrelated parts such that removing even one part completely destroys the system's function. In other words, the system as a whole does not function until an entire, complex system of interrelated parts is in place. This renders it impossible, or at least statistically highly improbable, to have come about through small changes and natural selection, since the separate component parts have no value to the organism. See, e.g., Michael Behe, Darwin's Black Box (1996). They also note that the fossil record does not show gradual development of complicated species from simpler species, as Darwin predicted, but rather the sudden emergence of new species at various times, without apparent precursors (with a few possible exceptions, which are themselves contested). Modern paleontologists describe this sudden appearance of new organisms as "punctuated equilibrium." See, e.g., Stephen Jay Gould and Niles Eldredge, Punctuated Equilibrium Comes of Age, 366 Nature 223 (1993). But critics charge that this is a label, not an explanation. For an engaging statement of the argument in favor of intelligent design, see Philip Johnson, Darwin on Trial (1991).

Defenders of natural selection give essentially the same response to the "irreducible complexity" argument that Darwin originally gave. A leading cell biologist who is a professing Christian states:

> The crux of the design theory is the idea that by themselves, the individual parts or structures of a complex organ are useless. The evolutionist says no, that's not true. Those individual parts can indeed be useful, and it's by working on those "imperfect and simple" structures that natural selection eventually produces complex organs. . . .
>
> In the case of the eye, biologists have realized that any ability, no matter how slight, to sense light would have had adaptive value. Bacteria and algae, after all, manage to swim to and from the light with nothing more than an eyespot—a lensless, nerveless cluster of pigments and proteins. Zoologists have discovered numerous gradations of light-sensing systems in nature. . . . The human eye . . . could indeed have been formed by evolution, one step at a time, from a series of simpler but still functioning organs[.]

Kenneth R. Miller, Finding Darwin's God: A Scientist's Search for Common Ground Between God and Evolution 135-136 (1999).

So far, this may sound like a squabble about what counts as evidence, or about how to read the evidence. But underlying these issues are serious moral and philosophical questions, which give the debate its energy. There are deep connections between scientific and philosophical understandings of the world. The switch from Ptolemaic to Copernican astronomy had profound implications for the centrality of humankind in the cosmic order. The shift from Newtonian to Einsteinian physics corresponds (roughly) to a change from a modern to a postmodern view of truth.

What are the philosophical implications of Darwinism and the alternatives? Natural selection, by offering a naturalistic explanation for the apparent design of organisms, certainly removed one common reason for believing in a divine being. Indeed, many leading evolutionists join Richard Dawkins in asserting that "Darwin made it possible to be an intellectually fulfilled atheist." Richard Dawkins, The Blind Watchmaker 6 (1986). If nature came about purely by chance, it is also much more difficult to believe in any normative quality to the universe. How could natural law, for example, be based on an understanding of the nature of reality, if nature itself has no purpose? Dawkins writes that "[t]he universe we observe has precisely the properties we should expect if there is, at bottom, no design, no purpose, no evil and no good, nothing but blind, pitiless indifference." Richard Dawkins, River Out of Eden 133 (1995). Another leading biologist, William Provine, claims that "[m]odern science directly implies that there are no inherent moral or ethical laws, no absolute guiding principles for human society. . . . We must conclude that when we die, we die, and that is the end of us." William Provine, Evolution and the Foundation of Ethics, 3 MBL Science 25 (1988). On the other hand, if the wonders of the biological universe are evidence of the workings of intelligent design, it becomes more plausible to believe not only in God but also in a universe of purpose and meaning. This could be the difference between nihilism and moral order.

The connection between evolution and moral philosophy was evident in the last century, when the idea of "survival of the fittest" helped to inspire a ruthless brand of capitalist competition, eugenics, scientific (or pseudoscientific) racism, and other social movements loosely called "Social Darwinism." Justice Oliver Wendell Holmes, Jr., an enthusiast for eugenics, wrote the Court's decision that allowed states to compel the sterilization of mentally retarded people, culminating in the famous phrase: "Three generations of imbeciles are enough." Buck v. Bell, 274 U.S. 200, 207 (1927). William Jennings Bryan was no scientist, but he foresaw trouble if the idea of the survival of the fittest were applied to human behavior. See Kazin, A Godly Hero, 274-275.

To be sure, many people (including many scientists) believe, and a number of scientists argue, that God chose natural selection as the mechanism for bringing new species into being. Indeed, some argue that the elegance and power of the mechanism actually point toward God. Miller, Finding Darwin's God at 248-253, 291-292; Howard J. Van Til, God and Evolution: An Exchange, First Things 32 (June/July 1993). In response to the spectre of Social Darwinism, they argue that natural selection often favors altruism—or at least cooperation—over selfishness. Miller, Finding Darwin's God at 245-248. Nevertheless, the ways of harmonizing natural selection and traditional religion are not straightforward, and to many people—both scientists and believers—the two are irreconcilable.

Lest you suppose that the creationist views we have described are found only on the periphery of American society, consider the observation of Stephen L. Carter, The Culture of Disbelief: How American Law and Politics Trivialize Religious Devotion 159-160 (1993): "Survey data indicate that 82 percent of American adults believe that God created human beings. This figure includes the 44 percent of adults who accept the Genesis account of creation and the 38 percent who believe that God guided evolution."

2. Secular Purpose. *Epperson* was the first decision to enforce the prohibition (eventually part of the Lemon v. Kurtzman test) against laws whose purpose is to advance religion.

(a) Was the purpose of the law religious? What exactly was the purpose of Arkansas's law? This is an unusually difficult question because the law was adopted by popular initiative in 1928. The age of the law is one obstacle. More important, popular votes are done by secret ballot, and there are no published hearings, committee reports, and debates as we sometimes have with statutes. Justice Fortas cites an advertisement that appeared in the Arkansas Gazette (n. 16). But this little ad ran only twice in Little Rock during the two weeks before the election. And at least one study of the initiative concludes that fundamentalists did not vote in disproportionate numbers for the law. See Larson, Trial and Error 115. As we have noted, Bryan, at least, aimed in large part to prevent the harmful social effects that he thought evolutionary beliefs caused. Whether or not he was right, wasn't this a secular purpose? It is also possible, as Justice Black suggested, that the purpose was simply to avoid controversy. In view of these complications, do you think the Court gives sufficient care to its finding that the "sole reason" for the law was "sectarian" conviction?

(b) What is wrong with a religious purpose? Suppose we succeed in uncovering the voters' reasons for supporting the initiative. Why is it illegitimate for them to vote based on religious considerations? In a general election people often vote for or against particular candidates because they are members of a particular church. Jews voted in large numbers for vice-presidential candidate

Joseph Lieberman in 2000; George W. Bush scored disproportionately high among Protestant evangelicals in 2000 and 2004. Indeed, citizens have a First Amendment right (free speech, free exercise) to support candidates for this reason. Why should they be forbidden to have similar thoughts when voting for an initiative? Is it because the initiative, unlike the candidate election, produces a law? Suppose that most people supported the initiative not because evolution contradicted their own religious beliefs, but because they wanted to spare their fundamentalist friends (a local minority) from a certain amount of unpleasantness. Is this a purpose to advance religion, in *Schempp*'s sense?

(c) **Should improper purpose alone invalidate a law?** Is it a mistake to conclude that purpose alone, unattended by any bad effect, can violate the Establishment Clause? There is nothing unconstitutional about not teaching evolution. Arkansas could have dropped biology from its curriculum because the equipment was too expensive. It is just the purpose that condemns the law. Consider this parallel. In 1962, Jackson, Mississippi, maintained five segregated swimming pools. When ordered to integrate the pools, the city closed them instead. The Supreme Court upheld its action against an equal protection challenge. There was nothing unconstitutional about not having swimming pools—the effect was felt by blacks and whites alike. And a bad purpose alone would not invalidate the law. Palmer v. Thompson, 403 U.S. 217 (1971). Why is a naked purpose to aid religion (if that is in fact what happened in *Epperson*) worse than a naked purpose to avoid integration?

3. Neutrality in the Curriculum. The *Schempp* test, which the Court applies in *Epperson*, is a measure of neutrality—a law should not advance or inhibit religion. But what is the neutral position in *Epperson*? To forbid the teaching of evolution surely takes sides in this controversy. But to teach evolution (at least to teach it as fact or as the best-supported scientific theory) takes sides, also. The next case was provoked by an incident in which a schoolchild recited that "God created the World, and God created man." His teacher graded this answer "unsatisfactory." Alan Freeman and Elizabeth Mensch, Religion as Science/Science as Religion: Constitutional Law and the Fundamentalist Challenge, 2 Tikkun 64-65 (1987). In that case the authority of the state's public educational system was deployed against a specific religious claim, and one who persisted in disputing the official version of the truth was punished with low marks.

Is it necessary for the state to be neutral about an issue of this sort? After all, the First Amendment does not forbid the establishment of scientific orthodoxy. Maybe these questions should be resolved on the basis of the school authorities' best judgment about pedagogy. But if that is the case, why should the courts intervene at all? Why intervene only on the side of evolution, as in *Epperson*?

4. Religious Involvement in Policy Making. Does *Epperson* hold that it is unconstitutional for public schools to adapt their curriculum in order to avoid offending the sensibilities of a significant religious group in the community? Why? Would it be unconstitutional for the school board to agree to a request by Jewish parents to remove *The Merchant of Venice* from the 10th grade curriculum? Would it be unconstitutional for the school board in a predominantly Roman Catholic community to decline to teach about contraception? See Mercer v. Michigan State Bd. of Educ., 379 F. Supp. 580 (E.D. Mich. 1974), aff'd, 419 U.S. 1081 (1974). After the riots in early 2006 over depictions of Mohammed in newspaper cartoons, could a school board decline to adopt a history textbook that contains a drawing of Mohammed because it knows this would offend many Muslim students? Does *Epperson* disqualify religious citizens from participating effectively in democratic policy making? We return to this question in section V-D.

5. Teaching Creationism.   Would it be more, or less, constitutionally objectionable for the state, instead of barring evolution, to decide that creationism should be taught as an alternative theory? That is the issue in the next case.

EDWARDS v. AGUILLARD, 482 U.S. 578 (1987):   Louisiana passed an Act for "Balanced Treatment for Creation-Science and Evolution-Science in Public School Instruction." The Act, in the Court's words, "forbids the teaching of the theory of evolution in public schools unless accompanied by instruction in 'creation science.' No school is required to teach evolution or creation science. If either is taught, however, the other must also be taught. The theories of evolution and creation science are statutorily defined as 'the scientific evidences for [creation or evolution] and inferences from those scientific evidences.'" In response to an Establishment Clause challenge, the state officials "defended on the ground that the purpose of the Act is to protect . . . academic freedom" in instruction concerning the origins and development of life. The Court struck down the Act on its face under the "secular purpose" prong of *Lemon.*

"The Court has been particularly vigilant in monitoring compliance with the Establishment Clause in elementary and secondary schools. Families entrust public schools with the education of their children, but condition their trust on the understanding that the classroom will not purposely be used to advance religious views that may conflict with the private beliefs of the student and his or her family. Students in such institutions are impressionable and their attendance is involuntary. The State exerts great authority and coercive power through mandatory attendance requirements, and because of the students' emulation of teachers as role models and the children's susceptibility to peer pressure. . . .

"In this case, appellants have identified no clear secular purpose for the Louisiana Act. . . . True, the Act's stated purpose is to protect academic freedom. [But] requiring schools to teach creation science with evolution does not advance academic freedom. The Act does not grant teachers a flexibility that they did not already possess to supplant the present science curriculum with the presentation of theories, besides evolution, about the origin of life. . . . In *Wallace,* the State characterized its new law as one designed to provide a 1-minute period for meditation. We rejected that stated purpose as insufficient, because a previously adopted Alabama law already provided for such a 1-minute period. Thus, in this case, as in *Wallace,* '[a]ppellants have not identified any secular purpose that was not fully served by [existing state law] before the enactment of [the statute in question].'"

The Court also rejected the state's claim that that the Act furthered the goal of "fairness" in teaching all the evidence about the origin of human beings: "If the Louisiana Legislature's purpose was solely to maximize the comprehensiveness and effectiveness of science instruction, it would have encouraged the teaching of all scientific theories about the origins of humankind. But under the Act's requirements, teachers who were once free to teach any and all facets of this subject are now unable to do so. Moreover, the Act fails even to ensure that creation science will be taught, but instead requires the teaching of this theory only when the theory of evolution is taught. Thus we agree with the Court of Appeals' conclusion that the Act does not serve to protect academic freedom, but has the distinctly different purpose of discrediting 'evolution by counter-balancing its teaching at every turn with the teaching of creationism. . . . '

"[W]e need not be blind in this case to the legislature's preeminent religious purpose in enacting this statute. There is a historic and contemporaneous link between the teachings of certain religious denominations and the teaching of evolution. It was this link that concerned the Court in Epperson v. Arkansas. The Court found that there can be no legitimate state interest in protecting particular religions from scientific views 'distasteful to them,' and concluded 'that the First Amendment does not permit the State to require that teaching and learning must be tailored to the principles or prohibitions of any religious sect or dogma.'

"These same historic and contemporaneous antagonisms between the teachings of certain religious denominations and the teaching of evolution are present in this case. The preeminent purpose of the Louisiana Legislature was clearly to advance the religious viewpoint that a supernatural being created humankind. The term 'creation science' was defined as embracing this particular religious doctrine by those responsible for the passage of the Creationism Act. Senator [Bill Keith, the sponsor of the Act, brought to the hearings an expert who testified] that the theory of creation science included belief in the existence of a supernatural creator. . . . The state senator repeatedly stated that scientific evidence supporting his religious views should be included in the public school curriculum to redress the fact that the theory of evolution incidentally coincided with what he characterized as religious beliefs antithetical to his own. The legislation therefore sought to alter the science curriculum to reflect endorsement of a religious view that is antagonistic to the theory of evolution.

"[T]he purpose of the Creationism Act was to restructure the science curriculum to conform with a particular religious viewpoint. Out of many possible science subjects taught in the public schools, the legislature chose to affect the teaching of the one scientific theory that historically has been opposed by certain religious sects. As in Epperson, the legislature passed the Act to give preference to those religious groups which have as one of their tenets the creation of humankind by a divine creator. The 'overriding fact' that confronted the Court in Epperson was 'that Arkansas' law selects from the body of knowledge a particular segment which it proscribes for the sole reason that it is deemed to conflict with . . . a particular interpretation of the Book of Genesis by a particular religious group.' Similarly, the Creationism Act is designed either to promote the theory of creation science which embodies a particular religious tenet by requiring that creation science be taught whenever evolution is taught or to prohibit the teaching of a scientific theory disfavored by certain religious sects by forbidding the teaching of evolution when creation science is not also taught. The Establishment Clause, however, 'forbids alike the preference of a religious doctrine or the prohibition of theory which is deemed antagonistic to a particular dogma.' Because the primary purpose of the Creationism Act is to advance a particular religious belief, the Act endorses religion in violation of the First Amendment."

Justice Scalia, joined by Chief Justice Rehnquist, dissented: "Our cases have . . . confirmed that when the Lemon Court referred to 'a secular . . . purpose,' it meant 'a secular purpose.' . . . Thus, the majority's invalidation of the Balanced

Treatment Act is defensible only if the record indicates that the Louisiana Legislature had no secular purpose.

"It is important to stress that the purpose forbidden by *Lemon* is the purpose to 'advance religion.' Our cases in no way imply that the Establishment Clause forbids legislators merely to act upon their religious convictions. We surely would not strike down a law providing money to feed the hungry or shelter the homeless if it could be demonstrated that, but for the religious beliefs of the legislators, the funds would not have been approved. Also, political activism by the religiously motivated is part of our heritage. Notwithstanding the majority's implication to the contrary, we do not presume that the sole purpose of a law is to advance religion merely because it was supported strongly by organized religions or by adherents of particular faiths. To do so would deprive religious men and women of their right to participate in the political process. Today's religious activism may give us the Balanced Treatment Act, but yesterday's resulted in the abolition of slavery, and tomorrow's may bring relief for famine victims.

"Similarly, we will not presume that a law's purpose is to advance religion merely because it 'happens to coincide or harmonize with the tenets of some or all religions,' Harris v. McRae (1980), or because it benefits religion, even substantially. We have, for example, turned back Establishment Clause challenges to restrictions on abortion funding, *Harris*, and to Sunday closing laws, McGowan v. Maryland (1961), despite the fact that both 'agre[e] with the dictates of [some] Judaeo-Christian religions[.]' Thus, the fact that creation science coincides with the beliefs of certain religions, a fact upon which the majority relies heavily, does not itself justify invalidation of the Act. . . .

"[In addition,] we have consistently described the Establishment Clause as forbidding not only state action motivated by the desire to *advance* religion, but also that intended to 'disapprove,' 'inhibit,' or evince 'hostility' toward religion. . . . Thus, if the Louisiana Legislature sincerely believed that the State's science teachers were being hostile to religion, our cases indicate that it could act to eliminate that hostility without running afoul of *Lemon*'s purpose test. . . .

"If one adopts the obviously intended meaning of the statutory term 'academic freedom,' there is no basis whatever for concluding that the purpose they express is a 'sham.' To the contrary, the Act pursues that purpose plainly and consistently. It requires that, whenever the subject of origins is covered, evolution be 'taught as a theory, rather than as proven scientific fact' and that scientific evidence inconsistent with the theory of evolution (viz., 'creation science') be taught as well. [The Act] treats the teaching of creation the same way. It does not mandate instruction in creation science; forbids teachers to present creation science 'as proven scientific fact'; and bans the teaching of creation science unless the theory is (to use the Court's terminology) 'discredit[ed] . . . at every turn' with the teaching of evolution. It surpasses understanding how the Court can see in this a purpose 'to restructure the science curriculum to conform with a particular religious viewpoint[.]' . . .

"It is undoubtedly true that what prompted the legislature to direct its attention to the misrepresentation of evolution in the schools (rather than the inaccurate presentation of other topics) was its awareness of the tension between evolution and the religious beliefs of many children. But even appellees concede that a valid secular purpose is not rendered impermissible simply because its pursuit is prompted by concern for religious sensitivities."

NOTES AND QUESTIONS

1. Secular Purpose. The Court again holds a statute unconstitutional because it lacks a secular purpose, without inquiring fully into its effect. In virtually every other area of constitutional law, a law must have a forbidden effect in order to be invalid. Why is the Establishment Clause different?

2. Secular Effect. Because the Court decides the case based on the "purpose" prong, technically it never determines if the effect of the Balanced Treatment Act would be to promote religious teaching. That question may have two parts. First, does the statute promote creationism? The Court rejected the state's argument that the statute was neutral ("balanced") between creationism and evolutionary theories; the majority pointed out, among other things, that the statute singled out creationism, among various possible antievolution theories, to elevate to equal status with evolution. Is there a good answer to that argument?

Second, assuming the statute promotes creationism, is creationism religious teaching? If a teacher presents creation as having been done by the God of the book of Genesis, that clearly seems religious. But what if a teacher merely refers to "a divine creator," or "intelligent design," or "a designing force"? Suppose, for example, a teacher urges the thesis, set forth above, that the "irreducible complexity" of living systems indicates an intelligent designer, or presents this as a scientific alternative to natural selection? See, e.g., David K. DeWolf et al., Teaching the Origins Controversy: Science, or Religion, or Speech?, 2000 Utah L. Rev. 39; Jay D. Wexler, Darwin, Design, and Disestablishment: Teaching the Evolution Controversy in Public Schools, 56 Vand. L. Rev. 751 (2003). Should the Court in *Aguillard* have waited, as Justice Scalia urged, to see how the Act was applied? If in any particular case, the question is when instruction passes from science over to religion, where is that line?

3. The Intelligent Design Controversy. The theory of intelligent design has caused much controversy recently. In 2004 a Pennsylvania school board adopted a policy that "[s]tudents will be made aware of gaps/problems in Darwin's theory and of other theories of evolution including, but not limited to, intelligent design." Teachers were also required to read a statement in biology class that

> [b]ecause Darwin's Theory is a theory, it continues to be tested as new evidence is discovered. The Theory is not a fact. Gaps in the Theory exist for which there is no evidence. A theory is defined as a well-tested explanation that unifies a broad range of observations. . . . With respect to any theory, students are encouraged to keep an open mind. The school leaves the discussion of the Origins of Life to individual students and their families.

The policy and the required statement were challenged by a group of teachers and parents as a violation of the Establishment Clause, and after a bench trial, the district court struck them down. Kitzmiller v. Dover Area School Dist., 400 F. Supp. 2d 707 (M.D. Pa. 2005). The court's lengthy opinion marshaled a host of arguments for why it is unconstitutional to teach intelligent design (or "ID"). We provide summary quotes of several of the arguments here. Which are consistent with Supreme Court precedent on these issues? Which are consistent with the best interpretation of the First Amendment?

(a) "An objective observer would know that ID and teaching about 'gaps' and 'problems' in evolutionary theory are creationist, religious strategies that evolved from earlier forms of creationism," such as the statutes struck down in *Epperson* and *Aguillard*. For example, a strategic document of the Discovery Institute, the leading institutional proponent of ID, states that the movement's ultimate goal "is to replace science as currently practiced with 'theistic and Christian science'[:] 'to replace materialistic explanations with the theistic understanding that nature and human beings are created by God.'"

(b) The policy and disclaimer promote creationist religion by "singl[ing] out evolution from the rest of the science curriculum and inform[ing] students that evolution, unlike anything else that they are learning, is 'just a theory,' which plays on the 'colloquial or popular understanding of the term ["theory"] and suggest[s] to the informed, reasonable observer that evolution is only a highly questionable "opinion" or a "hunch,"'" when in fact it is grounded in extensive evidence.

(c) The anti-evolution criticism based on the irreducible complexity of certain physiological systems has been "refuted" by several studies "showing that there are intermediate structures with selectable functions that could have evolved into the allegedly irreducibly complex systems." For example, "the alleged irreducible complexity of the blood-clotting cascade has been disproven by peer-reviewed studies dating back to 1969, which show that dolphins' and whales' blood clots despite missing a part of the cascade." Moreover, "even if [the assertion of] irreducible complexity had not been rejected, it still does not support ID as it is merely a test for evolution, not design."

(d) The textbook from which ID was to be taught originally referred to "creation" throughout, but after the *Aguillard* decision, these references were simply replaced systematically with "intelligent design," without any other change in content. "This compelling evidence strongly supports Plaintiffs' assertion that ID is creationism re-labeled."

(e) "ID is not science and cannot be adjudged a valid, accepted scientific theory as it has failed to publish in peer-reviewed journals, engage in research and testing, and gain acceptance in the scientific community" and because it "does not satisfy the ground rules of science which require testable hypotheses based upon natural explanations."

(f) "ID's religious nature is evident because it involves a supernatural designer. . . . [B]ecause its basic proposition is that the features of the natural world are produced by a transcendent, immaterial, non-natural being, ID is a religious proposition regardless of whether that religious proposition is given a recognized religious label."

(g) "ID's backers have sought to avoid the scientific scrutiny which we have now determined that it cannot withstand by advocating that the *controversy*, but not ID itself, should be taught in science class. This tactic is at best disingenuous, and at worst a canard. The goal of the IDM is not to encourage critical thought, but to foment a revolution which would supplant evolutionary theory with ID."

Advocates of intelligent design claim that many of these statements are false. These proponents assert, among other things, that the "irreducible complexity" argument has been accepted by a number of scientists and that it does constitute evidence of design; that the designing force they posit is not necessarily supernatural; that judges should be leery of dismissing a developing theory as non-science; and that the religious beliefs or ultimate motives of ID proponents are not relevant to the theory's scientific status. See, e.g., David K. DeWolf et al., Traipsing Into Evolution (Discovery Institute Press 2006).

4. Neutrality in the Curriculum: Science and Other Subjects.   Both Richard Dawkins the evolutionist and Philip Johnson the ID proponent believe that the naturalistic focus of science—referred to by the judge in the *Dover* case—conflicts with religious or spiritual explanations of life (they simply differ on which of the alternatives is correct). If that is so, what is "neutral" about teaching the naturalistic view in public schools and forbidding its competitors?

One response to this question is that there is no necessary conflict between religion and science properly defined. Science is committed only to "methodological naturalism"—to seeking natural explanations for events. It is not committed to "ontological naturalism," the proposition that natural things and events are all that exist. Science is a powerful method of acquiring knowledge, but it does not (or should not) claim that it is the only method, or that its domain, the testable features of the natural world, is the whole of knowledge. Religious doctrines may conflict with science when they make assertions about the natural world—for example, that it was created 6,000 years ago—but in general, science takes no position on religious questions such as whether a divine being exists and set into motion processes such as natural selection.

Is this a satisfactory resolution of the perceived conflict between science and religion? Does it provide a means by which the public school curriculum can be neutral on religious matters? If this resolution is satisfactory, are schools doing a good job of communicating it to students and parents? Should biology teachers issue statements like this on how science and religion relate, and if so, how would you write such a statement?

Would all assertions of evolutionary theorists in the evolution-creation debate pass the test above? Consider the following quote from Stephen Jay Gould, The Panda's Thumb: More Reflections in Natural History (1992):

> Orchids manufacture their intricate devices from the common components of ordinary flowers, parts usually fitted for very different functions. If God had designed a beautiful machine to reflect his wisdom and power, surely he would not have used a collection of parts generally fashioned for other purposes. Orchids were not made by an ideal engineer; they are jury-rigged from a limited set of available components. Thus, they must have evolved from ordinary flowers.

Isn't this the logical equivalent of the intelligent design argument? Is it any more or less "scientific" than ID?

Such questions arise not only with respect to the origins of life. Religious traditions around the world have teachings on numerous other subjects covered in school curriculums. Why is it "neutral" if the school teaches secular views on these subjects—often, as with evolution, secular views that directly contradict religious teachings—but does not present the religious views as serious alternatives? Is it possible for a school to present religious views "neutrally," especially given the wide range of religious views and the limited time in the curriculum? If neither the omission of religious views nor their inclusion is perfectly neutral, what is the solution to the problem?

5. Challenges to the Public School Curriculum

If the school curriculum may not contain religious materials, such as Bible reading or "scientific creationism," may it contain materials that students believe are contrary to their religion? Are the standards the same for antireligious as for religious materials? Should they be? Conflicts of this sort arise with some frequency. See George Dent, Religious Children, Secular Schools, 61 S. Cal. L. Rev. 863 (1988). Challenges have been raised to the public school curriculum by parents and groups who claim that it is not neutral and that it infringes on religious freedom rights. This section considers a variety of such challenges.

MOZERT v. HAWKINS COUNTY BOARD OF EDUCATION
827 F.2d 1058 (6th Cir. 1987)

LIVELY, Chief Judge.

Early in 1983 the Hawkins County, Tennessee Board of Education adopted the Holt, Rinehart and Winston basic reading series (the Holt series) for use in grades 1-8 of the public schools of the county. In grades 1-4, reading is not taught as a separate subject at a designated time in the school day. Instead, the teachers in these grades use the reading texts throughout the day in conjunction with other subjects. In grades 5-8, reading is taught as a separate subject at a designated time in each class. However, the schools maintain an integrated curriculum which requires that ideas appearing in the reading programs reoccur in other courses. . . .

At a pretrial hearing the parties made certain stipulations. Counsel for the defendants stipulated that the plaintiffs' religious beliefs are sincere and that certain passages in the reading texts offend those beliefs. However, counsel steadfastly refused to stipulate that the fact that the plaintiffs found the passages offensive made the reading requirement a burden on the plaintiffs' constitutional right to the free exercise of their religion. Similarly, counsel for the plaintiffs stipulated that there was a compelling state interest for the defendants to provide a public education to the children of Hawkins County. However, counsel stipulated only to a narrow definition of the compelling state interest—one that did not involve the exclusive use of a uniform series of textbooks.

The plaintiff Vicki Frost is the mother of four children, three of whom were students in Hawkins County public schools in 1983. [She] testified that the word of God as found in the Christian Bible "is the totality of my beliefs." [She said] that she had spent more than 200 hours reviewing the Holt series and had found numerous passages that offended her religious beliefs. She stated that the offending materials fell into seventeen categories which she listed. These ranged from such familiar concerns of fundamentalist Christians as evolution and "secular humanism" to less familiar themes such as "futuristic supernaturalism," pacifism, magic and false views of death.

In her lengthy testimony Mrs. Frost identified passages from stories and poems used in the Holt series that fell into each category. Illustrative is her first category, futuristic supernaturalism, which she defined as teaching "Man As God." Passages that she found offensive described Leonardo da Vinci as the human with a creative mind that "came closest to the divine touch." Similarly, she felt that a passage entitled "Seeing Beneath the Surface" related to an occult theme, by describing the use of imagination as a vehicle for seeing things not discernible through our physical eyes. . . .

[For a time, the school that Frost's children attended arranged an alternative reading program for them. But in 1983 the school board ordered all students to attend classes using the Holt series. Frost sued. The district court held that the school board had violated the plaintiffs' free exercise rights. It directed that objecting students be excused from reading classes where the textbooks were used, and awarded the parents about $50,000 to cover sums they had spent on private schools and on this lawsuit.]

III

The first question to be decided is whether a governmental requirement that a person be exposed to ideas he or she finds objectionable on religious grounds constitutes a burden on the free exercise of that person's religion as forbidden by the First Amendment. This is precisely the way the superintendent of the Hawkins County schools framed the issue in an affidavit filed early in this litigation. In his affidavit the superintendent set forth the school system's interest in a uniformity of reading texts. The affidavit also countered the claims of the plaintiffs that the schools were inculcating values and religious doctrines contrary to their religious beliefs, stating: "Without expressing an opinion as to the plaintiffs' religious beliefs, I am of the opinion that plaintiffs misunderstand the fact that exposure to something does not constitute teaching, indoctrination, opposition or promotion of the things exposed. While it is true that these textbooks expose the student to varying values and religious backgrounds, neither the textbooks nor the teachers teach, indoctrinate, oppose or promote any particular value or religion."

[The plaintiffs contended that the constitutional problem was created by the repeated nature of the offensive references.] The district court suggested that it was a matter of balance, apparently believing that a reading series that presented ideas with which the plaintiffs agree in juxtaposition to those with which they disagree would pass constitutional muster. While balanced textbooks are certainly desirable, there would be serious difficulties with trying to cure the omissions in the Holt series, as plaintiffs and their expert witnesses view the texts.

However, the plaintiffs' own testimony casts serious doubt on their claim that a more balanced presentation would satisfy their religious views. Mrs. Frost testified that it would be acceptable for the schools to teach her children about other philosophies and religions, but if the practices of other religions were described in detail, or if the philosophy was "profound" in that it expressed a world view that deeply undermined her religious beliefs, then her children "would have to be instructed to [the] error [of the other philosophy]." It is clear that to the plaintiffs there is but one acceptable view—the Biblical view, as they interpret the Bible. Furthermore, the plaintiffs view every human situation and decision, whether related to personal belief and conduct or to public policy and programs, from a theological or religious perspective. Mrs. Frost testified that many political issues have theological roots and that there would be "no way" certain themes could be presented without violating her religious beliefs. She identified such themes as evolution, false supernaturalism, feminism, telepathy and magic as matters that could not be presented in any way without offending her beliefs. The only way to avoid conflict with the plaintiffs' beliefs in these sensitive areas would be to eliminate all references to the subjects so identified. However, the Supreme Court has clearly held that it violates the Establishment Clause to tailor a public school's curriculum to satisfy the principles or prohibitions of any religion. Epperson v. Arkansas.

The testimony of the plaintiffs' expert witness, Dr. Vitz, illustrates the pitfalls of trying to achieve a balance of materials concerning religion in a reading course. He found "markedly little reference to religion, particularly Christianity, and also remarkably little to Judaism" in the Holt series. His solution would be to "beef up" the references to these two dominant religions in the United States. However, an adherent to a less widely professed religion might then object to the slighting of his or her faith. Balance in the treatment of religion lies in the eye of the beholder. Efforts to achieve the particular "balance" desired by any individual or group by the addition or deletion of religious material would lead to a forbidden entanglement of the public schools in religious matters, if done with the purpose or primary effect of advancing or inhibiting religion.

[In Sherbert v. Verner, and other cases about the denial of unemployment compensation (see Section III-A), there was governmental compulsion to engage in conduct that violated the plaintiffs' religious convictions. That element is missing in the present case. The requirement that students read the assigned materials and attend reading classes, in the absence of a showing that this participation entailed affirmation or denial of a religious belief, or performance or non-performance of a religious exercise or practice, does not place an unconstitutional burden on the students' free exercise of religion.

[Wisconsin v. Yoder might also] be read to support the proposition that requiring mere exposure to materials that offend one's religious beliefs creates an unconstitutional burden on the free exercise of religion. [But] Tennessee's school attendance laws offer several options to those parents who want their children to have the benefit of an education which prepares for life in the modern world without being exposed to ideas which offend their religious beliefs. [Parents can either send their children to church schools or private schools, as many of them have done, or teach them at home. Tennessee law prohibits state interference in the education process at church schools. And the statute permitting home schooling by parents or other teachers prescribes nothing with respect to curriculum or the content of class work.]

IV

The Supreme Court has recently affirmed that public schools serve the purpose of teaching fundamental values "essential to a democratic society." These values "include tolerance of divergent political and religious views" while taking into account "consideration of the sensibilities of others." Bethel School Dist. No. 403 v. Fraser (1986). The Court has noted with apparent approval the view of some educators who see public schools as an "assimilative force" that brings together "diverse and conflicting elements" in our society "on a broad but common ground." Ambach v. Norwick (1979), citing works of J. Dewey, N. Edwards and H. Richey. The critical reading approach furthers these goals. Mrs. Frost stated specifically that she objected to stories that develop "a religious tolerance that all religions are merely different roads to God." Stating that the plaintiffs reject this concept, presented as a recipe for an ideal world citizen, Mrs. Frost said, "We cannot be tolerant in that we accept other religious views on an equal basis with ours." While probably not an uncommon view of true believers in any religion, this statement graphically illustrates what is lacking in the plaintiffs' case.

The "tolerance of divergent . . . religious views" referred to by the Supreme Court is a civil tolerance, not a religious one. It does not require a person to accept any other religion as the equal of the one to which that person adheres. It merely requires a recognition that in a pluralistic society we must "live and let live." If the Hawkins County schools had required the plaintiff students either to believe or say they believe that "all religions are merely different roads to God," this would be a different case. . . .

. . . Since we have found none of the prohibited forms of governmental compulsion in this case, we conclude that the plaintiffs failed to establish the existence of an unconstitutional burden. Having determined that no burden was shown, we do not reach the issue of the defendants' compelling interest in requiring a uniform reading series or the question, raised by the defendant, of whether awarding damages violated the Establishment Clause. . . .

The judgment of the district court granting injunctive relief and damages is reversed, and the case is remanded with directions to dismiss the complaint. No costs are allowed. The parties will bear their own costs on appeal.

CORNELIA G. KENNEDY, Circuit Judge, concurring.

I agree with Chief Judge Lively's analysis and concur in his opinion. However, even if I were to conclude that requiring the use of the Holt series or another similar series constituted a burden on appellees' free exercise rights, I would find the burden justified by a compelling state interest.

Appellants have stated that a principal educational objective is to teach the students how to think critically about complex and controversial subjects and to develop their own ideas and make judgments about these subjects. Several witnesses testified that the only way to achieve these objectives is to have the children read a basal reader, participate in class discussions, and formulate and express their own ideas and opinions about the materials presented in a basal reader. Thus, appellee students are required to read stories in the Holt series, make personal judgments about the validity of the stories, and to discuss why certain characters in the stories did what they did, or their values and whether those values were proper. Appellee parents testified that they object to their children reading the Holt readers, being exposed to controversial ideas in the classroom, and to their children making critical judgments and formulating their own ideas about anything for which they believe the Bible states a rule or position.[1]

In Bethel School Dist. v. Fraser, the Supreme Court stated . . . that the state through its public schools must "inculcate the habits and manners of civility as values in themselves conducive to happiness and as indispensable to the practice

---

1. Appellee parents have indicated that they would not object to much of the material in the Holt readers if it were balanced by material supporting their religious beliefs. To the extent they assert a burden from the omission of material, I question how an omission can constitute a burden.

of self-government in the community and the nation." Teaching students about complex and controversial social and moral issues is just as essential for preparing public school students for citizenship and self-government as inculcating in the students the habits and manners of civility.

The evidence at trial demonstrated that mandatory participation in reading classes using the Holt series or some similar readers is essential to accomplish this compelling interest and that this interest could not be achieved any other way. Several witnesses for appellants testified that in order to develop critical reading skills, and therefore achieve appellants' objectives, the students must read and discuss complex, morally and socially difficult issues. Many of these necessarily will be subjects on which appellees believe the Bible states the rule or correct position. Consequently, accommodating appellees' beliefs would unduly interfere with the fulfillment of the appellants' objectives.

Additionally, Hawkins County Public Schools have a compelling interest in avoiding religious divisiveness. The Supreme Court has emphasized that the avoidance of religious divisiveness is nowhere more important than in public education, for "[t]he government's activities in this area can have a magnified impact on impressionable young minds. . . ." Grand Rapids School Dist. v. Ball. The opt-out remedy would permit appellee students to be released from a core subject every day because of their religion. Thus, although some students in the Hawkins County schools are presently released from class during the school day for special instruction, these students are not released because they have a religious objection to material being presented to the class. The present case is distinguishable from this Court's decision in Spence v. Bailey (6th Cir. 1972), inasmuch as the student in *Spence* was permitted to not participate in the school's R.O.T.C. program, a non-core subject. There is less divisiveness in excusing someone from military training than in excusing them from discussing a multitude of ideas. Accordingly, the opt-out remedy ordered by the court is inconsistent with the public schools' compelling interest in "promoting cohesion among a heterogeneous democratic people." McCollum v. Board of Educ. (1948) (Frankfurter, J., concurring).

BOGGS, Circuit Judge, concurring.

I concur with my colleagues that Hawkins County is not required by the Constitution to allow plaintiffs the latitude they seek in the educational program of these children. However, I reach that result on a somewhat different view of the facts and governing principles here. It seems that the court's opinion rests first on the view that plaintiffs' objection is to any exposure to contrary ideas, and that no one's religious exercise can be burdened simply by compelled exposure. Second, the opinion rests on the view that no burden can exist here because plaintiffs were not compelled to engage in any conduct prohibited by, or refrain from any practice required by, their religious beliefs.

I do not believe these attempted distinctions will survive analysis. I believe a deeper issue is present here, is implicitly decided in the court's opinion, and should be addressed openly. The school board recognizes no limitation on its power to require any curriculum, no matter how offensive or one-sided, and to expel those who will not study it, so long as it does not violate the Establishment Clause. Our opinion today confirms that right, and I would like to make plain my reasons for taking that position.

For myself, I approach this case with a profound sense of sadness. At the classroom level, the pupils and teachers in these schools had in most cases reached a working accommodation. Only by the decisions of higher levels of political authority, and by more conceptualized presentations of the plaintiffs' positions, have we reached the point where we must decide these harsh questions today. The school board faced what must have seemed a prickly and difficult group of parents, however dedicated to their children's welfare. In a similar situation, the poet Edwin Markham described a solution:

> *He drew a circle that shut me out—*
> *Heretic, Rebel, a thing to flout.*
> *But Love and I had the wit to win:*
> *We drew a circle that took him in!*

As this case now reaches us, the school board rejects any effort to reach out and take in these children and their concerns. At oral argument, the board specifically argued that it was better for both plaintiffs' children and other children that they not be in the public schools, despite the children's obvious desire to obtain some of the benefits of public schooling.

Plaintiffs' requests were unusual, but a variety of accommodations in fact were made, with no evidence whatsoever of bad effects. Given the masses of speculative testimony as to the hypothetical future evils of accommodating plaintiffs in any way, had there been any evidence of bad effects from what actually occurred, the board would surely have presented it.

II

Returning to the treatment of plaintiffs' free exercise claim, I believe this is a more difficult case than outlined in the court's opinion. I disagree with the first proposition in the court's opinion, that plaintiffs object to any exposure to any contrary idea. I do not believe we can define for plaintiffs their belief as to what is religiously forbidden to be so comprehensive, where both they and the district court have spoken to the contrary. A reasonable reading of plaintiffs' testimony shows they object to the overall effect of the Holt series, not simply to any exposure to any idea opposing theirs. The district court specifically found that the objection was to exposure to the Holt series, not to any single story or idea.

Ultimately, I think we must address plaintiffs' claims as they actually impact their lives: it is their belief that they should not take a course of study which, on balance, to them, denigrates and opposes their religion, and which the state is compelling them to take on pain of forfeiting all other benefits of public education.

Their view may seem silly or wrong-headed to some, but it is a sincerely held religious belief. By focusing narrowly on references that make plaintiffs appear so extreme that they could never be accommodated, the court simply leaves resolution of the underlying issues here to another case, when we have plaintiffs with a more sophisticated understanding of our own and Supreme Court precedent, and a more careful and articulate presentation of their own beliefs.

III

[I also] disagree with the court's view that there can be no burden here because there is no requirement of conduct contrary to religious belief. That view both slights plaintiffs' honest beliefs that studying the full Holt series would be conduct contrary to their religion, and overlooks other Supreme Court Free Exercise cases which view "conduct" that may offend religious exercise at least as broadly as do plaintiffs.

On the question of exposure to, or use of, books as conduct, we may recall the Roman Catholic Church's "Index Librorum Prohibitorum." This was a list of those books the reading of which was a mortal sin, at least until the second Vatican Council in 1962. I would hardly think it can be contended that a school requirement that a student engage in an act (the reading of the book) which would specifically be a mortal sin under the teaching of a major organized religion would be other than "conduct prohibited by religion," even by the court's fairly restrictive standard. Yet, in what constitutionally important way can the situation here be said to differ from that? Certainly, a religion's size or formality of hierarchy cannot determine the religiosity of beliefs. Similarly, and analogous to our case, church doctrine before 1962 also indicated that portions of the banned books could be used or read in a context to show their error, and that references to, or small portions of, the books did not fall under the same ban. Again, it seems inconceivable that we would determine that a Catholic child had forfeited the right to object to committing a mortal sin by reading Hobbes because he was willing, in another context, to read small portions or excerpts of the same material.

[Nevertheless, I would not require the school district here to accommodate the requests of those students and parents.] A constitutional challenge to the content of instruction (as opposed to participation in ritual such as magic chants, or prayers) is a challenge to the notion of a politically-controlled school system. Imposing on school boards the delicate task of satisfying the "compelling interest" test to justify failure to accommodate pupils is a significant step.[9] It is a substantial imposition on the schools to require them to justify each instance of not dealing with students' individual, religiously compelled, objections (as opposed to permitting a local, rough and ready, adjustment), and I do not see that the Supreme Court has authorized us to make such a requirement. . . .

Therefore, I reluctantly conclude that under the Supreme Court's decisions as we have them, school boards may set curricula bounded only by the Establishment Clause, as the state contends. Thus, contrary to the analogy plaintiffs suggest, pupils may indeed be expelled if they will not read from the King James Bible, so long as it is only used as literature, and not taught as religious truth. Contrary to the position of amicus American Jewish Committee, Jewish students may not assert a burden on their religion if their reading materials overwhelmingly provide a negative view of Jews or factual or historical issues important to Jews, so long as such materials do not assert any propositions as religious truth, or do not otherwise violate the Establishment Clause.

---

9. I do not think there is any evidence that actually accommodating pupils in practice need be as difficult as the state contends. Indeed, the state espouses a theory of rigidity (and finds alleged experts to support it) that seems a bit ludicrous in this age of individualized attention to many kinds of student language and interest. There was no evidence of actual confusion or disruption from the accommodation that did take place.

NOTES AND QUESTIONS

1. Mere Exposure to Objectionable Materials. The court of appeals held that the board's policy imposed no burden on the Frost children's free exercise rights because it did not require them to perform an act or affirm a belief that they objected to. That makes the case different from *Barnette* (performing an act) and *Torcaso* (affirming a belief). But how does this distinguish the case from Lee v. Weisman, where the Court held that a requirement to stand silently during a prayer was unconstitutional coercion? Remember that the prayers in *Weisman* were 30 seconds apiece, compared with the repeated exposure of the Frost children. See John H. Garvey, Cover Your Ears, 43 Case W. Res. L. Rev. 761 (1993). Is this a return to the regime of Commonwealth v. Cooke, where students could be required to read the Bible as long as they did not have to believe it? Is mere exposure to religious material different from mere exposure to material the student thinks is contrary to his religion?

Suppose one's faith teaches that it is sinful even to read the material in question, as did the Catholic Church about books on the Index Librorum Prohibitorum (and as Thomas Wall's priest instructed the boy in *Cooke*)? Is this attitude too squeamish to warrant the law's attention?

Consider a less extreme belief. Suppose my religion teaches me to avoid this material not because exposure is sinful in itself but because it can lead me into the path of sin. Should the law excuse people whom it puts in that predicament? Think about the practice of issuing movie ratings (PG-13) and parental discretion warnings for TV programs—don't we do these things because most parents think their children should be shielded from certain material? Does the *Mozert* court really mean not that mere exposure is harmless, but that exposure to *this* material is harmless? Compare Dent, 61 S. Cal. L. Rev. at 886-894; with Nadine Strossen, "Secular Humanism" and "Scientific Creationism": Proposed Standards for Reviewing Curricular Decisions Affecting Students' Religious Freedom, 47 Ohio St. L.J. 333 (1986). For further discussion of the issues in *Mozert*, see Stephen Bates, Battleground: One Mother's Crusade, the Religious Right, and the Battle for Control of Our Classrooms (1993); Nomi Maya Stolzenberg, "He Drew a Circle That Shut Me Out": Assimilation, Indoctrination, and the Paradox of a Liberal Education, 106 Harv. L. Rev. 581 (1993).

2. Skewing Against Religion? Judge Boggs argues that the plaintiffs' complaint was not really about specific passages in the Holt-Rinehart reader, but with its overall balance. They contended that the book consistently presented material from a point of view that was hostile to their own, without any countervailing readings. If this were true, would it raise a constitutional question? Is Judge Boggs correct that there is "no limitation on [a school board's] power to require any curriculum, no matter how offensive or one-sided, and to expel those who will not study it, so long as it does not violate the Establishment Clause?" Does that mean it is constitutional for public schools to impose a one-sided curriculum that is opposed to religion, but not a one-sided curriculum that favors religion? Is that consistent with the idea, reflected in the *Lemon* test, that the government may "neither advance *nor* inhibit religion"?

Consider an analogous question outside the context of public schools. In American Family Ass'n v. City and County of San Francisco, 277 F.3d 1114 (9th Cir. 2002), the Ninth Circuit held that it was not unconstitutional for the

San Francisco Board of Supervisors to issue statements condemning "major religious organizations," including specifically "the Religious Right," for taking positions that it deemed "hateful," "immoral," "erroneous and full of lies," and accusing these groups of being partly causally responsible for "horrible crimes committed against gays and lesbians." It also urged "local television stations not to broadcast advertising campaigns aimed at 'converting' homosexuals." The plaintiffs claimed, among other things, that this violated the Establishment Clause by officially disapproving of religion (under the "no endorsement" test set forth in decisions like *Lynch* and *Allegheny*, see p. 510 above). The Ninth Circuit rejected this claim on the ground that although the statements "may contain over-generalizations about the Religious Right," their primary effect was one of encouraging equal rights for gays and discouraging hate crimes, and any statements from which disapproval can be inferred [were] only incidental and ancillary." 277 F.3d at 1123. The court also rejected the organizations' free speech claim on the ground that "public officials may criticize practices that they would have no constitutional ability to regulate, so long as there is no actual or threatened imposition of government power or sanction." Are these rationales consistent with the endorsement test? Would it be constitutional for a city to issue a statement praising religious groups for their devotion to "truth" and "goodness"? Is there one standard—coercion—for challenging government speech disapproving of religion, and a more plaintiff-friendly standard—endorsement—for challenges to government speech approving of religion? Is *Mozert* based on a similar double standard?

3. Remedies for Free Exercise Versus Establishment Violations. Notice the district court's remedy in *Mozert*. How was it different from the remedy in *Weisman*? Is the difference related to the nature of the First Amendment claim? Why should we fix an Establishment Clause violation by eliminating the offensive material from the entire program, whereas for a free exercise violation we give an opt-out right? Is an Establishment Clause violation more serious? Is it because one law is unconstitutional on its face and the other is unconstitutional as applied?

4. Problem: Sex Education Classes in Public Schools. Suppose that Roman Catholic parents object to their child being required by the public school to attend sex education classes in which methods of contraception are taught. After *Mozert*, may the parents raise a free exercise claim for their child to be excused?

Suppose that the parents argue that an excusal right is insufficient because their children will be subjected to peer pressure and ridicule. Are they entitled to a factual hearing on their claim? If their claim were substantiated on the record, should they be given relief? Of what sort? Compare the plaintiff's allegations in *Schempp*.

The courts have generally held that students have a constitutional right to be excused from objectionable portions of sex education classes, but no right to prevent the schools from offering the classes. See, e.g., Smith v. Ricci, 89 N.J. 514, 446 A.2d 501 (1982); Medeiros v. Kiyosaki, 478 P.2d 314 (Haw. 1970). What, if anything, distinguishes *Mozert* from the sex education cases with respect to the excusal issue? With respect to efforts to eliminate sex education classes, the courts sometimes state that for public schools to eliminate such courses because they offend the religious views of some persons would violate the Establishment Clause. *Smith*, 446 A.2d at 506; *Medeiros*, 478 P.2d at 318-319. Do you agree?

Brown v. Hot, Sexy & Safer Productions, Inc., 68 F.3d 525 (1st Cir. 1995), involved a 90-minute mandatory high school assembly on AIDS and sex education, presented by a company that contracted with the school. Two 15-year-old students filed suit, along with their parents, for damages and a declaratory judgment that requiring them to attend violated their constitutional rights. The case arose on the defendants' motion to dismiss the complaint, and so the court accepted the following allegations as true:

> Plaintiffs allege that Landolphi [the performer and the company's owner] gave sexually explicit monologues and participated in sexually suggestive skits with several minors chosen from the audience. Specifically, the complaint alleges that Landolphi: 1) told the students that they were going to have a "group sexual experience, with audience participation"; 2) used profane, lewd, and lascivious language to describe body parts and excretory functions; 3) advocated and approved oral sex, masturbation, homosexual sexual activity, and condom use during promiscuous premarital sex; 4) simulated masturbation; 5) characterized the loose pants worn by one minor as "erection wear"; 6) referred to being in "deep sh—" after anal sex; 7) had a male minor lick an oversized condom with her, after which she had a female minor pull it over the male minor's entire head and blow it up; 8) encouraged a male minor to display his "orgasm face" with her for the camera; 9) informed a male minor that he was not having enough orgasms; 10) closely inspected a minor and told him he had a "nice butt"; and 11) made eighteen references to orgasms, six references to male genitals, and eight references to female genitals. Plaintiffs maintain that the sexually explicit nature of Landolphi's speech and behavior humiliated and intimidated [them]. Moreover, many students copied Landolphi's routines and generally displayed overtly sexual behavior in the weeks following the Program, allegedly exacerbating the [plaintiffs'] harassment. The complaint does not allege that either of the minor plaintiffs actually participated in any of the skits, or were the direct objects of any of Landolphi's comments.

The district court granted the motion to dismiss and the court of appeals affirmed. The court held that the mandatory assembly was a "neutral requirement that applied generally to all students" and thus satisfied the Free Exercise Clause under Employment Division v. Smith. It also rejected the argument that the plaintiffs stated a "hybrid claim" of religious exercise and parental control over education. The court distinguished the exemption of Amish children from compulsory schooling in *Yoder*, quoting *Yoder*'s statement that the Amish had "'convincingly demonstrated . . . the interrelationship of belief with their mode of life, the vital role that belief and daily conduct play in the continued survival of Old Order Amish communities . . . , and the hazards presented by the [attendance law].'" By contrast, the court said, "Here, the plaintiffs do not allege that the one-time compulsory attendance at the Program threatened their entire way of life."

In what sense was the program in *Hot, Sexy & Safer* "neutral and generally applicable"? If the program had been conducted from a religious point of view, would it have been deemed "neutral"?

———————————

NOTE ON TEACHING ABOUT RELIGION
IN PUBLIC SCHOOLS

Justice Brennan, concurring in *Schempp* (374 U.S. at 300), said:

> The holding of the Court today plainly does not foreclose teaching about the Holy Scriptures or about the differences between religious sects in classes in literature or history. Indeed, whether or not the Bible is involved, it would be impossible to teach meaningfully many subjects in the social sciences or the humanities without some mention of religion.

Are schools today failing to live up to this challenge? A number of studies of elementary and secondary public school curricula were conducted in the late 1980s, all concluding that public school curricula systematically avoid mention of religion. Two of the studies were conducted under the auspices of prominent separationist organizations. O. L. Davis Jr., et al., Looking at History: A Review of Major U.S. History Textbooks (People for the American Way, 1986); Charles Haynes, Teaching About Religious Freedom (Americans United Research Foundation, 1985); Paul Vitz, Religion and Traditional Values in Public School Textbooks: An Empirical Study (National Institute of Education Project, 1985). There was also a study, reported in the *New York Times* (July 2, 1987 at A16), by the Association for Supervision and Curriculum Development.

Charles Haynes, author of one of the studies, summarized his conclusions thus: "According to recent studies, a reader of most U.S. history and government texts would gain little insight into the history of religious liberty in America and might well conclude that religion in general has been of little or no consequence in our nation's history." Religious Freedom in America 6 (Americans United Research Foundation, 1986). Paul Vitz, a psychology professor at New York University, stated: "These studies make it abundantly clear that public school textbooks commonly exclude the history, heritage, beliefs, and values of millions of Americans. . . . Above all, those who are committed to their religious tradition—at the very least as an important part of the historical record—are not represented." Paul Vitz, Censorship: Evidence of Bias in Our Children's Textbooks 77 (1986).

Vitz directs attention particularly toward social studies textbooks in the early grades. These books are designed to introduce children to American social, economic, and political life as it exists today; they begin with accounts of the family and school setting and move outward, to neighborhood, community, region, country, and world. The emphasis is on ordinary life in all its variety. The Vitz study analyzed the 40 leading textbooks for grades 1 to 4 and found that "not one of the forty books totaling ten thousand pages had one text reference to a primary religious activity occurring in representative contemporary American life." *Id.* at 11. According to the study, the few indirect references were frequently misleading, especially in the sense of downplaying religious motivations. Examples include a story about life in a Spanish urban ghetto, entitled "El Barrio," which stated: "Religion is important for people in El Barrio. Churches have places for dances and sports events." Another textbook defines *Pilgrims* as "people who make long trips." (The theme of Pilgrims and Thanksgiving was frequently covered, but the major books made no mention of the Pilgrims' religious motivations or the fact that it was God they were thanking—implying in one instance that they were thanking the Indians.) Another textbook stated that "Mardi Gras is the end of winter celebration." Literary works were bowdlerized to eliminate religious references: an Isaac Bashevis Singer story about a Jewish boy in an Eastern European village was edited so that his statement, "Thank God," became "Thank goodness," and his "prayer to God" became a "prayer." Religious references tended to be foreign and exotic; Native American religious practices received more attention than Protestantism, Catholicism, or Judaism. Only one of 60 social studies books depicted any form of present-day Protestant practice: a photo of Episcopal monks worshiping together.

Fifth-grade American history textbooks, according to the Vitz study, contained relatively frequent references to religion in the colonial period, and very few in later periods. There was no discussion of religion's role in major social or political movements, such as abolition, women's suffrage, prohibition, immigration, education, pacifism, or social welfare. Of the ten leading fifth-grade history textbooks, all of which covered Dr. Martin Luther King, Jr., only one mentioned his religious beliefs (and it failed to explain what those religious beliefs were or what connection he saw between them and his civil rights work).

According to the Vitz study, the sixth-grade world history and culture textbooks contained little discussion of ancient Jewish history (there was much more coverage of Islam than of Judaism) and no reference in the major works to Jewish history between the Diaspora and the Holocaust. The life and historical impact of Jesus were given little coverage; four of the major textbooks did not mention his life or teaching at all. One major history textbook (published by Streck-Vaughn) summarized Jesus's impact as follows: "Jesus became a teacher. He preached that there was only One God. He told those who would listen that they must honor God by treating others with love and forgiveness." (Interestingly, the theme of "One God" was not central to Jesus's teaching; it is a much more common theme in Judaism and Islam.) Mohammed received much more extensive coverage. The rise of Islam was generally treated as an important event; the rise of Christianity was barely treated at all. One book (Laidlaw) devoted an 11-page section to Mohammed and Islam, plus scattered coverage, but only a few lines on one page to Christianity. Only one book (McGraw-Hill) had any significant coverage of the rise of Christianity or the early church. Later, Protestantism and the Reformation were disregarded; one prominent textbook (Riverside) "has twenty pages on Tanzania, nineteen pages on the history of the Netherlands, and sixteen pages on ancient Crete, but it makes no reference to Martin Luther or Calvin, and there is almost nothing on Protestantism." Only one major text (McGraw-Hill) explained the religious issues that prompted the break with the Roman Catholic Church. Sections on the modern period contained discussions of religious elements in foreign cultures, but not in the American culture. "Role models"—biographical sketches of noteworthy individuals—were exclusively secular, and if they happened to be religious as well, the religious aspect was ignored. (Joan of Arc was featured in one book without mention of God, religion, or the fact that she is a saint; Anne Hutchinson was portrayed as a protofeminist rather than as a religious dissenter.)

A more recent study of the treatment of religion in public school textbooks concluded that there has been "some improvement" but that "textbooks are still woefully inadequate in their treatment of religion." Warren Nord and Charles Haynes, Taking Religion Seriously Across the Curriculum 77, 78 (1998).

The results of these studies might be compared to standard analyses of sex and ethnic bias. These analyses have identified six types of bias in textbooks. The following summary is from S. McCune and M. Matthews, eds., Implementing Title IX and Attaining Sex Equity: A Workshop Package for Post-secondary Educators (1978):

1. *Invisibility.* By failing to mention women or members of minority groups, textbooks can imply that they are of less value, importance, and significance to society.
2. *Stereotyping.* By assigning traditional and rigid roles or attributes to a group, textbooks stereotype and limit the abilities and potential of that group.
3. *Imbalance/Selectivity.* Textbooks often present only one interpretation of an issue, ignoring complex and differing viewpoints.
4. *Unreality.* Textbooks often present an unrealistic portrayal of history and modern life, glossing over controversial topics, such as discrimination and prejudice.
5. *Fragmentation/Isolation.* By separating issues related to minority groups and women from the main body of text, the books imply that these issues are less important and not part of the dominant culture.
6. *Linguistic bias.* Language can be used to denigrate the experience and perspective of disadvantaged groups.

Assuming these studies are valid, why do you suppose this has occurred? Does it reflect hostility toward religion among the educational elite or a desire to avoid controversy? Or is it a response to constitutional necessity? Is there a constitutionally appropriate way to teach about religion in the public schools?

If it is true that there is a pattern of schools excluding even "objective" discussions about religious ideas, does it amount to anything worse than an incomplete education? Conservative Christian critics of the public schools have tried to argue that a secular school curriculum itself establishes a religion: that of "secular humanism." They rely on the Supreme Court's footnote in Torcaso v. Watkins (p. 473) listing secular humanism among those organized religious groups that do not believe in a deity. But this Establishment Clause challenge to the secular curriculum met the same fate as the free exercise "opt-out" challenge in *Mozert* : It succeeded in the district court, but failed at the appellate level. Smith v. Board of School Commissioners, 827 F.2d 684 (11th Cir. 1987). *Smith* and the issues it raises concerning the definition of "religion" are examined in detail in Part VI. Here, however, is a brief summary.

In *Smith*, a federal district court entered a permanent injunction prohibiting the use of 44 textbooks in the Mobile, Alabama, public schools. The textbooks, which had been approved by state and local authorities, covered the subjects of home economics, history, and social studies. The district judge held that the books, as taught in the curriculum, advanced the religion of "secular humanism" in violation of the Establishment Clause. Smith v. Board of School Comm'rs, 655 F. Supp. 939 (S.D. Ala. 1987).

The district court found that the home economics textbooks indoctrinated impressionable students into a "highly relativistic and individualistic" approach "to making moral decisions," in which "the validity of the moral choices is only to be decided by the student." The court drew this conclusion from statements in the books to the effect that moral choices are "purely personal," that "only you can decide," and that the prime question in deciding the morality of an action is the effect it will have on others. The court found that such teaching "undermines and competes" with "theistic points of view" under which "certain actions are in and of themselves immoral, whatever the consequences, and that, in addition, actions will have extra-temporal consequences."

The district court also found that the history and social studies books omitted events with religious significance and "uniformly ignore[d] the religious aspect of most American culture." Specifically, the books ignored the religious elements in events such as the arrival of the Puritans and the Great Awakening and in movements such as those for abolition, temperance, women's suffrage, and civil rights. The court found that the books presented religion as only "a private matter," a view "humanists have been seeking to instill for fifty years."

On appeal, the Eleventh Circuit reversed, holding that even if "secular humanism" is a "religion" for purposes of the Establishment Clause, none of the books conveyed a message of endorsement of secular humanism or disapproval of theism. With respect to the home economics textbooks, the court of appeals said that they merely "attempt to instill in Alabama public school children such values as independent thought, tolerance of diverse views, self-respect, maturity, self-reliance and logical decision-making." The court said that "many of the books specifically acknowledge that religion is one source of moral values and none preclude[s] that possibility." With respect to the history and social studies books, the court said that the mere omission of some facts with religious significance could not prove that the state was showing approval of secular humanism or hostility toward religion. At most, the court said, the books were "inadequate from an educational standpoint," which was a matter within the discretion of school administrators and did not pose a constitutional issue. The court of appeals concluded that the district court's ruling "turns the establishment clause's requirement of 'lofty neutrality' on the part of public schools into an affirmative obligation to speak about religion," a result "clearly inconsistent with the requirements of the establishment clause." Is this analysis consistent with *Epperson*?

6. *Alternatives to Public Education*

As the foregoing materials suggest, education is a lot more than the three *R*s. We depend on elementary and secondary schools to inculcate the values and ideals necessary for the next generation to become responsible citizens in our democratic society. The Supreme Court has referred to the "importance of public schools in the preparation of individuals for participation as citizens, and in the preservation of the values on which our society rests." Ambach v. Norwick, 441 U.S. 68, 76 (1979). It has stated that one objective of public education is "to inculcate fundamental values necessary to the maintenance of a democratic system." Bethel School Dist. v. Fraser, 478 U.S. 675, 681-683 (1986).

Yet the First Amendment is premised on the idea that there are many different but legitimate ways of understanding the world. How can that be squared with a system of public education that is designed to inculcate certain socially approved values? Public schools are operated and controlled by elected school boards, and therefore can be expected to reflect the needs and opinions of the society. What are the rights of those who dissent from the majority view?

As we saw in Section IV-B above, the Supreme Court long ago held that parents have the constitutional right to send their children to nonpublic schools, assuming those schools provide an adequate education. Pierce v. Society of Sisters, 268 U.S. 510 (1925). You should review *Pierce* (p. 366) and the notes accompanying it. As emphasized there, the role and legitimacy of nonpublic schooling has been a controversial issue for a century and a half, often mixed with tensions between Protestants and Roman Catholics.

After *Pierce*, the constitutional questions concerning private religious schools have been whether the state may provide them assistance (see Part IV), and how extensively the state may regulate them. The latter issue arises in the next case.

KENTUCKY STATE BOARD FOR ELEMENTARY AND SECONDARY EDUCATION v. RUDASILL
589 S.W.2d 877 (Ky. 1979)

LUKOWSKY, Justice.

This case requires us to establish the perimeter within which the Commonwealth may regulate the curriculum and instruction in private and parochial schools. The trial court held that the Commonwealth's textbook approval, teacher certification, and school accreditation requirements ... violated the first amendment to the federal constitution and section 5 of the Kentucky constitution. ...

This action was initiated by several pastors and their churches, parents of children enrolled in non-public schools of those churches, and the Kentucky Association of Christian Schools, Inc. [church schools]. The parties sought a declaratory judgment that the Commonwealth's standards for approval of private church schools were invalid. The church schools further sought and received below both temporary and permanent injunctive relief preventing the Commonwealth from imposing its approval standards upon the church schools and from prosecuting under the compulsory attendance laws, the church schools or the parents sending children to those schools. The church schools expressly recognized the state's interest in reasonable health, fire, and safety standards for those schools. ...

[State statutes and regulations] require that the church school teachers be certified and ... that textbooks used in the church schools be from the state list of approved textbooks. Attendance at church schools which are not so approved does not qualify the students there enrolled for the exemption from compulsory attendance in the public schools provided by [statute].

Section 5 of the Constitution of Kentucky provides in part "nor shall any man be compelled to send his child to any school to which he may be conscientiously opposed; ..."[2] [W]e have the history of section 5 and of this

2. "Sec. 5 Right of religious freedom.—No preference shall ever be given by law to any religious sect, society or denomination; nor to any particular creed, mode of worship or system of ecclesiastical polity; nor shall any person be compelled to attend any place of worship, to contribute to the erection or maintenance of any such place, or to the salary or support of any minister of religion;

clause to aid the court in divining the intent of the constitutional draftsmen. ....[3]

The Kentucky constitutions of 1792, 1799, and 1850 each contained a bill of rights which provided for religious liberty. The language of these sections remained virtually unchanged until the present constitution was adopted in 1891. The delegates to the Constitutional Convention of 1890 did not casually adopt verbatim the language of the bill of rights as it was found in the previous three Kentucky constitutions. Instead, . . . they drafted a comprehensive bill of rights for the new constitution. . . .

The language guaranteeing religious liberty in the Commonwealth reported by the Committee on Preamble and Bill of Rights did not include the clause "nor shall any man be compelled to send his child to any school to which he may be conscientiously opposed." The clause was specifically adopted by the convention and was the subject of comprehensive pointed debate.

[The primary] debate [was] between the advocates of "no man shall be compelled to send his child or children to any school" [hereinafter referred to as the Knott amendment] and of "no man shall be compelled to send his child to any school to which he may be conscientiously opposed" [hereinafter referred to as the Beckner amendment]. . . . [T]he convention adopted the Beckner language which is present in section 5.

The debate over section 5 centered on whether compulsory education should be constitutionally proscribed. The first seeds of intent were sown in the first debate:

> *Mr. Beckner.* As is well-known, there is a large element of a great religious organization, to which many persons in Kentucky belong, opposed to the American system of public schools. Their opposition arises from the fact that there is no religious instruction given in those schools. They are as conscientious in their opposition to those schools as I am in my belief in that system. I am anxious for this Convention to do whatever can be done to render our system of public schools acceptable to all our people. . . . This amendment simply provides that in the future there shall be no provision made requiring those who are conscientiously opposed to sending their children to public schools to do so. We do not know what may arise in the future in the zeal of those who come after us; and they may attempt to compel persons who are conscientiously opposed to the public schools to send their children to them, fixing pains and penalties for refusal.

Even at this early point in the exchange of ideas the Beckner amendment became the compromise position between those who would proscribe the concept of compulsory education and those who would leave the Commonwealth absolutely unfettered. . . .

The Beckner amendment represented the position that while the state has an interest in the education of its citizens which could be furthered through

---

nor shall any man be compelled to send his child to any school to which he may be conscientiously opposed; and the civil rights, privileges or capacities of no person shall be taken away, or in anywise diminished or enlarged, on account of his belief or disbelief of any religious tenet, dogma or teaching. No human authority shall, in any case whatever, control or interfere with the rights of conscience." (Emphasis added.)

3. We note at the outset that it is obvious that Section 5 of the Kentucky Constitution is more restrictive of the power of the state to regulate private and parochial schools than is the first amendment to the federal constitution as it has been applied to the states. See Wisconsin v. Yoder. . . .

compulsory education, the rights of conscience of those who desired education of their children in private and parochial schools should be protected. It was anticipated that without express protection of private and parochial education the state might try to prevent children from attending other than public schools. It must be recognized that this debate took place many years before the decision in Pierce v. Society of Sisters, which held the state could not require public school attendance to the exclusion of private and parochial schools. Obviously, the concern of the drafters of the Beckner amendment was well founded. . . .

Having concluded that the power to require universal education was not vitiated by the Beckner amendment to section 5, it becomes essential to identify the limits of this state power where the boundary between the state's interest in quality education and the individual's conscientious objection to public education is indistinct. May the Commonwealth control the manner in which private or parochial schools teach the young? Again, we look to the debates:

> *Mr. Beckner:* [M]y amendment simply says that those who have children shall not be required to send them to schools to which they may be conscientiously opposed. It does not hamper the Legislature in any way but allows it to provide that they shall send them to some school. . . . If it be the duty of the State to provide education for all its children, and to see that we have intelligent citizens, and to provide the means for becoming intelligent, then the State ought to be left free to see that the children are sent to schools.

The Beckner amendment supporters clearly intended that the legislature be allowed to compel attendance at some school, the choice of which the child's parents could make as a matter of conscience, but the purpose of which would be to educate children to be citizens. . . .

The use of the word "school" in its ordinary sense by the drafters also supports this conclusion: "In its ordinary meaning the word 'school' denotes a place for systematic instruction in any branch or branches of knowledge." City of Chicopee v. Jackubowski (Mass. 1964) . . . "A school the court holds to be an institution consisting of a teacher and pupils . . . gathered together for instruction in any branch of learning, the arts or the sciences." Benvenue PTA v. Nash Co. Bd. of Education (N.C. App. 1969). While the legislature could permit education in the home, it has not done so.

The light shed by the purpose of compulsory education expressed by the advocates of the Beckner amendment aids in the definition of the state's interest in private and parochial education. The delegates perceived that universal education might be required in order to prepare children of the Commonwealth to intelligently participate as citizens in a democracy, i.e., to exercise the elective franchise, but not to uniformly develop them socially and morally in the same educational mold.[9] . . .

We therefore conclude that the delegates in adopting the Beckner amendment intended to permit the Commonwealth to prepare its children to intelligently exercise the right of suffrage by compelling attendance at a formal school, public or private or parochial, for a legislatively determined period each year.

---

9. State controlled homogeneous schools have provided a fertile field for the growth of totalitarian governments. See, e.g., A. Hitler, Mein Kampf, Reynal & Hitchcock Ed. (1941).

The question now becomes to what extent does the state's interest in educating its citizens to vote in a democracy permit the Commonwealth to control "a school" outside of the free public system.

The [statutory scheme] provides that private and parochial schools shall (1) be taught in the English language; (2) "offer instruction in the several branches of study required to be taught in the public schools;" and (3) operate for a term not shorter than the public schools. From our examination of section 5, it is clear that [this] does not offend the bill of rights provided that the "several branches of study" are rationally related to the education of children to exercise their right of suffrage and to participate in the democratic system.[10]

The Commonwealth argues that the KRS 158.080 requirement to "offer instruction in the several branches of study" means that the "Instruments of instruction, such as teachers and books, be of reasonable Quality." Therefore, it is posited, the statute "clearly contemplates that standards may be prescribed . . . with which a school must comply in order to be approved." Section 5 does not allow the Commonwealth to reach this far.

It cannot be said as an absolute that a teacher in a non-public school who is not certified under KRS 161.030(2) will be unable to instruct children to become intelligent citizens. Certainly, the receipt of "a bachelor's degree from a standard college or university" is an indicator of the level of achievement, but it is not a sine qua non the absence of which establishes that private and parochial school teachers are unable to teach their students to intelligently exercise the elective franchise.

The Commonwealth's power to prescribe textbooks for use in private and parochial schools is likewise limited by Section 5. The textual materials used in the public schools are at the very heart of the conscientious opposition to those schools. To say that one may not be compelled to send a child to a public school but that the state may determine the basic texts to be used in the private or parochial schools is but to require that the same hay be fed in the field as is fed in the barn. Section 5 protects a diversified diet.

Pursuant to section 5 of the Constitution, the Commonwealth must "approve" a private or parochial school . . . unless it demonstrates the educational institution in question is not a "school" as contemplated by the constitutional convention or does not serve to educate the children of Kentucky to enjoy their right of suffrage. Insofar as 704 KAR 10.022 [the state regulation] applies the state accreditation standards to the private and parochial schools of Kentucky, it must fall.

If the legislature wishes to monitor the work of private and parochial schools in accomplishing the constitutional purpose of compulsory education, it may do so by an appropriate standardized achievement testing program. If the results show that one or more private or parochial schools have failed to reasonably accomplish the constitutional purpose, the Commonwealth may then withdraw approval and seek to close them for they no longer fulfill the purpose of "schools."

---

10. Obviously, such basic studies as reading, writing, spelling, grammar, history, mathematics and civics are so related. This is not to say that other subjects may not bear a more remote but still rational relationship.

NOTES AND QUESTIONS

1. Regulation of Religious Schools. With *Rudasill*, contrast Nebraska ex rel. Douglas v. Faith Baptist Church, 207 Neb. 802, 301 N.W.2d 571, appeal dismissed for want of a substantial federal question, 454 U.S. 803 (1981). In that case the Nebraska Supreme Court rejected a constitutional challenge to state accreditation requirements, including requirements that all teachers receive teaching certificates from the State Board of Education, that the school submit periodic reports to the State Board, and that the curriculum be approved by the State Board. The school employed some teachers who were ineligible for teaching certificates because they had not received baccalaureate degrees. The school also refused to submit its curriculum (a pervasively Bible-oriented, self-paced curriculum called PACE) for approval, despite assurances from state education officials that it would be approved, or to submit the periodic reports.

The school's position was "that the operation of the school is simply an extension of the ministry of the church, over which the State of Nebraska has no authority to approve or accredit." Moreover, the school contended that the State Board "is not capable of judging the philosophy of the defendant's school" and that they could not submit to inspections of the school "because the State has no right to inspect God's property."

The school submitted evidence that, as measured by standardized achievement tests, its students "were accomplishing the average amount of progress" for Nebraska students. Expert witnesses for the school testified that "the mere fact that a person held a baccalaureate degree"—one of the requirements for teacher certification—did not mean that he or she would be a good teacher.

The Nebraska Supreme Court upheld the accreditation requirements on the ground that they were "reasonable":

> We are not suggesting as an absolute that every person who has earned a baccalaureate degree in teaching is going to become a good teacher, any more than one who has obtained the appropriate training and education will become a good engineer, lawyer, beauty operator, welder, or pipefitter. However, we think it cannot fairly be disputed that such a requirement is neither arbitrary nor unreasonable; additionally, we believe it is also a reliable indicator of the probability of success in that particular field.

While agreeing with the "reasonableness" standard, Justice Krivosha dissented from the majority's result:

> Under our holding today, Eric Hoffer could not teach philosophy in a grade school, public or private . . . and Thomas Edison could not teach the theories of electricity. . . . The experience of time has failed to establish that requiring all teachers to earn a baccalaureate degree from anywhere results in providing children with a better education. While it may be appropriate for a state to set such requirements in a public school where state funds are expended, . . . I find no basis in law or fact for imposing a similar requirement in a private school.

The case received national attention when the pastor, Everett Sileven, refused to comply and was jailed as a result. State officials padlocked the church property to prevent the school from continuing to operate.

2. Problems.   Should the state be able to require that a religiously affiliated school:

(a) Teach evolution?

(b) Refrain from discriminating on the basis of sex or pregnancy in hiring teachers? See Dayton Christian Schools v. Ohio Civil Rights Comm'n, 766 F.2d 932 (6th Cir. 1985) (dismissal of pregnant teacher based on religious belief that mothers of young children should not work), rev'd on other grounds, 477 U.S. 619 (1986).

(c) Teach patriotism? Shortly after September 11, 2001, a newspaper story described an Islamic high school in America whose principal taught students vitriolic criticism of Israel (a "cursed population," according to an article by him in the school newsletter) and of American support for Israel. Marc Fisher, Muslim Students Weigh Questions of Allegiance, Wash. Post., Oct. 16, 2001, at B1. Suppose a teacher taught students that the September 11 attacks, or armed *jihad* against the United States, were good things. Could the government prohibit such teaching?

WISCONSIN v. YODER
406 U.S. 205 (1972)

[The basic facts of *Yoder* are set forth at p. 133. Members of the Old Order Amish religion refused to send their children to public or private school once the children reached age 14. The parents were fined $5 each for violating the state law requiring school attendance until age 16.]

Mr. Chief Justice BURGER delivered the opinion of the Court.

. . . The trial testimony showed that respondents believed, in accordance with the tenets of Old Order Amish communities generally, that their children's attendance at high school, public or private, was contrary to the Amish religion and way of life. They believed that by sending their children to high school, they would not only expose themselves to the danger of the censure of the church community, but, as found by the county court, also endanger their own salvation and that of their children. The State stipulated that respondents' religious beliefs were sincere.

. . . The history of the Amish sect was given in some detail, beginning with the Swiss Anabaptists of the 16th century who rejected institutionalized churches and sought to return to the early, simple, Christian life de-emphasizing material success, rejecting the competitive spirit, and seeking to insulate themselves from the modern world. As a result of their common heritage, Old Order Amish communities today are characterized by a fundamental belief that salvation requires life in a church community separate and apart from the world and worldly influence. This concept of life aloof from the world and its values is central to their faith.

A related feature of Old Order Amish communities is their devotion to a life in harmony with nature and the soil, as exemplified by the simple life of the early Christian era that continued in America during much of our early national life. Amish beliefs require members of the community to make their living by farming or closely related activities. Broadly speaking, the Old Order

Amish religion pervades and determines the entire mode of life of its adherents. Their conduct is regulated in great detail by the Ordnung, or rules, of the church community. Adult baptism, which occurs in late adolescence, is the time at which Amish young people voluntarily undertake heavy obligations, not unlike the Bar Mitzvah of the Jews, to abide by the rules of the church community. . . .

Formal high school education beyond the eighth grade is contrary to Amish beliefs, not only because it places Amish children in an environment hostile to Amish beliefs with increasing emphasis on competition in class work and sports and with pressure to conform to the styles, manners, and ways of the peer group, but also because it takes them away from their community, physically and emotionally, during the crucial and formative adolescent period of life. During this period, the children must acquire Amish attitudes favoring manual work and self-reliance and the specific skills needed to perform the adult role of an Amish farmer or housewife. They must learn to enjoy physical labor. Once a child has learned basic reading, writing, and elementary mathematics, these traits, skills, and attitudes admittedly fall within the category of those best learned through example and "doing" rather than in a classroom. And, at this time in life, the Amish child must also grow in his faith and his relationship to the Amish community if he is to be prepared to accept the heavy obligations imposed by adult baptism. In short, high school attendance with teachers who are not of the Amish faith—and may even be hostile to it—interposes a serious barrier to the integration of the Amish child into the Amish religious community. Dr. John Hostetler, one of the experts on Amish society, testified that the modern high school is not equipped, in curriculum or social environment, to impart the values promoted by Amish society.

The Amish do not object to elementary education through the first eight grades as a general proposition because they agree that their children must have basic skills in the 'three R's' in order to read the Bible, to be good farmers and citizens, and to be able to deal with non-Amish people when necessary in the course of daily affairs. They view such a basic education as acceptable because it does not significantly expose their children to worldly values or interfere with their development in the Amish community during the crucial adolescent period. While Amish accept compulsory elementary education generally, wherever possible they have established their own elementary schools in many respects like the small local schools of the past. In the Amish belief higher learning tends to develop values they reject as influences that alienate man from God. . . .

There is no doubt as to the power of a State, having a high responsibility for education of its citizens, to impose reasonable regulations for the control and duration of basic education. See, e.g., Pierce v. Society of Sisters. Providing public schools ranks at the very apex of the function of a State. Yet even this paramount responsibility was, in *Pierce*, made to yield to the right of parents to provide an equivalent education in a privately operated system. . . . As that case suggests, the values of parental direction of the religious upbringing and education of their children in their early and formative years have a high place in our society. . . .

It follows that in order for Wisconsin to compel school attendance beyond the eighth grade against a claim that such attendance interferes with the practice of a legitimate religious belief, it must appear either that the State does not deny the free exercise of religious belief by its requirement, or that there is a state interest of sufficient magnitude to override the interest claiming protection under the Free Exercise Clause. Long before there was general acknowledgment of the need for universal formal education, the Religion Clauses had specifically and firmly fixed the right to free exercise of religious beliefs. . . .

. . . [O]nly those interests of the highest order and those not otherwise served can overbalance legitimate claims to the free exercise of religion. . . . E.g., Sherbert v. Verner.

II

We come then to the quality of the claims of the respondents. . . . [W]e must be careful to determine whether the Amish religious faith and their mode of life are, as they claim, inseparable and interdependent. A way of life, however virtuous and admirable, may not be interposed as a barrier to reasonable state regulation of education if it is based on purely secular considerations; to have the protection of the Religion Clauses, the claims must be rooted in religious belief. . . . Thus, if the Amish asserted their claims because of their subjective evaluation and rejection of the contemporary secular values accepted by the majority, much as Thoreau rejected the social values of his time and isolated himself at Walden Pond, their claims would not rest on a religious basis. Thoreau's choice was philosophical and personal rather than religious, and such belief does not rise to the demands of the Religion Clauses.

. . . [T]he record in this case abundantly supports the claim that the traditional way of life of the Amish is not merely a matter of personal preference, but one of deep religious conviction, shared by an organized group, and intimately related to daily living. That the Old Order Amish daily life and religious practice stem from their faith is shown by the fact that it is in response to their literal interpretation of the Biblical injunction from the Epistle of Paul to the Romans, "be not conformed to this world. . . . " This command is fundamental to the Amish faith. Moreover, for the Old Order Amish, religion is not simply a matter of theocratic belief. As the expert witnesses explained, the Old Order Amish religion pervades and determines virtually their entire way of life, regulating it with the detail of the Talmudic diet through the strictly enforced rules of the church community.

The record shows that the respondents' religious beliefs and attitude toward life, family, and home have remained constant—perhaps some would say static—in a period of unparalleled progress in human knowledge generally and great changes in education. The respondents freely concede, and indeed assert as an article of faith, that their religious beliefs and what we would today call "life style" have not altered in fundamentals for centuries. Their way of life in a church-oriented community, separated from the outside world and "worldly" influences, their attachment to nature and the soil, is a way inherently simple and uncomplicated, albeit difficult to preserve against the pressure to conform. Their rejection of telephones, automobiles, radios, and television, their mode of dress, of speech, their habits of manual work do indeed set them apart from much of contemporary society; these customs are both symbolic and practical.

As the society around the Amish has become more populous, urban, industrialized, and complex, particularly in this century, government regulation of human affairs has correspondingly become more detailed and pervasive. The

Amish mode of life has thus come into conflict increasingly with requirements of contemporary society exerting a hydraulic insistence on conformity to major-itarian standards. . . . The conclusion is inescapable that secondary schooling, by exposing Amish children to worldly influences in terms of attitudes, goals, and values contrary to beliefs, and by substantially interfering with the religious development of the Amish child and his integration into the way of life of the Amish faith community at the crucial adolescent stage of development, contra-venes the basic religious tenets and practice of the Amish faith, both as to the parent and the child. . . .

III

[W]e turn, then, to the State's broader contention that its interest in its system of compulsory education is so compelling that even the established religious practices of the Amish must give way. . . . The State advances two primary arguments in support of its system of compulsory education. It notes, as Thomas Jefferson pointed out early in our history, that some degree of educa-tion is necessary to prepare citizens to participate effectively and intelligently in our open political system if we are to preserve freedom and independence. Further, education prepares individuals to be self-reliant and self-sufficient participants in society. We accept these propositions.

However, the evidence adduced by the Amish in this case is persuasively to the effect that an additional one or two years of formal high school for Amish children in place of their long-established program of informal vocational edu-cation would do little to serve those interests. Respondents' experts testified at trial, without challenge, that the value of all education must be assessed in terms of its capacity to prepare the child for life. It is one thing to say that compulsory education for a year or two beyond the eighth grade may be necessary when its goal is the preparation of the child for life in modern society as the majority live, but it is quite another if the goal of education be viewed as the preparation of the child for life in the separated agrarian community that is the keystone of the Amish faith.

The State attacks respondents' position as one fostering "ignorance" from which the child must be protected by the State. No one can question the State's duty to protect children from ignorance but this argument does not square with the facts disclosed in the record. Whatever their idiosyncrasies as seen by the majority, this record strongly shows that the Amish community has been a highly successful social unit within our society, even if apart from the conventional "mainstream." Its members are productive and very law-abiding members of society; they reject public welfare in any of its usual modern forms. The Congress itself recognized their self-sufficiency by authorizing exemption of such groups as the Amish from the obligation to pay social security taxes. . . .

The State, however, supports its interest in providing an additional one or two years of compulsory high school education to Amish children because of the possibility that some such children will choose to leave the Amish community, and that if this occurs they will be ill-equipped for life. . . . However, on this record, that argument is highly speculative. There is no specific evidence of the loss of Amish adherents by attrition, nor is there any showing that upon leaving the Amish community Amish children, with their practical agricultural training and habits of industry and self-reliance, would become burdens on society because of educational shortcomings. Indeed, this argument of the State appears to rest primarily on the State's mistaken assumption, already noted, that the Amish do not provide any education for their children beyond the eighth grade, but allow them to grow in "ignorance." To the contrary, [the Amish] continue to provide what has been characterized by the undisputed testimony of expert educators as an "ideal" vocational education for their children in the adolescent years.

There is nothing in this record to suggest that the Amish qualities of reliability, self-reliance, and dedication to work would fail to find ready markets in today's society. . . . [N]or is there any basis in the record to warrant a finding that an additional one or two years of formal school education beyond the eighth grade would serve to eliminate any such problem that might exist. . . .

IV

[Wisconsin] argues that a decision exempting Amish children from the State's requirement fails to recognize the substantive right of the Amish child to a secondary education, and fails to give due regard to the power of the State as parens patriae to extend the benefit of secondary education to children regardless of the wishes of their parents. [But it] is the parents who are subject to prosecution here for failing to cause their children to attend school, and it is their right of free exercise, not that of their children, that must determine Wisconsin's power to impose criminal penalties on the parent. The dissent argues that a child who expresses a desire to attend public high school in conflict with the wishes of his parents should not be prevented from doing so. There is no reason for the Court to consider that point since it is not an issue in the case. The children are not parties to this litigation. The State has at no point tried this case on the theory that respondents were preventing their children from attending school against their expressed desires, and indeed the record is to the contrary.[21] . . .

Our holding in no way determines the proper resolution of possible competing interests of parents, children, and the State in an appropriate state court proceeding in which the power of the State is asserted on the theory that Amish parents are preventing their minor children from attending high school despite their expressed desires to the contrary. Recognition of the claim of the State in such a proceeding would, of course, call into question traditional concepts of parental control over the religious upbringing and education of their minor children recognized in this Court's past decisions. It is clear that such an intrusion by a State into family decisions in the area of religious training would give rise to grave questions of religious freedom comparable to those raised here and those presented in Pierce v. Society of Sisters. On this record we neither reach nor decide those issues.

The State's argument proceeds without reliance on any actual conflict between the wishes of parents and children. It appears to rest on the potential that exemption of Amish parents from the requirements of the compulsory-

---

21. . . . [T]he wishes of the one child who testified corresponded with those of her parents. . . . Frieda Yoder [testified] that her personal religious beliefs guided her decision to discontinue school attendance after the eighth grade. The other children were not called by either side.

education law might allow some parents to act contrary to the best interests of their children by foreclosing their opportunity to make an intelligent choice between the Amish way of life and that of the outside world. The same argument could, of course, be made with respect to all church schools short of college. There is nothing in the record or in the ordinary course of human experience to suggest that non-Amish parents generally consult with children of ages 14-16 if they are placed in a church school of the parents' faith.

Indeed it seems clear that if the State is empowered, as parens patriae, to "save" a child from himself or his Amish parents by requiring an additional two years of compulsory formal high school education, the State will in large measure influence, if not determine, the religious future of the child. . . . [T]his case involves the fundamental interest of parents, as contrasted with that of the State, to guide the religious future and education of their children. . . .

V

. . . [T]he Amish in this case have convincingly demonstrated the sincerity of their religious beliefs, the interrelationship of belief with their mode of life, the vital role that belief and daily conduct play in the continued survival of Old Order Amish communities and their religious organization, and the hazards presented by the State's enforcement of a statute generally valid as to others. Beyond this, they have carried the even more difficult burden of demonstrating the adequacy of their alternative mode of continuing informal vocational education in terms of precisely those overall interests that the State advances in support of its program of compulsory high school education. In light of this convincing showing, one that probably few other religious groups or sects could make, and weighing the minimal difference between what the State would require and what the Amish already accept, it was incumbent on the State to show with more particularity how its admittedly strong interest in compulsory education would be adversely affected by granting an exemption to the Amish. . . .

Mr. Justice DOUGLAS, dissenting in part.

I agree with the Court that the religious scruples of the Amish are opposed to the education of their children beyond the grade schools, yet I disagree with the Court's conclusion that the matter is within the dispensation of parents alone. . . .

. . . If the parents in this case are allowed a religious exemption, the inevitable effect is to impose the parents' notions of religious duty upon their children. Where the child is mature enough to express potentially conflicting desires, it would be an invasion of the child's rights to permit such an imposition without canvassing his views. . . .

Religion is an individual experience. It is not necessary, nor even appropriate, for every Amish child to express his views on the subject in a prosecution of a single adult. Crucial, however, are the views of the child whose parent is the subject of the suit. Frieda Yoder has in fact testified that her own religious views are opposed to high-school education. I therefore join the judgment of the Court as to respondent Jonas Yoder. But Frieda Yoder's views may not be those of Vernon Yutzy or Barbara Miller. I must dissent, therefore, as to respondents Adin Yutzy and Wallace Miller. . . .

... Our opinions are full of talk about the power of the parents over the child's education. See *Pierce*; Meyer v. Nebraska (1923). And [yet] the education of the child is a matter on which the child will often have decided views. He may want to be a pianist or an astronaut or an oceanographer. To do so he will have to break from the Amish tradition.

It is the future of the student, not the future of the parents, that is imperiled by today's decision. If a parent keeps his child out of school beyond the grade school, then the child will be forever barred from entry into the new and amazing world of diversity that we have today. The child may decide that that is the preferred course, or he may rebel. It is the student's judgment, not his parents', that is essential if we are to give full meaning to what we have said about the Bill of Rights and of the right of students to be masters of their own destiny. If he is harnessed to the Amish way of life by those in authority over him and if his education is truncated, his entire life may be stunted and deformed. The child, therefore, should be given an opportunity to be heard before the State gives the exemption which we honor today.

NOTES AND QUESTIONS

1. Who Decides for the Child?   *Yoder* and other cases about private or home schooling can be thought of as questions about who decides what education a child will receive.

(a) The child?   Generally we let adults make significant life choices such as education and career for themselves. But children are different. Is it wise or feasible to recognize the children themselves as having the constitutional right to determine their education and upbringing? What if they choose the easy path of few demands and little work?

(b) The parents?   Why should the parents have a free exercise right to control the education of their children? Isn't Justice Douglas right: Doesn't that have the effect of limiting and controlling the children's range of options, with respect to religion and everything else? What are the limits on this freedom?

(c) The government?   If children are implausible repositories of constitutional authority, and if parents are imperfect, does that imply that the government should have a controlling hand in directing the upbringing of children? What are the advantages and disadvantages of governmental control versus parental control? For vigorous arguments in favor of parental control, see Stephen G. Gilles, On Educating Children: A Parentalist Manifesto, 63 U. Chi. L. Rev. 937 (1996); Stephen G. Gilles, Liberal Parentalism and Children's Educational Rights, 26 Capital U. L. Rev. 9 (1997); John H. Garvey, What Are Freedoms For? ch. 7 (1996). For a vigorous argument in favor of governmental control, see James Dwyer, Religious Schools Versus Children's Rights (1998).

What about a "balance of power" in which both parents and government have some control over the child's upbringing and education, in the hope that each will offer the child something distinctive and will check abuses by the other? See, e.g., Ira C. Lupu, The Separation of Powers and the Protection of Children, 61 U. Chi. L. Rev. 1317 (1994). Is that an attractive model? If so, what kind of educational system does it suggest? Is this a potential explanation for why America allows private schools but favors public schools through financial support and other means?

2. Home Schooling. Lupu argues, using his model of checking parental authority, that home schooling by parents should be more restricted than should attendance at private schools. *Id.* at 1353-1359. (Can you see why?) That too was a common reaction of state education regulators in the 1970s and 1980s when the number of home-schooling families began to increase substantially. Several states effectively barred home schooling for many parents by requiring that any teacher qualified under the state compulsory education laws be state-certified and/or have a college degree. Home-schooling families had only limited success in challenging such regulations in court, but they were much more successful in getting legislatures to accommodate them by statute. See Neal Devins, Fundamentalist Christian Educators v. State: An Inevitable Compromise, 60 Geo. Wash. L. Rev. 818 (1992). One court success for home schoolers came in Michigan, where the state supreme court struck down the state's teacher certification requirement as applied to home schoolers on the ground that (among other things) statistics showed no difference in students' performance because of teacher certification. People v. deJonge, 442 Mich. 266, 501 N.W.2d 127, 144 (1993). Earlier, however, the same court had refused to exempt private religious schools from the teacher certification requirement. Sheridan Road Baptist Church v. Department of Educ., 396 N.W.2d 373 (Mich. 1986). Are these two decisions consistent?

3. Religious Versus Secular Educational Rights. *Yoder* indicated that religious objections to the state's educational requirements have greater constitutional weight than secular objections, for example, those of a follower of Thoreau. This is one answer of the general question (see Part III) whether the Constitution gives special protection to religiously grounded conduct. Some states accord considerable freedom to all home-schooling parents; others give greater freedom to those who home-school for religious reasons. Which system is more consistent with First Amendment values?

7. Sunday Closing Laws

Of the laws given to Moses on Mt. Sinai, the third (or the fourth—there are two ways of counting) was this:

> Remember the Sabbath day, to keep it holy. Six days you shall labor, and do all your work; but the seventh day is a Sabbath to the Lord your God; in it you shall not do any work, you, or your son, or your daughter, your manservant, or your maidservant, or your cattle, or the sojourner who is within your gates; for in six days the Lord made heaven and earth, the sea, and all that is in them, and rested the seventh day; therefore the Lord blessed the Sabbath day and hallowed it.

Exodus 20:8-11. This command is still widely observed in America, though our legal system is not theocratic and our society is not predominantly Jewish. In our observance of the Sabbath, we sometimes distinguish between the religious overtones of the obligation and the natural human desire for periodic rest. We can see both strains in the history of the practice.

The most important step in translating the command of Exodus to our culture was the Christian adoption of the Sabbath sometime around the second century. Christians met each week to pray, read the scriptures, and dine together in the manner of the Jewish Sabbath—on the first day of the week rather than the last, because that was the day of Jesus's resurrection. The Christian focus was on worship rather than rest from labor, and this was a religious obligation, not a civil one. In the fourth century there arose an independent rule of Roman law that Sunday should be observed as a day of rest. Constantine decreed in 321 that city people and craftsmen should rest on "the venerable day of the sun"—a holiday observed by the popular Mithraist cult. The religious practice of worship and the civil practice of rest converged as the empire became officially Christian. Willy Rordorf, Sunday 154-173 (1968); Leo Pfeffer, Church, State, and Freedom 270-271 (1967).

In the seventeenth century, religious Sunday observance was an established practice in England, supported by the Church of England and Puritan dissenters alike. Both brought it to the colonies. The earliest American law on the subject, in Virginia in 1610, required church attendance but said nothing about rest:

> Every man and woman shall repair in the morning to the divine service and sermons preached upon the Sabbath day, and in the afternoon to divine service, and catechising, upon pain for the first fault to lose their provision and the allowance for the whole week following; for the second, to lose the said allowance and also be whipped; and for the third to suffer death.

William Blakely, American State Papers Bearing on Sunday Legislation 33 (1970). But there grew up alongside such rules of compulsory worship, in Virginia and elsewhere, rules about rest on Sunday. Massachusetts in 1650 punished anyone who "profane[d] the Lord's day by doing any servile work" with a fine of ten shillings or a whipping. *Id.* at 36. At the end of the eighteenth century, out of concern for religious liberty, states began to repeal their church attendance laws. They left in place their Sunday closing laws properly speaking—the restrictions on work and play, which, it was said, served secular as well as religious interests. Here is how Massachusetts justified its law in 1797:

> [T]he observance of the Lord's day is highly promotive of the welfare of a community, by affording necessary seasons for relaxation from labor and the cares of business; for moral reflections and conversation on the duties of life, and the frequent errors of human conduct; for public and private worship of the Maker, Governor and Judge of the world; and for those acts of charity which support and adorn a Christian society[.]

Support for Sunday closing began to erode in the nineteenth century, partly for commercial reasons. Travel (eventually on trains) became more feasible, and this stimulated related businesses such as hotels and restaurants. More stores sold more manufactured goods. Public amusements (baseball!) became a popular pastime. Those who ran these businesses, and their customers, liked Sunday sales. But the traditional rules still had support in several quarters. One was religious sabbatarians. Another was organized labor: Unions favored Sunday closing as a way of shortening the work week. Thus Justice Field wrote in 1885: "Laws setting aside Sunday as a day of rest are upheld, not from any right of the government to legislate for the promotion of religious observances, but from its right to protect all persons from the physical and moral debasement which comes from uninterrupted labor." Soon Hing v. Crowley, 113 U.S. 703, 710 (1885). See Alan Raucher, Sunday Business and the Decline of Sunday Closing Laws: A Historical Overview, 36 J. Church & State 13, 15-16 (1994).

As the cultural consensus behind blue laws[*] dissolved, some were repealed. Where that did not happen, opponents of the laws went to court—a possibility that opened up on the federal level after the Free Exercise Clause and the Establishment Clause were applied to the states in the 1940s. But the laws survived challenges under both clauses.

McGOWAN v. MARYLAND
366 U.S. 420 (1961)

Mr. Chief Justice WARREN delivered the opinion of the Court.

Appellants are seven employees of a large discount department store located on a highway in Anne Arundel County, Maryland. They were indicted for the Sunday sale of a three-ring loose-leaf binder, a can of floor wax, a stapler and staples, and a toy submarine in violation of Md. Ann. Code, Art. 27, § 521. Generally, this section prohibited, throughout the State, the Sunday sale of all merchandise except the retail sale of tobacco products, confectioneries, milk, bread, fruits, gasoline, oils, greases, drugs and medicines, and newspapers and periodicals. Recently amended, this section also now excepts from the general prohibition the retail sale in Anne Arundel County of all foodstuffs, automobile and boating accessories, flowers, toilet goods, hospital supplies and souvenirs. It now further provides that any retail establishment in Anne Arundel County which does not employ more than one person other than the owner may operate on Sunday. . . . Appellants were convicted and each was fined five dollars and costs. . . .

Appellants argue that the Maryland statutes violate the "Equal Protection" Clause of the Fourteenth Amendment [because the classifications] concerning which commodities may or may not be sold on Sunday are without rational and substantial relation to the object of the legislation. [This claim is without merit.] The constitutional safeguard is offended only if the classification rests on grounds wholly irrelevant to the achievement of the State's objective. State legislatures are presumed to have acted within their constitutional power despite the fact that, in practice, their laws result in some inequality. A statutory discrimination will not be set aside if any state of facts reasonably may be conceived to justify it.

It would seem that a legislature could reasonably find that the Sunday sale of the exempted commodities was necessary either for the health of the populace or for the enhancement of the recreational atmosphere of the day—that a family which takes a Sunday ride into the country will need gasoline for the automobile and may find pleasant a soft drink or fresh fruit; . . . that newspapers and drug products should always be available to the public. . . .

---

[*] Sunday closing laws are sometimes referred to as to as "blue laws," though it is not clear why. One theory is that the term refers to the color of the paper that the New Haven colony printed its first legal code on in 1665. Another is that the term implies a kind of Puritanical strictness. The expression "true blue" betokens constancy and fidelity, and during the reign of Charles II it became a term of reproach, signifying that one had a little too much of those virtues. David Laband and Deborah Heinbuch, Blue Laws 8 (1987).

The final questions for decision are whether the Maryland Sunday Closing Laws conflict with the Federal Constitution's provisions for religious liberty. First, appellants contend here that the statutes ... prohibit the free exercise of religion in contravention of the First Amendment[.] But appellants allege only economic injury to themselves; they do not allege any infringement of their own religious freedoms due to Sunday closing. In fact, the record is silent as to what appellants' religious beliefs are. Since the general rule is that "a litigant may only assert his own constitutional rights or immunities," we hold that appellants have no standing to raise this contention. . . .

Secondly, appellants contend that the statutes violate the guarantee of separation of church and state in that the statutes are laws respecting an establishment of religion contrary to the First Amendment, made applicable to the States by the Fourteenth Amendment. If the purpose of the "establishment" clause was only to insure protection for the "free exercise" of religion, then what we have said above concerning appellants' standing to raise the "free exercise" contention would appear to be true here. However, the writings of Madison, who was the First Amendment's architect, demonstrate that the establishment of a religion was equally feared because of its tendencies to political tyranny and subversion of civil authority. [Memorial and Remonstrance ¶8.]

The essence of appellants' "establishment" argument is that Sunday is the Sabbath day of the predominant Christian sects; that the purpose of the enforced stoppage of labor on that day is to facilitate and encourage church attendance; that the purpose of setting Sunday as a day of universal rest is to induce people with no religion or people with marginal religious beliefs to join the predominant Christian sects; that the purpose of the atmosphere of tranquility created by Sunday closing is to aid the conduct of church services and religious observance of the sacred day. . . . There is no dispute that the original laws which dealt with Sunday labor were motivated by religious forces. But what we must decide is whether present Sunday legislation, having undergone extensive changes from the earliest forms, still retains its religious character. . . .

The American colonial Sunday restrictions arose soon after settlement. Starting in 1650, the Plymouth Colony proscribed servile work, unnecessary traveling, sports, and the sale of alcoholic beverages on the Lord's day and enacted laws concerning church attendance. The Massachusetts Bay Colony and the Connecticut and New Haven Colonies enacted similar prohibitions, some even earlier in the seventeenth century. The religious orientation of the colonial statutes was equally apparent. For example, a 1629 Massachusetts Bay instruction began, "And to the end the Sabbath may be celebrated in a religious manner. . . . "

But, despite the strongly religious origin of these laws, beginning before the eighteenth century, nonreligious arguments for Sunday closing began to be heard more distinctly and the statutes began to lose some of their totally religious flavor. In the middle 1700's, Blackstone wrote, "[T]he keeping one day in the seven holy, as a time of relaxation and refreshment as well as for public worship, is of admirable service to a state considered merely as a civil institution. It humanizes, by the help of conversation and society, the manners of the lower classes; which would otherwise degenerate into a sordid ferocity and savage selfishness of spirit; it enables the industrious workman to pursue his occupation in the ensuing week with health and cheerfulness." 4 Bl. Comm. 63. . . .

More recently, further secular justifications have been advanced for making Sunday a day of rest, a day when people may recover from the labors of the week just passed and may physically and mentally prepare for the week's work to come. In England, during the First World War, a committee investigating the health conditions of munitions workers reported that "if the maximum output is to be secured and maintained for any length of time, a weekly period of rest must be allowed. . . . On economic and social grounds alike this weekly period of rest is best provided on Sunday." . . .

[The Establishment] Clause does not ban federal or state regulation of conduct whose reason or effect merely happens to coincide or harmonize with the tenets of some or all religions. In many instances, the Congress or state legislatures conclude that the general welfare of society, wholly apart from any religious considerations, demands such regulation. Thus, for temporal purposes, murder is illegal. And the fact that this agrees with the dictates of the Judaeo-Christian religions while it may disagree with others does not invalidate the regulation. So too with the questions of adultery and polygamy. Davis v. Beason; Reynolds v. United States. The same could be said of theft, fraud, etc., because those offenses were also proscribed in the Decalogue. . . .

In light of the evolution of our Sunday Closing Laws through the centuries, and of their more or less recent emphasis upon secular considerations, it is not difficult to discern that as presently written and administered, most of them, at least, are of a secular rather than of a religious character, and that presently they bear no relationship to establishment of religion as those words are used in the Constitution of the United States. . . .

We now reach the Maryland statutes under review. The title of the major series of sections of the Maryland Code dealing with Sunday closing—Art. 27, §§ 492-534C—is "Sabbath Breaking"; § 492 proscribes work or bodily labor on the "Lord's day," and forbids persons to "profane the Lord's day" by gaming, fishing et cetera; § 522 refers to Sunday as the "Sabbath day." [M]any of the exempted Sunday activities in the various localities of the State may only be conducted during the afternoon and late evening; most Christian church services, of course, are held on Sunday morning and early Sunday evening. [C]ertain localities do not permit the allowed Sunday activities to be carried on within one hundred yards of any church where religious services are being held. This is the totality of the evidence of religious purpose which may be gleaned from the face of the present statute and from its operative effect. [And there is evidence pointing in the other direction. Although § 492 talks of profaning the Lord's day,] other sections permit the activities previously thought to be profane. Prior denunciation of Sunday drunkenness is now gone. Contemporary concern with these statutes is evidenced by the dozen changes made in 1959 and by the recent enactment of a majority of the exceptions. . . .

But this does not answer all of appellants' contentions. We are told that the State has other means at its disposal to accomplish its secular purpose, other courses that would not even remotely or incidentally give state aid to religion. . . . However relevant this argument may be, we believe that the factual basis on which it rests is not supportable. It is true that if the State's interest were simply to provide for its citizens a periodic respite from work, a regulation demanding that everyone rest one day in seven, leaving the choice of the day to the individual, would suffice.

However, the State's purpose is not merely to provide a one-day-in-seven work stoppage. In addition to this, the State seeks to set one day apart from all others as a day of rest, repose, recreation and tranquility—a day which all members of the family and community have the opportunity to spend and enjoy together, a day on which there exists relative quiet and disassociation from the everyday intensity of commercial activities, a day on which people may visit friends and relatives who are not available during working days. . . . It would seem unrealistic for enforcement purposes and perhaps detrimental to the general welfare to require a State to choose a common day of rest other than that which most persons would select of their own accord. For these reasons, we hold that the Maryland statutes are not laws respecting an establishment of religion.[22]

NOTES AND QUESTIONS

1. The Current State of Affairs.   Nowadays Sunday closing laws are threatened more by legislatures than by courts. When *McGowan* was decided in 1961, 34 states had general Sunday closing laws, and all but three states restricted Sunday activities in some way. (The most common was, and is, a limit on the sale of alcohol.) Today Sunday restrictions exist in fewer than half the states. Some make them a local option. Closing laws are most common in the east and south, least in the west. Where they do exist, they are, as *McGowan* illustrates, riddled with exceptions. David Laband and Deborah Heinbuch, Blue Laws 47-137 (1987).

2. Secular Purpose.   Once again, as in the school prayer and curriculum cases, the crucial question is whether Sunday closing laws have a religious or secular purpose. The appellants in *McGowan* said the law was designed to encourage church attendance, get people to join Christian sects, and aid the conduct of church services. What evidence was there for this conclusion? What contrary evidence? Is the purpose question one of historical fact (what were the motives or intentions of those who enacted the law)? What did the Court say in Wallace v. Jaffree (p. 496) and Epperson v. Arkansas (p. 548)? *McGowan* concedes "that the original laws which dealt with Sunday labor were motivated by religious forces." Can that purpose have changed? How? Can we say that the old law has a new purpose because secular justifications now discourage the legislature from repealing it?

What light do the recent amendments to the Maryland law cast on its purpose? Did amendments to some parts of the law impart a new purpose to the whole thing? Why would the state make a special exception for "any retail establishment in Anne Arundel County which does not employ more than one person other than the owner?" Does Maryland's willingness to make such an exception show that it has abandoned the religious purposes alleged by the appellees?

In addition to attacking the purpose of the law, appellants claimed that Maryland had other means at its disposal that would have given less aid to religion, and that the Establishment Clause obliged the state to use those means. Why does the Court reject this claim? Have you seen such an argument before?

---

22. The Constitution itself provides for a Sunday exception in the calculation of the ten days for presidential veto. U.S. Const., Art. I, § 7.

Where? In free exercise cases before Employment Division v. Smith, there was a "less restrictive alternative" requirement. But *McGowan* is an Establishment Clause case, and appellants are urging the use of a "less beneficial alternative." If the state really has a secular purpose, why should we try to minimize the benefit that its laws confer (incidentally) on religion?

NOTE ON ACCOMMODATING SABBATH OBSERVERS

In addition to the question of the permissibility of Sunday closing laws, related issues have arisen concerning the accommodation of those who observe the Sabbath on a day when government or private businesses are operating (whether that is Saturday, Sunday, or another day). These issues have been considered earlier in this book; you may wish to refer back to them as you consider the questions below.

1. Free Exercise Exemptions from Sunday Closing Laws. Braunfeld v. Brown (p. 176) rejected a free exercise claim for exemption from a Sunday closing law, brought by business owners who closed on Saturday for their Sabbath and who therefore were put at an economic disadvantage by the law. Review *Braunfeld* and the notes following it, especially note 2 on p. 179 (discussing whether Sunday closing laws impose a significant burden on Saturday worshipers).

2. Is Accommodation for Sabbath Observers Unconstitutional Favoritism? Recall Estate of Thornton v. Caldor, 472 U.S. 703 (1985) (p. 7), in which the Court struck down a Connecticut law giving employees the absolute right to designate their Sabbath as a day off. Why did the Court hold that the law violated the Establishment Clause? Consider the following issues:

(a) Exempting religion from private constraints. If we begin with a traditional Sunday closing law, Connecticut's law giving employees their Sabbath off represents a liberalizing trend. The traditional law gives less protection to religious liberty at a higher cost: It offers no help to employees who observe the Sabbath on some day other than Sunday, and it requires employers to shut down altogether for one day out of seven. Connecticut's law gave everyone a day off, and extended to Jews, Muslims, and Seventh Day Adventists the Sabbath relief that mainline Christian groups always had. And the law accomplished this at a lower cost to employers: It allowed them to stay open every day (though they would naturally have to pay more for Sunday workers because Sabbath observance creates a labor shortage). Why was this an establishment of religion? Was it because the law made employers pay more for labor than they would have done in an unregulated market, and did so for religious reasons? Was it because the law imposed a new cost on nonreligious employees—when it came to choosing days off they now got second pick? Does the First Amendment allow the government to intrude on these private dealings and resolve them in favor of the religious actor? Can it justify this action as an effort to promote religious freedom? Or is that freedom merely a freedom from *government* constraints? Compare Pruneyard Shopping Center v. Robins, 447 U.S. 74 (1980) (government can order private property owner to admit third-party speakers). Does the Establishment Clause give the government less room to promote religious freedom than it has to promote freedom of speech?

What really bothered the Court? Was it that the law forced some people to pay for a religious practice that they disagreed with? Or was it that the law would give us more sabbatarianism than we would ordinarily have? What is the normal amount? Was the benefit that this law conferred valuable enough to induce people to join Sabbath-observing churches? Would it induce preexisting members to become more observant? Is the elimination of private obstacles to the practice of religion consistent with the idea that government should remain neutral in such matters?

(b) **What now?**   Suppose Thornton had waited to be fired (rather than quit) for refusing to work on his Sabbath. Under Sherbert v. Verner, Connecticut is required to pay him unemployment compensation so that he can stick by his principles. Not only Connecticut but also Caldor, Inc., would have to pay under this scenario. When a company lays off an employee and he draws unemployment compensation, the company's contribution rate to the unemployment compensation fund goes up. But under *Thornton*, Connecticut is forbidden to protect itself against this financial drain by making it illegal to fire Thornton. Does *Sherbert* read too much into the Free Exercise Clause? Or does *Thornton* read too much into the Establishment Clause? If the government can't make an employer accommodate an employee's Sabbath preference, why can it raise the employer's insurance rate for refusing to accommodate (where that results in the employee's separation)?

(c) **Title VII religious accommodation.**   Title VII of the Civil Rights Act of 1964 requires employers to make "reasonable accommodations" to the religious needs of their employees, including employees' Sabbath practices, if they can do so without "undue hardship." 42 U.S.C. §§ 2000e(j), 2000e-2(a)(1). The Supreme Court has not passed on the constitutionality of this provision. You may remember that in Trans World Airlines v. Hardison (p. 248), it held that Title VII does not require an employer to bear more than a de minimis cost to enable an employee to observe his Sabbath. The Court specifically said that employers are not obliged to let sabbatarians choose their days off ahead of more senior people, nor to pay premium wages to get replacements. Do these limits make Title VII constitutional? Why? Is it because they ensure that Title VII will be of little help to sabbatarians, and less aid is more constitutional? Is it because the Establishment Clause demands that third parties (here employers and more senior employees) not be forced to support religion?

B. REGULATION OF PRIVATE RELIGIOUS SPEECH

Much religious activity consists of speech and other expressive conduct covered by the Speech and Press Clauses as well as the Religion Clause. To the extent that free exercise or nonestablishment principles differ from free speech and press principles, this creates legal difficulties. The Supreme Court addressed the relation between these modes of protection in Lee v. Weisman (p. 498):

> The First Amendment protects speech and religion by quite different mechanisms. Speech is protected by insuring its full expression even when the government

participates, for the very object of some of our most important speech is to persuade the government to adopt an idea as its own. The method for protecting freedom of worship and freedom of conscience in religious matters is quite the reverse. In religious debate or expression the government is not a prime participant, for the Framers deemed religious establishment antithetical to the freedom of all. The Free Exercise Clause embraces a freedom of conscience and worship that has close parallels in the speech provisions of the First Amendment, but the Establishment Clause is a specific prohibition on forms of state intervention in religious affairs with no precise counterpart in the speech provisions. The explanation lies in the lesson of history that was and is the inspiration for the Establishment Clause, the lesson that in the hands of government what might begin as a tolerant expression of religious views may end in a policy to indoctrinate and coerce. A state-created orthodoxy puts at grave risk that freedom of belief and conscience which are the sole assurance that religious faith is real, not imposed.

1. Free Speech Principles

Constitutional theorists as diverse as Alexander Meiklejohn, Robert Bork, and Cass Sunstein have maintained that the freedoms of speech and press are primarily about political deliberation—the formation of public policy. Alexander Meiklejohn, Free Speech and Its Relation to Self-Government (1948); Robert Bork, Neutral Principles and Some First Amendment Problems, 47 Ind. L.J, 1, 26-28 (1971); Cass Sunstein, Democracy and the Problem of Free Speech (1993). But we must not forget that religious speakers and publicists have played at least as large a role in the development of these principles as have those with political aims—so much so that in the words of Justice Scalia, "a free-speech clause without religion would be Hamlet without the prince." Capitol Square Review & Advisory Bd. v. Pinette, 515 U.S. 753, 760 (1995).

When William Caxton brought the printing press to England in 1476, one of the burning issues of the day was whether the Bible should be translated and published in the vernacular. (Publication in the vernacular had a dangerous democratizing and Protestantizing effect in a world in which few outside the clergy could read the Latin Vulgate translation.) William Tyndale fled to the Continent to publish his English translation and smuggled copies into England from there. Many other pamphleteers—both political and religious—followed a similar path. (John Locke had to go to Holland to publish his major works.)

Henry VIII was quick to recognize the potential—and danger—of this new medium, the printing press. He showered favors on printers who pleased the Crown and prosecuted those who did not. As often as not, the occasions for Henry's intervention were theological. In 1529, he banned a number of Protestant works, issuing the following proclamation:

> certain heretical and blasphemous books lately made, [have been] privily sent into this realm by the disciples, fautors, and adherents of said Martin Luther, and other heretics. . . . [T]he king's subjects are likely to be corrupted, unless his highness (as Defender of the Faith) do put to his most gracious help and royal authority . . . wherefore his highness chargeth and straitly commandeth all and every his lords spiritual and temporal, judges, justices of peace, sheriffs, mayors, bailiffs, constables, etc. [to see that] no person or persons do from henceforth

presume to bring into this realm, or do sell, receive, take, or detail any book or work, printed or written, which is made, or hereafter shall be made against the faith catholic, or against the holy decrees, laws, and ordinances of holy church, or in reproach, rebuke, or slander of the king, his honorable council, or his lords spiritual or temporal.

F. Siebert, Freedom of the Press in England 1476-1776, at 167 (1952). Finding punishments—even death—insufficient to deter the publication of heresy, Henry instituted a licensing system for printers the following year:

> [N]o manner of person or persons take upon hym or them to printe any boke or bokes in englishche tong, concernynge holy scripture . . . ontyll such tyme as the same boke or bokes be examyned and approued by the ordinary of the diocese, where the said bokes shal be printed.

Id. at 46. This is the classic form of regulation, known as a "prior restraint," which is now prohibited by the First Amendment. It had certain advantages over subsequent punishment, most notably that it could avoid the inconvenience (to the Crown) of jury trial.

The most determined resisters to this scheme of royal censorship were the Puritans—theological forebears of the Massachusetts colonists. In the 1640s, the Independents and the Levellers (radical Protestant movements related to Puritanism), led by the great poet John Milton, author of *Paradise Lost*, conducted a concerted campaign against the licensing of the press. Milton's Areopagitica, A Speech for the Liberty of Unlicensed Printing, to the Parliament of England (1644), is generally credited with the proposition that we have nothing to fear from uncensored speech, because truth will always overcome falsehood:

> And though all the winds of doctrine were let loose to play upon the earth, so Truth be in the field, we do injuriously by licensing and prohibiting to misdoubt her strength. Let her and Falsehood grapple; who ever knew Truth put to the worse, in a free and open encounter?

John Milton, Complete English Poems, Of Education, Areopagitica 613 (Campbell ed., 1990).

In this country, too, religious speakers have figured in a large percentage of cases establishing the contours of speech and press freedom. The chief foundations were laid in a series of cases involving Jehovah's Witnesses, whose aggressive proselytization and solicitation door to door and on street corners during the 1930s and '40s irritated people across America and triggered a host of restrictions from local authorities. In an "unprecedented burst of litigation" from 1938 through 1946, the Court decided 23 cases on the merits involving Jehovah's Witnesses, and it ruled for the Witnesses in most of them. See Peters, Judging Jehovah's Witnesses at 185 (p. 482). Notice how many of the seminal cases discussed below involved the Witnesses.

Now we turn to the actual rules. The law pertaining to speech and press could—and does—occupy a whole course. We cannot provide a comprehensive summary here. But it is convenient to divide the rules according to the role played by the government, particularly the government as regulator (through criminal and other sanctions) and the government as property owner (through decisions about who can speak on public property or use public resources for their communication).

a. Government as Regulator

When the government uses its police power to regulate speech, there is no ambiguity about the "public-private" line, which corresponds to the "wall of separation between church and state." In this context, the speech is unquestionably "private," and the government's power is accordingly limited. Even so, the government is not powerless to regulate private speech, and there are a number of constitutional doctrines that seek to define the limits.

i. Prior Restraints

The first rule of freedom of speech and press—the rule against prior restraints—grew directly out of the experience of press licensing that so outraged Milton and his Puritan friends.

LOVELL v. CITY OF GRIFFIN
303 U.S. 444 (1938)

Mr. Chief Justice HUGHES delivered the opinion of the Court.

Appellant, Alma Lovell, was convicted in the recorder's court of the City of Griffin, Ga., of the violation of a city ordinance and was sentenced to imprisonment for fifty days in default of the payment of a fine of fifty dollars. . . .

The ordinance in question is as follows:

> Section 1. That the practice of distributing, either by hand or otherwise, circulars, handbooks, advertising, or literature of any kind, whether said articles are being delivered free, or whether same are being sold, within the limits of the City of Griffin, without first obtaining written permission from the City Manager of the City of Griffin, such practice shall be deemed a nuisance, and punishable as an offense against the City of Griffin.
> Section 2. The Chief of Police of the City of Griffin and the police force of the City of Griffin are hereby required and directed to suppress the same and to abate any nuisance as is described in the first section of this ordinance.

The violation, which is not denied, consisted of the distribution without the required permission of a pamphlet and magazine in the nature of religious tracts, setting forth the gospel of the "Kingdom of Jehovah." Appellant did not apply for a permit, as she regarded herself as sent "by Jehovah to do His work" and that such an application would have been "an act of disobedience to His commandment." . . .

. . . The ordinance is not limited to "literature" that is obscene or offensive to public morals or that advocates unlawful conduct. There is no suggestion that the pamphlet and magazine distributed in the instant case were of that character. The ordinance . . . is not limited to [methods of distribution] which might be regarded as inconsistent with the maintenance of public order or as involving disorderly conduct, the molestation of the inhabitants, or the misuse or littering of the streets. The ordinance prohibits the distribution of literature of any kind at any time, at any place, and in any manner without a permit from the City Manager.

We think that the ordinance is invalid on its face. Whatever the motive which induced its adoption, its character is such that it strikes at the very foundation of the freedom of the press by subjecting it to license and censorship. The struggle for the freedom of the press was primarily directed against the power of the licensor. It was against that power that John Milton directed his assault by his "Appeal for the Liberty of Unlicensed Printing." And the liberty of the press became initially a right to publish "*without* a license what formerly could be published only *with* one." While this freedom from previous restraint upon publication cannot be regarded as exhausting the guaranty of liberty, the prevention of that restraint was a leading purpose in the adoption of the constitutional provision. Legislation of the type of the ordinance in question would restore the system of license and censorship in its baldest form. . . .

As the ordinance is void on its face, it was not necessary for appellant to seek a permit under it. She was entitled to contest its validity in answer to the charge against her.

NOTE AND QUESTIONS

What Is Wrong with a Prior Licensing System?   Lovell was not denied a permit. She never applied for one. And the Court held that she didn't have to. The unconstitutional action in this case was the process the city required speakers to go through, not the outcome. What is wrong with a permit process? Blackstone explained that a scheme of prior licensing "subject[s] the freedom of sentiment to the prejudices of one man, and make[s] him the arbitrary and infallible judge of all controverted points in learning, religion, and government." By contrast, the punishment of "dangerous or offensive writings" is accomplished by means of a "fair and impartial trial," with a jury of ordinary citizens. William Blackstone, 4 Commentaries on the Laws of England 150-153 (1769).

The same concern is present in *Lovell;* by vesting the permit power in the city manager, the ordinance rendered free speech activity in Griffin, Georgia, subject to the "prejudices of one man." In another sense, however, Blackstone's worries seem anachronistic. To Blackstone, liberty was sufficiently protected when enforcement was channeled through a jury of ordinary citizens. This protects sentiments with popular support from censorship at the hands of the king, but it does less to protect the expression of unpopular views—and the Jehovah's Witnesses were certainly unpopular—from censorship at the hands of the community. The rule against prior restraints is designed to protect popular sovereignty against government—not to protect unpopular minorities from majority oppression. See Akhil Reed Amar, The Bill of Rights 23-24 (1998). Important as it is, therefore, the rule against prior restraints cannot be our only means of protecting religious dissenters.

ii. Overbreadth and Vagueness

The rule against prior restraints is primarily procedural in nature; it deals with the manner in which the government may regulate speech, rather than the substantive reach of governmental authority. The rules against overbreadth and vagueness are similar. See Henry Monaghan, First Amendment "Due Process," 83 Harv. L. Rev. 518 (1970). The overbreadth doctrine allows a free speech plaintiff to challenge a law on the ground that it would be unconstitutional as applied to someone else, even if his own conduct could constitutionally be punished. Gooding v. Wilson, 405 U.S. 518 (1972). For example, violence in the course of a political protest can be punished, but even a violent demonstrator is permitted to challenge his prosecution if the ordinance under which he is charged is so broad that it would apply to many lawful peaceful protests. The overbreadth doctrine is an exception to the usual rule of constitutional adjudication, which denies standing to challenge the constitutionality of a law on a basis that does not apply to oneself.

The vagueness doctrine renders unconstitutional any law that restricts speech in a way that fails to define the offense with reasonable clarity. The idea is that such a law is likely to induce people to exercise excessive caution, not knowing exactly where the boundary between permitted and forbidden speech may lie. See Anthony Amsterdam, The Void-for-Vagueness Doctrine in the Supreme Court, 109 U. Pa. L. Rev. 67 (1960). For example, it would probably be unconstitutional to prohibit any billboards that might "offend" significant segments of the community. How can a speaker tell, in advance, what might be forbidden under such a law?

iii. Content Discrimination

Perhaps the most important rule limiting the government's power to restrict speech in its capacity as regulator is the rule against content-based discrimination. See Geoffrey Stone, Content Regulation and the First Amendment, 25 Wm. & Mary L. Rev. 189 (1983). Such discrimination is subjected to strict scrutiny, which is usually tantamount to invalidation. The prohibition is particularly strict—approaching the absolute—when the regulation discriminates on the basis not just of content but of viewpoint. These are not always easy to distinguish, but an example may help. If the government prohibits commercial but not political billboards, it has discriminated on the basis of content—the subject matter—but not on the basis of viewpoint. See Metromedia, Inc. v. San Diego, 453 U.S. 490 (1981). If government permits performers to wear military uniforms in movies or plays only if "the portrayal does not tend to discredit" the armed forces, that is discrimination based on viewpoint. Schacht v. United States, 398 U.S. 58 (1970). Or if it restricts abortion "protests" in front of a clinic while allowing abortion defenders, this is viewpoint discrimination. Cf. Hill v. Colorado, 530 U.S. 703 (2000).

Content-neutral regulations—such as time, place, and manner restrictions—are subject to a lesser degree of scrutiny and are often, though not always, upheld. For example, the state can regulate the decibel level of rock bands in Central Park (Ward v. Rock Against Racism, 491 U.S. 781 (1989)), and it can prohibit picketing in front of a particular residence (Frisby v. Schultz, 487 U.S. 474 (1988)). These restrictions apply to all messages equally, no matter what the content. But the state cannot forbid all street demonstrations except for labor demonstrations (Police Dep't v. Mosley, 408 U.S. 92 (1972)) or single out particular messages for prohibition (R.A.V. v. City of St. Paul, 505 U.S. 377 (1992) (striking down "hate speech" ordinance).

In this connection consider Cantwell v. Connecticut, 310 U.S. 296 (1940) (p. 124). A Jehovah's Witness was prosecuted for breach of the peace after playing a phonograph record sharply attacking the Roman Catholic Church to people on the street. The Court overturned his conviction, stating:

> In the realm of religious faith, and in that of political belief, sharp differences arise. In both fields the tenets of one man may seem the rankest error to his neighbor. To persuade others to his own point of view, the pleader, as we know, at times, resorts to exaggeration, to vilification of men who have been, or are, prominent in church or state, and even to false statement. But the people of this nation have ordained in the light of history, that, in spite of the probability of excesses and abuses, these liberties are, in the long view, essential to enlightened opinion and right conduct on the part of the citizens of a democracy.
>
> Although the contents of the record not unnaturally aroused animosity, we think that, in the absence of a statute narrowly drawn to define and punish specific conduct as constituting a clear and present danger to a substantial interest of the State, the petitioner's communication, considered in the light of the constitutional gurantees, raised no such clear and present menace to public peace and order as to render him liable to conviction of the common law offense in question.

Compare *Cantwell* with the following decision:

PECK v. SONY MUSIC CORP.

68 Fair Empl. Prac. Cas. 1025 (S.D. N.Y. 1995)

STANTON, District Judge.

Plaintiff Shirley Peck sues defendant Sony Music Corp. ("Sony"), claiming that Sony terminated her employment in violation of Title VII of the Civil Rights Act. She alleges that she was subjected to religious harassment and discharged in retaliation for her complaints about that harassment.

Sony moves for summary judgment, arguing that the conduct of which Peck complains did not create a hostile environment as a matter of law. Sony further argues that Peck was discharged for nondiscriminatory reasons unrelated to her complaints about the alleged harassment. . . .

According to Peck, James Nevius [her co-worker or supervisor] regularly made comments to her concerning religion, including statements that Peck was a sinner and would go to hell. (See, e.g., Peck Dep. at 99-102 (on five or six occasions, Nevius told Peck that "no matter what I did to him, that God would love me"), 104 (Nevius made that statement "maybe two or three times a week"), 105 (Nevius offered to answer any questions that Peck might have concerning religion), 117 (Nevius treated Peck's co-workers differently in that "He did not go back there and scream at them and tell them they had to repent. He did not go back there and tell them that he was the supreme God"), 120, 155-156, 159 (Nevius sang religious songs when Peck was nearby), 144 (Nevius told Peck that she was a sinner), 152 (Nevius "came back there screaming at me and telling me I have to repent, I have to cooperate, I have to repent, 'You are a sinner'"), 154-155 (Nevius told Peck "at least every two weeks" that she was a "sinner and had to repent")). That course of conduct culminated in a prayer session Nevius and another Sony employee held over Peck's work area. (Peck Dep. at 37, 172-173.) Peck's termination was substantially contemporaneous with her complaint about the prayer session. (See Peck Dep. at 173-179.)

Drawing all inferences in Peck's favor, there is evidence from which a trier of fact could conclude that her "workplace was permeated with discriminatory intimidation that was sufficiently severe or pervasive to alter the conditions of her work environment, [and] that a specific basis exists for imputing the conduct that created the hostile environment to the employer," Murray v. New York Univ. College of Dentistry (2d Cir. 1995), or that Peck was discharged in retaliation for her complaints about Nevius' conduct.

Sony's motion for summary judgment is denied.

NOTES AND QUESTIONS

1. *Peck* **and** *Cantwell.*   How does *Peck* differ from *Cantwell* ? Was Nevius's speech more offensive than Cantwell's? Was it more repeated? (Would it have mattered if Cantwell had played the record many times, or every day?) Does the difference come down to the fact that Cantwell's unwilling listeners were on the street, and Nevius's were in the workplace? Would the restriction of Nevius's speech pass the constitutional standard set forth in *Cantwell?* Does it satisfy the requirements of the vagueness and overbreadth doctrines? Would a reasonable person in Nevius's position know how far he could go? Even if Nevius's own conduct was egregious enough to warrant punishment, might the statute apply to constitutionally protected workplace behavior?

2. **Religious Harassment Under Title VII.**   Title VII of the 1964 Civil Rights Act, 42 U.S.C. § 2000e-2(a)(1), forbids employers to discriminate in the "terms, conditions, or privileges of employment" on the basis of race, sex, or religion. The term *discrimination* has been interpreted to include the practice of maintaining a work environment where employees harass each other on the basis of religion. And harassment can include speech as well as conduct. In 1991, Title VII was amended to allow damages for emotional distress and punitive damages. These provisions taken together can create a First Amendment problem:

> Harassment law suppresses speech not by directly penalizing employees who say offensive things, but by threatening employers with liability if they do not punish such employees themselves. . . . Companies, fearing liability, implement policies prohibiting a particular kind of speech and providing for disciplinary measures. Employees, fearing discipline, avoid expressing the proscribed speech. . . .
>
> The incentive for employers to suppress speech is particularly great because the employer is liable for its employees' offensive speech—with the passage of the Civil

Rights Act [of 1991], possibly also liable for emotional distress damages and punitive damages—but derives no benefit from it.

Eugene Volokh, Freedom of Speech and Workplace Harassment, 39 UCLA L.
Rev. 1791, 1809-1810 (1992).

Harassment often takes the form of speech. Clearly at some point that speech
is unprotected and can be made criminal (say, repeated crank phone calls).
Liability for workplace harassment under antidiscrimination laws, though,
poses an additional First Amendment problem: It is limited to certain messages—ones of dislike or hate based on race, sex, religion, and so forth. Does
singling out such messages for restriction in the workplace violate the fundamental principle of neutrality between different viewpoints and messages? Or is
it justified by the strong interest in ensuring that persons of all different races,
sexes, and faiths can participate fully in economic life?

Of course, it takes more than isolated instances of misbehavior to create a
hostile workplace. The conduct has to be severe or pervasive, Meritor Savings
Bank v. Vinson, 477 U.S. 57, 67 (1986), and the employer is not liable unless it
fails to take "reasonable care" to investigate a complaint of harassment.
Burlington Indus. v. Ellerth, 524 U.S. 742, 763-765 (1998). But as Volokh notes,
"the only practical way for an employer to avoid liability based on the sum of
all offensive statements is by instituting a policy that will bar each individual statement." 39 UCLA L. Rev. at 1812. But cf. Thomas C. Berg, Religious Speech
in the Workplace: Harassment or Protected Speech?, 22 Harv. J.L. & Pub. Pol'y
959, 992-993 (1999) ("[M]any instances of harassment through 'accumulated'
effect involve an accumulation of conduct by a single employee or a small
group. . . . [I]t is possible for an employer to tell each individual employee to
exercise restraint and not repeat abusive comments over and over again.")

In 1993 the Equal Employment Opportunity Commission (EEOC) proposed
guidelines to help employers identify and root out harassment based on religion.
Guidelines on Harassment Based on Race, Color, Religion, Gender, National
Origin, Age or Disability, 58 Fed. Reg. 51,266 (1993). The proposal created a
furor in Congress and was eventually dropped. Among the objections were that

> [f]irst, the definition [of harassment] included speech that showed an "aver-
> sion" or that was "intimidating" as well as speech that showed hostility. [This]
> suggested additional grounds of illegality that might reach speech that was no
> more than strongly critical of the beliefs of another faith. . . .
>
> Most importantly, the Guidelines contained no discussion of limits on harass-
> ment liability, and no examples of religious speech or action that the EEOC would
> view as outside the statute and regulations or as constitutionally protected. . . . As a
> result, the EEOC Guidelines would have inevitably pushed the law toward over-
> enforcement and toward unacceptable restrictions on workplace religious speech.

Berg, 22 Harv. J.L. & Pub. Pol'y at 988. For further discussion of the problem of
religious harassment, see Theresa M. Beiner and John M. A. DiPippa, Hostile
Environments and the Religious Employee, 19 U. Ark. Little Rock L.J. 577
(1997); Laura S. Underkuffler, "Discrimination" on the Basis of Religion: An
Examination of Attempted Value Neutrality in Employment, 30 Wm. & Mary L.
Rev. 581, 615-619 (1989).

3. Harassment: The New Blasphemy?   One of the clearest forms of content-based regulation of religious speech was the hoary law against blasphemy. At common law the crime of blasphemy was one of the four branches of criminal libel, along with sedition, obscenity, and defamation. See Robert C. Post, Cultural Heterogeneity and Law: Pornography, Blasphemy, and the First Amendment, 76 Cal. L. Rev. 297 (1988); Note, Blasphemy, 70 Colum. L. Rev. 694 (1970).

In one famous prosecution, an apostate Universalist minister named Abner Kneeland was charged under a Massachusetts law, enacted in 1782, forbidding any person to "wilfully blaspheme the holy name of God, by denying, cursing, or contumeliously reproaching God, his creation, government, or final judging of the world, or by cursing or reproaching Jesus Christ." Commonwealth v. Kneeland, 37 Mass. (200 Pick.) 206 (1838). The conviction was upheld in an opinion by Chief Justice Shaw, essentially on the ground that the "wilfulness" requirement cured any constitutional defect. (Is there any equivalent protection under Title VII? Must harassment be "wilful"?) Justice Morton dissented on the ground that it cannot violate the law to express religious opinions unless "the object be to calumniate, or wantonly or maliciously to cause pain or injury to others, by wounding their feelings or corrupting their principles." How different is that from the modern law of religious harassment? In both contexts, speech regarding certain subjects (race, sex, religion) is singled out and punished if it "wounds the feelings" of others. Is the difference that blasphemy laws apply only to antireligious speech, while harassment laws apply to a wider range of speech? Is it that harassment laws apply both to pro- and to anti-religious speech? Either way, isn't this content-based speech regulation?

Could we justify the regulation of religious speech under Title VII by saying that it serves a more important state interest than did the blasphemy law? It protects people with unconventional religious convictions from the emotional distress of confrontation and ridicule in the workplace. The government has a particularly strong interest in assuring that people of all faiths have equal employment opportunities. Does this justification differ from the argument Justice Morton made in *Kneeland*? Some critics say that harassment laws impose legal sanctions for politically unpopular messages—"political incorrectness"—and punish dissent from currently dominant beliefs about racial, gender, and religious equality. What would Justice Morton say?

4. Problems on Religious Harassment.   Is there actionable harassment in the following situations?

(a) A business owner who is a devout Christian regularly puts religious statements on company publications, such as an employee newsletter, a general workplace bulletin board, and employees' paychecks, and plays Christian music on the office PA system. A non-Christian employee fears that these practices indicate that a non-Christian cannot be promoted in the company. What result? See Brown Transport Corp. v. Pennsylvania Human Relations Comm'n, 578 A.2d 555 (Pa. Commw. Ct. 1990) (finding liability in similar circumstances).

(b) An employee who is a Jehovah's Witness writes three personal letters to a coworker, asserting that the coworker has done immoral things and needs to ask God for forgiveness or else "you'll be damned to eternal punishment." The letters upset the coworker a great deal. Must the employer fire the religious employee or else be liable for religious harassment? If the employer does fire the religious employee, could *she* sue under Title VII? On what theory? Cf.

Chalmers v. Tulon Co., 101 F.3d 1012 (4th Cir. 1996) (upholding employer's firing of letter-writer).

5. Religious "Hate Speech" Outside the Workplace. The prohibition of content-based restrictions of speech may be weaker—although it still exists—in other Western democracies. In Sweden in 2003, a Pentecostal Christian minister gave a sermon to his congregation in which he stated that legalizing same-sex partnerships "will simply create disasters," that the "consequences" of homosexuality are seen "through the spread of AIDS," and continued:

> The Bible takes up here and teaches about these abnormalities. And sexual abnormalities are a deep cancerous tumour on the whole body of society. The Lord knows that sexually twisted people will even rape animals. . . .
>
> Defilers of boys. Already when the Bible was written the Lord knew what would happen. We have experienced it here and are still experiencing it and are horrified over it. And Paul speaks in First Corinthians one and ten of perverted humans. And perverted humans is translated from the original text that says "one who lies with boys" . . . One who lies with boys is one of the perverted people the Bible is speaking of then. Now I would like to stress that all homosexuals are not paedophiles. And all homosexuals are not perverted. But the door is nevertheless being opened to forbidden areas and allowing sin to take a hold in one's thoughts. . . . And being faithful in a homosexual relationship is in no way a better relationship than changing partners every day. It is not a better relationship. It is equally despicable in the eyes of God.
>
> Voluntarily I leave cleanliness and receive uncleanliness. They made a conscious exchange, says Paul. Homosexuality is something sick. A healthy and clean thought has been exchanged for a contaminated thought. . . . Is homosexuality something one chooses, the answer is yes. You choose it. You are not born into it. You quite simply choose this. You exchange it.

See Office of the Prosecutor General v. Ake Green, Case No. B 1050-05, available at http://www.writely.com/View.aspx?docid=ahjqqjkcw4tc. The minister was convicted and sentenced to a month in jail under a Swedish law punishing anyone who, in a disseminated communication, "threatens or expresses contempt for a national, ethnic or other such group of persons with allusion to race, colour, national or ethnic origin, religious belief or sexual orientation." See *id.* The law was based on legislative findings "that homosexuals are a vulnerable group in society, that homosexuals are often exposed to crime due to their sexual orientation, and that national socialist and other [racist extremist] groups . . . agitate against homosexuals and homosexuality." *Id.*

However, the conviction was reversed by the Supreme Court of Sweden (*id.*) based not on the Swedish Constitution, but on the European Convention for the Protection of Human Rights, art. 9, which protects everyone's "freedom of thought, conscience and religion," including the right "to manifest his religion or belief, in worship, teaching, practice and observance," subject "only to such limitations as are necessary in a democratic society in the interests of public safety, for the protection of public order, health or morals, or for the protection of the rights and freedoms of others." The court reasoned that the sermon "did not involve such hateful statements that are usually referred to as *hate speech*," since even the "most far-reaching" statement—"where sexual abnormalities are described as a cancerous tumor"—"seen in the light of what he said in connection with his sermon, is not of such a nature as can be regarded as promoting or justifying hatred of homosexuals." The court noted that the Rev. Green "made his statements in a sermon before his congregation on a theme that is in the Bible." In such circumstances, the court said, the European Court of Human Rights likely "would find that the limitation [criminal liability would place on Green's religious freedom] is not proportionate and thereby would constitute a violation of the European Convention." *Id.*

Given the First Amendment rules against viewpoint-based punishment of speech, the result in America would almost certainly have been the same. Wouldn't American constitutional law go further, protecting even a statement that explicitly called for "hatred of homosexuals"? European law often takes a less speech-protective stance than American law. For example, Germany (reacting to its Nazi past) bans the formation of racist groups, and Britain has relatively restrictive libel laws. Should American constitutional law give more weight to the harms caused by "hate speech"?

b. Government as Property Owner: "Forum" Law

Many free speech cases involve private persons speaking on government property—in parks, in airports, on the streets—or using governmental media of communication. These raise a different set of issues, because the government has more power to determine what will take place on its property or with its resources than it does to reward or punish purely private behavior. Think about the metaphor of the "wall of separation between church and state." On which side of the "wall" do public forums, such as parks and sidewalks, fall? There was a time in American law when the government could control the use of its property the way private owners can control theirs. As a homeowner I can invite my friends to dinner and snub people I don't like. I can do the same thing when I give away money or hire a lawyer. Perhaps the government should have the same authority. This is the approach of the following decision.

COMMONWEALTH v. DAVIS
162 Mass. 510, 39 N.E. 113 (1895)

HOLMES, J.

[Davis was convicted for giving a sermon on the Boston Common in violation of a city ordinance that said: "No person shall, in or upon any of the public grounds, make any public address, discharge any cannon or firearm, expose for sale any goods, wares or merchandise, erect or maintain any booth, stand, tent or apparatus for the purposes of public amusement or show, except in accordance with a permit from the mayor."] There is no evidence before us to show that the power of the legislature over the common is less than its power over any other park dedicated to the use of the public, or over public streets, the legal title to which is in a city or town. As representative of the public, it may and does exercise control over the use which the public may make of such places[.] For the legislature absolutely or conditionally to forbid public speaking in a highway or public park is no more an infringement of the rights of a member of the public than for the owner of a private house to forbid it in his house. When no proprietary rights interfere, the legislature may end the right of the public to enter upon the public place by putting an end to the dedication to public uses. So it may take the less step of limiting the public use to certain purposes.

. . . It is argued that the ordinance really is directed especially against free preaching of the gospel in public places, as certain western ordinances, seemingly general, have been held to be directed against the Chinese. But we have no reason to believe, and do not believe, that this ordinance was passed for any other than its ostensible purpose, namely, as a proper regulation of the use of public grounds.

NOTES AND QUESTIONS

1. *Davis* **in the Supreme Court.** The U.S. Supreme Court unanimously affirmed the state court ruling, showing even less sympathy for the constitutional claim than Justice Holmes did. Davis v. Massachusetts, 167 U.S. 43 (1897). In the Supreme Court, Davis complained that the ordinance imposed what we would call a prior restraint because it required speakers on the common to get a permit from the mayor. The Court responded: "The right to absolutely exclude all right to use, necessarily includes the authority to determine under what circumstances such use may be availed of, as the greater power contains the lesser."

Davis is no longer good law. The government now has to observe some constitutional constraints even when it is dealing with its own property. It must observe due process when it terminates welfare benefits or fires employees. Goldberg v. Kelly, 397 U.S. 254 (1970); Cleveland Bd. of Educ. v. Loudermill, 470 U.S. 532 (1985). And it must respect the First Amendment in its handling of public property. One thing this means is that the government must not discriminate in favor of its friends. The rule of neutrality applies in the public forum just as it does in private spaces. But that is not the government's only obligation. Even neutral laws may be unconstitutional if they limit speech too much. That is one message of International Society for Krishna Consciousness v. Lee, below.

2. **Government Property.** *Davis* rests on the premise that different First Amendment rules apply to the government when it acts as a proprietor rather than as a regulator. There are other areas of the law where states can do things with their own property that they can't do by simple regulation. Consider the market participant exception to the dormant Commerce Clause, which allows states trading on their own account to discriminate against foreign buyers and sellers. Reeves v. Stake, 447 U.S. 429 (1980); Hughes v. Alexandria Scrap Corp., 426 U.S. 794 (1976). Should we give more protection to free speech and free exercise than we do to free trade? Consider some closer First Amendment analogies. If the National Endowment for the Humanities offers a $10,000 prize for the best patriotic essay written by a high school student, it can surely reject entries that condemn democracy, even though this is viewpoint regulation. Should we distinguish, for First Amendment purposes, between what the government does with its money and what the government does with its land? See National Endowment for the Arts v. Finley, 524 U.S. 596 (1998).

There is some ambiguity in Holmes's analogy to private property owners. Why should it matter if the ordinance was really directed "against free preaching of the gospel"? A private property owner can allow A but not B to put a sign in her yard. Why can't the government? Did the U.S. Supreme Court agree with Holmes on this point? What is the meaning of its observation that "the greater power contains the lesser"?

If Holmes is right—if the government need not allow members of the public to use the park for free speech purposes—then would it violate the Establishment Clause to grant permission to Davis? When the government permits private religious speakers to use government property for the propagation of religious opinions, is this a forbidden subsidy under Lemon v. Kurtzman?

INTERNATIONAL SOCIETY FOR KRISHNA CONSCIOUSNESS v. LEE
505 U.S. 672 (1992)

Chief Justice REHNQUIST delivered the opinion of the Court.

[The International Society for Krishna Consciousness (ISKCON) is a religious corporation whose members perform a ritual known as sankirtan—going into public places, disseminating religious literature, and soliciting funds. A regulation adopted by the Port Authority prevented ISKCON from performing its ritual in the terminal areas of Kennedy, La Guardia, and Newark airports. The regulation said:

> The following conduct is prohibited within the interior areas of buildings or structures at an air terminal if conducted by a person to or with passers-by in a continuous or repetitive manner:
>
> (a) The sale or distribution of any merchandise, including but not limited to jewelry, food stuffs, candles, flowers, badges and clothing.
> (b) The sale or distribution of flyers, brochures, pamphlets, books or any other printed or written material.
> (c) The solicitation and receipt of funds.

The regulation allowed solicitation and distribution on the sidewalks outside the terminal buildings. ISKCON sued to enjoin enforcement of the regulation. Lee was the police superintendent for the Port Authority. The district court granted an injunction. The court of appeals held that the ban on solicitation was reasonable, but that the ban on distribution was not. Both sides petitioned the Supreme Court for review.]

It is uncontested that the solicitation at issue in this case is a form of speech protected under the First Amendment. But it is also well settled that the government need not permit all forms of speech on property that it owns and controls. Where the government is acting as a proprietor, managing its internal operations, rather than acting as lawmaker with the power to regulate or license, its action will not be subjected to the heightened review to which its actions as a lawmaker may be subject. . . .

These cases reflect, either implicitly or explicitly, a "forum based" approach for assessing restrictions that the government seeks to place on the use of its property. Under this approach, regulation of speech on government property that has traditionally been available for public expression is subject to the highest scrutiny. Such regulations survive only if they are narrowly drawn to achieve a compelling state interest. The second category of public property is the designated public forum, whether of a limited or unlimited character—property that the State has opened for expressive activity by part or all of the public. Regulation of such property is subject to the same limitations as that governing a traditional public forum. Finally, there is all remaining public property. Limitations on expressive activity conducted on this last category of property must survive only a much more limited review. The challenged regulation need only be reasonable, as long as the regulation is not an effort to suppress the speaker's activity due to disagreement with the speaker's view. . . .

The suggestion that the government has a high burden in justifying speech restrictions relating to traditional public fora made its first appearance in Hague v. CIO (1939). Justice Roberts, concluding that individuals have a right to use "streets and parks for communication of views," reasoned that such a right flowed from the fact that "streets and parks . . . have immemorially been held in trust for the use of the public and, time out of mind, have been used for purposes of assembly, communicating thoughts between citizens, and discussing public questions." [Since then we have identified other qualities that characterize a public forum: It] is property that has as "a principal purpose . . . the free exchange of ideas." Moreover, consistent with the notion that the government—like other property owners—"has power to preserve the property under its control for the use to which it is lawfully dedicated," the government does not create a public forum by inaction. Nor is a public forum created "whenever members of the public are permitted freely to visit a place owned or operated by the Government." The decision to create a public forum must instead be made "by intentionally opening a nontraditional forum for public discourse." Finally, we have recognized that the location of property also has bearing because separation from acknowledged public areas may serve to indicate that the separated property is a special enclave, subject to greater restriction. United States v. Grace (1983).

These precedents foreclose the conclusion that airport terminals are public fora. Reflecting the general growth of the air travel industry, airport terminals have only recently achieved their contemporary size and character. But given the lateness with which the modern air terminal has made its appearance, it hardly qualifies for the description of having "immemorially . . . time out of mind" been held in the public trust and used for purposes of expressive activity. [And during this period airports have not generally] been made available for speech activity. Nor can we say that these particular terminals . . . have been intentionally opened by their operators to such activity; the frequent and continuing litigation evidencing the operators' objections belies any such claim. In short, there can be no argument that society's time-tested judgment, expressed through acquiescence in a continuing practice, has resolved the issue in petitioners' favor. . . .

The restrictions here challenged, therefore, need only satisfy a requirement of reasonableness. [U]nder this standard the prohibition on solicitation passes muster.

We have on many prior occasions noted the disruptive effect that solicitation may have on business. "Solicitation requires action by those who would respond:

The individual solicited must decide whether or not to contribute (which itself might involve reading the solicitor's literature or hearing his pitch), and then, having decided to do so, reach for a wallet, search it for money, write a check, or produce a credit card." United States v. Kokinda (1990). Passengers who wish to avoid the solicitor may have to alter their paths, slowing both themselves and those around them. The result is that the normal flow of traffic is impeded. This is especially so in an airport, where "[a]ir travelers, who are often weighted down by cumbersome baggage . . . may be hurrying to catch a plane or to arrange ground transportation." Delays may be particularly costly in this setting, as a flight missed by only a few minutes can result in hours worth of subsequent inconvenience.

In addition, face-to-face solicitation presents risks of duress that are an appropriate target of regulation. The skillful, and unprincipled, solicitor can target the most vulnerable, including those accompanying children or those suffering physical impairment and who cannot easily avoid the solicitation. The unsavory solicitor can also commit fraud through concealment of his affiliation or through deliberate efforts to shortchange those who agree to purchase. Compounding this problem is the fact that, in an airport, the targets of such activity frequently are on tight schedules. This in turn makes such visitors unlikely to stop and formally complain to airport authorities. As a result, the airport faces considerable difficulty in achieving its legitimate interest in monitoring solicitation activity to assure that travelers are not interfered with unduly.

The Port Authority has concluded that its interest in monitoring the activities can best be accomplished by limiting solicitation and distribution to the sidewalk areas outside the terminals. This sidewalk area is frequented by an overwhelming percentage of airport users. [T]he resulting access of those who would solicit the general public is quite complete. In turn we think it would be odd to conclude that the Port Authority's terminal regulation is unreasonable despite the Port Authority having otherwise assured access to an area universally traveled. . . .

For the foregoing reasons, the judgment of the Court of Appeals sustaining the ban on solicitation in Port Authority terminals is affirmed.

[Joining in the Chief Justice's opinion were Justices White, O'Connor, Scalia, and Thomas. This provided a majority to affirm the ban on solicitation, the subject of ISKCON's petition. On Lee's cross-petition, Justice O'Connor voted with the other four members of the Court—Justices Kennedy, Blackmun, Stevens, and Souter—to strike down the ban on distribution. Here is a portion of her opinion.]

Justice O'CONNOR, concurring in No. 91-155 and concurring in the judgment in No. 91-339.

In my view, however, the regulation banning leafletting . . . cannot be upheld as reasonable on this record. [We have noted on other occasions] that leafletting does not entail the same kinds of problems presented by face-to-face solicitation. [T]he distribution of literature does not require that the recipient stop in order to receive the message the speaker wishes to convey; instead the recipient is free to read the message at a later time. With the possible exception of avoiding litter, see Schneider v. State (1939), it is difficult to point to any problems intrinsic to the act of leafletting that would make it naturally incompatible with a large, multipurpose forum such as those at issue here. [T]he regulation at issue in this case effects an absolute prohibition and is not supported by any independent justification outside of the problems caused by the accompanying solicitation. . . .

Of course, it is still open for the Port Authority to promulgate regulations of the time, place, and manner of leafletting which are "content-neutral, are narrowly tailored to serve a significant government interest, and leave open ample alternative channels of communication." For example, during the many years that this litigation has been in progress, the Port Authority has not banned sankirtan completely from JFK International Airport, but has restricted it to a relatively uncongested part of the airport terminals, the same part that houses the airport chapel. In my view, that regulation meets the standards we have applied to time, place, and manner restrictions of protected expression.

NOTES AND QUESTIONS

1. Traditional, Designated, and Nonpublic Forums.   *Lee* divides public property into three categories: traditional public forums (streets, sidewalks, and parks), designated public forums (other property that the government has intentionally opened up for expressive activity), and nonpublic forums (everyplace else). Stricter First Amendment rules apply in the first two than in the third.

Why are airport terminals "nonpublic"? The Court suggests that they are not traditional public forums because air travel (and therefore the airport) is a recent phenomenon. If airports are like streets and sidewalks, why should it matter how old they are? Justice Kennedy, concurring in *Lee*, suggested that the appropriate question was whether "expressive activity would be appropriate and compatible with" the "physical characteristics" and the existing use of the property—the sort of question we call a functional test. Did the Court focus on age because it takes a certain number of years to acquire a First Amendment easement? Is tradition important for some other reason?

A designated public forum comes into being only when the government intentionally creates it. Why does the government's intention matter? Because that is the usual way of granting an easement? Was Justice Holmes right after all in saying that the government is like a private owner of property? What kind of intention must the government have? The Port Authority certainly intended to allow *some* talking, buying, and selling in its airports. Why can it exclude *this kind* of speech and solicitation?

2. Standards of Review for Various Forums.   In traditional and designated public forums, the Court observes, regulation of speech is subject to strict scrutiny: It must be narrowly drawn to achieve a compelling state interest. This is true if the government bans speech altogether or bans a certain kind of speech defined by its content. But a different rule applies—even in a public forum—to non-content-based laws that regulate the time, place, or manner of speech. Such laws are given a kind of intermediate scrutiny. They must be "'narrowly tailored to serve a significant governmental interest, and . . . leave open ample alternative channels for communication.'" Ward v. Rock Against

Racism, 491 U.S. 781, 791 (1989).* *Ward* allowed New York City to regulate the volume of rock concerts in Central Park. But in Schneider v. State, 308 U.S. 147 (1939), another Jehovah's Witness case, the Court struck down several city ordinances against handing out leaflets. The cities were trying to prevent litter. The Court said:

> We are of opinion that the purpose to keep the streets clean and of good appearance is insufficient to justify an ordinance which prohibits a person rightfully on a public street from handing literature to one willing to receive it. . . . This constitutional protection does not deprive a city of all power to prevent street littering. [It can still punish] those who actually throw papers on the streets.

In nonpublic forums, the First Amendment standards are much more forgiving. The government can discriminate on the basis of subject matter. It can, for example, accept cigarette ads but not political ads for display on public transportation. (Though it may not, as we shall see, engage in discrimination among different viewpoints concerning a subject matter. Lamb's Chapel v. Center Moriches School Dist., 508 U.S. 384 (1993).) Regulations in a nonpublic forum need only be reasonable and viewpoint-neutral. This test is linguistically similar to the low-level review of the Equal Protection Clause but, as *Lee* shows, enforced with more vigor. Is the government, as proprietor of a nonpublic forum, once again like an owner of private property? Does *Lee* signal a return to the theory of *Davis* for venues other than streets and parks? Could a private owner forbid leafletting on her property? Why can't the Port Authority do so at airports? Is its decision really unreasonable? Does leafletting slow down pedestrian traffic? Does it cause litter?

2. Religious Free Speech: Does Free Exercise Add More Protection?

So far, we have focused only on the Free Speech Clause. We have seen that religious speakers often invoke these principles for protection against state action. But much religious speech is also an "exercise of religion." Does it get any extra protection?

MURDOCK v. PENNSYLVANIA
319 U.S. 105 (1943)

Mr. Justice DOUGLAS delivered the opinion of the Court.

The City of Jeannette, Pennsylvania, has an ordinance, some forty years old, which provides in part:

> That all persons canvassing for or soliciting within said Borough, orders for goods, paintings, pictures, wares, or merchandise of any kind, or persons

---

*In recent cases the Court has distinguished between content-neutral laws and content-neutral *injunctions* that regulate time, place, and manner. It subjects the latter to a kind of intermediate scrutiny that looks harder at means. The Court asks whether the injunction "burden[s] no more speech than necessary to serve a significant government interest." Madsen v. Women's Health Ctr., 512 U.S. 753, 765 (1994).

delivering such articles under orders so obtained or solicited, shall be required to procure from the Burgess a license to transact said business and shall pay to the Treasurer of said Borough therefor the following sums according to the time for which said license shall be granted.

For one day $1.50, for one week seven dollars ($7.00), for two weeks twelve dollars ($12.00), for three weeks twenty dollars ($20.00), provided that the provisions of this ordinance shall not apply to persons selling by sample to manufacturers or licensed merchants or dealers doing business in said Borough of Jeannette.

Petitioners are "Jehovah's Witnesses." They went about from door to door in the City of Jeannette distributing literature and soliciting people to "purchase" certain religious books and pamphlets, all published by the Watch Tower Bible & Tract Society. The "price" of the books was twenty-five cents each, the "price" of the pamphlets five cents each. In connection with these activities petitioners used a phonograph on which they played a record expounding certain of their views on religion. None of them obtained a license under the ordinance. Before they were arrested each had made "sales" of books. There was evidence that it was their practice in making these solicitations to request a "contribution" of twenty-five cents each for the books and five cents each for the pamphlets but to accept lesser sums or even to donate the volumes in case an interested person was without funds. In the present case some donations of pamphlets were made when books were purchased. Petitioners were convicted and fined for violation of the ordinance. . . .

The First Amendment, which the Fourteenth makes applicable to the states, declares that "Congress shall make no law respecting an establishment of religion, or prohibiting the free exercise thereof; or abridging the freedom of speech, or of the press. . . . " It could hardly be denied that a tax laid specifically on the exercise of those freedoms would be unconstitutional. Yet the license tax imposed by this ordinance is in substance just that.

Petitioners spread their interpretations of the Bible and their religious beliefs largely through the hand distribution of literature by full or part time workers. They claim to follow the example of Paul, teaching "publickly, and from house to house." Acts 20:20. They take literally the mandate of the Scriptures, "Go ye into all the world, and preach the gospel to every creature." Mark 16:15. In doing so they believe that they are obeying a commandment of God. . . .

The alleged justification for the exaction of this license tax is the fact that the religious literature is distributed with a solicitation of funds. . . . But the mere fact that the religious literature is "sold" by itinerant preachers rather than "donated" does not transform evangelism into a commercial enterprise. If it did, then the passing of the collection plate in church would make the church service a commercial project. . . .

We do not mean to say that religious groups and the press are free from all financial burdens of government. We have here something quite different, for example, from a tax on the income of one who engages in religious activities or a tax on property used or employed in connection with those activities. It is one thing to impose a tax on the income or property of a preacher. It is quite another thing to exact a tax from him for the privilege of delivering a sermon. The tax imposed by the City of Jeannette is a flat license tax, the payment of which is a condition of the exercise of these constitutional privileges. The power to tax the exercise of a privilege is the power to control or suppress its enjoyment. . . .

It is contended, however, that the fact that the license tax can suppress or control this activity is unimportant if it does not do so. But that is to disregard the nature of this tax. It is a license tax—a flat tax imposed on the exercise of a privilege granted by the Bill of Rights. A state may not impose a charge for the enjoyment of a right granted by the federal constitution. . . . It is true that the First Amendment, like the commerce clause, draws no distinction between license taxes, fixed sum taxes, and other kinds of taxes. But that is no reason why we should shut our eyes to the nature of the tax and its destructive influence. The power to impose a license tax on the exercise of these freedoms is indeed as potent as the power of censorship which this Court has repeatedly struck down. Lovell v. Griffin (1938). [T]he issuance of the permit or license is dependent on the payment of a license tax. And the license tax is fixed in amount and unrelated to the scope of the activities of petitioners or to their realized revenues. It is not a nominal fee imposed as a regulatory measure to defray the expenses of policing the activities in question. It is in no way apportioned. It is a flat license tax levied and collected as a condition to the pursuit of activities whose enjoyment is guaranteed by the First Amendment. Accordingly, it restrains in advance those constitutional liberties of press and religion and inevitably tends to suppress their exercise. That is almost uniformly recognized as the inherent vice and evil of this flat license tax.

The taxes imposed by this ordinance can hardly help but be as severe and telling in their impact on the freedom of the press and religion as the "taxes on knowledge" at which the First Amendment was partly aimed. They may indeed operate even more subtly. Itinerant evangelists moving throughout a state or from state to state would feel immediately the cumulative effect of such ordinances as they become fashionable. The way of the religious dissenter has long been hard. But if the formula of this type of ordinance is approved, a new device for the suppression of religious minorities will have been found. This method of disseminating religious beliefs can be crushed and closed out by the sheer weight of the toll or tribute which is exacted town by town, village by village. The spread of religious ideas through personal visitations by the literature ministry of numerous religious groups would be stopped.

The fact that the ordinance is "nondiscriminatory" is immaterial. The protection afforded by the First Amendment is not so restricted. A license tax certainly does not acquire constitutional validity because it classifies the privileges protected by the First Amendment along with the wares and merchandise of hucksters and peddlers and treats them all alike. Such equality in treatment does not save the ordinance. Freedom of press, freedom of speech, freedom of religion are in a preferred position.

NOTES AND QUESTIONS

1. *Murdock*: Special Protection for Religious Speech? *Murdock* was decided during the heyday of the idea of "preferred freedoms"—the idea that certain enumerated freedoms are entitled to the special protection of the law. How did this work? Did this special protection extend to all exercises of the freedoms of speech, press, and religion? Does the exemption from license taxes apply to commercial door-to-door sales of cosmetics, brushes, or socks? (Apparently not.) What differentiates Murdock from a commercial salesman? He made his living selling religious tracts, just as clergy earn their living making sermons. Is the distinction one of personal motive—that although he wished to make money, his real motive was to spread the gospel? What if he were selling something other than religious literature, but for the same motive? Some people sell candy to support good causes. Could the license fee apply? Or what if Murdock were distributing literature of a nonreligious nature? The Court implied that the same constitutional protections apply to "freedom of press, freedom of speech, freedom of religion." Does that mean a person selling newspaper subscriptions would be exempt from the tax? Does it matter if the salesperson really *believes* in the publication? How could the police, who administer such ordinances, tell the difference? (Consider the Flannery O'Connor short story "Good Country People," in which a Bible salesman admits that he doesn't believe in "all that crap." Would he be protected under *Murdock*?)

The municipal ordinance in *Murdock*, on its face, was neutral as to content. If the key to free speech analysis is whether a law regulates content, why was the tax held unconstitutional as applied to Jehovah's Witnesses? The Court offered four suggestions.

(a) **Tax directly on preaching?**   One was that the license tax as applied was a direct tax on religious activity: "It is one thing to impose a tax on the income or property of a preacher. It is quite another thing to exact a tax from him for the privilege of delivering a sermon." Suppose Pennsylvania applied its income tax to a preacher who made his living by delivering sermons? Or its property tax to a stack of Bibles awaiting sale in a warehouse? Exactly when is the relation between the tax and the prayer so close that we should call it "direct"? The Court used to apply a similar rule to state taxes on interstate commerce. It abandoned that approach in Complete Auto Transit, Inc. v. Brady, 430 U.S. 274 (1977).

(b) **Cumulative effect?**   The second suggestion the Court made was that license taxes could have a severe cumulative effect on Jehovah's Witnesses: If Murdock had to pay a $7 license fee in each town he visited, it could add up. And the tax was due even if he sold no tracts. But Murdock offered no proof that he was an itinerant evangelist. Suppose Jeannette was his hometown? See Follett v. McCormick, 321 U.S. 573 (1944). Suppose Jeannette charged a sales tax rather than a license tax, so that Murdock would always have money (from the sale proceeds) with which to pay it? Notice the Court's emphasis on *itinerant* evangelists. Does a cumulative license tax favor well-established churches over "religious dissenters?" Are Episcopalians, Catholics, and Jews as likely to pay such a tax?

(c) **Prior restraint?**   The Court's third suggestion was that the license tax was a prior restraint: "It is . . . collected as a condition to the pursuit of [First Amendment activity.] Accordingly, it restrains in advance those constitutional liberties of press and religion and inevitably tends to suppress their exercise." Do you think there should be a First Amendment difference between taxes paid in advance and taxes paid at the end of the year?

(d) **Disproportionate impact?**   The Court observed toward the end of its opinion that Jeannette's tax was "nondiscriminatory." On its face it was.

It applied to peddlers of all kinds—not just First Amendment peddlers. But the Court also noted that the law had a harsher effect on religious minorities. Does this kind of discrimination matter after Employment Division v. Smith? The drug law in that case had a harsher effect on Native Americans, who were forbidden to practice a sacramental rite. Or does *Murdock* state a stricter rule applicable to religious activity that is also protected under the Free Speech Clause?

Consider in this connection Larson v. Valente, 456 U.S. 228 (1982) (see p. 251). The Minnesota charitable solicitations statute required charities to register with the state and file annual reports of income and expenditures. Religious organizations were exempt, but only if they received more than half of their contributions from members (the "50 percent rule"). The state informed the Unification Church that it did not qualify for the exemption, and the church sued. The Court held that the 50 percent rule was a denominational preference, unconstitutional under the Establishment Clause unless it could survive strict scrutiny. (It didn't.)

> Appellants urge that [the rule] is merely "a law based upon secular criteria which may not identically affect all religious organizations." [But the fifty percent rule] is not simply a facially neutral statute, the provisions of which happen to have a "disparate impact" upon different religious organizations. On the contrary, [it] makes explicit and deliberate distinctions between different religious organizations. [It] effectively distinguishes between "well-established churches" that have "achieved strong but not total financial support from their members," on the one hand, and "churches which are new and lacking in a constituency, or which, as a matter of policy, may favor public solicitation over general reliance on financial support from members," on the other hand.

The Court mentioned legislative history suggesting that the 50 percent rule was designed to get at "the Moonies" without hurting mainstream denominations like Catholics. Is there any such evidence in *Murdock*? Can any inference be drawn from the fact that cities across America at this point in time adopted a wide variety of strategies to protect against unpopular evangelizing by Jehovah's Witnesses—many of which were struck down by the Court? Or does the case stand for the proposition that unintended disproportionate effects are enough?

2. The Limits of *Murdock* : Neutral Sales Taxes on Religious Publications. In Jimmy Swaggart Ministries v. Board of Equalization, 493 U.S. 378 (1990) (p. 191), a unanimous Court held that the state of California could apply its 6 percent sales tax to the sales of Bibles, religious pamphlets, and religious recordings by the Swaggart evangelistic organization in California (sales both at evangelistic meetings in California and through mail orders from California purchasers). Swaggart argued that *Murdock* and a companion decision, Follett v. McCormick, 321 U.S. 573 (1944), barred the government from taxing the distribution of religious materials. The *Swaggart* Court, however, said that *Murdock* and *Follett* had rested on "the particular nature of the challenged taxes—flat license taxes that operated as a prior restraint on the exercise of religious liberty." 493 U.S. at 386. By contrast, the sales tax and registration

> do not act as prior restraints—no fee is charged for registering, the tax is due regardless of preregistration, and the tax is not imposed as a precondition of

disseminating the message. Thus, unlike the license tax in *Murdock*, which was "in no way apportioned" to the "realized revenues" of the itinerant preachers forced to pay the tax, the tax at issue in this case is akin to a generally applicable income or property tax[.]

Id. at 390. (As you may recall, a similar distinction had been advanced the Term before in *Texas Monthly v. Bullock* (p. 243), where the plurality opinion concluded that exempting religious publications alone from sales taxes actually violated the Establishment Clause.)

The Court also said that this was not a case where "collection and payment of the tax violates [the taxpayer's] sincere religious beliefs"; it "merely decrease[d] the amount of money [Swaggart] ha[d] to spend on its religious activities," a burden that alone was "not constitutionally significant." (See p. 176ff. above, concerning "burdens on religion.") The Court did leave open the constitutionality of "a more onerous tax rate, [that] even if generally applicable, might effectively choke off an adherent's religious practices" and cited *Murdock*'s concern for the cumulative effect on traveling evangelists of flat taxes "exacted town by town"; but it said that "we face no such situation in this case." 493 U.S. at 392.

Is the distinction between *Murdock* and *Swaggart* persuasive? Or did *Swaggart* overrule *Murdock* without admitting it? See Garvey, What Are Freedoms For? ch. 11.

HEFFRON v. INTERNATIONAL SOCIETY FOR KRISHNA CONSCIOUSNESS
452 U.S. 640 (1981)

Justice WHITE delivered the opinion of the Court.

The question presented for review is whether a State, consistent with the First and Fourteenth Amendments, may require a religious organization desiring to distribute and sell religious literature and to solicit donations at a state fair to conduct those activities only at an assigned location within the fairgrounds even though application of the rule limits the religious practices of the organization.

I

Each year, the Minnesota Agricultural Society (Society), a public corporation organized under the laws of Minnesota, operates a State Fair on a 125-acre state-owned tract located in St. Paul, Minn. The Fair is conducted for the purpose of "exhibiting . . . the agricultural, stock-breeding, horticultural, mining, mechanical, industrial, and other products and resources of the state, including proper exhibits and expositions of the arts, human skills, and sciences." The Fair is a major public event and attracts visitors from all over Minnesota as well as from other parts of the country. During the past five years, the average total attendance for the 12-day Fair has been 1,320,000 persons. The average daily attendance on weekdays has been 115,000 persons and on Saturdays and Sundays 160,000.

The Society is authorized to make all "bylaws, ordinances, and rules, not inconsistent with law, which it may deem necessary or proper for the government of the fair grounds. . . . " Under this authority, the Society promulgated Minnesota State Fair Rule 6.05 which provides in relevant part that

> [s]ale or distribution of any merchandise, including printed or written material except under license issued [by] the Society and/or from a duly-licensed location shall be a misdemeanor.

As Rule 6.05 is construed and applied by the Society, "all persons, groups or firms which desire to sell, exhibit or distribute materials during the annual State Fair must do so only from fixed locations on the fairgrounds." Although the Rule does not prevent organizational representatives from walking about the fairgrounds and communicating the organization's views with fair patrons in face-to-face discussions, it does require that any exhibitor conduct its sales, distribution, and fund solicitation operations from a booth rented from the Society. Space in the fairgrounds is rented to all comers in a nondiscriminatory fashion on a first-come, first-served basis with the rental charge based on the size and location of the booth. The Rule applies alike to nonprofit, charitable, and commercial enterprises. [There typically are more applicants for booths than there are spaces.]

One day prior to the opening of the 1977 Minnesota State Fair, respondents International Society for Krishna Consciousness, Inc. (ISKCON), an international religious society espousing the views of the Krishna religion, and Joseph Beca, head of the Minneapolis ISKCON temple, filed suit against numerous state officials seeking a declaration that Rule 6.05, both on its face and as applied, violated respondents' rights under the First Amendment, and seeking injunctive relief prohibiting enforcement of the Rule against ISKCON and its members. Specifically, ISKCON asserted that the Rule would suppress the practice of Sankirtan, one of its religious rituals, which enjoins its members to go into public places to distribute or sell religious literature and to solicit donations for the support of the Krishna religion.

II

[T]he activities of ISKCON, like those of others protected by the First Amendment, are subject to reasonable time, place, and manner restrictions. "We have often approved restrictions of that kind provided that they are justified without reference to the content of the regulated speech, that they serve a significant governmental interest, and that in doing so they leave open ample alternative channels for communication of the information." Virginia Pharmacy Bd. v. Virginia Citizens Consumer Council (1976). The issue here, as it was below, is whether Rule 6.05 is a permissible restriction on the place and manner of communicating the views of the Krishna religion, more specifically, whether the Society may require the members of ISKCON who desire to practice Sankirtan at the State Fair to confine their distribution, sales, and solicitation activities to a fixed location.

[The Court held that Rule 6.05 in general satisfies these criteria and that the plaintiffs were not entitled to an exception.]

The justification for the Rule should not be measured by the disorder that would result from granting an exemption solely to ISKCON. That organization and its ritual of Sankirtan have no special claim to First Amendment protection as compared to that of other religions who also distribute literature and solicit funds.[15] None of our cases suggest that the inclusion of peripatetic solicitation as part of a church ritual entitles church members to solicitation rights in a public forum superior to those of members of other religious groups that raise money but do not purport to ritualize the process. Nor for present purposes do religious organizations enjoy rights to communicate, distribute, and solicit on the fairgrounds superior to those of other organizations having social, political, or other ideological messages to proselytize. These nonreligious organizations seeking support for their activities are entitled to rights equal to those of religious groups to enter a public forum and spread their views, whether by soliciting funds or by distributing literature.

ISKCON desires to proselytize at the fair because it believes it can successfully communicate and raise funds. In its view, this can be done only by intercepting fair patrons as they move about, and if success is achieved, stopping them momentarily or for longer periods as money is given or exchanged for literature. This consequence would be multiplied many times over if Rule 6.05 could not be applied to confine such transactions by ISKCON and others to fixed locations. Indeed, the court below agreed that without Rule 6.05 there would be widespread disorder at the fairgrounds. The court also recognized that some disorder would inevitably result from exempting the Krishnas from the Rule. Obviously, there would be a much larger threat to the State's interest in crowd control if all other religious, nonreligious, and noncommercial organizations could likewise move freely about the fairgrounds distributing and selling literature and soliciting funds at will.

Given these considerations, we hold that the State's interest in confining distribution, selling, and fund solicitation activities to fixed locations is sufficient to satisfy the requirement that a place or manner restriction must serve a substantial state interest. By focusing on the incidental effect of providing an exemption from Rule 6.05 to ISKCON, the Minnesota Supreme Court did not take into account the fact that any such exemption cannot be meaningfully limited to ISKCON, and as applied to similarly situated groups would prevent the State from furthering its important concern with managing the flow of the crowd. In our view, the Society may apply its Rule and confine the type of transactions at issue to designated locations without violating the First Amendment.

Justice BRENNAN, with whom Justice MARSHALL and Justice STEVENS join, concurring in part and dissenting in part.

[The dissent argued that the Rule was not sufficiently justified as applied to the free distribution of literature, and included this footnote:]

I am somewhat puzzled by the Court's treatment of the Sankirtan issue. Respondents' complaint, based on 42 U.S.C. §1983, alleges that Rule 6.05, on its face and as applied, violates both the Free Exercise and the Free Speech Clauses. In their brief and in oral argument, however, respondents emphasize that they do not claim any special treatment because of Sankirtan, but are willing

15. Respondents . . . concede that whatever exemption they were entitled to under the First Amendment would apply to other organizations seeking similar rights to take part in certain protected activities in the public areas of the fairgrounds.

to rest their challenge wholly upon their general right to free speech, which they concede is identical to the right enjoyed by every other religious, political, or charitable group. There is therefore no need for the Court to discuss Sankirtan.

Having chosen to discuss it, however, the Court does so in a manner that is seemingly inconsistent with prior case law. The parties have stipulated that members of ISKCON have a unique "duty to perform a religious ritual known as *Sankirtan*, which consists of going out into public places, to disseminate or sell religious literature and to solicit contributions to support the publishing, religious, and educational functions of Krishna Consciousness." The Court, however, disparages the significance of this ritual. . . .

Our cases are clear that governmental regulations which interfere with the exercise of specific religious beliefs or principles should be scrutinized with particular care. See, e.g., Sherbert v. Verner. As we stated in Wisconsin v. Yoder, "there are areas of conduct protected by the Free Exercise Clause of the First Amendment and thus beyond the power of the State to control, even under regulations of general applicability." I read the Court as accepting these precedents, and merely holding that even if Sankirtan is "conduct protected by the Free Exercise Clause," it is entitled to no greater protection than other forms of expression protected by the First Amendment that are burdened to the same extent by Rule 6.05.

[Justice Blackmun filed a separate dissenting opinion, in which he said that, "like Justice Brennan," he "would not reach the question whether respondents can claim an exemption from the operation of Rule 6.05 because of their adherence to the doctrine of Sankirtan."]

NOTES AND QUESTIONS

1. Religious Speech and Free Exercise Protections. What is Justice Brennan suggesting? If ISKCON had made an independent free exercise argument, based on the religious duty to engage in the ritual of Sankirtan, would it have prevailed? Remember that *Heffron* was decided before Employment Division v. Smith, and that the legal standard applicable to burdens on the exercise of religion (strict scrutiny under *Sherbert*) was more stringent than that applied to content-neutral time, place, and manner speech regulations. So it is possible that ISKCON could have prevailed on its free exercise claim, even though it lost as a pure free speech claimant.

Even after *Smith*, speech that also constitutes the discharge of a religious obligation might sometimes receive greater protection. For example, the religious exercise/speech might be protected under the Religious Freedom Restoration Act (RFRA) (if federal law is involved) or a state equivalent. Alternatively, it might be a "hybrid" right—a combination of speech and free exercise. As we saw in Section III-A, if the hybrid-rights doctrine means anything, it is that a non-free-exercise constitutional claim (speech, parental control over education) that is insufficient on its own can be strengthened, and perhaps become successful, when a free exercise claim is added to it: that is, when the speech or the parental decision-making is religiously motivated.

Is it appropriate to apply such doctrines to religious speech? One central theme in the law of freedom of speech is that the government must not favor the expression of one viewpoint over others. If the hybrid-rights approach is taken seriously, does it violate the principle of viewpoint neutrality by giving an additional legal claim to religious viewpoints? Is a statute like RFRA, which grants distinctive protection to religious exercise, inappropriate to apply when the religious exercise is speech?*

Suppose that two persons protest on the grounds of a federal government building, one against abortion on the ground that it violates God's will, the other against American foreign policy on secular grounds. Both are arrested by U.S. marshals for assembling on federal property without authorization. The religious protester raises the Religious Freedom Restoration Act as a defense, arguing that the limit on assembly does not serve a compelling governmental interest. The secular protester cannot raise this defense. Would recognizing the religious protester's RFRA defense, with no corresponding defense for the secular protester, be unconstitutional under the speech clause?

Suppose the situation involves two protesters presenting the same facially secular antiabortion message ("Abortion takes a life"), but one protester is religiously *motivated* and the other is not. Is accommodation for the religious claimant more acceptable in that case, on the ground that the distinction is not based on the *content* of the message?

Recall Justice White's concurring argument in Texas Monthly v. Bullock (p. 243) that the Texas sales tax exemption for religious publications violated the Free Press Clause by "discriminat[ing] on the basis of the content of publications." The First Amendment's Free Speech Clause likewise prohibits different treatment on the basis of the content of speech (at least in most cases), and especially on the basis of the viewpoint reflected in speech. As we will see in the next set of readings, religious speakers have invoked the Free Speech Clause to challenge policies that singled out religious expression for restriction in public parks and public schools. See, e.g., Capitol Square Review Bd. v. Pinette, 515 U.S. 753 (1995); Lamb's Chapel v. Center Moriches School Dist., 508 U.S. 384 (1993). Shouldn't the principle work the other way too, to prevent singling out religious expression for exemption? See Alan Brownstein, State RFRA Statutes and Freedom of Speech, 32 U.C. Davis L. Rev. 605 (1999) (arguing that free speech principles forbid special protection for religiously motivated speech as well as for speech with religious content).

If the content-neutrality principles of free speech law forbid accommodations specifically for religious speech, might that severely undermine the principle of accommodation? Could not many forms of religious activity seeking accommodation—for example, wearing a beard or a certain kind of headdress or using drugs at a worship service—be characterized as speech or expression? If there is a conflict between the content and viewpoint neutrality of free speech principles and the special status of religious exercise under the Religion Clause, how

---

*Although RFRA's text does not address this issue, its legislative history did say that "where religious exercise involves speech, as in the case of distributing religious literature, reasonable time, place, and manner restrictions are permissible consistent with [free speech] jurisprudence." S. Rep. No. 103-111, reprinted in 1993 U.S. Code Cong. & Admin. News 1892, 1903.

should we resolve the conflict? Should free speech equality override free exercise accommodation, or should it be the other way around?

2. Restrictions on Door-to-Door Canvassing.   In Watchtower Bible and Tract Society of New York v. Village of Stratton, 536 U.S. 150 (2002), the Court ruled for the Jehovah's Witnesses again in their challenge to an ordinance that required door-to-door solicitors obtain a prior permit from the village and show it upon request; the permit was free but required the applicant to disclose his or her name, thereby forefeiting the ability to canvass anonymously. In striking down the law, the Court said that it covered advocacy of a wide range of "unpopular causes unrelated to commercial transactions or to any special interest in protecting the electoral process," and "impose[d] an objective burden on some speech of citizens holding religious or patriotic views," for example, "persons whose religious scruples will prevent them from applying for such a license." *Id.* at 167. Is this reasoning consistent with Heffron v. ISKCON?

3. Problems: Special Protection for Religious Speech?

(a) The Big Sandy Independent School District, in Texas, enforces a dress code restricting the hair length of male students. There is no evidence that the purpose of the restriction is discriminatory. Courts have generally rebuffed constitutional challenges by students who assert a free speech right to express themselves by wearing long hair. Several members of the Alabama and Coushatta Tribes challenge the restrictions, asserting that wearing long hair is deeply rooted in the tribe's traditional religious beliefs. Assuming that can be proved—and that either the hybrid-rights doctrine or a state equivalent of RFRA applies—what should be the result? Would It violate the viewpoint-neutrality requirements of the Free Speech Clause to exempt students with religious objections to the hair length rule, without also exempting students whose objection is based on taste, style, or politics? Would it violate the Establishment Clause? Is the case any different because the conduct in question is not "pure speech"? (The students believe they should wear their hair long because of the sacredness of the body, independent of any message this may communicate to others.) See Alabama and Coushatta Tribes v. Big Sandy Ind. Sch. Dist., 817 F. Supp. 1319 (E.D. Tex. 1993).

(b) High-security prisons generally do not allow inmates to form groups and hold discussion sessions. Can they deny the right of inmates to participate in worship services? Or must they make exceptions for communal worship? If they do, is it a form of viewpoint discrimination? Should acts of worship be treated as merely one variety of speech? Would such treatment be consistent with the Court's approval of RLUIPA, the statute protecting prisoners' religious exercise, in Cutter v. Wilkinson (p. 239)?

(c) An acting student at a public university, who was a devout Mormon, refused to use certain words that she considered profane or blasphemous, and as a result she was constructively expelled from the program. In a constitutional challenge, she was prepared to introduce expert testimony that the use of such language is not essential for professional preparation in dramatics. She contended that the university's action violated her freedom not to be compelled to speak. She relied on Bd. of Educ. v. Barnette (p. 479) (holding it unconstitutional to force an objecting student to say the Pledge of Allegiance). That argument was rejected. Should it have been? Can *Barnette* be distinguished? She also raised a "hybrid" claim under *Smith*, based on her conviction that the use of the language in question would violate her religious beliefs. If the university agreed not to compel a student to utter words in violation of her religious conscience, would it be constitutionally required to excuse students from *any* acting roles they did not wish to perform? See Axson-Flynn v. Johnson, 151 F. Supp. 2d 1326 (D. Utah 2001), rev'd on other grounds, 356 F.3d 1277 (10th Cir. 2004).

(d) Suppose that two private groups seek permits to put up Christmas-related displays in a city park—one a crèche, the other a set of secular figures such as Santa and snowmen. Both are blocked by a content-neutral ordinance limiting the size and duration of private displays. Can the group erecting the crèche have any greater constitutional rights than the other? Does it matter that under Establishment Clause decisions such as *County of Allegheny* (p. 519), displays of crèches under city sponsorship are limited in ways that displays of secular figures are not?

3. Religious Speech in Public Forums: Does the Establishment Clause Require Greater Restrictions?

The Establishment Clause prohibits too close an association between religious activity and government. The question posed by the next set of readings is whether this places special limitations on the right of private speakers to express explicitly religious messages on government property.

WIDMAR v. VINCENT
454 U.S. 263 (1981)

Justice POWELL delivered the opinion of the court.

[The University of Missouri at Kansas City (UMKC) provides facilities for the meetings of more than 100 officially recognized student organizations. Students pay an activity free of $41 per semester to help defray the costs. Cornerstone, an organization of evangelical Christian students from various denominations, was allowed for several years to meet in classrooms and in the student center. The meetings, open to the public, attracted up to 125 students. They typically included prayer, hymns, Bible commentary, and discussion of religious views and experiences. In 1972 the board of curators adopted a regulation forbidding the use of University buildings "for purposes of religious worship or religious teaching." The University thereafter informed Cornerstone that it could no longer meet on campus. Several members sued. The district court upheld the regulation. The Eighth Circuit reversed.]

Through its policy of accommodating their meetings, the University has created a forum generally open for use by student groups. Having done so, the University has assumed an obligation to justify its discriminations and exclusions under applicable constitutional norms. The Constitution forbids a State to enforce certain exclusions from a forum generally open to the public, even if it was not required to create the forum in the first place. . . .

Here the UMKC has discriminated against student groups and speakers based on their desire to use a generally open forum to engage in religious worship and discussion. These are forms of speech and association protected by the First Amendment. In order to justify discriminatory exclusion from a public forum based on the religious content of a group's intended speech, the University must therefore satisfy the standard of review appropriate to content-based exclusions. It must show that its regulation is necessary to serve a compelling state interest and that it is narrowly drawn to achieve that end.

[The] University claims a compelling interest in maintaining strict separation of church and State. It . . . argues that it cannot offer its facilities to religious groups and speakers on the terms available to other groups without violating the Establishment Clause of the Constitution of the United States. We agree that the interest of the University in complying with its constitutional obligations may be characterized as compelling. It does not follow, however, that an "equal access" policy would be incompatible with this Court's Establishment Clause cases [decided under the three-part *Lemon* test].

In this case two prongs of the test are clearly met. Both the District Court and the Court of Appeals held that an open-forum policy, including nondiscrimination against religious speech, would have a secular purpose and would avoid entanglement with religion.[11] But the District Court concluded, and the University argues here, that allowing religious groups to share the limited public forum would have the "primary effect" of advancing religion. . . .

We are satisfied that any religious benefits of an open forum at UMKC would be "incidental" within the meaning of our cases. Two factors are especially relevant.

First, an open forum in a public university does not confer any imprimatur of state approval on religious sects or practices. As the Court of Appeals quite aptly stated, such a policy "would no more commit the University . . . to religious goals" than it is "now committed to the goals of the Students for a Democratic Society, the Young Socialist Alliance," or any other group eligible to use its facilities.

Second, the forum is available to a broad class of nonreligious as well as religious speakers; there are over 100 recognized student groups at UMKC. The provision of benefits to so broad a spectrum of groups is an important index of secular effect. If the Establishment Clause barred the extension of general benefits to religious groups, "a church could not be protected by the police and fire departments, or have its public sidewalk kept in repair." At least in the absence of empirical evidence that religious groups will dominate UMKC's open forum, we agree with the Court of Appeals that the advancement of religion would not be the forum's "primary effect." . . .

Our holding in this case in no way undermines the capacity of the University to establish reasonable time, place, and manner regulations. . . . The basis for our decision is narrow. Having created a forum generally open to student groups, the University seeks to enforce a content-based exclusion of religious speech. Its exclusionary policy violates the fundamental principle that a state regulation of speech should be content-neutral, and the University is unable to justify this violation under applicable constitutional standards.

Justice STEVENS, concurring in the judgment.

. . . Because every university's resources are limited, an educational institution must routinely make decisions concerning the use of the time and space

---

11. [T]he University would risk greater "entanglement" by attempting to enforce its exclusion of "religious worship" and "religious speech." Initially, the University would need to determine which words and activities fall within "religious worship and religious teaching." . . . There would also be a continuing need to monitor group meetings to ensure compliance with the rule.

that is available for extracurricular activities. In my judgment, it is both necessary and appropriate for those decisions to evaluate the content of a proposed student activity. I should think it obvious, for example, that if two groups of 25 students requested the use of a room at a particular time—one to view Mickey Mouse cartoons and the other to rehearse an amateur performance of Hamlet— the First Amendment would not require that the room be reserved for the group that submitted its application first. . . . Judgments of this kind should be made by academicians, not by federal judges, and their standards for decision should not be encumbered with ambiguous phrases like "compelling state interest."

Justice WHITE, dissenting.

In affirming the decision of the Court of Appeals, the majority rejects petitioners' argument that the Establishment Clause of the Constitution prohibits the use of university buildings for religious purposes. A state university may permit its property to be used for purely religious services without violating the First and Fourteenth Amendments. With this I agree. The Establishment Clause, however, sets limits only on what the State may do with respect to religious organizations; it does not establish what the State is *required* to do. I have long argued that Establishment Clause limits on state action which incidentally aids religion are not as strict as the Court has held. The step from the permissible to the necessary, however, is a long one. In my view, just as there is room under the Religion Clauses for state policies that may have some beneficial effect on religion, there is also room for state policies that may incidentally burden religion. In other words, I believe the States to be a good deal freer to formulate policies that affect religion in divergent ways than does the majority. See Sherbert v. Verner (Harlan, J., dissenting). The majority's position will inevitably lead to those contradictions and tensions between the Establishment and Free Exercise Clauses warned against by Justice Stewart in *Sherbert*.

A large part of respondents' argument, accepted by the majority, is founded on the proposition that because religious worship uses speech, it is protected by the Free Speech Clause of the First Amendment. Not only is it protected, they argue, but religious worship *qua* speech is not different from any other variety of protected speech as a matter of constitutional principle. I believe that this proposition is plainly wrong. Were it right, the Religion Clauses would be emptied of any independent meaning in circumstances in which religious practice took the form of speech.[3]

There may be instances in which a State's attempt to disentangle itself from religious worship would intrude upon secular speech about religion. In such a case, the State's action would be subject to challenge under the Free Speech Clause of the First Amendment. This is not such a case. This case involves religious worship only; the fact that that worship is accomplished through speech does not add anything to respondents' argument. That argument must rely upon the claim that the State's action impermissibly interferes with the free

---

3. Indeed, while footnote 6 of the majority opinion suggests that no intelligible distinction may be drawn between worship and other forms of speech, footnote 9 recognizes that the Establishment Clause "requires" that such a line be drawn. The majority does not adequately explain why the State is "required" to observe a line in one context, but prohibited from voluntarily recognizing it in another context. [Footnote relocated—EDS.]

exercise of respondents' religious practices. Although this is a close question, I conclude that it does not.

[There are a variety of plausible analogies to this case.] Respondents argue, and the majority agrees, that by permitting any student group to use its facilities for communicative purposes other than religious worship, the University has created a "public forum." With ample support, they argue that the State may not make content-based distinctions as to what groups may use, or what messages may be conveyed in, such a forum. . . . Moreover, it is clear that there are bounds beyond which the University could not go in enforcing its regulation: I do not suppose it could prevent students from saying grace before meals in the school cafeteria, or prevent distribution of religious literature on campus.

Petitioners, on the other hand, argue that allowing use of their facilities for religious worship is constitutionally indistinguishable from directly subsidizing such religious services. They argue that the fact that secular student groups are entitled to the in-kind subsidy at issue here does not establish that a religious group is entitled to the same subsidy. They could convincingly argue, for example, that a state university that pays for basketballs for the basketball team is not thereby required to pay for Bibles for a group like Cornerstone. . . .

. . . Because [these analogies] lead to different results, however, they are of limited help in reaching a decision here. . . . In my view, therefore, resolution of this case is best achieved by returning to first principles. This requires an assessment of the burden on respondents' ability freely to exercise their religious beliefs and practices and of the State's interest in enforcing its regulation.

Respondents complain that compliance with the regulation would require them to meet "about a block and a half" from campus under conditions less comfortable than those previously available on campus. I view this burden on free exercise as minimal. Because the burden is minimal, the State need do no more than demonstrate that the regulation furthers some permissible state end. The State's interest in avoiding claims that it is financing or otherwise supporting religious worship—in maintaining a definitive separation between church and State—is such an end.

NOTES AND QUESTIONS

1. The Free Speech Right. What triggers UMKC's free speech obligation in this case? Is the campus a traditional public forum (like a park or street)? If it is not, then why is strict scrutiny appropriate? Suppose that an evangelical group of townies (not students) wanted to meet on the campus. Would they have a First Amendment right to do so?

Suppose that we protect free speech rights for students because this is part of their education. See John H. Garvey, What Are Freedoms For? 97-111 (1996). Does this mean that the University could deny space to meetings that had no educational value? Could it make judgments based on content in allocating limited classroom space—for example, prefer Hamlet over Mickey Mouse (or vice versa?), as Justice Stevens suggests? Must it have a compelling reason for doing so? Could it decide that religious worship has no educational value?

2. No Establishment Violation.   *Widmar* was arguably the breaking point in the development of modern Establishment Clause doctrine. In the decade between *Lemon* and *Widmar*, with one minor exception, the Court handed down a string of decisions greatly narrowing the permissible range of government benefits to religious institutions. The theory was that the Establishment Clause precludes the government from providing assistance to the propagation of religious messages, even on a neutral basis. If the government provided assistance to a religiously affiliated organization, it had to be restricted to the strictly secular aspects of the organization's work, and if enforcement of such a restriction required significant monitoring, this would violate the entanglement prong. See Section IV-C. If that view were applied unflinchingly to the facts in *Widmar*, the case would have come out the other way.

On the other hand, from the perspective of the public forum doctrine, *Widmar* seemed an easy and obvious case—the other way. The Court had already held that public universities could not exclude radical student political groups on the basis of the content of their speech. Healy v. James, 408 U.S. 169 (1972). How could it exclude students who wanted to pray and discuss the Bible? None of the usual Establishment Clause concerns seemed pertinent: The program was neutral, no taxpayers saw their money transferred to religious groups, and no one would say that a university "endorses" a student group when it simply allows the group to meet. That was precisely the misconception the Court dispelled in *Healy* : that recognizing a university student group would give it the "college's stamp of approval." 408 U.S. at 182. A university does not "endorse" everything it permits on a neutral basis. Accordingly, even the most fervently separationist Justices, who also were the most fervently committed to freedom of speech, voted in favor of the religious student group.

Yet in principle the *Widmar* decision was diametrically opposed to the *Lemon* line of cases. Free meeting space is a form of subsidy; no attempt was made to ensure that Cornerstone's use of the classroom space was limited to its secular activities (if it had any). It is no answer under *Lemon* and *Nyquist* to say that the aid was provided on a neutral basis. The Establishment Clause stands as a bar to the subsidy of religion. If equal *funding* "advances" religion, why would equal access to *facilities* be any different?

When two inconsistent principles apply to the same legal terrain, usually one crowds out the other. In the years after *Widmar*, the Court began to see more and more cases through the lens of "equal access" rather than the lens of "no aid." Recall, for example, Mueller v. Allen, Witters v. Washington Dept. of Services, Mitchell v. Helms, and Zelman v. Simmon-Harris (Part IV-D). At first, the Court did not appear to notice the deep doctrinal contradiction this created. *Witters* (1986) was unanimous. It was not until Rosenberger v. University of Virginia (1995) that the Court seriously faced up to the inconsistency between "equal access" norms and "no aid" norms. Review that decision (discussed at pp. 403 and 435) to see how the Court dealt with the problem.

3. Legislative Accommodation in Reverse?   The Court has consistently held that the government may make accommodations for the exercise of religion, even when this is not required by the Free Exercise Clause. See Part III-C. In effect, the state has discretion to promote the constitutional value of free exercise beyond its strict, judicially enforceable minimum. Is there any parallel on the Establishment Clause side? May the state maintain a stricter separation between church and state than the Establishment Clause requires? Can it do so even if this would violate other parts of the First Amendment, such as freedom of speech? The Court rejected such an argument in *Widmar*, 454 U.S. at 275-276. Would *Widmar* have been a good case in whcih to recognize such a principle?

4. Distinguishing Religious Worship from Speech. In his dissenting opinion Justice White argued that "religious worship" is a special category, not fully protected by the free speech and equal protection guarantees of the First and Fourteenth Amendments. If "religious worship" were protected "speech," he reasoned, "the Religion Clauses would be emptied of any independent meaning in circumstances in which religious practice took the form of speech." The majority responded in a lengthy footnote:

> This is a novel argument. The dissent does not deny that speech *about* religion is speech entitled to the general protections of the First Amendment. It does not argue that descriptions of religious experiences fail to qualify as "speech." Nor does it repudiate last Term's decision in *Heffron*, which assumed that religious appeals to nonbelievers constituted protected "speech." Rather, the dissent seems to attempt a distinction between the kinds of religious speech explicitly protected by our cases and a new class of religious "speech act[s]," constituting "worship." There are at least three difficulties with this distinction.
>
> First, the dissent fails to establish that the distinction has intelligible content. There is no indication when "singing hymns, reading scripture, and teaching biblical principles" cease to be "singing, teaching, and reading"—all apparently forms of "speech," despite their religious subject matter—and become unprotected "worship."
>
> Second, even if the distinction drew an arguably principled line, it is highly doubtful that it would lie within the judicial competence to administer. Merely to draw the distinction would require the university—and ultimately the courts—to inquire into the significance of words and practices to different religious faiths, and in varying circumstances by the same faith. Such inquiries would tend inevitably to entangle the State with religion in a manner forbidden by our cases.
>
> Finally, the dissent fails to establish the *relevance* of the distinction on which it seeks to rely. The dissent apparently wishes to preserve the vitality of the Establishment Clause. But it gives no reason why the Establishment Clause, or any other provision of the Constitution, would require different treatment for religious speech designed to win religious converts, see *Heffron*, than for religious worship by persons already converted. It is far from clear that the State gives greater support in the latter case than in the former.

Do you understand the significance of this debate? If the Free Speech Clause applies, the government must not "single out" religious speech—something it necessarily does under both Free Exercise and Establishment Clauses—without compelling justification. But free speech doctrine carves out certain categories—obscenity, fighting words, commercial speech, defamation—for lesser or no protection. Apparently, Justice White would treat "worship" in that way. Under his approach, religious worship would be entitled to constitutional protection under the Free Exercise Clause, but not under the Free Speech Clause. Sometimes this would result in more protection (*Sherbert*) and sometimes less (*Widmar*). The relevant question in *Widmar* would not be whether the university was being neutral (the free speech question) but whether it was imposing a substantial burden on the exercise of religion. Would that be a better way to deal with these cases?

Is Justice White's position here consistent with his concurring opinion in Texas Monthly v. Bullock (see p. 243) in which he argued that favoring religious magazines violated the Free Press Clause? Why would it be permissible to disfavor religious groups in *Widmar*, but unconstitutional to favor religious groups in *Texas Monthly*? Is it because of the Press Clause? Is it because religious magazines are not engaged in "worship"?

5. Problems: Faculty Speech. Suppose an evangelical faculty member at UMKC wanted to give an extracurricular lecture about the influence that Jesus had on his own life and work. He invited students in his own class, but also opened it to other students and faculty, and stated that attendance would not affect academic credit. Other faculty had been allowed to make such talks about their interests, both personal and professional. After *Widmar*, could the university deny classroom space to the faculty member? What if the faculty member referred to the lecture as an "optional class"? Could the university forbid him to make observations about his personal beliefs in the course of his regular class lectures? See Bishop v. Aronov, 926 F.2d 1066 (11th Cir. 1991).

Are high school teachers more constrained? Suppose a teacher keeps a Bible at his desk and reads to himself while students are taking a test? Is this unconstitutional? May the principal forbid him to do so? Roberts v. Madigan, 921 F.2d 1047 (10th Cir. 1990); Doe v. Duncanville Ind. Sch. Dist., 70 F.3d 402 (5th Cir. 1995).

CAPITOL SQUARE REVIEW & ADVISORY BOARD v. PINETTE
515 U.S. 753 (1995)

Justice SCALIA announced the judgment of the Court and delivered the opinion of the Court with respect to Parts I, II, and III, and an opinion with respect to Part IV, in which THE CHIEF JUSTICE, Justice KENNEDY and Justice THOMAS join.

I

Capitol Square is a 10-acre, state-owned plaza surrounding the Statehouse in Columbus, Ohio. For over a century the square has been used for public speeches, gatherings, and festivals advocating and celebrating a variety of causes, both secular and religious. Ohio Admin. Code Ann. § 128-4-02(A) makes the square available "for use by the public . . . for free discussion of public questions, or for activities of a broad public purpose," and Ohio Rev. Code Ann. § 105.41 gives the Capitol Square Review and Advisory Board responsibility for regulating public access. To use the square, a group must simply fill out an official application form and meet several criteria, which concern primarily safety, sanitation, and non-interference with other uses of the square, and which are neutral as to the speech content of the proposed event. . . . Such diverse groups as homosexual rights organizations, the Ku Klux Klan and the United Way have held rallies. The Board has also permitted a variety of unattended displays on Capitol Square: a State-sponsored lighted tree during the Christmas season, a privately-sponsored menorah during Chanukah, a display showing the progress of a United Way fundraising campaign, and booths and exhibits during an arts festival. [In

November 1993, the Ohio Ku Klux Klan applied for permission to place a cross on the square from December 8 to 24. The Board denied the application, and the Klan sued. The Board defended its action on the ground that the permit would violate the Establishment Clause. The district court ordered the Board to grant a permit, and the Sixth Circuit affirmed.]

II

. . . Respondents' religious display in Capitol Square was private expression. Our precedent establishes that private religious speech, far from being a First Amendment orphan, is as fully protected under the Free Speech Clause as secular private expression. *Heffron.* Indeed, in Anglo-American history, at least, government suppression of speech has so commonly been directed precisely at religious speech that a free-speech clause without religion would be Hamlet without the prince. Accordingly, we have not excluded from free-speech protections religious proselytizing or even acts of worship. Petitioners do not dispute that respondents, in displaying their cross, were engaging in constitutionally protected expression. They do contend that the constitutional protection does not extend to the length of permitting that expression to be made on Capitol Square.

It is undeniable, of course, that speech which is constitutionally protected against state suppression is not thereby accorded a guaranteed forum on all property owned by the State. The right to use government property for one's private expression depends upon whether the property has by law or tradition been given the status of a public forum, or rather has been reserved for specific official uses. If the former, a State's right to limit protected expressive activity is sharply circumscribed: it may impose reasonable, content-neutral time, place and manner restrictions (a ban on all unattended displays, which did not exist here, might be one such), but it may regulate expressive *content* only if such a restriction is necessary, and narrowly drawn, to serve a compelling state interest. These strict standards apply here, since the District Court and the Court of Appeals found that Capitol Square was a traditional public forum.

Petitioners do not claim that their denial of respondents' application was based upon a content-neutral time, place, or manner restriction. To the contrary, they concede—indeed it is the essence of their case—that the Board rejected the display precisely because its content was religious. Petitioners advance a single justification for closing Capitol Square to respondents' cross: the State's interest in avoiding official endorsement of Christianity, as required by the Establishment Clause.

III

[In this section the Court noted the similarities between this case and Lamb's Chapel v. Center Moriches School Dist., 508 U.S. 384 (1993), and Widmar v. Vincent, two decisions in which private groups with religious interests were held to have an equal right to meet on the property of public schools.]

IV

Petitioners argue that one feature of the present case distinguishes it from *Lamb's Chapel* and *Widmar* : the forum's proximity to the seat of government, which, they contend, may produce the perception that the cross bears the State's approval. They urge us to apply the so-called "endorsement test," see, e.g., Allegheny County v. ACLU; Lynch v. Donnelly, and to find that, because an observer might mistake private expression for officially endorsed religious expression, the State's content-based restriction is constitutional.

We must note, to begin with, that it is not really an "endorsement test" of any sort, much less the "endorsement test" which appears in our more recent Establishment Clause jurisprudence, that petitioners urge upon us. "Endorsement" connotes an expression or demonstration of approval or support. Our cases have accordingly equated "endorsement" with "promotion" or "favoritism." We find it peculiar to say that government "promotes" or "favors" a religious display by giving it the same access to a public forum that all other displays enjoy. And as a matter of Establishment Clause jurisprudence, we have consistently held that it is no violation for government to enact neutral policies that happen to benefit religion. See, e.g., Bowen v. Kendrick; Witters v. Washington Dept. of Services; Mueller v. Allen; McGowan v. Maryland. Where we have tested for endorsement of religion, the subject of the test was either expression *by the government itself, Lynch,* or else government action alleged to *discriminate in favor* of private religious expression or activity, *Allegheny County.* The test petitioners propose, which would attribute to a neutrally behaving government *private* religious expression, has no antecedent in our jurisprudence, and would better be called a "transferred endorsement" test.

"[T]here is a crucial difference between government speech endorsing religion, which the Establishment Clause forbids, and private speech endorsing religion, which the Free Speech and Free Exercise Clauses protect." Board of Education v. Mergens (1990). Petitioners assert, in effect, that that distinction disappears when the private speech is conducted too close to the symbols of government. But that, of course, must be merely a subpart of a more general principle: that the distinction disappears whenever private speech can be mistaken for government speech. That proposition cannot be accepted, at least where, as here, the government has not fostered or encouraged the mistake.

Of course, giving sectarian religious speech preferential access to a forum close to the seat of government (or anywhere else for that matter) would violate the Establishment Clause (as well as the Free Speech Clause, since it would involve content discrimination). And one can conceive of a case in which a governmental entity manipulates its administration of a public forum close to the seat of government (or within a government building) in such a manner that only certain religious groups take advantage of it, creating an impression of endorsement *that is in fact accurate.* But those situations, which involve governmental favoritism, do not exist here. Capitol Square is a genuinely public forum, is known to be a public forum, and has been widely used as a public forum for many, many years. Private religious speech cannot be subject to veto by those who see favoritism where there is none.

The contrary view, most strongly espoused by Justice Stevens, . . . exiles private religious speech to a realm of less-protected expression heretofore inhabited only by sexually explicit displays and commercial speech. Young v. American Mini Theatres (1976); Central Hudson Gas & Electric Corp. v. Public Serv.

Comm'n (1980). It will be a sad day when this Court casts piety in with porn-ography, and finds the First Amendment more hospitable to private expletives, see Cohen v. California (1971), than to private prayers. This would be merely bizarre were religious speech simply as protected by the Constitution as other forms of private speech; but it is outright perverse when one considers that private religious expression receives preferential treatment under the Free Exercise Clause. It is no answer to say that the Establishment Clause tempers religious speech. By its terms that Clause applies only to the words and acts of government. It was never meant, and has never been read by this Court, to serve as an impediment to purely private religious speech connected to the State only through its occurrence in a public forum.

Since petitioners' "transferred endorsement" principle cannot possibly be restricted to squares in front of state capitols, the Establishment Clause regime that it would usher in is most unappealing. . . . Policy makers would find themselves in a vise between the Establishment Clause on one side and the Free Speech and Free Exercise Clauses on the other. Every proposed act of private, religious expression in a public forum would force officials to weigh a host of imponderables. How close to government is too close? What kind of building, and in what context, symbolizes state authority? If the State guessed wrong in one direction, it would be guilty of an Establishment Clause violation; if in the other, it would be liable for suppressing free exercise or free speech (a risk not run when the State restrains only its own expression),

Justice O'CONNOR, with whom Justice SOUTER and Justice BREYER join, concurring in part and concurring in the judgment.

I join Parts I, II, and III of the Court's opinion and concur in the judgment. . . . I see no necessity to carve out, as the plurality opinion would today, an exception to the endorsement test for the public forum context. . . . I conclude on the facts of this case that . . . the reasonable observer would not interpret the State's tolerance of the Klan's private religious display in Capitol Square as an endorsement of religion. [Justice O'Connor argued that because the cross was displayed in a place that had been used by other private groups and because it carried a sign disclaiming any state endorsement, the "reasonable observer" would conclude that there was no state endorsement.]

Justice STEVENS, dissenting.

The Establishment Clause . . . "prohibits government from appearing to take a position on questions of religious belief or from 'making adherence to a religion relevant in any way to a person's standing in the political community.' " Lynch v. Donnelly (O'Connor, J., concurring). At least when religious symbols are involved, the question of whether the state is "appearing to take a position" is best judged from the standpoint of a "reasonable observer." It is especially important to take account of the perspective of a reasonable observer who may not share the particular religious belief it expresses. A paramount purpose of the Establishment Clause is to protect such a person from being made to feel like an outsider in matters of faith, and a stranger in the political community. If a reasonable person could perceive a government endorsement of religion from a private display, then the State may not allow its property to be used as a forum for that display. No less stringent rule can adequately protect non-adherents from a well-grounded perception that their sovereign supports a faith to which they do not subscribe.[5]

In determining whether the State's maintenance of the Klan's cross in front of the Statehouse conveyed a forbidden message of endorsement, we should be mindful of the power of a symbol standing alone and unexplained. Even on private property, signs and symbols are generally understood to express the owner's views. The location of the sign is a significant component of the message it conveys. . . . The very fact that a sign is installed on public property implies official recognition and reinforcement of its message. That implication is especially strong when the sign stands in front of the seat of the government itself. The "reasonable observer" of any symbol placed unattended in front of any capitol in the world will normally assume that the sovereign—which is not only the owner of that parcel of real estate but also the lawgiver for the surrounding territory—has sponsored and facilitated its message. . . .

Because structures on government property—and, in particular, in front of buildings plainly identified with the state—imply state approval of their message, the Government must have considerable leeway, outside of the religious arena, to choose what kinds of displays it will allow and what kinds it will not. Although the First Amendment requires the Government to allow leafletting or demonstrating outside its buildings, the state has greater power to exclude unattended symbols when they convey a type of message with which the state does not wish to be identified. I think it obvious, for example, that Ohio could prohibit certain categories of signs or symbols in Capitol Square—erotic exhibits, commercial advertising, and perhaps campaign posters as well—without violating the Free Speech Clause. Moreover, our "public forum" cases do not foreclose public entities from enforcing prohibitions against all unattended displays in public parks, or possibly even limiting the use of such displays to the communication of non-controversial messages. Such a limitation would not inhibit any of the traditional forms of expression that have been given full constitutional protection in public fora.

The State's general power to restrict the types of unattended displays does not alone suffice to decide this case, because Ohio did not profess to be exercising any such authority. Instead, the Capitol Square Review Board denied a permit for the cross because it believed the Establishment Clause required as much, and we cannot know whether the Board would have denied the permit on other grounds.

Accordingly, we must evaluate the State's rationale on its own terms. But in this case, the endorsement inquiry under the Establishment Clause follows from the State's power to exclude unattended private displays from public property. Just as the Constitution recognizes the State's interest in preventing its

5. Justice O'Connor agrees that an "endorsement test" is appropriate and that we should judge endorsement from the standpoint of a reasonable observer. But her reasonable observer is a legal fiction [who] knows and understands much more than meets the eye. [This] strips of constitutional protection every reasonable person whose knowledge happens to fall below some "ideal" standard. . . . I would extend protection to the universe of reasonable persons and ask whether some viewers of the religious display would be likely to perceive a government endorsement. [To say] that "there is always someone" who will feel excluded by any particular governmental action ignores the requirement that such an apprehension be objectively reasonable. A person who views an exotic cow at the zoo as a symbol of the Government's approval of the Hindu religion cannot survive this test.

property from being used as a conduit for ideas it does not wish to give the appearance of ratifying, the Establishment Clause prohibits government from allowing, and thus endorsing, unattended displays that take a position on a religious issue.

NOTES AND QUESTIONS

1. Neutrality and Religious Expression.   The general rule in public forum law is that the government may not engage in content discrimination in a traditional public forum. The Board argued in *Pinette* that this rule did not apply to religious speech—indeed, that the government was forbidden to treat religious speakers like other speakers. Why should this be? There are, as Justice Scalia observes, some categories of speech that get less protection (even in public forums) because of their content, such as pornography and commercial advertising. Does the Establishment Clause imply that religious speech has a low value like those categories? Don't the Free Speech and Free Exercise Clauses imply the contrary? Does the history of speech and press freedom—remember Milton—support that idea?

What work does the Establishment Clause do in Justice Scalia's view? Is it congruent with the Free Speech and Free Exercise Clauses? Does it always permit what they require? Is it more accurate to say that the Establishment Clause is not even involved in *Pinette*, where the offending action is done by a private party (the KKK)? Or does the Establishment Clause impose on the government an affirmative obligation to control public religious displays?

Justice Scalia was the author of the Court's opinion in Employment Division v. Smith. Would it be accurate to say that he favors a rule of neutrality for both the Free Exercise and the Establishment Clauses? In looking at free exercise law, we have seen that neutrality plays a very important role, but that there are a number of rules that cannot be reduced to or subsumed under a metarule of neutrality. Is this also true of the Establishment Clause for Justice Scalia? How can you explain his support for legislative accommodations, as in *Texas Monthly, Amos,* and *Kiryas Joel* ?

Why does Justice O'Connor not join Part IV of Justice Scalia's opinion? Are there some private religious displays that she would not permit? Some other public places where she would not permit *this* display? What distinguishes them from this case?

2. Endorsement and the Public Forum.   Justice Stevens's dissenting opinion suggests that this is another crèche case, like Lynch v. Donnelly, but with a cross instead of a manger. He argues that Justice O'Connor's "endorsement" rule should govern both. Who owned the crèche in *Lynch*? In *Allegheny*? Who owned the park in *Lynch*? Does it matter for First Amendment purposes?

The endorsement test asks whether the government is, by its actions, "making a statement" about religion. In a case like this, the government might not *do* anything; rather, it might just refrain from taking down the KKK's cross. This omission might be meaningful. We might say that silence means consent. How would we know how to interpret the Board's silence? Is the relevant question what the Board meant by it, or what some complaining party thought the Board meant, or what some ideal observer might think? If the latter, how can a trial court know when an ideal observer would perceive an endorsement? Is this the subject of proof? Should the ideal observer know about the public forum rule? If he did, what intention would he attribute to a Board that did nothing about a religious display?

Could the Board forbid all freestanding, semipermanent structures around the capitol? Even in a traditional public forum like the plaza? Cf. Clark v. Community for Creative Non-Violence, 468 U.S. 288 (1983). Could the Board forbid some categories of symbols around the capitol? Suppose the American Nazi Party wanted to erect a 10-foot swastika for two weeks to celebrate the birthday of Adolf Hitler? Suppose an Ohio State fraternity wanted to put up the word "bullshit" in 10-foot-high three-dimensional letters around the time of final exams? Must the Board allow these displays if it permits the United Way to erect its traditional display showing the progress of its fund-raising campaign? Must it allow them if the state has put up statues honoring Robert Taft and John Glenn on the plaza lawn? If the state may exercise some discretion with regard to semipermanent structures, might it be *permitted* to deny a place to religious exhibits? If it were permitted to deny a place, then wouldn't it endorse religion by choosing the option of allowing a cross to stand?

4. Religious Speech in Public Schools

In section A we saw the Court adopt a strict bar against government sponsorship of religious activities or exercises in public schools. But public schools can also be forums for free speech by individuals, including students, faculty, or even, at appropriate times, outside groups. What principles apply?

BOARD OF EDUCATION v. MERGENS
496 U.S. 226 (1990)

Justice O'Connor delivered the opinion of the Court, except as to Part III, in which Chief Justice Rehnquist and Justices White and Blackmun joined.

[In 1985 Bridget Mergens met with the principal of Westside High School and requested permission to form a Christian club at the school. The club was to have the same privileges and meet on the same terms as other student groups (there were about 30 of them), but would not have a faculty sponsor. The purpose of the club would have been to read and discuss the Bible, to have fellowship, and to pray together. Membership was to be voluntary and open to all students. The principal denied the request. School Board Policy 5610 required all school clubs to have a faculty sponsor and forbade the formation of any clubs sponsored by political or religious organizations. Mergens and several other students sued, claiming that the principal's decision violated the Equal Access Act, 20 U.S.C. §§ 4071-4074. The Act provides (§ 4071(a)):

It shall be unlawful for any public secondary school which receives Federal financial assistance and which has a limited open forum to deny equal access or a fair opportunity to, or discriminate against, any students who wish to conduct a meeting within that limited open forum on the basis of the religious, political, philosophical, or other content of the speech at such meetings.

A "limited open forum" exists whenever a school "grants an offering to or opportunity for one or more non-curriculum related student groups to meet on school premises during non-instructional time" (§ 4071(b)). If the meeting is religious, school employees may attend only in a "non-participatory capacity" (§ 4071(c)). The Act concludes by saying that it does not "limit the authority of the school . . . to maintain order and discipline on school premises [or] protect the well-being of students and faculty" (§ 4071(e)).

[It was undisputed that Westside was a public secondary school receiving federal financial assistance. The Supreme Court began its opinion with a question of statutory interpretation. The crucial question was whether the school maintained a "limited open forum"—that is, whether it permitted one or more "non-curriculum related student groups" to meet on campus before or after classes.]

II

Unfortunately, the Act does not define the crucial phrase "non-curriculum related student group." Our immediate task is therefore one of statutory interpretation. We begin, of course, with the language of the statute. The common meaning of the term "curriculum" is "the whole body of courses offered by an educational institution or one of its branches." Webster's Third New International Dictionary (1976). Any sensible interpretation of "non-curriculum related student group" must therefore be anchored in the notion that such student groups are those that are not related to the body of courses offered by the school. The difficult question is the degree of "unrelatedness to the curriculum" required for a group to be considered "non-curriculum related."

[W]e think that the term "non-curriculum related student group" is best interpreted broadly to mean any student group that does not *directly* relate to the body of courses offered by the school. In our view, a student group directly relates to a school's curriculum if the subject matter of the group is actually taught, or will soon be taught, in a regularly offered course; if the subject matter of the group concerns the body of courses as a whole; if participation in the group is required for a particular course; or if participation in the group results in academic credit. We think this limited definition of groups that directly relate to the curriculum is a commonsense interpretation of the Act that is consistent with Congress' intent to provide a low threshold for triggering the Act's requirements.

For example, a French club would directly relate to the curriculum if a school taught French in a regularly offered course or planned to teach the subject in the near future. . . . On the other hand, unless a school could show that groups such as a chess club, a stamp collecting club, or a community service club fell within our description of groups that directly relate to the curriculum, such groups would be "noncurriculum related student groups" for purposes of the Act. The existence of such groups would create a "limited open forum" under the Act and would prohibit the school from denying equal access to any other student group on the basis of the content of that group's speech. [Westside includes a number of noncurriculum-related student groups among the

30 recognized clubs, including Subsurfers (a club for students interested in scuba diving) and the Chess Club.]

III

Petitioners contend that even if Westside has created a limited open forum within the meaning of the Act, its denial of official recognition to the proposed Christian club must nevertheless stand because the Act violates the Establishment Clause of the First Amendment, as applied to the States through the Fourteenth Amendment. Specifically, petitioners maintain that because the school's recognized student activities are an integral part of its educational mission, official recognition of respondents' proposed club would effectively incorporate religious activities into the school's official program, endorse participation in the religious club, and provide the club with an official platform to proselytize other students.

We . . . think the logic of *Widmar* applies with equal force to the Equal Access Act. As an initial matter, the Act's prohibition of discrimination on the basis of "political, philosophical, or other" speech as well as religious speech is a sufficient basis for meeting the secular purpose prong of the *Lemon* test. Congress' avowed purpose—to prevent discrimination against religious and other types of speech—is undeniably secular. Even if some legislators were motivated by a conviction that religious speech in particular was valuable and worthy of protection, that alone would not invalidate the Act, because what is relevant is the legislative purpose of the statute, not the possibly religious motives of the legislators who enacted the law. Because the Act on its face grants equal access to both secular and religious speech, we think it clear that the Act's purpose was not to " 'endorse or disapprove of religion.' "

Petitioners' principal contention is that the Act has the primary effect of advancing religion. Specifically, petitioners urge that, because the student religious meetings are held under school aegis, and because the State's compulsory attendance laws bring the students together (and thereby provide a ready-made audience for student evangelists), an objective observer in the position of a secondary school student will perceive official school support for such religious meetings.

We disagree. [T]here is a crucial difference between *government* speech endorsing religion, which the Establishment Clause forbids, and *private* speech endorsing religion, which the Free Speech and Free Exercise Clauses protect. We think that secondary school students are mature enough and are likely to understand that a school does not endorse or support student speech that it merely permits on a nondiscriminatory basis. . . .

Second, we note that the Act expressly limits participation by school officials at meetings of student religious groups, and that any such meetings must be held during "non-instructional time." The Act therefore avoids the problems of "the students' emulation of teachers as role models" and "mandatory attendance requirements," McCollum v. Board of Education (1948) [p. 649]. To be sure, the possibility of *student* peer pressure remains, but there is little if any risk of official state endorsement or coercion where no formal classroom activities are involved and no school officials actively participate. Moreover, petitioners' fear of a mistaken inference of endorsement is largely self-imposed, because the school itself has control over any impressions it gives its students. To the extent a school makes clear that its recognition of respondents' proposed club is not an endorsement of the views of the club's participants, students will reasonably understand that the school's official recognition of the club evinces neutrality toward, rather than endorsement of, religious speech.

Third, the broad spectrum of officially recognized student clubs at Westside, and the fact that Westside students are free to initiate and organize additional student clubs, counteract any possible message of official endorsement of or preference for religion or a particular religious belief. . . . Under the Act, a school with a limited open forum may not lawfully deny access to a Jewish students' club, a Young Democrats club, or a philosophy club devoted to the study of Nietzsche. . . .

Petitioners' final argument is that by complying with the Act's requirements, the school risks excessive entanglement between government and religion. The proposed club, petitioners urge, would be required to have a faculty sponsor who would be charged with actively directing the activities of the group, guiding its leaders, and ensuring balance in the presentation of controversial ideas. Petitioners claim that this influence over the club's religious program would entangle the government in day-to-day surveillance of religion of the type forbidden by the Establishment Clause.

Under the Act, however, faculty monitors may not participate in any religious meetings, and non-school persons may not direct, control, or regularly attend activities of student groups. Moreover, the Act prohibits school "sponsorship" of any religious meetings, which means that school officials may not promote, lead, or participate in any such meeting. Although the Act permits "[t]he assignment of a teacher, administrator, or other school employee to a meeting for custodial purposes," such custodial oversight of the student-initiated religious group, merely to ensure order and good behavior, does not impermissibly entangle government in the day-to-day surveillance or administration of religious activities. Indeed, as the Court noted in *Widmar*, a denial of equal access to religious speech might well create greater entanglement problems in the form of invasive monitoring to prevent religious speech at meetings at which such speech might occur.

Accordingly, we hold that the Equal Access Act does not on its face contravene the Establishment Clause. Because we hold that petitioners have violated the Act, we do not decide respondents' claims under the Free Speech and Free Exercise Clauses.

Justice KENNEDY, joined by Justice SCALIA, concurring in part and concurring in the judgment.

[Justice Kennedy argued that the proper Establishment Clause rule was "no coercion," not "no endorsement."] I should think it inevitable that a public high school "endorses" a religious club, in a commonsense use of that term, if the club happens to be one of many activities that the school permits students to choose in order to further the development of their intellect. But no constitutional violation occurs if the school's action is based upon a recognition of the fact that membership in a religious club is one of many permissible ways for a student to further his or her own personal enrichment. The inquiry . . . must be whether the government imposes pressure upon a student to participate in a religious activity.

Justice STEVENS, dissenting.

. . . High school students may be adult enough to distinguish between those organizations that are sponsored by the school and those which lack school sponsorship even though they participate in a forum that the school does sponsor. But high school students are also young enough that open fora may be less suitable for them than for college students. The need to decide whether to risk treating students as adults too soon, or alternatively to risk treating them as children too long, is an enduring problem for all educators. The youth of these students, whether described in terms of "impressionability" or "maturity," may be irrelevant to our application of the constitutional restrictions that limit educational discretion in the public schools, but it surely is not irrelevant to our interpretation of the educational policies that have been adopted. We would do no honor to Westside's administrators or the Congress by assuming that either treated casually the differences between high school and college students when formulating the policy and the statute at issue here.

For these reasons, I believe that the distinctions between Westside's program and the University of Missouri's program [in Widmar v. Vincent] suggest what is the best understanding of the Act: An extracurricular student organization is "non-curriculum related" if it has as its purpose (or as part of its purpose) the advocacy of partisan theological, political, or ethical views. A school that admits at least one such club has apparently made the judgment that students are better off if the student community is permitted to, and perhaps even encouraged to, compete along ideological lines. This pedagogical strategy may be defensible or even desirable. But it is wrong to presume that Congress endorsed that strategy—and dictated its nationwide adoption—simply because it approved the application of *Widmar* to high schools. And it seems absurd to presume that Westside has invoked the same strategy by recognizing clubs like the Swimming Timing Team and Subsurfers which, though they may not correspond directly to anything in Westside's course offerings, are no more controversial than a grilled cheese sandwich.

NOTES AND QUESTIONS

1. Constitutional Issues: Endorsement and Neutrality (Equal Treatment).   In both *Mergens* and *Widmar*, the Court invokes the *Lemon* test, and especially the second prong: Does equal access have the primary effect of advancing religion? *Mergens* also shows the influence of the so-called endorsement test: It asks whether "an objective observer in the position of a secondary school student will perceive official school support for such religious meetings." Why might this be true in *Mergens* if it was not in *Widmar*?

(a) Endorsement and students' age.   One possibility is that the students are younger, and this may affect their perception. Does youth make students more likely to see government approval where there is none? Is it true that teenagers have a high regard for authorities and generally go along with what their elders want them to think? Think about Tinker v. Des Moines School District, 393 U.S. 503 (1969), where the Court held that students had the right to wear black armbands to school to peacefully protest the Vietnam War. Would high school students suppose that the school condemned the war because it allowed the Tinker children to wear armbands? See Ruti Teitel, The Unconstitutionality of Equal Access Policies and Legislation Allowing Organized Student-Initiated Religious Activities in the Public High Schools: A Proposal for a Unitary First Amendment Forum Analysis, 12 Hastings Const. L.Q. 529 (1985).

Does the difference in age matter because it affects the school's educational policies? The state exercises more control over the curriculum in high schools than it does in colleges. May it also exercise more control over scholastic extra-curricular activities? If it may, does its failure to do so signify approval, or at least acceptance? Is that enough to violate the Establishment Clause?

(b) **How equal must "equal access" be?** In finding no endorsement, *Mergens* emphasizes that permitting the Bible club to meet would treat it equally with other clubs. But the Act seems to contemplate some inequalities. Other groups are permitted to invite outside speakers. Does the Christian club have the right to invite a minister? The Equal Access Act applies to student meetings "during non-instructional time." Suppose Westside High School designates sixth period as "activity period," when all student groups meet. Does the Christian club have a right to meet during that period? Must the school include a club picture in the yearbook?

Clubs usually have faculty sponsors, but the Act treats that issue differently for the religious club. How? If a religious faculty member wants to be involved in a club, does restricting him from doing so violate his rights? If other student groups prefer to dispense with faculty sponsors, are they being discriminated against?

2. Other Issues, Statutory and Constitutional. Several provisions of the Act raise issues of interpretation. And although these provisions are religion-neutral, they may raise constitutional questions as applied to religious clubs.

(a) **What is a "limited open forum"?** When does a school maintain a "limited open forum"? Is this the same as a designated public forum, or is the statutory obligation wider than the constitutional one? Suppose a school has a football team but no other student organizations. Is a football team a "non-curriculum related student group" that triggers the right of equal access? Douglas Laycock, Equal Access and Moments of Silence: The Equal Status of Religious Speech by Private Speakers, 81 Nw. U. L. Rev. 1 (1986), analyzes these issues fully and was cited throughout Justice O'Connor's *Mergens* opinion.

Note that the existence of even one non-curriculum related club triggers the Act's requirement of equal access. Compare this to the degree of departure from generally applicable laws necessary to trigger strict scrutiny under Employment Division v. Smith (Section III-A-5). The Equal Access Act's one-club trigger resembles the constitutional holding in Fraternal Order of Police v. Newark (p. 167), in which a single exception from the no-beard rule rendered the city's refusal to allow Muslim police officers to wear beards in accordance with their religious faith subject to strict scrutiny. Does the Equal Access Act go beyond what the Free Speech and Free Exercise Clauses require? If so, does that point to a violation of the Establishment Clause? What if the Equal Access Act protected only religious student clubs?

(b) **Secular clubs.** The Act protects political and philosophical as well as religious groups. One of the principal nonreligious applications of the Act has been to permit students to form gay rights clubs. At East High School in

Salt Lake City, Utah, for example, students formed the Gay/Straight Alliance and sought permission to meet under the Equal Access Act. In response, the school board voted to ban all noncurriculum-related clubs from meeting on public school campuses. See East High Gay/Straight Alliance v. Board of Educ., 81 F. Supp. 2d 1166 (D. Utah 1999). Although the school board's action was sustained in federal district court, the cancellation of all noncurricular clubs generated political pressure to reverse the decision. In the fall of 2000, the school board revoked its policy against noncurriculum-related clubs, and the Gay/Straight Alliance received authorization to meet.

Are there any student clubs that a public school would be justified in excluding? Ku Klux Klan? Al-Qaeda? Students for Pharmaceutical Freedom? If you were the lawyer for a school board, could you think of any way to exclude such groups without violating the Equal Access Act or the First Amendment?

(c) **Discrimination concerning offices and membership.** Can schools forbid student clubs to discriminate on the basis of race, sex, and religion? Could Westside require the Christian club to admit members who do not accept Jesus as their lord? Hsu v. Roslyn Union Free Sch. Dist., 85 F.3d 839 (2d Cir. 1996), held that a school policy forbidding religious discrimination in selection of club officers could apply to the offices of secretary and activities coordinator in a religious club, but not to the offices of president, vice president, and music director. On what basis could a court draw such a line? Since the Equal Access Act only guarantees a religious club equal treatment, why can't a religious non-discrimination requirement for all clubs apply fully to the religious club? Is it significant that secular clubs are allowed to confine their leadership positions to people who share their underlying philosophy? If the religious club cannot demand a statement of religious belief from its secretary or activities coordinator, does that violate its right to associate for expressive purposes under Boy Scouts of American v. Dale (see p. 176)?

Student chapters of the Christian Legal Society (CLS) require that officers and voting members sign a statement of doctrinal beliefs, and that they observe a "code of conduct" that excludes "unrepentant homosexual conduct" and other sexual relations outside of marriage. A state law school, relying on its policy forbidding school recognition for student groups that discriminate based on religion or sexual orientation, denied the CLS chapter funds otherwise available to student groups and also denied it access to a number of school media (bulletin boards, e-mail lists, etc.), although it permitted the group to meet in classrooms. Does the CLS chapter's "code of conduct" violate the rule against sexual-orientation discrimination? Does denying the chapter access to media violate the "equal access" principle of Widmar et al. by discriminating based on the group's viewpoint? Does excluding CLS from funds and media access unless it allows officers and members without regard to homosexual conduct violate CLS's right of expressive association under Boy Scouts of America v. Dale? Is there any constitutional distinction between funds and access to media? See Christian Legal Soc. Chapter, Univ. of Cal. Hastings v. Kane, 2006 WL 997217 (N.D. Cal. 2006) (granting summary judgment dismissing CLS's constitutional challenges).

(d) **No nonschool leaders: a disparate effect on Catholics?** Section 4071(d) states that for a group to be student-initiated and thus fall within the Act, "nonschool persons may not direct, conduct, control, or regularly attend" its meetings. Note that this allows groups to conduct worship services if and only if those services are led by students. Does this provision deny protection to religious groups who believe that worship must be led by clergy? See, e.g., Michael deHaven Newsom, Common School Religion: Judicial Narratives in a Protestant Empire, 11 S. Cal. Interdisc. L. J. 219, 318-19 (2002). Should there be exemption from this rule for a Catholic student fellowship's celebration of mass, which must be conducted by a priest? Does the Act's concept of "student initiation" reflect an individualist bias?

GOOD NEWS CLUB v. MILFORD CENTRAL SCHOOL
533 U.S. 98 (2001)

Justice THOMAS delivered the opinion of the Court.

This case presents two questions. The first question is whether Milford Central School violated the free speech rights of the Good News Club when it excluded the Club from meeting after hours at the school. The second question is whether any such violation is justified by Milford's concern that permitting the Club's activities would violate the Establishment Clause. We conclude that Milford's restriction violates the Club's free speech rights and that no Establishment Clause concern justifies that violation.

I

The State of New York authorizes local school boards to adopt regulations governing the use of their school facilities. . . . In 1992, respondent Milford Central School (Milford) enacted a community use policy adopting [several purposes] for which its building could be used after school. Two of the stated purposes are relevant here. First, district residents may use the school for "instruction in any branch of education, learning or the arts." Second, the school is available for "social, civic and recreational meetings and entertainment events, and other uses pertaining to the welfare of the community, provided that such uses shall be nonexclusive and shall be opened to the general public."

Stephen and Darleen Fournier . . . are sponsors of the local Good News Club, a private Christian organization for children ages 6 to 12. [I]n September 1996 the Fourniers submitted a request to Dr. Robert McGruder, interim superintendent of the district, in which they sought permission to hold the Club's weekly after-school meetings in the school cafeteria. The next month, McGruder formally denied the Fourniers' request on the ground that the proposed use—to have "a fun time of singing songs, hearing a Bible lesson and memorizing scripture"—was "the equivalent of religious worship." According to McGruder, the community use policy, which prohibits use "by any individual or organization for religious purposes," foreclosed the Club's activities.

. . . The Club [provided] the following description of its meeting:

> The Club opens its session with Ms. Fournier taking attendance. As she calls a child's name, if the child recites a Bible verse the child receives a treat. After attendance, the Club sings songs. Next Club members engage in games that involve, inter alia, learning Bible verses. Ms. Fournier then relates a Bible story and explains how it applies to Club members' lives. The Club closes with prayer. Finally, Ms. Fournier distributes treats and the Bible verses for memorization.

McGruder and Milford's attorney reviewed the materials and concluded that "the kinds of activities proposed to be engaged in by the Good News Club were not a discussion of secular subjects such as child rearing, development of character and development of morals from a religious perspective, but were in fact the equivalent of religious instruction itself." [The school board thus rejected the Club's request.]

[The Club sued in federal court, seeking an injunction requiring the school to allow it to use school facilities and alleging that the denial of its application violated, among other things, its free speech rights. Although the Club received a preliminary injunction and met in school facilities for a year, the district court eventually vacated the injunction and granted summary judgment for Milford. The court of appeals affirmed.]

II

. . . Because the parties have agreed that Milford created a limited public forum when it opened its facilities in 1992, . . . we simply will assume [that such a forum exists].

When the State establishes a limited public forum, the State is not required to and does not allow persons to engage in every type of speech. The State may be justified "in reserving [its forum] for certain groups or for the discussion of certain topics." Rosenberger v. Univ. of Virginia [p. 435]. The State's power to restrict speech, however, is not without limits. The restriction must not discriminate against speech on the basis of viewpoint, and the restriction must be "reasonable in light of the purpose served by the forum."

III

[W]e find it quite clear that Milford engaged in viewpoint discrimination when it excluded the Club from the after-school forum. In *Lamb's Chapel*, the local New York school district similarly had adopted [the] "social, civic or recreational use" category as a permitted use in its limited public forum. The district also prohibited use "by any group for religious purposes." Citing this prohibition, the school district excluded a church that wanted to present films teaching family values from a Christian perspective. We held that, because the films "no doubt dealt with a subject otherwise permissible" under the rule, the teaching of family values, the district's exclusion of the church was unconstitutional viewpoint discrimination.

Like the church in *Lamb's Chapel*, the Club seeks to address a subject otherwise permitted under the rule, the teaching of morals and character, from a religious standpoint. . . . The only apparent difference between the activity of Lamb's Chapel and the activities of the Good News Club is that the Club chooses to teach moral lessons from a Christian perspective through live storytelling and prayer, whereas Lamb's Chapel taught lessons through films. This distinction is inconsequential.

Despite our holdings in *Lamb's Chapel* and *Rosenberger*, the Court of Appeals, like Milford, believed that its characterization of the Club's activities as religious in nature warranted treating the Club's activities as different in kind from the other activities permitted by the school. [The court of appeals said that] the Club "is doing something other than simply teaching moral values." The

"Christian viewpoint" is unique, according to the court, because it contains an "additional layer" that other kinds of viewpoints do not. That is, the Club "is focused on teaching children how to cultivate their relationship with God through Jesus Christ," which it characterized as "quintessentially religious." With these observations, the court concluded that, because the Club's activities "fall outside the bounds of pure 'moral and character development,'" the exclusion did not constitute viewpoint discrimination.

We disagree that something that is "quintessentially religious" or "decidedly religious in nature" cannot also be characterized properly as the teaching of morals and character development from a particular viewpoint. [As the dissenting appellate judge said,] "[W]hen the subject matter is morals and character, it is quixotic to attempt a distinction between religious viewpoints and religious subject matters." . . . [W]e can see no logical difference in kind between the invocation of Christianity by the Club and the invocation of teamwork, loyalty, or patriotism by other associations to provide a foundation for their lessons. . . .

IV

Milford argues that, even if its restriction constitutes viewpoint discrimination, its interest in not violating the Establishment Clause outweighs the Club's interest in gaining equal access to the school's facilities. . . .

We have said that a state interest in avoiding an Establishment Clause violation "may be characterized as compelling," and therefore may justify content-based discrimination. *Widmar.* However, it is not clear whether a State's interest in avoiding an Establishment Clause violation would justify viewpoint discrimination. We need not, however, confront the issue in this case, because we conclude that the school has no valid Establishment Clause interest.

As in *Lamb's Chapel,* the Club's meetings were held after school hours, not sponsored by the school, and open to any student who obtained parental consent, not just to Club members. As in *Widmar,* Milford made its forum available to other organizations. . . .

Milford attempts to distinguish *Lamb's Chapel* and *Widmar* by emphasizing that Milford's policy involves elementary school children. According to Milford, children will perceive that the school is endorsing the Club and will feel coercive pressure to participate, because the Club's activities take place on school grounds, even though they occur during non-school hours.[6] This argument is unpersuasive.

First, we have held that "a significant factor in upholding governmental programs in the face of Establishment Clause attack is their neutrality towards religion." *Rosenberger;* see also Mitchell v. Helms. . . . The Good News Club seeks nothing more than to be treated neutrally and given access to speak about the same topics as are other groups. [Thus] Milford faces an uphill battle in arguing that the Establishment Clause compels it to exclude the Good News Club.

Second, to the extent we consider whether the community would feel coercive pressure to engage in the Club's activities, cf. Lee v. Weisman, the relevant community would be the parents, not the elementary school children. . . . Because the children cannot attend without their parents' permission, they

6. . . . [A]lthough Milford repeatedly has argued that the Club's meeting time directly after the schoolday is relevant to its Establishment Clause concerns, the record does not reflect any offer by the school district to permit the Club to use the facilities at a different time of day.

cannot be coerced into engaging in the Good News Club's religious activities. Milford does not suggest that the parents of elementary school children would be confused about whether the school was endorsing religion.

Finally, even if we were to inquire into the minds of schoolchildren in this case, we cannot say the danger that children would misperceive the endorsement of religion is any greater than the danger that they would perceive a hostility toward the religious viewpoint if the Club were excluded from the public forum. This concern is particularly acute given the reality that Milford's building is not used only for elementary school children. Students, from kindergarten through the 12th grade, all attend school in the same building. There may be as many, if not more, upperclassmen than elementary school children who occupy the school after hours. For that matter, members of the public writ large are permitted in the school after hours pursuant to the community use policy. Any bystander could conceivably be aware of the school's use policy and its exclusion of the Good News Club, and could suffer as much from viewpoint discrimination as elementary school children could suffer from perceived endorsement.

We cannot operate, as Milford would have us do, under the assumption that any risk that small children would perceive endorsement should counsel in favor of excluding the Club's religious activity. We decline to employ Establishment Clause jurisprudence using a modified heckler's veto, in which a group's religious activity can be proscribed on the basis of what the youngest members of the audience might misperceive. There are countervailing constitutional concerns related to rights of other individuals in the community. In this case, those countervailing concerns are the free speech rights of the Club and its members. . . . [7]

Justice SCALIA, concurring.

I join the Court's opinion but write separately to explain further my views on two issues.

I

First, . . . so-called "peer pressure," if it can even been considered coercion, is, when it arises from private activities, one of the attendant consequences of a freedom of association that is constitutionally protected. What is at play here is not coercion, but the compulsion of ideas—and the private right to exert and receive that compulsion (or to have one's children receive it) is protected by the Free Speech and Free Exercise Clauses, not banned by the Establishment Clause. A priest has as much liberty to proselytize as a patriot. . . .

II

. . . [R]espondent has agreed that groups engaged in the endeavor of developing character may use its forum. . . . When the [Good News] Club attempted to teach Biblical-based moral values, however, it was excluded because its

---

7. . . . Justice Souter suggests that we cannot determine whether there would be an Establishment Clause violation unless we know when, and to what extent, other groups use the facilities. When a limited public forum is available for use by groups presenting any viewpoint, however, we would not find an Establishment Clause violation simply because only groups presenting a religious viewpoint have opted to take advantage of the forum at a particular time.

activities "d[id] not involve merely a religious perspective on the secular subject of morality" and because "it [was] clear from the conduct of the meetings that the Good News Club goes far beyond merely stating its viewpoint."

From no other group does respondent require the sterility of speech that it demands of petitioners. The Boy Scouts could undoubtedly buttress their exhortations to keep "morally straight" and live "clean" lives, by giving reasons why that is a good idea—because parents want and expect it, because it will make the scouts "better" and "more successful" people, because it will emulate such admired past Scouts as former President Gerald Ford. The Club, however, may only discuss morals and character, and cannot give its reasons why they should be fostered—because God wants and expects it, because it will make the Club members "saintly" people, and because it emulates Jesus Christ. The Club may not, in other words, independently discuss the religious premise on which its views are based—that God exists and His assistance is necessary to morality. It may not defend the premise, and it absolutely must not seek to persuade the children that the premise is true. The children must, so to say, take it on faith.

This is blatant viewpoint discrimination. Just as calls to character based on patriotism will go unanswered if the listeners do not believe their country is good and just, calls to moral behavior based on God's will are useless if the listeners do not believe that God exists. Effectiveness in presenting a viewpoint rests on the persuasiveness with which the speaker defends his premise and in respondent's facilities every premise but a religious one may be defended.

... The right to present a viewpoint based on a religion premise carrie[s] with it the right to defend the premise.

Justice STEVENS, dissenting.

The Milford Central School has invited the public to use its facilities for educational and recreational purposes, but not for "religious purposes." Speech for "religious purposes" may reasonably be understood to encompass three different categories. First, there is religious speech that is simply speech about a particular topic from a religious point of view. The film in *Lamb's Chapel* [fit in] this category. Second, there is religious speech that amounts to worship, or its equivalent. Our decision in *Widmar* concerned such speech. Third, there is an intermediate category that is aimed principally at proselytizing or inculcating belief in a particular religious faith.

[W]hile a public entity may not censor speech about an authorized topic based on the point of view expressed by the speaker, it has broad discretion to "preserve the property under its control for the use to which it is lawfully dedicated." [T]he question is whether a school can, consistently with the First Amendment, create a limited public forum that admits the first type of religious speech [above] without allowing the other two.

Distinguishing speech from a religious viewpoint, on the one hand, from religious proselytizing, on the other, is comparable to distinguishing meetings to discuss political issues from meetings whose principal purpose is to recruit new members to join a political organization. If a school decides to authorize after school discussions of current events in its classrooms, it may not exclude people from expressing their views simply because it dislikes their particular political opinions. But must it therefore allow organized political groups—for example, the Democratic Party, the Libertarian Party, or the Ku Klux Klan—to hold meetings, the principal purpose of which is not to discuss the current-events topic from their own unique point of view but rather to recruit others to join their respective groups? I think not. Such recruiting meetings may introduce divisiveness and tend to separate young children into cliques that undermine the school's educational mission.

School officials may reasonably believe that evangelical meetings designed to convert children to a particular religious faith pose the same risk. . . . [Thus] a school [may] allow discussion of topics such as moral development from a religious (or nonreligious) perspective without thereby opening its forum to religious proselytizing or worship. Moreover, any doubt on a question such as this should be resolved in a way that minimizes "intrusion by the Federal Government into the operation of our public schools," *Mergens* (Stevens, J., dissenting).

[The record here shows that] the school district did not intend to exclude all speech from a religious point of view. See Appendix (testimony of the superintendent for Milford schools indicating that the policy would permit people to teach "that man was created by God as described in the Book of Genesis" and that crime was caused by society's "lack of faith in God"). Instead, it sought only to exclude religious speech whose principal goal is to "promote the gospel." In other words, the school sought to allow the first type of religious speech while excluding the second and third types. As long as this is done in an even handed manner, I see no constitutional violation in such an effort.

Justice SOUTER, with whom Justice GINSBURG joins, dissenting.

I

Lamb's Chapel . . . built on the accepted rule that a government body may designate a public forum subject to a reasonable limitation on the scope of permitted subject matter and activity, so long as the government does not use the forum-defining restrictions to deny expression to a particular viewpoint on subjects open to discussion. . . .

[But the lower courts correctly held] on the basis of undisputed facts that Good News's activity was essentially unlike the presentation of views on secular issues from a religious standpoint held to be protected in *Lamb's Chapel*. . . .

Good News's classes open and close with prayer. In a sample lesson considered by the District Court, children are instructed that "[t]he Bible tells us how we can have our sins forgiven by receiving the Lord Jesus Christ. It tells us how to live to please Him. . . . If you have received the Lord Jesus as your Saviour from sin, you belong to God's special group—His family." The lesson plan instructs the teacher to "lead a child to Christ," and, when reading a Bible verse, to "[e]mphasize that this verse is from the Bible, God's Word" and is "important—and true—because God said it." The lesson further exhorts the teacher to "[b]e sure to give an opportunity for the 'unsaved' children in your class to respond to the Gospel" and cautions against "neglect[ing] this responsibility." . . .

It is beyond question that Good News intends to use the public school premises not for the mere discussion of a subject from a particular, Christian point of view, but for an evangelical service of worship calling children to commit themselves in an act of Christian conversion. The majority avoids this reality only by resorting to the bland and general characterization of Good News's activity as "teaching of morals and character, from a religious standpoint." . . . Otherwise, indeed, this case would stand for the remarkable proposition that any public school opened for civic meetings must be opened for use as a church, synagogue, or mosque.

II

[Justice Souter also argued that summary judgment was inappropriate on the Establishment Clause issue. On that issue, he said, there should be] affidavits showing, for example, whether Good News conducts its instruction at the same time as school-sponsored extracurricular and athletic activities conducted by school staff and volunteers; whether any other community groups use school facilities immediately after classes end and how many students participate in those groups; and the extent to which Good News, with 28 students in its membership, may "dominate the forum" in a way that heightens the perception of official endorsement. We will never know these facts. . . .

What we know about this case looks very little like *Widmar* or *Lamb's Chapel.* The cohort addressed by Good News is not university students with relative maturity, or even high school pupils, but elementary school children as young as six. The Establishment Clause cases have consistently recognized the particular impressionability of schoolchildren, and the special protection required for those in the elementary grades in the school forum. . . .

Nor is Milford's limited forum anything like the sites for wide-ranging intellectual exchange that were home to the challenged activities in *Widmar* and *Lamb's Chapel.* . . .

The timing and format of Good News's gatherings, on the other hand, may well affirmatively suggest the imprimatur of officialdom in the minds of the young children. The club is open solely to elementary students (not the entire community, as in *Lamb's Chapel*), only four outside groups have been identified as meeting in the school, and Good News is, seemingly, the only one whose instruction follows immediately on the conclusion of the official school day. Although school is out at 2:56 P.M., Good News apparently requested use of the school beginning at 2:30 on Tuesdays "during the school year," so that instruction could begin promptly at 3:00, at which time children who are compelled by law to attend school surely remain in the building. Good News's religious meeting follows regular school activities so closely that the Good News instructor must wait to begin until "the room is clear," and "people are out of the room," before starting proceedings in the classroom located next to the regular third- and fourth-grade rooms. In fact, the temporal and physical continuity of Good News's meetings with the regular school routine seems to be the whole point of using the school. When meetings were held in a community church, 8 or 10 children attended; after the school became the site, the number went up three-fold.

Even on the summary judgment record, then, . . . there is a good case that Good News's exercises blur the line between public classroom instruction and private religious indoctrination, leaving a reasonable elementary school pupil unable to appreciate that the former instruction is the business of the school while the latter evangelism is not.

NOTES AND QUESTIONS

1. Discrimination by Viewpoint Versus by Subject Matter. Does it matter whether denying the Good News Club's request was viewpoint discrimination or subject matter discrimination? The distinction relates to the Court's public forum doctrine. For traditional public forums, such as parks and streets, the distinction is irrelevant: The government must generally permit speech on all topics, subject only to content-neutral restrictions on its time, place, or manner. But the viewpoint versus subject-matter distinction matters in the two other kinds of forums: nonpublic and designated public. For a nonpublic forum, the government may impose reasonable restrictions on access to preserve the facilities' intended use—a deferential standard—but it still may not discriminate based on the viewpoint of speech.

Milford's after-hours access policy was a designated or "limited" public forum, limited by subject matter ("social," "civic," and "moral" concerns). If a group's speech falls within the subject matter that the government has chosen for such a forum, its speech may not be restricted without a compelling reason. The government enjoys discretion in determining the subject matter of the forum in the first place—but only if the restriction does not discriminate on the basis of viewpoint. The problem is that whether an exclusion is by subject matter or by viewpoint seems to turn in large part on the government's definition of the forum—which, in Professor Laycock's words, can make the government's decision to censor "self-justifying." Laycock, 86 Nw. U. L. Rev. at 46. But in *Good News Club*, as in the *Lamb's Chapel* decision that it cites, the Court held that the government could not simply define religious speech as outside the forum's subject matter.

2. Worship Versus Speech? Justice Souter calls it "beyond question" that "Good News intends to use the public school premises not for the mere discussion of a subject from a particular, Christian point of view, but for an evangelical service of worship." What difference does that make? Should school authorities attempt to draw such a line? Justice Souter's argument is reminiscent of Justice White's dissent in *Widmar* (see pp. 622, 624). Does Justice Souter propose overruling *Widmar*?

3. Problem: Church Services in School Buildings. In many parts of the country it is common for local congregations to hold worship services in public school facilities, such as auditoriums or gymnasiums, on the weekend. A school is often one of few facilities in a residential neighborhood with parking and sufficiently large rooms for a congregation, and both real estate costs and zoning barriers can make it difficult for new churches to build their own facilities. The Second Circuit, which was reversed in both *Lamb's Chapel* and *Good News Club*, had also held that a school that opens its facilities to community groups may exclude a church service as well. Bronx Household of Faith v. Community School Dist. No. 10, 127 F.3d 207 (2d Cir. 1997). Can that ruling survive after *Good News Club*? Does it matter if, as is often the case, the church publicly advertises its school-based worship service in the newspapers or by means of a large sign visible from nearby streets? Does it matter that a congregation's use of facilities every weekend of the year might significantly limit other groups' access?

4. Special Programs for Religious Speech: The Release Time Cases. In one sense, the issue in *Good News Club*—religious instruction to elementary school students immediately at the end of the school day—brings the subject of the Establishment Clause in public schools back to its modern origins in the late 1940s. The Court's first decision on this, McCollum v. Board of Education, 333 U.S. 203 (1948), dealt with a "release time" program, under which religious teachers from the Protestant, Catholic, and Jewish faiths taught classes in their respective faiths to public school students, grades four to nine, in regular public school classrooms, once a week, at the end of the school day. Parents could sign their child up for the religion class they wanted, and the child was then required to attend; absences were reported to the child's public school teacher. Students who did not take the classes remained in school, essentially in a study hall. The local ecumenical religious council paid the instructors, but the school had the right to approve and supervise them.

The Court held that the program violated the Establishment Clause. Employing the "wall of separation" language from Everson v. Board of Education (decided the previous year), the Court said that the facts showed

> the use of tax-supported property for religious instruction and the close cooperation between the school authorities and the religious council in promoting religious education. . . . Pupils compelled by law to go to school for secular education are released in part from their legal duty upon the condition that they attend the religious classes. This is beyond all question a utilization of the tax-established and tax-supported public school system to aid religious groups to spread their faith.

Two years later, however, in Zorach v. Clauson, 343 U.S. 306 (1952), the Court approved, by a 6-3 vote, a New York release time program that allowed public school students to leave the school grounds during the school day and go to religious centers for instruction or devotional exercises. As in McCollum, students were released on written request of their parents; those not released stayed in the classroom; and churches made weekly attendance reports to the schools. Justice Douglas, who had joined in striking down the McCollum program, wrote the Court's opinion and made these observations:

> This "released time" program involves neither religious instruction in public school classrooms nor the expenditure of public funds. . . . The case is therefore unlike McCollum. . . . The nullification of this law would have wide and profound effects. A Catholic student applies to his teacher for permission to leave the school during hours on a Holy Day of Obligation to attend a mass. A Jewish student asks his teacher for permission to be excused for Yom Kippur. A Protestant wants the afternoon off for a family baptismal ceremony. In each case the teacher requires parental consent in writing. In each case the teacher, in order to make sure the student is not a truant, goes further and requires a report from the priest, the rabbi, or the minister. The teacher in other words cooperates in a religious program to the extent of making it possible for her students to participate in it. Whether she does it occasionally for a few students, regularly for one, or pursuant to a systematized program designed to further the religious needs of all the students does not alter the character of the act.
>
> We are a religious people whose institutions presuppose a Supreme Being. We guarantee the freedom to worship as one chooses. . . . When the state encourages religious instruction or cooperates with religious authorities by adjusting the schedule of public events to sectarian needs, it follows the best of our traditions. For it then respects the religious nature of our people and accommodates the public service to their spiritual needs.

(a) **On-campus versus off-campus classes?** Is *Zorach* distinguishable from *McCollum*, or do the two decisions reflect inconsistent approaches to the question whether public schools may cooperate with churches concerning religious instruction? The distinction that *Zorach* offers is whether the classes occurred on or off of the public school campus. Why does that matter? If the fact that the classes were in the schools was the key to invalidating the *McCollum* program, then is *McCollum* effectively overruled by decisions such as *Mergens* and *Good News Club*?

(b) **Special program versus equal access.** Almost certainly the key distinction between the invalidated *McCollum* release time program and the permissible meetings from *Widmar* through *Good News Club* is that the former "permitt[ed] school facilities to be used for instruction by religious groups, but not by others," thereby "appear[ing] to sponsor the views of the [religious speaker]." *Widmar*, 454 U.S. at 271 n.10. The emphasis in the recent decisions is on equal access to a forum open to religious and nonreligious groups. But if that is so, then shouldn't *Zorach* be overruled (since the program there was likely solely for religion)? The quotation from *Zorach* suggests that the program might be seen as a permissible accommodation specifically for religious needs (see Section III-C), and that is how the Court has since described it. Texas Monthly v. Bullock, 489 U.S. 1, 18 n.8 (1989) (plurality opinion). Recall the test for religious accommodations from the *Texas Monthly* plurality. Did the program in *Zorach* remove a significant state-imposed deterrent to religious exercise? Did it impose significant burdens on nonbeneficiaries?

Release time programs and equal access for groups like Good News Club are both responses to a persistent conflict in the public schools: Some parents want their children to receive religious education as part of school, while others do not, and many believe that religious education must not be conducted by public servants. While release time was the most prominent solution in the 1940s, equal access is most prominent today. Which solution is better for students and parents who want religious instruction? Which is better for those who do not want it? Which solution is better for the goals of understanding and tolerance in the public schools?

The divergent results in *McCollum* and *Zorach* may also suggest that release time programs can plausibly be fit into either of two categories: either private speech accommodated by the school (like the equal-access cases), or school sponsorship and promotion of such speech, effectively making it the school's own (like the official-prayer cases). In fact, there are a number of situations in which a court may have to decide whether a certain religious expression is the government's or a private citizen's. That is the subject of the next section.

C. THE LINE BETWEEN GOVERNMENT SPEECH AND PRIVATE SPEECH

As sections A and B show, the Court has distinguished two categories of religious speech in the public schools: (1) speech by the government (or sponsored or favored by the government) and (2) speech by individuals or private groups that the government simply permits on the same terms as other individuals' speech. The categories seem simple, but the line between them can be indistinct.

SANTA FE INDEPENDENT SCHOOL DISTRICT v. DOE
530 U.S. 290 (2000)

Justice STEVENS delivered the opinion of the Court.

Prior to 1995, the Santa Fe High School student who occupied the school's elective office of student council chaplain delivered a prayer over the public address system before each varsity football game for the entire season. This practice, along with others, was challenged in District Court as a violation of the Establishment Clause of the First Amendment. While these proceedings were pending in the District Court, the school district adopted a different policy that permits, but does not require, prayer initiated and led by a student at all home games. The District Court entered an order modifying that policy to permit only nonsectarian, non-proselytizing prayer. The Court of Appeals held that, even as modified by the District Court, the football prayer policy was invalid. We granted the school district's petition for certiorari to review that holding.

I

Respondents are two sets of current or former students and their respective mothers. One family is Mormon and the other is Catholic. The District Court permitted [them] to litigate anonymously to protect them from intimidation or harassment. . . . In their complaint the Does alleged that the District had engaged in several proselytizing practices, such as promoting attendance at a Baptist revival meeting, encouraging membership in religious clubs, chastising children who held minority religious beliefs, and distributing Gideon Bibles on school premises. They also alleged that the District allowed students to read Christian invocations and benedictions from the stage at graduation ceremonies, and to deliver overtly Christian prayers over the public address system at home football games.

[T]he District Court [first] entered an interim order [providing] that "non-denominational prayer" consisting of "an invocation and/or benediction" could be presented [at the graduation ceremony] by a senior student or students selected by members of the graduating class. The text of the prayer was to be determined by the students, without scrutiny or preapproval by school officials. References to particular religious figures "such as Mohammed, Jesus, Buddha, or the like" would be permitted "as long as the general thrust of the prayer is non-proselytizing."

In response to that portion of the order, the District adopted a series of policies over several months dealing with prayer at school functions. . . .

The August policy, which was titled "Prayer at Football Games," was similar to the July policy for graduations. [Each policy] authorized two student elections, the first to determine whether "invocations" should be delivered, and the second to select the spokesperson to deliver them. [Each policy] contained two parts, an initial statement that omitted any requirement that the content of the invocation be "nonsectarian and non-proselytizing," and a fallback provision that automatically added that limitation if the preferred policy should be enjoined. On August 31, 1995, according to the parties' stipulation, "the district's high school students voted to determine whether a student would deliver prayer at varsity football games. . . . The students chose to allow a student to say a prayer at football games." A week later, in a separate election, they selected a student "to deliver the prayer at varsity football games."

The final policy (October policy) [for football games] is essentially the same as the August policy, though it omits the word "prayer" from its title, and refers to "messages" and "statements" as well as "invocations."[5] It is the validity of that policy that is before us.[6] . . .

II

[I]n Lee v. Weisman, we held that a prayer delivered by a rabbi at a middle school graduation ceremony violated [the Establishment] Clause. Although this case involves student prayer at a different type of school function, our analysis is properly guided by the principles that we endorsed in *Lee*. . . .

In this case the District first argues that [the Establishment Clause] is inapplicable to its October policy because the messages are private student speech, not public speech. It reminds us that "there is a crucial difference between *government* speech endorsing religion, which the Establishment Clause forbids, and *private* speech endorsing religion, which the Free Speech and Free Exercise Clauses protect." *Mergens* (opinion of O'Connor, J.). We certainly agree with that distinction, but we are not persuaded that the pre-game invocations should be regarded as "private speech."

These invocations are authorized by a government policy and take place on government property at government-sponsored school-related events. . . . Although the District relies heavily on Rosenberger v. Univ. of Virginia and similar cases involving [government-created] forums [for individuals' speech], it is clear that the pre-game ceremony is not the type of forum discussed in those cases. The Santa Fe school officials simply do not "evince either 'by policy or by practice,' any intent to open the [pre-game ceremony] to 'indiscriminate use,' . . . by the student body generally." Rather, the school allows only one

---

5. Despite these changes, the school did not conduct another election, under the October policy, to supersede the results of the August policy election.

6. It provides:

STUDENT ACTIVITIES: PRE-GAME CEREMONIES AT FOOTBALL GAMES

The board has chosen to permit students to deliver a brief invocation and/or message to be delivered during the pre-game ceremonies of home varsity football games to solemnize the event, to promote good sportsmanship and student safety, and to establish the appropriate environment for the competition.

Upon advice and direction of the high school principal, each spring, the high school student council shall conduct an election, by the high school student body, by secret ballot, to determine whether such a statement or invocation will be a part of the pre-game ceremonies and if so, shall elect a student, from a list of student volunteers, to deliver the statement or invocation. The student volunteer who is selected by his or her classmates may decide what message and/or invocation to deliver, consistent with the goals and purposes of this policy.

If the District is enjoined by a court order from the enforcement of this policy, then and only then will the following policy automatically become the applicable policy of the school district. [The fallback policy was substantively identical, except that the following sentence was added at the end: "Any message and/or invocation delivered by a student must be nonsectarian and nonproselytizing."]

student, the same student for the entire season, to give the invocation. The statement or invocation, moreover, is subject to particular regulations that confine the content and topic of the student's message. . . .

Granting only one student access to the stage at a time does not, of course, necessarily preclude a finding that a school has created a limited public forum. Here, however, Santa Fe's student election system ensures that only those messages deemed "appropriate" under the District's policy may be delivered. That is, the majoritarian process implemented by the District guarantees, by definition, that minority candidates will never prevail and that their views will be effectively silenced.

Recently, in Board of Regents v. Southworth (2000), we explained why student elections that determine, by majority vote, which expressive activities shall receive or not receive school benefits are constitutionally problematic:

> To the extent the referendum substitutes majority determinations for viewpoint neutrality it would undermine the constitutional protection the program requires. The whole theory of viewpoint neutrality is that minority views are treated with the same respect as are majority views. Access to a public forum, for instance, does not depend upon majoritarian consent. . . .

Like the student referendum for funding in *Southworth*, this student election does nothing to protect minority views but rather places the students who hold such views at the mercy of the majority.[13] Because "fundamental rights may not be submitted to vote; they depend on the outcome of no elections," Bd. of Educ. v. Barnette, the District's elections are insufficient safeguards of diverse student speech. . . .

Moreover, the District has failed to divorce itself from the religious content in the invocations. . . . Contrary to the District's repeated assertions that it has adopted a "hands-off" approach to the pre-game invocation, the realities of the situation plainly reveal that its policy involves both perceived and actual endorsement of religion. In this case, as we found in Lee v. Weisman, the "degree of school involvement" makes it clear that the pre-game prayers bear "the imprint of the State and thus put school-age children who objected in an untenable position." . . .

The District has attempted to disentangle itself from the religious messages by developing the two-step student election process. The text of the October policy, however, exposes the extent of the school's entanglement. The elections take place at all only because the school "board *has chosen to permit* students to deliver a brief invocation and/or message." The elections thus "shall" be conducted "by the high school student council" and "[u]pon advice and direction of the high school principal." The decision whether to deliver a message is first made by majority vote of the entire student body, followed by a choice of the speaker in a separate, similar majority election. . . .

13. . . . The fact that the District's policy provides for the election of the speaker only after the majority has voted on her message identifies an obvious distinction between this case and the typical election of a "student body president, or even a newly elected prom king or queen" [quoting the dissent].

In addition to involving the school in the selection of the speaker, the policy, by its terms, invites and encourages religious messages. The policy itself states that the purpose of the message is "to solemnize the event." A religious message is the most obvious method of solemnizing an event. Moreover, the requirements that the message "promote good sportsmanship" and "establish the appropriate environment for competition" further narrow the types of message deemed appropriate, suggesting that a solemn, yet nonreligious, message, such as commentary on United States foreign policy, would be prohibited. Indeed, the only type of message that is expressly endorsed in the text is an "invocation"—a term that primarily describes an appeal for divine assistance. In fact, as used in the past at Santa Fe High School, an "invocation" has always entailed a focused religious message. . . . The results of the elections described in the parties' stipulation make it clear that the students understood that the central question before them was whether prayer should be a part of the pre-game ceremony.[14]

The actual or perceived endorsement of the message, moreover, is established by factors beyond just the text of the policy. Once the student speaker is selected and the message composed, the invocation is then delivered to a large audience assembled as part of a regularly scheduled, school-sponsored function conducted on school property. The message is broadcast over the school's public address system, which remains subject to the control of school officials. It is fair to assume that the pre-game ceremony is clothed in the traditional indicia of school sporting events, which generally include not just the team, but also cheerleaders and band members dressed in uniforms sporting the school name and mascot. The school's name is likely written in large print across the field and on banners and flags. . . . It is in a setting such as this that "[t]he board has chosen to permit" the elected student to rise and give the "statement or invocation."

In this context the members of the listening audience must perceive the pre-game message as a public expression of the views of the majority of the student body delivered with the approval of the school administration. . . .

. . . When a governmental entity professes a secular purpose for an arguably religious policy, the government's characterization is, of course, entitled to some deference. But it is nonetheless the duty of the courts to "distinguis[h] a sham secular purpose from a sincere one." Wallace v. Jaffree (O'Connor, J., concurring).

According to the District, the secular purposes of the policy are to "foste[r] free expression of private persons . . . as well [as to] solemniz[e] sporting events, promot[e] good sportsmanship and student safety, and establis[h] an appropriate environment for competition." We note, however, that the District's approval of only one specific kind of message, an "invocation," is not necessary to further any of these purposes. Additionally, the fact that only one student is permitted to give a content-limited message suggests that this policy does little to "foste[r] free expression." Furthermore, regardless of whether one considers a sporting event an appropriate occasion for solemnity, the use of an invocation to

---

14. Even if the plain language of the October policy were facially neutral, "the Establishment Clause forbids a State to hide behind the application of formally neutral criteria and remain studiously oblivious to the effects of its actions." See also Church of Lukumi Babalu Aye v. Hialeah (making the same point in the Free Exercise context).

foster such solemnity is impermissible when, in actuality, it constitutes prayer sponsored by the school. And it is unclear what type of message would be both appropriately "solemnizing" under the District's policy and yet non-religious.

Most striking to us is the evolution of the current policy from the long-sanctioned office of "Student Chaplain" to the candidly titled "Prayer at Football Games" regulation. This history indicates that the District intended to preserve the practice of prayer before football games. The conclusion that the District viewed the October policy simply as a continuation of the previous policies is dramatically illustrated by the fact that the school did not conduct a new election, pursuant to the current policy, to replace the results of the previous election, which occurred under the former policy. . . .

The delivery of such a message—over the school's public address system, by a speaker representing the student body, under the supervision of school faculty, and pursuant to a school policy that explicitly and implicitly encourages public prayer—is not properly characterized as "private" speech.

III

The District next argues that its football policy is distinguishable from the graduation prayer in *Lee* because it does not coerce students to participate in religious observances. . . .

The reasons just discussed explaining why the alleged "circuit-breaker" mechanism of the dual elections and student speaker do not turn public speech into private speech also demonstrate why these mechanisms do not insulate the school from the coercive element of the final message. In fact, this aspect of the District's argument exposes anew the concerns that are created by the majoritarian election system. The parties' stipulation clearly states that the issue resolved in the first election was "whether a student would deliver prayer at varsity football games," and the controversy in this case demonstrates that the views of the students are not unanimous on that issue.

One of the purposes served by the Establishment Clause is to remove debate over this kind of issue from governmental supervision or control.

The District further argues that attendance at the commencement ceremonies at issue in *Lee* "differs dramatically" from attendance at high school football games, which it contends "are of no more than passing interest to many students" and are "decidedly extracurricular," thus dissipating any coercion. [W]e may assume that the District is correct in arguing that the informal pressure to attend an athletic event is not as strong as a senior's desire to attend her own graduation ceremony.

There are some students, however, such as cheerleaders, members of the band, and, of course, the team members themselves, for whom seasonal commitments mandate their attendance, sometimes for class credit. The District also minimizes the importance to many students of attending and participating in extracurricular activities as part of a complete educational experience. As we noted in *Lee*, "[l]aw reaches past formalism." . . . High school home football games are traditional gatherings of a school community; they bring together students and faculty as well as family and friends from years present and past to root for a common cause. . . . For many [students], the choice between whether to attend these games or to risk facing a personally offensive religious ritual is in no practical sense an easy one. The Constitution, moreover, demands that the school may not force this difficult choice upon these students for "[i]t is a tenet of the First Amendment that the State cannot require one of its citizens to forfeit his or her rights and benefits as the price of resisting conformance to state-sponsored religious practice." *Id.*

Even if we regard every high school student's decision to attend a home football game as purely voluntary, we are nevertheless persuaded that the delivery of a pre-game prayer has the improper effect of coercing those present to participate in an act of religious worship. . . .

[N]othing in the Constitution as interpreted by this Court prohibits any public school student from voluntarily praying at any time before, during, or after the school day. But the religious liberty protected by the Constitution is abridged when the State affirmatively sponsors the particular religious practice of prayer.

IV

Finally, the District argues repeatedly that the Does have made a premature facial challenge to the October policy that necessarily must fail. The District emphasizes, quite correctly, that until a student actually delivers a solemnizing message under the latest version of the policy, there can be no certainty that any of the statements or invocations will be religious. . . .

This argument, however, assumes that we are concerned only with the serious constitutional injury that occurs when a student is forced to participate in an act of religious worship because she chooses to attend a school event. But the Constitution also requires that we keep in mind "the myriad, subtle ways in which Establishment Clause values can be eroded," Lynch v. Donnelly (O'Connor, J., concurring), and that we guard against other different, yet equally important, constitutional injuries. One is the mere passage by the District of a policy that has the purpose and perception of government establishment of religion. Another is the implementation of a governmental electoral process that subjects the issue of prayer to a majoritarian vote. . . .

This case comes to us as the latest step in developing litigation brought as a challenge to institutional practices that unquestionably violated the Establishment Clause. One of those practices was the District's long-established tradition of sanctioning student-led prayer at varsity football games. The narrow question before us is whether implementation of the October policy insulates the continuation of such prayers from constitutional scrutiny. It does not. Our inquiry into this question not only can, but must, include an examination of the circumstances surrounding its enactment. . . .

The District, nevertheless, asks us to pretend that we do not recognize what every Santa Fe High School student understands clearly—that this policy is about prayer. . . . We refuse to turn a blind eye to the context in which this policy arose, and that context quells any doubt that this policy was implemented with the purpose of endorsing school prayer.

Therefore, the simple enactment of this policy, with the purpose and perception of school endorsement of student prayer, was a constitutional violation. We need not wait for the inevitable to confirm and magnify the constitutional injury. . . .

This policy likewise does not survive a facial challenge because it . . . empowers the student body majority with the authority to subject students of minority views to constitutionally improper messages. The award of that power alone, regardless of the students' ultimate use of it, is not acceptable. . . . Simply by establishing this school-related procedure, which entrusts the inherently non-governmental subject of religion to a majoritarian vote, a constitutional violation has occurred. No further injury is required for the policy to fail a facial challenge.

Chief Justice REHNQUIST, with whom Justice SCALIA and Justice THOMAS join, dissenting.

The Court distorts existing precedent to conclude that the school district's student-message program is invalid on its face under the Establishment Clause. But even more disturbing than its holding is the tone of the Court's opinion; it bristles with hostility to all things religious in public life. . . .

We do not learn until late in the Court's opinion that respondents in this case challenged the district's student-message program at football games before it had been put into practice. . . . [T]he question is not whether the district's policy *may be* applied in violation of the Establishment Clause, but whether it inevitably will be.

The Court, venturing into the realm of prophecy, decides that it "need not wait for the inevitable" and invalidates the district's policy on its face. To do so, it applies the most rigid version of the oft-criticized test of Lemon v. Kurtzman. . . .

Even if it were appropriate to apply the *Lemon* test here, the district's student-message policy should not be invalidated on its face. The Court applies *Lemon* and holds that the "policy is invalid on its face because it establishes an improper majoritarian election on religion, and unquestionably has the purpose and creates the perception of encouraging the delivery of prayer at a series of important school events." The Court's reliance on each of these conclusions misses the mark.

First, the Court misconstrues the nature of the "majoritarian election" permitted by the policy as being an election on "prayer" and "religion."[2] To the contrary, the election permitted by the policy is a two-fold process whereby students vote first on whether to have a student speaker before football games at all, and second, if the students vote to have such a speaker, on who that speaker will be. It is conceivable that the election could become one in which student candidates campaign on platforms that focus on whether or not they will pray if elected. It is also conceivable that the election could lead to a Christian prayer before 90 percent of the football games. If, upon implementation, the policy operated in this fashion, we would have a record before us to review whether the policy, as applied, violated the Establishment Clause or unduly suppressed minority viewpoints. But it is possible that the students might vote not to have a pre-game speaker, in which case there would be no threat of a constitutional violation. It is also possible that the election would not focus on prayer, but on public speaking ability or social popularity. And if student campaigning did begin to focus on prayer, the school might decide to implement reasonable campaign restrictions.

But the Court ignores these possibilities by holding that merely granting the student body the power to elect a speaker that may choose to pray, "regardless of

2. The Court attempts to support its misinterpretation of the nature of the election process by noting that the district stipulated to facts about the most recent election. Of course, the most recent election was conducted under the *previous* policy—a policy that required an elected student speaker to give a pregame invocation. There has not been an election under the policy at issue here, which expressly allows the student speaker to give a message as opposed to an invocation.

the students' ultimate use of it, is not acceptable." The Court so holds despite the fact that any speech that may occur as a result of the election process here would be *private*, not *government*, speech. The elected student, not the government, would choose what to say. [This] essentially invalidates all student elections. A newly elected student body president, or even a newly elected prom king or queen, could use opportunities for public speaking to say prayers. Under the Court's view, the mere grant of power to the students to vote for such offices, in light of the fear that those elected might publicly pray, violates the Establishment Clause.

Second, with respect to the policy's purpose, the Court holds that "the simple enactment of this policy, with the purpose and perception of school endorsement of student prayer, was a constitutional violation." But the policy itself has plausible secular purposes: "[T]o solemnize the event, to promote good sportsmanship and student safety, and to establish the appropriate environment for the competition." Where a governmental body "expresses a plausible secular purpose" for an enactment, "courts should generally defer to that stated intent." *Jaffree* (O'Connor, J., concurring). . . .

[T]he Court dismisses the secular purpose of solemnization by claiming that it "invites and encourages religious messages." The Court so concludes based on its rather strange view that a "religious message is the most obvious means of solemnizing an event." But it is easy to think of solemn messages that are not religious in nature, for example urging that a game be fought fairly. And sporting events often begin with a solemn rendition of our national anthem, with its concluding verse "And this be our motto: 'In God is our trust.'" Under the Court's logic, a public school that sponsors the singing of the national anthem before football games violates the Establishment Clause. Although the Court apparently believes that solemnizing football games is an illegitimate purpose, the voters in the school district seem to disagree. Nothing in the Establishment Clause prevents them from making this choice.[3]

The Court bases its conclusion that the true purpose of the policy is to endorse student prayer on its view of the school district's history of Establishment Clause violations and the context in which the policy was written. . . . But the context—attempted compliance with a District Court order—actually demonstrates that the school district was acting diligently to come within the governing constitutional law. . . . Thus, the policy cannot be viewed as having a sectarian purpose.

The Court also relies on our decision in *Lee v. Weisman* to support its conclusion. In *Lee,* we concluded that the content of the speech at issue, a graduation prayer given by a rabbi, was "directed and controlled" by a school official. In other words, at issue in *Lee* was *government* speech. Here, by contrast, the potential speech at issue, if the policy had been allowed to proceed, would be a message or invocation selected or created by a student. That is, if there were speech at issue here, it would be *private* speech. . . .

Had the policy been put into practice, the students may have chosen a speaker according to wholly secular criteria—like good public speaking skills or social

---

3. The Court also determines that the use of the term "invocation" in the policy is an express endorsement of that type of message over all others. A less cynical view of the policy's text is that it permits many types of messages, including invocations. That a policy tolerates religion does not mean that it improperly endorses it. . . .

popularity—and the student speaker may have chosen, on her own accord, to deliver a religious message. Such an application of the policy would likely pass constitutional muster. . . .

Finally, the Court seems to demand that a government policy be completely neutral as to content or be considered one that endorses religion. This is undoubtedly a new requirement. . . .

[S]chools do not violate the First Amendment every time they restrict student speech to certain categories. But under the Court's view, a school policy under which the student body president is to solemnize the graduation ceremony by giving a favorable introduction to the guest speaker would be facially unconstitutional. Solemnization "invites and encourages" prayer and the policy's content limitations prohibit the student body president from giving a solemn, yet non-religious, message like "commentary on United States foreign policy."

The policy at issue here may be applied in an unconstitutional manner, but it will be time enough to invalidate it if that is found to be the case. I would reverse the judgment of the Court of Appeals.

NOTES AND QUESTIONS

1. The Scope of *Santa Fe*.   The Court catalogs a series of objectionable features in the Santa Fe prayer practice. If some of these features were different, would the practice be permissible?

(a) What if the policy referred only to a "message or statement," not specifically mentioning an "invocation"?

(b) What if, at two out of ten home football games, the speaker acting under the policy had given a secular message rather than a prayer? See Adler v. Duval County Sch. Bd., 206 F.3d 1070 (11th Cir. 2000) (en banc) (upholding countywide policy for electing student graduation speakers when, in one year, 7 of 17 graduation messages were secular).

(c) What if, instead of providing for an election, the school designated the class valedictorian to speak at the graduation ceremony, and she gave a prayer? See Doe v. Madison School Dist. No. 321, 147 F.3d 832 (9th Cir.) (upholding such a policy), vacated on mootness grounds, 177 F.3d 789 (1999) (en banc). What if the school designated the student council president, and he prayed?

In decisions after Doe v. Madison School Dist., the Ninth Circuit has held that when a school principal refused to allow a valedictorian speaker to engage in "proselytizing" religious speech at the graduation ceremony, the refusal did not violate the student's free speech rights and indeed "was necessary to avoid violating the Establishment Clause." Cole v. Oroville Union High School Dist., 228 F.3d 1092, 1101 (9th Cir. 2000); Lassonde v. Pleasanton High School, 320 F.3d 979 (9th Cir. 2003). In *Lassonde*, for example, the valedictorian's proposed speech would have urged fellow students " 'to seek out the Lord, and let Him guide you [because t]hrough His power, you can stand tall in the face of darkness, and survive the trends of "modern society"'; he also proposed to say, "'For the wages of sin is death; but the gift of God is eternal life through Jesus Christ our Lord.' Have you accepted the gift, or will you pay the ultimate price?' " 228 F.3d at 981. In both cases, the court held that "allowing the speech would have had an impermissibly coercive effect on dissenters, requiring them to participate in a religious practice even by their silence"; and that the speech would be attributable to the school district because the district "authorized the valedictory speech [a]s part of the graduation program, the graduation program was financed by the district, and the principal had supervisory control over the graduation and had the final authority to approve the content of student speeches." *Id.* at 983-84.

Is the result in these decisions required by *Santa Fe*? By Lee v. Weisman (p. 498)? Is it consistent with *Good News Club* (p. 641)? Should the school have discretion to reject such speech even if the Establishment Clause does not require it to do so? Does it matter if the school also rejects a valedictorian's "controversial" or "proselytizing" speech that is nonreligious, such as partisan political statements?

2. Problem: Injunction Against Religion in Alabama Public Schools. In a widely reported case involving public schools in DeKalb County, Alabama, the plaintiffs alleged that the school board had engaged in officially organized or school-sponsored religious activities at various school events, programs, and meetings. The district court enjoined the schools from a range of conduct with respect to religious activity at graduation ceremonies, at school assemblies, in classrooms, among student clubs, and concerning the distribution of literature by nonschool groups. The court found that school officials had made repeated efforts to sponsor religious activity at school events, including activity by students, and to evade restrictions on such activity. See Chandler v. James, 958 F. Supp. 1550 (N.D. Ala. 1997); 985 F. Supp. 1062 (N.D. Ala. 1997). The entry of the injunction prompted widespread protests by students in the DeKalb schools, who claimed that their right to religious expression on school grounds was being unconstitutionally suppressed.

On appeal, the Eleventh Circuit vacated the injunction, finding that it was not supported by the Establishment Clause, and in fact violated students' free speech rights, insofar as it restricted "genuinely student-initiated" religious speech without restricting student speech with non-religious content. Chandler v. James, 180 F.3d 1254 (11th Cir. 1999). But the Supreme Court remanded for reconsideration in the light of *Santa Fe*. How should the court of appeals have ruled on remand? See Chandler v. Siegelman, 230 F.3d 1313 (11th Cir. 2000). Here is a summary of the key provisions of the injunction; what do you think about each one? If you think a provision is problematic, how would you rewrite it?

The first part of the injunction generally enjoined the schools from conduct in the various school contexts listed below. In each context, the court enjoined the schools from "aiding, abetting, commanding, counseling, inducing, ordering, procuring, or permitting, school organized or officially sanctioned religious activity" in its programs. Which verb in that list, if any, trod on students' free-speech rights?

(a) Classroom settings. The injunction then applied this general rule to "classroom activities and instructional settings." However, the order specifically permitted "the educational use of religious texts in the classroom . . . in an objective and academic manner"; permitted "students' voluntary expression of their own religious belief in the form of homework, reports," etc.; and permitted a student religious group to "quietly engage in religious activity during non-instructional time" under the Equal Access Act.

(b) Graduation exercises. Next, the order applied the general rule to graduation exercises, including prayers by students. However, the order specifically permitted "a brief personal expression by a student which contains religious references during a commencement exercise or student address . . . provided that such expression . . . does not invite audience participation or response." The section also enjoined officials "from printing baccalaureate announcements . . . or other materials regarding baccalaureate services on the commencement programs of [the s]chools."

(c) Public address system. Next, the injunction applied the general bar to the delivery of "religious or devotional messages (including scriptural readings) over any public-address system during the instructional day (including the homeroom period [or] daily announcements[)]." The order specifically allowed students to announce "meetings of non-curricular religious clubs, provided that the announcements themselves do not contain a prayer or devotional." Other sections placed similar limits on religious activity at school assemblies and sports events, and on distribution of religious literature by nonschool groups.

Issues concerning the line between government-sponsored speech and individuals' speech arise in other public institutions besides schools. In 1997, the Clinton White House promulgated guidelines regarding religious activity in the federal workplace. Do you agree with the Guidelines' conclusions? Are they consistent with the approach of *Santa Fe*?

GUIDELINES ON RELIGIOUS EXERCISE AND RELIGIOUS EXPRESSION IN THE FEDERAL WORKPLACE

http://clinton2.nara.gov/WH/New/html/19970819-3275.html
(Aug. 14, 1997)

The following Guidelines, addressing religious exercise and religious expression, shall apply to all civilian executive branch agencies, officials, and employees in the Federal workplace. . . . These Guidelines principally address employees' religious exercise and religious expression when the employees are acting in their personal capacity within the Federal workplace and the public does not have regular exposure to the workplace. The Guidelines do not comprehensively address whether and when the government and its employees may engage in religious speech directed at the public. . . .

[E]xecutive departments and agencies ("agencies") shall permit personal religious expression by Federal employees to the greatest extent possible, consistent with requirements of law and interests in workplace efficiency as described in this set of Guidelines. Agencies shall not discriminate against employees on the basis of religion, require religious participation or non-participation as a condition of employment, or permit religious harassment. And agencies shall accommodate employees [in the] exercise of their religion in the circumstances specified in these Guidelines. . . .

A. Religious Expression

As a matter of law, agencies shall not restrict personal religious expression by employees in the Federal workplace except where the employee's interest in the expression is outweighed by the government's interest in the efficient provision of public services or where the expression intrudes upon the legitimate rights of other employees or creates the appearance, to a reasonable observer, of an official endorsement of religion. . . . As a general rule, agencies may not regulate employees' personal religious expression on the basis of its content or viewpoint. In other words, agencies generally may not suppress employees' private religious speech in the workplace while leaving unregulated other private employee speech that has a comparable effect on the efficiency of the workplace—including ideological speech on politics and other topics.

(1) EXPRESSION IN PRIVATE WORK AREAS

Employees should be permitted to engage in private religious expression in personal work areas not regularly open to the public to the same extent that they may engage in nonreligious private expression, subject to reasonable content- and viewpoint-neutral standards and restrictions: such religious expression must be permitted so long as it does not interfere with the agency's carrying out of its official responsibilities. *Examples:* (a) An employee may keep a Bible or Koran on her private desk and read it during breaks. (b) An agency may restrict all posters, or posters of a certain size, in private work areas, or require that such posters be displayed facing the employee, and not on common walls; but the employer typically cannot single out religious or anti-religious posters for harsher or preferential treatment.

(2) EXPRESSION AMONG FELLOW EMPLOYEES

Employees should be permitted to engage in religious expression with fellow employees, to the same extent that they may engage in comparable nonreligious private expression, subject to reasonable and content-neutral standards and restrictions: such expression should not be restricted so long as it does not interfere with workplace efficiency. Though agencies are entitled to regulate such employee speech based on reasonable predictions of disruption, they should not restrict speech based on merely hypothetical concerns, having little basis in fact, that the speech will have a deleterious effect on workplace efficiency. *Examples:* (a) In informal settings, such as cafeterias and hallways, employees are entitled to discuss their religious views with one another, subject only to the same rules of order as apply to other employee expression. If an agency permits unrestricted nonreligious expression of a controversial nature, it must likewise permit equally controversial religious expression. (b) Employees are entitled to display religious messages on items of clothing to the same extent that they are permitted to display other comparable messages. So long as they do not convey any governmental endorsement of religion, religious messages may not typically be singled out for suppression. (c) Employees generally may wear religious medallions over their clothes or so that they are otherwise visible. . . .

(3) EXPRESSION DIRECTED AT FELLOW EMPLOYEES

Employees are permitted to engage in religious expression directed at fellow employees, and may even attempt to persuade fellow employees of the correctness of their religious views, to the same extent as those employees may engage in comparable speech not involving religion. Some religions encourage adherents to spread the faith at every opportunity, a duty that can encompass the adherent's workplace. As a general matter, proselytizing is as entitled to constitutional protection as any other form of speech—as long as a reasonable observer would not interpret the expression as government endorsement of religion. Employees may urge a colleague to participate or not to participate in religious activities to the same extent that, consistent with concerns of workplace efficiency, they may urge their colleagues to engage in or refrain from other personal endeavors. But employees must refrain from such expression when a fellow employee asks that it stop or otherwise demonstrates that it is unwelcome. (Such expression by supervisors is subject to special consideration as discussed in Section B(2) of these guidelines.) *Examples:* . . . (b) One employee invites another employee to attend worship services at her church, though she knows that the invitee is a devout adherent of another faith. The invitee is shocked, and asks that the invitation not be repeated. The original invitation is protected, but the employee should honor the request that no further invitations be issued. (c) In a parking lot, a non-supervisory employee hands another employee a religious tract urging that she convert to another religion lest she be condemned to eternal damnation. The proselytizing employee says nothing further and does not inquire of his colleague whether she followed the pamphlet's urging. This speech typically should not be restricted. [But] such expression should not be permitted if it is part of a larger pattern of verbal attacks on fellow employees (or a specific employee) not sharing the faith of the speaker. Such speech, by virtue of its excessive or harassing nature, may constitute religious harassment or create a hostile work environment. . . .

(4) EXPRESSION IN AREAS ACCESSIBLE TO THE PUBLIC

Where the public has access to the Federal workplace, all Federal employers must be sensitive to the Establishment Clause's requirement that expression not create the reasonable impression that the government is sponsoring, endorsing, or inhibiting religion generally, or favoring or disfavoring a particular religion. This is particularly important in agencies with adjudicatory functions. However, even in workplaces open to the public, not all private employee religious expression is forbidden. For example, Federal employees may wear personal religious jewelry absent special circumstances (such as safety concerns) that might require a ban on all similar nonreligious jewelry. Employees may also display religious art and literature in their personal work areas to the same extent that they may display other art and literature, so long as the viewing public would reasonably understand the religious expression to be that of the employee acting in her personal capacity, and not that of the government itself. . . .

B. RELIGIOUS DISCRIMINATION

Federal agencies may not discriminate against employees on the basis of their religion, religious beliefs, or views concerning religion. . . .

(2) COERCION OF EMPLOYEE'S PARTICIPATION OR NONPARTICIPATION
   IN RELIGIOUS ACTIVITIES

A person holding supervisory authority over an employee may not, explicitly
or implicitly, insist that the employee participate in religious activities as a condition of continued employment, promotion, salary increases, preferred job
assignments, or any other incidents of employment. Nor [generally] may a
supervisor insist that an employee refrain from participating in religious activities outside the workplace. . . . This prohibition leaves supervisors free to
engage in some kinds of speech about religion. Where a supervisor's religious
expression is not coercive and is understood as his or her personal view, that
expression is protected in the Federal workplace in the same way and to the
same extent as other constitutionally valued speech. . . . Therefore, supervisors
should be careful to ensure that their statements and actions are such that
employees do not perceive any coercion of religious or non-religious behavior . . . and should, where necessary, take appropriate steps to dispel such mis-
perceptions. *Examples:* (a) A supervisor may invite co-workers to a son's
confirmation in a church, a daughter's bat mitzvah in a synagogue, or to his
own wedding at a temple. [But a] supervisor should not say to an employee:
"I didn't see you in church this week. I expect to see you there this
Sunday." . . . (e) At a lunch-table discussion about abortion, during which a
wide range of views are vigorously expressed, a supervisor shares with those
he supervises his belief that God demands full respect for unborn life, and
that he believes it is appropriate for all persons to pray for the unborn. Another
supervisor expresses the view that abortion should be kept legal because God
teaches that women must have control over their own bodies. Without more,
neither of these comments coerces employees' religious conformity or conduct.
Therefore, unless the supervisors take further steps to coerce agreement with
their view or act in ways that could reasonably be perceived as coercive, their
expressions are protected in the Federal workplace in the same way and to the
same extent as other constitutionally valued speech. . . .

(3) HOSTILE WORK ENVIRONMENT AND HARASSMENT

The law against workplace discrimination protects Federal employees from
being subjected to a hostile environment, or religious harassment, in the form of
religiously discriminatory intimidation, or pervasive or severe religious ridicule
or insult, whether by supervisors or fellow workers. . . . [See pp. 600-603.]

D. ESTABLISHMENT OF RELIGION

Supervisors and employees must not engage in activities or expression that a
reasonable observer would interpret as Government endorsement or denigra-
tion of religion or a particular religion. Activities of employees need not be
officially sanctioned in order to violate this principle; if, in all the circumstances,
the activities would leave a reasonable observer with the impression that Government was endorsing, sponsoring, or inhibiting religion generally or favoring
or disfavoring a particular religion, they are not permissible. . . . *Examples:* (a) At
the conclusion of each weekly staff meeting and before anyone leaves the room,
an employee leads a prayer in which nearly all employees participate. All employees are required to attend the weekly meeting. The supervisor neither explicitly

recognizes the prayer as an official function nor explicitly states that no one need participate in the prayer. This course of conduct is not permitted unless under all the circumstances a reasonable observer would conclude that the prayer was not officially endorsed.

D. RELIGION AND DEMOCRACY

1. Religious Voices in Politics: Case Law

One of the most contentious questions in political theory in recent years has been the proper role of religious argument in political deliberation. Some theorists maintain that in a liberal democracy, laws must be based on secular arguments. In constitutional law, this thesis potentially is reflected in several different parts of the *Lemon* test. First is the idea that law must have a "secular purpose," which may mean a purpose based on secular arguments. For discussion, see Andrew Koppelman, Secular Purpose, 88 Va. L. Rev. 87 (2002). Second is the idea that law may not have the primary effect of "advancing religion." If a law promotes or enforces a religious tenet, that may be forbidden. Under the "entanglement" portion of the effects part, the Supreme Court has sometimes spoken of "political division along religious lines" as either a warning signal or an independent constitutional violation. Other theorists maintain that it is either impossible or undesirable to enforce these limits as a matter of constitutional law, but that as a dictate of good citizenship citizens should observe the requirement of secular argument, at least in public settings.

On the other hand, some argue that in a liberal democracy all citizens are equally entitled to advocate laws based on reasons they find persuasive, with no epistemological, ideological, or metaphysical limitations. According to this view, laws cannot be unconstitutional, or otherwise objectionable, merely because their supporters are motivated by religiously informed judgments or make arguments based on religious ideas or authorities.

Consider first the different ways in which the Supreme Court has viewed religious influences on political decisions:

LEMON v. KURTZMAN
403 U.S. 602 (1971)

[This case involved two state programs that subsidized the salaries of teachers of secular subjects in religious schools. Other portions of the opinion are found at p. 372. This except is from Chief Justice Burger's opinion for the Court.]

A broader base of entanglement of yet a different character is presented by the divisive political potential of these state programs. In a community where such a large number of pupils are served by church-related schools, it can be assumed that state assistance will entail considerable political activity. Partisans of parochial schools, understandably concerned with rising costs and sincerely dedicated to both the religious and secular educational missions of their schools, will inevitably champion this cause and promote political action to achieve their goals. Those who oppose state aid, whether for constitutional, religious, or fiscal reasons, will inevitably respond and employ all of the usual political campaign techniques to prevail. Candidates will be forced to declare and voters to choose. It would be unrealistic to ignore the fact that many people confronted with issues of this kind will find their votes aligned with their faith.

Ordinarily political debate and division, however vigorous or even partisan, are normal and healthy manifestations of our democratic system of government, but political division along religious lines was one of the principal evils against which the First Amendment was intended to protect. The potential divisiveness of such conflict is a threat to the normal political process. To have States or communities divide on the issues presented by state aid to parochial schools would tend to confuse and obscure other issues of great urgency. We have an expanding array of vexing issues, local and national, domestic and international, to debate and divide on. It conflicts with our whole history and tradition to permit questions of the Religion Clauses to assume such importance in our legislatures and in our elections that they could divert attention from the myriad issues and problems that confront every level of government. The highways of church and state relationships are not likely to be one-way streets, and the Constitution's authors sought to protect religious worship from the pervasive power of government. The history of many countries attests to the hazards of religion's intruding into the political arena or of political power intruding into the legitimate and free exercise of religious belief.

McDANIEL v. PATY
435 U.S. 618 (1978)

[Seven years after *Lemon*'s caution against "political division along religious lines," the Court in *McDaniel* struck down, on free exercise grounds, a long-standing provision in the Tennessee state constitution excluding clergy from serving in the state legislature. The lead opinion, written (like *Lemon*) by Chief Justice Burger, rejected the argument that clergy legislators would "necessarily exercise their powers and influence to promote the interests of one sect or thwart the interests of another thus pitting one against the others." The Court said that "the American experience provides no persuasive support for [this] fear."]

Mr. Justice BRENNAN, concurring in the judgment.
. . . That public debate of religious ideas, like any other, may arouse emotion, may incite, may foment religious divisiveness and strife does not rob it of constitutional protection. The mere fact that a purpose of the Establishment Clause is to reduce or eliminate religious divisiveness or strife, does not place religious discussion, association, or political participation in a status less preferred than rights of discussion, association and political participation generally. "Adherents of particular faiths and individual churches frequently take strong positions on public issues including . . . vigorous advocacy of legal or constitutional positions. Of course, churches as much as secular bodies and private citizens have that right." Walz v. Tax Commission.

. . . The Establishment Clause . . . may not be used as a sword to justify repression of religion or its adherents from any aspect of public life.

Our decisions under the Establishment Clause prevent government from supporting or involving itself in religion or from becoming drawn into ecclesiastical disputes. These prohibitions naturally tend, as they were designed to, to avoid channelling political activity along religious lines and to reduce any tendency toward religious divisiveness in society. Beyond enforcing these prohibitions, however, government must not go. The antidote which the Constitution provides against zealots who would inject sectarianism into the political process is to subject their ideas to refutation in the marketplace of ideas and their platforms to rejection at the polls.

NOTES AND QUESTIONS

1. Religion, Politics, and Divisiveness. It may be true, as *Lemon* says, that the Establishment Clause was meant to head off "political division along religious lines." But how can that provide an answer to any particular issue? On most issues—aid to religious schools among them—there are religious groups on both sides of the question. While it may reduce religious friction, in a sense, to remove the question from democratic politics, how does that determine which of the contending sides should prevail?

More fundamentally, does the "no divisiveness" theory imply that citizens whose ideas of justice and the common good are shaped by religious convictions can or must be excluded from democratic discourse? In most contexts, the democratic response to sharp disagreement is to bring all sides of the conflict into civil debate on equal terms. Why are issues that divide Americans along religious lines any different? See Richard W. Garnett, Religion, Division, and the First Amendment, 94 Georgetown L.J. _____ (forthcoming 2006); Edward M. Gaffney, Political Divisiveness Along Religious Lines: The Entanglement of the Court in Sloppy History and Bad Public Policy, 24 St. Louis U. L.J. 205 (1980).

2. Does the Court Have a Consistent View? Are the statements about divisiveness in *Lemon* consistent with those in *McDaniel* approving religious activism in politics? Justice Brennan's proposed distinction is that political divisiveness along religious lines may justify "prevent[ing] government from supporting . . . religion" but cannot justify "repression of religion or its adherents from any aspects of public life." Does this distinction adequately explain the two decisions?

Consider also Epperson v. Arkansas (p. 548), where the Court struck down a state law prohibiting the teaching of evolution. The Court noted the religiously based attacks on evolution and concluded that the law could not be justified by any "considerations of state policy other than the religious views of some of [the state's] citizens. It is clear that fundamentalist sectarian conviction was and is the law's reason for existence." 393 U.S. at 107-108. Is *Epperson*'s rationale consistent with *McDaniel*?

The participation of religious groups and the role of religious arguments has been especially controversial with regard to highly charged moral and cultural issues, such as abortion, homosexuality, and the death penalty. In each of the following examples, identify the Court's implicit view of the role of religion in politics.

ROE v. WADE
410 U.S. 113 (1973)

[From Justice Blackmun's opinion for the Court:]

... Texas urges that, apart from the Fourteenth Amendment, life begins at conception and is present throughout pregnancy, and that, therefore, the State has a compelling interest in protecting that life from and after conception. We need not resolve the difficult question of when life begins. When those trained in the respective disciplines of medicine, philosophy, and theology are unable to arrive at any consensus, the judiciary, at this point in the development of man's knowledge, is not in a position to speculate as to the answer.

It should be sufficient to note briefly the wide divergence of thinking on this most sensitive and difficult question. There has always been strong support for the view that life does not begin until live birth. This was the belief of the Stoics. It appears to be the predominant, though not the unanimous, attitude of the Jewish faith. It may be taken to represent also the position of a large segment of the Protestant community, insofar as that can be ascertained; organized groups that have taken a formal position on the abortion issue have generally regarded abortion as a matter for the conscience of the individual and her family. As we have noted, the common law found greater significance in quickening. Physicians and their scientific colleagues have regarded that even with less interest and have tended to focus either upon conception, upon live birth, or upon the interim point at which the fetus becomes "viable," that is, potentially able to live outside of the mother's womb, albeit with artificial aid. Viability is usually placed at about seven months (28 weeks) but may occur earlier, even at 24 weeks. The Aristotelian theory of "mediate animation," that held sway throughout the Middle Ages and the Renaissance in Europe, continued to be official Roman Catholic dogma until the 19th century, despite opposition to this "ensoulment" theory from those in the Church who would recognize the existence of life from the moment of conception. The latter is now, of course, the official belief of the Catholic Church. As one brief amicus discloses, this is a view strongly held by many non-Catholics as well, and by many physicians. Substantial problems for precise definition of this view are posed, however, by new embryological data that purport to indicate that conception is a "process" over time, rather than an event, and by new medical techniques such as menstrual extraction, the "morning-after" pill, implantation of embryos, artificial insemination, and even artificial wombs. ...

In view of all this, we do not agree that, by adopting one theory of life, Texas may override the rights of the pregnant woman that are at stake.

HARRIS v. McRAE
448 U.S. 297 (1980)

[At issue in this case was the constitutionality of the Hyde Amendment, a law prohibiting Medicaid reimbursements for abortions. We include only the portion of Justice Stewart's opinion for the Court that addresses the religious basis for the legislation. This section of the opinion was unanimous.]

The appellees also argue that the Hyde Amendment contravenes rights secured by the Religion Clauses of the First Amendment. It is the appellees' view that the Hyde Amendment violates the Establishment Clause because it incorporates into law the doctrines of the Roman Catholic Church concerning the sinfulness of abortion and the time at which life commences. . . .

It is well settled that "a legislative enactment does not contravene the Establishment Clause if it has a secular legislative purpose, if its principal or primary effect neither advances nor inhibits religion, and if it does not foster an excessive governmental entanglement with religion." Applying this standard, the District Court properly concluded that the Hyde Amendment does not run afoul of the Establishment Clause. Although neither a State nor the Federal Government can constitutionally "pass laws which aid one religion, aid all religions, or prefer one religion over another," it does not follow that a statute violates the Establishment Clause because it "happens to coincide or harmonize with the tenets of some or all religions." McGowan v. Maryland. That the Judaeo-Christian religions oppose stealing does not mean that a State or the Federal Government may not, consistent with the Establishment Clause, enact laws prohibiting larceny. Id. The Hyde Amendment, as the District Court noted, is as much a reflection of "traditionalist" values towards abortion, as it is an embodiment of the views of any particular religion. In sum, we are convinced that the fact that the funding restrictions in the Hyde Amendment may coincide with the religious tenets of the Roman Catholic Church does not, without more, contravene the Establishment Clause.

WEBSTER v. REPRODUCTIVE HEALTH SERVICES
492 U.S. 490 (1989)

[This case involved the constitutionality of certain restrictions on abortion, preceded by a legislative finding that life begins at conception. The Court upheld the restrictions. Only Justice Stevens addressed the Establishment Clause issues in the case on their merits.]

Justice STEVENS, dissenting.

I am persuaded that the absence of any secular purpose for the legislative declarations that life begins at conception and that conception occurs at fertilization makes the relevant portion of the preamble invalid under the Establishment Clause of the First Amendment to the Federal Constitution. This conclusion does not, and could not, rest on the fact that the statement happens to coincide with the tenets of certain religions, see McGowan v. Maryland; Harris v. McRae, or on the fact that the legislators who voted to enact it may have been motivated by religious considerations. Rather, it rests on the fact that the preamble, an unequivocal endorsement of a religious tenet of some but by no means all Christian faiths, serves no identifiable secular purpose. That fact alone compels a conclusion that the statute violates the Establishment Clause. Wallace v. Jaffree.

My concern can best be explained by reference to the position on this issue that was accepted by the leaders of the Roman Catholic Church for many years. The position is summarized in a report, entitled "Catholic Teaching On Abortion," prepared by the Congressional Research Service of the Library of Congress. It states in part:

"The disagreement over the status of the unformed as against the formed fetus was crucial for Christian teaching on the soul. It was widely held that the soul was not present until the formation of the fetus 40 or 80 days after conception, for males and females respectively. Thus, abortion of the 'unformed' or 'inanimate' fetus (from anima, soul) was something less than true homicide, rather a form of anticipatory or quasi-homicide. This view received its definitive treatment in St. Thomas Aquinas and became for a time the dominant interpretation in the Latin Church. . . .

"For St. Thomas, as for mediaeval Christendom generally, there is a lapse of time—approximately 40 to 80 days—after conception and before the soul's infusion. . . .

"For St. Thomas, 'seed and what is not seed is determined by sensation and movement.' What is destroyed in abortion of the unformed fetus is seed, not man. This distinction received its most careful analysis in St. Thomas. It was the general belief of Christendom, reflected, for example, in the Council of Trent (1545-1563), which restricted penalties for homicide to abortion of an animated fetus only."

If the views of St. Thomas were held as widely today as they were in the Middle Ages, and if a state legislature were to enact a statute prefaced with a "finding" that female life begins 80 days after conception and male life begins 40 days after conception, I have no doubt that this Court would promptly conclude that such an endorsement of a particular religious tenet is violative of the Establishment Clause.

In my opinion the difference between that hypothetical statute and Missouri's preamble reflects nothing more than a difference in theological doctrine. The preamble to the Missouri statute endorses the theological position that there is the same secular interest in preserving the life of a fetus during the first 40 or 80 days of pregnancy as there is after viability—indeed, after the time when the fetus has become a "person" with legal rights protected by the Constitution. To sustain that position as a matter of law, I believe Missouri has the burden of identifying the secular interests that differentiate the first 40 days of pregnancy from the period immediately before or after fertilization when, as Griswold v. Connecticut (1965) and related cases establish, the Constitution allows the use of contraceptive procedures to prevent potential life from developing into full personhood. Focusing our attention on the first several weeks of pregnancy is especially appropriate because that is the period when the vast majority of abortions are actually performed.

As a secular matter, there is an obvious difference between the state interest in protecting the freshly fertilized egg and the state interest in protecting a 9-month-gestated, fully sentient fetus on the eve of birth. There can be no interest in protecting the newly fertilized egg from physical pain or mental anguish, because the capacity for such suffering does not yet exist; respecting a developed fetus, however, that interest is valid. In fact, if one prescinds the theological concept of ensoulment—or one accepts St. Thomas Aquinas' view that ensoulment does not occur for at least 40 days—a State has no greater secular interest in protecting the potential life of an embryo that is still "seed" than in protecting the potential life of a sperm or an unfertilized ovum.

There have been times in history when military and economic interests would have been served by an increase in population. No one argues today, however, that Missouri can assert a societal interest in increasing its population as its secular reason for fostering potential life. Indeed, our national policy, as reflected in legislation the Court upheld last Term, is to prevent the potential life that is produced by "pregnancy and childbirth among unmarried adolescents." If the secular analysis were based on a strict balancing of fiscal costs and benefits, the economic costs of unlimited childbearing would outweigh those of abortion. There is, of course, an important and unquestionably valid secular interest in "protecting a young pregnant woman from the consequences of an incorrect decision." Although that interest is served by a requirement that the woman receive medical and, in appropriate circumstances, parental, advice, it does not justify the state legislature's official endorsement of the theological tenet embodied in §§ 1.205.1(1), (2). . . .

Bolstering my conclusion that the preamble violates the First Amendment is the fact that the intensely divisive character of much of the national debate over the abortion issue reflects the deeply held religious convictions of many participants in the debate.[16] The Missouri Legislature may not inject its endorsement of a particular religious tradition into this debate, for "[t]he Establishment Clause does not allow public bodies to foment such disagreement." See County of Allegheny v. ACLU (Stevens, J., concurring in part and dissenting in part).

In my opinion the preamble to the Missouri statute is unconstitutional for two reasons. To the extent that it has substantive impact on the freedom to use contraceptive procedures, it is inconsistent with the central holding in Griswold. To the extent that it merely makes "legislative findings without operative effect," it violates the Establishment Clause of the First Amendment. Contrary to the theological "finding" of the Missouri Legislature, a woman's constitutionally protected liberty encompasses the right to act on her own belief that—to paraphrase St. Thomas Aquinas—until a seed has acquired the powers of sensation and movement, the life of a human being has not yet begun.

BOWERS v. HARDWICK

478 U.S. 186 (1986)

[In this case, the Court upheld a Georgia statute making sodomy a crime against a challenge under the privacy doctrine of the Due Process Clause. The majority made no reference to the religious origins of the law, commenting only that "[p]roscriptions against that conduct have ancient roots," and mentioning common law and statutes. In a separate concurrence, however, Chief Justice Burger observed that "[c]ondemnation of those practices is firmly rooted in Judaeo-Christian moral and ethical standards." The Chief Justice also cited Roman law, Blackstone's Commentaries, and other English and American legal sources. He concluded: "To hold that the act of homosexual sodomy is somehow protected as a fundamental right would be to cast aside millenia of moral teaching."]

16. No fewer than 67 religious organizations submitted their views as amici curiae on either side of this case. Amici briefs on both sides, moreover, frankly discuss the relation between the abortion controversy and religion. See generally, e.g., Brief for Agudath Israel of America as Amicus Curiae, Brief for Americans United for Separation of Church and State et al. as Amici Curiae, Brief for Catholics for a Free Choice et al. as Amici Curiae, Brief for Holy Orthodox Church as Amicus Curiae, Brief for Lutheran Church-Missouri Synod et al. as Amici Curiae, Brief for Missouri Catholic Conference as Amicus Curiae. Cf. Burke, Religion and Politics in the United States, in Movements and Issues in World Religions 243, 254-256 (C. Fu & G. Spiegler eds., 1987).

Justice BLACKMUN, dissenting.

... The assertion that "traditional Judeo-Christian values proscribe" the conduct involved cannot provide an adequate justification for [the anti-sodomy law]. That certain, but by no means all, religious groups condemn the behavior at issue gives the State no license to impose their judgments on the entire citizenry. The legitimacy of secular legislation depends instead on whether the State can advance some justification for its law beyond its conformity to religious doctrine. See, e.g., McGowan v. Maryland; Stone v. Graham (1980). Thus, far from buttressing his case, [the prosecutor's] invocation of Leviticus, Romans, St. Thomas Aquinas, and sodomy's heretical status during the Middle Ages undermines his suggestion that § 16-6-2 represents a legitimate use of secular coercive power. A State can no more punish private behavior because of religious intolerance than it can punish such behavior because of racial animus. "The Constitution cannot control such prejudices, but neither can it tolerate them. Private biases may be outside the reach of the law, but the law cannot, directly or indirectly give them effect." Palmore v. Sidoti (1984).

LAWRENCE v. TEXAS
539 U.S. 558 (2003)

[Lawrence overruled Bowers v. Hardwick, holding that private, noncommercial, consensual sexual relations between adults were protected against criminalization by the "liberty" component of the Due Process Clause. The majority stated, among other things:]

The [historical] condemnation [of homosexual behavior] has been shaped by religious beliefs, conceptions of right and acceptable behavior, and respect for the traditional family. For many persons these are not trivial concerns but profound and deep convictions accepted as ethical and moral principles to which they aspire and which thus determine the course of their lives. These considerations do not answer the question before us, however. The issue is whether the majority may use the power of the State to enforce these views on the whole society through operation of the criminal law.

[The Constitution protects] personal decisions relating to marriage, procreation, contraception, family relationships, child rearing, and education. . . . "These matters, involving the most intimate and personal choices a person may make in a lifetime, choices central to personal dignity and autonomy, are central to the liberty protected by the Fourteenth Amendment. At the heart of liberty is the right to define one's own concept of existence, of meaning, of the universe, and of the mystery of human life. Beliefs about these matters could not define the attributes of personhood were they formed under compulsion of the State." Planned Parenthood v. Casey (1992) [reaffirming the right to abortion].

. . . The Texas statute furthers no legitimate state interest which can justify its intrusion into the personal and private life of the individual.

ATKINS v. VIRGINIA
536 U.S. 304 (2002)

[In *Atkins* the Court held that executing the mentally retarded violated the Eighth Amendment proscription against cruel and unusual punishments because "a national consensus" had developed against the practice. The majority opinion relied primarily on the increasing number of states barring executions of the retarded and the infrequency of such executions in states where it was theoretically permitted. In a footnote, the Court added:]

Additional evidence makes it clear that this legislative judgment reflects a much broader social and professional consensus. For example, several organizations with germane expertise have adopted official positions opposing the imposition of the death penalty upon a mentally retarded offender. See Brief for American Psychological Association et al. as *Amici Curiae;* Brief for AAMR et al. as *Amici Curiae.* In addition, representatives of widely diverse religious communities in the United States, reflecting Christian, Jewish, Muslim, and Buddhist traditions, have filed an *amicus curiae* brief explaining that even though their views about the death penalty differ, they all "share a conviction that the execution of persons with mental retardation cannot be morally justified." Brief for United States Catholic Conference et al. as *Amici Curiae* 2. Moreover, within the world community, the imposition of the death penalty for crimes committed by mentally retarded offenders is overwhelmingly disapproved. Brief for European Union as *Amicus Curiae* 4. Finally, polling data shows a widespread consensus among Americans, even those who support the death penalty, that executing the mentally retarded is wrong. Although these factors are by no means dispositive, their consistency with the legislative evidence lends further support to our conclusion that there is a consensus among those who have addressed the issue.

NOTES AND QUESTIONS

1. Religious Tenets and Legislation. The fact that governmental action is consistent with long-standing moral teachings of major religions could relate to its constitutionality in any of several ways. It might: (1) enhance the likelihood that the action is constitutionally legitimate, (2) make the action more suspect, or (3) be treated as irrelevant. Which option does the Court follow in each of the excerpts above? Are the different results explicable because the cases are distinguishable in some way? Which approach is correct, and why?

2. What Makes a Law too "Religious"? If religious arguments in politics are constitutionally problematic, what evidence is necessary to demonstrate the problem? Is it that religious groups predominate among the advocates of the measure? (What if religious groups are on both sides? Does that tend to support or undermine its constitutionality?) Is it that religious arguments seem important to the debate? (What if religious arguments are made on both sides?) Is it that nonreligious arguments seem implausible? Is that true of the arguments about abortion? Homosexuality? What about dancing?

CLAYTON v. PLACE

690 F. Supp. 850 (W.D. Mo. 1988), rev'd, 884 F.2d 376 (8th Cir. 1989)

CLARK, District Judge.

[Plaintiffs—schoolchildren, parents, and taxpayers of the Purdy R-II School District—sued the school board and superintendent claiming that the school district's rule against holding school dances violated the Establishment Clause. Rule 502.29 provided:

SECRET ORGANIZATIONS—SCHOOL DANCES

No fraternities, sororities, secret societies, or organizations shall be permitted, nor shall any student organization be permitted to elect its own membership. School dances are not authorized and school premises shall not be used for purposes of conducting a dance.

The court made the following findings of fact.]

18. During the 1985-86 school year, [a] group of students and parents sought to change Rule 502.29. At a January meeting with Superintendent Place, when questioned by the parents about the reasons for the prohibition, Superintendent Place stated words to the effect "why should this surprise you, this is a conservative, religious community." When asked if it were the Baptists that opposed dancing, Superintendent Place stated, "Let's just say protestants." . . .

20. At the February 10, 1986 school board meeting, plaintiffs . . . appeared to request a reconsideration of Rule 502.29 in order to sponsor a dance by the newly formed SADD (Students Against Drunk Driving) chapter. At the meeting the school board members discussed all of the telephone calls they had been receiving concerning the dance issue. The board members now state the callers gave no reasons for maintaining the rule. Reverend Ted Davis and his wife were present at the meeting to state their opposition to a change in the rule. When Reverend Davis was asked for his reasons, board president Garrett stated that he did not have to tell anyone his reasons. Garrett stated "you'd better hope there's never separation of God and school" in response to a question about the separation of church and state. Rev. Davis then asked for time to respond to the rule change at the next school board meeting.

21. When school board member Terry was contacted by plaintiff Fox, he stated that he had voted for dance in the past but caught so much "flak" from the ministers that he would vote against it this time. School board member Keeling stated to Fox that he did not believe in dancing because he was taught it was wrong.

22. Board member Keeling told plaintiff Marlene Mareth that his background disfavored dancing; board member Negre stated his church is opposed to dancing.

23. After the February meeting the Ministerial Alliance met to plan the opposition to changing the rule. The group consists of ministers from the First Baptist, the First Christian, the First Free Will Baptist, the First Assembly of God, and the Macedonia Baptist Churches. There are no Catholic, Lutheran, Presbyterian, Methodist, Jewish or Mormon members in the Ministerial Alliance. The members agreed to "get" their church members to attend the March school board meeting to oppose a change in the rule.

24. The First Baptist Church minister, Rev. Winfrey, spoke to his congregation about the upcoming dance issue at the school board. He encouraged the congregation to attend the meeting and oppose the change in the rule to allow dancing. The church congregation has prayed for member Blakely's soul [one of the plaintiffs] for trying to change the rule in the school.

25. To become a member of the First Assembly of God, a person must agree to be separate from worldliness—which includes dancing. The minister of that congregation, Rev. Dement, testified that if a member of his congregation engaged in social dancing he would have no choice but to refer him/her to the Presbyters for counseling. He encouraged his congregation to attend the March meeting and made known his views against dancing.

26. Prior to the March meeting, the minister of the Free Will Baptist Church, Ted Davis, contacted every school board member except Stephens to voice his opposition to school dancing. Davis informed his church that there was a petition to be signed concerning dancing as they left the service the Sunday before the March meeting; he believes and preaches that social dancing is sinful, scripturally prohibited, and possibly satanic. He has discussed this view with church members, has preached against dancing from the pulpit and would have a private counseling session with a member of his congregation who engaged in social dancing.

27. The topic at Sunday school on the Sunday before the Board meeting at the Macedonia Free Will Baptist Church, was the change in the rule. Board member Henderson was present and stated that there would be no dancing as long as he was on the school board and encouraged everyone to go to the meeting to show their opposition to any change in the rule. Later at the church service, Gary Pinnell rose and asked everyone to show their support for the rule. Rev. Neal, a member of the Ministerial Alliance, believes social dancing is inappropriate behavior, has discussed his beliefs with board members Henderson and Negri, and has "mentioned" his belief in church services.

28. The largest crowd ever attended the March 10, 1986 board meeting. At the meeting on the dance issue, a presentation was made by Joan Fox, Rev. Davis and Gary Pinnell. No direct mention was made of religion per se at the meeting; however, the letter from the Ministerial Alliance was read in its entirety. At the end of Rev. Davis' talk, he asked the 250-400 people in attendance to stand in opposition to changing the rule. The overwhelming majority of people stood in opposition to changing the rule. Later in closed session, the Board did not take a formal vote, but left the rule intact. . . .

CONCLUSIONS OF LAW

[The court quoted the three-part *Lemon* test for Establishment Clause issues.] *Lemon*'s purpose requirement aims at preventing the relevant governmental decisionmaker from abandoning neutrality and acting with the intent of promoting a particular point of view in religious matters. Defendants argue that dancing in this case is not a religious issue. That assertion has no basis in the evidence presented to this Court. . . .

The entire board candidly admits that they followed the will of the majority; but they were not candid in their opinions on the religious reasoning of the majority. The board members were not particularly credible, either in demeanor or in the substance of their testimony. [I]t is inconceivable that no one in the Purdy area has ever expressed the view, within the board members' hearing, that dancing is either immoral, sinful or against any religion. It is inconceivable that certain board members were totally unaware that dancing was against the tenets of some Purdy residents' religion. It is equally unbelievable that the board placed no religious significance to a statement given by the ministerial alliance, a group of ministers whose combined ministry included some of the board members. This Court is skeptical that it heard the complete story concerning the board members' deliberations of the rule and the religious significance of the opposition to dancing in Purdy. The school board adopted the reasoning of the "majority" of townspeople, including the strongly-held religious views. . . .

Condemnation of dancing is not firmly rooted in Judeo-Christian moral or ethical standards. Allowing students to engage in dancing within the school building does not conflict with our historical traditions. See Bowers v. Hardwick. Although the intent of the decision-makers who promulgated the rule cannot be ascertained, the school board in keeping the rule abandoned neutrality with the intent to promote a particular view in religious matters. . . . It is clear to the Court that the reasons propounded by the majority were a mere pretext for the real religious reasoning. Thus, there is no valid secular purpose to having Rule 502.29.

Even if the defendants could show a valid secular purpose, the primary effect of this rule is to endorse the tenets of that particular religious group in Purdy who believe that social dancing is sinful. "Endorsement sends a message to non-adherents that they are outsiders, not full members of the political community, and an accompanying message to adherents that they are insiders, favored members of the political community." [Lynch v. Donnelly (O'Connor J., concurring).] In the present matter, the school board is placing the state's imprimatur on one particular religious belief. The testimony at trial was that a tenet of the Purdy Assembly of God religion is a separation from worldliness, including dancing. The evidence was that a tenet of the Purdy Free Will Baptist Church is that social dancing is sinful. By prohibiting dancing in the Purdy School, the school board has assumed the role of monitoring adherence to that particular tenet. . . . The right to dance may not be a tenet of the Methodist, Catholic, Lutheran or Mormon Church, but the children of these faiths cannot be made to feel that their religions are inferior because their churches do not prohibit (and in some cases, actually sponsor) dances. The public stamp of approval cannot be placed on one faith—even if it is the majority in that particular school system. It is no defense to urge that the religious practices here may be relatively minor encroachments on the First Amendment. The administration of religious training is properly in the domain of the family and church. The First Amendment prohibits public schools from serving that function. The primary effect of Rule 502.29 is to advance the religious beliefs of a particular religion.

The third prong set out in [Lemon] is whether there is excessive administrative or political entanglement. There is no question that the dance issue is deeply divisive in the Purdy area, nor is there any question that it has been a divisive issue for many years. . . . Religious groups of course have an absolute right to make their views known and to participate in public discussion of issues. The ministers who participated in this public debate can in no way be criticized by the state for that participation; however, those views may not prevail if they conflict with the constitutional mandate forbidding the establishment of a religion. . . .

It would be inappropriate for this Court to order the district to sponsor school dances; however, a district rule prohibiting students from holding dances on school property infringes on the First Amendment rights of the students and must be invalidated.

NOTE AND QUESTIONS

Clayton **on Appeal.** On appeal the Eighth Circuit reversed. The court noted that dancing itself is a secular activity, that a prohibition on dancing "carries . . . absolutely no religious component," and that the rule does not prevent students from dancing "should they choose to do so." 884 F.2d 376, 379 (8th Cir. 1989). As to the alleged religious motivation for the rule, the court stated that "[w]e simply do not believe elected government officials are required to check at the door whatever religious background (or lack of it) they carry with them before they act on rules that are otherwise unobjectionable under the controlling *Lemon* standards." "[T]his approach to constitutional analysis," the court said, "would have the effect of disenfranchising religious groups when they succeed in influencing secular decisions." *Id.* at 380. Which of the two rulings is correct?

2. Religious Voices in Politics: Commentary

There have been relatively few judicial decisions considering in any detail the role of religious voices in politics. Harris v. McRae, by firmly rejecting an establishment challenge to abortion-funding restrictions, has doubtless discouraged litigants from claiming that religious-moral activism in enacting a law makes the law suspect under the Establishment Clause. However, even if a religious basis for a law does not render the law unconstitutional, some have argued that it is a basis for criticizing the law as a matter of political morality. In recent years, there has been extensive debate among scholarly commentators on this moral and philosophical question—the question, as Professor Kent Greenawalt puts it, whether "a good member of our liberal democracy [would] rely on his or her religious convictions" in voting for political candidates or, if he or she is a political decision maker, in voting on legislation. Kent Greenawalt, Religious Convictions and Political Choice 4 (1988). This section presents several different views on the constitutional and moral questions concerning reliance on religious views as a basis for legislation.

THE PLACE OF RELIGIOUS ARGUMENT IN A FREE AND DEMOCRATIC SOCIETY
Robert Audi
30 San Diego L. Rev. 677, 690-702 (1993)*

[In a liberal democratic] society the use of secular reason must in general be the main basis of sociopolitical decision. . . . This seems to apply especially to decisions that result in coercion, whether through law or even through restrictive social policies not backed by legal sanctions. If I am coerced on grounds that cannot motivate me, as a rational informed person, to do the thing in question, I cannot come to identify with the deed and will tend to resent having to do it.

---

* Professor Audi's position is developed more fully in Robert Audi, Religious Commitment and Secular Reason (2000).—EDS.

Even if the deed should be my obligation, still, where only esoteric knowledge—
say, through revelation that only the initiated experience—can show that it is,
I will tend to resent the coercion. And it is part of the underlying rationale of
liberalism that we should not have to feel this kind of resentment—that we give
up autonomy only where, no matter what our specific preferences or particular
world view, we can be expected, given adequate rationality and sufficient information, to see that we would have so acted on our own.

[Audi then explains why it is important that the reasons for coercive legislation be not just "public"—the kind of reasons that in principle could be
accepted by all citizens—but also "secular," as opposed to religious.] For one
thing, a liberal democracy must make special efforts to prevent religious domination of one group by another. There are, in turn, at least two reasons for this.
One is that the authority structure common in many religions can make a desire
to dominate other groups natural and can provide a rationale for it. (What could
be more important or beneficial to others than saving their souls?) Another
reason is that the dictates of a religion often extend to the religious as well as
the secular conduct of persons, so that if domination occurs it undermines even
religious freedom. (To save people's souls they must not only cease performing
evil deeds but worship appropriately.) Religious freedom is a kind quite properly
given high priority by a liberal democracy. And, if religious considerations
threaten it more than nonpublic influences in general, additional reasons
exist for a liberal democracy to constrain the role of those considerations.

Another ground for [a requirement] of specifically secular reason . . . is connected with the authority which religious principles, directives, and traditions are
commonly felt to have. Where religious convictions are a basis of a disagreement,
it is, other things being equal, less likely that the disputants can achieve resolution or even peacefully agree to disagree. If God's will is felt to be clear, there
may seem to be only one way to view the issue. This can apply as much to prima
facie nonreligious problems such as physical health care as it does to specifically
religious practices. Granted, a nonreligious source of conviction can also be felt
to be infallible, and it may also be nonpublic. But not every nonpublic source of
views and preferences poses the authority problem, or the special threat to religious freedom, that can arise from certain kinds of unconstrained religious convictions. Particularly when people believe that extreme measures, such as bravely
fighting a holy war, carry an eternal reward, they tend to be ready to take them.
Being ready to die, they may find it much easier to kill.

So far, I have been imagining coercion by laws or institutional policies. But in
my view, the same sorts of considerations imply that individual as well as institutional conduct—the more common domain of discussions of religion and
politics—should be constrained in a related way. More specifically, I believe
that just as we separate church and state institutionally, we should, in certain
aspects of our thinking and public conduct, separate religion from law and
public policy matters, especially when it comes to passing restrictive laws. This
separation in turn implies the need for motivational as well as rationale principles. If, for example, some group has religious reasons for favoring circumci-
sion, they should not argue for a legal requirement of it without having
evidentially adequate secular reasons for such a law. Nor should they offer secular reasons that are not evidentially convincing to them or, for that reason or any
other, cognitively motivating, such as statistics about cervical cancer in women

married to men who are not circumcised. To do this would be to allow these reasons to serve as—or even to use them as—secular rationalizations that cloak the underlying religious motivation for seeking the legislation.

[I identify] two principles to express these constraints upon conscience. First, the principle of secular rationale says that one has a prima facie obligation not to advocate or support any law or public policy that restricts human conduct unless one has, and is willing to offer, adequate secular reason for this advocacy or support. A secular reason is roughly one whose normative force does not evidentially depend on the existence of God or on theological considerations, or on the pronouncements of a person or institution qua religious authority. The second, the principle of secular motivation, adds the idea that one also has a prima facie obligation to abstain from such advocacy or support unless one is sufficiently motivated by adequate secular reason. This [requires] that some secular reason [be] motivationally sufficient, roughly in the sense that one would act on it even if, other things remaining equal, other reasons were eliminated. . . .

It is important to emphasize two points about the proposed principles. First, the principle of secular motivation provides that one may also have religious reasons and be motivated by them. . . . The principles even allow a person to judge the religious reasons to be more important than the secular ones, or be more strongly motivated by them, or both. The rationale and motivation principles do not rule out a major role for religious considerations, even in public political advocacy. They simply provide a measure of protection against their domination in contexts in which they should be constrained. . . .

[Indeed, reasoning from] the assumption of at least a broadly Western theism, we can say this much: God would surely provide a route to moral truth along rational secular paths—as I think Aquinas, for one, believed God has done. Given how the world is—for instance, with so much evil that even many theists are tempted by the atheistic conclusion that such a realm could not have been created by God—it would seem cruel for God to do otherwise. . . .

[I] should think, moreover, that in some cases good secular arguments for moral principles may be better reasons to believe those principles divinely enjoined than theological arguments for the principles, based on scripture or tradition. For the latter arguments seem more subject than the former to extraneous cultural influences, more vulnerable to misinterpretation of texts or their sheer corruption across time and translation, and more liable to bias stemming from political or other nonreligious aims. This turns one traditional view of the relation between ethics and religion on its head; it may be better to try to understand God through ethics than ethics through theology. . . .

It is possible that a person believes, on authority or revelation, that God commands a certain kind of action, yet has no understanding of why it should be divinely commanded or otherwise obligatory. This might hold for persons of little education, particularly on matters where the available arguments, if there are any, are difficult to grasp. My principles do not deny such a person a right to act, even publicly, in favor of the commanded conduct. But, they also suggest an obligation to seek secular grounds for that conduct if it promotes any law or policy restricting freedom. On the other hand, if religious authorities are the source of the person's belief, we may certainly ask that the relevant people should themselves try to provide a readily intelligible secular rationale if they are promoting laws or public policies that restrict liberty. This may be what they would reasonably wish regarding their counterparts who promote practices incompatible with their own. The kind of commitment to secular reason that I propose may constrain the use of some religious arguments, but it can protect people against coercion or pressure brought by conflicting religious arguments from others. . . .

My position as applied to individual conduct is above all one that lays out what we ought to do in something like an ideal case. It describes an aspect of civic virtue, not a limitation of civil (or other) rights. I have not meant to suggest that, for example, there is no right to base one's vote on a religious ground. But surely we can do better than guide our civic conduct merely within the constraints imposed by our rights. If ethics directs us merely to live within our rights, it gives us too minimal a guide for daily life. . . .

There are, to be sure, various models of democracy, and some are highly permissive. I have been thinking of a liberal democracy, not just any system in which the people govern themselves. I am indeed particularly thinking of a constitutional democracy. My claim is that a substantially weaker separation of church and state than I have defended is not fully consonant with the ideals of liberal democracy, at least as it is best understood. I think that sound ethics itself dictates that, out of respect for others as free and dignified individuals, we should always have and be sufficiently motivated by adequate secular reasons for our positions on those matters of law or public policy in which our decisions might significantly restrict human freedom. If you are fully rational and I cannot convince you of my view by arguments framed in the concepts we share as rational beings, then even if mine is the majority view I should not coerce you. Perhaps the political system under which we live embodies a legal right for the majority to do so, for certain ranges of conduct; perhaps there is even a moral right to do so, given our mutual understanding of majority rule. But the principles I am suggesting still make a plausible claim on our allegiance. They require partial secularization of our advocacy, argumentation, and decisions, in certain contexts and for certain purposes. But they do not restrict our ultimate freedom of expression, and they leave us at liberty to fulfill our cherished religious ideals in all the ways compatible with a system in which those with differing ideals are equally free to pursue theirs.

FIVE REASONS TO REJECT THE CLAIM THAT RELIGIOUS ARGUMENTS SHOULD BE EXCLUDED FROM DEMOCRATIC DELIBERATION

Michael W. McConnell
1999 Utah L. Rev. 639

II. The Supposed Divisiveness, Intolerance, and Absolutism of
    Religious Argument Neither Distinguishes It From Secular
    Ideology Nor Provides a Justification for Exclusion
    From Democratic Politics

One of the principal arguments for constraining religious political activism (either formally, through constitutional limits, or informally, through general cultural perception) is that religious beliefs, being derived from perceived ultimate truths and ultimate loyalties, are especially prone to extremism and intolerance. As constitutional scholar Bill Marshall has explained, "[a] believer who sees those who oppose or question her beliefs as aligned with the 'powers of chaos' is likely to treat the public square as a battleground rather than as a forum for debate." The consequence, he says, is that religion, if "unleashed [note the metaphor] as a political force," may lead to "a particularly acrimonious divisiveness among different religions," and may be "easily transformed into movements of intolerance, repression, hate, and persecution." . . .

It is undeniable that religiously motivated political activism is sometimes heated and uncompromising. But the categories here—"religious" and "secular"—are so grossly over-inclusive and under-inclusive as to be untenable. Some religious political activism is undoubtedly strident, divisive, and uncompromising; but much religiously motivated political action is loving, gracious, and humble. And not a little secular political activism—especially in this day of identity politics—is as divisive, intolerant, and uncompromising as anything seen on the religious side of the line. As Michael Walzer says (in a slightly different context): "Religion is a mixed bag, exactly like secular ideology." Indeed, in the current political climate, many of the most heated political controversies involve a clash between largely religious forces of cultural traditionalism and largely secular forces of cultural deconstruction. It would be difficult to say which side in these conflicts was more strident, more intolerant, or more absolutist. . . .

The argument based on the greater divisiveness and absolutism of religious political activism thus falls short on empirical grounds. But perhaps more importantly, it falls short on normative grounds as well. First, it overlooks the value of democratic participation by citizens who are animated by deep moral commitments. Such people may be overzealous at times, but they also can spur the conscience of the nation. It is no accident that virtually every significant social reform movement in our history has been led by religious activists. [D]emocratic politics needs the spice of religious activism, lest it be nothing but interest group politics, bureaucratic policy-working, and compromise among the powers that be. A politics dominated by religious and other ideological activists would be frightening, but a politics without them would be stultifying.

The argument based on divisiveness and absolutism also falls short, normatively, because it undervalues the democratic process as a means for peaceful resolution of conflict. No more effective mechanism for fostering compromise and mutual accommodation has ever been found than a system in which every group and interest is permitted to argue its case, and decisions are based on voting and coalition building. Democratic participation creates an incentive for sectarians of all stripes to express their opinions in language that will attract outsiders, to enter into conversation with potential allies from other groups, to craft compromises and coalitions. We are more likely to accept the results of a process in which we were able to play a part, even if we do not prevail. By contrast, when particular groups are excluded from democratic participation, they become alienated and radicalized. They do not "get out of politics." They engage in a different kind of politics, politics outside of the system. When certain issues, like abortion, are "taken out of politics" by the Supreme Court, they do not cease to be the subjects of controversy, but the venue for controversy shifts from legislative hall to street demonstration, and the most extreme voices in the movement gain ascendancy over those with an incentive to reach acceptable middle-ground solutions. . . .

III. The Principle of Secular Rationale Rests on a False
Distinction Between Generally Accessible Public Reason
and Religious Ideas

Those who advocate exclusion of religiously based argument from democratic deliberation commonly justify this position on the ground that, in a liberal society, restrictive laws should be based only on reasons that are "accessible" to all citizens. This claim is related, but not identical, to the idea of "public reason," most closely associated with John Rawls. Arguments are "accessible" if they are subject to reasoned assessment on the basis of evidence that is, at least in principle, available to everyone. They need not be persuasive to everyone. I may not agree with the premises of Keynesian economics, but that does not make Keynesian arguments inaccessible.

The distinction between accessible arguments and arguments based on religion rests on a controversial view of epistemology that has been sharply disputed by some theorists. These theorists contend that religious beliefs rest on the same sorts of experience, and can be evaluated according to the same criteria of evidence, as any other beliefs—or, conversely, that seemingly objective forms of knowledge, like science, rest ultimately on the same sort of faith claims that undergird religious beliefs. Faith and reason are not opposites; both are essential to every form of argument. I will leave these arguments to specialists in epistemology, at least for the present. But the very existence of this serious argument suggests that it is a mistake to import into democratic theory an exclusionary principle that is so hotly debated. The underlying theory of democracy is that the people should make judgments about contestable matters. When democratic deliberation is deprived of certain categories of argument on the basis of controversial epistemological judgments, that theory is violated. Part of what goes on in democratic deliberation is debate over criteria for evaluation of competing claims. Whom do we believe and why? Citizens may not know what "epistemology" means, but they make epistemological judgments all the time. That role should not be taken away from them by epistemological pre-screening devices like the principle of secular rationale.

In any event, like the argument about divisiveness, the accessibility argument is fatally under-inclusive and over-inclusive. Inaccessible arguments are common in democratic discourse. There is nothing wrong with arguing on the basis of personal experience, even though such arguments are predicated on evidence available only to oneself. Some forms of knowledge are said to be accessible only to certain groups. Consider, for example, the argument at the time of the Clarence Thomas hearings that men "just don't get it" about sexual harassment, or the argument that only victims of discrimination can really understand the nature of American racism. All forms of identity politics rest on loyalties that some, but not all, citizens share. Most moral arguments rest, ultimately, on premises or intuitions that are not subject to empirical, scientific, or logical verification. They are held for much the same reason, and on the basis of much the same internal evidence, as religious beliefs. It seems improbable that advocates of the "accessibility" standard will rule all of these arguments out of bounds.

Moreover, the criterion of "accessibility" does not exclude most religious political argument. It would apply most aptly to religious traditions based upon a "leap of faith," since those who have not made the leap are unable to perceive the truth on the other side, or to religious traditions that assert that revelation is vouchsafed only to a few (to the hierarchy, or the elect). But most religions in this country are not of those kinds. The Roman Catholic tradition, for example, typically participates in public debate on the basis of some version of natural law, which is perceived through the application of reason to nature. There is nothing inaccessible about that. The fundamentalist tradition typically presents arguments based on the Holy Bible, rejecting arguments based on emotion, tradition, or extra-Biblical revelation to religious authorities. It is difficult to imagine a more accessible view. To be sure, not everyone agrees with the Bible, just as not everyone believes in Keynesian economics. But the Bible is available to everyone. All you have to do is pick it up and read. The argument for exclusion of inaccessible justifications does not take us very far toward an argument for exclusion of religious justifications if it does not apply to Roman Catholicism or fundamentalism—the two religious views most secular liberals are most concerned about.

A slightly different version of the accessibility thesis is based on the idea that, in a democracy, arguments must be made on the basis of commonly held premises, and not premises that are special or unique to particular groups. Reason, it is said, is common to all humanity, while religious beliefs are unique to particular groups. To allow laws to be predicated on religious beliefs, then, would be to favor those religious groups.

This version of the argument rests on a flawed dichotomy between reason and religion. Secular political arguments are not based on "reason" (though they may employ reason, just as religious arguments may employ reason); they are based on ideological positions, or points of view. If I argue against rent control on the ground that it decreases the supply of housing and ultimately hurts the very people it is intended to help, my argument is based not on "reason," but on microeconomic theory. Microeconomic theory, like religion, is a disputed matter among the American population. So is every other ideological position, whether secular or religious. It is hopelessly utopian to think that laws in a pluralistic republic can be based on shared premises, common to the entire populace, and silly to think that democratic theory (which is all about how to resolve disagreements) would insist on such a thing. But once it is recognized that every world view is held by some and disputed by others, there is no sound reason to rule one family of world views—religions—out of bounds for democratic argument. Democracy is better served by allowing every citizen an equal right to argue for collective public ends on the basis of whatever arguments he or she finds persuasive, without prior limitations based on the epistemological, methodological, or ideological premises of their arguments. Then we allow other citizens to accept or reject those arguments, based on their own opinions. . . .

V. The Principle of Secular Rationale Is Incompatible with the Very Principles of Equal Citizenship That Are Its Supposed Basis

This leads to the final point. The principle of secular rationale is designed to guarantee equal status as citizens to all members of this polity. When laws are based on religious rationales, it is argued, this degrades nonbelievers from the ranks of equal citizen. Laws should be based on principles that can be accepted, in principle, by all reasonable people. To present an argument to a fellow citizen that one knows he has no basis for accepting is an insult.

Insufficient attention has been paid, I believe, to the fact that religious believers are equal citizens, too. It is no more legitimate to dictate that they base their public advocacy on secular notions than it would be to insist that secular citizens present arguments grounded in religious authority. The principle of secular rationale degrades religious persons from the status of equal citizen.

In a pluralistic republic, the people will adhere to many different and practically irreconcilable world views. Some may be libertarians, some utilitarians, some feminists, some free marketeers. None share the others' premises. If it were true that the enactment of laws based on premises that one does not share is a degradation of equal citizenship status, then there could be no such thing as a regime of equal citizens, because all political losers would be second class citizens. Fortunately, that is not a valid conclusion. We are equal citizens not because we agree with the principles of the laws that are enacted, or even because those premises are accessible. We are equal citizens because we have an equal right to put forward our ideas in the public arena, and for those ideas to fail or prevail on the basis of whether our fellow citizens agree with them. Such a system is not compatible with the notion that some world views must be excluded from the outset.

NOTES AND QUESTIONS

1. Evaluating the Two Positions. The positions of Professors Audi and McConnell on religion and politics stand poles apart. Audi argues for substantial limits on religious bases for legislating, while McConnell argues against any special limits on religious bases. Which provides a better model for religious activity in politics in modern America? There are several possible criteria for answering that question. Which view, Audi's or McConnell's, is more consistent with:

   a. American traditions and history?
   b. Democracy ("liberal" or "constitutional" democracy)?
   c. Religious liberty?
   d. Equality among religions?
   e. Preserving social peace and encouraging tolerance among persons and groups?

2. Other Positions. Some other leading scholars take positions that fall between, or involve some combination of, the views of Audi and McConnell.

(a) Religious motivation but secular advocacy: Kent Greenawalt. Kent Greenawalt makes a distinction between an individual's grounds for deciding and the grounds he or she advocates to others. Greenawalt argues, contrary to Audi, that a citizen or legislator may "rely on religious grounds for moral judgments that affect law and public policy," because "all people must draw from their personal experiences and commitments of value to some degree" and it would be unfair and unrealistic to ask deeply religious people to disregard their own personal (religious) commitments. Kent Greenawalt, Religious Convictions and Political Choice 216, 145 (1988). However, contrary to McConnell, Green-awalt argues that "[p]ublic discourse about political issues with those who do not share religious premises should be cast in other than religious terms," because "a crucial premise about a liberal society is that citizens of extremely diverse religious views can build principles of political order and social justice that do not depend on particular religious beliefs." *Id.* at 217.

Audi would say (and McConnell might too) that it smacks of dishonesty to present "secular rationalizations that cloak the underlying religious motivation for seeking the legislation" (p. 679 above). Greenawalt anticipates this criticism and responds:

> [P]olitical discourse mainly involves advocacy of positions arrived at, not full revelation of all the bases by which a decision is reached. We do not expect a speaker to reveal all the personal judgments that have led him to his position; we expect him to put forward considerations that will appeal to others. Effective argument appeals to grounds that the audience will accept. . . . Thus, the course that I have suggested not only relates to liberal principles; it is also a maxim about effective advocacy for religious persons. Since most religious people cannot clearly identify where religious conviction leaves off and other values and factual judgments begin, they will usually suppose that the position they take will be the right one even apart from religious conviction, and they will not be insincere if they make arguments in nonreligious terms.

Id. at 220-221. Is this a satisfactory response?

(b) "Ecumenical" as opposed to "sectarian" arguments: Michael Perry. Professor Michael Perry has written frequently on the role of religion in politics, and has been open to rethinking his position at various stages. In one of his books on the subject, Perry argued for the legitimacy (indeed the necessity) of a certain kind of religious argument in politics: what he calls "ecumenical" political arguments. Perry defines ecumenical arguments in terms of their two "cardinal" virtues: "public intelligibility and public accessibility."

> The virtue of public intelligibility . . . is the habit of trying to elaborate one's position in a manner intelligible or comprehensible to those who speak a different religious or moral language. . . .
>
> [T]he virtue of public accessibility is the habit of trying to defend one's position in a manner neither sectarian nor authoritarian. A defense of a disputed position is sectarian if (and to the extent) it relies on experiences or premises that have little if any authority beyond the confines of one's own moral or religious community. A defense is authoritarian if it relies on persons or institutions that have little if any authority beyond the confines of one's own community. . . .
>
> The standard or criterion of public accessibility is not uncontroversial, of course. . . . But it is difficult to understand how *religious* convictions can play a . . . role in American politics that is not only not divisive but [is] constructive, unless some such standard is honored.

Michael J. Perry, Love and Power: The Role of Religion and Morality in American Politics 105-107 (1991) (emphases in original). Perry also emphasizes the importance of "fallibilism"; that is, a willingness to subject one's religious beliefs to the judgment of "self-critical rationality." *Id.* at 100.

Does Perry's distinction between ecumenical and sectarian arguments differ meaningfully from Audi's distinction between religious and secular arguments? Can you think of a familiar religious position on a political issue that could be called "ecumenical"? Is the ecumenical/sectarian distinction in the eye of the beholder? Is it unfair to those who see their religious beliefs as not revisable, and as stemming directly from, say, the Bible or the statements of the Pope and the Catholic bishops? See David M. Smolin, Regulating Religious and Cultural Conflict in Post-Modern America: A Response to Professor Perry, 76 Iowa L. Rev. 1067, 1076-1077, 1080 (1991) (criticizing Perry's criteria for "us[ing] his own vision of good religion as the standard for admission to political and legal debate"; arguing that "Perry's ecumenical politics is actually an explicit justification for liberalism's traditional exclusion of nonliberal cultural groups" such as fundamentalist Christians). But cf. Daniel O. Conkle, Different Religions, Different Politics: Evaluating the Role of Competing Religious Traditions in American Politics and Law, 10 J.L. & Relig. 1, 16 (1993-1994) (arguing that although religious fundamentalism has the constitutional right to influence politics, its "contributions to our public life are appropriately viewed with skepticism" because it rejects the "deliberative, dialogic decision-making process" that is crucial to our constitutional democracy).

3. Religion and Judicial Decision Making

We have seen that clergy (and other religious people) have a constitutional right to serve in the legislature, subject to some limits on what they can do and perhaps on what reasons they can rely upon. Should we have the same rules for religious people serving as judges? Are there things about the job of judge that make the introduction of religious concerns more problematic than it is in the legislature? Do judges have the same rights as legislators? As ordinary citizens?

IDAHO v. FREEMAN
507 F. Supp. 706 (D. Idaho 1981)

CALLISTER, District Judge.

[Idaho and Arizona challenged Congress's action extending the ratification period of the Equal Rights Amendment, and sought an injunction protecting their right to rescind their own prior ratification of the Amendment. The National Organization for Women (NOW), an intervenor, moved to disqualify Judge Callister pursuant to 28 U.S.C. § 455(a).*]

NOW's motion to disqualify asserts that the Court's appearance of impartiality might reasonably be questioned because of the following allegations:

1. The First Presidency of the Church of Jesus Christ of Latter-day Saints (the Church) has stated its position opposing the passage of the Equal Rights Amendment, and has encouraged members of the Church to work in appropriate arenas to defeat the ratification of the Amendment.

* [Section 455(a) provides: "Any justice [or] judge . . . of the United States shall disqualify himself in any proceeding in which his impartiality might reasonably be questioned."—EDS.]

2. The First Presidency has also opposed the extension of the ratification period as "unnecessary, unwise and unprecedented."

3. The Church or its members have been active politically in various parts of the United States in opposing the ratification of the Amendment.

4. In certain states, e.g., Virginia, Florida and Nevada, anti-ERA lobbying efforts were organized and supported by Church Regional Representatives who were purportedly asked by Church leaders to undertake these tasks.

5. Judge Marion J. Callister is a member of the Church and at the time of filing of this case was serving as a Regional Representative.

6. As a Regional Representative, it was Judge Callister's duty to assist the general leadership of the Church in the operation of Church programs in the region to which he was assigned. It is presumed that he faithfully carried out all of his duties including carrying forth the Church's opposition to the ERA.

7. The Church considers its position on the ERA to be of the utmost importance and those who back the ERA are subject to sanctions, including excommunication, as is evidenced by proceedings taken against the leader of the group "Mormons for ERA."

Furthermore, NOW contends that its view of the circumstances, as creating a reasonable question of the Court's impartiality, is shared by numerous newspaper editorialists, and that this fact adds weight to the conclusion that the Court should disqualify himself.

[I]n a motion to disqualify based on section 455(a), it is the Court's responsibility to consider all pertinent facts relating to the surrounding circumstances of the case, and after such a review determine if in the mind of a disinterested observer the Court's impartiality might reasonably be questioned. A review of pertinent facts is critical at this time not only to ascertain if disqualification is necessary, but also to establish an appropriate context in which to interpret the facts alleged by NOW in its memoranda, many of which are not altogether accurate[31] or relevant[32] to the issue at hand.

At the outset, two critical observations should be made. The first is that the Church of Jesus Christ of Latter-day Saints is not directly nor indirectly involved

31. One allegation that is not accurately presented by NOW in their memoranda is that all members of the Church's clergy are under an obligation to obtain permission from Church leaders before accepting or running for political office. This is not the case. What was referenced by NOW as the "Political Manifesto of the General Authorities" applies only to those officers that serve in full-time positions. Local lay officers, such as a Regional Representative, do not need Church authorities' permission before accepting any line of work. The basis of this rule is that to accept any other work would interfere with full-time service in the Church. In this particular case the Court did not have to obtain Church authorities' permission before accepting his appointment to the federal bench, nor has he ever had to obtain such permission before entering into a field of work.

32. Allegations of fact that have no bearing on the question of disqualification:

(1) The excommunication of the founder of the group "Mormons for ERA," has no bearing or relevance to the present disqualification motion. The Church court action taken against Ms. Sonia Johnson and her eventual excommunication were based on the following charges: (a) preaching false doctrine, (b) condemning Church leadership, and (c) hindering the Church's missionary efforts. Ms. Johnson was not excommunicated because of her belief in the ERA nor because she has actively supported it. The fact that she "can only conclude that the true reason for my excommunication was my public support for the Equal Rights Amendment and public exposure of the Church's anti-ERA political activities" has no bearing on the case, and because it is self-serving, it is of questionable credibility. The Court would note, however, that no evidence has been presented, nor is the Court aware of anyone who has been excommunicated from the Church for supporting the ERA. . . .

in the pending litigation as a party or as an amicus curiae, nor has the Church ever attempted to promote its position on the ERA by litigation.[33] It should also be recognized that the only relationship the Church has with this case is tangential at best, i.e., the Church has taken a moral stand against the possible impact of the broad and ambiguous wording of the Equal Rights Amendment. While the Church has been opposed to the propriety of the extension of the ratification period, it had never attempted to take an authoritative, legal position concerning the issues involved in this case, i.e., the proper procedure for amendment of the Constitution of the United States.

The second, and probably the most important observation, is that NOW, in its final reply memorandum, clarified its position that the disqualification they seek is not based solely on the Court's membership in the Church. They concede that disqualification based only on membership would be highly improper. In bringing a motion to disqualify, NOW focuses instead on the particular position once held by the Court as creating a reasonable question as to impartiality. While it is a matter of record that the Court no longer holds the position of Regional Representative, NOW contends that because that position was held by the Court at the time of the filing of the case, and for six months thereafter, it created an incurable taint. Therefore, the focal point of this inquiry should be whether there is anything particular about the holding of the position of a Regional Representative in the Church that would require disqualification under the standard outlined. Questions which focus on religious beliefs or membership affiliation are presumed not to be relevant.

We turn now to a consideration of an office in the Church and in particular the office of Regional Representative. The officers of the Church of Jesus Christ of Latter-day Saints consist almost exclusively of a lay clergy, including the Regional Representatives, who serve without financial remuneration or compensation. There are a few exceptions, however, relating to those General Authorities of the Church who serve full time, and usually have general or Church-wide jurisdiction as opposed to local authorities who have such local jurisdiction as their callings provide. The Church recognizes the particular time constraints placed on a lay clergy and indicates that an officer's priorities should be to first provide financial support for their families, then spend what time is necessary to meet the emotional, spiritual and interpersonal needs of the family, and then give such time as is reasonable to Church service. When members are called to serve, there is no designation as to the duration of time that the call will last, and when a release is made, it is understood that the release does not reflect a malfeasance or nonfeasance of that office, but allows another the opportunity to serve. Furthermore, offices in the Church are seen as opportunities to serve and undertaken without compulsion.

33. NOW raises the point that under the Code of Judicial Conduct of the American Bar Association a judge should refrain from serving as an officer in any organization whose interest might come before the Court, e.g., Anti-Defamation League of B'nai Brith, Sierra Club, and NAACP, since these organizations frequently appeal to the courts in furtherance of their stated goals. First, it should be pointed out that these organizations are all single-issue organizations and not churches. Second, it cannot be claimed that the Church uses the courts as a means of furthering its goals. Finally, it is incredible to believe that NOW would seriously maintain that the Code of Judicial Conduct should be read as requiring judges not to participate as active members or officers in their respective churches.

The position of a Regional Representative is somewhat of an anomaly. While occasionally referred to as a General Authority, it is in fact a local calling with limited jurisdiction. A brief job description would include the following: His most important duty is training stake presidencies[35] in leadership skills and church priesthood programs. They also consult with stake presidencies in setting appropriate goals and evaluating their progress. Other duties include: coordinating multi-stake activities; reviewing proposed stake and ward boundaries and submitting recommendations to area supervisors. Besides those duties outlined above, he has the responsibility of reporting performance and progress of stakes. The Regional Representative duties and responsibilities, however, relate only to the region to which he is assigned, and then has only limited jurisdiction even within his region. Furthermore, a Regional Representative is considered to have only limited line authority. For example, a Regional Representative does not serve as an intermediary between stake presidents and the general Church leadership. The Regional Representative is not involved in specific matters concerning Church courts and related activities, nor in counseling members in personal matters. These are handled by local leaders such as stake presidents, or bishops, and then if needed are referred by those leaders to the area supervisor, thus bypassing the Regional Representative. Also, a Regional Representative is not to call or release any local leaders; again, that is handled by area and General Authorities. A Regional Representative has no responsibility or control over local property held by the stakes or local units; those responsibilities lie exclusively with local leaders. Finally, all information coming down from the General Authorities is not necessarily passed through the Regional Representative, thus they are not considered an informational conduit for the general leadership.

NOW, in its memorandum, argues that holding the position of Regional Representative creates an appearance that those who hold that position are responsible for Church policy in that area and are required to promote the Church's stand on the ERA. In support of this contention they point to the activities of three Regional Representatives in Virginia, Nevada, and Florida who have been active in anti-ERA lobbying efforts. NOW alleges that their activities are at the request of Church leaders. NOW also indicates that certain political activities occurred in Idaho which brought about the rescission of Idaho's prior ratification of the ERA, and that the Church was somehow related to the activities. Whether these assertions are true or not is not within the knowledge of the Court and thus will be presumed to be true. But, it must be pointed out that organizing political lobbying efforts is not part of the responsibilities of a Regional Representative, and thus if such activity were undertaken he would most likely be acting in his capacity as a citizen and not in his Church capacity. This is doubly true considering he has no direct control or dominion over the general membership. In the Church there are well over 250 Regional Representatives. To conclude that because three Regional Representatives were involved in lobbying against the ERA that this taints all others who hold the same position is not

35. The local Church structure is generally as follows: The smallest units of the Church are Branches and Wards which consist of about two to five hundred members and presided over by a Branch president or bishop and their counselors. A stake consists of five to 10 wards or branches and is presided over by a stake president and two counselors.

a reasonable conclusion. Furthermore, NOW's allusion to the political activities in Idaho near the time of the move to rescind the prior ratification has no bearing on this case because the Court did not accept his assignment as a Regional Representative until after the Idaho legislature had acted and the matter was essentially a dead issue. In addition, the Court did not participate in such activities either before or after his calling as a Regional Representative.

The Court . . . has never publicly, either in a secular or ecclesiastical setting, stated any opinion or made his feelings known regarding the Equal Rights Amendment; nor has the Court, in any way, inserted himself improperly in the political process. The calling of Regional Representative is one of limited jurisdiction and circumscribed responsibility. At no time during the time that the Court served as a Regional Representative was he ever required or requested to promote the Church's position on the ERA. While the Court attempted to faithfully carry out his duties as a Regional Representative, those duties did not relate to the ERA. . . .

NOW has made it clear through their memorandum that they feel that the Court's appearance of impartiality can be questioned, and that under due process they have a right to an impartial forum. . . . While it is true that due process guarantees a party the right to an impartial forum, this should not be read as giving a party the judge of their choice. . . . The circumstances of this case do not permit a reasonable disinterested observer, knowing all the facts, to decide that the Court's appearance of impartiality might reasonably be questioned. To grant NOW's motion under these circumstances would be an inappropriate application of section 455(a).

NOTES AND QUESTIONS

1. The Federal Recusal Statute. The federal recusal statute, 28 U.S.C. § 455, has two provisions relevant to our purposes. Section 455(b)(1) disqualifies a judge from sitting on a case "where he has a personal bias or prejudice concerning a party." It is concerned with a state of mind that would prevent the judge from deciding fairly. Section 455(a), invoked in *Freeman*, provides for disqualification where the judge's "impartiality might reasonably be questioned." It is concerned with the appearance of justice, not with the inner workings of the judge's mind. In Liljeberg v. Health Services Acquisition Corp., 486 U.S. 847 (1988), the Court found a violation of § 455(a) where the judge, as a trustee of Loyola University, had a financial interest in the outcome of a case before him but was unaware of the conflict. Reasonable people might think that the judge would be inclined to favor one side. That's enough, even if they are wrong. See John H. Garvey and Amy V. Coney, Catholic Judges in Capital Cases, 81 Marq. L. Rev. 303, 331-350 (1998).

How is NOW's claim different from this? NOW argues that the Mormon Church actively opposes the ERA; that Judge Callister is a member of the Mormon Church—indeed, a Regional Representative; and that he therefore is generally understood (whatever may actually be the case) to share the Church's opposition to the ERA. Is the Mormon Church's teaching about the ERA not binding on Church members? Does Judge Callister not agree with the Church's teaching? Suppose the Church required its members to oppose the ERA, and that Judge Callister did so. Would he be disqualified under § 455(a) if his opposition was not publicly known? (Near the end of his opinion he states, "The Court . . . has never publicly . . . made his feelings known regarding the Equal Rights Amendment.") Would he be disqualified if his views had been made known? What are the legal issues in the underlying lawsuit? Could one who opposes the ERA decide them either way?

Is there a constitutional difference between disqualification under § 455(a) and under § 455(b)(1)? Suppose that Judge Callister held a religious belief that, he conceded, required him to decide the case in favor of one side or the other. Consider this example. The Roman Catholic Church teaches that capital punishment is morally repugnant except in very rare cases, which probably do not arise in the United States. It also teaches that faithful Catholics should adhere to this teaching. Suppose Judge Callister were a Catholic, and were assigned to sit in a capital case. In the sentencing phase of the trial, his faith would (arguably) forbid him to impose a death sentence decided upon by the jury. Could the government move to disqualify him for "a personal bias or prejudice concerning a party"?

Could the judge recuse himself as a means of avoiding the moral dilemma of either contravening the capital-punishment law or contravening his faith? Or is recusal a kind of "passing the buck," a failure to shoulder the task of judging according to law? See, e.g., Adam Liptak, On Moral Grounds, Some Judges Are Opting Out of Abortion Cases, N.Y. Times, Sept. 4, 2005, at A21. Would the judge face such a dilemma if he were not imposing a capital sentence but rather were reviewing it on habeas corpus? See Garvey and Coney, 81 Marq. L. Rev. at 329-331, 335-339.

2. The Religious Test Clause. Does the Constitution protect Judge Callister against disqualification, as it protected the right of Paul McDaniel (the clergyman in McDaniel v. Paty, p. 666) to serve as a legislator? McDaniel, a state delegate, could not invoke the protection of the Religious Test Clause, which applies only to federal offices. Can Freeman, a federal judge invoke it? The Religious Test Clause should be read together with the Oath Clause, which immediately precedes it. Here is what they say (U.S. Const. art. VI, cl. 3).

> The Senators and Representatives before mentioned, and the Members of the several State Legislatures, and all executive and judicial Officers, both of the United States and of the several States, shall be bound by Oath or Affirmation, to support this Constitution; but no religious Test shall ever be required as a Qualification to any Office or public Trust under the United States.

Presumably, it would be unconstitutional for the Senate to adopt a rule that it would not confirm any Mormon nominees to the federal bench. Is the clause also violated when a judge is disqualified from sitting in one particular case? See Feminist Women's Health Center v. Codisopti, 69 F.3d 399 (9th Cir. 1995); Garvey and Coney, 81 Marq. L. Rev. at 348-349. Could an individual Senator properly vote not to confirm a nominee because of the nominee's religious affiliation? For example, could a Senator sharing the political views of NOW vote against a Mormon nominee out of fear that the nominee's religious beliefs would prejudice him or her against equal rights for women? May (should) members of the Judiciary Committee question nominees about their religious beliefs? May they ask whether the nominee subscribes to his or her church's teaching on the subjects of abortion, capital punishment, or the role of women in society? Such questions have arisen in connection with several recent nominees to the Supreme Court and lower federal courts. May senators ask Islamic judicial nominees whether they can reconcile their faith with loyalty to the United States? May they ask, "Are you an atheist"? Cf. Baird v. State Bar, 401 U.S. 1 (1971); Schware v. Board of Bar Examiners, 353 U.S. 232 (1957); Sanford Levinson, The Confrontation of Religious Faith and Civil Religion: Catholics Becoming Justices, 39 DePaul L. Rev. 1047 (1990); Winston Calvert, Note, Judicial Selection and the Religious Test Clause, 82 Wash. U. L.Q. 1129 (2004).

3. Religious Thinking and Opinion Writing. There is a wide difference between saying that judges should not decide cases where their religious convictions forbid them to enforce the law (the devout Catholic judge doing capital sentencing) and saying that judges should not think religiously when deciding cases. Is it ever proper for a judge to rely on a religious proposition?

Consider first Chief Justice Burger's opinion in Bowers v. Hardwick, 478 U.S. 186 (1986), which we discussed at p. 671. The issue in *Bowers* was whether sodomy was a fundamental right protected by the Due Process Clause. According to the Court's precedents, the test for identifying fundamental liberties was this: They are "those liberties that are 'deeply rooted in this Nation's history and tradition.' " *Id.* at 192. To bolster his argument against a right to sodomy, the Chief Justice said:

> Decisions of individuals relating to homosexual conduct have been subject to state intervention throughout the history of Western civilization. Condemnation of those practices is firmly rooted in Judeao-Christian moral and ethical standards. Homosexual sodomy was a capital crime under Roman law.

Is the second sentence an example of religious thinking? Burger refers not to his own but to other people's religion. And he does not insist that the biblical conviction is true or proper, only that it is a datum tending to show that sodomy has been generally condemned (throughout the Nation's "history and tradition"). The same could be said of the Court's reference in *Atkins* (p. 672) to the views of religious organizations who reject capital punishment of mentally retarded offenders. This is more the sociology of religion than religion itself. May a judge consider religion in this way when deciding cases? See Kent Greenawalt, Private Consciences and Public Reasons 141-150 (1995); Scott C. Idleman, The Role of Religious Values in Judicial Decision Making, 68 Ind. L.J. 433, 480-481 (1993); Thomas C. Berg and William G. Ross, Some Religiously Devout Justices: Historical Notes and Comments, 81 Marq. L. Rev. 383, 388, 405 (1998).

Recall the passage from Roe v. Wade quoted above (p. 668), where the Court assessed the justifications for anti-abortion laws:

> The [state argues] that the fetus is a "person" within the language and meaning of the Fourteenth Amendment. [If this is so] the appellant's case, of course, collapses, for the fetus' right to life would then be guaranteed specifically by the Amendment. [But the] Constitution does not define "person" in so many

words. [The] predominant, though not the unanimous, attitude of the Jewish faith [is that life does not begin until live birth. This] may be taken to represent also the position of a large segment of the Protestant community. [The Roman Catholic Church] recognize[s] the existence of life from the moment of conception.

May a judge rely on a religious belief to answer this question? What other sources of information and grounds for belief are available to tell us about the status and value of fetal life? Is it possible to distinguish these from religious convictions? See Greenawalt, Religious Convictions and Political Choice chs. 7-8. Recall Justice Stevens's dissenting argument in Webster v. Reproductive Health Services (p. 669) that it is a violation of the Establishment Clause for a legislature—and presumably a court—to rely on theological assumptions in deciding when human life begins.

Consider also some commentators' reflections on this question. Kent Greenawalt notes a reason why judges should be more constrained than legislators are in relying on religious beliefs:

> Of all officials, judges are the most carefully disciplined in restraining their frame of reference. Asking them to try to decide exclusively, or nearly exclusively, on the basis of authoritative materials is not too great an imposition. Indeed, that is how, in the main, judges now see their responsibilities. . . .
>
> In the rare circumstances when a judge might properly rely in a self-conscious way on controversial religious or comprehensive views, . . . should that appear in a judicial opinion? Since different judges will have different views, such reasons would have no comfortable place in a majority opinion. [And] I believe that even when the opinion represents the voice of a single judge, the opinion should symbolize the aspiration of interpersonal reason and be limited to public reasons.

Private Consciences and Public Reasons at 149-150. In the same vein, Justice Scalia has stated that as a judge, "I would certainly not have the power to invalidate [laws] because they are contrary to the natural law. I have been appointed to apply the Constitution and positive law. God applies the natural law. . . . I'm a worldly judge. I just do what the Constitution tells me to do." Scalia/Rome Address—Of Democracy, Morality, and the Majority, Origins (Catholic News Service Documentary Service), June 27, 1996, at 90.

On the other hand, Stephen Carter makes an argument suggesting that it might frequently be legitimate for a judge to rely on personal religious premises in deciding:

> It is a bit late in the day to argue that when judges decide cases involving such issues as reproductive freedom or reapportionment, they are searching for rights that are already there, just waiting to be discovered. . . . [I]t is quite evident that the judge cannot make such decisions without relying, at least in part, on her own moral knowledge. . . .
>
> . . . The question, then, is whether one can make sense of a rule prohibiting judges from relying on their own moral knowledge if it happens to have a religious basis. . . .
>
> [Such a rule does not make sense. O]nce a judge's moral understanding is permitted to play a role, the liberal argument cannot distinguish religiously based knowledge from other moral knowledge.

Stephen L. Carter, The Religiously Devout Judge, 64 Notre Dame L. Rev. 932, 935, 944 (1989). Finally, Scott Idleman argues that

> [i]f the judge's purpose in adverting to religious values is primarily to advance or endorse religion, either in general or specifically over irreligion, then she will almost certainly violate the Establishment Clause. But if instead she adverts to religious values for the purpose of reaching a well-informed, impartial decision—that is, one which takes account of all sources of social, economic, political, and ethical input, including religious insight—then this should suffice as a legitimate secular purpose and the clause would not be violated.

Idleman, 68 Ind. L.J. at 483. Which of these positions is most persuasive?

4. Institutional Participation in Policy Making

In sections D-1 through D-3 we have considered whether the constitution imposes any constraints on individual religious actors (priests, ministers, rabbis, imams, members of their congregations) making political decisions or serving in public office—or whether on the contrary it protects them in their right to serve, and to rely on their religious convictions in political matters. In this assignment we ask much the same questions about religious institutions: What role may they play in public affairs?

This issue has two aspects. First, churches and other religious organizations often participate in debates about government policy in their "private" capacity—as speakers and opinion leaders on subjects ranging from abortion to foreign aid. In doing so they are protected by the freedoms of speech, religion, and association. (Think of the role the Rev. Martin Luther King's Southern Christian Leadership Conference played in the civil rights movement in the 1960s.) Yet there is one significant legal constraint on the political activity of religious organizations: the restrictions imposed by the federal tax code on electioneering and lobbying by tax-exempt organizations, including religious organizations and secular charities.

Second, religious groups might play an *official* role in government. In much of the world this is nothing unusual. In Iran and Jordan, religious groups are allocated seats in parliament and sometimes cabinet positions. In Israel and India there are religious courts established to decide questions of marriage, divorce, custody, and inheritance. Asher Maoz, Enforcement of Religious Courts' Judgments Under Israeli Law, 33 J. Church & State 473 (1991). In Denmark the National (Evangelical Lutheran) Church functions in some ways as a branch of government under the Minister of Ecclesiastical Affairs and the Queen. The English, whose behavior has had the greatest influence on our own, allot seats in the House of Lords to bishops of the Church of England. The English also maintained ecclesiastical courts with jurisdiction over marriage and probate matters until 1857, when the Matrimonial Causes Act and the Court of Probate Act transferred such issues to secular courts. Is there anything wrong with religious organizations performing similar functions in the United States?

We begin with the first subject: the effect that tax laws have on the political and expressive activity of religious organizations.

BRANCH MINISTRIES v. ROSSOTTI

211 F.3d 137 (D.C. Cir. 2000)

BUCKLEY, Senior Judge:

Four days before the 1992 presidential election, Branch Ministries, a tax-exempt church, placed full-page advertisements in two newspapers in which it urged Christians not to vote for then-presidential candidate Bill Clinton because of his positions on certain moral issues. The Internal Revenue Service concluded that the placement of the advertisements violated the statutory restrictions on organizations exempt from taxation and, for the first time in its history, it revoked a bona fide church's tax-exempt status because of its involvement in politics. Branch Ministries and its pastor, Dan Little, challenge the revocation on the grounds that (1) the Service acted beyond its statutory authority, (2) the revocation violated its right to the free exercise of religion guaranteed by the First Amendment and the Religious Freedom Restoration Act, and (3) it was the victim of selective prosecution in violation of the Fifth Amendment. Because these objections are without merit, we affirm the district court's grant of summary judgment to the Service.

I. BACKGROUND

A. TAXATION OF CHURCHES

The Internal Revenue Code ("Code") exempts certain organizations from taxation, including those organized and operated for religious purposes, provided that they do not engage in certain activities, including involvement in "any political campaign on behalf of (or in opposition to) any candidate for public office." 26 U.S.C. § 501(a), (c)(3). Contributions to such organizations are also deductible from the donating taxpayer's taxable income. *Id.* § 170(a). Although most organizations seeking tax-exempt status are required to apply to the Internal Revenue Service ("IRS" or "Service") for an advance determination that they meet the requirements of section 501(c)(3), a church may simply hold itself out as tax exempt and receive the benefits of that status without applying for advance recognition from the IRS. *Id.* § 508(c)(1)(A).

The IRS maintains a periodically updated "Publication No. 78," in which it lists all organizations that have received a ruling or determination letter confirming the deductibility of contributions made to them. Thus, a listing in that publication will provide donors with advance assurance that their contributions will be deductible under section 170(a). If a listed organization has subsequently had its tax-exempt status revoked, contributions that are made to it by a donor who is unaware of the change in status will generally be treated as deductible if made on or before the date that the revocation is publicly announced. [Citing IRS regulations.] Donors to a church that has not received an advance determination of its tax-exempt status may also deduct their contributions; but in the event of an audit, the taxpayer will bear the burden of establishing that the church meets the requirements of section 501(c)(3).

B. FACTUAL AND PROCEDURAL HISTORY

Branch Ministries, Inc. operates the Church at Pierce Creek ("Church"), a Christian church located in Binghamton, New York. In 1983, the Church requested and received a letter from the IRS recognizing its tax-exempt status. On October 30, 1992, four days before the presidential election, the Church placed full-page advertisements in *USA Today* and the *Washington Times*. Each bore the headline "Christians Beware" and asserted that then-Governor Clinton's positions concerning abortion, homosexuality, and the distribution of condoms to teenagers in schools violated Biblical precepts. [Each ad stated at the bottom: "Tax-deductible donations for this advertisement gladly accepted. Make donations to: The Church at Pierce Creek. [Mailing address]."]

The advertisements . . . produced hundreds of contributions to the Church from across the country. . . .

The advertisements also came to the attention of the Regional Commissioner of the IRS, who notified the Church on November 20, 1992 that he had authorized a church tax inquiry based on "a reasonable belief . . . that you may not be tax-exempt or that you may be liable for tax" due to political activities and expenditures. The Church denied that it had engaged in any prohibited political activity and declined to provide the IRS with certain information the Service had requested. . . . Following [a fuller examination and] two unproductive meetings between the parties, the IRS revoked the Church's section 501(c)(3) tax-exempt status on January 19, 1995, citing the newspaper advertisements as prohibited intervention in a political campaign.

The Church commenced this lawsuit soon thereafter [alleging the above claims]. After allowing discovery on the Church's selective prosecution claim, the district court granted summary judgment in favor of the IRS. [The Church appealed.]

II. ANALYSIS

The Church advances a number of arguments in support of its challenges to the revocation. We examine only those that warrant analysis.

A. THE STATUTORY AUTHORITY OF THE IRS

[The court first held that the IRS had statutory authority to revoke the Church's exemption based on sections 501(c)(3) and 170(c)(2)(B), (D). The first of those provides exemption from income taxes to]

> corporations . . . organized and operated exclusively for religious . . . purposes . . . which do[ ] not participate in, or intervene in (including the publishing or distributing of statements), any political campaign on behalf of (or in opposition to) any candidate for public office.

Similarly, section 170(c) allows taxpayers to deduct from their taxable income donations made to a corporation

> organized and operated exclusively for religious . . . purposes . . . which is not disqualified for tax exemption under section 501(c)(3) by reason of attempting to . . . intervene in (including the publishing or distributing of statements), any political campaign on behalf of (or in opposition to) any candidate for public office.

The Code, in short, specifically states that organizations that fail to comply with the restrictions set forth in section 501(c) are not qualified to receive the tax exemption that it provides. . . .

B. FIRST AMENDMENT CLAIMS AND THE RFRA

The Church claims that the revocation of its exemption violated its right to freely exercise its religion under both the First Amendment and the RFRA. To sustain its claim under either the Constitution or the statute, the Church must first establish that its free exercise right has been substantially burdened. We conclude that the Church has failed to meet this test.

The Church asserts, first, that a revocation would threaten its existence. The Church maintains that a loss of its tax-exempt status will not only make its members reluctant to contribute the funds essential to its survival, but may obligate the Church itself to pay taxes.

The Church appears to assume that the withdrawal of a conditional privilege for failure to meet the condition is in itself an unconstitutional burden on its free exercise right. This is true, however, only if the receipt of the privilege (in this case the tax exemption) is conditioned

> upon conduct proscribed by a religious faith, or . . . denie[d] . . . because of
> conduct mandated by religious belief, thereby putting substantial pressure on
> an adherent to modify his behavior and to violate his beliefs.

Jimmy Swaggart Ministries v. Bd. of Equalization [p. 191]. Although its advertisements reflected its religious convictions on certain questions of morality, the Church does not maintain that a withdrawal from electoral politics would violate its beliefs. The sole effect of the loss of the tax exemption will be to decrease the amount of money available to the Church for its religious practices. The Supreme Court has declared, however, that such a burden "is not constitutionally significant." *Id.*

In actual fact, even this burden is overstated. Because of the unique treatment churches receive under the Internal Revenue Code, the impact of the revocation is likely to be more symbolic than substantial. As the IRS confirmed at oral argument, if the Church does not intervene in future political campaigns, it may hold itself out as a 501(c)(3) organization and receive all the benefits of that status. All that will have been lost, in that event, is the advance assurance of deductibility in the event a donor should be audited. See 26 U.S.C. § 508(c)(1)(A). Contributions will remain tax deductible as long as donors are able to establish that the Church meets the requirements of section 501(c)(3).

Nor does the revocation necessarily make the Church liable for the payment of taxes. As the IRS explicitly represented in its brief and reiterated at oral argument, the revocation of the exemption does not convert bona fide donations into income taxable to the Church. Furthermore, we know of no authority, and counsel provided none, to prevent the Church from reapplying for a prospective determination of its tax-exempt status and regaining the advance assurance of deductibility—provided, of course, that it renounces future involvement in political campaigns.

We also reject the Church's argument that it is substantially burdened because it has no alternate means by which to communicate its sentiments about candidates for public office. In Regan v. Taxation With Representation (1983) (Blackmun, J., concurring), three members of the Supreme Court stated that the availability of such an alternate means of communication is essential to the constitutionality of section 501(c)(3)'s restrictions on lobbying. The Court subsequently confirmed that this was an accurate description of its holding. See FCC v. League of Women

Voters (1984). In *Regan*, the concurring justices noted that "TWR may use its present §501(c)(3) organization for its nonlobbying activities and may create a §501(c)(4) affiliate to pursue its charitable goals through lobbying."

The Church has such an avenue available to it. As was the case with TWR, the Church may form a related organization under section 501(c)(4) of the Code [(which exempts] "[c]ivic leagues or organizations not organized for profit but operated exclusively for the promotion of social welfare"). Such organizations are exempt from taxation; but unlike their section 501(c)(3) counterparts, contributions to them are not deductible. See *id.* §170(c). Although a section 501(c)(4) organization is also subject to the ban on intervening in political campaigns, it may form a political action committee ("PAC") that would be free to participate in political campaigns. 26 C.F.R. §1.527-6(f), (g) ("[A]n organization described in section 501(c) that is exempt from taxation under section 501(a) may, [if it is not a section 501(c)(3) organization], establish and maintain such a separate segregated fund to receive contributions and make expenditures in a political campaign.").

At oral argument, counsel for the Church doggedly maintained that there can be no "Church at Pierce Creek PAC." True, it may not itself create a PAC; but as we have pointed out, the Church can initiate a series of steps that will provide an alternate means of political communication that will satisfy the standards set by the concurring justices in *Regan*. Should the Church proceed to do so, however, it must understand that the related 501(c)(4) organization must be separately incorporated; and it must maintain records that will demonstrate that tax-deductible contributions to the Church have not been used to support the political activities conducted by the 501(c)(4) organization's political action arm.

That the Church cannot use its tax-free dollars to fund such a PAC unquestionably passes constitutional muster. The Supreme Court has consistently held that, absent invidious discrimination, "Congress has not violated [an organization's] First Amendment rights by declining to subsidize its First Amendment activities." *Regan*; see also Cammarano v. United States (1959) ("Petitioners are not being denied a tax deduction because they engage in constitutionally protected activities, but are simply being required to pay for those activities entirely out of their own pockets.").

Because the Church has failed to demonstrate that its free exercise rights have been substantially burdened, we do not reach its arguments that section 501(c)(3) does not serve a compelling government interest or, if it is indeed compelling, that revocation of its tax exemption was not the least restrictive means of furthering that interest.

Nor does the Church succeed in its claim that the IRS has violated its First Amendment free speech rights by engaging in viewpoint discrimination. The restrictions imposed by section 501(c)(3) are viewpoint neutral; they prohibit intervention in favor of all candidates for public office by all tax-exempt organizations, regardless of candidate, party, or viewpoint. Cf. *Regan* (upholding denial of tax deduction for lobbying activities, in spite of allowance of such deduction for veteran's groups).

C. SELECTIVE PROSECUTION (FIFTH AMENDMENT)

The Church alleges that the IRS violated the Equal Protection Clause of the Fifth Amendment by engaging in selective prosecution. In support of its claim, the Church has submitted several hundred pages of newspaper excerpts reporting political campaign activities in, or by the pastors of, other churches that have retained their tax-exempt status. These include reports of explicit endorsements of Democratic candidates by clergymen as well as many instances in which favored candidates have been invited to address congregations from the pulpit. The Church complains that despite this widespread and widely reported involvement by other churches in political campaigns, it is the only one to have ever had its tax-exempt status revoked for engaging in political activity. It attributes this alleged discrimination to the Service's political bias.

To establish selective prosecution, the Church must "prove that (1) [it] was singled out for prosecution from among others similarly situated and (2) that [the] prosecution was improperly motivated, i.e., based on race, religion or another arbitrary classification." United States v. Washington (D.C. Cir. 1983). This burden is a demanding one because "in the absence of clear evidence to the contrary, courts presume that [government prosecutors] have properly discharged their official duties." United States v. Armstrong (1996).

At oral argument, counsel for the IRS conceded that if some of the church-sponsored political activities cited by the Church were accurately reported, they were in violation of section 501(c)(3) and could have resulted in the revocation of those churches' tax-exempt status. But even if the Service could have revoked their tax exemptions, the Church has failed to establish selective prosecution because it has failed to demonstrate that it was similarly situated to any of those other churches. None of the reported activities involved the placement of advertisements in newspapers with nationwide circulations opposing a candidate and soliciting tax deductible contributions to defray their cost. . . .

Because the Church has failed to establish that it was singled out for prosecution from among others who were similarly situated, we need not examine whether the IRS was improperly motivated in undertaking this prosecution.

NOTES AND QUESTIONS

Branch Ministries presents a dramatic conflict between a church's understanding of its mission and the government's understanding of the role of charitable organizations.

1. Restrictions on Tax-Exempt Organizations. Sections 501(c)(3) and 170(c)(2) of the federal tax code (26 U.S.C.) contain two key restrictions on the political activity of tax-exempt organizations—that is, organizations whose income is exempt under § 501(c)(3), and whose supporters may deduct their charitable contributions to the organization under § 170(c)(2). The *electioneering* restriction, at issue in *Branch Ministries,* prohibits such an organization from "participat[ing] or interven[ing] in any political campaign [for or against] any candidate for public office." The *lobbying* restriction prohibits an exempt organization from devoting "a substantial part of [its] activities" to "attemptin[g] to influence legislation."

(a) The rationales. The lobbying and electioneering restrictions were added to the tax code in 1934 and 1954, respectively. Although the legislative records are sparse, several rationales for the provisions have been suggested. The sponsor of the lobbying restriction "asserted that the intent [was] to exclude from exempt status sham organizations that were merely a 'front' for lobbying for private interests." Edward M. Gaffney, On Not Rendering to Caesar: The Unconstitutionality of Tax Regulation of Activities of Religious Organizations Relating to Politics, 40 DePaul L. Rev. 1, 23 (1990) (quoting 78 Cong. Rec. 5959 (1934)). Somewhat analogously, the electioneering restriction might ensure that nonprofit organizations "do not become conduits through which otherwise nondeductible political contributions become deductible." Steffen N. Johnson, Of Politics and Pulpits: A First Amendment Analysis of IRS Restrictions on the Political Activities of Religious Organizations, 42 B.C. L. Rev. 875, 893 (2001). If these are the purposes, do the restrictions need to be as broad as they are?

A second rationale often suggested is that the government should not compel taxpayers, through tax exemptions, to "subsidize" particular candidates or legislation with which they disagree. See Deirdre Dessingue, Prohibition in Search of a Rationale: What the Tax Code Prohibits; Why; To What End?, 42 B.C. L. Rev. 903, 917-918 (2001) (discussing the argument). This rationale raises the question, which we have discussed before, whether tax exemptions should be viewed as exemptions or as subsidies. See p. 386 above. Even if the exemption is a subsidy, can a taxpayer complain about exemption for such a wide array of organizations as §501(c)(3) covers, just because he disagrees with the views of some of those organizations? Remember that in Walz v. Tax Commission (p. 386) and Rosenberger v. University of Virginia (p. 403), the Court held that including religious organizations among a wide range of recipients of tax exemptions and other assistance did not violate the Establishment Clause's prohibition on compelled support of religion. And Regents of Univ. of Wisconsin v. Southworth, 529 U.S. 217 (2000), held that broader First Amendment restrictions on compelling taxpayers to support ideological causes were not violated when a university used mandatory student fees to fund a wide range of student organizations speaking from different viewpoints.

(b) The churches' perspective.   While the government asserts interests in keeping exempt activities separate from lobbying and electoral politics, the perspective of a church, as one of the affected organizations, is often quite different:

> Can demands that religious associations and believers concern themselves only with spiritual, private matters . . . be squared either with our history or with the prophetic, evangelical, and world-transforming zeal that for so many animates their faith and motivates their actions? [The exemption] scheme invites government to label as something else—as electioneering, endorsement, lobbying, etc.— what may be, for a religious association, worship, evangelism, or prophecy.

Richard W. Garnett, A Quiet Faith? Taxes, Politics, and the Privatization of Religion, 42 B.C. L. Rev. 771, 783-784 (2001). In this light, was the *Branch Ministries* court correct to find that "a withdrawal from electoral politics" would not violate the Church's beliefs? What if the Church had asserted a belief in the necessity of political involvement?

(c) The approval of restrictions: *Regan*.   As *Branch Ministries* indicates, the Supreme Court in Regan v. Taxation with Representation, 461 U.S. 540 (1983), upheld the lobbying restriction on the ground that it does not burden the free speech rights of exempt organizations. The *Regan* majority said that "[t]he Code does not deny TWR the right to receive deductible contributions to support its non-lobbying activity, nor does it deny TWR any independent benefit on account of its intention to lobby. Congress has merely refused to pay for the lobbying out of public monies. This Court has never held that the Court must grant a benefit such as TWR claims here to a person who wishes to exercise a constitutional right." *Id.* at 546.

Was the majority correct? Justice Blackmun and two other Justices, concurring in *Regan*, countered that

> [i]f viewed in isolation, the lobbying restriction . . . violates the principle . . . "that the Government may not deny a benefit to a person because he exercises a constitutional right." Section 501(c)(3) does not merely deny a subsidy for lobbying activities; it deprives an otherwise eligible organization of its tax-exempt status and its eligibility to receive tax-deductible contributions for all its activities, whenever one of those activities is "substantial lobbying."

Id. at 552. This is why, as *Branch Ministries* notes, the concurring Justices believed it crucial that a charitable organization could set up an "affiliate" under § 501(c)(4). Because of that option, "[a] § 501(c)(3) organization's right to speak is not infringed, because it is free to make known its views on legislation through its § 501(c)(4) affiliate without losing tax benefits for its nonlobbying activities." *Id.* at 553. Accord FCC v. League of Women Voters, 468 U.S. 364, 400 (1984).

Assume that the ability to create a (c)(4) affiliate means that an organization merely is denied tax-exempt funds for lobbying—that its lobbying is not penalized with the loss of an independent benefit. Why does that dispose of the constitutional claim? Doesn't the restriction still discourage lobbying (which is an important political and expressive activity)? After all, if the organization changed its speech from lobbying on particular legislation to something more vague in content—an abstract discussion of a political issue—then it could support that speech with tax-deductible contributions.

Regan did not involve the other restriction on exempt organizations: the prohibition on electioneering. Nor did it involve a claim by a church, as in *Branch Ministries*. In the next two notes, we consider these potential distinguishing features.

2. Are the Electioneering Restrictions More Burdensome? While an organization's exemption may be revoked only for "substantial" lobbying, it may be revoked for even a single instance of intervening in a campaign (as was the case with the Church at Pierce Creek). Does this make it more difficult for a church or other organization to avoid committing a violation—so difficult that the burden becomes unconstitutionally onerous?

The simple alternative of setting up a § 501(c)(4) organization is not sufficient in the context of electioneering as opposed to lobbying. As the court in *Branch Ministries* notes, the § 501(c)(4) entity "is also subject to the ban on intervening in political campaigns"; support for a candidate requires in turn the formation of another entity, a political action committee or "PAC." (Nor can the (c)(3) organization itself set up the PAC.) "The members of the church thus can send their political message [in electoral campaigns], but [only] at the cost of maintaining several corporate entities." Alan L. Feld, Rendering Unto Caesar or Electioneering for Caesar? Loss of Church Tax Exemption for Participation in Electoral Politics, 42 B.C. L. Rev. 931, 936 (2001). In realistic terms, doesn't such government-mandated complexity place a real burden on First Amendment activity?

The definition of "interven[ing for or against] a candidate" might also be so broad that it cuts deeply into exempt organizations' political speech. The Church at Pierce Creek essentially said, "Do not vote for Bill Clinton," which violated the restriction under any reading. But the IRS has interpreted the language much more broadly. It prohibits an organization from "indirectly" endorsing a candidate, even through the means of distributing information about candidates' voting records or stands on issues. In distinguishing permissible voter education from impermissible electioneering, the IRS considers, among other things, (1) whether the materials are "biased" in presenting candidates' views, (2) whether the materials are distributed regularly or only during the election cycle, and (3) whether they cover a broad as opposed to a narrow range of issues.

The last of these factors has especially triggered criticism. "It is by no means clear why the Sierra Club, for example, should not be able to engage in voter education on environmental matters without having to take on a host of other matters that may be of lesser moment to that organization." Gaffney, 40 DePaul L. Rev. at 27. Another commentator adds:

> If the church is to be the church, it cannot be controlled by the state in determining the questions it deems important and worthy of consideration. If free exercise means anything, religious organizations must be free to say "this is what matters," and the church must not be forced to hide the questions that do matter in the morass of questions that do not.

Randy Lee, When a King Speaks of God, When God Speaks to a King: Faith, Politics, Tax-Exempt Status, and the Constitution in the Clinton Administration, 63 Law & Contemp. Probs. 391, 409-410 (2000). For an example of the kind of self-censorship such rules encourage, see Office of the General Counsel, U.S. Conference of Catholic Bishops, Political Activity Guidelines for Catholic Organizations (Mar. 15, 2004), available at http://www.usccb.org/ogc/guidelines.shtml#44 (advising Catholic organizations to use "extreme caution" in distributing voter education materials prepared by any other organization, to reconsider whether to print candidates' responses to issues questionnaires if some candidates do not respond, and warning against "wording of questions that evidences a bias [for or against a particular answer] on certain issues").

3. Are Churches Different?   The political-activity restrictions do not distinguish between religious and other exempt organizations. Is there a difference?

(a) The (c)(4) alternative and religious organizations.   The *Branch Ministries* court assumes that a § 501(c)(4) affiliate or a PAC is just as good an option for churches as for other nonprofit organizations, and that therefore the Pierce Creek Church's religious freedom was not burdened. Is that true? Consider the following argument:

> It is essential to the church's identity and mission, and to the moral authority of its pronouncements, that it speak as "church" through its religious structures and

leaders. No church can be restricted to speaking on political issues solely through functionaries employed by a political affiliate without violating its faith and calling. . . .

In any event, section 501(c)(4) is of no practical use to a preacher who cannot be required to announce at the beginning of a sermon whether he is speaking for a 501(c)(3) church or a 501(c)(4) clone.

Gaffney, 40 DePaul L. Rev. at 34-35 (quoting God Alone Is Lord of the Conscience: A Policy Statement Adopted by the 100th General Assembly of the Presbyterian Church (U.S.A.) 36 (1988)). Let us use the Roman Catholic Church as an example. As long as the Church can communicate its position on electoral issues, does it matter whether that communication comes through an official of a Catholic (c)(4) affiliate or PAC rather than, say, a bishop of a diocese?

(b) An exemption for religious organizations?   Even if the political-activity restrictions significantly burden religious exercise, they apply to exempt organizations generally. Aren't they therefore constitutional under the rule of Employment Division v. Smith? What if the Religious Freedom Restoration Act continues to apply to federal law: do the political-activity restrictions serve compelling interests? (Consider the rationales for the restrictions mentioned above.) Lobbying about legislation and pronouncements about elections are forms of speech. Could a religious organization therefore raise a "hybrid" claim of free speech and free exercise in order to obtain an exemption from the restrictions? See p. 173 above. Or does the fact that the religious activity here is speech *forbid* any exemption for religious organizations alone? See Section V-B-2.

(c) A special limit on religious organizations?   The political-activity restrictions, as applied to churches, are sometimes defended on the ground that they "serve the useful purpose of separating the spheres of religion and electoral politics." Feld, 42 B.C. L. Rev. at 939. Is this a constitutionally legitimate justification?

4. Selective Prosecution?   Didn't the Pierce Creek Church have a point when it said that it was being singled out for activity that is common in political campaigns? Candidates for office regularly appear in church pulpits, and organizations like the Christian Coalition and the U.S. Conference of Catholic Bishops put out information on the positions of various candidates. Consider this example:

Three days after the [federal government] argued [in district court] against the tax-exempt status of Branch Ministries, President Clinton spoke during a worship service at Baltimore's New Psalmist Baptist Church. The service was carried live on television. During his address, just two days before the 1998 election, President Clinton introduced several Democratic candidates for office to the assembly of nearly two thousand people. . . . [He] cited the accomplishments of many of these individuals and explained how he needed Democrats in Congress to help further his agenda. He added that "on Tuesday, you're in control of the arithmetic again and you can vote."

In his sermon that day, Reverend Walter Thomas of New Psalmist blamed "organized evil" for the dismantling of affirmative action and exhorted the crowd, "Every time you turn around, somebody's at you, somebody's trying to

destroy you, somebody's killing your program." Building on this theme, President
Clinton stressed that the 1998 election was about "whether the people who believe
they should divide America can leave you out because you stay home."

Lee, 63 Law & Contemp. Probs. at 394-396. The *Branch Ministries* court held
that the case before it was unique because it involved "the placement of advertisements in newspapers with nationwide circulations opposing a candidate and
soliciting tax deductible contributions to defray their cost." Was the court correct?

Churches that effectively endorse a particular political candidate (or engage
in too much legislative lobbying) may lose their tax exemptions, but beyond that
they have a free speech right to speak and agitate on questions of public policy.
Matters may be different, however, if a church is given a formal or official role in
governmental decision making.

LARKIN v. GRENDEL'S DEN, 459 U.S. 116 (1982):   Grendel's Den, a restaurant located on Harvard Square in Cambridge, Massachusetts, applied for a
liquor license. However, a church next door, the Holy Cross Armenian Catholic
Parish church, objected to the issuance of a license, pursuant to a Massachusetts
statute (ch. 138, § 16C) stating that premises within "five hundred feet of a
church or school shall not be licensed for the sale of alcoholic beverages if
the governing body of such church or school files written objection thereto."
The back walls of the two buildings were 10 feet apart. After its license application was denied on this basis, Grendel's Den sued in federal court. The Supreme
Court ultimately held that the statute violated the Establishment Clause:
"[Section] 16C delegates to private, non-governmental entities power to veto
certain liquor license applications. This is a power ordinarily vested in agencies
of government. We need not decide whether, or upon what conditions, such
power may ever be delegated to nongovernmental entities; here, of two classes of
institutions to which the legislature has delegated this important decisionmaking power, one is secular, but one is religious."
Applying the *Lemon* test, the Court continued: "The purpose of § 16C . . . is to
'protect[ ] spiritual, cultural, and educational centers from the "hurly-burly"
associated with liquor outlets.' . . . However, these valid secular objectives can be
readily accomplished by other means—either through an absolute legislative
ban on liquor outlets within reasonable prescribed distances from churches,
schools, hospitals and like institutions, or by ensuring a hearing for the views
of affected institutions at licensing proceedings where, without question, such
views would be entitled to substantial weight."
Turning to the "primary effect" prong, the Court said: "The churches' power
under the statute is standardless, calling for no reasons, findings, or reasoned
conclusions. That power may therefore be used by churches to promote goals
beyond insulating the church from undesirable neighbors; it could be employed
for explicitly religious goals, for example, favoring liquor licenses for members
of that congregation or adherents of that faith. . . . In addition, the mere appearance of a joint exercise of legislative authority by Church and State provides a
significant symbolic benefit to religion in the minds of some by reason of the
power conferred."

Finally, under the entanglement prong, "[T]he core rationale underlying the Establishment Clause is preventing 'a fusion of governmental and religious functions.' The Framers did not set up a system of government in which important, discretionary governmental powers would be delegated to or shared with religious institutions.

"Section 16C substitutes the unilateral and absolute power of a church for the reasoned decisionmaking of a public legislative body acting on evidence and guided by standards, on issues with significant economic and political implications. The challenged statute thus enmeshes churches in the processes of government and creates the danger of '[p]olitical fragmentation and divisiveness along religious lines,' *Lemon*. Ordinary human experience and a long line of cases teach that few entanglements could be more offensive to the spirit of the Constitution."

Justice Rehnquist dissented: "In its original form, § 16C imposed a flat ban on the grant of an alcoholic beverages license to any establishment located within 500 feet of a church or a school. This statute represented a legislative determination that worship and liquor sales are generally not compatible uses of land. . . .

"Over time, the legislature found that it could meet its goal of protecting people engaged in religious activities from liquor-related disruption with a less absolute prohibition. Rather than set out elaborate formulae or require an administrative agency to make findings of fact, the legislature settled on the simple expedient of asking churches to object if a proposed liquor outlet would disturb them. . . . The flat ban, which the majority concedes is valid, is more protective of churches and more restrictive of liquor sales than the present § 16C.

"[This is] the sort of legislative refinement that we should encourage, not forbid in the name of the First Amendment. If a particular church or a particular school located within the 500 foot radius chooses not to object, the state has quite sensibly concluded that there is no reason to prohibit the issuance of the license. Nothing in the Court's opinion persuades me why the more rigid prohibition would be constitutional, but the more flexible not. . . .

"The Court is apparently concerned for fear that churches might object to the issuance of a license for 'explicitly religious' reasons, such as 'favoring liquor licenses for members of that congregation or adherents of that faith.' . . . But our ability to discern a risk of such abuse does not render § 16C violative of the Establishment Clause."

NOTES AND QUESTIONS

1. What Was Wrong in *Grendel's Den*? Is *Grendel's Den* consistent with McDaniel v. Paty (p. 666)? *McDaniel* rejects the rule that ministers cannot hold public office; *Grendel's Den* strikes down a law giving churches (synagogues, etc.) a limited equivalent of public office (that is, veto power over certain zoning decisions). Why does the Free Exercise (or Free Speech) Clause not protect churches as it did the Rev. McDaniel? Is it because of a difference between giving power to a group and to an individual?

Is *Grendel's Den* consistent with *McDaniel* because the Massachusetts law gave churches (and almost no one else) a special right to object to a license, while

McDaniel simply got the same right as everyone else to be a legislator? We have seen numerous cases in which the Court allows the state to treat religious organizations the same as other organizations (in regulating them, providing financial assistance, or providing facilities for expression). Would the result in *Grendel's Den* have been the same if the Massachusetts law allowed an objection by any nonprofit organization located within 500 feet of a proposed liquor establishment?

Such a broader, religion-neutral law might still be challenged on constitutional grounds. In two decisions, old but not overruled, the Court struck down zoning ordinances conditioning building permits upon the consent of adjoining or nearby property owners. Eubank v. Richmond, 226 U.S. 137 (1912); Washington ex rel. Seattle Title Trust v. Roberge, 278 U.S. 116 (1928). As the Court more recently put it, these cases held that such a "standardless delegation of power to a limited group of property owners" violated due process by allowing those private parties to engage in arbitrary action. City of Eastlake v. Forest City Enterprises, 426 U.S. 668, 678 (1976) (distinguishing the *Eubank* and *Roberge* ordinances from a law submitting zoning changes to entire municipal electorate through referendum). Under this approach, again there is no unique barrier to religious organizations vetoing nearby land uses.

Parts of the Court's opinion, however, suggest that there is something uniquely wrong about a church having authority to veto a liquor license. Why might that be so? The Court suggests that the church might enforce religious ideas, or that it might "favor[ ] liquor licenses for members of that congregation or adherents of that faith." But don't *Eubank* and *Roberge* suggest that any landowner might engage in such arbitrary and unfair action? Why does the Court think that Holy Cross Church is more likely than a secular nonprofit organization to engage in that sort of favoritism?

In note 10 of *Grendel's Den* the Court observes that at the time of the Revolution, Americans feared "the danger of political oppression through a union of civil and ecclesiastical control." In the next paragraph of text the Court warns of "the danger of '[p]olitical fragmentation and divisiveness along religious lines.'" Are churches likelier than other groups to exercise political control in an oppressive fashion? See also William P. Marshall, The Other Side of Religion, 44 Hastings L.J. 843 (1993); Lee v. Weisman (p. 498) (Blackmun, J., concurring) ("[R]eligious faith puts its trust in an ultimate divine authority above all human deliberation. . . . Democratic government will not last long when proclamation replaces persuasion as the medium of political exchange.") Is this an accurate description of religious ways of thinking? If it is, why do we give churches tax exemptions?

2. Churches' Role in Marriage. The New York Domestic Relations Law states that "[n]o marriage shall be valid unless solemnized by . . . [a] clergyman or minister of any religion," or certain other public officials. N.Y. Dom. Rel. Law § 11 (McKinney 1997). The Religious Corporations Law defines who is a clergyman: "a person having authority from . . . the governing ecclesiastical body of the denomination [or from a freestanding] church or synagogue to preside over and direct the [group's] spiritual affairs." N.Y. Relig. Corp. Law § 2 (McKinney 1997). Ranieri v. Ranieri, 146 A.D.2d 34, 539 N.Y.S.2d 382 (Sup. Ct. 1989), held that a marriage solemnized by a minister of the Universal Life Church, Inc., was void because his "title and status [were too] casually and cavalierly acquired."

See also Ravenal v. Ravenal, 72 Misc. 2d 100, 338 N.Y.S.2d 324 (Sup. Ct. 1972); State v. Lynch, 301 N.C. 479, 272 S.E.2d 349 (N.C. 1980); Cramer v. Commonwealth, 214 Va. 561, 202 S.E.2d 911 (Va. 1974). Does *Grendel's Den* call into question the usual method for solemnizing marriages in most states?

Why does New York delegate to churches the task of solemnizing marriages? Is it because our society has long viewed marriage as both a contract and a sacrament? This has long been the view of the Roman Catholic Church and the Protestant Episcopal Church. See Roman Catholic Code of Canon Law, canon 1055 (1983); Constitutions and Canons for the Government of the Protestant Episcopal Church in the United States of America, Title I, canon 18 (1988). It worked its way into English matrimonial law at an early date. II Frederick Pollock & Frederick Maitland, The History of English Law 364-399 (2d ed. 1968); see also John Witte, From Sacrament to Contract: Marriage, Religion, and Law in the Western Tradition (1997). We do not have, as the English once did, a separate system of courts to enforce that law. But it would hardly be surprising if we, inheriting much of their religion and their law as we have, should retain some vestiges of this cooperative system run by church and state.

We asked above whether the Court in *Grendel's Den* forbade churches to take part in governmental decisionmaking because churches might enforce religious ideas. Can that happen in marriage cases? The Episcopal Church forbids its ministers to solemnize any marriage unless at least one of the parties is baptized. Constitution and Canons for the Government of the Protestant Episcopal Church in the United States of America, Title I, canon 18, § 2(d). That is clearly a religious judgment. Should we extend public authority to an institution that makes such distinctions?

Is the real difference between marriage and zoning that in the former case no one has to have his fate decided by a church? New York allows engaged couples who think nothing of religion to have their marriages solemnized by a mayor, recorder, police magistrate, city clerk, judge, or any of the leaders of the Society for Ethical Culture. N.Y. Dom. Rel. Law § 11.1-3. Grendel's Den had no alternative to a decision by Holy Cross Church. Could we let churches decide divorce cases too, if we warned the parties when they got married in the church that this would be the consequence?

3. Problems: Other Cases of Delegation. What result under *Grendel's Den* in the following cases?

(a) Kosher certification. A Baltimore city ordinance creates an unpaid Bureau of Kosher Meat and Food Control appointed by the Mayor (three Orthodox Rabbis and three laymen selected from a list submitted by the Council of Orthodox Rabbis of Baltimore and the Orthodox Jewish Council of Baltimore). The ordinance makes it a misdemeanor to sell as "kosher" food not approved by the Bureau. Barghout v. Bureau of Kosher Meat & Food Control, 66 F.3d 1337 (4th Cir. 1995).

(b) Religious college security officers. A North Carolina law authorizes the attorney general to commission as police officers members of campus security forces at both public and private colleges. Officer Jones, a security officer employed by Campbell University, a Baptist school, arrested a student near the campus for driving while impaired, and the student was convicted in county court. State v. Pendleton, 339 N.C. 379, 451 S.E.2d 274 (N.C. 1994).

4. Religious Delegation and Drawing Governmental Boundaries: *Kiryas Joel.*
The Court invoked *Grendel's Den* when it struck down the special public school
district at issue in Board of Educ., Kiryas Joel School Dist. v. Grumet, 512 U.S.
687 (1994). You can review the facts of *Kiryas Joel* at p. 252.

Justice Souter's plurality opinion concluded that the creation of the Kiryas
Joel school district, whose lines were drawn to include only members of the
Satmar Hasidic Jewish community, effectively "delegate[d] civic power to" a
religious community, which was constitutionally the same as the delegation of
power to a formal religious institution in *Grendel's Den*:

> [T]he village boundaries [were drawn] to exclude all but Satmars, [and] the
> New York Legislature was well aware that the village remained exclusively Satmar
> in 1989 when it adopted Chapter 748. . . .
>
> Because the district's creation ran uniquely counter to state practice, following
> the lines of a religious community where the customary and neutral principles
> would not have dictated the same result, we have good reasons to treat this district
> as the reflection of a religious criterion for identifying the recipients of civil
> authority.

The plurality distinguished McDaniel v. Paty, the decision forbidding the exclusion of clergy from public office: "That individuals who happen to be religious
may hold public office does not mean that a State may deliberately delegate
discretionary power to an individual, institution, or community on the ground
of religious identity."

Justice Scalia, dissenting, argued that *Grendel's Den* should be limited to invalidating "the grant of governmental power directly to a religious institution":

> [The] history of the populating of North America is in no small measure the
> story of groups of people sharing a common religious and cultural heritage striking
> out to form their own communities. It is preposterous to suggest that the civil
> institutions of these communities, separate from their churches, were constitution-
> ally suspect. . . . [Under the plurality's decision,] there is no reason why giving
> power to a body that is overwhelmingly dominated by the members of one sect
> would not suffice to invoke the Establishment Clause. That might have made the
> entire States of Utah and New Mexico unconstitutional at the time of their admis-
> sion to the Union,[1] and would undoubtedly make many units of local government
> unconstitutional today.

Justice Kennedy, concurring in *Kiryas Joel,* also focused on the religious criterion used for drawing the district line:

> [T]he Establishment Clause forbids the government to use religion as a line-
> drawing criterion. In this respect, the Establishment Clause mirrors the Equal
> Protection Clause. Just as the government may not segregate people on account
> of their race, so too it may not segregate on the basis of religion. The danger of
> stigma and stirred animosities is no less acute for religious line-drawing than for
> racial.

---

1. A census taken in 1906, 10 years after statehood was granted to Utah, and 6 years before it was
granted to New Mexico, showed that in Utah 87.7% of all church members were Mormon, and in
New Mexico 88.7% of all church members were Roman Catholic.

512 U.S. at 728. This suggests that the proper analogy to *Kiryas Joel* is not Larkin v. Grendel's Den, but Miller v. Johnson, 515 U.S. 900 (1995). In that case the Court held that a state plan to create voting districts on the basis of race must pass strict scrutiny. Should religious gerrymanders be subject to the same scrutiny as racial ones?

The Court said in *Miller* that racial districting "engages in the offensive and demeaning assumption that voters of a particular race, because of their race, 'think alike, share the same political interests, and will prefer the same candidates at the polls.'" 515 U.S. at 911-912. Is it offensive to suggest that members of the same religious group think alike? *Miller* also said that a well-behaved legislature, in drawing up districts, would show "respect for political subdivisions or communities defined by actual shared interests." *Id.* at 916. Isn't that what New York did? Is there some reason why we should discourage political recognition of religious groups *even though* they have shared interests?

The *Kiryas Joel* plurality dissented in *Miller*,* arguing that "[t]o accommodate the reality of ethnic bonds, legislatures have long drawn voting districts along ethnic lines. Our Nation's cities are full of districts identified by their ethnic character—Chinese, Irish, Italian, Jewish, Polish, Russian, for example." *Id.* at 944-945 (Ginsburg, J., dissenting). Why does this principle not cover the Satmars? They immigrated after World War II from Satu-Mare (St. Mary), Romania, where the Grand Rebbe Joel Teitelbaum established the sect early in this century. (The Village of Kiryas Joel is named for him.) Are they disqualified because their Jewishness includes religious beliefs as well as an ethnic identity? The *Kiryas Joel* dissenters joined the majority in *Miller*. Why would they allow religious districting but not racial districting? For comparison of the two, see Thomas C. Berg, Race, Religion, Segregation, and Districting: Comparing *Kiryas Joel* with *Shaw/Miller*, 26 Cumb. L. Rev. 365 (1996); cf. Jeffrey Rosen, *Kiryas Joel* and *Shaw v. Reno*: A Text-Bound Interpretivist Approach, 26 Cumb. L. Rev. 387 (1996).

As Rosen's article notes, around the time of the *Kiryas Joel* litigation, newspapers reported several acts of coercion and intimidation by the village's leaders against dissidents. See 26 Cumb. L. Rev. at 393-96; Ira C. Lupu, Uncovering the Village of Kiryas Joel, 96 Colum. L. Rev. 104 (1996). Is the risk of such coercion within the community—not the separation from those outside the community— the stronger reason to be worried about such single-religion towns? Note that the accounts of intimidation were not entered into the record in the litigation, which challenged the school district on its face rather than as it had been implemented, and did not challenge the village's creation at all. Abner Greene, *Kiryas Joel* and Two Mistakes About Equality, 96 Colum. L. Rev. 1, 19-20 (1996). Should such acts nevertheless affect the Court's attitudes toward jurisdictions like this?

---

*Justice Breyer replaced Justice Blackmun in the summer of 1994.

VI

WHAT IS "RELIGION"?

When the First Amendment was ratified in 1791, the vast majority of Americans were Protestant Christians. They would not have seen much ambiguity in the word *religion*. George Mason and James Madison defined it thus in the Virginia Declaration of Rights: "the duty which we owe to our Creator, and the manner of discharging it" (see p. 45). A century later, Justice Stephen J. Field put the same idea in similar words: "The term 'religion' has reference to one's views of his relations to his Creator, and to the obligations they impose of reverence for his being and character, and of obedience to his will." Davis v. Beason (p. 119).

Today people are less likely to agree that these are the essential elements of religion. One reason is that there are many more religious denominations (and informal groups) than there were a century or two ago. Some, like Buddhists, do not believe in a personal and creative God. Others, though they believe in a God or gods, do not consider that we owe him (her, them) duties.

A second important reason for the current ambiguity of the term *religion* is to some extent independent of these sociological changes. Once the Free Exercise Clause was ratified and the practice of religion given the status of a right, there came to be reasons unrelated to theology for claiming that one was "religious." "Granting religious exemptions from generally applicable legal rules frequently invites strategic behavior—that is, lying about one's religious convictions in order to gain the advantage of the religious immunity." Mayer G. Freed and Daniel D. Polsby, Race, Religion, and Public Policy: Bob Jones University v. United States, 1983 Sup. Ct. Rev. 1, 22. It is not frivolous, though it may be wrong, to argue for giving LSD the same protection the law affords to sacramental wine. Or for affording the Neo-American Church (whose church key is the bottle opener, and whose motto is "Victory over Horseshit") the same tax immunities as the Greek Orthodox Church. United States v. Kuch, 288 F. Supp. 439 (D.D.C. 1968).

It is tempting, and it suits our liberal sensibilities, to say that no one (least of all the law) should presume to judge the authenticity of another person's religion. Provided a claimant is sincere, some maintain, we should allow *her* to say what her religious beliefs are. But we do not do this with other freedoms mentioned in the Constitution. The First Amendment protects freedom of speech in the same breath as freedom of religion, and courts do not hesitate to define "speech"— it includes poems and flag burning, and maybe nude dancing, but not obscenity or intentional libel. So too with the fundamental liberties protected by the Due Process Clause—they include abortion and child rearing, but not the practice of optometry or assisted suicide. "Religion" in the Constitution is a legal category. It is natural that the courts should say what its outer limits are. If we let private claimants define the scope of their rights, there would be no stopping them. *Every* act would get the benefits and immunities of the First Amendment.

It thus seems inevitable that the courts (and maybe other branches of government) must sometimes say what counts as "religion" in our legal system. But how can we square this with the Establishment Clause? Does it not forbid the government to compile a list of approved religions? Or is this a false problem? The Establishment Clause forbids laws only within a certain range (those "respecting an establishment of religion"). We can't condemn a law for falling within that range without first defining the term "religion." It seems to follow from Marbury v. Madison, 5 U.S. (1 Cranch) 137 (1803), that the courts should give it some content.

We will begin by looking at the Supreme Court's effort to define "religion" in cases from the Vietnam War era involving conscientious objections to the military draft. Here its conclusions are quite generous. We will then see how this broad definition works in other contexts.

A. THE DRAFT CASES

The two cases that follow present issues of statutory, not constitutional, interpretation. But it is fairly obvious in both that the First Amendment drove the Court to conclusions it might not otherwise have reached. The cases thus shed considerable light on the constitutional meaning of the term "religion."

UNITED STATES v. SEEGER
380 U.S. 163 (1965)

Mr. Justice CLARK delivered the opinion of the Court.

These cases involve claims of conscientious objectors under § 6(j) of the Universal Military Training and Service Act, 50 U.S.C. App. § 456(j), which exempts from combatant training and service in the armed forces of the United States those persons who by reason of their religious training and belief are conscientiously opposed to participation in war in any form. . . . The parties raise the basic question of the constitutionality of the section which defines the term "religious training and belief," as used in the Act, as "an individual's belief in a relation to a Supreme Being involving duties superior to those arising from any human relation, but [not including] essentially political, sociological, or philosophical views or a merely personal moral code." The constitutional attack is launched under the First Amendment's Establishment and Free Exercise Clauses and is twofold: (1) The section does not exempt nonreligious conscientious objectors; and (2) it discriminates between different forms of religious expression in violation of the Due Process Clause of the Fifth Amendment. . . .

No. 50: Seeger was convicted in the District Court for the Southern District of New York of having refused to submit to induction in the armed forces. . . . He first claimed exemption as a conscientious objector in 1957 after successive annual renewals of his student classification. Although he did not adopt verbatim the printed Selective Service System form, he declared that he was conscientiously opposed to participation in war in any form by reason of his "religious" belief; that he preferred to leave the question as to his belief in a Supreme Being open, "rather than answer 'yes' or 'no' "; that his "skepticism or disbelief in the existence of God" did "not necessarily mean lack of faith in anything whatsoever"; that his was a "belief in and devotion to goodness and virtue for their own sakes, and a religious faith in a purely ethical creed." He cited such personages as Plato, Aristotle and Spinoza for support of his ethical belief in intellectual and moral integrity "without belief in God, except in the remotest sense." His belief was found to be sincere, honest, and made in good faith; and his conscientious objection to be based upon individual training and belief, both of which included research in religious and cultural fields. Seeger's claim, however, was denied solely because it was not based upon a "belief in a relation to a Supreme Being" as required by §6(j) of the Act. . . . He was convicted and the Court of Appeals reversed, holding that the Supreme Being requirement of the section distinguished "between internally derived and externally compelled beliefs" and was, therefore, an "impermissible classification" under the Due Process Clause of the Fifth Amendment.

[The facts in the companion cases are omitted.]

BACKGROUND OF §6(j)

[Our governments have always recognized the moral dilemma posed by the call to arms for people of certain religious faiths. The American colonies, and later the states, adopted various methods of ameliorating this difficulty. When the federal government conscripted soldiers for the Civil War it exempted] those conscientious objectors who were members of religious denominations opposed to the bearing of arms and who were prohibited from doing so by the articles of faith of their denominations. In that same year the Confederacy exempted certain pacifist sects from military duty.

The need for conscription did not again arise until World War I. The Draft Act of 1917 afforded exemptions to conscientious objectors who were affiliated with a "well-recognized religious sect or organization [then] organized and existing and whose existing creed or principles [forbade] its members to participate in war in any form. . . ." [Congress broadened the exemption in the 1940 Selective Training and Service Act] by making it unnecessary to belong to a pacifist religious sect if the claimant's own opposition to war was based on "religious training and belief." . . .

Between 1940 and 1948 two courts of appeals[1] held that the phrase "religious training and belief" did not include philosophical, social or political policy. Then in 1948 the Congress amended the language of the statute and declared that "religious training and belief" was to be defined as "an individual's belief in a relation to a Supreme Being involving duties superior to those arising from any

---

1. See United States v. Kauten (2d Cir. 1943); Berman v. United States (9th Cir. 1946).

human relation, but [not including] essentially political, sociological, or philosophical views or a merely personal moral code." The only significant mention of this change in the provision appears in the report of the Senate Armed Services Committee recommending adoption. It said simply this: "This section reenacts substantially the same provisions as were found in subsection 5(g) of the 1940 act. Exemption extends to anyone who, because of religious training and belief in his relation to a Supreme Being, is conscientiously opposed to combatant military service or to both combatant and non-combatant military service. (See United States v. Berman [sic], 156 F.2d 377, certiorari denied, 329 U.S. 795.)" S. Rep. No. 1268, 80th Cong., 2d Sess. 14.

INTERPRETATION OF § 6(j)

1. [None of the parties before us] claims to be an atheist or attacks the statute on this ground. The question is not, therefore, one between theistic and atheistic beliefs. We do not deal with or intimate any decision on that situation in these cases. . . . Our question, therefore, is the narrow one: Does the term "Supreme Being" as used in §6(j) mean the orthodox God or the broader concept of a power or being, or a faith, "to which all else is subordinate or upon which all else is ultimately dependent"? Webster's New International Dictionary (Second Edition). . . .

2. [Congress borrowed its 1948 language from the opinion of] Chief Justice Hughes in United States v. MacIntosh (1931) (emphasis supplied)]: "The essence of religion is belief in a relation to *God* involving duties superior to those arising from any human relation." [But Congress deliberately broadened Hughes's language] by substituting the phrase "Supreme Being" for the appellation "God." . . . Moreover, the Senate Report on the bill specifically states that §6(j) was intended to re-enact "substantially the same provisions as were found" in the 1940 Act. That statute, of course, refers to "religious training and belief" without more. . . . Within that phrase would come all sincere religious beliefs which are based upon a power or being, or upon a faith, to which all else is subordinate or upon which all else is ultimately dependent. The test might be stated in these words: A sincere and meaningful belief which occupies in the life of its possessor a place parallel to that filled by the God of those admittedly qualifying for the exemption comes within the statutory definition. This construction avoids imputing to Congress an intent to classify different religious beliefs, exempting some and excluding others, and is in accord with the well-established congressional policy of equal treatment for those whose opposition to service is grounded in their religious tenets. . . .

4. Moreover, we believe this construction embraces the ever-broadening understanding of the modern religious community. The eminent Protestant theologian, Dr. Paul Tillich, whose views the Government concedes would come within the statute, identifies God not as a projection "out there" or beyond the skies but as the ground of our very being. . . . In his book, Systematic Theology (1957), Dr. Tillich says:

I have written of the God above the God of theism. . . . In such a state [of self-affirmation] the God of both religious and theological language disappears. But something remains, namely, the seriousness of that doubt in which meaning within meaninglessness is affirmed. The source of this affirmation of meaning within meaninglessness, of certitude within doubt, is not the God of traditional theism but the "God above God," the power of being, which works through those who have no name for it, not even the name God.

. . . Dr. David Saville Muzzey, a leader in the Ethical Culture Movement, states in his book, Ethics As a Religion (1951), that "[e]verybody except the avowed atheists (and they are comparatively few) believes in some kind of God," and that "The proper question to ask, therefore, is not the futile one, Do you believe in God? but rather, What *kind* of God do you believe in?" Dr. Muzzey attempts to answer that question:

Instead of positing a personal God, whose existence man can neither prove nor disprove, the ethical concept is founded on human experience. It is anthropocentric, not theocentric. Religion, for all the various definitions that have been given of it, must surely mean the devotion of man to the highest ideal that he can conceive. And that ideal is a community of spirits in which the latent moral potentialities of men shall have been elicited by their reciprocal endeavors to cultivate the best in their fellow men. What ultimate reality is we do not know; but we have the faith that it expresses itself in the human world as the power which inspires in men moral purpose.

Thus the "God" that we love is not the figure on the great white throne, but the perfect pattern, envisioned by faith, of humanity as it should be, purged of the evil elements which retard its progress toward "the knowledge, love and practice of the right."

These are but a few of the views that comprise the broad spectrum of religious beliefs found among us. But they demonstrate very clearly the diverse manners in which beliefs, equally paramount in the lives of their possessors, may be articulated. They further reveal the difficulties inherent in placing too narrow a construction on the provisions of § 6(j) and thereby lend conclusive support to the construction which we today find that Congress intended.

5. [I]n resolving these exemption problems one deals with the beliefs of different individuals who will articulate them in a multitude of ways. In such an intensely personal area, of course, the claim of the registrant that his belief is an essential part of a religious faith must be given great weight. . . . The validity of what he believes cannot be questioned. Some theologians, and indeed some examiners, might be tempted to question the existence of the registrant's "Supreme Being" or the truth of his concepts. But these are inquiries foreclosed to Government. As Mr. Justice Douglas stated in United States v. Ballard [p. 193]: "Men may believe what they cannot prove. They may not be put to the proof of their religious doctrines or beliefs. Religious experiences which are as real as life to some may be incomprehensible to others." Local boards and courts in this sense are not free to reject beliefs because they consider them "incomprehensible." Their task is to decide whether the beliefs professed by a registrant are sincerely held and whether they are, in his own scheme of things, religious.

But we hasten to emphasize that while the "truth" of a belief is not open to question, there remains the significant question whether it is "truly held." This is the threshold question of sincerity which must be resolved in every case. It is, of course, a question of fact—a prime consideration to the validity of every claim for exemption as a conscientious objector. . . .

APPLICATION OF §6(j) TO THE INSTANT CASES

[There is no question here] of the applicant's sincerity. He was a product of a devout Roman Catholic home; he was a close student of Quaker beliefs from which he said "much of [his] thought is derived"; he approved of their opposition to war in any form; he devoted his spare hours to the American Friends Service Committee and was assigned to hospital duty.

In summary, Seeger professed "religious belief" and "religious faith." He did not disavow any belief "in a relation to a Supreme Being"; indeed he stated that "the cosmic order does, perhaps, suggest a creative intelligence." He decried the tremendous "spiritual" price man must pay for his willingness to destroy human life. In light of his beliefs and the unquestioned sincerity with which he held them, we think the Board, had it applied the test we propose today, would have granted him the exemption. We think it clear that the beliefs which prompted his objection occupy the same place in his life as the belief in a traditional deity holds in the lives of his friends, the Quakers. We are reminded once more of Dr. Tillich's thoughts:

> And if that word [God] has not much meaning for you, translate it, and speak of the depths of your life, of the source of your being, or your ultimate concern, of what you take seriously without any reservation. Perhaps, in order to do so, you must forget everything traditional that you have learned about God. . . . Tillich, The Shaking of the Foundations (1948) (emphasis supplied).

It may be that Seeger did not clearly demonstrate what his beliefs were with regard to the usual understanding of the term "Supreme Being." But as we have said Congress did not intend that to be the test. We therefore affirm the judgment in No. 50.

NOTES AND QUESTIONS

1. A Little History About Draft Exemptions. As you should remember from Section III-C, when the First Congress debated what would become the Second Amendment, there was a discussion of creating an explicit constitutional exemption from service in the state militias. See p. 231. The Select Committee proposed, and the House passed (by a vote of 24 to 22), this provision: "no person religiously scrupulous shall be compelled to bear arms." 1 Annals of Cong. 778 (J. Gales ed., 1834) (Aug. 17, 1789). It was rejected in the Senate, and so did not become part of the Bill of Rights. The fate of this clause sheds some light on the First Amendment. It was the only time the First Congress specifically addressed the question of religious exemptions from generally applicable laws. As discussed in the earlier section, the militia-exemption debate is inconclusive on whether religious exemptions were ever constitutionally required, but it does indicate that they were generally thought constitutionally permissible. As the Court indicates in *Seeger*, the Draft Acts passed during the Civil War and the First and Second World Wars exempted religious conscientious objectors. The 1917 version, which required membership in a "well-recognized [pacifist] religious sect or organization," was upheld against a First

Amendment challenge in the Selective Draft Law Cases, 245 U.S. 366 (1918). The defendants in one of those cases (the well-known anarchists Emma Goldman and Alexander Berkman, who were convicted of conspiracy to impede registration) argued that it violated the Establishment and Free Exercise Clauses for Congress "to foster and aid well-recognized churches or sects."

> You may have two persons of exactly the same religious conviction of opposition to participating in war in any form. They may believe firmly, "Thou shalt not kill." Both . . . derive their convictions from the same source, their conscience; but one of them belongs to a certain particular sect and the other does not. [But the first is exempted, while the second is made a felon.] If this is not making a law "respecting an establishment of religion" and "prohibiting the free exercise thereof," "establishing inequality" and "making religious distinctions," no such law can be devised.

No. 702 Pl. in Err. Br. 37, 39 (O.T. 1917). The Court rejected the argument, but gave no explanation: "[W]e pass without anything but statement the proposition that an establishment of a religion or an interference with the free exercise thereof repugnant to the First Amendment resulted from the exemption clauses of the act . . . , because we think its unsoundness is too apparent to require us to do more." 245 U.S. at 389-390. Several years later the Court held that the exemption, though permissible, was not constitutionally required. United States v. MacIntosh, 283 U.S. 605, 624 (1931). See also Gillette v. United States, 401 U.S. 437, 461-462 (1071), discussed below at p. 724.

2. What Is "Religion"? Notice how the eighteenth- and nineteenth-century efforts to define religion (in the Virginia Declaration of Rights and in Davis v. Beason) focus on a conjunction of several essential elements: God, duty, acts of obedience. *Seeger* and the next decision, Welsh v. United States, not only reject these elements but also this definitional approach. Is this a mistake? What is the alternative?

(a) A "higher power"? In limiting the exemption to religious objectors, Congress spoke of "a relation to a Supreme Being involving duties superior to those arising from any human relation." *Are* peoples' duties to God (if there is a God) more compelling than their duties to other people? Are the consequences of violating our duties to God more serious? Some suppose that the penalty for violating God's commands is eternal torment or the loss of eternal bliss. Is this why the First Amendment gives special protection to religious freedom? Does it explain why Congress showed special concern for religious pacifists? Jesse H. Choper, Defining "Religion" in the First Amendment, 1982 U. Ill. L. Rev. 579; Michael S. Paulsen, God Is Great, Garvey Is Good: Making Sense of Religious Freedom, 72 Notre Dame L. Rev. 1597 (1997).

How would this theory work for strict Calvinists, who believe that there is no cause-and-effect relation between our actions and our salvation? For those Jews who do not believe in a life after death? For Catholics, who believe in the forgiveness of sins? How would it work outside the context of conscientious objection? Prayer and fasting may be obligatory at certain times (Sunday, Yom Kippur, Ramadan); at others they are seen as virtuous actions that may win merit, but not matters of duty. Would a standard that focused on duties to God and extratemporal consequences protect them under these circumstances?

Perhaps it is too western to imagine that any genuine religion will include a belief in the one omnipotent God of Jews, Christians, and Muslims. See, e.g.,

Eduardo Penalver, The Concept of Religion, 107 Yale L. J. 791, 812-814 (1997).
Can we say that all religious people make some supernatural assumptions or
believe in some higher power? What about a belief that the true reality is deep
within rather than above us? Must the higher power be in some sense transcendent or spiritual? Should we say that Scientology is not a religion? Cf. Hernandez v.
Commissioner, 490 U.S. 680 (1989). What about practices like Ethical Culture?
See Torcaso v. Watkins (p. 473), at n.11.

   (b) "Ultimate concern"?   *Seeger* does not actually contradict the statutory
assumption that a religion must have a Supreme Being. It surmounts this difficulty by interpreting §6(j) very broadly: "Supreme Being" in §6(j) does not
mean the orthodox God. It could be a "being" or a "power," but it might be
nothing more than a "faith" to which all else is subordinate. The Court finds
support for this conclusion in the work of the influential liberal Protestant
theologian Paul Tillich. Tillich would have said that everyone has a God: God
is "your ultimate concern, . . . what you take seriously without any reservation."
The Shaking of the Foundations 57 (1948).

   Traditional definitions of religion focus on the content of a creed—God, duty,
worship, etc. *Seeger* eschews that in favor of a psychological approach. What matters most is how deeply a person believes, not who or what or why. This approach
has several appealing features. One is that it avoids the parochialism of content-
based definitions. If any authentic religion must have a God, we must omit Buddhism and Confucianism from the list, and that seems wrong. Another is that it
provides a limiting principle—not every sincere claim for exemption, immunity,
or special treatment will qualify as religious in this scheme. Note, Toward a
Constitutional Definition of Religion, 91 Harv. L. Rev. 1056 (1978).

   But this psychological approach also presents a number of difficulties. Can a
person have only one ultimate concern? Suppose Joe, a Quaker, skipped a
Sunday meeting to spend time with his newborn child. Would he forfeit his
claim of religious pacifism if his family sometimes took precedence over his
religion? And why must an ultimate concern be a moral, ethical, or religious
principle? There are people who eat, drink, and sleep baseball. Are their base-
ball-related activities protected by the Free Exercise Clause? What about a drug
addict, whose chief concern each day is to get a supply of heroin? If the psychological approach of *Seeger* and *Welsh* is truly content-free, these questions present
real difficulties.

   Suppose we address this problem by saying that ultimate concerns must at a
minimum be moral or ethical principles. Is there a danger that the test may
sometimes be too strict, rather than too loose? Traditional religions provide
answers and rules not just for life's major events (birth, death, marriage) but
also for mundane issues such as what to eat, how to cook, what to wear, how to
stand at prayer. These practices are not always absolute duties (not, psychologically speaking, ultimate concerns). Indeed, sometimes they are not duties at all,
but matters of religious commitment above and beyond duty. Are they therefore
not religious? Can the government forbid the sale of kosher food or the sale of
rosaries without even triggering a free exercise inquiry? Kent Greenawalt,
Religion as a Concept in Constitutional Law, 72 Cal. L. Rev. 753 (1984). If we
extend protection to such activities, must we give the same treatment to all forms
of behavior with equal psychological significance? A Seventh-Day Adventist's
objection to Saturday work is clearly religious. See Sherbert v. Verner.

Does *Seeger* require us to say that a mother's desire to spend Saturday with her children is also "religious"?

(c) A "family resemblance"?   Can we hold on to the idea that "religion" has substantive content, without requiring all religions to subscribe to certain creedal propositions (God, duty, worship, etc.)? Consider how it is with "games"— baseball, chess, solitaire, Monopoly. They don't all have things in common: not all require skill or athleticism, not all involve competition or amusement. Instead there is a kind of family resemblance, "a complicated network of similarities overlapping and criss-crossing." Ludwig Wittgenstein, Philosophical Investigations ¶66 (3d ed. 1958). Kent Greenawalt has suggested that it is like that with "religion." What, then, are the features that create the family resemblance? Greenawalt mentions the following:

> a belief in God; a comprehensive view of the world and human purposes; a belief in some form of afterlife; communication with God through ritual acts of worship and through corporate and individual prayer; a particular perspective on moral obligations derived from a moral code or from a conception of God's nature; practices involving repentance and forgiveness of sins; "religious" feelings of awe, guilt, and adoration; the use of sacred texts; an organization to facilitate the corporate aspects of religious practice and to promote and perpetuate beliefs and practices.

72 Calif. L. Rev. at 767-768. Are there others? How many of these must a practice exhibit to qualify as "religious"? Africa v. Pennsylvania, 662 F.2d 1025 (3d Cir. 1981). The Washington Ethical Society stresses spiritual values and inward peace; it holds Sunday services with singing and meditation; it uses "Leaders" to conduct services. Is it a religion? Washington Ethical Soc'y v. District of Columbia, 249 F.2d 127 (D.C. Cir. 1957). What about Alcoholics Anonymous? Paul Salamanca, The Role of Religion in Public Life and Official Pressure to Participate in Alcoholics Anonymous, 65 U. Cin. L. Rev. 1093 (1997). What about the Communist Party? The Ku Klux Klan?

WELSH v. UNITED STATES
398 U.S. 333 (1970)

Mr. Justice BLACK announced the judgment of the Court and delivered an opinion in which Mr. Justice DOUGLAS, Mr. Justice BRENNAN, and Mr. Justice MARSHALL join.

The petitioner, Elliott Ashton Welsh II, was convicted by a United States District Judge of refusing to submit to induction into the Armed Forces in violation of 50 U.S.C. App. § 462(a), and was on June 1, 1966, sentenced to imprisonment for three years. [The facts are similar, though not identical, to those in United States v. Seeger.[2]] In filling out their exemption applications both Seeger and Welsh were unable to sign the statement that, as printed in the

---

2. [Footnote in original:] An amendment to the [Universal Military Training and Service] Act in 1967, subsequent to the Court's decision in the *Seeger* case [and to Welsh's conviction], deleted the reference to a "Supreme Being" but continued to provide that "religious training and belief" does not include "essentially political, sociological, or philosophical views, or a merely personal moral code."

Selective Service form, stated "I am, by reason of my religious training and belief, conscientiously opposed to participation in war in any form." Seeger could sign only after striking the words "training and" and putting quotation marks around the word "religious." Welsh could sign only after striking the words "my religious training and." On those same applications, neither could definitely affirm or deny that he believed in a "Supreme Being," both stating that they preferred to leave the question open. But both Seeger and Welsh affirmed on those applications that they held deep conscientious scruples against taking part in wars where people were killed. Both strongly believed that killing in war was wrong, unethical, and immoral, and their consciences forbade them to take part in such an evil practice. [I]n both cases the Selective Service System concluded that the beliefs of these men were in some sense insufficiently "religious" to qualify them for conscientious objector exemptions under the terms of §6(j). Seeger's conscientious objector claim was denied "solely because it was not based upon a 'belief in a relation to a Supreme Being' as required by §6(j) of the Act," while Welsh was denied the exemption because his Appeal Board and the Department of Justice hearing officer "could find no religious basis for the registrant's beliefs, opinions and convictions." Both Seeger and Welsh subsequently refused to submit to induction into the military and both were convicted of that offense.

[The Government seeks to distinguish our holding in *Seeger* in two ways. First,] Welsh was far more insistent and explicit than Seeger in denying that his views were religious. For example, in filling out their conscientious objector applications, Seeger put quotation marks around the word "religious," but Welsh struck the word "religious" entirely and later characterized his beliefs as having been formed "by reading in the fields of history and sociology." [But] few registrants are fully aware of the broad scope of the word "religious" as used in §6(j), and accordingly a registrant's statement that his beliefs are nonreligious is a highly unreliable guide for those charged with administering the exemption. Welsh himself presents a case in point. Although he originally characterized his beliefs as nonreligious, he later upon reflection wrote a long and thoughtful letter to his Appeal Board in which he declared that his beliefs were "certainly religious in the ethical sense of the word." He explained:

> I believe I mentioned taking of life as not being, for me, a religious wrong. Again, I assumed Mr. [Brady (the Department of Justice hearing officer)] was using the word "religious" in the conventional sense, and, in order to be perfectly honest did not characterize my belief as "religious."

The Government also seeks to distinguish *Seeger* on the ground that Welsh's views, unlike Seeger's, were "essentially political, sociological, or philosophical views or a merely personal moral code." [But we] do not think that §6(j)'s exclusion of those persons with "essentially political, sociological, or philosophical views or a merely personal moral code" should be read to exclude those who hold strong beliefs about our domestic and foreign affairs or even those whose conscientious objection to participation in all wars is founded to a substantial extent upon considerations of public policy. The two groups of registrants that obviously do fall within these exclusions from the exemption are those whose beliefs are not deeply held and those whose objection to war does not rest at all upon moral, ethical, or religious principle but instead rests solely upon considerations of policy, pragmatism, or expediency. . . .

Welsh stated that he "believe[d] the taking of life—anyone's life—to be morally wrong." In his original conscientious objector application he wrote the following:

> I believe that human life is valuable in and of itself; in its living; therefore I will not injure or kill another human being. This belief (and the corresponding "duty" to abstain from violence toward another person) is not "superior to those arising from any human relation." On the contrary: it is essential to every human relation. I cannot, therefore, conscientiously comply with the Government's insistence that I assume duties which I feel are immoral and totally repugnant.

Welsh elaborated his beliefs in later communications with Selective Service officials. On the basis of these beliefs and the conclusion of the Court of Appeals that he held them "with the strength of more traditional religious convictions," we think Welsh was clearly entitled to a conscientious objector exemption. Section 6(j) requires no more. That section exempts from military service all those whose consciences, spurred by deeply held moral, ethical, or religious beliefs, would give them no rest or peace if they allowed themselves to become a part of an instrument of war.

Mr. Justice HARLAN, concurring in the result.

Candor requires me to say that I joined the Court's opinion in *Seeger* only with the gravest misgivings as to whether it was a legitimate exercise in statutory construction, and today's decision convinces me that in doing so I made a mistake which I should now acknowledge. [The] liberties taken with the statute both in *Seeger* and today's decision cannot be justified in the name of the familiar doctrine of construing federal statutes in a manner that will avoid possible constitutional infirmities in them. . . . I therefore find myself unable to escape facing the constitutional issue that this case squarely presents: whether § 6(j) in limiting this draft exemption to those opposed to war in general because of theistic beliefs runs afoul of the religious clauses of the First Amendment. . . .

[Congress could, if it wished], eliminate all exemptions for conscientious objectors. Such a course would be wholly "neutral" and, in my view, would not offend the Free Exercise Clause, for reasons set forth in my dissenting opinion in Sherbert v. Verner. However, having chosen to exempt, it cannot draw the line between theistic or non-theistic religious beliefs on the one hand and secular beliefs on the other. [This violates the corresponding principle of neutrality found in the Establishment Clause. If the exemption is to be given application, it must encompass the entire] class of individuals it purports to exclude, those whose beliefs emanate from a purely moral, ethical, or philosophical source.[9] The common denominator must be the intensity of moral conviction with which a belief is held. Common experience teaches that among "religious" individuals

9. [Despite what we held in Sherbert v. Verner, I do not believe that the Free Exercise Clause requires a State to conform a neutral secular program to the dictates of religious conscience of any group. A State may constitutionally create exceptions to its program to accommodate religious scruples. But any such exception,] in order to satisfy the Establishment Clause of the First Amendment, would have to be sufficiently broad to be religiously neutral. This would require creating an exception for anyone who, as a matter of conscience, could not comply with the statute. Whether, under a statute like that involved in *Sherbert*, it would be possible to demonstrate a basis in conscience for not working Saturday is quite another matter.

some are weak and others strong adherents to tenets and this is no less true of individuals whose lives are guided by personal ethical considerations. . . .

[The] authorities assembled by the Government, far from advancing its case, demonstrate the unconstitutionality of the distinction drawn in § 6(j) between religious and nonreligious beliefs. Everson v. Board of Education; the Sunday Closing Law Cases [i.e., McGowan v. Maryland]; and Board of Education v. Allen all sustained legislation on the premise that it was neutral in its application and thus did not constitute an establishment, notwithstanding the fact that it may have assisted religious groups by giving them the same benefits accorded to nonreligious groups. To the extent that Zorach v. Clauson [p. 239] and Sherbert v. Verner stand for the proposition that the Government may (*Zorach*), or must (*Sherbert*), shape its secular programs to accommodate the beliefs and tenets of religious groups, I think these cases unsound. . . .

[I] am prepared to accept the prevailing opinion's conscientious objector test, not as a reflection of congressional statutory intent but as patchwork of judicial making that cures the defect of under-inclusion in § 6(j) and can be administered by local boards in the usual course of business. Like the prevailing opinion, I also conclude that petitioner's beliefs are held with the required intensity and consequently vote to reverse the judgment of conviction.

Mr. Justice WHITE, with whom THE CHIEF JUSTICE and Mr. Justice STEWART join, dissenting.

[I largely agree with Justice Harlan on the question of statutory interpretation. But I disagree with his further conclusion that Congress violated the Establishment] Clause in exempting from the draft all those who oppose war by reason of religious training and belief. . . . If there were no statutory exemption for religious objectors to war and failure to provide it was held by this Court to impair the free exercise of religion contrary to the First Amendment, an exemption reflecting this constitutional command would be no more an establishment of religion than the exemption required for Sabbatarians in Sherbert v. Verner, or the exemption from the flat tax on book sellers held required for evangelists, Follett v. McCormick (1944). Surely a statutory exemption for religionists required by the Free Exercise Clause is not an invalid establishment because it fails to include nonreligious believers as well; nor would it be any less an establishment if camouflaged by granting additional exemptions for nonreligious, but "moral" objectors to war.

On the assumption, however, that the Free Exercise Clause of the First Amendment does not by its own force require exempting devout objectors from military service, it does not follow that § 6(j) is a law respecting an establishment of religion within the meaning of the First Amendment. It is very likely that § 6(j) is a recognition by Congress of free exercise values and its view of desirable or required policy in implementing the Free Exercise Clause. That judgment is entitled to respect. Congress has the power "To raise and support Armies" and "To make all Laws which shall be necessary and proper for carrying into Execution" that power. Art. I, § 8. The power to raise armies must be exercised consistently with the First Amendment which, among other things, forbids laws prohibiting the free exercise of religion. It is surely essential therefore—surely "necessary and proper"—in enacting laws for the raising of armies to take account of the First Amendment and to avoid possible violations of the Free Exercise Clause. . . .

We have said that neither support nor hostility, but neutrality, is the goal of the religion clauses of the First Amendment. "Neutrality," however, is not self-defining. If it is "favoritism" and not "neutrality" to exempt religious believers from the draft, is it "neutrality" and not "inhibition" of religion to compel religious believers to fight when they have special reasons for not doing so, reasons to which the Constitution gives particular recognition? It cannot be ignored that the First Amendment itself contains a religious classification. The Amendment protects belief and speech, but as a general proposition, the free speech provisions stop short of immunizing conduct from official regulation. The Free Exercise Clause, however, has a deeper cut: it protects conduct as well as religious belief and speech. . . . We should thus not labor to find a violation of the Establishment Clause when free exercise values prompt Congress to relieve religious believers from the burdens of the law at least in those instances where the law is not merely prohibitory but commands the performance of military duties that are forbidden by a man's religion.

NOTES AND QUESTIONS

1. **The Scope of *Welsh*.** What does *Welsh* stand for? The plurality opinion does not try, as *Seeger* did, to show that the petitioner believed in a "Supreme Being." It does argue that Welsh's beliefs were "religious"—notwithstanding his own disavowal of that term. Is this interpretation of "religious" consistent with § 6(j)? The plurality concludes its opinion by saying that anyone with "deeply held moral, ethical, or religious beliefs" against war is entitled to an exemption. Section 6(j) says it does not allow exemptions on the basis of "a merely personal moral code." Is Justice Black driven to this position by the First Amendment? Does he think it would be unconstitutional to say that a religion must include a belief in a Supreme Being? Is this the holding of the Court?

Had the Court *already* made that decision in Torcaso v. Watkins (p. 473)? At the end of his opinion for the Court in *Torcaso*, Justice Black said that "neither a State nor the Federal Government . . . can aid those religions based on a belief in the existence of God as against those religions founded on different beliefs." And in the accompanying footnote 11 he observed, "Among religions in this country that do not teach what would generally be considered a belief in the existence of God are Buddhism, Taoism, Ethical Culture, Secular Humanism, and others." Were these observations essential to the decision in *Torcaso*?

Justice Harlan concurs in rewriting the statute as a form of constitutional relief. He maintains that religion is a proper ground for exemption only when it is subsumed in a larger class whose defining trait can be stated in secular terms. A proper exemption here might include all people with intense moral objections to war. Whether exemptions must be this broad is a subject we have dealt with in Section III-C. Has the Court approved narrower ones? Does it matter that other people must be drafted to fill in for conscientious objectors? Does a requirement of alternative service cure this problem?

2. **The Effect of Wisconsin v. Yoder.** Two years after *Welsh* the Court held in Wisconsin v. Yoder (p. 133) that Amish children were entitled to an exemption from compulsory school attendance laws after eighth grade. But the Court

VI. What Is "Religion"?

emphasized that this was a "religious" exemption, and not everyone could qualify for it (406 U.S. at 215-216):

> A way of life, however virtuous and admirable, may not be interposed as a barrier to reasonable state regulation of education if it is based on purely secular consider-ations. . . . Thus, if the Amish asserted their claims because of their subjective evaluation and rejection of the contemporary secular values accepted by the major-ity, much as Thoreau rejected the social values of his time and isolated himself at Walden Pond, their claims would not rest on a religious basis. Thoreau's choice was philosophical and personal rather than religious, and such belief does not rise to the demands of the Religion Clauses.

Was Thoreau actually different from the Amish? Here is what he said about his decision to live at Walden Pond:

> I went to the woods because I wished to live deliberately, to front only the essential facts of life, and see if I could not learn what it had to teach, and not, when I came to die, discover that I had not lived. . . . I wanted to live deep and suck out all the marrow of life, . . . to drive life into a corner, and reduce it to its lowest terms. . . . For most men, it appears to me, are in a strange uncertainty about it, whether it is of the devil or of God, and have *somewhat hastily* concluded that it is the chief end of man here to "glorify God and enjoy him forever."

Henry David Thoreau, Walden 83-84 (Oxford ed. 1997) (emphasis in original). Is there a difference between looking for an answer to a religious question, as Thoreau might have been doing, and living out a religious answer, as the Yoders were doing? Is Thoreau different from Welsh? Were his beliefs "deeply held"? Did they rest on "moral, ethical, or religious" principles?

3. Selective Conscientious Objection. Section 6(j) provided an exemption to "persons who by reason of their religious training and belief are conscien-tiously opposed *to participation in war in any form*" (emphasis added). In Gillette v. United States, 401 U.S. 437 (1971), the Court held that it did not relieve people who objected to a particular war, rather than to war in general. One of the petitioners in *Gillette* (Negre) was a devout Catholic who discriminated, in accordance with Catholic teaching, between "just" and "unjust" wars. He claimed that it was a violation of the Establishment Clause to favor some kinds of religious objections over others—objectors to all wars versus objectors to "unjust" wars. Is this distinction (based on the content of a religious creed) different from the one that bothered the Court in *Seeger* and *Welsh*? Is it dif-ferent from the complaint that Emma Goldman and Alexander Berkman raised about the 1917 version of the exemption, which excused only those who belonged to a "well-recognized [pacifist] religious sect or organization"? Is there a government interest sufficiently compelling to justify such a distinc-tion? For an extensive review of the background of the selective conscientious-objection issue, see Charles J. Reid, Jr., John T. Noonan, Jr., on the Catholic Conscience and War: *Negre v. Larsen*, 76 Notre Dame L. Rev. 881 (2001).

4. A Taffy Pull. There is an ongoing debate among free speech experts about whether it is possible to extend the coverage of the Free Speech Clause *too* far. Some say we may suffer a net loss of freedom when we extend the con-cept of "speech" to commercial advertising, pornography, and video games.

Consider the observations of Vincent Blasi, The Pathological Perspective and the First Amendment, 85 Colum. L. Rev. 449, 479 (1985):

> In pathological periods, courts need to present the forces of repression with strict, immutable legal constraints. That kind of implacable judicial posture is easier to assume when the basic reach of the first amendment is modest and compatible with widely shared intuitions regarding the natural ambit of the commitment to expressive liberty.

There may be, in other words, a kind of inverse relation between coverage and protection. They are like taffy: the wider we stretch the meaning of "speech," the thinner the barrier between us and the government. See also Frederick Schauer, Free Speech: A Philosophical Enquiry 134-135 (1982).

Seeger and *Welsh* stretch the meaning of "religion" past the boundaries we have long been accustomed to. The Court was driven, in part, by a desire to expand the domain of religious freedom. Did it succeed? Twenty years after *Welsh* the Court greatly thinned out the protection afforded by the Free Exercise Clause. Compare Employment Division v. Smith with Sherbert v. Verner. Is there a connection between these two lines of decisions? The defenders of strict scrutiny in *Smith* suggested that the Court should reserve it for laws affecting conduct "central" to a person's religion. Justice Scalia said that it was improper for courts to make such decisions about coverage. See p. 137 above.

B. DEFINING RELIGION IN OTHER CONTEXTS

Seeger and the plurality in *Welsh* gave the term "religion" a meaning so broad that it could embrace any kind of deeply held conscientious conviction. It is not hard to understand the impetus for this approach. In the late 1960s the United States was embroiled in the Vietnam War, a very unpopular conflict opposed by many people of good sense and good will. And the issue at stake for would-be conscientious objectors was of the utmost gravity—killing other human beings. It would not be surprising if, under these circumstances, judges reached for an interpretation that offered the maximum degree of protection.

Suppose we transpose this reading to other contexts. Would it work as well for tax exemptions as for draft exemptions? What effect would it have on the curriculum of public schools, where the government may not teach religion? Would it be unconstitutional to teach any doctrine that people hold with deep conscientious conviction? What about the rule that forbids financial aid to religion? Would the establishment clause forbid the government to fund any kind of "ultimate concern?" Consider the next case.

SMITH v. BOARD OF SCHOOL COMMISSIONERS
827 F.2d 684 (11th Cir. 1987)

JOHNSON, Circuit Judge:
[This case was a continuation of Wallace v. Jaffree (p. 496), which held unconstitutional Alabama's moment-of-silence law. Smith and others (Appellees)

intervened in that action to request that the injunction against religious activity be extended to "the religions of secularism, humanism, evolution, materialism, agnosticism, atheism and others." The district court agreed. It found that use of 44 textbooks violated the Establishment Clause of the First Amendment, and enjoined their use in the Alabama public schools. This appeal followed.]

The Supreme Court has never established a comprehensive test for determining the "delicate question" of what constitutes a religious belief for purposes of the first amendment, and we need not attempt to do so in this case, for we find that, even assuming that secular humanism is a religion for purposes of the establishment clause, Appellees have failed to prove a violation of the establishment clause through the use in the Alabama public schools of the textbooks at issue in this case.

The religion clauses of the first amendment require that states "pursue a course of complete neutrality toward religion." Wallace v. Jaffree. [The court set forth the three criteria of Lemon v. Kurtzman.]

The parties agree that there is no question of a religious purpose or excessive government entanglement in this case and our review of the record confirms that conclusion. Our inquiry, therefore, must center on the second *Lemon* criterion: whether use of the challenged textbooks had the primary effect of either advancing or inhibiting religion. . . .

The district court found that the home economics, history, and social studies textbooks both advanced secular humanism and inhibited theistic religion. Our review of the record in this case reveals that these conclusions were in error. As discussed below, use of the challenged textbooks has the primary effect of conveying information that is essentially neutral in its religious content to the school children who utilize the books; none of these books convey a message of governmental approval of secular humanism or governmental disapproval of theism.

A. HOME ECONOMICS TEXTBOOKS

The district court found that the home economics textbooks required students to accept as true certain tenets of humanistic psychology, which the district court found to be "a manifestation of humanism." In particular, the district court found that the books "imply strongly that a person uses the same process in deciding a moral issue that he uses in choosing one pair of shoes over another," and teach that "the student must determine right and wrong based only on his own experience, feelings and [internal] values" and that "the validity of a moral choice is only to be decided by the student." The district court stated that "[t]he emphasis and overall approach implies, and would cause any reasonable thinking student to infer, that the book is teaching that moral choices are just a matter of preferences, because, as the books say, 'you are the most important person in your life.' " The district court stated that "[t]his highly relativistic and individualistic approach constitutes the promotion of a fundamental faith claim" that "assumes that self-actualization is the goal of every human being, that man has no supernatural attributes or component, that there are only temporal and physical consequences for man's actions, and that these results, alone, determine the morality of an action." . . . It concluded that, while the state may teach certain moral values, such as that lying is wrong, "if, in so doing it advances a reason for the rule, the possible different reasons must be explained evenhandedly" and "the state may not promote one particular reason over another in the public schools."

In order to violate the primary effect prong of the *Lemon* test through advancement of religion, it is not sufficient that the government action merely accommodates religion. . . . Nor is it sufficient that government conduct confers an indirect, remote or incidental benefit on a religion, or that its effect merely happens to coincide or harmonize with the tenets of a religion:

> [T]he Establishment Clause does not ban federal or state regulation of conduct whose reason or effect merely happens to coincide or harmonize with the tenets of some or all religions. In many instances, the Congress or state legislatures conclude that the general welfare of society, wholly apart from any religious considerations, demands such regulation. Thus, for temporal purposes, murder is illegal. And the fact that this agrees with the dictates of the Judaeo-Christian religions while it may disagree with others does not invalidate the regulation. So too with the questions of adultery and polygamy. The same could be said of theft, fraud, etc., because those offenses were also proscribed in the Decalogue.

McGowan v. Maryland. In order for government conduct to constitute an impermissible advancement of religion, the government action must amount to an endorsement of religion.

Examination of the contents of these textbooks, including the passages pointed out by Appellees as particularly offensive, in the context of the books as a whole and the undisputedly nonreligious purpose sought to be achieved by their use, reveals that the message conveyed is not one of endorsement of secular humanism or any religion. Rather, the message conveyed is one of a governmental attempt to instill in Alabama public school children such values as independent thought, tolerance of diverse views, self-respect, maturity, self-reliance and logical decision-making. This is an entirely appropriate secular effect. Indeed, one of the major objectives of public education is the "inculcat[ion of] fundamental values necessary to the maintenance of a democratic political system." Ambach v. Norwick (1979). It is true that the textbooks contain ideas that are consistent with secular humanism; the textbooks also contain ideas consistent with theistic religion. However, as discussed above, mere consistency with religious tenets is insufficient to constitute unconstitutional advancement of religion.

Nor do these textbooks evidence an attitude antagonistic to theistic belief. The message conveyed by these textbooks with regard to theistic religion is one of neutrality: the textbooks neither endorse theistic religion as a system of belief, nor discredit it. Indeed, many of the books specifically acknowledge that religion is one source of moral values and none preclude that possibility. While the Supreme Court has recognized that "the State may not establish a 'religion of secularism' in the sense of affirmatively opposing or showing hostility to religion, thus 'preferring those who believe in no religion over those who do believe,'" Abington School Dist. v. Schempp, that Court also has made it clear that the neutrality mandated by the establishment clause does not itself equate with hostility towards religion. Rather, the separation of church and state mandated by the first amendment "rests upon the premise that both religion and government can best work to achieve their lofty aims if each is left free from the other within its respective sphere." . . .

B. HISTORY AND SOCIAL STUDIES TEXTBOOKS

The district court's conclusion that the history and social studies textbooks violated the establishment clause was based on its finding that these books failed to include a sufficient discussion of the role of religion in history and culture. . . . Use of the social studies books was found unconstitutional because the books failed to integrate religion into the history of American society, ignored the importance of theistic religion as an influence in American society and contained "factual inaccuracies . . . so grave as to rise to a constitutional violation."

. . . We do not believe that an objective observer could conclude from the mere omission of certain historical facts regarding religion or the absence of a more thorough discussion of its place in modern American society that the State of Alabama was conveying a message of approval of the religion of secular humanism. [N]or can we agree with the district court's conclusion that the omission of these facts causes the books to "discriminate against the very concept of religion." Just as use of these books does not convey a message of governmental approval of secular humanism, neither does it convey a message of government disapproval of theistic religions merely by omitting certain historical facts concerning them.

The district court's reliance on Epperson v. Arkansas [p. 548] to support its conclusion that omission of certain material regarding religion in this case constituted a first amendment violation is misplaced. *Epperson* involved an Arkansas statute that made it a crime to teach the theory of evolution in the public schools. The Supreme Court found that the law violated the establishment clause under the purpose prong of the *Lemon* test: the state forbade the teaching of evolution because it conflicted with a particular religious doctrine. The Court stated that "the First Amendment does not permit the State to require that teaching and learning must be tailored to the principles or prohibitions of any religious sect or dogma." Thus, "[t]he State's undoubted right to prescribe the curriculum for its public schools does not carry with it the right to prohibit, on pain of criminal penalty, the teaching of a scientific theory or doctrine where that prohibition is based upon reasons that violate the First Amendment."

There is no question in this case that the purpose behind using these particular history and social studies books was purely secular. Selecting a textbook that omits a particular topic for nonreligious reasons is significantly different from requiring the omission of material because it conflicts with a particular religious belief. . . . There simply is nothing in this record to indicate that omission of certain facts regarding religion from these textbooks of itself constituted an advancement of secular humanism or an active hostility towards theistic religion prohibited by the establishment clause.

[I]mplicit in the district court's opinion is the assumption that what the establishment clause actually requires is "equal time" for religion. Thus, the district court states that, while the state may teach certain moral values, it cannot advance any reason for those values unless "the possible different reasons [are] explained evenhandedly," and finds that history may not be taught constitutionally in the schools unless the textbooks contain more references to the place of religion in history.

"Separation is a requirement to abstain from fusing functions of Government and religious sects, not merely to treat them all equally." McCollum v. Board of Education (1948) (Frankfurter, J., concurring). The public schools in this country are organized

> on the premise that secular education can be isolated from all religious teaching so that the school can inculcate all needed temporal knowledge and also maintain a strict and lofty neutrality as to religion. The assumption is that after the individual has been instructed in worldly wisdom he will be better fitted to choose his religion.

Everson v. Bd. of Education (Jackson, J., dissenting). The district court's opinion in effect turns the establishment clause requirement of "lofty neutrality" on the part of the public schools into an affirmative obligation to speak about religion. Such a result clearly is inconsistent with the requirements of the establishment clause.

The judgment of the district court is reversed and the case is remanded for the sole purpose of entry by the district court of an order dissolving the injunction and terminating this litigation.

NOTE AND QUESTIONS

What Is a Religion?   At first blush it seems odd for the plaintiff to claim (and the court to provisionally accept) that secular humanism is a religion. Ordinary English speakers would call it a rejection of religion—a belief that we can get along fine without a God. Justice Clark said in Abington School Dist. v. Schempp (p. 486) that "the State may not establish a 'religion of secularism' in the sense of affirmatively opposing or showing hostility to religion." But was he just speaking metaphorically? He surely did not mean that the government establishes a religion whenever it opposes a particular religious claim. That would be a very thin notion of religion. What more would we need to fill it out?

One difference that may occur to you between secular humanists and Methodists, say, is that Methodists are organized as a group, into congregations and conferences, whereas secular humanist seems more like a personality type. But there actually is a group called the American Humanist Association (AHA). It publishes a magazine called *The Humanist*. Paul Kurtz, one of its members and the author of the Humanist Manifesto II (1973), testified at the *Smith* trial that the AHA's membership was of two minds about whether their system of belief was a religion. What would make it one? Is it enough that the group opposes a particular religious claim? Is the National Abortion Rights Action League a religion? The National Association of Biology Teachers? Maybe a group has to hold views on a certain range of subjects, or engage in certain rituals, in order to qualify. The AHA does hold views on many of the subjects that traditional religions address: the existence of God, the origin of life, the finality of death, the source of moral authority, the understanding of human nature.

See Mary Harter Mitchell, Secularism in Public Education: The Constitutional Issues, 67 B.U. L. Rev. 603, 622-627 (1987). But its views are designed to refute the claims of traditional religion. Does this disqualify it from First Amendment protection? Consider the observation in footnote 11 of Torcaso v. Watkins: "Among religions in this country which do not teach what would generally be considered a belief in the existence of God are Buddhism, Taoism, Ethical Culture, Secular Humanism and others[.]"

What is the difference between Elliot Ashton Welsh II's theology and the perspective taken in these textbooks? If secular humanism (whatever that means) is religion enough to warrant draft exemption, why isn't it religion enough to create problems when it is espoused in textbooks in public school?

MALNAK v. YOGI
592 F.2d 197 (3d Cir. 1979)

PER CURIAM.

This appeal requires us to decide whether the district court erred in determining that the teaching of a course called the Science of Creative Intelligence Transcendental Meditation (SCI/TM) in the New Jersey public high schools, under the circumstances presented in the record, constituted an establishment of religion in violation of the first amendment of the United States Constitution.... The course under examination here was offered as an elective at five high schools during the 1975-76 academic year and was taught four or five days a week by teachers specially trained by the World Plan Executive Council United States, an organization whose objective is to disseminate the teachings of SCI/TM throughout the United States. The textbook used was developed by Maharishi Mahesh Yogi, the founder of the Science of Creative Intelligence. It teaches that "pure creative intelligence" is the basis of life, and that through the process of Transcendental Meditation students can perceive the full potential of their lives.

Essential to the practice of Transcendental Meditation is the "mantra"; a mantra is the sound aid used while meditating. Each mediator has his own personal mantra which is never to be revealed to any other person. It is by concentrating on the mantra that one receives the beneficial effects said to result from Transcendental Meditation.

To acquire his mantra, a meditator must attend a ceremony called a "puja." Every student who participated in the SCI/TM course was required to attend a puja as part of the course. A puja was performed by the teacher for each student individually; it was conducted off school premises on a Sunday; and the student was required to bring some fruit, flowers and a white handkerchief. During the puja the student stood or sat in front of a table while the teacher sang a chant and made offerings to a deified "Guru Dev." Each puja lasted between one and two hours.

The district court found, [and we agree,] that the SCI/TM course has a primary effect of advancing religion and religious concepts, and that the government aid given to teach the course and the use of public school facilities constituted excessive governmental entanglement with religion. Lemon v. Kurtzman. ...

ADAMS, Circuit Judge, concurring in the result. . . .

[You might suppose that we could easily dispose of this case on the authority of Engel v. Vitale and Abington School Dist. v. Schempp. Not so. In those cases] the State, through the edict of a state agency or by statute, [sought] to require that school districts engage in a particular form of obviously religious activity. Such religious partisanship, even though nonsectarian, is forbidden by the establishment clause. . . .

In contrast, appellants here unwaveringly insist that the Puja chant has no religious meaning whatsoever and is, in fact, a "secular Puja," quite common in Eastern cultures. [Students who chose to take the courses] were specifically told that the chant had no religious meaning; and they stated in affidavits that they did not understand it to have such meaning.

[Neither *Engel* nor *Schempp* provides much insight into] the constitutional definition of religion. Both the prayer in *Engel* and the Bible readings in *Schempp* are unquestionably and uncompromisingly Theist. Even under the most narrow and traditional definition of religion, prayers to a Supreme Being and readings from the Bible would be considered "religious." But the important question presented by the present litigation is how far the constitutional definition of religion extends beyond the Theistic formulation[.]

THE MODERN DEFINITION OF RELIGION

The original definition of religion prevalent in this country was closely tied to a belief in God. James Madison called religion "the duty which we owe to our creator, and the manner of discharging it." [Memorial and Remonstrance (p. 49). This] was the position of the Supreme Court at the end of the nineteenth century. [Davis v. Beason. The] traditional definition was grounded upon a Theistic perception of religion. It is not clear, however, given the absence of any concentration in SCI/TM on a "Supreme Being," that it may be considered a religion under this traditional formulation.*

. . . Under the modern view, "religion" is not confined to the relationship of man with his Creator, either as a matter of law or as a matter of theology. Even theologians of traditionally recognized faiths have moved away from a strictly Theistic approach in explaining their own religions. Such movement, when coupled with the growth in the United States, of many Eastern and non-traditional belief systems, suggests that the older, limited definition would deny "religious" identification to faiths now adhered to by millions of Americans. The Court's more recent cases reject such a result.

[United States v. Seeger held that] beliefs holding the same important position for members of one of the new religions as the traditional faith holds for more orthodox believers are entitled to the same treatment as the traditional beliefs. [But it is one thing to conclude] that a particular group or cluster of ideas is religious; it is quite another to explain exactly what indicia are to be looked to in making such an analogy and justifying it. There appear to be three useful indicia that are basic to our traditional religions and that are themselves related to the values that undergird the first amendment.

---

* [Relocated text—EDS.]

The first and most important of these indicia is the nature of the ideas in question. This means that a court must, at least to a degree, examine the content of the supposed religion, not to determine its truth or falsity, or whether it is schismatic or orthodox, but to determine whether the subject matter it comprehends is consistent with the assertion that it is, or is not, a religion. [O]ne of the conscientious objectors whose appeal was coupled with *Seeger* submitted a long memorandum, noted by the Court, in which he defined religion as the "sum and essence of one's basic attitudes to the fundamental problems of human existence." [And the Court itself in *Seeger* quoted the Protestant theologian Dr. Paul Tillich, who expressed his view on the essence of religion in the phrase "ultimate concern."] Nor is it difficult to see why this philosophy would prove attractive in the American constitutional framework. One's views, be they orthodox or novel, on the deeper and more imponderable questions—the meaning of life and death, man's role in the Universe, the proper moral code of right and wrong—are those likely to be the most "intensely personal" and important to the believer. They are his ultimate concerns. As such, they are to be carefully guarded from governmental interference, and never converted into official government doctrine. The first amendment demonstrates a specific solicitude for religion because religious ideas are in many ways more important than other ideas. New and different ways of meeting those concerns are entitled to the same sort of treatment as the traditional forms.

Thus, the "ultimate" nature of the ideas presented is the most important and convincing evidence that they should be treated as religious.[40] Certain isolated answers to "ultimate" questions, however, are not necessarily "religious" answers, because they lack the element of comprehensiveness, the second of the three indicia. A religion is not generally confined to one question or one moral teaching; it has a broader scope. It lays claim to an ultimate and comprehensive "truth." Thus the so-called "Big Bang" theory, an astronomical interpretation of the creation of the universe, may be said to answer an "ultimate" question, but it is not, by itself, a "religious" idea. Likewise, moral or patriotic views are not by themselves "religious," but if they are pressed as divine law or a part of a comprehensive belief-system that presents them as "truth," they might well rise to the religious level.

The component of comprehensiveness is particularly relevant in the context of state education. A science course may touch on many ultimate concerns, but it is unlikely to proffer a systematic series of answers to them that might begin to resemble a religion[.]

A third element to consider in ascertaining whether a set of ideas should be classified as a religion is any formal, external, or surface signs that may be analogized to accepted religions. Such signs might include formal services, ceremonial functions, the existence of clergy, structure and organization, efforts at propagation, observation of holidays and other similar manifestations

---

40. It should not be reasoned from this that those teachings of accepted religious groups that do not address "ultimate" matters are not entitled to religious status. Many religions are sufficiently comprehensive to include rules or views on very ordinary matters such as diet, periods for rest, and dress. These are not themselves "ultimate concerns," but they are intimately connected to a religion that does address such concerns. Once a belief-system has been credited as a "religion" through an examination of its "ultimate" nature, its teachings on other matters must also be accepted as religious.

associated with the traditional religions. Of course, a religion may exist without any of these signs, so they are not determinative, at least by their absence, in resolving a question of definition. But they can be helpful in supporting a conclusion of religious status given the important role such ceremonies play in religious life.[45] . . .

A Unitary Definition for Both Religion Clauses

[Some scholars argue that] the broader definition of religion developed in the free exercise cases should be applied under the establishment clause. Professor Tribe of Harvard has advanced the argument that the free exercise clause should be read broadly to include anything "arguably religious," but that the establishment clause should not be construed to encompass anything "arguably non-religious"[:]

> Clearly, the notion of religion in the free exercise clause must be expanded beyond the closely bounded limits of theism to account for the multiplying forms of recognizably legitimate religious exercise. It is equally clear, however, that in the age of the affirmative and increasingly pervasive state, a less expansive notion of religion was required for establishment clause purposes lest all "humane" programs of government be deemed constitutionally suspect. Such a twofold definition of religion—expansive for the free exercise clause, less so for the establishment clause—may be necessary to avoid confronting the state with increasingly difficult choices that the theory of permissible accommodation . . . could not indefinitely resolve.

[Laurence H. Tribe, American Constitutional Law (1978).]

Despite the distinguished scholars who advocate this approach, a stronger argument can be made for a unitary definition to prevail for both clauses. This would seem to be the preferable choice for several reasons. First, it is virtually required by the language of the first amendment. As Justice Rutledge put it over thirty years ago:

> "Religion" appears only once in the Amendment. But the word governs two prohibitions and governs them alike. It does not have two meanings, one narrow to forbid "an establishment" and another, much broader, for securing "the free exercise thereof." "Thereof" brings down "religion" with its entire and exact content, no more and no less, from the first into the second guaranty, so that Congress and now the states are as broadly restricted concerning the one as they are regarding the other.

[*Everson* (Rutledge, J., dissenting).] Moreover, the policy reasons put forward by the supporters of a dual definition, in my view at least, are unpersuasive.

The advocates of a dual definition appear to be motivated primarily by an anxiety that too extensive a definition under the establishment clause will lead to "wholesale invalidation" of government programs. Behind this fear lurks,

---

45. Appellants have urged that they do not consider SCI/TM to be a religion. But the question of the definition of religion for first amendment purposes is one for the courts, and is not controlled by the subjective perceptions of believers. Supporters of new belief systems may not "choose" to be non-religious, particularly in the establishment clause context. . . . [Relocated footnote—Eds.]

I believe, too broad a reading of the teachings of *Seeger, Welsh,* and Torcaso [v. Watkins.] The selective service case did not hold that Seeger, Welsh and the other conscientious objectors were advancing views sufficient to qualify as a religion or religions, only that their views were based on religious belief. Were a school, or government agency, to advance the cause of peace, or opposition to war, such an official position would not qualify as a "religion" even though some citizens might come to adopt that very view because of their own religious beliefs. All programs or positions that entangle the government with issues and problems that might be classified as "ultimate concerns" do not, because of that, become "religious" programs or positions. Only if the government favors a comprehensive belief system and advances its teachings does it establish a religion. It does not do so by endorsing isolated moral precepts or by enacting humanitarian economic programs.

In this regard it should be noted that the modern definition of religion does not extend so far as to include those who hold beliefs—however passionately— regarding the utility of Keynesian economics, Social Democracy or, for that matter, Sociobiology. These ideas may in some instances touch on "ultimate concerns," but they are less analogous to religious views than they are to the political or sociological ideas that they are. Thus *Torcaso* does not stand for the proposition that "humanism" is a religion, although an organized group of "Secular Humanists" may be. An undefined belief in humanitarianism, or good intentions, is still far removed from a comprehensive belief system laying a claim to ultimate truth and supported by a formal group with religious trappings.

Moreover, the establishment clause does not forbid government activity encouraged by the supporters of even the most orthodox of religions if that activity is itself not unconstitutional. The Biblical and clerical endorsement of laws against stealing and murder do not make such laws establishments of religion. Similarly, agitation for social welfare programs by progressive churchmen, even if motivated by the most orthodox of theological reasons, does not make those programs religious. The Constitution has not been interpreted to forbid those inspired by religious principle or conscience from participation in this nation's political, social and economic life.

Finally, in addition to these doubts whether "doctrinal chaos" would in fact result from resort to the new definition in the establishment clause context, the practical result of a dual definition is itself troubling. Such an approach would create a three-tiered system of ideas: those that are unquestionably religious and thus both free from government interference and barred from receiving government support; those that are unquestionably non-religious and thus subject to government regulation and eligible to receive government support; and those that are only religious under the newer approach and thus free from governmental regulation but open to receipt of government support. That belief systems classified in the third grouping are the most advantageously positioned is obvious. No reason has been advanced, however, for favoring the newer belief systems over the older ones. If a Roman Catholic is barred from receiving aid from the government, so too should be a Transcendental Meditator or a Scientologist if those two are to enjoy the preferred position guaranteed to them by the free exercise clause. . . .

For these reasons, then, I think it is correct to read religion broadly in both clauses and agree that the precedents developed in the free exercise context are properly relied upon here. Having reached this conclusion, two final questions remain: Does SCI/TM qualify as a religion under the criteria discussed above and, if it does, does the teaching and funding of this course constitute an establishment of that religion.

[APPLYING THESE PRINCIPLES TO THIS CASE]

Although Transcendental Meditation by itself might be defended—as appellants sought to do in this appeal—as primarily a relaxation or concentration technique with no "ultimate" significance, the New Jersey course at issue here was not a course in TM alone, but a course in the Science of Creative Intelligence. Creative Intelligence, according to the textbook in the record, is "at the basis of all growth and progress" and is, indeed, "the basis of everything." Transcendental Meditation is presented as a means for contacting this "impelling life force" so as to achieve "inner contentment." Creative Intelligence can provide such "contentment" because it is "a field of unlimited happiness," which is at work everywhere and visible in such diverse places as in "the changing of the seasons" and "the wings of a butterfly." That the existence of such a pervasive and fundamental life force is a matter of "ultimate concern" can hardly be questioned. It is put forth as the foundation of life and the world itself.

[Although SCI/TM] is not as comprehensive as some religions—for example, it does not appear to include a complete or absolute moral code—it is nonetheless sufficiently comprehensive to avoid the suggestion of an isolated theory unconnected with any particular world view or basic belief system. SCI/TM provides a way—indeed in the eyes of its adherents *the way*—to full self realization and oneness with the underlying reality of the universe. Consequently, it can reasonably be understood as presenting a claim of ultimate "truth."

This conclusion is supported by the formal observances and structure of SCI/TM Although there is no evidence in the record of organized clergy or traditional rites, such as marriage, burial or the like, there are trained teachers and an organization devoted to the propagation of the faith. And there is a ceremony, the Puja, that is intimately associated with the transmission of the mantra. . . .

Like the majority, I am convinced that the conclusion that SCI/TM is a religion is largely determinative of this appeal. There is nothing per se unconstitutional about offering [an objective] course in religion or religious writings. [But a] careful review of the transcript, and the content of the course, reveals nothing other than an effort to propagate TM, SCI, and the views of Maharishi Mahesh Yogi.

NOTES AND QUESTIONS

1. "Creator" Versus "God"?   The premise of Judge Adams's concurrence—and of *Seeger*, and most modern attempts to define "religion" legally—is that the concept of God or a deity is too narrow to encompass the increasingly wide range of views that Americans hold on spiritual matters. The language of the 1776 Virginia Declaration of Rights—religion is "the duty that we owe to our creator, and the manner of discharging it"—was intended to be more expansive than the God of the Bible, reflecting in part the deist ideas influential among many leading Virginians (Jefferson and, to a lesser extent, Madison). Is the Virginia definition serviceable today? Does it exclude anything that should count as "religious"? Does it include anything that should not count?

2. The Three-Part Definition.   Judge Adams in *Malnak* proposes a different way to expand the definition beyond traditional theism. His three-part test became a holding in Africa v. Pennsylvania, 662 F.2d 1025, 1032 (3d Cir. 1982) (Adams, J.): "First, a religion addresses fundamental and ultimate questions having to do with deep and imponderable matters. Second, a religion is comprehensive in nature; it consists of a belief-system as opposed to an isolated teaching. Third, a religion can often be recognized by the presence of certain formal and external signs."

(a) Ultimate concern.   The first factor is a concern with ultimate or fundamental problems—"the meaning of life and death, man's role in the universe, the proper moral code of right and wrong." Judge Adams implies that ultimate concerns deal with certain subjects. Is this consistent with *Seeger*? With the First Amendment rule against content-based distinctions (p. 599)? Isn't the very question "What matters are of ultimate concern?" committed to individual conscience under the First Amendment?

Transcendental meditation got a boost from the Beatles, who followed the Maharishi Mahesh Yogi to a weekend seminar in Wales in 1967, the year they released *Sgt. Pepper's Lonely Hearts Club Band.* It became a popular relaxation technique. Many would say it was just a fad like tai chi or jazzercise. Perhaps it is taking it too seriously to call it a religion. According to one way of understanding *Seeger*, TM could be your ultimate concern if you felt strongly enough about it. But Judge Adams says that a religion must deal with certain questions. Hence the importance of SCI, which is "the basis of all growth and progress." Does this scientific overlay make TM a religion? Could one make any concern ultimate by restating it at a high enough level of generality?

One problem with the *Seeger* test is its implication that some traditional religious practices (for example, kosher food, praying the rosary) are not covered by the First Amendment because they are not ultimate concerns. Judge Adams would avoid this difficulty by saying that any belief system, once it is accredited as a religion, can get coverage for all its activities. Why? If the point of coverage is, as *Seeger* is sometimes read to suggest, that some activities have deep psychological importance, why protect those that don't? Conversely, if the First Amendment protects drinking wine at masses and seders, why not at bachelor parties? If on the other hand, as Judge Adams argues, teachings on ultimate matters get protected because of their subject matter, where in the order of importance should we put sumptuary rules? And if they qualify not on their own merits but derivatively—because they are practiced by a group that also holds ultimate religious concerns—how close must the connection be?

(b) Comprehensiveness.   You should reconsider at this point Smith v. Board of School Commissioners (p. 725). Smith asked for, and the district court issued, an injunction against the teaching of the religions of evolution, secularism, and materialism (among others) in the Alabama public schools. Biology and physics do consider ultimate and fundamental questions like "man's role in the Universe." Does this make them religious? Judge Adams says that a religion "is not generally confined to one question or one moral teaching." This seems like a useful observation concerning the teaching of evolution in biology or the big bang theory in physics. But how do we know when these theories stand alone and when they are part of a larger worldview? Suppose, as is often the case, that a teacher's or a school board's views on evolution grow out of a more general belief in materialism—a conviction that physical stuff is all there is, that things come about with no supernatural help, that when we die we die, and so on. Does it then violate the Establishment Clause to teach evolution? Or is this like the case where the legislature adopts a ban on partial-birth abortion? It coincides with the beliefs of some religious people, and some of them voted for it, including for religious reasons; but the First Amendment nevertheless allows it because it is not *necessarily* connected to religion?

On the other hand, if public schools can teach stand-alone theories about creation and human development that are consistent with materialism, why not theories that are consistent with spiritual assumptions? Consider again the Court's decision in Edwards v. Aguillard (p. 555).

(c) Formal and external signs. In the *Africa* case itself, Judge Adams wrote for the court holding that a prisoner's claim for a special diet based on his naturist philosophy was not religious even though his group believed in the sacredness of all things, in the ideal of maintaining "purity" by (for example) eating only water and raw food, and in the need to be "in touch with life's vibration" through following the group's teaching. The court pointed to, among other things, the group's lack of "organizational structure" such as clergy, religious services, scripture, or holidays. *Africa*, 662 F.2d at 1035-1036. Should the absence of such external features be enough to show that the group is not religious? Should their absence or presence be relevant at all? See Penalver, 107 Yale L. J. at 818-820 (criticizing reliance on such features).

3. Two Definitions for Two Clauses? As Judge Adams notes, Professor Laurence Tribe once proposed defining religion in two different ways—broadly for free exercise purposes, narrowly for the Establishment Clause. American Constitutional Law 827-828 (1978).[*] Tribe forthrightly explained that he was tailoring the word to accomplish different objectives: It "must be expanded" in free exercise cases to account for new "legitimate" practices; it must be contracted in establishment cases "lest all 'humane' programs of government be deemed . . . suspect." This may be putting the cart before the horse. To a certain extent, the degree of protection we get from the First Amendment depends on the text, rather than the other way around. For example, the text forces us to use the word "religion" consistently in free exercise and establishment cases regardless of what we might want. And the word has a core of meaning that includes Judaism and excludes lawn-mowing. But Tribe is right to observe that meaning is closely tied to the purposes of the Religion Clauses. (Let us leave aside for the moment whether it determines or depends on them.) This suggests that the purposes of the two clauses may be congruent. They must at least not conflict.

Consider the suggestion Justice Blackmun made in Lee v. Weisman (p. 498): One point of the Establishment Clause is to protect the government against the irrational and exclusionary effects of religion. What kind of religion did

[*] Later editions of his treatise abandon the suggestion. American Constitutional Law 1186-1187 (2d ed. 1988).

Justice Blackmun have in mind? Would he say that Seeger's and Welsh's brand of religion was irrational? Would it be improper (incomprehensible?) for Seeger or Welsh to urge Congress to adopt his views? Could they be taught in a philosophy class at the University of Kentucky? Can a religion practiced by one individual be exclusionary? If Justice Blackmun, when he condemned religion as irrational and exclusionary, was thinking about churches with supernatural beliefs, how would he have voted on the exemption question in *Seeger* and *Welsh*?

Suppose we accept Justice Blackmun's argument in *Lee*; and suppose we also accept Justice Rutledge's observation that "religion" must have the same meaning in both clauses. What purpose should we attribute to the Free Exercise Clause? Can we construct a convincing argument for protecting the freedom to engage in an activity that is irrational and exclusionary? To put the point more bluntly, if religion is a "bad" thing in the eyes of the Establishment Clause, how can it be a "good" thing in the eyes of the Free Exercise Clause?

4. Commentary on the Definition Issue. The question of how to define "religion" in the First Amendment has generated a large body of commentary. In addition to the works already cited in this section, see, e.g., Arlin M. Adams and Charles J. Emmerich, A Nation Dedicated to Religious Liberty 90-91 (1990); Thomas C. Berg, The State and Religion in a Nutshell 287-301 (2d ed. 2004); Andrew W. Austin, Faith and the Constitutional Definition of Religion, 22 Cumb. L. Rev. 1 (1991-1992); Stanley Ingber, Religion or Ideology: A Need Clarification of the Religion Clauses, 41 Stan. L. Rev. 233 (1989); George C. Freeman, III, The Misguided Search for the Constitutional Definition of "Religion," 71 Geo. L.J. 1519 (1983); Penalver, 107 Yale L.J. 791; Timothy L. Hall, Note, The Sacred and the Profane: A First Amendment Definition of Religion, 61 Tex. L. Rev. 139 (1982).

NOTE ON INCOME TAXES AND THE DEFINITION OF RELIGION

1. Problem. Consider the facts set forth in Church of the Chosen People v. United States, 548 F. Supp. 1247 (D. Minn. 1982):

> Plaintiff Church of the Chosen People (North American Panarchate) also known as Demigod Socko Pantheon [(DSP)] . . . seeks a refund in the amount of $472 [in federal income taxes] on the basis that the plaintiff [corporation] qualified as a tax exempt organization under § 501(c)(3) of the Internal Revenue Code. . . . According to Richard John Baker (Baker), an attorney for and Archon [spiritual leader] of the DSP, the plaintiff's primary purpose and activity is the preaching of a doctrine called The Gay Imperative. The plaintiff defines The Gay Imperative as "[t]he philosophic fundamental whereby the Gods direct that ever increasing numbers of persons expand their affectional preferences to encompass loving Gay relationships to hasten their full development for the control of overbreeding, and to ensure the survival of the human species and the multitude of terrestrial ecologies." Baker testified that "gay relationships" are positive, self-fulfilling emotional and physical bonds between two members of the same gender. . . . A major goal of the doctrine is the control of "overbreeding" or population growth.
>
>   . . . The Gay Imperative includes the belief that there are three equally valid human pair-bonds: male-male, female-female, and male-female. According to

Baker, each can be viewed as a leg of a triangle; all are necessary to the species. Baker stated that religions that the IRS views as mainstream promulgate doctrines that state only male-female relationships are valid in the eyes of God and that other relationships are perversions. . . . Baker testified that individuals have a duty to develop "viewpoints" and "ideologies" to counterbalance mainstream or traditional religions. An often-stated goal of the plaintiff is the conversion of "breeders" [persons who wished to have children] to the plaintiff's beliefs and espoused lifestyle.

The plaintiff's organization or structure is pyramidal. Archons occupy the highest governing positions in the DSP. . . . According to Baker, Archons are divinely appointed and are not required to complete any formal training. . . . [All members] are only required to take one vow, which is to preach The Gay Imperative. . . .

[T]he plaintiff has no published literature explaining its traditions. . . . During the years in question, the plaintiff conducted only two ceremonies. One of the ceremonies was a memorial to a gay victim; the other was the dedication of an archacy or subunit of the geographic area known as a Panarchate. The plaintiff held no regular religious services although it declared certain parts of an annual Gay Pride Week a "Festival of the Chosen." The plaintiff claims to have performed one marriage between two members of the same sex. . . .

. . . The plaintiff's sacerdotal functions are "[a]ll bodily functions normal to the adult human[.]" . . . Baker testified that the main activity of the plaintiff's adherents is preaching The Gay Imperative which can be done anywhere on the planet and encompasses all of daily life. This "preaching," according to Baker, involves attaining a state of consciousness that can be exhibited anywhere including walking down the street or at poker games. No words are required to "preach" the doctrine.

No clear distinction existed between the plaintiff's business affairs and those of Baker and McConnell [the other Archon]. The plaintiff's income from donations and the sale of religious artifacts was used to pay the rent at 2929 South 40th Street, Minneapolis, Minnesota, in 1977. Baker and McConnell used the residence as their personal residence and only one room was occasionally used for church administrative matters. On a few occasions the residence was used for social gatherings by the plaintiff's adherents. The rent was not prorated to reflect a division between personal and church use. The plaintiff's revenues also were used to pay the utilities and telephone bills for the residence. In addition, the plaintiff paid for subscriptions to Time magazine, local newspapers, and other periodicals in Baker's and McConnell's names.

Recall section 501(c)(3) of the Internal Revenue Code (p. 696). It provides an exemption from income tax for (among others)

[c]orporations . . . organized and operated exclusively for religious . . . purposes . . . no part of the net earnings of which inures to the benefit of any private shareholder or individual, no substantial part of the activities of which is carrying on propaganda, or otherwise attempting, to influence legislation . . . and which does not participate in, or intervene in (including the publishing or distributing of statements), any political campaign on behalf of any candidate for public office.

Does the Church of the Chosen People qualify for an exemption under these provisions? Under the definition of "religion" set forth in the *Malnak* and *Africa* decisions?

2. The Tax-Code "Religious" Exemption. Section 501(c)(3) exempts not only "religious" organizations but also other charitable organizations—scientific, literary, educational, sporting, and others. (And 26 U.S.C. § 170(c) allows donors to deduct contributions to these groups.) The Constitution does not require the religious exemption. See Hernandez v. Commissioner, 490 U.S. 680 (1989); United States v. Lee, 455 U.S. 252 (1982). But it probably does not forbid it either. The exemption of many secular organizations makes this case like Walz v. Tax Commission (see p. 383), and deflects the kind of objection Justice Harlan raised in *Welsh*. But what about the narrower problem the Court sought to avoid in *Seeger*—the fact that the "religious" category does not encompass every group that wants to be there?

The district court, referring to the *Africa* test, held that the Church of the Chosen People did not qualify for the exemption. Do you agree? If so, was it because the organization's focus on sexual preference and orientation did not deal with an "ultimate" question? Isn't sexual identity a fundamental question about human nature? Most religions teach that homosexual activity is evil. Plaintiff taught that it is good. If one side of that debate is considered "religious," shouldn't the other be as well?

Is the Church not "religious" because its views are not "comprehensive" but focus only on one issue? Were Seeger's and Welsh's beliefs comprehensive in nature? We know what they thought about war: how about love and marriage? Doesn't *Seeger* imply that a religion should have only one ultimate concern? Whence the requirement of comprehensiveness?

Is it a problem that the Church lacked "external manifestations analogous to other religions"—scriptures, trained clergy, ceremonies, significant membership? Why must a religion have these attributes? *Seeger* and *Welsh* imply that religion can be an individual thing, but a one-person religion would lack these attributes. The statute itself (§ 501) is limited to organizations, so only groups can claim the exemption. Is *this* a problem?

Or was the problem with the Church of the Chosen People more simple: the fact that it did some things that appeared to "inure to the [financial] benefit of" the individuals involved? If so, this was not the first or the last case in which an individual or commercial concern appeared to create a "religious" entity solely to claim tax-exempt status. At one point a U.S. Tax Court panel was driven to state: "Our tolerance for taxpayers who establish churches solely for tax avoidance purposes is reaching the breaking point." Miedaner v. Commissioner, 81 T.C. 272, 282 (1983) (denying exemption to author who transferred royalty rights in his book to a church whose assets he used for personal benefit and to avoid taxes on royalties).

3. Defining a "Church." Though the tax code gives special treatment to a fairly wide variety of religious organizations, churches are treated better than other groups for some purposes. They automatically qualify as "maximum deduction" organizations; that is, ones to which people can contribute up to 50 percent of their adjusted gross income and still get a deduction. 26 U.S.C. § 170(b)(1)(A)(i). Private foundations do not. Churches are also excused from having to apply for exemption under § 501(c)(3) (though they must, if asked, show that they meet the requirements). The code does not define what is a "church." The IRS has developed a list of criteria that it uses as a rough and ready guide:

> (1) a distinct legal existence; (2) a recognized creed and form of worship; (3) a definite and distinct ecclesiastical government; (4) a formal code of doctrine and

discipline; (5) a distinct religious history; (6) a membership not associated with any other church or denomination; (7) an organization of ordained ministers; (8) ordained ministers selected after completing prescribed studies; (9) a literature of its own; (10) established places of worship; (11) regular congregations; (12) regular religious services; (13) Sunday schools for religious instruction of the young; (14) schools for the preparation of its ministers.

Lutheran Social Serv. of Minn. v. United States, 758 F.2d 1283, 1286-1287 (8th Cir. 1985); Charles M. Whelan, "Church" in the Internal Revenue Code: The Definitional Problems, 45 Fordham L. Rev. 885 (1977). Cf. St. Martin Lutheran Church v. South Dakota, 451 U.S. 772, 783-784 & n.15 (1981). Does this pose an even narrower Establishment Clause problem than the definition of the word "religious"? Do criteria 5 and 10 favor mainline religions over new groups? Does criterion 13 favor Christians over Muslims and Jews? Do criteria 3, 7, 8, and 14 favor hierarchical over democratic forms of organization? Would the Establishment Clause permit the IRS to use these criteria if a group did not have to satisfy them all?

4. Taxes and the Definition of Religion.   Is "religion" defined more narrowly in tax cases than in draft cases, or cases like Malnak v. Yogi? If so, why? Is there a greater likelihood of strategic behavior in tax cases? Is there something like the draft law's requirement of alternative service? How are the costs of exemption redistributed in tax cases? In draft cases? In others? How should this affect a court's thinking?

TABLE OF CASES

TABLE OF STATUTES

TABLE OF AUTHORITIES

References to principal authorities are in italics.

Abbott, W.M., The Documents of Vatican II (1966), 335

Adams, A.M., and C.J. Emmerich, A Nation Dedicated to Religious Liberty (1990), 738

Adams and Hanlon, *Jones v. Wolf:* Church Autonomy and the Religion Clauses of the First Amendment, 128 U. Pa. L. Rev. 1211 (1980), 299

Ahlstrom, S., A Religious History of the American People (1972), 111

Alexander, Good God, Garvey! The Inevitability and Impossibility of a Religious Justification of Free Exercise Exemptions, 17 Drake L. Rev. 35 (1992), 272

____, Liberalism, Religion, and the Unity of Epistemology, 30 San Diego L. Rev. 763 (1993), 434

Amar, A.R., The Bill of Rights (1998), 72, 598

Amar, V.D., State RFRAs and the Workplace, 32 U.C. Davis L. Rev. 513 (1999), 249

Amsterdam, The Void-for-Vagueness Doctrine in the Supreme Court, 109 U. Pa. L. Rev. 67 (1960), 599

Arrington, L.J., Great Basin Kingdom: An Economic History of the Latter-Day Saints (1958), 121

Audi, R., The Place of Religious Argument in a Free and Democratic Society, 30 San Diego L. Rev. 677 (1993), 677

____, Religious Commitment and Secular Reason (2000), 677

Austin, Faith and the Constitutional Definition of Religion, 22 Cumb. L. Rev. 1 (1991-1992), 738

Aynes, R.L., The Blaine Amendment, in Religion and Law: An Encyclopedia (Finkelman ed., 2000), 363

Bates, S., Battleground: One Mother's Crusade, the Religious Right, and the Battle for Control of Our Classrooms (1993), 568

Becker, The Politics of Women's Wrongs and the Bill of "Rights": A Bicentennial Perspective, 53 U. Chi. L. Rev. 453 (1992), 459

Behe, Darwin's Black Box (1996), 551

Beiner and DiPippa, Hostile Environments and the Religious Employee, 19 U. Ark. Little Rock L.J. 577 (1997), 602

Berg, Anti-Catholicism and Modern Church-State Relations, 33 Loy. U. Chi. L.J. 121 (2001), 370, 379

____, The Constitutional Future of Religious Freedom Legislation, 20 U. Ark. Little Rock L. Rev. 715 (1998), 159, 160

____, Minority Religions and the Religion Clauses, 82 Wash. U. L.Q. 919 (2004), 416

____, The New Attacks on Religious Freedom Legislation, and Why They Are Wrong, 21 Cardozo L. Rev. 415 (1999), 158

____, Religion, Race, Segregation, and Districting: Comparing *Kiryas Joel* with *Shaw/Miller*, 26 Cumb. L. Rev. 365 (1996), 265-266, 709

____, Religious Speech in the Workplace: Harassment or Protected Speech?, 22 Harv. J.L. & Pub. Pol'y 959 (1999), 602

____, The State and Religion in a Nutshell (2d ed. 2004), 738

____, Vouchers and Religious Schools: The New Constitutional Questions, 72 U. Cin. L. Rev. 151(2003), 415

Berg and Ross, Some Religiously Devout Justices: Historical Notes and Comments, 81 Marq. L. Rev. 383 (1998), 692

Berman and Witte, The Transformation of Western Legal Philosophy in Lutheran Germany, 62 S. Cal. L. Rev. 1573 (1989), 117

Beschle, The Conservative as Liberal: The Religion Clauses, Liberal Neutrality, and the Approach of Justice O'Connor, 62 Notre Dame L. Rev. 151 (1987), 524

Blackstone, W., Commentaries on the Laws of England (1769), 15, 16, 598

Wexler, Darwin, Design, and Disestablishment: Teaching the Evolution Controversy in Public Schools, 56 Vand. L. Rev. 751 (2003), 558

Whelan, "Church" in the Internal Revenue Code: The Definitional Problems, 45 Fordham L. Rev. 885 (1977), 741

Williams, E., *The Essential Rights and Liberties of Protestants (1744), 36*

Williams, R., The Bloody Tenent of Persecution for Cause of Conscience, in Polishook, Roger Williams, John Cotton, and Religious Freedom (1967), 475

Williams and Williams, Volitionalism and Religious Liberty, 76 Cornell L. Rev. 769 (1991), 190

Witte, J., From Sacrament to Contract: Marriage, Religion, and Law in the Western Tradition (1997), 707

____, *The Essential Rights and Liberties of Religion in the American Constitutional Experiment, 71 Notre Dame L. Rev. 371 (1986), 29, 66*

Wittgenstein, L., Philosophical Investigations (3d ed. 1958), 719

Wolterstorff, A Religious Argument for the Civil Right to Freedom of Religious Exercise, Drawn from American History, 36 Wake Forest L. Rev. 535 (2001), 37-38

The Writings of George Washington (Fitzpatrick ed. 1939), 46

Yudof, M., When Government Speaks (1983), 472

Zelinsky, Are Tax "Benefits" for Religious Institutions Constitutionally Dependent on Benefits for Secular Entities?, 42 B.C. L. Rev. 805 (2001), 386

Zollman, C., American Church Law (1917), 285

INDEX